Ryan Johnson

28 October 2011

Hammersmith

D1336762

COUSINS
ON
THE LAW OF
MORTGAGES

PROPERTY AND CONVEYANCING LIBRARY

COUSINS

ON

THE LAW OF MORTGAGES

THIRD EDITION

by

EDWARD F. COUSINS B.A., LL.M.

The Adjudicator to HM Land Registry
Chief Commons Commissioner
Deputy Chancery Master
Bencher of Lincoln's Inn
Of Gray's Inn and King's Inns, Dublin, Barrister

with

IAN CLARKE, LL.B.

Of Lincoln's Inn, Barrister
A Deputy Adjudicator to HM Land Registry

Contributors

MICHELLE STEVENS-HOARE, LL.B., LL.M. (Property)
Of The Middle Temple, Barrister
A Deputy Adjudicator to HM Land Registry

STUART HORNETT LL.B., M.Phil
Of The Middle Temple, Barrister

EDWARD ROWNTREE B.A. (OXON)
Of Lincoln's Inn, Barrister

and

SARA E. BENBOW LL.B.
Of The Middle Temple, Barrister

SWEET & MAXWELL THOMSON REUTERS

LONDON • 2010

First Edition 1989
Second Edition 2001

Published in 2010 by Thomson Reuters (Legal) Limited (Registered in England & Wales,
Company No 1679046. Registered Office and address for service: 100 Avenue Road,
London NW3 3PF) trading as Sweet & Maxwell

*For further information on our products and services,
visit www.sweetandmaxwell.co.uk*

Typeset by Interactive Sciences Ltd, Gloucester
Printed in Great Britain by TJ International Ltd, Padstow, Cornwall

*No natural forests were destroyed to make this product;
only farmed timber was used and re-planted.*

A CIP catalogue record for this book is available from the British Library.

ISBN-13 978-0-42191-410-0

Thomson Reuters and the Thomson Reuters logo are trademarks of Thomson Reuters.
Sweet & Maxwell ® is a registered trademark of Thompson Reuters (Legal) Limited

Preface to the First Edition

The decision to publish this book was prompted by a perceived continuing and unfulfilled demand for a new practitioner's text on the law of mortgages.

Initially, it was envisaged that this project would involve the publication of a third edition of that valuable and now unobtainable work, *Waldock on the Law of Mortgages* (1949), the first edition of which having been written by Professor Hanbury and Mr Waldock and published in 1939. But, at an early stage of this venture, owing to the considerable developments which have occurred in the field of mortgages since the publication of the second edition of Waldock, it was found necessary to revise, reconstruct and rewrite substantial sections of this work.

It is in these circumstances that the *Law of Mortgages* was conceived, written, and now finally published, with all due acknowledgment to those remaining parts based upon (and hopefully, without any detraction from) the second edition of Waldock. It is my desire that this work will provide a useful and concise guide to practitioners and academics in the field of mortgages. I have attempted to set out the law as at June 30, 1989.

Finally, my thanks are due to colleagues and friends for their kindly criticisms and suggestions. I must also extend my thanks to my wife and children for their forbearance, large sections of this book having been written whilst on holiday in France and Spain during the Summers of 1987 and 1988.

Preface to the Second Edition

The first edition of this work was published in late 1989. As the preface to that edition stated, the decision to publish was prompted by the unfulfilled demand for a new practitioners' text. That original decision has been vindicated in two ways. First, the sales of the work since publication have been very healthy. Secondly, there has been a strong demand from practitioners for the text to be updated to reflect the wide changes in both statute law and case law that has occurred since 1989.

It is in these circumstances that the second edition has been published with all due acknowledgment to the hard work put in by Ian Clarke, Michelle Stevens-Hoare and Edward Rowntree.

Unfortunately it has not proved possible in this work to treat fully the provisions of the Financial Services and Markets Act 2000 as to mortgage regulation. The scope of the regulatory regime has still not been finalised in subordinate legislation and guidance and many provisions of the Act are still not yet in force.

The thrust of the Act is that no unauthorised person will be able to carry out any regulated activity. Authorised persons will only be able to carry out regulated activities for which they have been granted permission. A "regulated activity" is one which is regulated by the Financial Services Authority under the Act.

It is currently anticipated that the FSA's regime of mortgage regulation will come into effect no later than August 31, 2002. This date is referred to as "N3" in the latest Consultation Paper (CP98) published in June 2001 entitled "The Draft Mortgage Sourcebook, including Policy Statement on CP70". This is to be nine months after the 2000 Act (including Part II) finally comes into force. That date is referred to as "N2" in the Consultation Paper and is to be no later than November 30, 2001. The date for response to this Consultation Paper is September 14, 2001.

Thus, any detailed treatment of the Act and its subordinate legislation and guidance at this stage will be premature.

I must also extend my thanks to Peter Kennealy, Thomas Bourke and the other members of staff and the *stagières* at the European University Institute, San Domenico di Fiesole, Firenze, for all their help and assistance provided to me earlier this year. I spent happy times in the Library of the EUI revising this work having accompanied my wife whilst she held a Visiting Fellowship at the Institute.

11 Stone Buildings
Lincoln's Inn

July 2001

Preface to the Third Edition

It is more than 21 years since this work first appeared, and 9 years since the second edition was produced. Since then there have been a number of developments in the field of mortgage law which have provided the incentive for this new edition. There has also been considerable encouragement from users for the text to be updated to reflect such changes. It is gratifying to know that this work continues to be well regarded by both the judiciary and practitioners versed in the field.

I should state that there have been substantial changes made in the conceptual framework of the work, and a re-ordering of the textual format to assist exposition and to reflect the legal developments which have occurred since the last edition. New chapters have also been included relating to Subrogation, Priority, Consumer Credit Law, and the Law of Insolvency as it affects both the mortgagor and the mortgagee.

It is in these circumstances that this third edition has come to fruition.

I should express my gratitude to those who have assisted in its publication, notably Ian Clarke and the Contributors. I also wish to give especial thanks to David Rees, an Assistant Land Registrar at the Land Registry, Telford Office, who has provided me with gentle textual suggestions on the land registration aspects of mortgage law.

It is hoped that this work will continue to be of use to all those involved in the law of mortgages.

This edition is dedicated to the patience and tolerance of my new wife, Sarah, who found an unexpected intruder, in the shape of the somewhat frenetic writing activity, interposed into what was intended to be a tranquil and peaceful summer holiday.

I have endeavoured to state the law as at November 1, 2010.

Hampstead
London NW3

November 2010

CONTENTS

TABLE OF CASES

TABLE OF STATUTES

TABLE OF STATUTORY INSTRUMENTS

CHAPTER 1

THE NATURE OF A MORTGAGE

INTRODUCTION

There have been many attempts, both judicial and academic, to describe a **1–01** mortgage. Two of the most famous attest to the difficulty of carrying out that task in a satisfactory manner. Lord Macnaghten was moved to say, in the case of *Samuel v Jarrah Timber and Wood Paving Corp*,[1] that no-one, by the light of nature, ever understood an English mortgage of real estate; while Maitland described it as "one long *suppressio veri* and *suggestio falsi*".[2]

Although the essence of a mortgage transaction is the charging of property as security[3] for performance of an obligation, the transaction had for centuries been carried out by conveying an estate in land to the mortgagee, thereby giving rise to the difficulty. These two facts were recognised by Lindley M.R. when he formulated his well-known description of a mortgage in the case of *Santley v Wilde*.[4] This was a case where the mortgage had been taken not merely as security for the loan but, additionally, as security for a one-third share of future profits, thus serving to demonstrate that mortgages can be raised to secure the performance of obligations other than the payment of debts.

The purpose of security is to afford to the obligee some additional means of **1–02** enforcing the performance of the obligation by, or extracting the money equivalent from, the obligor. Thus, a lender is often unwilling to rely solely on the borrower's personal credit and requires a greater certainty of repayment than the mere possibility of enforcing the claim in a claim for debt. The borrower can meet this requirement by offering personal security or suretyship. In that case, a third party (the surety or guarantor) undertakes to answer for the borrower's default by way of a personal commitment, and the lender has a claim in debt

---

[1] [1904] A.C. 323, 326.

[2] Maitland, *Equity* (2nd edn, 1969) p.182. In 1991, and following the publication of its Working Paper (No.99) on Land Mortgages in 1986, the Law Commission made wide-ranging recommendations for the simplification of the law of mortgages. The major recommendation was that the present system should be abolished and replaced by a simple concept, namely the formal land mortgage and the informal land mortgage. This Report *Transfer of Land—Land Mortgages* ((1991) Law. Com. No.204, HC 5) states that the law is complicated and has achieved " . . . a state of artificiality and complexity that is now difficult to defend" (para.2.1). Regrettably, the then government rejected such proposals on the basis that there was considered to be insufficient support (see the Press Notice from the Lord Chancellor's Department issued on March 19, 1998). In due course the Law Commission may reconsider these recommendations.

[3] See *Bristol Airport Plc v Powdrill* [1990] Ch. 744, 760 (definition of "security"). See also *Halliday v Holgate* (1867–68) L.R. 3 Exch. 299, 302 (categorisation of security).

[4] [1899] 2 Ch. 474, and see paras 30–25 et seq. below.

against him should the borrower default. The value of such security depends on differing commercial considerations and future events over which the lender may only (at best) have limited control. Therefore, the borrower or surety may seek to reinforce their respective undertakings by giving real security.

Real security[5] is obtained when property is appropriated specifically to the satisfaction of a particular debt, so that that debt is a primary charge on the property. The lender whose right is protected by a real security is entitled to take that security for the discharge of his own secured debt, even to the extent of exhausting it entirely and withdrawing it altogether from the pool of the borrower's assets available to the general creditor.[6] If, as is usual, the mortgagee takes a personal covenant from the mortgagor to repay and the security is insufficient to discharge the debt, he can seek to recover the balance and prove in the mortgagor's bankruptcy for such purpose.[7]

1-03   By giving real security, the mortgagor has a property with which he cannot deal freely because it is encumbered. However, he can release the property from its encumbrance by discharging his obligation to the mortgagee whatever the nature of the right which the mortgagee acquired. This right to redeem is part of the mortgagor's equity of redemption. A mortgage deed generally contains a stipulation that the mortgagor shall repay on a fixed date which is, say, six months from the execution of the deed. The result, at law, of the mortgagor's failure to comply with this stipulation is that the property becomes vested in the mortgagee. However, in equity the mortgagor will be allowed to redeem the property after his default.[8] This arises even though the parties may have made time the essence of the contract. This right to redeem will subsist until the mortgagee has exercised such powers as he may have to destroy the mortgagor's equity of redemption by statute, foreclosure, sale or release.[9] The mortgagor's right to redeem can also become statute-barred[10] if the mortgage is a mortgage of real property which comprises unregistered land,[11] or of a mixed fund,[12] but not if it is a mortgage of personal property only. The position in relation to registered land is different; in such circumstances a mortgagee in possession cannot extinguish a mortgagor's right to redeem.[13]

In spite of judicial reluctance to accept it, there is a well established principle that the mortgagor will not be permitted to surrender to the mortgagee his right

---

[5] Which may comprise a mortgage or possessory or non-possessory security, see *Halliday v Holgate* (1867–68) L.R. 3 Exch. 299, at 302.

[6] *White v Simmons* (1871) L.R. 6 Ch. App. 555.

[7] *Re London, Windsor and Greenwich Hotels Co (Quartermaine's Case)* [1892] 1 Ch. 639; *Re Bonacino, ex p. Discount Banking Co* (1894) 1 Mans. 59.

[8] *Seton v Slade, Hunter v Seton* (1802) 7 Ves. 265.

[9] *Weld v Petre* [1929] 1 Ch. 33, at 43.

[10] Limitation Act 1980 ss.16, 17. In order to rely on that section, the mortgagee must be in possession in his character as mortgagee: *Hyde v Dallaway* (1843) 2 H. 528. See para.6–29, below.

[11] See para.6–29, below. The position in relation to a chargee differs insofar as recovery of land under s.15 is concerned in that the period of limitation is not disapplied against a charge, see para.6–31: ibid., s.96(1).

[12] i.e. a mortgage of real property and a life policy, see *Charter v Watson* [1899] 1 Ch. 175.

[13] See Land Registration Act 2002 (LRA 2002) s.96(2); and see para.6–31.

to redeem by any term of the mortgage contract;[14] although he may enter into a separate contract to give the lender a collateral advantage.[15]

THE SUBSTANCE OF THE TRANSACTION[16]

In equity, it is a matter of substance, not of form, whether a transaction creates **1–04** a security or transfers absolute ownership. If the true purpose of the transaction is to create a security, it will not assist the mortgagee to disguise it as a conditional sale or a conveyance.[17] It is possible to demonstrate the sham nature of a written agreement masking its true nature by providing extrinsic evidence to that effect, such evidence being admissible in court. It is necessary to look at the agreement as a whole as there is no one clear touchstone.[18] Where an agreement was intended only to create a security, that fact may be proved afterwards by parol evidence even though it contradicts the plain language of a deed.[19] Thus, where a conveyance of property was accompanied by a parol agreement for the defeasance of the deed on payment of a sum of money, it was held to be a fraud, in equity, for the grantee to refuse to give up the deed in return for the payment being made.[20] Nor is it conclusive in the mortgagee's favour that the mortgagor makes two separate agreements, one to give security and one to purchase the mortgaged property. The court will declare the latter void if it appears that there was only one transaction.[21]

THE MORTGAGE AS SECURITY

A mortgage has been described as "a conveyance of land or an assignment of **1–05** chattels as a security for the payment of a debt or the discharge of some other obligation for which it is given."[22] This description brings out the essential features of a mortgage: the provision of *security* by a *transfer of property rights*.

---

[14] *Samuel v Jarrah Timber and Wood Paving Corporation* [1904] A.C. 323, per Lord Halsbury L.C. See generally, Ch.30, below.

[15] *Kreglinger v New Patagonia Meat and Cold Storage Co* [1914] A.C. 25; cf. *Noakes v Rice* [1902] A.C. 24 and *Bradley v Carritt* [1903] A.C. 253.

[16] This is of significance when considering a number of aspects, including any limitations on the mortgagor's right to redeem. See Ch.30, below.

[17] *England v Codrington* (1758) 1 Ed. 169; *Re Duke of Marlborough* [1894] 2 Ch. 133; cf. *Barnhart v Greenshields* (1853) 9 Moo. P.C.C. 18; *Re Kent and Sussex Sawmills* [1947] Ch. 177.

[18] See *Snook v London and West Riding Investments Ltd* [1967] 2 Q.B. 786; *Welsh Development Agency v Export Finance Co Ltd* [1992] B.C.C. 270; *Lloyds & Scottish Finance Ltd v Cyril Lord Carpet Sales Ltd* [1992] B.C.L.C. 609.

[19] *Lincoln v Wright* (1859) 4 De G. & J. 16; *Walker v Walker* (1740) 2 Atk 98; *Lord Irnham v Child* (1791) Bro. C 92.

[20] *Re Duke of Marlborough* [1894] 2 Ch. 133. See also *England v Codrington* (1758) 1 Eden 169; *Williams v Owen* (1840) 5 My & Cr 303, 306; *Douglas v Culverwell* (1862) 4 De G.F. & J. 20; *Barton v Bank of New South Wales* (1890) 15 App. Cas. 379; *United Dominion Trust Ltd v Beech, Savan, Tabner, and Thompson* [1972] 1 Lloyd's Rep. 546.

[21] *Lewis v Love (Frank)* [1961] 1 W.L.R. 261 where separate options to purchase were held to be void; cf. *Reeve v Lisle* [1902] A.C. 461. See para.30–10.

[22] *Santley v Wilde* [1899] 2 Ch. 474 per Lindley M.R.

Although mortgages are most commonly raised to secure a money debt, they may also be granted to secure other obligations.[23]

The mortgage transaction consists of a transfer of the legal or equitable title to property from the mortgagor to the mortgagee, to be held by the mortgagee until all his claims under the mortgage are satisfied. The mortgagor's right is to have the title restored to him on fulfilment of his obligation to the lender even if he does not do so until after the contractual date for that fulfilment.

Although in certain circumstances the mortgagee may assume possession of the property, his security does not depend on being in possession. If he wishes to apply the rents and profits to the satisfaction of the mortgage debt, his remedy is to appoint a receiver.[24] He cannot derive any personal profit from being in possession. Indeed, he is accountable to the mortgagor not only for the profits which he does make but also for those which he reasonably ought to have made.[25]

1–06   In order to protect both his own interests and those of persons who may deal with the borrower subsequent to the giving of security, the lender should ensure to the best of his ability that the borrower is not able to represent himself as being the owner of the property free from encumbrances. This means either taking the documents of title in addition to the conveyance,[26] or registering his mortgage in whatever way is appropriate.

The mortgagee's ultimate remedy is the destruction of the mortgagor's equity of redemption. This he can achieve by sale without the intervention of the court if there is an express or statutory power of sale, but not otherwise. This can also be achieved by foreclosure, but this can be decreed only by the court which has the power to order sale instead.[27]

CHARGES

1–07   The essential feature of distinction between a mortgage and a charge is that a mortgage is a security accompanied by a transfer of property rights, while a charge is an appropriation of property to the satisfaction of an obligation without any such transfer of title. The chargee only has certain rights over the property charged.[28] It therefore, should follow as a matter of principle that a mortgagee, but not a chargee, should have the right to foreclose or to go into possession, while both should have the right to appoint a receiver or to realise the security by

---

[23] *Santley v Wilde* [1899] 2 Ch. 474.

[24] Law of Property Act 1925 (LPA 1925) s.109.

[25] *White v City of London Brewery* (1889) 42 Ch.D. 237; *Shepherd v Spansheath* (1988) E.G.C.S. 35.

[26] Since the enactment of the Law of Property (Miscellaneous Provisions) Act 1989 s.2, a deposit of title deeds can no longer be construed as an act of part performance of the contract to create a legal mortgage. See para.14–03, below.

[27] LPA 1925 s.91. See paras 27–24 et seq.

[28] See *Jones v Woodward* (1917) 116 L.T. 378, 379; *London County and Westminster Bank Ltd v Tompkins* [1918] 1 K.B. 515. Sale must be by way of judicial process: *Swiss Bank Corp v Lloyds Bank Ltd* [1982] A.C. 584, at 595; *Carreras Rothmans Ltd v Freeman Matthews Transport Ltd* [1985] Ch. 207, at 227; *Re Charge Card Services Ltd* [1987] Ch. 150, at 176; [1989] Ch. 497 (on appeal); *Re BCCI (No.8)* [1998] A.C. 214; *Re Coslett Contractors Ltd* [1998] Ch. 495, at 507–508.

sale. Matters, however, are not as clear cut as this may suggest and differences do remain, especially between legal and equitable charges.

At law: The distinction, nevertheless, is clouded not only by judicial indif- **1–08** ference, referred to above, but also by the draftsmen of the 1925 property legislation. In the definition section of the Law of Property Act,[29] a mortgage is described as including "a charge or lien on any property for securing money or money's worth". A mortgagee includes "a chargee by way of legal mortgage" but not the holder of a lien or an equitable chargee.[30] Moreover, given that a chargee by deed by way of legal mortgage has the same rights as if he had a charge by way of legal mortgage[31] and that all charges of registered land created after October 12, 2003, operate as if created as a charge by deed by way of legal mortgage[32]; it can be seen that the distinction in reality no longer exists.[33] Further, while s.90 of the Act deals with orders for sale in reference to equitable mortgages, the section is actually entitled "Realisation of equitable charges by the court."

This confusion also reflects reality when looked at from the point of view of the borrower. The lender has, *at law*, rights which differ according to whether he is a mortgagee or a chargee. As Harman J. said in *Four-Maids Ltd v Dudley Marshall (Properties) Ltd*[34]:

> "The right of the mortgagee to possession in the absence of some contract has nothing to do with default on the part of the mortgagor. The mortgagee may go into possession before the ink is dry on the mortgage unless there is something . . . whereby he has contracted himself out of that right."

A chargee has no such right against the chargor, as he is never owner of the property at law. That same circumstance prevents him destroying the chargor's equity of redemption by foreclosure, which is a right confined to a mortgagee.

The borrower, however, may find himself put in the same position, in practice, **1–09** vis-à-vis the lender, whatever the lender's status. If he cannot discharge the obligation, his right to redeem is as effectively destroyed by sale as by fore-closure. He loses possession as a result either of the appointment of a receiver or the making of a possession order.

The similarity in the borrower's position, whether his lender is a mortgagee or a chargee, is reflected by the statutory provision created by the Law of Property Act 1925 allowing a legal mortgage to be created by means of a charge by deed expressed to be by way of legal mortgage.[35] In practice, therefore, a legal charge is no different from a legal mortgage. Although the document is described as a charge, the lender, regardless of his lack of title, has all the powers of a legal

---

[29] LPA 1925 s.205(1)(xvi).

[30] ibid.

[31] LPA 1925 ss.1(2)(c), 85(1), and see *Grand Junction Co Ltd v Bates* [1954] 2 Q.B. 160 at 168–169; *Regent Oil Co Ltd v JA Gregory (Hatch End) Ltd* [1966] Ch. 402 at 431.

[32] LRA 2002 s.51. This Act came into force on October 13, 2003, by virtue of the provisions of the Land Registration Act 2002 (Commencement No.4) Order 2003 (SI 2003/1725).

[33] Also, if by deed a chargee has the rights specified: LPA 1925 s.101, see s.205(1)(xvi).

[34] [1957] Ch. 317, at 320.

[35] LPA 1925 s.85(1).

mortgagee[36]: foreclosure, sale, possession, and the appointment of a receiver are all available to him.

1–10 In Equity: Save for charges by way of legal mortgage and certain maritime hypothecations,[37] charges are only enforceable in equity. These are considered elsewhere.[38]

STATUTORY CHARGES[39]

1–11 There are species of charges which are subsumed under the generic head of "statutory charges". They are to be distinguished from mortgages in that they are imposed by statute on land,[40] whereas mortgages arise out of the consensual act of the parties. The nature and effect of a statutory charge depend on the terms of the particular statute.

The following are some examples of statutory charges imposed on land:

Housing authorities: charges made in favour of local authorities relating to the expense of executing works following a failure to comply with repair notices.[41] The chargee has the powers and remedies of a mortgagee[42] and enjoys priority over other mortgagees and rent-chargees.[43] It is provided that with effect from the date of demand for the sum recoverable becomes operative the sum is a charge on the relevant premises until so recovered, and takes effect as a local land charge.[44]

Street works: charges upon premises of frontagers in favour of local authorities for expenses incurred by them in making up private streets.[45] Again, these are enforceable as local land charges.

Charging orders: charging orders on land by way of equitable execution;[46]

Business tenancies: charges in favour of landlords of business premises in respect of compensation for or the cost of improvements;[47]

---

[36] ibid., s.87.

[37] The latter are outside the scope of this work.

[38] See Ch.14.

[39] For a fuller exposition of Statutory Charges, see Ch.21.

[40] They therefore differ from a statutory legal charge under LPA 1925 s.117; see para.12–31.

[41] See now the Housing Act 2004 ss.49 and 50. The former provisions of the Housing Act 1985 ss.189, 190, 193, Sch.10, para.7, were repealed by the Housing Act 2004 s.266, Sch.16, with effect from April 6, 2006.

[42] ibid.

[43] *Paddington Borough Council v Finucane* [1928] Ch. 567; *Bristol Corp v Virgin* [1928] 2 K.B. 622.

[44] See Housing Act 2004 s.50(9), (10).

[45] See, e.g Highways Act 1980 ss.203, 212 and 305. As to the powers of local authorities, see *Payne v Cardiff RDC* [1932] 1 K.B. 241; *Poole Corpn v Moody* [1945] K.B. 350. As to registration as a local land charge, see Local Land Charges Act 1975 ss.5, 10.

[46] See Charging Orders Act 1979, and para.3–21 and Ch.20.

[47] See Landlord and Tenant Act 1927 s.12, Sch.1. These are registrable as Class A Land Charges, ibid., Sch.1, para.7. If they are not so registered then they are void against a purchaser for value of the land so charged.

Agricultural matters: charges in favour of landlords or tenants of agricultural holdings in respect of compensation payable;[48]

Right to buy: charges to secure the repayment of discounts given by local authorities to public sector tenants on the purchase of a house or flat in the event of early disposal of the property.[49]

Legal Services Commission: a statutory charge[50] is imposed on any property recovered or preserved (except insofar as the regulations provide otherwise[51]) where legal services have been funded by the Legal Services Commission as part of the Community Legal Service.[52] Similar provisions applied when funding was provided in like circumstances by the Legal Aid Board.[53]

Mental health: Under the Mental Health Act 1983 a general power of charging a patient's property was included in order to provide security for money advanced for the permanent improvement or benefit of any of the patient's property.[54] Part VII of that Act was repealed and replaced by the provisions of the Mental Capacity Act 2005 with effect from October 1, 2007. This has established a new Court of Protection with greater powers than before, and also the new statutory office of Public Guardian.[55] The Court of Protection is, inter alia, provided with the power to order that money expended as ordered or directed by the court on improving or benefiting any of the property of a person lacking capacity is to be charged on that property, either with or without interest, in favour of such person as may be just. No such charge, however, may confer any right of sale or foreclosure during the lifetime of the person lacking capacity.[56]

Registered land: Where a statutory charge is imposed on registered land after October 12, 2003, and a pre-existing charge is postponed to it,[57] notice of its creation must be given in accordance with the Land Registration Rules 2003.[58]   1–12

Human Rights: The Law Commission has expressed doubt over whether those statutory charges which take priority over pre-existing charges are compatible   1–13

---

[48] See Agricultural Holdings Act 1986 ss.85–87. These are registrable as Class A Land Charges, ibid. s.100, Sch.14, para.51. If they are not so registered they will be void against a purchaser for value of the land charged. See also paras 24–09 et seq.

[49] See Housing Act 1985 ss.36, 156; Housing Act 1988 s.79, Sch.11 paras 1, 2; Housing Act 1996 s.11.

[50] See Community Legal Service (Financial) Regulations 2000 (SI 2000/516) Pt III.

[51] Access to Justice Act 1999 s.10.

[52] ibid., s.10(7), and see *Morgan v Legal Aid Board* [2000] 1 W.L.R. 1657.

[53] Legal Aid Act 1988 s.16(6) (now repealed).

[54] Mental Health Act 1983 ss.96, 101. Any grant granted could not be realised by sale or foreclosure during the patient's lifetime: ibid., s.101(6).

[55] ibid., Pt 2.

[56] ibid., Sch.2.

[57] e.g. street works.

[58] SI 2003/1417, rr.105, 106; LRA 2002 s.50.

with art.1 of the First Protocol to the European Convention on Human Rights.[59]

CHARGES AND TRUSTS

1–14   A charge is created by the appropriation of specific property for the discharge of a debt or other obligation, there having been no change in ownership of the property either at law or in equity. It confers on the chargee the right to apply to the court for an order for sale or the appointment of a receiver. The charger has a right to redeem.[60] It does not confer the right to possession.[61] In the case of a trust there occurs the disposition of a beneficial interest in property to the beneficiary or beneficiaries under the trust who are thereby entitled to the trust property. Where a loan is made by the trustees of a trust, the terms of the trust deed should ensure that provision is made for the appropriation of sufficient security to satisfy the obligation.

STATUTORY LEGAL CHARGES

1–15   This is a special form of charge by way of a legal mortgage and certain covenants are implied.[62]

OTHER FORMS OF SECURITY

Possessory securities

1–16   **Pledge:**   A pledge (or pawn)[63] of chattels is effected either by actual[64] or constructive delivery, the latter being by delivery of documents.[65] It is a form of bailment. The creditor's rights arise through his *possession* under the contract of pledge. The right of the lender, or pledgee, is to retain the chattel until a proper tender of the amount due is made.[66] It is not a right of *ownership*. As against the borrower, or pledgor, he may deny him possession. If the debt remains unsatisfied, he may, after a reasonable time, sell the chattel. The borrower's right to

---

[59] *Land Registration for the Twenty-first Century—A Conveyancing Revolution* (2001) Law Com. No.271, para.7.41.

[60] *Carreras Rothmans Ltd v Freeman Mathews Treasure Ltd* [1985] Ch. 207.

[61] *Re Bond Worth Ltd* [1980] Ch. 228 at 248, per Slade J.; *Carreras Rothmans Ltd v Freeman Mathews Treasure Ltd* [1985] Ch. 207; *Tatung (UK) Ltd v Galex Telesure Ltd* (1989) 5 B.C.C. 325; *Compaq Computer Ltd v Abercon Group Ltd* [1993] B.C.L.C. 603 [1991] B.C.C. 484; and *Modelboard Ltd v Outer Box Ltd* [1992] B.C.C. 945.

[62] See para.12–31.

[63] These are interchangeable terms. Special rules apply, however, to "pawning" goods in, e.g. pawnbrokers where advances are made to the pledgor. Such transactions may be governed by the Consumer Credit Act 1974 as regulated consumer credit agreements, see s.6(2), (3), ss.114–121 (as amended), see paras 14–01 et seq.

[64] *Re Morritt, ex p. Official Receiver* (1886) 18 Q.B.D. 222.

[65] *Official Assignee of Madras v Mercantile Bank of India Ltd* [1935] A.C. 53.

[66] *Halliday v Holgate* (1867–68) L.R. 3 Ex. 299; *Yungmann v Briesemann* (1892) 67 L.T. 642.

redeem subsists, however, until the chattel is sold.[67] When the pledged goods are sold, any moneys remaining in the hands of the pledgee after satisfaction of the debt are held on trust for the pledgor and interest is payable on them.[68]

The lender thus has a special property in the chattel.[69] It is to be distinguished from a mortgage of chattels as, unlike a mortgagee, the lender is not at law the owner of it and therefore can never foreclose.[70] Foreclosure is the destruction of the equity to redeem property which at law is the property of the mortgagee and is therefore unavailable to a pledgee.[71] On the other hand, if a third party wrongfully removes the pledged chattel from his keeping, it is the lender who has the right to sue in conversion since that right arises from ownership and possession or from possession alone or from the immediate right to possession. While the chattel is in pledge the borrower has none of these remedies.

If the lender returns the chattel to the borrower before he has discharged the debt, the lender loses his special property[72] in the chattel unless there is a particular temporary purpose for the return. The lender is thereby relegated to the status of an unsecured creditor.[73]

Possessory liens: A possessory lien gives the lender even less of a right against **1–17** the borrower than a pledge. The right is a passive right to detain the chattel until a debt is satisfied.[74] There is, in general, no right to realise the security by sale or otherwise deal with the property,[75] though such a right can exist in special cases. An example of such a lien arises where a garage owner has the right to retain a vehicle until payment has been made for its repair.[76]

Common law liens[77]: If the lender is in possession of the borrower's chattels **1–18** under any of the following circumstances, he has, provided that his possession remains continuous, a lien on the chattels until his debt is satisfied. These occur if:

(1) he has expended labour, skill or money on them[78];
(2) he is compellable by law to receive, or to perform services in respect of them[79];

---

[67] *Carter v Wake* (1877) 4 Ch.D. 605.

[68] *Matthew v TM Sutton Ltd* [1994] 1 W.L.R. 1455.

[69] *Donald v Suckling* (1866) L.R. 1 Q.B.D. 585.

[70] *Carter v Wake* (1877) 4 Ch.D. 605. *Re Cosslett (Contractors) Ltd* [1988] Ch. 495, 508 per Millett L.J.

[71] *Donald v* Suckling (1866) L.R. 1 Q.B.D. 585.

[72] The term "special property" was criticised by Lord Mersey in *The Odessa* [1916] 1 A.C. 145, 158–159. Here it was stated that the pawnee's right to sell in truth created no property right whatsoever. He preferred the term "special interest". See also *Mathew v TM Sutton Ltd* [1994] 1 W.L.R. 1455, 1461 per Chadwick J.

[73] *Reeves v Capper* (1838) 5 Bing. N.C. 136; *North Western Bank v Poynter, Son and Macdonalds* [1895] A.C. 56.

[74] *Lickbarrow v Mason* (1787) 2 T.R. 63.

[75] *Smart v Sandars* (1848) 5 C.B. 895; *Re Hamlet International Plc* [1998] 2 B.C.L.C. 164.

[76] See, e.g. *Green v All Motors Ltd* [1917] 1 K.B. 625.

[77] They are also known as particular liens.

[78] *Chase v Westmore* (1816) 5 M. & S. 180.

[79] *Robins & Co v Gray* [1895] 2 Q.B. 501; *Marsh v Commissioner of Police* [1945] K.B. 43.

(3) he has saved them from loss or capture at sea.[80]

Such liens arise by operation of law.[81] They secure only the particular debt which accrues to the lender by reason of his dealings with the chattels in his possession.

1–19 *Contractual liens:* A similar right can be created by express contract or can arise by implication from trade or business usage.[82] Frequently, such contractual liens, as they are generally termed,[83] extend to cover the general balance between debtor and creditor, so that the indebtedness is not necessarily related to the chattel detained. Thus, a solicitor's lien on papers which come into his possession in the course of business,[84] or a factor's lien on chattels,[85] gives each the right to detain against the general balance of his account.

1–20 *Requirement for possession:* Whether the lien arises at common law, by contract or by implication, the rights under it depend on possession. Thus, if the lender returns the chattels to the borrower, or contracts on terms that the borrower may temporarily resume possession, or the lender hands the chattels to a third party with the intent to abandon possession, his lien is lost. As with a pledge, there is an exception to this rule where, for some specific and temporary purpose, he delivers the chattels to the borrower or to a third party.[86]

Non-possessory securities

1–21 **Equitable liens:** Like a lien at common law, an equitable lien can arise in respect of both real and personal property.[87] Unlike a common law lien, however, an equitable lien does not depend on possession of the property which is subject to the lien.[88] It is a type of equitable charge arising by operation of law arising irrespective of the parties' intentions,[89] except where its retention would be manifestly inconsistent with the terms of the agreement between the parties or the true nature of the transaction.[90] It also falls within the definition of "mortgage" for the purposes of the Law of Property Act 1925.[91] Further, the holder of an equitable lien has the power to realise his security by judicial sale[92] or the appointment of a receiver. This means that the holder of the equitable lien is

---

[80] *Hartfort v Jones* (1699) 1 Ld. Ray. 393.
[81] *Gladstone v Birley* (1817) 2 Mer. 401.
[82] *Rushforth v Hadfield* (1805) 7 East. 224.
[83] They are also known as general liens.
[84] *Ex p. Sterling* (1809) 16 Ves. 258.
[85] *Kruger v Wilcox* (1755) Amb. 252.
[86] *Reeves v Capper* (1838) 5 Bing. N.C. 136.
[87] *Re Stucley* [1906] 1 Ch. 67; *Barker v Stickney* [1919] 1 K.B. 121.
[88] *Goode v Burton* (1847) 1 Ex. 189; *Wrout v Dawes* (1858) 25 Beav. 369.
[89] *Re Beirnstein* [1925] Ch. 12, at 17–18; *Re Birmingham, (dec'd)* [1959] Ch. 523, 529.
[90] *Barclays Bank Plc v Estates and Commercial Ltd* [1997] 1 W.L.R. 415, 420–421; *UCB Group Ltd v Hedworth* [2003] EWCA Civ 1717. It can also arise by virtue of the doctrine of proprietary estoppel, see *Kinane v Alimamy Mackie-Conteh* [2005] EWCA Civ 45.
[91] LPA 1925 s.205(xvi).
[92] *Neate v Duke of Marlborough* (1838) 3 Myl. & Cr. 407.

treated in equity as a secured creditor of the purchaser and can apply to the court for a declaration of his interest and for an order for sale of the land. His debt will be satisfied from the proceeds of sale together with the costs of proceedings. If the holder of the lien is paid off by a third party, that party can claim the benefit of the lien by subrogation. However, subrogation may be displaced by a specific charge.[93] It is exceptional for the holder of a *common law* lien to have the power of sale.

Unpaid vendor's lien: The contrast is well illustrated by reference to the **1–22** position of a vendor under a specifically enforceable contract for the sale of land. Thus, at common law the vendor would have a lien on the land or the deeds for the unpaid purchase money until he had conveyed the land to the purchaser or let him into possession of it, or handed over the deeds. The equitable lien, however, persists irrespective of possession, so long as any part of the purchase money remains unpaid. It does not appear to depend upon a specifically enforceable contract to purchase the legal estate. It is liable to be defeated by a bona fide purchaser for value if it is not protected, as a general equitable charge in the case of unregistered land (as a Class C(iii) general equitable charge), or by notice or caution if the land is registered if the lien arose before October 13, 2003. After October 12, 2003, the provisions of the Land Registration Act 2002 apply and an unpaid vendor's lien cannot bind the estate in question against a disponee for valuable consideration unless protected by notice in the register by the vendor prior to the completion of the disposition by registration, or by a substantive registration as a charge.[94] However, the vendor's common law lien dependant on his possession is an overriding interest if the land is registered, and thus does not require to be so protected.[95]

Purchaser's lien: A purchaser also has an equitable lien for his deposit[96] and **1–23** costs of investigating title should he lawfully rescind the contract.[97] The lien arises by operation of law. It does not depend upon a specifically enforceable contract to purchase the legal estate, and will often arise where there is no specifically enforceable agreement.[98] It operates as an equitable charge and the holder is in equity a secured creditor of the vendor and can apply to the court for a declaration of his interest and for an order of sale of the land.[99] The lien can (and should) be protected in the same manner as are unpaid vendor's liens.

---

[93] *Coptic Ltd v Bailey* [1972] Ch. 446; *Orakpo v Manson Investments Ltd* [1978] A.C. 95; but see *Bank of Ireland Finance Ltd v DJ Daley Ltd* [1978] I.R. 83.

[94] LRA 2002 ss.29(1), (2), 48, and 123.

[95] ibid., Sch.3, para.2.

[96] *Whitbread & Co v Watt* [1902] 1 Ch. 835; but cf. *Combe v Swaythling* [1947] Ch. 625 (no lien where deposit paid to stakeholder).

[97] *Kitton v Hewett* (1904) W.N. 21; *Re Furneaux & Aird's Contract* (1906) W.N. 215; where the contract goes off because the vendor's title is defective, the lien extends to costs of proceedings to enforce specific performance, or of a vendor and purchaser summons.

[98] *Chattey v Farndale Holdings Inc* [1998] 75 P. & C.R. 298, at 305–307.

[99] *Lyus v Prowsa Developments Ltd* [1982] 1 W.L.R. 1044, at 1046–1047; *Chattey v Farndale Holdings Inc* [1998] 75 P. & C.R. 298, 318.

However, if the purchase goes off through the purchaser's fault, the lien is lost.[100]

1-24   *Statutory Lien:*   Statutory liens are conferred by specific statutes, such as airports,[101] and solicitors.[102]

1-25   **Equitable charge**[103]**:**   An equitable charge arises where specified property is appropriated to the discharge of an obligation without possession or any right of ownership being transferred to the charge.[104] In many ways an equitable chargee is in the same position as the holder of an equitable lien. He is in the position of a secured creditor.[105] His interest is liable to be defeated if it is not protected in the appropriate manner. Since he has no title, he cannot foreclose or go into possession.[106] Judicial and academic indifference to strictness of terminology has led to the two terms being treated as largely interchangeable,[107] and the most obvious distinction between them is that a lien arises by operation of law and a charge by act of parties. This makes little, if any, difference to the remedies available.[108] The distinction remains of considerable importance, however, when considering the registration provisions under the Companies Act 2006.[109]

There remains a fundamental difference between an equitable charge and an equitable mortgage, even if the distinction between a legal mortgage and legal charge has been largely assimilated. In equity, the distinction stems from the fact that a mortgagee acquires a legal or equitable title to the land in question; a chargee does not.[110] This gives rise to a difference in remedies available to the equitable mortgagee, on the one hand, and the equitable chargee, on the other.[111] Even so, more dicta have continued to blur the differences between the two.[112]

1-26   *Creation:*   An equitable charge may be created by making real or personal property expressly or constructively liable or specifically appropriated to discharge a debt or other obligation. It must be a present[113] charge of specific property, which may be in the chargor's possession or which may be to come into

---

[100] *Dinn v Grant* (1852) 5 De G. & Sm. 451.

[101] Civil Aviation Act 1982 s.88.

[102] Solicitors Act 1974 s.73.

[103] See also Ch.14.

[104] For judicial consideration of "mortgage" and equitable charge, see *London County & Westminster Bank Ltd v Tompkins* [1918] 1 K.B. 515 (CA).

[105] *National Provincial and Union Bank of England v Charnley* [1924] 1 K.B. 431, 445–446.

[106] *Tennant v Trenchard* (1869) L.R. 4 Ch. 537.

[107] See Ch.14.

[108] *Goode v Burton* (1847) 1 Ex. 189; *Re Richardson, Shillito v Hobson* (1885) 30 Ch.D. 396, per Fry L.J. at 403.

[109] See Companies Act 2006 s.860; and see *Re Wallis & Simmonds (Builders) Ltd* [1974] 1 W.L.R. 391; *Trident International Ltd v Barlow* [2000] B.C.C. 602.

[110] *Re Cosslett (Contractors) Ltd* [1998] Ch. 495, 508. See also *Re Charge Card Services Ltd* [1987] Ch. 150.

[111] A charge by deed carries with it the statutory powers specified in the LPA 1925 ss.101, 205(1)(xvi).

[112] *Re Bank of Credit and Commerce International SA (No.8)* [1998] A.C. 214, 225–227.

[113] *Williams v Burlington Investments Ltd* (1977) 121 Sol. Jo. 424.

his possession from a specified source.[114] No particular form is required,[115] although regard must be had to other requirements as to formalities.[116] A charge by deed carries with it the statutory powers specified in the Law of Property Act 1925 s.101.[117] A voluntary agreement for a future charge is not enforceable[118]; one given for value will attach according to its terms.[119]

Distress[120]: This is the least effective form of real security. The creditor does **1–27** not get ownership or possession or the rights of a chargee, and the class of transaction in which it affords the creditor protection in a bankruptcy is very limited. Most commonly it is exercised by a landlord, whose power of distress entitles him to take and eventually sell chattels brought by the tenant on to the demised premises to satisfy a claim for rent. A licence to seize and sell annexed to a contract of pledge is also valid, since it is not caught by s.9 of the Bills of Sale Act 1882.[121] However, in general, a licence to seize chattels given by contract expressly to secure a debt is a bill of sale for the purposes of that Act and is void because it cannot be made in the form required.[122]

---

[114] *Metcalfe v Archbishop of York* (1836) 6 Sim. 224; (1836) 1 My. & Cr. 547 (on appeal); *Buller v Plunkett* (1860) 1 John & H 441.

[115] *Cradock v Scottish Provident* (1893) 69 L.T. 280; (1894) 70 L.T. 718 (CA).

[116] Thus, for example, an equitable charge on land or an interest therein will have to satisfy the LPA 1925 s.53.

[117] LPA 1925 s.205(1)(xvi).

[118] *Re Earl of Lucan, Hardinge v Cobden* (1890) L.R. 45 Ch.D 470.

[119] *Wellesley v Wellesley* (1839) 4 Myl. & Cr. 561.

[120] See now the Tribunals, Courts and Enforcement Act 2007 Pt 3 (and in particular s.71, and see Sch.12), repeals the existing law on distress for rent insofar as landlords of commercial premises are concerned, and introduces a new statutory regime defined as "Commercial Rent Arrears Recovery" ("CRAR"). This new statutory procedural code is outside the scope of this work.

[121] *Re Townsend* (1886) 16 Q.B.D. 532.

[122] ibid.

CHAPTER 2

DEVELOPMENT OF THE LAW OF MORTGAGE[1]

AT COMMON LAW

Origins: The practice of giving rights over land as security for debt is of great **2–01** antiquity. Until the end of the 12th century the transaction was by way of lease by the mortgagor to the mortgagee, and was either a *vivum vadium* (live pledge, "vifgage") or a *mortuum vadium* (dead pledge, "mortgage" i.e. mort (dead), gage (pledge)). This depended on whether the income from the land was, or was not, used in the discharge of the debt. In default of repayment either on the appointed day or, following an order of the court, after a reasonable time, the mortgagee took the fee simple.[2] The Roman law of mortgages went through a similar evolution to that in England. By Justinian's time the use of hypothecation was almost universal. In England a mortgage is in substance if not in form a hypothecation and the charge by way of legal mortgage is in the process of ousting the mortgage, so that the distinction between a mortgage and charge has ceased to have any significant relevance.

Such transactions were not wholly satisfactory to the mortgagee since the *seisina ut de vadio* which he acquired was not protected by law and it was also doubtful whether a term of years could be enlarged into a fee simple. Mortgages of freehold land were therefore made by conveyance of the fee simple, subject to the mortgagor's right to re-enter and determine the mortgagee's estate if the money were repaid on the named date. This was very onerous for the mortgagor, who would lose the land and yet remain liable for the debt if he did not repay it on the due date.

The usual form of the mortgage by reconveyance did not remain fixed, and by **2–02** the beginning of the 17th century had developed into something resembling the modern pre-1926 form. It consisted of a conveyance of the fee simple with a covenant to reconvey if the money was paid on the due date. Mortgages by granting leases still existed, but their main use was for the purpose of raising portions terms. The effect of the mortgage, at common law, was not changed as a result of the change in form. The mortgagor still lost his land and remained

---

[1] For fuller treatments of the subject, see Pollock and Maitland, *The History of English Law* (2nd edn, 1911), Vol.2, p.119; Holdsworth, *History of English Law*; and the preface to Turner, *Equity of Redemption* (1931).

[2] The usury laws influenced the development of the forms of mortgage as a means of securing the lending of money. Lending at a fixed rate of interest to a borrower was rendered illegal by such laws and methods were developed to avoid the restrictions—hence the concept of the mortgagor granting a lease over his property in favour of the mortgagee.

liable for the debt if he failed to pay on the due date, unless the mortgage provided otherwise. An alternative form was a conveyance subject to a condition that the conveyance would be avoided if the debt was repaid on the due date.

2–03   The evolution of the creditor's rights: The important substantive, as distinct from formal, development was that the proprietary right of the creditor arose, not by virtue of a lease and the operation of a condition precedent, but by virtue of a grant and the operation of a condition subsequent. Although the mortgagee still went into possession under the latter form, his protection was no longer based on that possession but on the title derived from the grant. The form underwent an apparently minor alteration in that the reconveyance was no longer, in general, made on condition that the mortgagor was entitled to re-enter on discharging the debt, but, rather, subject to a proviso[3] that the mortgagee would reconvey the fee simple if the debt was paid on the due date. The advantage of this form was that proof of title depended on the reconveyance rather than on the date of payment of the money.

The pre-1926 position

2–04   Freeholds: Thus the modern pre-1926 form of mortgage was by way of conveyance of the fee simple to the mortgagee, defeasible by a condition subsequent on a date fixed by the parties. The mortgagee enjoyed the following advantages:

      (1) absolute priority, in the absence of fraud, misrepresentation or gross negligence, over all later encumbrances by virtue of his legal title which gave him a right in rem;

      (2) the right to custody of the title deeds;

      (3) the power to convey the legal estate to a purchaser, in exercising his express or statutory power of sale, without applying to the court;

      (4) the right to protect his security by going into possession;

      (5) the right to apply to the court for a decree of foreclosure which, if granted, would destroy the mortgagor's equity of redemption and immediately vest the fee simple in him.

2–05   Leaseholds: Similarly, leaseholds could be mortgaged by way of assignment of the term with a covenant to reassign. This, however, was not a popular form of mortgage because it created privity of estate between the landlord and the mortgagee.[4] The mortgagee thus became liable on all such covenants in the lease as ran with the land, including the obligation to pay rent. Consequently, the alternative method, whereby the mortgagor granted a sub-lease, one day shorter than the lease, with a proviso for cesser on redemption, was generally adopted. This became one of the two methods for the mortgage of leaseholds permitted by

---

[3] As a result of *Cromwel's Case* (1601) 2 Co Rep. 69(b) which decided that "proviso" makes a condition, the proviso for reconveyance subjected the mortgagee's estate to a condition subsequent.

[4] Under the doctrine in *Spencer's Case* (1583) 5 Co Rep. 16.

the 1925 legislation. As a sub-tenant, the mortgagee would not be in privity of estate with the landlord and would not be liable on the covenants in the lease.[5]

This method of creating mortgages of leaseholds, however, led to two difficul- **2–06** ties, both of which arose from the retention of a nominal reversion by the mortgagor. The mortgagee was not entitled to custody of the title deeds, nor could he, on exercising his power of sale, vest the whole of the mortgagor's lease in the purchaser. These were overcome by providing, in the mortgage deed, that the mortgagor declared himself a trustee of the nominal reversion for the mortgagee. Usually there was a clause permitting the mortgagee to appoint new trustees in place of the mortgagor. In this way the mortgagor could be compelled to assign his reversion to a purchaser, without the need for the court to order an assignment. The mortgagee, therefore, had effective control of the nominal reversion.[6]

THE INFLUENCE OF EQUITY

The development of the law of mortgages was also affected by the laws relating **2–07** to loans made at interest. Originally, as stated above,[7] loans at interest were illegal. However, from the 16th century onwards, maximum rates were fixed by the Usury Acts, with the result that the Court of Chancery took the view that a mortgage should be a security only.[8] It would no longer permit the mortgagee to profit from the fee simple, and would confine his benefit to the interest permitted by statute. Occupation, likewise, would yield no advantage to the mortgagee (except in the case of the now obsolete Welsh mortgage[9]) since he would be liable to the mortgagor for a full rent should he go into possession. Thus arose the modern type of mortgage under which the mortgagor remains in possession of the land and the conveyance of the fee simple is by way of security only.

The courts of equity, which had for many years relieved the mortgagor against forfeiture in special cases, at length established the rule that the mortgagor must be permitted to redeem his fee simple even though he did not pay on the due date.[10] The mortgagee had vested in him, as soon as the mortgage was made, an equitable interest whose measure was the difference between the value of the land and the amount of the debt, and one which he could enforce against anyone except a bona fide purchaser for value from the mortgagor without notice.

In addition to the contractual right to redeem at common law, which would rarely be exercised, the mortgagor obtained an equitable right to redeem which could not be exercised until the contractual date for redemption was past.[11] This

---

[5] *Bonner v Tottenham and Edmonton Permanent Investment Building Society* [1899] 1 Q.B. 161.

[6] *London and County Bank v Goddard* [1897] 1 Ch. 642.

[7] See fn.2, above.

[8] *Thornborough v Baker* (1675) 3 Swans. 628; (1676) 1 Ch Ca. 283.

[9] Coote, *Mortgages*, Ch.III.

[10] *Emanuel College, Cambridge v Evans* (1625) 1 Rep Ch. 18.

[11] *Brown v Cole* (1845) 14 Sim. 427.

right could be exercised only if the courts of equity thought it proper. Inequitable conduct on the part of the mortgagor would bar his right to redeem.

The equity of redemption

2-08   The equity of redemption is an interest which the mortgagor can convey, devise, entail, lease, mortgage or settle.[12] If the mortgagor dies intestate it will devolve subject to the intestacy rules.[13] It has been held that the equity of redemption in leasehold premises subject to a mortgage can pass to the Crown as bona vacantia where the mortgagor company has been dissolved.[14]

Prior to 1926, second and subsequent mortgages of freeholds would usually have been mortgages of the equity of redemption, since the legal fee simple would normally have been held by the first mortgagee. Until the enactment of the Conveyancing Act 1881, this led to the inconvenient situation whereby, on the mortgagee's death, the realty, that is, the legal estate, devolved on his devisee or heir who held it on trust for the persons entitled to the mortgage money, while the right to the money lent, being personalty, passed to the mortgagee's personal representatives. This complication was one of the factors which kept the mortgage by lease in being during the late 19th century.

As with subsequent mortgages of freeholds by conveyance, so subsequent mortgages of leaseholds by assignment were normally dealings with the equity of redemption. Subsequent mortgages of leaseholds made by sub-lease, however, did not involve any such dealing. Instead, further sub-leases were granted, each longer, usually by one day, than the sub-lease immediately before. Such mortgages, unlike subsequent mortgages by assignment, were legal, not equitable.

Destruction of the equity of redemption

2-09   Since an unfettered right to redeem would have nullified the intended effect of the mortgage transaction, that is, to enable the mortgagee to recover his capital, it was necessary to limit that right. The courts achieved this by a decree of forfeiture,[15] for which the mortgagee had to apply. The effect of such a decree was to destroy the equity of redemption,[16] including, of course, the right to redeem. The court, however, guarded against oppressive foreclosures by ordering a sale when the property was much more valuable than the debt, and the mortgagee then received only the balance due to him.[17]

---

[12] *Pawlett v Att.-Gen.* (1667) Hard. 465 at 469; *Fawcett v Lowther* (1751) 2 Ves Sen. 300.
[13] Administration of Estates Act 1925 ss.1, 3(1).
[14] *Re Wells* [1933] Ch. 29.
[15] *How v Vigures* (1628) 1 Rep Ch. 32.
[16] Subject to rights to reopen the foreclosure; see *Thornhill v Manning* (1851) 1 Sim.(N.S.) 451; *Coombe v Stewart* (1851) 13 Beav. 111 and *Lancashire & Yorkshire Reversionary Interest Co v Crowe* (1970) 114 S.J. 435.
[17] *Rhymney Valley District Council v Pontygwindy Housing Association Ltd* (1976) 73 L.S. Gaz. 405.

The equity of redemption is likewise destroyed if the mortgagee, acting under his statutory power, makes a binding contract of sale of the mortgaged property,[18] and the exercise of an express power of sale has the same effect.

While the equity of redemption cannot be defeated by a stipulation in the mortgage that it will be extinguished if the debt is not paid by a specified date, it is open to the mortgagor to agree to release his equity of redemption by means of a separate and independent transaction subsequent to the mortgage.[19] Transactions have, however, been set aside as clogging the equity of redemption where such a provision was part of the mortgage deed or contemporaneous with it.[20]

Finally, the mortgagor is barred from bringing an action to redeem any mortgaged land of which the mortgagee has been in possession for 12 years,[21] unless during that period the mortgagee in possession either receives a payment of principal or interest, or signs an acknowledgment of the mortgagor's title. An acknowledgment signed after the lapse of the 12-year period is of no effect if no payment has been received during that time.

Law of Property Act 1925: The Modern Position[22]

Transitional provisions[23]

The 1925 legislation abolished two forms of mortgage: it was no longer possible **2–10** to create legal mortgages of freeholds by conveyance of the fee simple, or legal mortgages of leaseholds by assignment.

The transitional provisions which are contained in the Law of Property Act 1925 Sch.1, Pts VII and VIII, include saving clauses which state that the subsisting rights of the parties are not to be affected by changes in mortgage forms.[24] In particular they expressly prescribe that a mortgagee of a legal estate made before January 1, 1926, and not protected by a deposit of title deeds or by registration of a land charge should not obtain any benefit by reason of its conversion into a legal mortgage, against a bona fide purchaser without notice, but was to retain, as against him, the status of an equitable interest.[25] It was therefore advisable to register pre-1926 mortgages which were not protected by a deposit of title deeds.

---

[18] *Waring v London and Manchester Assurance Co* [1935] Ch. 310; *Property and Bloodstock Ltd v Emerton* [1968] Ch. 94; *Duke v Robson* [1973] 1 W.L.R. 267; and see para.26–62.

[19] *Reeve v Lisle* [1902] A.C. 461 and see para.30–11.

[20] *Fairclough v Swan Brewery Co Ltd* [1912] A.C. 562.

[21] In relation to land adversely occupied prior to October 13, 2003, or, since that date, unregistered land: Limitation Act 1980 ss.16, 17. Different principles apply to registered land after October 12, 2003: Land Registration Act 2002 s.96. See below, para.6–31.

[22] This is set out in more detail in Ch.12.

[23] These transitional provisions relating to freehold and leasehold mortgages in existence on January 1, 1926, are now of historical interest only as there can be few, if any, remaining mortgages that have not now been redeemed.

[24] Law of Property Act 1925 s.39 provides for the effecting of the transition from the law prior to the commencement of the Law of Property Act 1922, to the law enacted by that Act (as amended), by means of the provisions in Sch.1.

[25] ibid., Sch.1, Pt VII, para.6 does not apply to mortgages or charges registered or protected under the Land Registration Act 1925.

2–11 **Freeholds:**   The effect of the provisions of Pt VII on pre-1926 legal mortgages of freeholds was that:

(1) A first mortgage became a lease for 3,000 years without impeachment of waste, but subject to a provision for cesser on redemption corresponding to the right of redemption subsisting on January 1, 1926.[26]

(2) Second and subsequent mortgages were similarly converted into leases for one, two or more days longer than the term vested in the first mortgagee.[27]

(3) The legal fee simple was vested in the mortgagor or in the tenant for life, statutory owner, trustee for sale, personal representative or other person of full age who, if all money owing on the security of the mortgage or mortgages had been discharged on January 1, 1926, would have been entitled to have the fee simple conveyed to him.[28]

(4) A sub-mortgage was converted into a lease for a term less by one day than the mortgage from which it was derived.[29]

2–12 **Leaseholds:**   The corresponding provisions in respect of leaseholds are contained in Pt VIII of Sch.1 and affect pre-1926 mortgages as follows:

(1) A first mortgage by assignment of a lease was converted into a sublease for a term of ten days less than the principal lease subject to a provision for cesser corresponding to the existing right of redemption.[30]

(2) Second and subsequent mortgages were similarly converted into subleases for terms at least one day less than the principal lease.[31]

(3) The provision as to the vesting of the principal lease corresponds to that for vesting of the legal fee simple, the person in whom it is to be vested being the person who would have been entitled to have the term assigned or surrendered to him.[32]

(4) A sub-mortgage was converted into a lease for a term less by one day than that of the mortgage from which it was derived.[33]

(5) The provisions of the Law of Property Act 1922 Sch.15 paras 2 and 5 (which converted perpetually renewable leases to terms of 200 years) and the Law of Property Act 1925 s.149(6) (which converted leases for lives or marriages into terms of 90 years determinable after the death or marriage of the original lessee) apply to mortgage terms, with certain variations provided by the Law of Property Act 1925 Sch.1, Pt VIII, s.6.

---

[26] ibid., para.1.
[27] ibid., para.2.
[28] ibid., 1925 Sch.1, Pt VII, para.3.
[29] ibid., para.4.
[30] ibid., Pt VIII, para.1.
[31] ibid., para.2.
[32] ibid., para.3.
[33] ibid., para.4.

Legal mortgages

Freeholds: Under the 1925 legislation legal mortgages of freeholds may now   **2–13**
be created only by[34]:

(1) a demise for a term of years absolute, subject to a provision for cesser
on redemption; or
(2) a charge by deed expressed to be by way of legal mortgage.

As a consequence, legal mortgages can only be vested by deed. In relation to
registered land, mortgages by demise or sub-demise (i.e. (1) above) have been
incapable of creation after October 12, 2003.[35]

Demise for a term of years absolute: By the first method, a long term,   **2–14**
generally 3,000 years, is granted. The provision for cesser is that the term shall
cease when the loan is repaid, but since on repayment the term becomes a
satisfied term and ceases automatically, the provision is superfluous.[36]

Although the mortgagor now retains the legal estate, and is thus owner of the
property both at law and in equity, the mortgagee does not suffer any disadvantage. Save in relation to registered land after October 12, 2003,[37] the
mortgagor can create successive legal mortgages by granting a series of leases
each one day longer than the preceding lease.[38] The substantial rights of the
mortgagees will be their interests in the equity of redemption, not their nominal
rights as reversioners.

Unlike a mortgagee by reconveyance, a mortgagee by demise before 1926 had   **2–15**
no right to the title deeds, a fact which made mortgages by lease unpopular.
However, the 1925 legislation provides expressly that a mortgagee by demise
should have the same right to the title deeds as if he had the fee simple.[39] Even
so, mortgages by demise or sub-demise were considered to be absolute prior to
the enactment of the Land Registration Act 2002.[40]

A purported conveyance of the fee simple by way of first mortgage now
operates as a demise for 3,000 years without impeachment for waste, subject to
cesser on redemption.[41] Each subsequent mortgage takes effect as a similar term
one day longer than that granted to the immediately prior mortgagee.[42]

Charge by way of legal mortgage: The second method does *not* create a term   **2–16**
in the mortgagee, but he is given the same powers, protection and remedies as if

---

[34] ibid., s.85(1).

[35] Land Registration Act 2002 ss.23(1), 126 and Sch.10, Pt 1, paras 2 and 133 and Sch.11
para.2(1)(b), amending Law of Property Act 1925 s.85(3). See Ch.13.

[36] See *Knightsbridge Estates Trust v Byrne* [1939] Ch. 441, 461; affirmed [1940] A.C. 613.

[37] See fn.35, above.

[38] A second legal mortgage for a term of the same length as, or shorter than, the first is still valid
since it is binding on the lessor by estoppel. *Neale v Mackenzie* (1836) 1 M. & W. 747.

[39] Law of Property Act 1925 s.85(1).

[40] *Land Registration for the Twenty-First Century—A Conveyancing Revolution* (2001), Law Com.
No.271, para.4.7.

[41] ibid., s.85(2)(a). Save in relation to registered land after October 12, 2003.

[42] ibid., s.85(2)(b). As to registered land, see fn.41, above.

he had a term of 3,000 years without impeachment for waste. In order to have effect at law, the charge must be by deed and be expressed to be by way of legal mortgage,[43] although it is not necessary to use the phrase as one complete expression, and perhaps in the case of unregistered land, not at all.[44] Indeed, after October 12, 2003, all charges created by means of a registrable disposition take effect upon registration as charges by deed by way of legal mortgage.[45] Thus, the distinction between a legal mortgage and a charge has therefore ceased to have any real relevance. Although the chargee does not in fact have a legal term of years vested in him in the charged property, the effect is that he is as fully protected as if he had such.[46] The chargee is therefore empowered to create tenancies and enforce covenants.[47] The legal charge is in effect a mortgage and the terminology is somewhat of a misnomer and confusing. The legal charge is generally considered to be more readily intelligible than the ordinary form of mortgage,[48] which has in the past attracted much academic and judicial criticism.[49] It also provides a convenient method of mortgaging freeholds and leaseholds together.

2–17   Since the charge creates no sub-lease in favour of the mortgagee, it is generally considered that it does not amount to a breach of covenant against sub-letting.[50] However, if, as is usual, the covenant also prohibits parting with possession, there will be a breach if the mortgagee enforces his right to possession.

2–18   **Leaseholds:**   Mortgages of leaseholds can be created only in two ways[51]:

    (1) by sub-demise for a term of years absolute subject to cesser on redemption, the term being at least one day shorter than that vested in the mortgagor;

    (2) by charge by deed expressed to be by way of legal mortgage.

After October 12, 2003, the prohibition contained in the Land Registration Act 2002 concerning the creation of mortgages by demise or sub-demise applies in relation to registered land.[52]

---

[43] ibid., s.87(1).

[44] *Cityland and Property (Holdings) Ltd v Dabrah* [1968] Ch. 166, 168, 171. In any event not in the case of registered land: ibid.

[45] Land Registration Act 2002 s.51.

[46] See *Grand Junction Co Ltd v Bates* [1954] 2 Q.B. 160; *Weg Motors v Hales* [1962] Ch. 49, 74; *Cumberland Court (Brighton) Ltd v Taylor* [1964] Ch.29.

[47] See *Regent Oil Co Ltd v JA Gregory (Hatch End)* [1966] Ch. 402.

[48] Law of Property Act 1925 Sch.4 provides statutory forms of mortgage and transfer, but they are not commonly used nowadays.

[49] *Samuel v Jarrah Timber and Wood Paving Corp* [1904] A.C. 323, per Lord Macnaghten at 326; *Salt v Marquess of Northampton* [1892] A.C. 1, per Lord Bramwell at 18; Maitland, *Equity* (2nd edn, 1949), p.182.

[50] *Gentle v Faulkner* [1900] 2 Q.B. 267; *Grand Junction Co Ltd v Bates* [1954] 2 Q.B. 160. If a licence is required by the lease, it shall not unreasonably be withheld; LPA 1925 s.86(1). Similarly, a covenant against assignment is not hindered by the mention of a legal charge. However, normally there is inserted into the lease a covenant against charging.

[51] ibid., s.86(1).

[52] See paras 3–03 et seq.

Sub-demise for a term of years absolute: Because the sub-term is shorter **2–19** than the original term, the mortgage will not operate as an assignment, and mortgages of leaseholds by assignment are not permitted by the 1925 legislation. It is, in fact, usual to make the sub-term ten days shorter than the original term, so that subsequent mortgages can be accommodated.[53] However, the rule has been preserved that a subsequent lease can take effect in reversion on a lease of the same or greater length.[54] Consequently, all the subsequent mortgages could be secured by terms of the same length and would take effect according to whatever rules determine their respective priorities.

A post-1925 purported mortgage by assignment of a lease takes effect as a sub-demise for a term of years absolute subject to cesser on redemption. A first or only mortgagee takes a sub-term 10 days shorter than the original term and each subsequent mortgage takes a term one day longer than the immediately prior mortgage term, if this is possible.[55] The sub-term must, however, always be at least one day shorter than the original term.

Clearly, the foregoing has no application to registered land after October 12, 2003.[56]

Charge by way of legal mortgage: The position with regard to leaseholds is **2–20** identical to that of freeholds in that the chargee is not in fact granted a term of years. He is similarly protected as the chargee of a freehold interest and is given the same rights and remedies as if he had a sub-term one day shorter than the term vested in the mortgagor.[57] Charges created after October 12, 2003, over registered land by means of a registrable disposition have effect as if by deed by way of legal mortgage.[58]

Equitable Mortgages

For the position as to equitable mortgages of equitable and legal interests, see Ch.15.

---

[53] Although they can all be of the same length; *Neale v Mackenzie* (1836) 1 M. & W. 747.
[54] Law of Property 1925 s.149(5); enacting the common law rule in *Re Moore & Hulm's Contract* [1912] Ch. 105.
[55] ibid., s.86(2).
[56] Land Registration Act 2002 s.23.
[57] ibid., s.87(1).
[58] Land Registration Act 2002 s.51.

CHAPTER 3

CREATION OF MORTGAGES

CREATION

Prior to October 13, 2003

Under the Law of Property Act 1925 freeholds could no longer be mortgaged by **3–01** the conveyance of the fee simple. In relation to unregistered land, s.85(1) of that Act provided that a freehold estate was only capable of being mortgaged by either a demise of a term of years absolute subject to a provision for cesser on redemption or by a charge by deed expressed to be by way of legal mortgage.[1] Sections 85(3) and 86(3) of that Act applied the provisions of that Act as regards the creation of mortgages over land registered under the Land Registration Act 1925. Section 205(1)(xxii) of the Law of Property Act 1925, states that "registered land" had the same meaning as in the Land Registration Act 1925: that is, land or any estate in land the title to which is registered under the Land Registration Act 1925 (as amended). "Registered land" included any easement, privilege, right or benefit appendant or appurtenant to it.[2] A "registered charge" included a mortgage or encumbrance registered as a charge under the Land Registration Act 1925.[3]

There were two ways in which a mortgage of registered land could have been created, namely, the registered charge and the unregistered mortgage (i.e. a mortgage of land as if it were not registered).[4] These two methods can still be utilised in respect of unregistered land and were used as to registered title until the enactment of the Land Registration Act 2002.

Post October 12, 2003

By virtue of s.23 of the Land Registration Act 2002 in principle there are two **3–02** methods for creating a mortgage, namely, under subss.(1)(a) and (1)(b). The owner's powers in relation to a registered estate, whether freehold or leasehold,

---

[1] See Ch.2, paras 2–13 ff. Leaseholds similarly could only be mortgaged by a sub-demise or a charge expressed to be by way of legal mortgage: s.86(1).
[2] Land Registration Act 1925 s.3(xxiv).
[3] ibid., s.3(xxiii).
[4] Formerly there was a third, that is a mortgage created by deposit of the title deeds. This has now become obsolete, see para.4.25.

enable the owner (as previously) to execute a charge by deed by way of legal mortgage, or by charging the estate with the payment of money.[5] The effect is identical, as on completion of registration the charge takes effect as a charge by deed by way of legal mortgage "if it would not otherwise do so".[6] It is therefore now impossible to create a legal charge of a registered estate other than by the execution of a charge. Once created in this manner and completed by registration the legal charge gains the protection of the rules relating to priority.[7]

CHARGE BY WAY OF LEGAL MORTGAGE[8]

3–03   The legal charge has considerable advantages over the alternative method of creation of a legal mortgage by a sub-demise for a term of years absolute (which still remains available for unregistered land). It merely states that the property has been charged with a debt by way of legal mortgage and there is no conveyance of any estate to the mortgagee. To be effective at law the statutory legal charge must comply with the following requirements:

(1) be made by deed;

(2) be expressed to be by way of legal mortgage, and the deed must contain a statement that the charge is made by way of legal mortgage; and

(3) in relation to a registered estate, be completed by registration in accordance with the provisions of Sch.2 to the Land Registration Act 2002.

The effect of such a charge of freeholds is that the chargee obtains the same protection, powers and remedies as if he had a term of 3000 years without impeachment of waste.[9] It provides an easy way to mortgage freeholds and leaseholds together, and also the grant of a legal charge on a lease probably does not amount to a breach of any covenant in that lease against sub-letting for the reason that a charge creates no actual sub-lease in favour of the mortgagee. Instead it gives him the same rights as if he had a sub-lease.[10] The mortgage by demise effectively became otiose well before the enactment of the provisions of the Land Registration Act 2002.[11]

---

[5] It is now impossible to create a mortgage by demise or sub-demise, Land Registration Act 2002 s.23(1)(a). See Ch.13.

[6] ibid., s.51.

[7] ibid., ss.28, 29.

[8] See further para.12–30.

[9] Law of Property Act 1925 s.87(1).

[10] Quaere if the covenant in the lease also prohibits the tenant from parting with possession of the property, then a breach of covenant will arise if the mortgagee enforces his right to possession.

[11] *Transfer of Land—Land Mortgages* (1991) Law Com. No.204, para.2–13 and *Land Registration for the Twenty-first Century—A Conveyancing Revolution* (2001) Law Com. No.271, para.4–7.

Registered Land[12]

The Form of Mortgage

Prior to October 13, 2003

Subject to any entry to the contrary being entered on the register, the proprietor **3–04** of any registered land could mortgage by deed or otherwise the land or any part of it in any manner which would have been permissible if the land had not been registered, and (subject to the considerations set out below) to like effect.[13] While unregistered, such a mortgage only took effect in equity as a minor interest and was capable of being overridden by a registered disposition for valuable consideration unless duly protected by entry on the register by a notice or caution against dealings.[14]

Equitable mortgage or charge[15]:   An equitable charge could also be created **3–05** over registered land similar to a general equitable charge in the case of unregistered land. Such a charge took effect as a minor interest and could be protected by entry of a notice or caution against dealings.[16] Until September 27, 1989, a good security in equity could have been created by the deposit of title deeds of the freehold or leasehold interest. After September 26, 1989, an equitable mortgage of, or charge on land or any interest in land can only be made in writing.[17]

Liens[18]:   Section 66 of the Land Registration Act 1925 provided an alternative **3–06** method of creating a security in registered land. Prior to April 3, 1995, it was a common method of securing a loan by creating a lien by deposit of the land certificate with the mortgagee. The section provided as follows:

> "The proprietor of any registered land or charge may, subject to the overriding interests, if any, to any entry to the contrary on the register, and to any estates, interests, charges, or rights registered or protected on the register at the date of the deposit, create a lien on the registered land or charge by deposit of the land certificate or charge certificate; and such lien shall, subject as aforesaid, be equivalent to a lien created in the case of unregistered land by the deposit of documents of title or of the mortgage deed by an owner entitled for his own benefit to the registered estate, or a mortgagee beneficially entitled to the mortgage, as the case may be."

Rules 239 and 240 of the Land Registration Rules 1925 formerly provided two methods of creating a mortgage by deposit of the land certificate. Rule 239 provided a formal method by which a notice of deposit could be entered on the

---

[12] For registered charges, see below para.13–10.

[13] Land Registration Act 1925 s.106(1), (4), as substituted by the Administration of Justice Act 1977 s.26(1).

[14] Land Registration Act 1925 s.106(2), as substituted by the Administration of Justice Act 1977 s.26(1) and see para.3–16.

[15] For equitable mortgages and charges, see further Ch.14, below.

[16] Land Registration Act 1925 ss.49(1)(c), 59(2).

[17] Law of Property (Miscellaneous Provisions) Act 1989 s.2

[18] See also para.11–49.

register[19] or a notice or caution could be registered.[20] Similarly an applicant for registration as proprietor of land or of a charge could create a lien on it equivalent to that created by deposit of a certificate whether the land or charge was already registered or not. Rule 240 set out the procedure for creating a mortgage by way of written notice of intended deposit of the land certificate when issued. The notice did not have to be in any specified form, but r.241 provided that certain particulars had to be given. Rule 242(1) provided that both operated as cautions against dealings under s.54 of the Land Registration Act 1925.

3–07   Resultant upon changes in the law following the enactment of the Law of Property (Miscellaneous Provisions) Act 1989 s.2,[21] and also changes introduced into the Land Registration Rules 1925,[22] the efficacy of liens created or notices of deposit entered then had to be considered against the background of three distinct periods. These were (1) prior to September 27, 1989[23]; (2) between September 27, 1989 and April 2, 1995; (3) post April 2, 1995.

3–08   As to the first period, it was possible to create liens by deposit of the land certificate or charge certificate. Such a lien was a contract to create a charge protected by a notice of deposit.[24] As to the second period, a deposit made in such a manner was valid only if there was compliance with the formal requirements of s.2 of the Law of Property (Miscellaneous Provisions) Act 1989.[25] Thus, a notice relating to an equitable mortgage created after September 27, 1989, which is not in writing would be cancelled.[26] If there was such compliance, a notice of deposit or intended deposit could be entered. As regards the third period, it was no longer possible to protect a lien by notice of deposit or intended deposit. Assuming compliance with s.2 of the 1989 Act, the lien could only then be protected by a notice which should have been registered by the equitable mortgagee or chargee in the Charges Register of the title. The mortgagee would have only been able to exercise his power of sale once the charge had been registered as a legal charge.

Post October 12, 2003

3–09   As a result of the revocation of s.66 of the Land Registration Act 1925 and its associated rules, to which reference has been made, it is no longer possible to register a notice of deposit or intended deposit. A proprietor of a registered estate,

---

[19] Land Registration Rules 1925 r.239.
[20] *Re White Rose Cottage* [1965] Ch. 240.
[21] See para.3–08.
[22] By the Land Registration Rules 1925 r.4(1), 4(4), SI 1995/140. These revoked rr.240 to 243, and substituted a new r.240. These changes were brought about as a result of the decision in *United Bank of Kuwait v Sahib* [1997] Ch. 107.
[23] This was the date when Law of Property (Miscellaneous Provisions) Act 1989 s.2 came into force.
[24] *Birch v Ellames* (1794) 2 Anst. 427 at 431; *Carter v Wake* (1877) 4 Ch.D. 605 at 606; *Re Wallis & Simmonds (Builders) Ltd* [1974] 1 W.L.R. 391 at 395; *Swiss Bank Corporation v Lloyds Bank Ltd* [1982] A.C. 584 at 594–595; *Thames Guaranty v Campbell* [1985] Q.B. 210 at 232, 233; *Re Alton Corporation* [1985] B.C.L.C. 27 at 33.
[25] See *United Bank of Kuwait v Sahib* [1997] Ch. 107.
[26] See *United Bank of Kuwait v Sahib* [1997] Ch. 107.

however, is still able to create an equitable security over registered land in any manner permitted by the general law.[27] An equitable charge so created should be protected by entering a notice on the register in order to protect its priority against subsequent registered dispositions.[28] Until it is registered, a mortgage or charge of registered land does not operate at law until the relevant registration requirements are met, as set out in Sch.2 to the Land Registration Act 2002. Thus, until registration it takes effect in equity only and is capable of being overridden by registration of a registrable disposition for valuable consideration unless protected in the register. Transitional provisions under the Land Registration Act 2002 make provision for the preservation of the effect of notices entered before October 13, 2003, under the provision contained in s.49(1) of the Land Registration Act 1925 (now repealed).[29]

Effect of registration of charge: Once registered, the charge will take effect **3–10** as a charge by deed by way of legal mortgage.[30] By virtue of the provisions of s.29(1) of the Land Registration Act 2002 priority will be conferred upon the registered proprietor under a registered disposition for valuable consideration over any interest affecting the estate immediately before the disposition whose priority is not protected at the time of registration.[31] The priority of any interest, however, created prior to that registered charge is protected if:

(1) it is a registered charge or the subject of a notice in the register,
(2) it is an overriding interest falling within the provisions of Sch.3 to the Land Registration Act 2002, or
(3) it appears from the register to be excepted from the effect of registration.[32]

In the case of a disposition of a leasehold estate, the priority of an interest is protected if the burden of the interest is incident to the estate.

In the case of charges, if a registrable disposition of a registered charge is made for valuable consideration, completion of the disposition by registration has the effect of postponing to the interest under the disposition any interest affecting the charge immediately before the disposition whose priority is not protected at the time of registration.[33] The priority of an interest is protected in a similar manner to that set out above.[34]

In essence, the position is the same as that under the Land Registration Act 1925 and it means that the proposed chargee must be careful to obtain an official search of the register with priority in the usual way and to take account of any overriding interest which might take priority over its security. It also means that it is necessary to ensure that the charge is properly registered within the priority

---

[27] See Land Registration Act 2002 s.23(1)(a).
[28] ibid., ss.28, 29(1), (2), 30 and 32.
[29] See Land Registration Act 2002 s.134, Sch.12 para.2; and see s.34(1).
[30] See Land Registration Act 2002, s.51, and see further para.13–02.
[31] ibid., s.29(1).
[32] ibid., s.29(2)(a)(i), (ii) and (iii).
[33] ibid., s.30(1).
[34] ibid., s.30(2).

period guaranteed by the official search. It is to be noted that the Land Registration Act 2002 does not change the position under the general law that a beneficial interest existing behind a trust of land may be overreached by the payment of mortgage moneys to not less than two trustees of the land or to a trust corporation, thereby securing priority for the charge.

3–11   Equitable charges on land[35]**:**   An instrument which creates an equitable charge and contains an agreement to create a legal mortgage, but is ineffective in its compliance with the formalities for a legal mortgage, will still create a valid equitable charge.[36] A distinction should, however, be drawn between equitable charges and equitable mortgages. The distinction is still of importance insofar as the remedies available to the equitable mortgagee are more extensive than those available to the equitable chargee. An equitable charge of the legal estate is capable of being the subject of an entry in the register; being the entry of a notice and (if appropriate) a restriction. An equitable charge of an equitable share (being an interest under a trust of land) cannot be protected by entry of a notice and only a restriction in standard Form A may be applied for (as it is not a charging order, to which the exception in r.93(k) of the Land Registration Rules 2003 applies), if such a restriction does not already appear in the register.

3–12   Liens: There is no provision contained in the Land Registration Act 2002 for a lien to arise by deposit of the land certificate. Section 66 of the Land Registration Act 1925 was repealed and not replaced.[37]

IMPLIED COVENANTS

Prior to October 13, 2003

3–13   Where a registered charge was created on any land s.28(1) of the Land Registration Act 1925 provided that two covenants were implied on the part of the chargor at the time of creation of the charge, unless there was an entry on the register negativing such implication.

They were:

(a)   a covenant with the proprietor for the time being of the charge to pay the principal sum charged, and interest, if any, thereon, at the appointed time and rate; and

(b)   covenant, if the principal sum or any part thereof is unpaid at the appointed time, to pay interest half-yearly at the appointed rate as well

---

[35] See further Ch.14.

[36] See *Walsh v Lonsdale* (1882) L.R. 21 Ch.D. 9 which interprets the transaction as a valid equitable mortgage of the legal estate. N.B. for this to occur there would have to be compliance with the provisions of the Law of Property (Miscellaneous Provisions) Act 1989 s.2.

[37] Any deposit registered before April 3, 1995, and still subsisting continues to operate as a caution against dealings, see Land Registration Act 2002 Sch.12 para.3.

after as before any judgment is obtained in respect of the charge on so much of the principal sum as for the time being remains unpaid.

An additional implied covenant was provided, in the case of leasehold land, by s.28(2) of the Land Registration Act 1925. That was to pay the rent and observe the covenants and conditions contained in the lease, and to indemnify the chargee against all proceedings or claims arising out of breaches of the covenants or conditions. If the mortgagee desired to enter and perform the covenant himself, he had to stipulate for the power to do so, as s.28(2) did not confer that power on him.

The completion by registration of an instrument of charge negating or modifying the provisions of s.28 (and/or ss.29 and 34) was deemed to be a sufficient negative or contrary entry on the register.[38] It was important for trustees, fiduciary owners, and tenants for life of settled land to make such entries in order to avoid personal liability to pay the mortgage debt.

Covenants for title were also implied on the part of the chargor who was expressed to charge with full or limited title guarantee under the Law of Property (Miscellaneous Provisions) Act 1994. They could be modified or extended.[39]

Post October 12, 2003

Section 28(1) of the Land Registration Act 1925 was repealed by the provisions **3–14** of the Land Registration Act 2002 and not re-enacted.[40] The provisions of the Law of Property (Miscellaneous Provisions) Act 1994 continue to remain in force.[41]

PROTECTION OF THE MORTGAGEE

Prior to October 13, 2003

Under the Land Registration Act 1925 mortgages were capable of being created **3–15** by transactions either on or off the register. A registered charge was one the title to which had been examined by the registrar and completed by registration, and its protection derived from the entry on the charges register. Securities off the register were capable of being protected by one of the methods discussed below, but they were not entered on the charges register and no certificate was issued in respect of them.

Advances made by a mortgagee on the security of registered land should have been protected in the case of a legal charge by the completion of the substantive

---

[38] Land Registration Rules 1925 r.140. See *Fairmile Portfolio Management Ltd v Davies Arnold Cooper* [1998] 42 L.S. Gaz. R. 34.
[39] Law of Property (Miscellaneous Provisions) Act 1994 ss.1, 8(1) and see paras 12–19 et seq.
[40] For the express personal covenant to pay, see Ch.27.
[41] See para.3–13.

registration of the mortgagee as the registered proprietor of the charge.[42] A legal estate did not exist until registration of the charge.[43] A registered charge could not constitute an overriding interest as it was entered on the register itself, nor was it a minor interest as it was created by registered disposition.[44]

Subject to any entry to the contrary on the register, it had always been possible for the registered proprietor of land to mortgage the land or any part thereof in any manner which would have been permissible if the land had not been registered and with like effect. Thus, it had always been possible for the registered proprietor to make an unregistered dealing with registered land or a disposition off the register. A mortgage so created was capable of being protected by an appropriate entry in the register but until completed by registration so as to take effect as a registered disposition it would not become a registered legal charge.[45]

3–16 **Other entries in the register:** The law relating to the protection of mortgages of registered land was substantially amended by s.26 of the Administration of Justice Act 1977, which substituted a new s.106 into the Land Registration Act 1925 for that originally inserted. After August 29, 1977,[46] it was no longer possible to protect a mortgage on the register by a special form of mortgage caution.[47] This was a rarely used procedure in any event. Section 106 (as amended) provided that:

> "106.—(1) The proprietor of any registered land may, subject to any entry to the contrary on the register, mortgage, by deed or otherwise, the land or any part of it in any manner which would have been permissible if the land had not been registered and, subject to this section, with the like effect.
>
> (2) Unless and until the mortgage becomes a registered charge—
>
> (a) it shall take effect only in equity, and
> (b) it shall be capable of being overridden as a minor interest unless protected as provided by subsection (3) below.
>
> (3) A mortgage which is not a registered charge may be protected on the register by—
>
> (a) a notice under section 49 of this Act
> (b) any other such notice as may be prescribed, or
> (c) a caution under section 54 of this Act."

Thus, unless and until a mortgage became a registered charge, it took effect only in equity and was capable of being overridden as a minor interest unless it had been protected by entry on the register as provided.[48] In the case of a mortgage

---

[42] Land Registration Act 1925 s.26(1).

[43] *Grace Rymer Investments Ltd v Waite* [1958] Ch. 831; *ES Schwab & Co Ltd v McCarthy* (1975) 31 P. & C.R. 196. Land Registration Act 1925 s.106(2).

[44] Land Registration Act 1925 s.3(xvi), (xv).

[45] Land Registration Act 1925 s.106(1), (2).

[46] The date the Administration of Justice Act 1977 came into force.

[47] As from August 29, 1977, the registrar could convert any mortgage protected by mortgage caution into a registered charge.

[48] Land Registration Act 1925 s.106(2), as substituted by the Administration of Justice Act 1977 s.26(1).

which was not a registered charge, such protection included the registration of a notice or caution against dealings.[49]

Section 101(1) of the Land Registration Act 1925 dealt with the power of any **3–17** person, whether the proprietor or not, having a sufficient interest in, or power over, registered land, to dispose of it, or create interests or rights in it. By s.101(2), all such interests or rights took effect as minor interests and were capable of being overridden by registered dispositions for valuable consideration. Section 101(3) dealt with the protection of minor interests, which were expressed to take effect only in equity. This was achieved by entry in the register of such notices, cautions, inhibitions and restrictions as the 1925 Act or rules made thereunder provided.

Land and charge certificates: Section 64 of the Land Registration Act 1925 **3–18** made provision for production of certificates to the registrar and the noting of certificates. Subsection (1) provided that as long as a land certificate or charge certificate was outstanding, it had to be produced to the registrar upon registration of most dealings with the registered title. Sub-section (2) provided that a note of every such entry or transmission should be officially entered on the certificate, and gave the registrar the same powers of compelling the production of certificates as the 1925 Act gave him in respect of other documents.

Section 65 provided that the land certificate had to be deposited at the Land **3–19** Registry for as long as the registered charge existed. The charge certificate was issued to the chargee as his certificate of title.[50]

In order for the registered chargee to avoid the possibility of losing his security as a result of temporarily giving up the certificate, he was well advised to produce it to the registrar himself. Rule 244 of the Land Registration Rules 1925 provided that if, while a notice of deposit or intended deposit is on the register, the certificate was left at the Land Registry for any purpose, it was to be dealt with, notwithstanding the notice, and was to be returned to the person leaving it or as he might in writing direct.

If a notice of deposit was entered on the register under the substituted r.239 of the Land Registration Rules 1925 the mortgagee had the additional protection conferred on a cautioner by s.55(1) of the Land Registration Act 1925. He was entitled to notice of any intended disposition or entry on the register and would have had 14 days in which to appear and to apply that the caution be continued or the dealing should not be registered. The caution also entitled the mortgagee to notice of any application for a replacement certificate and thus prevented his being prejudiced by such an application based on a false representation to the effect that the original had been lost or destroyed.

Post October 12, 2003

Section 106 of the Land Registration Act 1925 (as amended) was revoked by the **3–20** Land Registration Act 2002 and the provision was not re-enacted. Further, it is

---

[49] Land Registration Act 1925 s.106(3), as substituted ibid.; see LRA 1925 s.49(1)(c) (for a notice), s.54 (for a caution).
[50] Land Registration Rules 1925 r.262.

to be noted charge certificates are no longer issued, such practice of issuing charge certificates having been abolished by the Land Registration Act 2002. Instead, the chargee receives a Title Information Document containing an official copy of the register.[51]

Further, under the Land Registration Act 2002, the grant of a legal charge is a registrable disposition required to be completed by registration. Until completed by registration, it will take effect in equity rather than at law and in consequence, if its priority is to be retained as against a registrable disposition for valuable consideration, it will need to be protected by one of the means discussed above.

Section 48 of the Land Registration Act 2002 provides that registered charges upon the same registered estate, or upon the same registered charge, rank as between themselves in the order shown in the register. Rule 101 of the Land Registration Rules 2003 states that, except as shown by an entry in the register to the contrary, the order in which registered charges are entered in the register shows the order in which the registered charges rank as between themselves. This means that where the entry in respect of a registered charge appears in the charges register before that of another registered charge, the charge shown first in the order of charges in the register ranks in priority before the other charge. This general rule does not apply where there is an entry to the contrary in the register, e.g. where:

(1) priority has been altered under r.102 of the 2003 Rules; or
(2) a statutory charge has overriding priority under s.50 of the Land Registration Act 2002.

Rule 102 provides a mechanism whereby the priority of registered charges can be altered. Application must be made in Form AP1 by or with the consent of the proprietor or person entitled to be registered as proprietor of any registered charge whose priority is adversely affected by the alteration. No such consent is required from a person who has executed the instrument which alters the priority of the charges. The registrar may accept a conveyancer's certificate that they hold any necessary consents. If the application is in order the registrar must make an entry in the register in such terms as he considers appropriate to give effect to the application.

Rule 116A provides that the registrar may, on application, make an entry in the register referring to an agreement which it is claimed relates to the priorities between a registered charge and a charge which is the subject of a notice in the register.

CHARGING ORDERS[52]

3–21   A charging order made by the court under the Charging Orders Act 1979 takes effect as an equitable charge. As such, where it relates to registered land, it

---

[51] See also para.13–21.
[52] For charging orders, see further Ch.20.

cannot be registered as a registered legal charge, but it may be capable of being the subject of an entry in the register, depending upon whether it affects the legal estate or only an equitable share in a property.

(1) An interim or final charging order against the legal estate i.e. one made against a sole proprietor who is the sole legal and beneficial owner or against joint proprietors expressly as "trustees", may be protected by entry of an agreed notice or a unilateral notice. An application to the court for such a charging order may be similarly protected.

(2) An interim or final charging order against a beneficial interest, i.e. one made against the equitable share of a joint proprietor, cannot be protected by entry of a notice, but may be protected by entry of a standard restriction in Form K. This is an exception to the general rule concerning derivative interests, which cannot be protected by a restriction in this way. Separate charging orders made against joint proprietors in the same court proceedings will not be treated by the registrar as charging the legal estate and separate applications for a restriction in Form K would instead need to be made. Application for entry of a standard restriction in Form A may also be made, if such a restriction does not already appear in the register, to reflect the severance of any beneficial joint tenancy as a result of the charging order. An application to the court for such a charging order cannot be protected in the register.

CHARGES BY COMPANIES[53]

Registration of a charge of registered land at the Companies Registry is not **3–22** sufficient protection. It should also be completed by registration at the Land Registry, if it is to take effect at law and be protected in the register.

In the case of a UK company (i.e. one registered in England and Wales, Scotland or Northern Ireland under the Companies Acts or in Northern Ireland under the Companies (Northern Ireland) Order 1986) or a UK limited liability partnership (i.e. one incorporated in England and Wales or Scotland under the Limited Liability Partnerships Act 2000 or in Northern Ireland under the Limited Liability Partnerships Act (Northern Ireland) 2002), registration of the charge at the Companies Registry should precede an application for registration to the Land Registry.

As from October 1, 2009, r.111 of the Land Registration Rules 2003 provides that when making an application for registration of a charge created by a UK company or a UK limited liability partnership, the applicant must produce to the registrar the appropriate certificate that the charge has been registered at the Companies Registry. If the certificate is not produced, the registrar must enter a note in the register stating that no evidence of registration of the charge in

---

[53] See further, below para.23–44.

accordance with s.860 or s.878 of the Companies Act 2006 (as appropriate) has been lodged.

As from October 1, 2009, r.111A of the Land Registration Rules 2003 provides that an application for registration of a charge created by an overseas company (i.e. one incorporated outside the UK), must be accompanied by evidence to satisfy the registrar that the charge has been registered in the Companies Registry under Pt 3 of the Overseas Companies (Execution of Documents and Registration of Charges) Regulations 2009, or the charge must include a statement that the charge, when created, did not require to be so registered. In default of this, the registrar must enter a note in the register to the effect that no evidence has been lodged either that the charge has been so registered or that such registration was not required.

CHAPTER 4

PARTIES TO MORTGAGES

ABSOLUTE OWNERS

General

As a general proposition, an absolute owner of property, whether real or personal, **4–01** who is not subject to any incapacity[1] may mortgage that property in exercise of the full powers of alienation with which he is invested.[2] This general rule is now reflected in s.23 of the Land Registration Act 2002, which confers an express power on the owner of a registered estate: (a) to make a disposition of any kind permitted by the general law in relation to an interest of that description, other than a mortgage by demise or sub-demise[3]; and (b) to charge the estate at law with the payment of money.

Exceptions: There are a number of common law and statutory exceptions to **4–02** the general rule permitting an absolute owner to mortgage property. As a matter of private law, restrictions on alienation contained within settlements, contracts and leases can also affect the right of an absolute owner to charge his own property.

Common law: At common law, it has long been established that the assign- **4–03** ment of the salaries and pensions of persons in the service of the Crown offends public policy.[4] The basis for the doctrine appears to be that it is wrong to charge pay given to induce persons to keep themselves ready for the service of the Crown.[5] It extends to the salaries of those serving in the Armed Forces,[6]

---

[1] See below, paras 4–09 et seq.
[2] See Coke on Littleton, 223a.
[3] The exception of mortgages by way of demise and sub-demise reflects the prospective abolition of such mortgage under the Act; *Wolstenholme & Cherry's Annotated Land Registration Act 2002* at 3–023.
[4] *Stone v Liddudale* (1795) 2 Anst. 533.
[5] *Ex p. Higgins* (1882) 21 Ch.D. 85.
[6] *Stone v Liddudale*, ibid.

parliamentary counsel,[7] civil servants, police officers, school teachers and fire-men.[8] However, there has been judicial reluctance to extend the doctrine[9] and, to come within it, the pay must come from national, not local funds.[10]

4–04   Statute: The common law prohibition on the assignment of pay, half pay and pensions of those serving in the Armed Forces is reinforced by statute which makes any assignment or charge over such property void.[11] There are other specific statutory prohibitions relating to police officers, fireman and similar public servants and also restrictions in social security legislation on the assigna-bility of child and national insurance benefits.[12] These prohibitions may be important in the context of family maintenance settlements and awards.[13]

4–05   Restrictions on alienation: Freehold and leasehold property fall to be con-sidered separately.

4–06   *Freehold:*   One of the essential incidents of ownership of a freehold estate is the ability to sell or dispose of the property, so that a condition against alienation inconsistent with this right, leading to the forfeiture of the estate, will be void for being contrary to public policy.[14] An absolute condition preventing alienation by way of mortgage will not therefore be enforceable.[15] However, this only applies if the breach of covenant or condition gives rise to forfeiture or loss of the estate, not if it merely sounds in damages or gives rise to the right to an injunction.[16]

4–07   *Leasehold:*   Leases of commercial and residential property frequently contain absolute or qualified restrictions on alienation to varying degrees. An express covenant against charging the property (though rare in modern leases) will be enforceable and breached if a mortgage or fixed charge is granted over the leasehold estate (although any such covenant is likely to be qualified to permit charging with the consent of the landlord, such consent not to be unreasonably withheld). A covenant against assignment or sub-letting has been held to be breached by a mortgage by way of sub-demise or by way of assignment.[17] However, it is suggested that care is required when applying such authorities because each alienation clause must be interpreted having regard to its own wording and context. A mortgage that results in the alienation of the legal estate is nonetheless likely to be a breach of a covenant against assignment, but it is

---

[7] *Cooper v Reilly* (1829) 2 Sim 560.

[8] *Lucas v Lucas* [1943] P. 68.

[9] *Re Mirams* [1891] 1 Q.B. 594.

[10] *Re Mirams,* ibid. (clergyman outside rule); *Lynch v Subjic Times* May 18, 1987 (assignment of dentist's salary permissible).

[11] Army Act 1955 s.203; Air Force Act 1955 s.203; Naval and Marine Pay and Pensions Act 1865 s.4.

[12] Social Security Administration Act 1992 s.187(1).

[13] *Roberts v Roberts* [1986] 1 W.L.R. 437.

[14] See generally Megarry & Wade, *The Law of Real Property* (2008) 7th edn at 3–063.

[15] *Ware v Cann* (1830) 10 B&C 433.

[16] *Caldy Manor Estates Ltd v Farrell* [1974] 3 All E.R. 753.

[17] *Serjeant v Nash, Field & Co* [1903] 2 K.B. 300.

difficult to see how the creation of an equitable mortgage or charge would similarly be a breach, absent express prohibition.

Co-owners

Where land is owned by more than one person, such persons may be beneficially   **4–08**
interested in the land either jointly or as tenants in common. In such a case the legal estate in the land will be held by not more than four of the co-owners as joint tenants upon trust for the co-owners as joint tenants or tenants in common.[18]

As trustees of a trust of land the co-owners have, in relation to the land, all the powers of an absolute owner pursuant to statute[19] and thus may mortgage the land under their statutory powers. Where the same persons are both the trustees and the beneficiaries, they may mortgage by virtue of their powers as absolute owners and need not rely upon the statutory powers. A purported mortgage by one co-owner operates as a severance of any joint tenancy in equity and operates to charge or transfer (as the case may be) the sole co-owner's share.[20]

Where a legal mortgage of land is made to several persons, the legal estate vests in the mortgagees or the first four named as joint tenants upon trust. By virtue of s.111 of the Law of Property Act 1925[21] where the mortgage is made to several mortgagees jointly or the mortgage money is expressed to belong to them on a joint account, then unless a contrary intention is expressed in the mortgage instrument, the mortgage moneys are (as between the mortgagees and the mortgagor) deemed to be and remain moneys belonging to the mortgagees on joint account. Thus, persons dealing in good faith with several mortgagees may assume that the mortgagees are entitled to the mortgage moneys on a joint account unless a contrary intention is expressed in the instruments relating to the mortgage.[22]

Persons subject to disabilities

Bankrupts: Upon an individual becoming bankrupt, the entirety of his estate   **4–09**
(with some exceptions) vests, without conveyance, in the Official Receiver upon his becoming trustee and thereafter in his trustee in bankruptcy.[23] Thus, a bankrupt retains no interest in his general assets at the date of the bankruptcy which he can mortgage.[24]

---

[18] Law of Property Act 1925 (LPA 1925) ss.34, 36; Settled Land Act 1925 s.36; Trustee Act 1925 s.34 (all as amended).

[19] Trustee Act 1925 s.16(1); Trusts of Land and Appointment of Trustees Act 1996 (TLATA 1996) s.6(1).

[20] *Ahmed v Kendrick* (1988) 56 P. & C.R. 120.

[21] Replacing the Conveyancing Act 1881 s.61.

[22] LPA 1925 s.113(1)(*a*)

[23] See below para.34–08.

[24] See generally Ch.34.

Minors

4–10 **Borrowing powers:** The law applicable to contracts by minors[25] is now governed by the Minors' Contracts Act 1987, which applies to any contracts made by minors after June 9, 1987. The effect of the Act is to substantially restore the common law position that existed prior to the Infants Relief Act 1874, which invalidated certain contracts made by minors and prohibited actions to enforce contracts, even if they were ratified after majority. The 1987 Act also disapplies the Betting and Loans (Infants) Act 1892 s.5 which invalidated contracts to repay loans advanced during minority.

Under s.1 of the 1874 Act, all contracts with minors for the repayment of money lent, or for goods supplied or to be supplied (other than contracts for "necessaries" which were binding on the minor), and all accounts stated with minors, were rendered absolutely void. It did not, however, invalidate any contract into which a minor might enter by statute or the rules of common law or equity except those which under the existing law were voidable. The disapplication of that section will, therefore, result in the contracts in question again becoming subject to the rules of common law.

The disapplication of s.2 of the 1874 Act means that on a minor reaching the age of majority, his ratification of an otherwise unenforceable contract entered into by him as a minor, is effective. However, s.2, while not abolishing the common law rules, imposed a bar on proceedings to enforce ratification (whether or not there was new consideration) of a minor's contract, by providing that no action should be brought for that purpose. The removal of this procedural bar serves to reinstate the relevant rules of common law or equity.

Further, the 1987 Act disapplies s.5 of the Betting and Loans (Infants) Act 1892, which rendered void any new agreements by a minor, after attaining his majority, to repay a loan made to him while a minor. It also invalidates any negotiable instrument given in connection with such an agreement. In doing so, the 1987 Act makes any such new agreement and any such negotiable agreement effective.

Further, s.3(1) of the 1987 Act extends the power of the court, if it is just and equitable to do so, to require a minor who has acquired property under an unenforceable contract to restore it. This is the case even where there has been no fraud on the part of the minor.[26] The power will also be exercisable where the minor has, on the ground of his minority, repudiated the contract under which he acquired the property. The courts power is limited to ordering the transfer of property acquired under the contract, or property representing it.[27]

---

[25] The Family Law Reform Act 1969 reduced the age of majority to 18 (s.1).

[26] Under the old law that power was confined to cases where the minor induced the other party to enter into the contract by fraud.

[27] According to the Law Com. Report No.134, the words property representing property are to be interpreted as referring to the general principle of tracing. Thus, if the minor has sold or exchanged the goods acquired under the contract, he can be compelled to pay over the price, or hand over the goods received in exchange. But if he has consumed or otherwise dissipated the goods or their proceeds, he cannot be required to pay to the seller a sum equivalent to the purchase price, or to the value of the goods.

A minor cannot hold a legal estate in land, and consequently cannot be a legal mortgagor.[28] Thus, although a minor may be a member of a building society and may give all necessary receipts,[29] he cannot execute a valid mortgage to secure advances made to him by the society.[30] An equitable mortgage made by a minor is unenforceable, but a minor can ratify it upon attaining his majority.[31] Where the mortgage was made to secure moneys lent for the purchase of "necessaries" the mortgage is voidable and not absolutely void.[32] As the disposition is voidable and not void it is binding if the minor fails to repudiate it within a reasonable time after attaining his majority.[33] Where a minor has executed such a mortgage and subsequently upon attaining full age charges the premises with a further advance and has confirmed the earlier mortgage, he cannot redeem without paying off the sum advanced during his infancy.[34]

Where a minor is beneficially entitled to any property, the court may direct the trustees to raise money by mortgage of the property or order them to apply the capital or income for the minor's maintenance, education or benefit.[35] Powers of management of a minor's lands may be conferred on the trustees appointed for the purpose or if there are none so appointed, then the trustees of the trust under which the minor is entitled. The specified powers do not include a power to mortgage, but the power generally to deal with the land in a proper and due course of management may comprehend such a power.[36] Personal representatives also have power of mortgaging property during the minority of a beneficiary.[37] Under the Settled Land Act 1925, a binding disposition of a minor's land may be made by the statutory owner which permits sales, exchanges, leases and mortgages on certain terms.[38]

Lending powers: The repeal of the Infants Relief Act 1874 by the Minors' **4–11** Contracts Act 1987 means that a contract of loan can be enforced by a minor.

Mortgages to minors: Since the Law of Property Act 1925, a minor cannot be **4–12** an estate owner. Thus, he cannot hold a legal estate in land[39] and thus cannot be a legal mortgagee. Prior to January 1, 1997, any attempt to grant or transfer a

---

[28] LPA 1925 s.1(6). After December 31, 1996, a purported conveyance to a minor operates as a declaration of trust in the minors favour (TLATA 1996 Sch.1 para.1(2)). If the conveyance is to a minor and a person of age, it operates to vest the legal estate in the adult on trust for himself and the minor (ibid., Sch.1 para.1(2)). Prior to then, a conveyance to an infant gave rise to an agreement for valuable consideration to execute a settlement (LPA1925 s.19(1), Settled Land Act 1925 s.27(1)) which, on January 1, 1997, became a declaration of a trust of land for the minor (TLATA 1996, Sch.1 para.1(4)).

[29] Building Societies Act 1986 s.5 Sch.2 para.5(3)(a); but cannot vote or hold office: *Nottingham Permanent Benefit Building Society v Thurstan* [1903] A.C. 6.

[30] ibid., but the Society in this case was entitled to a loan on the property for the purchase moneys.

[31] *Gardner v Wainfur* (1920) 89 L.J.Ch. 98.

[32] *Martin v Gale* (1876) 4 Ch.D. 428 at 431; *Edwards v Carter* [1893] A.C. 360.

[33] *Edwards v Carter* [1893] A.C. 360.

[34] *Gardner v Wainfur* (1919) 89 L.J.Ch. 98.

[35] Trustee Act 1925 s.53.

[36] Settled Land Act 1925 s.102.

[37] Administration of Estates Act 1925 ss.33 and 39 (as amended by Trustee Act 2000).

[38] Settled Land Act 1925 s.102.

[39] LPA 1925 s.1(6).

legal mortgage or charge to one or more persons who were all minors was not effective to pass the legal estate and in the meantime the mortgagor or transferor held the beneficial interest in the mortgage debt, if any, on trust for the persons intended to benefit.[40] If the mortgage was made to a minor or minors together with a person or persons of full age it operated to vest the legal estate in the person of full age as if the minors were not named but subject to the infant's beneficial interest.[41]

In relation to mortgages or conveyances made on or after January 1, 1997, the Trusts of Land and Appointment of Trustees Act 1996 has made the following changes to the law. Where a person purports to convey a legal estate to a minor, the conveyance will not pass the legal estate but will operate as a declaration of trust for the minor.[42] A conveyance made jointly to a minor and a person of full age operates to vest the legal estate in the person of full age subject to a statutory trust in favour of himself and the minor.[43]

Where a minor is beneficially entitled to any property, the court may direct the trustees to raise money by mortgage of the property in order to apply the capital or income for the minor's maintenance, education or benefit.[44] Personal representatives also have powers of mortgaging property during the minority of a beneficiary.[45] Under the Settled Land Act 1925 a binding disposition of a minors land may be made by the statutory owner which permits sales, exchanges, leases and mortgages on certain terms.[46]

4–13   **Persons suffering from mental disorder:**   The law relating to the property and affairs of persons suffering from mental incapacity underwent a major overhaul in the form of the Mental Capacity Act 2005.[47] The Act, among other things, sets out principles and tests to determine whether and when a person lacks mental capacity[48]; contains provisions for the making of lasting powers of attorney[49] and advance decisions[50]; and confers power on a newly constituted superior court of record, the Court of Protection, to make declarations and decisions concerning a person's welfare, property and affairs. There is a specific new power in s.16 which allows the Court of Protection to appoint deputies to make similar decisions about the welfare, property and affairs of mentally incapacitated persons.[51] This replaces the previous regime of appointing receivers under the Mental Health Act 1983.

The Act does not alter or codify the substantive law of contract or any other private law relations between persons with mental incapacity and third parties.

---

[40] LPA 1925 s.19(4), (6). See also s.19(1) and the Settled Land Act 1925 s.27(1).
[41] LPA 1925 s.19(5), (6) proviso.
[42] LPA 1925 s.2(6) and Sch.1 para.1(1).
[43] LPA 1925 s.2(6) and Sch.1 para.1(2).
[44] Trustee Act 1925 s.53.
[45] Administration of Estates Act 1925 ss.33 and 39.
[46] Settled Land Act 1925 s.102 as amended by the Trustee Act 2000 Sch.2(II) para.15.
[47] The Act came fully into force on October 1, 2007. It repealed and replaced Pt 7 of the Mental Health Act 1983.
[48] Mental Capacity Act 2005 ss.1–4.
[49] ibid., ss.9–14.
[50] ibid., ss.25–26.
[51] ibid., ss.15–21A.

This is still the subject of the common law. Indeed, nothing in the Act expressly overrules any common law rules.

Section 16 of the 2005 Act confers on the Court of Protection the power to appoint a deputy over the property and affairs of a person suffering from mental incapacity. The court can make such further orders or directions and confer such powers on the deputy as it thinks necessary or expedient,[52] but the powers conferred should be as limited in scope and duration as possible as is reasonably practicable in the circumstances.[53] Section 18 lists the express powers which can be conferred on a deputy, including the power to dispose of or charge property.[54] Section 22 of the Law of Property Act 1925, concerning conveyances on behalf of persons suffering from mental disorder, has been amended to reflect this change. Schedule 2 para.9(2) of the 2005 Act permits the court to order that any expenditure that it has ordered may be a charge on that property, with our without interest, in favour of such person as it considers just.

At common law, any contract or deed executed by a person suffering from such mental disorder as to render him incapable of understanding its effect when its nature and contents are explained to him is potentially voidable,[55] but not void.[56] The original rule at law was that a contract with a person of an unsound mind was void, because there could be no *consensus ad idem*. This was later qualified by a rule that a person could not plead his own insanity in order to avoid a contract he had made. This later gave way to a further rule that such a plea was permissible if it could be shown that the other contracting party knew of the insanity.[57] In order for the contract to be avoided, the person denying its validity must prove not only the mental incapacity of the person who is alleged to be a party to the contract, but also that the other contracting party had actual knowledge of the incapacity at the time,[58] or that he knew of facts and matters such as to put him on constructive notice of the incapacity.[59] At one time there was some doubt as to whether this rule applied to mortgages entered into by persons who lacked mental capacity,[60] but later authority assumed it would do,[61] and there can be no reason to think that under the modern law, mortgages should not be treated in the same way as any other deed or contract.

However, a deed executed during a lucid interval for valuable consideration is binding, provided the person suffering from the mental disorder understood its

---

[52] ibid., s.16(5).

[53] ibid., s.16(4)(b).

[54] ibid., s.18(1)(a).

[55] *Hart v O'Conner* [1985] 1 A.C. 1000; *Irvani v Irvani* [2000] 1 Lloyds Rep. 412, C.A.

[56] The view expressed in last edition of this work was that a deed executed by a person of unsound mind would be absolutely void, based on *Price v Berrington* (1849) 7 Hare 394 at 402; on appeal (1851) 3 Mac. & G. 486. Although there is more recent authority supporting this view (e.g. *Re Beaney* [1978] 1 W.L.R. 770), the better view now seems to be as stated at para.4–13—see Vol.30(2) Halsbury's Laws (4th edn, 2005) Mental Health at 602.

[57] *Hart v O'Conner*, ibid., at 1018–1019

[58] *Hart v O'Conner*, ibid.; *Beavan v McDonnell* (1854) 9 Exch. 309; *Imperial Loan Co Ltd v Stone* [1892] 1 Q.B. 599.

[59] *York Glass Co Ltd v Jubb* (1925) 134 LT 36 at 41 (C.A.)

[60] *Snook v Watts* (1848) 11 Beav. 105.

[61] *Campbell v Hooper* (1855) 3 Sm. & G. 153

nature and effect.[62] Similarly, a deed executed before the supervention of mental disorder is binding.[63]

Where, however, a deputy has been appointed under s.16 of the 2005 Act, the mentally disordered person probably cannot exercise any power of disposition, inter vivos, over his property even during a lucid interval, by reason of the fact that upon the making of such an order his property passes out of his control to the deputy and any disposition made by him is inconsistent with that passing of control, and consequently is void,[64] although much might turn on the precise scope of the appointment under s.16(4).

Married persons and civil partners.

4–14   The courts have a special jurisdiction over property disputes between husband and wife and the parties to a civil partnership which is dealt with elsewhere in this work.[65]

Partnerships

4–15   An ordinary partner has an implied authority under the Partnership Act 1890[66] as an agent of the partnership and the other partners to pledge or mortgage partnership property and to give good receipt thereof. This implied authority, however, only arises when the dealing is for the purpose of raising money for the carrying on in the usual way of the partnership business and is in accordance with the partnership objects. It does not arise if the partner so acting has in fact no authority to act for the firm, and the person with whom he is dealing either knows that he has no authority, or does not know or believe him to be a partner. At common law, the implied authority does not arise in the case of a mortgage by deed of partnership property[67] in the absence of special authority,[68] although whether this remains the law must be doubtful having regard to the statutory abolition of the common law rule requiring the authority by one person to another to deliver an instrument as a deed on his behalf to be given by deed.[69]

4–16   **Mortgage of personal property:**   Provided that there is no notice of fraud or want of authority, a partner[70] may mortgage or pledge the personal property of the partnership for the ordinary purposes of the firm.[71] But such a transaction will

---

[62] *Towart v Sellers* (1817) 5 Dow. 231; *Selby v Jackson* (1844) 6 Beav. 192; *Jenkins v Morris* (1880) 14 Ch.D. 674; *Drew v Nunn* (1879) 4 Q.B.D. 661.

[63] *Affleck v Affleck* (1857) 3 Sm. & G. 394.

[64] *Re Marshall; Marshall v Whateley* [1920] 1 Ch. 284.

[65] See Ch.19.

[66] See s.5, and see *Re Bourne; Bourne v Bourne* [1906] 2 Ch. 427.

[67] *Harrison v Jackson* (1797) 7 Term. Rep. 207.

[68] *Steightz v Egginton* (1815) Hoh. N.P. 141.

[69] Law of Property (Miscellaneous Provisions) Act 1989 s.1(1)(c).

[70] A limited partner does not have power to bind the firm, see the Limited Partnerships Act 1907 s.6(1).

[71] See the Partnership Act 1890 s.5.

not be binding upon the firm if made in order to secure the partner's personal debt without the knowledge and consent of the other partners.[72] The mortgagee must prove such knowledge and consent[73] or circumstances in which such knowledge and consent might reasonably be inferred. If it can be shown that the mortgagee is unaware[74] that the security is partnership property, then the transaction will not be set aside.[75] The authority to mortgage partnership property continues after dissolution for the purpose of winding up the affairs of the partnership and to complete any unfinished transactions at that date.[76]

Mortgage of real property: Where partners hold the legal estate of the **4–17** partnership property, either freehold or leasehold, as beneficial owners they are empowered to mortgage the legal interest as joint tenants holding the same as statutory trustees of a trust of land.[77] At common law, it was long established that one partner was unable to bind the other partners by executing a mortgage deed of partnership property without the concurrent and express authority under seal to do so.[78] However, s.1(1)(c) of the Law of Property (Miscellaneous Provisions) Act 1989 abolished the common rule that required the authority by one person to another to execute a deed to itself be given by way of deed. Since most of the common law authorities on the point relied on this rule to justify the exception to the normal rule in the case of partners executing mortgages by deed, it would seem to follow that the exception is no longer good law. However, in some of the authorities, a more general justification for the exception was propounded, namely that it would be wrong in principle to allow a partner to burden the estate of other partners without special authority.[79] However, this was before the law relating to the general agency of partners was fully developed and it must be doubtful if the special exception for deeds remains good law. Where there is an equitable mortgage,[80] or the mortgage itself is not required to be effected by deed, the general rule set out above with regard to the implied authority vested in a partner will apply.

Lending power of partners: A partner has authority to lend the firm's money **4–18** on mortgage when such a transaction is part of the firm's ordinary business.[81]

Mortgage of share of partnership: A share in a partnership is a right to share **4–19** in the profits and, in the event of dissolution, to share in the division of the assets.

---

[72] *Re Litherland, Ex p. Howden* (1842) 2 Mont.D. & De G. 574.

[73] *Shirreff v Wilks* (1800) 1 East. 48.

[74] *Snaith v Burridge* (1812) 4 Taunt. 684.

[75] *Reid v Hollinshead* (1825) 4 B. & C. 867.

[76] Partnership Act 1890 s.38; *Butchart v Dresser* (1853) 4 De G.M. & G. 542; *Re Bourne, Bourne v Bourne* [1906] 2 Ch. 427.

[77] LPA 1925 ss.34 and 36(1); Settled Land Act 1925 s.36(4). See also the Trustee Act 1925 ss.16, 17; LPA 1925 s.28(1).

[78] *Harrison v Jackson* (1797) 7 Term Rep. 207; *Steiglitz v Egginton* (1815) 1 Holt N.P. 141; *Elliot v Davis* (1800) 2 Bos. & P. 338; *Cumberlege v Lawson* (1857) 1 C.B.(N.S.) 709

[79] *Harrison v Jackson,* ibid.

[80] As to which see Ch.14.

[81] *Re Land Credit Co of Ireland, Weikersheim's Case* (1873) 8 Ch. App. 831; but see *Niemann v Niemann* (1889) 43 Ch.D. 198.

It is, in the nature of things, a somewhat speculative form of security, but a partner may freely mortgage his share to cover his private debts. On the other hand, a partner is by statute precluded from introducing a new partner into the firm without the consent of all the existing partners.[82] The fact that a mortgagee is not normally introduced into the partnership materially increases the hazards of taking a partnership share as security for he has no voice whatever in the management of the business. His rights are set out in s.31 of the Partnership Act 1890, and are broadly as follows:

(1) During the partnership he is not entitled either to interfere in the management of the partnership business or to require accounts of partnership transactions or to inspect books. He is entitled to the profits but must accept the account of profits agreed between the partners.
(2) On dissolution, he is entitled to receive the mortgagor's share of the assets and, for the purpose of ascertaining that share, he is entitled to an account from the other partners as from the date of dissolution.

A mortgagee is thus in a very weak position in regard to maladministration of the partnership business. Section 31 does not, of course, preclude him from impugning transactions between the partners which are designed to overreach him. It is only a genuine partnership transaction with which he has no right to concern himself.[83]

It is to be observed that, as a mortgage of a partnership share is essentially a mortgage of a chose in action, it is not a bill of sale despite the fact that, on dissolution, the mortgagee is entitled to share in the personal chattels of the partnership.[84] The mortgage does not, therefore, require registration as a bill of sale. Notice of the mortgage should, however, be given to the other partners in order to bind them to pay over the share to the mortgagee and to establish his priority against other assignees as the mortgagee takes subject to the equities subsisting between the partners.[85]

In the event that a partner charges his share of the partnership property for his own separate debt, the other partners have the statutory right to dissolve the partnership at their option.[86]

Limited liability partnerships

4-20   A limited liability partnership ("LLP") is a body corporate, with legal personality separate from that of its members, which is formed by being incorporated under the Limited Liability Partnerships Act 2000.[87] A limited liability partnership has unlimited capacity.[88] An LLP is a creature of statute. It is not a

[82] Partnership Act 1890 s.24(7).
[83] *Watts v Driscoll* [1901] 1 Ch. 294.
[84] *Re Bainbridge* (1878) 8 Ch.D. 218.
[85] See para.22–82.
[86] Partnership Act 1890 s.33(2).
[87] Limited Liability Partnership Act 2000 ss.1(2), 18.
[88] ibid., s.1(3).

partnership and does not itself have limited liability but does give its members limited liability. The general law of partnership does not apply to LLPs, save to the extent that the 2000 Act specifically provides to the contrary.[89]

LLPs are in their nature similar to corporations. It is therefore not unsurprising that, subject to certain modifications, the law relating to the registration of company charges, now contained within the Companies Act 2006,[90] applies to LLPs.[91]

CORPORATIONS

Borrowing powers of corporations

The historical position under the Companies Acts. Prior to the coming into force of s.31 of the Companies Act 2006, the Companies Acts had always required that the objects of the company should be stated in the company's memorandum of association. From an early stage, the courts developed the principle that a company had no power to do an act not expressly or impliedly authorised by its memorandum.[92] Thus, a company had no power to mortgage or charge its property unless authorised by its objects clause. **4–21**

However, in the case of companies incorporated under the Companies Acts for trading or commercial purposes, there was an implied power to mortgage the company's property even though the memorandum of association was silent provided that there was no positive prohibition preventing it[93] and provided the proposed transaction was in the ordinary course of the company's business and in the furtherance of its objects.[94] Such an implication would not be made in the case of a non-trading company which could mortgage its property only if it is expressly authorised to do so by its memorandum of association.

These principles potentially rendered all unauthorised transactions ultra vires and void.[95] However, in the case of any party to a transaction dealing with a company in good faith, such transaction being decided upon by the directors, the said party was not bound to inquire as to the capacity of the company to enter into it or as to any limitation on the powers of the directors under the memorandum or articles of association. In other words, it was deemed to be a transaction which was within the capacity of the company to enter, unless the contrary was proved.[96]

---

[89] ibid., s.1(5).

[90] See paras 23–44 ff.

[91] Limited Liability Partnerships Regulations 2001 reg.4 Sch.2, Pt 1.

[92] *Ashbury Railway Carriage and Iron Co v Riche* (1875) L.R. 7 H.L. 653.

[93] *Patent Ivory Manufacturing Co Howard v Patent Ivory Manufacturing Co* (1888) 38 Ch.D. 156; *General Auction Estate and Monetary Co v Smith* [1891] 3 Ch. 432.

[94] *Blackburn Building Society v Cunliffe Brooks & Co* (1882) 22 Ch.D. 61 at 70.

[95] See generally *Palmer's Company Law* at 2.612.

[96] See the European Communities Act 1972 s.9(1) as repealed by Companies Act 1985 s.35 prior to its repeal, substitution by the Companies Act 1989 s.108(1); see further *Buckley on the Companies Act* (2000).

4–22   **Section 35(1) Companies Act 1985:**   The ultra vires doctrine was substantially eroded by s.35(1) of the Companies Act 1985.[97] This brought about a simplification in the law so that, with effect from February 4, 1991, a company's capacity to borrow will not be affected by anything in its memorandum of association[98] and, furthermore, those dealing with the company are not bound to enquire whether any transaction is permitted by the company's memorandum of association or as to any limitation on the powers of the board of directors to bind the company or authorise others to do so.[99] This change was brought about by the Companies Act 1989 and does not affect any act done by a company prior to February 4, 1991.[100] Accordingly, consideration of the old ultra vires law will remain relevant when considering transactions entered into before that date, which could conceivably include older mortgages and charges executed by the company.

4–23   **Companies Act 2006:**   For companies incorporated after October 1, 2009, the company memorandum has been relegated to being no more than part of its application for initial registration.[101] It is no longer even part of the constitution of the company.[102] Furthermore, s.31 of the Companies Act 2006 now provides that unless a company's articles specifically restrict its objects, the objects of the company are unrestricted, so third parties can assume that a company has no constitutional limits on its capacity. This does not apply to charitable companies.[103] For existing companies, object clauses in their memorandum will be imported into the articles of association,[104] so that existing objects clauses will become limitations on director's authority. Any company can therefore now remove any existing objects clauses by amending the articles of the company.

4–24   **Other corporations:**   A public utility company incorporated by a special Act of Parliament has the powers conferred by the special Act and the Companies Clauses Consolidation Act 1845[105] which enables such a company to raise money by way of mortgage of property subject to certain conditions.[106] Further, a corporation created by Royal Charter, prima facie, is empowered to mortgage on the basis that it has all the rights and powers possessed by an ordinary person.[107]

4–25   **Registration:**   The requirements for a company to register any transaction whereby it charges its property is dealt with in detail elsewhere in this work.[108]

---

[97] Inserted by s.108 Companies Act 1989.
[98] Companies Act 1985 s.35(1), as amended by the Companies Act 1989 s.108(1).
[99] Companies Act 1985 s.35B.
[100] SI 1990/2569 art.7(1).
[101] Companies Act 2006 s.8.
[102] ibid., s.17.
[103] ibid., s.31(4).
[104] ibid., s.28.
[105] ibid., s.38. See also generally *Palmers Company Law* (25th edn).
[106] Companies Clauses Consolidation Act 1845 ss.38–55. In the case of nationalised corporations the powers of the particular body to raise money by way of mortgage are contained in the statute creating the particular body.
[107] *Jenkin v Pharmaceutical Society of Great Britain* [1921] 1 Ch. 392 at 398.
[108] See paras 23–44 ff.

Such a transaction must be registered under s.860 of the Companies Act 2006 and a failure to do so is a criminal offence.[109] A charge shall be void against the liquidator and any creditor of the company unless the prescribed particulars of the charge are delivered to or received by the registrar of companies for registration within 21 days after the date of its creation.[110] When the charge becomes void the money secured thereby shall immediately become payable.[111]

Public Authorities

Local Authorities

Borrowing and mortgaging powers: The powers of local authorities to bor-   **4–26** row money are now contained in the Local Government Act 2003.[112] Section 1 of the Act confers a statutory power on a local authority to borrow money for any purpose relevant to its functions under any enactment or for the purpose of the prudent management of its financial affairs. Section 2 restricts the power of borrowing in two ways. Section 2(1)(a) and s.3 of the Act restrict the amount of borrowing to that which the local authority can afford to borrow according to that authority's own review procedures. Section 2(1)(b) and s.4 restrict borrowing to any specific borrowing limit set by the Secretary of State under Regulations. Section 5 of the Act permits temporary borrowing on certain terms.

Section 13(1) of the 2003 Act stipulates that a local authority may not mortgage or charge any of its property as security for money which it has borrowed or otherwise owes unless all moneys borrowed by a local authority and any interest accrued thereon is charged indifferently on all its revenues.[113] All securities created by a local authority ranks equally without priority.[114] Section 6 of the 2003 replicates previous statutory provisions and provides that a person lending money to a local authority is not bound to inquire whether the authority has power to borrow and will not be prejudiced by the absence of that power.

Lending powers: This subject is dealt with in detail elsewhere in this work.[115]   **4–27** A local authority or county council may, subject to any economic restraints imposed on such authorities, advance money for the purpose of acquiring, constructing, altering, enlarging, repairing or improving houses, for converting buildings into houses or flats, for acquiring houses for that purpose or for paying off a loan for such purposes.[116] The mortgage can only be made if secured against an estate comprising either a fee simple absolute in possession or a term of years absolute for a term not less than 10 years in excess of the period fixed for repayment.[117]

---

[109] Companies Act 2006 s.860(4).
[110] Companies Act 2006 s.874.
[111] ibid., s.874(3).
[112] The Act came into force on November 27, 2003.
[113] This condition was also contained in s.47(1) of the Local Government and Housing Act 1989.
[114] Local Government Act 2003 s.13(4).
[115] See Ch.18.
[116] Housing Act 1985 s.435(1).
[117] Housing Act 1985 s.436.

Other Public Authorities

4–28   Other public authorities have statutory powers, where required, both to advance money on mortgage or to mortgage property. Such powers are conferred by the statutes creating or regulating the authority in question. Thus, internal drainage boards[118] may raise money on mortgage. The Agricultural Mortgage Corporation Limited had power to make advances by way of mortgage.[119] The National Trust may also borrow money by way of mortgage of its alienable property.[120] National Health Service Trusts are prohibited from mortgaging or charging their assets.[121]

Housing Associations[122]

4–29   By virtue of the Housing Act 1985 a Housing Association[123] is a society, body of trustees, or company established for the purpose of, or amongst whose objects or powers are included those of, providing, constructing, improving, or managing, or facilitating or encouraging the construction or improvement of houses or hostels, being a society, body of trustees or company who do not trade for profit or whose constitution or rules prohibit the issue of any capital with interest or dividend exceeding the rate for the time being prescribed by the Treasury, whether with or without differentiation as between share and loan capital.[124] A housing association may be either an industrial and provident society,[125] a company registered under the Companies Acts,[126] or unincorporated. It may also be a charity.[127] Its borrowing powers are determined by its legal status. It may or may not be registered under the Housing Associations Act 1985 and the land which it acquires may or may not be grant-aided.[128]

The Housing Corporation

4–30   The Housing Corporation[129] was established by Pt I of the Housing Act 1964. Its functions were extended by the Housing Act 1974 and are now consolidated in the Housing Associations Act 1985 as amended by the Housing Act 1996. It is

---

[118] See the Land Drainage Act 1991 s.35.

[119] See the Agricultural Credits Act 1928 ss.1, 2, now repealed by the Agriculture and Forestry (Financial Provisions) Act 1991 s.1(1), (2), Sch. Pt I.

[120] See the National Trust Act 1907 s.22.

[121] National Health Service Act 2006 Sch.5, para.3(3).

[122] As to the history and the development of the various types of housing associations see (Craddock), (1959) 23 Conv. (N.S.) 3.

[123] This includes a housing society.

[124] Housing Associations Act 1985 s.1(1).

[125] See below para.4–32.

[126] See above para.4–21.

[127] See para.4–44.

[128] See the Housing Associations Act 1985 s.9(1) Sch.1.

[129] In Wales, the body is known as Housing For Wales and was created by the Housing Act 1988. It has all the functions conferred upon it by the Housing Associations Act 1985 and, from December 1988, has had vested in it all the property in Wales previously held by the Housing Corporation.

a body corporate with perpetual succession and has a common seal. The objects of the Housing Corporation are to promote and assist the development of registered housing associations and unregistered self-build societies, to facilitate the proper performance of the functions of such associations and to publicise their aims and principles. Further, it is to establish and maintain a register of housing associations and to exercise supervision and control over them and to undertake the provision of dwellings for letting or sale and of hostels and the management of dwellings or hostels provided by the Corporation.[130] The Housing Corporation has certain borrowing powers[131] and it is also empowered to make loans to certain specified borrowers.[132] By virtue of s.9 of the 1985 Act a registered housing association may, not, inter alia, mortgage any land, and an unregistered association may not, inter alia, mortgage grant-aided land, except with the consent of the Housing Corporation.[133]

Building societies

The law relating to the lending of money and granting of mortgages by building societies is dealt with in detail elsewhere in this work.[134]   **4–31**

Industrial and provident societies

Industrial and provident societies are societies for the carrying on of any industry,   **4–32** business or trade and may be registered under the Industrial and Provident Societies Act 1965 if they are a bona fide co-operative society or are conducted for the benefit of the community.[135] The 1965 Act was a consolidating Act, and it has been supplemented by further Acts since that date, including the Industrial and Provident Societies Act 1967. The regulatory and record-keeping functions formerly performed by the Registrar of Friendly Societies were transferred to the Financial Services Authority by the Financial Services and Markets Act 2000.[136]

Generally, the rules of each society must provide whether it may enter into loans or receive money on deposit from members or other persons, and if so, under what conditions, on what security and to what amounts.[137] Such mortgages and charges over the property of industrial and provident societies do not require registration with the Chief Registrar of Friendly Societies. A mortgagee is not bound to inquire as to the relevant authorisation for the mortgage by the society

---

[130] ibid., s.75 (as amended).
[131] ibid., ss.92, 93 (as amended).
[132] ibid., s.79(1) permits loans to registered social landlords, unregistered self-build societies, subsidiaries of the Corporation and other bodies in which the Corporation has an interest.
[133] If, however, the association is a registered charity and the mortgage requires consent or an order under the Charities Act 1993, such consent under the Housing Associations Act is not required.
[134] See Ch.17.
[135] Industrial and Provident Societies Act 1965 s.1 and Sch.1.
[136] For a review of the statutory regime, see *Re Devon & Somerset Farmers Ltd* [1994] Ch. 57.
[137] Industrial and Provident Societies Act 1965 s.1 and Sch.1.

and the society's receipt is a good discharge for all moneys arising from such a transaction.[138]

Fixed and floating charges may be created by industrial and provident societies on their personal chattels free from the provisions of the Bills of Sale Acts 1878 and 1882 if an application is lodged within 14 days at the central office established under the Friendly Societies Act 1896 to record the charge.[139] Although industrial and provident societies can grant fixed and floating charges over their property, it has been held that the provisions of s.72A(1) of the Insolvency Act 1986 relating to the appointment of administrators or those relating to receivers and manages do not apply to industrial and provident societies because, although such societies are in many ways similar to a company, the statutory insolvency framework for companies incorporated under the Companies Acts and for societies registered under the 1965 Act were separate.[140]

A registered industrial and provident society may by its rules provide for advances of money to members on the security of real or personal property or, if the society is registered to carry on banking business, in any manner customary in the conduct of such business.[141] Further, advances can be made to members of agricultural, horticultural or forestry societies for agricultural, horticultural or forestry purposes without security.[142]

Friendly societies

4–33 Friendly Societies are governed by a statutory regime contained in the Friendly Societies Act 1974 and the Friendly Societies Act 1992. They are now regulated by the Financial Services Authority.[143] Generally, provided that a registered society or branch rules permit it to hold land and buildings, such land can be mortgaged.[144]

The trustees of a registered society or branch may, with the consent of the committee or of a majority of the members present and entitled to vote in a general meeting,[145] invest the funds of the society or branch or any part thereof, inter alia, upon any security expressly directed by the rules of the society or branch, not being a personal security but only as authorised by the provisions of the Friendly Societies Act 1974 with respect to loans[146] and in any investments authorised by law for investment of trust funds.[147] The Act also makes provisions for loans to members out of a separate loan fund.[148]

---

[138] ibid., s.30(1).
[139] ibid., s.1.
[140] See *Re Dairy Farmers of Britain Ltd* [2010] 2 W.L.R. 311.
[141] Industrial and Provident Societies Act 1965 s.21.
[142] ibid., s.12.
[143] Friendly Societies Act 1992 s.1 as amended by the Financial Services and Markets Act 2000.
[144] Friendly Societies Act 1974 s.53 which implies a power to borrow, and see s.23(2).
[145] Friendly Societies Act 1974 s.46(1).
[146] ibid., ss.48 and 49.
[147] ibid., s.46(1)(d), (e).
[148] ibid., s.49.

Clubs

Clubs which are incorporated have powers to borrow in accordance with their **4–34** memoranda and articles of association and the Companies Act 2006. The property of unincorporated clubs is usually held by trustees on behalf of the members. The trustee's powers to alienate property and borrow are governed by the club's rules and/or the instrument creating the trust or by the applicable statutory provisions (e.g. as trustees of land) or any order of the court. The rules of an incorporated club or the memorandum and articles of association of an incorporated club may permit the issue of debentures. Debentures issued by unincorporated clubs should not include personal chattels or furniture since, even if they were registered under the Bills of Sales Acts,[149] they would be void for non-compliance with the statutory form.[150] There is no power, absent express provision in the rules or constitution of the club, for the committee of the club or the majority of members to alienate club property against the wishes of the minority, unless it is authorised by implication by the rules and is consistent with the purposes of the club.[151] This would include granting charges or mortgages over club property.

FIDUCIARY OWNERS

By way of general introduction, all fiduciary owners must exercise such powers **4–35** of mortgage as may be vested in them strictly in accordance with their fiduciary obligations. The same principle applies in relation to powers of borrowing and lending. In exercising either power, "a fiduciary must act in good faith; he must not make a profit out of his own trust; he must not place himself in a position where his duty and his interest may conflict, he may not act for his own benefit or the benefit of a third person without the informed consent of his principal".[152] A trustee must also exercise his powers in accordance with duty of care contained in s.1 of the Trustee Act 2000.

Fiduciary mortgagees do not usually enter into covenants to repay the borrowing under a mortgage. Such a covenant would expose the trustee to a personal liability that might exceed the value of the trust fund. It is prudent for any personal covenant to be limited to funds and property under the control of the trustee.[153]

Personal Representatives

Common law: At common law, unless the terms of the will required an **4–36** immediate and absolute sale, personal representatives have always been able to

---

[149] Bills of Sale Act (1878) Amendment Act 1882 s.8 and Ch.22.

[150] ibid., s.9.

[151] See the Scottish case of *Murray v Johnstone* [1896] R. 981 and *Ashton and Reid on Club Law* (2005) at 8–05.

[152] *Bristol & West Building Society v Mothew* [1998] Ch. 1, per Millet L.J. at 18.

[153] *Re Robinson's Settlement* [1912] 1 Ch. 717.

raise money by mortgaging the deceased's personal estate for the payment of debts, funeral and testamentary expenses and the proper expenses of administering the estate.[154]

4–37   Statute: By virtue of ss.2 and 39 of the Administration of Estates Act 1925 (as amended by the Trusts of Land and Appointment of Trustees Act 1996 ("TLATA 1996")), personal representatives have an express statutory power to mortgage both the real and personal estate of the deceased. With regard to the deceased's real estate, by s.2 of the Act, a personal representative has the same powers of disposition as a personal representative had before 1926.[155] With regard to both the real and personal estate of the deceased, by s.39 of the Act, personal representatives have, for the purposes of administration or during the minority of any beneficiary or the subsistence of any life interest or until the period of distribution arrives, the same powers and discretions, which includes the power to raise money by way of mortgage or charge, whether or not by the deposit of documents, as a personal representative had before 1926 with regard to personal estate.[156] The Act (as amended) also confers on a personal representative all the powers contained in Pt 1 of TLATA relating to trustees of land.[157]

4–38   Protection of the mortgagee: In the case of land, the power to mortgage may be exercised by the personal representatives by way of legal mortgage. Although the position at common law prior to 1925 was otherwise, such a mortgage is not invalidated on the basis that the mortgagee had notice that all the debts, liabilities, funeral, testamentary and administration duties and legacies of the deceased had been provided for.[158] Furthermore, at common law there is a presumption that when a representative raises money on the property of the deceased, it is for the purpose of paying estate debts or an administration cost.[159] But if there is evidence to suggest the contrary, then the presumption no longer applies and in some circumstances, the mortgagee might be fixed with actual or constructive notice of a breach of trust by the representative, although the effect on the validity of the mortgage will depend on whether the mortgage is before or after 1925.[160]

4–39   Formalities: In the case of a mortgage of real estate[161] all the personal representatives must concur or an order of the court must be obtained.[162] An

---

[154] *Mead v Orrery* (1745) 3 Atk. 235; *Scott v Tyler* (1788) 2 Dick 712 and see Williams, Mortimer and Sunnucks, *Executors Administrators and Probate* (19th edn, 2008) at 54–30.

[155] Administration of Estates Act 1925 s.2(1). In relation to deaths after 1925, s.2 replaces with amendments the Land Transfer Act 1897 s.2(2), and the Conveyancing Act 1911 s.12.

[156] Administration of Estates Act 1925 s.39(1)(i), as amended by TLATA 1996 Sch.1.

[157] ibid., s.39(1)(ii), (iii), as amended by TLATA 1996 Sch.1.

[158] ibid., s.36(8).

[159] *Re Venn and Furze* [1894] 2 Ch. 101; *Re Henson* [1908] 2 Ch. 356.

[160] See *Williams, Mortimer and Sunnucks,* ibid., at 54–41 to 54–49 for a full discussion of the principles.

[161] Real Estate includes chattels real, and leasehold: see the Administration of Estates Act 1925 ss.3(1) and 55(1)(xix).

[162] ibid., ss.2(2) and 55(1)(ii). See *Harrison v Wing* (1988) 56 P. & C.R. 358 (executors not bound as not all concurring in a lease).

exception arises, however, where probate is granted to one or some of two or more persons named as executors, whether or not power is reserved to the other or others to prove, when a mortgage may be made by the proving executor or executors for the time being.[163] If a personal representative exceeds his powers, he will be personally liable on any covenant given in the mortgage, but the mortgagee cannot prove for any shortfall against the other assets of the estate.[164]

Private trustees of land[165]

Mortgage of trust property: The Trusts of Land and Appointment of Trustees   **4–40**
Act 1996, which came into force on January 1, 1997, applies to all trusts comprising or including land[166] with the exception of land which was settled land prior to 1997 and land which is subject to the Universities and College Estates Act 1925.[167] With effect from the date of commencement, settlements, trusts for sale and bare trusts have been abolished and replaced with trusts of land.

The trustees of a trust of land are vested with both the legal estate of the land and with the powers of management of that land. Section 6 of TLATA provides trustees of land when exercising their functions as trustees with the powers of an absolute owner of land. The section further bestows upon them the power to convey land to the beneficiaries when they are absolutely entitled to it and the power to purchase land. All these powers must be exercised however, with regard to the rights of the beneficiaries under the trust of land[168] and cannot be exercised in contravention of, or of any order made in pursuance of any enactment or any rule of law or equity.

It follows that the trustees are not authorised to act in breach of trust. So, where the beneficiaries are all of age and the land is held by their nominees or the property is held on a constructive or resulting trust, any disposition of the trust property other than to the beneficiaries or with their concurrence will amount to a breach of trust since such trusts do not necessarily have all the incidents normally associated with the relationship between trustee and beneficiary.[169] A purchaser for money or money's worth,[170] however, need not be concerned with the nature of the trust upon which the land is held; if a disposition of land requires the consent of more than two persons to the exercise of any function by the trustees, the consent of any two of them is sufficient in favour of the purchaser.[171]

---

[163] ibid., s.2(2). But see *Fountain Forestry Ltd v Edwards* [1975] Ch. 1.

[164] *Farhall v Farhall* (1871) 7 Ch. App. 123.

[165] See also *Lewin on Trusts* (18th edn, 2008), paras 37–13 et seq.

[166] TLATA 1996 s.1(2).

[167] TLATA 1996 s.1(3).

[168] Trustees should, so far as practicable, consult the beneficiaries who are *sui iuris* and, so far as consistent with the general interest of the trust, give effect to the wishes of the beneficiaries or the majority of the beneficiaries: TLATA 1996 s.11, subject to certain exceptions set forth in s.11(3).

[169] See *Berkely v Poulett* [1977] 1 E.G.L.R. 86 and 93 and *Target Holdings Ltd v Redferns* [1996] A.C. 421 at 434 et seq.

[170] TLATA 1996 s.23(1); LPA 1925 s.205(1)(xxi).

[171] TLATA 1996 s.10(1).

Similarly, where the trustees are authorised by any other statutory provision to act but subject to any restriction, limitation or condition imposed by the relevant statute, the trustees cannot exercise their powers under s.6 in order to circumvent that other statutory provision. For example, regard would have to be had to trustees' powers of investment or delegation.

In addition, trustees' powers are further circumscribed by the following factors. The power bestowed by s.6 is in relation to their functions as trustees (i.e. the exercise by them of their powers and obligations). However, those powers and obligations must be exercised in a fiduciary capacity in the best interests of the trust.[172] Furthermore, s.6 only provides the trustees with power in exercising their functions in relation to land and thus in trusts comprising a mixed fund of personalty and land, it can only apply to the trustees' exercise of their functions with regard to the latter.

Trustees of land must act unanimously,[173] unless the trust instrument appointing them expressly so provides,[174] or the court so orders.[175]

4-41   **Investments:**   The general power of investment conferred by s.3 of the Trustee Act 2000 includes the power to invest in loans secured on land.[176]

Private trustees of personalty

4-42   **Mortgage of trust property:**   In the case of trust property other than land held for non-charitable purposes, a private trustee may not mortgage trust property unless he is expressly or impliedly authorised to do so by the instrument creating the trust,[177] or pursuant to a power conferred by statute or pursuant to a court order.[178]

By virtue of s.57 of the Trustee Act 1925, where trustees are authorised by the trust instrument (if any) creating the trust, or by law, to pay or apply capital moneys subject to the trust for any purpose or in any manner, they have, and are deemed always to have had, power to raise, inter alia, money by way of mortgage of all or any part of the trust property for the time being in possession.[179] This power is available notwithstanding anything to the contrary in the instrument creating the trust, but it does not apply to trustees of property held for charitable purposes, or to trustees of settled land not being also statutory owners.[180] Further,

---

[172] *Cowan v Scargill* [1985] Ch. 270 at 286; *Harries v The Church Commissioners for England* [1992] 1 W.L.R. 1241 at 1246; *Edge v Pensions Ombudsman* [1998] Ch. 513.

[173] *Luke v South Kensington Hotel Co* (1879) 11 Ch.D. 121 at 125.

[174] *Re Butlins Settlement Trusts* (1974) 118 S.J. 757.

[175] TLATA 1996 s.14.

[176] For a full discussion of these powers and when and in what manner they should be exercised see *Lewin on Trusts* (18th edn, 2008) at 35–79 et seq.

[177] *Re Bellinger* [1898] 2 Ch. 534; *Re Suenson-Taylor's Settlement Trusts* [1974] 1 W.L.R. 1280.

[178] See the Trustee Act 1925 s.57. In the case of settled land, see the Settled Land Act 1925 s.64.

[179] Trustee Act 1925 s.16(1). Possession includes receipt of rents and profits or the right to receive the same, if any; ibid., s.68(10).

[180] ibid., s.16(2).

trustees of land have, in relation to land, all the powers of a statutory owner.[181]

With regard to settled land, however, any powers to mortgage which are conferred upon the trustees are exercisable not by them, unless they are the statutory owners for the time being, but by the tenants for life or statutory owner by way of additional powers if conferred by the Settled Land Act 1925. By virtue of s.17 of the Trustee Act 1925, a mortgagee advancing money on a mortgage purporting to be made under any trust or power vested in trustees is not concerned to see that the money is wanted, or that no more than is wanted is raised, or otherwise as to its application. However, as the mortgage money is capital money the mortgagee must not pay it to fewer than two trustees unless the trustee is a trust corporation.[182]

Power to lend money on mortgage: Trustees are only able to lend money on   **4–43** mortgage if authorised by the trust instrument in the case of personal property, or pursuant to the statutory power to do so under the Trustee Act 2000 in the case of real property (either freehold or leasehold), unless expressly prevented from doing so by the instrument creating the trust. A tenant for life has no power to mortgage or charge the legal estate for his own benefit or use. If he wishes to do so he can mortgage his own beneficial interest.

Charitable trustees[183]

Powers of mortgage: Charitable trustees have all the powers of trustees of   **4–44** land.[184] However, no mortgage of land held by or on trust for a charity (save for those held by an exempt charity) can be granted without an order of the court or of the Charity Commissioners unless the trustees have obtained and considered proper written advice concerning the matters set forth in s.38(3) of the Charities Act 1993 prior to granting the mortgage.[185]

Those matters are:

"(3) (a) whether the proposed loan is necessary in order for the charity trustees to be able to pursue the particular course of action in connection with which the loan is sought by them;
(b) whether the terms of the proposed loan are reasonable having regard to the status of the charity as a prospective borrower; and
(c) the ability of the charity to repay on those terms the sum proposed to be borrowed."

[181] LPA 1925 s.28(1).

[182] LPA 1925 s.27(2); Law of Property (Amendment) Act 1926 s.7 and Sch. In order to avoid the difficulty of the beneficiaries having to join in giving a receipt for the mortgage monies, or to investigate whether or not the trustees were the duly appointed trustees of the trust in question (see *Re Blaiberg & Abrahams* [1899] 2 Ch. 340) it became the common practice to insert a joint account clause where two or more persons lent money. After 1881 such a clause is now unnecessary.

[183] See also *Tudor on Charities* (9th edn, 2003), Ch.7.

[184] TLATA 1996 ss.1, 2(6) and 6(8)

[185] Charities Act 1993 s.38(1).

The written advice that the trustees must consider must be provided by a person who is reasonably believed by the trustees to be qualified to give that advice by reason of his ability in and practical experience of financial matters and who has no financial interest in the making of the loan. He may be an officer or employee of the charity or its trustees.[186]

4–45 Form of mortgage: The mortgage must contain a statement to the effect that the land is held by or on trust for a charity, whether the charity is an exempt charity and whether the mortgage is one for which general or special authority is given under s.36(9)(a) of the Act (authority by statute or scheme legally established; disposition to another charity in accordance with the trusts of that charity at less than the best price reasonably obtainable; grant of a lease otherwise than for the best rent reasonably obtainable to a beneficiary for purposes of the charity) and indicate whether the statutory restrictions apply. If they do apply, the mortgage must contain a statement that they have been complied with.[187] If the mortgage so states it is conclusively presumed in favour of a purchaser for money or money's worth (or his successors-in-title) that the facts so stated were true.[188] If the statement is omitted the mortgage is only valid in favour of the purchaser acting in good faith.[189]

Save where the charitable trustees wish to transfer their assets to another charity or amend the charity's objects,[190] charitable trustees can act by a simple majority[191] and may exceed four in number in instances where the trust is of land.

4–46 Mortgages of personalty: Where the property of the charity to be mortgaged comprises assets other than land, the trustees' power to mortgage is governed by the instrument regulating the charity.

LIMITED OWNERS

Tenants for life and statutory owners

4–47 Generally: After January 1, 1997, it is not possible to create a settlement for the purpose of the Settled Land Act 1925, nor is one deemed to be made.[192] Even so an important class of persons having power to raise money by way of a legal

---

[186] ibid., s.38(4).
[187] ibid., s.39.
[188] ibid., s.39(3).
[189] ibid., s.39(4).
[190] In which case the concurrence of the Charity Commissioners is required together with a two-thirds vote in favour by the charity trustees: ibid., s.74.
[191] *Re Whitley* [1910] 1 Ch. 600.
[192] TLATA 1996 s.2(1).

mortgage over the settled property is the tenant for life or statutory owner under settlements created before that date and thus governed by the Settled Land Act 1925 as trustees or parties interested under the settlement.[193] Settlements existing on January 1, 1997, will continue to exist until there is no relevant property (land and chattels) and will be governed by the law that applied as at that date. The requisite vesting instrument must have been made vesting the legal estate in the settled land in the tenant for life or statutory owner,[194] and the loan must be required for certain specified purposes. Where there is no tenant for life or person otherwise having, either under the Act or by the settlement, the powers of a tenant for life, then the trustees of the settlement may exercise those powers for the purposes of the Act as statutory powers.[195] A settlement includes any instrument or instruments whereby a fee simple or term of years absolute is limited in trust for an infant, or for any person contingently or where the land stands charged with family charges.[196] The tenant for life also has the power to create a settlement for the express purpose of overreaching equitable interests and powers.[197] There are two classes of purpose for which a mortgage may be made, namely, purposes paramount to the settlement, and purposes for giving effect to equitable interests under the settlement. It should be noted, however, that in the absence of a contrary provision in the settlement itself,[198] a tenant for life has no power to mortgage or charge the legal estate for his own benefit or use. If he wishes to do so he can mortgage his own beneficial interest.

Mortgages paramount to equitable interests under the settlement: The **4–48** tenant for life or statutory owner has power by a legal mortgage[199] to raise money for certain specified purposes, namely where money is required[200] for any of the following purposes:

(1) discharging an encumbrance[201] on the settled land or parts thereof[202];

(2) paying for any improvement authorised by the Act or by the settlement[203];

(3) equality of exchange;

---

[193] See the Settled Land Act 1925 s.107.

[194] ibid., s.13.

[195] See the Settled Land Act 1925 ss.23, 26 and 117(1)(xxvi).

[196] ibid., s.1(1)(ii)(d), (iii).

[197] ibid., s.72 and LPA 1925 s.2. An estate owner also has the powers of a tenant for life; in particular the power to make overreaching conveyances under the Settled Land Act 1925 s.21.

[198] See *Re Egerton's Settled Estates* [1926] Ch. 574.

[199] Or charge by way of legal mortgage, see the Settled Land Act 1925 s.117(1)(xi).

[200] "Required" means reasonably required having regard to the circumstances, see *Re Clifford* [1902] 1 Ch. 87; *Re Bruce* [1905] 2 Ch. 372 at 376.

[201] i.e. of a permanent nature and not any annual sum payable only during a life or lives or during a term of years absolute or determinable, see the Settled Land Act 1925 s.71(2).

[202] This includes, e.g. local charges for making up streets, see *Re Smith's Settled Estate* [1901] 1 Ch. 689; *Re Pizzi* [1907] 1 Ch. 67.

[203] See the Settled Land Act 1925 s.83 and Sch.3.

(4) redeeming a compensation rent charge[204] in respect of the extinguishment of manorial incidents and affecting the settled land[205];

(5) satisfying any claim under the Landlord and Tenant Act 1927 for compensation for an improvement[206];

(6) paying a coast protection charge or expenses incurred in carrying out work under a works scheme under the Coast Protection Act 1949[207];

(7) paying certain expenses and making certain payments under the Landlord and Tenant Act 1954[208];

(8) paying certain sums recoverable under the Town and Country Planning Act 1990[209];

(9) paying expenses incurred by a tenant for life or statutory owner in connection with proceedings for enfranchising leaseholds or obtaining extensions of leases under the Leasehold Reform Act 1967, and paying compensation in connection with exercise of certain overriding rights of a landlord under that Act[210];

(10) paying the costs of any transaction authorised under the foregoing heads or by ss.69 or 70 of the Settled Land Act 1925.[211]

Thus, the tenant for life may raise the money so required on the security of the settled land or any part thereof, and the money so raised shall be capital money for that purpose, and may be paid or applied accordingly. For this purpose it must be paid to the trustees of the settlement.[212] As has already been noted the mortgage must be a legal mortgage, which includes a charge by way of legal mortgage, and the tenant for life or statutory owner cannot make an equitable mortgage.[213]

4–49 Overreaching effects of paramount mortgage of settled land: A legal mortgage made by the tenant for life or statutory owner under the statutory powers is effectual to give the mortgagee a title to discharge free from all the limitations, powers, and provisions of the settlement and from all estates, interests and charges subsisting or to arise thereunder, but subject to and with the exception of:

---

[204] Such power is conferred by LPA 1922 s.139(3); the Manorial Incidents (Extinguishment) Rules 1925 (S.R. & O. 1925 No. 810), r.15; and also see the Manorial Incidents (Extinguishment) (Amendment) Rules 1935 (S.R. & O. 1935 No.1241), r.2.

[205] Settled Land Act 1925 s.71(1)(i)ñ(iii), (vi), (ix). Other purposes were also specified by s.71(1) namely, the raising of money by mortgage for extinguishing manorial incidents, for compensating the stewards on the extinguishment of manorial incidents and discharging expenses incurred in connection with the extinguishment for commuting any additional rents made payable on the conversion of a perpetually renewable leasehold interest into a long term and for satisfying any claims for compensation by an agent of the lessor in respect of loss of fees on conversion (see s.71(1)(iv) (v), (vii), (viii)). They are either repealed or spent by virtue of the Statute Law (Repeals) Act 1969 s.1, Sch., Pt III.

[206] Landlord and Tenant Act 1927 s.13(2) (as amended by TLATA 1996 Sch.4).

[207] Coast Protection Act 1949 s.11(2)(a).

[208] Landlord and Tenant Act 1954 Sch.2 para.6.

[209] Town and Country Planning Act 1990 s.328.

[210] Leasehold Reform Act 1967 s.6(5), Sch.2 para.9(1).

[211] Settled Land Act 1925 s.71(1)(ix).

[212] ibid., s.75.

[213] ibid., s.72(1).

(1) all legal estates and charges by way of legal mortgage having priority to the settlement;

(2) all legal estates and charges by way of legal mortgage which has been conveyed or created for securing money actually raised at the date of the deed; and

(3) all leases and grants at fee-farm rents or otherwise, and all grants of easements, rights of common, or other rights or privileges which: (a) were before the date of the mortgage granted or made for value in money or money's worth, or agreed so to be, by the tenant for life or statutory owner, or by any of his predecessors in title, or any trustees for them, under the settlement, or under any statutory power, or are at that date otherwise binding on the successors in title of the tenant for life or statutory owner; and (b) are at that date protected by registration under the Land Charges Act 1925 if capable of registration thereunder.[214]

Notwithstanding registration under the Land Charges Act 1925 of an annuity within the meaning of Pt II of that Act or of a limited owner's charge or a general equitable charge within the meaning of that Act, a mortgage under the Settled Land Act 1925 operates to overreach such annuity or charge.[215]

Shifting encumbrances: By virtue of s.69 of the Settled Land Act 1925, where **4–50** there is an encumbrance[216] affecting any part of the settled land (whether capable of being overreached on the exercise by the tenant for life of his powers under the Act or not) then *Re Knight's Settled Estates*[217] illustrates that the tenant for life, with the consent of the encumbrancer, may charge that encumbrance on any other powers of the settled land, or on all or any part of the capital money or securities representing capital money subject or to become subject to the settlement, whether already charged therewith or not, in exoneration of the first mentioned part and the tenant for life may by a legal mortgage or otherwise make provision accordingly.

Variation and consolidation of securities: By s.70 where an encumbrance **4–51** affects any part of the settled land, the tenant for life may, with the consent of the encumbrancer, vary the rate of interest charged and any other provisions of the instrument, if any, creating the encumbrance and, with the like consent, charge that encumbrance on any part of the settled land, whether already charged therewith or not, or on all or any part of the capital money or securities representing capital money subject or to become subject to the settlement, by way of additional security, or of consolidation of securities. The tenant for life may by a legal mortgage or otherwise make provision accordingly.

---

[214] ibid., s.72(2).
[215] ibid., s.72(3).
[216] "Encumbrance" in this section includes any annual sum payable during a life or lives or during a term of years absolute or determinable, but in any such case an additional security must be effected so as only to create a charge or security similar to the original charge or security, see s.70(2).
[217] [1918] 1 Ch. 211.

4–52 Costs: The court may direct that a tenant for life may also raise by a legal mortgage of the settled land or any part thereof, any costs, charges or expenses to be paid out of the property subject to the settlement.[218] The costs of the summons for leave to raise by mortgage such costs, may be added and raised.[219]

4–53 Additional powers under the settlement: The settlement may confer powers to mortgage additional to or larger than those conferred by the Settled Land Act 1925,[220] but any power of mortgaging conferred on the trustees of the settlement or other persons for any purpose, whether or not provided for by the Act, is exercisable by the tenant for life or statutory owner, as if it were an additional power conferred on the tenant for life,[221] and operates as if it were conferred by the Act on the tenant for life.[222]

4–54 Additional powers authorised by order of the court: By virtue of s.64 of the Settled Land Act 1925 the court has a statutory jurisdiction to authorise the tenant for life to effect any transaction affecting or concerning the settled land, or any part thereof, or any other land not otherwise authorised by the Act or the settlement[223] if in the opinion of the court it would be for the benefit of the settled land, or any part thereof for the persons interested under the settlement.[224] But it must be a transaction which could have been validly made by an absolute owner.[225] The transactions which may be authorised include any sale, exchange, assurance, grant, lease, surrender, re-conveyance, release, reservation, or other disposition; any purchase or other acquisition; any covenant, contract or option; any application of capital money and any compromise or other dealing or arrangement.[226] Thus, the court has authorised a tenant for life to raise a mortgage on the settled land to pay off his debts which had arisen from the expenses of maintaining the land.[227] Further, this jurisdiction empowers the court to sanction a proposed scheme on behalf of those who are unable to consent (for example an infant) which alters the beneficial interest under the settlement,[228] having as its object or effect to reduce liability for tax, including estate duties,

---

[218] See the Settled Land Act 1925 ss.92 and 114.

[219] *Re Pizzi* [1907] 1 Ch. 67 at 71.

[220] Settled Land Act 1925 s.109(1).

[221] ibid., s.108(2).

[222] ibid., s.109(2).

[223] See *Re Symons* [1927] 1 Ch. 344 at 354.

[224] See *Re Cleveland Literary and Philosophical Society's Land* [1931] 2 Ch. 247.

[225] Settled Land Act 1925 s.64(1) as amended by the Settled Land and Trustee Acts (Court's General Powers) Act 1943 s.2. Certain words were repealed by the Statute Law (Repeals) Act 1969 s.1, Sch., Pt III. By virtue of s.1 of the 1943 Act the jurisdiction of the court was extended to enable it, in particular circumstances, to make an order authorising expenses of management to be treated as a capital outgoing notwithstanding that in other circumstances the expense could not have been so treated. This provision was amended and made permanent by the Emergency Laws (Miscellaneous Provisions) Act 1953 s.9.

[226] See the Settled Land Act 1925 s.64(2), as amended, and s.109(1).

[227] *Re White-Popham Settled Estates* [1936] Ch. 725.

[228] See *Re Simmons* [1956] Ch. 125.

which could not normally be effected under the general law prior to the enactment of the Variation of Trust Acts 1958.[229]

Tenant for life as trustee—limits on powers: The tenant for life not only has **4–55** the estate[230] vested in him on trust for himself and the other beneficiaries under the settlement but also he is in the position of a trustee in relation to the exercise of his statutory powers.[231] Thus, the tenant for life will be restrained by injunction from creating a mortgage which is prejudicial or unjust to the interests of the beneficiaries[232] and the court will treat the creation of any such mortgage as a breach of trust. Thus, a tenant for life is not entitled to attempt to preserve a heavily encumbered estate by mortgaging it if, by doing so, he prejudices the interests of existing equitable encumbrances.[233] However, provided that the tenant for life acts in good faith and has proper regard to his statutory duty under the Act in relation to the interests of all parties entitled under the settlement, the court will not normally interfere with the discretion of a tenant for life as to the exercise of those powers.[234]

If, however, a trustee fails to see that he is acting unjustly despite being honest and acting within the letter of his trust, it is the duty of the court to interfere.[235]

Payment of capital money to trustees and protection of mortgages: Since **4–56** money raised by virtue of the statutory powers is capital money it must be paid either to the trustees of the settlement, for the purposes of the Settled Land Act 1925 of whom there must be not fewer than two persons as trustees of the settlement unless the trustee is a trust corporation[236] or into court, at the option of the tenant for life.[237] The tenant for life must also give notice to each of the trustees of the settlement of his intention to mortgage or charge the land, and, if known, to the solicitor for the trustees.[238] This, however, must be a notice of each specific transaction contemplated by the tenant for life[239] and a general notice does not suffice.[240] A mortgagee dealing in good faith with the tenant for life is not concerned to make any enquiry with regard to the giving of the notice.[241] Further, a mortgagee paying his advance to the trustees is not concerned to see

---

[229] See, e.g. *Chapman v Chapman* [1954] A.C. 429.
[230] Settled Land Act 1925 s.16(1); and see *Re Boston's Wills Trust* [1956] Ch. 395 at 405.
[231] See the Settled Land Act 1925 s.107.
[232] *Hampden v Earl of Buckinghamshire* [1893] 2 Ch. 531 at 543, 544.
[233] ibid.
[234] ibid.; and see *Re Richardson* [1900] 2 Ch. 778 at 790.
[235] *Hampden v Earl of Buckinghamshire* [1893] 2 Ch. 531 at 544; *Re Gladwin's Trust* [1919] 1 Ch. 232; and see *Re Charteris, Charteris v Biddulph* [1917] 2 Ch. 379 at 394. The title of the estate mortgaged by the tenant for life is not affected by this provision, but it causes the tenant for life to be personally bound as a trustee, see *Re Marquis of Ailesbury's Settled Estates* [1892] 1 Ch. 506 at 535, 536.
[236] Settled Land Act 1925 s.94.
[237] ibid., ss.75(1), 94.
[238] ibid., s.101(1).
[239] See *Re Ray's Settled Estates* (1884) 25 Ch.D. 464.
[240] i.e. under the Settled Land Act 1925 s.101(2).
[241] Settled Land Act 1925 s.101(5).

that the money advanced is required for any purpose under the Act or that no more than is wanted is raised.[242]

4–57 **Mortgages to give effect to equitable interests:** Further, by virtue of s.16 of the Settled Land Act 1925, the estate owner is a statutory trustee of the settled land for giving effect to the equitable interests. Thus, where:

> "(*a*) any principal sum is required to be raised on the security of the settled land, by virtue of any trust, or by reason of the exercise of an equitable power affecting the settled land, or by any person or persons who under the settlement is or are entitled or together entitled to or has to have a general power of appointment over the settled land, whether subject to any equitable charges or powers of charging subsisting under the settlement or not; or
>
> (*b*) the settled land is subject to any equitable charge for securing money actually raised and affecting the whole estate the subject of the settlement;
>
> the estate owner shall be bound, if so requested in writing, to create such legal estate or charge by way of legal mortgage as may be required for raising the money or giving effect to the equitable charge."[243]

It is therefore possible to raise money under this provision for portions.

But this is subject to the proviso that so long as the settlement remains subsisting, any legal estate or charge by way of legal mortgage so created shall take effect and must be expressed to take effect subject to any equitable charges or powers of charging subsisting under the settlement which have priority to the interests or powers of the person or persons by or on behalf of whom the money is required to be raised, or legal effect is required to be given to the equitable charge, unless the persons entitled to the prior charges or entitled to exercise the powers consent in writing to the same being postponed. But it is not necessary that such consent be expressed in the instrument creating such estate or charge by way of legal mortgage.[244] Further, effect may be given by means of a legal mortgage[245] to an agreement for a mortgage, or a charge or lien, whether or not arising by operation of law, if the agreement, charge or lien ought to have priority over the settlement.[246]

The Act also provides for the means of settling doubts as to whether any and what legal estate ought to be created under the foregoing provisions[247] by application to the court for directions and for vesting orders in case of refusal or neglect by the tenant for life, or any other difficulty.[248]

---

[242] ibid., ss.95 and 110(1) and the Trustee Act 1925 s.17.

[243] ibid., s.16(1)(iii); See also the Land Registration Act 1925 s.90; and the Land Registration Rules 1925 r.144. While charge rank in order of priority as registered under the Land Registration Rules 2003 r.101, the rule making power under the Land Registration Act 2002 has not been exercised to give effect to any analogous rules under that Act to replace the former provisions under the Land Registration Act 1925.

[244] Settled Land Act 1925 s.16(1)(iii) proviso; Land Registration Rules 1925 r.156 (as to which see fn.243).

[245] Which includes a legal charge, see the Settled Land Act 1925 s.117(1)(xi).

[246] Settled Land Act 1925 s.16(4).

[247] i.e. Under the Settled Land Act 1925 s.16.

[248] ibid., s.16(6), (7).

Overreaching effect of mortgage and protection of mortgagee: Provided   **4–58**
that the mortgage or legal charge is expressed to be made pursuant to s.16 of the
Settled Land Act 1925, it takes effect in priority to all the trusts of the settlement
and equitable interests and powers subsisting or to arise under the settlement
except those to which it is expressly made subject, and shall so take effect
whether the mortgagee or chargee has notice of any such trusts, interests or
powers, and further the mortgagee or chargee shall not be concerned to see that
a case has arisen to authorise the mortgage or charge or that no money than was
wanted was raised.[249] But, if the deed is to take effect under the Act and to
overreach the beneficial interests there is one important condition which must be
observed. The mortgagee or chargee must require that any capital money payable
in respect of the transaction must be paid either:

(1) to or by the direction of all the trustees of the settlement who must be
     either two or more in number or a trust corporation[250]; or
(2) into court.[251]

This rule applies notwithstanding anything to the contrary in the settlement.

Mortgage of land subject to family charges: The meaning of settled land was   **4–59**
extended by the Settled Land Act 1925[252] to include, not only the normal case of
land limited in trust for any person in possession, but to various other cases
where land is not vested in some person absolutely and beneficially.

Thus, land is settled land where it is subject to family charges, such as an
annuity or jointure rent charge and charges for portions. In the circumstances the
estate owner subject to such family charges only has the powers of a tenant for
life[253] and can only create a legal mortgage free from such charges if the Settled
Land Act procedure as to the appointment of trustees and the execution of a
vesting deed are observed.[254] In a limited class of case provided by s.1 of the Law
of Property (Amendment) Act 1926 (which allows settled land to be dealt with
as if it were not settled) the estate owner may make a legal mortgage subject to
such charges as if the land had not been settled land and without compliance with
the Settled Land Act procedure.

Mortgage to tenant for life: A mortgage or charge of the settled land may be   **4–60**
made to the tenant for life.[255] In such a case the trustees of the settlement have,
in addition to their powers as trustees, all the powers of a tenant for life as to
negotiating and completing the transaction.[256]

Mortgage by trustees where tenant for life has ceased to have a substantial   **4–61**
interest: If it is shown to the satisfaction of the court that the tenant for life:

---

[249] ibid., s.16(2).
[250] ibid., s.18(1)(b), (c); L.P.A. 1925, s.2(1)(i).
[251] ibid., s.18(1)(b).
[252] ibid., s.1(1).
[253] ibid., s.1(1)(v).
[254] ibid.
[255] ibid., s.13.
[256] ibid., s.68(2).

(1) has ceased to have a substantial interest in the land by reason of bankruptcy, assignment, encumbrance, or otherwise; and

(2) either consents to an order being made or has unreasonably refused to exercise any of the powers conferred on him by the Settled Land Act 1925;

then by virtue of s.24(1) of the Settled Land Act 1925:

> "the court may, upon the application of any person interested in the settled land or the part thereof affected, make an order authorising the trustees of the settlement to exercise in the name and on behalf of the tenant for life, any of the powers . . . in relation to the settled land or the part thereof affected, either generally and in such manner and for such period as the court may think fit, or in a particular instance."

Once such an order has been made it prevents the tenant for life from exercising any of the powers affected by the order.[257] But a person dealing with the tenant for life is not affected by it unless and until it has been registered under the Land Charges Act 1972 as an order affecting land. Such an order does not vest the legal estate nor the statutory powers in the trustees who do not become the statutory owner. The order merely authorises the trustees to exercise the statutory powers on behalf of the tenant for life and in his name. Further, the provision does not apply to statutory owners and is limited to tenants for life.[258]

4–62   **Mortgage of tenant for life's beneficial interest:**   It is possible for the tenant for life to mortgage his beneficial interest in the trust fund. Such an interest is necessarily equitable, but as it is an equitable thing in action within the meaning of s.136 of the Law of Property Act 1925, it is capable of legal assignment.[259] However, a mortgage of an equitable interest is normally by way of an equitable mortgage.

Tenants in tail

4–63   **Power of tenant in tail to mortgage:**   A tenant in tail in possession will normally have the legal estate, either freehold or leasehold, in the entailed property vested in him as estate owner on the trusts of the settlement.[260] In such circumstances he has the statutory power of a tenant for life to mortgage. Where he has only an equitable interest in the land entailed, which is the usual case,[261] he has special statutory powers of disposing of his equitable interest in the entailed land[262] apart from the general powers of disposition conferred on limited

---

[257] ibid., s.24(2), and see the Land Charges Act 1972 s.6.

[258] *Re Craven Settled Estates* [1926] Ch. 985.

[259] *Re Pain* [1919] 1 Ch. 38; *Earle Ltd v Hemsworth R.D.C.* (1928) 44. T.L.R. 605.

[260] Settled Land Act 1925 ss.4(2), 6(b), 7(1)–(4), 9(2), 20(1)(i), 117(1)(xxviii).

[261] See the Law of Property Act 1925 s.1. (1), (3).

[262] See the Fines and Recoveries Act 1833 s.15, and the Law of Property (Amendment) Act 1924 s.9, Sch.9, by which the Fines and Recoveries Act 1833 remains in force only as regards dealings with entailed interests as equitable interests.

owners under the Settled Land Act 1925 Pt II, ss.38 to 72. The tenant in tail[263] can put an end to the settlement by barring the entail[264] and, having done so by virtue of his legal estate becomes the absolute owner in equity by virtue of his legal estate and can mortgage. Unless the legal estate in the entailed land is vested in the tenant in tail[265] he can only mortgage the equitable interest in the land. By virtue of his special statutory powers of disposition the tenant in tail in possession may execute by deed a mortgage in the form of a conveyance of his equitable interest in fee simple or any less interest in the land.[266] If, however, the tenant in tail is not in possession, unless the mortgage is made with the consent of the protector of the settlement,[267] it will only convey to the mortgagee an equitable interest in the nature of a base fee. This is unimpeachable during the survival of the issue of the tenant in tail but is voidable upon the death of the survivor of that issue by the person next entitled in remainder on the estate tail.[268]

Extent of disentailment by mortgage: When a tenant in tail mortgages the   **4–64** land entailed under his special statutory powers pursuant to the Fines and Recoveries Act 1833,[269] generally the entail is wholly barred in equity to the extent of the interest created by the mortgage, irrespective of any intention to the contrary express or implied in the mortgage deed.[270] If the mortgage only creates an interest *pur autre vie*, a term of years, a charge unsecured by a term of years, or a greater interest, then the entail is barred only so far as is necessary to give effect to the mortgage, notwithstanding any intention express or implied to the contrary.[271]

Agreement to disentail: The 1833 Act also provides that a disposition by a   **4–65** tenant in tail in contract is of no force and that the courts are not to give effect to defective dispositions.[272] However, if it would seem that an agreement by a tenant in tail to disentail for the purpose of executing a legal mortgage may be specifically enforced against the tenant in tail himself.[273] But it cannot be specifically enforced against the issue in tail if the tenant in tail dies before conveying,[274] unless the remainder man was a party to the mortgage transaction.[275]

---

[263] As to the circumstances of family charges constituting a settlement, see the Settled Land Act 1925 s.1(1)(v) and the power of a person beneficially entitled to land subject to such family charges to convey or create a legal estate subject to the charges, see the Law of Property (Amendment) Act 1926 s.1.

[264] See the Fines and Recoveries Act 1833 s.15.

[265] See above, fn.2.

[266] See the Fines and Recoveries Act 1833 ss.15, 40.

[267] ibid., ss.22–28, 32.

[268] ibid., s.34.

[269] ibid., s.15.

[270] See the Fines and Recoveries Act 1833 s.21.

[271] ibid., s.21, proviso.

[272] ibid., ss.40, 47.

[273] *Bankes v Small* (1887) 36 Ch.D. 716.

[274] See *Att.-Gen. v Day* (1749) 1 Ves.Sen. 218 at 224; *Hinton v Hinton* (1755) 2 Ves.Sen. 631 at 634.

[275] See *Pryce v Bury* (1853) 2 Drew 11.

CHAPTER 5

TRANSFER AND DEVOLUTION OF RIGHTS UNDER THE SECURITY

INTER VIVOS TRANSFER OF THE MORTGAGE

General

A mortgagee, like any other owner, has a right to alienate his interest either **5–01** absolutely or by way of sub-mortgage,[1] save in the case of a local authority mortgage,[2] without the need for the agreement of the mortgagor.[3] His interest comprises two distinct titles; his title to the mortgage debt and his title to the mortgaged property. Conceivably, therefore, he may assign the debt without the title and vice versa. Accordingly, before 1926 it was the practice expressly to provide both for the assignment of the debt and the conveyance of the security and presumably this is still necessary when the transfer is not effected by deed. In the case of a deed executed after December 31, 1925, and insofar as it concerns unregistered land, s.114(1) of the Law of Property Act 1925 provides that—subject to the expression of a contrary intention[4]—the deed shall operate to transfer:

> "(a) the right to demand, sue for, recover, and give receipts for, the mortgage money or the unpaid part thereof and the interest then due, if any, and thenceforth to become due thereon; and

[1] The chargee under a registered charge may not create a legal sub-mortgage (see Land Registration Act 2002 s.23(3)) but can create a sub-charge by way of charge on the indebtedness secured by the primary charge (i.e. s.23(2)).

[2] Local Government Act 1986 ss.7–9 and the Local Authorities (Disposal of Mortgages) Regulations 1986 (SI 1986/1028)

[3] *Re Tahiti Cotton Co, Ex p. Sargent* (1874) L.R. 17 Eq. 273 at 279, per Jessel M.R.; but it is not yet settled whether a building society mortgage (as opposed to the mortgage debt) is transferable without either an express contract to that effect or the actual concurrence of the mortgagor and in any event the transferee may not be able to exercise the power of sale; see *Taylor v Russell* [1892] A.C. 247 at 255. See also *Re Rumney & Smith* [1897] 2 Ch. 351; *Sun Building Society v Western Suburban & Harrow Road Permanent Building Society* [1920] 2 Ch. 144; reversed on other grounds [1921] 2 Ch. 438. It would seem to be difficult to separate the rights arising from membership of the building society from the rights arising under the mortgage. Since the Building Societies Act 1986 a transfer of a building society mortgage may be made under an amalgamation of transfer of engagements between societies. In such circumstances a mortgagor will be bound by the rules of the amalgamated or transferee society, (see ss.93(4), 94(8) both as amended by the Building Societies Act 1997). It is also now possible to transfer business from a building society to a commercial company (see s.97 as amended). See also Ch.17.

[4] *Paragon Finance Plc v Pender* [2005] 1 WLR 3412—s.114 of the Law of Property Act 1925 (LPA 1925) does not apply in relation to the transfer of a registered charge (the Court of Appeal upholding the decision of Peter Smith J. at first instance) where, on registration, the transferee takes

(b) the benefit of all securities for the same and the benefit of and the right to sue on all covenants with the mortgagee, and the right to exercise all powers of the mortgagee[5]; and

(c) all the estate and interest in the mortgaged property then vested in the mortgagee subject to redemption or cesser, but as to such estate and interest subject to the right of redemption then subsisting."[6]

In short, and subject to the above caveat, if the transfer is by deed, then without these details being set out, the transferee[7] steps into the shoes of the mortgagee.[8] If, as is unlikely, a case should arise where the debt and the security have not been assigned together, the consequences are as follows. Where the debt alone is transferred, the assignor remains the mortgagee and is the person to exercise the powers and remedies attached to that position. He must therefore be the party joined in redemption of foreclosure proceedings but he is a trustee of the powers and remedies for his assignee and must hand over to the assignee any money he obtains by exercising them.[9] When the security alone is transferred, the assignee becomes entitled to hold the security until he is redeemed by payment of the debt charged thereon. Moreover, as mortgagee, he may foreclose and thus holds the beneficial interest in the debt to the extent that it can be satisfied out of the security[10] but the assignee cannot sue on the covenant.

Form of transfer

5–02   Again, subject to the caveat arising in *Paragon v Pender* (above), s.114(1) applies equally to mortgages of realty and personalty with the exception of mortgages of bills of sale. Its provisions are comprehensive and render a transfer by deed a completely effective instrument. Therefore, in practice a transfer is nearly always carried out either by deed or by the newer method of transfer, i.e. a receipt endorsed upon the mortgage deed, to which method s.115 of the Law of Property Act 1925 gives the same effect as a transfer by deed.[11]

5–03   It is, however, necessary to consider the minimum requirements of form for an effective transfer of mortgages of land. Moreover, it will be assumed that the assignor intends to transfer the debt and the security together. If the debt only is

---

free of encumbrances and other matters not protected on the register which bound the transferor (see ss.23(2)(a), 27(3), 30 (in relation to priorities) and 52(1) of the Land Registration Act (LRA) 2002). In the case of unregistered land the transferee steps into the shoes of the transferor. As to registered land, the transfer has effect in equity only until registration (see also *Meretz Investments NV v ACP Ltd* [2007] Ch. 197 per Lewison J. at first instance and affirmed on appeal [2008]Ch. 244).

[5] Express assignment of the benefit of covenants is therefore no longer necessary. Statutory powers are in any case exercisable by any person from time to time deriving title under the mortgagee: LPA 1925 s.205(1)(xvi).

[6] LPA 1925 s.114(1).

[7] "Transferee" includes his personal representatives and assignees (ibid., s.114(2)).

[8] Quaere whether this is the position where further advances are then made by the transferee to the mortgagor after transfer in the absence of a supplement deed between the parties.

[9] *Morley v Morley* (1858) 25 Beav. 253.

[10] *Jones v Gibbons* (1804) 9 Ves. 407; cf. *Phillips v Gutteridge* (1859) 4 De G. & J. 531.

[11] LPA 1925 s.155(6); all that is necessary is that the receipt should on its face appear to have been given to a person not entitled to the immediate equity of redemption. Such a transfer made before 1926 would not have passed the legal estate: *Re Beachey, Heaton v Beachy* [1904] 1 Ch. 67.

transferred, the assignment must be in writing and notice given to the mortgagor for the purpose of enabling the assignee to sue in his own name.[12]

A legal mortgage of land or a charge by way of legal mortgage requires, **5–04** strictly speaking, a deed for its transfer in every case because otherwise the legal title will not pass. There is no difficulty in the registered proprietor of a registered charge transferring the mortgage—such a transfer is a registrable disposition where the transfer will take effect at law only upon registration pursuant to s.27(3)(a) of the Land Registration Act 2002.[13] Again, transfers of legal charges on registered land must not only be by deed[14] but must be in the prescribed form[15] and the name of the transferee must be entered on the register as the new proprietor of the charge.[16]

The transfer of an equitable mortgage need not, of course, be by deed, **5–05** although in practice it usually is so effected. However, transfers of equitable mortgages are caught by s.53 of the Law of Property Act 1925, and therefore such transfers ought always to be made by an instrument in writing. Section 53 applies equally to an equitable security by deposit of title deeds prior to the enactment of the Law of Property (Miscellaneous Provisions) Act 1989 as the deposit creates an equitable mortgage which can only be assigned by a disposition in writing under s.53.[17] A mortgage which is not a registered charge can be transferred, discharged or surrendered by the same instruments as if the land had not been registered. Where such a mortgage is protected by a unilateral notice, the assignee can apply to be registered in addition to the registered beneficiary.[18]

It is, of course, critical to bear in mind that a contract for the transfer of an equitable mortgage must comply with s.2 of the Law of Property (Miscellaneous Provisions) Act 1989 as regards the interest in land—failure to comply renders the contract void.

Subrogation[19]

Such are the rules to which, strictly, transfers should conform. However, it is idle **5–06** to pretend that a transfer will be impossible without keeping to these rules given that equitable doctrines concerning the merger and non-merger of charges frequently allow a transfer to be effected by mere payment of the mortgage debt—that is to say that in the absence of an actual transfer a person advancing moneys to a mortgagor who uses the same to pay off a mortgage debt will stand (absent any reason for refusing the remedy) subrogated to the rights under the

---

[12] LPA 1925 s.136.
[13] See LRA 2002 ss.23(2), 27(3), 30 and 52(1).
[14] See LPA 1925 s.52 and LRA 2003 ss. 27(3) and 30.
[15] Land Registration Rules 2003, r.116 and see also the three forms (TR3 (Transfer of Charge); TR4 (transfer of a portfolio of charges) or AS2 (assent of charges) and LRA 2002 Sch.2 para.10 and Land Registration Rules 2003, rr.81, 84(4) and 88.
[16] See paras 13–24 et seq.
[17] *Re Richardson, Shillito v Hobson* (1885) L.R. 30 Ch.D. 396.
[18] Land Registration Rules 2003 r.88.
[19] Subrogation is considered in detail in Ch.7.

security. The availability of subrogation as an equitable remedy to reverse or prevent unjust enrichment arises when A is enriched at the expense of B and such an enrichment is unjust[20]—it does not turn on the intention of the parties or upon the lender showing some fault on the part of the mortgagor. In *Cheltenham & Gloucester Plc v Appleyard*[21] Neuberger L.J. (as he then was) set out a series of propositions which operate as the starting point for present day analysis. While there must be no reason of policy for refusing the remedy,[22] subrogation is not based on any argument of common intention of the parties respectively enriched and deprived.[23] An intention that A should be unsecured may operate to prevent subrogation to any security.[24]

5–07   Thus, if a stranger discharges the mortgage debt, he will—unless he has manifested a contrary intention—be presumed to intend to keep the mortgage alive for his own benefit,[25] that is to say, his legal relations with a defendant who would otherwise be unjustly enriched are regulated as if the benefit of the charge had been assigned to him. The person so discharging the debt will not, however, be treated as an assignee vis-à-vis someone who would not be unjustly enriched.

5–08   Moreover, the presumption is a strong one because in one case it was held to apply although the person discharging the debt had actually contracted with the mortgagor to be given a new mortgage.[26] The result is that under this doctrine a transfer may be obtained by merely paying over the mortgage moneys, the effectiveness of the transfer being assured by the fact that in equity the person discharging the debt is *subrogated* to the rights of the mortgagee.[27]

In circumstances where the funds put forward by the lender are used in part payment of a first charge, the lender stands subrogated to the rights of the first charge as against subsequent charges but the first charge does not lose his priority over the lender.[28]

5–09   If the mortgagee holds the deeds, the person paying him will obtain delivery of the deeds. On the other hand, this apparently simple method is not usually employed because the transferee cannot thus obtain the legal estate and because there are strong reasons for making the mortgagor concur in a proper deed of transfer. Therefore, in the normal case, transfers are effected by deed, or by an endorsed receipt under s.115 of the Law of Property Act 1925.[29]

---

[20] *Banque Financière de la Cité v Parc (Battersea) Ltd* [1999] 1 A.C. 221; [1998] 2 W.L.R. 475.

[21] [2004] 13 E.G. 127 (C.S.). See also *Halifax Mortgage Services v Muirhead* (1997) 76 P. & C.R. 418; *Halifax Plc v Omar* [2002] 2 P. & C.R. 26; *Eagle Star Insurance Co Ltd v Karasiewicz* [2002] EWCA Civ 940; *Filby v Mortgage Express (No.2) Ltd* [2004] 2 P. & C.R. DG16; *Primlake Ltd v Matthews Associates* [2009] EWHC 2774 (Ch).

[22] For example, *Orakpo v Manson Investments* [1978] A.C. 95.

[23] *Banque Financière de la Cité v Parc (Battersea) Ltd* [1998] 2 W.L.R. 475 per Lord Hoffmann at 483E–G.

[24] *Banque Financière,* above; *Paul v Speirway (in liq.)* [1976] Ch. 220; *Boscawen v Bajwa* [1996] 1 W.L.R. 328.

[25] *Chetwynd v Allen* [1899] 1 Ch. 353.

[26] *Butler v Rice* [1910] 2 Ch. 277 at 282, 283.

[27] See *Cracknall v Janson* (1879) 11 Ch.D. 1; *Patten v Bond* (1889) 60 L.T. 583; *Ghana Commercial Bank v Chandiram* [1960] A.C. 732 at 744, 745.

[28] *National Westminster Bank Plc v Mayfair Estates Property Investment Ltd* [2007] EWHC 287 (Ch).

[29] See below, paras 6–02 et seq.

It follows, and has been made clear,[30] that the subrogated security can be **5–10** enforced to recover the discharged secured debt together with interest. However, no order for possession should be made until the sums that would have been due under the subrogated security have been determined, including, if necessary, consideration of any repayments as had been made by the mortgagor being attributed to the subrogated security and any subsequent events (for example agreements to vary the amount of payments or extend time).[31] Further, the principle that a subrogator is under a duty not to destroy or prejudice any right or remedy of the subrogatee and that he would be liable to compensate the subrogate if he did,[32] applies equally where a prior encumbrancer had been paid off by a subsequent encumbrant.[33]

Transfers initiated by the mortgagor: Law of Property Act 1925 section 95

Another form of transfer requires special mention, namely transfers which are **5–11** not initiated by the mortgagee but are instigated by the person redeeming. It is a common occurrence for a mortgagor, who is pressed for payment, or who can obtain his money more cheaply elsewhere, to discharge the mortgage with the money of a stranger, who will require the mortgage to be transferred to him.[34] The primary rule is that a stranger has no right to redeem and cannot obtain a transfer except by contract with the mortgagee.[35] Section 95 of the Law of Property Act 1925, however, creates an exception to this rule when a stranger discharges the debt through the mortgagor. Subsection (1) provides[36] that, where a mortgagor is entitled to redeem and the mortgage debt is discharged, he may require the mortgagee, instead of reconveying or surrendering, to assign the mortgage debt and convey the mortgaged property to any third person as the mortgagor shall direct and the mortgagee is bound to assign and convey accordingly. This right is exercisable, not only by the original mortgagor, but by any person from time to time deriving title under him and by any person with any right to redeem. Mesne encumbrancers[37] are therefore entitled to call for a

---

[30] *Western Fronts Savings Ltd v Rock* [1993] N.P.C. 89; *Primlake Ltd v Matthews Associates* (above) and *Kali & Burlay v Chawla* [2008] B.P.I.R. 415.

[31] *Halifax Mortgage Services Ltd v Muirhead* [1997] N.P.C. 171, (1997) 76 P. & C.R 418.

[32] *MacGillary on Insurance Law* (11th edn, 2008), para.22–55.

[33] *Faireharm Investments Ltd v Citibank International Plc, The Times*, February 20, 1998.

[34] A stranger assisting a mortgagor to pay off the first mortgagee cannot safely take a new mortgage from the mortgagor because of the danger that the mortgagor has created mesne encumbrances; in the case of land he would be safeguarded by searching the register, but even so, if he discovers an encumbrance he must have a registered transfer instead of a new mortgage to preserve his priority: cf. *Teevan v Smith* (1882) 20 Ch. 724 at 728.

[35] *James v Biou* (1819) 3 Swanst. 234.

[36] Notwithstanding any stipulation to the contrary in the mortgage.

[37] This follows from the definition of mortgagor in LPA 1925 s.205(1)(xvi). Accordingly, the right is exercisable by an equitable mortgagee or chargee or the holder of an equitable lien: see *Everitt v Automatic Weighing Machine Co* [1892] 3 Ch. 506.

transfer and subsection (2) expressly states that, where there are several encumbrancers, each encumbrancer and the mortgagor may call for a transfer, notwithstanding the existence of intervening encumbrances but that in case of conflict the right is exercisable according to their priorities.

Limitations

5–12   There are, however, two important limitations on the exercise of the right given by s.95, the first of which is that a mortgagee in possession cannot be compelled to make a transfer unless he is brought into court for that purpose.[38] The reason for this is that a mortgagee who goes into possession will not be allowed to give up possession without the leave of the court if he makes a transfer and goes out of possession. He remains absolutely liable to account, as mortgagee in possession, for all rents and profits which have, or ought to have, been received after the transfer.[39] Even if the mortgagor were to concur in releasing him from liability this would not be sufficient when there were any mesne encumbrancers, for the latter would not be bound by the release. It is only under the direction of the court that a mortgagee in possession can safely transfer.[40] The second limitation is that a person does not qualify to exercise the right by merely tendering the mortgage moneys he must become entitled to a surrender or a reconveyance.[41] Therefore, if the mortgagee has notice that the mortgagor is not entitled to a reconveyance to himself absolutely he cannot be compelled to transfer the mortgage to the mortgagor's nominee absolutely.[42] This limitation is important in connection with mesne encumbrancers, for a prior mortgagee must give effect to the rights of any intervening mortgagees of whose mortgages he has notice[43] and, therefore, a mortgagee cannot under s.95 be compelled to transfer to a third party, when he has notice of a mesne encumbrancer whose consent has not been obtained.[44]

Effect of transfer by a mortgagee

5–13   When a mortgage is transferred without the concurrence of the mortgagor, the transferee takes subject to any equity which, at the date of the transfer, the mortgagor might have asserted in taking the mortgage account; for the debt, being a chose in action, can only be assigned subject to existing equities. It is true that in the transfer of a legal mortgage the transferee obtains a legal title, but it

---

[38] LPA 1925 s.95(3).

[39] *Re Prytherch, Prytherch v Williams* (1889) 42 Ch.D. 590; and see *Hinde v Blake* (1841) 11 L.J.Ch. 26.

[40] *Hall v Heward* (1886) 32 Ch.D. 430.

[41] But subs.(2) expressly allows a mortgagor to call for a transfer, notwithstanding mesne encumbrances, overruling *Teevan v Smith* (1882) 20 Ch.D. 724, to this extent; for the reasons given in the text, subs.(2) is, however, of limited application.

[42] *Alderson v Elgey* (1884) 26 Ch.D. 567.

[43] *Corbett v National Provident Institution* (1900) 17 T.L.R. 5.

[44] (1915) 84 L.J.Ch. 814.

is apparent upon the face of the title that it is a security only for a debt and that the real transaction is an assignment of a debt (thus the amount of the debt and not the nature of the security is of paramount importance).[45] As was said by Loughborough L.C. in *Matthews v Wallwyn*,[46] it is not consonant to the general course of equity to consider the estate as more than a security for a debt. The result is that, as a rule, a transferee's only right is to the sum actually owing by the mortgagor to the mortgagee at the date of the transfer and after allowing the mortgagor the benefit of any set-off or other equity which he had against the mortgagee.[47] For example, in *Turner v Smith*,[48] a mortgagor put into the hands of her solicitor a sum sufficient to pay off the mortgage. The solicitor subsequently himself took a transfer of the mortgage, having concealed from his client that he had never paid it off; he then transferred it again to the defendant for value, but the mortgagor was held entitled to redeem without further payment because the transferee could be in no better position than the solicitor at the date of the assignment.

Attendant Risks

The moral of this story is that a man takes a transfer of a mortgage at his peril **5–14** if he does not obtain an acknowledgment from the mortgagor of the sum actually due. Indeed, the transfer of a mortgage is an unsafe investment unless the mortgagor concurs or joins in the transfer as a party to the transaction[49] whereby he enters into a new covenant for the payment of the debt and interest. The risk is well illustrated by the case of *Parker v Jackson*.[50] Real property was mortgaged for £700 and the mortgage then transferred to the mortgagor's solicitor. Before he took the transfer the solicitor had sold other property of his client such that he held in his hands £2,000 of his client's money. He did not appropriate the money to the discharge of the mortgage nor did he pay it over to the client. Without informing his client he transferred the mortgage again and became bankrupt. Farwell J. held that the fact that the money had not been appropriated to the mortgage debt was immaterial and that the transferee could be redeemed without payment. Although a transferee is as a rule entitled to no more than the sum actually due at the date of the transfer—plus subsequent interest—the mortgagor may sometimes estop himself from relying on his equity. For example,

---

[45] *Matthews v Wallwyn* (1798) 4 Ves. 118; *Chambers v Goldwin* (1804) 9 Ves. 254.

[46] ibid., at 126. It seems, however, that a legal estate may be a protection to a transferee if the original mortgage was voidable on equitable grounds; he will, if he is a bona fide purchaser, be able to hold the estate as a security for money due under the mortgage at the date of the transfer: *Judd v Green* (1875) 45 L.J.Ch. 108; *Nant-y-glo and Blaina Ironworks Co Ltd v Tamplin* (1876) 35 L.T. 125. These decisions, both by Bacon V.C., are criticised in *Halsbury's Laws of England* (4th edn, re-issue 1999), Vol.32, para.581.

[47] *Bickerton v Walker* (1885) 31 Ch.D. 151 at 158. He cannot, in general add the costs of the transfer to the mortgage debt. The mortgagee must pay such costs himself (see *Re Radcliffe* (1856) 22 Beav. 201).

[48] [1901] 1 Ch. 213.

[49] See *Matthews v Wallwyn* (1798) 4 Ves. 118 at 126(a). In the case of a transfer of statutory mortgage the covenant will be implied if the transferee is joined in the transfer (LPA 1925 s.118(3)).

[50] (1936) 155 L.T. 104.

where a mortgage is executed containing an acknowledgment of the receipt of the sum expressed to be advanced, the mortgagor cannot afterwards claim that only a lesser sum was actually advanced, as against a transferee who acted on the faith of the receipt and was not aware of any special circumstances to put him upon inquiry.[51] This does not mean that where there is such a receipt the concurrence of the mortgagor is superfluous as there will always remain the risk that the mortgage was paid off, either in part or in full, between the date of the mortgage and that of the transfer. The mortgagor will not be permitted to deny a deceit practiced by the transferor on the transferee where he, the mortgagor, has enabled that deceit.[52]

There is a further danger. A debtor who has no notice of an assignment of the debt is entitled to pay it to the assignor.[53] Consequently, a transferee takes subject not only to the equities existing in favour of the mortgagor at the date of the transfer but also to any equities which arise after that date and before notice of the transfer.[54] Payments made by the mortgagor to the mortgagee after but without notice of the transfer are binding as against the transferee.[55] If the whole debt is thus discharged the mortgagor may redeem from the transferee without further payment.[56] Indeed, any agreement made for value to discharge the debt will be effective against the transferee in the absence of collusion.[57] The result is that if a transferee makes the initial mistake of not obtaining the concurrence of the mortgagor, it is vital that notice of the transfer should at once be given.

Rights transferred

5–15   Since a transferee takes the mortgage subject to the state of the accounts at the date of transfer he is, unless a contrary intention is expressed, entitled to arrears of interest.[58] In accordance, however, with the general rule that arrears may not be capitalised except by agreement, a transferee has no right to treat the arrears as part of the principal merely because he has had to pay the aggregate sum to obtain his investment.[59] This right may be obtained if the mortgagor is made to join in the transfer and to assent to the capitalisation of the arrears because it will be assumed that his assent was given in return for forbearance by the creditor.[60]

---

[51] *Bickerton v Walker* (1885) 31 Ch.D. 151; LPA 1925 s.68. cf. also *Dixon v Winch* [1900] 1 Ch. 736, where the mortgagor's equity was lost on the ground of imputed notice.

[52] *Bickerton v Walker* (1885) 31 Ch.D. 151—where the transferee enabled the mortgage advance to be described as larger than it fact was.

[53] *Stocks v Dobson* (1853) 4 De G.M. & G. 11.

[54] *Williams v Sorrell* (1799) 4 Ves. 389.

[55] *Dixon v Winch* [1900] 1 Ch. 736 at 742, per Cozens-Hardy J.

[56] *Norrish v Marshall* (1821) 5 Madd 475; *Re Lord Southampton's Estate* (1880) 16 Ch.D. 178.

[57] In *Norrish v Marshall* (above), the mortgagor paid in goods, not money.

[58] *Cottrell v Finney* (1874) 9 Ch. App. 541.

[59] *Ashenhurst v James* (1845) 3 Atk. 270; *Matthews v Wallwyn* (1798) 4 Ves. 118; *Halifax Mortgage Services v Muirhead* [1997] N.P.C. 171, (1997) 76 P. & C.R. 418.

[60] cf. *Porter v Hobbard* (1677) Freem. Ch. 30. But a mesne encumbrancer will not be bound by such an agreement, if the prior mortgagee had notice of his encumbrance: *Digby v Craggs* (1762) Amb. 612.

If the transfer is properly drawn it will contain such an agreement for capitalisation in express terms, although it seems that the court will also infer the agreement from the mere fact of the mortgagor's concurrence.[61]

It should also be noted that the sum paid to the mortgagee on a transfer does **5–16** not determine the amount to which the transferee is entitled as against the mortgagor. The market value of a mortgage is not necessarily the amount due on the security because the soundness of the security and the general credit of the debtor materially affect its attractiveness as an investment.[62] Therefore, a transferee who purchases his mortgage at a price less than the amount of the mortgage debt may stand on his rights as assignee of the mortgagee and claim the full amount of the debt from the mortgagor,[63] not least because the assignee takes the risk of obtaining recovery and is entitled to the benefit of the bargain he has struck. This is true whether the transferee is a stranger,[64] a mesne encumbrancer,[65] or a person otherwise beneficially interested in the estate.[66] However, the mortgagor himself and his personal representatives, who succeed to his liability on the contract for payment, cannot, of course, buy up the first mortgage at an undervalue and hold it against mesne encumbrancers, for they have no right to keep the mortgage alive at all and it is wholly extinguished on the transfer being taken.[67] Again, in special circumstances a transferee may not be permitted to hold the mortgage as security for more than its purchase price on the ground that he is in a fiduciary relation with the mortgagor. Thus a trustee,[68] solicitor,[69] agent[70] or any other person whose position gives him special opportunities of buying up the mortgage and of knowing its real value, will hold the mortgage subject to redemption only at the price for which he bought it.[71]

Transfer part of mortgage debt

If the mortgagee wishes to transfer part of the mortgage debt rather than the **5–17** whole, it is necessary either to execute a transfer of the whole debt and mortgaged property to a trustee for both the transfer and transferee, or for the mortgagee to execute a declaration of trust. The reason for this is that the mortgagee's powers of redemption, foreclosure, or sale are indivisible and the execution of a trust deed or declaration of trust are the only methods available to accommodate this state of affairs.

---

[61] *Agnew v King* [1902] 1 I.R. 471.

[62] See *Anon.* (1707) 1 Salk 155.

[63] *Davis v Barrett* (1851) 14 Beav. 542.

[64] *Phillips v Vaughan* (1685) 1 Vern. 336.

[65] *Darcy v Hall* (1682) 1 Vern. 49.

[66] e.g. a reversioner (*Davis v Barrett* (1851) 14 Beav. 542); but a life tenant under the Settled Land Act 1925 would be in a fiduciary position.

[67] *Otter v Lord Vaux* (1856) 6 De G.M. & G. 638; *Morrett v Paske* (1740) 2 Atk. 52; see below, para.5–27.

[68] *Darcy v Hall* (1682) 1 Vern. 49.

[69] *Macleod v Jones* (1883) 24 Ch.D. 289.

[70] *Carter v Palmer* (1841) 8 Cl. & F. 657.

[71] *Hobday v Peters (No.1)* (1860) 28 Beav. 349. Similarly a surety: *Reed v Norris* (1837) 2 My. & Cr. 361.

Transfer of registered charge

5–18   In the case of the transfer of a registered charge the proprietor of such a charge may transfer it by use of the prescribed form.[72] Completion of the transfer then occurs when the registrar enters the transferee in the register as the proprietor.[73] Provided that he had no notice of any irregularity or invalidity in the original charge, a registered transferee for valuable consideration and his successors in title should not be affected thereby.[74] Once registration has been effected, the term granted rests in the proprietor for the time being of the charge without any consequence or assignment.[75] But until the registration formalities have been completed, the transferee of the charge does not become the proprietor. The effect of this is that until registration is completed the transferee cannot exercise his statutory powers, for example, the power to appoint a receiver.[76]

Transfers of local authority mortgages

5–19   Since the enactment[77] of s.7 of the Local Government Act 1986, a local authority wishing to transfer any interests in land which they hold as mortgagee must obtain the prior written consent of the mortgagor.

The Act makes specific provision for the local authority to ensure that the mortgagor has the opportunity to make an informed decision whether or not to give consent. Thus the consent must specify the name of the transferee, it may be withdrawn by notice in writing at any time before the date of the transfer and it ceases to have effect if the transfer does not take place within six months after the consent is given.[78] Further, the Local Authorities (Disposal of Mortgages) Regulations 1986[79] impose requirements in the case of transfers taking place on or after September 1, 1986. In particular, the mortgagor's consent must be in the form set out in the Schedule to the Regulations and the local authority must supply the mortgagor with information specified by the Regulations. A transfer made without consent is void.[80] It is to be presumed that failure to comply with the requirements set out in s.7 and in the regulations has the same effect. There is also special provision in the case of transfers which appear on their face to be valid. Thus, it is provided[81] that a transfer made following an initially valid consent is valid even if the consent has expired or been withdrawn by the date of the transfer provided that the transfer contains a certificate by the transferor that consent has not been withdrawn or ceased to have effect. In such a case, however,

---

[72] Form TR3 (transfer of charge); Form TR4 (transfer of a portfolio of charges) or AS2 (Assent of Charges) as prescribed by Land Registration Rules 2003 r.116

[73] LRA 2002 s.27(3)(a) and Sch.2 para.10.

[74] ibid., s.29(1).

[75] ibid., s.30.

[76] *Lever Finance Ltd v Trustee of the Property of Needleman* [1956] Ch. 375.

[77] Applying to all transfers made *after* April 1, 1986 (unless pursuant to a contract made before that date).

[78] Local Government Act 1986 s.7(1) and (2).

[79] SI 1986/1028.

[80] Local Government Act 1986 s.7(3).

[81] ibid., s.7(4), (5).

the mortgagor is entitled to have the transfer set aside and the mortgage re-vested in the transferor by serving notice to that effect on the local authority within six months of the transfer.

Sub-mortgages

A sub-mortgage is in essence a transfer of a mortgage subject to a proviso for **5–20** redemption. In other words, it is a mortgage of a mortgage and it arises when a mortgagee wishes to borrow money upon the security of a profitable mortgage and it avoids the calling in the whole of the loan. Therefore, the rules set out above apply mutatis mutandis to sub-mortgages.

Registered land

Insofar as registered land is concerned, the only possible registration is of a **5–21** charge and the only sub-mortgage is a charge which charges with payment of money the indebtedness secured by the registered charge.[82]

Unregistered land

Given the divergences between the three types of sub-mortgage of unregistered **5–22** land (transfer by legal mortgage; sub-mortgage by sub-demise and charge by way of legal mortgage) it important to take care when considering the effect of a sub-mortgage. Given that the parties to a sub-mortgage can agree between themselves the form that the sub-mortgage is to take, the essential document is that which creates the sub-mortgage.[83] The mere existence of a sub-mortgage, regardless of the construction of the contractual documents, either divest a principal mortgagee of his right to possession or suspend that right during the currency of the sub-mortgage.[84] The critical question will be as to what rights the document provides to the sub-mortgagee, first, in relation to the original mortgage debt; second, in relation to the property charged by the original mortgagee; and third, what rights are provided to the sub-mortgagor over the property originally charged.

Insofar as the transfer of a sub-mortgage is concerned, in circumstances where the principal mortgage is by way of legal mortgage or an equitable mortgage, a transfer of the sub-mortgage is effected by an assignment of the benefit of the legal charge or equitable mortgage. In circumstances where the principal mortgage is a legal mortgage by demise, a transfer of the sub-mortgage is effected by an assignment of the sub-mortgage term subject to redemption under the sub-mortgage. Reliance on s.114 of the Law of Property Act 1925 will be sufficient where the sub-mortgage is a security on a legal charge, equitable mortgage or

---

[82] LRA 2002 s.23(2)(a) and (b).
[83] *Credit & Mercantile Plc v Marks* [2005] Ch. 81.
[84] ibid.

legal mortgage by demise. Notice should, of course, be given to the principal mortgagor and the sub-mortgagor.

5–23   After 1925, however, if the original mortgage was of the legal estate and created by demise, the sub-mortgage cannot be effected by assignment of the estate. It can only be created by *the transfer* of the mortgage debt, together with either a separate sub-demise of the estate or with a separate legal charge or equitable mortgage of the estate.[85] This means that the simple form of transfer provided by s.114[86] is not appropriate.[87] Otherwise the effect of the transaction is the same as if a transfer were made subject to a proviso for redemption.[88] In all other cases the sub-mortgage can be effected by a transfer of the benefit of the head mortgage by a deed under s.114.[89] Whatever its form, a sub-mortgage should contain an express covenant for payment of the moneys due under the sub-mortgage and a proviso for redemption of the sub-mortgage. Further, the original mortgagor should join in the transaction or be given immediate notice of it in order to avoid the problems which can arise under cases such as *Norrish v Marshall* and *Parker v Jackson*.[90]

If the terms of the agreement put the sub-mortgagee in the position of a transferee of the principal mortgage, he may exercise his rights under the principal or sub-mortgage. Upon exercise of the power of sale under the principal mortgage (on default) he will extinguish the rights of redemption under both mortgages

Therefore, a sub-mortgage makes the sub-mortgagee a transferee of the original mortgage subject to an equity of redemption in the mortgagee. As such, he may exercise all the powers of the original mortgagee and may sell, foreclose, dispose of the fee simple or lease under ss.88(5) or 89(5) of the Law of Property Act 1925 or otherwise realise the mortgaged property.[91]

For example: A mortgages Blackacre for £1,000 to B. Owing to arrears of interest the mortgage debt stands at £1,500 when B sub-mortgages to C for an advance of £500. A, the mortgagor, is made to concur and C thus holds a mortgage for £1,500 as security for his advance of £500.

If he subsequently wishes to realise his security, C has two choices. He may either realise his sub-mortgage alone, or the original mortgage which necessarily involves terminating the sub-mortgage as well. If he sells his sub-mortgage to X for £600 and his own account against B remains at £500, he must pay over the

---

[85] LPA 1925 s.86(1), (3).

[86] Which has no application, in any event, to registered land—*Paragon Finance Plc v Pender* and *Meretz Investments NV v ACP* (above).

[87] It can, however, be used, since s.86(2) provides that an attempt to mortgage a term of years by assignment shall take effect as a sub-demise.

[88] See Key & Elphinstone, *Precedents in Conveyancing* (15th edn, 1953–54), Vol.2, p.230.

[89] Some doubt has been expressed, however, as to the appropriateness of this method, see (1948) 12 Conv. (N.S.) 171 (H. Woodhouse).

[90] *Norrish v Marshall* (1821) 5 Madd. 475; *Parker v Jackson* (1936) 155 L.T. 104. A sub-mortgagee being in the position of a transferee, takes subject to the state of the accounts between the mortgagor and the mortgagee at the date of the sub-mortgage. If the mortgagor's concurrence is not obtained notice must be given to him to avoid the consequences of any equities arising after the date of the transfer.

[91] A sub-mortgage, which transfers the original power of sale to the sub-mortgagee, appears at the same time to deprive the original mortgagee of the power, see *Cruse v Nowell* (1856) 25 L.J.Ch. 709.

surplus to B while X becomes transferee of the mortgage. If, on the other hand, he sells Blackacre itself for £2,000, he pays himself his £500, then discharges A's debt to B, deducting £500 from B's claim, and finally hands over any surplus to A. On the same principle, he may foreclose on the mortgagee without disturbing the original mortgagor or making him a party. If he forecloses on the mortgagor, the mortgagee must be joined as a party and given an opportunity to redeem.

Registered land

A mortgage debt may be charged at law by the proprietor of a registered charge   **5–24**
with the repayment of money by way of a sub-charge.[92] However, a registered chargee may not grant a legal sub-mortgage by way of a transfer by way of mortgage, nor a sub-mortgage by sub-demise, nor a charge by way of legal mortgage.[93] At law the sub-chargee must be registered as the proprietor of the sub-charge for it to be effective.[94] Section 30(1) of the Land Registration Act 2002 provides that if a registrable disposition is made for valuable consideration, completion of the disposition by registration has the effect of postponing to the interest under the disposition any interest affecting the charge immediately before the disposition whose priority was not protected at the time of registration—effecting sub-charges and sub-chargees accordingly. Section 53 of the Land Registration Act 2002 provides that the registered proprietor of a sub-charge has the same powers as the sub-chargor in relation to the property which is the subject of the principal or any intermediate charge. A sub-charge must be transferred and discharged in the same form and same manner as any other registered charge.

INTER VIVOS TRANSFER OF EQUITY OF REDEMPTION

In the absence of any express provisions or statutory enactment to the contrary,[95]   **5–25**
a mortgagor can at any time transfer the mortgaged property without the mortgagee's consent. However, he remains personally liable on the covenant to pay despite such transfer.[96]

A mortgagor is only able to convey his property unencumbered if:

(1) the mortgagee consents to the transfer; or
(2) the mortgagor redeems the mortgage; or

---

[92] LRA 2002 s.23(2).

[93] ibid., ss.23(2)(b) and 23(3). By s.24 the power to sub-charge may be exercised by a person entitled to be registered as the proprietor of a registered charge.

[94] ibid., s.25 and Sch.2 para.11.

[95] Under the Small Dwellings Acquisition Acts 1899 to 1923, the mortgagor was restricted from transferring the mortgaged property. These Acts have now been repealed by the Housing (Consequential Provisions) Act 1985. But the Housing Act 1985 s.456 and Sch.18 (as amended), contain provisions applicable to existing mortgages made under the previous legislation. Most building society mortgages contain restrictions on transfer.

[96] See paras 27–42 et seq.

(3) a declaration is obtained from the court by the mortgagor that the property is free from encumbrances upon sufficient money being paid into court.[97]

DEVOLUTION ON DEATH

5–26   In *Thornborough v Baker*[98] Lord Nottingham settled conclusively that, whatever the nature of the property mortgaged, a mortgagee's interest in his mortgage is personalty, the mortgagee's principal right being to the money and his right to the land being only a security for that money. The result was that until 1882 freehold estates in mortgage caused difficulty upon the mortgagee's intestacy, as the estate passed to the heir-at-law while the debt belonged to the personal representatives.[99] Further, since the estate was in equity only a security, the heir-at-law held it on trust for the personal representatives.[100] The Conveyancing Act 1881[101] (superseded by the Land Transfer Act 1897[102]) however, provided that a mortgaged estate should pass to the personal representatives as if it were a chattel real notwithstanding any testamentary disposition to the contrary. The point is now merely of historical interest, though it may arise in an occasional search on title.

The Law of Property Act 1925 removes all difficulties by its initial provision that mortgages of freehold cannot be created by the conveyance of the title but must be effected through terms of years, the result being that both the security and the debt are in their own nature personalty. Furthermore, the Administration of Estates Act 1925[103] has instituted a single system of devolution upon intestacy for both realty and personalty. On the death of a mortgagee, the mortgage and the debt devolve on his personal representatives (without registration[104]) who, until the mortgage is discharged, or until they have assented in favour of the persons next entitled, may exercise all the powers of the mortgagee.[105] The personal representatives are deemed by s.1(2) of the Administration of Estates Act 1925 to be the heirs and assigns of the mortgagee with all the power conferred on the mortgagee in relation to mortgages made prior to 1926 and as they derive title under the original mortgagee can exercise the statutory powers of the mortgagee.[106] If the mortgage is specifically bequeathed, the executors will at the appropriate moment vest the debt and such mortgage term as remains in the

---

[97] LPA 1925 s.50(1), (2); see para.26–52.

[98] (1675) 3 Swann. 628.

[99] ibid.

[100] *Re Loveridge, Drayton v Loveridge* [1902] 2 Ch. 859.

[101] s.30.

[102] s.1(1).

[103] ss.1(1), 3(1).

[104] LRA 2002 s.27(5)(a)—subject to any interest to which the charge was subject at the date of the death of the deceased. On the grant of representation the personal representatives may apply to be registered as proprietor (see Land Registration Rules r.163).

[105] In the case of the death of one of several mortgagees, see the operation of the joint account clause in the case where two or more persons lend money.

[106] See LPA 1925 s.205(1)(xvi).

beneficiary,[107] the beneficiary taking as personalty. If not the executors will dispose of the same as part of the residuary estate. If the deceased dies intestate, the mortgage devolves under the usual statutory trusts. The basic principle in *Thornborough v Baker*[108] is, however, still of importance. The benefit of the mortgage passes under a general bequest of personalty but not a general devise of realty.[109] This rule is on the assumption that the equity of redemption is still subsisting. If the equity of redemption is destroyed by foreclosure or by the mortgagee having been in possession for the statutory period without acknowledging the debt, a conversion takes place and his interest acquires the nature of the property mortgaged so that in the case of freehold it becomes realty.[110]

Assent by personal representatives

Although a mortgage term is "an estate or interest in real estate" for the purposes of s.36(1) of the Administration of Estates Act 1925, a mortgage debt is not. Thus there is some doubt as to whether an assent by personal representatives is sufficient to pass both the legal estate and the debt. But as such a debt passes if there is a clear intention that it should,[111] it seems that no difficulty would arise in most cases.

5–27

DEVOLUTION ON INSOLVENCY

Insolvency of mortgagee

In the case of an individual insolvency of an individual mortgagee[112] any mortgage, like the rest of the bankrupt's estate, vests (with certain exceptions) in his trustee.[113] Thus his trustee may exercise all the mortgagee's powers and remedies including the right to sue for foreclosure.[114]

In the case of registered land the trustee is entitled to be registered as the proprietor in the place of the bankrupt but he may deal with the charge before registration.[115]

5–28

---

[107] Administration of Estates Act 1925 s.36(1).

[108] (1675) 3 Swann. 628.

[109] Even a specific devise of Blackacre will not give the devisee the beneficial interest in a mortgage held by the testator if he also held a reversionary interest in the property: the devisee will get the reversionary interest only: *Bowen v Barlow* (1872) L.R. 8 Ch. 171.

[110] See *Garrett v Evers* (1730) Mos. 364; *Thompson v Grant* (1819) 4 Madd. 438; *Re Loveridge, Pearce v Marsh* [1904] 1 Ch. 518.

[111] *Re Culverhouse* [1896] 2 Ch. 251.

[112] For a more detailed analysis of the positions of both the mortgagee and mortgagor on insolvency, see further *Muir Hunter on Personal Insolvency* (most recent release March 2010).

[113] Insolvency Act 1986 s.306.

[114] *Waddell v Toleman* (1878) 9 Ch.D. 212.

[115] ibid., s.37; Land Registration Rules 1925 r.170.

Where an incorporated mortgagee has been dissolved, all property and rights whatsoever vested in or held in trust for the company immediately before it dissolution are deemed to be bona vacantia and devolve to the Crown.[116]

Insolvency of mortgagor

5–29 The impact on the mortgagee of the insolvency of the mortgagor is considered elsewhere.[117]

---

[116] Companies Act 2006 s.1012.
[117] See below Ch.34.

CHAPTER 6

EXTINGUISHMENT OF THE SECURITY

DISCHARGE OF THE MORTGAGE OR CHARGE

Once the debt secured by the mortgage has been paid in full, the mortgagor is **6–01**
entitled to have the mortgaged property returned free of the security.[1] The precise
character of the instrument necessary to release the security depends on the
nature of the mortgage, though the Law of Property Act 1925 has made it largely
a matter of an appropriate receipt. Prior to 1926, when mortgages of freehold
were usually made by conveyance of the legal estate, redemption involved a deed
of reconveyance executed by the mortgagee without which the mortgagor's chain
of title would be incomplete.[2] Again, because mortgages of a leasehold estate
were made, as a rule, by sub-demise redemption necessitated an express surrender of the sub-lease because the Satisfied Terms Act 1845 did not apply to
terms created out of leaseholds.[3] Equitable mortgages, on the other hand, did not
require any instrument of reconveyance because the receipt of the mortgage
moneys automatically terminated the equity.[4] Nevertheless it was in fact quite
common to have a reconveyance even in these cases. In one class of mortgage,
however, namely building society mortgages, special legislation[5] was enacted
enabling the discharge of such mortgages to be effected by a receipt indorsed on
or annexed to the mortgage deed. In these cases the receipt operated as an
automatic reconveyance of the property mortgaged.

Unregistered land

Indorsed (or statutory) receipt: Law of Property Act 1925 section 115

The Law of Property Act 1925 has simplified the machinery of redemption by **6–02**
extending this principle to all mortgages of land except those of registered land.
Thus, under s.115 a receipt for the mortgage moneys indorsed on, written at the

---

[1] Law of Property Act 1925 (LPA 1925) s.116.
[2] *Webb v Crosse* [1912] 1 Ch. 323.
[3] *Re Moore & Hulm's Contract* [1912] 2 Ch. 105.
[4] *Firth & Sons v IR Commissioners* [1904] 2 K.B. 205.
[5] Building Societies Act 1986 s.13(7), Sch.4 para.2, re-enacting (with modifications) s.37 of the
Building Societies Act 1962 which itself consolidated earlier legislation, particularly Building
Societies Act 1874: See Ch.17.

foot of, or annexed to the mortgage instrument and executed by the mortgagee[6] operates:

(1) in the case of a mortgage by demise or sub-demise as an automatic surrender of the term, so that the term is merged in the reversion, which is immediately expectant on the term;

(2) in other cases, as an automatic reconveyance of the mortgaged interest to the person who, immediately before the execution of the receipt, was entitled to the equity of redemption.

The result is that an indorsed receipt at once exonerates the property from the mortgage but does not alter the position of anyone with an interest in the property paramount to the discharged mortgage. Thus it operates to discharge the mortgagor in respect of all claims against the mortgaged property. In one case where the mortgagee had made an arithmetical error in calculating the redemption figure it was held that the mortgage had been validly discharged.[7]

Payment by persons not entitled to the immediate equity

6-03   A mortgage is not always redeemed by the person immediately entitled to the equity of redemption[8] but sometimes by a person—for example, a third or later mortgagee—who is entitled to have the charge kept alive against the second encumbrancer. In such cases, if the receipt were allowed to effect a surrender of the term or reconveyance of the security, the charge would be extinguished. Accordingly, s.115 provides that if the receipt clearly indicates[9] that the money was not paid by the person entitled to the immediate equity of redemption the indorsement is to operate as a *transfer* of the mortgage by deed to the person actually named as the payer.[10] Of course, if the latter does not wish to keep the charge alive his intention not to take a transfer can be stated in the receipt by means of a declaration to this effect, in which case the indorsement will have its usual effect. Section 115, in fact, takes care to preserve the law as to merger of charges intact and by subs.(3) prevents a mortgagor from making use of these provisions to redeem and keep alive a first mortgage against a later encumbrance

---

[6] The receipt need not be under seal; all that the statute requires is that it should be executed under the hand of the mortgagee: *Simpson v Geoghehan* [1934] W.N. 232. The production by a solicitor or licensed conveyancer of his client's indorsed receipt is a sufficient authority to the debtor to make his payment to the solicitor or licensed conveyancer; see the LPA 1925 s.69 (as amended by the Administration of Justice Act 1985 s.34(1)).

[7] *Erewash Borough Council v Taylor* (1979) C.L. 1831 C.C.

[8] In the case of several encumbrances, the person *immediately* entitled to the equity of redemption is, of course, the second encumbrancer.

[9] There need not be an express statement to that effect, provided that the fact sufficiently appears: *Simpson v Geoghehan* [1934] W.N. 232.

[10] LPA 1925 s.115(2). See also *Cumberland Court (Brighton) Ltd v Taylor* [1964] Ch. 29 where it was held that although the receipt had operated as a transfer of the charge to the *vendor* (as the receipt was dated *after* the conveyance), there was no defect in title as there was an estoppel from the recitals in the conveyance which was "fed" on transfer and passed the interest in the property to the purchaser.

which he himself has created. This was forbidden in *Otter v Lord Vaux*[11] and subs.(3), perhaps *ex abundanti cautela*, warns that this case is still good law.

Partial redemption

Section 155 reserves for a person who redeems an absolute right to demand a reconveyance in place of the indorsed receipt.[12] This right will not, however, be frequently exercised because a reconveyance only increases the cost of redemption. There are, however, occasions when a reconveyance is still not merely convenient but a necessity. For example, if a mortgagor is redeeming only as to part of the debt, so that only a portion of the mortgaged property is being exonerated, an indorsed receipt cannot be employed. Section 115 in terms confines the use of a receipt to occasions when *all* moneys charged upon the property under the mortgage are being repaid. In cases, therefore, of partial redemption a reconveyance is essential.

6–04

Use of a simple receipt: Law of Property Act 1925 section 5 and section 116

Although the extended use of the indorsed (or statutory) receipt has simplified the conveyancing side of redemption, it is important to remember that in the case of mortgages of legal estates ss.5 and 116 of the Law of Property Act 1925 afford an alternative[13] means of discharging the mortgage[14] if it has been created by demise. Section 5 affirms the provisions of the Satisfied Terms Act 1845 and extends them to sub-terms created out of leaseholds. Section 116 expressly brings mortgage terms and sub-terms within the same principle so that (provided that there is written evidence) mortgages by demise or sub-demise may now be discharged by a mere payment of the mortgage debt, the term thereby being automatically merged in the reversion. Here again merger does not take place if the person making payment has a right to have the charge kept alive and he may in these circumstances obtain a transfer of the mortgage instead. However, it must be said that conveyancers in practice do not rely on such an "ordinary" receipt and prefer the statutory form, as the ordinary form is only prima facie evidence of payment.

6–05

Practice after redemption

After redemption the title deeds should be returned to the mortgagor. If there is another person, such as a subsequent mortgagee, with a better title the Law of Property Act 1925 s.96(2) (as amended) provides that the mortgagee whose mortgage is surrendered or otherwise extinguished is not liable on account of

6–06

---

[11] (1856) 6 De G.M. & G. 638. For the rules regarding merger of charges see paras 6–10 et seq.

[12] LPA 1925 s.115(4).

[13] And prior to the Finance Act 1971 s.64, (which abolished stamp duty on mortgages), a cheaper means of discharging the mortgage.

[14] Either a mortgage by demise or a charge by way of legal mortgage, see *Edwards v Marshall-Lee* (1975) 235 E.G. 901.

delivering the deeds to the person not having the best right thereto unless he has notice of the better right. It is further expressly provided that notice does not include statutory notice implied by reason of registration under the Land Charges Act 1972.

Registered land

6–07   Mortgages of registered land are outside s.115 of the Law of Property Act 1925. Prior to the coming into effect of the Land Registration Act 2002, the discharge of registered mortgages was expressly provided for under s.35 of the Land Registration Act 1925 which provided for the discharge of a mortgage by a notification in the register that the charge had been cancelled, either at the request of the mortgagee or upon sufficient proof that the mortgage has been paid off.

The section has been repealed by the 2002 Act and has not been directly replaced. However, the old rules under the Land Registration Rules 1925[15] have been largely replicated in rr.114 and 115 of the Land Registration Rules 2003 which implicitly recognise the principal that upon proof of discharge, a charge will be removed from the register and will no longer have any effect.

Rule 114(1) of the Land Registration Rules provides that "a discharge of a registered charge must be in Form DS1" and r.114(2) requires release of part of the registered estate to be in Form DS3. Any discharge or release of in Form DS1 or DS3 must be executed as a deed or authenticated in a manner approved by the registrar.[16] The application to register a discharge must be made in Form AP1 or DS2,[17] which provides for documents and information to be given in support of the application.

Notwithstanding these requirements, the registrar is entitled to accept and act upon any other proof of satisfaction of a charge that he may regard as sufficient.[18] The Rules also make provision for the discharge or release of registered charges in electronic form, a method used by many institutional lenders.[19]

Discharge of equitable mortgages

6–08   The statutory method of discharge is inappropriate in the case of equitable mortgages. Although not strictly necessary, there is usually a reconveyance of the property to the mortgagor even though a simple receipt will suffice.

Discharge of legal choses in action

6–09   In the case of the discharge of a legal chose in action, a statutory receipt or reassignment is necessary.

---

[15] Land Registration Rules 2003 r.151.
[16] Land Registration Rules 2003 r.114(3).
[17] Land Registration Rules 2003 r.114(5)
[18] Land Registration Rules 2003 r.114(4).
[19] Land Registration Rules 2003 r.115, see para.13–27.

MERGER OF A MORTGAGE OR CHARGE

Equitable doctrine of merger—a question of intention

The purchase of an equity of redemption by the mortgagee or the redemption of   **6–10**
a mortgage by a person entitled to redeem seems, at first sight, certain to put an
end to the mortgage and such, in fact, was the result at common law.[20] In equity,
however, the merger, both of charges and of estates, was purely a question of
intention[21] and did not occur automatically on the union in one hand of a charge
with an estate, or of a lesser estate with a greater. Indeed, so free from technical-
ities were the equitable rules that the intention to extinguish a charge might
produce a merger, although the estate was outstanding in a trustee such that there
would be no merger at common law.[22] Equitable principles now prevail[23] and, in
any case, s.185 of the Law of Property Act 1925[24] expressly provides that "there
is no merger by operation of law only of any estate the beneficial interest in
which would not be deemed to be merged or extinguished in equity" while s.116
recognises that the discharge of the mortgage debt does not necessarily extinguish the mortgage.

Rationale behind the equitable principle

The main object of keeping alive a charge which has been paid off is that it may   **6–11**
afford a protection against subsequent encumbrances.[25] The doctrine of equity is
based on the principle that a later encumbrancer has no claim to benefit gratui-
tously from a transaction to which he himself contributes nothing.[26] For when
merger takes place the result is that a second encumbrancer is raised to the
position of first encumbrancer without any effort of his own. Equity therefore
does not, except in one case, consider a charge to be extinguished by the mere
fact of its being paid off but makes merger a question of intention.

The one exception is that where a mortgagor himself pays off an encumbrance
he can in no circumstances set it up as a protection against a later mortgage which
he has himself created.[27] Not even an express declaration of intention in the deed
of discharge will avail him to keep the encumbrance alive. The reason is that a
second mortgage, as between the parties, is a grant of the mortgagor's entire
interest in the property, saving only the rights of the prior encumbrancer, and the
mortgagor cannot derogate from his grant by holding the first mortgage against

---

[20] Either by analogy to the merger of estates or on the principle that a man cannot be his own
debtor.
[21] *Forbes v Moffatt* (1811) 8 Ves. 384.
[22] *Astley v Milles* (1827) 1 Sim. 298, 344; *Forbes v Moffatt* (1811) 18 Ves.Jr. 384 at 390.
[23] Senior Courts Act 1981 s.49(1), re-enacting the Judicature Act 1873 s.25(11) and the Supreme
Court (Consolidation) Act 1925 s.44.
[24] Re-enacting s.25(4) of the Judicature Act 1873.
[25] See above, para.6–03.
[26] cf. Fletcher-Moulton L.J., in *Manks v Whiteley* (1912) 1 Ch. 735 at 764.
[27] *Otter v Lord Vaux* (1856) 6 De G.M. & G. 638.

the second mortgagee.[28] This is the position even in the case where a third party provides the mortgagor with the necessary money to redeem the mortgage.[29]

A purchaser of the equity of redemption is not, however, under this disability for the same considerations do not apply. He may pay off a charge and take a transfer of the mortgage. He can then keep it alive to protect himself against a subsequent encumbrance which he has not himself created because he has no personal contract with the subsequent encumbrancer.[30] Consequently, in the case of a purchaser of the equity of redemption the general rule applies and merger depends on intention.

Establishing intention: presumptions

6–12   The intention to extinguish a charge is a question of fact to be established by the evidence. There are, however, certain presumptions as to intention which are made by the court, and which decide the onus of proof.[31] The principle on which all these presumptions are based is that a person intends a charge to be kept alive or merged, according as to whether it is of advantage or of no advantage to him that the charge be kept alive.[32] The result is that:

(a)   If a life tenant or any other limited owner (not a tenant in tail)[33] acquires or pays off a charge there is a presumption against merger because merger would operate as a gift of the charge to those in remainder.[34]

(b)   If a person entitled in possession to either a fee simple or a fee tail acquires a charge on the estate, whether by devolution or by paying off the chargee, the presumption is in favour of merger unless the estate is defeasible by the operation of a condition. In general, there is no advantage in a man having a charge on his own estate, and the removal of the charge simplifies the title.

(c)   If a person entitled in remainder to a fee simple or a fee tail acquires a charge, no merger takes place until the estate comes into possession. When this occurs, the question of merger depends on the intention which the owner of the estate is presumed to have had *at the time when he acquired the charge*. Therefore, the presumption is against merger, (if he acquired the charge by paying it off himself) because he cannot have intended to benefit the inheritance at a time when it was uncertain

---

[28] A mortgagor " . . . cannot derogate from his own bargain by setting up the mortgage so purchased against a second mortgagee" per Lord Haldane L.C. in *Whiteley v Delaney* [1914] A.C. 132 at 145. See also *Frazer v Jones* (1846) 5 Hare 475.

[29] *Parkash v Irani Finance Ltd* [1970] Ch. 101; *Adams v Angell* (1877) 5 Ch.D. 634; *Thorne v Cann* (1895) A.C. 11; *Whiteley v Delaney* [1914] A.C. 132.

[30] *Burrell v Earl Egremont* (1844) 7 Beav. 205.

[31] per Parker J. in *Manks v Whiteley* (1911) 2 Ch. 448 at 458.

[32] A tenant in tail is for this purpose an absolute owner because he has it in his power to become owner of the whole fee.

[33] *Burrell v Lord Egremont* (1844) 7 Beav. 205; *Lord Gifford v Lord Fitzhardinge* (1899) 2 Ch. 32.

[34] *Donisthorpe v Porter* (1762) 2 Eden 162.

that he would ever succeed to it.[35] On the other hand, if he acquired the charge by devolution, he is presumed to have intended it to merge in the inheritance and merger takes place when the inheritance comes into possession.[36]

The above presumptions as to the intention of a person who pays off a charge are derived from the nature of his interest in the encumbered property. All are founded on the principle that he intends what is for his own benefit and does not intend to confer gratuitous benefits on strangers. It is evident that at the time when a charge is acquired, there may exist other circumstances which make it clearly beneficial for the person acquiring the charge to keep it alive. If this is so, the court presumes that he does not intend to extinguish his charge. This presumption will displace the ordinary presumption in favour of merger when an absolute owner pays off a charge on his estate. For example, the circumstance that a charge acquired by the owner of an estate has priority over other encumbrances, raises a presumption that he intends to keep it alive as a protection against the other charges.[37] This does not, as we have seen, apply to encumbrances created by the owner of the estate himself because he can never keep alive a charge against his own encumbrancers.[38] However, a purchaser of an equity of redemption may keep alive a charge, which he acquires, to protect himself against mesne encumbrances, if such was his intention at the time when he acquired the charge.[39] Similarly, a prior mortgagee, who takes a release of the equity of redemption, may keep his own charge alive against later mortgagees. In these cases, as in others, merger is a matter of intention.[40]

Toulmin v Steere[41]

It would, therefore, be expected that when the purchaser of an equity of redemp- **6–13**
tion pays off a charge, the existence of mesne encumbrances would automatically raise a presumption against merger under the general rule that the intention is to be gathered from what is advantageous to the owner of the charge. However, the decision of Sir William Grant in *Toulmin v Steere*[42] suggests that if the purchaser of an equity of redemption has actual or constructive notice of mesne encumbrances when he pays off a charge on the estate the court will not presume an intention to keep alive the prior charge, so that the presumption is in favour of merger.[43] If this is correct, the intention to keep the charge on foot must be

---

[35] *Horton v Smith* (1857) 4 K. & J. 624.
[36] ibid.
[37] *Forbes v Moffatt* (1811) 8 Ves. 384.
[38] *Otter v Lord Vaux* (1856) 6 De G.M. & G. 638.
[39] *Whiteley v Delaney* [1914] A.C. 132.
[40] *Adams v Angell* (1877) 5 Ch.D. 634.
[41] (1817) 3 Mer. 210.
[42] ibid.
[43] Sir William Grant's decision actually went further than this and denied that even actual intention could in such a case keep the charge alive. This part of his decision has been clearly overruled by *Adams v Angell* (1877) 5 Ch.D. 634 and *Thorne v Cann* (1895) A.C. 11.

affirmatively proved, either by an express declaration to that effect in the deed of discharge, or otherwise by circumstances surrounding the transaction.[44]

The authority of *Toulmin v Steere*, however, is very doubtful. It has been severely criticised by eminent judges,[45] and runs counter to the general principle on which presumptions in favour of and against merger are based. There is no good reason for denying to a purchaser of an equity of redemption the benefit of a presumed intention to keep his charge alive in circumstances when it is clearly to his advantage to do so. Knowledge of the mesne encumbrances is irrelevant because he can never be under any obligation to confer a gratuitous benefit on third parties. Indeed, notice of the puisne encumbrances only assists the presumption against merger, because it is sheer madness for the owner of an estate, who acquires a prior charge, to extinguish it when he knows of mesne encumbrances. *Toulmin v Steere* was considered by the House of Lords in *Thorne v Cann*,[46] in *Liquidation Estates Purchase Co v Willoughby*[47] and in *Whiteley v Delaney*.[48] It is probably not going too far to say that the case has not been expressly overruled only because of the great reputation of the judge who decided it and the accident that, for the decision of the cases before the House of Lords, it was unnecessary to do so.[49] In *Thorne v Cann* the court, in deciding that the purchaser of an equity of redemption intended to keep alive the charge which he had acquired, found indications of his intention, not only in the form of the instruments, but in the circumstances surrounding the transaction. It is difficult to believe that the existence of mesne encumbrances is not a circumstance from which such an indication of intention can be derived.[50] After this decision, and the language of Lord Haldane in *Whiteley v Delaney*, it is safe to say that *Toulmin v Steere* will no longer be followed, and that the existence of mesne encumbrances raises a presumption against merger in all cases.

Conclusion

6–14   The foregoing presumptions do no more than establish the onus of proof and do not prevail when there is sufficient evidence that the actual intention was otherwise. Such evidence is usually to be found in the instrument under which the property and the benefit of the charge become united in the same hand. Thus, if it is intended to keep a charge on foot, the proper course is to insert in the instrument an express declaration to that effect, for this will usually be conclusive of the intention.[51] The form of the instrument itself may indicate the intention either to keep alive or merge the charge; for example, if the instrument is in terms

---

[44] *Thorne v Cann* (1895) A.C. 11.

[45] e.g. James L.J. in *Stevens v Mid-Hants Rly Co* (1873) L.R. 8 Ch. 1064 at 1069; Lords Herschell and Macnaghten in *Thorne v Cann* (1895) A.C. 11 at 16, 18; Fletcher-Moulton L.J. in *Manks v Whiteley* (1912) 1 Ch. 735 at 759.

[46] [1895] A.C. 11.

[47] [1898] A.C. 321.

[48] [1914] A.C. 132, in particular at 144, 145.

[49] In *Liquidation Estates Purchase Co v Willoughby* and *Whiteley v Delaney* the cases were decided on other grounds; in *Thorne v Cann* an actual intention was established.

[50] Lindley L.J. in *Liquidation Estates Purchase Co v Willoughby*, thought that the dicta in *Thorne v Cann* have overruled *Toulmin v Steere* (1896) 1 Ch. 726 at 734.

[51] *Re Gibbon* [1909] 1 Ch. 367.

a transfer of the charge, it suggests that the charge is to be kept alive; but if the instrument is merely a reconveyance of the security, the merger of the charge appears to be the intention. In neither case, however, is the form of the transaction decisive unless the surrounding circumstances point to the same conclusion.[52] Similarly, the fact that the charge is assigned to a trustee to be held for the owner of the estate is not by itself sufficient evidence of an intention to keep the charge alive. In one case, however, the circumstances point conclusively to an intention to extinguish the charge, namely, when a mortgagee takes a conveyance of the equity of redemption in consideration not only of releasing his own debt but of paying off all other encumbrances.[53]

In determining the question of merger or no merger, evidence of intention is therefore usually derived either from the language or the circumstances of the instrument by which the charge is acquired. It appears, however, that the court will allow parol evidence of intention to be given, for in *Astley v Milles*[54] the solicitor, who had prepared the instruments by which a charge was acquired, was permitted to depose that the actual intention of the parties had been to keep the charge on foot. When the evidence establishes an intention to extinguish, this is decisive, since a charge, once merged, is destroyed forever. If, on the other hand, a charge has been kept alive either by express declaration or by reason of the circumstances of its acquisition, this will not be conclusive if a subsequent change of intention is proved. For example, when property is afterwards mortgaged or settled without the deeds noticing the charge, an intention to cancel the charge will be inferred.[55]

DESTRUCTION OR LOSS OF MORTGAGED PROPERTY

If the mortgaged property is lost or destroyed the benefit of the security may also be lost. This can arise for instance, in a case where a mortgaged leasehold is forfeited,[56] but not where the lease is surrendered.[57] The mortgagor's personal liability on the covenant remains.[58]   **6–15**

DISCHARGE OR MODIFICATION BY STATUTE

Under the Housing Act 1985

The Housing Act 1985 Pt XVII contained special provisions with regard to the discharge or modification of liabilities under a mortgage or instalment purchase   **6–16**

---

[52] *Hood v Phillips* (1841) 3 Beav. 513.
[53] *Brown v Stead* (1832) 5 Sim. 535.
[54] (1827) 1 Sim. 298 at 345.
[55] *Tyler v Lake* (1831) 4 Sim. 351; *Hood v Philipps* (1841) 3 Beav. 513.
[56] But see LPA 1925 s.146(4) which empowers a mortgagee to apply for relief from forfeiture.
[57] *E S Schwab & Co Ltd v McCarthy* (1975) 31 P. & C. R. 196
[58] *London and South of England Building Society v Stone* [1983] 1 W.L.R. 1242 (C.A.) and see above [16–110].

agreement. The legislation was designed to provide for the removal by demolition or closure of unfit houses incapable of being rendered fit at reasonable expense and also to provide for slum clearance with provision made for the payment of compensation to a mortgagee in such circumstances. Those provisions have been repealed in relation to demolition orders made after March 31, 1990.[59] Now, under s.584A of the 1985 Act, a mortgagee in possession is paid compensation referable to the diminution in the compulsory purchase value of the property. For a mortgagee not in possession, the position applies as it does for compulsory purchase.

Under the Leasehold Reform Act 1967[60]

6–17   **The purpose of the Act:**   The purpose of this Act is to enable tenants of dwelling-houses held on long leases who fulfil the requisite residential qualification to acquire the freehold or an extended lease provided that the premises are within the appropriate rateable value limits and the tenancy is a long tenancy at a low rent. Where the tenant gives notice of his desire to have the freehold or an extended lease, the landlord is bound (subject to the Act) to convey to him the fee simple absolute or a new tenancy for a term expiring 50 years after the existing tenancy. In such circumstances, mortgages of both the landlord's and the tenant's interest in the premises may be affected.

6–18   **Discharge of the landlord's estate:**   The Act therefore provides for the discharge of mortgages on the landlord's estate. A conveyance executed to give effect to the tenant's right to acquire the freehold shall as regards any charge on the landlord's estate (however created or arising) to secure the payment of money or the performance of any other obligation by the landlord or any other person, not being a charge subject to which the conveyance is required to be made or which would be overreached apart from this section, be effective by virtue of this section to discharge the house and premises from the charge and from the operation of any order made by the court for the enforcement of the charge, and to extinguish any term of years created for the purposes of the charge, and shall do so without the persons entitled to or interested in the charge or in any such order or term of years becoming parties to or executing the conveyance.[61]

6–19   **Section 12:**   Where in accordance with s.12(1) the conveyance to a tenant will be effective to discharge the house and premises from a charge to secure the payment of money then except as otherwise provided by s.12 it shall be the duty of the tenant to apply the price payable for the house and premises, in the first instance, in or towards the redemption of any such charge (and, if there are more than one, then according to their priorities).[62] If any amount payable in accordance with s.12(2) to the person entitled to the benefit of a charge is not so paid

---

[59] Local Government and Housing Act 1989 ss.165(1) and 194(4).
[60] For detailed consideration of this Act and enfranchisement generally, see *Hague, Leasehold Enfranchisement* (5th edn, 2009).
[61] Leasehold Reform Act 1967 s.12(1).
[62] ibid., s.12(2).

nor paid into court, in accordance with s.13 of the Act, then for the amount in question the house and premises shall remain subject to the charge and to that extent s.12(1) of the Act shall not apply.[63] Where the house and premises are discharged by s.12 of the Act from a charge (without the obligations secured by the charge being satisfied by the receipt of the whole or part of the price) the discharge of the house and premises shall not prejudice any right or remedy for the enforcement of those obligations against other property comprised in the same or any other security, nor prejudice any personal liability as principal or otherwise of the landlord or any other person.[64]

Payment by tenant: The tenant acquiring the freehold may pay into court on   **6–20** account of the price for the house and premises the amount, if known, of the payment to be made in respect of the charge or, if that amount is not known, the whole of the price or such less amount as the tenant thinks right in order to provide for that payment.[65] This can occur if:

(a)   for any reason difficulty arises in ascertaining how much is payable in respect of the charge; or

(b)   for any reason mentioned in s.13(2) difficulty arises in making a payment in respect of the charge.

Such difficulty is envisaged in the following cases:

(a)   because a person who is or may be entitled to receive payment cannot be found or ascertained; or

(b)   because any such person refuses or fails to make out a title, or to accept payment and give a proper discharge, or to take any steps reasonably required of him to enable the sum to be ascertained and paid; or

(c)   because a tender of the sum payable cannot, by reason of complications in the title to it or the want of two or more trustees or for other reasons, be effected, or not without incurring or involving unreasonable costs or delay.[66]

The tenant must pay the purchase price into court if before execution of the conveyance written notice is given to him:

(i)   that the landlord or a person entitled to the benefit of a charge on the house and premises so requires for the purpose of protecting the rights of persons so entitled, or for reasons related to any application made or to be made under s.36 of the Act, or to the bankruptcy or winding up of the landlord; or

---

[63] ibid., s.12(2).
[64] ibid., s.12(6).
[65] ibid., s.13.
[66] ibid., s.13(2).

(ii) that steps have been taken to enforce any charge on the landlord's interest in the house and premises by the bringing of proceedings in any court, or by the appointment of a receiver, or otherwise.[67]

Where payment is made into court by reason only of a notice under s.13(3) and the notice is given with reference to proceedings in a court specified in the notice other than the county court, payment shall be made into the court so specified.[68]

In certain cases the court is able to grant relief in respect of mortgages on the landlord's estate in order to avoid or mitigate any financial hardship that might otherwise be caused by the rights conferred on tenants by the Act.[69]

Under the Landlord and Tenant Act 1987

6–21   The Act provides for the compulsory acquisition of the landlord's interest and entitles qualifying tenants of blocks of flats to apply to the court for an acquisition order.[70] This contains provision for the discharge of mortgages on the landlord's interest, if such order is made.[71]

Under the Leasehold Reform, Housing and Urban Development Act 1993

6–22   **Exercise of rights under Chapter I:**   Chapter I of the 1993 Act gives certain lessees of residential flats the right to acquire the freehold of their block, subject to various qualifications and conditions. When the lessees acquire the freehold under the provisions of the Act, by virtue of s.35 of the Act, the conveyance to the nominee purchaser has the effect of discharging any mortgage to which the section applies[72] and from any order made by the court for the enforcement of the mortgage[73] and also extinguishes any term of years created for the purposes of the mortgage.[74] The reciprocal obligation on the part of the nominee purchaser is that it must apply the purchase consideration towards discharge of the mortgage and there are detailed provisions in the Act which make provision for cases where the purchase price is insufficient to pay the sum in full or there is a dispute over it.[75]

6–23   **Exercise of rights under Chapter II:**   Chapter II of the Act confers rights on individual lessees of residential flats the right to extend their leases for up to 90 years. The exercise of this right does not discharge any mortgage on the landlord's interest, but s.58 of the Act does confer statutory authorisation to, and

---

[67] ibid., s.13(3).

[68] ibid. The court for the purposes of s.13(1) and (unless the landlord's notice specifies another court) s.13(3), is the county court, see s.20(1).

[69] ibid., s.36.

[70] Landlord and Tenant Act 1987 Pt III.

[71] ibid., s.32, Sch.1. See further *Woodfall's Law of Landlord and Tenant* (1994).

[72] Any mortgage to secure payment of money or performance by the person from whom the interest is acquired and which is not overreached apart from the section—s.35(2)

[73] Leasehold Reform, Housing and Urban Development Act 1993 s. 35(1)(a).

[74] ibid., s.35(1)(b)

[75] ibid., Sch.8.

enforceability of, any extension lease against a mortgagee notwithstanding that the original lease was granted subsequent to the mortgage.

Under the Commonhold and Leasehold Reform Act 2002

Section 28 of the 2002 Act makes provision of the extinguishment of charges over common parts, to the extent that they relate to common parts, upon registration of a commonhold proprietor's interest of the common parts of the relevant premises.   **6–24**

Under the Land Registration Act 2002 (in the event of adverse possession)

Upon registration of an adverse possessor's title under Sch.6 of the 2002 Act, the estate is generally vested in him free of any registered charge affecting the estate immediately before registration.[76]   **6–25**

Under the Rent Act 1977

The Act makes provision for the variation of the terms of regulated mortgages, dealt with elsewhere in this work.[77]   **6–26**

Under the Consumer Credit Act 1974

The Act contains provisions for the refusal of enforcement orders and other matters affecting mortgages, dealt with elsewhere in this work.[78]   **6–27**

Under the Lands Clauses Consolidation Act 1845 (and compulsory purchase legislation)

Section 108 of the 1845 Act provides that it shall be lawful for the promoters of the undertaking to purchase or redeem the interest of the mortgagee of any such lands which may be required for the purposes of the special Act, and that whether they shall have previously purchased the equity of redemption of such lands or not, and whether the mortgagee thereof be entitled thereto in his own right or in trust for any other party, and whether he be in possession of such lands by virtue of such mortgage or not, and whether such mortgage affect such lands solely, or jointly with any other lands not required for the purposes of the special Act. Detailed provision is also made in the Compulsory Purchase Act 1965 in cases where the mortgaged land is worth less than the mortgage debt.[79]   **6–28**

---

[76] Land Registration Act 2002 Sch.6 para.9(3), (4).
[77] See above, para.16–88.
[78] See above, Ch.14 and para.16–87.
[79] Compulsory Purchase Act 1965 ss.16 & 17.

EXTINCTION OF MORTGAGE BY LAPSE OF TIME

Loss of the mortgagor's right to redeem by lapse of time

Unregistered land

6–29   A mortgagor can lose his right to redeem a mortgage by lapse of time. In *Lewis v Plunkett*[80] Farwell J. held that where the owner of a legal estate executes a mortgage and hands over the mortgage and other title deeds to the mortgagee, but fails to pay any interest on the mortgage or give any acknowledgment to the mortgage debt for more than 12 years, the mortgagee loses all title to the land and the mortgagor can recover possession of the mortgage and other title deeds.

Where the security is land,[81] s.16 of the Limitation Act 1980 ("the 1980 Act") provides that when a mortgagee:

> "has been in possession of any of the mortgaged land for a period of twelve years, no action to redeem the land of which he has been so in possession shall be brought after the end of that period by the mortgagor or any person claiming through him."

Section 17 of the 1980 Act further provides for the extinguishment of the mortgagor's title in the following terms:

> "Subject to section 18 of this Act . . . at the expiration of the period prescribed by this Act for any person to bring an action to recover land (including a redemption action) the title of that person to the land shall be extinguished."

Section 16 means that time begins to run against the mortgagor at once from the mortgagee's entry into possession, whether or not the right of redemption has yet arisen.[82] It begins to run in respect of any part of which the mortgagee is in possession even though the mortgagor remains in possession of the rest of the land.[83] In order to satisfy the section, the mortgagee must enter into and stay in possession in his capacity as mortgagee, not in some other capacity. The effect of barring the mortgagor's title is to vest the legal estate in the mortgagee.[84]

Formerly, the fact that the mortgagor was under a disability made no difference, as actions for redemption were not actions to recover land within s.16 of the Real Property Limitation Act 1833 which made allowance for disability.[85] Section 22 of the Limitation Act 1939, however, extended the allowance for disability to all cases where the Act imposed a limitation and therefore to actions for

---

[80] [1937] Ch. 303.

[81] "Land" is defined in s.38(1) of the Limitation Act 1980 as including "corporeal hereditaments, tithes and rentcharges and any legal or equitable estate therein . . . but except as provided above in this definition does not include any incorporeal hereditament."

[82] *Re Metropolis and Counties Permanent Investment Building Society* [1911] 1 Ch. 698. However, the mortgagee must have entered in the character of mortgagee: *Hyde v Dallaway* (1843) 2 Hare 528.

[83] *Kinsman v Rouse* (1881) 17 Ch.D. 104.

[84] Limitation Act 1980 s.17. See *Kibble v Fairthorne* [1895] 1 Ch. 219; *Zaman v Zoha* [2005] EWHC 3539 (Ch).

[85] ibid.

redemption of mortgages of land.[86] This is now incorporated into s.28 of the 1980 Act which applies to ss.16 and 17 of the 1980 Act.

Acknowledgment and part payment: By s.29(4) of the 1980 Act the running **6–30** of time under the Limitation Act 1980, is stopped if the mortgagee:

"either:

(a) receives any sum in respect of the principal or interest of the mortgage debt; or

(b) acknowledges the title of the mortgagor, or his equity of redemption."

The 12-year period then runs from the date of the last payment or acknowledgment. A receipt, to have this effect, must be of money paid "in respect of the principal or interest", so that the receipt of rents or proceeds of sale by a mortgagee in possession without accounting for them to the mortgagor will not stop the period from running. An acknowledgment must be in writing, signed either by the mortgagee or his agent, and must be made to the owner of the equity of redemption or his agent.[87] The actual form of the instrument is immaterial so long as it contains an unequivocal recognition of the fact that the estate is mortgaged.[88]

Where there are two or more mortgagors, an acknowledgment to one is deemed to be made to all and so stops time from running against any of them.[89] However, an acknowledgment by one of two or more mortgagees does not bind the other mortgagees. Section 31 of the 1980 Act provides:

"(3) Where two or more mortgagees are by virtue of the mortgage in possession of the mortgaged land, an acknowledgement of the mortgagor's title or of his equity of redemption by one of the mortgagees shall only bind him and his successors and shall not bind any other mortgagee or his successors.

(4) Where in a case within subsection (3) above the mortgagee by whom the acknowledgement is given is entitled to a part of the mortgaged land and not to any ascertained part of the mortgage debt the mortgagor shall be entitled to redeem that part of the land on payment, with interest, of the part of the mortgage debt which bears the same proportion to the whole of the debt as the value of the part of the land bears to the whole of the mortgaged land."

The effect of this somewhat difficult language appears to be that:

(a) An acknowledgment by one mortgagee can in no case bind the other mortgagees.

(b) Where the mortgage moneys are not held by the mortgagees on a joint account an acknowledgment by one binds him and the mortgagor may redeem him as to his share thus acquiring an equitable right to his

---

[86] Preston & Newsom, *Limitation of Actions* (1953), p.219.

[87] Limitation Act 1980 s.30. cf. *Wright v Pepin* [1954] 1 W.L.R. 635, where the authority was inferred. There had been an acknowledgment by the mortgagor's solicitor which was held sufficient.

[88] cf. *Stansfield v Hobson* (1853) 3 De G.M. & G. 620.

[89] Limitation Act 1980 s.31(5).

interest in the mortgage. The other mortgagees hold their shares in the mortgage free of the equity of redemption.

(c) Where the mortgage moneys are held on a joint account (i.e. no ascertained share) but the mortgagees have entered separately into possession of distinct parts of the mortgaged land an acknowledgment by one binds him and exposes him to redemption of the part of which he is in possession. As he is not entitled to any ascertained part of the mortgaged debt the price of redemption is worked out by attributing to him a share of the mortgage debt corresponding to the proportion of the mortgaged land which his part bears to the whole.

(d) Where the mortgage moneys are held on a joint account and the mortgagees are jointly in possession an acknowledgment by one is wholly ineffective to stop the running of the period in favour of all.[90]

Once the right of redemption has been barred by the mortgagee's continuance in possession for the statutory period, no subsequent acknowledgment can revive it for s.17 of the 1980 Act expressly extinguishes the title to the equity of redemption.[91]

Registered land

6–31 Sections 16 and 17 of the 1980 Act now only apply to unregistered land. Section 96(2) of the Land Registration Act 2002 disapplies them in relation to any registered estate and so no statutory limitation period exists for a redemption action by a mortgagor of registered land. As noted above, this substantially changes the law and so a mortgagee will not be able to rely on any period in possession to found a claim by adverse possession under Sch.6 of the 2002 Act because he will either be a tenant under a lease (if the mortgage was made by demise or sub-demise prior to October 13, 2003)[92] or has the same rights as if he were such a person if the charge is by way of legal mortgage.[93] However, it is to be noted that s.96(1) of the 2002 Act does not disapply s.15 of the 1980 Act (recovery of land). Thus the scheme under Sch.6 does not apply to a chargee whose right to recover possession or to foreclose remains subject to the provisions of the 1980 Act.[94]

Personalty

6–32 **No statutory limitation period:** Although the Limitation Act 1939 placed foreclosure actions for mortgaged personalty on the same footing as for realty, barring them after 12 years, it did not subject actions to redeem mortgaged

---

[90] cf. *Richardson v Younge* (1871) L.R. 6 Ch. 478.

[91] cf. *Young v Clarey* [1948] Ch. 191; and under the former law; *Re Alison* (1879) 11 Ch.D. 284.

[92] LPA 1925 ss.85, 86.

[93] ibid., s.87.

[94] See *Land Registration for the Twenty-first Century*, Law Com. No.271 paras 14.12–14.14.

personalty to the limitations governing actions to redeem realty. The Law Revision Committee justified this differential treatment of realty and personalty in regard to redemption on the ground that whereas a mortgagee of land does not ordinarily take possession except by way of enforcing his security, the mortgagee of personalty may have possession of the property from the outset. It was for this reason that the Committee thought that serious practical difficulties might arise if the statutory limitations were applied to the redemption of mortgaged personalty. It had in mind particularly the case of bonds or shares deposited with a bank by way of equitable mortgage and left with the bank more or less indefinitely to cover an overdraft.[95] Consequently, the Limitation Act 1939, like previous Statutes of Limitation, left actions to redeem personalty without any statutory limit. Moreover, it was well established under the former statutes that equity will not, by analogy, extend to personalty statutory limitations whose operation is expressly restricted to land.[96] This position remains unchanged under the 1980 Act. Thus a situation can arise in which sums due under a mortgage can be statute barred for many years but the security remains redeemable. [97]

Laches: Since no Statute of Limitation operates, whether directly or by analogy, to bar actions to redeem personalty, lapse of time will defeat such actions only on the general principle of laches—"*quitas vigilantibus non dormientibus succurrit*" ("equity aids the vigilant and not the indolent"). The rules on which the court acts in refusing its assistance to stale demands cannot be stated with precision because in cases where no Statute of Limitation applies judges have refrained from fixing a definite period within which equitable remedies must be brought. In *Weld v Petre*,[98] although counsel invited the court to say that no action to redeem personalty would be entertained after 20 years, the court refused to lay down any rigid rule. A defence based on lapse of time depends in equity primarily on the balance of justice or injustice in affording or refusing relief.[99] Under such a test each case will clearly be governed by its own special circumstances. Thus in *Erlanger v New Sombrero Phosphate Co*[100] Lord Blackburn said:

6–33

> "I think, from the nature of the inquiry, it must always be a question of more or less, depending on the degree of diligence which might reasonably be required, and the degree of change which has occurred, whether the balance of justice or injustice is in favour of granting the remedy or withholding it."

The doctrine of laches thus really provides two distinct grounds on which a remedy may be refused:

---

[95] Fifth Interim Report (1936), Cmd. 5334, p.15.

[96] *London & Midland Bank v Mitchell* [1899] 2 Ch. 161; *Weld v Petre* [1929] 1 Ch. 33. But in the case of a mixed fund of personalty and realty it was held in one case that the right to redeem personalty was barred as the equity was indivisible, see *Charter v Watson* [1899] 1 Ch. 175.

[97] See *Dr Anthony Stephen De Silva Farmer v Moseley (Holdings) Ltd (trading as RTK Marine)* [2001] 2 B.C.L.C. 527

[98] [1929] 1 Ch. 33.

[99] *Lindsay Petroleum Co v Hurd* (1874) L.R. 5 P.C. 221.

[100] (1878) 3 App. Cas. 1218 at 1279.

(a) conduct by the claimant which suggests that he has waived his right; or

(b) a change in the circumstances of the defendant which renders it practically unjust to enforce the remedy.

The leading case on the application of the doctrine to the right to redeem personalty is *Weld v Petre*[101] in which it was held that:

(a) Mere inaction by the mortgagor, laches in the narrow sense, is not sufficient evidence of an intention to waive his rights and will not bar the right to redeem under the doctrine of laches. Thus, Russell J. at first instance[102] expressly said: "Equity should not, in my opinion, deprive mortgagors of their right to redeem if, when they assert it, the debt has been or can be repaid, the security is available and no one's position has been altered in the meanwhile. If these circumstances co-exist, the mortgagor should be allowed to redeem unless his right has been destroyed by statute, foreclosure, sale or release."

(b) Where the mortgagee (i) has not altered his position by expending money on the property in the reasonable belief that the property was now his own; (ii) has not, by reason of the delay, lost any evidence which will make it difficult for him to render his accounts; and (iii) has not otherwise altered his position to his prejudice, the mortgagor will be admitted to redeem.

(c) The fact that on the death of the mortgagee the mortgaged property has been included in the mortgagee's assets and estate duty paid in respect of it is not a sufficient ground for refusing relief to the mortgagor.

BARRING A MORTGAGEE'S REMEDIES UNDER THE LIMITATION ACT 1980

6–34 The limitations imposed by the the 1980 Act on the enforcement of a mortgagee's remedies require to be considered under five main heads:

(1) personal actions on the contract for payment;
(2) actions to recover principal sums of money secured by mortgage or charge;
(3) actions for foreclosure and possession;
(4) actions to enforce mortgages of future interests; and
(5) actions for the recovery of arrears of interest.

In addition, the rules laid down for these actions are affected by the general provisions of the Act relating to disability, acknowledgment, part payment, fraud, concealment and mistake.

---

[101] [1929] 1 Ch. 33.
[102] ibid., at 42.

Personal actions on the contract for payment

When the mortgage is not under seal an action on the express or implied promise **6–35** to pay the debt is one "founded on simple contract" within s.5 of the 1980 Act and, as such, is barred "after the expiration of six years from the date when the cause of action accrued", i.e. after the date for repayment.[103] It was, however, well settled under the old law that the barring of the personal action on the contract after six years did not preclude the subsequent enforcement of the remedies against the security. The reason was that the statute only barred the action and did not extinguish the debt.[104] The position in regard to the debt is still the same under the 1980 Act so that the remedies against the security are not touched by s.5 but fall under s.20, being barred only after 12 years. When the mortgage is under seal the action on the covenant for payment is one "upon a specialty" within s.8 of the 1980 Act. The period of limitation is thus 12 years.[105]

Actions to recover principal sums of money secured by mortgage or charge

Section 20(1) of the 1980 Act provides: **6–36**

> "(1) No action shall be brought to recover—
>
> (a) any principal sum of money secured by a mortgage or other charge on property (whether real or personal); or
> (b) proceeds of the sale of land;
>
> after the expiration of twelve years from the date on which the right to receive the money accrued."

Thus, quite apart from the limits imposed on contractual actions to recover the principal, the Act specifically bars any action to recover the principal by enforcing the security after the elapse of 12 years. The extension of this statutory limitation on enforcing securities to mortgages of personalty, as explained above, was an innovation. The limitation of 12 years now applies to all forms of property. However, the right to receive any principal sum of money secured by a mortgage or other charge shall not be treated as accruing so long as that property comprises any interest or any life insurance policy which has not matured or been determined.[106]

When time begins to run

The relevant date from which time runs under s.20(1) is "the date on which the **6–37** right to receive the money accrued". This is not necessarily the date upon which

---

[103] This will depend on whether the covenant gives the date for repayment and whether a demand is necessary.

[104] *London & Midland Bank v Mitchell* [1899] 2 Ch. 161.

[105] It is not sufficient for the obligation to be merely acknowledged or evidenced by the security, it must be created or secured by it: *Re Compania de Electricidad de la Provincia de Buenos Aires Ltd* [1980] Ch. 146.

[106] Limitation Act 1980 s.20(3).

the cause of action accrues.[107] Presumably, much will turn on the precise wording and terms of the mortgage instrument. Where a charge is imposed on a bankrupt's estate under s.313 of the Insolvency Act 1986, the right to receive the money does not accrue until the date of an order for sale.[108]

Limitation period for recovery of sale after shortfall

6–38   Although the terms of the section appear straightforward, for many years there was uncertainty over whether once a property had been repossessed and sold, an action by the mortgagor for the recovery of any shortfall was governed by s.20 an subject to a 12-year limitation period or whether such a claim was in simple contract and governed by the limitation period applicable to that action (six years for simple contract and 12 years for a speciality).[109] The issue turned on whether the words "any principal sum of money secured by a mortgage", refers only to a principal sum secured by a mortgage when the action is brought or whether it is sufficient that the principal be secured by a mortgage at the start of the 12-year limitation period, whatever may have happened thereafter.

In two decisions decided in the same year, the Court of Appeal held that, other than in exceptional cases, s.20, not s.5 or s.8, applied to actions to recover any shortfall on a mortgage following a sale and that the 12-year limitation period applied in relation to the recovery of the principal. However, in relation to interest, the limitation period was six years.[110] The reasoning in *Bristol & West v Bartlett* was based on what Longmore L.J. called a "much more natural" reading of s.20(1).[111] The court would not read words into the statute that the principal must continue to be secured by a mortgage at the time when the action is brought.

Bristol & West v Bartlett was expressly approved of by the House of Lords in *West Bromwich Building Society v Wilkinson*,[112] in which the lenders sought to argue that the previous Court of Appeal decisions were wrongly decided. In that case, proceedings were brought to recover a shortfall upon sale just within a 12-year period after the property was sold but outside a 12-year period from the first default by the mortgagors. The terms of the mortgage were unusual and the mortgagee sought to argue that, as a matter of construction, the mortgage deed did not give rise to a cause of action nor a "right to receive money" on default, only upon sale. This construction was rejected by the House of Lords. The mortgagees further argued that because the 1980 Act only barred the exercise of the remedy and did not destroy the underlying obligation, the time to ask the question whether the principal sum was secured by a mortgage was when

---

[107] *Hornsey Local Board v Monarch* (1889) 23 Q.B.D. 1. The House of Lords did not find it necessary to decide the question in *West Bromwich Building Society v Wilkinson*, [2005] 1 W.L.R. 2303 at [21].

[108] *Gotham v Doodes* [2007] 1 W.L.R. 86.

[109] This point was described as seriously arguable by the Court of Appeal in *Hopkinson v Tupper*, unreported, January 30, 1997.

[110] *Bristol & West v Bratlett* [2003] 1 W.L.R. 284; *Scottish Equittable Plc v Thompson* [2003] H.L.R 690.

[111] At [30].

[112] [2005] 1 W.L.R. 2303, per Lord Hoffman at [10].

the claimant wished to bring the action. Lord Hoffman rejected this contention:

> "Putting aside actions for the recovery of land, where questions of title are involved, English law attributes periods of limitation by reference to the cause of action which the claimant seeks to enforce. Thus there are periods of limitation for personal injury actions, defamation actions, other actions in tort, actions founded on simple contract, actions on a specialty and so on. This method of classification suggests that ordinarily time will run from the moment when the cause of action designated by the appropriate rule has arisen. It would be strange if the lender could then stop time running by his own act in exercising the power of sale. If, therefore, the cause of action when it arose was a claim to a debt secured on a mortgage, I do not think section 20 ceases to apply when the security is subsequently realised."[113]

Charging orders

In *Yorkshire Bank Finance v Mulhall*[114] the Court of Appeal held that neither   **6–39**
ss.20(1) nor 20(5) of the 1980 Act applied to ordinary charging orders and that, it being accepted that s.24(1) did not apply, there was no statutory limitation period that applied to the enforcement of a charging order. The court held that the previous Court of Appeal decision of *Ezekiel v Orakpo*[115] was binding authority for the proposition that that redemption by the chargor was not "an action brought to recover any principal sum of money secured by a . . . charge on property" within s.20(1) and that that principle applied equally to s.20(5).

Actions for foreclosure and possession

Foreclosure

Foreclosure actions are dealt with by the 1980 Act as actions to recover the   **6–40**
property rather than to recover the debt by realising the security and are outside the provisions of s.20.

Section 20(4) of the 1980 Act provides:

> "(4) Nothing in this section shall apply to a foreclosure action in respect of mortgaged land, but the provisions of this Act relating to actions to recover land shall apply to such an action."

A foreclosure action will therefore be subject to the limitation period contained in s.15 of the 1980 Act, which prescribes a 12-year limitation period for an action to recover land. Formerly, the Real Property Limitation Acts did not specify foreclosure actions as actions to recover land but it was settled in a series of decisions that land foreclosure actions, for purposes of the limitation of actions, are actions to recover land.[116] These decisions were not perhaps entirely logical

---

[113] ibid., at [10].
[114] [2009] 1 P. & C. R. 16.
[115] [1997] 1 W.L.R. 340.
[116] e.g. *Heath v Pugh* (1881) 6 Q.B.D. 345; *Pugh v Heath* (1881) 7 A.C. 235; *Harlock v Ashberry* (1882) 19 Ch.D. 539.

because foreclosure is not, either in law or in equity, an action to recover the mortgagor's interest. It is an action to complete the mortgagee's title to an interest already vested in him by removing the stop on the title imposed by equity.[117] Moreover, a foreclosure action always invites redemption and is in substance an action to recover the amount of the debt by realising the security. The courts, however, looked primarily to the fact that in equity the mortgagor remains beneficial owner and that a foreclosure order absolute for the first time vests the beneficial ownership in the mortgagee.[118] On this basis, they decided to treat foreclosure actions as actions to recover land. They had a strong inducement to do so in that some of the provisions postponing the running of the statutory period applied, owing to the erratic policy of the Acts, to actions for the recovery of land but not to actions for the recovery of money charged on land.[119] Although the 1980 Act maintains the distinction between foreclosure and other remedies, happily the distinction has lost most of its importance owing to the rules relating to actions for the recovery of money charged on property having been assimilated to those governing actions to recover land.

6–41   The applicable limitation period: In the case of land,[120] s.20(4), re-enacting the former law, declares that foreclosure actions are not within s.20 at all but are governed by the provisions of the Act relating to actions to recover land, in particular by s.15. The period prescribed by s.15(1) in ordinary cases is 12 years from the date on which the right of action accrued under the mortgage.[121] In the case of personalty where formerly there was no statutory limit on foreclosure actions, the Act does not carry logic to the extent of applying the provisions relating to recovery of chattels. Instead, s.20(2) simply enacts that foreclosure actions in respect of mortgaged personalty shall be barred after 12 years from the date on which the right to foreclose accrued. The general rule is thus the same both for land and personalty: foreclosure actions are barred 12 years after the right to foreclose accrued.

6–42   Accrual of the cause of action: The right to foreclose accrues when the mortgagor is in default on the proviso for redemption and the mortgagee's estate has become absolute at law.[122] Although any default which touches the terms of the proviso for redemption gives rise to the right of foreclosure, the right usually accrues on a default in the covenant to pay the mortgage moneys on the date specified. Where, however, the moneys are repayable on demand the right accrues immediately on the execution of the mortgage unless the demand has been made a condition precedent to the enforcement of the mortgage.[123] Such are

---

[117] See paras 27–24 et seq.

[118] See *Heath v Pugh* (1881) 6 Q.B.D. 345 at 360.

[119] A good example is the case of future interests discussed, below, para.22–35.

[120] "Land" includes corporeal hereditaments, tithes and rentcharges and any legal or equitable estate or interest therein, including an interest in the proceeds of the sale of land held upon trust for sale, but except as provided above in this definition does not include an incorporeal hereditament, as defined by s.38(1).

[121] Sch.1 para.10 prescribes 30 years in the case of the Crown and spiritual or eleemosynary corporations sole.

[122] See para.16–92.

[123] See *Re Brown's Estate* [1893] 2 Ch. 300; *Lloyds Bank v Margolis* [1954] 1 W.L.R. 644.

the basic rules concerning the first accrual of the right of foreclosure and the date when the statutory period begins to run. The 1980 Act, however, contains several provisions which, for the purposes of the limitation of actions, suspend the accrual of the right of action of a mortgagee. The most important of these provisions, covering future interests, disabilities, acknowledgments and part payment, apply generally to all remedies and are dealt with separately below. One provision, however, affects foreclosure alone. If a mortgagee, whether of land[124] or of personalty,[125] has been in possession of the mortgaged property after the right of foreclosure has accrued the right is deemed not to have accrued until he has been dispossessed or has discontinued his possession.

A mortgagee who exercises his rights and obtains a foreclosure order absolute acquires, it was decided in *Heath v Pugh*,[126] an entirely new title so that time only runs against his new right to eject the mortgagor as from the date of the order being made absolute.

Possession

The applicable limitation period: A mortgagee's right to take possession of   **6–43**
the security is also a right to recover land and is subject to the 12-year limitation period contained in s.15 of the 1980 Act. Section 38(7) makes clear that "a right of action to recover land" includes "a right to enter into possession". Therefore, the right to possession will be extinguished 12 years after the right accrued by virtue of s.17 of the 1980 Act.

Accrual of the cause of action: Unless qualified by the mortgage instrument,   **6–44**
a mortgagee has an immediate right to possession and so time begins to run immediately from the execution of a legal mortgage. Most modern mortgages however qualify the right mortgagee's right to possession so as to arise only upon default. Accordingly, if the mortgage provides for quiet enjoyment by the mortgagor until default, it operates as a redemise to him from the mortgagee and the period only begins to run from the date of the default.[127]

Need for adverse possession: Schedule 1 of the 1980 Act contains specific   **6–45**
provisions with respect to actions to recover land.
Paragraph 3 of Sch.1 provides:

> "Where any person brings an action to recover land, being an estate or interest in possession assured otherwise than by will to him, or to some person through whom he claims, and—(a) the person making the assurance was on the date when the assurance took effect in possession of the land . . . and (b) no person has been in possession of the land by virtue of the assurance; the right of action shall be treated as having accrued on the date when the assurance took effect."

Paragraph 8 of Sch.1 provides:

---

[124] Limitation Act 1980 Sch.1 para.1.
[125] ibid., s.20(2).
[126] (1881) 6 Q.B.D. 345.
[127] *Wilkinson v Hall* (1837) 3 Bing N.C. 508.

"No right of action to recover land shall be treated as accruing unless the land is in the possession of some person in whose favour the period of limitation can run (referred to below in this paragraph as 'adverse possession'); and where under the preceding provisions of this Schedule any such right of action is treated as accruing on a certain date and no person is in adverse possession on that date, the right of action shall not be treated as accruing unless and until adverse possession is taken of the land."

This provision becomes relevant in cases where a mortgagee has delayed in taking possession proceedings after default by the mortgagor, whether through inadvertence or as a result of a conscious commercial decision driven by the likelihood of there being a shortfall on sale (most notably in periods of low property prices). In *Ashe v National Westminster Bank Plc*[128] the Court of Appeal held that para.3 of Sch.1 embraced claims by legal mortgagees against mortgagors in possession and that the provisions of para.8 of Sch.1 applied to all actions to recover land, including an action by a mortgagee, so that a mortgagor will have to show he has been adversely possessing the property for 12 years in order to defeat the mortgagee's claim to possession. However the Court of Appeal went on to hold that, in the normal case, the mortgagee's lack of enforcement of its right to possession and lack of objection to or tolerance of the mortgagor's possession would not amount to an implied permission for the mortgagor to remain.[129]

6–46 **Equitable mortgages:** As an equitable mortgagee has no right to possession except by special agreement, the date when the right accrues can only be ascertained from the agreement if such an agreement exists.[130]

6–47 **Acknowledgement and part payment:** The running of the statute against the right to enter into possession is, as with other remedies, interrupted by acknowledgment or part payment or by disability. In practice, this means that the 12-year limitation period will usually run from the date of default or the date of the last payment, whichever is the later, provided of course that the date of the last payment was not after the expiry of the original or any newly accrued limitation period.

Actions to enforce mortgages of future interests

The decision in *Hugill v Wilkinson*

6–48 The distinction between actions for foreclosure of land and actions to recover money charged on land was formerly of particular importance in regard to the mortgage of future interests. Section 2 of the 1874 Act provided that the operation of the statute against actions to recover land should, in the case of a

---

[128] [2008] 1 W.L.R. 710.
[129] ibid., at [82]–[87]. For what is required for adverse possession generally, see *Pye (JA) (Oxford) Ltd v Graham* [2003] 1 A.C. 419.
[130] *Ocean Accident & Guarantee Corp. v Ilford Gas Co* [1905] 2 K.B. 493.

future interest, be postponed until the interest fell into possession. In *Hugill v Wilkinson*,[131] North J. decided that foreclosure actions, being actions to recover land, also had the benefit of s.2 with the result that foreclosure of a mortgage of a remainder was not barred until 12 years after the remainder became vested in possession. There was, however, no similar provision to effect a postponement in the case of actions to recover money charged on land. Consequently, in the absence of acknowledgment, part payment or disability a mortgagee's other remedies were barred 12 years after the mortgagor's default in redeeming even though the security might not yet have fallen into possession.[132] This meant that in charges, properly so called, where foreclosure was not an available remedy, the creditor might lose his charge on a future interest altogether 12 years after his charge first became payable.[133] Moreover, owing to the particular language of s.2, its operation was confined to land in the strict sense and it did not, like other sections, extend to the proceeds of sale of land. The result, as previously mentioned, was that the unlucky mortgagee of a future interest in proceeds of sale found that his security was land for the purpose of attracting the 12 years' limit imposed on foreclosure actions for the recovery of land, but not "land" for the purpose of working a postponement under s.2.[134] On the other hand, the mortgagee of a future interest in pure personalty had nothing to worry about because to him no statute of limitations applied at all.[135]

The decision in *Hugill v Wilkinson*[136] was a literal application of s.2 of the 1874 Act in the light of the decisions that foreclosure is an action to recover land. The principle of the case was not, however, really the same as that of s.2. Foreclosure operates between mortgagee and mortgagor where the right to foreclose arises immediately on the mortgagor's default whether the property be present or future and there is no legal obstacle to the prosecution of the action. Foreclosure, as stated, is really an action to terminate the equity of redemption. Even if it is regarded as an action to recover the mortgagor's interest, it is not, where the security is a future interest, a future right of action for the recovery of the land but an immediate right of action to recover the mortgagor's present right to future possession. The fact that foreclosure of a future interest does not vest in the mortgagee an immediate right to the rents and profits is immaterial. Foreclosure does effectively vest in him an immediate title to the property mortgaged. This point was taken by Cozens-Hardy M.R. in *Wakefield and Barnsley Union Bank Ltd v Yates*[137]: "the object of foreclosure is to destroy the mortgagor's right to redeem and it is only as an incident that the right to receive the rents and profits arises." The Court of Appeal in that case refused to regard the fact that the mortgaged property was a reversion after a 21 years' lease as any reason for postponing the running of the statute. Yet, for purposes of the limitation of actions, leasehold reversions are treated as future interests in the

---

[131] ibid.
[132] *Re Owen* [1894] 3 Ch. 220.
[133] *Re Witham* [1922] 2 Ch. 413.
[134] *Re Hazeldine's Trusts* [1908] 1 Ch. 34; *Re Fox* [1913] 2 Ch. 75.
[135] See *Re Witham* [1922] 2 Ch. 413, where part of the property was personalty.
[136] (1888) 38 Ch.D. 480. For a discussion of this case see Preston & Newsom, *Limitation of Actions* (1953), pp.110–114.
[137] [1916] 1 Ch. 452 at 458.

same category as the remainder in *Hugill v Wilkinson*. Consequently, the decision of the Court of Appeal in *Yates'* case is scarcely consistent with that of North J. in *Hugill v Wilkinson*, although the latter case was referred to in *Yates'* case without disapproval.

The modern position

6–49   On the other hand, the principle of *Hugill v Wilkinson*, if open to question on technical grounds, has practical advantages. There is much to be said for a rule which does not constrain a mortgagee to realise his security before the asset to which the mortgagor looked as the means for repaying his debt has materialised. At any rate the Law Revision Committee approved the principle of *Hugill v Wilkinson*[138] such that s.18(3) of the Limitation Act 1939 incorporated it in statutory form and it is now repeated in s.20(3) of the 1980 Act. This provides as follows:

> "The right to receive any principal sum of money secured by a mortgage or other charge and the right to foreclose on the property subject to the mortgage or charge shall not be treated as accruing so long as the property comprises any future interest or any life insurance policy which has not matured or been determined."

The effect of this provision is that time does not run against remedies to enforce mortgages comprising any future interest until the future interest falls into possession and a life insurance policy that has not yet matured or been determined is treated as a future interest for this purpose. Section 20(3) applies to all remedies for the recovery of money charged on real or personal property and to foreclosure of mortgages of personalty. It does not, however, apply to foreclosure of mortgages of "land" which falls under s.15 and Sch.1, which govern actions for the recovery of land.

Future interests in land

6–50   Section 15 substantially re-enacts the provisions of the former Acts relating to the postponement of the statutory period of limitation in the case of future interests in land. But the primary rule is now contained in Sch.1 para.4 to the 1980 Act which provides:

> "The right of action to recover any land shall, in a case where—
>
> (a) the estate or interest claimed was an estate or interest in reversion or remainder or any other future estate or interest; and
> (b) no person has taken possession of the land by virtue of the estate or interest claimed;
>
> be treated as having accrued on the date on which the estate or interest fell into possession by the determination of the preceding estate or interest."

Section 15(2) qualifies this rule in cases where the holder of a preceding estate, other than a term of years, has been dispossessed during its continuance by

---

[138] Fifth Interim Report (1936), Cmnd. 5334, p.14.

allowing to the person entitled to the future interest either 12 years from the dispossession or six years from the date when his own interest vested in possession, whichever is longer. Certain other points of detail are covered in the Act to which detailed reference should be made.

The effect of section 15 of the Act

The result is that s.15 makes provision for the postponement of the operation of **6–51** the statute in actions for the recovery of land comparable to the general provision for postponement in s.20(3) in regard to actions for the recovery of money charged on real and personal property. Ironically enough, it is doubtful whether the benefit of postponement under s.6 extends to actions to foreclose mortgages of future interests in land owing to the questionable authority of the decision in *Hugill v Wilkinson*.[139] If the decision in *Wakefield and Barnsley Union Bank Ltd v Yates*[140] is correct, foreclosure actions are not within s.15 and Sch.1. Further, there is nothing in the 1980 Act to bring them within that section. Yet the intention plainly was that in the case of land foreclosure, actions should have the benefit of postponement no less than the actions now covered by s.20(3). The Law Revision Committee assumed that *Hugill v Wilkinson* was good law and recommended its extension in the manner effected by the predecessor to s.20(3).[141]

The position in regard to foreclosure of future interests in land is, therefore, scarcely satisfactory. The courts may be inclined, in interpreting the 1980 Act, to overlook the difficulty of reconciling *Hugill v Wilkinson* with *Yates'* case and simply give foreclosure actions the benefit of postponement under s.15 on the basis of the decisions holding foreclosure actions to be actions for the recovery of land.[142] If this is not done, an arbitrary distinction will be created between foreclosure of mortgages of land and other actions to enforce mortgages of realty and personalty, a distinction which would be the precise opposite of that which the Law Revision Committee intended to remove.[143]

If *Hugill v Wilkinson* is followed in applying the 1980 Act, the status of *Yates'* case necessarily comes into question particularly in regard to the position of a second mortgagee. Under the similar provisions of the earlier Acts it had been decided that:

(a) The existence of a prior mortgage, under which possession has not been taken, does not make a second mortgage a mortgage of a future interest so that it does not postpone the operation of the statute against a second mortgagee's right to foreclose.[144]

---

[139] (1888) 38 Ch.D. 480.
[140] [1916] 1 Ch. 452. This question was left open by the House of Lords in *Fairweather v St Marylebone Property Co Ltd* [1963] A.C. 510 at 523
[141] *Hugill v Wilkinson* had been mentioned without disapproval in more than one case, e.g. *Re Witham* [1922] 2 Ch. 413.
[142] As is assumed in Oughton, *Limitation of Actions* (1998).
[143] See Preston & Newsom, *Limitation of Actions* (1953), p.113.
[144] *Kibble v Fairthorne* [1895] 1 Ch. 219.

(b) The same is true, if the prior mortgagee goes into possession after the creation of the second mortgage.[145]

(c) Similarly the existence of a 21 years' lease under which possession has been taken before the execution of a mortgage does not postpone the running of the statute against the right to foreclose.[146]

All these decisions are obviously good sense. It would be absurd to postpone the running of the statute against a second mortgagee merely because of the existence of a prior mortgage term, even when the prior mortgagee has taken possession. A second mortgagee obtains the mortgagor's right to redeem the first mortgagee and there is nothing to stop him either from foreclosing the mortgagor or redeeming the first mortgagee whenever he chooses. What case is there for postponement? *Yates'* case has a particular importance owing to mortgages now being made by demise and it is believed to be fundamentally sound. It certainly has to be accepted if any sense is to be made of the position of a second mortgagee. Yet, if foreclosure is regarded as an action for the recovery of land, *Yates'* case is not easy to square with the general principles of the Limitation Acts under which a reversion upon a term of years is treated as a future interest. The courts are likely to uphold both *Yates'* case and *Hugill v Wilkinson*, but by what process of reasoning remains to be seen.

In any event, the 1980 Act seems to have created minor anomalies. Thus, s.20(3) postpones the operation of the statute so long as the property mortgaged "comprises any future interest". These words can only mean that, where present and future interests are mortgaged together, s.20(3) protects the mortgagee's remedies in respect of *all* the property against the operation of the statute until the future interest falls into possession. No such provision is to be found in regard to foreclosure of mortgages of land, although a single mortgage comprising both a present interest in land and a future interest in realty or personalty is by no means impossible.

Again, s.15(3) excludes from the category of future interests estates or interests which fall into possession after an entail capable of being barred. There is no similar provision under s.20, although entails of personalty are now permissible.

Actions for the recovery of arrears of interest

Six-year limitation period

6–52   So long as the right to the principal remains alive, the right to interest also continues, since interest is accessory to principal. But s.20(5) of the 1980 Act requires actions for the recovery of arrears of interest payable in respect of sums secured by mortgage or charge to be brought within six years of the date when

---

[145] *Samuel Johnson & Sons Ltd v Brock* [1907] 2 Ch. 533.
[146] *Wakefield & Barnsley Union Bank Ltd v Yates* [1916] 1 Ch. 452.

the interest became due.[147] In other words, the maximum amount of interest recoverable in such an action is six years' arrears, even if the principal sum can be recovered within 12 years. The difference in time limits means that the way the mortgagee accounts for payments as between principal and interest may make a difference to what is recoverable in certain actions.[148] The same limit is imposed on actions to recover arrears by way of damages, in cases where there is no covenant for payment of interest and the court gives interest by way of damages.[149]

Exceptions

There are, however, two qualifications on the general limit of six years by s.20(6)   **6–53**
and (7) of the Act:

(a) Where a prior encumbrancer has been in possession of the property mortgaged, a subsequent encumbrancer, if he brings his action within one year of the discontinuance of the prior mortgagee's possession, may recover all interest which fell due during the period of that possession. The reason, of course, is that the prior encumbrancer's possession disables the second mortgagee from keeping down the interest of his own mortgage out of the rents and profits.[150]

(b) Where the mortgaged property comprises any future interest or life insurance policy and it is a term of the mortgage that arrears of interest shall be treated as part of the principal debt secured by the mortgage, then the interest is deemed not to be due until the right to receive the principal is deemed to accrue. This means that when the statute does not run against the mortgagee of future property until the property falls into possession, all arrears of interest accruing during the time when the property was still future are deemed to accrue only on the date when the property vested in possession. Consequently all such arrears are recoverable within six years of that date.

This is not, however, a general exception in favour of a mortgagee of future property. It is only when the mortgage provides for capitalisation of arrears of interest that the second exception operates. In other cases the six years' limit runs against the right to interest from the date when the interest was actually due whether or not the running of the statute against the right to the principal is postponed under s.20(3).

The six years' limit under s.20(5) applies to an action to recover arrears of interest, which includes an action to recover the principal with the interest

---

[147] *Bristol & West v Bartlett* [2003] 1 W.L.R. 284; *Scottish Equitable Plc v Thompson* [2003] H.L.R. 690.
[148] See *Bristol & West v Bartlett*, ibid., at 33.
[149] cf. *Mellersh v Brown* (1890) 45 Ch.D. 225.
[150] Unless the prior mortgagee pays over surplus rents and profits to the second mortgagee, which rarely happens.

thereon.[151] On the basis of the decisions taken under the similar provision in s.42 of the Real Property Limitation Act 1833, the six years' limit would also apply to all proceedings by the mortgagee to enforce the mortgage, for it was settled that no more than six years' arrears of interest might go into the mortgagee's account in proceedings for foreclosure, judicial sale or the appointment of a receiver.[152] The 1980 Act, however, by wholly excluding foreclosure of mortgages of land from the provisions of s.20(4) appears inadvertently to have enacted that more than six years' arrears of interest may be claimed in foreclosure of land. Thus, while only six years' arrears will be allowed in computing the mortgagor's personal debt, the full amount of the arrears will, in the case of land, be allowed in actions against the security.[153]

Arrears of interest in redemption actions

6–54   In any event, it is well settled that the six years' limit does not apply in actions *by the mortgagor* for redemption[154] and this is so even when the mortgagee has instituted proceedings for foreclosure and the mortgagor counterclaims for redemption.[155] A mortgagor who has lost his estate at law will only be allowed to redeem it in equity on the terms of discharging all his obligations under the mortgage. The mortgagor's neglect to pay the interest is just as culpable as the mortgagee's failure to enforce his rights. The rule is the same where the mortgagee has sold the security under a power of sale and the mortgagor seeks to recover the surplus proceeds of sale, for this is in essence an action for redemption. The mortgagee may thus retain out of the proceeds the full amount of the arrears.[156] The position is, however, not entirely clear when the property has been sold not in pursuance of the mortgagee's power of sale but under a paramount power outside the mortgage and the proceeds of sale have been paid into court. In *Re Stead's Mortgaged Estates*[157] the property had been sold under the Land Clauses Acts and the mortgagee petitioned to have the amount of his debt with full arrears of interest paid out to him. Malins V.C. only allowed him six years' arrears. However, in *Re Lloyd*[158] the Court of Appeal allowed the mortgagee his full arrears when the property had been sold in an administration suit and the proceedings for payment out of court were initiated by the mortgagor. The court expressed no view as to the correctness of *Re Stead's Mortgaged Estates* and treated the mortgagor's claim as in substance one for redemption. The only observable difference between the two cases was in the party who took the first step in the proceedings for payment out. This difference can scarcely be material because in foreclosure the mortgagor's counterclaim for redemption,

[151] *Bristol & West v Bratlett* [2003] 1 W.L.R. 284; *Scottish Equitable Plc v Thompson* [2003] H.L.R. 690.
[152] *Sinclair v Jackson* (1853) 17 Beav. 405; *Re Lloyd* [1903] 1 Ch. 385.
[153] McGee, *Limitation Periods* (5th edn, 2006), paras 13–062 to 13–068.
[154] *Elvy v Norwood* (1852) 5 De G. & Sm. 240; *Edmunds v Waugh* (1866) L.R. 1 Eq. 418 *Ezekiel v Orakpo* [1997] 1 W.L.R. 340.
[155] *Dingle v Coppen* [1899] 1 Ch. 726; *Holmes v Cowcher* [1970] 1 W.L.R. 834 *Ezekial v Orakpo*, above.
[156] *Edmunds v Waugh* (1866) L.R. 1 Eq. 418; *Holmes v Cowcher*, above.
[157] (1876) 2 Ch.D. 713.
[158] [1903] 1 Ch. 385.

although made under the pressure of the mortgagee's proceedings, is outside the six years' limitation on arrears of interest. Indeed, if this is the difference between the cases, money may lie in court because neither party wishes to take the first step in the proceedings. It is therefore hoped that *Re Lloyd* will be regarded as having impliedly overruled *Re Stead's Mortgaged Estates*.

EXTENSIONS AND INTERRUPTIONS TO LIMITATION PERIODS UNDER THE ACT

Disability

It is beyond the scope of this work to consider in detail the rules governing the extension of the period of limitation by reason of the disability of the person entitled to sue.[159] The main rule laid down in s.28 is that if, on the date when the right of action accrued the person to whom it accrued was under a disability, the action may be brought within six years of the cessation of the disability. The disability must therefore subsist on the date when the right of action accrues which, in the case of a mortgagee's remedies is normally the date when the mortgagor defaults on the covenant for redemption. It is not enough if the disability arises after the date fixed for redemption.[160]

6–55

Section 28(4) contains a provision with a special bearing on remedies to enforce a mortgage of land. Notwithstanding any disability, no action to recover land (including, of course, foreclosure) or to recover money charged on land may be brought more than 30 years after the right of action accrued. In other words, there is an absolute limit of 30 years even in cases of disability.

Acknowledgments and part payments

The Act provides in ss.29–31 for the fresh accrual of actions—and thus for the extension of the statutory period—when an acknowledgment or part payment is made. It lays down slightly different rules for the remedies against the security and those in respect of the personal debt, so that the two forms of remedy have to be considered separately.

6–56

Remedies against the security

Section 29(1) to (3), which applies equally to realty and personalty, enacts that when there has accrued to a mortgagee any right of action to recover the mortgaged property, including a foreclosure action, and:

6–57

---

[159] See McGee, *Limitation Periods* (5th edn, 2006) paras 19.001–19.032.
[160] *Purnell v Roche* [1927] 2 Ch. 142. In this case the remedies of a lunatic mortgagee were held not to have been saved by the disability, although interest had been paid after the disability supervened. Now, however, under s.29(3) of the 1980 Act, in a foreclosure or other action by the mortgagee, payment of principal or interest by the person in possession of the property causes the accrual of the right of action to be deemed to be postponed until the date of such payment, and facts similar to those in *Purnell v Roche* would today give a different result.

(1) the person in possession of the land acknowledges the title of the mortgagee[161]; or

(2) the person in possession or the person liable for the mortgage debt makes any payment in respect of the debt whether principal or interest;

the right shall be deemed to have accrued on the date of the acknowledgment or payment.

An *acknowledgment* is thus effective only when made by the person in possession or an agent on his behalf, while a *payment* is effective not only when made by the person in possession but also when made by the person liable for the mortgage debt. Both acknowledgments and payments, when effective, bind "all other persons in possession during the ensuing period of limitation."[162] In other words, the mortgagee's remedies against the property are protected against everybody for a further period of 12 years from the date of the acknowledgment or payment. Section 31, which establishes these rules, refers only to mortgages and mortgagees. There is no definition clause in the Act, which extends the meaning of "mortgage" to cover a charge. It is therefore arguable that acknowledgments and part payments under s.31 do not extend a chargee's remedies against the security. The argument gains point from the fact that s.20, which does cover charges, refers specifically to "a mortgage or other charge". The omission of charges[163] from the operation of s.31 can hardly have been intended and the courts may resort to the definition of mortgage in s.205(1)(xvi) of the Law of Property Act 1925, in order to avoid this result.[164]

6–58 Mortgagor dispossessed by third party: If, after the execution of the mortgage, a third party obtains possession and occupies the property under such conditions that time begins to run in his favour against the mortgagor, the mortgagee's rights will be unaffected so long as the mortgagor continues to make payments in respect of the debt (whether of principal or interest). In such a case the protection afforded by s.29(3) of the 1980 Act is absolute.[165] If, on the other hand, the mortgagor was already dispossessed at the date of the mortgage and time was already running against him, the execution of the mortgage does not confer on the mortgagee a new right of entry, so that subsequent payments by the mortgagor cannot prevent time from running in favour of his disseisor.[166]

Remedies in respect of the personal debt

6–59 Subject to s.29(6), s.29(5) enacts that where any right of action has accrued to recover any debt or other liquidated pecuniary claim or any claim to the personal

---

[161] Or as agent on his behalf, see, e.g. *Wright v Pepin* [1954] 1 W.L.R. 635.

[162] Limitation Act 1980 s.31(1) and (2).

[163] A charge by way of legal mortgage is presumably in the same position as a legal mortgage by virtue of LPA 1925 ss.88 and 89.

[164] "Mortgage" in the Law of Property Act 1925, "includes any charge or lien on any property for securing money or money's worth."

[165] See *Doe d. Palmer v Eyre* (1851) 17 Q.B.D. 366; *Ludbrook v Ludbrook* [1901] 2 K.B. 96.

[166] *Thornton v France* [1897] 2 Q.B. 143.

estate of a deceased person or to any share or interest in any such estate and the person liable or accountable for the claim acknowledges the claim or makes any payment in respect of it, the right shall be treated as having accrued on and not before the date of the acknowledgment or payment. This is subject to the provision that a payment of a part of the rent or interest due at any time shall not extend the period for claiming the remainder then due, but any payment of interest shall be treated as a payment in respect of the principal debt.[167]

The effect of an acknowledgment is different from that of a payment. A *payment* binds all persons liable in respect of the debt, including, of course, the successors of the person paying.[168] But an *acknowledgment* only binds the acknowledgor and his successors, i.e. his personal representatives and any person on whom the liability for the debt devolves on his death or bankruptcy or by disposition of property or by the terms of a settlement or otherwise.[169]

The effect of acknowledgment or payment made after the relevant period of limitation has run

Formerly there existed a rule of law that where the effect of the expiration of the **6–60** prescribed period of limitation was merely to bar the remedy and not the right, an acknowledgment or payment could cause a right of action to accrue once again even though it was made after the expiry of the prescribed period of limitation unless the statute had extinguished the right itself. It is now provided by s.29(7) that a current period of limitation may be repeatedly extended under the section by further acknowledgments or payments but that a right of action once barred shall not be revived by any subsequent acknowledgment or payment.[170]

Extinction of title after expiration of time

Section 17 extinguishes the title of a mortgagee of land who fails to exercise his **6–61** remedies within the prescribed period and so a subsequent acknowledgment or payment does not revive his rights against the security.[171]

There is no corresponding provision which extinguishes the title of a mortgagee of personalty, so that a subsequent acknowledgment or payment appears to revive the mortgage as well as the personal debt.[172] This difference between

---

[167] Limitation Act 1980 s.29(6).

[168] ibid., s.31(7).

[169] ibid., s.31(6), (9). Section 31(6) and (7) re-enact s.25(5) and (6) of the 1939 Act but omit provisos which formerly existed to both subsections. Those limited the effect of an acknowledgement or payment made *after* the expiration of the period of limitation prescribed the commencement of an action to recover a debt or other liquidated pecuniary claim and were repealed by the Limitation Amendment Act 1980, ss.6(3), 13(2), and Sch.2.

[170] This is subject to the Limitation Act 1980 s.29(6). This change came as a result of the recommendation made by the Law Reform Committee in its 21st Report (Final Report on Limitations of Actions) (Cmnd. 6923), para.2.71.

[171] *Kibble v Fairthorne* [1895] 1 Ch. 219. After the mortgagee's remedies have been barred against the land, the mortgagor is entitled to the return of the deeds: *Lewis v Plunket* [1937] Ch. 306.

[172] It is true that s.3(2) extinguishes the title to chattels after an action for conversion has been barred, but this does not cover the case of mere inactivity by mortgagor and mortgagee.

realty and personalty in regard to the effect of acknowledgments and payments on a mortgagee's rights is to be explained more by reference to the history of the drafting of the relevant provisions than on rational grounds.

In any event, acknowledgments and payments made after the statutory period has once run may operate to revive the personal action for the mortgage debt. Section 5 bars the remedy for simple contract and s.8 in the case of specialty debts but neither extinguishes the debt. The right to the debt is therefore revived and under s.31[173] it is revived not only against the person making the acknowledgment or payment but against his successors and all persons liable in respect of the debt, respectively, with one exception. The exception is that the revival of the debt by a limited owner under a settlement antedating the acknowledgment or payment does not bind other persons taking under that settlement.[174]

Conditions of an effective acknowledgment or payment

6–62 Payment: Payment need only be proved as a fact. However, where a payment is clearly referable to an admitted part of the debt it operates as an acknowledgment of that liability and nothing more.[175] Extrinsic evidence can be taken into account in determining whether the payment made was referable to the whole sum of just the part.[176]

6–63 Acknowledgment: An acknowledgment to have the effects described above, must, however, be in writing signed by the person making it.[177]

The acknowledgment or payment has further to be made by the person specified in s.29, that is:

(1) in the case of an acknowledgment of the mortgage, by the person in possession;
(2) in the case of a payment keeping the mortgage alive, by the person in possession or by the person liable for the mortgage debt;
(3) in the case of an acknowledgment or payment keeping the personal debt alive, by the person liable or accountable for the debt.

The acknowledgment or payment may also be made by the agent of the person required to make it.[178] A payment made by the Benefits Agency can constitute a payment made on behalf of the mortgagor for these purposes.[179] An acknowledgment made in without prejudice communications is inadmissible in evidence.[180]

---

[173] Limitation Act 1980 s.31(6), (7).

[174] cf. *Gregson v Hindley* (1846) 10 Jur. 383.

[175] *Surrendra Overseas Ltd v Government of Sri Lanka* [1977] 2 All E.R. 481, considered in *John Howard Ashcroft v Bradford & Bingley Plc* [2010] EWCA Civ 223; [2010] N.P.C. 30

[176] *Dungate v Dungate* [1965] 1 W.L.R 1477.

[177] Limitation Act 1980 s.30(1).

[178] ibid., s.30(2). cf. *Wright v Pepin* [1954] 1 W.L.R. 635 (acknowledgment by mortgagor's solicitor held to be sufficient).

[179] *Bradford & Bingley v Cutler* [2008] EWCA 74, *The Times* February 22, 2008.

[180] *Ofulue v Bossert* [2009] 1 A.C. 990.

The "person in possession": The "person in possession" for the purposes of **6–64** s.29 is the person in possession of the interest mortgaged. It does not include a tenant from the mortgagor and a payment of rent by a tenant direct to the mortgagee does not bind the mortgagor unless made at the latter's express direction. A tenant is not the implied agent of the mortgagor for making acknowledgments or payments to the mortgagee.[181] On the other hand, a receiver, whether appointed by the court or by the mortgagee under a power, is in law the agent of the mortgagor and entitled to make payments on the mortgagor's behalf. Consequently, a receiver's acts do bind the mortgagor.[182]

The "person liable or accountable": The "person liable or accountable" for **6–65** the debt means a person liable or accountable in connection with the discharge of the mortgage debt. A surety[183] or a co-mortgagor[184] is clearly such a person, and their payments bind the mortgagor.

It is otherwise with a third party who is liable to make payments to the mortgagee in connection with the mortgaged property but not in relation to the discharge of the mortgage debt. The case of rent paid by a tenant to the mortgagee has already been mentioned above. Payments of rent at the request of the mortgagee convert him into a mortgagee in possession but do not constitute payments by the mortgagor. If an insurance policy is assigned by way of mortgage and notice is given to the insurers, the latter become liable to pay the moneys to the mortgagee. A payment under the policy is not, however, a payment in respect of the debt and does not keep the mortgagee's remedies alive against other securities comprised in the mortgage.[185] Similarly, if a beneficiary mortgages his interest in a trust fund, a payment by the trustees direct to the mortgagee in pursuance of their duty to give effect to all interests of which they have notice does not bind the mortgagor.[186]

The "person liable or accountable" is not limited to persons contractually liable to the mortgagee. It is enough if the person paying is "concerned to answer the debt".[187] In *Bradshaw v Widdrington*[188] a father borrowed money on mortgage for the benefit of his son who executed a bond for the money in favour of his father. Payments by the son in respect of mortgage interest were held sufficient to keep the mortgage alive since, as between him and the mortgagor, he was bound to discharge the mortgage debt. There need not even be a contractual obligation for the discharge of the debt between the mortgagor and the person making payment. All that is necessary is that the person paying should, by reason of the relations between himself and the mortgagor, be entitled in law to

---

[181] *Harlock v Ashberry* (1882) 19 Ch.D. 539. A payment of rent made by a tenant of mortgaged property to a mortgagee in consequence of a notice by the mortgagee requiring the rent to be paid to him is not a receipt of any sum in respect of the mortgage debt and accordingly not a payment to prevent the barring by the Limitation Act of a foreclosure action.

[182] *Chinnery v Evans* (1864) 11 H.L.C. 115 at 134.

[183] *Lewin v Wilson* (1886) 11 A.C. 639.

[184] *Re Earl Kingston's Estate* [1869] 3 I.R. 485.

[185] *Re Lord Clifden* [1900] 1 Ch. 774.

[186] *Re Edwards' Will Trusts* [1937] Ch. 553.

[187] *Lewin v Wilson* (1886) 11 A.C. 639 at 644.

[188] [1902] 2 Ch. 430.

discharge the debt.[189] Thus, when the property mortgaged is settled, a payment by any one beneficiary is sufficient to save the mortgagee's remedies against the property.[190] The rule appears to be that whenever a number of persons stand in peril of suit by a creditor so that all benefit by the discharge of the liability, a payment by one keeps the creditor's remedies alive.[191]

Assignments of the equity of redemption

6–66   Logically, the same rule should apply in assignments of the equity of redemption so that a payment either by the mortgagor[192] or by the assignee[193] would keep the mortgagee's remedies alive. It has in fact been so decided in the case of an equity of redemption assigned *free from encumbrances* when the original mortgagor is, as between himself and his assignee, bound to discharge the mortgage debt.[194] If, however, the assignment is made *subject to encumbrances*, the position is not free from doubt. In *Newbould v Smith*[195] the Court of Appeal held that payments by the original mortgagor would not bind the assignee. This decision is inconsistent with the language of Westbury L.C. and Lord Cranworth in *Chinnery v Evans*[196] and it seems to have been doubted by the House of Lords in *Newbould v Smith* itself, the court finding other reasons for dismissing the appeal. The decision, although the Court of Appeal was a strong one, is submitted to be entirely unacceptable. A mortgagee who receives regular payments of interest from his mortgagor should not be concerned to inquire into the latter's dealings with the equity of redemption. Any other rule would be very alarming to mortgagees.[197]

To whom the acknowledgment payment is to be made

6–67   Finally, an acknowledgment or payment must be made to the person whose remedies are to be kept alive, i.e. to the person entitled to the mortgage or to his agent. Who is the right person to receive an acknowledgment or payment naturally depends on the dealings with the mortgage debt and on the notices of those dealings given to the mortgagor. If the mortgagee has died, his personal representatives are the persons concerned to receive acknowledgments or payments.[198] Similarly, if the mortgage debt has been settled, the trustees are the right persons to be paid. A payment direct to the proper beneficiary is regarded

---

[189] *Bradshaw v Widdrington* [1902] 2 Ch. 430 at 439, per Buckley J.

[190] *Barclay v Owen* (1889) 60 L.T. 220. A life tenant, who is also the mortgagee of the settled property, is presumed to be keeping down the interest on his own encumbrance so that the statute does not run against his mortgage: *Wynne v Styan* (1847) 2 Ph. 303.

[191] *Re Lacey* [1907] 1 Ch. 330 at 346, per Farwell L.J.; also *Roddam v Morley* (1857) 1 De G. & J. 1.

[192] *Bradshaw v Widdrington* [1902] 2 Ch. 430.

[193] *Dibb v Walker* [1893] 2 Ch. 429.

[194] *Bradshaw v Widdrington*, above.

[195] (1886) 33 Ch.D. 127, affirmed (1889) 14 A.C. 423 but on other grounds, the House of Lords reserving their opinion on this point.

[196] (1864) 11 H.L.C. 115.

[197] ibid., at 139, per Lord Cranworth.

[198] *Barclay v Owen* (1889) 60 L.T. 220.

as paid to him as agent for the trustees[199] and may be sufficient to prevent time from running.

Institution of proceedings by the mortgagee

If an action is begun by the mortgagee within the statutory period such will **6–68** prevent his rights from being barred even though the hearing does not take place before time has run out.[200] It must be remembered that the institution of proceedings does not have the same effect as an acknowledgment and saves the remedies only for that action, so that upon the discontinuance of the action the benefit of the saving will not be available in a subsequent action.[201] On the other hand, if a judgment for foreclosure absolute is obtained, the effect is to vest a new title in the mortgagee so that although the mortgagor may remain continuously in possession, the statutory period begins to run afresh from the decree.[202]

Fraud, concealment and mistake

Section 32 of the 1980 Act provides that: **6–69**

(1) where the action is based on the fraud of the defendant, his agent or any person through whom he claims and his agent;

(2) any fact relevant to the claimant's right of action has been deliberately concealed by fraud; or

(3) the action is for relief from the consequences of a mistake;

the period shall not begin to run until the plaintiff either discovered or could with reasonable diligence have discovered the fraud, concealment or mistake.

The section at the same time saves the rights of bona fide purchasers.[203]

---

[199] *Re Somerset* [1894] 1 Ch. 231.
[200] *Wrixon v Vize* (1842) 3 Dr. & W. 104 at 123.
[201] *Pratt v Hawkins* (1846) 15 M. & W. 399.
[202] *Heath v Pugh* (1881) 6 Q.B.D. 345 affirmed (1882) 7 App. Cas. 235. Unless, of course, the action is struck out.
[203] Limitation Act 1980 s.32(3) and see McGee, *Limitation Periods* (5th edn, 2006), paras 20–002 to 20–039.

CHAPTER 7

SUBROGATION

NATURE OF SUBROGATION

This chapter is concerned with the remedy of subrogation that arises as a result **7–01** of the operation of law. This is to be contrasted with contractual subrogation. In the context referred to in this chapter, subrogation is not a right or a cause of action, but an equitable restitutionary remedy against a party who would otherwise be unjustly enriched. The doctrine will only operate when the court is satisfied that reason and justice demand it takes effect.[1] Where one party has conferred a benefit on another, such as the provision of funds to pay money owed by them to a third party and it is just in all the circumstances if there is no reason to prevent it, the provider of the benefit should be allowed to succeed to the rights or assets the third party had in respect of that money owed. The remedy of subrogation enables a later lender whose funds were used to satisfy the obligation to an earlier lender to "stand in the shoes" of the earlier lender and enforce its security as if it had the benefit of the earlier lender's charge. Put another way, subrogation is a remedy that "gives effect to a property right which already exists in equity, i.e. the right to be regarded as chargee of the property in question".[2] As a simple expression of the relevant principles the formula set out by Walton J. some 35 odd years ago has proved remarkably resilient:

> "[W]here A's money is used to pay off the claim of B, who is a secured creditor, A is entitled to be regarded in equity as having had an assignment to him of B's rights as a secured creditor. . . . It finds one of its chief uses in the situation where one person advances money on the understanding that he is to have certain security for the money that he has advanced, and for one reason or another, he does not receive the promised security. In such a case he is nevertheless to be subrogated to the rights of any other person who at the relevant time had any security over the same property and whose debts have been discharged in whole or in part by the money so provided by him."[3]

---

[1] *Orakpo v Manson Investments* [1978] A.C. 95; [1977] 3 W.L.R. 229 at 110, approved in *Bankers Trust Co v Namdar* [1997] E.G. 20(C.S.); [1997] N.P.C. 22.

[2] *Halifax Plc v Omar* [2002] EWCA Civ 121; [2002] 2 P. & C.R. 377 at [81].

[3] *Burtson Finance v Speirway Ltd (in liq.)* [1974] 3 All E.R. 735. This section was cited with approval by Oliver J. in *Paul v Speiway Ltd (in liq.)* [1976] Ch. 220, by Jonathan Parker L.J. in *Halifax v Omar* [2002] EWCA Civ 121; [2002] 2 P. & C.R. 377; by Lord Hutton in *Banque Financière de la Cité v Parc (Battersea)* [1999] 1 A.C. 221; and by Neuberger L.J. (as he then was) in *Cheltenham & Gloucester Plc v Appleyard* [2004] EWCA Civ 291; [2004] 13 E.G. 127 (C.S.)—the principle was "nowhere better stated".

Thus, in simple terms, if the lender's moneys are used to discharge an earlier security, the lender is subrogated to the rights under that earlier security and obtains priority over encumbrances which followed that security.[4] It is critical that the lender can show that the money which was used to discharge the earlier indebtedness was in fact his.[5] In practice this means that the mortgage discharged using the lender's funds is not kept alive[6] but the lender having the right of subrogation has the same rights as if it had been and had been assigned to him.[7]

The nature of subrogation was set out by Millet L.J. in *Boscawen v Bajwa*:

> "Subrogation ... is a remedy, not a cause of action.... It is available in a wide variety of different factual situations in which it is required in order to reverse the defendant's unjust enrichment. Equity lawyers speak of a right of subrogation, or of an equity of subrogation, but this merely reflects the fact that it is not a remedy which the court has a general discretion to impose whenever it thinks it just to do so. The equity arises from the conduct of the parties on well settled principles and in defined circumstances which make it unconscionable for the defendant to deny the proprietary interest claimed by the plaintiff. A constructive trust arises in the same way. Once the equity is established the court satisfies it by declaring that the property in question is subject to a charge by way of subrogation in the one case or a constructive trust in the other."[8]

SUBROGATION AND THE LAW OF MORTGAGES

7–02 In the context of the law of mortgages, a lender who finds that the effect or scope of an intended mortgage does not operate as he expected, may look to claim that he is subrogated to the rights of a vendor such as the vendor's lien,[9] a vendor's mortgagee,[10] a discharged mortgagee rights under the former mortgage, or an earlier (but subsisting) mortgagees rights.[11]

Using the remedy of subrogation, it may be possible for a lender who otherwise has no charge or an equitable charge whose priority has, or could be, defeated, to establish:

---

[4] See for example *UCB Group Ltd v Hedworth* [2003] EWCA Civ 1717; [2003] 3 F.C.R. 739 in which it is made clear that there is no conceptual difficulty with subrogation at one remove provided the standard requirements are met; see para.7–10 below.

[5] See *Filby v Mortgage Express (No.2) Ltd* [2004] EWCA Civ 759; [2004] 2 P. & C.R. DG16.

[6] See Lord Hoffmann in *Banque Financière* (below) at 236.

[7] Neuberger L.J. (in *Appleyard* (below)) approved Evans L.J.'s view in *Halifax Mortgage Service Ltd v Muirhead* (1997) 76 P. & C.R. 418 at 427 that the subsequent lender cannot obtain a greater rate of interest than that which he had contracted for. The practical approach apparently approved by the court (*Kali & Burlay v Chawla* [2007] EWHC 2357 (Ch)) is as follows: (i) the overarching assumption is that the right to interest is part of the remedy of subrogation; (ii) the rate is usually that which was formerly charged by the creditor; (iii) the rate may be capped at that for which the new creditor contracted; and (iv) interest is usually charged from when the debt was paid off or any later moment when the new creditor's right to subrogation arose.

[8] *Boscawen v Bajwa* [1996] 1 W.L.R. 328 at 335B–D.

[9] *Boodle Hatfield & Co v British Films Ltd* (1986) 2 B.C.C. 99,221.

[10] *Boscawen v Bajwa* [1996] 1 W.L.R. 329.

[11] See Ch.5 paras 5–06 to 5–10 for further consideration of the manner in which the remedy of subrogation operates to effectively transfers the ability to rely on an previous or continuing mortgagees right to a new lender.

(i) a right against a legal and/or beneficial owner or co-owner, who was unaware of the transaction involving the lender which provided moneys to fund a purchase[12] or to discharge some or all of a valid mortgage[13];

(ii) priority over the overriding interest of a beneficial owner and/or occupier which was subject to an earlier mortgage[14];

(iii) priority over charges created prior to the date of its mortgage, where the funds provided were used to discharge an earlier mortgage with priority;

(iv) its entitlement to security for at least part of its advance, where it had constructive notice of a right to set aside the transactions creating its mortgage on the basis of pre-existing mortgages which its funds were used to redeem[15];

(v) entitlement to the benefit of the "unpaid" vendor's lien where the advance made is used to pay the purchase price and without the advance the purchase price would not have been paid[16];

(vi) entitlement to be subrogated to an earlier lender's right to be subrogated to the rights of another.[17]

GENERAL PRINCIPLES

Subrogation arises by operation of law in a wide range of different cases. This work is not concerned with contractual subrogation. Subrogation is a flexible remedy but that does not detract from its principled foundation. As with any restitutionary remedy, the fundamental questions which need to be answered in establishing a claim for such relief in the context of mortgages are whether the borrower, owner or earlier lender/secured creditor would be enriched at the claiming lender's expense, whether the enrichment would be unjust, and whether there are policy reasons to deny subrogation as a remedy.   **7–03**

> "The test as to whether the courts will apply the doctrine of subrogation to the facts of any particular case is entirely empirical. It is, I think, impossible to formulate any narrower principle than that the doctrine will be applied only when the courts are satisfied that reason and justice demand that it should be."[18]

Neuberger L.J. undertook an important and wide-ranging review of the case-law in *Cheltenham & Gloucester v Appleyard*.[19] While acknowledging that there was a limit to the extent to which any general rules could be extracted in relation to   **7–04**

---

[12] *Equity & Law Home Loans Ltd v Prestridge* [1992] 1 W.L.R. 137.

[13] *Butler v Rice* [1910] 2 Ch. 277.

[14] *Eagle Star Insurance Co Ltd v Karasiewicz* [2002] EWCA Civ 940.

[15] *UCB Corporate Services Ltd v Williams* [2002] EWCA Civ 555; [2003] 1 P. & C.R. 168, *Fibly v Mortgage Express (No.2) Ltd* [2004] EWCA Civ 759; [2004] 2 P. & C.R. DG16.

[16] *UCB Group Ltd v Hedworth* [2003] EWCA Civ 1717; [2003] 3 F.C.R. 739, *Halifax v Omar* [2002] EWCA Civ 121; [2002] 2 P. & C.R. 377.

[17] *UCB Group Ltd v Hedworth* above, *Castle Philips Finance v Piddington* (1995) 70 P. & C.R. 592.

[18] *Orakpo v Manson Investments Ltd* [1978] A.C. 95; [1977] 3 W.L.R. 229 at 110 per Lord Salmon.

[19] Above.

equitable subrogation given the very nature of the remedy (varying as it does from case to case with the object of effecting a fair and just balance between the rights of the parties) he set out a series of 13 points of general application. They wholly justify setting out in full:

(i) Subrogation is more than a single concept; its nature is sometimes contractual and sometimes equitable.

(ii) As a remedy subrogation is primarily aimed at preventing unjust enrichment.[20]

(iii) Subrogation is a flexible remedy, which must still be applied in a principled fashion.[21]

(iv) A classic case of subrogation is that described by Walton J. in *Burston Finance.*[22]

(v) The characteristic case of subrogation involving a lender who expected to receive security (in the proprietary sense) claiming subrogation to another security does not define the full extent of the remedy, it can apply to personal rights.[23]

(vi) A lender of money who gets some security is not barred from claiming to be subrogated to another security.

(vii) A lender who obtains all the security which he bargained for cannot claim to be subrogated to another security or other rights.

(viii) The fact that the lender's own negligence was the cause of his failure to obtain the security he bargained for is irrelevant.[24]

(ix) The fact that the borrower and the lender did not have a common intention that the lender should have security is not fatal to a lender's subsequent claim for subrogation. However the intention of the parties to the arrangement on which a claim for subrogation is based may be highly relevant.

(x) A lender cannot invoke subrogation so as to put himself in a better position than he would have been in had he obtained all the rights for which he bargained.

(xi) It is difficult, and may be impossible, for a lender to invoke subrogation where he has obtained security which gives him all the rights and remedies of security to which he claims to be subrogated, or is a security into which the original security would naturally merge.

(xii) The capital sum in respect of which a lender is subrogated cannot normally be greater than the amount of the secured debt that has been discharged.[25]

[20] Per Lord Diplock in *Orakpo v Manson Investments Ltd* [1978] AC 95; Millett L.J. in *Boscawen v Bajwa* [1996] 1 W.L.R. 328; and Lords Hoffman and Clyde *in Banque Finacière* (above) at 231G–H and 237D–E respectively.

[21] Per Millett L.J. in *Boscawen* (above) at 338G–339C.

[22] [1974] 1 W.L.R. 1648

[23] Per Lord Hoffman in *Banque Financière* [1999] 1 AC 221 at 229C where the lender bargained for a negative form of protection in the form of an undertaking which he did not get. This did not prevent his claim to be subrogated to a security (in essence as personal remedy).

[24] *Anfield (UK) Ltd v (1) Bank of Scotland Plc & ors* [2010] EWHC 2374.

[25] Per Lord Diplock in *Orakpo* (above) at 104G and per Evans L.J. in *Halifax Mortgage Services v Muirhead* (above) at 426.

(xiii) Normal equitable principles apply to subrogated rights. Accordingly, the usual equitable defences are available to defend a claim for subrogation;

(xiv) Priority as between the person with the subrogated right and the other parties are to be determined in accordance with normal equitable principles.

In the context of mortgages, consider where a lender advances money in anticipation of security over Blackacre for the money advanced and, for some reason or another, he does not receive the promised security.[26] In this case, the lender may be subrogated to the rights of any other person, B, who previously owned Blackacre and was paid in whole or part using the advance, or who previously had security over Blackacre and whose debt has been discharged, in whole or in part, by the money advanced from the lender.[27] By means of subrogation, the lender's relations with the purchaser and the original mortgagor and/or the borrower who would otherwise be unjustly enriched, are regulated as if the benefit of the purchase or sale, or of the redeeming of the charge had been assigned to him.[28]

In practice these principles have allowed mortgagees a remedy, sometimes overcoming interest would take priority to the interest granted them, in the following situations:

(i) To avoid the problems inherent in any attempt to enforce his own subsequent charge caused by having constructive notice of the equity of a party to the subsequent charge to have that subsequent charge set aside[29];

(ii) to obtain priority over other intermediate charges where the funds provided by the pursuant to the subsequent mortgage were misappropriated by the purchaser's solicitors[30];

(iii) To acquire priority over the rights of a wife or civil partner in a matrimonial home which rights would otherwise have taken effect as an overriding interest against the subsequent charge and the lender's rights[31];

(iv) to be subrogated to the right of the vendor to claim the unpaid vendors' lien on property where the purchase monies would have remained

---

[26] The reasons for failing to obtain the intended security may be various: *Nottingham Permanent Benefit Building Society v Thurstan* [1903] A.C. 6 at 10 (mortgagor was a minor); *Filby v Mortgage Express (No.2) Ltd* [2004] EWCA Civ 759; [2004] 2 P. & C.R. DG16 at [9] (mortgagor's signature was forged).

[27] *Halifax Plc v Omar* [2002] EWCA Civ 121; [2002] 2 P. & C.R. 377 at [4]; *Burston Finance Ltd v Speirway Ltd (in liq.)* [1974] 1 W.L.R 1648; [1974] 3 All E.R. 735 at 1652B–C per Walton J.; *Banque Financière de la Cité v Parc (Battersea) Ltd* [1999] 1 A.C. 221; [1998] 2 W.L.R. 475 at 245C–D per Lord Hutton; *Halifax Plc v Omar* [2002] 2 P. & C.R. 377 at [79]–[80] per Jonathan Parker L.J.

[28] *Banque Financière de la Cité v Parc (Battersea) Ltd* [1999] 1 A.C. 221 at 231G–232B per Lord Hoffmann.

[29] *UCB Corporate Services Ltd v Williams* [2002] EWCA Civ 555 and *Filby v Mortgage Express (No.2) Ltd* (above).

[30] *Boscawen v Bajwa* (above).

[31] *Eagle Star Insurance Co Ltd v Karasiewicz* [2002] EWCA Civ 940.

unpaid but of the subsequent lender's funds advanced by reason of fraud[32];

(v) to be subrogated to an earlier chargee's right to subrogation to the lien which the vendor would have had if the price had remained unpaid.[33]

Subrogation thus effectively provides lenders with an alternative route to obtaining security in place of the anticipated security for some or all of the money advanced, which they will then be able to rely on in the event of a subsequent default by their borrower. In a typical re-mortgage situation, it enables the later lender to "stand in the shoes" of the earlier lender and enforce its security as if it had the benefit of the earlier charge. In the case of a purchase it allows the lender to "stand in the shoes" of a vendor and enforce the unpaid vendor's lien which was discharged with its moneys. The common phrase that the lender "steps into the shoes" of another does not mean that the other's earlier charge or lien is kept alive and it does not necessarily mean the later lender has an entitlement to everything to which the earlier lender was entitled. Often the earlier mortgage will have been discharged and as between the actual parties to it there will be no basis for it to subsist. Rather it means that the later lender has the same rights as if the earlier charge or lien had been kept alive and the benefit of it assigned to the later lender,[34] at least to the extent of the enrichment received at the later lender's expense.

7–05   Subrogation in the restitutionary sense is not dependant on the agreement or intentions of the parties or those affected. Neuberger L.J. clarified the position in *Cheltenham & Gloucester Plc v Appleyard* when he stated[35]:

> "The absence of a common intention on the part of the borrower and the lender that the lender should have security is by no means fatal to a lender's subsequent claim for subrogation."[36]

Subrogation by operation of law is also not dependent on the knowledge or consent of the mortgagor. As a matter of policy it need not be, as his position is in no way altered when rights that existed against him can still be enforced, albeit by another person or entity.[37]

Consequently, all that needs to be shown is that the claiming lender's money was in fact used to discharge the earlier loan or liability, so that the borrower(s) or others holding the property or rights over it are thereby enriched at the claiming lender's expense[38] and the claiming lender has not received the anticipated security. The law then enables the claiming lender, by subrogation, to rely

---

[32] *Halifax Plc v Omar* [2002] EWCA Civ 121, [2002] 2 P. & C.R. 377.

[33] *UCB Group Ltd v Hedworth* [2003] EWCA Civ 1717; [2003] 3 F.C.R. 739.

[34] *Banque Financière de la Cité v Parc (Battersea) Ltd* [1999] 1 A.C. 221 per Lord Hoffmann.

[35] *Cheltenham & Gloucester Plc v Appleyard* [2004] EWCA Civ 291; [2004] 13 E.G. 127 (C.S.).

[36] ibid., per Neuberger L.J. at 40.

[37] *Butler v Rice* [1910] Ch. 277 at 282–3; *Castle Phillips Finance v Piddington* [1995] 1 F.L.R. 783; (1995) 70 P. & C.R. 592 at 599 per Peter Gibson L.J.

[38] *Filby v Mortgage Express (No.2) Ltd* [2004] EWCA Civ 759; [2004] 2 P. & C.R. DG16 at [62].

on the rights or interests of the enriched party to obtain the anticipated security, or as much of it as is reflected in those rights or interests.

The fact that the later lender obtains some valid security does not prevent him from seeking further security.[39] Subrogation is unavailable however, if A obtains the security he bargained for,[40] or where the lender has specifically bargained on the basis that he would receive no security.[41] **7–06**

It is irrelevant that the claiming lender (or its solicitors) failed to take proper precautions to ensure it obtained a valid security.[42] It is also not a bar to subrogation that A's failure to obtain the security was attributable to his own negligence.[43] **7–07**

Unjust Enrichment

The basis of the remedy of subrogation is the reversal or prevention of unjust enrichment. It is not a means of enabling the agreement or intentions of the parties to be realised when they failed to make a binding arrangement. It follows that subrogation in the context of mortgages is directed to ensuring that no one gains a new or less encumbered proprietary interest at the expense of a lender. At the expense of the lender in this context is reference to the lender being unsecured where it was anticipated by the lender at least that its lending would be secured. As Lord Hoffman put it: **7–08**

> "This type of subrogation operates as a restitutionary remedy to prevent a defendant's unjust enrichment through the claimant's failure to obtain a valid (or fully valid) security on an occasion when an earlier, valid security is discharged."[44]

Therefore, dependant as it is on unjust enrichment, subrogation cannot be invoked so as to put the lender in a better position than that in which he would have been if he had obtained all the rights for which he bargained, nor does it ensure he necessarily obtains all the rights he bargained for.[45]

The claiming lender is entitled to precisely the same security or rights as the original chargee or vendor to whose rights he is subrogated, subject to any limiting factors that he bargained for. The capital sum in respect of which the claiming lender is subrogated cannot be greater than the amount of the secured **7–09**

---

[39] ibid., at [37], [70].
[40] ibid., 759 at [38].
[41] *Paul v Speirway Ltd (in liq.)* [1976] Ch. 220; [1976] 2 W.L.R. 715.
[42] *Banque Financière de la Cité v Parc (Battersea) Ltd* [1999] 1 A.C. 221.
[43] *Cheltenham & Gloucester Plc v Appleyard* [2004] EWCA Civ 291; [2004] 13 E.G. 127 (C.S.) at [39] per Neuberger L.J.
[44] *Banque Financière de la Cité v Parc (Battersea) Ltd* [1999] 1 A.C. 221 at 231G–232B per Lord Hoffman; *Birmingham Midshires Mortgages Services Ltd v Sabherwal (Equitable Interest)* (2000) 80 P. & C.R. 256 at 264 per Robert Walker L.J.; *Cheltenham & Gloucester Plc v Appleyard* [2004] EWCA Civ 291; [2004] 13 E.G. 127 (C.S.) at [33] per Neuberger L.J.; *Filby v Mortgages Express (No.2) Ltd* [2004] EWCA Civ 759; [2004] 2 P. & C.R. DG16 at [62] per May L.J.
[45] *Cheltenham & Gloucester Plc v Appleyard* [2004] EWCA Civ 291; [2004] 13 E.G. 127 (C.S.) at [41] per Neuberger L.J.; *Filby v Mortgages Express (No.2) Ltd* [2004] EWCA Civ 759; [2004] 2 P. & C.R. DG16 at [62] per May L.J.

debt or purchase price which has been discharged by use of its funds,[46] nor can it acquire a better rate of interest by subrogation than it bargained for.[47]

So the lender claiming to be entitled to a mortgage by subrogation is not entitled to more than he had or would have agreed to accept under his own mortgage. Nor is he entitled to more than the entitlement of the original holder of the rights to which he is subrogated. It follows that the calculation of what sums are secured in favour of a mortgagee by subrogation necessarily involves the calculation of both the total sum, including interest, that the claiming lender would be entitled to in respect of the capital that is secured by subrogation, and the total sum that the original holder of the subrogated rights would have been entitled to in respect of the same capital sum. An order for possession of residential property should not be made until both sums have been identified, since it is not until that point that the court will know what sum to treat as outstanding when considering the exercise of its discretion.

In *Anfield (UK) Ltd v Bank of Scotland* the Court considered the position of a lender who through its own negligence failed to register and perfect its own security as against a subsequent lender who stood to be enriched by the failure to register the earlier charge. The court confirmed that the original lender could rely on subrogation in that situation. Subrogation in that situation did not turn entirely on the existence of an unfulfilled mutual intention as between the two lenders. The relevant consideration was the non-fulfilment of the original lender's expectation as to security.

SUB-SUBROGATION

7–10 Subrogation of an entitlement that was itself acquired by subrogation is possible and not uncommon in the context of mortgages where borrowers may remortgage several times. By way of example, suppose Lender 1 lent A £50,000 to purchase a property, subsequently Lender 2 advanced £100,000, £50,000 of which was used to redeem the first advance. Lender 3 advances £150,000 of which £100,000 is used to repay Lender 2 and £20,000 is used to repay unsecured joint loans. A then defaults in the repayment of his instalments due to Lender 3. If the charge given to Lender 2 was invalid, but the charge to Lender 1 was valid, Lender 2 will have been subrogated to the rights of Lender 1 and Lender 3 is entitled, on the principle of "sub-subrogation" or "subrogation at one remove", to take over the security previously enjoyed by Lender 2 including its entitlement by subrogation to Lender 1.[48]

In *Castle Phillips v Piddington*, Peter Gibson L.J. held that Barclays, having been entitled to the Lloyds security by subrogation when Castle Phillips discharged the debt to Barclays, thinking that it was obtaining an effective security

---

[46] *Cheltenham & Gloucester Plc v Appleyard* [2004] EWCA Civ 291; [2004] 13 E.G. 127 (C.S.) at [43] per Neuberger L.J.

[47] *Halifax Mortgage Services Ltd v Muirhead* [1997] N.P.C. 171; (1997) 76 P. & C.R. 418 at 427, approved in *Cheltenham & Gloucester Plc v Appleyard* [2004] EWCA Civ 291; [2004] 13 E.G. 127 (C.S.) at [76] per Neuberger L.J.

[48] *Castle Phillips Finance v Piddington* (1995) 70 P. & C.R. 592 at 600 per Peter Gibson L.J.

for its own money, became entitled to the same security as Barclays had been entitled to.[49]

Subrogation to the Unpaid Vendor's Lien

Pending the payment of purchase money, a vendor enjoys a form of security over the subject matter of the sale, i.e. an unpaid vendor's lien in the land.[50] To the extent that the lender's money reaches the vendor, the vendor may claim to be subrogated to the unpaid vendor's security.[51]   **7–11**

In *Halifax v Omar*, the Court of Appeal held that Halifax, having advanced mortgage money to a fraudulent mortgagor, was subrogated to the equitable charge that would otherwise have been held by a vendor who had received the bulk of Halifax's money.

> "[A] claimant who is subrogated to a security right is treated in equity as if had that security: thus in a case such as the instant case, where the security takes the form of an unpaid vendor's lien, he is, as the judge correctly concluded, an equitable chargee to the extent that his money was used to pay the purchase price for the property."[52]

To the extent that loan money has been advanced as part of the purchase price, a lender may be subrogated to any lien acquired by the vendor and satisfied with the money advanced.[53]

Bars to Subrogation

Subrogation is not available if A does not actually put forward money for the discharge of an existing debt, but instead merely facilitates the release of money for this purpose by providing a guarantee of its repayment.[54] In *Bankers Trust v Namdar*, Jonathan Parker L.J. stated that: **7–12**

> "[t]he guarantee was not an asset of the Bank but a continuing obligation assumed by the Bank. I do not follow how the creation of a continuing obligation owed by the Bank, not giving rise to an asset of the Bank, can be traced into what is asserted to

---

[49] See *Kali & Burlay v Chawla* [2007] EWHC 237 (Ch). This has been affirmed in *UCB Group Ltd v Hedworth (No.2)* [2003] EWCA Civ 1717; [2004] 1 P. & C.R. DG21 at [137]–[147] per Jonathan Parker L.J.

[50] For the Unpaid Vendor's Lien see para.1–22.

[51] *Nottingham Permanent Benefit Building Society v Thurstan* [1903] A.C. 6 at 10 per Earl of Halsbury L.C.; *Bank of Ireland Finance Ltd v DJ Daly Ltd* [1978] I.R. 79 at 82; *Boodle Hatfield & Co v British Films Ltd* (1986) 2 B.C.C. 99,225–99,226 (unsecured advance to client to firm of solicitors in order to facilitate completion of purchase before clearance of client's cheque).

[52] *Halifax Plc v Omar* [2002] 2 P. & C.R. 377 at [84] per Jonathan Parker L.J.

[53] *Nottingham Permanent Benefit Building Society v Thurstan* [1903] A.C. 6 at 10.

[54] *Bankers Trust Co v Namdar* [1997] EWCA Civ 1015; [1995] N.P.C. 139, per Peter Gibson L.J.

be an asset of the Bank, viz, the monies paid to it to discharge the secured debt".[55]

7-13   Nor will A be subrogated to the rights of another, if the benefit which he has conferred on B was conferred as a gift.[56]

The inability to rely on subrogation as a remedy may be excluded, restricted or modified by contract between the relevant parties.[57]

7-14   Subrogation will be denied if granting the remedy would result in the indirect enforcement of a transaction which the law has declared to be ineffective. The case law draws a distinction between loans that are declared void and loans that are declared unenforceable. Where a loan is declared to be unenforceable, the House of Lords in *Orakpo v Manson Investments Ltd*[58] took the view that subrogation was not allowed. However, where a loan is declared to be void, subrogation has been held to be permitted.[59] This seems to be because allowing subrogation when a loan is declared void does not offend against the policy of any statute.

7-15   Normal equitable principles and defences also apply to subrogated rights. Thus, as Neuberger L.J. made clear in *Cheltenham & Gloucester Plc v Appleyard*:

> "the familiar equitable defences can be raised against a claim for subrogation, and priority as between the person with the subrogated right and other parties are to be determined in accordance with normal equitable principles".[60]

So, for example, the equitable right of subrogation can be overridden by a bona fide purchaser for value of the legal estate without notice,[61] estoppel, change of position, laches, or limitation and election.

Further, it should be noted that subrogation can be excluded or modified by contract.[62] In *Boodle Hatfield v British Films Ltd*, Nicholls J. stated:

> "[a]s to the argument that the plaintiffs obtained all they bargained for, it is important to remember that subrogation applied in this case unless excluded. Accordingly, the question is not: did the plaintiffs bargain for the transfer to them of the vendor's security rights? Rather it is: did the bargain made by the plaintiffs with the defendant

---

[55] Jonathan Parker L.J. also held that it is not possible to trace from the guarantee to the moneys released and thought the idea "a misconceived proposition". Citing *Lipkin Gorman v Karpnale Ltd* [1991] 2 A.C. 548 at 573; [1991] 3 W.L.R. 10 per Lord Goff: "It is well established that a legal owner is entitled to trace his property into its product, provided that the latter is indeed identifiable as the product of his property. . . . Of course, 'tracing' or 'following' property into its product involves a decision by the owner of the original property to assert his title to the product in place of his original property." Jonathan Parker L.J. then went on to say that in the case of a guarantee there is no "original property" of the Bank, but only the creation of a contingent liability and it cannot be said that a Bank decided to assert title to the moneys paid to it in place of any original property of the Bank. "In no meaningful sense can it be said that the guarantee is represented by the monies paid to it."

[56] Goff and Jones, *Law of Restitution* (6th edn, Sweet & Maxwell, 2002) at para.3–013.

[57] *Banque financière de la cité v Parc (Battersea) Ltd* [1999] 1 A.C. 221; *Re Rusjon Ltd (in liquidation)* [2008] 2 B.C.L.C. 234, [2007] EWHC 2943.

[58] *Orakpo v Manson Investments Ltd* [1978] A.C. 95.

[59] *Nottingham Permanent Benefit Building Society v Thurstan* [1903] A.C. 6.

[60] *Cheltenham & Gloucester Plc v Appleyard* [2004] EWCA Civ 291; [2004] 13 E.G. 127 (C.S.) at [44] per Neuberger L.J.

[61] *Halifax Plc v Omar* [2002] EWCA Civ 121; [2002] 2 P. & C.R. 26 at [62].

[62] *Boodle Hatfield & Co (a firm) v British Films Ltd* (1986) 2 B.C.C. 99,221.

exclude that transfer, either expressly or impliedly? Unless this is kept in mind, consideration of whether the plaintiffs obtained what they bargain for is likely to mislead rather than assist in a case where, at the time, in the course of one short conversation neither party directed his mind to the crucial question."[63]

[63] *Boodle Hatfield & Co (a firm) v British Films Ltd* (1986) 2 B.C.C. 99,221 at 99,226 per Nicholls J.

CHAPTER 8

CONSOLIDATION

The effect of this equitable doctrine is that, in certain circumstances, a mortgagee **8–01** is able to enlarge his security beyond the property which he took to secure his debt.

RIGHT TO CONSOLIDATE

If a mortgagee holds two or more distinct mortgages, he may have the right to **8–02** refuse to allow the mortgagor to redeem one mortgage unless he redeems all of them. Whereas equity normally extends the right to redeem, the application of the maxim "he who seeks equity must do equity"[1] results, where the doctrine of consolidation comes into play, in a restriction of that right on the basis that a partial redemption may expose the mortgagee to a deficiency in his security. It is not a doctrine that has received universal acclaim[2] and it is open to question whether (in the context of a consumer mortgage) it can survive the application of the Unfair Terms in Consumer Contracts Regulations 1999.[3] Normally, the mortgagee will wish to exercise the right when one of the mortgaged properties depreciates in value so that by itself it is insufficient to satisfy the security; but he may do so even if each property is, by itself, a sufficient security for the debt.

The basis of the long-established right to consolidate is the practice of courts of equity in redemption actions. After the mortgagor is in default, he needs the assistance of equity in order to redeem and equity demands, in such a case, that he shall not be able to redeem an estate which is sufficient security for the debt while leaving the mortgagee with another estate which is not.[4] This would suggest that the mortgagee can exercise the right only when one of the properties mortgaged depreciates. It is, however, settled law that the right exists in any circumstances where the mortgagor has to assert his equitable title. Thus it applies in a forfeiture action since in such an action the mortgagor has to redeem then or not at all.[5] It applies also when the mortgagee has sold one property under his power of sale and the mortgagor is claiming to be paid the surplus remaining

---

[1] *Willie v Lugg* (1761) 2 Eden 78; *White v Hillacre* (1839) 3 Y. & C. Ex. 597; *Chesworth v Hunt* (1880) 5 C.P.D. 266; *Cummins v Fletcher* (1880) 14 Ch.D. 699.

[2] *Pledge v White* [1896] A.C. 187 at 192.

[3] SI 1999/2083.

[4] *Jennings v Jordan* (1881) 6 App.Cas. 698, H.L.; *Griffith v Pound* (1890) 45 Ch.D. 553.

[5] *Cummins v Fletcher* (1880) 14 Ch.D. 699; *Watts v Symes* (1851) 1 De G. M. & G. 240.

after the discharge of that mortgage; the effect of the doctrine is then to give the mortgagee the right to retain that surplus so as to satisfy a debt secured on another property.[6] Unlike the right to tack,[7] the right to consolidate is independent of the possession of the legal estate.

ABOLITION AND EXPRESS PRESERVATION OF THE DOCTRINE

8–03 The doctrine may cause difficulty to a purchaser of mortgaged property since the mortgage may be liable to be consolidated against him although he has no means of knowing that to be the case. Consequently, the operation of the doctrine was abolished by statute for all mortgages made after December 31, 1881, except where a contrary intention is expressed in the mortgage. Section 93 of the Law of Property Act 1925 now provides that:

> "(1) A mortgagor seeking to redeem any one mortgage is entitled to do so without paying any money due under any separate mortgage made by him, or by any person through whom he claims, solely on property other than that comprised in the mortgage which he seeks to redeem.
>
> This subsection applies only if and so far as a contrary intention is not expressed in the mortgage deeds or one of them.
>
> (2) This section does not apply where all the mortgages were made before 1st January, 1882.
>
> (3) Save as aforesaid nothing in this Act, in reference to mortgages, affects any right of consolidation or renders inoperative a stipulation in relation to any mortgage made before or after the commencement of this Act reserving a right to consolidate."

The intention to exclude the statutory rule may be effectively manifested either by a clause in the mortgage deed that s.93(1) is not to apply to the security,[8] or by a clause providing for the preservation of the right to consolidate.[9] In circumstances where an equitable mortgagee has undertaken to execute a legal mortgage in such form and with such powers and provisions as the mortgagee may require, that undertaking will not entitle the mortgagee to have the statutory rule excluded.[10]

REQUIREMENTS FOR CONSOLIDATION

8–04 If either all the mortgages were made before January 1, 1882, or the parties have excluded s.93(1), the mortgagee's right to consolidate can be exercised subject to the following conditions:

---

[6] *Selby v Pomfret* (1861) 3 De G. F. & J. 595; *Cracknall v Janson* (1879) 11 Ch.D. 1 (CA).

[7] For the doctrine of Tacking see para.11–67.

[8] Which, in practice, most mortgagees require.

[9] *Hughes v Britannia Permanent Benefit Building Society* [1906] 2 Ch. 606. In *Re Salmon, Ex p. the Trustee* [1903] 1 K.B. 147 it was held that a clause excluding the statute (at that time s.17 of the Conveyancing Act 1881) and contained in the first of several mortgages would preserve the right to consolidate; compare *Griffith v Pound* (1890) 45 Ch.D. 553; a clause in a later mortgage is ineffective as to earlier mortgages.

[10] *Whitley v Challis* [1892] 1 Ch. 64; *Farmer v Pitt* [1902] 1 Ch. 954.

(1) the legal dates of redemption of all the mortgages sought to be consolidated have passed[11];

(2) all mortgages must have been made by the same mortgagor;

(3) the security must be in existence at the time that the mortgagee claims to consolidate;

(4) at one and the same time all the mortgages must have been vested in some person and all the equities of redemption in some other person.

These conditions are now considered in turn.

Condition (1)

The right to consolidate is an equitable right and does not override the legal right to redeem on the contractual date. Thus for equity to intervene and permit consolidation, the legal date for redemption must have passed.

Condition (2)

The right can come into existence only if the mortgages were originally made by the same mortgagor,[12] with one possible exception. That exception is where one mortgage is made by B and the other mortgage is made by persons claiming by devolution from him on his death.[13] Thus, the right does not exist where one mortgage is made by B and the other jointly by A and B[14]; nor when B as beneficiary makes one and A, as B's trustee, makes the other[15]; nor when B as principal debtor makes one and A as surety makes the other[16]; nor when B makes one as security for a private debt, and A and B as partners make the other as security for a partnership debt.

Various other differences between the mortgages are irrelevant to the existence   **8–05** of the right to consolidate. First, it does not matter that the mortgages were originally made to different mortgagees.[17] Second, the right is not affected by either the nature of the mortgage or the nature of the property mortgaged, except that no right to consolidation can arise in respect of personal chattels as defined by the Bills of Sale Acts 1878.[18] Thus, two legal mortgages, or two equitable mortgages,[19] or a legal and an equitable mortgage can be consolidated,[20] as can

---

[11] *Cummins v Fletcher* (1880) 14 Ch.D. 699.

[12] *Sharp v Rickards* [1909] 1 Ch. 109.

[13] *White v Hillacre* (1839) 3 Y. & C. Ex. 597.

[14] *Jones v Smith* (1794) 2 Ves. Jun. 372; *Thorneycroft v Crockett* (1848) 2 H.L.C. 239; *Cummins v Fletcher* (1880) 14 Ch.D. 699; *Re Raggett, Ex p. Williams* (1880) 16 Ch.D. 117.

[15] *Re Raggett, Ex p. Williams* (1880) 16 Ch.D. 117.

[16] *Aldworth v Robinson* (1840) 2 Beav. 287.

[17] Provided that they are united in the same mortgagee when the right to consolidation is claimed: *Pledge v White* [1896] A.C. 187.

[18] *Chesworth v Hunt* (1880) 5 C.P.D. 266.

[19] *Tweedale v Tweedale* (1857) 23 Beav. 341.

[20] *Cracknall v Janson* (1879) 11 Ch.D. 1, C.A.; *Watts v Symes* (1851) 1 De G. M. & G. 240.

a mortgage of realty and a mortgage of personalty other than personal chattels.[21]

Condition (3)

Where a mortgagee holds two mortgages and one has ceased to exist because its subject matter has determined, as may be the case when it is a mortgage of a lease[22] or a life interest,[23] the mortgagee may not apply any surplus on the other to make good the deficiency on the one whose subject-matter has determined. As soon as it has determined, the debt is no longer secured and is a simple contract debt.

This does not apply when a security has ceased to exist because the mortgagee has realised it. The right to consolidate is not affected by realisation.[24]

This rule may be illustrated by the following examples. Consider these events and assume that all other conditions for consolidation are satisfied:

(a)   B mortgages a leasehold interest in Blackacre to L for £10,000;
(b)   B mortgages a freehold interest in Whiteacre to L for £40,000;
(c)   L realises his security in Whiteacre for £50,000;
(d)   The leasehold interest in Blackacre determines;
(e)   L gives B notice to pay off the debt on Blackacre, with a view to becoming entitled to exercise his power of sale.

If the events (a), (b), (e) happen in that order, L can consolidate against B and can refuse a tender by B of the money secured against Blackacre.[25]

If the events (a), (b), (d), (c) happen in that order, L can consolidate and apply the surplus on realisation of his security in Whiteacre to the payment of the debt secured on Blackacre, since both securities were in existence when L claimed to consolidate.[26]

If the events (a), (b), (c), (d) happen in that order, the security on Blackacre no longer exists at the time L realises his security in Whiteacre. The debt formerly secured on Blackacre has now become a simple contract debt and in respect of it, L is in the same position as any other of B's unsecured creditors. If there are such creditors L cannot, against them, claim to apply the surplus from Whiteacre to the payment of the Blackacre debt.[27]

Both mortgages must be vested solely in L at the time when he wishes to exercise his right to consolidate, so, if in either of the first two rules above, the mortgage in one property was vested in L and M jointly at the time L wished to exercise the right, he would not be permitted to do so.[28]

[21] *Cracknall v Janson*, above. *Tassell v Smith* (1858) 2 De G. & J. 713 was overruled by *Jennings v Jordan* (1881) 6 App. Cas. 698 which held that consolidation cannot occur so as to prejudice the purchaser of an equity of redemption by virtue of a mortgage created after the sale.
[22] *Re Raggett, Ex p. Williams* (1880) 16 Ch.D. 117.
[23] *Re Gregson, Christison v Bolam* (1887) 36 Ch.D. 223.
[24] *Selby v Pomfret* (1861) 3 De G. F. & J. 595; *Cracknall v Janson* (1879) 11 Ch.D. 14 (CA).
[25] *Griffith v Pound* (1890) 45 Ch.D. 553.
[26] *Selby v Pomfret*, above; *Cracknell v Janson*, above.
[27] *Re Gregson, Christison v Bolam* (1887) 36 Ch.D. 223; *Talbot v Frere* (1878) 9 Ch.D. 568.
[28] *Riley v Hall* (1898) 79 L.T. 244.

Condition (4)

For the purposes of the first three rules, only the right to consolidate against the original mortgagor needs to be discussed. The fourth rule, however, involves consideration of the right to consolidate against an assignee of a mortgagor, as well as the right to consolidate against the original mortgagor.

CONSOLIDATION AGAINST THE ORIGINAL MORTGAGOR

Consider the following transactions: **8–06**

    (a) B mortgages Blackacre to L;
    (b) B mortgages Blackacre to M;
    (c) B mortgages Whiteacre to M;
    (d) L buys M's mortgage on Whiteacre;
    (e) K buys both mortgages;
    (f) B assigns the equity of redemption in one of the properties to N.

Provided the conditions previously discussed are all satisfied, M will have the right to consolidate against B if the events (b) and (c) occur before (f), while L will have the same right if the events (a), (c) and (d), occur before (f). The equities of redemption are in B's hand throughout and whoever acquires both mortgages can consolidate against him. This applies equally if, instead of L buying M's mortgage, K buys both mortgages.

If, however, the equities are severed before both mortgages come into one hand, as in the sequences (b), (f), (c), or (a), (c), (f), (d) (or e); there can be no right to consolidate against B because B never owns both equities of redemption at the same time that either L or K owns both mortgages.[29] Subsequent transactions may, as explained below, create a right to consolidate against N.

It is for the mortgagee of the two properties to decide whether he wishes to take advantage of his right to consolidate. The mortgagor cannot compel him to do so against his will. In *Pelly v Wathen*,[30] after the events (a) and (c), B created a second mortgage of both properties in favour of P. It was held that P was entitled, if he wished, to redeem only one of the first mortgages even though he had the right to consolidate against B if he redeemed both.

The right to consolidate is not lost because the mortgagee does not choose to exercise it. If, following the events (a), (c) and (e), K gives notice to B that he requires payment of the mortgage on Blackacre he can refuse a tender by B if it is insufficient to discharge both mortgages.[31]

---

[29] *Harter v Coleman* (1882) 19 Ch.D. 630; *Minter v Carr* [1894] 3 Ch. 498.
[30] (1849) 7 Hare 351; on appeal (1851) 1 De G. M. & G. 16; cf. *Re Thompson's Estates* [1912] 1 I.R. 194.
[31] *Griffith v Pound* (1890) 45 Ch.D. 553.

CONSOLIDATION AGAINST THE MORTGAGOR'S ASSIGNEE OR SUCCESSOR-IN-TITLE

8–07 The principle is that an assignee of the equity of redemption succeeds to whatever rights the mortgagor had at the time of the assignment[32] and takes subject to the existing equities.[33] The simple example is where a person purchases the freehold or leasehold interest of the mortgagor subject to one or more mortgages. However, a person acquiring the equity of redemption under a will or intestacy,[34] by virtue of the mortgagor's bankruptcy,[35] will be in the same position.

Consider the following transactions:

(a) B mortgages Blackacre to L;
(b) B mortgages Whiteacre to L;
(c) B mortgages Whiteacre to L and M;
(d) B mortgages Whiteacre to M;
(e) L buys M's mortgage;
(f) B assigns both equities of redemption to N;
(g) B assigns the equity of redemption in Blackacre to N.

In the events (a) and (b), L can consolidate against B and he will have the same right in the events (a), (c), (d), or (a), (d), (e), since B has both equities of redemption and at the same time L has both mortgages. As soon as (f) occurs, L can consolidate against N. The same is true if (g) occurs, because N takes the assignment subject to the existing right to consolidate. If N wishes to redeem Blackacre, L can force him to redeem Whiteacre at the same time though N will, if he redeems, be entitled to have Whiteacre transferred to him.[36]

In the events (a), (d), (f) and (e) it would appear that there is no right to consolidate since, after the occurrence of (a) and (d) the two mortgages were in different hands. There would have been no right to consolidate against B and therefore no right to consolidate against N. On general principles, N should not be prejudiced by the subsequent transaction between L and M. It is, however, an old-established rule[37] that in such circumstances the assignee of both equities must be deemed to have taken the assignment with the knowledge that the two mortgages might come into one hand, with the result that the mortgagee would have the right to consolidate against him.[38] This leads to the possibility that a mortgagee whose security was inadequate could improve his position at the expense of the mortgagor's general creditors if the mortgagor became bankrupt. If, in the sequence of events (a), (d), (f), (f) takes place because N is B's trustee

---

[32] *Willie v Lugg* (1761) 2 Eden 78.
[33] *Harter v Coleman* (1882) 19 Ch.D. 630.
[34] *Harris v Tubb* (1889) 42 Ch.D. 79.
[35] *Selby v Pomfret* (1861) 3 De G. F. & J. 595; *Re Salmon, Ex p. the Trustee* [1903] 1 K.B. 147.
[36] *Cracknall v Janson* (1871) 11 Ch.D. 1, C.A.; *Mutual Life Assurance Society v Langley* (1886) 32 Ch.D. 460 (CA).
[37] *Bovey v Skipwith* (1671) 1 Cas. in Ch. 201; *Tweedale v Tweedale* (1857) 23 Beav. 341; *Vint v Padget* (1858) 2 De G. & J. 611.
[38] As was decided, albeit with reluctance, in *Pledge v White* [1896] A.C. 187.

in bankruptcy, either L or M, if he thought his security to be inadequate, would be able to enlarge it by buying up the other's mortgage and consolidating against N and would be unaffected by B's bankruptcy.[39] It would be otherwise if the sequence were (a), (f), (d). There could be no consolidation of two mortgages, one created before and one after the start of the bankruptcy.

It might be thought that the same result would occur as a result of the sequence (a), (d), (g) and (e); that is, that B assigns only one equity of redemption. If N is exposed to the risk of consolidation against himself when he buys both equities, the fact that he has bought only one should not make any difference. The decision in *Beevor v Luck*[40] to that effect is, however, no longer considered to be good law, the practical reason being the risk that would be associated with the purchase of any equity of redemption. In this example, N when he took the equity of redemption in Blackacre would have no means of finding out from L that Whiteacre had been mortgaged to M by B and that, in consequence M, by buying L's mortgage, would be able to consolidate against him. As was said in *Pledge v White*,[41] a person in the position of N can see, if he buys two properties mortgaged by the same mortgagor, that there is a risk of the mortgages coming into the same hand. However, if he buys one property, he can be aware of this risk only if B tells him that he has mortgaged other property.

Where the sequence of events is (a), (g), (d), (e) there can clearly be no consolidation, since the equities of redemption in the two properties have been severed before there is even a potential right to consolidate.[42]

CONSOLIDATION AFTER THE ASSIGNMENT OF THE EQUITY OF REDEMPTION

The general principle that the assignor of an equity of redemption should not be able to prejudice his assignee's position by subsequent transactions with third parties was qualified in *Jennings v Jordan*[43] where it was suggested that the assignee might be affected by an express contractual term reserving to the assignor the right to consolidate future mortgages. That case was decided before the Conveyancing Act 1881 came into operation, and mortgage deeds did not then, as they commonly do now, contain clauses excluding the statutory prohibition on, or preserving the right of, consolidation.   **8–08**

The question therefore arises whether an assignee of an equity of redemption is liable, by reason of such a contractual term, to have consolidated against him mortgages created by the assignor which were not in existence at the time of the assignment. In *Andrews v City Permanent Building Society*[44] it was held that, while a second mortgagee would not by virtue of the equitable doctrine be liable to have mortgages consolidated against him which were not in existence when he took the second mortgage, he was so liable if the first mortgage contained an

---

[39] *Selby v Pomfret* (1861) 3 De G. F. & J. 595.
[40] (1867) L.R. 4 Eq. 537.
[41] [1896] A.C. 187.
[42] *Jennings v Jordan* (1881) 6 App.Cas. 698 (HL).
[43] (1881) 6 App.Cas. 698 at 702.
[44] (1881) 44 L.T. 641.

express stipulation for a right to consolidate later mortgages. The liability arises whether or not the second mortgagee has notice of the stipulation because the mortgage contract prevents him from redeeming free of that right.

The same point arose in *Hughes v Britannia Permanent Benefit Building Society*[45] where the much-criticised Kekewich J. arrived at what is generally considered to be the right decision. He held that the second mortgagee is affected by the contractual stipulation but treated it as if it reserved the right to tack further advances and applied the rule in *Hopkinson v Rolt*,[46] that is, that a mortgagee with notice of an intervening mortgage could not tack further advances. The rule has been criticised on the ground that a paramount right to tack created by a first mortgage should not be capable of being defeated by the action of a second mortgagee in giving notice of his charge, but, whatever substance there is in that criticism, it is settled law that a second mortgagee can prevent consolidation of later mortgages against him by giving actual notice to the first mortgagee. Registration of the second mortgage is not notice for this purpose where a mortgage is expressly made for securing further advances.[47]

REGISTRATION OF THE RIGHT TO CONSOLIDATE

Prior to October 13, 2003

8–09   Where the land affected by the right to consolidate was registered land, the Land Registration Act 1925 and the Land Registration Rules 1925 r.154 applied.

Section 25(3)(ii) of the Land Registration Act 1925 stated that any provision contained in a charge which purported to affect any registered land or charge other than that in respect of which the charge is to be expressly registered shall be void.

Rule 154 of the Land Registration Rules 1925 provided:

> "(1) Where a charge, whether affecting the whole or part of the land comprised in a title, reserves the right to consolidate, it shall not on that account be registered against any other land than that expressly described in it.
> (2) But where the right reserved is to consolidate with a specified charge, or an application in writing is made to register the right in respect of a specified charge, the Registrar shall require the production of the land certificate of all the titles affected, and, on the production thereof, shall enter in the register a notice that the specified charges are consolidated."

Since the Land Registration Act 1925 s.65 required that on registration of a charge or mortgage, the land certificate was to be deposited at the registry until the charge or mortgage was cancelled, it must be to the charge certificate, and not the land certificate, to which r.154(2) should have referred.

---

[45] [1906] 2 Ch. 606.

[46] (1861) 9 H.L.C. 514; see Megarry and Wade, *The Law of Real Property* (7th edn, 2008), para.25–060.

[47] Law of Property Act (LPA) 1925 s.94(2) (as amended by the LPA 1969 s.16(2), Sch.2, Pt I; and the Law of Property (Amendment) Act 1926 s.7).

The right to consolidate did not depend on the entry of any notice under r.154.

After October 12, 2003

Rule 110 of the Land Registration Rules 2003 provides that a chargee who has **8–10** a right of consolidation in relation to a registered charge may apply in Form CC to the Registrar for an entry to be made in respect of that right in the individual register in which the charge is registered. On receipt of such an application, the Registrar must make an entry in the individual register in such terms as he considers appropriate to give effect to the application. Absent such an application, the Registrar will not make a note of consolidation of charges merely because the right to consolidate appears on the face of the charge, and the practice of HM Land Registry is such that no requisition will be raised in those circumstances.

CHAPTER 9

MARSHALLING AND RELATED RIGHTS

MARSHALLING

The doctrine of marshalling, contribution and the equity of exoneration may each **9–01** affect the incidence of the mortgage debt as between various properties over which it is secured. Each will be considered in turn.

If B has two creditors, L and M, and L has recourse to only one security in order to satisfy his debt, while M has recourse to more than one, M will not be permitted to satisfy his debt in a way that prejudices L.[1] Although the application of this doctrine will, like the application of the doctrine of consolidation, enlarge the creditor's security beyond that for which he contracted, it is not a right which the creditor needs actively to assert since in any case where it should apply the court will automatically apply it without it being claimed as relief in any proceedings.[2]

An illustration of the doctrine is given by the following facts: **9–02**

    (a)   B mortgages Blackacre to M;
    (b)   B mortgages Whiteacre to M;
    (c)   B mortgages Whiteacre to L.

The effect of the doctrine is that L may claim, against B, that B should satisfy M's debt out of Blackacre so far as possible leaving Whiteacre for the satisfaction of his own debt.[3] The doctrine applies to all types of property[4] and also applies whether the security is by way of mortgage, charge or lien.[5] It only operates as against the mortgagor; any creditor can still elect to which of his various securities he will have recourse. The doctrine does not give the party to whom it is available any equitable right of property.[6]

---

[1] *Lanoy v Duke of Athol* (1742) 2 Atk. 444; *Aldrich v Cooper* (1803) 8 Ves. 382; *Trimmer v Bayne (No.2)* (1803) 9 Ves. 209, approved, *Webb v Smith* (1885) 30 Ch.D. 192; *Averall v Wade* (1835) L. & G. temp. Sugden 252.

[2] *Gibbs v Ougier* (1806) 12 Ves. 413; Senior Courts Act 1981 s.49(2).

[3] *Lanoy v Duke of Athol*, above; *South v Bloxam* (1865) 2 H. & M. 457.

[4] See, for example, *Heyman v Dubois* (1871) L.R. 13 Eq. 158 (insurance policies).

[5] *Re Westzinthus* (1833) 5 B. & Ad. 817; *Re Fry* [1912] 2 Ch. 86. But not where the creditor's right as against the second fund is merely one of set-off: *Trimmer v Bayne*, above; *Webb v Smith*, above.

[6] *Commonwealth Trading Bank v Colonial Mutual Life Assurance Society Ltd* [1970] Tas S.R. 120.

Suppose, in the above events, B had mortgaged the two properties to M to secure a loan of £25,000, and later mortgaged Whiteacre to L to secure a loan of £15,000, and suppose each of the two properties to be worth £20,000. If the doctrine of marshalling did not exist, then the primary rule[7] as to the satisfaction of M's debt would operate and it would be satisfied as to £12,500 out of each property, leaving only £7,500 of the equity in Whiteacre for L. Thus, although the two properties would, between them, be sufficient to satisfy the total debts owing to L and M, L's would be only half satisfied.

If the securities are marshalled, M's debt is satisfied as to £20,000 out of Blackacre and as to the remaining £5,000 out of Whiteacre, leaving £15,000 equity in Whiteacre to satisfy L.

Conditions for marshalling

9–03   There are four conditions which must be satisfied:

(1) the right exists only where the prior mortgagee holds two securities (of whatever nature) which belong to the same owner;

(2) subject to (3), the right exists against the common mortgagor and against all persons claiming through him;

(3) the right is not enforced to the prejudice of third parties claiming as purchasers;

(4) a puisne encumbrancer's right to marshall does not affect the prior mortgagee's right to realise his securities in whatever manner or order he decides.

Condition (1)

9–04   The two securities must originally have belonged to the same owner.[8] Thus, where the two securities were a ship and its cargo and belonged to different owners, marshalling was not permitted.[9] It is not necessary for the securities to have been created at the same time or to have been given in respect of each of the same debt. However, if two securities are given, one in respect of each of two debts, marshalling is not permitted unless the debts are those of the same person.[10] As with consolidation, the right does not exist where one security is given by one person and the other security by the same person jointly with someone else.

If, in the example given above, M had satisfied his debt out of Whiteacre, L's right to marshall would be enforced by being subrogated to M's rights against Blackacre.[11]

---

[7] i.e. that the debt is satisfied out of the two properties rateably to their values.

[8] *Douglas v Cooksey* (1868) 2 I.R.Eq. 311.

[9] *The Chioggia* [1898] P. 1, distinguishing *The Edward Oliver* (1867) L.R. 1. A. & E. 379; contra *Webb v Smith* (1885) 30 Ch.D. 192, which is considered incorrect on this point.

[10] *Ex p. Kendall* (1811) 17 Ves. 514.

[11] *Mason v Bogg* (1837) 2 My. & Cr. 443; *Wallis v Woodyear* (1855) 2 Jur.N.S. 179; *Dolphin v Aylward* (1870) L.R. 4 H.L. 486.

Condition (2)

The right may be exercised against the common mortgagor[12] or against persons **9–05**
claiming the property or part of it under him unless those persons take by charge
or assignment.[13] They are not subject to the right even if they are volunteers.[14]

As the right is exercisable against the common mortgagor's personal representatives[15] and his trustee in bankruptcy,[16] a puisne encumbrancer may be able
to enlarge his security at the expense of the general creditors. The common
mortgagor's judgment creditors[17] and real and personal representatives[18] are
exposed to the operation of the doctrine.

The right is not lost by reason of the two funds or securities later becoming
vested in different persons.[19]

Condition (3)

The court will not interfere with a mortgagee in the exercise of his remedies. **9–06**
Thus, if, in the example above M chooses to satisfy his debt first out of
Whiteacre, L's debt will be thrown on Blackacre, of which he becomes second
mortgagee, and if L pays off the unsatisfied part of M's debt, he becomes first
mortgagee.[20] If M realises both securities, he holds the aggregate proceeds on
trust to pay himself first, then L.[21]

Nor will the rule be applied with its full rigour against persons claiming part
of the property (whether by assignment or charge) for value[22] or as volunteers[23]
unless the other part had already been disposed of with a right to exoneration
against the double creditor's mortgage. Ordinarily in those circumstances the
parts of the property the subject of apportionment are the first mortgage debt
between the two parts of the property.[24]

The right to marshall does not operate to the disadvantage of third parties **9–07**
claiming as purchasers.[25] This can be illustrated by considering what would
happen if there was a fourth event added to the series above,[26] that is:

---

[12] *Haynes v Forshaw* (1853) 11 Hare. 93.

[13] *Barnes v Racster* (1842) 1 Y. & C.Ch.Cas. 401; *Flint v Howard* [1893] 2 Ch. 54 (CA).

[14] *Dolphin v Aylward* (1870) L.R. 4 H.L. 486; *Hales v Cox* (1863) 32 Beav. 118.

[15] *Flint v Howard* [1893] 2 Ch. 54, 73.

[16] *Re Cornwall, Baldwin v Belcher* (1842) 3 Dr. & War. 173; *Re Tristram, Ex p. Hartley* (1835) 1
Deac. 288; *Re Holland, Ex p. Alston* (1868) 4 Ch.App. 168; *Heyman v Dubois* (1871) L.R. 13 Eq.
158.

[17] *Gray v Stone and Funnell* (1893) 69 L.T. 282; unless that creditor has a charge of the estate: *Re
Fox* (1856) S.I. Ch. R 541.

[18] *Lanoy v Duke of Athol* (1742) 2 Atk. 444; *Flint v Howard* [1893] 2 Ch. 54 (CA).

[19] *Lanoy v Duke of Athol*, above.

[20] *Manks v Whitely* [1911] 2 Ch. 448, affirmed [1914] A.C. 132; and see *Noyes v Pollock* (1886)
32 Ch.D. 53.

[21] *South v Bloxham* (1865) 2 Hem. & M. 457.

[22] *Barnes v Racster* (1842) 1 Y&C Ch. Cas. 401; *Flint v Howard* [1893] 2 Ch. 54, 73.

[23] *Dolphin v Aylward* (1870) L.R. 4 H.L. 486, 501.

[24] *Barnes v Racster*, above; but see *Finchley Shaw* (1854) 19 Beav. 500; affirmed (1856) 5 H.L.
Cas. 905, 922 and *Haynes v Forshaw* (1853) 11 Hem. 93.

[25] *Baglioni v Cavalli* (1900) 83 L.T. 500.

[26] See para.9–02 above.

(d)   B mortgages Blackacre to N.

This does not affect L's right to marshall against B; but if M satisfies himself primarily out of Whiteacre, which is the only property to which L can resort, L can no longer throw his debt on Blackacre.[27] It is irrelevant that N had notice of the previous transactions[28] or that he was a volunteer.[29]

There are only two cases in which L's right can affect N. In *Re Mower's Trusts*[30] it was held that N was bound by L's pre-existing right to marshall because his mortgage was expressly made subject to the payment of the two earlier mortgages. In *Stronge v Hawkes*[31] there was an erroneous recital to the effect that the prior mortgagee had been paid off, so L thought that he was the prior mortgagee. N, taking with notice of the error and of L's consequent incorrect belief, was held to be subject to L's right to marshall.

Condition (4)

9–08   The mere fact that N's second mortgage overrides L's right of marshalling does not altogether destroy the effect of the doctrine, as the following example shows:

(a)   B mortgages Blackacre and Whiteacre to M for £20,000;
(b)   B mortgages Whiteacre to L for £10,000;
(c)   B mortgages Blackacre to N for £10,000.

Suppose that, on realisation, each property was found to be worth £20,000. If L were allowed to marshall, the effect would be that M would satisfy his entire debt out of Blackacre, L would satisfy his out of Whiteacre, leaving £10,000 equity in Whiteacre to which N would have no recourse.

The rule does not permit this. The court preserves the right of all the encumbrancers, so far as possible, by apportioning M's charge, as between L and N, rateably between the two properties. There is no marshalling, strictly speaking; the rateable division simply prevents the loss from lying where it falls as a result of the way in which M elects to satisfy his debt. If M, in the above example, were to satisfy his debt entirely out of Whiteacre, N's debt would be satisfied out of Blackacre and L would get nothing; with the converse result if he satisfied it entirely out of Blackacre.[32]

Suppose, in the example above, M chose to satisfy his debt primarily out of Whiteacre and that Whiteacre was worth £10,000 and Blackacre £30,000. The court would treat the matter as if M had satisfied his debt rateably out of the two properties, that is, £5,000 out of Whiteacre (notionally leaving £5,000 equity)

---

[27] *Barnes v Racster* (1842) 17 Y. & C. Ch. 401.
[28] *Baglioni v Cavalli* (1900) 93 L.T. 500; *Flint v Howard* [1893] 2 Ch. 54, C.A.; *Smyth v Toms* [1918] 1 I.R. 338.
[29] *Dolphin v Aylward* (1870) L.R. 4 H.L. 486.
[30] (1869) L.R. 8 Eq. 110.
[31] (1859) 4 De G. & J. 632.
[32] *Barnes v Racster* (1842) 1 Y. & C. Ch. 401; *Flint v Howard* [1893] 2 Ch. 54 (CA); *Bugden v Bignold* (1843) 2 Y. & C .Ch. 377.

and £15,000 out of Blackacre (notionally leaving £15,000 equity). To the extent of the £5,000 which he would have had out of Whiteacre had M in fact satisfied his debt rateably, L will be subrogated to N's rights in Blackacre.[33]

As M satisfied his debt so as to leave no equity in Whiteacre and £20,000 in Blackacre, that £20,000 will go first towards the rights to which L is subrogated (£5,000) then towards the satisfaction of N's debt (£10,000) leaving a surplus of £5,000 which L is entitled to claim as against B.

CONTRIBUTION AND EXONERATION

A right of exoneration, if enforced, has the effect of varying the incidence of a **9–09** liability as between two or more properties. Primarily, that incidence is determined by the doctrine of contribution[34] which is based on the principle that where two properties or funds are equally liable to pay a debt, one shall not escape because the creditor has chosen to satisfy himself entirely out of the other.[35]

Contribution

If two or more properties, whether or not all owned by the same person, are **9–10** mortgaged for or subject equally to one debt,[36] they will, under the doctrine of contribution, be rateably liable for it, the value of each property being reduced by the amount of any other encumbrance affecting it. Thus, if Blackacre and Whiteacre are each worth £20,000, and if Blackacre is mortgaged to secure a debt of £10,000, after which Blackacre and Whiteacre are mortgaged together to secure a debt of £15,000, the value of Blackacre for the purpose of determining its rateable share of the later debt is £10,000. Since Whiteacre is otherwise unencumbered its value for that purpose is £20,000. Thus Blackacre will bear one third and Whiteacre two thirds of the later debt. A right of contribution can be defeated by a right to marshall if the security is the only security of those seeking to marshall.[37]

Exoneration

Circumstances exist, however, in which the doctrine of contribution does not **9–11** apply and the person entitled to one property or fund has a right to be exonerated at the expense of the other.

[33] *Cracknall v Janson* (1879) 11 Ch.D. 1.

[34] Perhaps most commonly encountered as between guarantors and co-sureties. See generally *Wolmershausen v Gullick* [1893] 2 Ch. 514.

[35] See *Re Pittortou (A Bankrupt)* [1985] 1 W.L.R. 58. See also *Re Richards (A Bankrupt), Bateman v Williams* [2009] EWHC 1760 (Ch), [2009] B.P.I.R. 973.

[36] See *Leonino v Leonino* (1878–79) L.R. 10 Ch.D. 460; *Dunlop v Dunlop* (1882) L.R. 21 Ch.D. 583, 590. Where a property is expressly made liable for the debt it secures, it will not be liable to contribute with other properties subject to a general charge: *Wisden v Wisden* (1854) 2 Sm.& G. 396.

[37] *Bartholomew v May* (1737) 1 Atk 487.

Consider the following series of transactions:

(a) B mortgages Blackacre and Whiteacre to L;
(b) B assigns Blackacre to M;
(c) B assigns Whiteacre to N.

Suppose only events (a) and (b) occur. B as mortgagor is personally liable and therefore the property remaining in his hands (Whiteacre) is the primary fund for payment.[38] If B has paid the debt there is no equity to compel any contribution to be made out of Blackacre unless the assignment to M was expressly made subject to the prior mortgage.[39]

If, however, L has enforced payment out of Blackacre, M is entitled to be exonerated out of Whiteacre, whether the assignment to him was voluntary or for value.[40]

If events (a), (b) and (c) occur, the doctrine of contribution cannot be displaced by the above argument, neither M nor N being personally liable. The earlier assignee, M, will have a right to exoneration if:

(i) the assignment to him contains a covenant against encumbrances, or for further assurance; or
(ii) when he took the assignment it was represented to him, even orally, by B, that Blackacre was free from encumbrances,[41]

and, in either case, that the later assignee, N was not a purchaser of the legal estate in Whiteacre for value and without notice.

It would appear that M has no right of exoneration on the second of these two grounds if he himself is a volunteer.

The right of exoneration may also exist as a result of the following series of transactions:

(a) B mortgages Blackacre and Whiteacre to L;
(b) both properties vest in A subject to B's mortgage which is paramount to A's title;
(c) A assigns Blackacre to M.

9–12 Since A did not create the mortgage, the doctrine of contribution is not displaced by the existence of any personal liability; so if A pays off the mortgage, he is entitled to contribution from M, unless he made the assignment to M on the basis that Blackacre was free from encumbrances. In that case, M has a right to exoneration, which will enable him to marshal against Whiteacre unless and

---

[38] *Re Darby's Estate, Rendall v Darby* [1907] 2 Ch. 465.
[39] *Re Mainwaring's Settlement Trusts, Mainwaring's Trustee in Bankruptcy v Verden* [1937] Ch. 96.
[40] *Re Best, Parker v Best* [1924] 1 Ch. 42; *Ker v Ker* (1869) 4 Ir.R.Eq. 15.
[41] *McCarthy v M'Cartie* [1904] 1 I.R. 100; see *Finch v Shaw, Colyer v Finch* (1854) 19 Beav. 500.

until it comes into the hands of a purchaser for value of the legal estate without notice.[42]

In addition, the right of exoneration also exists where:

(a) B incurs a debt to C;

(b) that debt is secured against Blackacre, being the jointly owned property of B and D.

In those circumstances, and in the absence of any evidence to the contrary, D has secured B's debt as a surety and is entitled to be exonerated by B. D has the same entitlement where Blackacre is mortgaged in order to raise money for the benefit of B, for example, for its application in his own, separate, business. The principle is often encountered in connection with that of a spouse providing security for pre-existing or new debts in relation to the other spouse's business. The principle has thus operated where Blackacre (jointly owned between the spouses) is charged to secure the debts of the husband; in the absence of a shared contrary intention, the wife (being in a position of a surety) is entitled not only as between the two joint owners but as between him or herself and the creditor, to have the secured indebtedness discharged so far as possible out of the husband's interest in the property before recourse is had to her interest.[43]

---

[42] *Ocean Accident & Guarantee Corporation Ltd and Hewitt v Collum* [1913] 1 I.R. 337.

[43] *Re Pittortou (A Bankrupt)* [1985] 1 W.L.R. 58; see also *Paget v Paget* [1898] 1 Ch. 470; *Hall v Hall* [1911] 1 Ch. 487.

CHAPTER 10

SECOND AND SUBSEQUENT MORTGAGES

GENERAL

Before 1926 second and subsequent mortgages of freehold land were necessarily **10–01** equitable by virtue of the practice of effecting the first mortgage by a conveyance to the mortgagee subject to cesser on redemption. This was also the case with leasehold land if the first mortgage was made by assignment. Subsequent mortgages of leasehold land, however, could be legal mortgages if the first mortgage was made by sub-demise, each successive mortgage being by sub-demise for a term one day longer than the term of the previous mortgage. It is now possible for second and subsequent mortgages of both freehold and leasehold land to be legal since any number of mortgages can be by deed expressed to be by way of legal mortgage which are themselves legal estates.[1]

Clearly, a second or subsequent mortgage carries with it an obvious commer- **10–02** cial risk by reason of its lesser priority. This chapter aims to consider some of the risks and factors peculiar to second and subsequent mortgages. In that regard, it is worth noting that the conventional wisdom is that a second or subsequent mortgagee is particularly exposed to the risk that:

(i) a prior mortgagee will tack further advantages onto his security,[2] i.e. make further advances to the mortgagor which will rank in priority to the second or subsequent mortgage and thus deplete the security afforded to the later mortgagee. Before 1926, two classes of mortgagee had the right to tack further advances, namely an equitable mortgagee who acquired the legal estate, and a legal mortgagee who made a further advance. The right to tack is now regulated by s.94 of the Law of Property Act 1925 and is considered in depth elsewhere;

(ii) a prior mortgagee may insist that any redemption of the prior mortgage on Blackacre by a second or later mortgagee should not proceed in isolation but instead should be consolidated and redeemed with his other charges on Blackacre/Whiteacre, in which latter property the second or later mortgagee may have no interest.[3] The later encumbrancer in those circumstances may face difficulty in "redeeming up"

[1] Law of Property Act (LPA) 1925 ss.85(1), 86(1) and 86(2).
[2] For the doctrine of tacking see paras 11–67 et seq.
[3] In *Re Salmon, Ex p. The Trustee* [1903] 1 K.B. 147 consolidation was allowed in respect of three mortgages, the first two on the same property, the third being on that and other property, the trustee not being allowed to redeem a third mortgage without redeeming the first and second mortgages. The judge expressed his unfamiliarity with the question and, while the decision has been accepted as

on a sale of Blackacre or securing acceptable commercial terms to acquire the prior mortgage on that property. However, in the absence of an express preservation of the right to consolidate, the right is now lost[4];

(iii) (in relation to unregistered land) the second mortgagee will not hold the documents of title. This is considered further below.[5] However, given the dominance of registered conveyancing, this concern is perhaps little more than historic; and

(iv) the prior mortgagee may sell the mortgaged property or foreclose. The latter remedy is now obsolete; as to the risk posed by the former, while a mortgagee who exercises his power of sale is not a trustee of that power for the mortgagor, he does owe a duty not only to act in good faith but also to take reasonable care to obtain the true market value of the mortgaged property at the date at which he sells it. In the case of a building society mortgagee this is enshrined as a statutory duty.[6] It therefore ought to follow that, provided a second or subsequent mortgagee makes reasonable enquiries and takes reasonable precautions to satisfy himself that there is sufficient equity in the property to secure his advance, he should not be at much risk of loss on a sale by a prior mortgagee. In practice, he often suffers loss resulting from the accumulated interest on the prior mortgage.

MANNER AND FORM

10–03   As to the manner in which land may be mortgaged, there is now a distinction—albeit perhaps only theoretical—between registered and unregistered land. In relation to unregistered land, any mortgage (of whatever priority) may still be created by demise or sub-demise[7] or by a charge expressed to be by way of legal mortgage. In relation to registered land, the ability to create any mortgage by demise or sub-demise has been prospectively abolished with effect from October 13, 2003.[8]

As to the form of a second or subsequent mortgage, such a mortgage must be executed in the same manner as a first mortgage; there is no particular form required for a second or later encumbrance per se. Under the Land Registration Rules 2003 r.103, a form for the creation of any registered charge may be in Form CH1.

authority for the propositions that: (i) the doctrine can be excluded by a provision in any one of the mortgage deeds; and (ii) that the right to consolidate exists where the mortgages become vested after the mortgagor's bankruptcy, it has never been subsequently cited as determining that the doctrine applies to successive mortgages of the same property. As a decision it is probably wrong—a view shared by Megarry & Wade, *The Law of Real Property* (7th edn, 2008) para.25–066.

[4] LPA 1925 s.93(1). Consolidation is considered in depth at paras 8–01 et seq.

[5] But see para.10–09 below.

[6] See paras 17–01 et seq.

[7] LPA 1925 s.85(2) (as amended).

[8] Land Registration Act (LRA) 2002 s.23(1)(a). Mortgages by demise or sub-demise (whether of registered or unregistered land) are practically obsolete in any event, mortgages being habitually being charges by deed expressed to be by way of legal mortgage: see LPA 1925 s.85(1).

As a matter of practice, a second or subsequent mortgage, in addition to **10–04** reciting the mortgagor's ownership and the agreement for the loan, should recite the state of the prior mortgage. This provides the mortgagee with a remedy under the implied covenants for title[9] given by the mortgagor in the event that the sum owing is greater than the sum recited. The demise or charge should be expressly made subject to any prior mortgage, and it is usual for the power of sale to be made exercisable on interest under a prior mortgage being in arrears for a specified number of days. There should also be a power for the subsequent mortgagee to settle and pass the accounts of prior mortgagees and a charge of the costs of so doing upon the mortgaged property.

Parties

The capacity of a specific person or entity to enter into a mortgage and the form **10–05** in which such any such mortgage must be executed is considered elsewhere.[10] There are generally no particular considerations which apply in relation to second or subsequent mortgages. However, the following (albeit historic) issues are worthy of note in the context of second and subsequent mortgages.

Trustees

Prior to February 1, 2001, when the Trustee Act 2000 came into force,[11] trustees **10–06** could lend moneys secured on any mortgage of freehold property in England, Wales or Northern Ireland, or of any leasehold property of which the unexpired term was over 60 years but only obtained the protection of s.8 of the Trustee Act 1925[12] if they complied with the provisions of s.8(1). Since s.8(1)(b) of that Act required them to show that the amount of the loan did not exceed two-thirds of the value of the property, second mortgages by properly advised trustees were rare.

Since January 31, 2001, there is no longer any statutory rule of thumb as to **10–07** what proportion of the value of a property can properly be advanced by trustees on mortgage.[13] Whether this makes second or subsequent mortgages by trustees any less rare is perhaps doubtful.

Building societies

Formerly, s.32(1) of the Building Societies Act 1962 prohibited a building **10–08** society from advancing money on the security of real property subject to a prior

---

[9] See above paras 3–13 et seq.

[10] See paras 4–01 et seq.

[11] Trustee Act 2000 (Commencement) Order 2001, SI 2001/49.

[12] This section provided for the circumstances when a trustee would not be chargeable with breach of trust by reason only of the proportion borne by the amount of the loan to the value of the property at the time the loan was made.

[13] Trustee Act 2000 s.40, Sch.2 Pt II para.18 and Sch.4 repeal s.8 of the Trustee Act 1925 but not so as to affect the operation of that section in relation to loans or investments made before February 1, 2001: see s.40, Sch.3 para.2.

mortgage, except as provided by Sch.5 to the Act or where the prior charge was in favour of the society. Section 32(2) fixed the directors jointly and severally with the liability for making good any loss occasioned to the society by the advance. The power of a building society to lend on second or subsequent mortgage was greatly extended by Pt III of the Building Societies Act 1986. Building society law and mortgage lending is considered elsewhere.[14]

PROTECTION OF THE SECOND (OR SUBSEQUENT) MORTGAGEE

Unregistered land

10–09   A second or subsequent legal mortgagee will not, in general, have the title deeds, since they will normally be in the possession of the first mortgagee. A second or subsequent mortgagee has the right to inspect and make copies of the title deeds.[15] In the unlikely event that the first mortgagee does not have custody of the title deeds, any mortgagee should take them into its possession.

10–10   Section 2(4) of the Land Charges Act 1972 provides that a puisne mortgage (that is "a legal mortgage which is not protected by a deposit of documents relating to the legal estate affected") shall be registered as a class C(i) land charge and, if not registered, is void against a purchaser for value of any interest in the land.[16] Accordingly, a legal second (or later) mortgage should be protected by the entry of such a charge in the Land Charges Register.

10–11   Equitable mortgages are registrable as general equitable charges. A class C(iii) land charge should accordingly be entered in relation to an equitable second or subsequent mortgage. A failure to so renders the charge void against a purchaser for value of any interest in the land.[17]

Registered land[18]

10–12   The implementation of the Land Registration Act 2002 on October 13, 2003,[19] altered the relevant statutory provisions and scheme of protection in relation to registered land and effectively abolished land and charge certificates since the Act makes no provision for them. The two schemes make it necessary to consider the provisions under that Act and the Land Registration Act 1925.

Before October 13, 2003

10–13   **Legal mortgages:** If a first charge was entered into and registered, the land certificate will have been deposited at HM Land Registry in accordance with s.65

---

[14] Below paras 17–01 et seq.
[15] LPA 1925 ss.96(1), 205(1)(xvi).
[16] Land Charges Act 1972 s.4(5).
[17] ibid.
[18] For Priority of Mortgages, see also paras 11–01 et seq.
[19] Land Registration Act (Commencement No.4) Order 2003, SI 2003/1725.

of the Land Registration Act 1925. A second legal mortgage could be registered, however, and a charge certificate issued in respect of it. There was thus a paper trail which provided an element of protection to the mortgagee since its absence may give rise to practical difficulties in any transfer or disposition.

As for the order of priority, s.29 of the 1925 Act provided that, subject to any entry to the contrary in the register, priorities among legal mortgages were determined by the order in which they were entered on the register and not according to the order in which they were created. Form 45 formerly contained stipulations altering the priority of charges under s.29. However, that form has now been revoked.[20]   **10–14**

Equitable mortgages: Before September 27, 1989,[21] when it was possible to create an equitable charge by deposit of the land certificate, the land certificate would be held by the prior mortgagee and protection would have been registered by way of a notice under the Land Registration Act 1925 s.49 (which permitted the entry of a notice in the register to protect the equitable charge[22]) if the depositee was willing to make the land certificate available. Otherwise, the encumbrance had to be protected by caution under the Land Registration Act 1925 s.54. Equitable charges by deposit did not survive the implementation of s.2 of the Law of Property (Miscellaneous Provisions) Act 1989.[23]   **10–15**

After October 12, 2003

Legal mortgages: Land and charge certificates are abolished. Under the 2002 Act, the legal mortgagee applies to register his charge using Form AP1 together with (if he has chosen to use the standard form charge) Form CH1 or the mortgage deed and, in either case, obtains the registration of the charge in the Charges Register.   **10–16**

Priority remains governed by the order in which such charges are entered in the register.[24] This can be varied by the parties' agreement.[25]   **10–17**

Equitable mortgages: Registered land remains capable of being subject to equitable mortgages and charges; they must be protected by the entry of an agreed or unilateral notice against the registered estate affected. A failure to do so would leave the charge vulnerable to a loss of priority to a later registrable disposition for valuable consideration completed by registration,[26] such as legal mortgage which is properly registered.   **10–18**

Equitable mortgages enjoy priority inter se according to their date of creation.[27]   **10–19**

---

[20] Land Registration Rules 1925 Sch.1. See above para.4–05.
[21] When the Law of Property (Miscellaneous Provisions) Act 1989 s.2 came into force.
[22] This was the preferable but not exclusive method of protection—see *Re White Rose Cottage* [1965] Ch. 940.
[23] *United Bank of Kuwait Plc v Sahib* [1997] Ch. 107 (CA).
[24] LRA 2002 s.48(1); Land Registration Rules 2003 r.101.
[25] Land Registration Rules 2003 r.102.
[26] LRA 2002 s.29(1).
[27] ibid., s.28.

Notice

10–20   Irrespective of whether the land is registered or not, the subsequent encumbrancer should serve notice of his encumbrance on all prior chargees.[28] By this route, the subsequent encumbrancer can protect himself from the tacking[29] of further advances onto the security of the earlier charge(s)[30] *unless* the prior chargee is under an obligation to make further advances.[31] In the case of unregistered land, notice also would render the prior encumbrancer liable in the event that he delivered documents of title to the mortgagor on discharge of his mortgage.[32]

Sale by a prior encumbrancer

10–21   Section 105 of the Law of Property Act 1925 provides that a mortgagee who exercises his power of sale holds the purchase money on trust, after prior mortgages have been paid off, to pay:

(i) all expenses incidental to the sale;
(ii) to himself, the principal, interest and costs due under the mortgage;
(iii) the surplus, if any, to the person entitled to the mortgaged property.

10–22   These words are defined so as to include subsequent mortgagees and the prior mortgagee is a trustee of the surplus for those subsequent mortgagees of whose encumbrances he has notice. Registration as a land charge is notice for this purpose in relation to unregistered land[33] and, in relation to registered land, it is now provided that for the purposes of s.105, a mortgagee in relation to the application of proceeds of sale of registered land is taken to have notice of anything in the registered immediately before the disposition on sale.[34]

REMEDIES OF THE SECOND (OR SUBSEQUENT) MORTGAGEE

10–23   A second (or subsequent) encumbrancer has all the remedies that his security— whether legal or equitable—brings with it and are considered in depth elsewhere.[35] Practically, however, his remedies in relation to the property will be

---

[28] In the case of unregistered land, mere registration of the later encumbrance as a land charge will not give the requisite notice unless it was registered when the prior charge was created or when the prior chargee undertook the last search of the register: LPA 1925 s.94(2). For registered land, see Land Registration Rules 2003 r.107 for the manner in which such notice ought to be served.

[29] See paras 11–67 et seq.

[30] LPA 1925 s.94(1)(b) (unregistered land); LRA 2002 s.49(1) (registered land).

[31] ibid., s.94(1)(c); ibid., s.49(3) *and*, in the case of registered land, the obligation to do so is noted in the register.

[32] LPA 1925 s.96(2).

[33] ibid., s.198(1)

[34] LRA 2002 s.54.

[35] See Chs 26, 27 and 28.

limited[36] when a prior mortgagee is exercising the right in question; thus, if the first mortgagee is in possession or has appointed a receiver, the second (or later) mortgagee may find his practical remedies curtailed. The court can (and does) order possession in favour of a second mortgagee "subject to the rights of the first mortgagee"[37] but it has been observed that a warrant of possession may not lie in such circumstances.[38] Likewise, the second mortgagee can always effect a sale of the security but, unless he takes a transfer of the prior security or sells with the prior mortgagee's agreement or obtains an order under s.50 of the Law of Property Act 1925,[39] he can only effect a transfer of the property subject to prior encumbrances.

---

[36] He can always sue on the personal covenant.

[37] *Cassel Arenz & Co v Taylor* (1968) 209 *Estates Gazette* 357; see also *Universal Showcards and Display Manufacturing v Brunt* (1984) 128 Sol. Jo. 581.

[38] *Berkshire Capital Funding Ltd v Street* (1999) 27 P. & C.R. 321, D23; [1999] 2 E.G.L.R. 92.

[39] A sale with the proceeds paid into court and a direction that that the transfer be free from the prior encumbrance.

Chapter 11

PRIORITY OF MORTGAGES

Introduction

As a mortgagor is able to obtain successive advances secured on the same interest **11–01** in real property, circumstances may arise in which the value of the property is insufficient to satisfy all the securities. Accordingly, there is a need for rules which regulate priorities among the various mortgagees to provide for the order of recovery from the limited funds available. Unlike the unsecured creditors of a bankrupt, mortgagees of a bankrupt do not share rateably if there is insufficient to satisfy all sums secured. Questions as to priorities may also arise as between a mortgagee and a tenant or beneficial owner who claims their interests are not subject to a mortgage.

The simplest way of regulating priorities is by order of creation and that has long been the starting point. However, that is far from the whole picture. While such an approach would be fair in many cases, it would not be fair when, by the misconduct of the mortgagor or an earlier mortgagee, the existence of that earlier mortgage was concealed from a later mortgagee. Further, there is tension between that approach and the modern vision of land registration involving a register that gives a complete and accurate snap-shot of the estates in land and interests in, over and attaching to them. That tension will dissipate if and when e-conveyancing becomes the norm.

The remaining significance of the principles

The introduction of the Land Registration Act 2002 addressed the priority of **11–02** legal mortgages relating to registered land. Other relevant statutory provisions including the Law of Property Act 1925 provide for priorities, in the sense of protection against the claims of third parties, in relation to puisne and equitable mortgages and general equitable charges and the registration of mortgages granted by companies. Nevertheless, the pre-1925 Act principles remain significant. Further, the pre-1926 principles remain pertinent when considering the following: priorities between unregistered charges of registered land; mortgages of equitable interests, in particular those subject to a trust of land; agreements between mortgagors (or other encumbrances) affecting priorities; the setting aside of a mortgage for wrongdoing by the debtor when the mortgagee relies on its position as a purchaser for value without notice; and mortgages of personalty.

Real property

11–03 For mortgages (including sub-mortgages) of real property, the basic rule of priority, that of ranking in order of the date of creation ("*qui prior est tempore, potior est jure*"), was modified in two ways. The first can be summed up by the phrase "where the equities are equal, the law prevails". In *Bailey v Barnes* Lindley L.J. said that equality meant "the non-existence of any circumstance which affects the conduct of one of the rival claimants, and makes it less meritorious than that of the other".[1] The reference to "law" in this context is to legal interests as distinct from equitable interests. The result of this is that, where a legal and an equitable mortgagee have, for all other purposes, equal claims, the legal mortgagee will rank first even though his mortgage was created later.

The second modification was that any priority, whether depending on earlier creation or superiority as a legal interest, could be lost if the conduct of the mortgagor or the prior mortgagee was inequitable. As a result priorities of mortgages of real property were regulated by general equitable principles, subject to the two following exceptions.

(1) The first exception related to registration. The principle of the registration system was that an earlier transaction by A would be void against a later purchaser, B, unless A's deed was registered before B's. The efficacy of this system was initially[2] severely reduced by the insistence of the courts of equity on applying the doctrine of notice, so that B took subject to A's encumbrance if he knew of its existence, irrespective of registration. That interference with the integrity of the registration system no longer subsists and as registration, in particular compulsory registration of title, has extended across the whole of the jurisdiction the scope for such principles to intervene has been dramatically curtailed.

(2) The second exception was tacking, a device whereby a later mortgagee can gain priority over an earlier mortgagee by amalgamating his debt with that owed to a still earlier mortgagee. The opportunities for this device to be used were significantly reduced by the 1925 legislation and its operation is now regulated entirely by statute.[3]

Personalty

11–04 The rules regulating priorities of mortgages of personalty developed rather differently to those regulating real property. Legal mortgages of personal chattels are only regulated by the Bills of Sale Acts 1878 and 1882.[4] Mortgages of choses in action are governed by the general law of assignment though sub-mortgages,

---

[1] [1894] 1 Ch. 25 at 36 (CA).
[2] Between 1703 and 1735, registers of transactions in land were set up for Yorkshire and Middlesex.
[3] Law of Property Act (LPA) 1925 s.94 and Land Registration Act (LRA) 2002 s.49.
[4] See Ch.22.

which are mortgages of mortgage debts and therefore choses in action are treated as interests in land and are subject to the same rules of priority as mortgages.[5]

Mortgages of equitable interests in personalty were subject to the rule in **11–05** *Dearle v Hall*.[6] In its original form the rule provided that priority depended on the order in which notice of the mortgages or other transactions was received by the owner of the legal estate or interest in the subject-matter. This was subject to an exception where, if at the time the subsequent mortgagee lent the money, he had actual or constructive notice of the earlier transaction in which case he was postponed to it. Although the rule now applies to equitable interests in land subject to a trust of land and its proceeds of sale,[7] it did not do so before 1926.

A SUMMARY OF PRINCIPLES OF PRIORITY AFTER 1925

The Law of Property Act 1925 reduced the number of legal estates and put the **11–06** titles of limited owners "behind the curtain" as equitable interests. The registration system set up by the Land Charges Act 1925 was intended to provide a register of interests which would bind the legal estate in the hands of a subsequent purchaser. Consequently, equitable interests which are overreached and become charges on the proceeds of sale of the land have no place in such a register. It therefore follows that the rules for determining priority must depend on whether the interest mortgaged is legal (in which case it is capable of binding the land in the hands of a subsequent purchaser) or equitable, and not on whether the mortgage itself is legal or equitable.

The effect of the 1925 legislation, is that the priority of a mortgage of a legal estate in land depends either on possession of the title deeds, or on registration, while priority of a mortgage of any equitable interest, whether in realty or personalty, is governed by the rule in *Dearle v Hall* as altered by the Law of Property Act 1925 s.137(1).

It is worthy to note that ordinarily where there are two mortgages of the same property, the mortgages may vary the order of priority without the mortgagor's consent.[8] It is of course open to a mortgagor who wishes to have secured debt satisfied in a particular order, to require the inclusion of a specific term in the mortgage which prevents the order of priority being changed.[9]

The Land Registration Act 2002 provides a complete statutory framework for **11–07** priorities between competing registered interests generally and priorities between registered charges against a registered estate particularly. Generally, priority is based on the date of creation, subject to a special rule which gives registrable

[5] *Taylor v London & County Banking Co*; *London and County Banking Co v Nixon* [1901] 2 Ch. 231.

[6] 38 E.R. 475; (1828) 3 Russ. 1.

[7] LPA 1925 s.137 (as amended by Trusts of Land and Appointment of Trustees Act 1996 s.25(1), Sch.3 paras 4 and 15).

[8] *Cheah Theam Swee v Equiticorp Finance Group Ltd* [1992] 1 A.C. 472; [1992] 2 W.L.R. 108.

[9] *Cheah Theam Swee,* above. See also *Re Portbase Clothing Ltd* [1993] Ch. 388; [1993] 3 W.L.R. 14.

dispositions for valuable consideration (of which mortgages are an example) when completed by registration priority over interests which are not protected in one of several particular ways as at the date of registration of the registrable disposition.[10] As between registered charges their priority is based (subject to any entry to the contrary in the register) on the order in which they appear in the register, which reflects the date of registration, and not the date of creation.[11] There are two exceptions to that approach. First, mortgagees can agree upon a different priority between themselves,[12] and second, certain statutory charges have overriding priority.[13]

PRIORITY UNDER THE LAND REGISTRATION ACT 2002

Generally

11–08   In relation to registered land, the Land Registration Act 1925 made provision for registration and for loss of priority in the absence of registration in some circumstances. The Land Registration Act 2002 repealed the Land Registration Act 1925. It did not render the previous law of priorities obsolete in relation to registered land but instead grafted, on to the pre-existing law, a statutory framework for priorities between registered interests and the impact of registered dispositions on the priority of other interests. Given the extent to which freehold and leasehold title within the jurisdiction are now registered, in reality that statutory framework will be the determining law in most instances where questions over priorities arise.

11–09   The 2002 Act establishes a "basic rule" which is subject to a very significant exception, or "special rule", which addresses the impact of a registrable disposition of a registered estate or charge for valuable consideration, when completed by registration on any unregistered interest which is not protected as an overriding interest by actual occupation or otherwise protected.

11–10   The basic rule is that the priority of an interest affecting a registered estate or charge is not affected by a disposition of the estate or charge but ranks according to the date of creation.[14] However, under the special rule the priorities are reversed for the benefit of a registered disponee for valuable consideration where there is an interest with priority that is unprotected for the purposes of the special rule when the disponee's interest under the disposition was completed by registration. This special rule represents a substantial qualification which benefits those who acquire an interest upon the registration of a registrable disposition for valuable consideration. Registrable dispositions include the grant of a legal charge, the transfer of a legal charge, the grant of a sub-charge (but not the creation of a legal charge which is a local land charge).[15] Registrable dispositions

---

[10] LRA 2002 ss.28–30.
[11] LRA 2002 s.48.
[12] Land Registration Rules 2003 r.102.
[13] See Access to Justice Act 1999 s.10(7), LRA 2002 s.50. See paras 21–01 to 21–04.
[14] LRA 2002 s.28.
[15] LRA 2002 ss.27(1), (2)(3) and (5)(c).

must be completed by registration. Such dispositions, if made for valuable consideration, will, once registered, operate to postpone any pre-existing interest affecting the estate or charge unless that interest is protected for the purposes of the special rule of priority. A disposition is not for valuable consideration if the consideration is nominal or marriage consideration.[16]

An interest is protected for the purposes of the special rule of priority if it is a registered charge, the subject of a notice in the register, is an overriding interest within Sch.3 to the 2002 Act, appears from the register to be excepted from the effect of registration or is a burden incident to a leasehold estate which is the subject matter of the disposition.[17]

There is an exception to the special rule in relation to statutory Inland Revenue   **11–11**
charges; a purchaser in good faith for money or monies worth takes free from the statutory charge if it was not registered.[18]

It follows that the concept of notice or knowledge of a pre-existing interest has   **11–12**
limited relevance to priorities affecting registered charges under the 2002 Act. Such concepts may arise in the context of the Inland Revenue statutory charge and some overriding interests and also in the case of bankruptcy of a registered proprietor.

Priority of competing registered charges

The general rule under the 2002 Act is that registered charges affecting the same   **11–13**
registered estate rank in priority according to the order in which they are shown in the register, which reflects the order in which they were registered, not the date they were created.[19] The proper use of searches with priority and the Day List provides protection to those contemplating and registering charges over registered land. It will be appreciated that when e-conveyancing is fully operational the date of creation of a new charge will coincide with its date of registration.

Where parties agree to alter the priority of registered charges, such an agree-   **11–14**
ment must be recorded in an instrument and an application may be made to the Land Registry by or with the consent of the person whose charge is to be adversely affected.[20] Where the statutory provisions give rise to a statutory charge apparently or arguably taking priority over any existing charges affecting the same estate, the 2002 Act imposes a duty on the Registrar to notify the prior chargee of any such statutory charge that is entered on the register.[21] If the Registrar is satisfied the statutory charge has priority, he must register it showing that priority, but if the Registrar is not satisfied and considers it is arguable the charge has priority, he may make an entry recording the claimed priority. In either instance the prior chargee is notified.

---

[16] LRA 2002 s.132(1).
[17] LRA 2002 ss.29 and 30.
[18] LRA 2002 s.31, Inheritance Tax Act 1984 ss.237 and 238.
[19] LRA 2002 s.48.
[20] Land Registration Rules 2003 r.102.
[21] LRA 2002 s.50, Land Registration Rules 2003 r.106(1).

11–15   The effect of ss.29(1), (2)(a)(i)–(ii) of the Land Registration Act 2002 is that, until protected on the register by registration, unregistered mortgages take effect only in equity. The priority of competing equitable charges depends upon the basic rule so that their priority will be determined by the order in which they were created. Of course the priority of equitable charges (including a charge created by a registrable disposition which has not been completed by registration) not protected by notice or as an overriding interest will be defeated by the registration of a legal charge or mortgage effected for valuable consideration.

PRIORITY—GENERAL RULES

Priorities between legal and equitable mortgages of land

Two successive legal mortgages

11–16   Legal mortgages of land before 1926 were almost invariably created by a conveyance of the fee simple with a proviso for reconveyance on redemption and therefore the opportunity for any priority question to arise rarely occurred.

Successive legal mortgages could arise from the grant of successive terms of years, in which case priority would normally be determined by the order of creation on the basis that the first lease would be a lease in possession, to which the second, as a lease in reversion, would be postponed.[22]

The earlier mortgagee could, as in *Jones v Rhind*,[23] lose priority by parting with the title deeds. In that case, S mortgaged a leasehold property first to J, then to R, handing over the deeds to R when he made the second mortgage. R had no notice of the first mortgage and he was held to have priority over J. In *Mason v Rhodes*,[24] W created three mortgages; an equitable mortgage to G, followed by legal mortgages to B and then to R. R, who had no notice of B, arranged to pay off G, and received the title deeds. It was held on appeal that R had priority over M (B's trustee in liquidation) to the extent of G's security.

One source of successive legal mortgages came from the portions term contained in a strict settlement. The trustees of the portions term were empowered to raise money for the younger children by mortgaging for a long term, usually 1,000 years. In *Hurst v Hurst*[25] it was held that a tenant for life, who had power under the settlement to create portions terms, could not do so to the prejudice of the mortgagees with whom he had covenanted not to exercise that power, even though the portions term was not made subject to the mortgage term.

Legal mortgage followed by equitable mortgage

11–17   Where there is a legal mortgage which is subsequently followed by an equitable mortgage, the legal mortgagee has a claim to priority based on both the earlier

---

[22] *Ex p. Knott* 32 E.R. 1225; (1806) 11 Ves. Jr. 609.

[23] (1869) 17 W.R. 1091; applying *Perry-Herrick v Attwood* (1857) 2 De G. & J. 21. See also *Abbey National Building Society v Cann* [1991] 1 A.C. 56; [1990] 2 W.L.R. 832.

[24] (1885) 53 L.T. 322.

[25] 51 E.R. 822; (1852) 16 Beav. 372.

creation and the superiority of the legal estate.[26] However, this double protection is not impenetrable and can be lost. Usually the cases on such loss of protection are considered under the three headings of estoppel (or misrepresentation), fraud and gross negligence in relation to the title deeds.

Loss of priority by estoppel: The principles of proprietory estoppel and **11–18** estoppel by convention may operate to alter priority by depriving a mortgagee of priority of which he otherwise had the benefit.[27] Accordingly, where a mortgagee or potential mortgagee who is aware another is advancing money on the basis he will receive a first legal charge either encourages that advance or acquiesces in that advance taking some of the benefit of it, they will be estopped from assisting or taking a first legal charge himself. Similarly, an estoppel may arise where there is an understanding or an assumption between the two mortgagees about the priorities that arise or that one of them has. However the use of estoppel by convention is likely to be limited as it will only arise in respect of an understanding or assumption about a current state of affairs not a future position.

Historically the so-called estoppel cases have fallen into two classes. The first, involved the prior mortgagee putting into the hands of a mortgagor a document containing within it a statement that money has been received by the prior mortgagee. As against an innocent person who lends money on the property on the faith of that receipt, he cannot deny that the money has been received.[28]

The second class of estoppel case involved a situation where the mortgagee has provided the mortgagor with the title deeds. Possession of the title deeds without more amounted to a representation (either express or implied), that the person holding them is entitled to deal freely with the property. Thus where a mortgagee authorised the mortgagor to raise money on the security of the property and gives him control of the title deeds, he represented to innocent third parties who advanced money that the mortgagor had the proper authority to deal with the property. He cannot claim priority against such a third party, or rely on any limitation of the mortgagor's apparent authority unless the third party has notice.[29] Thus, where the prior legal mortgagee returned the deeds to the mortgagor so that he could raise a further loan, his legal mortgage was postponed to a later equitable mortgagee's interest because he lent without notice of the earlier mortgage. The fact the mortgagor exceeded the limit that he was actually authorised to borrow was irrelevant.[30] This similarly arose where the mortgagor had undertaken to inform the later mortgagee of the existing mortgage, but failed to do so.[31] It is apparent that an estoppel would not arise in the context of registered land where possession of the title deeds could not be said to give rise

[26] *Peter v Russell* 25 E.R. 85; (1716) Gilb. Ch. 122.
[27] *Scottish & Newcastle Plc v Lancashire Mortgage Corp Ltd* [2007] EWCA Civ 684; [2007] N.P.C. 2007.
[28] *Bickerton v Walker* (1885) 31 Ch.D. 151; cf. *Rice v Rice* 61 E.R. 646; (1854) 2 Drew. 73.
[29] *Rimmer v Webster* [1902] 2 Ch. 163; *Fry v Smellie* [1912] 3 K.B. 282; *Abigail v Lapin* [1934] A.C. 491, PC (Aus); *Brocklesby v Temperance Permanent Building Society* [1895] A.C. 173; *Lloyds Bank v Cooke* [1907] 1 K.B. 794; *Edmunds v Bushell* (1865–66) L.R. 1 Q.B. 97.
[30] *Perry-Herrick v Attwood* (1857) 2 De G. & J. 21; *Abbey National Building Society v Cann* [1991] 1 A.C. 56.
[31] *Briggs v Jones* (1870) L.R. 10 Eq. 92.

to a representation about the ability to deal with the property since it is the Register not possession of the title deeds that defines the person whether the powers of a legal owner.

In any event priority will not be lost where the title deeds are left with another for safe-keeping or without reference to any transaction regarding the property.[32] The pre-1926 rule as to questions of priority affecting equitable interests depending on possession of deeds is preserved.[33]

11–19 **Loss of priority by fraud and/or gross negligence:** The fraud and gross negligence cases are considered together. In *Peter v Russell*[34] it was held that a prior mortgagee who deliberately assists or connives in a scheme of the mortgagor designed to defeat later encumbrancers, is postponed to them. The same applies if the fraud is that of the party's solicitor, provided that the solicitor–client relationship existed at the time of the fraud. In *Evans v Bicknell*,[35] Lord Eldon held that a prior mortgagee would be postponed if his conduct in relation to the deeds displayed such gross negligence that it amounted to a fraudulent intention.

However, in *Colyer v Finch*[36] the court concluded that in order to deprive a first mortgagee of his legal priority, the party claiming by title subsequent must satisfy the court that the first mortgagee has been guilty of either fraud or gross negligence in obtaining or retaining the title deeds, but for which he would have had the deeds in his possession. *Clarke v Palmer*[37] seems to have been decided in accordance with this principle. X, the first mortgagee, negligently failed to obtain the title deeds, after which the mortgagor further mortgaged part of the property to Y, then all of it to Z. Z knew of Y but neither of them knew of X, who was, on account of his gross negligence, postponed to both of them.

11–20 In reviewing the authorities, two particular cases stand out as difficult to reconcile[38]; *Northern Counties of England Fire Insurance Co v Whipp*[39] and *Walker v Linom*.[40]

11–21 *Northern Counties:* In his analysis of the authorities in *Northern Counties of England Fire Insurance Co v Whipp*,[41] Fry L.J. held *Clarke v Palmer* to have been rightly decided. He considered six types of case. In the first three, the prior legal mortgagee retains priority:

> (1) Where he has a reasonable excuse for not obtaining the deeds. This has been extended in *Grierson v National Provincial Bank of England*

---

[32] *Shropshire Union Railways and Canal Co v R.* (1874–75) L.R. 7 H.L. 496; *Re Vernon, Ewens & Co* (1886) 33 Ch.D. 402; cf. *Waldron v Sloper* 61 E.R. 425; (1852) 1 Drew. 193.

[33] *Beddoes v Shaw* [1937] Ch. 81; LPA 1925 s.13.

[34] (1716) 1 Eq. Cas. Abr. 321.

[35] 31 E.R. 998; (1801) 6 Ves. Jr. 174 at 189.

[36] 10 E.R. 1159; (1856) 5 H.L. Cas. 905.

[37] (1882) 21 Ch.D. 124.

[38] See para.11–21.

[39] (1884) 26 Ch.D. 482 (CA).

[40] [1907] 2 Ch. 104.

[41] (1884) 26 Ch.D. 482 (CA).

Ltd[42] where F, a leaseholder, deposited his lease with another bank as security for a loan and then granted a legal mortgage to G which was made expressly subject to the prior equitable mortgage. He then redeemed the equitable mortgage and deposited the lease with the defendant bank, who knew nothing of G, as security for a loan. It was held that G retained priority over the defendant bank.

(2) Where he reasonably believes that he has been given all the deeds though he has not, in fact, been given all of them. *Walker v Linom*,[43] which is discussed later, is against this proposition.

(3) Where he has lent them to the mortgagor who has given a reasonable excuse for requiring them as in *Peter v Russell*[44] and *Martinez v Cooper*.[45]

In the remaining three, priority would be lost by the prior legal mortgagee:

(4) Where the legal mortgagee has made no inquiry for the deeds, he will be postponed to a prior equitable estate or to a subsequent equitable owner who used diligence in inquiring for the deeds. In the first case, of which he cites *Worthington v Morgan*[46] as an example, his reasoning was that the conduct of the mortgagee in making no inquiry was evidence of fraudulent intent to escape notice of a prior equity. In the second case, exemplified by *Clarke v Palmer*,[47] he considered that a subsequent mortgagee who was misled by the mortgagor taking advantage of fraudulent conduct on the part of the legal mortgagee could, against him, take advantage of the fraudulent intent.

(5) and (6) These are the cases, already dealt with under estoppel, such as *Perry-Herrick v Attwood*[48] and *Briggs v Jones*,[49] where the legal mortgagee has conferred apparent authority on the mortgagor to deal with the property without restriction, although there were conditions as between mortgagee and mortgagor of which a third party would be unaware.

In arriving at his decision in *Northern Counties of England Fire Insurance Co v Whipp*,[50] Fry L.J. relied a line of authorities starting with *Evans v Bicknell*,[51] but seems to have ignored the plain words of *Colyer v Finch*.[52] He has used a later passage which refers to "gross negligence, so gross as to be tantamount to **11–22**

---

[42] [1913] 2 Ch. 18.
[43] [1907] 2 Ch. 104; see para.11–23 and *Cottey v National Provincial Bank of England* (1904) 48 S.J. 589.
[44] 1 Eq. Cas. Abr. 321.
[45] (1826) 2 Russ. 198.
[46] 60 E.R. 987; (1849) 16 Sim. 547.
[47] (1882) 21 Ch.D. 124.
[48] (1857) 2 De G. & J. 21.
[49] (1870) L.R. 10 Eq. 92.
[50] (1884) 26 Ch.D. 482 (CA).
[51] (1801) 6 Ves. 174.
[52] (1856) 5 H.L.C. 905, in the headnote and at 928.

fraud"[53] in order to reconcile those two cases and make fraud a requirement for postponement.

11–23   *Walker v Linom*[54]:   In *Walker v Linom*, Parker J. reviewed the authorities, particularly the judgment of Fry L.J. referred to above, and concluded that the principle should be stated as follows:

> "Any conduct on the part of the holder of the legal estate in relation to the deeds which would make it inequitable for him to rely on his legal estate against a prior equitable estate of which he had no notice ought also to be sufficient to postpone him to a subsequent equitable estate the creation of which has only been rendered possible by the possession of deeds which but for such conduct would have passed into the possession of the owner of the legal estate."[55]

In that case, W conveyed land to solicitor trustees to hold on the trusts of his marriage settlements. The title deeds, except for the conveyance to W, were handed over to the trustees who failed to discover the omission. They were found to have been negligent but not dishonest in that failure which had enabled W, using the conveyance, to mortgage the property to X, who then sold it to Y. The court held that the trustees were postponed to Y.

11–24   Although that decision is inconsistent with Fry L.J.'s judgment in *Northern Counties v Whipp*,[56] it is suggested that Parker J.'s formulation of the principle is correct, the more so since Hall V.C. did not find any fraudulent conduct in *Clarke v Palmer*[57] but still postponed the prior mortgagee on the grounds of his negligence.

11–25   The attempt to reconcile the decisions in the *Northern Counties* case and *Walker v Linom*,[58] on the basis that the first refers to negligence in failing to retain and the second to negligence in failing to obtain the title deeds, cannot be supported. As Waldock[59] has pointed out, it is not satisfactory to argue that by carelessly failing to keep the title deeds the legal mortgagee could prejudice only himself and his carelessness would thus not tend to convict him of fraud. The owner of the legal estate is the one person who could not be prejudiced by misuse of the title deeds. Normally the person prejudiced is one who enters into a transaction with the person who should not have them. The prejudice arises whether the deeds fall into the wrong hands by failure to retain or failure to obtain.

It may be, as Waldock suggests, that Fry L.J. was influenced by the doctrine of constructive fraud.[60] Commenting on the decision in *Ratcliffe v Barnard*,[61] Jeune P. said in *Oliver v Hinton*[62]:

---

[53] ibid., at 929.
[54] [1907] 2 Ch. 104.
[55] ibid., at 114.
[56] (1884) 26 Ch.D. 482.
[57] (1882) 21 Ch.D. 124.
[58] [1907] 2 Ch. 104.
[59] *Waldock on Mortgages* (2nd edn, 1950) p.397.
[60] ibid. and see *Le Lievre v Gould* [1893] 1 Q.B. 491.
[61] (1871) 6 Ch.App. 652 (CA).
[62] [1899] 2 Ch. 264 at 275.

"I think that what he [James L.J.] meant was . . . negligence so gross as would justify the Court of Chancery in concluding that there had been fraud in an artificial sense of the word—such gross negligence, for instance, as omitting to make any inquiry as to the title to the property."

It is also clear from the judgments in *Derry v Peek*,[63] that fraud and gross negligence are to be regarded as two different causes of action and from the above cases that each of them constitutes a valid and independent ground for postponing a prior legal mortgagee.

Equitable mortgage followed by legal mortgage

Where the prior interest is equitable, it was liable to be defeated by a bona fide **11–26** purchaser for value of the legal estate without notice of that prior equitable interest.[64] A mortgagee is a purchaser for this purpose and a person who, although not the purchaser of a legal estate, has a better title to the legal estate than the equitable mortgagee, can also displace his priority.

The onus is on the legal mortgagee to show that he is a bona fide[65] purchaser[66] without notice. It is not sufficient for him to show lack of actual notice; if he fails to make inquiries such as would normally be made by a reasonably prudent man of business he is fixed with constructive knowledge of what he would have discovered by making them. Not only the failure to enquire for the title deeds but also the inability of the mortgagor to produce them or to provide a reasonable excuse for their non-production would amount to constructive notice of some prior interest.

Notice—the use of agents: In addition, where a mortgagee employed an agent **11–27** to carry out the transaction, the knowledge of prior interests which his agent obtained, or should have obtained, was imputed to him so as to prevent him being a purchaser without notice.[67] Originally this rule was applied very strictly, it being possible to impute to the purchaser the knowledge acquired by his agent in an entirely separate transaction on behalf of some other principal.[68] By s.3(2) of the Conveyancing Act 1882, however, the doctrine of imputed notice was restricted to cases in which the agent's knowledge was obtained in the same transaction as that which led to the question of notice being raised.[69] This provision is re-enacted by the Law of Property Act 1925 by virtue of s.199(1)(ii)(b).

The duty to enquire: The words "ought reasonably to enquire" did not fix the **11–28** purchaser with any legal duty to inquire but rather meant that he "ought, as a matter of prudence [to make the inquiries], having regard to what is usually done

---

[63] (1889) 14 App. Cas. 337.
[64] *Re Hardy, Ex p. Hardy* (1832) 2 Deac. & Ch. 393.
[65] *Att.-Gen. v Biphosphated Guano Co* (1879) L.R. 11 Ch.D. 327.
[66] A mortgagee is a purchaser; *Pilcher v Rawlins* (1871–72) L.R. 7 Ch. 259.
[67] *Sheldon v Cox* (1764) 2 Eden. 224; *Berwick & Co v Price* [1905] 1 Ch. 632; *Kennedy v Green* (1834) 3 My. & K. 699.
[68] *Hargreaves v Rothwell* (1836) 1 Keen 154.
[69] *Re Cousins* (1886) 31 Ch.D. 671.

by men of business under similar circumstances".[70] It was generally considered that the following inquiries ought reasonably to have been made:

(1) Inspection of the land. Failure to inspect land occupied by a third party would fix the purchaser with knowledge of the third party's rights.[71]

(2) Investigation of the title for the statutory period applicable to an open contract. Failure to investigate would fix the purchaser with knowledge of all that he would have discovered by doing so, even if he had stipulated for a shorter contractual root of title.[72]

(3) Examination of deeds executed within the statutory period if they actually affected the title. Failure to do so would fix a purchaser with notice of their contents.[73] If, however, the character of the deed was such that it was uncertain whether it would affect the title, he was permitted to rely on an assurance that it did not.[74]

(4) Inquiry into the terms of any trust affecting the land, the existence of which he knew. Knowledge of the trust fixed him with knowledge of the interests of the beneficiaries.[75]

11–29   **Actual notice:** Whether the purchaser had actual notice was a fact to be established by evidence. The decided cases are, however, at variance as to whether information must be given by a person interested in the property in order to fix the purchaser with notice.[76]

11–30   **"Gross negligence" and actual notice:** In spite of the principle that a subsequent purchaser of a legal estate would be fixed with notice of a prior encumbrance if the mortgagor was unable to produce the title deeds, the courts found it necessary to develop a separate doctrine of "gross negligence" in relation to their non-production, which in effect (in circumstances where it applied) amounted to actual notice of the prior interest.

In *Hewitt v Loosemore*[77] and *Hunt v Elmes,*[78] it was said that to deprive a man of the protection of the legal estate, he must have been guilty of either fraud or gross and wilful negligence. In *Oliver v Hinton*[79] Lindley M.R. followed these authorities, holding that a purchaser for value of a legal estate, without notice of a prior equitable encumbrance, would not be permitted to assert the superiority of the legal estate if he had, himself, been guilty of such gross negligence as to render it unjust to deprive the equitable encumbrancer of his priority. An attempt

---

[70] *Bailey v Barnes* [1894] 1 Ch. 25, per Lindley L.J. at 35.

[71] *Hunt v Luck* [1902] 1 Ch. 428.

[72] *Re Nisbet and Potts' Contract* [1906] 1 Ch. 386.

[73] *Bisco v Earl of Banbury* (1676) 1 Ch.Cas. 287.

[74] *English and Scottish Mercantile Investment Trust v Brunton* [1892] 2 Q.B. 700.

[75] *Perham v Kempster* [1907] 1 Ch. 373.

[76] *Barnhart v Greenshields* (1853) 9 Moo.P.C. 18 at 36; explained in *Reeves v Pope* [1914] 2 K.B. 284; cf. *Lloyd v Banks* (1868) L.R. 3 Ch. 488, where the court was dealing with notice under the rule in *Dearle v Hall*. The effect of notice, to trustees, of dealings with equitable interests is regulated by the LPA 1925 s.137(3).

[77] (1851) 9 Hare. 449.

[78] 45 E.R. 745; (1860) 2 De G. F. & J. 578.

[79] [1899] 2 Ch. 264.

to describe the requisite degree of negligence was made in *Hudston v Viney*[80] where Eve J. said:

> "It must at least be carelessness of so aggravated a nature as to amount to the neglect of precautions which the ordinary reasonable man would have observed, and to indicate an attitude of mental indifference to obvious risks."

It is not clear why such conduct would not be held to fix the purchaser of the legal estate with constructive notice of the prior encumbrance,[81] and in view of the repeated failure of the courts to give anything but the most general description of "gross negligence," one must sympathise (pace Lord Chelmsford) with the views of Rolfe B. in *Wilson v Brett*[82]:

> "I said that I could see no difference between negligence and gross negligence—that it was the same thing with the addition of a vituperative epithet".

In *Oliver v Hinton*,[83] X deposited the deeds of some property with O, then two years later purported to convey it to H. H's agent asked to see the deeds but X replied that he could not as they also related to other property. At first instance it was held that O retained priority because H had constructive notice of the prior encumbrance. The Court of Appeal affirmed the decision, but on the basis that H's agent had acted with such gross carelessness that it would be unjust to deprive O of priority.

Summary: However unnecessary the doctrine of postponement by gross negli- **11–31** gence may be, it is undoubtedly part of the law and the decided cases are authority for the following propositions as to when a prior equitable mortgagee will be postponed[84]:

(1) the weight of the authorities favours the view that the degree of negligence needed to bring about a postponement is the same whether the prior mortgagee is a legal or an equitable mortgagee, though a contrary view had been expressed[85];

(2) a prior equitable mortgagee will be postponed if:

    (a) his title depends on the deeds and he fails to acquire any of them,[86] and

    (b) he has a right to obtain them, and not only fails to do so, but fails to give a reasonable explanation for the failure[87];

(3) A prior equitable mortgagee will not be postponed if:

---

[80] [1921] 1 Ch. 98 at 104.
[81] *Le Neve v Le Neve* (1748) 3 Atk. 646.
[82] (1843) 11 M. & W. 113 at 116.
[83] [1899] 2 Ch. 264.
[84] *Taylor v Russell* [1891] 1 Ch. 8 at 14–20; [1892] A.C. 244 at 262.
[85] *National Provincial Bank v Jackson* (1886) 33 Ch.D. 1 (CA).
[86] See *Rice v Rice* (1854) 2 Drew. 73 at 81 per Kindersley V.C.; *Farrand v Yorkshire Banking Co* (1889) 40 Ch.D. 182.
[87] *Worthington v Morgan* (1849) 16 Sim. 547; *Colyer v Finch* (1856) 5 H.L.C. at 905; *Clarke v Palmer* (1882) 21 Ch.D. 124.

(a) he inquired for the deeds and was given a reasonable excuse for their non-production,[88]

(b) he received some of the deeds but reasonably believed he was receiving all of them.[89] The same applies if it was represented to him that the packet of deeds handed to him contained all the necessary deeds and he honestly believed that to be true. He would not lose priority by failure to examine them,[90]

(c) he lent the deeds to the mortgagor on a reasonable representation of his requiring them and was diligent in inquiring for them,[91] and

(d) he allowed the deeds to be in the custody of someone in a fiduciary relationship to him who fraudulently or negligently parted with them.[92] But he would be postponed by estoppel[93] if the fiduciary had authority to deal with them.

If he was a second mortgagee and, at the time of making the advance the deeds were in the hands of a prior mortgagee, he would not be deprived of his priority by failure to give notice of his interest to the earlier encumbrance, even though that resulted in the deeds being returned to the mortgagor on discharge of the earlier mortgage. The same applied if the deeds had not come into existence at the time of the mortgage, as where the leasehold was mortgaged before the head lessor executed the lease.

Where a mortgagee left deeds in the hands of his trustee with authority to deal with them, he was not protected against subsequent equitable encumbrances by setting limits on that authority.[94] However, beneficiaries who so act are protected if the trustee exceeds his apparent authority.[95]

Two successive equitable mortgages[96]

11–32 As is the case with successive legal mortgages, priority normally depended on the order of creation but with the additional condition that, for that rule to apply, the equities had to be equal. Inequitable behaviour on the part of the prior

---

[88] *Hewitt v Loosemore* (1851) 9 Hare. 449 *Agra Bank v Barry* (1874) L.R. 7 H.L. 135; *Barnett v Weston* (1806) 12 Ves. 130; *Manners v Mew* (1885) 29 Ch.D. 725.

[89] *Ratcliffe v Barnard* (1870–71) L.R. 6 Ch. 652.

[90] *Dixon v Muckleston* (1872) App. 8 Ch. 155; *Colyer v Finch* (1856) 5 H.L.C. 905.

[91] *Peter v Russell* (1716) 1 Eq. Cas. Abr. 321; *Martinez v Cooper* (1826) 2 Russ 198; *Layard v Maud* (1867) L.R. 4 Eq. 397.

[92] *Shropshire Union Railways and Canal Co v R.* (1875) L.R. 7 H.L. 496; *Re Vernon Ewens & Co* (1886) 33 Ch.D. 402; *Re Richards* (1890) 45 Ch.D. 589; *Hill v Peters* [1918] 2 Ch. 273. In *Carritt v Real and Personal Advance Co* (1889) 42 Ch.D. 263 it was held that where trustees advanced trust moneys on mortgage, the beneficiaries were not postponed to a subsequent equitable encumbrancer simply because they allowed the deeds to be taken by the trustees, who had subsequently misused them.

[93] *Rimmer v Webster* [1902] 2 Ch. 163; see also *Heid v Reliance Finance Corp Pty* (1984) 49 A.L.R. 229, High Court of Australia.

[94] *Perry-Herrick v Atwood* (1857) 2 De G. & J. 21. And see *Abbey National Building Society v Cann* [1991] 1 A.C. 56.

[95] *Capell v Winter* [1907] 2 Ch. 376.

[96] *Rice v Rice* (1853) 2 Drew. 73; cf. *Rimmer v Webster* [1902] 2 Ch. 163. See also *Heid v Reliance Finance Corp Pty* (1984) 49 A.L.R. 229, High Court of Australia.

mortgagee could cause him to be postponed. Generally this consisted of miscon-duct in relation to the title deeds, which has already been discussed.

Priority of mortgages of equitable interests in personalty: *Dearle v Hall*

As between equitable interests, there is a rule that where the equities are equal the **11–33** first in time prevails. However, *Dearle v Hall*[97] established a different approach. which focused on notice and followed similar thinking to that related the pre-1926 principles related to possession or control of title deeds. In *Dearle v Hall,* a person having a beneficial interest in a fund, assigned parts of that interest to D and S respectively for valuable consideration and then, advertising the fund as unencumbered, sold his entire beneficial interest to H. H made enquiries of the trustees and, learning of no prior encumbrance, completed the purchase and gave the trustees notice to pay the dividends of the fund to him. It was held that H gained priority over the prior interests of D and S. Sir Thomas Plumer M.R. relied on *Ryall v Rolle*[98] where it was said that if a person had a right to possession and failed to exercise it, leaving the property in possession of another and thereby enabling him to gain a false and delusive credit, he must take the consequences. This may include loss of priority to a subsequent purchaser who does exercise his right in the appropriate way, that is, by giving notice to the owner of the legal estate or interest in the property. In affirming that decision,[99] Plumer M.R. held that D and S, by neglecting to give the trustees notice of the assignments to them, could not assert the priority arising from the earlier creation of their interests, against H.

Before *Dearle v Hall* there had never been a case in which a prior mortgagee of an equitable interest in personalty had been postponed to a subsequent mortgagee except where there was fraud on the part of the prior mortgagee.[100] Although the rule in *Dearle v Hall* was approved by the House of Lords in *Foster v Cockerell*,[101] the reasons for its adoption were not clearly and consistently expressed and those reasons were subsequently criticised in *Ward v Dun-combe*.[102] The rule itself, however, continued to be accepted and was developed in a series of cases dealing with the nature of notice, the manner in which it was given or received and the effect of the subsequent encumbrancer's knowledge of a prior mortgage. As the rule applied to equitable interests in all forms of personalty, it regulated the priorities of successive mortgages of equitable inter-ests in land, such interests being treated as interests in personalty by virtue of the doctrine of conversion[103] prior to the abolition of that doctrine.[104] It does not

---

[97] (1828) 3 Russ. 1; affirmed on appeal, ibid., at 55. The appeal in the similar case of *Loveridge v Cooper* (1828) 3 Russ. 30, was heard together with that in *Dearle v Hall.*

[98] (1750) 1 Ves.Sen. 348.

[99] *Dearle v Hall* (1828) 3 Russ. 1.

[100] *Cooper v Fynmore* (1828) 3 Russ. 60, per Plumer V.C.

[101] (1835) 3 Cl. and F. 456.

[102] *Ward v Duncombe sub nom. Re Wyatt* [1892] 1 Ch. 188 (CA), at 209; [1893] A.C. 369 at 392, per Lord Macnaghten; *BS Lyle Ltd v Rosher* [1959] 1 W.L.R. 8 (HL).

[103] *Lee v Howlett* (1856) 2 Kay. & J. 531.

[104] Trust of Land and Appointment of Trustees Act 1996, s.3.

apply "until a trust has been created" and this has been held to exclude its application to interests of purchasers under a contract of sale or a lease.[105]

11–34 In *Dearle v Hall*, it was not necessary to consider what would have been the situation if H had known, at any time, of the existing interests of D and S, because he had no such knowledge, either actual or constructive. It was later decided[106] that the subsequent encumbrancer who gave notice first would gain priority provided that, at the time he advanced the money, he had no such knowledge. He was not adversely affected if he later acquired such knowledge and then gave notice, that being the very event which would cause him to give notice.[107]

What amounts to notice?

11–35 Although the rule is expressed in terms of gaining priority by giving notice, it is in fact the receipt of the notice by the trustee or other legal owner, not the giving of notice by the subsequent encumbrancer, that affords priority.[108] Thus, in *Lloyd v Banks*[109] priority was given to the earlier encumbrancer over a later encumbrancer who gave notice when the trustee's knowledge of the earlier encumbrancer had been derived from a newspaper report. Knowledge on which a reasonable man or an ordinary man of business would act in the execution of the trust, would be sufficient. Oral notice would be sufficient provided that it was clear and distinct[110]; however this does not include knowledge imparted in the course of a casual conversation.[111] It does not appear that the decision in *Lloyd v Banks* would apply so as to give a later encumbrancer priority over an earlier encumbrancer who had not given notice.[112] As Megarry puts it, "stronger measures are needed to upset the natural order of the mortgages than are needed to maintain it".[113]

11–36 **"To the legal owner":** It was laid down in *Addison v Cox*[114] that notice, to be effective, must be given to the legal owner of the fund. Notice given to an executor or administrator who renounces probate is therefore ineffective,[115] as is notice given to a trustee before his appointment. In *Ipswich Permanent Money*

---

[105] *Property Discount Corporation Ltd v Lyon Group Ltd* [1981] 1 W.L.R. 300.

[106] *Spencer v Clarke* (1878) 9 Ch.D. 137; *Mutual Life Assurance Society v Langley* (1886) 32 Ch.D. 460; *Re Holmes* (1885) 29 Ch.D. 786. These cases show that the later encumbrancer who gives notice first obtains priority provided he does not know of the earlier encumbrance when he advances the money; his state of knowledge when he gives notice to the trustees is immaterial.

[107] *Wortley v Birkhead* (1754) 2 Ves. Sen. 571.

[108] *Calisher v Forbes* (1871) 7 Ch.App. 109; *Johnstone v Cox* (1881) 19 Ch.D. 17 (CA). See also *Colonial Mutual General Insurance Co Ltd v AWZ Banking Group (New Zealand) Ltd* [1995] 1 W.L.R. 1140.

[109] (1868) 3 Ch. App. 488.

[110] *Browne v Savage* (1859) 4 Drew 635; cf. *Re Worcester* (1868) 3 Ch. App. 555 where a statement of a directors' meeting was held sufficient notice.

[111] *Re Tichener* (1865) 35 Beav. 317.

[112] *Arden v Arden* (1885) 29 Ch.D. 702.

[113] Megarry & Wade, *The Law of Real Property* (7th edn, 2008), para.26–19.

[114] (1872) 8 Ch.App. 76.

[115] *Re Dallas* [1904] 2 Ch. 385.

Club Ltd v Arthy,[116] this was done and held to be effective on the principle of *Lloyd v Banks* but it is thought that the effect would be only to preserve existing priorities rather than to prefer a later encumbrancer to one earlier who had not given notice.

Where the legal owner is a bank, notice is given when, in the ordinary course of business, it would be read. In *Calisher v Forbes*,[117] X left notice with the bank after closing hours, while Y gave notice immediately the bank opened the following day. It was held that the two notices were to be treated as having been received simultaneously, with the result that the charges ranked in order of creation.[118] Had the charges been created simultaneously, A and B would have shared the fund rateably.[119] Notice given to the solicitors of the trustees was held to be effective in *Foster v Cockerell*,[120] but later decisions held that this will be the case only where the solicitors are agents to receive notice on the trustees' behalf.[121]

Funds in court

Where the fund is in court, notice given to the trustees before the fund was paid into court is effective and it is the duty of the trustees to inform the court of such notice.[122] A notice given to the trustees after payment into court is not effective and only a stop order[123] will be effective to regain priority.   **11–37**

Trustees

Where there is more than one trustee, it is advisable to give notice to all, since that notice will continue to be effective even if they all retire or die without communicating the notice to their successors.[124] If notice is given to only one trustee, it will be effective against all encumbrances created during his trusteeship, even after his death or retirement.[125] It will not be effective against an encumbrance created after his trusteeship has come to an end unless he has communicated that notice to at least one of the remaining trustees.[126] The creator   **11–38**

---

[116] [1920] 2 Ch. 257.

[117] (1871) 7 Ch.App. 109.

[118] *Boss v Hopkinson* (1870) 18 W.R. 725. If notices bearing different dates are received on the same day, the notice dated earlier ranks first.

[119] *Re Metropolitan Rail Co, Re Tower Hill Extension Act, Re Rawlins' Estate, Ex p. Kent* (1871) 19 W.R. 596.

[120] (1835) 3 Cl. & Fin. 456.

[121] *Saffron Walden Second Benefit Building Society v Rayner* (1880) 14 Ch.D. 406; *Arden v Arden* (1885) 29 Ch.D. 702 at 709.

[122] *Livesey v Harding* (1856) 23 Beav. 141; *Brearcliffe v Dorrington* (1850) 4 De G. & Sm. 122.

[123] CPR, Sch.1, RSC, Ord. 50.

[124] *Re Wasdale, Brittin v Partridge* [1899] 1 Ch. 163. For the complications which occur when there are two trustees and successive encumbrancers give notice to one only, see Fisher and Lightwood, *The Law of Mortgage* (13th edn, 2010), para.39.17.

[125] *Ward v Duncombe* [1893] A.C. 369 at 394, per Lord MacNaughton.

[126] *Timson v Ramsbottom* (1837) 2 Keen 35; criticised in *Ward v Duncombe* [1893] A.C. 369 and followed in *Re Phillips Trusts* [1903] 1 Ch. 183. Although criticised in *Ward v Duncombe* it was accepted by Lord Herschell in the same case, at 381, as it has been in *Meux v Bell* (1841) 1 Hare 73; *Re Hall* (1880) 7 L.R.Ir. 180; *Re Wyatt, White v Ellis*, [1892] 1 Ch. 188, CA.

of the earlier encumbrance will have to give a fresh notice in order to protect himself.

11–39   If the mortgagor is a trustee, his knowledge does not constitute notice so as to affect priorities. Clearly it would be in his interest to conceal his knowledge from subsequent encumbrancers.[127] Where the mortgagee is a trustee, his knowledge does constitute notice, as it is in his interest to disclose the existence of an existing encumbrance.[128]

At any given time a trustee is entitled to pay out the capital or income of a trust fund to those persons of whose interests he is aware. So, while notice is not essential to the validity of a mortgage[129] (as between the mortgagor and mortgagee), a mortgagee who gives notice to a trustee protects his own interests by so doing. A trustee will be presumed to have knowledge of such interests as would have been revealed to him by inspection of the documents handed over to him.[130]

11–40   A trustee is not liable to a prior assignee of whose interest he is unaware,[131] if he pays out the fund or any part thereof to a subsequent encumbrancer of whom he is aware. He is bound only to pay out to all those of whose existence he knows.[132] If he is a successor trustee, he is not bound to make inquiry of his predecessor as to what notices he received. In *Low v Bouverie*,[133] it was decided that a trustee was under no duty to answer enquiries from a beneficiary or a prospective mortgagee as to the extent to which the property was encumbered. If he was questioned, he was bound only to answer to the best of his knowledge and belief and did not have to make enquiries to ascertain whether or not his existing knowledge was adequate.

The effect of these principles somewhat reduces the value of the rule in *Dearle v Hall*, since a purchaser who received an honest but incorrect reply from a trustee as to the non-existence of prior encumbrances would have no remedy if these existed, unless the trustee was estopped from denying such non-existence. The purchaser's situation has, in this respect, been somewhat improved by the Law of Property Act 1925 s.137(8).

Judgment creditors

11–41   The rule in *Dearle v Hall* does not apply to a judgment creditor[134] or assignee in bankruptcy[135] of an encumbrancer to enable him, by giving notice, to gain a priority which he has lost by failure to do so, since they stand in his shoes and take subject to prior equities.[136] Nor can a volunteer gain priority over earlier

---

[127] *Browne v Savage* (1859) 4 Drew 635 at 641; *Lloyds Bank v Pearson* [1901] 1 Ch. 865.
[128] *Newman v Newman* (1885) 28 Ch.D. 674.
[129] *Burn v Carvalho* (1839) 4 My. & Cr. 690; *Gorringe v Irwell India-Rubber and Gutta-Percha Works* (1886) 34 Ch.D. 128, CA.
[130] *Hallows v Lloyd* (1888) 39 Ch.D. 686.
[131] *Phipps v Lovegrove* (1873) L.R. 16 Eq. 80.
[132] *Hodgson v Hodgson* (1837) 2 Keen 704.
[133] [1891] 3 Ch. 82.
[134] *Scott v Lord Hastings* (1858) 4 K. & J. 633, *United Bank of Kuwait v Sahib* [1997] Ch. 107.
[135] *Re Anderson* [1911] 1 K.B. 896.
[136] *Re Atkinson* (1852) 2 De G. M. & G. 140.

encumbrances by giving notice,[137] although he can protect his priority against later encumbrances by doing so.

Right to tack

It is not altogether clear whether the right to tack applies to mortgages of **11–42** equitable interests in personalty. In *West v Williams*[138] it was held that it did, where the mortgage was expressed to be made to cover further advances. In *Re Weniger's Policy*[139] it was decided that notice of further advances must be given to the trustees if the mortgage did not cover them.

PRIORITY PURSUANT TO THE 1925 LEGISLATION

Mortgages of legal estates in unregistered land[140]

The Law of Property Act 1925 provides, by s.85(1), that a legal mortgage of a **11–43** fee simple can be created only by a demise for a term of years absolute or by a charge by deed expressed to be by way of legal mortgage. Both these methods of creation admit the possibility of successive legal mortgages of a legal estate, in which case a system of priorities based on the superiority of the legal estate is inappropriate.

In the rare pre-1925 cases where successive legal mortgages were created by the grant of successive terms of years, priority would normally have been determined by the order of creation. This exposed a later mortgagee or purchaser who had made all reasonable inquiries to the risk that the mortgagor was fraudulently concealing a prior encumbrance. *Grierson v National Provincial Bank of England Ltd*[141] affords a good example of the difficulties caused by fraudulent concealment. The mortgagor created an equitable mortgage by deposit followed by a legal mortgage by conveyance of the fee simple. The legal mortgagee discovered the existence of the prior equitable mortgagee but did not inform the equitable mortgagee of his own interest. When the equitable mortgage was paid off the deeds were returned to the mortgagor, who negotiated another equitable mortgage by deposit with the bank. Although there was no way in which the bank could have discovered the existence of the concealed legal mortgage, it was held that priority went in order of creation.

Protection by deposit of deeds

Where a mortgage of a legal estate in unregistered land is protected by deposit **11–44** of title deeds, it is not capable of being registered as a land charge. Priorities

---

[137] *Justice v Wynne* (1860) 12 I.Ch.Rep. 289.
[138] [1899] 1 Ch. 132.
[139] [1910] 2 Ch. 291.
[140] A mortgage of unregistered land triggers a requirement for compulsory registration of the underlying legal estate: LRA 2002 s.4.
[141] [1913] 2 Ch. 18. See above, para.11–21.

between such mortgages are regulated by the pre-1926 rules. It appears that a "protected" mortgage is one which was originally protected, rather than one which has been continuously protected.[142] In light of the Law of Property (Miscellaneous Provisions) Act 1989,[143] mortgages by deposit of deeds will no longer confer any security.

Protection by registration

11–44   Mortgages which are not protected by a deposit of title deeds and were created after 1925 are registrable as land charges. They are of two types: "puisne mortgages" and general equitable charges. The Land Charges Act 1972 s.2(4) defines these as follows. A puisne mortgage is a legal mortgage not protected by a deposit of documents relating to the legal estate affected. A general equitable charge is any equitable charge on land which:

> (1) is not included in any other class of land charge; and
> (2) is not secured by a deposit of documents relating to the legal estate affected; and
> (3) does not arise, or affect any interest arising, under a trust of land or a settlement.

11–45   Failure to register: The Land Charges Act 1972 s.4(5) deals with the effect of the failure to register such charges and states as follows:

> "A land charge of class B and a land charge of class C (other than an estate contract) created or arising on or after 1st January 1926 shall be void as against a purchaser of the land charged with it, or of any interest in such land, unless the land charge is registered in the appropriate register before the completion of the purchase."

The other provisions relevant to priorities between unprotected mortgages are s.13 of the Law of Property Act 1925 which notes that:

> "This Act shall not prejudicially affect the right or interest of any person arising out of or consequent on the possession by him of any documents relating to a legal estate in land, nor affect any question arising out of or consequent upon any omission to obtain or any other absence of possession by any person of any documents relating to a legal estate in land."

Additionally s.97 of the Law of Property Act 1925 (as amended by s.18(1) and Sch.3 para.1 of the Land Charges Act 1972) reads:

> "Every mortgage affecting a legal estate in land made after the commencement of this Act, whether legal or equitable (not being a mortgage protected by the deposit of documents relating to the legal estate affected) shall rank according to the date of registration as a land charge pursuant to the Land Charges Act 1972."

11–46   Effect of the statutory provisions: Priorities between unprotected mortgages are regulated by the above provisions, and three possibilities exist:

---

[142] Megarry and Wade, *The Law of Real Property* (7th edn, 2008), paras 26–006, 26–010.
[143] s.2; *United Bank of Kuwait v Sahib* [1997] Ch. 107; [1996] 3 W.L.R. 372.

(1) If the first mortgage is registered before the second is made, then the first has priority over the second even if the first is equitable and the second is legal. By s.198(1) of the Law of Property Act 1925, registration under the Land Charges Acts of any instrument or matter required or authorised to be registered under the Act is deemed to constitute actual notice of the interest registered to all persons and for all purposes connected with the land affected, as from the date of registration or other prescribed date, so long as the registration continues to be in force. This prevents the subsequent legal mortgagee from claiming to be a purchaser without notice of the prior equitable interest.

(2) If the first mortgage is made but remains unregistered, it will be void, by reason of s.4(5) of the Land Charges Act 1972, against a later mortgagee. This is so regardless of the legal or equitable character of the two mortgages.

(3) In both of the above cases, the same conclusions are reached regarding priorities regardless of whether s.4(5) of the Land Charges Act 1972, or s.97 of the Law of Property Act 1925 is applied.

Consider, however, the following sequence of events: **11–47**

(a) L mortgages Blackacre to A;
(b) L mortgages Blackacre to B;
(c) A registers;
(d) B registers.

The effect of s.4(5) of the Land Charges Act 1972 would be to make A's mortgage void against B; thus the order of priority places B's mortgage ahead of A's. On the other hand, s.97 of the Law of Property Act 1925 provides for priority to run according to order of registration, in which case the order is reversed accordingly. Earlier commentators disagree as to which of these two solutions is to be adopted and there is no settled judicial decision on the point.[144]

The arguments advanced in favour of the first view are as follows:

(a) If A's mortgage is void against B, it has no existence with respect to B and thus it is difficult to see how its subsequent registration can adversely affect B.

(b) Section 97 of the Law of Property Act 1925 refers not simply to registration, but to registration as "a land charge pursuant to the Land Charges Act." It is thus possible to interpret s.97 of the Law of Property Act 1925 as incorporating by reference the rule in s.4(5) of the Land Charges Act 1972, in which case no conflict arises.

---

[144] The problem was considered by Megarry ((1940) 7 C.L.J. 243) who, while stating that the subject is not one for dogmatism, comes down in favour of the first solution which is also adopted by Waldock, *Mortgages* (2nd edn, 1950), pp.410 et seq. and by Fisher and Lightwood, *The Law of Mortgage* (13th edn, 2010), para.35.13.

(c) In relation to each of the five registers set up by the Land Charges Act 1972, it is provided that in respect of each type of encumbrance, failure to register will make it void against a subsequent purchaser. It is thought improbable that s.97 of the Law of Property Act 1925 was intended to destroy the symmetry of the scheme, and therefore established a different rule for land charges.

(d) In the same way that, of two irreconcilable provisions in one Act, the later prevails, the provisions of the Land Charges Act 1925, the later statute, should prevail over those of the Law of Property Act 1925 where the provisions appear to create an irreconcilable conflict.

However, the arguments against this can be summarised as follows:

(a) The simple reading of s.97 of the Law of Property Act 1925, is that the first mortgage to be registered has priority.[145]

(b) The general opinion appears to be that priority will depend on the date of registration as mentioned in s.97, because that section deals expressly with priority of mortgages, whereas the Land Charges Act 1972 s.4(5) deals with the avoidance of charges as against purchasers, and mortgagees are only brought in by reference to the Land Charges Act 1972 s.17(1).[146]

11–48 It is submitted that the most practical and elegant solution is found by adopting solution (b) above, according to which argument the two statutes do not conflict, thus avoiding the unlikely conclusion that Parliament simultaneously enacted contradictory statutes, one expressly referring to the other.[147]

Insoluble problems involving three or more registrable mortgages have been discussed by the courts[148]; in practice the solution to these problems has been found by resorting to the doctrine of subrogation. However, this solution is totally arbitrary, since there is no reason for breaking into the circle in which the priorities run at one place rather than another—whatever is done, one creditor will lose a priority which he arguably has over another. It appears that the judicially favoured approach would be to take the mortgages in order of creation and begin by subrogating the latest mortgages to the earliest.[149]

No such difficulties arise where one mortgage is protected and the other is not. If only the first mortgage is protected, its priority runs from the date of its creation and it will have priority over the second, subject to the rules, discussed earlier, regarding loss of priority due to fraud or gross negligence. If only the second mortgage is protected, one of two situations can arise. Where the first mortgage is registered before the second is created, its priority ranks from the date of the registration by virtue of s.97 of the Law of Property Act 1925. Where

---

[145] Hargreaves, (1950) 13 M.L.R. 534 and Megarry and Wade, *The Law of Real Property* (7th edn, 2008), para.26–28, both regard the argument for this interpretation as unconvincing.

[146] *Emmet & Farrand on Title* (looseleaf), para.25.207.

[147] See Megarry and Wade, *The Law of Real Property* (7th edn, 2008), para.26–028.

[148] ibid.; (1968) Conv.(N.S.) pp.325 et seq. (W.A. Lee).

[149] Megarry and Wade, *The Law of Real Property* (7th edn, 2008), paras 26–28 and 26–03; (1961) 71 Yale L.J. 53 (G. Gilmore).

it is not, it is void against the second mortgage for want of registration. The second mortgage takes priority from the date of its creation and therefore ranks first even if the first mortgage is subsequently registered.

Liens[150]

Prior to April 3, 1995, it was possible to create a lien over registered land by depositing the land certificate with a mortgagee.[151] Such a lien operated as a contract to create a charge,[152] but following the enactment of s.2 of the Law of Property (Miscellaneous Provisions) Act 1989, such a contract would only have been valid if it was made in writing and in compliance with provisions of that section.[153] Accordingly, r.239 of the Land Registration Rules 1925 was amended,[154] in order that it was no longer possible to protect a lien by notice of deposit or intended deposit of the land certificate as was previously the case. An entry which existed on the register before April 3, 1995, operated as a caution until it was cancelled.[155] Under the Land Registration Act 2002, a lien created in accordance with the 1989 Act may be protected against subsequent dealings by the entry of a notice in the charges register of the title affected.[156]

11–49

Mortgages of equitable interests

Priorities among mortgages of equitable interests in land arising under a trust, are regulated by the rule in *Dearle v Hall* as amended by ss.137 and 138 of the Law of Property Act 1925 (as further amended by the Trusts of Land and Appointment of Trustees Act 1996).[157] According to that rule, priority depends on the order in which notice of the mortgages is received by the trustees. By s.137(10), the rule does not apply until a trust has been created. It is considered that this provision excludes the interest of a purchaser under a contract of sale or lease.[158] Section 137(3) provides that the notice must be in writing, whereas under the original rule oral notice was sufficient.[159]

Section 137(2) specifies the persons to whom notice must be given, namely; the trustees of the settlement if the interest is in settled land; the trustees of the trust of land if the interest arises under such trust; and, in any other cases, the

11–50

---

[150] See above, paras 1–16 et seq.

[151] LRA1925 s.66; *Thames Guaranty Ltd v Campbell* [1985] Q.B. 210 at 232.

[152] *Thames Guaranty Ltd,* above; *Re Alton Corporation* [1985] B.C.L.C. 27 at 33.

[153] *United Bank of Kuwait v Sahib* [1987] Ch. 107.

[154] And rr.240–243 revoked by Land Registration Rules 1995, SI 1995/140 r.4(1), 4(4).

[155] Land Registration Rules1925 r.239(1) (as amended by Land Registration Rules 1995 SI 1995/140, r.4).

[156] LRA 2002 ss.32–34.

[157] LRA 1925 s.102(2) formerly made provisions for priorities between certain dealings of equitable interests in registered land to be determined in accordance with the lodging of priority cautions and inhibitions in the Minor Interests Index. This subs. has now been repealed by the LRA 1986 s.5(1). Consequently, s.137(1) now determines questions of priority both in respect of registered and unregistered land. For the way in which existing entries are to be treated, see 1986 Act, s.5(2)–(4) and LRA 2002 Sch.12 paras 1, 2 and 3.

[158] Megarry and Wade, *The Law of Real Property* (7th edn, 2008), para.26–40 and *Property Discount Corp Ltd v Lyon Group Ltd* [1981] 1 W.L.R. 300.

[159] *Browne v Savage* (1859) 4 Drew 635; *Re Worcester* (1868) 3 Ch. App. 555.

estate owner (i.e. the owner of the legal estate) of the land affected. Under the old law it was advisable to give notice to all the trustees[160] and the 1925 legislation does not alter this position.

Section 137(4) sets out the procedure to be adopted where the valid notice cannot be served, either because there are no trustees, or because its service would involve unreasonable costs or delay. The purchaser may require the endorsement of a memorandum on the instrument creating the trust, or (where the trust is created by statute or operation of law) on the document under which the equitable interest is acquired or which evidences its devolution. Such an endorsement has the same effect as serving a notice on the trustees.

11–51   By s.138 of the Law of Property Act 1925, a trust corporation may be nominated to receive the notice. Where this is the case, notice to the trustees is ineffective. Notice does not affect priorities until it is delivered to the corporation.

The Law of Property Act 1925 s.137(8), (9), brings about a change in the law relating to the duty to produce notices. In the case of *Low v Bouverie*[161] it was held that trustees were not bound to answer inquiries by a prospective mortgagee or a beneficiary regarding the extent to which a beneficiary's share was encumbered. By s.137(8) any person interested in the equitable interest may require the trustee to produce all such notices. Section 137(9) places a corresponding liability on the estate owner.

PRIORITY BETWEEN MORTGAGEE AND BENEFICIAL OWNER

11–52   Disputes between mortgagees and beneficial owners who claim not be bound by the mortgage are frequent. Even when the alleged beneficial owner establishes their interest, they have to also establish that the mortgagee takes subject to it and the primary mechanism for achieving that position is to establish that the beneficial interest is an overriding interest. The statutory provisions relating to overriding interests changed following the enactment of the Land Registration Act 2002. However, understanding the pre-2002 Act position is helpful and those provisions remain relevant in some cases even now.[162]

Decision in *William & Glyn's Bank v Boland*

11–53   In the case of *Williams and Glyn's Bank v Boland*,[163] the husband was registered as sole proprietor of the matrimonial home in which he and his wife lived, and towards the purchase of which she had contributed substantially. She had not

---

[160] *Lloyds Bank v Pearson* [1901] 1 Ch. 865; *Timson v Ramsbottom* (1837) 2 Keen 35; *Re Wasdale, Brittin v Partridge* [1899] 1 Ch. 163; *Ward v Duncombe* [1892] 1 Ch. 188 (CA).

[161] [1891] 3 Ch. 82 at 99; *Woodhouse AC Israel Cocoa SA v Nigerian Produce Marketing Co Ltd* [1972] A.C. 741 (HL).

[162] *HSBC Bank Plc v Dyche* [2009] EWHC 2954 (Ch); [2010] 2 P & CR 4.

[163] [1981] A.C. 487, varying the decision of the Court of Appeal at [1979] Ch. 312, which allowed the appeal of Mr and Mrs Boland against the decision of Templeman J. at (1978) P. & C.R. 448. This appeal was heard together with *Williams and Glyn's Bank v Brown* in which at first instance H.H. Judge Clapham applied Templeman J.'s decision, making an order for possession in favour of the Bank.

protected the equitable interest thus acquired by any entry on the register. The husband, without her consent, mortgaged the house to the bank to secure his business indebtedness and the bank made no inquiries of her. The question considered by the court was whether that equitable interest constituted an over-riding interest by which the mortgagee bank was bound.

Section 70(1)(g) of the Land Registration Act 1925 (now repealed) provided that the class of overriding interests included: **11–54**

> "The rights of every person in actual occupation of the land or in receipt of the rents and profits thereof, save where enquiry is made of such person and the rights are not disclosed . . . "

Lord Wilberforce found no difficulty in concluding that a spouse, living in a house, had an actual occupation which is capable of conferring protection upon his or her rights as an overriding interest.[164] In so concluding, he rejected arguments that to come within the section, the occupation must have been inconsistent with the rights of the vendor.[165] He then went on to consider whether such equitable interests were "minor interests" as defined by s.3(xv) of the Land Registration Act 1925. Although holding that the interests of co-owners under statutory trusts[166] are minor interests, he considered that any such interests, if protected by actual occupation, acquired the status of an overriding interest, being, as s.70 of the Land Registration Act 1925 required, interests subsisting in reference to land.[167]

Effect of *Boland*

This decision, as Lord Wilberforce recognised, had important consequences for conveyancers, which he formulated in these words: **11–55**

> "What is involved is a departure from an easy-going practice of dispensing with enquiries as to occupation beyond that of the vendor and accepting the risks of doing so. To substitute for this a practice of more careful enquiry as to the facts of occupation, and, if necessary, as to the rights of occupiers can not, in my view of the matter, be considered as unacceptable except at the price of overlooking the wide-spread development of shared interest in ownership."[168]

The Law Commission considered that the law in this field had been left in a most unsatisfactory state.[169] Their subsequent report made three recommendations.   **11–56**

---

[164] ibid., at 506. A person in actual occupation of part of land comprised in a registered disposition could enforce against the new registered proprietor any overriding interest which he had either in the land or part of the land occupied by him or in the remainder of the land comprised in the disposition in question. See *Ferrishurst Ltd v Wallcite Ltd* [1999] Ch. 355. This position no longer prevails under the Land Registration Act 2002.

[165] Disapproving *Caunce v Caunce* [1969] 1 W.L.R. 286 and *Bird v Syme-Thompson* [1979] 1 W.L.R. 440 at 444, and approving *Hodgson v Marks* [1971] Ch. 892 at 934 (CA) per Russell L.J.

[166] Defined in LPA 1925 s.35.

[167] *Elias v Mitchell* [1972] Ch. 652, cf. *Cedar Holdings Ltd v Green* [1981] Ch. 129; for cases in which it was held that equitable interests other than those of tenants in common could be overriding interests if protected by actual occupation, see *Bridges v Mees* [1957] Ch. 475; *Hodgson v Marks* [1971] Ch. 892 (CA).

[168] [1981] A.C. 487 at 508, 509.

[169] Law Commission Report No.115, Cmnd. 8636 (1982), at paras 2.52–2.54, *The Implications of Williams and Glyn's Bank v Boland*.

One dealt with overcoming the conveyancing problems faced by purchasers and mortgagees,[170] and the others for protecting and establishing the interests of married co-owners in the matrimonial home.[171] To date, this report has not been acted upon. Indeed, Sch.3 to the Land Registration Act 2002 preserves the status of overriding interest (now defined under this Act as "unregistered interests which override registered dispositions") for most interests of persons in actual occupation, subject to some modifications. Under that statutory scheme, which replaces the provisions considered in *Boland*, an overriding interest cannot include an interest under the Settled Land Act 1925 or a leasehold estate in land taking effect more than three months after grant which have not taken effect by the date of the disposition.

Enquiries to be made

11–57   A problem which soon became apparent following *Boland* was that no guidance had been given as to the extent and nature of the inquiries which would be necessary in order to ascertain the existence of persons in occupation and their equitable rights. In *Malory Enterprise Ltd v Cheshire Homes (UK) Ltd*,[172] the court concluded that the test was whether the occupation was sufficient to put a person inspecting on notice that there was a person in occupation. It follows that an actual inspection is contemplated, but not one that involves in-depth scrutiny of everything present.

11–58   At various points, criticism was made of the fact that s.70(1)(g) did not limit the scope of such inquiries by reference to any concept of "reasonable inquiry".[173] The section did not specify who must make the inquiry, although it was subsequently accepted that in most cases this could properly be done by the solicitor acting for the purchaser,[174] nor did it specify when inquiry or disclosure ought to be made. It was clear, however, that the inquiry must be made of the person whose rights would otherwise amount to an overriding interest.[175]

The difficulties facing a purchaser in making adequate inquiries have been discussed extensively.[176] In unregistered conveyancing, it had been decided in *Caunce v Caunce*[177] that notice of the presence of the wife in the matrimonial

---

[170] That co-ownership interests in land should be registrable at HM Land Registry and should be protected against purchasers and mortgagees if, and only if, they were so registered.

[171] That: (i) the interest of every married co-owner in the matrimonial home should carry with it a right to prevent any dealing being made without that co-owner's consent or a court order; and (ii) as a general rule married couples should, in the absence of agreement to the contrary, have an equal ownership of the matrimonial home.

[172] [2002] EWCA Civ 151; [2002] Ch. 216.

[173] Law Com. Report No.158, H.C. 267 (1987), para.2.59 and para.2.57, the Report recommended that all categories of overriding interest be made explicitly subject to the jurisdiction of the courts to postpone them in favour of subsequent purchasers and lenders on general grounds of fraud or estoppel.

[174] *Winkworth v Edward Baron Development Co Ltd* [1986] 1 W.L.R. 1512.

[175] *Hodgson v Marks* [1971] Ch. 892; *Kling v Keston Properties* (1985) 49 P. & C.R. 212 at 220.

[176] (1979) 95 L.Q.R. 501 (R.J. Smith); [1980] Conv. 85, 311 and 318; [1980] Conv. 361 (J. Martin); *Kling v Keston Properties*, above, at 222; (1986) 136 New L.J. 771 (P. Luxton); *Kingsnorth Finance Co v Tizard* [1986] 1 W.L.R. 783; K. Gray, *Elements of Land Law* (5th edn, 2009), paras 8.2.76–8.2.77; *Emmet & Farrand on Title* (loose-leaf), paras 5.137–5.138.

[177] [1969] 1 W.L.R. 286.

home was not, of itself, notice of any interest that she might have. That decision came under judicial attack[178] and was not followed in *Kingsnorth Trust Ltd v Tizard*.[179] In that case it was held that the mortgagee had not made such inquiries as ought reasonably to have been undertaken and was therefore fixed with constructive notice of the wife's interest.[180] It was held that two facts in particular fixed Kingsnorth with constructive notice of the wife's interest. First, T's informing the surveyor that he was married but separated from his wife, who lived nearby, although he had described himself as single on the application form. Second, the evidence of occupation by teenage children. In addition, however, the judge took the view that, in the circumstances, the pre-arranged inspection was not within the category of "such . . . inspections . . . as ought reasonably to have been made."[181]

After the decision in *Boland*, institutional mortgagees in many cases sought to protect themselves against the rights of occupiers by requiring them to sign forms of acknowledgement, consent or waiver. This device was, for a number of reasons, less effective than mortgagees would have wished. In the first place, it was inadequate to give protection against the rights of an equitable co-owner who was in constructive occupation.[182] Next, some persons may not be capable of giving a valid consent to the release of their rights.[183] Most importantly, however, an occupier who gives such a consent may seek to claim that the consent was vitiated by duress or undue influence.[184]

Two subsequent decisions[185] have gone some way to restricting the effect of **11–59** *Boland*, in that where it is established that a person who subsequently seeks to assert an overriding interest, knew that the registered proprietor was acquiring the property with the assistance of a mortgage, an intention has been imputed to that person to the effect that their overriding interest should be postponed to the prior interest of the mortgagee.

Further, in *Equity & Law Loans v Prestidge*[186] the intention imputed to the second defendant (O) who sought to assert her prior beneficial interest was held to be the same with regard to a second mortgage (of which O was genuinely ignorant) which redeemed and replaced the first mortgage (of which O was aware) on no less favourable terms. The court held that the charge in favour of the second mortgage enjoyed priority to O's interest, up to the amount for which consent was to be imputed to her in relation to the first mortgage.

---

[178] *Williams and Glyn's Bank v Boland* [1981] A.C. 487 at 505–506.

[179] [1986] 1 W.L.R. 783.

[180] LPA 1925 s.199(1)(ii)(a) and s.205(1)(xxi) ("purchaser" includes "mortgagee").

[181] [1986] 1 W.L.R. 783 at 795.

[182] See *Strand Securities v Caswell* [1965] Ch. 958 (CA), for discussion of what constitutes occupation for the purposes of LRA 1925 s.70(1)(g).

[183] The Law Commission recognised this, referring in its Report No.115, Cmnd. 8636 (1982) at para.42(1)(b) to patients and minors.

[184] See paras 31–16 et seq. and para.31–29.

[185] *Bristol and West Building Society v Henning* [1985] 1 W.L.R. 783 (which did not expressly consider *Boland*, above); *Paddington Building Society v Mendlesohn* [1985] 1 W.L.R. 778 (which did).

[186] [1992] 1 W.L.R. 137 in which *Bristol and West Building Society v Henning*, above, was followed.

Thus, *Boland* will not unduly concern banks or building societies on purchase transactions in such circumstances since there can be few cases in which the equitable co-owner of a property will be unaware that the acquisition is being financed at least in part by way of mortgage.

Land Registration Act 2002

11–60   The successor to s.70(1)(g) of the Land Registration Act 1925, being para.2 of Sch.3 to the Land Registration Act 2002,[187] retained the essential protection given for those in occupation whose rights were not protected on the register and dealt with most of other criticisms made but not all. It provides that unregistered interests which override registered dispositions include:

> " . . .

>> (2) An interest belonging, at the time of the disposition, to a person in actual occupation, so far as relating to land of which he is in actual occupation,[188] except for—

>>> (a) an interest under a settlement made by virtue of the Settled Land Act 1925;
>>> (b) an interest of a person of whom inquiry was made before the disposition and who failed to disclose the right when he could reasonably have been expected to do so;
>>> (c) an interest—

>>>> (i) which belongs to a person whose occupation would not have been obvious on a reasonably careful inspection of the land at the time of the disposition, and
>>>> (ii) of which the person to whom the disposition is made does not have actual knowledge at that time;

>>> (d) a leasehold estate in land granted to take effect in possession after the end of the period of three months beginning with the date of the grant and which has not taken effect in possession at the time of the disposition."

The exact terms of the statutory provisions should be noted. Accordingly it is a pre-requisite to reliance on an inquiry that the inquiry is made of the person with the interest. Further reliance on an inspection depends on carrying out a "reasonably careful inspection".

By virtue of transitional provisions within para.8 of Sch.12 to the Land Registration Act 2002, the overriding status of certain pre-existing former overriding interests under s.70(1)(g) of the Land Registration Act 1925 is preserved.

Time at which the interest is to be determined

11–61   In *Abbey National Building Society v Cann*,[189] the House of Lords made clear that the relevant date for determining the existence of overriding interests

---

[187] The successor provision to LRA 2002 s.70(1)(g).

[188] Thus potentially limiting the effect of the rights established to land actually occupied if and to the extent it differs from the scope of the registered title.

[189] [1991] 1 A.C. 56 (HL).

affecting the estate transferred or created was the date of registration of the estate, and not the date of transfer or creation of that estate. However, in order to successfully claim an overriding interest against a transferee or chargee of by virtue of s.70(1)(g), the person claiming that interest had to have been in occupation at the time of the creation or transfer of the legal estate. The argument that a *scintilla temporis* could somehow arise in a conveyancing transaction, thereby allowing an individual in possession prior to the registration of a charge to acquire an overriding interest which would bind the mortgagee, was emphatically rejected.

In *Lloyds Bank Ltd v Rossett*[190] the House of Lords confirmed that, where a wife claimed that she had a beneficial interest in a house registered in her husband's sole name, and that her interest had priority over the rights of the mortgagee under a legal charge executed without her knowledge, then in order to claim the protection afforded to overriding interests by s.70(1)(g) the wife must have been in actual occupation of the house when the relevant estate was transferred or created, not the date when it was registered. In *Chhokar v Chhokar and Parmar*,[191] the purchaser, who had bought the house at an undervalued price, attempted to prevent the wife (who had contributed to the purchase price) acquiring an overriding interest by her occupation. However, the court held that the purchaser nevertheless took subject to that interest because the wife was in actual occupation at the time when registration of the purchaser's title was sought. While it is clear that in the case of a first registration of title it is the date of registration which is decisive,[192] there appears to be no firm rule in the case of a transfer of an existing registered title under the Land Registration Act 1925.

For the purpose of the Land Registration Act 2002 para.2 of Sch.3 to the Land Registration Act 2002 defines overriding interests as "an interest belonging at the time of the disposition to a person in actual occupation". It then goes on to refer to inquiries made before the disposition and reasonably careful inspection at the time of the disposition. In *Thompson v Foy*[193] Lewison J. commented obiter upon the meaning of those words in the context of a potential overriding interest. He concluded that the wording of Sch.3 clearly pointed to the need for actual occupation, with the inspection treated as being at the point in time the disposition between the parties took place (i.e. completion by execution of documentation and the provision of money). He also gave some support for the suggestion that it was necessary for actual occupation at the date of registration as well. It should also be noted that he pointed to the need to consider where the interest claimed relates to only part of the registered estate, whether the actual occupation related to that same part. **11–62**

[190] [1991] 1 A.C. 107 (HL).
[191] [1984] F.L.R. 313; (1984) 14 Fam.Law 269 (CA).
[192] *Re Boyle's Claim* [1961] 1 W.L.R. 339. For discussion of what is actually decided by this case; Megarry and Wade, *Law of Real Property* (7th edn, 2008) para.7–096. So far as the proposition in the text is concerned, the case has been followed in *Schwab and Co v McCarthy* (1975) 31 P. & C.R. 196 at 204 and *Kling v Keston Properties* (1985) 49 P. & C.R. 212 at 218.
[193] [2009] EWHC 1076 (Ch); [2010] 1 P&CR 16.

Overreaching of interests

11–63 It was not necessary to consider in *Boland* whether the interests of the beneficial owners were overreached, as the mortgage money was paid to a sole registered proprietor. In that case, Lord Wilberforce said:

> "Undivided shares in land can only take effect in equity behind a trust for sale upon which the legal owner is to hold the land. Dispositions of the land, including mortgages, may be made under this trust and, provided there are at least two trustees or a trust corporation, 'overreach' the trusts. This means the 'purchaser' takes free from them whether or not he has notice of them, and the trusts are enforceable against the proceeds of sale." [194]

This is to be contrasted with the position in *City of London Building Society v Flegg*. [195]

City of London Building Society v Flegg

11–64 The question of overreaching interests did arise in *City of London Building Society v Flegg*. The registered proprietors of Bleak House were a Mr and Mrs Maxwell-Brown, the daughter and son-in-law of Mr and Mrs Flegg, who had contributed over half of the purchase price, having sold their own home in order to do so and with the intention that all four should live together. The Maxwell-Browns raised their contribution by means of a mortgage and later, without the knowledge or consent of the Fleggs, executed three more charges, the third being for the purpose of discharging all the earlier charges. The Fleggs had been in occupation throughout and no inquiries had ever been made of them as to whether they claimed any interest in the property. The Maxwell-Browns defaulted on the mortgage repayments and the mortgagee sought possession. The House of Lords overturned a much-criticised Court of Appeal decision and held that the Fleggs' interests under the trust for sale were overreached. Lord Templeman [196] considered that this was brought about by ss.27 and 28 [197] of the Law of Property Act 1925, while Lord Oliver's more extensive analysis also referred to ss.2 and 26 of the same Act. [198] Although the decision of the House of Lords was welcomed, [199] the basis of it has since been questioned. [200] Even so, it is quite clear that the equitable interest of a beneficiary under a trust of land may be overreached if the mortgage is granted by not less than two trustees of that trust (or by a trust corporation) and the capital moneys are paid to them. [201] Thus, from the mortgagee's point of view, fail-safe practice dictates a refusal to deal with a sole

---

[194] [1981] A.C. 487 at 503.
[195] [1986] Ch. 605 (CA); reversed [1988] A.C. 54, restoring the decision of the judge at first instance.
[196] [1988] A.C. 54 at 71–72.
[197] s.28 now repealed by Trusts of Land and Appointment of Trustees Act 1996 Sch.4. See ibid., s.6 for powers of trustees of land.
[198] ibid., at 80–81, 83, 90–91.
[199] See, e.g. *Emmet & Farrand on Title* (looseleaf) para.11.088.
[200] [1987] Conv. 451 (W.J. Swadling); [1988] Conv. 141 (P. Sparkes); [1980] Conv. 313 (draft Editorial Practice Note) entitled "Occupational Hazards."
[201] Reinforced in *Lloyds Bank v Carrick* [1996] 4 All E.R. 680 (CA).

proprietor (unless a trust corporation) and the appointment of a second trustee, with all mortgage monies being paid to both. Such caution however rarely manifests itself in practice.

However, it should also be noted that even where two trustees grant or transfer and interest to one of themselves and receive payment from that person, albeit in a difference capacity any pre-existing interest will not be overreached.[202] Transactions involving a transfer from two legal owners to one of themselves are common (particularly in the context for divorce and other forms of family breakdown) and accordingly caution should be exercised as it cannot be assume any underlying beneficial interest has been overreached.

Restrictions and overreaching

Section 42(1)(b) of the Land Registration Act 2002 allows beneficiaries to enter **11–65** a restriction on the proprietorship register, effectively requiring over-reaching steps to be taken on sale of a property which is held on trust, before the purchaser can be registered as the new proprietor. The relevant form of standard restriction is Form A of Sch.4 to the Land Registration Rules 2003.

PRIORITY BETWEEN MORTGAGEE AND TENANT

The position of tenants is considered at various points elsewhere in this work. In **11–66** particular, see Chapters 26, 27 and 32 and paras 26–13, 27–11 and 32–03 to 32–11.

TACKING

Tacking has been described as a special way of obtaining priority for a secured **11–67** loan by amalgamating it with another secured loan of higher priority.[203] Before 1926 there were two forms of tacking, of which one was abolished by the 1925 legislation,[204] and the law relating to the other was amended. The Law of Property Act 1925 provided a statutory code for tacking that related to unregistered land and provided for three methods of tacking. However, tacking in connection with charges registered pursuant to the Land Registration Act 1925 depended on the common law, subject to only the minor statutory intervention. As a result of the Land Registration Act 2002 there is now a complete statutory code for registered land. That code provides for four methods of tacking, three of which largely coincide with those under the 1925 Act. An understanding of the system for unregistered land will assist in understanding how the 2002 Act is likely to be approached by the courts.

---

[202] *HSBC Bank Plc v Dyche* [2010] 2 P. & C.R. 4.
[203] Megarry and Wade, *The Law of Real Property* (7th edn, 2008), para.26–050.
[204] "Tabula in naufragio"—a plank in a shipwreck.

Registered land

An advance in the absence of notice of a subsequent charge

11–68 Prior to the 2002 Act, a first mortgagee could make a further advance secured by his first legal charge unless he had notice of a subsequent charge. As a consequence it became established practice for lenders taking subsequent charges over property, to notify all prior lenders of their new charge. That practice has been given statutory effect so that a proprietor of a registered charge against a registered estate may make further advances secured by his registered charge, unless and until a subsequent chargee provides him with notice of a subsequent charge.[205] Until such notice is received, in accordance with the applicable rules, all advances rank in priority to the subsequent chargee's advances.

The Land Registration Rules 2003 do not provide for a prescribed form of notice, but they do provide for the date on which the notice having been served in particular ways (which reflect common means of service in CPR r.6.3) ought to have been received.[206] Provision is made for service by post, document exchange (DX), fax and email. The postal address to be used to take the benefit of those provisions is, unsurprisingly, the prior chargee's address as shown in the Register. Although there is no prohibition on any particular means of sending notice, only those methods detailed in the Rules have the benefit of a provision which in effect deems service providing the subsequent chargee with certainty.

A further advance pursuant to an obligation

11–69 Where a prior chargee makes a further advance pursuant to an obligation to do so, and at the time the subsequent charge was created the obligation was entered in the register in accordance with the Land Registration Rules 2003, the further advance will have priority over the subsequent charge.[207] The 2003 Rules provide for three means by which the application for an obligation to make a further advance to be shown on the register may be made.[208] Where such an application is made, the Registrar must make an entry on the register in such terms as he considers appropriate.

Agreement to a maximum amount

11–70 Where the parties to a prior charge, the prior chargee and borrower, had agreed a maximum amount that the charge would secure and that agreement was entered on the register, in accordance with the 2003 Rules, at the time the subsequent charge was created, then further advances by the prior chargee up to the maximum amount will have priority as against the subsequent chargee.[209] The 2003

---

[205] LRA 2002 s.49(1).
[206] Land Registration Rules 2003 r.107.
[207] LRA 2002 s.49(3).
[208] Land Registration Rules 2003 r.108.
[209] LRA 2002 s.49(4). It should be noted that the wording of the subsection is not explicit about limiting the further advance to a sum up to the agreed maximum.

Rules provide for three means by which the application for an obligation to make a further advance to be shown on the register may be made.[210] Where such an application is made the Registrar must make an entry on the register in such terms as he considers appropriate. Where such an entry is made and the parties to the prior charge agree a new maximum amount, a further entry may be made on the register and would be operative as against subsequent chargees whose charges were created after the date of the further entry in the register.

There is power under the 2002 Act to disapply this method of tacking, or to provide for specific conditions to apply to particular types of charge simply by the making of rules to that effect.[211] As yet no such rules have been made.

Further advance by agreement

The 2002 Act preserves the ability to tack where a subsequent chargee agrees a prior chargee's further advance can take priority.[212] Any such agreement must be entered on the register in the manner provided for by the 2003 Rules.[213] Such agreements are characterised in the Rules as an alteration of priority. An application to record such an agreement must be made by or with the consent of any proprietor of a registered charge whose priority will be adversely affected. A conveyancer's certificate that the necessary consents are held may be accepted by the registrar.   **11–71**

Unregistered land

The law as to tacking affecting unregistered land is now set out in s.94 of the Law of Property Act 1925. There are three methods of tacking available. Those methods largely overlap with those now available for registered land, save that the agreed maximum advance is not available for unregistered land. Section 94 reads: **11–72**

> "(1) After the commencement of this Act, a prior mortgagee shall have a right to make further advances to rank in priority to subsequent mortgages (whether legal or equitable)—
>
> (a) if an arrangement has been made to that effect with the subsequent mortgagees; or
>
> (b) if he had no notice of such subsequent mortgages at the time when the further advance was made by him; or
>
> (c) whether or not he had such notice as aforesaid, where the mortgage imposes an obligation on him to make such further advances.
>
> This subsection applies whether or not the prior mortgage was made expressly for securing further advances.
>
> (2) In relation to the making of further advances after the commencement of this Act a mortgagee shall not be deemed to have notice of a mortgage merely by reason that it was registered as a land charge[214] if it was not so registered at the time when

---

[210] Land Registration Rules 2003 r.109.
[211] LRA 2002 s.49(5).
[212] LRA 2002 s.49(6).
[213] Land Registration Rules 2003 r.102.
[214] Repealed by LPA 1969 s.16(2), Sch.2 Pt 1.

the original mortgage was created or when the last search (if any) by or on behalf of the mortgagee was made, whichever last happened.

This subsection only applies where the prior mortgage was made expressly for securing a current account or other further advances.

(3) Save in regard to the making of further advances as aforesaid, the right to tack is hereby abolished:

Provided that nothing in this Act shall affect any priority acquired before the commencement of this Act by tacking, or in respect of further advances made without notice of a subsequent encumbrance or by arrangement with the subsequent encumbrancer.

(4) This section applies to mortgages of land before or after the commencement of this Act, but not to charges on registered land."

11–73   Section 94(1) extended the doctrine of tacking in two ways. It made the nature of the prior mortgage immaterial, and it applied to any prior mortgagee. Thus, if B successively mortgages the property to L, M, N and M again, then M has the right to tack, subject to any provisions as to notice. Section 94(1)(a) preserved the pre-1926 position on tacking with the consent of subsequent mortgagees. Section 94(1)(b) again preserves the pre-1926 position as laid down in *Hopkinson v Rolt*,[215] but, by virtue of s.198 of the Law of Property Act 1925, registration of the subsequent mortgage as a land charge constitutes deemed actual notice. Section 94(1)(c) reversed the principle of *West v Williams*[216] in that, where there is an obligation to make further advances, notice to the prior mortgagee does not affect his right to tack. Therefore a mortgagee must make a search whenever he makes a further advance, unless the mortgage is made expressly to secure further advances or a current account. He is not affected by an unregistered mortgage unless he has actual notice of it.

Section 94(1) permits tacking of further advances to rank in priority to subsequent mortgages. Therefore, the mortgagee who wishes to tack is bound by other intervening interests which are registered. It is suggested that the failure to give priority over such interests is a flaw in drafting.[217] Emmet[218] refers to the situation where an estate contract has been registered between dates of the original and a further advance. The mortgagee would be deemed to make the further advance with notice of the estate contract. It would therefore seem that he could be compelled to release his security in favour of the purchaser on receiving only the amount of the original advance if it was the case that the purchase price was insufficient to repay both the original and the further advance. The risk involved in not searching before making a further advance is discussed by Rowley,[219] as is the meaning of the words "for securing a current account or other further advances".[220]

Section 94(2)[221] provides an exception to the rule laid down by s.198(1) of the Law of Property Act 1925 that registration constitutes deemed actual notice. If

[215] (1861) 9 H.L.C. 514.
[216] [1899] 1 Ch. 132.
[217] Maitland, *Equity* (8th edn, 1949), p.214.
[218] *Emmet on Title* (loose-leaf), para.25–212.
[219] (1958) 22 Conv. (N.S.) 44 at 56.
[220] ibid., at 49.
[221] As amended by the Law of Property (Amendment) Act 1926. The amendment safeguards a mortgage registered before the principal mortgage was created.

the prior mortgage is made expressly for securing a current account or further advances, registration of a subsequent charge is not equivalent to actual notice of that charge to the prior mortgagee and he can tack against that charge provided that he had no actual notice of it at the time of the further advance. He takes, of course, subject to any charges which were registered at the time of the original advance. The reason for this exception to s.198 is to make it unnecessary for a bank to have to search the register before cashing each cheque drawn by a borrower who has a secured overdraft, although the exception applies whenever the mortgagee contemplates further advances on the same security.

Protecting a subsequent mortgagee

Consequently, a subsequent mortgagee who wishes to protect himself from loss **11–74** of priority by tacking, should give notice to all prior mortgagees in case their mortgages are in a form which allows them to tack further advances against registered encumbrances. Giving notice to the immediately prior mortgagee also fixes him with the duty to hand over the deeds when that mortgage is discharged.

The position of banks

Banks are affected by the rule in *Clayton's Case*,[222] the effect of which is that **11–75** where there is an unbroken account between the parties, or "one blended fund" as in the case of a current account at a bank, in the absence of any express appropriation each payment is impliedly appropriated to the earliest debt that is not statute-barred. Thus, where a prior mortgage is made to secure a current account with a bank and notice of a subsequent mortgage is received, subsequent payments reduce the overdraft existing at the time of the notice and these improve the position of the later mortgagee.[223] The bank can avoid this result by closing the account, and if it wishes, opening a new account into which the mortgagor's subsequent payments can be made.[224] The parties can agree to exclude the rule, which can also be displaced if an intention to exclude it appears from the circumstances.[225] For obvious reasons this rule is habitually excluded.

Tacking—The Former Common Law Principles

Tabula in naufragio

The form of tacking which was abolished in 1926[226] was the *tabula in naufragio* **11–76** ("plank in the shipwreck"). A mortgagee could benefit from this method of

---

[222] (1816) 1 Mer. 572.
[223] *Deeley v Lloyds Bank* [1912] A.C. 756 (HL).
[224] *Re Sherry* (1884) 25 Ch.D. 692.
[225] *Re James R. Rutherford & Sons* [1964] 1 W.L.R. 1211.
[226] LPA 1925 s.94(3), without affecting priority acquired before the passing of the Act.

tacking, when a borrower (B) created a legal mortgage in favour of L, followed by successive equitable mortgages in favour of M and N. If N then took a transfer of L's mortgage ("the plank") he would, provided he had no notice of M's mortgage when he advanced his money,[227] obtain the priority over M that L had, if B defaulted ("the shipwreck") in respect of all moneys owed to him. Tacking in this manner depended on the superiority of the legal estate[228]; provided the equities between M and N were equal,[229] N's possession of[230] or best right to call for the legal estate[231] upset the natural priorities which were governed by order of creation. Prior legal estates, or rights to call for legal estates which were sufficient to bring the doctrine into operation, included a term of years,[232] a judgment giving legal rights against the land,[233] an express declaration of trust by the owner of the legal estate in favour of the mortgagee who sought to tack,[234] or a transfer of the legal estate to a trustee for such a mortgagee.[235] The right to tack was lost as soon as the mortgagee parted with the legal estate[236] and did not arise unless the legal estate and the mortgage were held in the same right.[237]

Notice acquired after the advance was made by N, but before he got in the legal estate, did not prevent him tacking.[238] Notice to L, the holder of the legal estate, was immaterial, so M could not prevent N tacking by giving notice to L of his mortgage.[239] This opened the possibility of L and N conspiring to cheat M.[240] If a legal estate was held on trust for M, and N has notice of the trust, he was bound by it and could not get that estate in, so as to tack.[241]

Tacking of further advances

11–77   The more important form of tacking was the tacking of further advances. The mortgagor might wish to raise further sums on the property at a later date (as where he was developing a building estate), or the mortgagee might contemplate a variation in the state of the mortgagor's account and be prepared to make further advances. Where B mortgaged the property first to L, then to M, then took a further advance from L, it was possible, in certain circumstances, for L's

[227] *Brace v Duchess of Marlborough* (1728) 2 P.Wms. 491.

[228] *Bailey v Barnes* [1894] 1 Ch. 25 at 36, per Lindley L.J.; "a curious example of the deference paid by equity to the legal estate".

[229] *Lacey v Ingle* (1847) 2 Ph. 413; *Rooper v Harrison* (1855) 2 K. & J. 86, in which it was held that, if the mortgagee subsequently parts with the legal estate, he lost the right to tack.

[230] *Wortley v Birkhead* (1754) 2 Ves.Sen. 571.

[231] *Wilkes v Bodington* (1707) 2 Vern. 599; *Ex p. Knott* (1806) 11 Ves. 609.

[232] *Willoughby v Willoughby* (1756) 1 Term. Rep. 763; *Maundrell v Maundrell* (1804) 10 Ves. 246; *Cooke v Wilton* (1860) 29 Beav. 100.

[233] *Morret v Paske* (1740) 2 Atk. 52.

[234] *Wilmot v Pike* (1845) 5 Hare 14.

[235] *Earl of Pomfret v Lord Windsor* (1752) 2 Ves.Sen. 472; *Stanhope v Earl Verney* (1761) 2 Eden 81; *Pease v Jackson* (1868) 3 Ch.App. 576; *Crosbie-Hill v Sayer* [1908] 1 Ch. 866.

[236] *Rooper v Harrison* (1855) 2 K. & J. 86.

[237] *Harnett v Weston* (1806) 12 Ves. 130.

[238] *Taylor v Russell* [1892] A.C. 244.

[239] *Peacock v Burt* (1834) 4 L.J.Ch. 33.

[240] *West London Commercial Bank v Reliance Permanent Building Society* (1885) 29 Ch.D. 954.

[241] *Sharples v Adams* (1863) 32 Beav. 213; *Mumford v Stohwasser* (1874) L.R. 18 Eq. 556; *Taylor v London and County Banking Co* [1901] 2 Ch. 231; *Saunders v Dehew* (1692) 2 Vern. 271.

further advance to be tacked on to the original advance, displacing M's priority.

Where L had no notice of the mortgage in favour of M, tacking was allowed provided one of two conditions was satisfied:

(1) Where L was either a legal mortgagee[242] or an equitable mortgagee with the best right to call for the legal estate.[243] As with the *tabula in naufragio*, priority resulted from the superiority of the legal estate.

(2) Where the mortgage to L expressly provided for the security to be extended to cover further advances, whether or not such further advances were obligatory. This form of tacking was independent of the legal estate. Originally the courts had held that where M had notice that L's mortgage was expressed to cover further advances, he took subject to L's right to tack further advances.[244] However, this line of authority was overruled by a divided House of Lords[245] and the rule that notice of a subsequent encumbrance prevented the first mortgagee from tacking further advances, was applied even where the first mortgage contained a covenant to make further advances.[246] Nonetheless, in that case, the creation of M's mortgage released L from the obligation to make any further advances, since further advances to him could no longer have the same priority as the original mortgage.

Tacking could also take place if M agreed that further advances to L should have priority over his mortgage. This was a matter of contract between the parties and it was immaterial whether L was a legal or equitable mortgagee.

---

[242] *Wyllie v Pollen* (1863) 3 De G.J. & S. 596.

[243] *Wilkes v Bodington* (1707) 2 Vern. 599; *Wilmot v Pike* (1845) 5 Hare. 14; *Taylor v London and County Banking Co* [1901] 2 Ch. 231; see also *McCarthy & Stone Ltd v Hodge & Co* [1971] 1 W.L.R. 1547.

[244] *Gordon v Graham* (1716) 2 Eq.Cas.Abr. 598.

[245] *Hopkinson v Rolt* (1861) 9 H.L.C. 514; see also *London & County Banking Co Ltd v Ratcliffe* (1881) 6 App.Cas. 722; *Bradford Banking Co v Briggs & Co Ltd* (1886) 12 App.Cas. 29; *Union Bank of Scotland v National Bank of Scotland* (1886) 12 App.Cas. 53; *Matzner v Clyde Securities Ltd* [1975] 2 N.S.W.L.R. 293; *Central Mortgage Registry of Australia Ltd v Donemore Pty Ltd* [1984] 2 N.S.W.L.R. 128.

[246] *West v Williams* [1899] 1 Ch. 132 (CA).

CHAPTER 12

LEGAL MORTGAGES OF UNREGISTERED LAND[1]

INTRODUCTION

Since January 1, 1926, there have only been two methods of creating a legal **12–01** mortgage of an estate in fee simple: either by demise for a term of years absolute, subject to a provision for cesser on redemption, or by a charge by deed expressed to be by way of legal mortgage.[2] In relation to legal mortgages of a term of years absolute, they have (since that date) only been capable of creation by the grant of a sub-demise for a term of years absolute for a term shorter (by at least one day) than that vested in the mortgagor, subject to a provision for cesser on redemption or by a charge by deed expressed to be by way of legal mortgage.[3] To the extent that the lessor's licence to sub-demise is necessary, that licence cannot be unreasonably refused.[4]

LEGAL MORTGAGES BY DEMISE

Freehold land

The device of causing mortgages to operate as leases with a nominal reversion in **12–02** the mortgagor is a conveyancing device to keep equities off the title, in accordance with the general principles underlying the 1925 legislation. The transitional provisions of the 1925 legislation caused subsequent mortgages to take effect for terms longer by one, two or more days than the principal mortgage term.[5] The Law of Property Act 1925 s.85(2) causes a purported second or subsequent mortgage by conveyance of the fee simple (including an absolute conveyance with the deed of defeasance on redemption) to operate similarly. It was seen to be necessary, however, to remove various uncertainties as to the positions of the parties to the mortgage. This was effected in the case of mortgages of freehold land, by ss.85 and 88 of the Law of Property Act 1925. These sections provide as follows:

---

[1] There is no prescribed form for the creation of a charge of registered land. For mortgages where title to the land is registered, see Ch.13.
[2] In both cases a legal mortgage can only be created by deed, see Law of Property Act 1925 (LPA 1925) s.85(1).
[3] ibid., s.86(1).
[4] ibid.
[5] LPA 1925 Sch.1, Pt VII.

(i) a first mortgagee has the same right to documents of title as if his security included the fee simple (s.85(1))[6];

(ii) on a sale by a mortgagee under a power of sale, the conveyance to the purchaser operates to vest in him the whole of the mortgagor's estate, including the nominal reversion (s.88(1));

(iii) the mortgagor's nominal reversion will be vested in the mortgagee on a foreclosure order by the court which also terminates his equity of redemption. Such vesting also occurs when his equity of redemption becomes barred by lapse of time (s.88(2), (3));

(iv) s.88(5) operates to extend the provisions of s.88(1), (2), (3) to a sub-mortgagee so as to enable him to acquire the nominal reversions of both his immediate mortgagor and the original mortgagor;

(v) on discharge of a mortgage debt, the mortgage term becomes a satisfied term and ceases automatically (s.116). This applies equally to sub-mortgages since s.5 of the Law of Property Act 1925 restates the provisions of the Satisfied Terms Act 1845 so that they apply to underleases.

12–03   Section 85(2) (which does not apply to registered land)[7] provides that any purported conveyance of an estate in fee simple by way of mortgage made after January 1, 1926, shall (to the extent of the estate of the mortgagor) operate as a demise of the land in question for a term of years absolute without impeachment for waste but subject to cesser on redemption. In the case of a first mortgage it operates for a term of 3,000 years. In the case of second and subsequent mortgages it operates for a term one day longer than the term vested in the mortgagee with immediate priority. Subsection (2) also provides that any conveyance includes an absolute conveyance with a deed of defeasance and any other assurance which would operate to vest the fee simple in the mortgagee is a deed to which the subsection applies.

12–04   The replacement of the mortgage by conveyance with the mortgage by demise saves the mortgagor the cost of two conveyances, on mortgaging the property and upon redemption. Further, because of the provisions respecting satisfied terms, it is unnecessary to terminate the mortgage term by an express surrender. Normally, a properly executed receipt for the mortgage money is sufficient to put an end to the term.

The possibility of a series of legal mortgages of the same land altered the old rule whereby a legal mortgage automatically gave the mortgagee priority. This was lost only by his own fraud, misrepresentation or gross negligence. Priority against subsequent purchasers in circumstances where the mortgage is not protected by the deposit of the title deeds is achieved by registration of the mortgage as a land charge.[8] Formerly priority could also be secured by deposit of title

---

[6] Thus addressing the former position that unless the deeds were obtained at the time of the advance, a first mortgagee (because he did not have the fee simple) had no right to the deeds: *Wiseman v Westland* (1826) 1 Y.J. 117.

[7] LPA 1925 s.85(3), as amended. Otherwise the methods of mortgaging freeholds prescribed in s.85 (demise or by deed by way of legal charge) apply to registered land and regardless of whether the land is held subject to a trust for sale or otherwise: s.85(3).

[8] Class C(i)—Land Charges Act 1972 s.4(5).

deeds.[9] Mortgages of unregistered land may give rise to an obligation to register the title to the land in question.[10]

Statutory mortgage: A mortgage of freehold land can also be granted by deed **12–05** expressed to be by way of statutory mortgage. This is in a prescribed form modified as the circumstances require to suit the particular loan.[11] This is a special form of charge by way of legal mortgage and certain covenants are implied.

Leasehold land

In practice, the 1925 legislation did not bring about substantial changes in the **12–06** way in which leaseholds were mortgaged because mortgages by assignment, which were converted into mortgages by sub-demise as a result of that legislation,[12] were in any case rare. This state of affairs arose from the operation of the rule in *Spencer's Case*,[13] whereby the burden of a covenant which touched and concerned the land affected an assignee of a term. The position was obviously unattractive to mortgagees who looked to the land as security and did not wish to be liable under the covenants.

By s.86(1) of the Law of Property Act 1925, the proper form of the mortgage is for the mortgagor of the land to make an underlease for a term shorter than that of the lease forming the subject-matter of the mortgage. Although an underlease for a concurrent term would be valid,[14] the first mortgagee's term is made shorter, usually by 10 days, so as to leave room for further legal mortgages of the same lease, each of which would be for a term one day longer than the term of the immediately prior mortgage.[15] Section 86(2) puts this on a statutory basis in respect of successive mortgages of leases which purport to be created by assignment. Sections 86(1) and 89(1), (2), (3), (5) of the Law of Property Act 1925 make the same provisions in favour of a mortgagee or sub-mortgagee of leasehold land as are made by the corresponding subsections of ss.85 and 88 regarding freehold land.

Section 86(3) of the 1925 Act provides that sub-mortgages shall be made in the same way as other mortgages of leaseholds. If one person has advanced money on the security of a lease and wishes to raise money on the mortgaged property without calling in the mortgage, he can sub-mortgage the property to another by creating a mortgage term in the form of an underlease 10 days shorter than the lease.

---

[9] For the position as to deposit of title deeds and the effect of s.2 of the Law of Property (Miscellaneous Provisions) Act 1989, see paras 14–03 et seq.

[10] See paras 13–04 et seq.

[11] See s.117(1), Sch.IV, Form 1; Form 4 is a combined form for statutory transfer and mortgage; and see para.12–31.

[12] LPA 1925 s.86(2).

[13] (1583) 5 Co. Rep. 16.

[14] It would, however, operate as an assignment with the consequences identified above: *Beardman v Wilson* (1868) L.R. 4 C.P. 57.

[15] A failure to do so is not fatal since a lease may take effect in reversion upon another lease of the same or greater length: LPA 1925 s.149(5).

12–07 *Statutory mortgage:* A mortgage of leasehold land can similarly be granted by deed expressed to be by way of statutory mortgage. This is in a prescribed form modified as the circumstances require to suit the particular loan.[16] The same applies to a mortgage of freehold land.[17]

12–08 *Forfeiture of the leasehold interest:* Clearly, since a mortgagee by sub-demise derives his title from a lessee who, in turn, may have his interest determined by forfeiture, a mortgage by sub-demise represents a species of security which is vulnerable to destruction according to the actions or inaction of the mortgagor/ lessor. A mortgagee by sub-demise may, however, seek relief from forfeiture,[18] as may an equitable mortgagee but not an equitable chargee.[19] Consideration of the law concerning relief from forfeiture is beyond the scope of this work.[20]

Contents of a deed of mortgage by demise

Generally

12–09 Mortgages by demise for a term of years absolute are becoming increasingly rare, especially in the case of residential lending where mortgagees tend to lend on pro forma documentation. As such mortgages, however, do continue to be granted in the commercial field it is necessary to have some regard to their contents.

Certain matters must be included in a deed[21] of mortgage by demise as a matter of formality and do not require detailed consideration here.[22] These include the date of the mortgage, a statement of the parties and a recital of the loan agreement. Further, the Law of Property Act 1925 grants to the mortgagee by deed certain statutory powers that obviate the need for these to be created by express covenants. These are: the power to grant leases while in possession (s.99(2)); to realise a security by sale (ss.101(1), 103); and to appoint a receiver (ss.101(1)(iii), 109).

Testatum

12–10 This states that the mortgagee has paid to the mortgagor the sum agreed to be lent, and that the mortgagor acknowledges its receipt. The receipt is not, as between the parties, conclusive as to the amount paid,[23] and it is open to the mortgagor to show that a smaller amount was actually advanced and to claim redemption on payment of that amount. Section 67(1) provides that a receipt for

---

[16] See s.117(1), Sch. IV, Form 1; Form 4 is a combined form for statutory transfer and mortgage.

[17] See para.12–31.

[18] LPA 1925 s.146(2).

[19] *Bland v Ingrams Estates Ltd* [2001] Ch. 767.

[20] Reference should be made to *Woodfall: Landlord and Tenant.*

[21] Which must be used in order to create a legal mortgage: see LPA 1925 ss.85, 86 and 53.

[22] For detailed consideration, see also Appendix 1, paras A-01 et seq. of the 2nd edn of this work.

[23] *Mainland v Upjohn* (1889) L.R. 41 Ch.D. 126. It does however bind the parties to the mortgage vis-à-vis third parties: *Bickerton v Walker* (1886) L.R. 31 Ch.D. 151.

consideration money or securities in the body of a deed shall be a sufficient discharge for the same to the person paying or delivering the same, without any further receipt for the same being endorsed on the deed.

Whereas the receipt may be inconclusive as between the parties to the deed, they themselves are estopped from denying its truth as against third parties.[24] The fact that one party to the deed is solicitor to the other does not fix a third party with any constructive notice or put him on inquiry. Where a solicitor, however, takes a security from a client and the deed does not express the real nature of the transaction, extrinsic evidence is required to prove the amount of the debt and the bona fides of the transaction.[25]

Covenant for repayment

The express covenant to pay: This is an express covenant by the mortgagor to pay the principal, together with interest at a stated rate. The mortgagor's personal obligation to repay the principal sum is a speciality debt[26] and therefore is similar to the remedies against the land, subject to the 12-year limitation period.[27] The six-year period appropriate to actions founded on simple contracts applies to the personal remedy on a simple contract debt charged on land in a document not under seal. It also applies to a simple contract debt which is merely recited in a deed and in which there is no express or implied promise to repay. The six-year period is also the appropriate period of limitation for claims as to interest.[28] The limitation period runs not from the date of the instrument but from the date of breach of the covenant, i.e. the date when the right to receive the money accrued on the default of the mortgagor under the terms of the deed.[29]

12–11

It is usual to stipulate that the principal be repaid on a date shortly after the execution of the deed. The date fixed is normally six months from the date of the deed. Usually the mortgagor does not provide for the mortgagor to repay prior to the date fixed for repayment. A loan made subject to the bank's standard banking terms and conditions does not thereby result in it being repayable on demand.[30]

Unless the mortgage otherwise provides, the statutory powers of sale and appointment of a receiver do not arise until this date is past and usually after a demand has been made. Further, there is normally a distinct covenant for payment of interest if the principal sum remains unpaid after the due date. If this is included the dates of payment and the rate of interest should be stated. It is unclear whether this is necessary as it has been held that where there is a covenant to pay principal and interest the covenant is to pay two distinct sums of

12–12

---

[24] *Powell v Browne* (1907) 97 L.T. 854; *Bickerton v Walker* (1886) L.R. 31 Ch. D. 151; and see LPA 1925 ss.68(1), 205(1)(xxi) for the effect of a receipt in favour of a purchaser.

[25] *Lewes v Morgan* (1817) 5 Price 42; *Bateman v Hunt* [1904] 2 K.B. 530.

[26] *Sutton v Sutton* (1883) L.R. 22 Ch. D. 511.

[27] Limitation Act 1980 s.20(1). See paras 6–36 et seq.

[28] *See Bristol & West Plc v Bartlett, Paragon Finance Finance Plc v Banks, Halifax Plc v Grant* [2002] EWCA Civ 1181.

[29] *See Bristol & West Plc v Bartlett, Paragon Finance Finance Plc v Banks, Halifax Plc v Grant* [2002] EWCA Civ 1181, approved in *West Bromwich Building Society v Wilkinson* [2005] UKHL 44.

[30] *Cryne v Barclays Bank* [1987] B.C.L.C. 548.

money and can be enforced by two separate actions notwithstanding that the obligations are contained in the same instrument.[31] In the absence of an express covenant to pay interest, interest is still payable (even though the mortgage is only equitable[32]), save in limited circumstances.[33]

In most modern mortgages the amount repayable is greater than the principal sum advanced. The reason for this is that interest (either compound or simple) is usually added to the principal sum lent and the repayments made by the mortgagor are calculated over the term of the mortgage. The advance can also be index linked so that the principal sum increases parallel with inflation.[34] Premiums and bonuses can also be added thereby increasing the amount repayable by the mortgagor.

12–13   Consideration, however, must be given to a number of aspects relating to collateral benefits and penalties[35]; the provisions of consumer law relating to extortionate credit bargains under the Consumer Credit Act 1974—now defined as "unfair relationships" under the Consumer Credit Act 2006[36]; and unfair contract terms.[37]

12–14 Punctual payment: A covenant to secure punctual payment is often inserted. This is expressed to be for the payment of a higher rate of interest, reducible on punctual payment, to the agreed rate.[38] A written agreement specifying the rate of interest can be varied by a parol agreement made for good consideration to reduce the rate.[39] If the covenant to secure punctual payment is made in a form whereby the agreed rate of interest is to be increased if payment is not made punctually, it will be unenforceable as a penalty.[40] Covenants to secure punctual

---

[31] *Dickenson v Harrison* (1817) 4 Price 282.

[32] *Anon* (1813) 4 Taunt. 876; *Cityland & Property (Holdings) v Dabrah* [1968] Ch. 162, 182. See also *Re Drax, Sark v Drax* [1903] 1 Ch. 781.

[33] See para.33–11.

[34] See para.33–11; and see *Cityland and Property (Holdings) Ltd v Dabrah* [1968] Ch. 166; *Multiservice Bookbinding Ltd v Marden* [1979] Ch. 84; *Nationwide Building Society v Registrar of Friendly Societies* [1983] 1 W.L.R. 1226.

[35] *Lordsvale Finance Plc v Bank of Zambia* [1996] Q.B. 752.

[36] Under the provisions of the Consumer Credit Act 1974 ss.67–73 (as amended) certain types of mortgages could be rescinded under certain circumstances; see also ss.137–140; these were known as cancellable regulated agreements. The Consumer Credit Act 2006 repealed ss.137–140 of the 1974 Act with effect from April 6, 2007 by Sch.4 of the 2006 Act which has introduced new provisions into the 1974 Act regulating unfair relationships between creditors and debtors by the introduction of a new s.140A and 140B into the 1974 Act, see ss.19–22 of the 2006 Act, and see para.16–49, below. For the transitional provisions, see para.16–50, below. The new test applies to all credit agreements including agreements already in existence and regulated by the 1974 Act. Quaere whether a first legal charge over residential land is an exempt agreement under the 1974 Act, as amended by the 2006 Act (see s.16(6C)), being a mortgage which is regulated under the Financial Services and Markets Act 2000. For the financial limits, see para.16–18, and see para.16–12, below. Also it is to be noted that the limitation of £25,000 as to extortionate credit agreements is no longer operative.

[37] For unfair contract terms and the Unfair Terms in Consumer Contracts Regulations 1999, SI 1999/2083, in particular regs 5(1), 6, and see paras 16–08 et seq. The Unfair Contract Terms Act 1977 does not apply to contracts for the disposition of interests in land, see s.1(2), Sch.1, para.1(b).

[38] In the light of the Unfair Terms on Consumer Contracts Regulations 1999 and the view of the Circuit Judge in *Falco Finance Ltd v Gough* [1999] C.C.L.R. 16, this approach must be open to question. Quaere whether there is a distinction under the 1999 Regulations between a clause that offers a concession on compliance and a higher rate in the event of default.

[39] *Lord Milton v Edgworth* (1773) 5 Bro. P.C. 313.

[40] *Holles v Wyse* (1693) 2 Vern. 389; *Strode v Parker* (1694) 2 Vern. 316; *Lordsvale Finance Plc v Bank of Zambia* [1996] Q.B. 752.

payment are strictly construed. If the payment is not made on the specified day, the mortgagee is entitled to demand the full rate. The fact that on one occasion he has accepted the reduced rate when payment was made late does not estop him from demanding the full rate in respect of a subsequent delayed payment.[41] Unless the covenant so stipulates, one late payment by the mortgagor will not deprive him of the benefit of the covenant in respect of future payments made punctually.[42]

Payment by instalments: It is not necessary to stipulate that the principal be repaid on one fixed date. The principal may be made repayable by instalments, with a stipulation that its repayment shall not be otherwise enforced provided that the instalments and interest[43] are duly paid. Where repayment of the principal by instalments is agreed, the parties are assumed to intend that, on default of regular payment of instalments, the whole debt shall become immediately payable. This may be provided for by one of the following covenants: **12–15**

(a) to pay the principal sum on a given date, with a proviso that if the sum is to be paid by the instalments stipulated, the lender will not require payment otherwise;

(b) to pay in instalments with a proviso that if default is made in the payment of any instalment, the whole debt is to become immediately payable. Such a proviso is binding and will not be relieved against as a penalty.[44]

This is not the case where, on default, additional interest for the full term of the loan is repayable.[45]

If interest is calculated for the term and added to the premium, the mortgage should provide for a discount in the event of early redemption.[46] How the discount is calculated may be prescribed in the mortgage agreement or may be calculated by reference to "the Rule of 78", which is a formula under which the sum of interest is spread over the period of the loan so that, in general terms, it is at a constant rate. Calculating the discount simply by reference to the period of the loan which is unexpired may cause difficulties since, although the interest will have been spread evenly throughout the term, it is (in fact) greater as a proportion of the payments made in the earlier years. The Consumer Credit Acts 1974 and 2006 apply to regulated agreements.[47]

[41] *Maclaine v Gatty* [1921] 1 A.C. 376.

[42] *Stanhope v Manners* (1763) 2 Eden. 197.

[43] As to total charges for credit and the true costs of borrowing provisions, rates of interest, extortionate credit bargains, and unfair relationships under the Consumer Credit Acts 1974 and 2006, see fn.34, above.

[44] *Sterne v Beck* (1863) 1 De. G.J. and Sm. 595; *Wallington v Mutual Society* (1880) 5 App. Cas. 685; *Cityland Property (Holdings Ltd) Dabrah* [1968] Ch. 166.

[45] *Oresundsvarvet Aktiebolag v Marcos Diamantis Lemos (The Angelic Star)* [1988] 1 Lloyd's Rep. 122. See also *General Credit & Discount Co v Glegg* (1883) 22 Ch.D. 549 (stipulation for "commission" on late instalments).

[46] Otherwise the premium may amount to an unreasonable collateral advantage (see *Cityland*, above) since there is otherwise no entitlement for a discount: *Harvey v Municipal Permanent Investment Building Society* (1884) L.R. 26 Ch.D. 273.

[47] See paras 16–01 et seq. and in particular para.16–03, and fn.36, above.

12–16   **Payment on demand:**   It is also possible to stipulate simply that the principal be repayable on demand or immediately after notice, in which case it is implied that the mortgagor has a reasonable time in which to comply with the demand.[48] The mortgage may, in such a case, provide that a demand is deemed to have been duly made once certain formalities have been observed.

12–17   **Implied covenant to pay:**   The promise to pay, however, may be implied in the absence of an express covenant to pay.[49] It depends upon the construction of the particular agreement,[50] as does the implication whether the promise to pay takes effect as a simple contract to repay the principal and interest giving rise to a six year period of limitation or as a covenant to repay a speciality debt, in which case the 12-year period applies.[51] In the case of a third party charge where the mortgagor's property was security for the loan and the covenant repay was by the third party the presumption was rebutted.[52]

12–18   **Variable interest rates:**   In the absence of contractual provision, the rate of interest cannot be varied. As a matter of practice, commercial mortgagees make provision to vary the rates of interest chargeable from time to time.[53] This power (which is usually unfettered) cannot, however, be exercised improperly, capriciously or for ulterior motives for it would otherwise defeat the legitimate expectation of the parties.[54] The Unfair Terms in Consumer Contracts Regulations[55] may also apply.[56] Interest rates which are expressed to prevail even after judgment (i.e. the doctrine of merger is excluded[57] or does not apply[58]) may be subject to those regulations.[59]

Covenants for title

12–19   **Covenants implied by demise as beneficial owner prior to July 1, 1995[60]:**   By demising the property as beneficial owner, the mortgagor gave the

---

[48] See *Cripps (Pharmaceuticals) Ltd v Wickenden* [1973] 1 W.L.R. 944; *Williams & Glyn's Bank Ltd v Barnes* [1981] Com. L.R. 205; *Bank of Baroda v Panessar* [1987] Ch. 335; *Cryne v Barclays Bank* [1987] B.C.L.C. 548; *Lloyds Bank Plc v Jeffrey Lampert* [1999] Lloyds Rep. Bank 138.

[49] *Sutton v Sutton* (1883) L.R. 22 Ch.D. 511 at 515 per Jessel M.R.; *King v King* (1735) 3 P. Wm.; *Ezekiel v Orakpo* [1997] 1 W.L.R. 340 at 346.

[50] *National Provincial Bank Ltd v Liddiard* [1941] Ch. 158; *Tam Wing Chuen v Bank of Credit and Commerce Hong Kong Ltd* [1996] 2 B.C.L.C. 69; *Re Bank of Credit and Commerce International SA (No.8)* [1998] A.C. 214.

[51] *Sutton v Sutton* (1883) L.R. 22 Ch.D. 511 at 516, and see paras 6–34 et seq.

[52] *Fairmile Portfolio Management Ltd v Davies Arnold Cooper* [1998] E.G.L.S. 149.

[53] Which provision does not infringe the Consumer Credit Act 1974: *Lombard Tricity Finance Ltd v Paton* [1989] 1 All E.R. 919.

[54] *Abu Dhabi National Tanker Co Procut Star Shipping Ltd (The Product Star) (No.2)* [1993] 1 Lloyd's Rep. 397, 404; *Nash v Paragon Finance Plc* [2001] EWCA Civ 1466. This may extend to unreasonable rates: ibid. See also fnn. 34 and 40, above, and paras 33–11 et seq. below.

[55] SI 1999/2083.

[56] See para.16–12.

[57] *Economic Life Assurance Society v Usborne* [1902] A.C. 147.

[58] e.g. statutory legal charges: LPA 1925 s.117(2). *Ealing LBC v El Isaac* [1980] 1 W.L.R. 932, 937; *Director General of Fair Trading v First National Bank Plc* [2002] 1 A.C. 481.

[59] ibid.

[60] This is the commencement date of ss.1 and 2 of the Law of Property (Miscellaneous Provisions) Act 1994.

covenants implied by s.76 of the Law of Property Act 1925 in the mortgagee's favour. These are fully set out in Sch.2, Pts III and IV. The following comprises a summary:

(a) full power to convey and, in the case of a leasehold property, that the lease is in full force, unforfeited, unsurrendered, has not become void or voidable, and that all covenants and conditions have been observed, and in the case of a mortgage of a leasehold property to indemnify the mortgagee for future rents and covenants;

(b) quiet enjoyment if entry is made on default;

(c) freedom from encumbrances other than those to which the mortgage is expressly made subject;

(d) further assurance.[61]

Section 7 provides that the benefit of the covenants runs with the estate or interest of the disponee. They are therefore capable of being enforced by any person in whom that estate or interest is (in whole or in part) for the time being vested. The burden of the covenant on the part of the disponer is absolute and his liability is therefore more extensive than under the covenants implied under s.76 of the Law of property Act 1925.

Title guarantee after June 30, 1995: Of considerable importance to the law of **12–20** mortgages is the effect of the provisions of the Law of Property (Miscellaneous Provisions) Act 1994 on title guarantee. This followed the recommendations of the Law Commission[62] and was enacted to remedy a perceived series of defects in the law as existing at the time.

Under the 1994 Act covenants for title may be implied into any instrument effecting or purporting to effect a disposition of property and expressed to be made with full or limited title guarantee. A disposition includes a mortgage or charge or lease.[63] Such covenants will only be implied if the disposition is expressed to be made with full or limited title guarantee. It is a matter of negotiation for the parties and does not arise out of the disponer's capacity. Often the instrument making the disposition may extend the operation of the implied covenants.[64] Section 8(3) further provides that where the disposition is expressed to be made at the direction of a person the implied covenants apply to him as if he were the person making the disposition. Such instances arise where a nominee conveys at the direction of the beneficial owner, or a vendor conveys to a third party at the direction of the purchaser.

---

[61] Section 76 has been repealed as regards dispositions made after July 1, 1995. See the Law of Property (Miscellaneous Provisions) Act 1994 (Commencement No.2) Order 1995, SI 1995/1317. Certain transitional provisions exist for mortgages granted after that date pursuant to mortgages made before that date, see ibid., ss.11–12.

[62] *Transfer of Land—Land Mortgages* (1991) Law com. No.204, para.2–13 and *Land Registration for the Twenty-first Century—A Conveyancing Revolution* (2001) Law Com. No.271, para.4–7.

[63] "Instrument" includes an instrument which is not a deed; "disposition" includes the creation of a term of years; and "property" includes a thing in action, and any interest in real or personal property: s.1(4).

[64] ibid., s.8(1).

12–21 *Full title guarantee:*   The covenants implied[65] are that the disponor has:

     (i) the right to dispose of the property as he purports to do (with the concurrence of any other mortgagor)[66];

    (ii) that he will at his own cost do all that he reasonably can do to give the mortgagee the title he purports to give[67];

   (iii) that the property is free from all charges and encumbrances and free from all rights exercisable by third parties other than those of which the disponer does not and could not reasonably be expected to know[68]; and

   (iv) in the case of leasehold land that the lease is subsisting at the time of the disposition and that there are no subsisting breaches of any condition or tenant's obligations which would render the lease liable to forfeiture[69];

    (v) in addition, in the case where the disposition is a mortgage of a leasehold interest or in the case where the property is subject to a rentcharge, the mortgagor further impliedly covenants that he will fully and promptly observe and perform all obligations (in addition to the above covenants) under the lease imposed on him in his capacity as tenant or (as the case may be) imposed by the owner of any rent-charge.[70] The covenants set out above (i), (iii) and (iv) do not impose liability on the disponor in respect of any matter to which the mortgage is made subject[71] or for anything which is within the actual knowledge of the mortgagee or which is a necessary consequence of facts within his actual knowledge.[72]

12–22 *Limited title guarantee:*   Where a disposition is made with limited title guarantee the position is almost identical. The disponor impliedly enters into the same covenants in so far as they are applicable save for one important qualification— namely, the disponer does *not* enter into (iii) above.[73] Instead a covenant is implied that he has not, since the last disposition or value, created any charge or encumbrance or granted any third party rights which are subsisting at the time that the disposition is made, or allowed the property to become charged or encumbered in that way, and that he is not aware that anyone else has done so.[74]

---

[65] ibid., s.1(2).
[66] ibid., s.2(1).
[67] ibid.
[68] ibid., s.3(1). There are also certain statutory charges for which the mortgagor is not liable, e.g. council tax, ibid., s.3(2).
[69] ibid., s.4(1).
[70] ibid., s.5.
[71] ibid., s.6(1).
[72] ibid., s.6(1).
[73] ibid., s.1(2)(b).
[74] ibid., s.3(3).

The habendum: This states the length of the term, that the lease is granted   **12–23**
without impeachment of waste, and that there is a proviso for cesser on
redemption.

Proviso for cesser on redemption: This normally states that if the mortgagor   **12–24**
on a given day pays to the mortgagee the mortgage debt and interest, the
mortgage term shall cease.[75] An alternative proviso is that the mortgagee will, at
any time thereafter and at the mortgagor's request and cost, surrender the term to
the mortgagor or at his direction. A mortgagor cannot usually claim to be allowed
to redeem before the day specified in the contract for payment of the principal,
though he may do so if, before that date, the mortgagee has taken steps to recover
payment. In the case of a legal charge a similar proviso is used to the effect that
on payment on the date set for repayment the mortgage will discharge the
security.

Where there is a stipulation in a mortgage that the principal loan is not to be
called in for a given period, there is usually a corresponding stipulation preventing the mortgagor from repaying or redeeming the mortgage, without the mortgagee's consent, until the period has expired. However, the second stipulation if
standing by itself may be held invalid as a clog on the equity of redemption, at
any rate where the mortgagor is precluded from redeeming for an unreasonable
length of time.

Covenants to repair and insure[76]**:**   A mortgagee by deed has, by s.108(1) of   **12–25**
the Law of Property Act 1925, a limited statutory power to insure the premises
for loss or damage by fire to the extent specified in the mortgage deed or, if no
amount is specified, up to two-thirds of the amount required to reinstate the
property in the event of its total destruction. The power is exercisable as soon as
the mortgage is made.[77] This enables the mortgagee to protect his security.

This power is excluded in the circumstances set out in s.108(2). These are the
following:

    (i) where there is a declaration in the mortgage deed that no insurance is
       required;
   (ii) where the insurance is kept up by or on behalf of the mortgagor in
       accordance with the mortgage deed. This the usual position;
  (iii) where the mortgage deed is silent on the question of insurance and the
       insurance is kept up by or on behalf of the mortgagor, with the consent
       of the mortgagee, to the amount authorised by the section.

By s.101(1)(ii), the premiums paid are a charge on the mortgaged property with
the same priority and bearing the same rate of interest as the mortgage money.
The premiums are a charge and cannot be recovered from the mortgagor as a
debt, hence the mortgagor in practice has to covenant to insure, and breach of that
covenant causes the mortgagee's power of sale to become exercisable.

[75] LPA 1925 ss.85(1), 86(1).
[76] See further para.32–02.
[77] s.101(1)(ii).

The mortgagee has no right to the policy monies if the mortgagor further insures on his own account independent of the mortgage security, and, dependent upon the term of the insurance policy, the mortgagee may receive less than anticipated. This position would arise in the circumstances where the mortgagee's insurance contained a clause limiting his liability in the event that the mortgage security was the subject of any other insurance.[78] However, in the case where the mortgagor insures having covenanted to do so, on the true construction of the covenant as a matter of law the covenant operates to grant to the mortgagee a charge over the proceeds. This position arises even if the insurance is taken out in the name of the mortgagor.[79]

Although a mortgagor is not obliged by statute to keep the mortgaged property in repair, it is usual for him to covenant to do so.[80] Formerly, if the mortgage was a controlled mortgage[81] and the mortgagor failed to keep the property in a proper state of repair (measured by the general condition of the property at the date of the mortgage and not requiring that anything be done other than preserving that condition[82]) he lost his protection against the mortgagee's right to foreclose, sell or otherwise enforce his security.

12–26   Restriction on mortgagor's statutory powers of leasing[83]:   These powers, which are conferred by s.99 of the Law of Property Act 1925, can be restricted or excluded by agreement[84] except in respect of mortgages of agricultural land[85] or where such exclusion or restriction would operate to prevent the carrying out of an order to grant a new tenancy of business premises.[86] The usual form of covenant is one not to grant a lease without the written consent of the mortgagee. However, this does not prevent the mortgagor creating a lease which, as between himself and the tenant, is binding by estoppel. Such leases are not validated against the mortgagee.[87] If the powers are excluded, a mortgagee can on an application for permission by the mortgagor to lease the mortgaged land act entirely in his own interests—he owes no equitable duty to the mortgagor in this regard and can unreasonably withhold his consent.[88]

---

[78] *Halifax Building Society v Keighley* [1931] 2 K.B. 248; and see *Re Doherty* [1925] 2 I.R. 246.

[79] *Colonial Mutual General Insurance Co Ltd v ANZ Banking Insurance Group (New Zealand) Ltd* [1995] 1 W.L.R. 1140.

[80] But the mortgagee does have the right to have the security preserved from deterioration, see below paras 16–19 et seq.

[81] The provisions of the Rents Acts relating to controlled mortgages were repealed by the Housing Act 1980 s.152, and Sch.26.

[82] *Woodfield v Bond* [1922] 2 Ch. 40.

[83] See further below para.32–10.

[84] *Iron Traders Employers' Insurance Association Ltd v Union Land and House Investors Ltd* [1937] Ch. 313; *Dudley and District Benefit Building Society v Emerson* [1949] Ch. 707; *Rust v Goodale* [1957] Ch. 33.

[85] See Agricultural Holdings Act 1986 s.100, Sch.14 para.12(1), (2).

[86] Landlord and Tenant Act 1954 s.36(4).

[87] ibid., s.152. Leases granted by a mortgagor prior to November 1, 1993, and which were unauthorised by the mortgagee may, if extended under the Leasehold Reform, Housing & Urban Development Act 1993 s.56 (individual enfranchisement) be deemed to bind the mortgagee: ibid., s.58(1). Grants after that date in those circumstances do not bind the mortgagee: ibid., s.58(2).

[88] *Citibank International Plc v Kessler* (1999) 78 P. & C.R. D7.

Mortgagees' right to consolidate: Section 93(1) of the Law of Property Act   **12–27**
1925, provides that a mortgagor seeking to redeem any one mortgage is entitled
to do so without paying any moneys due under any separate mortgage made by
him, or by any other person through whom he claims, on property other than that
comprised in the mortgage which he seeks to redeem. However, this subject to
the proviso that no contrary intention is expressed in any one of the mortgage
deeds and that at least one mortgage was made after 1881. It is therefore usual
for the mortgage deed to contain a clause excluding the operation of s.93,
although the restriction can equally well be excluded by a clause expressly
preserving the mortgagee's right to consolidate.

Covenant against registration of title: The mortgagor usually covenants that   **12–28**
no third party shall be registered as owner of the mortgaged property, under the
Land Registration Act 2002, without the mortgagee's consent. Whilst such a
clause may provide the mortgagee with recourse against the mortgagor in the
event of breach, it will also require the registration of a caution against first
registration under the Land Registration Act 2002.[89] Clearly the provisions in
that Act concerning compulsory registration cannot be excluded or ignored, not
least because of the effect on the mortgagee's title.[90]

Attornment clause: There is some doubt as to whether such a clause now has   **12–29**
any value.[91] It was at one time usual for the mortgagor to attorn tenant: (i) at a
nominal yearly rent; or (ii) at a rent reserved equivalent to the amount of interest
payable annually; or (iii) at a full rack rent.
    The reason for creating the landlord–tenant relationship was to give the
mortgagee the rights of a landlord as well as his right qua mortgagee; and in case
(ii) above, to provide the right of distress as an additional security.[92] Although
such a clause would not confer the right of distress unless registered as a bill of
sale,[93] its invalidity as a bill of sale does not destroy the landlord-tenant relationship.[94] Nor does it invalidate the mortgage.[95]
    It is possible for a mortgagor to attorn tenant to a second mortgagee although
he has already attorned tenant to the first mortgagee[96] and while the first
mortgagee's rights under the mortgages are unaffected by the second attornment,
that second attornment is valid by estoppel.

---

[89] As registration of cautions against first registration, see LRA 2002 Pt 2, Ch.2, ss.15–22.
[90] See LRA 2002 ss.6, 7.
[91] *Steyning and Littlehampton Building Society v Wilson* [1951] Ch. 1018. In this case such clauses
were described as being "entirely obsolete" (per Danckwerts J.); cf. *Regent Oil Co Ltd v J.A. Gregory
(Hatch End) Ltd* [1966] Ch. 402. See also paras 26–11, 27–01.
[92] As to the law on distress see now the Tribunals, Courts and Enforcement Act 2007 Pt 3, (and
in particular s.71, and see Sch.12), repeals the existing law on distress for rent in so far as landlords
of commercial premises are concerned, and introduces a new statutory regime defined as "Commercial Rent Arrears Recovery" ("CRAR"). This new statutory procedural code is outside the scope of
this work.
[93] *Re Willis, Ex p. Kennedy* (1888) 21 Q.B.D. 384.
[94] *Mumford v Collier* (1890) 25 Q.B.D. 279; *Kemp v Lester* [1896] 2 Q.B. 162.
[95] *Re Burdett* (1888) 21 Q.B.D. 162.
[96] *Re Kitchin, ex parte Punnett* (1880) 16 Ch.D. 226, CA.

It has also been held that such a clause enables a mortgagee to enforce covenants given by a mortgagor's successor in title by virtue of the doctrine of privity of estate.[97] It was further held in the same case, that such a clause in a charge by way of legal mortgage created, not a tenancy at will, but a tenancy during the continuance of the security. This continued so long as the property was occupied by the mortgagor or persons deriving title under him, and subject to the mortgagee's right to determine the tenancy on giving the requisite period of notice.

Where the clause requires that notice be given for determination of the tenancy, the mortgagee may not re-enter until that notice has been given.[98] In the case where the clause does not require notice to be given, commencement of possession proceedings operates as a determination[99] and thereafter no tenancy exists. In such circumstances Rent Act protection is not available and no statutory tenancy comes into existence.[100] It has also been held that an attornment clause does not of itself create an agricultural tenancy for the purposes of the Agricultural Holdings Act 1948. Thus a notice to determine the tenancy created is not subject to the restrictions on the service of a notice to quit contained in that Act.[101]

On the other hand it has been held that s.16 of the Rent Act 1957 (now s.5 of the Protection from Eviction Act 1977 (as amended)) might apply where the rent reserved by the attornment clause was a full rack rent or where the mortgagor was required to reside on the premises.[102] It is therefore advisable, in order to safeguard against such protection being available to the mortgagor, for the clause to be in a form enabling the mortgagee to take possession without notice.

CHARGE BY WAY OF LEGAL MORTGAGE

12–30   The Law of Property Act 1925 provides that legal mortgages of both freeholds (s.85(1)) and leaseholds (s.86(1)) may be effected by a charge by deed expressed to be by way of legal mortgage. Section 87(1) provides that a chargee by deed expressed to be by way of legal mortgage shall have the same protection, powers and remedies as if he were a mortgagee by demise or sub-demise.

By s.205(1)(xvi), "mortgage" includes any charge or lien on any property for securing money or money's worth, and "mortgagee" includes a chargee by way of legal mortgage. Nevertheless, a deed of charge does not convey any proprietary right to the chargee, so the mortgagor retains the full title instead of being left with only the nominal reversion. The charge, instead of demising the

---

[97] *Regent Oil Co Ltd v J.A. Gregory (Hatch End)* [1966] Ch. 402. In this case it was also held that such a clause was effective to create a legal estate in a legal charge as it was in a legal mortgage; and see fn.86, above.

[98] *Hinkley and Country Building Society v Henny* [1953] 1 W.L.R. 352.

[99] *Woolwich Equitable Building Society v Preston* [1938] Ch. 129; *Portman Building Society v Young* [1951] 1 All E.R. 191.

[100] *Portman Building Society v Young* [1951] 1 All E.R. 191.

[101] *Steyning and Littlehampton Building Society v Wilson* [1951] Ch. 1018.

[102] See *Alliance Building Society v Pinwell* [1958] Ch. 788, applied in *Peckham Mutual Building Society v Registe* (1981) 42 P. & C.R. 186. See further below paras 16–24 and see *Bolton Building Society v Cobb* [1996] 1 W.L.R. 1.

property merely states that the mortgagor (with full or limited title guarantee) charges it by way of legal mortgage with the payment of the principal, interest and any other money secured by the charge. In addition, the charge differs substantially from a mortgage by demise in that it contains no proviso for redemption.

The words (with full or limited title guarantee) inserted into the charge fix the mortgagor with the same implied covenants as if the mortgage were by demise.[103]

It has been suggested that it is uncertain whether the chargee can foreclose in the absence of a proviso for redemption or discharge. Foreclosure has been judicially described as the removal, by the court, of a stop put by the court itself on the mortgagee's title,[104] which would otherwise be absolute by reason of a breach of condition on the part of the mortgagor. A legal chargee, however, has no title from which a stop can be removed. Apparently, not even an express proviso for redemption could confer on him the right to foreclose. Sometimes a provision is inserted into the deed that, for the purposes of the charge, the legal right to redemption is to cease after the contract date.

It seems, however, that the words of ss.88(2) and 89(2) of the Law of Property Act 1925 clearly mean that a legal chargee has the right to foreclose although there is no mortgage term. The only matter left uncertain is the event upon which that right arises. The provisions referred to above have the effect of fixing that date in accordance with the interpretation that the right arises as soon as the borrower is in default.

STATUTORY LEGAL CHARGES

There is a special form of charge by way of legal mortgage of freehold and **12–31** leasehold land expressed to be a statutory mortgage.[105] This charge states the names of the parties, the sum lent, the rate of interest, the receipt of the money by the mortgagor, and the fact that the mortgagor charges the named property with the principal and interest. It is now practically obsolete.

A mortgage when made in statutory form implies the following covenants[106]:

(a) that the mortgagor will on the day stated pay to the mortgagee the stated mortgage debt with interest meanwhile at the stated rate; and thereafter will continue to pay interest at that rate, so long as the debt or any part of it remains unpaid, in half-yearly instalments, and this whether or not a judgment has been obtained under the mortgage[107];

---

[103] See above paras 12–20 et seq.

[104] *Carter v Wake* (1877) 4 Ch.D. 605.

[105] 1925 s.117(1), Sch.IV Form 1. Form 2 applies where a mortgagor does not join; Form 3 applies where a covenantor joins; and Form 4 is a combined form for statutory transfer and mortgage; and Form 5 sets out a receipt on discharge of the statutory charge.

[106] ibid., s.117(2).

[107] Thus statutorily preventing merger.

(b) that if the mortgagor on the stated day pays to the mortgagee the
mortgage debt and interest due, the mortgagee shall at the borrower's
request and cost at any time thereafter discharge the mortgaged property or transfer the benefit of the mortgage as the mortgagor may
direct.

DISCHARGE AND TRANSFER OF LEGAL MORTGAGES OF LAND

12–32 For discharge of legal mortgages of unregistered and registered land, see Chapter
6.[108] For transfer of mortgages of unregistered and registered land, see Chapter
5.[109]

---

[108] See below paras 6–01 et seq.
[109] See below paras 5–01 et seq.

CHAPTER 13

MORTGAGES OF REGISTERED LAND

GENERALLY

Historical perspective

On January 1, 1990, the last remaining areas in England and Wales became **13–01** subject to compulsory first registration of title to land upon the happening of a disposition giving rise to a requirement to register.[1] The policy behind the Land Registration Acts 1925–1986 was for all unregistered titles to be brought, in the fullness of time, into the land registration system and that policy has (with the heralded advent of electronic conveyancing) received a new impetus under the Land Registration Act 2002. Since the grant of security over land is a commonplace occurrence, it has (in certain circumstances) been defined as a triggering event giving rise to a requirement to register since the amendment to s.123 of the Land Registration Act 1925[2] took effect on April 1, 1998. The "triggers" for compulsory registration under the Land Registration Act 2002 are no less sensitive and the grant of a legal mortgage by demise or a legal mortgage by deed by way of legal charge will give rise to the requirement to register title to the unregistered land over which the mortgage is granted.[3] Clearly, voluntary registration of title is unaffected by these provisions[4] and various fee incentives and discounts have been retained.[5]

The Land Registration Act 2002

On October 13, 2003, the Land Registration Act 2002 was brought into force[6] **13–02** and applies to dispositions on or after that date.

Section 23(1) of the Land Registration Act 2002 provides the registered proprietor of a registered estate with owner's powers in relation to the registered estate, namely:

---

[1] Registration of Title Order 1989, SI 1989/1347.
[2] By the Land Registration Act (LRA) 1997 ss.1, 5(4).
[3] LRA 2002 s.4.
[4] See ibid., s.3.
[5] Land Registration Fee Order 2003, SI 2003/2092.
[6] Land Registration Act 2002 (Commencement No.4) Order 2003, SI 2003/1725.

(1) to make a disposition of any kind permitted by the general law other than a mortgage by demise or sub-demise;

(2) to charge the estate at law with the payment of money.

There are therefore two methods by which a legal mortgage of a registered estate may be created:

(1) the methods applicable under the general law that have not been prohibited by s.23(1)(a), that is a charge by way of legal mortgage; and

(2) by charge made to secure payment of money even where the deed does not use the words "charge by way of legal mortgage".

There is no practical difference between the two methods as s.51 of the Land Registration Act 2002 provides that on completion of the relevant registration requirements a charge created by means of a registrable disposition of a registered estate will have the same effect as a charge by deed by way of legal mortgage even if it would otherwise not have done so. In the case of *Cityland and Property (Holdings) Limited v Dabrah*[7] it was held by Goff J. that having regard to the provisions of ss.25(1) and 27(1) of the Land Registration Act 1925 (now repealed) there was no necessity for those words to appear in the charge itself. He rejected the submission that as the charge was not expressed to be "by way of legal mortgage" that it was not effective as a legal mortgage.

The need for completion of the charge by registration is paramount. Section 27(2)(f) of the Land Registration Act 2002 provides that the grant of a legal charge is a registrable disposition which is required to be completed by registration. Section 27(1) provides that a registrable disposition does not take effect at law until the relevant registration requirements are met. Thus until registered a mortgage or charge of registered land does not operate at law until the relevant registration requirements are met as set out in Sch.2 to the 2002 Act. Until registration it takes effect in equity only and is capable of being overridden by registration of a registrable disposition for valuable consideration unless protected in the register.[8] It may be protected in the register by:

(1) substantive registration—this is the highest form of protection;

(2) entry of a notice under s.34 of the Land Registration Act 2002;

(3) being an interest excepted from the effect of registration (e.g. if the land is registered with a qualified title and the qualification in the register relates to the mortgage); or

(4) being an interest which overrides a registered disposition, as listed in Sch.3 to the Land Registration Act 2002 (e.g. if the mortgagee is in actual occupation of the land);

(5) entry of a restriction under s.42 of the Land Registration Act 2002 and r.92 of the Land Registration Rules 2003;

---

[7] [1968] Ch. 166.
[8] See below para.13–15.

(6) if the entry was made prior to October 13, 2003, by entry of a caution against dealings or a notice under the Land Registration Act 1925.

In the case of some legal interests, such as a legal charge, the entry of a person in the register as the proprietor can only be registered in relation to the registered estate on which they are dependent and cannot be registered with an independent registered title.[9]

In the case of entry of a restriction or a caution against dealings, referred to in (5) and (6) above, although the restriction or caution does not in itself protect the priority of the mortgage for the purposes of the special rule of priority conferred by the 2002 Act upon registrable dispositions for valuable consideration, it may prevent that disposition being completed by registration and thereby gaining the benefit of the special rule of priority.

Prior to October 13, 2003, although a legal mortgage would usually be substantively registered, it could be protected by entry of a notice or caution against dealings if substantive registration was unavailable (e.g. if the consent of a prior chargee, pursuant to a restriction in the register, was not forthcoming). Under the transitional provisions contained in Sch.12 to the Land Registration Act 2002 existing notices are treated as if they were agreed notices under the 2002 Act. These transitional provisions also ensure that s.55 (effect of cautions against dealings) and s.56 (general provisions as to cautions) of the Land Registration Act 1925 will continue to have effect in respect of existing cautions even though those provisions have been repealed. Rules 218 to 223 of the Land Registration Rules 2003 set out transitional provisions governing how existing cautions are to be dealt with, including the withdrawal and cancellation of such cautions. **13–03**

Triggering the Compulsory First Registration of Land

Title to an unregistered legal estate in land[10] may be registered voluntarily at any time as a separate legal registered title[11] irrespective of when it was acquired by the applicant. In specified circumstances, however, it is the subject of compulsory registration of title.[12] Mortgages of unregistered land may trigger the compulsory registration of the land charged. There has been provision since the Land Registration Act 1925 for voluntary registration of land in England and Wales.[13] On December 1, 1990, however, the whole of England and Wales became the subject of compulsory registration of land in specified circumstances.[14] The dispositions relating to unregistered land triggering compulsory first registration **13–04**

---

[9] LRA 2002 s.59.
[10] See Law of Property Act (LPA) 1925 s.1(1), (4). A charge by way of legal mortgage is included as a legal estate in land as it is capable of subsisting or of being conveyed or created at law, ibid., s.1(1), (2), (3). A "charge" for the purposes of LRA 2002 means any mortgage, charge or lien for securing money or money's worth, see s.132.
[11] LRA 2002 ss.2(a)(1), 3(1)(a).
[12] ibid., s.4.
[13] LRA 1925 ss.4, 8.
[14] Registration of Title Order 1989, SI 1989/1347.

were the subject of wide extension under the provisions of the Land Registration Act 1997[15] which came into effect on April 1, 1998.[16] This policy has continued following the enactment of the Land Registration Act 2002, one of the underlying objectives of which is to bring all land into the system of registration. Fee incentives were brought into force so as to encourage voluntary first registrations,[17] and these remain.[18] The effect of these changes means that unregistered mortgages of unregistered land will exponentially decrease in importance. Conversely, mortgages of registered land will grow in number and importance, not least because the "triggering events" for compulsory first registration under the Land Registration Act 1925[19] were easily triggered and have been made more so following the bringing into force of the Land Registration Act 2002.[20]

Prior to October 13, 2003

13–05 **Dispositions which triggered the obligation to register:** If any of the following dispositions of unregistered land occurred on or after April 1, 1998[21] and prior to the commencement of the Land Registration Act 2002 on October 13, 2003, s.123A of the Land Registration Act 1925 imposed a requirement to effect first registration upon the transferee or estate owner.

The specified dispositions[22] were:

    (1) the conveyance of the freehold estate for valuable (which included a disposition with a negative value) or other consideration (including by way of gift) or in pursuance of any order of a court (a "qualifying conveyance" in the terminology of the Land Registration Act 1925);

    (2) a qualifying grant of a term of years for more than 21 years from the date of grant;

    (3) a qualifying assignment of a term of years with more than 21 years to run from the date of assignment;

    (4) any disposition by an assent of a freehold estate or a term of years with more than 21 years to run from the date of disposition;

    (5) a legal mortgage of a freehold estate or a legal mortgage of a term of years absolute which, on the date of the mortgage, had more than 21 years to run, where the mortgage is protected by the deposit of documents relating to the mortgaged estate and it ranks ahead in priority to all other mortgages.

---

[15] In a joint publication from the Law Commission and HM Land Registry (1995) Law. Com. No.235 certain recommendations as to land registration were made. These were implemented by the 1997 Act.

[16] LRA 1997 Act s.1. This section has substituted and inserted new sections into LRA 1925 ss.123 and 123A, and see SI 1997/303.

[17] Land Registration Fee Order 2003, SI 2003/2092.

[18] Land Registration Fee Order 2009, SI 2009/845.

[19] See s.123 as substituted by LRA 1997 s.1.

[20] On October 13, 2003; see the Land Registration Act 2002 (Commencement No.4) Order 2003, SI 2003/1725.

[21] Being the date upon which the amendments to LRA 1925 s.123 effected by LRA1997 s.1 were brought into force: SI 1997/3036.

[22] LRA 1925 s.123(1), (2) (as substituted).

For the purposes of these provisions, "assignment" excluded an assignment or surrender of a lease to the owner of the immediate reversionary interest where the term would merge; and "term of years absolute" excluded a PPP lease.

Effect of the requirement to register: Once a disposition had occurred which triggered the requirement for compulsory first registration, the transferee in instances (a)–(d) above, or the mortgagor in the circumstances specified in (e) or, in either case, their successors in title or assigns were required to effect the first registration of the estate in question within the applicable period (being two months or such longer period as the registrar might allow) of the disposition.[23] A mortgagee under a mortgage which gave rise to the obligation to effect registration could apply for the legal estate charged by the mortgage to be registered whether or not the mortgagor consented.[24] Pending registration *within the applicable period* (or its retrospective extension),[25] the disposition operated in accordance with its terms.[26]   **13–06**

The provisions of the Land Registration Act 1925 applied to any dealing with land which took place between the disposition which gave rise to the obligation to effect first registration and the application for first registration of title to the land as if it had taken place after the date of first registration.[27]

Failure to register within the applicable period: A failure to effect registration within the applicable period caused the title to any legal estate transferred by the disposition to revert to the transferor on bare trust for the transferee or (in the case of a disposition purporting to grant a legal estate or create a legal mortgage) for the same to operate as a contract to grant or create that estate or mortgage for valuable consideration, regardless of whether the formal requirements for such a contract were satisfied.[28]   **13–07**

If the applicable period was extended by the registrar retrospectively, the provisions specifying the consequences of failure did not apply and the disposition was "revived" and had effect as if the applicable period never lapsed, thus effectively creating a legal mortgage for the extended period.[29]

Any later disposition by way of replacement for one which had become void under the provisions of s.123A would (a) (in the absence of agreement to the contrary) be at the disponor or mortgagor's cost,[30] and (b) would trigger the same obligation to effect registration as that occasioned by the void disposition.[31]

Clearly there was a serious danger for the mortgagee in the event of a failure to comply with these provisions. If the mortgage (constituting a notional estate   **13–08**

---

[23] ibid., s.123A(1) (as substituted).
[24] Land Registration Rules 1925 r.19 (as substituted by the Land Registration Rules 1997 r.2(1); Sch.1 para.3.
[25] LRA 1925 s.123A(6) (as substituted).
[26] ibid., s.123A(4) (as substituted).
[27] Land Registration Rules 1925 r.73(1) (as substituted by the Land Registration Rules 1997 r.2(1); Sch.1 para.17.
[28] LRA 1925 s.123A(5) (as substituted).
[29] ibid., s.123A(6) (as substituted).
[30] ibid., s.123A(8), (9) (as substituted).
[31] ibid., s.123A(7) (as substituted). See *Proctor v Kidman* (1986) 51 P. & C.R. 67, 72.

contract) was not registered as a land charge[32] and the mortgagee was not in possession it would not bind a purchaser of the legal estate for money or money's worth. Any such purchaser would take free from it if a disposition of the legal estate is made during the period of non-registration.

After October 12, 2003

13–09 **Dispositions which trigger the obligation to register:** Section 4 of the Land Registration Act 2002 extends the scope of the events which give rise to an obligation to register. Now the following events give rise to compulsory first registration:

> (1) the transfer (other than by operation of law[33]) of a qualifying estate in land (being a freehold estate or a term of years which, at the time of transfer, grant or creation has more than seven years to run[34]) for valuable (which includes a disposition with a negative value[35]) or other consideration (including by way of gift) or in pursuance of any order of a court or by means of a vesting assent (as defined in the Settled Land Act 1925);
>
> (2) the transfer (other than by operation of law) of a qualifying estate giving effect to a partition of land subject to a trust of land;
>
> (3) the transfer (other than by operation of law) of a qualifying estate by a deed that appoints (or by virtue of s.83 of the Charities Act 1993 has effect as if it appointed) a new trustee;
>
> (4) the transfer (other than by operation of law) of a qualifying estate by a vesting order under s.44 of the Trustee Act 1925 that is consequential on the appointment of a new trustee;
>
> (5) the transfer of an unregistered legal estate in land in circumstances where s.171A of the Housing Act 1985 applies (disposal by landlord which leads to a person no longer being a secure tenant);
>
> (6) the grant out of a qualifying estate of an estate in land for a term of years for more than seven years from the date of grant for valuable or other consideration (including by way of gift) or in pursuance of any order of a court;
>
> (7) the grant out of a qualifying estate of an estate in land for a term of years absolute to take effect in possession after the end of the period of three months beginning with the date of the grant;
>
> (8) the grant of a lease in pursuance of Pt 5 of the Housing Act 1985 (right to buy);
>
> (9) the grant of a lease out of an unregistered legal estate in land in such circumstances as are mentioned in sub-para.(2);

---

[32] Land Charges Act 1972 s.4(6).
[33] LRA 2002 s.4(3).
[34] ibid., s.4(2).
[35] ibid., s.4(6).

(10) the creation of a protected first legal mortgage of a qualifying estate.[36]
A "protected first legal mortgage" arises where the mortgage is protected by the deposit of documents relating to the mortgaged estate and
it ranks, on creation, ahead in priority to all other mortgages.[37]

For the purposes of sub-paras (1) and (6) above, "transfer" or "grant" includes
the constitution of certain trusts where the settlor does not retain the whole of the
beneficial interest or the uniting of the bare legal title and the beneficial interest
in a property held under a trust in relation to which the settlor did not, on
constitution retain the whole of the beneficial interest.[38]

Thus, a transfer[39] (other than by operation of law[40]) of a charge by way of legal **13–10**
mortgage (being a "qualifying estate") for valuable or other consideration,[41] by
way of gift or in pursuance of an order of any court or by means of an assent
(including a vesting assent) should trigger the requirement to register under
s.4(1)(a) because a mortgage created by this method is outside the exclusion
given by s.4(4)(a).[42]

Section 4(1)(g) provides that the requirement to register applies on, inter alia,
"the creation of a protected first legal mortgage of a qualifying estate". A
"qualifying estate" is defined as including an unregistered legal estate[43] which is
(a) a freehold estate in land, or (b) a leasehold estate in land for a term which, at
the time of the transfer, grant or creation, has more than seven years to run.[44]

A legal mortgage is protected if it takes effect on its creation as a mortgage to
be protected by the deposit of documents relating to the mortgaged estate, and is
one which, on its creation, ranks in priority ahead of any other mortgages
affecting the mortgaged estate.[45] Since most, if not all, first mortgages of
unregistered land require the mortgagor to deliver up documents of title in
addition to executing the necessary form or mortgage, one must anticipate that
the overwhelming majority of first legal mortgages of unregistered land will be
"protected" and thus will trigger the requirement to register.

Dispositions expressly excepted from the compulsory registration of title

(a) *assignment of a mortgage term:*   Section 4(4)(a) of the Land Registration **13–11**
Act 2002 provides that s.4(1)(a) (which requires registration on the transfer of a
"qualifying estate" for valuable or other consideration, by way of gift or in
pursuance of an order of any court, or by means of an assent (including a vesting
assent)) does not apply to "the assignment of a mortgage term". There is no
definition of the phrase "mortgage term" in either the Land Registration Act

---

[36] ibid., s.4(1)(g).
[37] ibid., s 4(8).
[38] ibid., s.4(7).
[39] As to that which may comprises a triggering transfer, see ibid., s 4(7).
[40] ibid., s.4(3).
[41] Which occurs even if the estate transferred has a negative value: ibid., s.4(6).
[42] But see below para.13–11, and in particular fn.47.
[43] As defined in the Law of Property Act 1925: LRA 2002 s.132(1).
[44] LRA 2002 s.4(2).
[45] ibid., s.4(8).

2002 or the Law of Property Act 1925 but it would appear, by the use of that phrase, that the exception afforded by this provision is intended to be confined to mortgages by demise or sub-demise and to circumstances where the mortgagee assigns the mortgage by transferring the mortgage term.[46]

A charge by way of legal mortgage is outside the definition of "qualifying estate" since it does not fall within the definition of "freehold estate in land" (a mortgage cannot be said to constitute such an estate) and does not comprise a leasehold estate within s.4(2)(b) (and thus a "qualifying estate") since the powers and remedies of the mortgagee whose security is granted by this route only arise *as if* a demise or sub-demise had been granted.[47]

13–12   (b) *the assignment or surrender of a lease to the owner of the immediate reversion where the term is to merged in that reversion:*   Section 4(4)(b) provides that s.4(1)(a) (see above) does not apply to the assignment or surrender of a lease to the owner of the immediate reversion where the term is to merge in that reversion.

13–13   (c) *the grant of an estate to a person as a mortgagee:*   Section 4(5) provides that s.4(1)(c) (which requires registration on the grant of a qualifying estate for a term of years absolute of more than seven years from the date of the grant, and for valuable or other consideration, by way of gift or in pursuance of an order of the court) does not apply to the grant of an estate to a person as a mortgagee.

13–14   **Duty to apply for registration of title:**   Once the requirement for registration applies, "the responsible estate owner", or his successor in title, being the transferee or grantee of the estate in question[48] or, in the case of a protected first legal mortgage under s.4(1)(g), the mortgagor,[49] or his successor in title, must apply to the registrar for registration within two months beginning with the date upon which the relevant event occurs or such longer period as the registrar may allow.[50] The registrar may by order provide that the period for registration ends on such later date as he may specify in the order if he is satisfied on an application being made to him that there is good reason for doing so.[51]

Where an application for first registration is made under r.21 of the Land Registration Rules 2003, or by the owner of an estate that is subject to a legal charge falling within s.4(1)(g), the registrar must enter the mortgagee of the legal charge falling within s.4(1)(g) as the proprietor of that charge if he is satisfied of

---

[46] *Land Registration for the Twenty-first century—A Conveyancing Revolution* (2001), Law Com No.271, para.3.25; notes to the Land Registration Bill para.25.

[47] LPA 1925 s.87. Quaere whether the transfer of a charge by way of legal mortgage would in fact be a trigger for first registration. Although it may be arguable that such a charge falls outside the definition of a "mortgage term" for the purposes of s.4(4)(a) of the LRA 2002 it would not appear to fall within the definition of a "qualifying estate" for the purposes of s.4 (see para.13–11). The transfer of such a charge, not being the *transfer of a qualifying estate* (albeit a charge secured upon a qualifying estate—but where that underlying qualifying estate was not itself being transferred), would not therefore trigger compulsory registration.

[48] ibid., s.6(3).

[49] ibid., s.6(2).

[50] ibid., s.6(4).

[51] ibid., s.6(5).

that person's entitlement.[52] A mortgagee under a mortgage which gave rise to the obligation to effect first registration under s.4(1)(g) of the Land Registration Act 2002 is, however, safeguarded in the event of any default by the mortgagor as he may make an application to the Registrar in the name of the mortgagor for the legal estate charged by the mortgage to be registered whether or not the mortgagor consents.[53] The registrar is bound to enter the mortgagee of the legal charge under r.21.

Where a charge or mortgage subsists at the time of first registration, it must be disclosed in the application for first registration. The charge will be registered under r.22 of the Land Registration Rules 2003 (in the case of a protected first legal mortgage) or under r.34 (in the case of a subsequent legal charge).

Where a charge or mortgage has been created contemporaneously with the disposition of the property which has triggered first registration, under r.38 of the 2003 Rules this will need to be completed by registration as a "dealing" taking place prior to completion of the first registration. In such a case, the charge should be lodged for registration with the application for first registration and it will be registered on completion of the first registration; under r.38(2) the registration of the charge has effect from the time of the making of the application for first registration.

Effect of non-compliance with the requirement of registration under section 6:   13–15
Section 7 of the Land Registration Act 2002 contains materially identical terms to those contained in the Land Registration Act 1925 s.123A. Section 7(1) provides that if the requirement for first registration is not complied with the transfer, grant or creation becomes void as regards the transfer, grant or creation of the legal estate. In the case of a disposition within s.4(1)(g) of the Land Registration Act 2002, namely the creation of a protected first legal mortgage of a qualifying estate, the grant or creation has effect as a contract to grant or create that mortgage for valuable consideration.[54] In these circumstances the mortgagee will only hold an equitable interest under the mortgage.

If, however, the applicable period is extended by the registrar retrospectively on an application being made to him by any interested person,[55] the provisions specifying the consequences of failure do not apply and the position is restored. It has the effect as if the applicable period had never lapsed.[56]

If the legal estate is retransferred, regranted or recreated because of a failure to comply with the requirements of registration the mortgagor is liable to the other party for all the proper costs of and incidental to the retransfer, regrant or recreation of the legal estate and is liable to indemnify the other party in respect of any other liability reasonably incurred by him because of the failure to comply with the requirement of registration.[57]

---

[52] Land Registration Rules 2003 r.22.
[53] ibid., r.21.
[54] LRA 2002 s.7(2).
[55] ibid., s.6(5).
[56] ibid., s.7(3).
[57] ibid., s.8.

13–16 In the case of a voluntary first registration of title[58] the registrar must enter the mortgagee of a legal mortgage as the proprietor of that charge if on first registration of the legal estate charged by that charge he is satisfied of that person's entitlement. This applies to a legal mortgage which is either a charge on the legal estate being registered, or a charge on such charge. Absent the element of compulsion, however, s.3(5) of the Land Registration Act 2002 provides that an application may not be made for the voluntary registration of title in respect of a leasehold estate vested in the applicant as a mortgagee where there is a subsisting right of redemption. Despite the absence of express statutory authority,[59] it appears that HM Land Registration will entertain an application by a mortgagee for voluntary first registration of the mortgaged estate where the title deeds have been lost or destroyed, subject to the evidence relied upon.[60] An application for registration of a leasehold estate vested in the mortgagee qua mortgagee where there is a subsisting right of redemption is not permitted.[61]

REGISTERED CHARGES

Before October 13, 2003

13–17 By s.25(1) (as amended) of the Land Registration Act 1925, the proprietor of any registered land could by deed:

> "(a) charge the registered land with the payment at an appointed time of any principal sum of money with or without interest;
> (b) charge the registered land in favour of a building society under the Building Societies Act 1986,[62] in accordance with the rules of that society."

13–18 *Form of registered charge:* By virtue of s.25(2) of the Land Registration Act 1925, a charge could be:

> "in *any form* provided that:
>
> (1) the registered land comprised in the charge is described by reference to the register or in any other manner sufficient to enable the registrar to identify the same without reference to any other document;
> (2) the charge does not refer to any other interest or charge affecting the land which

---

[58] i.e. not falling within rr.22 or 38 of the Land Registration Rules 2003; r.38 relates to dealings taking place after a prior disposition that is subject to compulsory registration of title.

[59] ibid., s.3 makes no express provision and, by virtue of s.3(5), it would seem that a mortgagee cannot bring himself within s.3(2). Indeed, in the light of r.27 of the Land Registration Rules 2003 (application where there is a requirement to register) requiring evidence that the applicant is within s.3(2), it may be argued that there is a contrary indication, suggesting that a mortgagee cannot apply.

[60] Land Registry Practice Guide 2, November 2008.

[61] LRA 2002 s.3(5).

[62] In the Land Registration Act 1925, the Acts referred to are the Building Societies Acts 1874 to 1894. The reference to the Building Societies Act 1986 was inserted by the Building Societies Act 1986 s.120; Sch.18 para.2.

(a) would have priority over the same and is not registered or protected on the register

(b) is not an overriding interest."

Further, the Land Registration Act 1925 s.25(3) invalidated any provision in a charge which purported to:

"(1) take away from the proprietor the power of transferring it by registered disposition or of requiring its cessation to be noted on the register; or

(2) affect any registered land or charge other than that in respect of which the charge is to be expressly registered."

By s.26(1) of the Land Registration Act 1925, it was provided that "the charge shall be completed by the registrar entering on the register the person in whose favour the charge is made as the proprietor of such charge, and the particulars of the charge".

Section 63(1) of the Land Registration Act 1925 further provided that, on the **13–19** registration of a charge, a charge certificate should be prepared, and must have been delivered either to the proprietor or, if he so preferred, deposited in the Land Registry. By s.63(4), the preparation, issue, indorsement and deposit in the Land Registry of the certificate should have been effected without cost to the proprietor.

Rule 262 (as amended) of the Land Registration Rules 1925 dealt with the form of the charge certificate. It was required to certify that the charge had been registered and to contain:

(a) either the original or an office copy of the charge;

(b) a description (if no description was contained in the charge) of the land affected;

(c) the name and address of the proprietor of the charge;

(d) a list of the prior incumbrances, if any, appearing on the register.

It was required to have the Land Registry seal affixed and could contain such further particulars as the registrar thought fit, and notes of subsequent dealings could be entered on the charge certificate, or if more convenient, a new certificate was issued. The registrar also issued a charge certificate to the chargee, while the chargor was required to deposit the land certificate at the Land Registry, where it remained until the charge was cancelled.

After October 12, 2003

Powers of disposition of a registered charge: The powers of disposition of the **13–20** owner in relation to a registered charge is expressly provided for in ss.23(2) and 24 of the Land Registration Act 2002. These consist of:

(1) power to make a disposition of any kind permitted by the general law in relation to a interest of that description, other than a legal sub-mortgage[63]; and

---

[63] In s.23(2)(a) a legal sub-mortgage means: (a) a transfer by way of mortgage, (b) a sub-mortgage by sub-demise, and (c) a charge by way of legal mortgage.

(2) power to charge at law with the payment of money indebtedness secured by the registered charge.

13–21　The principle under the Land Registration Act 1925 as to the fact that a registered charge of a registered estate should be executed by deed has not been altered by the provisions of the Land Registration Act 2002. The requirements of electronic conveyancing, however, will obviate the requirement to execute a deed, and the procedure of using deeds will be eliminated altogether.[64] There is no prescribed form, however, for the creation of a charge of registered land and there is no requirement under the Land Registration Act 2002 for the charge to be executed in a standard form provided that it complies with the general law as to the execution of deeds.[65] There is, however, provision for the use of Form CH1, which is the Land Registry form of charge deed.[66] Alternatively if lenders utilise their own forms of charge they are encouraged by the Land Registry to seek the approval of the Land Registry for their use. The application to register the charge itself should be made on Form AP1 which should accompany Form CH1 or the lender's own form of charge. The detailed procedure for making the application for registration of the charge can be found in the Land Registry Practice Guide number 29. It is also to be noted that no charge certificate is issued, such practice of issuing charge certificates having been abolished by the Land Registration Act 2002. Instead, the chargee receives a Title Information Document containing an official copy of the register. The lender may also wish to ensure that other matters are entered in the register at the time of the registration of the charge itself, such as one of the appropriate standard restrictions against the registered title, or the lender's obligation to make further advances, and questions of consolidation.

Section 123 of the Land Registration Act 2002 defines a "charge" as "any mortgage, charge or lien for securing money or money's worth", and a "registered charge" is a charge the title to which is entered in the register. The definition, therefore, encompasses statutory charges and charges to secure the performance and obligation together with the mortgage of real property.

SUB CHARGES

Before October 13, 2003

13–22　Where there was a registered charge granted over registered land, the proprietor of that charge could create a sub-charge in the same form and manner as a registered charge.[67] Rules 163–166 of the Land Registration Rules 1925 dealt with the powers of the proprietor of a charge or sub-charge and dispositions of sub-charges and the formalities of registration. Rule 163(2) provided that the

---

[64] See para.13–01.

[65] See Law of Property Act (Miscellaneous Provisions) Act 1989 s.1.

[66] See Land Registration Rules 2003 r.101 where it is stated that "a legal charge of a registered estate may be in Form CH1". Form CH1 is contained in Sch.1 to the Land Registration Rules 2003.

[67] See LRA 1925 s.36, Land Registration Rules 1925 r.163(1).

proprietor of the sub-charge had the powers as the proprietor of the principal charge. Section 106 of the Land Registration Act 1925 provided that the proprietor of registered land could also sub-mortgage the charge by deed or otherwise, in any way that would have been permissible to do so had the land not been registered.

After October 12, 2003

Since the enactment of the Land Registration Act 2002 there has been an **13–23** important change to the registration of sub-charges and sub-mortgages. A sub-charge of registered land can now only be made by way of a charge on the indebtedness of the primary charge that is registered as security.[68] The registered proprietor of the sub-charge has, in relation to the property subject to the principle charge or any intermediate charge, the same powers as the sub-chargor.[69] It is therefore impossible to create a sub-charge by transfer of the mortgage, demise or a charge by deed by way of legal mortgage. The sub-charge is a registered disposition which must be completed by registration.[70] Once registered it is protected in the case of a subsequent registered disposition for value of the registered estate over which it operates and it also has the benefit of the rule as to priority in relation to earlier unprotected interests.[71]

TRANSFER OF REGISTERED CHARGES

Before October 13, 2003

Section 33 of the Land Registration Act 1925 contained provisions governing the **13–24** transfer of registered charges. A transfer of a registered charge of registered land had to be in the prescribed form and completed by entry on the register in the name of the new proprietor.[72] Under Rule 153 of the Land Registration Rules 1925,[73] the use of Forms TR3 or TR4 was required.

After October 12, 2003

In the case of a statutory transfer of a charge by way of legal mortgage of **13–25** freehold or leasehold land made by a statutory legal charge it may be transferred by deed expressed to be made by way of a statutory transfer in one of the statutory forms as may be appropriate with such variations and additions, if any, which the circumstances may require.[74] In so far as land registration is concerned, in the case of a registrable transfer of a registrable charge, since the enactment of the Land Registration Act 2002, the transferee, or his successor in

---

[68] See LRA 2002 ss.23(2)(a) and (b), and 23(3).
[69] "Sub-charge" means a charge under LRA 2002 s.23(2)(b); and see s.132(1). ibid., s.53.
[70] ibid., s.27(1), (3).
[71] ibid., ss.28, 30.
[72] LRA 1925 s.33(2).
[73] As amended by the Land Registration Rules 1999 r. 2(1), Sch.1 para.14.
[74] See LPA 1925 s.118(1), Sch.4, Form 2, Form 3, and Form 4.

title, must be entered in the register as the proprietor of the charge.[75] The transfer must be in the prescribed form.[76]

DISCHARGE OF CHARGES OF REGISTERED LAND

Before October 13, 2003

13–26   The procedure for discharge of registered charges and the procedure for doing so under the Land Registration Act 1925 was altered by the provisions of the Land Registration Rules 1999 and 2000. Forms DS1 or DS3 were mandatory[77] save in cases where there was an arrangement which permitted electronic discharge.[78]

After October 12, 2003

13–27   Rules 114 and 115 of the Land Registration Rules 2003 make provision (respectively) for documentary discharge and electronic discharge.[79] An application for discharge in documentary form must be made on the prescribed form[80] and should be executed as a deed.[81] The discharge of the mortgage itself does not result in the cancellation. It is achieved by the alteration to the register on the receipt of the additional form of application accompanying the discharge.[82] While the majority of mortgagees use the Electronic Notification of Discharge system (END)—thus simply communicating the fact of discharge to the registrar electronically and subsequently applying for him to alter the register—use of the Electronic Discharge system (ED)—where the mortgagee himself alters the register—is becoming more widespread. Again the discharge is achieved by the alteration to the register on the receipt of the additional form for which there is an electronic version.[83] The ED system is a fully electronic form of automatic discharge of the charge with no involvement on the part of the staff of the Land Registry.

The ED system has recently been supplemented by the introduction of e-DS1s, which is an electronic form of discharge submitted through the Land Registry Portal. The e-DS1 acts as both the evidence of discharge and the application to cancel the charge from the register. Currently, the e-DS1 service is designed for corporate chargees and their agents only.

---

[75] See LRA 2002 s.27(4), Sch.2 paras 9, 10.

[76] Land Registration Rules 2003 r.116, and see Sch.1, Form TR4 or Form AS2.

[77] In Forms DS1 or DS3, Land Registration Rules 1925 r.151, as substituted and amended by Land Registration Rules 1999 r.2(1), Sch.1 para.13; and Land Registration Rules 2000 r.2(1), Sch.1 para.1.

[78] Land Registration Rules 1925 r.151A, as inserted by Land Registration Rules 2000 r.2(1); Sch.1 para.2.

[79] Land Registration Rules 2003 r.115.

[80] Prescribed forms are required by r.114, namely DS1 (discharge of whole), or DS3 (release of part of land).

[81] See the Land Registry Practice Guide No.31—*Discharges of charges.*

[82] Namely, Form AP1 or DS2 in the case of the cancellation of the whole, or DS3 in the case of the release of part of the land from the registered charge.

[83] Form DS2E.

CHAPTER 14

EQUITABLE MORTGAGES AND CHARGES OF LAND

GENERALLY

The essential distinction between a mortgage and a charge is that a mortgage is **14–01** a conveyance of property, legal or equitable, subject to a right of redemption, whereas nothing is conveyed by a charge which merely provides the chargee with certain rights over the property charged.[1] Thus the rights accorded to an equitable chargee are not as extensive as those accorded to an equitable mortgagee.

Equitable mortgages: An equitable mortgage is a specifically enforceable **14–02** contract to create a legal mortgage.[2] It does not convey any legal estate or interest to the mortgagee, but creates a charge on the property charged, the charge amounting to an equitable interest. It is enforceable under the courts' equitable jurisdiction as an executory assurance equivalent to an actual assurance.[3] An equitable mortgage may be made by a mortgage of an equitable interest; by an agreement to create a legal mortgage; or by a mortgage which fails to comply with the formalities for a legal mortgage. A deposit of title deeds is not effective to create an equitable mortgage over land.[4]

Equitable charges: An equitable charge is an interest in a security created **14–03** without any transfer of title of possession to the beneficiary which can be created by an informal transaction for value and over any kind of property.[5] Thus, it is a security which only confers an equitable interest in the land upon the chargee and does not create a legal estate. In the absence of any express provision contained in the charge it does not amount to an agreement for a legal mortgage. It can be created expressly, or may arise where a mortgagor purports to mortgage a greater estate in the property than that which he possesses. The 1925 property legislation did not affect the form of equitable mortgages of equitable interests, and such mortgages can still be made by a conveyance of the whole equitable interest with a proviso for re-conveyance. Provided that the meaning is plain, the actual form of words used to create the equitable mortgage is immaterial.[6] It

---

[1] *Jones v Woodward* (1917) 116 L.T. 378 at 379; *London County and Westminster Bank Ltd v Tompkins* [1918] 1 K.B. 515, at 528.
[2] *Swiss Bank Corp v Lloyds Bank Ltd* [1982] A.C. 584.
[3] See *Downsview Nominees Ltd v First City Corp Ltd* [1993] A.C. 295 at 311.
[4] See *United Bank of Kuwait Plc v Sahib* [1997] Ch. 107.
[5] *Re Cosslett (Contractors) Ltd* [1998] Ch. 495.
[6] See *William Brandt's Sons & Co v Dunlop Rubber Co Ltd* [1905] A.C. 454 at 462.

must, however, be made in writing and signed by the mortgagor or his agent so authorised in writing.[7]

A contract to create a legal mortgage must comply with the formal requirements of s.2 of the Law of Property Act (Miscellaneous Provisions) Act 1989 in that it must be made in writing, signed by both parties and incorporate all the agreed terms. This provision made a fundamental change to the existing law which meant that it was no longer possible from September 27, 1989, to create an informal mortgage by depositing the title deeds to a property as security for a loan with no written memorandum. A mortgage so created had been enforceable on the basis of the doctrine of part performance which was aggregated by the Act.[8]

A contract made since September 27, 1989, for a mortgage of or a charge on land or any interest in land can be made only in writing and by incorporating all the terms which the parties have expressly agreed in one document or, where contracts are exchanged, in each.[9] The document incorporating the terms or, where contracts are exchanged, one of the documents incorporating them (but not necessarily the same one) must be signed by or on behalf of each party to the contract.[10]

CREATION

14–04   The provisions of the 1925 legislation did not alter the substantive law relating to equitable mortgages created over equitable interests in land. These mortgages are by definition equitable as the mortgagor only holds an equitable interest. The procedure for the creation of such mortgages is by conveyance or assignment of the whole equitable interest as security for the advance with a proviso for reconveyance or re-assignment on payment. There is no necessity for a deed. However, the creation of an equitable mortgage over an equitable interest in land *subsisting* at the time of the disposition is governed by the provisions of s.53(1)(c) of the Law of Property Act 1925. It must be in writing, signed by or on behalf of the mortgagor, and not merely evidenced in writing.[11]

Thus, provided that there is such a written document where it is intended to create an equitable mortgage over a subsisting equitable interest and the meaning is plain no particular form of words is necessary.[12] However, it is advantageous

---

[7] Law of Property Act (LPA) 1925 s.53(1)(c).

[8] See *Russel v Russel* (1783) 1 Broc. CC 269; *Re Alton Corp* [1985] B.C.L.C. 27 at 33; and *United Bank of Kuwait Plc v Sahib* [1997] Ch. 107.

[9] See *Commission for the New Towns v Cooper (GB) Ltd* [1995] Ch. 259; *Firstpost Homes Ltd v Johnson* [1995] 1 W.L.R. 1567.

[10] s.2(3) [s.21(1), (6) (as amended by the Trusts of Land and Appointment of Trustees Act 1996 s.25(2), Sch.4)].

[11] ibid., s.205(1)(ii), (xx); equitable mortgages of personalty are also governed by the same provision. It has been doubted that the provisions of s.53(1)(c) apply to mortgages of equitable interests which have come into existence through an implied or resulting trust.

[12] ibid., s.53(1)(c); and see *William Brandt's Sons & Co v Dunlop Rubber Co Ltd* [1905] A.C. 454 at 462. If the equitable mortgage is preceded by a contract for its disposition consensually made between the parties then the provisions of s.2 of the Law of Property (Miscellaneous Provisions) Act 1989 will apply.

for the equitable mortgage to have been created by deed so as to give rise to the mortgagee's statutory power of sale or to appoint a receiver.[13] An example of an equitable mortgage over an equitable interest occurs when beneficiaries holding under a trust of land wish to mortgage their interest. The beneficiaries must effect the same by conveyance and re-conveyance in writing. Another example that can arise is where one of two joint holders of a legal estate purports to create a legal mortgage by pretending to be solely entitled or by forging or obtaining by improper means the co-owner's signature. Such an act not only severs any beneficial joint tenancy but also operates to charge in equity the forging party's share of the beneficial interest.

The overreaching provisions usually apply where there has been a conveyance of the legal estate subject to a mortgage of an equitable interest under a trust for land. The proceeds of sale are utilised to satisfy the mortgage advance.[14]

EQUITABLE CHARGES OF EQUITABLE INTERESTS

An equitable charge over an equitable interest is again necessarily equitable as **14–05** the chargor only holds an equitable interest. An equitable charge of an equitable (or legal interest) in land is created when a particular asset is expressly or constructively made liable or specifically appropriated in satisfaction of a partic- ular debt or other obligation owed by the chargor or a third party entitling the chargee to seek to discharge that liability from that asset. It creates a transmis- sible interest in the land but without any transfer of title or possession (either actually or notionally) to the chargee in law or in equity.[15]

The creation of an equitable charge over an equitable interest is again gov- erned by the provisions of s.53(1)(c) of the Law of Property Act 1925. No special wording is required for its creation provided that the parties demonstrate the appropriate intention that the asset should form the subject matter of the secu- rity.[16] Again, it is advantageous for the equitable charge to be created by deed so as to give rise to the chargee's statutory power of sale.[17] The equitable chargee by deed is in exactly the same position as the equitable mortgagee in relation to sale or the appointment of a receiver out of court as the statutory definition of a

---

[13] ibid., s.10(1).

[14] LPA 1925 s.2(1)(iii), and see *City of London Building Society v Flegg* [1988] A.C. 54, 83 and 91.

[15] *London County and Westminster Bank v Tompkins* [1918] 1 K.B. 515 at 528; *Re Cosslett (Contractors) Ltd* [1998] Ch. 495 at 507–508, per Millett L.J.; *Carreras Rothmans Ltd v Freeman Mathews Treasure Ltd* [1985] Ch. 207 at 227. See also *Swiss Bank Corp v Lloyds Bank Ltd* [1982] A.C. 584, affirmed [1982] A.C. 584 at 595; *Re Charge Card Services Ltd* [1987] Ch. 150, affirmed [1989] Ch. 497; *Re Bank of Credit and Commerce International SA (No.8)* [1998] A.C. 214; *Bland v Ingram Estates Ltd* (2001) 24 E.G. 163.

[16] *Cradock v Scottish Provident Institution* (1893) 69 L.T. 380, affirmed (1894) 70 L.T. 718; *National Provincial and Union Bank of England v Charnley* [1924] 1 K.B. 431 at 440 and 445–456, and 459–460; *Mathews v Goodday* (1861) 31 L.J. Ch. 282. If the equitable charge is preceded (unusually) by a contract for its disposition consensually made between the parties then the provisions of s.2(1) of the Law of Property (Miscellaneous Provisions) Act 1989 will apply. For an unreported case on the provisions of s.2(3) of the 1989 Act and s.53(1)(a) of the 1925 Act, see *De Serville v Agree Ltd*, unreported, April 26, 2001.

[17] LPA1925 s.101(1).

mortgage extends to a charge.[18] If otherwise than by deed his remedies are inferior. Examples of equitable charges arise where a voluntary settlement or will charges land with the payment of money.[19] It is also possible for an equitable charge to arise by operation of law where one of two joint owners enters into a mortgage having forged the signature of the other co-owner.[20] Another instance can arise where a person holding a beneficial interest in land purports to charge the legal estate when he has no capacity to do so.

EQUITABLE MORTGAGES AND CHARGES OF LEGAL INTERESTS IN LAND

Equitable mortgages and charges arising from contract

14–06 Equitable securities in legal estates are executory contracts to grant legal mortgages,[21] or charges[22] in the strict sense. While a mortgage is a conveyance of property subject to a right of redemption, a charge is not a conveyance but gives the chargee certain rights over the property charged. An equitable mortgage of a legal interest creates an equitable interest in the land but does not convey any *legal* estate or interest to the creditor.[23]

A typical contract creating an equitable charge over a legal interest arises where one party enters into a written contract to charge his realty with the payment of a sum of money to another,[24] but only conferring on the creditor an equitable interest in the land charged. Such a contract does not amount to an agreement to grant a legal mortgage. However, the provisions of s.2 of the Law of Property (Miscellaneous Provisions) Act 1989 will apply as it is a contract for the sale or a disposition of an interest in land.[25] It may take priority over a subsequently acquired legal estate if duly registered.[26]

The essential difference, therefore, is that the equitable mortgage gives rise to a specifically enforceable agreement to create a legal mortgage enforceable under

---

[18] s.205(1)(xvi); and see paras 1–13 to 1–15.

[19] *Re Lloyd, Lloyd v Lloyd* [1903] 1 Ch. 385 at 404; *Re Owen* [1894] 3 Ch. 220. An equitable charge carries no right of foreclosure nor possession; the remedy is only by sale or mortgage of such interest, or the appointment of a receiver, see para.16–27.

[20] *First National Securities Ltd v Hegarty* [1985] 1 Q.B. 850; and see LPA 1925 ss.63(1), 53(1)(a).

[21] *London County and Westminster Bank v Tompkins* [1918] 1 K.B. 515.

[22] There have been many attempts to define "charge"; see *Re Sharland, Kemp v Rozey (No.2)* (1896) 74 L.T. 64; *National Provincial and Union Bank of England v Charnley* [1924] 1 K.B. 431; cf. *Thomas v Rose* [1968] 1 W.L.R. 1797.

[23] See s.205(1)(x) (amended by the Trusts of Land and Appointment of Trustees Act 1996 s.25(2), Sch.4).

[24] *Montagu v Earl of Sandwich* (1886) 32 Ch.D. 525; but the express contract to give a charge was construed as a contract to give a mortgage, so the security was enforceable by foreclosure. See also *Craddock v Scottish Provident Institution* (1893) 69 L.T. 380, affirmed (1894) 70 L.T. 718, where an annuity was secured by a deed appointing a receiver of rents and profits. Romer J. held this deed to be a good equitable charge, but decreed foreclosure, not sale. See also *National Provincial and Union Bank of England v Charnley* [1924] 1 K.B. 431 at 440, 445 and 459.

[25] See *United Bank of Kuwait Plc v Sahib* [1995] 2 W.L.R. 94, affirmed on different grounds [1997] Ch. 107.

[26] As a Class C (iii) land charge (general equitable charge), see the Land Charges Act 1972 ss.2(1), (4)(iii) (as amended).

the court's equitable jurisdiction.[27] An order can then be made vesting a legal term of years in the mortgagee. An alternative is for the mortgagee to apply to the court for an order for foreclosure. An action for specific performance does not arise in the case of an equitable charge as there is no express or implied agreement to execute a legal mortgage. The remedy is for an order for sale.[28]

CHARGING ORDERS

For Charging Orders, see Ch.20, below   **14–07**

---

[27] *Swiss Bank Corp v Lloyds Bank Ltd* [1982] A.C. 584, affirmed [1982] A.C. 584; *Downsview Nominees Ltd v First City Corp Ltd* [1993] A.C. 295 at 311.
[28] *Mathews v Goodday* (1861) 31 L.J. Ch. 282.

CHAPTER 15

MORTGAGES OVER MISCELLANEOUS INTERESTS IN OR RELATED TO LAND

FIXTURES

As a general principle of land law, whatever, is attached to the land becomes part **15–01** of it (*"quicquid planatur solo, solo cedit"*). That principle provides a good starting point for the consideration of the relationship between fixtures and mortgages of the land to which they are affixed. Subject to express provision to the contrary and limited other exceptions fixtures affixed to the mortgaged property form part of the security.[1] Accordingly, where fixtures pass by mortgage to the mortgagee, a trustee in bankruptcy of mortgagor will not be entitled to them.[2]

The rule applies to all fixtures which are the subject matter of legal or an equitable mortgages[3] of freehold or leasehold title.[4] Fixtures which are annexed to the land at the date of the mortgage or become so during its continuance form part of the security along with the land, whether or not they are specified in the terms of the mortgage.[5] Although fixtures can be expressly excluded from a mortgage the express identification of some fixtures as forming part of the security will not generally result in an inference that other unspecified fixtures were excluded from it.[6] Rights of foreclosure, possession and statutory rights of sale extend to the interest in any fixtures or personal chattels affected by the mortgage.[7]

---

[1] Law of Property Act 1925 (LPA 1925) ss.62(1), 205(1)(ii).

[2] *Clark v Crownshaw* (1823) B & Ad 804 and *Ashton v Blackshaw* (1870) L.R. 9 Eq. 510.

[3] *Re Lusty, Ex p. Lusty v Official Receiver* (1889) 60 L.T. 160.

[4] *Meux v Jacobs* (1875) L.R. 7 H.L. 481; *Southport and West Lancashire Banking Co v Thompson* (1887) 37 Ch.D. 64. Approved in *National Provincial and Union Bank of England v Charnley* [1924] 1 K.B. 431.

[5] *Mather v Fraser* (1856) 2 K. & J. 536; *Walmsley v Milne* (1859) 7 CB (ns) 115; *Longbottom v Berry* (1869) L.R. 5 Q.B. 123; *Holland v Hodgson* (1872) L.R. 7 C.P. 328; *Smith v Maclure* (1884) 32 W.R. 459; *Reynolds v Ashby & Son* [1904] A.C. 466; *Ellis v Glover and Hobson Ltd* [1908] 1 K.B. 388; *Vaudeville Electric Cinema v Muriset* [1923] 2 Ch. 74; *Hulme v Brigham* [1943] 1 K.B. 152 (a case where free-standing printing machines were held not to be fixtures despite the fact that the driving mechanism was fixed to the floor. See also *TSB Bank Plc v Botham* [1996] E.G.C.S. 149, *sub nom. Botham v TSB Bank Plc* (1996) 73 P. & C.R. D1 at D2, where it was held that items contained in a dwelling house were to be construed as fixtures.

[6] *Hamp v Bygrave* (1982) 266 Estates Gazette 720

[7] LPA 1925 ss.88(4), 89(4). *Cross v Barnes* (1877) 36 L.T. 693, *Re Rogerstone Brick & Store Co Ltd* (1919) 1 Ch. 110.

Fixtures which a tenant is entitled to retain as against his landlord pass with the mortgage of the leasehold interest granted by the tenant.[8] Thus the exceptions as to fixtures arising in the law of landlord and tenant do not apply as such in the case of mortgaged property.[9] However, where a landlord mortgages tenanted property, an exception exists. Trade fixtures which customarily belong to the tenant[10] will not pass with the mortgage of the reversion. As between landlord and his mortgagee, the landlord is entitled to permit such fixtures to be introduced or removed provided there is no express stipulation to the contrary and the security is not materially diminished.[11]

15–02   If chattels which are bailed under a hire or hire-purchase agreement, or are agreed to be sold under a conditional sale agreement, become fixtures (other than trade fixtures) they become subject to the mortgage even if affixed after it was created.[12] Where such chattels are trade fixtures, the owner or creditor has no right against a prior legal mortgagee, without notice of the agreement, to sever and remove them. However, he has such a right against a subsequent equitable mortgagee with or without notice.[13] This right is displaced by the right of a legal mortgagee of the land who has taken possession under his security. It is not so displaced by the right of an equitable mortgagee whose mortgage was created after the hire, hire-purchase or conditional sale agreement was entered into, even if the mortgagee took without notice of the agreement.[14] This position applies even when an equitable mortgagee has appointed a receiver who has entered into possession.[15] It should be noted where a hire purchase agreement or similar entitles the owner to enter and seize chattels in the event of default and the chattels have been affixed to land an equitable interest in the land in favour of the owner arises.[16] It appears by analogy such an interest is not capable of being protected as a land charge.[17] It is not a registrable estate under the Land Registration Act 2002 but is potentially protectable by a notice.

RENEWABLE LEASES, ENFRANCHISEMENTS AND ACCRETIONS

15–03   A first mortgagee is entitled to the benefit and value of anything that the mortgagor[18] or a subsequent mortgagee,[19] adds to the property so that the

---

[8] *Meux v Jacobs* (1875) L.R. 7 H.L. 481.

[9] *Climie v Wood* (1868) L.R. Exch. 257, affirmed (1869) L.R. 4 Exch. 328; *Monti v Barnes* [1901] 1 K.B. 205.

[10] *Sanders v Davis* (1885) 15 Q.B.D. 218.

[11] *Ellis v Glover and Hobson Ltd* [1908] 1 K.B. 388, *Mancetter Developments Ltd v Garmanson Ltd* [1986] Q.B. 1212.

[12] As to whether a chattel has become a fixture, see *Holland v Hodgson* (1872) L.R. 7 C.P. 328; *Crossley Bros v Lee* [1908] 1 K.B. 86.

[13] *Hobson v Gorringe* [1897] 1 Ch. 182; *Reynolds v Ashby and Son* [1904] A.C. 466; *Ellis v Glover and Hobson Ltd* [1908] 1 K.B. 388.

[14] *Re Samuel Allen & Sons Ltd* [1907] 1 Ch. 575

[15] ibid.

[16] *Reynolds v Ashby & Sons* [1904] A.C. 466, *Kay's Leasing Corp Pty Ltd v CSR Provident Fund Nominees Pty Ltd* [1962] V.R. 429

[17] *Poster v Slough Estate Ltd* [1969] 1 Ch. 495, *Shiloh Spinner Ltd v Harding* [1973] A.C. 691.

[18] *Re Kitchin, Ex p. Punnett* (1880) L.R. 16 Ch.D. 226.

[19] See *Maxwell v Ashe* (1752) 1 Bro. C.C. 444n; *Moody v Matthews* (1802) 7 Ves 174; *Sims v Helling* (1851) 21 L.J.Ch. 76; *Hughes v Howard* (1858) 25 Beav. 575; *Landowners West of England & South Wales Land Drainage and Inclosure Co v Ashford* (1880) L.R. 16 Ch.D. 411.

addition constitutes part of the mortgage security. It follows where a leasehold interest is extended or renewed, whether by the mortgagor or the mortgagee, the renewed or extended lease forms part of the mortgage security under the mortgage in place at the time of renewal or extension.[20] The mortgage affecting the extended or renewed lease will be subject to the same terms and confer the same rights on the mortgagee as the mortgage that was in place. It matters not whether the lease renewal or extension is achieved by the exercise of an option, accretion of adjoining land to an existing lease, a vesting order upon the grant of relief from forfeiture or by enfranchisement. It will result in the new or extended lease being mortgaged security for the benefit of the mortgagee.[21]

Where a mortgagor acquires an extended tenancy under the current statutory schemes conferring the right to an extended lease,[22] there is express statutory provision for the extension of the security to the extended lease.[23] Further,[24] the mortgagee who was entitled to possession of the title deeds relating to the original lease has a statutory right in the same terms in respect of those relative to the extended lease.[25]

By way of contrast, if the addition to the mortgagor's property is the freehold **15–04** reversion of a leasehold interest which forms the mortgaged security, that freehold estate will not necessarily form part of the security once acquired without more. The statutory route by which the freehold estate is acquired is of relevance in determining whether the freehold falls within the security or not.

A freehold estate acquired by a tenant under the Leasehold Reform Acts 1967[26] does not merge with his leasehold estate if the lease is mortgaged. Merger cannot occur when the charge and the land are owned by different persons, since the charge is an intervening interest in separate ownership. Unless the parties agree to restructure the mortgage, the leasehold interest alone will continue to be the mortgaged security and the freehold estate will be free of that mortgage in the hands of the leaseholder/mortgagor.

Since collective enfranchisement under the Leasehold Reform, Housing and Urban Development 1993 does not result in an individual leaseholder acquiring

---

[20] *Re Biss, Biss v Biss* [1903] 2 Ch. 40; *Rakestraw v Brewer* (1729) 2 P Wms 511; *Leigh v Burnett* (1885) L.R. 29 Ch. D. 231.

[21] *Re Kitchen, Ex p. Punnett* (1880) L.R. 16 Ch. D. 226, *Tucker v Farm and General Investment Trust Ltd* [1966] 2 Q.B. 421, *Chelsea Estates Investment Trust Co Ltd v Marche* [1955] Ch. 328, Leasehold Reform Act 1967 ss.14–16 (the 1967 Act), Leasehold Reform, Housing and Urban Development Act 1993 ss.58–58A (the 1993 Act) and *Belgravia Insurance Co Ltd v Meah* [1964] 1 Q.B. 436

[22] ibid., ss.14–16.

[23] See also the Leasehold Reform, Housing and Urban Development Act 1993 s.58(4), as regards the right of a tenant to the grant of a new lease of a flat. If the existing lease is subject to a mortgage the new lease takes effect subject to the mortgage in substitution for the existing lease.

[24] Under the 1967 Act s.14(6) and under the 1993 Act s.58(5).

[25] Under the 1993 Act s.58(5)–(6). The lessee/mortgagor is obliged to deliver the new lease to the mortgagee within a month of receiving the same from HM Land Registry. If the lessee/mortgagor fails to deliver the lease within the time provided the mortgage takes effect as if it included a term to deliver the lease (or counterpart) and enforcement action can be taken for the breach of that term.

[26] The 1967 Act ss.8–13, as amended by the 1979 Act.

the freehold estate there is no question of the individual's mortgagor acquiring an interest in the freehold by virtue of the enfranchisement. It is worth noting that mortgage term cannot be enfranchised.[27] If a freehold estate acquired by individual or collective enfranchisement was mortgaged prior to enfranchisement it must be transferred free from the existing incumbrances. Statutory provision is made for the automatic discharge of the mortgage by the payment of the premium due to the mortgagee or into court.[28]

The enlargement of a long lease into a freehold results in the freehold being subject to all the same covenants, provisions and obligations as the term would have been if enlargement had not occurred. Accordingly, a mortgage over a long lease takes effect over the freehold created by the enlargement of that lease.[29] Similarly, the exercise by a leaseholder's mortgagee of an option, in a lease, to acquire a freehold will result in the freehold being mortgaged on the same terms as the leasehold. Although the option was exercised by the mortgagee, ultimately he is not entitled to retain the benefit of the freehold estate per se. In other words, on redemption the mortgagor is entitled to get back the whole of his security. Thus on payment of principal, interest, costs and the purchase price of the reversion the mortgagor is entitled to a conveyance of the freehold.[30] Where a long lease that is mortgaged is enlarged into a fee simple it will be the fee simple that is the subject of the mortgage thereafter.[31]

MORTGAGES OF LEASEHOLDS AND REVERSIONARY INTERESTS

Relief from forfeiture

15–05   When a lease is determined by forfeiture, any derivative interests are determined along with the lease. A mortgage or a charge over a lease is such a derivative interest and accordingly is determined by forfeiture.[32] The fact that the mortgagee's interest in the lease is determined upon forfeiture commonly results in an early approach to a mortgagee by a lessor contemplating forfeiture for non-payment of sums due under the lease. The mortgagee's position is protected to a large extent by statute; however early intervening to avoid forfeiture proceedings will often be more attractive. For the avoidance of doubt the determination of the lease and the mortgagee's interest does not relieve the mortgagor of liability under his personal covenants.

---

[27] *Re Fairview, Church Street, Bromyard* [1974] 1 W.L.R. 579.
[28] Under the 1967 Act s.12; under the 1993 Act s.35.
[29] LPA 1925 s.153.
[30] *Nelson v Hannam* [1943] Ch. 59; *Citibank NA v MBIA Assurance SA* [2007] EWCA Civ 11; [2007] All E.R. (Comm) 475.
[31] LPA 1925 s.153(8).
[32] *G.W. Ry v Smith* (1876) L.R. 2 Ch.D. 235 at 253; *Viscount Chelsea v Hutchinson* [1994] 2 E.G.L.R. 61.

The mortgagee's position is protected in any event by his ability to intervene **15–06**
and seek relief from forfeiture which can operate retrospectively to restore the
lease. The court is empowered to grant relief from forfeiture on an application
being made to it by the mortgagee. The decision whether to grant relief from
forfeiture is essentially a matter for the discretion of the court.[33] There are two
forms of relief available to the court: the grant of a new lease to the mortgagee[34]
or the making of a retrospective vesting order vesting the original lease in the
mortgagor.[35] The court's discretionary powers to grant relief arise under s.146 of
the Law of Property Act 1925, ss.210 & 212 the Common Law Procedure Act
1952 or s.38 of the Senior Court Act 1981, s.138 of the County Courts Act 1984
and the High Court's inherent jurisdiction. Most applications for relief are made
pursuant to s.146 of the Law of Property Act 1925.

Subsection 146(4) of the Law of Property Act 1925[36] provides that where a **15–07**
lessor is proceeding by action or otherwise to enforce a right of re-entry or
forfeiture under any covenant, proviso or stipulation in a lease, or for non-
payment of rent, an underlessee (which includes a mortgagee[37] but not an
equitable chargee[38]) may apply for relief from forfeiture either in the lessor's
action (if any) or in any action brought by such person for that purpose. In effect
the mortgagee has the same rights as, and stands in the shoes of, the lessee under
the lease. For such a right to arise the mortgage must be by legal charge or sub-
demise.[39] It has been established that for the purposes of subs.146(4) mortgagee
does not include an equitable chargee holding under a charging order.[40]

Where a mortgagee makes an application under s.146(4) the court can make an
order vesting the whole term of the lease or any lesser term of the property
comprised in the lease or any part thereof in the mortgagee upon such conditions
as to the execution of any deed or other document, payment of rent, costs,
expenses, damages, compensation, giving security or otherwise as the court in
the circumstances of each case may think fit.[41] Various conditions can be
imposed by the court which include making good any subsisting breaches[42] or
performing the covenants of the existing lease. However, "in no case shall any
such under-lessee be entitled to require a lease to be granted to him for any longer

[33] See *Escalus Properties Ltd v Dennis* [1996] Q.B. 231; *Mohammadi v Anston Investments Ltd*
[2003] EWCA Civ 981; [2004] L. & T.R. 6.
[34] LPA 1925 s.146(2). For the procedural aspects in the High Court and County Court, see paras
26–09 et seq.
[35] ibid.,LPA 1925 s.146(4). For the procedural aspects in the High Court and County Court, see
paras 26–09 et seq.
[36] Replacing Conveyancing Act 1892 s.4, and as amended by the Law of Property (Amendment)
Act 1929 s.1.
[37] *Belgravia Insurance Co Ltd v Meah* [1964] 1 Q.B. 436.
[38] *Bland v Ingrams Estate Ltd* [2001] Ch. 767.
[39] See *Re Good's Lease* [1954] 1 W.L.R. 309; *Grand Junction Co Ltd v Bates* [1954] 2 Q.B. 160;
Chelsea Estate Investments Trust Co Ltd v Marche [1955] Ch. 328. Since October 13, 2003, the
creation of land mortgages by sub-demise have been abolished, see LRA 2002 s.23.
[40] *Bland v Ingrams Estates Ltd* [2001] Ch. 767.
[41] LPA 1925 s.146(2).
[42] *Ewart v Fryer* [1901] 1 Ch. 499 and *Chelsea Estates Investment Trust Co Ltd v Marche* [1955]
Ch. 338

term than he had under his original sub-lease".[43] Such relief gives rise to the creation of a *new* lease in favour of the mortgagee directly and the new lease becomes the substituted security and is subject to the mortgagors' right of redemption and the rights of subsequent mortgagees for an account of the proceeds of sale of the mortgaged property by such mortgagee.[44] In effect therefore, a vesting order of this sort creates a new direct relationship between mortgagee and lessee while the relationship between mortgagee and mortgagor remains.

As noted above by way of contrast, as an application under s.146(2) results in the retrospective restoration of the forfeited lease, which will once again be subject to the mortgage.[45] In those circumstances the mortgagee has no direct liability to the lessor under the lease and there will be no intervening period during which any liability for mesne profits could have arisen.[46]

15–08   A number of aspects arise for consideration with regard to these statutory provisions. The most important of these are the following. First, the court is only able to grant relief under s.146(4) where the lessor is proceeding by action or otherwise. A landlord is no longer "proceeding" once he obtains possession pursuant to a lawfully executed court order. A landlord who has peaceably re-entered without legal process is still "proceeding", despite having achieved physical re-entry.[47] The mortgagee can continue to seek relief at any point prior to the execution of a court order for possession. Delay in seeking relief or intervening events may of course have an impact on whether the court will exercise its discretion.

Second, pending relief being granted, a sub-tenant (including a mortgagee) is to be regarded as a trespasser in the interregnum period between the forfeiture of the lease and the grant of relief.[48] Third, as stated above, the grant is of a new lease and is not retrospective.[49] Further, a lease so granted need not be on the same terms as the original lease.[50]

Fourth, the mortgagee cannot seek relief under the provisions of s.146(2) of the Law of Property Act 1925 if the head lease is forfeited for non-payment of rent or where the provisions of s.146 are excluded.[51]

---

[43] LPA 1925 s.146(4). An apparent conflict exists between these provisions, but it has been decided that the court will not grant a sub-lessee a term longer than his sub-lease; see *Ewart v Fryer* [1901] 1 Ch. 499 at 515 and see *Factors Sundries Ltd v Miller* [1952] 1 All E.R. 630 at 634. It must be noted that a sub-lease can be extended by the provisions relating to security of tenure under the Rent Act 1977; see *Cadogan v Dimovich* [1984] 1 W.L.R. 609.

[44] See *Chelsea Estates Investments Trust Co Ltd v Marche* [1955] Ch. 328; *Cadogan v Dimovich* [1984] 1 W.L.R. 609; *Official Custodian for Charities v Mackey* [1985] Ch. 168 at 164; and see also *Official Custodian for Charities v Mackey (No.2)* [1985] 1 W.L.R. 1308; *Hammersmith and Fulham LBC v Tops Shop Centres Ltd* [1990] Ch. 237. For a recent case where relief under s.146(4) was refused to an equitable chargee, but allowed in a claim for *indirect* relief by the chargee based upon an implied obligation, see *Bland v Ingram's Estate Ltd* [2001] Ch. 767.

[45] *Escalus Properties Ltd v Robinson* [1996] Q.B. 231.

[46] *Escalus Properties Ltd v Robinson* [1996] Q.B. 231 and *Bland v Ingrams Estate Ltd* [2001] Ch. 767.

[47] *Billson v Residential Apartments Ltd* [1992] A.C. 494.

[48] *Official Custodian for Charities v Mackey* [1985] Ch. 168; *Viscount Chelsea v Hutchinson* [1994] 2 E.G.L.R. 61; *Pellicano v MEPC Plc* [1994] E.G.L.R. 104.

[49] See fn.29 above.

[50] *Hammersmith and Fulham LBC v Tops Shop Centres Ltd* [1990] 2 Ch. 237.

[51] LPA 1925 s.146(8) and (9).

Further, of considerable importance is the effect that the Landlord and Tenant **15–09** (Covenants) Act 1995[52] has on a new lease created by order of the court on or after January 1, 1996, and on the continued enforceability of the covenants contained in any forfeited lease granted before that date by the mortgagee of the reversion. Where a lease was granted before January 1, 1996, the mortgagee of the security is entitled to enforce and take advantage of covenants having reference to the subject matter of the lease, covenanted for by the lessee including the rights of re-entry.[53] He can also re-enter for breaches of covenant committed before the mortgage unless they had been waived or released at the time of the mortgage.[54]

A mortgagee in possession of property subject to a lease granted before January 1, 1996 can enforce any tenant covenant of a tenancy or any right of re-entry enforceable by the mortgagor.[55] Similarly, a mortgagee in possession of the tenant's interest can enforce a "landlord's covenant"[56] against the landlord.[57]

Any tenant covenant of a tenancy, or a right of re-entry contained in a tenancy enforceable against the tenant in respect of any property demised by the tenancy is also enforceable against any mortgagee in possession of the tenant's interest.[58] Covenants which are express to be personal or unenforceable for non-registration are not enforceable against a mortgagee in possession.[59]

An equitable chargee under a charging order over a lease has no direct ability **15–10** to apply for relief against forfeiture but may pursue relief indirectly. Chargors are subject to an implied obligation to take reasonable care to preserve the chargee's security. An equitable chargee can therefore require the chargor to initiate and pursue a claim for relief where such a claim can properly be made.[60]

GOODWILL

The general principle that anything added to the property becomes part of the **15–11** property in the context of mortgages extends to goodwill which will generally

[52] As the Law Commission Working Paper No.99, *Land Mortgages* pointed out at para.3.74 that as a result of a principle of privity of contract this had the effect of making the mortgagee liable on the covenants of the new lease throughout the term of the lease. See also the Law Commission Working Paper No.95, *Landlord and Tenant—Privity of Contract and Estate: duration of liability of parties to leases* (1986) where it was concluded that the principle of privity of contract should be abrogated. See also the recommendations of the Law Commission (1988) Law Com. No.174 which eventually resulted in the enactment of the Landlord and Tenant (Covenants) Act 1995 (which implemented these recommendations and other unpublished recommendations of the Law Commission, subject to modifications). The main provisions of this Act apply to all tenancies granted after January 1, 1996.
[53] See LPA 1925 s.141(1), (2). The expression "mortgagee" includes a "chargee", Landlord and Tenant (Covenants) Act 1995 s.15(6).
[54] LPA 1925 s.141(3).
[55] ibid., s.15(1). "tenant covenant" is defined by ibid., s.28(1).
[56] ibid., s.28(1).
[57] ibid., s.15(3).
[58] ibid., s.15(4).
[59] ibid., s.15(5).
[60] *Bland v Ingrams Estates Ltd* [2001] Ch. 767.

attach to mortgaged premises for the benefit of the mortgagee.[61] For instance, the goodwill of a public house business[62] attaches to the mortgaged property, with the result that the mortgagee will be entitled to an assignment of the licence,[63] but not to the proceeds of sale of those rights.[64] There is some authority supporting the proposition that the mortgage security will include the actual business carried on from the premises.[65] However, if the terms of the security show that the intention of the mortgagor and mortgagee was to limit the mortgage to the original property and not the goodwill of the business, it will not form part of the security.[66] Further, where goodwill arises from the mortgagor's personal reputation acquired from his expertise rather than the premises the mortgagee is not entitled to the benefit of the goodwill.[67]

COMPULSORY ACQUISITION OF LAND AND COMPENSATION

15–12 Where mortgaged property is to be compulsorily acquired both the mortgagor and the mortgagee are entitled to a notice to treat. Where the acquiring authority pays a lump sum into court in respect of both interests, the court will apportion the sum between them. It is, however, usual for the acquiring authority to treat with the mortgagor for the full value, leaving him to discharge the mortgage. The exception to that approach would be where the mortgagee is in possession. Where the acquiring authority wish to, and the mortgagee has not given notice of intention to redeem, it may redeem the mortgage immediately upon payment of the principal, interest, costs and six months' additional mortgage or six months' notice to pay.[68] Upon payment, the mortgagee's obligation to convey arises. Where a property is in negative equity only the value of the property, as agreed between mortgagee, mortgagor and acquiring authority (or as determined by the Lands Tribunal), will be paid and the mortgagee must convey his whole interest in the land to the acquiring authority.[69]

The mortgagee is entitled to the money paid as compensation for the licence of a mortgaged public house as part of the mortgage security.[70] There are special statutory provisions entitling the acquiring authority to redeem the mortgagee's interest in the land. It is necessary to refer to a specialist work in this field.[71]

---

[61] *Cooper v Metropolitan Board of Works* (1884) L.R. 25 Ch. D. 472. See also *Chissum v Dewes* (1828) 5 Russ. 29; *King v Midland Rly Co* (1868) 17 W.R. 113; *Pile v Pile, Ex p. Lambton* (1876) L.R. 3 Ch. D. 36; *Re Kitchin, Ex p. Punnett* (1880–81) L.R. 16 Ch. D. 226.

[62] *Re Kitchin, Ex p. Punnett* (1880–81) L.R. 16 Ch. D. 226, and *West London Syndicate v IRC* (1898) 2 Q.B. 507.

[63] *Rutter v Daniel* (1882) 30 W.R. 724 (on appeal 30 W.R. 801); *Re O'Brien* (1883) 11 L.R. Ir. 213; *Garrett v St Marylebone, Middlesex Justices* (1884) 12 Q.B.D. 620.

[64] *Re Carr* [1918] 2 I.R. 448.

[65] *County of Gloucester Bank v Rudry Merthyr Steam and House Coal Colliery Co* [1895] 1 Ch. 629.

[66] *Whitley v Challis* [1892] 1 Ch. 64; *Palmer v Barclays Bank Ltd* (1971) 23 P. & C.R. 30.

[67] *Cooper v Metropolitan Board of Works* (1884) L.R. 25 Ch. D. 472.

[68] Clauses Consolidation Act 1845 s.108, Compulsory Purchase Act 1965 s.14.

[69] Lands Clauses Consolidation Act 1845 s.110, Compulsory Purchase Act 1965 s.15(1).

[70] *Law Guarantee and Trust Society Ltd v Mitcham and Cheam Brewery Co Ltd* [1906] 2 Ch. 98; *Noakes v Noakes & Co Ltd* [1907] 1 Ch. 64; *Dawson v Braime's Tadcaster Breweries Ltd* [1907] 2 Ch. 359.

[71] See, e.g. *Compulsory Purchase and Compensation* (7th edn) Barry Denyer-Greene.

INSURANCE MONEYS AND MORTGAGE INDEMNITY POLICIES

Although a mortgagor is not obliged by statute to keep the mortgaged property **15–13** in repair, it is usual for him to covenant to do so.[72] All moneys received by virtue of any insurance of the mortgaged property effected under the provisions of the Law of Property Act 1925 or for the maintenance of which the mortgagor is liable under the mortgage deed must, if the mortgagee so requires, be applied by the mortgagor in making good the loss or damage in respect of which the money is received.[73]

However, the mortgagee has no right to the policy moneys if the mortgagor **15–14** insures on his own account.[74] In the case where the mortgagor insures having covenanted to do so, subject to express wording to the contrary the covenant will be construed as the grant to the mortgagee of a charge over the proceeds, but he will be accountable to the mortgagor for any surplus. This position arises even if the insurance is taken out in the name of the mortgagor by way of a partial equitable assignment.[75]

Frequently mortgagees take out a mortgage indemnity policy with an insur- **15–15** ance company. This is designed to protect the mortgagee against the inability or failure by the mortgagor to make the repayments due under the mortgage, at a time when the proceeds of sale are less than the outstanding debt on sale of the mortgaged property. Despite the fact that it is the mortgagor who is debited with the premium and the policy is usually described as additional security in the general conditions applicable to the mortgage, the proceeds of such a policy belong to the mortgagee and not the mortgagor. They do not discharge any part of the debt owed by the mortgagor.[76]

INCORPOREAL HEREDITAMENTS AND OTHER RIGHTS

Incorporeal hereditaments are rights related to property which are included as **15–16** part of real property in English land law. However, they are to be distinguished from corporeal land as they are rights of an intangible nature and consist of rights not interests in physical matter. Examples of incorporeal rights include franchises (such as markets and fairs)[77]; manorial rights; easements; profits (such as rights of common); rentcharges; annuities; advowsons; tithes and other property rights of an intangible nature separated from the ownership of corporeal property but closely connected with it.

Although the treatment of incorporeal hereditaments as part of the realty may be an accident of history, their status forms part of the land law. As such they

---

[72] See above para.12–25.
[73] LPA 1925 s.108(3).
[74] *Halifax Building Society v Keighley* [1931] 2 K.B. 248; *Re Doherty* [1925] 2 I.R. 246.
[75] *Colonial Mutual General Insurance Co Ltd v ANZ Banking Insurance Group (New Zealand) Ltd* [1995] 1 W.L.R. 1140.
[76] *Mortgage Corp v McNicholas*, unreported, September 22, 1992; *Woolwich Building Society v Brown* [1996] C.L.C. 625.
[77] See *Pease and Chitty's Law of Markets and Fairs* (5th edn, Cousins and Anthony, 1998).

constitute "land" for the purposes of the Law of Property Act 1925.[78] Further, as their existence depends on a grant, they can only be conveyed by deed. They may therefore be the subject matter of a legal mortgage. Advowsons are an exception to the ability to mortgage such rights as since they were excluded from the definition of "land" for the purposes of the Law of Property Act 1925.[79]

AGRICULTURAL MORTGAGES AND CHARGES

15–17   The general law of mortgages and bills of sale is applicable to mortgages and charges of farms and stock in appropriate cases subject to number of specific adjustments.[80] Generally, there is a bar on the exclusion or restriction of the statutory power of leasing. In addition there are special provisions contained in the Agricultural Credits Act 1928 for short-term credit by way of agricultural mortgages and charges in favour of a bank on farming stock.[81]

MORTGAGE OF MINES AND MINERALS

15–18   Generally, property consisting of or including mines and minerals can be subject to legal mortgages and charges provided that there is in existence a legal interest in the property in question to which the mortgage can relate. Given the wasting nature of such assets the mortgage deed of such property frequently includes provision for the creation of a sinking fund or repayment of the advance by instalments designed to ensure the security does not exceed the capital outstanding at any time. Another provision often inserted in the mortgage deed is permission, in the case of default, for the mortgagee to enter upon the mortgaged property, work the mine and to make all proper expenditure for that purpose. In the case of any deficiency it may be then be charged against the property.[82]

The mortgagee's statutory power of sale includes (and subject to any contrary intention expressed in the mortgage deed) the power to sell the mortgaged property or any part of it with the exception or reservation of all or any of the mines or minerals, or to sell all or any mines and minerals apart from the surface.[83]

---

[78] LPA 1925 ss.1(2), 205(I)(ix).
[79] See Beneficies Act 1898 ss.1(1)(b), 7; Beneficies Act 1898 (Amendment Measure) 1923 s.4; the Patronage (Beneficies) Measure 1986 repealed s.1 of the Beneficies Act 1898, see LPA 1925 s.201(1).
[80] See below paras 24–01 to 24–04.
[81] See Ch.24, below paras 24–13 et seq.
[82] *Norton v Cooper* (1854) 5 De. G.M. & G. 728.
[83] See LPA 1925 s.101(2)(ii), (4).

CHAPTER 16

CONSUMER PROTECTION

INTRODUCTION

The object of this chapter is to consider the regulatory landscape providing **16–01** protection for the consumer, comprising the Consumer Credit Act 1974 ("the CCA 1974")[1] and the Unfair Terms in Consumer Contracts Regulations 1999 ("the 1999 Regulations").[2]

The Unfair Terms in Consumer Contracts Regulations 1999

The 1999 Regulations derive from the EC Council Directive on Unfair Terms and **16–02** Consumer Contracts[3] which was initially implemented into English law by the Unfair Terms in Consumer Contracts Regulations 1994 ("the 1994 Regulations"). These regulations were repealed and replaced by the 1999 Regulations, which more closely follow the European Directive and enlarged the number of "qualifying bodies" which may apply to the courts for injunctive relief against the use or recommendation for use of unfair terms. The repealed regulations apply to contracts made between July 1, 1995, and September 30, 1999, the day before the coming into force of the 1999 Regulations on October 1, 1999.[4] They apply to contracts concerning the grant or transfer of an interest in land.[5]

---

[1] As amended by the Consumer Credit Act 2006.

[2] SI 1999/2083 (as amended), repealing the Unfair Terms in Consumer Contracts Regulations 1994, SI 1994/3159 and implementing the EC Directive on Unfair Terms in Consumer Contracts 93/13 EEC, [1993] OJ L95/29.

[3] Directive 93/13, [1993] OJ L95/21. While the 1999 Regulations follow the Directive almost word for word, their interpretation must also aim to give effect to the purpose behind the Directive: *Von Colson and Kammann v Land Nordrhein-Westfalen (C-14/83)* [1984] E.C.R. 1891; *Marleasing SA v La Comercial Internacionale de Alimentacion SA (C-106/89)* [1990] E.C.R. I-4135. To that, it is germane to note that the preamble to the Directive makes clear that its purposes are: (i) to reduce distortions in competition between sellers of goods and suppliers of services caused by differences in rules governing terms in consumer contracts; (ii) to create effective uniform legal protection for consumers from the imposition of unfair contract terms, especially (but not exclusively) where this concerns transactions with suppliers in Member States other than their own; and (iii) to enhance the awareness of consumers as to the rules of law which govern consumer contracts in Member States other than their own, for otherwise they may be deterred from entering direct transactions with suppliers in other Member States.

[4] The 1999 Regulations, regs 1 and 2. The uncertainty as to the temporal extent is considered in para.16–08 below.

[5] See para.16–12 below.

The 1999 Regulations subject a very wide range of types of terms in consumer contracts to two requirements. First, the terms should be "fair"; second, when in writing they should be written in "plain, intelligible language" (sometimes referred to as a requirement on "transparency"). As between the parties to any contract which fails the first test of fairness, that term is not binding on the consumer, while the term which fails the requirement of transparency is to be interpreted *contra proferentum* and may be subject to the test of fairness even if it relates to the contract's price to its main subject matter. At the higher level, the 1999 Regulations now empower the Director General of Fair Trading and a number of other bodies to bring proceedings from injunction to prevent the use of a term which is considered to be unfair or unclear.[6] This overarching regulatory control by the Director General of Fair Trading and others is outside the scope of this work and is not considered further.

The Consumer Credit Act 1974

16–03 The CCA 1974 provides a statutory code for the provision of credit and, save for the Bills of Sales Acts 1878–1882[7] (which deal with mortgages of personal property), replaces all prior legislation.[8] The CCA 1974 can apply to an agreement notwithstanding that the liability thereunder is secured by a mortgage or charge on land or relates to an advance for the purchase of land. However, certain land mortgage transactions are "exempt agreements" under the CCA 1974[9] and thus first legal residential mortgages[10] and "regulated home purchase plans"[11] are regulated by the Financial Services Authority ("the FSA") under the Financial Services and Markets Act 2000 ("the FSMA"). Accordingly, the market in relation to the provision of credit secured on land is regulated by both the FSA and the Office of Fair Trading (under the CCA 1974), with (on occasions) an element of overlap. Moreover, it is possible for some land mortgage transactions to fall outside both statutory regimes if they can take advantage of the exemptions under the CCA 1974 and are not within the scope of the regulatory provisions under the FSMA.[12] As for other exemptions from the CCA 9174 s.16A exempts "high net worth" debtors, s.16B exempts credit agreements entered into for the debtor's business purposes and s.16C makes provision in relation to "buy to let" properties. Such exempt agreements (apart from those

[6] See, for example, *Director General of Fair Trading v First National Bank Plc* [2002] 1 A.C. 481.

[7] See para.22–14, below.

[8] Such as the Moneylenders Acts 1900–1927, the Pawnbrokers Acts 1972–1960 and the Hire Purchase Act 1965.

[9] See paras 16–20 et seq. below.

[10] i.e. "regulated mortgage contracts" within the Regulated Activities Order 2001 (SI 2001/554) art.61 is amended by SI 2001/3544 art.8 and SI 2006/2383 art.17.

[11] Within the Regulated Activities Order 2001, SI 2001/554 art.63F(3)(a) as added with effect from April 6, 2007 by SI 2006/2383 art.18.

[12] CCA 1974 s.16 exempts certain land mortgage transactions where the creditor is a local authority, or housing authority from the provisions of the CCA. It also allows (by order) certain other land mortgage transactions to be affected by certain creditors (banks, building societies, insurers) and to be exempted by order. See SI 1989/869, as amended and paras 16–20 et seq. below.

regulated by the FSA)[13] are nevertheless not excepted from the "unfair credit relationship" provisions.[14]

The European Dimension

Directive 2008/48/EC on credit agreements for consumers[15] ("the 2008 Directive") was adopted by the European Council on April 23, 2008, and repeals[16] the existing directive on consumer credit (Directive 87/102/EEC).[17] The 2008 Directive is a "full harmonisation" directive that aims to promote both further integration of consumer credit markets and higher levels of consumer protection.[18] The 2008 Directive applies to almost all types of consumer credit from £160 to £60,260, with (as considered immediately below) the main exclusion being land mortgages.[19] **16–04**

Directive 2008/48/EC: The preambles to the 2008 Directive define inter alia the intended application of the new European Community consumer credit framework. In light of the English courts' now established approach to the interpretation of domestic legislation implementing European Directives,[20] some regard should be had to the preambles to the 2008 Directive. In particular, preamble (14) provides that: **16–05**

> "Credit agreements covering the granting of credit secured by real estate should be excluded from the scope of this Directive. That type of credit is of a very specific nature.[21] Also, credit agreements the purpose of which is to finance the acquisition or retention of property rights in land or in an existing or projected building should be excluded from the scope of this Directive.[22] However, credit agreements should not be excluded from the scope of this Directive only because their purpose is the renovation or increase of value of an existing building."

---

[13] CCA 1974 ss.140A(5), 16(6C).

[14] ibid., ss.16(7A), 16A(8), 16B(6), 16C(11).

[15] 2008 OJ L133/66.

[16] 2008 Directive art.29, effective from May 12, 2010.

[17] 1987 OJ L42/48.

[18] Preambles (1) to (10) and arts 1 and 22

[19] art.2.2(a) and preamble (14)

[20] *Litster v Forth Dry Dock and Engineering Co Ltd* [1990] 1 A.C. 546; *Marleasing SA v LA Comercial Internacionale de Alimentacion SA* [1992] 1 C.M.L.R. 305 (E.C.J.); *Khatun v London Borough of Newham and the Office of Fair Trading* [2004] EU.L.R. 116; [2004] 1 E.G.L.R. 34 (Newman J.) considering whether the Unfair Terms in Consumer Contracts Regulations 1999 ("the 1999 Regulations") could be construed as giving effect to the Unfair Contract Terms Directive (93/13/EEC) ("the 1993 Directive").

[21] In contrast to the position under the 1993 Directive, articulated by the Court of Appeal in *Khatun v London Borough of Newham and the Office of Fair Trading* [2005] Q.B. 37. Laws L.J. (with whom Auld and Wilson L.JJ. agreed) held at [68]–[70] that there was no distinction drawn between real and personal property and that, as a result, the 1993 Directive and the 1999 Regulations applied to contracts for the grant or transfer of an interest in land.

[22] Again, in contra-distinction to the position under the 1993 Directive and the 1999 Regulations. The ECJ in *Freiburger Kommunalbauten GMbH Baugesellschaft & Co KG v Hofstetter* [2004] 2 C.M.L.R. 13 assumed that a contract for the purchase of a building to be constructed fell within the scope of the 1993 Directive, and before the Court of Appeal in *UK Housing Alliance (North West) Ltd v Francis* [2010] 3 All E.R. 519 counsel conceded that the 1999 Regulations applied to a sale and leaseback (that is, "property rights in land or an existing building"). See also the Court of Appeal decision in *Khatun* (above).

The body text of the Directive is similarly clear about the limits to its application. Article 2.2 provides that the 2008 Directive shall not apply inter alia to:

(a) credit agreements which are secured either by a mortgage or by another comparable security commonly used in a Member State on immovable property or secured by a right related to immovable property;

(b) credit agreements the purpose of which is to acquire or retain property rights in land or in an existing or projected building;

(c) credit agreements involving a total amount of credit[23] less than €200 or more than €75,000.

It is therefore not intended at Community level that land mortgages should fall within the scope of the 2008 Directive. Further, although the 2008 Directive will apply to credit agreements the purpose of which is simply to make improvements to an existing building, the new provisions should not apply to credit agreements in relation to the acquisition of property rights in land or in buildings.

The Consumer Credit (EU Directive) Regulations 2010

16–06   The Consumer Credit (EU Directive) Regulations 2010[24] ("the 2010 Regulations"), implement the 2008 Directive in the United Kingdom, and will come into force on February 1, 2011, with certain exceptions.[25] Part 2 of the 2010 Regulations contains amendments to the CCA 1974 and Pt 3 contains amendments to the considerable volume of secondary legislation made under the CCA 1974. Regrettably, there are at present no plans to consolidate the consumer credit legislation.[26]

The Department for Business Innovation and Skills ("DBIS") states[27] that "the key new elements in the new consumer credit regime" are:

(a) a duty on the lender to provide adequate explanations about the credit on offer to the consumer (regs 3 and 4);

(b) an obligation on the lender to check creditworthiness before offering or increasing credit (reg.5);

(c) requirements concerning credit reference databases (reg.40);

(d) a right for consumers to withdraw from a credit agreement within 14 days, without giving any reason (reg.13);

(e) requirements to inform consumers when debts are sold on (reg.36);

(f) requirements on credit intermediaries to disclose fees and links to creditors (reg.41); and

(g) a right to make partial early repayments of credit (regs 29–34, 59–62, and 77–84).

---

[23] Defined at art.3(l): "the ceiling or the total sums made available under the credit agreement".
[24] SI 2010/1010, as already amended by SI 2010/1969.
[25] See further regs 99–101; Explanatory Note to the 2010 Regulations.
[26] Explanatory Memorandum, para.7.7.
[27] See *http://www.bis.gov.uk/policies/consumer-issues/consumer-credit-and-debt/consumer-credit-regulation/ec-consumer-credit-directive/consumer-credit-directive-draft-regulations* [Accessed September 30, 2010].

DBIS adds further that the 2008 Directive "will amend existing consumer credit law in a number of areas, including advertising, consumer information, and the calculation of the total charge for credit."[28] To this end, four further pieces of secondary legislation assist in the implementation of the 2008 Directive in those specific areas: the Consumer Credit (Total Charge for Credit) Regulations 2010[29]; the Consumer Credit (Advertisements) Regulations 2010[30]; the Consumer Credit (Disclosure of Information) Regulations 2010[31]; and the Consumer Credit (Agreements) Regulations 2010.[32]

Given the tenor of the 2008 Directive, it is perhaps unsurprising that the 2010 Regulations have only very limited application to credit agreements secured on land. Save as regards the change to the "high net worth" opt out exception in s.16A of the CCA 1974,[33] where the 2010 Regulations do apply it is largely in relation the provision and disclosure of relevant information.[34]

The same is true of the four, additional sets of 2010 regulations. The Consumer Credit (Advertisements) Regulations 2010 do not apply to a credit advertisement insofar as it relates to a consumer credit agreement secured on land.[35] The Consumer Credit (Agreements) Regulations 2010 only apply to a consumer credit agreement secured on land where pre-contract credit information has been disclosed in compliance (or in purported compliance) with the Consumer Credit (Disclosure of Information) Regulations 2010.[36] The Consumer Credit (Disclosure of Information) Regulations 2010 only apply to a consumer credit agreement secured on land in the limited circumstances prescribed in reg.2(5). The Consumer Credit (Total Charge for Credit) Regulations 2010 do not apply to consumer credit agreements which are secured on land, or to prospective consumer credit agreements which are to be secured on land, except to the extent that the Consumer Credit (Disclosure of Information) Regulations 2010 apply to such agreements.[37]

Reform

The European Commission is expected to review the 2008 Directive in 2013 and, **16–07** if appropriate, put forward proposed amendments to the existing framework. DBIS proposes to carry out a review of the effectiveness of the domestic implementing legislation to a similar timescale.[38] In relation to land mortgages specifically, the status quo for agreements secured on land (and more specifically in relation to agreements for second mortgages) has, for the present, largely been retained. This is because the regulation of mortgage lending is under review and

---

[28] See further s.7 (key changes) of the Explanatory Memorandum to the five sets of 2010 regulations.
[29] SI 2010/1011.
[30] SI 2010/1012, as amended by SI 2010/1970.
[31] SI 2010/1013, as amended by SI 2010/1969.
[32] SI 2010/1014, as amended by SI 2010/1969.
[33] See para.16–21 below.
[34] Regs 53–56, 65(b), 66, 67, 75, 78.
[35] reg.11(5).
[36] reg.2.
[37] reg.3.
[38] Explanatory Memorandum, para.12.2.

it was not considered appropriate to make changes before the outcome of the review is known.[39] The review comprises, initially, a consultation exercise undertaken by HM Treasury in relation to buy-to-let and second mortgages. The Treasury published its paper "Mortgage regulation: a consultation" on November 25, 2009,[40] in which the government considered (i) the transfer of responsibility for the regulation of lending on second mortgages from the OFT to FSA; (ii) the extension of FSA regulation to buy-to-let mortgages; and (iii) consumer protection in the onward sale of regulated mortgage portfolios to unregulated entities. It seems the government will proceed with legislation to implement at least the first[41] of these proposals to coincide with the results of the FSA's own consultation, resulting in a single regulator for all residential mortgage lending.[42] The FSA's consultation paper "Mortgage Market Review: Responsible Lending" was published in July 2010,[43] and the responses to the proposals were expected, variously, between September 30 and November 16, 2010. The FSA intends to publish a policy statement in the first quarter of 2011.

THE UNFAIR TERMS IN CONSUMER CONTRACTS REGULATIONS 1999

Contracts governed by the Regulations

Timing of the contract

16–08 Between them, the 1994 and 1999 Regulations have been in force continuously since July 1, 1995. As to their temporal effect, their terms are ambivalent. As a matter of construction, the requirement of fairness arguably applies to all contracts whenever created, while the requirement of fairness may only apply to contracts made after they came into force.[44] The Directive states that it applies to all contracts concluded after December 31, 1994.[45] Since the domestic courts of a Member State must interpret national law to give effect to a directive, it would seem that the Regulations do not have retrospective effect at least prior to January 1, 1995. As to the "twilight period" between the commencement of the Directive and the coming into force of the 1994 Regulations (i.e. January 1, 1995 to June 30, 1995), the provisions of the Directive would only apply if it were to have direct effect in this jurisdiction. Mindful of the requirements to implement such a directive in this fashion,[46] the better view would seem to be that an English court has no obligation to give effect to the Directive between a "non-

---

[39] Explanatory Memorandum, para.4.3.

[40] Treasury paper, "Mortgage regulation: a consultation", December 2010.

[41] Further consultation will be undertaken as to the appropriate form of regulation of the two later, following the closure of the Treasury consultation on investment in the UK private rented sector.

[42] Treasury paper "Mortgage regulation: summary of responses", March 2010, paras 1.3–1.5.

[43] CP10/16, July 2010; see also "Mortgage Review Discussion Paper" DP09/3.

[44] See 1994 Regulations regs 5(1) and 6; 1999 Regulations regs 8(1) and 7.

[45] reg.10.

[46] See S. Prechal, *Directives in EC Law* (OUP, 2nd edn, 2005) pp.243 et seq; *Marshall I (152/84)* [1986] E.C.R. 723; *Faccini Dori (C-91/92)* [1994] E.C.R. 1-3325.

state business"[47] and a consumer in that period and only as between a "state business" and a consumer if the 1994 Regulation passes the conditions for direct effect.

The nature of the contract to which the Regulations apply

They apply in relation to unfair terms in contracts concluded between a seller or a supplier and a consumer. They do not apply to contractual terms which reflect: **16–09**

(a) mandatory statutory or regulatory provisions (including such provisions under the law of any member state or in Community legislation having effect in the United Kingdom without further enactment); or
(b) the provisions or principles of international conventions to which the Member States or the Community are party.[48]

"Consumer":   A "consumer" is defined as meaning any natural person[49] who, in contracts covered by the Regulations, is acting for purposes which are outside his trade, business or profession.[50] A borrower who had taken out a loan on a property that was partly residential and partly commercial has been held to be a consumer for the purposes of the Unfair Terms in Consumer Contracts Regulations 1999 with the consequence that an early redemption penalty imposed by the lender was unfair.[51]   **16–10**

"Seller or supplier":   A "seller or supplier" is defined as meaning any natural or legal person who, in contracts covered by the Regulations, is acting for purposes relating to his trade, business or profession,[52] whether publicly owned or privately owned.[53]   **16–11**

---

[47] On the inclusion of public bodies acting in the course of a business within the 1993 Directive generally, see below, para.15–024. The ECJ has taken a broad view of the concept of the State for the purposes of the doctrine of vertical direct effect: see *Foster v British Gas Plc (C-188/89)* [1990] E.C.R. I-3313 and Craig and de Búrca, *EU Law: Text, Cases, and Materials*, 4th edn (2008), pp.284–87.

[48] 1999 Regulations reg.4.

[49] i.e. not companies.

[50] As to whether an individual is a "consumer", see *Standard Bank London Ltd v Apostolakis (No.1)* [2000] I. L. Pr. 766 and *Standard Bank London Ltd v Apostolakis (No.2)* [2001] Lloyd's Rep. Bank 240; *Prostar Management Ltd v Twaddle* [2003] S.L.T. (Sheriff's Court) 11 and *Heifer International Inc v Christinansen* [2008] Bus. L.R. D 49; *Maple Leaf Macro Volatility Master Fund v Rouvroy* [2009] 1 Lloyd's Rep. 475; *Barclays Bank Plc v Kufner* [2009] 1 All E.R. (Comm.) 1.

[51] *Evans v Cherry Tree Finance Ltd* [2008] EWCA Civ 331. Tuckey L.J. considered that the purpose for which the natural person entered into the contract was an objective question of fact, at the time the contract was made. Whether a contract which was partly for trade would be within the Regulations was left open.

[52] A local authority discharging its statutory obligation to house the homeless has been within this definition: *Newnham LBC v Khatun* [2005] Q.B. 37. See also *Veedfald v Arhus Amtskommune* [2001] ECR 1-3569 at [15] on a similarly worded directive.

[53] ibid., art.3.

16–12   Contract for the sale or creation of an interest in land: In *Newnham LBC v Khatun, Zeb and Iqbal*,[54] the Court of Appeal held that, in construing the Directive as a measure aimed at providing the consumer with a high level of protection which did not expressly exclude land transactions and as part of a single corpus of law binding across the member states, there was no basis for importing into the application of the Directive the English law distinction between real and personal property. It concluded therefore that the Directive and the 1999 Regulations applied to contracts for the grant or transfer of an interest in land. Subsequently, the European Court of Justice in *Freiburger Kommunalbauten GMbH Baugesellschaft & Co KG v Hofstetter*[55] was content to assume that a contract for the purchase of a building to be constructed falls within the ambit of the 1993 Directive, although the issue of the application of the 1993 Directive to contracts relating to land was not before the court. The application of the Regulations to a sale and leaseback was conceded in *UK Housing Alliance (North West) Ltd v Francis*.[56] It must follow that the 1999 Regulations therefore apply to mortgages.

Unfair terms

16–13   What constitutes unfairness: Regulation 5(2) of the 1999 Regulations provides that a contractual term which has not been individually negotiated[57] is to be regarded as unfair if, contrary to the requirement of good faith, the *term* causes a significant imbalance[58] in the parties' rights[59] and obligations arising under the contract, to the detriment of the consumer. Moreover, notwithstanding that a specific term or certain aspects of it in a contract has or have been individually negotiated, the Regulations still apply to the rest of a contract if an overall assessment of the contract indicates that it is a pre-formulated standard contract.[60] Thus, a few bespoke terms will not save the remainder of a standard form contract from being subject to the Regulations.[61]

---

[54] [2005] Q.B. 37. See also *Kindlance v McBride*, unreported, 1997 N.I. Ch. D. (where on a summons for possession of mortgaged property it was held that the Regulations did apply to contracts of mortgage); *Falco Finance Ltd v Gough* (1999) 17 Tr. L. 526, Macclesfield Cty Ct and *Director General of Fair Trading v First National Bank* [2002] 1 A.C. 481.

[55] (C–237/02) [2004] 2 C.M.L.R. 13.

[56] [2010] Bus. L.R. 1034; [2010] 3 All E.R. 519. See also *Zealander v Laing Homes Ltd* (2000) 2 T.C.L.R. 724 (arbitration clause in a new-build contract); *Peabody Trust Governors v Reeve* [2008] EWHC 1432 (Ch) (contract of tenancy).

[57] And this, in reality, must be the case in relation to all or virtually all terms of a mortgage or other charge, if only because reg.5(2) provides that a term is always be regarded as not having been individually negotiated where it has been drafted in advance and the consumer has therefore not been able to influence the substance of the term.

[58] Thus, an unfair term may be adequately counterbalanced by others in the contract (e.g. a right to terminate without penalty when the terms is invoked).

[59] It thus may not matter that it has not been relied on or does not cause unfairness on the facts. It is the potential for unfairness that the Regulations will strike down. Thus, broadly drafted terms represent a particular risk.

[60] 1999 Regulations reg.5.

[61] Indeed, this may be the case if the standard form is advanced by the consumer, although the point was left open in *Bryen & Langley Ltd v Boston* [2005] EWCA Civ 973 (JCT contract).

The burden of demonstrating that a term was individually negotiated lies on the person advancing such a case.[62] The fact that the consumer or his legal representative has had the opportunity of considering the terms of an agreement does not mean that any single term has been individually negotiated; reg.5(2) imposes an absolute prohibition on a finding of individual negotiation if the consumer had not been able to influence the substance of the term.[63]

Any contractual term which provides that that a consumer bears the burden of proof in respect of showing whether a distance supplier or an intermediary complied with any or all of the obligations placed upon him resulting from the Directive and any rule or enactment made by the Financial Services Authority under the Financial Services and Markets Act 2000[64] implementing it shall always be regarded as unfair.

The unfairness of a contractual term falls to be assessed taking into account the nature of the goods or services for which the contract was concluded and by reference, at the time of conclusion of the contract,[65] to all the circumstances attending the conclusion[66] of the contract and to all the other terms of the contract or of any other contract on which it is dependent.[67]

The concept of "good faith" requires some elaboration in the context of this test.[68] While the first and basic element of the requirement of fairness is that the term "causes a significant imbalance in the parties' rights and obligations arising under the contract, to the detriment of the consumer", not all contract terms which cause such a significant imbalance are to be held unfair. Recital 16 of the Directive explains the special role of the requirement of good faith.

> "Whereas the assessment, according to the general criteria chosen, of the unfair character of the terms, in particular in sale or supply activities of a public nature providing collective services which take account of solidarity among users, must be *supplemented by a means of making an overall evaluation of the different interests involved; whereas this constitutes the requirement of good faith*; whereas, in making an assessment of good faith, particular regard shall be had to the strength of the bargaining positions of the parties, whether the consumer had an inducement to agree to the term and whether the goods or services were sold or supplied to the special order of the consumer; whereas the requirement of good faith may be satisfied by the seller or supplier where he deals fairly and equitably with the other party whose legitimate interests he has to take into account" (*emphasis added*).

It thus represents a factor which requires the court to have regard to the circumstances as a whole. In *Director General of Fair Trading v First National Bank Plc*[69] the House of Lords considered the requirement of good faith and the

---

[62] ibid., reg.5(4).

[63] *Housing Alliance (North West) Ltd v Francis* [2010] Bus. L. R. 1034; [2010] 3 All E.R. 519.

[64] Or by a designated professional body within the meaning of FMSA, s.326(2).

[65] This would allow the court to take into account circumstances prior to the contract being concluded but, it is submitted, not afterwards.

[66] Including whether it was signed under pressure of time or without an opportunity for the consumer to read it.

[67] 1999 Regulations reg.6(1).

[68] See also Collins, "Good Faith in European Contract Law" (1994) 14 O.J.L.S 229; quoted with approval in *OFT v Abbey National Plc* [2009] UKSC 6; [2010] 1 A.C. 696, [44] (Sup. Ct.).

[69] [2001] 1 A.C. 481.

test of unfairness more generally for the purposes of the Directive. Lord Bingham of Cornhill observed:

> "The requirement of good faith in this context is one of fair and open dealing. Openness requires that the terms should be expressed fully, clearly and legibly, containing no concealed pitfalls or traps. Appropriate prominence should be given to terms which might operate disadvantageously to the customer. Fair dealing requires that a supplier should not, whether deliberately or unconsciously, take advantage of the consumer's necessity, indigence, lack of experience, unfamiliarity with the subject matter of the contract, weak bargaining position or any other factor listed in or analogous to those listed in Schedule 2 to the [1994] Regulations.[70] Good faith in this context is not an artificial or technical concept; nor, since Lord Mansfield was its champion, is it a concept wholly unfamiliar to British lawyers. It looks to good standards of commercial morality and practice. Regulation [5(2)] lays down a composite test, covering both the making and the substance of the contract, and must be applied bearing clearly in mind the objective which the Regulations are designed to promote."[71]

16–14   **The list:**   Regulation 5(5) and Sch.2 of the 1999 Regulations provide for an indicative and illustrative list of what terms may be regarded as unfair. The list is broadly drawn and its scope has significant potential to encompass many "usual" mortgage provisions.

Subject to the saving provisions contain in para.2 of the Schedule which are considered below, it covers terms which have the object or effect of:

> "(a) excluding or limiting the legal liability of a seller or supplier in the event of the death of a consumer or personal injury to the latter resulting from an act or omission of that seller or supplier;
>
> (b) inappropriately excluding or limiting the legal rights of the consumer vis-a-vis the seller or supplier or another party in the event of total or partial non-performance or inadequate performance by the seller or supplier of any of the contractual obligations, including the option of offsetting a debt owed to the seller or supplier against any claim which the consumer may have against him;
>
> (c) making an agreement binding on the consumer whereas provision of services by the seller or supplier is subject to a condition whose realisation depends on his own will alone;
>
> (d) permitting the seller or supplier to retain sums paid by the consumer where the latter decides not to conclude or perform the contract, without providing for the consumer to receive compensation of an equivalent amount from the seller or supplier where the latter is the party cancelling the contract;

---

[70] These provisions do not appear in the 1999 Regulations but since the factors mentioned were taken from the preamble to the Directive, they remain relevant to the assessment of good faith under the current Regulations. Schedule 2 provided that:

"In making an assessment of good faith, regard shall be had in particular to—
  (a) the strength of the bargaining positions of the parties;
  (b) whether the consumer had an inducement to agree to the term;
  (c) whether the goods or services were sold or supplied to the special order of the consumer, and
  (d) the extent to which the seller or supplier has dealt fairly and equitably with the consumer."

[71] ibid., [17].

(e) requiring any consumer who fails to fulfil his obligation to pay a dispropor-
tionately high sum in compensation[72];

(f) authorising the seller or supplier to dissolve the contract on a discretionary
basis where the same facility is not granted to the consumer, or permitting the
seller or supplier to retain the sums paid for services not yet supplied by him
where it is the seller or supplier himself who dissolves the contract;

(g) enabling the seller or supplier to terminate a contract of indeterminate
duration without reasonable notice except where there are serious grounds for
doing so;

(h) automatically extending a contract of fixed duration where the consumer does
not indicate otherwise, when the deadline fixed for the consumer to express
his desire not to extend the contract is unreasonably early;

(i) irrevocably binding the consumer to terms with which he had no real
opportunity of becoming acquainted before the conclusion of the contract;

(j) enabling the seller or supplier to alter the terms of the contract unilaterally
without a valid reason which is specified in the contract;

(k) enabling the seller or supplier to alter unilaterally without a valid reason any
characteristics of the product or service to be provided;

(l) providing for the price of goods to be determined at the time of delivery or
allowing a seller of goods or supplier of services to increase their price
without in both cases giving the consumer the corresponding right to cancel
the contract if the final price is too high in relation to the price agreed when
the contract was concluded;

(m) giving the seller or supplier the right to determine whether the goods or
services supplied are in conformity with the contract, or giving him the
exclusive right to interpret any term of the contract;

(n) limiting the seller's or supplier's obligation to respect commitments undertaken by his agents or making his commitments subject to compliance with
a particular formality[73];

(o) obliging the consumer to fulfil all his obligations where the seller or supplier
does not perform his,

(p) giving the seller or supplier the possibility of transferring his rights and
obligations under the contract, where this may serve to reduce the guarantees
for the consumer, without the latter's agreement;

(q) excluding or hindering the consumer's right to take legal action or exercise
any other legal remedy, particularly by requiring the consumer to take
disputes exclusively to arbitration not covered by legal provisions, unduly
restricting the evidence available to him or imposing on him a burden of
proof which, according to the applicable law, should lie with another party to
the contract."

Schedule 2 para.2 provides for some clauses within the list not to be regarded as
unfair. Thus:

(a) para.(g) above is without hindrance to terms by which a supplier of
financial services reserves the right to terminate unilaterally a contract
of indeterminate duration without notice where there is a valid reason,
provided that the supplier is required to inform the other contracting
party or parties thereof immediately;

(b) para.(j) above is without hindrance to terms under which:

---

[72] Such as interest at 8% over base on non-payment of an invoice for 30 days or more: *Munkenbeck
& Marshall v Harold* [2005] EWHC 356 (TCC).

[73] e.g. "entire agreement clauses".

      (i)   a supplier of financial services reserves the right to alter the rate of interest payable by the consumer or due to the latter, or the amount of other charges for financial services without notice where there is a valid reason, provided that the supplier is required to inform the other contracting party or parties thereof at the earliest opportunity and that the latter are free to dissolve the contract immediately,

      (ii)   a seller or supplier reserves the right to alter unilaterally the conditions of a contract of indeterminate duration, provided that he is required to inform the consumer with reasonable notice and that the consumer is free to dissolve the contract;

  (c)   paras (g), (j) and (l) do not apply to:

      (i)   transactions in transferable securities, financial instruments and other products or services where the price is linked to fluctuations in a stock exchange quotation or index or a financial market rate that the seller or supplier does not control,

      (ii)   contracts for the purchase or sale of foreign currency, traveller's cheques or international money orders denominated in foreign currency;

  (d)   para.(l) is without hindrance to price indexation clauses, where lawful, provided that the method by which prices vary is explicitly described.

16–15   **Regulation 6—the partial exclusion of "core terms":**   Since the 1999 Regulations control unfair terms and not unfair contracts (in the sense of contract which represents a bad bargain), reg.6(2) of the 1999 Regulations operates to exclude from their scope (but only insofar as it is in plain, intelligible language) any assessment of the fairness of a term which relates (a) to the definition of the main subject matter of the contract, or (b) to the adequacy of the price or remuneration, as against the goods or services supplied in exchange.

     In *Director General of Fair Trading v First National Bank Plc*,[74] the House of Lords took a restrictive approach to the interpretation of the exclusion of "core terms" from this test of fairness. In the view of Lord Bingham of Cornhill:

> "The object of the Regulations and the Directive is to protect consumers against the inclusion of unfair and prejudicial terms in standard-form contracts into which they enter, and that object would plainly be frustrated if [reg.6(2)] were so broadly interpreted as to cover any terms other than those falling squarely within it. In my opinion the term, as part of a provision prescribing the consequences of default, plainly does not fall within it. It does not concern the adequacy of the interest earned by the bank as its remuneration but is designed to ensure that the bank's entitlement to interest does not come to an end on the entry of judgment."[75]

In determining whether a term falls within reg.6(2) by virtue of it being couched in terms which are plain and intelligible, a traditional, common law, approach to

---

[74] [2002] 1 A.C. 481 (HL).
[75] ibid., [12].

the construction of the term is inappropriate. Rather than relying on the construction of the contract in the traditional way (the intention of both the contracting parties as viewed objectively), the court will look at the reasonable expectation of the consumer in question albeit not to the exclusion of a consideration of the typical seller or supplier.[76]

So in *OFT v Foxtons Ltd*,[77] Mann J. held that in order to determine whether certain letting agency terms and conditions were expressed in plain and intelligible language, it was necessary to define the typical consumer. It was not in issue in that case that "professional" or "commercial" landlords doing business with F were not "consumers" for the purposes of the Regulations; the issue raised concerned the "consumer" landlords who had acquired one or two properties as an alternative to pensions and savings. The typical consumer was to be defined on an analogous footing to that on which the court approached the attributes of the reasonable man. When considering the term and whether it was "plain and intelligible", the court held that a term could fail that test even though it was not so vague as to be void for legal uncertainty.[78] Nor would a term fail the "plain and intelligible" requirement simply because it was capable of bearing different meanings:

> "Any lawyer worth his salt can usually contrive possible alternative meanings of contractual words, and the fact that this can be done does not of itself make any given language insufficiently plain and intelligible. For that to result the alternative wording, or uncertain effect, must be one of substance or significance, and not merely of legal contrivance."[79]

Nor does the fact that a term may arguably be implied into a written contract does not mean that there is doubt as to the meaning of the written terms themselves.[80]

As to reg.6(2)(b),[81] the Supreme Court in *OFT v Abbey National Plc*[82] held that it contains no indication that only an "essential", rather than "ancillary", price or remuneration was relevant for the purposes of that regulation and that any monetary price or remuneration payable under a contract fell within its scope. So (on the facts of that case) charges for unauthorised overdrafts were not the prices paid in exchange for the transactions in question, nor default charges designed to discourage customers from overdrawing on their accounts without prior arrangement, but were monetary consideration for the package of banking services supplied to current account customers. The evidence showed that these charges were an important part of the bank's charging structure and the court held it was irrelevant that the charges were contingent and that the majority of

---

[76] *OFT v Abbey National Plc* [2009] 2 W.L.R. 1286, [72] (CA); [2008] EWHC 875 (Comm). This aspect was not considered by the Supreme Court. See *Chitty on Contracts* (30th edn, para.15–031).

[77] [2009] EWHC 1681 (Ch).

[78] ibid., at [62].

[79] ibid., at [73].

[80] *County Homesearch Co (Thames & Chilterns) Ltd v Cowham* [2008] EWCA Civ 26; [2008] 1 W.L.R. 909 at [21].

[81] Excluding from consideration a term concerning the adequacy of the price or remuneration, as against the goods or services supplied in exchange.

[82] [2009] 3 W.L.R. 1215.

customers did not incur them when considering their fairness. Accordingly, the relevant charges constituted part of the price or remuneration for the banking services provided and, in so far as the terms giving rise to the charges were in plain and intelligible language, any assessment under the 1999 Regulations of the fairness of those terms which related to their adequacy as against the services supplied was excluded by reg.6(2)(b).

16–16   **Consequences of unfairness:** Regulation 8 of the 1999 Regulations puts the consequences simply: an unfair term in a contract concluded with a consumer by a seller or supplier shall not be binding on the consumer; that said, the remainder of the contract shall continue to bind the parties if it is capable of continuing in existence without the unfair term.

Intelligibility in written contracts

16–17   Regulation 7 of the 1999 Regulations obliges a seller or supplier to ensure that any written term of a contract is expressed in plain *and* intelligible language and provides that where there is doubt about the meaning of a written term, the interpretation which is most favourable to the consumer shall prevail.

While the existence or absence of plain terms and the intelligibility of a term will also be relevant to its fairness, this is a free-standing obligation under the 1999 Regulations. The OFT encourages the avoidance of legal jargon, a minimum of cross-references and legible font.

THE CONSUMER CREDIT ACT 1974: REGULATION OF CONSUMER CREDIT AGREEMENTS

16–18   The CCA 1974 was extensively amended and its scope broadened by the Consumer Credit Act 2006 ("CCA 2006"). In order to understand what is within the scope of the regulation imposed by the CCA 1974 (and, perhaps, as importantly, to appreciate what is outside its scope) it is necessary to consider the bespoke terminology employed by the Act. Historically, the CCA 1974 did not apply to agreements for providing credit in excess of £25,000.[83] The Consumer Credit Act 2006 repealed this limit for all agreements made after April 6, 2008,[84] unless the agreement is a "relevant agreement",[85] in which case the limit is abolished for agreements entered into after October 30, 2008.

---

[83] CCA 1974 s.8(2), as amended.

[84] CCA 2006 s.2(1)(b).

[85] Sch.1 to the Consumer Credit Act 2006 (Commencement No.4 and Transitional Provisions) Order 2008 (SI 2008/831) defines a "relevant agreement" as one securing a loan on land outside the United Kingdom, or where the loan is secured on mortgage on land within the United Kingdom, where less than 40% of the land is used by the debtor as a dwelling or, if the debtor(s) are trustees, by an individual who is a beneficiary of the trust or a person related to such an individual.

"Consumer Credit Agreement" and other Terminology

"Consumer credit agreement":   Section 8[86] provides that a consumer credit   **16–19**
agreement is an agreement between an individual[87] ("the debtor") and any other
person ("the creditor") by which the creditor provides the debtor with credit of
any amount. This definition and the removal of the former credit limit[88] would
(but for the exemptions specified below) catch credit agreements secured on
land.

Such an agreement is a "regulated consumer credit agreement" within the
meaning of the CCA 1974 if it is not an "exempt agreement" specified in or
under ss.16, 16A, 16B or 16C.[89] "Credit" includes a cash loan, and any other
form of financial accommodation[90] but not an item entering into the total charge
for credit. Such an item is not "credit" for the purposes of the Act even though
time is allowed for its payment.[91] "Fixed-sum credit" is provided under a
consumer credit agreement whereby the debtor is enabled to receive credit
(whether in one amount or by instalments).[92] This covers bank and building
society loans. A "restricted-use credit agreement" is a regulated consumer credit
agreement which, inter alia, finances a transaction between the debtor and a
person other than the creditor, such as an advance by a bank to the individual's
bankers for the purpose of the acquisition of or an interest in land.[93] A re-
mortgage is also a restricted-use credit agreement.[94] An "unrestricted-use credit
agreement" is a regulated consumer credit agreement that is not a restricted-use
credit agreement.[95]

A "debtor–creditor–supplier agreement" is a regulated consumer credit agreement[96] being (inter alia) a restricted-use credit agreement which falls within
s.11(1)(b) of the CCA 1974 and is made by the creditor under pre-existing
arrangements, or in contemplation of future arrangements, between himself and
the supplier.[97] In the mortgage context, this definition may be satisfied where the
lender has some connection with the land transaction in question which the loan

---

[86] As amended by CCA 2006 from (i) April 6, 2008, for purposes specified in SI 2008/831 art.3(a)
and Sch.2 subject to transitional provisions specified in SI 2008/831 art.4, and (ii) from October 31,
2008, as specified in SI 2008/831 art.3(2) and Sch.3, as amended by SI 2008/2444 art.2(2) and
(3).

[87] An "individual" includes (a) a partnership consisting of two or three persons not all of whom
are bodies corporate; and (b) an unincorporated body of persons which does not consist entirely of
bodies corporate and is not a partnership: CCA 1974 s.189(a).

[88] The former financial limit of £25,000 (raised from £15,000 on May 1, 1998 and from £5,000 on
May 20, 1985) has been removed generally, although retained for the purposes for the exemption for
credit advanced purely for business purposes: see ss.15(1) and 16B.

[89] CCA 1974 s.8(3).

[90] ibid., s.9(1). Where credit is provided otherwise than in sterling it shall be treated for the
purposes of this Act as provided in sterling of an equivalent amount: s.9(2).

[91] ibid., s.9(4).

[92] ibid., s.10(1)(b).

[93] ibid., s.11(1)(b). The mere fact that the debtor could apply the monies to another purpose does
not prevent what would otherwise be a restricted use credit agreement from being one: see CCA 1974
Sch.2, Pt II, example 12.

[94] ibid., s.11(1)(c).

[95] ibid., s.11(2). Also ss.12(c) and 13(c).

[96] Which is not necessarily tripartite: see *Dimind v Lovell* [2002] 1 A.C. 384.

[97] ibid., s.12(b).

is financing and will take a mortgage over the land in question as security. Within the "new-build" market, loans by vendors to facilitate a purchase coupled (post-purchase) by the grant of security are not uncommon.

"Land" includes an interest in land; "land improvement company" means an improvement company as defined by s.7 of the Improvement of Land Act 1899[98] and "land mortgage" includes any security charged on land.

"Security", in relation to an actual or prospective consumer credit agreement or consumer hire agreement or any linked transaction, means a mortgage, charge, pledge, bond, debenture, indemnity, guarantee, bill, note or other right provided by the debtor or hirer, or at his request (express or implied), to secure the carrying out of the obligations of the debtor or hirer under the agreement. A document providing security is a "security instrument".[99]

It has been suggested[100] that an occupier's consent to mortgage would thus constitute "security" for the purposes of the CCA 1974.

Exempt agreements

16–20   The material provisions are contained in ss.16, 16A, 16B and 16C of the CCA 1974. The effect of an agreement being exempt is that whilst it is not a consumer credit agreement for the principal regulatory purposes of the CCA 1974, it remains subject to the unfair credit relationship provisions under s.140A–40D.[101]

Section 16 provides for three types of exempt agreements where the credit is secured on land:

(a)   Certain consumer credit agreements secured by a land mortgage where the creditor is a local authority or where the creditor is one of the institutions listed in s.16(1) and where that creditor has been "specified" by the Exempt Agreements Order.[102] The list of institutions which may be so "specified", and hence whose land mortgages may be rendered exempt agreements by Order, includes "deposit-takers"[103] (i.e. banks), building societies, insurers,[104] friendly societies, organisations of employers or workers, charities and land improvement companies.

(b)   A consumer credit agreement secured by a land mortgage of a dwelling where the creditor is a housing authority.[105]

---

[98] Being any company authorised by any Act of Parliament to execute or advance money for the execution of improvements of land.

[99] CCA 1974 s.105(2).

[100] *Putnam* [1983] L. S. Gaz. 219.

[101] CCA 1974 s.16(7A).

[102] SI 1989/869, with numerous amendments.

[103] Defined in CCA 1974 s.16(10)(a).

[104] ibid., s.16(10)(b).

[105] ibid., s.16(6A), "housing authority" being defined in s.16(6B) as any authority or body within s.80(1) of the Housing Act 1985 (landlord condition for secure tenancies) other than a housing association or a housing trust which is a charity.

(c) The third type is a consumer credit agreement secured by a land mortgage or that is a "regulated home purchase plan" and where entering into the agreement as lender is a "regulated activity" for the purposes of the FSMA.[106]

The effect of this latter exemption is to remove from the control of the CCA 1974 (a) the majority of land mortgages where the borrower is an individual, the loan is secured by a first legal mortgage and the property mortgaged is used as a dwelling house by the borrower or his family; and (b) "regulated home purchase plans" as defined in the FSMA 2000 regime, provided that (in both cases) the creditors are subject to regulation by the FSA.

The type of consumer credit agreement for which s.16 may confer exemption:

(a) a debtor–creditor–supplier agreement financing:

    (i) the purchase of land, or
    (ii) the provision of dwellings on any land, and secured by a land mortgage on that land; or

(b) a debtor–creditor agreement secured by any land mortgage; or
(c) a debtor–creditor–supplier agreement financing a transaction which is a linked transaction in relation to:

    (i) an agreement falling within paragraph (a), or
    (ii) an agreement falling within paragraph (b) financing:

        (aa) the purchase of any land, or
        (bb) the provision of dwellings on any land,

    and secured by a land mortgage on the land referred to in paragraph (a) or, as the case may be, the land referred to in sub-paragraph (ii).[107]

Exemption for "high net worth" debtors

Section 16A and the order made under it[108] provides for the exemption of **16–21** consumer credit agreements for "high net worth" debtors and hirers. These are debtors or hirers that satisfy four conditions[109]: (a) they must be "natural persons"; (b) the agreement itself must include a signed "declaration", as specified by the Order that the debtor or hirer agrees to forgo the CCA 1974 "protection and remedies"; (c) a "statement of high net worth" in the specified form must have been made in relation to the debtor or hirer; and (d) this statement of high net worth must have been made during the year ending with the date of the agreement by a person of the specified description (and not the debtor)

[106] ibid., s.16(6C).
[107] ibid., s.16(2).
[108] Consumer Credit (Exempt Agreements) Order 2007 (SI 2007/1168).
[109] And if there are joint debtors, each must satisfy the conditions: CCA 1974 s.16A(5).

stating that in the opinion of that person the debtor has income assets above the prescribed levels.[110] As a result of the Consumer Credit (EU) Directive[111] and the Consumer Credit (EU Directive) Regulations 2010,[112] this exemption will, from February 1, 2011, only apply to consumer credit agreements for the provision of credit exceeding £60,260.[113]

Exemption relating to businesses

16–22 Section 16B of the CCA 1974 exempts from reg.(a) a consumer credit agreement by which the creditor provides the debtor or hirer with credit exceeding £25,000 or requires him to make payments exceeding that amount provided that the agreement is entered into by the debtor or hirer wholly or predominantly for the purposes of a business carried on, or intended to be carried on, by him.

An agreement which includes a declaration[114] made by the debtor or hirer to the effect that the agreement is entered into by him wholly or predominantly for the purposes of a business carried on, or intended to be carried on, by him is presumed[115] to have been entered into by him wholly or predominantly for such purposes.[116] That presumption does not apply if, when the agreement is entered into (a) the creditor or owner, or (b) any person who has acted on his behalf in connection with the entering into of the agreement knows, or has reasonable cause to suspect, that the agreement is not entered into by the debtor or hirer as stated in the declaration.

Exemption relating to investment properties

16–23 Section 16C exempts what would otherwise be a consumer credit agreement from regulation if, at the time the agreement is entered into, any sums due under it are secured by a land mortgage on land and less than 40 per cent[117] of the land is used, or is intended to be used, as or in connection with a dwelling:

(a) by the debtor or a person connected[118] with the debtor, or

(b) in the case of credit provided to trustees, by an individual who is the beneficiary of the trust or a person connected with such an individual.[119]

---

[110] Currently £150,000 per annum or assets of at least £500,000; ibid., art.5 and Sch.2.

[111] [2008] OJ L133/66.

[112] SI 2010/1010, amending art.2 of the Consumer Credit (Exempt Agreements) Order 2007, (SI 2007/1168).

[113] ibid., reg.92.

[114] In the prescribed form: Consumer Credit (Agreements) Regulations 2010 (SI 2010/1014).

[115] Rebuttably so, it is submitted.

[116] CCA 1974 s.16B(2).

[117] The area of any land which comprises a building or other structure containing two or more storeys is to be taken to be the aggregate of the floor areas of each of those storeys: ibid., s.16C(3).

[118] A person is "connected with" the debtor or an individual who is the beneficiary of a trust if he is: (a) that person's spouse or civil partner; (b) a person (whether or not of the opposite sex) whose relationship with that person has the characteristics of the relationship between husband and wife; or (c) that person's parent, brother, sister, child, grandparent or grandchild.

[119] CCA 1974 s.16C(2).

This is a significant exception, leaving buy-to-let mortgages outside the scope of the 1974 Act as well as those of land which is used or is intended to be used as stated above.

Effect of regulation by the Consumer Credit Act 1974

Agreements regulated by the CCA 1974 are subject to detailed regulation from their earliest stages (e.g. advertising and canvassing for business) through to enforcement in the event of default and the service of notices confirming satisfaction of the debt. Contracting out of the protection afforded by the CCA 1974 is prohibited.[120] The principal aspects most germane to mortgages are considered below.   **16–24**

Licensing of credit and hire businesses

Part III of the CCA 1974[121] provides that those who undertake "consumer credit business"[122] or "consumer hire business"[123] must hold a licence. An individual is not conducting such a business merely because he occasionally enters into transactions belonging to business of that type.[124] The licensing of businesses is entrusted to the OFT.   **16–25**

Aside from attracting potential criminal sanction,[125] a regulated agreement is not enforceable against the debtor or hirer by a person acting in the course of a consumer credit business or a consumer hire business (as the case may be) if that person is not licensed to carry on a consumer credit business or a consumer hire business (as the case may be) of a description which covers the enforcement of the agreement.[126] The OFT can sanction unlicensed trading, with the effect that the agreements in question are enforceable.[127]

Seeking business

Advertising: Part IV of the CCA 1974[128] regulates advertisements published by a person who carries on a business in the course of which he provides credit   **16–26**

---

[120] ibid., s.173.

[121] ibid., ss.21–42.

[122] Defined as any business being carried on by a person so far as it comprises or relates to (a) the provision of credit by him, or (b) otherwise his being a creditor, under regulated consumer credit agreements: ibid., CCA 1974 s.189(1).

[123] Defined as any business being carried on by a person so far as it comprises or relates to (a) the bailment or (in Scotland) the hiring of goods by him, or (b) otherwise his being an owner, under regulated consumer hire agreements: CCA 1974 s.189(1).

[124] CCA 1974 s.189(2). See *Shahabinia v Gyachi*, unreported, June 16, 1988 QBD; *R. v Marshall* (1990) 90 Cr. App. R. 73; *Conroy v Kenny* [1999] 1 W.L.R. 1340. See also (on Hire-Purchase Act 1964 s.29(2)) *GE Capital Bank Ltd v Rushton* [2006] 1 W.L.R 899. See also (on moneylending) *Re Griffin* (1890) 60 L.J.Q.B. 235, 237; *Litchfield v Dreyfus* [1906] 1 K.B. 584; *Newton v Pyke* (1908) 25 T.L.R. 127; *Kirkwood v Gadd* [1910] A.C. 422, 423, 426, 431, 432; *Newman v Oughton* [1911] 1 K.B. 792; *Fagot v Fine* (1911) 105 L.T. 583; *Edgelow v MacElwee* [1918] 1 K.B. 205; *Marshall v Goulston Discount (Northern) Ltd* [1966] Ch. 72; *Skelton Finance Co v Lawrence* (1976) 120 S.J. 147; *Wills v Wood* (1984) 128 S.J. 222.

[125] CCA 1974 ss.39, 167; Sch.1.

[126] ibid., s.40(1).

[127] ibid., s.40(2).

[128] ibid., ss.43–54.

to individuals secured on land.[129] It does not apply to an advertisement insofar as it is a communication of an invitation or inducement to engage in investment activity within the meaning of s.21 of the Financial Services and Markets Act 2000, other than an exempt generic communication.[130] Regulations have been made which prescribe the form and content of advertisements.[131]

16–27 **Antecedent negotiations:** "Antecedent negotiations" are any negotiations with the debtor or hirer (a) conducted by the creditor or owner in relation to the making of any regulated agreement, or (b) conducted by a credit-broker in relation to goods sold or proposed to be sold by the credit-broker to the creditor before forming the subject-matter of a debtor–creditor–supplier agreement within s.12(a) of the CCA 1974, or (c) conducted by the supplier in relation to a transaction financed or proposed to be financed by a debtor–creditor–supplier agreement within s.12(b) or (c) of that Act.[132]

Negotiations with the debtor in a case falling within (b) or (c) above are deemed to be conducted by the negotiator (i.e. the person by whom negotiations are conducted with the debtor or hirer) in the capacity of agent of the creditor as well as in his actual capacity.[133] Section 56(3) contains anti-avoidance provisions in relation to the statutory agency created by this section.

For the purposes of this Act, antecedent negotiations shall be taken to begin when the negotiator and the debtor or hirer first enter into communication (including communication by advertisement), and to include any representations made by the negotiator to the debtor or hirer and any other dealings between them.

Clearly therefore, the creditor may be liable for the negotiator's misrepresentations and any contractual undertakings given by him.

Entry into credit or hire agreements

16–28 Part V of the CCA 1974[134] regulates the manner in which any agreement is concluded unless the agreement is exempted from its application under s.74. The primary exemption for present purposes applies to "non-commercial agreements", which comprise any consumer credit agreements or a consumer hire agreements not made by the creditor or owner in the course of a business carried

---

[129] ibid., s.43(2). Because of the involvement of both the FSA and OFT in regulating land mortgages, they have produced *Credit Advertising: A guide to dually-regulated advertisements:* (OFT and FSA, September 2008).

[130] An "exempt generic communication" is a communication to which FSMA 2000 s.21(c) does not apply, as a result of an order (s.21(5)), because it does not identify a person as providing an investment or as carrying on an activity to which the communication relates.

[131] Consumer Credit (Advertisements) Regulations 2004 (SI 2010/1484) as prospectively amended by Consumer Credit (EU Directive) Regulations 2010 (SI 2010/1010) from February 1, 2011 (with transitional provisions). Unless pre-contract credit information has been disclosed in compliance with (or purported compliance with) the Consumer Credit (Disclosure of Information) Regulations 2010 (SI 2010/1013), SI 2010/1010 does not apply to agreements secured on land.

[132] CCA 1974 s.56(1).

[133] ibid., s.56(2). See also s.75 (debtor–creditor–supplier agreements).

[134] ibid., ss.55–74, as prospectively amended by the Consumer Credit (EU Directive) Regulations 2010 (SI 2010/1010) with effect from February 1, 2011.

on by him.[135] In instances where s.74 applies, the following provisions are relevant.

Form and content of agreements: The Consumer Credit (Agreements) Reg- **16–29**
ulations 1983[136] provide for the form and content of documents embodying regulated agreements. They are aimed at ensuring that the debtor or hirer is made aware of (a) the rights and duties conferred or imposed on him by the agreement, (b) the amount and rate of the total charge for credit (in the case of a consumer credit agreement), (c) the protection and remedies available to him under this Act, and (d) any other matters which, in the opinion of the Secretary of State, it is desirable for him to know about in connection with the agreement.[137] The combined effect of this section and s.61 is that a failure to comply with the Regulations renders any agreement improperly executed.

Calculating the "total charge for credit" is a complex process.[138] In practice (and particularly with advances made directly by the creditor to pay off arrears under a prior mortgage), this has caused difficulties.[139]

Withdrawal from prospective agreement: The cancellation provisions of **16–30**
ss.67 to 73 do not apply to land mortgages. However, s.57(4) applies s.57(1) to non-cancellable agreements, and, by s.57(1), the rights of the parties after withdrawal are the same as those conferred by s.69 where the agreement was cancellable. Accordingly, it is necessary to note that section's provisions in relation to a withdrawal from a prospective (albeit, non-cancellable agreement). The section provides that:

"(1) The withdrawal of a party from a prospective regulated agreement shall operate to apply this Part to the agreement, any linked transaction and any other thing done in anticipation of the making of the agreement as it would apply if the agreement were made and then cancelled under section 69.

(2) The giving to a party of a written or oral notice which, however expressed, indicates the intention of the other party to withdraw from a prospective regulated agreement operates as a withdrawal from it.

(3) Each of the following shall be deemed to be the agent of the creditor or owner for the purpose of receiving a notice under subsection (2)—

(a) a credit-broker or supplier who is the negotiator in antecedent negotiations, and

(b) any person who, in the course of a business carried on by him, acts on behalf of the debtor or hirer in any negotiations for the agreement.

(4) Where the agreement, if made, would not be a cancellable agreement, subsection (1) shall nevertheless apply as if the contrary were the case."

Linked transactions are defined by s.19 of the CCA 1974. Not only is the transaction and any linked transaction cancelled, but so is any offer by the debtor

---

[135] ibid., s.189(1).

[136] SI 1983/1553, as amended with effect on and after February 1, 2011, by the Consumer Credit (Agreements) Regulations 2010 (SI 2010/1014). These regulations have limited effect on agreements secured on land.

[137] CCA 1974 s.60.

[138] ibid., ss.9(4), 20(1) and the relevant regulations.

[139] ibid., ss.9(4), 20(1) and the relevant regulations. See *Watchtower Investments Ltd v Payne* [2002] EWCA Civ 522; *London North Securities v Meadows* [2005] EWCA Civ 956; *Southern Pacific Mortgage Ltd v Heath* [2010] Ch. 254.

or hirer or his relative, to enter into a linked transaction, unless in both cases the linked transaction is exempted by regulation by virtue of s.69(5). Section 69(4) provides that cancelled agreements are to be treated as if they had never been entered into.

If the relevant agreement is a debtor–creditor–supplier agreement financing the supply of goods or doing of work in an emergency, or financing the supply of goods which have become incorporated by act of the debtor or his relative in any land or thing not itself comprised in the agreement or any linked transaction, the cancellation or withdrawal affects only those provisions that relate to the provision of credit, or require payment of an item in the total charge for credit. But the obligation of the debtor to pay for the work or supply of goods is unaffected.[140]

16–31   Opportunity for withdrawal from prospective land mortgage: Before sending to the debtor or hirer, for his signature, an unexecuted agreement in a case where the prospective regulated agreement is to be secured on land (the "mortgaged land"), the creditor or owner shall give the debtor or hirer a copy of the unexecuted agreement which contains a notice in the prescribed form[141] indicating the right of the debtor or hirer to withdraw from the prospective agreement, and how and when the right is exercisable, together with a copy of any other document referred to in the unexecuted agreement.[142]

Unless these requirements and those set out below are complied with, the document is not properly executed.[143] The additional requirements are that (a) the unexecuted agreement is sent, for his signature, to the debtor or hirer by an appropriate method (which can be electronically)[144] not less than seven days after a copy of it was given to him under s.58(1), and (b) during the consideration period, the creditor or owner refrained from approaching the debtor or hirer (whether in person, by telephone or letter, or in any other way) except in response to a specific request made by the debtor or hirer after the beginning of the consideration period, and (c) no notice of withdrawal by the debtor or hirer was received by the creditor or owner before the sending of the unexecuted agreement.

Since an advance copy and copies under ss.62 and 63 of the CCA 1974, must be sent to each debtor,[145] no less than six copies may be required where there are joint mortgagors.[146] The special pause provisions do not, however, apply to a restricted-use credit agreement to finance the purchase of the mortgaged land, or to an agreement for a bridging loan in connection with the purchase of the mortgaged land or other land.[147]

---

[140] ibid., s.69(2).
[141] See Consumer Credit (Cancellation Notices and Copies of Documents) Regulations 1983 (SI 1983/1557) (as amended), particularly reg.4.
[142] ibid,. s.58(1).
[143] ibid., s.61(2).
[144] Consumer Credit Act 1974 (Electronic Communications) Order 2004 (SI 2004/3236).
[145] See CCA 1974 s.185.
[146] Some relief is afforded by the Consumer Credit (Cancellation Notices and Copies of Documents) Regulations 1983 SI 1983/1557 (as amended), reg.11.
[147] CCA 1974 ss.58(2), 61(2)(a).

Consequences of improper execution: In the absence of proper execution by   **16–32**
virtue of the contravention of any provision so providing that (as a result) the
agreement is not properly executed, the agreement is only enforceable against the
debtor or hirer on an order for the court[148] or with his consent.[149] Taking
possession is an enforcement of the agreement.[150] If an order is made, the
security may be enforced, but not otherwise.[151] If the application for an order
fails save on technical grounds only, the security is rendered invalid.[152]

In the case of an application for an enforcement order under (a) s.65(1)
(improperly executed agreements), or (b) s.105(7)(a) or (b) (improperly executed
security instruments), or (c) s.111(2) (failure to serve copy of notice on surety),
or (d) s.124(1) or (2) (taking of negotiable instrument in contravention of section
123),[153] s.127(1) provides that the court shall dismiss the application if, but only
if, it considers it just to do so having regard to:

(i) prejudice caused to any person by the contravention in question, and
the degree of culpability for it; and

(ii) the powers conferred on the court by subs.(2) and ss.135 (power to
impose conditions, or suspend operation of order) and 136 (power to
vary agreements and securities).

Section 127(2) allows the court to reduce or discharge any sum payable by the
debtor or hirer, or any surety, so as to compensate him for prejudice suffered as
a result of the contravention in question. In addition, the court may make a "time
order" under s.129.[154]

The court's discretion is wide[155] and the former provisions of the CCA 1974[156]
which rendered some agreements "irredeemably unenforceable"[157] have been
repealed with effect from April 6, 2007.[158]

---

[148] ibid., s. 65(1). See, in particular, *Wilson v First County Trust (No.2)* [2004] 1 A.C. 816 (HL) and
McGuffick v Royal Bank of Scotland [2010] Bus. L.R. 1108.
[149] ibid., s.173(3).
[150] ibid., s.65(2).
[151] ibid., s.113(2).
[152] ibid., ss.206, 113(3)(c).
[153] This list is extended from February 1, 2011, to include applications under s.55(2) (disclosure of
information) or s.61B(3) (duty to supply copy of overdraft agreement): by Consumer Credit (EU
Directive) Regulations 2010 (SI 2010/1010), Pt 2, regs 12 and 18, with transitional provisions.
[154] See para.16–47.
[155] For refusals to enforce, see *PB Leasing Ltd v Patel and Patel (t/a Plankhouse Stores)* [1995]
C.C.L.R. 82; *Smerdon v Ellis* [1997] C.L.Y. 960; *Re Dixon-Vincent* [1997] C.L.Y. 958; *Rendle v Hicks*
[1998] C.L.Y 2504; *Rahman v Brassil* [1998] C.L.Y. 2503 Cty Ct. For enforcement orders made, see
National Guardian Mortgage Corp v Wilkes [1993] C.C.L.R. 1 (but interest rate reduced); *Rank
Xerox v Hepple* [1993] C.C.L.R. 1 (but reduction of amount payable); *Hatfield v Hiscock* [1996]
C.C.L.R. 68; *London North Securities Ltd v Meadows* [2005] EWCA Civ 956 (but PPP not payable);
Wilson v Hurstanger Ltd [2007] EWCA Civ 299 (but some sums not payable); *Southern Pacific
Homeloans Ltd v Walker* [2010] Bus. L.R. 418; *McGuffick v Royal Bank of Scotland* [2010] Bus. L.R.
1108.
[156] CCA 1974 s.127(3)–(5).
[157] per Lord Hoffman in *Dimond v Lovell* [2002] 1 A.C. 384.
[158] Consumer Credit Act 2006 Sch.4 para.1 and SI 2007/123. Those provisions still apply to
agreements entered into before that date.

16–33 **Signing of agreement:**   Section 61 provides that a regulated agreement is not properly executed unless (a) a document in the prescribed form itself containing all the prescribed terms and conforming to regulations under s.60(1) is signed in the prescribed manner both by the debtor or hirer and by or on behalf of the creditor or owner, and (b) the document embodies all the terms of the agreement, other than implied terms, and (c) the document is, when presented or sent to the debtor or hirer for signature, in such a state that all its terms are readily legible. There must also be compliance with the additional requirements concerning prospective land mortgages.[159]

16–34 **Duty to supply copy of unexecuted and executed agreements:**   If the unexecuted agreement is presented personally to the debtor or hirer for his signature, but on the occasion when he signs it the document does not become an executed agreement, a copy of it, and of any other document referred to in it, must be there and then delivered to him.[160] If the unexecuted agreement is sent to the debtor or hirer for his signature, a copy of it, and of any other document referred to in it, must be sent to him at the same time.

Section 63(1) provides that if the unexecuted agreement is presented personally to the debtor or hirer for his signature, and on the occasion when he signs it the document becomes an executed agreement, a copy of the executed agreement, and of any other document referred to in it, must be there and then delivered to him. A copy of the executed agreement, and of any other document referred to in it, must be given to the debtor or hirer within the seven days following the making of the agreement unless (a) subs.(1) applies, or (b) the unexecuted agreement was sent to the debtor or hirer for his signature and, on the occasion of his signing it, the document became an executed agreement.[161]

Failure to comply with either s.62 or 63 renders the agreement improperly executed.[162]

Matters arising during the currency of a regulated agreement

16–35 **Duty to give notice before taking certain action:**   Section 76(1) provides that the creditor or owner is not entitled to enforce a term of a regulated agreement by (a) demanding earlier payment of any sum, or (b) recovering possession of any goods or land, or (c) treating any right conferred on the debtor or hirer by the agreement as terminated, restricted or deferred, except by or after giving the debtor or hirer[163] not less than seven days' notice in the prescribed form of his intention to do so. This subsection does not prevent a creditor from treating the right to draw on any credit as restricted or deferred and taking such steps as may be necessary to make the restriction or deferment effective[164] nor does it apply to a right of enforcement arising by reason of any breach by the debtor or hirer

---

[159] See para.16–31.
[160] ibid., s.62(1).
[161] ibid., s.63(2).
[162] ibid., ss.62(3), 63(5).
[163] Notice must also be given to any surety: ibid., s.111(1).
[164] ibid., s.76(4).

of the regulated agreement.[165] This latter requirement makes the provisions of the section less onerous from a mortgagee's perspective.

It should also be noted that s.76(1) only applies where (a) a period for the duration of the agreement is specified in the agreement, and (b) that period has not ended when the creditor or owner does an act as mentioned above but so applies notwithstanding that, under the agreement, any party is entitled to terminate it before the end of the period so specified.

Provision of information: Sections 77 (duty to give information to debtor   **16–36** under fixed-sum credit agreement), 77A (statements to be provided in relation to fixed-sum credit agreements), 78 (duty to give information to debtor under running-account credit agreement), 78A (duty to give information to debtor on change of rates of interest)[166] and 79 (duty to give hirer information) make provision for the supply of information to the debtor and to any surety.

Arrears and default: Sections 86B (notice of sums in arrears under fixed-sum   **16–37** credit agreements etc.), 86C (notice of sums in arrears under running-account credit agreements), 86D (failure to give notice of sums in arrears), 86E (notice of default sums) and 86F (interest on default sums) were inserted into the CCA 1974 by the Consumer Credit Act 2006. In addition to providing for the manner, timing and form of notices of sums in arrears,[167] they provide for the effect of non-compliance (an inability on the creditor to enforce and no liability on the debtor to pay interest or any sum falling due during non-compliance)[168] and for provision for notices in connection with any payment due on default (i.e. arising as a consequence of breach of the agreement) and interest payable on any such payment.

Notices: Sections 87–89 provide for a regime of default notices. Section 87   **16–38** provides that the service of a notice on the debtor or hirer in accordance with s.88 (a "default notice") is necessary before the creditor or owner can become entitled, by reason of any breach by the debtor or hirer of a regulated agreement (a) to terminate the agreement, or (b) to demand earlier payment of any sum, or (c) to recover possession of any goods or land, or (d) to treat any right conferred on the debtor or hirer by the agreement as terminated, restricted or deferred, or (e) to enforce any security.

This requirement does not prevent the creditor from treating the right to draw upon any credit as restricted or deferred, and taking such steps as may be necessary to make the restriction or deferment effective.[169] The doing of an act by which a floating charge becomes fixed is not enforcement of a security.[170]

---

[165] ibid., s.76(6).
[166] Inserted by Consumer Credit (EU Directive) Regulations 2010 (SI 2010/1010) reg.27 with effect from February 1, 2011.
[167] As to which the OFT has a role; s.86A.
[168] ibid., s.86D(3) and (4).
[169] ibid., s.87(2).
[170] ibid., s.87(3).

The default notice must be served in the prescribed form[171] and, where the breach is capable of remedy, giving a period of not less than seven days to remedy the same.[172]

Section 98 imposes a duty to give not less than seven days' notice in the prescribed form) of termination in non default cases, failing which the creditor or owner is not entitled to terminate. The requirement only applies where (a) a period for the duration of the agreement is specified in the agreement, and (b) that period has not ended when the creditor or owner does an act mentioned in subsection. It does apply notwithstanding that, under the agreement, any party is entitled to terminate it before the end of the period so specified.[173]

16–39 Statements: Section 97 obliges a creditor, if required, to provide a statement in the prescribed form indicating the amount required to discharge the indebtedness under the agreement and particulars as to how the sum is calculated. If the creditor is in default, he cannot enforce the agreement.[174]

At least annual statements must be provided under s.77A. Breach precludes enforcement and the debtor is relieved of liability to pay interest.[175]

A termination statement (confirming that the debt has been discharged and the agreement is at an end) can be requested under s.103 which provides a mechanism for a counter-notice in the dispute.

Certain statements made by the creditor are binding on him.[176] In the event of mistake, the court can grant relief.[177]

16–40 Variation: A unilateral variation[178] by the creditor—such as an increase in interest charged[179]—does not take effect unless notice in the prescribed form is given at least seven days beforehand.[180] Notice by a press announcement will suffice.[181] Where the variation is automatic—such as an increase or decrease in interest by virtue of changes to a third party's base rate—will not invoke the provisions of s.82.

Security

16–41 Form and content of securities: Section 105 provides that any security (save for one provided by debtor or hirer[182]) provided in relation to a regulated

[171] ibid., s.88(1). See Consumer Credit (Enforcement, Default and Termination Notices) Regulations 1983 (SI 1983/1561), as amended.
[172] ibid., s.88(2).
[173] ibid., s.98(2).
[174] ibid., s.97(3)(a).
[175] ibid., s.77(6).
[176] ibid., s.172.
[177] ibid., s.172(3).
[178] As to variation by agreement, see s.82(2). A mere indulgence does not amount to a variation: see *Broadwick Financial Services Ltd v Spencer* [2002] 1 All E.R. (Comm.) 46.
[179] See *Lombard Tricity Finance Ltd v Paton* [1989] 1 All E.R. 918; *Paragon Finance Plc v Nash* [2002] 1 W.L.R. 685.
[180] CCA 1974 s.82.
[181] Consumer Credit (Notice of Variation of Agreements) Regulations 1977 (SI 1977/328), as amended.
[182] ibid., s.105(6).

agreement shall be expressed in writing and permits regulations to prescribe the form and content of documents ("security instruments") to be made in compliance with that requirement. The regulations made are confined to guarantees and indemnities,[183] which are not properly executed unless in the prescribed form, containing all the prescribed terms and conforming to regulations and signed in the prescribed manner by or on behalf of the surety. They must also embody all the terms of the security, other than implied terms, and, when presented or sent for the purpose of being signed by or on behalf of the surety, be in such state that its terms are readily legible. When the document is presented or sent for the purpose of being signed by or on behalf of the surety, he must also be presented or sent a copy of the document.[184]

A security instrument is not properly executed unless (a) where the security is provided after, or at the time when, the regulated agreement is made, a copy of the executed agreement, together with a copy of any other document referred to in it, is given to the surety at the time the security is provided, or (b) where the security is provided before the regulated agreement is made, a copy of the executed agreement, together with a copy of any other document referred to in it, is given to the surety within seven days after the regulated agreement is made.

Consequences of improper execution or form: If, in contravention of **16–42** s.105(1), a security is not expressed in writing, or a security instrument is improperly executed, the security, so far as provided in relation to a regulated agreement, is enforceable against the surety on an order of the court only. If that application is dismissed (except on technical grounds only) s.106 (ineffective securities) applies to the security.

Section 106 provides that where, under any provision of the CCA 1974, it applies to any security provided in relation to a regulated agreement, then, subject to s.177 (saving for registered charges) (a) the security, so far as it is so provided, shall be treated as never having effect; (b) any property lodged with the creditor or owner solely for the purposes of the security as so provided shall be returned by him forthwith; (c) the creditor or owner shall take any necessary action to remove or cancel an entry in any register, so far as the entry relates to the security as so provided; and (d) any amount received by the creditor or owner on realisation of the security shall, so far as it is referable to the agreement, be repaid to the surety.

Saving for registered charges under the Land Registration Act 2002: With **16–43** one important exception, nothing in the CCA 1974 affects the rights of a proprietor of a registered charge (within the meaning of the Land Registration Act 2002), who (a) became the proprietor under a transfer for valuable consideration without notice of any defect in the title arising (apart from this section) by

---

[183] Consumer Credit (Guarantees and Indemnities) Regulations 1983 (SI 1983/1556), as amended.
[184] CCA 1974 s.105(4).

virtue of the CCA 1974,[185] or (b) derives title from such a proprietor.[186] The exception is that this saving provision does *not* apply to a proprietor carrying on a consumer credit business, a consumer hire business or a business of debt-collecting or debt administration.[187] Thus, those who should know better are unable to take advantage of the section.

Nothing the CCA 1974 affects the operation of s.104 of the Law of Property Act 1925 (protection of purchaser where mortgagee exercises power of sale).[188]

16–44   Indemnity: Where a land mortgage is enforced which, but for the provisions of s.177 would be treated as never having effect, the original creditor or owner is liable to indemnify the debtor or hirer against any loss thereby suffered by him.[189]

16–45   Enforcement of land mortgages: Section 126 provides that a land mortgage securing a regulated agreement is enforceable—in the absence of consent[190] and so far as provided in relation to the agreement—on an order of the court only. No sanction is provided for breach of this section.

Pledges

16–46   Sections 114–122 deal with pledges—principally pawns under a regulated agreement—and negotiable instruments. They do not apply to pledges of documents of title or bearer bonds[191] nor deeds or certificates of title relating to land.[192]

Time orders

16–47   Section 129 provides that:

> (1) Subject to subs.(3) below, if it appears to the court just to do so:
>
>   (a)   on an application for an enforcement order; or
>   (b)   on an application made by a debtor or hirer under this paragraph after service on him of:
>
>   (i)   a default notice, or
>   (ii) a notice under section 76(1) or 98(1); or
>
>   (ba) on an application made by a debtor or hirer under this paragraph after he has been given a notice under section 86B or 86C; or

---

[185] The purpose of this requirement is not clear.
[186] ibid., s.177(1).
[187] ibid., s.177(3).
[188] ibid., s.177(2).
[189] ibid., s.177(4).
[190] ibid., s.173(3).
[191] ibid., s.114(3); "documents of title" is not defined in the Act.
[192] See *Swanley Coal Co v Denton* [1906] 2 K.B. 873.

    (c)   in an action brought by a creditor or owner to enforce a regulated agreement or any security, or recover possession of any goods or land to which a regulated agreement relates,

the court may make an order under this section (a "time order").
  (2) A time order shall provide for one or both of the following, as the court considers just:

    (a)   the payment by the debtor or hirer or any surety of any sum owed under a regulated agreement or a security by such instalments, payable at such times, as the court, having regard to the means of the debtor or hirer and any surety, considers reasonable;

    (b)   the remedying by the debtor or hirer of any breach of a regulated agreement (other than non-payment of money) within such period as the court may specify.

Section 129A makes provision for when an application for a time order may be made under s.129(1)(ba). Section 130 makes supplementary provisions as to the making of and circumstances in which the court may make a time order.

In *Southern and District Finance Plc v Barnes*[193] the Court of Appeal gave guidance as to the considerations that arise when addressing an application for a time order. Leggatt L.J. stated that:

  (1) When a time order is applied for, or a possession order sought of land to which a regulated agreement applies, the court must first consider whether it is just to make a time order. That will involve consideration of all the circumstances of the case, and of the position of the creditor as well as the debtor.[194]

  (2) When a time order is made, it should normally be made for a stipulated period on account of temporary financial difficulty. If, despite the giving of time, the debtor is unlikely to be able to resume repayment of the total indebtedness by at least the amount of the contractual instalments, no time order should be made. In such circumstances it will be more equitable to allow the regulated agreement to be enforced.[195]

  (3) When a time order is made relating to the non-payment of money:

    (a) The "sum owed" means every sum which is due and owing under the agreement, but where possession proceedings have been brought by the creditor that will normally comprise the total indebtedness[196]; and

---

[193] (1995) 27 H.L.R. 691.

[194] This includes any previous history of default and intermittent payments and whether the evidence demonstrates a real prospect of the debtor making good his default: *First National Bank v Syed* [1991] 2 All E.R. 250.

[195] Nonetheless, the discretion is broad: *Director General of Fair Trading v First National Bank Plc* [2002] 1 A.C. 481, [28]. In *Southern and District Finance*, above, the payments were rescheduled over 15 years.

[196] See *Southern and District Finance*, above at 697; *Smith v Smith* [1891] 3 Ch. 550, 552.

(b) The court must consider what instalments would be reasonable both as to amount and timing, having regard to the debtor's means.

(4) The court may include in a time order any amendment of the agreement, which it considers just to both parties, and which is a consequence of a term of the order. If the rate of interest is amended, it is relevant that smaller instalments will result both in a liability to pay interest on accumulated arrears and, on the other hand, in an extended period of repayment. But to some extent the high rate of interest usually payable under regulated agreements already takes account of the risk that difficulties in repayment may occur.

(5) If a time order is made when the sum owed is the whole of the outstanding balance due under the loan, there will inevitably be consequences for the term of the loan or for the rate of interest or both.

(6) If justice requires the making of a time order, the court should suspend any possession order that it also makes, so long as the terms of the time order are complied with."[197]

Section 129 would therefore permit the court, on an application for possession of mortgaged premises, not only to reschedule existing arrears but to address payments and interest going forward and to vary them. A time order may, itself, be varied or revoked.[198]

Protection orders

16–48 Under s.131 of the CCA 1974, the court may, on the application of the creditor or owner under a regulated agreement, make such orders as it thinks just for protecting any property of the creditor or owner, or property subject to any security, from damage or depreciation pending the determination of any proceedings under this Act, including orders restricting or prohibiting use of the property or giving directions as to its custody.

Extortionate credit bargains and unfair credit relationships

16–49 The statutory provisions in ss.137–140 of the CCA 1974 regulating extortionate credit bargains were repealed with effect from April 6, 2007; ss.140A–140D now regulate unfair credit relationships. Whereas formerly, the threshold for judicial intervention was that the payments were "grossly exorbitant" or the bargain "grossly contravened" the principles of fair dealing[199] have been replaced by a requirement that the credit agreement is merely "unfair to the debtor".[200] The new provisions apply to any agreement entered into on or after April 6, 2007.

---

[197] ibid., at 698.
[198] CCA 1974 s.130(6).
[199] ibid., s.138(1).
[200] ibid., s.140A(1).

Transitional provisions: The court may make an order under ss.140A–D in **16–50** proceedings under s.140B(2) notwithstanding that the agreement in question pre-dates April 6, 2007, if those proceedings were commenced before April 6, 2008, and the agreement was not completed[201] prior to April 6, 2007, or became completed in that period.[202] Other transitional provisions apply and preserve the ability to make an order under ss.138–140 in specified circumstances.[203] The former provisions apply to any agreement which pre-date April 6, 2007, or which completed prior to April 6, 2008. It is therefore appropriate to consider both schemes. Before doing so, the equitable jurisdiction falls to be considered.

The equitable jurisdiction to set aside harsh and unconscionable bargains

The general equitable jurisdiction of the courts to set aside "harsh and uncon- **16–51** scionable" bargains was supplemented by s.1(1) of the Moneylenders Act 1900. Where a transaction was caught by this provision, the court had power to re-open it where there was evidence that the interest and other charges were excessive and that the transaction was harsh and unconscionable or otherwise such that the court of equity would give relief. Before 1900, courts of equity had set aside two classes of bargain: those with expectants (reversioners and heirs) and those which equity viewed as unconscionable.

Expectants: Where the bargain was with an expectant reversioner or heir **16–52** (being a person hoping to take a benefit under the will or intestacy of someone still alive),[204] the onus was on the purchaser to prove that the bargain struck was fair, just and reasonable and, if he failed to discharge that burden, the transaction would be set aside regardless of the relationship between the parties to the bargain. The jurisdiction in relation to the sale of or dealings with remainders and reversionary interests has been removed[205] but without affecting the court's jurisdiction to set aside or modify unconscionable bargains.[206]

Unconscionable bargains: The second class of bargain with which equity **16–53** would interfere arose where the court considered that the creditor had taken a grossly unfair advantage of the debtor thereby rendering the bargain unconscion-able.[207] In *Samuel v Newbold*[208] it was decided that this ground and that considered immediately above were quite distinct.

---

[201] An agreement is a completed agreement when no sum is or will become payable under it: Consumer Credit Act 2006 Sch.3 para.1(2).

[202] ibid., para.14.

[203] ibid., paras 15 and 16.

[204] *Earl of Aylesford v Morris* (1873) L.R. 8 Ch. App. 484; *Earl of Chesterfield v Janssen* (1750) 2 Ves. Sen. 125; *Nevill v Snelling* (1880) 15 Ch.D. 679.

[205] LPA 1925 s.124(1).

[206] ibid., s.177(2).

[207] [1979] Ch. 84. Here the court refused to apply the test of "reasonableness" to an indexation clause in the mortgage made between the parties. The test was whether the bargain was "unfair and unconscionable". Held: stipulation valid and enforceable, reflecting *Tresider-Griffin v Co-operative Insurance Society Ltd* [1956] 2 Q.B. 127. See also *Davis v Directloans Ltd* [1986] 1 W.L.R. 823.

[208] [1906] A.C. 461.

This distinct equitable doctrine applies where the complainant is suffering from certain kinds of disability or disadvantage, the bargain struck was itself oppressive to the complainant and the beneficiary of the bargain acted unconscionably in that he knowingly took advantage of the complainant. Where these requirements are met, it is up to the beneficiary of the bargain to satisfy the court that the transaction was "fair just and reasonable".[209] It is unclear whether the evidential burden shifts only when all three elements of the transaction are proved or whether unconscionable conduct can be presumed[210] or, indeed, whether the oppressive nature of the bargain could also be presumed.[211] The principles of notice which have developed in relation to undue influence apply equally to transactions which are unconscionable.[212] The doctrine has been applied in cases of the sale of property[213] and of mortgages.[214] It does not appear that the doctrine has any application to gifts.[215]

16–54 *Disability or disadvantage:* Either must be such as to significantly affect the ability of the complainant to make a judgment as to what may or may not me in his best interests. Illiteracy, a poor education,[216] age and poverty have all been recognised as sufficient categories of disability or disadvantage.[217]

16–55 *Oppressive terms:* The terms must be "overreaching and oppressive" such that they "shock the conscience of the court".[218] Mere imprudence is insufficient.[219]

16–56 *Unconscionable conduct:* In addition, the court looks for the behaviour of the stronger party to be morally culpable or reprehensible; mere inequality of bargaining power does not invoke the doctrine.[220] In addition the complainant must establish that the beneficiary of the transaction was aware that the complainant was actually under a disability or that he was in weak position; however,

---

[209] *Aylesford v Morriss* (1873) 8 Ch. App. 484, 490–491.

[210] There is authority that it can: see *Portman Building Society v Dusangh* [2000] 2 All E.R. (Comm.) 221, 234 (CA).

[211] As to which see *Cresswell v Potter* (1968) [1978] 1 W.L.R. 255N at 258. But see also *Chagos Islanders v The Attorney General* [2004] EWCA Civ 997, [562].

[212] *Portman Building Society v Dusangh,* above.

[213] *Cresswell v Potter,* above; *Singla v Bashar* [2002] EWHC 883; *Fry v Lane* (1888) 40 Ch. D. 312.

[214] *Multi-service Bookbinding Ltd v Marden* [1979] Ch. 84; *Alec Lobb (Garages) Ltd v Total Oil (Great Britain) Ltd* [1983] 1 W.L.R. 87; *Credit Lyonnais Nederland NV v Burch* [1997] 1 All E.R. 144; *Portman Building Society v Dusangh,* above.

[215] *Langton v Langton* [1995] 2 F.L.R. 890.

[216] The description in *Fry v Lane* of the "poor and ignorant" in modern parlance refers to members of the lower income bracket and those who are less highly educated: see *Cresswell v Potter,* above, at 257, 258; *Backhouse v Backhouse* [1978] 1 W.L.R. 243; *Credit Lyonnais Nederland NV v Birch,* above and *Steeples v Lea* [1998] 2 F.C.L. 144 (the latter two inferences being junior employees).

[217] See *Portman Building Society v Dusangh,* above at 228; *Singla v Bashir,* above at [7] and *Chagos Islanders v Attorney General,* above at [580].

[218] *Alex Love Garages Ltd v Total Oil Great Britain Ltd,* above at 95C–D; affirmed on appeal, [1985] 1 W.L.R. 173.

[219] *Portman Building Society v Dusangh,* at 228A–B. See also *Mitchell v James* [2001] All E.R. (D) 116; *Jones v Morgan* [2001] EWCA Civ 995; *Singla v Bashir,* above and *Chagos Islanders v The Attorney General,* above.

[220] *Boustany v Pigott* (1995) 69 P. & C.R. 298, 303.

the evidence in relation to this must be quite strong and is often required to establish more than this: see *Jones v Morgan*.[221]

The power of the courts of equity to set aside unconscionable bargains was reviewed in *Multiservice Bookbinding Limited v Marden*.[222] It is clear from that judgment that courts will not set aside bargains which are improvident or contain terms which are, by normal standards, unreasonable. A bargain cannot be unfair and unconscionable unless one of the parties to it has imposed the objectionable terms in a morally reprehensible manner and thus in a way that affects his conscience. The categories of unconscionable bargains are not limited.

A bargain may be set aside where advantage is taken of a poor, ignorant or weak-minded person, or one who is for some other reason in need of special protection. In *Fry v Lane*[223] it was held that there were three requirements to be satisfied if a bargain was held to be unconscionable: (i) poverty and ignorance of the plaintiff; (ii) sale at an undervalue; (iii) lack of independent advice. In *Cresswell v Potter*[224] Megarry J. explained "ignorant" as meaning "ignorant in the context of property transactions in general and conveyancing documents in particular". In *Backhouse v Backhouse*,[225] Balcombe J. considered that a party who had executed a document under the emotional strain of an impending or actual marriage breakdown, might be relieved as being in the position of unequal bargaining power under the principle enunciated by Lord Denning M.R. in *Lloyds Bank v Bundy*.[226] In *Samuel v Newbold*[227] it was said that a transaction might fall within the description because of the borrower's extreme necessity and helplessness, or because of the relationship in which he stood to the lender, or because of his situation in other ways. That was a case in which the circumstances of the transaction and the "monstrous" rate of interest charged (418 per cent) were each sufficient to characterise the bargain as harsh and unconscionable.

Drunkenness or addiction does not amount to a sufficient disability or disadvantage, however.[228] Moreover, the question of disability or disadvantage needs to be considered in the light of the transaction in question and the documentation and complexity involved.[229]

Extortionate credit transactions

The provisions of the Moneylenders Acts 1900–1927 were totally repealed on **16–57** May 19, 1985 and replaced by s.137–140 of the CCA 1974 which remain

---

[221] [2001] EWCA Civ 995.

[222] [1979] Ch. 84. Here the court refused to apply the test of "reasonableness" to an indexation clause in the mortgage made between the parties. The test was whether the bargain was "unfair and unconscionable". Held: stipulation valid and enforceable, reflecting *Tresider-Griffin v Co-operative Insurance Society Ltd* [1956] 2 Q.B. 127. See also *Davis v Directloans Ltd* [1986] 1 W.L.R. 823.

[223] (1888) 40 Ch.D. 312.

[224] Reported as a note (p.255) to *Backhouse v Backhouse* [1978] 1 W.L.R. 243.

[225] ibid.

[226] [1975] Q.B. 326 at 329.

[227] [1906] A.C. 461.

[228] *Irvani v Irvani* [2000] 1 Lloyd's Rep. 412.

[229] *Chagos Islanders v The Attorney-General*, above at [559]. As for the potential significance of legal advice, see: *Jones v Morgan* [2001] EWCA Civ 995.

relevant in the light of the transitional provisions discussed above. Section 137 provided:

"(1) If the court finds a credit bargain extortionate it may reopen the credit agreement so as to do justice between the parties.

(2) In this section and sections 138 to 140—

    (a) 'credit agreement' means any agreement [(other than an agreement which is an exempt agreement as a result of section 16(6C))]1 between an individual (the 'debtor') and any other person (the 'creditor') by which the creditor provides the debtor with credit of any amount, and

    (b) 'credit bargain'—

        (i) where no transaction other than the credit agreement is to be taken into account in computing the total charge for credit, means the credit agreement, or

        (ii) where one or more other transactions are to be so taken into account, means the credit agreement and those other transactions, taken together."

Section 138(1) defined "extortionate" while s.138(2) to (5) sets out the evidential matters which the court is to take into account in determining whether a credit bargain is extortionate:

"(1) A credit bargain is extortionate if it—

    (a) requires the debtor or a relative of his to make payments (whether unconditionally, or on certain contingencies) which are grossly exorbitant, or

    (b) otherwise grossly contravenes ordinary principles of fair dealing.

(2) In determining whether a credit bargain is extortionate, regard shall be had to such evidence as is adduced concerning—

    (a) interest rates prevailing at the time it was made,

    (b) the factors mentioned in subsections (3) to (5), and

    (c) any other relevant considerations.

(3) Factors applicable under subsection (2) in relation to the debtor[230] include—

    (a) his age, experience, business capacity and state of health; and

    (b) the degree to which, at the time of making the credit bargain, he was under financial pressure, and the nature of that pressure.

(4) Factors applicable under subsection (2) in relation to the creditor include—

    (a) the degree of risk accepted by him, having regard to the value of any security provided[231];

    (b) his relationship to the debtor; and

    (c) whether or not a colourable cash price was quoted for any goods or services included in the credit bargain.

---

[230] The cases of *Samuel v Newbold* [1906] A.C. 461, *Poncione v Higgins* (1904) 21 T.L.R. 11 and *Glaskie v Griffin* (1914) 111 L.T. 712 contain decisions on similar factors under the old provisions.

[231] For relevant decisions see *Kruse v Seeley* [1924] 1 Ch. 136; *Verner-Jeffreys v Pinto* [1929] 1 Ch. 401; *Reading Trust Ltd v Spero* [1930] 1 K.B. 492.

(5) Factors applicable under subsection (2) in relation to a linked trans-action include the question how far the transaction was reasonably required for the protection of debtor or creditor, or was in the interest of the debtor."

Whether the bargain is extortionate has to be determined as at the date of the agreement.[232] If the bargain as struck is not extortionate, the borrower will not be relieved merely because its terms become more onerous in the light of subsequent events.[233] The hurdles faced by a complainant were high and the case law demonstrates complainants' limited success.[234]   **16–58**

Thus, s.138 dealt with the matters to which the court shall have regard if evidence of them is adduced. It was for the party, not the court, to call the evidence, and the court could not call for any evidence or direct a party to do so against his wishes. Further, by s.139 it was only the debtor or a surety who could apply to re-open the transaction. On a literal reading of s.139(1)(b), that provision would appear to preclude the court from raising the matter of its own volition. However, in *First National Bank Plc v Syed*,[235] Dillon L.J. expressly considered whether the Court of Appeal should, in a case in which the debtor was unrepresented and had not raised the issue, make an order of its own motion directing the County Court to determine whether the agreement was extortionate. On the facts of the case, the court did not do so. However, it did leave open the possibility that in different circumstances, the court could choose to raise the issue of its own motion.

Although s.138 directed the court to have regard to evidence adduced of factors applicable to the debtor and to the creditor, it does not follow that any weight will necessarily be placed on such evidence. The older decisions strongly suggested that, before the bargain could be set aside, the court must find that the creditor knew of the circumstances which made the debtor particularly vulnerable and unfairly took advantage of them. Although abnormally high interest rates may be taken as conclusive evidence of unfair dealing (and regard must be had not only to prevailing rates but also the type and nature of the agreement and the circumstances in which it was made),[236] they may on the other hand be

---

[232] *Harris v Classon* (1910) 27 T.L.R. 30.

[233] *Multiservice Bookbinding Ltd v Marden* [1979] Ch. 84 and see *Davies v Directloans Ltd* [1986] 1 W.L.R. 823.

[234] In *Woodstead Finance v Petrou, The Times*, January 23, 1986, the Court of Appeal did not disturb a mortgage at an APR of 42.5% p.a. as this rate was normal for short-term loans. And see *A Ketley Ltd v Scott* [1981] I.C.R. 241; and *Davies v Directloans Ltd* [1986] 1 W.L.R. 823, where interest rates of 48% and 21.7% (APR), on agreements that were secured by a land mortgage, were upheld. Contrast, however, *Barcabe v Edwards* [1983] C.C.L.R. 11 Cty Ct, interest of 100% p.a. (APR 319%) on unsecured loan reduced to 40 per cent p.a.; *Devogate v Jarvis*, unreported 1987 Cty Ct, interest of APR 39% reduced to 30% where loan was well secured; *Shahabinia v Gyachi* (1988) Lexis interest rates on non-commercial loans of 104%, 78% and 156% reduced to 15%; *Prestonwell Ltd v Capon* (1988) Lexis, Cty Ct, interest rate of 42% flat reduced by half, the risk being low; *Castle Phillips & Co v Wilkinson* [1992] C.C.L.R. 83 Cty Ct interest rate of 4% per month (interest being deducted from the loan) on secured "bridging" loan reduced to 20% p.a.; *Batooneh v Asombang* [2003] EWHC 2111 (QB) (interest rate of 100% on informal commercial loan reduced to 25%); *County Leasing Ltd v East* [2007] EWHC 2907 (Ch) (reopening of business loan of over £370,000).

[235] [1991] All E.R. 250.

[236] *A Ketley Ltd v Scott* [1981] I.C.R. 241; *Grangwood Securities v Ellis*, unreported, November 9, 2000; *Batooneh v Asombang* [2003] EWHC 2111 (Ch); [2004] B.P.I.R. 1 (QBD); *Broadwick Financial Services Ltd v Spencer* [2002] EWCA Civ 35, [2002] 1 All E.R. (Comm) 446.

intended genuinely to reflect the risk involved in lending. As Darling J. said in *Jackson v Price*[237]: "If you had to lend a mutton chop to a ravenous dog, on what terms would you lend it?"

It was for the debtor to show, on the balance of probabilities, the existence of any fact on which he relied for the purpose of establishing any matter referred to in s.138(3) and, if it was relevant, the creditor's knowledge of that fact. If he failed to do so, the court would not take the matter into account; but if he succeeded, it was for the creditor by virtue of s.171(7) to show that, despite those facts, the bargain was not extortionate. In regard to s.138(4)(c), the 1974 Act did not provide a definition of the words a "colourable cash price" but this denoted a price artificially inflated so as to conceal the actual rate of charge.

16–59   The question whether a credit bargain was extortionate was considered in *Davies v Directloans Ltd*.[238] In that case, it was held impermissible and unnecessary to look outside the Act at earlier authorities, in order to ascertain the meaning of the word "extortionate" in s.138(1), and that it did not necessarily mean the same as "harsh and unconscionable".[239] Outside the Act a bargain cannot be unfair and unconscionable:

> "unless one of the parties to it has imposed the objectionable terms in a morally reprehensible manner, that is to say, in a way which affects his conscience"[240]

whereas within the Act it was not necessary or permissible to consider whether the creditor's behaviour had been morally reprehensible but only whether one or other of the conditions of s.138(1) is fulfilled. A fortiori, the creditor's conduct during negotiations need not be unlawful.

In determining whether a credit bargain was extortionate, s.138(2)(a) laid down that the prevailing rate of interest at the time the bargain was made was a factor to be considered. It was held that regard should be had to the true rate of interest, that is, the annual percentage rate of charge calculated in accordance with the Consumer Credit (Total Charge for Credit) Regulations 1980[241] even though the regulations did not apply to the loan in question. *Coldunell Limited v Gallon*[242] was primarily concerned with the question whether A can avoid a transaction with B on the grounds of undue influence exerted by C, and decided that for such avoidance it must be shown that C was acting as B's agent. At first instance the transaction in that case was set aside both on that ground and on the ground that the bargain was extortionate within the definition in s.138(1)(b). On appeal it was held that C was not B's agent, and the burden on B of showing the

---

[237] (1909) 26 T.L.R. 106 at 108.

[238] [1996] 1 W.L.R. 823.

[239] *Castle Phillips Finance Co Ltd v Khan* [1980] C.C.L.R. 1 at 3.

[240] per Browne-Wilkinson J. in *Multiservice Bookbinding Ltd v Marden* [1979] Ch. 84 at 110. This judgment was approved by the CA in *Alec Lobb (Garages) Ltd v Total Oil (Great Britain) Ltd* [1985] 1 W.L.R. 173. In the latter case, a majority of the CA was of the view that there was no general doctrine of "reasonableness" independent of undue influence and duress. Equity controls only unconscionable and not unreasonable bargains. See *Lloyds Bank v Bundy* [1975] Q.B. 326 at 339; *Nationwide Building Society v Registrar of Friendly Societies* [1983] 1 W.L.R. 1226; and *Davies v Directloans Ltd* [1986] 1 W.L.R. 823.

[241] SI 1980/51, as amended by SI 1985/1192, SI 1989/596, SI 1999/3177 and SI 2010/1010.

[242] [1986] Q.B. 1184. See also *Davies v Directloans Ltd*, above.

bargain not to be extortionate was discharged, so far as s.138(1)(b) was concerned, by demonstrating that the bargain was on its face a proper commercial bargain and that B had acted in the way that an ordinary commercial lender would be expected to act.

Section 139 was concerned with the methods by which the extortionate credit bargain may be reopened, and is set out below (excluding subss.(6) and (7) which apply to Scotland and the Northern Ireland, respectively):

"(1) A credit agreement may, if the court thinks just, be reopened on the ground that the credit bargain is extortionate—[243]

    (a) on an application for the purpose made by the debtor or any surety to the High Court, county court or sheriff court; or

    (b) at the instance of the debtor or a surety[244] in any proceedings to which the debtor and creditor are parties, being proceedings to enforce the agreement, any security relating to it, or any linked transaction; or

    (c) at the instance of the debtor or a surety in other proceedings in any court where the amount paid or payable under the credit agreement is relevant.

(2) In reopening the agreement, the court may, for the purpose of relieving the debtor or a surety from payment of any sum in excess of that fairly due and reasonable, by order—

    (a) direct accounts to be taken, or (in Scotland) an accounting to be made, between any persons,

    (b) set aside the whole or part of any obligation imposed on the debtor or surety by the credit bargain or any related agreement,

    (c) require the creditor to repay the whole or part of any sum paid under the credit bargain or any related agreement by the debtor or a surety, whether paid to the creditor or any other person,

    (d) direct the return to the surety of any property provided for the purposes of the security, or

    (e) alter the terms of the credit agreement or any security instrument.

(3) An order may be made under subsection (2) notwithstanding that its effect is to place a burden on the creditor in respect of an advantage unfairly enjoyed by another person who is a party to a linked transaction.

(4) An order under subsection (2) shall not alter the effect of any judgment.

(5) In England and Wales, an application under subsection (1)(a) shall be brought only in the county court in the case of—

    (a) a regulated agreement, or

    (b) an agreement (not being a regulated agreement) under which the creditor provides the debtor with fixed-sum credit or running-account credit."[245]

Section 140 provided as follows:

16–60

"Where the credit agreement is not a regulated agreement, expressions used in sections 137 to 139 which, apart from this section, apply only to regulated agreements, shall be construed as nearly as may be as if the credit agreement were a regulated agreement."

[243] The onus of proof in this regard was on the creditor: s.171(7).

[244] See, however, *First National Bank v Syed* [1991] 2 All E.R. 250.

[245] This section was amended and s.5A repealed by the High Court and County Courts Jurisdiction Order 1991 art.2(8) with effect from July 1, 1991. Notwithstanding the reference to "High Court" in s.139(1)(a), the effect of that order is to require applications under that section to be brought in the County Court. Article 2(1)(h) of the Order confirms the County Courts' jurisdiction with regard to applications under s.139(5)(a).

Section 139 applied to agreements whenever made.[246] However, the limitation period in which a claim for relief under s.139(2) can be brought was 12 years from the date of execution of the agreement in question.[247]

In the event that the debtor is adjudged bankrupt prior to any application, both his and his trustee's right to apply under s.139(1)(a) are precluded by s.343(6) of the Insolvency Act 1986, pursuant to which any challenge would have to be made by the trustee alone.[248] The trustee would be able, however, to intervene in any proceedings brought by the creditor under s.139.

Section 139(4) would appear to have precluded the court from reopening a credit bargain on which the creditor has obtained judgment. However, a court may be persuaded to re-open the judgment on appeal or, in limited circumstances, to set it aside. In *Shireknight Ltd v Wareing*[249] obiter dicta of Glidewell L.J. indicated that he considered that a mortgagee's order for possession might be set aside pursuant to an application under s.139.

Unfair credit relationships

16–61   **Jurisdiction:**   The court may make an order under s.140B in connection with a credit agreement[250] if it determines that the relationship between the creditor and the debtor[251] arising out of the agreement (or the agreement taken with any related agreement) is unfair to the debtor because of one or more of the following:

(a)   any of the terms of the agreement or of any related agreement;

(b)   the way in which the creditor has exercised or enforced any of his rights under the agreement or any related agreement;

(c)   any other thing done (or not done) by, or on behalf of, the creditor (either before or after the making of the agreement or any related agreement).

In deciding whether to make a determination, the court will have regard to all matters it thinks relevant (including matters relating to the creditor and matters relating to the debtor).[252] Logically, these matters must include those that were relevant under the previous regime.[253] The ability to have regard to matters pertaining after the agreement is made is new.

For the purposes of these provisions, the court will (except to the extent that it is not appropriate to do so) treat anything done (or not done) by, or on behalf

---

[246] Consumer Credit Act 1974 Sch.3 para.43.

[247] *Rahman v Sterling Credit Ltd* [2001] 1 W.L.R. 496.

[248] Insolvency Act 1986 s.343(2).

[249] [1999] G.C.C.R. 1677.

[250] "Credit agreement" means any agreement between an individual (the "debtor") and any other person (the "creditor") by which the creditor provides the debtor with credit of any amount.

[251] Which includes assignees and those who have rights and duties by operation of law and in the case of joint creditors or debtors, it includes any one or more of them: CCA 1974 s.140C(2).

[252] CCA 1974 s.140A(2).

[253] ibid., s.138(2), (3); see paras 16–57 et seq.

of, or in relation to, an associate[254] or a former associate of the creditor as if done (or not done) by, or on behalf of, or in relation to, the creditor.

Reviewable agreements: This provision thus applies to exempt agreements, **16–62** (save for those exempt under s.16(6C))[255] and non-commercial agreements. It is thus (like its predecessor) of more general application than the other provisions under the CCA 1974. It can also be used to examine and reopen any related agreement to the credit agreement.[256] It thus extends to agreements consolidated in the credit agreement, to agreements linked with the credit agreement or any agreement it consolidates and any security provided or linked to those transactions.[257] The CCA 1974 now expressly provides that a determination may be made under the unfair credit relationship provisions in relation to a relationship notwithstanding that the relationship has ended.[258]

Discretion: The court is not obliged to make an order and it may refuse to do **16–63** so. Delay in relation to an application in connection with a relationship that has ended,[259] a failure by the debtor to disclose his true financial position[260] or the obtaining of credit by false representations[261] are all relevant to the exercise of the court's discretion.

"Unfair relationship": It is the relationship arising out of the agreement **16–64** which must be unfair. Indeed, the most relevant terms are those which will go to what (in the language of the 1999 Regulations) comprise "the adequacy of the price or remuneration, as against the goods or services supplied in exchange",[262] i.e. the price of the credit and particularly the interest charged, which may (albeit subject to certain requirements) be outside the scope of those Regulations. The unfair credit relationship provisions—and their ability to consider related agreements etc.—thus have an independent and important role.

Interest: The old law made express reference to the need to consider the **16–65** "interest rates prevailing at the time [the agreement] was made".[263] Any consideration by the court of whether a relationship was unfair will require the same

---

[254] "Associate" is defined in s.184.

[255] See s.140A(5). Section 16(6C) exempts those agreements where (a) it is secured by a land mortgage and entering into the agreement as lender is a regulated activity for the purposes of the FSMA 2000; or (b) it is or forms part of a regulated home purchase plan and entering into the agreement as home purchase provider is a regulated activity for the purposes of that Act.

[256] CCA 1974 s.140C(4).

[257] ibid.

[258] ibid., s.140A(4). The courts have hitherto exercised their assumed jurisdiction to do this cautiously: *Davies v Directloans Ltd* [1986] 1 W.L.R. 823.

[259] *Davies v Directloans Ltd*, above.

[260] *A Ketley Ltd v Scott* [1981] I.C.R. 241.

[261] ibid., see also *First National Securities Limited v Bertrand*, unreported (1978) Cty Ct; *Premier Finance Co Ltd v Gravesande* [1983] C.C.L.R. 1 (Cty Ct).

[262] UTCCR 1999 reg.6.

[263] CCA 1974 s.138(2)(a).

exercise and, in doing so, it must make a comparison of "like with like".[264] An interest rate that a high-street bank may lend to a "AAA" rated debtor will have no bearing on that which will be charged for credit by a less risk-adverse lender to a debtor with a poor credit rating. There is also a price to be paid for the facility itself which may not necessarily properly be translated into a rate of interest.[265] Now that the regime allows events after the making of the agreement to be considered, a creditor's failure to reduce interest rates may properly be the subject of scrutiny.[266]

16–66   *Creditor's rights:*   The court is now required to review the way in which the creditor (or his "associate") has exercised or enforced his rights when performing its analysis.

16–67   *Activity/inactivity before or after the agreement:*   This extends to that of the creditor and his associates but not third parties to any related agreement (unless they are associates).

Powers of court in relation to unfair relationships

16–68   An order under s.140B in connection with a credit agreement may do one or more of the following:

> (a)   require the creditor, or any associate or former associate of his, to repay (in whole or in part) any sum paid by the debtor or by a surety by virtue of the agreement or any related agreement (whether paid to the creditor, the associate or the former associate or to any other person)[267];
>
> (b)   require the creditor, or any associate or former associate of his, to do or not to do (or to cease doing) anything specified in the order in connection with the agreement or any related agreement;
>
> (c)   reduce or discharge any sum payable by the debtor or by a surety by virtue of the agreement or any related agreement;
>
> (d)   direct the return to a surety of any property provided by him for the purposes of a security;
>
> (e)   otherwise set aside (in whole or in part) any duty imposed on the debtor or on a surety by virtue of the agreement or any related agreement;

---

[264] See the case law under the old provisions: *A Ketley Ltd v Scott* [1981] I.C.R. 241; *Barcabe v Edwards* [1983] C.C.L.R. 11 Cty Ct; *Premier Finance Co Ltd v Gravesande* [1983] C.C.L.R. 1; *Davies v Directloans Ltd* [1986] 1 W.L.R. 823; *Woodstead Finance v Petrou* [1986] C.C.L.R. 107 CA; *Broadwick Financial Services Ltd v Spencer* [2002] EWCA Civ 35, [2002] 1 All E.R. (Comm) 446. cf. *Batooneh v Asombang* [2003] EWHC 2111 (Ch) (interest rate of 100% on informal commercial loan reduced to 25%); *Castle Phillips & Co v Wilkinson* [1992] C.C.L.R. 83 Cty Ct. See also *Paragon Finance Plc v Nash* [2002] 1 W.L.R 665, *Paragon Finance Plc v Pender* [2005] 1 W.L.R. 3412, *Patel v Patel* [2009] EWHC 3264 (QB); [2010] 1 All E.R. (Comm) 864 and *Khodari v Tamimi* [2009] EWCA Civ 1109. As for bridging finance, see *Shaw v Nine Regions Ltd* [2009] EWHC 3514 (QB).

[265] *Blair v Buckworth* (1908) 24 T.L.R. 474, 476.

[266] CCA 1974 s.140A; cf. s.138(2)(a).

[267] ibid., s.140B(3) provides that an order under this section may be made notwithstanding that its effect is to place on the creditor, or any associate or former associate of his, a burden in respect of an advantage enjoyed by another person. It is thus not the case that the recipient must pay.

(f) alter the terms of the agreement or of any related agreement;

(g) direct accounts to be taken, or (in Scotland) an accounting to be made, between any persons.

Procedural matters

An order may be made in connection with a credit agreement only (a) on an **16–69** application made by the debtor or by a surety; (b) at the instance of the debtor or a surety in any proceedings in any court to which the debtor and the creditor are parties, being proceedings to enforce the agreement or any related agreement; or (c) at the instance of the debtor or a surety in any other proceedings in any court where the amount paid or payable under the agreement or any related agreement is relevant.[268]

That application must be brought in the County Court.[269]

Burden of proof: Section 140B(9) provides that if, in any such proceedings, the **16–70** debtor or a surety alleges that the relationship between the creditor and the debtor is unfair to the debtor, it is for the creditor to prove to the contrary. However, it would seem that the debtor must adduce prima facie evidence to raise the issue; a bare allegation would not suffice.[270]

Limitation: Limitation only arises in connection with claims brought; a defence **16–71** founded on the sections would be unaffected. Under the former provisions on extortionate credit, the limitation period for an action under was 12 years[271] unless it is for the repayment of a sum of money; in which case it was six years.[272] That no longer applies to the new unfair credit relationship provisions. In *Patel v Patel*,[273] the court held that there would have been a serious flaw in the legislation if the time limit for seeking an order under s.140B expired 12 years after the credit agreement giving rise to an unfair relationship was entered into. Instead, the court had to determine whether the relationship arising out of the agreement was unfair, not whether the relevant credit agreement was unfair. The critical question was the relevant date at which the fairness or unfairness had to be determined. In principle the determination had to be made having regard to the entirety of the relationship and all potentially relevant matters up to the time of making the determination. If the relationship had ended, then the determination had to be made as at the date when it ended; if the relationship was continuing, it had to be made as at the time of trial. Thus (at least during the currency of the relevant credit agreement) the cause of action is a continuing one, accruing from day-to-day.

[268] ibid., s.140b(2).
[269] ibid., s.140B(3). The definition of "Court" in s.189 does not apply: s.140C(3).
[270] *Coldunell v Gallon* [1986] Q.B. 1184, 1202.
[271] Limitation Act 1980 s.8(1); *Collin v Duke of Westminster* [1985] Q.B. 581.
[272] ibid., s.9(1); *Rahman v Sterling Credit Ltd* [2001] 1 W.L.R. 496. But see also *Nash v Paragon Finance Plc* [2002] 1 W.L.R. 685 and *Nolan v Wright* [2009] 3 All E.R. 823. See also *Re Priory Garage (Walthamstow) Ltd* [2001] B.P.I.R. 144 (limitation period applicable to claim to recover money under ss.238–241 of the Insolvency Act 1986).
[273] [2009] EWHC 3264 (QB); [2010] 1 All E.R. (Comm.) 864.

The Financial Services and Markets Act 2000

16–72   The primary importance for the purposes of this work in considering the FSMA is to assist in indentifying what agreements are not with the CCA 1974 by virtue of the exemption referred to above.[274] Unlike the CCA 1974, breach of which can render a regulated agreement unenforceable, breach of the relevant FSA Handbook has more limited and indirect consequences.[275]

In November 2000, the FSA consulted extensively on mortgage regulation and the approach to be adopted.[276] The government announced, following the consultation, that it intended to ensure that mortgage lending came within the scope of the FSMA. The details of the scope of the FSA's regulatory regimes and mortgages was confirmed in the response by HM Treasury in February 2001.

The Financial Services and Markets Act 2000 (Regulated Activities) Order 2001[277] ("the Regulated Activities Order") provides under Ch.15 that various activities in relation to mortgage contracts are regulated activities. These are:

> (1) entering into a "regulated mortgage contract" as a lender[278];
>
> (2) administering a "regulated mortgage contract" where the contract was entered into by way of business after the coming into force of this article[279];
>
> (3) entering a regulated home reversion plan as plan provider[280];
>
> (4) administering a regulated home reversion plan where the plan was entered into on or after April 6, 2007[281];
>
> (5) entering into a "regulated home purchase plan" as home purchase provider[282];
>
> (6) administering a "regulated home purchase plan", when the plan was entered into by way of business, on or after April 6, 2007[283];
>
> (7) entering into a "regulated sale and rent back agreement" as an agreement provider[284];
>
> (8) Administering a "regulated sale and rent back agreement", when the agreement was entered into on or after July 1, 2009.[285]

The Regulated Activities Order defines those phrases in the relevant articles.[286]

16–73   The most significant of the regulated activities is that of a "regulated mortgage contract", which is a contract under which credit is provided to an individual or

---

[274] See paras 16–20 et seq.
[275] See para.16–76 below.
[276] See p.70 "Mortgage Regulation: The FSA High Level Approach".
[277] SI 2001/544, as amended.
[278] ibid., art.61(1).
[279] ibid., art.61(2).
[280] ibid., art.63B.
[281] ibid., art.63B(2).
[282] ibid., art.63F(1).
[283] ibid., art.63F(2).
[284] ibid., art.63J(1).
[285] ibid., art.63J(2).
[286] ibid., arts 61(3), 63B(3), 63F(3) and 63J(3).

trustees and is secured by a first legal mortgage on land (other than timeshare accommodation, situated in the United Kingdom and at least 40 per cent of the land is used or is intended to be used as or in connection with a dwelling by the borrower, or, where the borrower comprises trustees, an individual who is a beneficiary of the trust or by a related person.[287] Thus, communal mortgages, buy-to-let mortgages and second charges are not within that definition. A "regulated home purchase plan" cannot be a "regulated mortgage contract"[288] but is subject to its own provisions.[289]

For the purposes of the relevant articles, "administering" means either or both of the notification to the borrower of changes in interest rates or payments due or other matters of which he is required to be notified and taking any necessary steps for the purposes of collecting or recovering payments due.

The Regulated Activities Order also contains a number of exclusions such that, in relation to a "regulated mortgage contract", a person who is not an authorised person is not in breach of the FSMA and does not carry on an activity of the kind specified by art.61(2) where he (a) arranges for another person, being an authorised person with permission to carry on an activity of that kind, to administer the contract, or (b) administers the contract himself during a period of not more than one month beginning with the day on which any such arrangement comes to an end.[290] Nor is it a breach of the FSMA for an authorised person to enter into an agreement with an unauthorised person to carry out an activity for which the authorised person is otherwise permitted to do.[291] Similar exclusions operate in relation to the other regulated activities mentioned above.

Exemptions

Simply because an activity is a regulated activity and the individual concerned **16–74** cannot take advantage of any of the exclusions mentioned above does not mean that the provisions of the FSMA necessarily apply. In addition to the exemptions discussed above and those that apply generally in respect of all regulated activities (other than insurance business),[292] the Financial Services and Markets Act 2000 (Exemption) Order 2001[293] ("the Exemption Order") specifically exempts the following from the requirements to be authorised to carry on mortgage lending or mortgage administration in connection with the activities listed above:

---

[287] Defined in art.61(4) as being the borrower or beneficiary's spouse or civil partner or a person (whether or not of the opposite sex) whose relationship with the borrower has the characteristics of the relationship between husband and wife or is the borrower's parent, brother, sister, child, grandparent or grandchild.

[288] ibid., art.61(3).

[289] ibid., art.63F.

[290] ibid., art.62.

[291] ibid., art.63.

[292] See Financial Services & Markets Act (Exemption) Order 2001 SI 2001/1201 Pt I which lists 17 institutions exempt from regulation, including the Bank of England, other central banks of any EEA state and various other national and international organisations.

[293] SI 2001/1201, as amended.

CHAPTER 17

BUILDING SOCIETY LAW AND MORTGAGE LENDING

GENERAL BACKGROUND

The law governing building societies and their power to make advances secured **17–01** on residential property forms an elaborate code. The code was initially established by the enactment of the Building Societies Act 1986 ("the 1986 Act") which repealed the Building Societies Act 1962. That Act was in the main a consolidating Act which drew together previous legislation, in particular the Building Societies Act 1874. Since then, the 1986 Act has been the subject of considerable amendment, principally by the Building Societies (Joint Account Holders) Act 1995, the Building Societies Distributions) Act 1997, and the Building Societies Act 1997 ("the 1997 Act"), In particular s.12(1) of the 1997 Act revoked Pt III of the 1986 Act, which had regulated advances, loans and other assets, and the power of a building society to lend on a second or subsequent mortgage, was greatly extended by Pt III of the 1986 Act. Further substantial amendments have since been made by the Financial Services and Markets Act 2000 ("the 2000 Act"), for instance, the substitution of a new Pt I in the 1986 Act dealing with the functions of the Financial Services Authority ("the FSA") in relation to building societies. There are also a number of statutory instruments governing the powers of building societies promulgated under the 1997 and 2000 Acts. The result is a complex amalgam of legislative provisions.

SUMMARY OF THE NATURE AND POWERS OF A BUILDING SOCIETY

Building society loans are governed by the general law of mortgages.[1] The main **17–02** difference between building society mortgages and other mortgages is the incorporation of the particular society's rules into the mortgage deed. The mortgage deed usually provides that the mortgagor shall be bound by any alteration of the rules, and, while a society has extensive powers to alter its rules,[2] such alteration

---

[1] *Provident Permanent Society v Greenhill* (1878) L.R. 9 Ch. D. 122.
[2] *Rosenberg v Northumberland Building Society* (1889) L.R. 22 Q.B.D. 373; *Wilson v Miles Platting Building Society* (1887) L.R. 22 Q.B.D. 381, n: *Bradbury v Wild* [1893] 1 Ch. 377. Also see Sch.2 para.6 to the 1986 Act.

must be one which could reasonably be considered as within the contemplation of the members of the society when the contract of membership was made.[3]

A building society is a mutual association incorporated under the 1986 Act[4] whose purpose or principal purpose is to make loans secured on residential property (as defined),[5] such loans being funded substantially by its members and its principal office must be in the United Kingdom.[6] A building society operates within the powers conferred on it by its memorandum.[7] The memorandum must state this purpose or principal purpose.[8] These powers can include the power to hold land as part of a building society's assets. Strict financial controls govern the structure of such assets and its subsidiaries. This is designed to ensure that the prescribed relationship between advances made by the society and secured on residential property and other assets is not breached.[9] However, failure to comply with these requirements will not affect the validity of any transaction.[10]

A building society may also have the power contained in its memorandum (if so conferred upon it) to raise funds and borrow money, such as to create a fixed charge over its property. A building society is restricted in relation to certain other transactions. It cannot act as a market maker in securities, commodities or currencies; trade in commodities or currencies or enter into any transaction involving derivative interests.[11] Further a building society cannot create a floating charge over the whole or part of its undertaking or property,[12] and any such charge is void.[13]

17–03   Following the enactment of the 2000 Act the regulation of building societies is now undertaken by the Financial Services Authority ("the FSA") and to some extent the Treasury. Such powers are also subject to the statutory requirements regarding the financial structure of a building society, where relevant.[14]

The 1986 Act contemplates the dissolution of building societies by members' consent,[15] or their winding up, voluntarily or by the court.[16] The rules of a society must specify the entitlement of the members to participate in the surplus assets in the event of dissolution by consent or winding up.[17] The substituted s.92 of the 1986 Act further provides as follows:

> "Where a building society is being wound up or dissolved by consent, a member to whom an advance has been made under a mortgage or other security, or under the

---

[3] *Hole v Garnsey* [1930] A.C. 472; *Lord Napier and Ettrick v RF Kershaw Ltd (No.2)* [1997] L.R.L.R. 1 (CA (Civ)); *Re IMG Pension Plan* [2009] EWHC 2785 (Ch); [2010] Pens. LR 23.

[4] The 1986 Act s.5(2)–(6) as amended by the Financial Services and Markets Act 2000 (Mutual Societies) Order SI 2001/2617 Sch.3(II) para.133(a).

[5] Building Society Act 1986 s.5(10) (substituted by the 1997 Act s.1(4)).

[6] ibid., s.5(1)(a) and (b) (substituted by 1997 Act s.1(3)).

[7] ibid., s.5(5) (substituted by the 1997 Act, s.1(3)).

[8] ibid., s.5(8), Sch.2 para.2(1) (substituted by the 1997 Act, s.43, Sch.7 para.56(3)).

[9] ibid., s.6 (substituted by the 1997 Act s.4), and s.6A (inserted by the 1997 Act s.5).

[10] ibid., s.6(5)(b) (substituted by the 1997 Act s.4).

[11] ibid., s.9A(1) (inserted by the 1997 Act s.10). This is subject to certain exceptions contained in subss.(2)–(5).

[12] ibid., s.9B(1) (inserted by the 1997 Act s.11).

[13] ibid., s.9B(2) (inserted by the 1997 Act s.11).

[14] ibid., ss.7, 8 (substituted by the 1997 Act ss.8, 9).

[15] ibid., ss.86(1)(a), 87.

[16] ibid., ss.86(1)(b), 88 and 89.

[17] ibid., Sch.2,para.3(4).

rules of the society, shall not be liable to pay any amount except at the time or times and subject to the conditions set out in the mortgage or other security, or in the rules, as the case may be."[18]

THE CHANGING NATURE OF BUILDING SOCIETIES

The original purpose of building societies, as stated in the preamble to the Building Societies Act 1836, was to enable persons of moderate means to buy small properties. In the early societies, funds were derived from subscriptions but societies also raised funds by the issues of shares and by receiving deposits or loans. The first known building society was formed in 1775 in Birmingham and like most early societies was "terminating", meaning the business was closed after all of its members had been housed. This changed when societies started accepting deposits from individuals who did not necessarily desire to borrow to buy a home, but simply wished to invest their money. No longer "terminating", these formed the basis of the "permanent" societies as they are now understood.   **17–04**

Following the liberalisation of their structure many building society shifted from financial institutions offering just savings accounts and mortgages to offering a full range of personal financial services.   **17–05**

A building society is a corporate body in the nature of a mutual institution and it differs from a bank in that sense. Those who hold savings accounts, or have had advances made on the security of mortgages, are usually members of the society. Consequently they have certain rights to vote and receive information, as well as to attend and speak at meetings. Each member has one vote, regardless of the amount of money invested or borrowed or how many accounts they hold. Each building society has a board of directors who run the society and who are responsible for setting its strategy. The board in effect act as trustees, holding the society's assets in trust for its members. Banks are companies normally listed on the stock market and are therefore owned by, and are operated for, their shareholders. Societies have no external shareholders requiring dividends. Their mutual status prevents them from being companies. A mutual society is run in the interests of its members, namely the savers and borrowers. The essential distinction, therefore, between a building society and bank lending institution is that the former does not have to pay dividends to its shareholders. This means that in principle the surplus or profit a society makes can be put back into the organisation to benefit its members.

The numbers of building societies have reduced with demutualisation and mergers across the financial sector. There are, however, currently still around 50 building societies in the United Kingdom holding assets of over £335 billion.[19] Building society law is, therefore, still of considerable relevance to a work on the law of mortgages.   **17–06**

---

[18] As substituted by the 1997 Act s.43, Sch.7 para.40.
[19] Building Societies' Association statistics.

THE 1986 ACT

17–07 The 1986 Act provided building societies with a comprehensive new legal framework for the first time since building society legislation was first consolidated in 1874.

The 1986 Act in its original form set out detailed provisions in relation to:

(1) the constitution of building societies;
(2) limits on raising funds other than from individuals and on lending other than fully secured on land, and restrictions on powers;
(3) the powers of control of the Buildings Societies Commission;
(4) protection of investors and complaints and disputes;
(5) management of building societies, accounts and audit;
(6) mergers and transfers of business.

The 1986 Act as originally enacted was prescriptive as to the powers of building societies and the way in which the powers were exercised. However, an important feature of the 1986 Act also included the wide-ranging power given to the Building Societies Commission and/or the Treasury to promulgate statutory instruments, subject to parliamentary approval. Since it came into force (many provisions came into force on January 1, 1987), the 1986 Act has been considerably amended and extended, especially as to the powers of building societies. Some of the main changes to the Act were made in 1988 shortly after its enactment, but subsequently there has been substantial revision to it by the 1997 Act, and now more recently by the 2000 Act.

THE 1997 ACT

17–08 The 1997 Act made a large number of substantive amendments to the 1986 Act. Its main purposes were to:

(1) remove the prescriptive powers accorded to building societies and to replace them with a permissive regime with a view to developing the commercial freedom of societies and enhancing the scope for increased competition and wider choice for customers;
(2) enhance the powers of control of the Buildings Societies Commission;
(3) introduce a package of measures to enhance the accountability of the boards of building societies to their members;
(4) make changes to the provisions relating to the transfer of a building society's business to a company structure.

The provisions of the 1997 Act came into force on various dates during 1997.

THE 2000 ACT

The 2000 Act was brought into effect over a period of time between November   **17–09**
2001 and August 2003. Specific provision relevant to building societies
included:

(1) transfer of all the functions of the Buildings Societies Commission to
    the newly established FSA;
(2) repeal of the current different statutory authorisation criteria for banks,
    building societies, insurance companies, investment firms and other
    such organisations and their replacement by a single unified statutory
    process;
(3) establishment of a single financial services and markets compensation
    scheme and a single financial services ombudsman scheme.

The provisions of the 1986 Act relating to the constitution, governance and
purpose of building societies in principle remain in place.

KEY ELEMENTS OF THE STATUTORY REGIME

Purpose of a building society

Section 5(1)(a) of the 1986 Act[20] provides that a building society may be   **17–10**
established under the 1986 Act if (and only if):

"Its purpose or principal purpose is that of making loans which are secured on
residential property and are funded substantially by its members."

"Residential property" is defined as being land at least 40 per cent of which is
normally used as, or in connection with, one or more dwellings, or which has
been, is being or is to be developed or adapted for such use.[21]
    The 1997 Act, conferred the freedom for building societies to pursue any
activities set out in their memorandum, subject only to compliance with the
lending limit, the funding limit, the restrictions on powers and the criteria of
prudent management, referred to below. In essence, it is these requirements,
together with the fact that most of a building society's customers are its members, which give to building societies their essential character and differentiate
them from other financial institutions.

Establishment and constitution

A new building society can be established by 10 or more people who have to   **17–11**
agree on the purpose or principal purpose of the society and the rules for its

---

[20] As substituted by the 1997 Act s.1(1).
[21] 1986 Act s.5(10) (substituted by the 1997 Act s.1(4)).

regulation in compliance with the Act, and the requirements of the FSA.[22] Schedule 2[23] of the 1986 Act makes provision for societies to have a memorandum setting out the purpose and powers of the society, and rules covering its internal regulation and arrangements concerning membership, meetings, resolutions, directors and other factors. This concept is similar to the memorandum and articles in the case of a limited company, the main difference being that the majority of a building society's customers are also its members. Most of the constitutional provisions are contained in Sch.2 of the 1986 Act.

Funding and the funding limit

17–12   Section 7[24] of the 1986 Act provides a formula whereby at least 50 per cent of the funds of a building society (or any subsidiary undertaking of the society) must be raised in the form of shares held by individual members of the society. This single funding limit replaced the two previous limits on funding—the 50 per cent limit in respect of non-retail funds and deposits and the 50 per cent limit on the amount due on deposits and loans. Section 1 of the Building Societies (Funding) and Mutual Societies (Transfer) Act 2007 (not yet in force) prospectively enables the Treasury to increase the limit on funding to a maximum of 75 per cent by order. That can only be done if there is an order in place giving the members equality with creditors in the event of dissolution or winding up. The Treasury would have no power by further order to reduce a funding limit increased by order under the new provisions.

Section 8[25] imposes restrictions on the categories of deposit accounts which an individual may hold with a building society, and prohibits a building society from accepting corporate bodies as shareholders (other than in respect of deferred shares). Funds raised from individuals cannot be by deposit and must be in the form of shares[26] with the exception only of current accounts; client or trustee accounts; qualifying time deposits; deposits at overseas branches; transferable instruments; and where the society has announced publicly that it intends to transfer its business to a company. The rights of existing individual depositors in respect of deposits made before the coming into force of the 1997 Act are preserved by transitional provisions in Sch.8 to the 1997 Act.[27]

A building society may not raise funds from a body corporate or from a bare trustee for a body corporate in the form of shares, except in the form of deferred shares. The rights of existing corporate shareholders are also preserved by the transitional provisions contained in para.8 of Sch.8 to the 1997 Act.

---

[22] ibid., s.5(2).
[23] Many of the provisions contained in Sch.2 have been substituted by statutory instruments made under the 1997 and 2000 Acts.
[24] As substituted by the 1997 Act s.7.
[25] As substituted by the 1997 Act s.9.
[26] ibid., s.8(1),
[27] Sch.8 paras 8, 9.

Restrictions on powers

Section 9A of the 1986 Act[28] imposes restrictions, subject to certain exceptions, **17–13**
on the powers of a building society or a subsidiary undertaking in relation to
acting as a market maker in securities, commodities or currencies; trading in
commodities or currencies; and entering into transactions involving derivatives.
The main exceptions relate to hedging transactions entered into by the society or
undertaking and certain transactions effected for customers of the society or
undertaking or where the amount involved does not exceed £100,000. A society
is required to do all that is reasonably practicable to secure that each of its
subsidiary undertakings complies with the restrictions.

Section 9B[29] prohibits a building society from creating a floating charge over
its assets and any such charge will be void.[30] Section 104A[31] allows the Secretary
of State, by order, to provide that appropriate provisions of the Companies Act
2006[32] shall apply in relation to the registration of fixed charges created by
building societies over their assets.

Part II of Sch.2 to the 1997 Act includes "safe harbour" provisions, in parallel
with those in the Companies Act 2006, whereby a building society's capacity is
not limited by its memorandum and, in favour of persons dealing with a society
in good faith, the powers of the directors to bind the society are free from any
such limitation.

Section 92A[33] requires a building society to seek the approval of members to
the acquisition or establishment by the society or a subsidiary undertaking of a
significant "non-core" business. This requirement applies only in the case of a
business where, in the opinion of the directors, a greater part of the business
relates to activities having no connection with loans secured on residential
property, and where the acquisition or establishment would cost 15 per cent or
more of the society's own funds (capital).

Investor protection scheme

Sections 24 to 30 of the 1986 Act[34] contained detailed provisions for a Statutory   **17–14**
Investor Protection Scheme and Building Societies Investor Protection Board.
However, under the 2000 Act the government has now established a single
financial services and markets compensation scheme known as the Financial
Services Compensation Scheme.[35]

---

[28] As inserted by the 1997 Act s.10.

[29] As added by the 1997 Act s.11.

[30] See fnn 13 and 14 above.

[31] As added by the 1997 Act s.42.

[32] Companies Act 2006 (Consequential Amendments, Transitional Provisions and Savings) Order
2009 (SI 2009/1941) Sch.1 para.87(7) (October 1, 2009).

[33] As inserted by the 1997 Act s.29.

[34] Repealed by the Financial Services and Markets Act 2000 (Mutual Societies) Order 2001 (SI
2001/2617).

[35] By s.337 of the 2000 Act the Building Societies Investor Protection Board has been abolished
and replaced by the Financial Services Compensation Scheme established under Pt XV of the Act,
and the supplemental provisions contained in s.339(2), (3). These sections came into force on
February 25, 2001 (SI 2001/516). Most of the provisions contained in Pt XV came into force on June
18, 2001 (SI 2001/1820).

FSA powers of control

17–15   Sections 36, 36A[36] and 37[37] of the 1986 Act give certain regulatory powers where a building society fails to comply with the principal purpose requirement, the lending limit or the funding limit. These powers now vest in the FSA.[38] The powers include a direction for the society to submit for approval a restructuring plan to bring it within the relevant statutory requirements, a direction to the society to call a general meeting to consider converting to company status, a prohibition order where a society has failed to carry out a restructuring plan, and, ultimately, to present a petition for the winding up of the society. A failure to comply does not, however, affect the validity of the transaction or other act by the building society.[39]

Sections 42B[40] and 42C[41] provide that if the FSA considers it expedient to do so in order to protect the investments of shareholders or depositors of a building society, it may either direct the society to transfer all its engagements to one or more other building societies, or to transfer its business to an existing company. The FSA may also direct that a transfer may proceed by board resolution only rather than by seeking the approval of the members of the society.

17–16   Section 46A[42] provides the method for referring a warning notice or a decision notice given by the FSA to the Financial Services and Markets Tribunal under ss.36(3), (5), (6), or (10) of the 1986 Act.

Sections 52, 52B[43] and 54 give the FSA extensive powers to obtain information or documents and s.53 deals with the confidentiality of information obtained by that body.

Sections 55 to 57 give the FSA power to appoint inspectors to investigate any aspect of the business of a particular building society, or its affairs generally, or to summon a meeting of members.

Management, directors and other officers

17–17   Part VII of the 1986 Act (ss.58–70) deals with the constitutional aspects of the management of building societies. Section 58 requires that there shall be at least two directors, and s.59 requires that every society shall have a chief executive and a secretary (who may be the same person), with appropriate knowledge and experience.

Sections 60 and 61 of the 1986 Act (as amended) set out detailed provisions for elections of directors. For all elections to the board of a building society, there must be a vote and each candidate must receive a positive endorsement from the

---

[36] As inserted by the 1997 Act s.14.
[37] As substituted by the 1997 Act s.15.
[38] See paras 17–01 and 17–03 above.
[39] s.5(4A) as inserted by the 1997 Act s.1(2).
[40] As inserted by the 1997 Act s.17.
[41] As inserted by the 1997 Act s.18.
[42] As substituted for ss.46–49 by the Financial Services and Markets Act 2000 (Mutual Societies) Order 2001 (SI 2001/2617).
[43] As inserted by the 1997 Act s. 43, Sch.7 para.18 for s.52A.

members. Except where voting in an election is conducted by postal ballot, a society is required to send proxy forms to all members entitled to receive notice of the meeting at which the election is to be held, and the directors must be elected on a poll. A director must retire at the age of 70 (or lower if required by the society in its rules) unless he or she is specifically re-elected each year. Other directors are elected for a three-year term. A society's rules may provide for a director to have a shareholding of not more than £1,000.

A nomination for a candidate for election as director may be made at any time. However, if the nomination is made after the last day of the financial year immediately preceding the election, the nomination is to be carried forward to the next election of directors after that, unless the candidate otherwise requires. The maximum number of members that a society's rules may require to join in nominating a person for election as a director of a building society varies from 10 to 50, depending on the society's total commercial assets (total assets *less* fixed assets and liquid assets). A person nominating a candidate may either be a shareholding member or borrowing member (and must have the relevant minimum shareholding or mortgage debt). The maximum length of an election address which a candidate can require a society to distribute to its members is 500 words.

Sections 62 to 70 of the 1986 Act (as amended) are concerned with dealings **17–18** between a building society and its directors (and persons connected with them). Directors must declare any interest in contracts and other transactions with their society. There are limitations on substantial property transactions involving directors, on loans to directors on favourable terms, and a general prohibition on accepting commission in connection with loans. A contract may be rendered voidable at the instance of a building society where the board had gone beyond its powers in a transaction with a director. Societies are required to keep a register containing details of transactions made with directors, and they have to record income received from the society by related outside businesses of directors, including conveyancing, surveying and valuations, accountancy and insurance.

Accounts and audit

Section 71 of the 1986 Act specifies the accounting records and systems of **17–19** control of its business and records and of inspection and report which a building society and its subsidiary undertakings must maintain. The directors and chief executive of each society are required to report annually to the Commission expressing their opinion as to whether the requirements of s.71 have been complied with by the society.

Sections 72A–72M[44] and ss.74–76 set out the requirements on the directors of a building society to prepare annual accounts, an annual business statement, a directors' report and a summary financial statement. The summary financial statement is sent to members. The full annual accounts must be available on

---

[44] As substituted by the Building Societies Act 1986 (International Accounting Standards and Other Accounting Amendments) Order 2004 (SI 2004/3380).

request. The form and detailed content of the annual accounts, etc., are prescribed in regulations made by the Commission. Sections 80, 81, 81A[45] and 81B[46] deal with the requirements concerning signing, issuing and submission of copies of a society's annual accounts, etc. to members and the Commission.

Section 77 (and Sch.11) of the 1986 Act set out detailed provisions concerning appointment, qualification, resignation and removal of auditors. The auditors of a building society are required to report to the members under, and comply with the provisions of, ss.78, 78A to 78D,[47] 79 to 81, and 81A, on the truth and fairness of the annual accounts and other documents and whether the documents comply with the provisions of the Act, and also fulfil certain obligations as to the signing of the balance sheet, laying and furnishing accounts and their publication.

Complaints and disputes

17–20 Under the 2000 Act, the government established a single financial services ombudsman scheme. Section 85 (and Sch.14) of the 1986 Act provide for the settlement of disputes between a building society and a member or members, in their capacity as such (rather than as customers), to be dealt with by the High Court or by in some indentified instances by arbitration if the building society rules provide.

LOANS SECURED ON LAND

17–21 The purpose or principal purpose of a building society is to make loans secured on residential property such loans being funded substantially by its members.[48]

Section 6 of the 1986 Act[49] provides that at least 75 per cent of the "business assets" of a building society (or of the society's group) must be loans fully secured on residential property.[50] The term "business assets" is not in fact used in s.6. They comprise total assets (or total group assets) *plus* provisions for bad and doubtful debts, *less* fixed assets, liquid assets and any long term insurance funds, and currently comprise mostly mortgage assets. The Treasury may reduce the limit by order to not less than 60 per cent.

Section 6A of the 1986 Act[51] defines "loans secured on land". The definition is primarily relevant to classification of assets (and not to powers) and to eligibility for borrowing membership. The land concerned has to be located in

---

[45] As substituted by the Building Societies Act 1986 (International Accounting Standards and Other Accounting Amendments) Order 2004 (SI 2004/3380).

[46] ibid.

[47] As inserted by the Building Societies Act 1986 (International Accounting Standards and Other Accounting Amendments) Order 2004 (SI 2004/3380).

[48] See above paras 17–02, 17–05.

[49] As substituted by the 1997 Act s.4.

[50] For the definition of "residential property", see para.17–12, above.

[51] As substituted by the 1997 Act s.5.

the United Kingdom or any other country or territory within the European Economic Area, the Channel Islands, the Isle of Man or Gibraltar. The Commission, with the consent of the Treasury, may by order extend the definition of a loan secured on land, and the application of any of the other provisions of the Act, to loans secured on land outside those countries or territories.

Section 6B defines "loans fully secured on land".[52] A loan which is secured   **17–22** on residential property or other land is fully secured on the land if the principal of, and interest accrued on, the loan does not exceed the value of the security and no, or no more than one, mortgage of the land over the society's (or undertaking's) mortgage is outstanding in favour of an outside person. The test of whether a loan is "fully secured" is to be satisfied "on the occasion on which" a loan is made or acquired. Provision is made for the re-classification of loans on the occurrence of certain events.

Section 5(10)[53] provides that "residential property" means land at least 40 per cent of which is either normally used as, or in connection with, one or more dwellings; or which has been, is being or is to be developed or adapted for such use.

DUTIES ON SALE

Section 12(2) of the 1997 Act provides that the common law duties of a   **17–23** mortgagee to take reasonable care to obtain a proper price or true market value when selling a mortgaged property in possession apply to building societies. This replaces the previous statutory duty under the now superseded provisions of s.12(1) of the 1986 Act.[54]

REDEMPTION, TRANSFER AND DISCHARGE OF A BUILDING SOCIETY MORTGAGE

Borrowers under building society mortgages have the same right to redeem as   **17–24** any other mortgagors.[55] The rules of a building society must provide for the manner in which advances are to be made and repaid, and the conditions on which the borrower may redeem the amount due from him before the end of the period for which the advance was made.[56] In the case of a "permanent" building society[57] the covenant for repayment is for the payment of an aggregate amount representing principal plus interest, by equal instalments over a stated period of years, together with any other sums which may become due under the rules of the society.

---

[52] As substituted by the 1997 Act ss.6, 46(1), Sch.8 para.6.

[53] As substituted by the 1997 Act s 1(4).

[54] And see the mortgagee's common law duty to "achieve the true market value" or the "best price reasonably obtainable at the time". See also *Reliance Permanent Building Society v Harwood-Stamper* [1944] Ch. 362.

[55] *Provident Permanent Society v Greenhill* (1878) L.R. 9 Ch. D. 122.

[56] 1986 Act Sch.2 para.3(4).

[57] One whose rules do not contemplate the termination of the society on any particular date.

Where an advance is made to a member of a "terminating" society,[58] the covenant provides for the payment of subscriptions, fines and all other sums due under the rules of the society until the advanced member shall have paid the full amount due from an investing member, plus periodical sums called redemption monies, which are, in fact, interest.[59] The advance is of a sum, usually less a discount, equal to the amount to which the member would have been entitled on the termination of the society had he remained an investing member.

Whether the society is "permanent" or "terminating", the mortgage normally contains a clause whereby default in the payment of any one instalment will render due immediately the entire amount advanced. Such a clause is not invalid as a penalty clause.[60] It is also probably not vulnerable to challenge under the Unfair Terms in Consumer Regulations 1999.[61]

TRANSFER

17–25 Under the general law the mortgagee is entitled to transfer his security either absolutely or by way of sub-mortgage, with or without the mortgagor's consent. But where the mortgagee is a building society, the relation between the mortgagor, as member, and the society, prevents this unless the mortgagor consents or special provision is made.[62] A transfer, however, may be made under an amalgamation or transfer of engagements.[63]

In the absence of special provision or the consent of the mortgagor it may be that the society can only assign the mortgage debt,[64] and even if a transfer is possible the transferee may not be able to exercise the power of sale and will not be in the same position as the society for the purpose of exercising the mortgagee's rights. Thus, in *Re Rumney and Smith*[65] it was held that trusts and powers for sale could be exercised only by the person authorised to do so by the instrument creating the trust or power.

---

[58] One whose rules contemplate the termination of the society on a fixed date or on the occurrence of a specified event, e.g. that the amount of each share has reached a specified sum.

[59] *Fleming v Self* (1854) 3 De. G.M. & G. 997, approved *Hack v London Provident Building Society* (1883) L.R. 23 Ch.D. 103.

[60] *Protector Endowment and Annuity Loan Co v Grice* (1879–80) L.R. 5 Q.B.D. 592, *BNP Paribas v Wockhard & EU Operations (Swiss) AG* [2009] EWHC 3116 (Comm)

[61] See above paras 16–01 and 16–37 to 16–40.

[62] *Sun Building Society v Western Suburban and Harrow Road Building Society* [1920] Ch. 144.

[63] See ss.93, 94 (as amended) and Sch.2 para.30 of the 1986 Act.

[64] *Re Rumney and Smith* [1897] 2 Ch. 351.

[65] [1897] 2 Ch. 351.

CHAPTER 18

LOCAL AUTHORITY MORTGAGES

BORROWING BY LOCAL AUTHORITIES

Power

As with all its powers, the power of a local authority to borrow is generally **18–01** conferred by statute.[1] However, a power to borrow may be implied where it is necessary to enable the local authority to carry out its statutory powers and obligations.[2] Any local authority has a specific power to borrow in connection with any purpose relevant to any of its statutory functions or for the purposes of prudent management of its financial affairs under Pt 1 of the Local Government Act 2003.[3] There are restrictions upon the source and terms upon which a local authority can borrow in the absence of specific Ministerial and Treasury approval.[4]

The ability of Housing Associations to borrow funds is referred to elsewhere in this work.[5]

Inability to grant charges over specific property

All moneys borrowed by a local authority together with interest thereon are **18–02** "charged indifferently on all the revenues of the authority",[6] and equally without any priority.[7] A local authority has no authority to grant mortgages or charges over specific property owned by it in order to secure borrowings. Any mortgage or charge purportedly granted by a local authority over its property will be ultra vires and unenforceable.[8] A person lending money to a local authority is not

---

[1] See, e.g. Local Government Act 1972 s.111; Highways Act 1980 ss.272(6), 279; Local Government Act 2003 s.1.

[2] *Baroness Wenlock v River Dee Co (No.3)* (1887) L.R. 36 Ch.D. 674.

[3] Local Government Act 2003 Ss.1–24, and in particular ss.1–5. Pt 1 repealed, Pt IV of the Local Government and Housing Act 1989, with effect from April 1, 2004; and see *Hazel v Hammersmith and Fulham London Borough Council* [1992] 2 A.C. 1.

[4] ibid.

[5] See Ch.4, para.4–29.

[6] Local Government Act 2003 s.13(3).

[7] Local Government Act 2003 s.13(4).

[8] Local Government Act 2003 s.13(1), (2); and see *A-G v Oldham Corporation* [1936] 2 All E.R. 1022.

bound to inquire whether the authority has power to borrow the money and will not be prejudiced by the absence of any such power.[9]

LENDING BY LOCAL AUTHORITIES

18–03   A local authority (as defined)[10] may, subject to political and economic restraints imposed on such authorities, advance money for the purposes related to the acquisition and improvement of housing. Part XIV of the Housing Act 1985 (as amended) sets out the purposes, terms and restrictions on such lending. Advances may be made for the purpose of acquiring, constructing, altering, enlarging, repairing or improving houses, for acquiring buildings for conversion into houses or flats, for carrying out such conversions, or for paying off loans for such purposes.

The powers of local authorities to make such advances are effectively controlled by central government by restrictions on borrowing[11] and the imposition of cash limits. Ministerial consent is required for the disposal of council dwellings, other than under the provisions governing "right to buy" or by way of a letting under a secure tenancy (or what would be a secure tenancy if it did not fall within one of the prescribed statutory exceptions). Local authority capital expenditure on housing is determined through the Housing Investment Programme, which involves submissions by local authorities relating to levels of expenditure planned for their areas. One of the heads of such expenditure is lending to private persons for house purchase and improvement.

Loans under the Housing Act 1985 s.435

18–04   Section 435(1)[12] of the 1985 Act gives local authorities power to make loans, or to make advances to repay previous loans, for the acquisition, construction, alteration, enlargement, improvement, or repair of houses, or for the conversion of buildings into houses or their acquisition for such conversion. Such loans must be secured by a mortgage. Before making an advance the local authority must be satisfied that the resultant house will be fit for human habitation, or in the case of a house to be acquired, is or will be made fit.[13] One purpose of this provision is to assist owner-occupiers who already have loans secured by a mortgage and to whom the original lender is unwilling to make a further advance; and it applies whether or not the original lender was a local authority. Because the local authority is empowered to make a loan which is large enough to pay off the

---

[9] Local Government Act 2003 s.6.

[10] See Housing Act 1985 s.4(e), as amended. A distinction is drawn for certain purposes between a local authority and a local authority which is not a local housing authority.

[11] For the lending powers of other public authorities and the borrowing powers of local authorities, see below, para.4–27.

[12] As amended by the Regulatory Reform (Housing Assistance) (England and Wales) Order 2002 (SI 2002/1860).

[13] Housing Act 1985 s.439, as amended by the Regulatory Reform (Housing Assistance) (England and Wales) Order 2002 (SI 2002/1860).

existing mortgage debt as well as to pay for improvements, the borrower is not faced with the difficulties of a second mortgage. In order to prevent the borrower from using the part of the loan not required to pay off the mortgage debt for purposes other than meeting his housing needs, it is provided[14] that no such advance shall be made unless the local authority is satisfied that the primary effect will be to meet the borrower's housing needs. Advances may be made to "any persons". "Person" is not defined in the Act but in view of the necessity for the local authority to be satisfied that housing needs are being met, it would seem that "persons" means "natural persons" and does not include bodies corporate. A local authority may, however, make loans to housing associations.[15]

The terms of advances are set out in s.436. The amount of the advance must **18–05** not exceed the value of the mortgaged security in the case of a house or houses to be acquired, or in any other case, the value which it is estimated the mortgaged security will bear when the construction, conversion, alteration, enlargement, repair or improvement has been carried out.[16] The advance together with interest must be secured by a mortgage on the property.[17] No advance may be made unless the estate proposed to be mortgaged is either a fee simple absolute in possession, or is an estate for a term of years absolute for a period of not less than 10 years in excess of the period fixed for repayment.[18] The mortgage must provide for repayment of the principal, either by instalments (of equal or unequal amounts) beginning on the date of the advance or a later date or at the end of a fixed period (with or without a provision allowing the authority to extend the period) or on the happening of a specific event before the end of that period and for the payment of instalments of interest[19] throughout the period beginning on the date of the advance and ending when the whole of the principal is repaid.[20] In either case, the balance outstanding is payable on demand if there is a breach of any of the conditions of the advance and the borrower may repay on any of the usual quarter days after giving a month's notice of his intention.[21]

The provisions as to local authority mortgage interest rates are set out in **18–06** s.438(1) and Sch.16 of the 1985 Act. The applicable rate will be the higher of a national rate set by the Secretary of State and a local rate determined by reference to a formula set by the Secretary of State. A local authority may give assistance[22] by way of waiver or reduction of payments of property requiring repair or

---

[14] ibid., s.439(3), re-enacting s.43(2A) of the Housing (Financial Provisions) Act 1958, as amended by the Regulatory Reform (Housing Assistance) (England and Wales) Order 2002 (SI 2002/1860)..

[15] Housing Associations Act 1985 ss.58 et seq.

[16] Housing Act 1985 s.436(3). There must be a valuation on behalf of the local authority. Except in cases of advances for acquiring houses, the advance may be made by instalments as the works proceed.

[17] Housing Act 1985 s.436(3).

[18] Housing Act 1985 s.436(2).

[19] For interest, see the Housing Act 1985 s.438 and Sch.16.

[20] Housing Act 1985 s.436(5). This is subject to s.441 (waiver or reduction of payments in case of property requiring repair or improvement) and s.446(1)(b) (assistance for first time buyers: part of loan interest free for up to five years).

[21] Housing Act 1985 s.436(6).

[22] Housing Act 1985 s.438(1).

improvement,[23] or by making a small element of a loan interest-free for first time buyers for the first five years of the loan.[24]

Advances may be made in addition to other assistance given by the local authority in respect of the same house under any other Act or any other provisions of the Housing Act 1985.[25]

Secure Tenant's Rights and Former Rights to Mortgages Associated with the Right to Buy

The secure tenant's "right to buy"

18–07   A secure tenancy is a tenancy of a dwelling-house[26] which is let as a separate dwelling and in respect of which

(a) the interest of the landlord belongs to one of a specified list of authorities or bodies[27]; and

(b) the tenant[28] is an individual and occupies the dwelling-house as his only or principal home; or, where the tenancy is a joint tenancy, that each of the joint tenants is an individual and at least one of them occupies the dwelling-house as his only or principal home.[29]

A secure tenant has the right to buy, at discounted prices, either:

(a) the freehold of his dwelling-house if the landlord owns the freehold; or

---

[23] ibid., s.441.

[24] ibid., s.446(1)(b).

[25] Housing Act 1985 s.435(4), e.g. under ss.460 et seq. of the 1985 Act (improvement and other grants).

[26] In this context "dwelling-house" means a house or part of a house: Housing Act 1985 s.112(1). For land let together with a dwelling-house, see s.112(2).

[27] i.e. a local authority, a development corporation, a housing action trust, an urban development corporation, (in the case of a tenancy falling within Housing Act 1985 s.80(2A)–(2E), the Homes and Communities Agency or the Welsh Ministers (as the case may be), the Regulator of Social Housing, a housing trust which is a charity, or a housing association to which this section applies by virtue of s.80(2) or housing co-operative to which s.80 applies: Housing Act 1985 s.80(1), (2) as amended by the Housing Act 1986, the Housing Act 1988 and the Housing Act 1996 (Consequential Provisions) Order 1996 (SI 1996/2325), the Housing and Regeneration Act 2008 (Consequential Provisions) Order 2008 (SI 2008/3002) and the Housing and Regeneration Act 2008 (Consequential Provisions) Order 2010 (SI 2010/866) Sch.2.

[28] The definition of a secure tenant includes a former secure tenant whose right to buy has been preserved following disposal of the reversion to a private landlord: see Housing Act 1985 ss.171A–171H and Sch.9A if protected in the register—it is not otherwise an interest which overrides, see Sch.9A para.6; Housing (Preservation of Right to Buy) Regulations 1993 (SI 1993/2241).

[29] Housing Act 1985 s.81.

(b)   a long lease of it at a low rent if the landlord does not own the freehold
or if the dwelling-house is a flat (whether or not the landlord owns the
freehold),[30]

provided that the relevant conditions and exceptions stated in ss.118 et seq. of the
Housing Act 1985 are satisfied.[31]

The former right to a mortgage to fund a "right to buy"

Under the consolidated scheme set out in the Housing Act 1985 the secure tenant   **18–08**
exercising a right to buy had a number of other ancillary rights that gave him
access to funding from his public landlord. Those rights were (subject to his
financial status) the right to a mortgage,[32] the right to be granted a shared
ownership lease[33] and the right to defer completion.[34] The provisions were
repealed with effect from October 11, 1993,[35] and were replaced by the right to
acquire of "mortgage to rent" terms.[36] That right to acquire on rent to mortgage
terms itself has now been determined by the provisions of the Housing Act 2004
with effect from July 18, 2005.[37] This means that unless the right was exercised
in pursuance of a notice served before that date the right was no longer exercisable. There was only a limited take-up of the right by the public in the 12 years
or so of its existence. Thus, the following text is now of historic interest only.

The right to acquire on rent to mortgage terms

Where a secure tenant had claimed to exercise his right to buy and had estab-   **18–09**
lished that right, while his notice claiming the right to buy was in force he also
had the right to acquire on "rent to mortgage" terms. This enabled the tenant
effectively to use public funds to assist in purchase and to acquire a share of the

---

[30] ibid., s.118(1) containing provisions formerly in the Housing Act 1980 s.1(1), (2), as amended.
Where a secure tenancy is a joint tenancy then, whether or not each of the joint tenants occupies the
dwelling-house as his only principal home, the right to buy belongs jointly to all of them or to such
one or more of them as may be agreed between them; but such an agreement is not valid unless the
person or at least one of the persons to whom the right to buy is to belong occupies the dwelling-
house as his only or principal home: s.118(2) reinforcing provisions formerly in s.4(1) of the 1980
Act.
[31] For details of the right to buy see further, s.119 and Sch.4 (qualifying period: now five
years—Housing Act 2004 c. 34 Pt 6 c.1 s.180(1)); s.120 and Sch.5, as amended by the Housing and
Planning Act 1986 s.1; s.121, as amended by the Housing Act 2004 s.4, and the Housing and
Regeneration Act 2008 (circumstances in which the right cannot be exercised); s.121A (where the
right is suspended), inserted by Housing Act 2004 s.192(2) with effect from June 6, 2005); s.121AA
(information to help tenants decide whether to exercise right to buy); ss.122–125E, as amended by
the Housing and Planning Act 1986 s.4 (the procedure for exercising the right); ss.126–131 and Sch.4
as amended.
[32] Housing Act 1985 ss.132–135 (repealed by Leasehold Reform, Housing and Urban Development Act 1993 c. 28).
[33] Housing Act 1985 ss.143–151.
[34] Housing Act 1985 s.142.
[35] Generally see *Woodfall*, para.27.068. The Housing Act 1985 as amended by the Leasehold
Reform, Housing and Urban Development Act 1993 ss.107, 108.
[36] Housing Act 1985 s.143 as substituted by Leasehold Reform, Housing and Urban Development
Act 1993 s.108.
[37] Housing Act 1985 s. 142A introduced by the Housing Act 2004 s.190.

dwelling house for a price that equated to a multiple of the rent payable when capitalised. This permitted him to fund the purchase by a mortgage where the interest payment did not exceed the rent that was payable. Where the right to buy was owned by a number of people jointly the right to acquire on "rent to mortgage" terms also belonged to them jointly.[38]

The right to acquire on "rent to mortgage" terms did not arise or was not exercisable in a number of circumstances. First, if the right to buy was not exercisable for any reason the right to acquire on "rent to mortgage" terms did not arise. A tenant who was or was entitled to receive housing benefit in respect of any part of a period commencing 12 months before the day the tenant claims to exercise the right to acquire and ending on the day the conveyance or grant was executed in pursuance of that right was also excluded from exercising the right.[39] A claim for housing benefit made or treated as made on behalf of the tenant in respect of any part of the same period which had not been determined and withdrawn would have resulted in exclusion of the right to acquire on "rent to mortgage" terms.[40]

The maximum initial capital payment that a tenant could have made in exercise of the right to acquire was 80 per cent of the purchase price. The minimum initial payment a tenant was required to make when exercising the right to acquire was calculated by reference to a formula.[41] The minimum initial payment was the product of multiplying the weekly rent for the dwelling house with the multiplier currently declared by the Secretary of State. The Secretary of State also declared a maximum figure for the rent that might have been used in determining the minimum initial payment. Where the actual rent exceeded the declared maximum the formula is adjusted so that the minimum initial payment was the product of multiplying the declared multiplier and the difference between the actual rent and the maximum rent figure and adding the maximum rent figure.

The figures declared by the Secretary of State were set at a level that it was believed would have resulted in a minimum initial payment which could have been raised on a 25 year mortgage funded by monthly mortgage payments equal to the monthly rent payable. If the minimum initial payment exceeded the maximum, the right to acquire on "rent to mortgage" terms is excluded.[42]

The procedure for exercising the right

18–10   A secure tenant claiming to exercise a right to acquire on "rent to mortgage" terms had to do so by serving on the landlord a written notice to that effect.[43] A landlord could not serve an effective notice to complete the purchase while a notice claiming the right to acquire on "rent to mortgage" terms was in force.[44] The service by a tenant of notice claiming to exercise the right to acquire on "rent

[38] Housing Act 1985 s.143(3).
[39] Housing Act 1985 s.143A(1)(a).
[40] Housing Act 1985 s.143A(1)(b).
[41] Housing Act 1985 s.143B,
[42] Housing Act 1985 s.143B(1).
[43] Housing Act 1985 s.144.
[44] Housing Act 1985 s.144(3).

to mortgage" terms after a notice to complete had been served by the landlord had the effect of deeming the withdrawal of the landlord's notice to complete.

Such a notice could have been withdrawn at any time by a further written notice.[45] Withdrawal from the exercise of a right to acquire on "rent to mortgage" terms did not inhibit the continued exercise of the right to buy.[46]

After receipt of a notice claiming the right to acquire on "rent to mortgage" terms the landlord was required to serve written notice admitting or denying the right as soon as practicable.[47] The notice had to admit the right and give further information or deny the right stating the reasons it was denied the tenant was entitled to claim the right. The further information the landlord was required to provide included the various elements that were required to calculate the initial payment, that figure and its relationship to the purchase price under the right to buy, the landlord's share in the property if the initial minimum payment was made and the discount on that assumption and the provisions the landlord considered appropriate for the subsequent purchase of the landlord's share in the property.

The tenant was then required to serve a written notice[48] on the landlord stating **18–11** either that he intended to pursue the right to buy exercising a right to acquire on "rent to mortgage" terms and the initial payment that he proposed to make or that he was proceeding with the right to buy but withdrawing the claim to the right to acquire on "rent to mortgage" terms, or that both rights were withdrawn. The tenant's notice was required to be served within 12 weeks of the landlord's notice. There was provision for a landlord to serve notice requiring the tenant to respond within 28 days if no response had been received within the 12 week period. A failure by the tenant to respond after a service of such a notice would result in the claim to the right to acquire being deemed withdrawn.

Where the right to acquire on "rent to mortgage" terms was being pursued, the **18–12** landlord had to serve a further notice confirming the landlord's share in the event of the initial payment proposed by the tenant and the initial discount on that assumption.[49]

The terms applicable to the acquisition

The terms of the conveyance or lease where the right to buy was accompanied by **18–13** the right to acquire on "rent to mortgage" terms had follow the terms required by the right to buy provisions[50] plus provisions dealing with the redemption of the landlord's share. Where the property purchased on "rent to mortgage" terms was leasehold, the tenant's covenants relating to service charges would be limited to a percentage that was proportionate to his percentage ownership of the property.

[45] Housing Act 1985 s.144(2).
[46] Housing Act 1985 s.144(4).
[47] Housing Act 1985 s.146.
[48] Housing Act 1985 s.146A.
[49] Housing Act 1985 ss.147 and 148.
[50] Housing Act 1985 s.151.

Purchase or redemption of the landlord's share

18–14 The conveyance or grant had include a covenant obliging the tenant to redeem the landlord's share immediately:

> (1) following a disposal by the tenant which was not an excluded disposal[51];
> (2) on the expiry of a year from the death of the person or last remaining person entitled to the property purchased.

In addition, the conveyance or grant had included provisions entitling the tenant or his successors to redeem the landlord's share at any time.

The redemption of the landlord's share would necessitate the payment by the tenant of the value of that share less the amount of the discount. A tenant could opt to redeem part of the landlord's share provided the payment required to redeem the share being purchased was not less than 10 per cent of the value of the dwelling house.[52]

If at the time of the redemption of the last of the landlord's interest the secure tenant, or one of them or certain of their spouses was the owner within the preceding two years, the purchasing tenant would have had the benefit of a final discount of 20 per cent. Upon partial redemption the purchasing tenant was entitled to a proportionate discount.[53]

Registration of title

18–15 On the grant of a lease out of unregistered land or the transfer of a local authority's title which lead to an individual no longer being a secure tenant (which included an acquisition pursuant to a right to buy or on a conveyance where the former secure tenant had, under a "rent to mortgage" acquisition, acquired a 100 per cent. interest in the dwelling-house) registration of the transaction was compulsory.[54]

Where the local authority landlord's title to the dwelling-house was not registered, on a transfer the landlord was required to give the tenant a certificate or a form approved by the Chief Land Registrar stating that the landlord was entitled to convey the freehold or make the grant subject only to such encumbrances, rights and interests as were stated in the conveyance or grant or

---

[51] Excluded disposals comprise the following: between spouses or civil partners; a vesting in a person taking under a will or intestacy; or a disposal in pursuance of an order under ss.24 or 24A of the Matrimonial Causes Act 1973, s.2 of the Inheritance (Provisions for Family and Dependants) Act 1975, s.17 of the Matrimonial and Family Proceedings Act 1984 para.1 of Sch.1 to the Children Act 1989 or Pts 2 or 3 of Sch.5, or para.9 of Sch.7 to the Civil Partnership Act 2004 and see Housing Act 1985 Sch.6A (inserted by the Leasehold Reform, Housing and Urban Development Act 1993 s.117), as amended.

[52] Housing Act 1985 Sch.6A.

[53] Housing Act 1985 Sch.6A.

[54] Housing Act 1985 s.154 and Land Registration Act 2002 s.4(1)(b) ,(f).

summarised in the certificate.[55] Such certificate was to be accepted by the Chief Land Registrar as sufficient evidence of the facts stated in it.[56]

Repayment of discount on early disposal

If a purchaser under the right to buy or the right to acquire on "rent to mortgage"   **18–16**
terms disposed[57] of the dwelling-house or his share within five years of the acquisition, the purchaser was required to repay the such part of the discount ignoring the value of any home improvements)[58] as the local authority considered appropriate, the maximum recoverable being reduced by one fifth for each complete year which has elapsed since the acquisition.[59] The liability to repay is a charge on the dwelling-house, taking effect as a charge created by statute as if it had been created by deed expressed to be by way of legal mortgage[60] and having priority immediately after any legal charge securing an amount: (i) left outstanding by the tenant in exercising the right to buy; (ii) advanced to him by an approved lending institution[61] for the purpose of enabling him to exercise that right; or (iii) further advanced to him by that institution. For the purpose of the Land Registration Act 2002, the definition of charge is any mortgage, charge or lien for securing money or moneys' worth and therefore includes the statutory local authority charge to secure repayment of the discount which must be protected on the register as any charge created by deed would need to be.[62]

---

[55] Housing Act 1985 s.154(2), (4).

[56] Housing Act 1985 s.154(5). The landlord must indemnify him if a claim is successfully made against him under s.77 of the Land Registration Act 2002.

[57] For relevant disposals see Housing Act 1985 s.159; *Re Milius* (1996) 1 E.G.L.R. 209.

[58] Housing Act 1985 s.155C.

[59] Housing Act 1985 s.155, as amended; Housing Act 1988 s.140; Leasehold Reform, Housing and Urban Development Act 1993 s.120(1) and (2), and the Housing Act 2004 s.185; *Pagemanor Ltd v Ryan* (2002) B.P.I.R. 593, affirmed on appeal. For exempted disposals see s.160.

[60] ibid., s.156(1). Land Registration Act 2002 s.132(1).

[61] e.g. a building society, bank, etc.: see s.156(4)–(6) as amended by the Housing Act 1996 Sch.18 para.22 and Sch.19, Government of Wales Act 1998, Financial Services and Markets Act 2000 (Consequential Amendments and Repeals) Order 2001 (SI 2001/3649), art.299, Housing and Regeneration Act 2008, s.307.

[62] Housing Act 1985 s.156(2); but the landlord may at any time by written notice served on an approved lending institution postpone the charge created by the liability to repay to a legal charge securing an amount advanced or further advanced to the tenant by that institution: s.156(2B).

made or done in pursuance of an order under section 40, as good as if made or done by the other spouse.

With regard to mortgages,[13] s.30(5) provides that if a spouse with matrimonial home rights is entitled to occupy a dwelling-house (or part thereof) and makes any payment in or towards satisfaction of a mortgage on that dwelling-house, the person to whom payment is made may treat it is payment by the mortgagor but that the fact that the payment has been made does not alter any claim that the paying spouse may have for an interest in the property. The fact that the property is owned by trustees does not prevent the application of subss.30(3), 30(4) and 30(5).[14]

Registration as a charge

Generally: Sections 31(1) and (2) of the Family Law Act 1996 provide that **19–06** where matrimonial home rights exist, they are a charge on the property-owning spouse's interest. Such a charge can only be registered against one property and, if more than one property is so charged, the Chief Land Registrar must cancel the first registered charge.[15] The sections only enable rights of occupation to be registered in relation to the matrimonial home, and not an investment or other property owned by a husband and wife.[16] If protected rights do not exist, an entry should not be maintained on the register for the collateral purpose of protecting some other unregistered rights or to in effect freeze the estate of the legal owner.[17] A charge has the same priority as if it were an equitable interest created at the latest of (a) the date on which the right was acquired; (b) the date of marriage; or (c) January 1, 1968.[18]

If the charge so created is a charge on an interest of the other spouse under a trust and, apart from either of the spouses, there are no persons (living or unborn) who are or could become beneficiaries under that trust, then the rights shall also be a charge on the estate or interest of the trustees of that other spouse.[19] The charge so created has the same priority as if it were an equitable interest created (under powers overriding the trusts) on the date when it arises.[20]

Where a spouse's matrimonial home rights are a charge on the estate or interest of the other spouse (or of trustees of the other spouse), an order under s.33 (occupation orders) binds the other spouse's successors-in-title save insofar as a contrary intention appears.[21] Merger by surrender of the estate charged into a larger estate will result in the superior estate remaining subject to the charge if, but for the merger, the person taking the estate or interest surrendered would be bound by the charge for so long as the estate or interest surrendered would have endured had it not been surrendered.[22]

---

[13] ibid., s.30(4) makes provision with regard to certain types of tenancy.
[14] ibid., s.30(6).
[15] ibid., Sch.4 para.2.
[16] *Barnet v Hassett* [1981] 1 W.L.R. 1385; *Clapich v Shah* [2003] EWHC 2423 (Ch).
[17] *Clapich v Shah*, ibid.
[18] ibid., s.31(3).
[19] ibid., s.31(4) and (5).
[20] ibid., s.31(6).
[21] ibid., s.34(1).
[22] ibid., s.31(9).

If a spouse's matrimonial home rights are a charge on the estate of the other spouse (or of trustees of that spouse) and the estate is subject to a mortgage then, if after the date of the creation of that mortgage ("the first mortgage"), the charge is registered under s.2 of the Land Charges Act 1972, the charge is deemed to be a mortgage subsequent to the first mortgage for the purposes of s.94 of the Law of Property Act 1925 (which regulates the rights of mortgagees to make further advances ranking in priority to subsequent mortgages).[23]

Even though the spouse's home rights are a charge on an estate or interest in the dwelling house, those rights are brought to and by the death of the spouse or the termination of the marriage, unless the court directs otherwise,[24] or the court makes an order to this effect under s.33(5) of the 1996 Act.

19-07 **Unregistered land:** Where the dwelling consists of unregistered land, the charge should be registered as a Class F land charge.[25] A spouse who is not in occupation of the matrimonial home and who has not obtained the leave of the court to enter and occupy it can nevertheless still register a Class F charge.[26] A charge under s.31(2) or (5) of the Family Law Act 1996 is not registrable under s.2 of the Land Charges Act 1972 unless it is a charge on the legal estate.[27]

19-08 **Registered land:** If the dwelling house comprises registered land, any land charge affecting the matrimonial home is to be protected by entry of a notice on the register[28] provided the charge is against the legal estate.[29] Notices registered under s.2(8) of the Matrimonial Homes Act 1983 or a notice or caution registered under s.2(7) of the Matrimonial Homes Act 1967 that are subsisting on the register on October 13, 2003, are unaffected by the new regime introduced under the Land Registration Act 2002.[30] A notice can only be registered against one property and, if more than one property is so subject, the Chief Land Registrar must cancel the first registered charge.[31] The spouse's matrimonial home rights are not overriding interests.[32] They entitle the person with the benefit of the notice to notice of any dealings with the land; they do not, however, give any entitlement to assert priority over any subsequently registered charge.[33]

Actions by mortgagees

19-09 A spouse, cohabitant or former spouse or cohabitant does not, by virtue of any matrimonial home rights or any rights bestowed by s.35 (former spouse with no rights to occupy) or s.36 (cohabitant or former cohabitant with no existing right

---

[23] ibid., s.31(12).
[24] ibid., s.31(8)
[25] Land Charges Act 1972, s.2(1), (7).
[26] *Watts v Waller* [1973] Q.B. 173.
[27] Family Law Act 1996 s.31(13).
[28] ibid., s.31(10), Land Registration Act 2002 s.34
[29] ibid., s.31(13).
[30] Land Registration Act 2002 s.134(2) and Sch.12 para.1.
[31] Family Law Act 1996 Sch.4 para.2.
[32] ibid., s.31(10).
[33] *Clark v Chief Land Registrar* [1994] Ch. 370 (CA).

to occupy) acquire any greater right to occupy the property as against a mortgagee than the property-owning spouse[34] unless those rights are a charge affecting the mortgagee on the estate or interest mortgaged.[35]

If a mortgagee of a dwelling house brings an action for the enforcement of its security, and at the relevant time either a Class F land charge (for unregistered land) or a notice (for registered land) is registered against the legal title, then if the person on whose behalf the charge is registered is not already a party to the proceedings, they must be served with notice of the court action.[36] The "relevant time" is, if an official search has been made and a certificate issued and proceedings commenced within the priority period, the date of the certificate[37] and in every other case, the time when the action is commenced.[38]

Release or postponement of matrimonial home rights

A spouse entitled to matrimonial home rights may, in writing, release those rights **19–10** in relation to the whole or part of the property.[39] Similarly, such a spouse may postpone those rights in writing.[40] A spouse's matrimonial home rights are deemed to have been released where contract is made for the sale of an estate or interest in a dwelling house or for the grant of lease and, on completion, there is delivered to the purchaser's solicitor an application by the spouse with those rights for the cancellation of the registration of the charge or (if sooner) the lodging of such an application at the Land Registry.[41]

Civil partnerships

The foregoing provisions of the Family Law Act 1996 apply to civil partnerships **19–11** registered under the Civil Partnership Act 2004.[42]

---

[34] Family Law Act 1996 s.54(2).
[35] ibid., s.54(4).
[36] ibid., s.56(1), (2).
[37] ibid., s.56(3).
[38] ibid., s.56(3).
[39] ibid., Sch.4 para.5(1).
[40] ibid., Sch.4 para.6.
[41] ibid., Sch.4 para.5(2).
[42] As amended by the Civil Partnership Act 2004 Sch.9.

CHAPTER 20

CHARGING ORDERS

NATURE OF A CHARGING ORDER

A charging order is a charge over a judgment debtor's property to secure a judgment debt created by the court exercising a statutory power. Under the Charging Orders Act 1979 it is open to a judgment creditor to apply to the High Court or County Court for a "charging order" over a specific asset of the debtor for the purpose of enforcing the obligation to make payment under the judgment or order they have in their favour.[1] It is an increasingly popular method utilised by creditors for the recovery of debts owed by debtors. Its attraction is that it creates an enforceable equitable security arising out of a judgment debt.   **20–01**

The court has discretion as to whether or not to make an order,[2] but the order, once made, provides the person with a money judgment or order with an enforceable security with proprietary attributes over the property of the judgment debtor. Sir Christopher Staughton described the interest created as: **20–02**

> " . . . a proprietary interest . . . and so binding on third parties. A charging order does not give a right to possession or foreclosure, but it seems to be an assignment of some proprietary right, effected by the order of the court".[3]

A charging order has the effect of imposing on some specified property of the judgment debtor a "charge for securing the payment of any money due or to become due under the judgment or order".[4]

By virtue of s.3(4) of the Charging Orders Act 1979 a charging order has the like effect and is enforceable in the same courts and in the same manner as an equitable charge created by the debtor by writing under his hand.[5] The judgment creditor can therefore invoke legal process for the purpose of realising his security to satisfy the judgment obtained, together with appropriate interest[6] and the cost of enforcing the charging order.[7] A charging order is enforceable by sale[8]   **20–03**

---

[1] Charging Orders Act 1979 s.1(1).
[2] ibid., s.1(5).
[3] *Croydon (Unique) Ltd v Wright* [2001] Ch. 318, at 328D.
[4] ibid., s.1(1).
[5] ibid., s.3(4); *Bland v Ingrams Estates Ltd (No.1)* [2001] Ch. 767 at 774F, per Nourse L.J.
[6] *Ezekiel v Orakpo* [1997] 1 W.L.R. 340 at 345H–346E, "such a charge would carry interest even though there were no words allowing interest in the charge itself" per Millet L.J., followed by *Yorkshire Bank Finance Ltd v Mulhall* [2008] EWCA Civ 1156; [2009] 2 All E.R. (Comm) 164.
[7] *Holder v Supperstone* [2000] 1 All E.R. 473, [1999] E.G. 145 (C.S.), at 479f–480b.
[8] CPR 73–10, PD73.

or the appointment of a receiver[9] and in the same manner as an equitable charge. Since January 1, 1997, a judgment creditor holding a charging order over a beneficial interest in land may apply under s.14 of the Trusts of Land and Appointment of Trustees Act 1996 for an order for sale of the legal estate.[10]

THE SCOPE OF A CHARGING ORDER

20–04   A charging order may be made against interests in land, government stocks, funds in court or other stock, with the exception of building society stocks or stocks of a body incorporated outside the jurisdiction where no stock register is maintained within the jurisdiction.[11] In addition interests in units of a unit trust in respect of which a register of unit holders in kept within the jurisdiction.[12] A charging order may extend to any interest or dividends payable in respect of an asset that is the subject of the order.[13]

20–05   A charging order may be made in respect of any interest (including land or under any trust) held by the debtor beneficially.[14] This power extends to the legal interest in land held on trust where the judgment is against the trustee in that capacity, and to any interest held on a bare trust for the debtor.[15] Similarly, the interest of a trustee which is itself held beneficially under a trust may be the subject matter of a charging order.[16] Also a charging order may be made where land is held by two or more debtors all of whom are liable to the creditor for the same debt and who together hold the whole beneficial interest under the trust unencumbered and for their own benefit.[17] Separate charging orders made against joint proprietors in the same court proceedings will not be treated by the registrar as charging the legal estate, and separate applications for a restriction in Form K would instead need to be made. Where the beneficial interest in a property is held by more than own person and a charging order does not relate to the interests of all of them only the beneficial interest of the debtor will be the subject of the charging order. It should also be noted that the imposition of a charging order on one joint beneficial tenant's interest may operate to sever the joint tenancy.[18]

---

[9] CPR Sch.1, RSC Ord. 51; the Senior Court Act 1981 s.37; the County Courts Act 1984 s.107.

[10] Prior to that date the judgment creditor was entitled to apply for such an order pursuant to the provisions of the Law of Property Act 1925 s.30, now repealed; and see *Midland Bank Plc v Pike* [1988] 2 All E.R. 434.

[11] Charging Orders Act 1979 s.2(2).

[12] ibid., s.2(2).

[13] ibid., s.2(3).

[14] ibid., ss.2(1)(a)(i), (ii), 2(2)(a). The procedure is particularly topical in relation to interests held in the matrimonial home.

[15] ibid., s.2(1)(b)(i), (ii).

[16] *Nelson v Greening & Sykes* [2008] 08 E.G. 158 CA.

[17] ibid., s.2(1)(b)(iii); and see *Clark v Chief Land Registrar* [1993] Ch. 370. A caution registered to protect a charging order does not confer priority. The rule in *Dearle v Hall* (1828) 3 Russ. 1 (notice to trustees) does not extend to a judgment creditor, see *United Bank of Kuwait v Sahib* [1995] 2 W.L.R. 94; affirmed [1997] Ch. 107. Further, a charging order takes effect subject to any prior mortgages affecting the estate or interest charged, whether legal or equitable.

[18] *Midland Bank Plc v Pike* [1988] 2 All E.R. 434.

OBTAINING A CHARGING ORDER AND THE SUBSEQUENT ORDER FOR SALE

Both the High Court and the County Court have power to make charging **20–06** orders.[19] Where the subject of the charging order is to be funds in court, the application should be made to the court in which the fund is lodged which court has exclusive jurisdiction. In addition the High Court has jurisdiction where the application is to enforce a maintenance order made in the High Court or the judgment is a High Court judgment for more than £2,000. Aside from applications relating to funds in court the County Court has jurisdiction in all matters, including those where the High Court has jurisdiction. In most instances the CPR require an application to made in the court that made the judgment or order it is based on.[20]

A judgment creditor wishing to secure his position with a charging order must **20–07** make an application for a charging order using a prescribed form.[21] A single application may be made in respect of a number of judgments against the same judgment debtor.[22] Such application is usually made without notice[23] and is initially dealt with without a hearing. That paper exercise usually results in an interim charging order. That operates as a charge on the property affected immediately. The judgment creditor must then ensure that the interim charging order is served on the judgment debtor, such other creditors as the court directs and anyone interested under a trust for land relating to the charge obtained. Where the subject matter of the application is stocks or units, then certain other bodies must be served with the interim order.

Service must be effected at least 21 days before the hearing at which the court will consider whether the interim order should be made final. At that hearing the judgment debtor, or any party interested in the property to which the order relates, may show cause why the final charging order should not be made or the conditions it should be subject to. Any evidence parties who wish to object intend to rely upon should be served on the judgment debtor at least seven days before the hearing. In addition the court should be informed of any relevant intervening event that may make the making of an order in appropriate or futile, such as the insolvency of the judgment debtor[24] or the sale of the property to a purchaser without notice of the order.[25] Once the matter has been heard the court must make the charging order final, confirm it, subject to conditions including the time it is to become enforceable, or discharge it.[26] If a final order results it should then be served on everyone the interim order was served on.

Usually a judgment creditor must commence a separate Pt 8 claim for an order **20–08** for sale to enable him to realise funds to satisfy his outstanding judgment.[27] Such

---

[19] Charging Orders Act 1979 s.1(2).
[20] CPR 73.3(2).
[21] CPR 73.
[22] CPR 73.3(3).
[23] CPR 73.3(1).
[24] *Roberts Petroleum Ltd v Bernard Kenny Ltd (in liq.)* [1983] 2 A.C. 192.
[25] *Howell v Montey* (1990) 61 P & CR 18.
[26] Charging Orders Act 1979 s.3(1), *Austin-Fell v Austin-Fell* [1990] Fam. 172, [1990] 3 W.L.R. 33.
[27] CPR 73.10(3) & (4).

a claim should be made to the court that made the charging order, unless that court lacks jurisdiction,[28] it must also be supported by evidence and accompanied by a copy of the charging order filed with the claim form. Such a claim is not an action to enforce a judgment, rather it is an action to recover a sum due to the claimant as a secured creditor and accordingly the judgment creditor is limited to only six years worth of interest if the delay between judgment and order for sale is greater than six years.[29] Further the costs of the claim to enforce by way of an order for sale are payable out of the proceeds of sale.[30] There is no statutory limitation period that applies to the enforcement of a charging order.[31]

THE DISCRETION TO MAKE AND ENFORCE A CHARGING ORDER

Generally

20–09 The court has discretion whether or not to make a charging order as a means of securing and/or enforcing a judgment.[32] The subsequent process undertaken by a judgment creditor, and any subsequent application made by the judgment debtor, or anyone else interested in the property or asset subject to the charging order, to discharge or vary a charging order, is also subject to judicial discretion.[33] Finally, if the judgment creditor proceeds to enforce the charging order by seeking an order for an immediate sale again the court will have a discretion. If the property affected by a charging order is jointly owned by others who are not a judgment debtor the power to the make an order for sale arises under s.14 of the Trust of Land and Appointment of Trustees Act 1996 since to do so is an exercise of the trustees power in relation to a trust of land. Accordingly the judicial discretion must be exercised in accordance with that Act.[34]

In exercising the discretion to make a charging order, the court must consider "all the circumstances of the case". The court, in particular, must have regard to the matters prescribed for consideration in s.1(5) of the Charging Orders Act 1979:

> "(5) In deciding whether to make a charging order the court shall consider all the circumstances of the case and, in particular, any evidence before it as to—
>
> (a) the personal circumstances of the debtor, and
> (b) whether any other creditor of the debtor would be likely to be unduly prejudiced by the making of the order."

---

[28] CPR 73.10.

[29] *Ezekiel v Orakpo* [1997] 1 W.L.R. 340.

[30] *Holder v Supperstone* [2000] 1 All E.R. 473 at 479–480.

[31] *Yorkshire Bank Finance v Mulhall* [2009] 1 P. & C.R. 16. See further Ch.6 para.6–39.

[32] Charging Orders Act 1979 s.1(5).

[33] ibid., s.3(5). This is only open to a "person interested in any property to which the order relates". According to *Banque National de Paris Plc v Montman Ltd* [2000] 1 B.C.L.C. 576 at 518a, this means a "proprietary interest or an interest akin thereto". In this case the interest claimed was the spouse's statutory "home rights".

[34] Trusts of Land and Appointment of Trustees Act 1996 s.15; *Close Invoice Finance Ltd v Pile* [2008] B.P.I.R. 1465; *Forrester Ketley & Co v Brent* [2009] EWHC 3441 (Ch); *National Westminster Bank Plc v Rushmer* [2010] EWHC 554 (Ch); [2010] 2 F.L.R. 362.

The making of the charging order itself simply gives the judgment creditor security and that security is confined to the judgment creditor's interest. In those circumstances it is not surprising that the circumstances of the debtor or even his family will not generally provide justification for refusing to make such an order. As Lord Brandon put it in *Roberts Petroleum Ltd v Bernard Kenny Ltd*:

> "The making of a charging order is a discretionary remedy, but a judgment creditor, although not entitled to such an order as of right, is justified in expecting that such an order will be made in his favour unless the judgment debtor can persuade the court that in all the circumstances of the case the order should not be made."[35]

An application to vary or discharge may be made by the judgment debtor or a **20–10** person interested in the property charged.[36] A person with a beneficial interest in the same property is a person interested for this purpose notwithstanding the fact that it is only the judgment debtor's interest in that is charged.[37] The court is able to exercise its discretion to discharge, against the wishes of the holder of a properly obtained and registered charging order, if in the all circumstances it concludes it is appropriate to do so.[38] The enforcement of any charging order by sale will necessarily involve an order for the sale of the whole property and therefore impact on the form of the co-owner's interest and their enjoyment of it. A judgment debtor will not obtain a discharge by payment of the judgment debt without payment of any interest and costs also due and secured.[39]

The court has a discretion as to whether the property should actually be sold **20–11** or not. Where the property charge is not an interest under a trust of land the court is only concerned with the competing interests of those in occupation and not their needs or welfare.[40]

Exercising discretion in a family home context

In the context of the family home the court looks to "strike a balance between the **20–12** normal expectation of the creditor and the hardship to the spouse or partner and children if an order is made".[41] There is no presumption one way or another, the wording of s.1(5) is taken to include the family within the personal circumstances of the debtor and therefore reads as treating the two categories with conflicting interests as being equally pertinent.[42]

---

[35] [1982] 1 W.L.R. 301 at 307. See also *First National Securities Ltd v Haggerty* [1985] Q.B. 850 at 866–867.

[36] Charging Orders Act 1979 s.3(5).

[37] *Harman v Glencross* [1986] Fam. 81, [1986] 2 W.L.R. 637.

[38] *Howell v Montey* [1991] 61 P. & C.R. 18—An interim charging order was obtained whilst a potential purchaser had the benefit of a priority period and the final order was obtained after contracts were exchanged. When the purchase completed and was not registered the charging order was registered. The Court nevertheless discharged the charging order enabling the purchaser to be registered free of that charging order.

[39] *Ezekial v Orakpo* [1997] 1 W.L.R. 340.

[40] *Pickering v Wells* [2002] EWHC 273 (Ch); [2002] 2 F.L.R. 798 where any suggestion that because of the Human Rights Act 1998 the occupants needs and welfare were relevant to the court's discretion was rejected. But see *Close Invoice Finance Ltd v Pile* [2008] EWHC 1580 (Ch); [2009] 1 F.L.R. 873 for a dissenting view.

[41] *Harman v Glencross* [1986] Fam. 81 at 104A per Fox L.J.

[42] ibid. at 57B per Ewbank J.

Where there are family members who are joint owners of a home upon which a charging order is sought, the court has a duty at least to consider whether they ought to be given notice of the hearing so that they can put forward any relevant matters to ensure, in accordance with the statute, all the circumstances of the case are before the court for its consideration.[43] The courts continue to recognise the rights of the creditor to be paid. As Ewbank J. put it in *Harman v Glencross*:

> "The factors of importance in coming to a decision seem to me to be these: in favour of the creditor, first, that he is owed a debt and he ought to be able to enforce it against any asset of the husband. Secondly, if the partnership had prospered the wife and children would have benefited, and it is said on his behalf, if the opposite happens and the business fails the wife must bear the loss as well as everybody else."[44]

Those factors must then be balanced and in *Harman v Glencross* the court went on to consider the wife's involvement or lack of involvement in the debt, the fact the creditor had not sought a charge when initially making the advance, the creditor's knowledge of the family and their situation and the fact of an impending divorce. Where ancillary relief proceedings are pending and the wife will be seeking a property transfer or capital out of the property charged the court will normally adjourn any application for charging order or order for sale or transfer the matter to the court cessed of the family proceedings for them to be heard together.[45] Dealing with the matters together has power through the ancillary relief proceedings to transfer the property to the wife which would defeat the charging order or to postpone a sale typically until the children reach 17 or 18.

20–13   Where an attempt is made to secure an order for sale to secure payment of the judgment debt an application affecting property with a beneficial owner who is not a judgment debtor will be made under s.14 of the Trust of Land and Appointment of Trustees Act 1996. For that reason in practical terms the exercise of discretion under Charging Orders Act 1979 coincides with the discretion under the Trust of Land and Appointment of Trustees Act 1996 where there are other beneficial owners.[46]

When an application is made for an order for sale and there is another beneficial owner the matters set out in s.15 of the Trust of Land and Appointment of Trustees Act 1996 must be considered. They include the intentions of those who created the trust, the purpose of the trust, the welfare of any minor occupants, the interests of any secured creditors and the interests and wishes of those beneficiaries of full age immediately entitled to their interest.[47] The courts have expressed the view that section 15 and an exercise of discretion in accordance with it is compliant with the Human Rights Act.[48]

---

[43] ibid. at 54G–H per Ewbank J.; [1986] Fam. 81 at 89D–E.

[44] ibid., at 59A–B.

[45] *Harman v Glencross* [1986] Fam. 81.

[46] Gray and Gray, *Elements of Land Law* (5th edn, OUP 2009) at 6.1.36.

[47] Trusts of Land and Appointment of Trustees Act ss.15(1) and 15(3) and *Mortgage Corporation v Shaire* [2001] Ch. 743 at 758F–G, 760E–F per Neuberger J.

[48] *Close Invoice Finance Ltd v Pile* [2008] B.P.I.R. 1465; *National Westminster Bank Plc v Rushmer* [2010] EWHC 554 (Ch); [2010] 2 F.L.R. 362.

Connection to bankruptcy proceedings

A creditor may seek a charging order against a debtor who is on the verge of bankruptcy. In view of the substantial preference given to the trustees in bankruptcy, even in the context of the family home, the courts are likely to grant the creditor his charging order if there are no other substantial creditors to be considered and the court's exercise of discretion is therefore focused on the creditor and the debtor or his family. Balcombe L.J. focused on the harsh realities in *Harman v Glencross* when he stated: **20–14**

> "[T]he court should consider whether there is any point in denying the judgment creditor his charging order, if the wife's rights of occupation could in any event be defeated by the judgment creditor making the husband bankrupt".[49]

The court does have to take account of any prejudice to other creditors and it may be the grant of a charging order or an order for sale on the basis of a charging order would allow the judgment creditor to gain an inappropriate advantage ahead of the other creditors. However, that does not mean the mere fact there is an unsecured creditor who wishes to be on a equal footing with the judgment creditor on the point of getting a charging order will prevent a charging order being made.[50]

Where a judgment debtor is bankrupt or in liquidation a charging order should not be made and if made should be discharged.[51]

Protection against third parties: registered title

As with any other charge or mortgage the holder of a charging order will be concerned to preserve their interest so that in the event of realisation it ranks ahead of other subsequently acquired interests in the same property, or indeed any pre-existing interest over which it is possible to secure priority. In the context of registered land, the Land Registration Act 2002 provides the rules as to priorities and protection.[52] **20–15**

A charging order over an interest in land which is a registered estate held legally and beneficially by a debtor can be protected by the entry of a notice in the charges register of the debtor's title.[53] A notice does not establish the validity of the underlying interest but it does protect such priority as that interest has, so that a disponee for valuable consideration acquiring by virtue of subsequent transfer, lease or mortgage, even if completed by registration will take their interest subject to the charging order.[54]

---

[49] [1986] Fam. 81 at 100B per Balcombe L.J.

[50] *Roberts Petroleum Ltd v Bernard Kenny Ltd (in liq.)* [1982] 1 W.L.R. 301; [1982] 1 All E.R. 685 (unaffected on this point by the reversal in the House of Lords) and *Nathan v Orchard* [2004] EWHC 344 (Ch).

[51] *Roberts Petroleum Ltd v Bernard Kenny Ltd (in liq.)* [1983] 2 A.C. 192, *Rainbow v Moorgate Properties* [1975] 1 W.L.R. 788; [1975] 2 All E.R. 821, and *Clarke v Coutts & Co* [2002] EWCA Civ 943; [2002] 26 E.G. 140 (C.S.).

[52] See Ch.11.

[53] Land Registration Act 2002 ss.32(1), 34(1).

[54] ibid., ss.32(3), 29(1), (2)(i).

20–16   If the debtor's beneficial interest is behind a trust of land a notice cannot be used to protect the charge created, since the interest is under a trust of land.[55] The charging order can be protected with the entry of a standard restriction in Form K in the proprietorship register of the debtor's title, since the 2002 Act expressly provides that a person entitled to a charging order under such an interest is a person having a right or claim to the trust property.[56] A restriction does not operate to establish the validity or priority of the interest. However, it provides protection by regulating the circumstances under which a disposition that is required to be completed by registration and would on completion would take priority may be so registered.[57] The protection achieved by the standard form of restriction applicable to charging orders affecting beneficial interests, is limited to a requirement for certification to be given to the Land Registry that the person with the benefit of the charging order has been given written notice of the transaction that is to be registered. It is arguable that the legal protection given is limited since the restriction is not explicit about the timing of the written notice and if a transfer has taken place and the money been paid to the judgment debtor before written notice has been given by the purchaser, he is entitled to register once notice has been given and his newly acquired title will take priority.[58] However, in practical terms purchasers will generally not proceed or part with their money until they are assured by undertakings or otherwise that all such entries in the register will be removed, with the result that notice tends to be given before completion between the parties or receipt of the money by the judgment debtor. The holder of the charging order then has a chance to ensure that part of the money realised is paid over in settlement of the debt. So, for practical purposes, the presence of such a restriction will generally have the desired effect.

20–17   Both an interim charging order and a final charging order can be protected in the register and the entry in respect of the interim charging order will in practical terms extend to a subsequent final charging order. Accordingly, best practice is to register as soon as the interim charging order is obtained.

20–18   In the case of *registered* land prior to October 13, 2003, when the order imposed a charge only on the interests of the beneficiaries a charging order could not be the subject of a notice in the charges register of the registered title.[59] A caution against dealings could be lodged instead, but this was subject to the consent of the registrar where the beneficial interest was already protected by a restriction.[60] However, the registration of a caution would confer no priority[61] and the charging order only operated as an equitable charge of a minor interest. When a charging order imposed a charge on the legal estate, protection could be

---

[55] ibid., s.33(a)(i).

[56] ibid., s.42(1)(c), s.42(4); Land Registration Rules 2003 r.93(k).

[57] Land Registration Act 2002 s.40(1).

[58] ibid., s.29.

[59] Land Registration Act 1925 s.49(1)(g) (inserted by the Charging Orders Act 1979 s.3(3)), and see *Perry v Phoenix Assurance Plc* [1988] 1 W.L.R. 940 at 945.

[60] Land Registration Act 1925 s.54(1) proviso (as amended). See also Land Registration Act 1925 ss.59(1), 65.

[61] See *United Bank of Kuwait v Sahib* [1995] 2 W.L.R. 94; affirmed [1997] Ch. 107.

effected by entry of a notice or a caution depending on whether or not the land certificate was produced.

Protection against third parties: unregistered title

The Land Charges Act 1972 applies to charging orders in the same manner as it **20–19** applies in relation to other orders or writs issued or made for the purposes of enforcing judgments.[62] In the case of unregistered land a charging order is capable of being registered over the legal estate as a land charge but only if it is a writ or order affecting land.[63] A complicating feature is that undivided shares in land are expressly excluded from the definition of land in s.17(1) of the Land Charges Act 1972. It follows, therefore, that in the case of *unregistered* land where land is held beneficially under a trust of land a charging order cannot be registered under the Land Charges Act 1972 when the order imposes a charge only on the interests of the beneficiaries. Different considerations would apply where the order imposes a charge on the estate held by the trustees. The logic for this is that beneficial interests held under a trust of land are themselves not registrable under s.6(1) of the Land Charges Act 1972.[64] A charging order also cannot be registered as a general equitable charge.[65]

Priority of charging orders

In summary, a charging order obtained will rank behind any prior legal or **20–20** equitable mortgages or charges over registered or unregistered land, whether registered or not. A charging order over registered land will also rank behind any prior overriding interests. A charging order that is unprotected by registration as a land charge or as an equitable charge by registration of a notice or a restriction as appropriate will lose its priority to a subsequent purchaser or mortgagee for value, regardless of notice, provided in the case of registered title that the subsequent transaction completed at registration. Where there are two charging orders against registered land, priority is determined by the date of creation. In the case of unregistered land the first in time will have priority in accordance with the general rule where equities are equal. It follows priority depends on the date the charging orders were made in both cases. However, since there is no requirement that the equities will be equal in the case of registered land, in that context priority will not be lost by factors such as "inequitable conduct" or "gross carelessness".[66]

---

[62] s.3(2).

[63] Land Charges Act 1972 s.6(1)(a).

[64] ibid., s.6(1)(A) (inserted by the Trusts of Land and Appointment of Trustees Act 1996 s.25(1), Sch.3 para.12(3), and see *Perry v Phoenix Assurance Plc* [1988] 1 W.L.R. 940 at 945).

[65] ibid., s.2(4), Class C(iii) (as amended the Trusts of Land and Appointment of Trustees Act 1996 s.25(1), Sch.3 para.12(2)).

[66] See discussion in *Registered Conveyancing for the Twenty-first Century* (Law Commission No.271), para.5.5.

CHAPTER 21

OTHER STATUTORY CHARGES

NATURE OF A STATUTORY CHARGE

In addition to charging orders (which are dealt with in the preceding chapter) **21–01** there are a number of statutory charges that may arise and take effect as a charge against the proprietary interests of an individual or in some cases a company. In essence a statutory charge arises without the agreement or any action on the part of the mortgagor to create it. They arise as a matter of statute on the occurrence of certain events. Such charges are to be distinguished from a mortgage in that a statutory charge is imposed by the statute itself on the land in question.[1]

The relevant statute will provide for the circumstances and/or means by which the statutory charge will arise, the nature of the charge, the extent of liability the charge relates to and the property to which it attaches. In some instances if a particular situation occurs the charge will arise automatically. In other instances the mortgagee is obliged to take certain steps, as laid out in the statute, such as the service of a notice. Further, in some, but not all instances, the statute will provide for the statutory charge to have priority over any existing charges[2] or will identify the charges over which it is to have priority.[3]

All statutory charges provide a statutory code for the securing of a variety of types of liability that may or may not be associated with the use of the charged property. Often it is the State in one guise or another that is entitled to recover the liability secured by the charge.

LEGAL SERVICES COMMISSION STATUTORY CHARGE

Wherever someone has had the benefit of public funds to pursue or defend **21–02** litigation and as a result they "recover or preserve" any property for himself or another, then unless the regulations provide otherwise, a statutory charge will be created that operates as a first charge over that property.[4] It is not necessary for the Legal Services Commission to take any steps for the charge to arise. The property may have been recovered or preserved in proceedings or any compromise or settlement of any dispute in respect of which the publicly funded services were provided.

---

[1] They therefore differ from a statutory legal charge under the Law of Property Act 1925 s.117.
[2] Access to Justice Act 1999 s.10(7).
[3] Housing Act 1985 ss.36 and 156.
[4] Access to Justice 1999 s.10(7).

The predecessor provisions dealing with the Legal Aid statutory charge have been considered by the courts on a number of occasions. Although those provisions expressly provided that "it is immaterial what the nature of the property is and where it is situated", there is no equivalent wording in the current provision. Current regulations provide that in most instances any charge is a charge in favour of the Legal Services Commission and contain detailed provision for the calculation of sums that are secured by the charge.[5]

21–03   Consideration by the courts of the predecessor provisions established that property recovered or preserved was widely defined, and included the preservation of a right to possession so that, even where the land the right to possession related to was in negative equity property would have been preserved and the statutory charge would arise.[6] Further it was established that where a settlement involved a party paying to retain the property, provided the value of the property exceeded the sum paid, it was preserved and the charge arose.

21–04   Ordinarily such a statutory charge can be protected on the register by way of registration as a charge and should be accompanied by an indication it is an overriding charge. However, where the litigant who had the benefit of public funds is not the legal owner or one of a number of legal owners the charge will only operate as a charge against his beneficial interest, which is an interest under a trust for land and accordingly may not registered as a charge against the registered title or be protected by a notice.[7] Rather it may be the subject of a restriction.[8] Since the statute provides for a first charge to arise it would appear the Legal Service Commission's charge takes priority over any pre-existing charges.

LOCAL, HOUSING AND STREET WORKS AUTHORITIES STATUTORY CHARGES

Housing authorities

21–05   Statutory charges related to the activities of Housing authorities may arise in a number of instances.

21–06   The recovery of discounts on the early sale of a property sold pursuant to a right of buy or a disposal of land held for housing stock are two examples.[9] In both cases, the statutory provisions provide that the charge arises and takes effect as if it had been created by deed and expressed to be by way of legal mortgage. It follows that the Housing Authority do not need to take any specific steps to cause the charge to arise. Once such a charge has arisen it can be protected in the

---

[5] Community Legal Service (Financial) Regulations 2000 (SI 2000/516).

[6] *McPherson v Legal Services Commission* [2008] EWHC 2865 (Ch), *Parkes v Legal Aid Board* [1997] 1 W.L.R. 1547 and *Curling v Law Society* [1985] 1 W.L.R. 470. However see *Legal Service Commission v Pugh* Ref 2006/1672 (Decision of the Adjudicator to HM Land Registry) where the "property recovered" was a right of way and it was decided that would not entitle the LSC to a charge of the property that benefited from that right of way.

[7] *McPherson v Legal Services Commission* [2008] EWHC 2865 (Ch)

[8] Land Registration Rules 2003 r.91 and Sch.4, Standard form restriction JJ.

[9] Housing Act 1985 ss.36 and 156, Housing Act 1988 s.79, Sch.11 paras 1 and 2; Housing Act 1996 s11.

same manner as an ordinary legal charge would be, namely as a registrable charge against the registered title acquired. Such charges take priority after any charge relating to any unpaid part of the purchase price and to any mortgage provided by an approved lender for the purpose of funding the purchase. There is also provision for the Housing Authority to give consent by written notice for its charge to rank behind a charge relating to subsequent borrowings from an approved lender for specific purposes.

Housing authorities have powers to require landowners to undertake necessary works where the condition of residential property is hazardous.[10] Where a Housing Authority incurs costs in enforcing those obligations or has to undertake any of the necessary works itself, it can seek to recover those sums from the landowner.[11] Once those sums are recovered as required by the statute and the time for appealing has expired, the demand becomes operative.[12] Upon the demand becoming operative, and until the money demanded is recovered, a charge arises as if it were a charge by deed.[13] The charge is registrable as a local land charge and the Housing Authority have the powers and remedies available under s.20 of the Law of Property Act 1925, which include powers of sale, lease, accepting surrenders of leases and the appointing of a receiver. It was established that the predecessor provisions provided for the charge that arose to take priority over existing charges and rent charges.[14] The current provisions are silent as to priority. **21–07**

A local authority which is involved in incurring expenses in addressing statutory nuisances or clean air issues under the Environmental Protection Act 1990 is entitled to recover the expenditure incurred along with interest thereon.[15] Such expenditure shall be a charge on the premises affected by the works provided the local authority has served a notice stating the amount recoverable, the statutory power to recover with interest and the fact of the charge along with the provisions for appeal and the coming into effect of the charge. The charge does not arise until the time for appealing has expired and/or any appeal has been finally determined.[16] The charge attracts all the powers and rights available under s.20 of the Law of Property Act 1925 along with the powers of sale, lease, accepting surrenders of leases and appointing a receiver as if the local authority was a mortgagee by deed.[17] The statute makes no particular provision as to registration and is silent on the question of priorities. **21–08**

Street works authorities

Where a local authority undertakes certain works making up private streets which affect premises fronting such a street they may recover the expenses incurred **21–09**

---

[10] Housing Act 2004 Pt 1.
[11] Housing Act 2004 s.49.
[12] Housing Act 2004 s.50(5)–(8).
[13] Housing Act 2004 s.50(9)—(11).
[14] *Bristol Corp v Virgin* [1928] 2 K.B. 622, *Paddington BC v Finucane* [1928] Ch. 567.
[15] Environmental Protection Act 1990 s.81A.
[16] Environmental Protection Act 1990 s.81A(4).
[17] Environmental Protection Act 1990 s.81A(8).

along with interest.[18] The authority has to undertake a process by which the expenses incurred are apportioned and once that is completed by the authority or the court the charge arises.[19] That charge is capable of registration as a local land charge and confers on the authority all the powers and remedies under the Law of Property Act 1925 including the powers of sale, leasing and appointment of a receiver.[20]

STATUTORY CHARGES ASSOCIATED WITH LANDLORDS AND TENANTS

Agricultural tenancies[21]

21–10   Where a landlord fails for one month to pay compensation due to his agricultural tenant (following agreement or determination) pursuant to the Agricultural Holdings Act 1986, the tenant may apply to the relevant Minister for an order charging the holding with the payment of the monies due.[22] The landlord has a similar ability to obtain a charge over the holding by application to the relevant Minister if the tenant has failed to pay monies due under the Act for a month.[23]

The statute expressly provides that a charge for the benefit of the tenant shall rank in priority to any other charge, however and whenever created or arising; save that charges created under the Act in favour of the tenant shall rank in order of creation.[24] The Act is silent as to priority affecting a charge in favour of the landlord and accordingly such a charge will not rank in priority to existing charges.

Business tenancies

21–11   Where compensation is payable for improvements or the costs of improvements pursuant to a notice under the Landlord and Tenant Act 1927, a charge may be obtained from the relevant Minister. The charge is registrable as a Class A land charge.[25]

CHARGING ORDERS IN RESPECT OF SOLICITOR'S COSTS

21–12   A court seised of a matter where a solicitor is acting, has power under the Solicitors Act 1974 to impose a charging order on "property recovered or preserved" by the solicitor, to secure payment of the solicitor's assessed costs.[26]

---

[18] Highways Act 1980 s.212(1).
[19] Highways Act 1980 s.212(2).
[20] Highways Act 1980 s.212(3).
[21] See also Ch.24.
[22] Agricultural Holdings Act 1986 s.85.
[23] Agricultural Holdings Act 1986 s.86. These are registrable as Class A Land Charges. ibid., s.100, Sch.14 para.51. If they are not so registered they will be void against a purchaser for value of the land charged.
[24] Agricultural Holdings Act 1986 s.87(6).
[25] Landlord and Tenant Act 1927 s.12, Sch.1.
[26] Solicitors Act 1974 s.73(1).

Such an order may be made before the costs are assessed[27] and may be made in respect of property that does not belong to the solicitor's client, provided it is recovered or preserved by the solicitor.[28] "Property" is not defined in the Act. However, since the language of the Act makes it clear that the court is imposing a charging order, it may be the definition of "property" for the purposes of the Charging Orders Act 1979 which is of some assistance.

STATUTORY CHARGES ASSOCIATED WITH LOCAL AUTHORITY CARE AND SERVICES

Local authority services

Under the Health and Social Services and Social Security Adjudications Act   **21–13**
1983, a statutory charge may be imposed for non-payment in respect of "Part III Accommodation". Part III Accommodation is a reference to accommodation provided by a local authority those in need by reason of age, illness or disability or other circumstances or to expectant or nursing mothers in need pursuant to ss.21–26 of the National Assistance Act 1948. Those most commonly accommodated within these provisions are elderly or disabled residents in care rather than nursing homes.

The 1983 Act makes provision for the local authority to require payment towards the costs of such accommodation, unless the resident has satisfied the local authority their means are insufficient.[29] Commonly a financial assessment is made of the residents' capital and income, including any property they own and the local authority will determine how much should be paid periodically for the accommodation. Wherever such an assessment is made and the money not paid, if the resident has a beneficial interest in a property the local authority may elect to create a charge over that interest.[30] The charge does not arise until the local authority makes a declaration in writing to that effect following an assessment and non payment.[31]

A joint beneficial interest will not be severed by the making of the charge, however the charge will be limited to the value of the resident's interest as if it had been severed. Where the resident dies without payment, the interest of any persons who acquired the resident's interest by survivorship will be charged but only up to the value of what the resident's share would have been if it had been severed.

CHARGES OVER THE PROPERTY OF PATIENTS

There has been a long standing ability of those responsible for the affairs of   **21–14**
patients under legislation relating to mental health to charge the patient's property.

---

[27] Solicitors Act 1974 s.73(1)(b).
[28] *Greer v Young* (1883) L.R. 24 Ch.D. 545.
[29] Health and Social Services and Social Security Adjudication Act 1983 s.17.
[30] Health and Social Services and Social Security Adjudication Act 1983 s.22.
[31] *Hertfordshire County Council v Wilson* 2004/0547 (Decision of Adjudicator to HM Land Registry).

Under the Mental Health Act 1983 the general power of charging a patient's property was relatively limited. It was confined to providing security for money advanced for the permanent improvement or benefit of any of the patient's property.[32] Any security provided could not be realised by sale or foreclosure during the lifetime of the patient.[33]

With effect from October 1, 2007, the Mental Capacity Act 2005 repealed and replaced the relevant parts of the Mental Health Act 1983. A new Court of Protection with much greater powers than before has now been established along with a new office of the Public Guardian.[34] The powers of the Court of Protection include the ability to order that money expended on improving or benefiting any property of a person lacking capacity pursuant to an order or direction of the court be charged on that property.[35] Such charges may provide for the liability to attract such interest as may be just but need not do so. As before, such charges cannot confer any right of sale or foreclosure during the lifetime of the person lacking capacity.

REGISTRATION OF STATUTORY CHARGES

21–15 Where the statutory charge created is a charge over the legal title of registered property, in order to ensure the charge is capable of enforcement and protected, the chargee should register it as a charge. A charge not so registered will be void against a purchaser for value of the land charged unless it takes effect on an overriding interest, for example para.6 of Sch.3 to the LRA 2002 by virtue of being a local land charge. Such registration would be in addition to registration as a local land charge. Where a statutory charge is imposed on registered land after October 12, 2003, and a pre-existing charge is postponed to it,[36] notice of its creation must be given in accordance with the Land Registration Rules 2003.[37] As discussed elsewhere in this work[38] where the interest charged is purely a beneficial interest a restriction entered against the relevant registered title.

Under the Inheritance Tax Act 1984 ("IHTA") a charge is imposed on specified property in respect of unpaid tax on the value transferred by a chargeable transfer. A disposition of that property takes effect subject to that charge[39] except where the disposal is registered land and the charge is not protected in the register *and* the purchaser is in good faith and the disposition is for consideration other than nominal consideration in money or money's worth.[40] Section 31 of the Land Registration Act 2002 preserves the Inland Revenue's priority in relation to charges not within this description in accordance with that Act by disapplying the provisions of ss.28–30 of the Land Registration Act 2002.

---

[32] Mental Health Act 1983 ss. 96, 101.
[33] Mental Health Act 1983 s. 101(6).
[34] Mental Capacity Act 2007 Pt 2.
[35] Mental Capacity Act 2007 Sch.2.
[36] e.g. street works.
[37] SI 2003/1417, rr.105, 106.
[38] See Ch.20 para.20–16.
[39] IHTA 1984, s.237(6).
[40] IHTA 1984, s.272.

CHAPTER 22

MORTGAGES OF PERSONALTY AND CHOSES IN ACTION

PART I: PERSONALTY

INTRODUCTION

Distinction between pledge, charge and mortgage

A debt may be secured on personal chattels by way of pledge, charge or mortgage. There are conceptual differences between a pledge on the one hand and a charge or mortgage on the other.[1]   **22–01**

Pledge

Delivery of possession of the chattels to the lender in exchange for a loan but without transfer of ownership is an essential element of a pledge.[2] Possession may be constructive, as where a document of title to the chattel rather than the chattel itself is delivered. Pledge is a form of bailment. The pledgor's right to possession is deferred to the repayment of the debt but he retains the right to deal with goods as title holder subject to the pledge. A pledge does not create in the pledgee any rights of ownership in the goods. The pledgee acquires a so-called "special property" in the chattel. This term has been criticised on the grounds that no proprietary right vests in him. However, the term appears to be too well established to be replaced by any supposedly more accurate expression.[3]   **22–02**

Charge

Where security over the chattels is given by way of charge (or, as it is also termed, hypothecation) no transfer of possession occurs. The chargee obtains a right, in preference to other creditors, to apply the chattels to the satisfaction of the debt. For the purpose of so doing he has the right to trace the chattels into the   **22–03**

---

[1] See generally Beale, Braide, Gulfer and Lomnicka, *The Law of Personal Property* (2007), Ch.2.

[2] See *Halsbury's Laws* (5th edn), Vol.77 (2010) at 112.

[3] The term "special property" was criticised by Lord Mersey in *The Odessa* [1916] 1 A.C. 145 at 158–159. Here it was stated that the pawnee's right to sell in truth create no property right whatsoever. He preferred the term "special interest". See also *Mathew v TM Sutton Ltd* [1994] 1 W.L.R. 1455 at 146, per Chadwick J.

hands of third parties other than those having a prior claim or purchasers of the legal title without notice of the charge. Since no transfer of ownership is brought about by the creation of a charge, the instrument creating it is not a bill of sale at common law.[4]

Mortgage

22–04   Where the chattel is mortgaged, however, it is by way of assignment of the legal title with a proviso, express or implied, for reassignment on redemption, and possession is irrelevant to the mortgagee's title. It is the passing of title that is the defining characteristic of a mortgage of a chattel and that which distinguishes it from a pledge. The legal title will pass when the parties intend it to pass and the transfer of that title requires neither delivery nor writing.

Form of mortgage of personalty

Indivisible legal title

22–05   The legal title to personal chattels cannot be divided. It is therefore not possible to create a mortgage of chattels by demise, nor can a second legal mortgage be created. All subsequent mortgages are mortgages of the equity of redemption, and must, as dispositions of equitable interests subsisting at the time of the disposition, comply with the requirements of s.53(1)(c) of the Law of Property Act 1925, of being in writing signed by or on behalf of the mortgagor.[5] A legal mortgage by way of statutory assignment of a chose in action must comply with the requirements of s.136 of the Law of Property Act 1925.

Consequence of parol, as opposed to written, mortgage

22–06   A legal mortgage of chattels may be created orally or in writing, but if possession is given by way of security without any express transfer of the title, it will be for the court to determine whether the intention of the parties was to create a mortgage or a pledge. If a mortgage of personal chattels is in writing, it will be subject to the statutory provisions relating to bills of sales, most notably the Bills of Sale Acts, which forms an important part of the law of mortgages of personalty and to which a significant part of this chapter is devoted. A parol mortgage is good at common law even without delivery, but absent delivery, the mortgagee has no priority over the general creditors of the debtor and so likely to be of little value.

---

[4] However, s.4 of the Bills of Sale Act 1878 defines "bill of sale" so as to include any agreement which *creates a charge or security* over personal chattels.

[5] s.205(1)(ii). For equitable mortgages of land and the application of s.53(1)(c), see above, paras 5–02, 5–03.

FRAUDULENT TRANSACTIONS

The main reason for securing debts by way of mortgage, rather than pledging **22–07** chattels, is that the debtor can retain the use and enjoyment of the mortgaged property while giving the creditor the desired security. The mortgagee's title does not depend on possession. While this arrangement may be satisfactory as between the creditor and the debtor, the retention of possession of the mortgaged chattel by the debtor opens the way to fraud in two main respects.[6]

In the first place, it is open to the debtor to enter into a collusive transaction whereby he is able to represent to his unsecured creditors that chattels are encumbencumbered and thus unavailable to satisfy his debts to them. This danger was realised long ago and the Fraudulent Conveyances Act 1571 avoided any assurance of chattels made with intent to delay, hinder or defraud creditors. Continued possession of mortgaged chattels by the mortgagor was taken as raising a presumption of fraud for the purposes of that statute. However, it now seems to be accepted that such possession, like any other surrounding circumstance, is a matter to be taken into account in deciding whether the assurance of chattels was made bona fide. The possession of chattels subject to a mortgage bill of sale by the mortgagor is, of course, entirely consistent with the mortgage contract and is, without more, insufficient to raise a presumption of fraud.[7]

In the second place, a bona fide mortgage of chattels by an individual can lead to fraud, since, where the mortgagor remains in possession, there is nothing to show that the chattels are encumbered. He can thus obtain credit to which he is not entitled by falsely representing himself to be their unencumbered owner mortgages or charges of chattels by companies require registration.[8] Since there are no essential documents of title to chattels (except for bills of lading and similar documents) it is difficult for the mortgagee to prevent the mortgagor from dealing with the chattels as if he were the legal owner. The legislation originally enacted to deal with this problem applied only in the case of bankruptcy. It transferred to the trustee in bankruptcy all goods in the possession, order or disposition of the bankrupt with a reputation of ownership. The provisions relating to reputed ownership formerly contained in s.38(c) of the Bankruptcy Act 1914 have been repealed.[9] The protection which that legislation afforded to general creditors was, in any case, limited, as all it did was to bring into the bankruptcy some chattels which would otherwise have been unavailable. Also, it did nothing to prevent them advancing credit on the strength of the ostensible

---

[6] Discussed in *Cookson v Swire* (1883–84) L.R. 9 App. Cas. 653, per Lord Blackburn at 664; also see *Re Tooth, Trustee v Tooth* [1934] 1 Ch. 616

[7] Insolvency Act 1986 ss. 423–425 enable the court, where a person has entered into a transaction at an undervalue with the purpose of defeating the claims of creditors or other persons, to make orders restoring the position to what it would have been, had the transaction not been entered into, thus protecting the interests of persons prejudiced. These sections should be compared with ss.238 and ss.339 of the Insolvency Act 1986, which confer similar powers on the court in relation to transactions at an undervalue and preferences. See also the Consumer Credit Act 1974 and the law relating to extortionate credit bargains, below, paras 14–08 et seq. It is also necessary to note the jurisdiction of the court to set aside or vary the terms of any extortionate credit company; see Insolvency Act 1986 s.244. There are similar provisions in the case of bankrupts, see s.343.

[8] Companies Act 2006 ss.860–861; see above paras 11–27 et seq.

[9] Insolvency Act 1985 s.235, Sch.10, Pt III.

ownership, nor did it in any way assist an execution creditor where there is no bankruptcy.

THE BILLS OF SALE ACTS

The earlier legislation

22–08   The first enactment designed to deal with the two problems mentioned above was the Bills of Sale Act 1854; the preamble provides, in part, as follows:

> " ... frauds are frequently committed upon creditors by secret bills of sale of personal chattels, whereby persons are enabled to keep up the appearance of being in good circumstances and possessed of property, and the grantees or holders of such bills of sale have the power of taking possession of the property of such persons, to the exclusion of the rest of their creditors."

The 1854 Act did not ascribe any particular meaning to the term "bill of sale", which is, at common law, a written instrument which effects a transfer of personal property.

The Act provided that every bill of sale of chattels, including mortgage bills of sale, whether absolute or conditional, whereby the grantee or holder was enabled to seize or take possession of any property comprised therein, should be registered. Want of registration would cause the bill to be avoided against the grantor's assignees in bankruptcy, against assignees for the benefit of creditors, and against execution creditors. Registration did not, however, amount to such a publication of change of ownership as would protect the grantee from the operation of the former "reputed ownership" rule in bankruptcy.[10] The Bills of Sale Act 1866 provided that registration should be renewed every five years.

The current Bills of Sale legislation

22–09   The major Acts which now apply are the Bills of Sale Act 1878 (the 1878 Act) and the Bills of Sale Act (1878) Amendment Act 1882. The Bills of Sale Acts 1890 and 1891 make some minor amendments to the main legislation. The main purpose of the 1878 Act,[11] like its predecessors, was the protection of creditors against having their rights prejudiced by secret assurances under which chattels were permitted to remain in the apparent possession of those who had in fact parted with them. It invalidated all unregistered bills of sale against execution creditors and the grantor's trustee in bankruptcy, but not between grantor and grantee.

---

[10] *Badger and Williarns v Shaw and Walker* (1860) 2 E. & E. 472. Partnership assets were outside the "reputed ownership" provisions, as no partner had an exclusive right to them: *Re Bainbridge, Ex p. Fletcher* (1878) L.R. 8 Ch.D. 218.

[11] *Manchester, Sheffield and Lincolnshire Railway Co v North Central Wagon Co* (1888) L.R. 13 App.Cas. 554, per Lord Herschell at 560.

The 1882 Act was designed to prevent the entrapment of the grantor by presenting him with an incomprehensible document to sign and thereby to protect him from having an oppressive bargain forced on him.[12] The 1882 Act changed the scope of the 1878 Act. From then on the 1878 Act applied only to bills of sale either by way of absolute assignment or those which enabled the grantee to take possession of personal chattels otherwise than as security for the payment of money. Such bills are termed "absolute" bills. The 1882 Act applies only to bills of sale given as security for loans ("security" bills). It invalidates such bills which do not conform to its provisions as between grantor and grantee, as well as between all other persons.

Both the 1878 and 1882 Acts are concerned with instruments that transfer property in goods, not transactions.[13]

Application and scope of the Bills of Sale Act 1878

Definition of "Bill of Sale"

The 1878 Act defines "bill of sale", in s.4, as including: **22–10**

> " . . . bills of sale, assignments, transfers, declarations of trust without transfer, inventories of goods with receipt thereto attached, or receipts for purchase moneys of goods, and other assurances of personal chattels, and also powers of attorney, authorities, or licenses to take possession of personal chattels as security for any debt, and also any agreement, whether intended or not to be followed by the execution of any other instrument, by which a right in equity to any personal chattels, or to any charge or security thereon, shall be conferred";

and as excluding:

> " . . . assignments for the benefit of the creditors of the person making or giving the same,[14] marriage settlements,[15] transfers or assignments of any ship or vessel or any share thereof, transfers of goods in the ordinary course of business of any trade or calling, bills of sale of goods in foreign parts or at sea, bills of lading, India warrants, warehouse-keepers' certificates, warrants or orders for the delivery of goods, or any other documents used in the ordinary course of business as proof of the possession or control of goods, or authorising or purporting to authorise, either by indorsement or by delivery, the possessor of such document to transfer or receive goods thereby represented";

and, additionally, the Bills of Sale Acts 1890 and 1891 exempt certain letters of hypothecation relating to imported goods.

---

[12] ibid.

[13] *Charlesworth v Mills* [1892] A.C. 231 at 235.

[14] In this exception "creditors" mean all the creditors: *General Furnishing and Upholstery Co v Venn* (1863) 2 H. & C. 153. It is sufficient if all the creditors have an opportunity of taking advantage of the deed by executing or assenting to it: *Boldero v London and Westminster Loan and Discount Co* (1879–80) L.R. 5 Ex. D. 47, although a time limit may be fixed within which a creditor must do so: *Hadley & Son v Beedom* [1895] 1 Q.B. 646.

[15] Informal ante-nuptial agreements are within the exemption: *Wenman v Lyon & Co* [1891] 2 Q.B. 192, but post-nuptial settlements are not: *Ashton v Blackshaw* (1870) L.R. 9 Eq. 510. Also see *Re Reis, Ex p. Clough* [1904] 2 K.B. 769.

Other charges exempted from the operation of the Bills of Sale Acts are:

(1) debentures issued by any mortgage, loan, or other incorporated company[16];

(2) any instrument of charge or other security issued by a company which is required to be registered in the company's register of charges;

(3) charges executed after September 14, 1967, by a society registered or deemed to be registered under the Industrial and Provident Societies Act 1965, and which has registered offices in England or Wales, provided that an application for recording the charge is made in accordance with ss.1(1) and 8(2) of the Industrial and Provident Societies Act 1965;

(4) an agricultural charge (as defined by s.5(7) of the Agricultural Credits Act 1928) created by a farmer on all or any of his farming stock and other agricultural assets, in favour of a bank; and debentures issued by a society registered under the Industrial and Provident Societies Act 1965, or by an agricultural marketing board, may be registered in like manner as an agricultural charge, if secured on farming stock and created in favour of a bank[17];

(5) mortgages of aircraft registered in the United Kingdom Nationality Register and made on or after October 1, 1972[18];

(6) a mortgage of a ship or vessel or any share thereof.[19]

Application to companies

22–11   Until very recently, there was uncertainty whether the Acts applied to bills of sale executed by companies. In *Re Standard Manufacturing Co*[20] it was held that debentures were excluded from the Acts because they had their own regime for registration under the Companies Acts. In later cases, the view was that *Re Standard* did not support the proposition that companies were excluded from the Acts altogether, merely that companies for whom specific provision was made for the registration of mortgages fell outside the Acts.[21] More recently, it was held at first instance that the Acts did not apply to companies at all[22] and that view has now been endorsed by the Court of Appeal in the decision of *Online Catering Limited v Acton*.[23] The court reached this conclusion for three reasons: first, the fact that, in Victorian times, the purpose of the Acts appeared to be aimed at protecting individuals because separate legislation had been passed for the registration of company charges; secondly, the language of the Acts themselves pointed to the exclusion of companies and thirdly, certain provisions in the

---

[16] Bills of Sale (1878) Amendment Act 1882 s.17.
[17] See above, para.10–07.
[18] See above, para.6–12.
[19] See above, para.6–11.
[20] [1891] 1 Ch. 627.
[21] *Great Northern Railway Co v Cole Co-operative Society* [1891] 1 Ch. 187.
[22] *NV Slavenburg's Bank v Intercontinental Natural Resources Ltd* [1980] 1 W.L.R. 1076.
[23] [2010] EWCA Civ 58.

Companies Acts also pointed to the fact that the Bills of Sale Acts are confined to individuals.[24]

Documents not transactions

By s.3 of the 1878 Act, its operation is restricted to bills of sale by which the **22–12** grantee or holder has power, with or without notice, immediately or at any future time, to seize or take possession of any personal chattels comprised in or made subject to such bill of sale. The Bills of Sale Acts deal with documents, not with transactions. Consequently, they do not apply where possession passes. Thus the Acts do not apply to the case when a pledge or lien is effected by physical change of possession and can be proved without reference to any document. This is so even when change in possession is accompanied by a collateral instrument regulating the rights of the parties as to the sale of the goods.[25] Possession can be constructive, as where a pledgor gives a delivery order to a warehouseman; this was held to be equivalent to actual possession by the pledgee.[26] The Acts do not require that any transaction shall be put into writing. Such transactions can be made orally.[27] They only require that *if* a transaction is put in writing and is of a particular character, then it shall be registered, otherwise it shall be void.[28]

If the transaction is complete without any writing, so that the property intended to be dealt with passes independently of the writing, the Acts do not apply to any document merely confirming or referring to the transaction.[29] The transaction is not invalidated because such a document is afterwards drawn up and not registered. Thus where a motor car, that was orally pledged as security for a debt owing, was handed over to the pledgee, the transaction was not brought within the Acts because the registration book was handed over at the same time.[30] If the transferee's title is dependant upon a document, whether that document is a transfer, an agreement to transfer, or a document of title made at that time as a record of the transaction, it will be a bill of sale[31] and the Acts will apply.

What constitutes a bill of sale?

There have been many cases in which tests have been suggested for determining **22–13** whether a document is or is not a bill of sale. Thus, a receipt will be a bill of sale if it is a reduction into writing of the agreement between the parties as to the giving of the security.[32] In *Charlesworth v Mills*[33] it was held that if a document,

---

[24] per Ward L.J. at [24].
[25] *Re Hardwick, Ex p. Hubbard* (1886) L.R. 17 Q.B.D. 690.
[26] *Grigg v National Guardian Assurance Co* [1891] 3 Ch. 206.
[27] *Reeves v Capper* (1838) 5 Bing. N.C. 136; *Flory v Denny* (1852) 7 Exch. 581.
[28] *United Forty Pound Loan Club v Bexton* [1891] 1 Q.B. 25.
[29] *Ramsay v Margrett* [1894] 2 Q.B. 18.
[30] *Waight v Waight and Walker* [1952] P. 282.
[31] *Marsden v Meadows* (1880–81) L.R. 7 Q.B.D. 80 at 85.
[32] *Newlove v Shrewsbury* (1888) L.R. 21 Q.B.D. 41, per Lord Esher M.R.
[33] [1892] A.C. 231.

even though a simple receipt for purchase money, was intended by the parties to it to be part of the bargain to pass the property in the goods, it was a bill of sale. In *Ramsay v Margrett*[34] Lopes L.J. posed the questions:

> (i) Was it necessary to look at the document to prove the plaintiff's title?
> (ii) Did the document transfer any property?

This test was applied in *Youngs v Youngs*[35] where a receipt to which an inventory of goods was attached was held to have been given as an assurance of title and to be part of the bargain which transferred the property.

In *Re Townsend, Ex p. Parsons*[36] it was held that a document giving a licence to take immediate possession of goods as security for a debt was a bill of sale within s.4 of the 1878 Act. However, where goods were pledged as security for a loan and delivered to the pledgee, a document signed by the pledgor, recording the transaction and regulating the pledgee's right to sell the goods, was held not to be a bill of sale since possession had already passed independently of the document.[37] The reasoning in *Charlesworth v Mills* was also applied to documents created after goods had been reduced into possession under a common law lien.[38]

Certain instruments conferring powers of distress are declared to be bills of sale by the provisions of s.6 of the 1878 Act. This was designed to confine powers of distress to their proper purpose, namely securing genuine leasehold rents. Before the Act, mortgages often contained an attornment clause whereby the mortgagor attorned tenant to the mortgagee at a rent equal to the mortgage interest, and the mortgagee was given power to distrain for arrears. Such a clause has been held not to be a bona fide lease[39] but a lease to secure money and thereby coming with the ambit of s.6 below:

> "Every attornment instrument or agreement, not being a mining lease, whereby a power of distress is given or agreed to be given by any person to any other person by way of security for any present future or contingent debt or advance, and whereby any rent is reserved or made payable as a mode of providing for the payment of interest on such debt or advance, or otherwise for the purpose of such security only, shall be deemed to be a bill of sale, within the meaning of this Act, of any personal chattels which may be seized or taken under such power of distress.
>
> Provided, that nothing in this section shall extend to any mortgage of any estate or interest in any land tenement or hereditament which the mortgagee, being in possession, shall have demised to the mortgagor as his tenant at a fair and reasonable rent."

---

[34] [1894] 2 Q.B. 18.
[35] [1940] 1 K.B. 760.
[36] *Re Townsend, Ex p. Parsons* (1886) L.R. 16 Q.B.D. 532.
[37] *Re Hardwick, Ex p. Hubbard* (1886) L.R. 17 Q.B.D. 690. In *Wrightson v McArthur and Hutchinsons (1919) Ltd* [1921] 2 K.B. 807, the contents of a room were constructively delivered by handing over the keys. A subsequently executed written licence to enter was held not to be a bill of sale. For attornment clauses, see above, para.3–36 and below, paras 16–24 et seq.
[38] *Great Eastern Railway Co v Lord's Trustee* [1909] A.C. 109.
[39] *Re Willis, Ex p. Kennedy* (1888) L.R. 21 Q.B.D. 384; cf. *Green v Marsh* [1892] 2 Q.B. 330.

In summary, the section deems powers of distress conferred by way of security for debt to be bills of sale, except in respect of:

(i) mining leases;
(ii) leases, by mortgagees in possession, to their mortgagors at a fair and reasonable rent.[40]

Thus, a lease of a public house containing a power of distress for the price of goods sold was held to be a licence to take possession of personal chattels as security for a debt; this was deemed to be a bill of sale and was held void for want of registration.[41] Documents containing attornment clauses such as that referred to above are not altogether void. The landlord-tenant relationship created by such a clause exists for the purpose of giving the mortgagee the right to sue for possession or to enforce a proviso for re-entry for non-payment of rent. As the clause is merely "deemed" to be, rather than actually made into, a bill of sale, it will not be void for non-compliance with the statutory form.

Definition of "Personal Chattels"

In order for a document to fall within the provisions of the Bills of Sale Acts, it **22–14** must not only be a bill of sale but it must also relate to personal chattels as defined by s.4 of the 1878 Act. The definition applies to both Acts. However, where a security bill comprises some personal chattels as defined together with some other property, it may be effectual with regard to that other property, although void, for non-compliance with the statutory form, as regards the personal chattels.[42] The 1878 Act defines "personal chattels" in s.4, as:

> " . . . goods, furniture, and other articles capable of complete transfer by delivery, and (when separately assigned or charged) fixtures and growing crops, but shall not include chattel interests in real estate, nor fixtures (except trade machinery as hereinafter defined),[43] when assigned together with a freehold or leasehold interest in any land or building to which they are affixed, nor growing crops[44] when assigned together with any interest in the land[45] on which they grow, nor shares or interests in

[40] *Re Roundwood Colliery Co Ltd* [1897] 1 Ch. 373 (CA).
[41] *Pulbrook v Ashby & Co* (1887) 56 L.J.Q.B. 376.
[42] *Re Burdett, Ex p. Byrne* (1886) L.R. 20 Q.B.D. 310, following *Pickering v Ilfracombe Railway Co* (1868) L.R. 3 C.P. 235, per Willes J. at 250; followed in *Re North Wales Produce and Supply Society* [1922] 2 Ch. 340. The case of *Davies v Rees* (1886) L.R. 17 Q.B.D. 408 (and affirmed ibid. at 499), was distinguished on the ground that it was a case where only personal chattels were mortgaged.
[43] By s.5, as machinery used in or attached to any factory or workshop, exclusive of (i) fixed motive power and its appurtenances; (ii) fixed power machinery; and (iii) steam, gas and water pipes.
[44] At common law, growing crops produced by agricultural labour (emblements, *fructus industriales*) or other growing crops (*fructus naturales*) after severance are "goods". However, s.4 makes all growing crops "personal chattels" provided they are separately assigned or charged.
[45] 1878 Act s.7 applies both to growing crops and fixtures and provides that they shall not be deemed to have been separately assigned or charged:
" . . . by reason only that they are assigned by separate words, or that power is given to sever them from the land or building to which they are affixed, or from the land on which they grow, without otherwise taking possession of or dealing with such land or building, or land, if by the same instrument any freehold or leasehold interest in the land or building to which such fixtures are affixed or in the land on which such crops grow, is also conveyed or assigned to the same persons or person."

the stock, funds, or securities of any government, or in the capital or property of incorporated or joint stock companies, nor choses in action, nor any stock or produce upon any farm or lands which by virtue of any covenant or agreement or of the custom of the country ought not to be removed from any farm where the same are at the time of making or giving of such bill of sale."

22–15 **Growing crops:**   Thus a document transferring or charging those growing crops which are personal chattels within s.4 of the principal Act is registrable as a bill of sale[46] unless:

(1) the crops are industrial growing crops assigned by a transfer made in the ordinary course of business[47] or contained in an agricultural charge;

(2) the crops are farming stock or produce which by virtue of any agreement, covenant or custom of the country (i.e. prevalent usage of reasonable duration in the neighbourhood where the land is situated) ought not to be removed from the farm; or

(3) the document is otherwise excluded from the definition of a bill of sale or is exempted from the Acts by some other provision.

A mortgage of growing crops (like a transfer of chattels) is a bill of sale if the mortgagee is able to realise his security in the growing crops independently from his security in the land.[48] It is only when growing crops are mortgaged incidentally in a mortgage of land and as part of the land that the Bills of Sale Acts are excluded. In such circumstances they are treated as personal chattels so as to exclude the Acts.[49] Therefore, a mortgage of crops after severance is a bill of sale.[50]

22–16 **Fixtures:**   Fixtures affixed to mortgaged land, whether affixed before or after the date of the mortgage, form part of the security in the land and pass automatically to the mortgagee as realty unless the mortgage shows a contrary intention.[51] As with growing crops, a mortgage of fixtures is a bill of sale only where the mortgagee can realise his security in the fixtures separate from that in the land.[52]

22–17 **Trade machinery:**   Trade machinery, as defined in s.5 of the 1878 Act, is deemed to be a personal chattel for the purposes of that Act. Any mode of disposition of it by its owner which would be a bill of sale as to any other personal chattels is deemed to be a bill of sale within the meaning of the 1878

---

[46] *Re Phillips, Ex p.National Mercantile Bank* (1880) L.R. 16 Ch.D. 104.
[47] *Stephenson v Thompson* [1924] 2 K.B. 240.
[48] ibid.
[49] *Re Gordon, Ex p. Official Receiver* (1889) 61 L.T. 299.
[50] *Re Phillips, Ex p. National Mercantile Bank* (1880) L.R. 16 Ch.D. 104.
[51] *Reynolds v Ashby* [1904] A.C. 466.
[52] *Re Yates* (1888) L.R. 38 Ch.D. 112. In *Small v National Provincial Bank* [1894] 1 Ch. 686, it was held that there was an intention to mortgage fixtures as chattels separately because fixtures grouped with movable chattels were clearly not part of the land. See also *Reeves v Barlow* (1883) L.R. 12 Q.B.D. 436. See also *Climpson v Coles* (1889) L.R. 23 Q.B.D. 465 as to building materials brought on to land where buildings are in course of erection. See also above, para.6–01.

Act. Fixed trade machinery not expressly mentioned in a mortgage of property may pass as part of the mortgaged premises. If there is no disposition of trade machinery as such, or any power to sell separately, the mortgage is not a bill of sale.[53] If on the true construction of the instrument there is a power to sell it separately, the instrument is a bill of sale so far as the trade machinery is concerned.[54]

Documents: Paper and documents, including documents making up a solici-   **22–18**
tors' file are capable of constituting personal chattels within the meaning of s.4 of the 1878 Act.[55]

Choses in action: Choses in action, shares and interests in stock are all   **22–19**
specifically excluded from the definition of personal chattels in s.4 of the 1878 Act. This includes shares in partnership assets even though they involve the right to specific chattels.[56] A mortgage of a reversionary interest in specific chattels settled as heirlooms has been held to be outside the Act,[57] as has a mortgage of rights under a hire purchase agreement where the chattels subject to the agreement was not mentioned.[58] However, a charge on a car in a garage until sale and afterwards on the purchase money was held to be within the Act. The reason for this is that the charge is primarily on the chattel which the chose of action represents, namely, the prospective proceeds of sale.[59]

Mortgage of after-acquired goods: In the previous edition of this work, it was   **22–20**
considered that there was a conflict of opinion as to whether future goods can be "personal chattels" for the purposes of the Acts. Waldock[60] took the view that chattels not yet in existence or which are not yet owned by a mortgagor are outside the definition since they are not "capable of complete transfer by personal delivery",[61] whereas *Holroyd v Marshall*[62] it was held that assignments of specific after-acquired property operate in equity to transfer an equitable title as soon as the assignee acquires the property. That conflict has seemingly now been resolved at first instance level at least. In *Chapman v Wilson*,[63] it was held that an assignment of after acquired property can be a bill of sale (whether as a licence to take possession of personal chattels or as an instrument creating a right in equity to any personal chattels) within the meaning of the Acts, but may well

---

[53] *Re Yates* (1888) L.R. 38 Ch.D. 112.
[54] *Small v National Provincial Bank* [1894] 1 Ch. 686.
[55] *Chapman v Wilson* [2010] EWHC 1746 (Ch).
[56] *Re Bainbridge* (1878) L.R. 8 Ch.D. 218.
[57] *Re Thynne* [1911] 1 Ch. 282.
[58] *Re Davis & Co, Ex p. Rawlings* (1888) L.R. 22 Q.B.D. 193.
[59] *National Provincial and Union Bank of England v Lindsell* [1922] 1 K.B. 21.
[60] Waldock, *Mortgages* (2nd edn, 1950), p.87.
[61] *Brantom v Griffits* (1877) 2 C.P.D. 212; *Thomas v Kelly* (1888) L.R. 13 App. Cas. 506, *per* Lord Macnaghten at 518, affirming *Kelly & Co v Kellond* (1888) L.R. 20 Q.B.D. 569 but cf. *Chapman v Wilson* [2010] EWHC 1746 (Ch), fn.79, below.
[62] (1862) 10 H.L.C. 191.
[63] [2010] EWHC 1746 (Ch.).

be void for non-compliance with one or more of ss.4, 5, 8, or 9 of the 1882 Act.[64]

After-acquired property is "specific" for the purpose of the doctrine in *Holroyd v Marshall* if it is described by sufficiently precise general words so to render the property intended to be comprised in the assignment ascertainable.[65] Regardless of the Bills of Sale Acts, assignments of after-acquired property create equitable mortgages which bind the property as soon as such property comes into the hands of the mortgagor.[66] A valid mortgage of personalty can be created even though the mortgagor does not know the exact nature of the chattels,[67] or where the personal property is not yet in existence, provided he has an actual or potential interest in the source of the property.[68] A security in an incomplete chattel may be created by way of a contract to complete the chattel and to assign both the materials appropriated for its completion and the chattel itself when finished.[69]

It has been suggested[70] on three grounds that whether a chattel is "capable of complete transfer by personal delivery" depends on its physical characteristics and not on its existence or ownership at the time the security is created. Those grounds are:

(1) The Bills of Sales Act 1878 (repealing and replacing the 1854 Act) added, in s.4, the following words to the definition of a bill of sale, "any agreement . . . by which a right in equity to any personal chattels, or to any charge or security thereon, shall be conferred". The purpose of this addition was to catch agreements giving equitable rights over after-acquired property.
(2) Section 5 of the 1882 Act, which is headed "Bill of sale not to affect after-acquired property", refers to "personal chattels . . . of which the grantor was not the true owner at the time of execution of the bill of sale". Unless after-acquired property is within the definition, the section is inherently contradictory;

---

[64] ibid., at [100]. In coming to this decision, Vos J. held that the House of Lords decision in *Thomas v Kelly* (1883) L.R. 13 App. Cas. 506 was not authority for the proposition that a security over after-acquired property cannot in any circumstances be a bill of sale; rather the *ratio* of that case was that the bill of sale under consideration was not in required form because the after-acquired property was not scheduled to the bill, contrary to s.9 of the 1882 Act. On proper analysis, Lord Macnaghten's view that the Acts did not apply at all to after acquired property was not supported by the other members of the House of Lords. Confusion had therefore been created by that case and the Court of Appeal's decision in *Welsh Development Agency v Export Finance Co Ltd* [1991] B.C.L.C. 936, in which obiter views were expressed to the effect that after acquired property was excluded from the Acts based on Lord Macnaghten's speech. The wording of ss.4 and 5 of the 1882 Act made clear that a bill of sale could list chattels to be later acquired and be valid against the grantor, even if it would be void against a trustee in bankruptcy.

[65] *Tailby v Official Receiver* (1888) L.R. 13 App. Cas. 523, HL; see also *Re Wait* [1927] 1 Ch. 606, *Syrett v Egerton* [1957] 1 W.L.R. 1130.

[66] *Industrials Finance Syndicate Ltd v Lind* [1915] 2 Ch. 345; mortgage of an expectancy in personalty under a will or intestacy is a valid equitable mortgage which matures when the property falls into possession.

[67] *Re Beattie, Ex p. Kelsall* (1846) De G. 352.

[68] *Langton v Horton* (1842) 1 Hare. 549.

[69] *Woods v Russell* (1822) S.B. & Ald. 942; *Reid v Fairbanks* (1853) 13 C.B. 692.

[70] See *Halsbury's Laws*, above.

(3) Even were the section not self-contradictory, it could, unless after-acquired property is within the definition of "personal chattels", readily be evaded by the taking of a bill shortly before the grantor acquired the assets.

The characteristics of a bill of sale

There are 14 characteristics of a bill of sale, and a bill which departs from any **22–21** of them is void, even if the legal effect of the bill is unaltered by the departure.[71] They are:

(1) the date of the bill;
(2) the names and addresses[72] of the parties;
(3) a statement of the consideration;
(4) an acknowledgment of receipt if the advance is a present advance;
(5) an assignment, by way of security, of personal chattels capable of specific description;
(6) securing of a fixed monetary obligation;
(7) statement of the sum secured,[73] the rate of interest[74] and the instalments by which repayment is to be made[75];
(8) agreed terms for maintenance[76] or defeasance of the security;
(9) a proviso limiting the grounds of seizure to those specified in s.7 of the 1882 Act;
(10) the description of the chattels to be in the schedule, not the body of the bill;
(11) execution by the grantor;
(12) attestation;
(13) name, address and description of the attesting witness;
(14) schedule describing the personal chattels.

---

[71] *Thomas v Kelly* (1886) L.R. 13 App. Cas. 506.
[72] *Altree v Altree* [1898] 2 Q.B. 267; bill invalidated by omission of address even though these could have been ascertained from another source with reasonable certainty.
[73] The amount ultimately payable must be certain: *Hughes v Little* (1886) L.R. 18 Q.B.D. 32.
[74] Which must be stated as a rate though not necessarily a percentage, *Lumley v Simmons* (1887) L.R. 34 Ch.D. 698, and not a lump sum: *Blankenstein v Robertson* (1890) L.R. 24 Q.B.D. 543.
[75] Both the amount repayable and the times of repayment must be certain: *Attia v Finch* (1904) 91 L.T. 70 (interest); *De Braam v Ford* [1900] 1 Ch. 142 (principal).
[76] These include covenants:
   (i) to repair and replace; *Furber v Cobb* (1887) L.R. 18 Q.B.D. 494;
   (ii) to insure; *Neverson v Seymour* (1907) 97 L.T. 788; *Topley v Crosbie* (1888) L.R. 20 Q.B.D. 350;
   (iii) not to remove the goods without consent; *Re Coton, Ex p. Payne* (1887) 56 L.T. 571; *Furbes v Cobb* (1887) L.R. 18 Q.B.D. 494;
   (iv) to pay rent, rates and taxes on the premises where the chattels are situated; *Goldstrom v Tallerman* (1886) L.R. 18 Q.B.D. 1; and to produce receipts therefore; *Furbes v Cobb* (1887) L.R. 18 Q.B.D. 494; *Cartwright v Regan* [1895] 1 Q.B. 900;
   (v) to permit the grantee to pay insurance premiums, rent, rates or taxes, and to add such payments to the security, on default by the grantor on such payments; *Coldstrom v Tallerman* (1886) L.R. 18 Q.B.D. 1; *Neverson v Seymour* (1907) 97 L.T. 788; *Topley v Crosbie* (1888) L.R. 20 Q.B.D. 350;
   (vi) for further assurance of title; *Re Cleaver, Ex p. Rawlings* (1887) L.R. 18 Q.B.D. 489.

Although superfluous material not altering the legal effect, such as recitals, will not avoid the bill,[77] it must not be such as to confuse the grantor or destroy the simplicity which the Act was designed to attain.

Maintenance of the security means the preservation of the security "in as good a plight and condition as at the date of the bill of sale",[78] whilst defeasance of the security involves a provision which limits the operation of the bill or stipulates for its discharge on a stated event. The scope for imposing defeasance clauses is very limited since s.10(3) of the 1878 Act provides that any defeasance not contained in the body of the deed is deemed to be part of the bill and must be written on the same document as the bill prior to registration. If this is not done the registration is void, which invalidates the bill as far as the personal chattels are concerned, though the covenant for payment remains valid. If the bill is a security bill, the defeasance must comply with the statutory form[79] and the conclusion of any covenant for defeasance which gives the grantee a power of seizure not in accord with ss.7 or 13 of the 1882 Act avoids the bill totally.[80]

Effect of non-registration under the 1878 Act

22–22   If a document which is a bill of sale within the 1878 Act fails to comply with the provisions relating to form and registration,[81] it is void against the grantor's execution creditors, or his trustee in bankruptcy or his assignee for the benefit of creditors. However, it is void only in so far as it comprises any chattels which at the time of the execution of process, the filing of the bankruptcy petition, or of the assignment, are in his possession or apparent possession.

Goods remain in the grantor's apparent possession until something is done which clearly takes them out of his possession.[82] Where two people live in the same house, they may each be in apparent possession, but the person who has the legal title is in possession. The nature of the relationship between them is irrelevant provided the two people have the common use of the chattels.[83] However, the principle does not apply to a domestic servant living with his master. It has been held that there was no common use of the chattels in the house

---

[77] *Roberts v Roberts* (1884) L.R. 13 Q.B.D. 794; *Re Morritt* (1886) L.R. 18 Q.B.D. 222.

[78] *Furber v Cobb* (1887) L.R. 18 Q.B.D. 494. However, the fact that two courts differ as to the construction of a bill does not lead to avoidance under this principle, *Edwards v Marston* [1891] 1 Q.B. 225.

[79] *Smith v Whiteman* [1909] 2 K.B. 437.

[80] *Davis v Burton* (1883) L.R. 11 Q.B.D. 537 (covenant giving a right of seizure for failure to produce rent receipts on demand); *Barr v Kingsford* (1887) 56 L.T. 861 (right of seizure for default in respect of a covenant not necessary for the maintenance of the security); *Lyon v Morris* (1887) L.R. 19 Q.B.D. 139 (express power to sell and seize immediately on default).

[81] Bills of Sale Act 1878 s.8.

[82] *Re Blenkhorn, Ex p. Jay* (1874) L.R. 9 Ch. App. 697; goods are still in the grantor's apparent possession although the broker's men are in her house, but no longer when the men start to pack up and load the goods into vans.

[83] *Ramsay v Margrett* [1894] 2 Q.B. 18; *French v Gething* [1922] 1 K.B. 236 (husband and wife); contra *Youngs v Youngs* [1940] 1 K.B. 760, (in which see the observations by Goddard L.J. as to the application of the doctrine of *Ramsay v Margrett*, above to a case where a woman was living with a man as his mistress); *Antoniadi v Smith* [1901] 2 K.B. 589 (mother-in-law and son-in-law).

in such circumstances.[84] Where two persons live in the same house and one purports to make a gift to the other, the gift will be avoided against the grantor's execution creditor or trustee in bankruptcy if there is no sufficient delivery. There must be such act of delivery or change of possession as would be unequivocally referable to an intention by the donor to transfer possession and title in the chattels to the donee.[85] Failure to comply with the requirements of form or registration does not invalidate an absolute bill of sale as between the parties to it.[86] Simply because an agreement contains provisions that go beyond the standard provisions of a bill of sale does not mean that it is not a bill of sale.[87] Conversely, even if a bill of sale falls foul of the Acts, it does not follow that it is wholly void for all purposes. If part of the bills concerns "personal chattels" outside the scope of the acts, that part is valid, even if the part concerning chattels included within the Acts is void.[88]

Application and effect of the Bills of Sale (1878) Amendment Act 1882

The 1882 Act applies to bills of sale given by way of security for the payment   **22–23** of money. It applies where the subject-matter of the bill of sale is "personal chattels" as defined by s.4 of the 1878 Act, provided that:

(a) those personal chattels should be capable of specific description, and should be specifically described therein[89];

(b) at the time of the execution, the grantor should be the true owner of those personal chattels.[90]

There are exceptions to these rules for growing crops, plant and trade machinery, and fixtures.[91]

The main provisions of the 1882 Act are:

(1) the restriction of the grantee's right of seizure to five specified causes[92];

(2) a brief and simple form of bill of sale, setting out clearly the consideration and terms of payment, incorporating by reference the statutory

---

[84] *Youngs v Youngs*, above. But cf. *Koppel v Koppel* [1966] 1 W.L.R. 802 (CA) (married man and housekeeper, where latter held to be living in house not as an ordinary paid domestic servant but as a person sharing a common establishment with the married man).

[85] *Hislop v Hislop* [1950] W.N. 124 (gift by writing not under seal and no physical delivery of the chattels); *Re Cole (A Bankrupt), Ex p. Trustees of the Property of the Bankrupt* [1964] Ch. 175, purported oral gift, no delivery).

[86] *Davis v Goodman* (1880) 5 C.P.D. 128; *Tuck v Southern Counties Deposit Bank* (1889) L.R. 42 Ch.D. 471.

[87] *Chapman v Wilson* [2010] EWHC 1746 (Ch) at [81].

[88] ibid. at 80–81; *Re Burdett, Ex p. Byrne* (1888) L.R. 20 QBD 310; *In re North Wales Produce and Supply Society Ltd* [1922] 2 Ch. 340.

[89] Bills of Sale Act (1878) Amendment Act (1882) s.4.

[90] ibid., s.5.

[91] ibid., s.6.

[92] ibid., s.7.

grounds of seizure and specifying the property comprised in the bill, was made obligatory[93];

(3) a bill of sale not in the prescribed form was made absolutely void in regard to the personal chattels comprised in it[94];

(4) a bill of sale in the prescribed form was made absolutely void, if not registered,[95] in contrast to the 1878 Act, under which unregistered absolute bills of sale remained valid between grantor and grantee;

(5) all bills of sale given in consideration of a sum less than £30 were made absolutely void[96];

(6) s.20 of the 1878 Act was repealed in regard to security bills of sale so that registration does not take goods comprised in security bills of sale out of the possession, order or disposition of a bankrupt grantor.[97]

The application of the Acts has been set out in the following frequently cited words:

> "Those statutes do not require that any transaction shall be put in writing; they only require that if a transaction be put in writing and be of a particular character, then it shall be registered, otherwise it shall be void".[98]

This principle, usually paraphrased as "the Acts strike at documents, not transactions" is reinforced by s.62(3) of the Sale of Goods Act 1979, which provides that nothing in that Act or the 1893 Act affects the enactments relating to bills of sale.

Nevertheless, the courts have regard to the substance of the transaction, and the intention of the parties is material in two respects. If a document is essential to the transaction whereby the property passes, it is a bill of sale.[99] However, it is not a bill of sale if it is a mere record and is not intended to be essential, as where it is a receipt acknowledging the change in ownership.[100] Also, if a document is intended to conceal the fact that a transaction is a loan on security, it is caught by the Acts. Similarly, where a document purported to set out a hire-purchase agreement but the parties had no intention that the intending purchaser should ever become the owner of the chattels, it is also caught.[101]

If a contract, according to the tenor of the document and the intention of the parties, is a contract of hire with an option to purchase, it is outside the Acts.[102]

---

[93] ibid., s.8, and see the Schedule which sets out the form.

[94] ibid., s.9.

[95] ibid., s.8.

[96] ibid., s.12.

[97] ibid., ss.3 and 15.

[98] *United Forty Pound Loan Club v Bexton* [1891] 1 Q.B. 28 n., per Fry L.J.

[99] *Youngs v Youngs* [1940] 1 K.B. 760.

[100] *Ramsay v Margrett* [1894] 2 Q.B. 18.

[101] *Maas v Pepper* [1905] A.C. 102; and see *Re Walden, Ex p. Odell* (1878) L.R. 10 Ch.D. 76; *Re Watson* (1890) L.R. 25 Q.B.D. 27; *North Central Wagon Finance Co v Brailsford* [1962] 1 W.L.R. 1288; *Mercantile Credit Co v Hamblin* [1965] 2 Q.B. 242.

[102] *McEntire v Crossley Bros Ltd* [1895] A.C. 457. See also *Helby v Mathews* [1895] A.C. 471, per Lord Mcnaughten at 482: *Modern Light Cars Ltd v Seals* [1934] 1 K.B. 32; *Pacific Motor Auctions Pty Ltd v Motor Credits (Hire Finance) Ltd* [1965] A.C. 867 (PC); for further discussions, see A. L. Diamond, (1960) 23 M.L.R. 399 at 516 and Crossley Vaines, *Personal Property* (5th edn, 1973), pp.371 et seq. and 467 et seq.

The provision in a hire-purchase agreement giving the owner the power to re-take possession of the property does not make the agreement into a bill of sale. It has been said that if a contract of sale is genuinely intended to operate according to its tenor, so that the hire-purchase agreement is executed by the legal owner of the property, the transaction cannot be impeached as a colourable cloak for a mortgage.[103] This is so even if the parties initially contemplated a transaction by way of bill of sale and genuinely changed their intention.[104]

Seizure and sale of goods

The grantee of a security bill of sale may only seize the chattels if one of the following conditions set out in s.7 apply:

22–24

"(i) If the grantor shall make default in payment of the sum or sums of money secured by the bill at the time therein provided for payment,[105] or in the performance of any covenant or agreement contained in the bill and necessary for maintaining the security;

(ii) If the grantor becomes bankrupt,[106] or suffers the goods to be distrained[107] for rent, rates or taxes;

(iii) If the grantor fraudulently removes or suffers the goods to be removed from the premises;

(iv) If the grantor upon demand in writing unreasonably refuses to produce his last receipts for rent, rates and taxes[108];

(v) If execution has been levied against the goods of the grantor under any judgment at law."

If even one instalment is unpaid, the grantee may seize the whole of the goods as security for the whole of the money, even though the bill of sale makes no such express provision. When the right to seize has accrued, the grantee may not remove or sell the goods until five clear days have elapsed.[109] Section 7 also provides that, during that period, the grantee may apply to the High Court for relief and the court, if satisfied that for any reason the cause of seizure no longer exists, can restrain the grantee from removing or selling them or make such other order as it thinks just. However, even after the five days have elapsed, the grantor can exercise his equitable right to redeem so long as the grantee has not sold the goods or foreclosed.[110]

---

[103] *Yorkshire Railway Wagon Co v McClure* (1882) L.R. 21 Ch.D. 309, *Manchester, Sheffield and Lincolnshire Railway Co v North Central Wagon Co* (1888) L.R. 13 App. Cas. 554.

[104] *Beckett v Tower Assets Co* [1891] 1 Q.B. 1. Each case must be determined according to the proper inference from the facts; see *Johnson v Rees* (1915) 84 L.J.K.B. 1276.

[105] *Re Wood, Ex p. Woolfe* [1894] 1 Q.B. 605.

[106] This means what it says and does not mean "commits an act of bankruptcy"; *Gilroy v Bowey* (1888) 59 L.T. 223.

[107] The Tribunals Courts and Enforcement Act 2007 inserts (from a date to be appointed) at this point, the words " . . . or taken control of using the power in Schedule 12" of that Act.

[108] What constitutes cause for seizure under this provision is dealt with in *Hammond v Hocking* (1884) L.R. 12 Q.B.D. 291; *Barr v Kingsford* (1887) 56 L.T. 861; *Ex p. Wickens* [1898] 1 Q.B. 543; *Re Wood, Ex p. Woolfe* [1894] 1 Q.B. 605.

[109] Bills of Sale Act (1878) Amendment Act 1882 s.13. After the five days have elapsed, the court can grant relief only under the general law applicable to mortgages: *Longden v Sheffield Deposit Bank* (1888) 24 S.J. 913.

[110] *Johnson v Diprose* [1893] 1 Q.B. 512.

Form and contents of a security bill of sale

22–25   The validity of a security bill of sale is dependent on it satisfying the conditions of ss.8 and 9 of the 1882 Act and the Schedule thereto. Section 8 states that:

> "Every bill of sale shall be duly attested,[111] and shall be registered under the principal Act within seven clear days after the execution thereof, or if it is executed in any place out of England then within seven clear days after the time at which it would in the ordinary course of post arrive in England if posted immediately after the execution thereof; and shall truly set forth the consideration for which it was given[112] otherwise such bill of sale shall be void in respect of the personal chattels comprised therein."

Consideration, for the purpose of s.8, means, not the sum secured by the bill, but that which the grantor receives for giving it.[113] The consideration can include the cost of preparation of the bill, paid to a solicitor, if the grantor has agreed to pay it.[114] "Truly" means with substantial accuracy according to either the mercantile or legal effect of the facts.[115] A clerical error will not invalidate a bill of sale if it appears otherwise from the document what the true consideration was[116]—an approximate statement will suffice if nearly accurate.[117] If the consideration is not truly set forth, the bill is avoided whether the untrue statement was made intentionally or accidentally. In many of the cases the untrue statement involved the concealment of a bonus or expenses to be paid to the moneylender within the statement of the consideration.[118] The avoidance is in respect of the personal chattels only. So the covenant for payment remains valid as a personal obligation even though the security is void as between the parties as well as against third parties.[119]

Section 9 of the 1882 Act provides that:

> "A bill of sale made or given by way of security for the payment of money by the grantor thereof shall be void unless made in accordance with the form in the Schedule to this Act annexed."

The Schedule is as follows:

> "This Indenture made   the day of   , between *A.B.* of   of the one part, and *C.D.* of   of the other part, witnesseth that in consideration of the sum of £ now paid to *A.B.* by *C.D.*, the receipt of which the said *A.B.* hereby acknowledges *[or*

---

[111] By one or more credible witnesses none of whom is a party; compare s.10 of the 1878 Act which provides that an absolute bill must be attested by a solicitor and that the attestation must state that before the bill was executed the solicitor explained its effect to the grantor.

[112] Which must not be less than £30, otherwise the bill is absolutely void, s.12 of the 1882 Act.

[113] *Ex p. Challinor* (1880) L.R. 16 Ch.D. 260; *Darlow v Bland* [1897] 1 Q.B. 125; *Criddle v Scott* (1895) 11 T.L.R. 222; *Henshall v Widdison* (1923) 130 L.T. 607.

[114] *London and Provinces Discount Co v Jones* [1914] 1 K.B. 147.

[115] *Credit Co v Pott* (1880) L.R. 6 Q.B.D. 295.

[116] *Roberts v Roberts* (1884) L.R. 13 Q.B.D. 794.

[117] *Hughes v Little* (1886) L.R. 18 Q.B.D. 32; "£32 or thereabouts" held to be in accordance with the requirements of s.8.

[118] *Richardson v Harris* (1889) L.R. 22 Q.B.D. 268; *Re Cowburn, Ex p. Firth* (1882) L.R. 19 Ch.D. 419; *Cohen v Higgins* (1891) 8 T.L.R. 8; *Parsons v Equitable Investment Co Ltd* [1916] 2 Ch. 527.

[119] *Heseltine v Simmons* [1892] 2 Q.B. 547.

whatever else the consideration may be], he the said *A.B.* doth hereby assign unto *C.D.,* his executors, administrators, and assigns, all and singular the several chattels and things specifically described in the schedule hereto annexed by way of security for the payment of the sum of £ , and interest thereon at the rate of per cent. per annum *[or whatever else may be the rate].* And the said *A.B.* doth further agree and declare that he will duly pay to the said *C.D.* the principal sum aforesaid, together with the interest then due, by equal payments of £ on the day of *[or whatever else may be the stipulated times or time of payment].* And the said *A.B.* doth also agree with the said *C.D.* that he will *[here insert terms as to insurance, payment of rent, or otherwise, which the parties may agree to for the maintenance or defeasance of the security].*

Provided always, that the chattels hereby assigned shall not be liable to seizure or to be taken possession of by the said *C.D.* for any cause other than those specified in section seven of the Bills of Sale Act (1878) Amendment Act 1882

In witness, &c

Signed and sealed by the said *A.B.* in the presence of me *E.F. [add witness's name, address, and description]."*

A bill given by way of security which is not substantially in accordance with the above form is void, not only as between grantor and grantee in respect of the assignment of personal chattels, but it is also void as a contract of loan in respect of the personal covenant to pay principal and interest.[120] This is so even if it purports to be an absolute bill.[121] The lender can recover his money only in an action for money had and received but will then be allowed only a reasonable rate of interest rather than the stipulated[122] rate. Where a bill is void in toto, this does not mean that the security of which it forms a part is void in toto. If the security comprises personal chattels and also property which does not fall within that description, and it is possible to sever the security on the personal chattels from the security on the other property, then the security will be void as to the personal chattels but good as to the other property.[123] However, a bill of sale will be bad if it includes in the schedule property other than personal chattels.[124]

The phrase "in accordance with the form in the Schedule" was considered in *Re Barber, Ex p. Stanford.*[125] It had already been decided that a material departure by way of addition would cause the bill to be avoided.[126] In *Re Barber, Ex p. Stanford* the point to be decided was the effect of inserting the words "as beneficial owner" after "doth hereby assign". This insertion altered the legal effect of the document, since by s.7 of the Conveyancing Act 1881[127] the words

---

[120] *Davies v Rees* (1886) L.R. 17 Q.B.D. 408; *Smith v Whiteman* [1909] 2 K.B. 437.

[121] *Madell v Thomas & Co* [1891] 1 Q.B. 230.

[122] *North Central Wagon & Finance Co Ltd v Brailsford* [1962] 1 W.L.R. 1288; *Davies v Rees,* above. In *Bradford Advance Co v Ayers* [1924] W.N. 152, 5 per cent per annum was taken as the appropriate rate of interest.

[123] *Re O'Dwyer* (1886) 19 L.R. Ir. 19, where the instrument comprised a bill of sale of personal chattels and a mortgage of freehold or leasehold property. In *Re Burdett, Ex p. Byrne* (1888) L.R. 20 Q.B.D. 310, a bill of sale of personal chattels and also of trade machinery was excepted under s.5 of the 1878 Act.

[124] *Cochrane v Entwistle* (1890) L.R. 25 Q.B.D. 116; but the mortgage will be effective as regards the other property.

[125] (1886) L.R. 17 Q.B.D. 259.

[126] *Davis v Burton* (1883) L.R. 11 Q.B.D. 537.

[127] Now Law of Property Act 1925 s.76.

incorporated a covenant for immediate possession on default, which was inconsistent with the provisions of s.7 of the 1882 Act. An invalid addition cannot be saved by a proviso that conditions not in accordance with the statutory form are to be disregarded, since this would be a departure of a kind "calculated to mislead those whom it is the object of the statute to protect".[128]

Registration: section 8

22–26   Sections 8 and 22 of the 1882 Act require bills of sale to be registered and lay down certain rules for due registration. On registration a true copy of the bill and an affidavit in support thereof must be filed with the registrar of bills of sale at the central office of the Royal Courts of Justice. The true copy of the bill must be accompanied by a copy of every schedule or inventory herein referred to; the affidavit must contain statements as to the time of making the bill, its due attestation and execution, the residence and occupation of the grantor and every attesting witness.[129] The registration must be renewed every five years,[130] as failure to do so avoids it even against the grantor.[131] However, an assignment or transfer need not be registered.[132] If registration is not made within seven days the court may, on being satisfied that the omission to register was due to mistake or inadvertence, extend the time for registration[133] but there is no power to extend the time for renewal of registration.[134]

Although all original registrations are in London, s.11 of the 1882 Act[135] directs the registrar to transmit copies of the bill of sale to the registrar of the county court in whose district the chattels are situated, if either the chattels are situated, or the grantor resides, outside the London bankruptcy district. The bill is not avoided by the failure of the registrar to transmit the copy to a county court registry.[136]

A bill of sale is vacated by an entry of satisfaction in the register.[137] On the filing of an affidavit showing that the grantee covenants to satisfaction being entered, the registrar orders a memorandum of satisfaction to be endorsed on the bill. There is provision for the rectification of inadvertent errors in the register, but an order cannot be made for an affidavit to be filed correcting errors in the bill of sale or supporting affidavit.[138] Any order made for rectifying the register is made subject to rights which have already accrued to third parties.[139] Because

---

[128] *Re Barber, Ex p. Stanford* (1886) L.R. 17 Q.B.D. 259.

[129] So that third parties can make all necessary inquiries before lending the grantor money or supplying him with goods on credit; *Jones v Harris* (1871) L.R. 7 Q.B. 157, a decision under the Bills of Sale Act 1854.

[130] Bills of Sales Act (1878) Amendment Act 1882, s.11.

[131] *Fenton v Blythe* (1890) L.R. 25 Q.B.D. 417.

[132] *Re Parker, Ex p. Turquand* (1885) L.R. 14 Q.B.D. 636; *Marshall and Snelgrove Ltd v Gower* [1923] 1 K.B. 356.

[133] Bills of Sale Act 1878 s.14.

[134] *Re Emery, Ex p. Official Receiver* (1888) L.R. 21 Q.B.D. 405.

[135] The same provision for absolute bills of sale is in s.10 of the Bills of Sale Act 1878.

[136] *Trinder v Raynor* (1887) 56 L.J.Q.B. 422.

[137] Bills of Sale Act 1878 s.15.

[138] *Crew v Cummings* (1888) L.R. 21 Q.B.D. 420.

[139] ibid. See also *Re Parsons, Ex p. Furber* [1893] 2 Q.B. 122.

the register is open to inspection and search[140] the grantor may find it difficult to obtain further credit. Under the Bills of Sale Act 1854, registration could be avoided by giving successive bills of sale of the same property for the same debt before the seven-day period had expired. This practice was stopped (except where the court is satisfied that the subsequent bill was given bona fide for the purpose of correcting a material error in the prior bills) by providing that the subsequent bill should be absolutely void to the extent of the repetition.[141]

Inventory and specific description

The Bills of Sale Act 1882 s.4 states that: 22–27

> "Every bill of sale shall have annexed thereto or written thereon a schedule contain-
> ing an inventory of the personal chattels comprised in the bill of sale; and such bill
> of sale, save as hereinafter mentioned, shall have effect only in respect of the
> personal chattels specifically described in the said schedule; and shall be void, except
> as against the grantor, in respect of any personal chattels not so specifically
> described."

The effect of this provision is that if the bill has no schedule at all it is absolutely void for all purposes, not being in accordance with the statutory form.[142] If it has a schedule in which some of the chattels are not "specifically described" it is void against third parties in respect of the chattels, but it remains valid for all purposes as between grantor and grantee. Thus a bill of sale which refers in the Schedule to some specifically-described existing chattels, and some after-acquired chattels, it is void against third parties in respect of the after-acquired chattels but otherwise valid. On the other hand, if the body of the bill contains a mortgage of after-acquired chattels it is absolutely void for non-compliance with the statutory form.[143]

There must be an inventory. A general description such as "stock-in-trade" is inadequate.[144] The chattels must be described as a businessman would describe them[145] and the degree of detail will vary from case to case.[146] A more detailed description will be necessary when the chattels mortgaged are part of a fluctuat-ing stock-in-trade. There is very little direct authority as to what constitutes a specific description, though it has been said that "specifically" involves a description which helps to separate a chattel from the rest of the things of the same class.[147]

---

[140] Bills of Sale Act 1878 ss.12, 16; Bills of Sale Act (1878) Amendment Act 1882 s.16.
[141] Bills of Sale Act 1878 s.9.
[142] *Griffin v Union Deposit Bank* (1887) 3 T.L.R. 608.
[143] *Thomas v Kelly* (1888) L.R. 13 App. Cas. 506.
[144] *Witt v Banner* (1887) L.R. 20 Q.B.D. 114.
[145] *Roberts v Roberts* (1884) L.R. 13 Q.B.D. 794, per Lindley L.J. at 806.
[146] *Davies v Jenkins* [1900] 1 Q.B. 133; *Carpenter v Deen* (1889) L.R. 23 Q.B.D. 566; *Hickley v Greenwood* (1890) L.R. 25 Q.B.D. 277; *Witt v Banner, supra*; *Herbert's Trustee v Higgins* [1926] Ch. 794: *Davidson v Carlton Bank Ltd* [1893] 1 Q.B. 82.
[147] *Witt v Banner*, above.

True ownership: section 5

22–28   Section 5 of the 1882 Act states that:

> "Save as herein-after mentioned,[148] a bill of sale shall be void, except as against the grantor, in respect of any personal chattels specifically described in the schedule thereto of which the grantor was not the true owner at the time of the execution of the bill of sale."

The term "true owner" includes an equitable owner or a trustee[149] and is not limited to "beneficial owner". If an owner of chattels has previously executed a mortgage bill of sale, he still owns the equity of redemption and remains the true owner for the purposes of a second bill granted subject to the first.[150] A mortgage bill of sale by a legal owner is valid even if third parties have prior equitable interests in the chattels. If the grantor has already made an absolute sale or gift of the chattels, he has transferred both the legal and equitable title and is not the true owner; it is irrelevant that the grantee has no notice of the sale or gift.[151] A hirer under a hire-purchase agreement being merely a bailee for use is not the true owner. Thus he cannot create a valid mortgage of the chattel until he has exercised his option to purchase.[152] A person beneficially entitled to chattels is the 'true owner' to the extent of his interest.[153] However, if two persons purport to assign goods jointly as grantor, the bill of sale will be valid only to the extent of the chattels which they own jointly.[154] A purported assignment "jointly and severally" of chattels, some of which belonged to the husband and some to the wife, was held absolutely void for non-compliance with the statutory form, which contemplates a single grantor.[155] But where a husband was correctly assigned as sole grantor and the wife was made a party to the bill of sale for collateral purposes, the bill was held to be valid.[156] Whenever a bill of sale is avoided as against third parties, a grantee cannot maintain title to the goods against such third parties, for example, the grantor's assignee under an assignment for the benefit of creditors, even though he has possession of the goods.[157]

Bankruptcy: section 15

22–29   By s.20 of the 1878 Act, chattels comprised in an absolute bill of sale are deemed not to be within the possession order and disposition of the grantor for the

---

[148] Bills of Sale Act (1878) Amendment Act 1882 s.6, creating exceptions to the avoidance provisions in ss.4 and 5 in respect of growing crops, or fixtures, separately assigned, or trade machinery.

[149] *Re Sarl, Ex p. Williams* [1892] 2 Q.B. 591.

[150] *Thomas v Searles* [1891] 2 Q.B. 408; *Usher v Martin* (1889) L.R. 24 Q.B.D. 272.

[151] *Tuck v Southern Counties Deposit Bank* (1889) L.R. 42 Ch.D. 471.

[152] *Lewis v Thomas* [1919] 1 K.B. 319.

[153] *Re Field, Ex p. Pratt* (1890) 63 L.T. 289.

[154] *Gordon v Goldstein* [1924] 2 K.B. 779, where a husband and wife purported to assign jointly chattels which belonged to the wife alone. The bill was held void against third parties under s.5.

[155] *Saunders v White* [1902] 1 K.B. 472.

[156] *Brandon Hia Ltd v Lane* [1915] 1 K.B. 250.

[157] *Newlove v Shrewsbury* (1888) 21 Q.B.D. 41.

purpose of bankruptcy proceedings. However, s.15 of the 1882 Act repealed this provision in respect of security bills and provided that the chattels comprised therein might be seized by the trustee in bankruptcy.[158] The provisions formerly contained in s.38 of the Bankruptcy Act 1914, which concerned the bankrupt's available property, are replaced by s.283 of the Insolvency Act 1986[159] which define the bankrupt's estate. Section 306 of the Insolvency Act 1986[160] provides for the vesting of the bankrupt's estate in the trustee by operation of law as soon as his appointment takes effect. Goods comprised in a security bill of sale can be distrained as for rates and taxes.[161] They are not currently protected against a distraining landlord,[162] who is entitled to exercise his right of distress during the five-day period provided by s.13 of the 1882 Act.[163]

Priority of bills of sale

It is possible to create successive security bills of sale because the grantor is still, **22–30** after the execution of the first bill, the owner of the equity of redemption and is therefore the "true owner".[164] Where successive security bills of sale cover the same chattels in whole or in part, they rank in order of their registration.[165] An unregistered security bill of sale is void as to the security.[166] However, where a grantor gives an absolute bill of sale, it remains valid between him and the grantee irrespective of registration, so that he has no title to, and ceases to be the true owner of, the chattels comprised therein. Since, by s.5 of the 1882 Act, a bill of sale of chattels not made by the true owner is void against third parties, an earlier absolute bill of sale, registered or not, has priority over a later registered bill of sale. The doctrine of notice, therefore, is irrelevant to the question of priorities.[167]

Section 10 of the 1878 Act applies whether the security created by the bill of sale is legal or equitable. A registered agreement to create a bill of sale will therefore prevail over a later, registered bill of sale. But if the legal title to chattels is acquired in good faith by someone who has no actual notice of the bill of sale, it will prevail over a registered equitable mortgage of chattels by bill of sale.[168] Registration merely fixes priorities between competing bills of sale and

---

[158] *Re Ginger* [1897] 2 Q.B. 461; approved, *Hollinshead v Egan* [1913] A.C. 564.

[159] Replacing s.130 of the Insolvency Act 1985, to which it corresponds.

[160] Replacing s.153 of the Insolvency Act 1985, to which it corresponds, and restating more precisely and clearly the law formerly contained in s.18(1) of the Bankruptcy Act 1914. See also below, para.23–07.

[161] Bills of Sale Act (1878) Amendment Act 1882 s.14.

[162] Law of Distress Amendment Act 1908 s.4, but prospectively repealed by the Tribunals, Courts and Enforcement Act 2007 Sch.14 para.20 from a date to be appointed.

[163] *London and Westminster Loan and Discount Co v London and North Western Railway Co* [1893] 2 Q.B. 49.

[164] *Thomas v Searles* [1891] 2 Q.B. 408.

[165] Bills of Sale Act 1878 s.10.

[166] Bills of Sale Act (1878) Amendment Act 1882 s.8.

[167] See *Edwards v Edwards* (1876) L.R. 2 Ch.D. 291, where the court refused to postpone the holder of a registered bill of sale to the holder of a prior unregistered bill of which he had express notice.

[168] *Joseph v Lyons* (1884) L.R. 15 Q.B.D 280.

is not a notice to all the world. A legal mortgage of chattels created by bill of sale will not prevail against a third party who obtains title to the chattels from the mortgagor in the ordinary course of the mortgagor's business.[169] The grantee of a bill of sale over the grantor's stock-in-trade impliedly authorises the grantor to carry on the business and bona fide purchasers of the chattels acquire a title valid against the grantee.[170] Nor does it matter that the bill of sale contains a covenant not to dispose of the chattels without consent.[171]

During the currency of the reputed ownership provisions, security bills comprising goods in trade or business were considered to be precarious securities. *Re Ginger*[172] decided that, if a mortgagee wished to remove the false reputation of ownership he must either publicise his title or, once one of the causes under s.7 has arisen, take possession before he gets notice of an act of bankruptcy. That disadvantage has been eliminated by the abolition of the reputed ownership provisions.[173]

Mortgages of Ships, Freight and Aircraft

22–31   The Merchant Shipping Act 1995 governs mortgages of ships.[174] A registered ship or share in a registered ship may be made security for the repayment of a loan or the discharge of any other obligation. The instrument creating any such security (referred to as a "mortgage") must be in the form prescribed by or approved under registration regulations. The registrar must register the mortgage executed in accordance with these provisions in the prescribed manner. It is known as a "registered mortgage".[175] Such registered mortgages must be registered in the order in which they are produced to the registrar for the purposes of registration. The rights of unregistered mortgagees are postponed to those of registered mortgagees.

Mortgages of ships which would otherwise require registration as bills of sale are exempt from the statutory provisions relating to bills of sale.[176] Until the mortgagee takes possession, the ship's earnings remain the property of the mortgagor. However, there is also usually included with the mortgage of a particular vessel a collateral mortgage of the freight on board made in favour of the same mortgagee. This will include the mortgagor's interests in the policies of insurance and earnings from freight. The mortgagee should complete this security by giving notice to the persons who are liable to pay the cost of the freight[177]

---

[169] If title is obtained otherwise than in the ordinary course of the mortgagor's business, the purchaser is postponed to the mortgagee: *Payne v Fern* (1880–81) L.R. 6 Q.B.D. 620.

[170] *National Mercantile Bank v Hampson* (1879–80) L.R. 5 Q.B.D. 177.

[171] *Walker v Clay* (1880) 49 L.J.Q.B. 560.

[172] [1948] 1 K.B. 705.

[173] By the Insolvency Act 1985 s.235, Sch.10 Pt III.

[174] ibid., see s.313(1). See also Bowtle and Kevin McGuiness, *The Law of Ship Mortgages*, 2001.

[175] ibid., s.16(1), Sch.1 para.7(1), (2), (3), para.14; and see the Merchant Shipping (Registration of Ships) Regulations 1993 (SI 1993/3138) regs 57, 58.

[176] Bills of Sale Act 1878 and the Bills of Sale Act (1878) Amendment Act 1882.

[177] *Mestaer v Gillespie* (1805) 11 Ves. 621 at 629; *Davenport v Whitmore* (1836) 2 My. & Cr. 177; *Gardner v Lachlan* (1838) 4 My. & Cr. 129; *Langton v Horton* (1842) 1 Hare 549.

but otherwise it is unnecessary to comply with the statutory provisions for the security to be valid.

A registered mortgage of a ship or of a share in a ship may be transferred by an instrument made in the form prescribed by or approved under the registration regulations.[178] Whether or not the mortgage is registered under the provisions set out above, a mortgage of a ship or share in a ship made by a *company* is in any event registrable under the Companies Act 2006. If is not properly registered in that sense it will be void against a liquidator or any creditor of the company.[179]

For a detailed analysis of mortgages of ships and the respective rights of a statutory mortgagee to freight, and the priorities between such a mortgagee and an assignee of freight it is necessary to consult a specialist work on the subject of shipping and freight.

An aircraft or hovercraft,[180] duly registered in the register maintained under **22–32** the relevant statutory provisions[181] may be made security for a loan or other valuable consideration.[182] Similarly an aircraft or hovercraft with any store of spares for it can be the subject matter of a mortgage for a loan or other valuable consideration. Provision is also made for the voluntary registration of any such mortgage.[183]

Mortgages of registered aircraft which would otherwise require registration as bills of sale are exempt from the statutory provisions relating to bills of sale from October 1, 1972. However, mortgages of unregistered aircraft still remain subject to those Acts. A mortgage made by a *company* is registrable under the Companies Act 2006 within 21 days at Companies House. Whether it not such a mortgage is registered pursuant to the relevant provisions affecting the subject matter it will be void against a liquidator or any creditor of the company if not registered at Companies House.[184]

---

[178] The Merchant Shipping Act 1995 s.16, Sch.1 paras 11, 12; the Merchant Shipping (Registration of Ships) Regulations 1993 (SI 1993/3138) reg.60 (as substituted).

[179] See the Companies Act 2006 ss.889 and 878.

[180] For the definition of "hovercraft" see the Hovercraft Act 1968 s.4(1). Hovercraft are classified as "aircraft" for mortgage purposes (although for most other purposes they rank as ships). The Mortgaging of Aircraft Order 1972 (SI 1972/1268) (as amended), applies to hovercraft by virtue of the Hovercraft (Application of Enactments) Order 1972 (SI 1972/971) art.5, Sch.2, Pt A. The Mortgaging of Aircraft Order 1972 was made under the provisions of the Civil Aviation Act 1968 s.16 (now repealed). However, it now takes effect as if it were made under the Civil Aviation Act 1982 s.86 (as amended) by virtue of the provisions of the Interpretation Act 1978 s.17(2)(b). See also the provisions of the Civil Aviation Act 1982 s.86 (as amended) which applies to hovercraft by virtue of the Interpretation Act 1978 ss17(2)(a), 23(2); and see the Hovercraft Act 1968 ss1(1)(h)(as amended), 1(3). The last hovercrafts in commercial service in the United Kingdom cover the route from Southsea to Ryde, Isle of Wight. This may be their last commercial application in this jurisdiction.

[181] Registered in the register maintained under the Civil Aviation Act 1982 s.60 (as amended) and the Air Navigation Order (No.2) 1995 (SI 1995/1970) art.3 (as amended). See the Mortgaging of Aircraft Order 1972 (SI 1972/1268) arts 2(2), 3 (as amended), see fn.1, above.

[182] ibid., arts 4–14(1). A registered mortgage takes priority over an earlier unregistered mortgage, ibid., art.14(2)–(5).

[183] The Bills of Sale Act 1878 and the Bills of Sale Act (1878) Amendment Act 1882, see Ch.12 below paras 12–05 et seq., and see the Mortgaging of Aircraft Order 1972 (SI 1972/1268) art.16(1).

[184] See the Companies Act 2006 ss.889 and 878.

There is no special form required for the transfer of a statutory mortgage of a ship or hovercraft.

PART II: CHOSES IN ACTION

GENERAL PRINCIPLES

"Chose in action"

22–33   There is no precise definition of the term "chose in action",[185] but it is generally regarded as including all forms of personalty not held in possession and which, if wrongfully withheld, must be recovered by action.[186] In contrast, a chose in possession is a tangible thing the possession of which will pass by delivery and can be seized and sold in execution of a judgment in a personal action.

Choses in action, therefore, cover diverse forms of incorporeal personalty varying from simple contract debts to such specialised property as shares in a company, patents, copyrights and trademarks. They also include equitable interests in a trust fund of personalty. Moreover, although they may not usually be regarded as including equitable interests in a trust fund of realty, it will be convenient to deal with those interests in this chapter, because their mortgages are governed by the same principles as choses in action. As it is not possible here to deal individually with every form of chose in action, the general principles of their mortgages are set out and then specific regard is directed to mortgages of equitable interests in trust funds, insurance policies, partnership shares and shares in a company all of which are particularly important in practice.

Mortgages of choses in action are expressly excluded from the operation of the Bills of Sale Acts.[187] They depend, in most cases, on the general law of assignment,[188] though the assignment of some choses in action is regulated by statute.[189]

The position at common law

22–34   At common law, the general rule was that no debt or other chose in action could be assigned without the debtor's consent. It was said that assignments would be:

---

[185] "Chose in action" is a known legal expression used to describe all personal rights of property which can only be claimed or enforced by action, and not by taking physical possession. *Torkington v Magee* [1902] 2 K.B. 427 at 430, per Channell J.

[186] *British Mutoscope and Biograph Co v Homer* [1901] 1 Ch. 671.

[187] See the definition of "goods" in s.4 of the Bills of Sale Act 1878.

[188] For a more detailed treatment, see *Chitty on Contracts* (30th edn, 2008), Ch.19; *Bailey* (1931) 47 L.Q.R. 516; (1932) 48 L.Q.R. 248 and 547; Marshall, *Assignment of Choses in Action* (1950); Biscoe, *Credit Factoring* (1973).

[189] Bills of lading: Bills of Lading Act 1855 s.1. Policies of life assurance: Policies of Assurance Act 1867 s.1. Policies of marine assurance: Marine Insurance Act 1906 s.50(2). Shares in a company: Stock Transfer Act 1963 and Companies Act 2006 ss.541, 544. Negotiable instruments: Bills of Exchange Act 1882. Patents: Patent Act 1977 s.30. Copyrights: Copyright, Designs and Patents Act 1988 s.8. See also Law of Property (Miscellaneous Provisions) Act 1994 s.1(4), which provides that covenants for title (whether full or limited title guarantee) may apply to assignments of choses in action.

"the occasion of multiplying contentions and suits of great oppression of the people, and the subversion of the due and equal execution of justice."[190]

This rule may have had its origin in the conceptual difficulties inherent in conceiving of the transfer of an intangible[191] but the possibility was recognised by statute in 1603.[192] At common law the Crown could both grant and receive choses in action by way of assignment,[193] and when the rules of the Law Merchant were incorporated into English law, mercantile choses in action became not only assignable but negotiable.[194] The difference is that, whereas an assignee takes subject to all defects in the assignor's title, a holder for value in due course gets a good title even though the person from whom he received it had not.

Apart from these exceptions, at common law the debtor had to be made a party **22–35** to the assignment which, therefore, amounted to a novation, that is, the creation of a new contract between the assignor and the assignee. This involves the consent of all three parties that the original contract be extinguished and replaced by a new one.[195] It is thus necessary for the new contract to be supported by consideration.[196] An alternative procedure appears to be by acknowledgment,[197] whereby the creditor asks his debtors to pay some third party, and the debtor agrees to do so and informs the third party.[198]

Assignment could also be made by power of attorney but this was normally revocable.[199]

The position in equity

Equity, however, freely permitted the assignment of both legal and equitable **22–36** choses in action.[200] The Judicature Act 1873 introduced a general form of statutory assignment, but before 1875 mortgages of choses in action, subject to the exceptions mentioned above, could be created only by equitable assignment. The equitable rules still govern mortgages of choses in action which do not comply with the statutory form and, as will be seen, *charges* of choses in action can only be created by equitable assignment. It is necessary, therefore, to consider two main methods of mortgaging choses in action: (i) by assignment in equity; and (ii) by statutory assignment.

---

[190] *Lampet's Case* (1612) 10 Co.Rep. 46 at 48(a).
[191] Holdsworth, *History of English Law*; *Bailey* (1931) 47 L.Q.R. 516.
[192] The statute 1 Jac. I, c. 15 permitted the assignment of the debts of a bankrupt.
[193] *Chitty on Contracts* (30th edn, 2008), para.19–001.
[194] Milnes Holden, *The History of Negotiable Instruments in England Law* (1955).
[195] *Wilson v Lloyd* (1873) L.R. 16 Eq. 60; *Miller's Case* (1876) 3 Ch.D. 391; *Perry v National Provincial Bank* [1910] 1 Ch. 464; *Meek v Port of London Authority* [1918] 2 Ch. 96.
[196] *Tatlock v Harris* (1789) 3 Term Rep. 174; *Cuxon v Chadley* (1824) 3 B. & C. 591; *Wharton v Walker* (1825) 4 B. & C. 163.
[197] Davies (1959) 75 L.Q.R. 220; *Yates* (1977) Conv. (N.S.) 49; Goff and Jones, *Law of Restitution* (5th edn, 1998), pp.691–693; *Chitty on Contracts* (30th edn, 2008), para.19–087.
[198] *Wilson v Coupland* (1821) 5 B. & Ald. 228; *Hamilton v Spottiswoode* (1849) 4 Ex. 200; *Griffin v Weatherby* (1862) L.R. 3 Q.B. 753. As to whether and in what circumstances consideration is required, see *Liversidge v Broadbent* (1859) 4 H. & N. 603; *Shamia v Joory* [1958] 1 Q.B. 448.
[199] Marshall, *Assignment of Choses in Action* (1950), pp.67–69.
[200] *Wood v Griffith* (1818) 1 Swanst. 43.

Mortgage By Equitable Assignment

22–37   Equity makes a distinction between the assignment of legal choses, such as contract debts, and equitable choses such as legacies and trust interests. While both forms of chose in action are equally assignable, the assignee of a chose in equity may sue in his own name provided he has given notice to the holder of the fund.[201] An equitable assignment is absolute and complete without notice having been given to the debtor or fundholder, for notice does not render the title perfect,[202] and the validity of the assignment is not affected by the death or bankruptcy of the assignor before the holder of the fund receives notice. Furthermore, until the debtor receives notice, he is entitled to continue paying the original creditor[203]; and once the debtor has notice of the assignment, he cannot do anything to take away or diminish the rights of the assignee as they stood at the time of the notice.[204] Priorities between successive assignments are determined by the order in which the debtor or trustee receives notice of the assignee's title, in accordance with the rule in *Dearle v Hall*.[205]

Essentials of an equitable assignment

22–38   An equitable assignment can be made by an agreement between a debtor and his creditor that a specific chose in action which is, or will be in the hands of a third person, or is due from them and belongs to the debtor, shall be applied in discharge of the debt. The form of an equitable assignment is considered below.[206]

Thus, in *Brice v Bannister*,[207] G, who owed a debt to P, was performing work for D who was paying him by instalments. Before the work was finished, and at a time when D had paid all the instalments then due, G directed D to pay £100 to P out of moneys due, or to become due, from D to G. G gave D written notice but he refused to be bound by it and continued to pay the money to G. It was held, by a majority of the Court of Appeal, that this was a valid assignment on which P was entitled to recover from D, notwithstanding D's payments to G, subsequent to the notice.

22–39   Alternatively, an equitable assignment can be made by an order[208] given by a debtor whereby the holder of the fund is directed or authorised to pay it to the creditor.[209] There must be an engagement to pay the debt out of a particular

---

[201] *Row v Dawson* (1749) 1 Ves.Sen. 331; *Walker v Bradford Old Bank* (1884) 12 Q.B.D. 511.

[202] *Ward v Duncombe* [1893] A.C. 369.

[203] *Stocks v Dobson* (1853) 4 De G. M. & G. 11.

[204] *Roxburghe v Cox* (1881) 17 Ch.D. 520.

[205] (1823) 3 Russ. 1; see paras 13–09 et seq. and see also LPA 1925 s.137(3) which provides that notice of an equitable assignment of trust interests is ineffective for the purpose of determining priority among competing interests unless in writing.

[206] See para.22–40.

[207] (1878) 3 Q.B.D. 569, CA (Bramwell, Cotton L.JJ.; Brett L.J. *dissentiente*).

[208] *Brown, Shipley & Co v Kough* (1885) 29 Ch.D. 848.

[209] *Row v Dawson* (1849) 1 Ves. Sen. 331; *Burn v Carvalho* (1839) 4 My. & Cr. 690; *Rodick v Gandell* (1852) 1 De G.M. & G. 763; *Diplock v Hammond* (1854) 5 De G.M. & G. 320; *William Brandt's Sons & Co v Dunlop Rubber Co* [1905] A.C. 454; *Palmer v Carey* [1926] A.C. 703, P.C.; *Cotton v Heyl* [1930] 1 Ch. 510; *Re Warren* [1938] Ch. 725; *Elders Pastoral Limited v Bank of New Zealand* [1990] 1 W.L.R. 1478.

fund.[210] A mere direction to pay money to a third person is not necessarily an assignment, for it may be a revocable mandate.[211] The direction itself gives the third person no right in the subject matter of the mandate and is revoked by any subsequent disposition of the property inconsistent with it.[212] Nevertheless, even in the case of an equitable chose, the assignor may for practical reasons have to be joined as a party when the assignment is not an absolute assignment of the whole debt. For, if the assignment is for part of the debt only, the assignor has to be joined in the action in order that the accounts may be correctly taken between the third parties, and that the debtor may be protected against a second action in respect of the same debt.[213] The modern practice in regard to joining an assignor is, unless the debtor waives the assignor's presence in court[214] to join him as a nominal claimant with an indemnity for costs, but, if he raises objection, to join him as a defendant.[215]

A cheque, being a bill of exchange is not an equitable assignment of the drawer's balance with his bankers.[216]

Where the assignment was absolute, the assignee could sue in his own sole name[217] before the Judicature Act 1873, and this position is unaltered. The provision for statutory assignment made by the Judicature Act 1873 s.25(6), did not "forbid or destroy equitable assignments or impair their efficacy in the slightest degree".[218]

If the assignment gives a right to payment out of a particular fund or property but does not transfer the fund or property, it is "by way of charge"[219] and so is an assignment of so much of a future debt as shall be sufficient to satisfy an uncertain future indebtedness.[220]

Form

Subject to s.53(1)(c) of the Law of Property Act 1925 (which provides that a **22–40** disposition of an equitable interest or trust subsisting at the time of the disposition must be in writing signed by the person disposing of the same or by his agent thereunto lawfully authorised in writing or by will), an equitable assignment is not required to be made in any particular form either from the point of view of

[210] *Watson v Duke of Wellington* (1830) 1 Russ. & M. 602; *Percival v Dunn* (1885) 29 Ch.D. 128; *Re Gunsbourg* (1919) 88 L.J.K.B. 479.
[211] *Malcom v Scott* (1843) 3 Hare 39; *Bell v London and North Western Railway* (1852) 15 Beav. 548; *Re Whitting, ex p. Hall* (1879) 10 Ch.D. 615.
[212] *Morrell v Wootten* (1852) 16 Beav. 197; cf. *London & Yorkshire Bank v White* (1895) 11 T.L.R. 570 and *The Zigurds* [1934] A.C. 209.
[213] *Re Steel Wing Co* [1921] 1 Ch. 349.
[214] *William Brandt's Sons v Dunlop Rubber Co* [1905] A.C. 454.
[215] *Bowden's Patents Syndicate v Smith* [1904] 2 Ch. 86; see also *Weddell v J.A. Pearce & Major* [1988] Ch.26 as to non-joinder under the (then) Rules of the Supreme Court. See also para.22–70.
[216] *Hopkinson v Forster* (1874) L.R. 19 Eq. 74.
[217] *Cator v Croydon Canal Co* (1841) 4 Y. & C. Ex. 593; *Donaldson v Donaldson* (1854) Kay. 711.
[218] *William Brandt's Sons & Co v Dunlop Rubber Co* [1905] A.C. 454 at 461, per Lord Macnaghten.
[219] *Tancred v Delagoa Bay and East Africa Rty Co* (1889) 23 Q.B.D. 239.
[220] *Jones v Humphreys* [1902] 1 K.B. 10; cf. *Mercantile Bank of London v Evans* [1899] 2 Q.B. 613.

evidence of or terminology. It may be verbal[221] and couched in any language provided that the interest in the debt[222] is unmistakably made over to the assignee.[223] It is immaterial that the amount of the debt has not been ascertained at the time of the assignment.[224] Nor is an equitable assignment incomplete merely because notice has not been given to the debtor. Highly desirable though it is for an assignee to notify the debtor of his interest in order to bind the debtor not to pay out to any third party, an equitable assignment is by itself a perfect conveyance as between assignor and assignee.[225] Moreover, notice of an equitable assignment, when given, may be informal and even indirect, except in the case of trust interests, where notice must be in writing under s.137(3) of the Law of Property Act 1925.

22-41   Equitable assignments are thus virtually unrestricted by formal requirements. Mortgages of choses in action may still be created by these informal assignments operating only in equity. It is necessary only to make the nature of the transaction plain.[226] Thus in *Tailby v Official Receiver*[227] it was said:

> "It has long been settled that future property, possibilities and expectancies are assignable in equity for value. The mode or form of assignment is absolutely immaterial provided that the intention of the parties is clear."

Conversely it may be clear that the transaction is not an assignment. In *Re Danish Bacon Co v Staff Pension Fund Trusts*[228] a revocable nomination which would not in any event become effective until the death of the nominator and this might never affect any property at all, was held not fairly capable of being called an assignment.

Parties to Proceedings

22-42   Whereas, prior to the Judicature Act 1873, an assignee of an equitable chose in action could sue in his own name provided that the assignment was absolute and notice had been given to the holder of the fund[229]; the assignee of a legal chose in action could not. This arises because equity, having exclusive control of equitable interests, can allow an assignee of an equitable chose[230] to sue directly.

---

[221] *Brown, Shipley & Co v Kough* (1885) 29 Ch.D. 848 at 854.

[222] Whereas there cannot be a statutory assignment of part of a debt or fund, there can be a good equitable assignment of a specified debt or fund: *Roddick v Gandell* (1852) 1 De G.M. & G. 763; *Palmer v Carey* [1926] A.C. 703, PC.

[223] *William Brandt's Sons Ltd v Dunlop Rubber Co* [1905] A.C. 454.

[224] *Crowfoot v Gurney* (1832) 9 Bing. 372 at 376.

[225] *Gorringe v Irwell India Rubber Works* (1886) 34 Ch.D. 128. An equitable assignment is good without notice against a trustee in bankruptcy: *Re Anderson* [1911] 1 K.B. 896, or against a judgment creditor: *Scott v Lord Hastings* (1858) 4 K. & J. 633; and see applied in *United Bank of Kuwait v Sahib* [1995] 2 W.L.R. 94, *Holt v Heatherfield Trust Ltd* [1942] 2 K.B. 1.

[226] *German v Yates* (1915) 32 T.L.R. 52.

[227] (1888) 13 App.Cas. 523 at 543 (assignment of future book debts in unspecified businesses not so vague as to be invalid).

[228] [1971] 1 W.L.R. 248.

[229] *Row v Dawson* (1749) 1 Ves. Sim. 331.

[230] A chose which could be sued for only in the Court of Chancery, e.g. an interest in a trust fund.

In the case of a legal chose,[231] he has to have the assignor nominally a party before the court in order to bind the assignor's rights in the legal chose at common law. Equity, in fact, treats the assignor of a legal chose as trustee of his rights for the assignee.

After the Judicature Act 1873 came into operation, the position was that assignments of legal choses in action not complying with the statute continued to be valid in equity[232] but both the assignor and the assignee had to be made parties to the proceedings.[233] If the assignor wishes to sue, he must join the assignee.[234]

It has been suggested that the rule requiring both the assignor and the assignee **22–43** to be party to proceedings for enforcement of an equitable assignment of a legal chose in action serves a useful purpose only where the assignor has not wholly disposed of his interest, since in such cases it ensures that all parties with an interest in the chose are brought before the court. Conversely, it has also been suggested that there is no need for the rule where, although the assignment is absolute, it takes effect only as an equitable assignment because, for example, it is not in writing.[235]

Mortgage by assignment under the Law of Property Act 1925 section 136

Section 25(6) of the Judicature Act 1873, introduced a new form of statutory **22–44** assignment not limited to particular forms of choses in action. This section was, with negligible variations of language, re-enacted in s.136 of the Law of Property Act 1925, which provides as follows:

> "(1) Any absolute[236] assignment by writing[237] under the hand of the assignor (not purporting to be by way of charge only) of any debt[238] or other legal thing in action, of which express notice in writing has been given to the debtor, trustee or other person from whom the assignor would have been entitled to claim such debt or thing in action, is effectual in law (subject to equities having priority over the right of the assignee) to pass and transfer from the date of such notice—
>
> (a) the legal right to such debt or thing in action;
> (b) all legal and other remedies for the same; and
> (c) the power to give a good discharge for the same without the concurrence of the assignor:
>
> Provided that, if the debtor, trustee or other person liable in respect of such debt or thing in action has notice—

---

[231] A chose which could be sued for only in the common law courts, e.g. a contract debt.

[232] *William Brandt's Sons & Co v Dunlop Rubber Co* [1905] A.C. 454.

[233] *Performing Rights Society Ltd v London Theatre of Varieties Ltd* [1924] A.C. 1; *Williams v Atlantic Assurance Co* [1933] 1 K.B. 81; *Holt v Heatherfield Trust Ltd* [1942] 2 K.B. 1.

[234] *Walter and Sullivan Ltd v Murphy & Sons Ltd* [1955] 2 Q.B. 584.

[235] *Chitty on Contracts* (30th edn, 2008), para.19–039. See also para.22–69.

[236] "Absolute" does not have the same meaning as in the Bills of Sale Act, where it means "not by way of security". *Lloyds Scottish Finance Limited v Cyril Lord Carpet Sales Limited* (1992) B.C.L.C. 609.

[237] No particular form of words is necessary: *Re Westerton* [1919] 2 Ch. 104; but an intention to transfer the interest must be shown: *Curran v Newpark Cinemas Ltd* [1951] 1 All E.R. 295; *Coulls v Bagot's Executor and Trustee Co Ltd* (1967) 119 C.L.R. 460.

[238] This means "the entire debt"; see *Re Steel Wing Co* [1921] 1 Ch. 349: see para.22–46.

> (a) that the assignment is disputed by the assignor or any person claiming under him; or
>
> (b) of any other opposing or conflicting claims to such debt or thing in action;
>
> he may, if he thinks fit, either call upon the persons making claim thereto to interplead concerning the same, or pay the debt or other thing in action into court under the provisions of the Trustee Act 1925.
>
> (2) This section does not affect the provisions of the Policies of Assurance Act 1867."[239]

22–45   Section 136 does not supersede the provisions of the Law Merchant or of particular statutes governing the assignment of special forms of property. Otherwise there appears to be little restriction on the kinds of choses in action which are assignable under the section. The words "any debt or other *legal* thing in action" have to be interpreted as not confined to legal choses properly so called. They cover any right which the common law did not look on as assignable because of it being a chose in action, but which equity dealt with as assignable.[240] This means that equitable as well as legal choses in action are assignable under the statute, but not rights such as contracts of personal service, which not even equity has ever regarded as being assignable.[241]

Absolute assignment

22–46   The opening words of the section at once raise the query whether statutory assignment is available at all for the creation of mortgages, for only absolute assignments not by way of charge are within its scope. It is, however, well established that an assignment in statutory form of a whole debt to a mortgagee, with the usual proviso for redemption and reconveyance, is an absolute assignment within s.136.[242] The same is true where an assignment is made apparently out and out, but, in fact, for purposes of security and the equity of redemption is merely implied,[243] or where a whole debt is assigned for the discharge of a liability subject to a trust for the repayment of any surplus to the assignor.[244]

In *Durham Bros v Robertson*,[245] S & Co charged £1,080 due to them from R on completion of certain buildings as security for advances, and assigned their interest in that sum to D until the money with added interest was repaid to them. Unlike the cases cited earlier, this was held not to be an absolute assignment since the debtor would be uncertain as to whom he should pay the money unless he inquired into the state of accounts between the assignor and the assignee. The

---

[239] See para.22–73.

[240] *Torkington v Magee* [1902] 2 K.B. 427, rvsd. [1903] 1 K.B. 644; *King v Victoria Insurance Co* [1896] A.C. 250; *Manchester Brewery v Coombs* [1901] 2 Ch. 608; *Re Pain* [1919] 1 Ch. 38; *G. & T. Earle Ltd v Hemsworth R.D.C.* (1928) 44 T.L.R. 605.

[241] *Tolhurst v Associated Portland Cement Manufacturers* [1903] A.C. 414.

[242] *Tancred v Delagoa Bay and East Africa Rty Co* (1889) 23 Q.B.D. 239.

[243] *Hughes v Pump House Hotel Co* [1902] 2 K.B. 190, CA.

[244] *Comfort v Betts* [1891] 1 Q.B. 737, CA; *Bank of Liverpool v Holland* (1926) 43 T.L.R. 29; *Camdix International Limited v Bank of Zambia* [1998] Q.B. 22, CA.

[245] [1898] 1 Q.B. 765, CA, applied in *Mutual General Insurance Co Ltd v ANZ Banking Group (New Zealand) Ltd* [1995] 1 W.L.R. 1140, JCPC.

assignment is absolute only where the debtor is entitled to pay the whole debt to the assignee without further inquiry unless he is notified otherwise.

In that case, Chitty L.J. said[246]:

> "The assignment of the debt was absolute: it purported to pass the entire interest of the assignor in the debt to the mortgagee, and it was not an assignment purporting to be by way of charge only. The mortgagor-assignor had a right to redeem, and on repayment of the advances a right to have the assigned debt reassigned to him. Notice of the assignment pursuant to the subsection would be given to the original debtor and he would thus know with certainty in whom the legal right to sue was vested."

The crucial point thus is whether the title of the assignee is absolute in the sense **22–47** that the debtor, until he is informed to the contrary by notification, is entitled to pay the whole debt to the assignee without inquiry. The object of the section, in excepting assignments by way of charge, was to protect the debtor against repeated actions in respect of the same debt and against the risks involved in making payments dependent on the state of accounts between other parties. The assignment of an entire debt by way of mortgage is not inconsistent with this object because, for the time being, the mortgagee became vis-à-vis the debtor the absolute owner of the debt. Uncertainty in the state of accounts *between assignor and assignee* does not prevent an assignment from being absolute if it does not affect the obligations of the debtor. So in *Hughes v Pump House Hotel Co*,[247] when debts had been assigned to a bank as continuing security to cover a current account, this was held to be a perfectly good statutory assignment.

A fortiori, a determinable interest of only part of a debt cannot be the subject of a statutory assignment.[248] This was illustrated by the facts of *Jones v Humphreys*,[249] in which a schoolmaster assigned to a moneylender so much and such part of his salary as should be necessary to pay £22 10s. or any further sums advanced. This is precisely what the statute means by a charge as distinct from an absolute assignment. Such a charge cannot be created by statutory assignment, but is good in equity as a partial assignment of the debt. The practical effect is that the enforcement of the charge entails the joining of the assignor as a party to the proceedings against the primary debtor, i.e. in the present case the headmaster of the school. It also now seems settled that part of a debt cannot be assigned under s.136 on the ground that such an assignment is not "absolute". Accordingly the mortgage even of a specified portion of a debt can only operate in equity.[250] This was held to be the case in *Walter and Sullivan Ltd v J. Murphy and Sons Ltd*[251] where A owed B £1,808, B owed C £1,558 and B gave A an irrevocable authority to pay £1,558 to C. This was held to be a good equitable

---

[246] ibid. at 772.

[247] [1902] 2 K.B. 190, CA.

[248] *Jones v Humphreys* [1902] 1 K.B. 10.

[249] ibid.

[250] *Forster v Baker* [1910] 2 K.B. 636; *Re Steel Wing Co* [1921] 1 Ch. 349; *G. & T. Earle Ltd v Hemsworth RDC* (1928) 44 T.L.R. 605 at 758; *Williams v Atlantic Assurance Co* [1933] 1 K.B. 81 at 100; though the point was not originally free from doubt: *Brice v Bannister* (1878) 3 Q.B.D. 569; *Skipper & Tucker v Holloway & Howard* [1910] 2 K.B. 630.

[251] [1955] 2 Q.B. 584, CA. See also *Three Rivers District Council v Governor & The Company of the Bank of England* [1996] Q.B. 292, CA.

assignment of the £1,558 by way of charge. It was also held that B and C were necessary parties to an action against A.

This rule has arisen because conflicting decisions might arise if either the existence or the amount of the debt was in dispute[252] and also because of the burden on the debtor which would be created if the creditor was allowed to split up the debt into several causes of action.[253]

Notice

22–48   Assignment under s.136 has two requirements of form:

(1) The assignment itself must be in writing under the hand of the assignor.
(2) Written notice of the assignment must be given to the debtor. As the section does not say from whom, etc. notice is to issue, it may be given by the assignor, the assignee or his successors in title.

22–49   The notice must be given, otherwise the assignee cannot sue in his own name,[254] but it can be given by the assignor, the assignee or their successors in title[255] at any time[256] before an action is brought. If there are joint debtors, notice must be given to both.[257] It is essential not only for a statutory assignment to be in writing, but also for the notice to be in writing. The requirement of notice in writing must be met even if the debtor cannot read and the assignment is brought to his attention in some other way.[258] Whereas notice of an equitable assignment simply operates to establish the right of the assignee against third parties, the notice of a statutory assignment is an integral part of the conveyance from the assignor to the assignee. The assignment takes effect from the date when the notice is received by the debtor and if no written notice is given, it takes effect in equity only.[259]

22–50   There is no need to state a date, but if the notice purports to identify the assignment by its date and the date is wrong, it will be invalid.[260] It has been suggested that the notice will be invalid unless the amount of the debt is correctly stated,[261] but, apart from any question of validity that might arise, it is prudent,

---

[252] *Re Steel Wing Co* [1921] 1 Ch. 349 at 357.

[253] *Durham Bros v Robertson* [1898] 1 Q.B. 765, CA.

[254] If the assignee does sue without having given notice, the claim is not a nullity but will be stayed since (bar certain special circumstances) an equitable assignee cannot enter judgment without the assignor being a party: *Weddle v J.A. Pearce and Major* [1988] Ch. 26. See also *Deposit Protection Board v Dalia* [1994] 2 A.C. 367 and para.22–69.

[255] *Bateman v Hunt* [1904] 2 K.B. 530.

[256] ibid. See also *Compania Columbiana de Seguros v Pacific Steam Navigation Co* [1965] 1 Q.B. 101; including a time after the death of the assignor; *Walker v Bradford Old Bank* (1884) 12 Q.B.D. 511; *Re Westerton* [1919] 2 Ch. 104 or assignee; *Bateman v Hunt* [1904] 2 K.B. 530.

[257] *Josselson v Borst and Gliksten* [1938] 1 K.B. 723.

[258] *Hockley and Papworth v Goldstein* (1920) 90 L.J.K.B. 111.

[259] *Holt v Heatherfield Trust Ltd* [1942] 2 K.B. 1.

[260] *Stanley v English Fibres Industries Ltd* (1899) 68 L.J.Q.B. 839; *W.F. Harrison & Co v Burke* [1956] 1 W.L.R. 419, CA; *Van Lynn Developments Ltd v Pelias Construction Co Ltd* [1969] 1 Q.B. 607, explaining the *Harrison* case at 612; see also (1956) 72 L.Q.R. 321.

[261] *W.F. Harrison & Co v Burke* [1956] 1 W.L.R. 419 at 421.

before executing the assignment, to obtain a written admission from the debtor as to the amount of the debt assigned,[262] so as to prevent any dispute, when the assignee comes to realise the security, as to how much was due when the assignment was taken. As a creditor can assign by directing his debtors to pay the assignee it would appear that a single written document could serve as both assignment and notice.[263]

Apart from the statutory requirement, the giving of notice forms an important part of the assignee's protection. First, it binds the debtor, trustee or other person from whom the assignor would have been entitled to claim the debt or thing in action, to pay it or convey it to the assignee.[264] Second, it gives priority over subsequent dealings between the debtor and the assignor. Whether an assignment is statutory or equitable, the assignee takes subject to equities between the debtor and the assignor which existed before the debtor received notice of the assignment.[265] Finally, it establishes priority over other assignees, since it is provided by the Law of Property Act 1925 s.137(1) that priority among successive assignees of choses in action is regulated by the dates on which the debtor received notice of the assignments.

Defective statutory assignments are considered below.[266]

22–51

Priority of assignments and the rule in Dearle v Hall

That final provision, which derives from the rule in *Dearle v Hall*,[267] applies to all mortgages of equitable interests in property of whatever description which are held by a trustee or other person having legal control of the property. The date of the notice itself is irrelevant to any question of priority. Where the notice is posted, it apparently takes effect when received, though it might be argued that, as between competing assignees, the first to post the notice should have priority. There is no express decision on the point.[268]

Once notice of an absolute assignment has been received by the debtor he is no longer liable to the assignor but to the assignee[269] and if he disregards such a notice and pays the assignor after having received it he will be liable to make a second payment to the assignee.[270] If the debtor made such a payment under a mistake of fact or law he may be able to recover it from the assignor.[271] If, however, a debtor pays his debt to the assignor by cheque but afterwards receives

22–52

---

[262] *Matthews v Walwyn* (1798) 4 Ves. 118.

[263] *Curran v Newpark Cinemas* [1951] 1 All E.R. 295.

[264] In the absence of notice, payment by the debtor to the assignor or a release by the assignor will be good against the assignee: *Stocks v Dobson* (1853) 4 De G.M. & G. 11.

[265] *Roxburghe v Cox* (1881) 17 Ch.D. 520.

[266] See para.22–65.

[267] (1828) 3 Russ. 1; see also *Loveridge v Cooper* (1823) 3 Russ 30. It seems that the rule originated earlier, but in the more restrictive form that the postponement of a prior assignee would occur only where the failure to give notice earlier was due to fraud or his gross negligence amounting to evidence of fraud. On this point see *Tourville v Naish* (1734) 3 P.Wms. 307 and *Stanhope v Verney* (1761) 2 Eden. 80.

[268] *Holt v Heatherfield Trust Ltd* [1942] 1 K.B. 1.

[269] *Cottage Club Estates v Woodside Estates (Amersham) Ltd* [1928] 2 K.B. 463.

[270] *Jones v Farrell* (1857) 1 D. & J. 208; *Brice v Bannister* (1878) 3 Q.B.D. 569.

[271] *Chitty on Contracts* (30th edn, 2008), at 29–026; *Kleinwort Benson v Lincoln City Council* [1999] 2 A.C. 349.

a notice that the debt has been assigned, he is not compelled to stop the cheque.[272]

Assignment "subject to equities"

22–53   The rule in *Dearle v Hall*[273] must not be confused with the provision in s.136 of the Law of Property Act 1925 that the assignee takes subject to equities existing when the assignment takes effect of which the assignee has notice.[274] "Equities" include defects in the assignor's title and certain claims which the debtor has against the assignor. Thus an assignee of a contract affected by mistake or illegality normally has no greater rights than the assignor would have had, though an exception exists in the field of life assurance. It was held in *Beresford v Royal Insurance Co*[275] (a case decided before the Suicide Act 1961 decriminalised suicide) that generally a life assurance policy could not be enforced by the representative of an assured who had committed suicide, since it was against public policy to allow his estate to benefit from his crime. However, where the assignment was made before the suicide, the assignee was permitted to recover, since the benefit did not go to the criminal or his estate.[276] If a debtor has the right to set aside a contract for misrepresentation, the assignee takes subject to that right, unless it is excluded or modified by statute[277] or contract.[278] The purpose of the provision that the assignee takes subject to equities is to prevent the debtor being prejudiced by the assignment. If a debtor has a claim against the assignor, it is immaterial whether the assignee knew of the claim when he took the assignment.[279] Correlatively the debtor cannot do anything to take away or diminish the rights of the assignee as they stood at the time of the notice, once he has received notice of the assignment.[280]

22–54   These two rules are illustrated by the case of *Bradford Banking Co Ltd v Briggs & Co Ltd*,[281] where it was held that an assignee of shares or debentures takes them subject to all equitable claims of the company which arose before notice of the assignment; but that, after notice, the company could not create any fresh equities. The rule that an assignee takes subject to equities is often excluded in debentures.

The ability of the debtor to rely, against the assignee, on a claim against the assignor depends on the way in which it arose. He can rely on a claim arising out

---

[272] *Bence v Shearman* [1898] 2 Ch. 582.

[273] (1828) 3 Russ. 1.

[274] *Ord v White* (1840) 3 Beav. 357; *Mangles v Dixon* (1852) 3 H.L.C. 702; *Phipps v Lovegrove* (1873) L.R. 16 Eq. 80; *Lawrence v Hayes* [1927] 2 K.B. 111.

[275] [1938] A.C. 586.

[276] *White v British Empire Mutual Life Assurance Co* (1868) L.R. 7 Eq. 394.

[277] cf. Bills of Exchange Act 1882 s.38(2); Marine Insurance Act 1906 s.50(2).

[278] *William Pickersgill & Sons Ltd v London and Provincial Insurance Co* [1912] 3 K.B. 614; *Re Agra and Masterman's Bank, ex p. Asiatic Banking Corp* (1867) 2 Ch.App. 391; *Re Blakely Ordinance Co, ex p. New Zealand Banking Corp* (1867) 3 Ch.App. 154.

[279] *Athenaeum Society v Pooley* (1858) 3 D. & J. 294; *Biggerstaff v Rowatt's Wharf Ltd* [1896] 2 Ch. 93.

[280] *Roxburghe v Cox* (1881) 17 Ch.D. 520 at 526.

[281] (1886) 12 App.Cas. 29.

of the contract assigned,[282] whenever the claim arose.[283] If the debtor's set-off
against the assignor exceeds the amount of the debt, the assignee will recover
nothing; but he is not liable to the debtor for the excess.[284] Among the equities
which bind the assignee is the debtor's right to rescind for misrepresentation,
provided, apparently, that the right has not been lost.[285]

If the claim arises out of some transaction other than the contract assigned, it
can be set up against the assignee only if it arose before notice of the assignment
was given to the debtor.[286] If it neither accrued due before notice was given, nor
arose out of the contract to be assigned, or a contract closely connected with it,
it cannot be set off.[287]

If an assignor does not acquire a right to the subject-matter of the assignment
the assignee can take nothing, for example, where an assignment was made of
money to become due under a building contract which the assignor failed to
perform.[288] Nor can the assignee recover more from the debtor than the assignor
could have done.[289]

Consideration

Generally: Whether consideration is necessary to support an assignment is a   **22–55**
question between the assignor and the assignee.[290] The debtor has to pay the debt
and his only concern is that all parties should be before the court, so that he does
not have to pay twice. He cannot refuse to pay the assignee because the
assignment was gratuitous.[291]

A statutory assignment of either an equitable or a legal chose in action is valid   **22–56**
whether or not consideration is given.[292] There are, however, three situations
where the existence or non-existence of consideration is relevant. First, where the
purported assignment is of some right which either does not exist or has not yet
been acquired by the assignor; second, where there is a voluntary equitable
assignment; and, third, where there is a defective statutory assignment.

---

[282] *Business Computers Ltd v Anglo African Leasing Ltd* [1977] 1 W.L.R. 578, in which the
authorities reviewed extend this principle to claims closely connected with the contract assigned. See
also *Newfoundland Government v Newfoundland Ry Co* (1888) 13 App. Cas. 199 at 213.

[283] *Graham v Johnson* (1869) LR. 8 Eq. 36; *William Pickersgill and Sons Ltd v London and
Provincial Insurance Co* [1912] 3 K.B. 614; *Banco Central SA and Trevelan Navigation Inc v Lingoss
& Falce and BFI Line; The Raven* [1980] 2 Lloyd's Rep. 266.

[284] *Young v Kitchin* (1878) 3 Ex.D. 127.

[285] *Stoddart v Union Trust Ltd* [1912] 1 K.B. 181. This decision has been criticised: see *Chitty on
Contracts* (30th edn, 2008), para.19–071.

[286] *Stephens v Venables* (1862) 30 Beav. 625; cf. *Watson v Mid Wales Ry* (1867) L.R. 2 P. 593. See
also *Roxburghe v Cox; Business Computers Ltd v Anglo African Leasing Ltd;* and *Newfoundland
Government v Newfoundland Ry Co* (1888) 13 App.Cas 199.

[287] *Business Computers Ltd v Anglo African Leasing Ltd* [1977] 1 W.L.R. 578 at 585; see also
Jeffryes v Agra & Masterman's Bank (1866) L.R. 2 Eq. 674; *Watson v Mid Wales Ry Co* (1867) L.R.
2 C.P. 593; *Christie v Taunton, Delmard, Lane & Co* [1893] 2 Ch. 175; *Re Pinto Leite & Nephews,
ex p. Desolivaes* [1929] 1 Ch. 221.

[288] *Tooth v Hallett* (1869) L.R. 4 Ch.App. 242.

[289] *Dawson v Great Northern and City Ry Co* [1905] 1 K.B. 260.

[290] *Re Rose* [1952] Ch. 499; *Letts v IRC* [1957] 1 W.L.R. 201; *Dalton (Smith's Administrative v IRC*
[1958] T.R. 45.

[291] *Walker v Bradford Old Bank* (1884) 12 Q.B.D. 511.

[292] *Harding v Harding* (1886) 17 Q.B.D. 442; *Re Westerton* [1919] 2 Ch. 104.

22–57   **Assignment of future property:**   A future chose in action cannot be the subject of an assignment, but only of an agreement to assign and such an agreement can be valid only when supported by consideration.[293] Rights which the prospective assignor has not yet acquired may fall into one of three categories. In the first are sums which are certain to become payable under an existing contract or other legal obligations and are treated as existing choses in action, even though the amounts which will be received are unascertained.[294] In the second are expectancies, as where the assignor hopes to receive sums under a contract not yet made, or to inherit from a person living at the date of the assignment.[295] The third, intermediate class, comprises rights which may become due under an existing obligation but it is uncertain whether they will do so, because the obligation may terminate or is subject to a condition. Rights in the first category can be assigned without consideration; those in the second cannot. The decisions as to those in the third class are impossible to rationalise, though it seems clear that even where there is an existing chose in action capable of assignment, the proceeds of the chose may be a mere expectancy.[296]

Assignments of rights of action

22–58   Prior to January 1, 1968 both maintenance[297] and champerty[298] were crimes. However, the Criminal Law Act 1967 abolished the criminal nature of these acts and also a party's tortious liability therefor. However, the Act expressly provided that "the abolition of criminal and civil liability... for maintenance... shall not affect any rule of... law as to the cases in which a contract is to be treated as contrary to public policy or otherwise illegal".[299] Accordingly, it would seem that agreements which, under the law before 1968 would have been unenforceable for either maintenance or champerty remain unenforceable as a matter of public policy.[300] This state of affairs also affects assignments of rights of action. Generally a bare right of litigation, such as the right to damages for a wrongful

---

[293] *Meek v Kettlewell* (1843) 1 Ph. 342; *Tailby v Official Receiver* (1888) 13 App.Cas. 523; *Glegg v Bromley* [1912] 3 K.B. 474; *Cotton v Heyl* [1930] 1 Ch. 510.

[294] *Shepherd v Federal Commissioners of Taxation* (1965) 113 C.L.R. 385.

[295] *Meek v Kettlewell* (1843) 1 Ph. 342; *Re Tilt* (1896) 74 L.T. 163; *Re Ellenborough* [1903] 1 Ch. 697; cf. *Kekewich v Manning* (1851) 1 De G.M. & G. 176.

[296] See e.g. *Grovewood Holdings Plc v James Capel & Co Ltd* [1995] Ch. 80. *Glegg v Bromley* [1912] 3 K.B. 474 (proceeds of a defamation action being brought by the assignor); *Norman v Federal Commissioner of Taxation* (1963) 109 C.L.R. 9 (interest payable in the future as a loan which was not for a fixed period; dividends on shares already held which may become due in the future). In the following cases the subject-matter has been held to be an existing chose in action: *Walker v Bradford Old Bank* (1864) 12 Q.B.D. 511 (sum standing to the assignor's credit at date of his death); *Hughes v Pump House Hotel Co* [1902] 2 K.B. 190 (sums payable to a builder under an existing contract). See also para.22–62.

[297] Where a person supports litigation in which he has no legitimate concern without just cause or excuse: see *Chitty on Contracts* (30th edn, 2008), para.16–050.

[298] Which has been described as "an aggravated form of maintenance" in which an individual stipulates for a share in the proceeds of the litigation: *Giles v Thompson* [1993] 3 All E.R. 328, CA. See *Chitty on Contracts* (30th edn, 2008), para.16–054.

[299] Criminal Law Act 1967 s.14(2).

[300] See *Chitty on Contracts* (30th edn, 2008), para.16–049.

act[301] is not assignable[302] on the principle that the law will not recognise any transaction savouring of maintenance or champerty.[303]

However, there is nothing unlawful in the purchase of property which the **22–59** purchaser can enjoy only by defeating existing adverse claims.[304] Moreover, it has been held that rights of action (even in tort) which are incidental and subsidiary to property may be validly assigned when the property is transferred.[305] The test that the House of Lords applied in *Trendtex Trading Corporation v Credit Suisse*[306] was that:

> "If the assignment is of a property right or interest and the cause of action is ancillary to that right or interest, or if the assignee had a genuine commercial interest in taking the assignment and enforcing it for his own benefit, [there is] no reason why the assignment should be struck down as an assignment of a bare cause of action or a savouring of maintenance".[307]

Thus in *Trendtex*, it was accepted that a creditor who had financed the transaction **22–60** giving rise to the right of action had a legitimate commercial interest in it and that an assignment to him would be valid unless the object of the assignment was other than to protect that creditor's interest. Where the right of action assigned is ancillary to the transfer of property, it is in every case a question whether the purchaser's real object in acquiring an interest in the property is precisely that or the acquisition is merely ancillary to the true purpose, namely the acquisition of a right to bring an action, either alone or jointly with the vendor.[308]

Thus the purchaser of a freehold reversion may take an assignment of the right to recover damages for dilapidations from the sub-tenant.[309] A creditor may assign his debt so as to enable another to sue for it.[310] A person may buy shares in a company merely for the purpose of challenging, by legal proceedings, acts of the directors as being ultra vires.[311] An assignment by an assured to his insurer of his rights against a contract breaker or tortfeasor is good, the enforcement of the cause of action being legitimately supported by the insurer's interest in recouping the amount of loss which he has paid under the policy as a result of the act, neglect or default of the contract breaker or tortfeasor.[312]

---

[301] e.g. for assault: *May v Lane* (1894) 64 L.J.Q.B. 236, 238, per Rigby L.J.

[302] *Dawson v Great Northern City Railway Company* [1905] 1 K.B. 260 at 271, per Stirling L.J.; *Fitzroy v Cave* [1905] 2 K.B. 364 at 371; *Defries v Milnes* [1913] 1 Ch. 98; *Holt v Heatherfield Trust Ltd* [1942] 2 K.B. 1; *Laurent v Sale & Co* [1963] 1 W.L.R. 829.

[303] *Rees v De Bernardy* [1896] 2 Ch. 437; *Laurent v Sale & Co*; *Grovewood Holdings Plc v James Capel & Co Ltd* [1995] Ch. 80; *Re Oasis Merchandising Services Ltd* [1998] Ch. 170; *Norglen Ltd v Reid Rains Prudential Ltd* [1999] 2 A.C. 1.

[304] *Dickenson v Burrell* (1866) L.R. 1 Eq. 337; *County Hotel & Wine Co Ltd v London & North Western Railway Co* [1918] 2 K.B. 251, affirmed on other grounds [1921] 1 A.C. 85; *Ellis v Torrington* [1920] 1 K.B. 399; *Candex International Ltd v Bank of Zambia* [1998] Q.B. 22.

[305] ibid.

[306] [1982] A.C. 679.

[307] per Lord Reid at 703.

[308] *Dickenson v Burrell* (1866) L.R. 1 Eq. 337; *Prosser v Edmonds* (1835) 1 Y. & C. Ex. 481; *Harrington v Long* (1833) 2 My. & Kay. 590; *Knight v Bowyer* (1858) 2 De G. & J. 421.

[309] *Williams v Protheroe* (1829) 5 Bing. 309; *Ellis v Torrington* [1920] 1 K.B. 399.

[310] *Fitzroy v Cave* [1905] 2 K.B. 364 (even though the wish of that other person to enforce debt arises from ill-feeling towards the debtor).

[311] *Bloxam v Metropolitan Rly Co* (1868) 3 Ch.App. 337 at 353.

[312] *Companie Columbiana de Seguros v Pacific Steam Navigation Co* [1965] 1 Q.B. 101.

22-61   A solicitor purchasing from his client the subject-matter of a suit is in a different position from other purchasers. After his employment as such in the suit[313] he cannot purchase the subject-matter from his client[314] although he may lawfully take a mortgage on it to secure costs and expenses already incurred.[315]

The assignment of right in action by an assignor to another party where the object and effect of the assignment was to enable the assignee to obtain public funding for the pursuit of the claim which would not otherwise have been available to the assignor is not contrary to public policy or unlawful.[316] Presumably the same principles apply where an assignor, who would otherwise be at risk of providing security for costs pursuant to the Civil Procedure Rules assigns the cause of action to an assignee who is not at such a risk.

Voluntary equitable assignments

22-62   **Generally:**   The general principle to be derived from the decided cases is that an assignment of an existing chose in action need not be supported by consideration provided that the assignor has done everything within his power to transfer the property in the manner appropriate to its nature.[317] In many cases the law will not treat a gift as valid unless it has been made in the prescribed way. Thus a gift of a chattel must be made either by deed of gift or by delivery of the chattel with the intent that the property shall pass.[318] In *Milroy v Lord*[319] the owner of shares in a company made a voluntary assignment of them by deed poll. This could not take effect as a gift since the legal title to the shares could be transferred only by execution of a proper instrument of transfer and registration of the transfer in the books of the company.

22-63   It was held that a voluntary settlement could not be valid and effectual unless the donor had done everything in his power which was necessary, having regard to the nature of the property comprised in the settlement, to transfer the property and render the settlement binding on him. That rule applies only to gifts which by law had to be made in a specified form.

22-64   **Form:**   The only formality required for the assignment of an equitable chose in action is that it must be in writing[320]: so a voluntary settlement in writing of an

---

[313] *Knight v Bowyer* (1858) 2 De G. & J. 421, CA; *Davis v Freethy* (1890) 24 Q.B.D. 519.

[314] *Wood v Downes* (1811) 18 Ves. 120; *Simpson v Lamb* (1857) 7 E. & B. 84; *Davis v Freethy* (1890) 24 Q.B.D. 519.

[315] *Anderson v Radcliffe* (1858) E.B. & E. 806.

[316] *Norglen Limited v Reid Rains Provincial Ltd* (1999) 2 A.C.

[317] *Kekewich v Manning* (1851) 1 De G.M. & G. 176; *Milroy v Lord* (1862) De F. & S. 264 *Harding v Harding* (1886) 17 Q.B.D. 442; *Re Griffin* [1899] 1 Ch. 408; *German v Yates* (1915) 32 T.L.R. 52; *Re Williams* [1917] 1 Ch. 1; *Holt v Heatherfield Trust* [1942] 2 K.B. 1; *Re Rose Midland Bank Executor-Trustee Co v Rose* [1949] Ch. 78; *Re McArdle* [1951] Ch. 669; *Re Rose Rose v IRC* [1952] Ch. 499; *Letts v IRC* [1957] 1 W.L.R. 201. *Brown and Root Technology Ltd v Sun Alliance and London Assurance Co Ltd* [1996] Ch. 51.

[318] *Re Breton's Estate* (1881) 17 Ch.D. 416; *Cochrane v Moore* (1890) 25 Q.B.D. 57; *Re Cole (A Bankrupt), ex p. Trustees of the Property of the Bankrupt* [1964] Ch. 175.

[319] (1862) 4 De G.F. & J. 264; and see Turner L.J. at 274 for a statement of the rule. cf. *Antrobus v Smith* (1805) 12 Ves. 39 where a gift of shares failed because it was made in writing not under seal, contrary to the company's articles.

[320] LPA 1925 s.53(1)(c).

equitable interest in a trust fund has been held binding on the settlor,[321] since he did not need to do anything else in order to transfer the property. Equitable assignments of legal choses in action are not required to be in writing.[322] Unless the nature of the property brings special rules into play, there are no formal requirements for the transfer of legal choses in action[323] and it is necessary only for the donor to do all within his power to effect the transfer. If that has been done, it is immaterial that further steps need to be taken by the donee[324] or by some other third party.[325]

Defective statutory assignments

A statutory assignment may be ineffective as such, though it may take effect as **22–65** an equitable assignment, if no written notice has been given to the debtor, or if it is not in writing, or if it is not an absolute assignment. Assignments which are conditional, or by way of charge, or are assignments of part of a debt, are not absolute and therefore defective by reason of non-compliance with s.136 of the Law of Property Act 1925.

Where the defect is want of notice, the assignment is effective although not supported by consideration.[326] Since it is not required by s.136 of the Law of Property Act 1925, that the assignor shall give the notice, he has done all within his power to transfer the property.

Where the defect is lack of writing, and the chose is equitable, the question of **22–66** consideration does not arise because the assignment is void unless in writing. If it is a legal chose, want of consideration does not, by itself, invalidate the transfer. In *German v Yates*[327] a voluntary oral assignment of a debt was held to bind the personal representatives of the assignor, and that the Judicature Act 1873[328] had not destroyed equitable assignments or impaired them in any way.[329] In that case, it was held that the assignment was a perfect gift. But the problem which may arise is whether an oral assignment was a perfect gift or merely a promise to make a gift in the future. A voluntary promise to assign an equitable interest is not an assignment, and the fact that is made by means of signed writing is irrelevant. In *Re McArdle, Decd*,[330] the following words were held to be incapable of being construed as an equitable assignment:

> "in consideration of your carrying out certain alterations and improvements to the property... we... agree that the executors shall ... repay to you from the estate when so distributed £488 in settlement of the amount."

[321] *Kekewich v Manning* (1851) 1 De G.M. & G. 176.

[322] See para.22–37.

[323] See *Fortescue v Barnett* (1834) 3 My. & K. 36, voluntary assignment, by deed, of a life insurance policy held binding on the assignor.

[324] *Re Paradise Motor Co Ltd* [1968] 1 W.L.R. 1125.

[325] *Re Rose, Midland Bank Executor and Trustee Co v Rose* [1949] Ch. 78; see also *Re Rose, Rose v IRC* [1952] Ch. 499.

[326] *Holt v Heatherfield Trust Ltd* [1942] 2 K.B. 1.

[327] (1915) 32 T.L.R. 52.

[328] The original provision enabling statutory assignments to be made was s.25(6) of the Judicature Act 1873.

[329] For a similar dictum see *William Brandt's Sons & Co v Dunlop Rubber Co* [1905] A.C. 454 at 462.

[330] [1951] Ch. 669.

The works referred to had been carried out and it was held that the document purported to be a contract to assign, not an assignment, and thus required consideration. Since the consideration was past, the contract was unenforceable. That case also suggests that a voluntary equitable assignment of part of a debt may be valid, but the reasoning by which that conclusion is arrived at has been criticised.[331]

22–67   Where the assignment is not absolute because it is conditional, its effectiveness depends on the condition. If this is such as to require some further act to be done by the donor, the assignment will be ineffective, being an imperfect gift.

22–68   Finally, where there is an assignment by way of charge the question of consideration will not normally arise because the assignment will nearly always be made to secure a debt and there will be consideration in the form of the assignee's advancing money or forbearance, or promising not to sue. For-bearance will amount to consideration only for a promise that is induced by it. Thus where a debtor executed a mortgage of an insurance policy in favour of his creditor, but the creditor did not know of the mortgage, it was held that his forbearance to sue for his antecedent debt was not consideration,[332] though it was said that he would have provided consideration if he had been told of the mortgage and forborne to sue on the strength of it. Forbearance may, it seems, be requested expressly[333] or impliedly.[334]

Assignments of particular choses in action

Trust property

22–69   The 1925 property legislation provides for the mortgaging of equitable interests, in both realty and personalty, by assignment of the equitable interest subject to a proviso for reassignment on redemption. An interest in trust property was always freely assignable in equity, and the assignee could sue in his own name and if the whole interest was assigned, the assignor did not have to be made a party,[335] though his joinder was essential if he retained any interest, as where the assign-ment was conditional or by way of charge.[336] The 1925 legislation did not alter this situation; it merely provided an alternative mode of assignment.

As between assignor and assignee the assignment is complete without notice to the trustee; notice is important for the reasons discussed earlier, which are to do with the interests of third parties.

---

[331] See R.E. Megarry, (1951) 67 L.Q.R. 295 for a critical commentary and also see D.M. Stone, (1951) 14 M.L.R. 356; Treitel, *Law of Contract* (11th edn, 2003), p.688.

[332] *Wigan v English and Scottish Law Life Assurance Society* [1909] 1 Ch. 291.

[333] *Crears v Hunter* (1887) 19 Q.B.D. 341.

[334] *Alliance Bank v Broom* (1864) 2 Dr. & Sm. 289.

[335] *Performing Rights Society v London Theatre of Varieties Ltd* [1924] A.C. 1.

[336] Modern authority suggests the joinder of the assignor is a procedural rather than substantive requirement and thus not a sine qua non: see *Weddell v J.A. Pearce-Major* [1988] Ch. 26; *Three Rivers District Council v Bank of England* [1996] Q.B. 292 and *Raiffeisen Zentralbank Osterreich AG v Five Star Trading LLC* [2001] Q.B. 825. This approach is not without its critics: see *Smith, The Law of Assignment* (2007), paras 6.13 et seq.

Form: The requirements of form arise, therefore, not from the provisions **22–70**
regulating statutory assignments but from s.53(1)(c) of the Law of Property Act
1925 which provides as follows:

> "A disposition of an equitable interest or trust subsisting at the time of the disposi-
> tion, must be in writing, signed by the person disposing of the same, or by his agent,
> thereunto lawfully authorised in writing or by will."

In addition, it is usual for an assignment of trust property to be created by deed,
since the assignee will then have the statutory powers conferred on a mortgagee
by deed.[337] Because of the uncertain nature of limited or contingent interests in
a trust property, the deed will contain various additional covenants and powers
giving the assignee greater protection:

    (1) Power for the assignee to protect his security by taking any proceed-
        ings, making any inquiries, giving any notices or obtaining any stop
        orders[338] necessary for that purpose.

    (2) The assignment of a policy of life insurance or of insurance against a
        particular contingency, together with the assignment of the trust inter-
        est, and covenants by the assignor to pay the premiums and maintain
        the security.

Stop Orders: Power is given to the court, under the Civil Procedure Rules[339] **22–71**
to make an order prohibiting the transfer, sale, delivery out, payment or other
dealing with funds paid into court or any part of such fund or the income thereof,
without notice to the applicant. In relation to funds in Court, a person:

    (1) who has a mortgage or charge on the interest of any person in funds in
        court; or

    (2) to whom that interest has been assigned; or

    (3) who is a judgment creditor of the person entitled to that interest,

may apply to the court by an application pursuant to CPR Pt 23 in any existing
proceedings, or, if there are none, by issuing a claim form. In relation to securities
other than securities held in Court, any person claiming to be beneficially entitled
to an interest may apply.[340] Stop orders have priority, among themselves, in the
order in which they were made,[341] but do not gain priority over existing incum-
brancers who have given notice to the trustees before the stop order was made.[342]
Express notice should also be given to the trustees.

---

[337] LPA 1925 s.101.
[338] CPR Pt 73.11. When a trust fund is paid into court, a "stop order" is equivalent to giving notice
to the trustees: *Pinnock v Bailey* (1883) 23 Ch.D. 497; *Montefiore v Guedalla* [1903] 2 Ch. 26, CA.
Express notice should be given to the trustees.
[339] CPR Pt 73.11.
[340] CPR Pt 73.12(1)(b).
[341] *Greening v Beckford* (1832) 5 Sim. 195; *Swayne v Swayne* (1849) 11 Beav. 463.
[342] *Livesey v Harding* (1857) 23 Beav. 141; *Re Anglesey* [1903] 2 Ch. 727. See also *White Book*,
2010, para.73.13.8.

22–72   **Notice to the trustees:**   While giving notice of the assignment to the trustees regulates priorities among assignees, it does not amount to taking possession of the trust interest unless the notice requires the payment of the income to be made to the assignee.[343] Until such notice is given, the trustees are entitled to continue to pay the income to the assignor and, in the interests of certainty, it is advisable to insert a declaration in the assignment to the effect that the assignor is entitled to receive the income until the assignee otherwise directs.[344]

Even if the assignee notifies the trustees that all available monies are to be paid over to him it does not necessarily follow that the trustees must do so.[345] If the amount available exceeds the debt to the assignee and the trustees have notice of other assignments, they should pay over only such a sum as will discharge the principal, interest and costs.[346] If trustees are uncertain of the amount of the debt, they may refuse to pay over anything, even to the assignee first in priority, until an account has been taken.[347] They are trustees for all interested parties and need not pay monies, even to persons apparently entitled to them, without making inquiries.

Policies of life assurance

22–73   Before the Policies of Assurance Act 1867, mortgages of such policies were governed by the general law of assignment. Since rights under life assurance policies are legal choses in action, the assignee could not, under the pre-1867 general law, sue in his own name. However, s.1 of the 1867 Act made this possible subject to compliance with the statutory formalities. The statutory provisions do not displace the previous law, so that an equitable assignment of a life assurance policy can still be made subject to the rules governing such assignments.

22–74   **Statutory requirements:**   There are two separate and distinct methods of assignment pursuant to statute. The first is in accordance with s.136 of the Law of Property Act 1925.[348] The second is under the Policies of Assurance Act 1867. An assignment under the 1867 Act must be made in writing, either by an endorsement on the policy or by a separate instrument in the form given by the Schedule to the Act[349] or to the purpose and effect thereof. It has been held that a letter to the purported assignee, requesting him to instruct his solicitor to prepare an assignment, was not a valid assignment, either in equity or by statute and in consequence, notice to the insurance company by the purported assignee, B, that he was holding the policies as security for a debt was not a valid notice

---

[343] *Re Pawson's Settlement* [1917] 1 Ch. 541; though cf. *Dearle v Hall* (1828) 3 Russ. 1 at 58, per Lyndhurst L.C.

[344] Key and Elphinstone, *Precedents in Conveyancing* (15th edn, 1953–54), Vol.2, p.23.

[345] They may do so: *Jones v Farrell* (1857) 1 De G. & J. 208.

[346] *Re Bell* [1896] 1 Ch. 1, CA.

[347] *Hockey v Western* [1898] 1 Ch. 350.

[348] See paras 22–45 et seq. Section 136(2) provides that nothing in s.136 affects the Policies of Assurance Act 1867 and the more familiar provisions under the LPA 1925 are more commonly used.

[349] Policies of Assurance Act 1867 s.5.

of assignment.[350] Likewise, an agreement to assign on request is not an assignment,[351] and a notice of the agreement is not a notice of the assignment. Consequently, the purported assignee did not, by informing the company of the agreement, gain priority over a prior equitable assignee, A, by deposit who had not given the company notice of such deposit. Indeed, the inability of the assignor to produce the policy was held to be constructive notice to B, in the circumstances of the case, of A's rights.[352] This accords with an earlier decision that, where the equities of two assignees are otherwise equal, possession of deeds gives the better equity.[353]

The assignee has no right to sue on the policy until written notice of the date and purport of the assignment has been given to the company. The policy must specify the place or places at which such notice may be given. The company is bound, on request and on payment of the prescribed fee, to give a written acknowledgment of receipt of notice, and that acknowledgment is conclusive, against the company, of such receipt.

Priority: The assignee takes subject to equities, including the right of the company to avoid the policy if full disclosure has not been made. **22–75**

The 1867 Act provides that priorities between competing assignees are regulated by the order in which notice is given to the company,[354] but notice of a dealing not amounting to an assignment is ineffective. The provision does not apply where a subsequent assignee has notice, whether actual, constructive, or imputed, of a prior assignment,[355] as where money is lent on the security of an insurance policy which, being in the hands of a prior assignee, is not handed over. The non-delivery of the policy is constructive notice of the prior assignment.[356] The subsequent assignee will obtain priority by giving notice first if he has no notice of the prior assignee, even though he was prevented from getting notice by fraudulent concealment of the prior assignment. **22–76**

Assignment by way of mortgage: Mortgages of life assurance policies are made by way of assignment with a proviso for reassignment. They normally contain covenants not to allow the policy to become void and to pay premiums and produce receipts therefore to the mortgagee, with power, in default, for the mortgagee to pay the premiums himself and charge them against the policy. The cost of paying premiums so as to keep the policy on foot is allowable, whether or not the policy contains an express provision to that effect.[357] A mortgagee by deed has the statutory power of sale given by s.101 of the Law of Property Act 1925. A receiver may also be appointed in appropriate circumstances. **22–77**

---

[350] *Crossley v City of Glasgow Life Assurance Co* (1876) 4 Ch.D. 421.

[351] *Spencer v Clarke* (1879) 9 Ch.D. 137.

[352] *Re Weniger's Policy* [1910] 2 Ch. 291.

[353] *Rice v Rice* (1853) 2 Drew. 73.

[354] Policies of Assurance Act 1867 s.3. If a written request for an acknowledgment is made, the company must give an acknowledgment of receipt of notice, in writing, and this is conclusive against the company: Policies of Assurance Act 1867 s.6. The policy must specify the place at which notice of assignment is to be given: Policies of Assurance Act 1867 s.4.

[355] *Re Lake, ex p. Cavendish* [1903] 1 K.B. 151.

[356] *Spencer v Clarke*, above; *Re Weniger's Policy*, above.

[357] *Gill v Downing* (1874) L.R. 17 Eq. 316.

Since a creditor has an insurable interest in his debtor's life to the extent of the debt,[358] it is permissible for the creditor to take out a policy in his own name on the life of the debtor, instead of the debtor taking it out and assigning it to the creditor. Unless the creditor can be placed in a position whereby he can take advantage of s.1 of the Contracts (Rights of Third Parties Act) 1999,[359] the debtor should not take out a policy in the name of the creditor as the creditor, not being a party to the policy, would have no rights under it.[360] Thus where S took out a policy in his own name for the benefit of G, to mature in 17 years' time, and died five years after taking it out, it was held that G could not benefit as he was not a party to the policy and no declaration of trust in his favour had been made; nor did the Law of Property Act 1925 s.56(1) operate so as to confer any benefit on him.

22–78   **Ownership of the policy:**   Depending on circumstances, the policy may be the property of the debtor, mortgaged to the creditor, or it may belong to the creditor absolutely. There are three possible arrangements to consider:

(1) The debtor takes out the policy and pays the premiums. The policy is part of the security and belongs to the debtor.
(2) The creditor takes out the policy in the debtor's name, and pays the premiums without having any agreement with the debtor to charge the premiums to him. The policy is treated as having been taken out for the creditor's own protection and belongs to him.[361] This is so even where the creditor purported, in his own accounts, to charge the debtor with the premiums but there was no agreement to do so.
(3) The creditor takes out the policy but the premiums are by agreement chargeable to the debtor. There are two possible views:

(a) the policy belongs to the debtor in equity, subject to security;
(b) the policy belongs to the creditor and the stipulation that the debtor pays the premiums is a bonus for the creditor.

There is a presumption in favour of (a) which can be rebutted by evidence showing that it was intended that the creditor should receive an outright bonus.[362]

Where the policy is part of the security, the debtor has a right to redeem and any stipulation purporting to take away that right is void.[363] Nor can the creditor claim the whole benefit of the policy if the debtor defaults in paying the

---

[358] *Morland v Isaac* (1855) 20 Beav. 389; see also *Freme v Brade* (1858) 2 De G. & J. 582; *Drysdale v Piggot* (1856) 8 De G.M. & G. 546; *Bruce v Garden* (1869) 5 Ch.App. 32; *Salt v Marquis of Northampton* [1892] A.C. 1 (HL).

[359] This Act applies to contracts entered into after May 11, 2000 and permits a third party to the contract to enforce it if the contract so provides or if it confers a benefit on him and (in the latter case) does not provide to the contrary. See *Chitty on Contracts* (30th edn, 2008), paras 18–01 et seq.

[360] *Re Sinclair's Life Policy* [1938] Ch. 799.

[361] *Bruce v Garden*, above.

[362] *Salt v Marquess of Northampton* [1892] A.C. 1 at 16.

[363] ibid.

premiums. He can only pay them himself to preserve the security and add them to the mortgage debt. He can acquire the security only by foreclosure.[364]

Suicide: Life assurance policies are particularly hazardous in that they may be **22–79** avoided by the suicide of the assured if they so provide (either expressly or by implication). Nor does the law allow the representatives of a wilful suicide to enforce a life policy,[365] and this rule has not been displaced by the Forfeiture Act 1982. That Act expresses the rule of public policy which may prevent a person who has unlawfully killed another from acquiring a benefit from the death of that other and, in certain circumstances, provides for relief where a person has been guilty of unlawful killing.[366] A mortgagee, being an assignee, cannot be in a better position than the representatives of the deceased assured unless the policy expressly provides for the preservation of rights of bona fide assignees for value.[367] Such provisions are not contrary to public policy, since they preserve the negotiability and hence the value to the assured, of the policy, and are frequently found in life policies.

Such a clause appeared in the policy the rights to which were in dispute in *Solicitors and General Life Assurance Society v Lamb*.[368] L mortgaged a life policy and other securities to R and committed suicide. R relied on the clause against the insurance company to force the payment of the policy monies to him and also realised the other securities. The total exceeded the mortgage debt and the company claimed the surplus as against L's widow, advancing two arguments. They claimed that either the debt to R should be satisfied first out of the other securities, or that it should be apportioned rateably between the debt and the other securities. Both arguments were rejected, the court holding that the clause was inserted in the interests of the assured and created no equity in favour of the insurers in regard to monies payable to assignees.

The same principles were applied in *White v British Empire Mutual Life Assurance Co*,[369] where the insurance company was the mortgagee. Other securities were also mortgaged to the company and it was held that, in the absence of any contractual provision entitling the company to repay itself out of the other securities, the widow of the assured could require the company to repay itself first out of the policy monies. The consequences of this decision in *Lamb's* case can be avoided if the clause provides for the preservation of the rights only of assignees who are independent third parties.[370]

---

[364] *Drysdale v Piggot* (1850) 8 De G.M. & G. 546.

[365] *Beresford v Royal Insurance Co* [1938] A.C. 586. The ratio was not on the basis of public policy but because, as a matter of principle, a man cannot by his own deliberate act cause a payment to be made. The principle was also applied to prevent recovery on a policy of life insurance where the assured was executed for felony, although the policy did not expressly provide for this contingency: *Amicable Society v Bolland* (1830) 4 Bligh. (N.S.) 194. Recovery is permitted if the suicide was insane: *Horn v Anglo-Australian & Universal Family Life Assurance Co* (1861) 30 L.J. Ch. 511.

[366] See, by example, *S (Deceased)* [1996] 1 W.L.R. 235; *Dunbar v Plant* [1998] Ch. 412.

[367] ibid. It has not been decided whether the security is avoided if the assured assigned the policy before committing suicide: *Hardy v Motor Insurers Bureau* [1964] 2 Q.B. 745, CA.

[368] (1864) 2 De G.J. & S. 251.

[369] (1868) L.R. 7 Eq. 394.

[370] *Royal London Mutual Insurance Society v Barrett* [1928] Ch. 411.

22–80   Discharge: A legal mortgage of a life assurance policy is discharged by reassignment, either in the form of an express reassignment or by way of statutory receipt. The printed form of a mortgage of a life policy of banks and building societies and other institutional lenders usually, however, provide for an express reassignment. Notice of the discharge should be given to the insurance company.

Shares in partnerships

22–81   A share in a partnership confers the right to a share in the profits and, on dissolution, in the assets.[371] It is a hazardous security, particularly as, by s.33 of the Partnership Act 1890, a partnership may, at the option of the other partners, be dissolved if any partner suffers his share of the partnership property to be charged under the Act for his separate debt. Further, under s.31 of that Act, the assignee has no right during the continuance of the partnership to interfere in the business or to receive accounts or to inspect the books.

A mortgagee is not usually introduced into the partnership and by s.24(7) a partner may not, without the consent of all the other partners, introduce another partner into the firm. Unless he is so introduced, he has no right to interfere in the management of the partnership business,[372] to require accounts of partnership transactions, or to inspect partnership books.[373] He is not, however, precluded from impugning transactions made between the partners which are designed to deprive him of his rights.[374]

He is entitled, on a dissolution, to receive the mortgagor's share of the assets, and, for the purpose of ascertaining that share, to an account as from the date of dissolution.[375]

A mortgagee can enforce his security by foreclosure[376] and if the mortgage is made by deed, he has the statutory powers of sale and appointment of a receiver.

Although the mortgagee is entitled to share in the personal chattels of the partnership on dissolution, the mortgage is a mortgage of a chose in action and not a bill of sale,[377] and accordingly does not require registration. Notice of the mortgage should, however, be given to the other partners so as to establish priority as against other mortgagees and to bind them to pay over the share to the mortgagee.

Stocks and shares

22–82   Mortgages of stocks and shares are not regulated by the Bills of Sale Acts, such choses in action being outside the definition of "personal chattels" in s.4 of the

---

[371] See *Lindley and Banks on Partnership* (18th edn, 2002), Ch.25.
[372] *Re Garwood's Trusts* [1903] 1 Ch. 236; Partnership Act 1890 s.31. See also para.4–19, above.
[373] *Bonnin v Neame* [1910] 1 Ch. 732.
[374] *Watts v Driscoll* [1901] 1 Ch. 294.
[375] ibid.
[376] *Whetham v Davey* (1885) 30 Ch.D. 574.
[377] *Re Bainbridge* (1878) 8 Ch.D. 218.

Bills of Sale Act 1878. Stocks and shares had been made assignable at law before the Judicature Act 1873 provided for the legal assignment of choses in action. A company incorporated under the Companies Act 2006 may, by its articles of association regulate the transfer of its shares in any manner. By s.770(1) of the Companies Act 2006, it is not lawful for a company to register a transfer of shares in the company otherwise than by operation of law without a proper instrument of transfer being delivered to it unless the transfer is an exempt transfer within the Stock Transfer Act 1982.

The Stock Transfer Act 1963[378] provides that, notwithstanding anything in the articles of association of a company or any enactment or instrument relating thereto, fully paid up registered securities may be transferred by means of an instrument under hand, signed only by the transferor, whose signature need not be attested.

Legal mortgages: Legal mortgages of shares are created by transfer with a   **22–83** proviso for re-transfer but it is not usual to mortgage shares in this way. Such a transaction gives the mortgagee both the rights and liabilities of a shareholder; thus he is subject to calls if the shares are not fully paid up and he may be compelled to vote in accordance with the wishes of the mortgagor[379]: on the other hand, he becomes entitled to the dividends. To the outside world (and even to the company, which is not obliged to enter notice of any trust in the register of members[380]) the mortgagee is the absolute owner. A "stop notice"[381] may therefore be appropriately served on the company.

Equitable mortgages: An equitable mortgage of shares is usually created by a   **22–84** deposit of the share certificates with the mortgagee, together with a memorandum of deposit. It normally contains, inter alia, a statement that the deposit is by way of security, covenants by the mortgagor not to incur a forfeiture, to pay principal and interest, an undertaking by him to execute a registered transfer, a proviso for redemption, a power of sale,[382] and a statement that the deposit is by way of security. While the mortgagor remains the registered owner, he must vote as the mortgagee directs.[383]

The deposit of the share certificates may also be accompanied by a transfer   **22–85** form executed by the mortgagor but with the date and the mortgagee's name left blank.[384] This allows the mortgagee to perfect his title by filling in the transfer and having it registered, provided that it is possible to transfer the shares merely by an instrument under hand.[385] Delivery of the blank transfer raises a presumption that the mortgagor has appointed the mortgagee his agent for the purpose of

---

[378] ss.1 and 2.
[379] *Puddephatt v Leith* [1916] 1 Ch. 200; *Musselwhite v C.H. Musselwhite & Sons Ltd* [1962] Ch. 964. *Michaels v Harley House (Marylebone) Ltd* [2000] Ch. 104.
[380] Companies Act 2006 s.126.
[381] See CPR Pt 73.16. See para.22–88.
[382] One may be implied: see *Stubbs v Slater* [1910] 1 Ch. 632.
[383] *Wise v Lansdell* [1921] 1 Ch. 420.
[384] *Barclay v Prospect Mortgages Ltd* [1974] 1 W.L.R. 837.
[385] *Ortigosa v Brown, Janson & Co* (1878) 47 L.J.Ch. 168.

completing the transfer.[386] If, however, the shares are required to be transferred by deed, only an agent appointed by an instrument under seal can execute the deed,[387] and in such a case the deposit will be accompanied by a deed of mortgage containing a power of attorney authorising the mortgagee to execute a transfer of the shares to himself or a purchaser.[388]

Difficulties may arise if the mortgagor gives the mortgagee a blank transfer under seal and the mortgagee later executes it without having been given a power of attorney under seal or redelivering it to the mortgagor for re-execution by him. For in such circumstances the mortgagor has never acknowledged the deed as his own. He may be estopped from denying its validity as against a bona fide purchaser for value from the mortgagee without notice.[389] A transfer of the certificates without registration does not pass the legal title to the shares.[390] Nevertheless, it is not a mere pledge but constitutes an equitable mortgage.[391] The equitable mortgagee can compel the mortgagor to execute a registered transfer of the shares and after default he is entitled to foreclose[392] or, after reasonable notice to the mortgagor, to sell the shares.[393]

22–86   Notice to company: Notice of the deposit of share certificates should be given to the company. This is not for the purpose of regulating priorities since by s.126 of the Companies Act 2006,[394] no trust may be entered on the register of a company.[395] Further, the rule in *Dearle v Hall*[396] does not apply to equitable mortgages of shares, priorities among which are governed by the same rules as applied to mortgages of land before 1926.[397]

The purpose of notice to the company, although not regulating priorities, is to cause the company to become aware of conflicting claims and perhaps to defer registration, even, when appropriate, until the court has determined the rights of the conflicting parties.[398] It is doubtful whether a company is legally bound to delay so far,[399] but equally it is not bound to register a transfer which effectuates a fraud.[400] A "stop notice"[401] (though rarely used) would be an alternative—and preferable—course. In *Ireland v Hart*,[402] a solicitor was the registered owner of

[386] *Colonial Bank v Cady* (1890) 15 App.Cas. 267.
[387] *Powell v London & Provincial Bank* [1893] 2 Ch. 555.
[388] *Hibblewhite v M'Morine* (1840) 6 M. & W. 200; *Société Générale de Paris v Walker* (1885) 11 App.Cas. 20; *Re Seymour, Fielding v Seymour* [1913] 1 Ch. 475.
[389] *Earl of Sheffield v London Joint Stock Bank* (1888) 13 App.Cas. 333; *Waterhouse v Bank of Ireland* (1891) 29 L.R.Ir. 384; *London Joint Stock Bank v Simmons* [1892] A.C. 201; *Fuller v Glyn Mills, Currie & Co* [1914] 2 K.B. 168.
[390] *Société Générale de Paris v Walker*, above.
[391] *Harrold v Plenty* [1901] 2 Ch. 314.
[392] ibid.
[393] *Deverges v Sandeman* [1902] 1 Ch. 579.
[394] formerly Companies Act 1985 s.360.
[395] *MacMillan Inc v Bishopsgate Trust (No.3)* [1996] 1 All E.R. 585.
[396] (1828) 3 Russ. 1.
[397] See para.22–89.
[398] *Moore v North Western Bank* [1891] 2 Ch. 599. See also *Simpson v Molson's Bank* [1895] A.C. 270.
[399] ibid.
[400] *Roots v Williamson* (1888) 38 Ch.D. 485.
[401] See CPR Pt 73.16. See para.22–88.
[402] [1902] 1 Ch. 522.

shares which he held in trust for his wife. He mortgaged them by deposit to H, who, being doubtful as to the mortgagor's financial stability, filled in his own name on the blank transfer which accompanied the deposit and applied for registration. In the meantime, the directors of the company had learnt of the wife's interest. They deferred their decision and the court held that the wife's prior interest prevailed over H's later interest. It is only where the later equitable mortgagee has a "present, absolute and unconditional right" to be registered that he will gain priority; and this appears to be restricted to the case where the company has formally accepted the transfer and only a ministerial act by an officer of the company is required to complete registration.

Notice to the company will also protect an equitable mortgagee against **22–87** equities raised by the company after the notice has been given to it.[403] Thus, if the company by virtue of its articles of association has a first and paramount lien or charge on every share issued for all debts due from the holder, notice to the company of an equitable mortgage will cause further advances on the security of the same shares to rank after the equitable mortgage.[404] Further, if the company has actual notice that a shareholder does not own shares beneficially and makes advances to him, it does not acquire a lien on those shares for the debt.[405]

Stop notices: The limited effect of notice can be circumscribed by the entry of **22–88** a "stop notice". Dealings with this security can be prevented by the service of a stop notice on the company under the Civil Procedure Rules.[406] The effect is that the person or body on whom the stop notice is served shall not register a transfer of the securities or take any other steps restrained by the stop notice until 14 days after sending the notice thereof by ordinary first-class post to the person on whose behalf the stop notice was filed, but shall not by reason only of that notice refuse to register the transfer or to take any other step, after the expiry of that period. By this route, the mortgagee at last secures himself a reasonable period in which to act. A mortgagor who, by putting a stop on registration, wrongfully obstructs the mortgagee in the exercise of his remedies is liable in damages for any resulting loss.[407]

Priorities: Since, by these rules, a bona fide purchaser of the legal estate **22–89** without notice of a prior equitable mortgage takes in priority to it, it is advisable for the equitable mortgagee to acquire the legal title by having the transfer registered. Priority in time is only displaced if a second equitable assignee takes without notice of the first equity and then becomes registered as the legal owner of the shares.[408] An equitable mortgagee who acquires that mortgage with notice of prior equity and then obtains the legal title does not obtain priority over prior equities and takes subject to them.[409] The relevant time, in respect of notice

---

[403] *Rainford v James, Keith and Blackman Co* [1905] 2 Ch. 147.
[404] *Bradford Banking Co Ltd v Briggs & Co Ltd* (1886) 12 App.Cas. 29, applying *Hopkinson v Rolt* (1861) 9 H.L.Cas 514; *Mackereth v Wigan and Iron Co Ltd* [1916] 2 Ch. 293.
[405] *Reardon v Provincial Bank of Ireland* [1896] 1 I.R. 532.
[406] CPR Pt 73.16 et seq.
[407] *Deverges v Sandeman* [1902] 1 Ch. 579.
[408] *Dodds v Hills* (1865) 2 H. & M. 424.
[409] *Earl of Sheffield v London Joint Stock Bank*, above.

acquired by the later mortgagee, is the time when he gave value for his interest. He is not adversely affected by notice acquired between the time he gave value and the time when he acquired the legal title.[410] This not only protects him against earlier equitable mortgages but against subsequent dealings between a fraudulent mortgagor and an innocent third party. In certain instances, where the circumstances are such that it would have been reasonable for an enquiry to have been made, notice may be imputed.[411] Thus, the non-production of the share certificates should put the third party on notice of a prior interest.[412] However, the court may well uphold the title of the third party if the mortgagor gives him a plausible excuse for not providing the certificates and the company registers the transfer to him. Even where the company's articles of association state that certificates must be produced before transfers are registered, the company is not bound to require their production.[413]

It has been held that a private company's lien arising out of a quasi-loan to a director had priority over a subsequent mortgage of the shares notwithstanding an agreement to postpone payment of the debt.[414]

Delivery of a blank form of transfer and wrongful transfer of shares:

22–90   *Legal mortgage:*   When a mortgagor of shares either transfers the legal title to shares to a mortgagee, or puts into his hands a blank transfer,[415] he enables the mortgagee to represent himself as being the beneficial owner of the shares. His beneficial interest is in the shares as security for the mortgage debt and if he transfers the shares he has the right only to assign the mortgage debt and his interest in the shares as security for it. The mortgagor, however, runs the risk of the mortgagee fraudulently transferring the shares to a third party, for value, without telling the transferee of his limited interest. When the mortgagee has perfected his legal title by registration of the transfer, the mortgagor can protect himself only by giving notice of his equity of redemption to the company as a result of which he may be able to intervene if the mortgagee attempts to make a fraudulent transfer or by entering a stop notice.

22–91   *Equitable mortgage:*   Where the mortgagee is an equitable mortgagee, the rights of the parties will be determined by estoppel and by whether the person to whom the mortgagee transferred the shares is a bona fide purchaser for value without notice. When a mortgagor delivers share certificates and a blank transfer form, he confers on the mortgagee the right to do one of three things, namely to:

(1) complete his own legal title by filling in his name and registering himself as owner;

---

[410] *Ortigosa v Brown, Janson & Co* (1878) 47 L.J. Ch. 168.
[411] *Earl of Sheffield v London Joint Stock Bank*, above.
[412] *France v Clark* (1884) 26 Ch.D. 257; *Fox v Martin* (1895) L.J.Ch. 473.
[413] *Rainford v James, Keith and Blackman Co* [1905] 1 Ch. 296; reversed on the facts [1905] 2 Ch. 147.
[414] *Champagne Perrier-Jouet SA v H.H. Finch Ltd* [1982] 1 W.L.R. 1359.
[415] See para.22–85.

(2) sell the shares as mortgagee and fill in the name of the purchaser, having first given due notice to the mortgagor;

(3) assign the mortgage.

Even though the mortgagor has placed the indicia of title in the mortgagee's hands, he is not estopped from denying the mortgagee's right to deal with the shares in any other way.

In *France v Clark*[416] F deposited share certificates with C, to secure a loan of £150, and also executed a blank transfer form. C then deposited both the certificates and transfer form with Q to secure his own debt to Q of £250. C died insolvent and Q then filled in his own name as transferee, sending on the transfer for registration. F gave notice to both the company and Q that he denied the validity of the transfer and it was not clear whether that notice was given before or after the registration in the name of C.

The Court of Appeal held that a transferee who takes a blank transfer and fills up the blanks in his own favour is not entitled to be treated as a bona fide purchaser for value without notice: and if he makes no inquiry he can take only the right that the mortgagee received from the mortgagor. Consequently, it was irrelevant whether the registration took place before or after the notice, as registration would give effect only to a prior valid transfer, but would not validate a document which, as between the mortgagee and his transferee, was of no effect. It was further held that the mortgagee had no authority to fill up the form for purposes foreign to the original contract, and thus Q had no title against F except as security for the £150 which F owed C. It would have been otherwise had the facts been such as to indicate that C had a general authority to deal with the shares; or if instead of shares they had been negotiable instruments such as bearer securities.

Debts

A mortgage of debts can be effected by a legal or equitable assignment with a proviso for redemption since public policy does not preclude such a mortgage.[417] Such a mortgage should relieve the mortgagee of any liability should the debt prove to be irrecoverable.[418]   **22–92**

Future debts: There cannot be a legal assignment of a future debt; if the same is made and supported by valuable consideration, it is treated as a contract to assign.[419] Such a contract is provable in the mortgagor's bankruptcy and from which the mortgagor is released on discharge.[420] A mortgage of "all the book debts due and owing and which may, during the continuance of the security, become due and owing" to the mortgagor is sufficient to pass the equitable   **22–93**

[416] (1883) 22 Ch.D. 830.
[417] *Linden Gardens Trust Ltd v Lenesta Sludge Disposals Ltd, St Martin's Corp v Sir Robert MacAlpine & Sons Ltd* [1994] 1 A.C. 85, HL.
[418] *Williams v Price* (1824) 1 Sim. & St. 581.
[419] *Holyroyd v Marshall* (1862) 10 H.L. Cas. 191.
[420] *Collyer v Isaacs* (1881) 19 Ch.D. 342; *Wilmot v Alton* [1897] 1 Q.B. 17; *Bank of Scotland v Maclead* [1914] A.C. 411; *Re Collins* [1925] Ch. 556.

interest in the book debts incurred after the assignment, whether in the business carried on by the mortgagor at the date of the assignment or in any other business.[421] Unless registered under the Bills of Sale Act 1878, such a mortgage of future debts by a person engaged in business is void as against the mortgagor's trustee in bankruptcy where the debt has not been paid before the presentation of the petition.[422]

22-94   A mortgage of an expectancy or a future thing in action, such as a beneficiary's interest under a discretionary trust or an expectancy under a will is unenforceable if supported by consideration, purely voluntary.[423] If supported by consideration, the mortgage operates as a contract to assign the specified property when it falls into the mortgagor's possession and passes an interest which will attach when the property is acquired.[424] Until that acquisition there was only a liability on the contract, provable in any bankruptcy.[425] The bankruptcy of the mortgagor, having effected a mortgage of an expectant share in the estate of a living person, has no bearing; such a mortgage operates as a good equitable charge and does not impose a mere personal liability on the mortgagor to charge the share upon it vesting in him.[426]

22-95   **Notice to the debtor:**   Until notice is given to the debtor, the mortgage remains equitable[427] although since notice to a body of trade debtors can have adverse commercial consequences on the mortgagor, such mortgages often contain provisions that notice will not be given unless the mortgagor is in default. Provision is often made for the mortgagee to collect the debts as the mortgagor's agent. In the absence of notice, payment by the debtor to the mortgagor will be a good release for the debtor as against the mortgagee.[428]

22-96   **Priority:**   The priority of such mortgages is governed by the date of receipt by the debtor of notice of the mortgages.[429]

Copyright

22-97   Copyright is transmissible by assignment, by testamentary disposition or by operation of law as personal or moveable property.[430] Accordingly, any original literary, dramatic, musical or artist work, any sound recordings, films, broadcasts and the typographical arrangement of published edition[431] may be mortgaged.

    An assignment or other transmission of a copyright may be total so that all of the rights are covered by the definition of the right to have been assigned for the

---

[421] *Tailby v Official Receiver* (1888) 13 App.Cas. 523. Sed quaere following *National Westminster Bank Plc v Spectrum Plus Ltd* [2005] 2 AC 680. See paras 23–24 et seq. below.
[422] Insolvency Act 1986 s.344. See also *Re Collins* [1925] Ch. 556.
[423] *Meek v Kettlewell* (1843) 1 Ph. 342
[424] *Raiffeisen Zentralbank Osterreich AG v Five Star Trading LLC* [2001] QB 825, [81].
[425] *Bank of Scotland v MacLeod* [1914] AC 311; *Re Collins* [1925] Ch. 556.
[426] *Re Lind, Industrial Finance Syndicate v Lind* [1915] 2 Ch. 345.
[427] Law of Property Act 1925 s.136(1).
[428] *Stocks v Dobson* (1853) 4 De G.M. & G. 11.
[429] See paras 22–52 et seq.
[430] Copyright, Designs and Patents Act 1988 s.90(1).
[431] CDPA 1988 s.1(1).

whole duration of the right, or may be partial, that is limited so as to apply to one or more but not all of the things a copyright owner has the exclusive right to do or to part but not the whole of the period for which the copyright is to subsist.[432]

Formality: An assignment of a copyright is not effective unless it is in writing   **22–98** and signed by or on behalf of the assignor. However, an equitable or informal mortgage of copyright can be created both by way of express agreement or by implication.[433]

Whereby, under agreement made in relation to future copyright and signed by or on behalf of the prospective owner of the copyright, the prospective owner purports to assign the future copyright (wholly or partially) to another person, then if, on the copyright coming into existence the assignee or other person claiming under him would be entitled as against all other persons to require the copyright to be vested in him, the copyright shall vest in the assignee or his successor in title.[434]

Patents

Any patent or application for a patent is personal property (without being a thing   **22–99** in action) and may be transferred, created or granted under s.30(1) of the Patents Act 1977. Any assignment or mortgage of a patent or any application for a patent or any right in a patent or any such application is void unless it is in writing and signed by or on behalf of the assignor or mortgagor.[435] Section 33 of the Patents Act 1977 requires a mortgage of a patent to be registered if it is to be effective against a person who later acquires the patent or an interest in the patent but it does not have knowledge of the unregistered mortgage or charge.

Trademarks

A registered trademark is transmissible by assignment, testamentary disposition   **22–100** or operation of law in the same way as other personal or moveable property.[436] An assignment or other transmission of a registered trademark may be absolute or partial, in the same way as copyright.[437] An assignment of a registered trademark or an assent relating to a registered trademark is not effective unless it is in signed writing by or on behalf of the assignor.[438] Anyone who becomes entitled by way of assignment to a registered trademark must apply for the registration of title under the Trademarks Act 1994.[439]

---

[432] CDPA 1988 s.90(2).
[433] *Performing Right Society Ltd v London Theatre of Varieties Ltd* [1924] A.C. 1 HL; *Western Front Ltd v Vestron Inc* [1987] FSR 66.
[434] CDPA 1988 s.9(1).
[435] Patents Act 1977 s.30(6).
[436] Trademarks Act 1994 s.24(1).
[437] See para.22–97 above.
[438] Trademarks Act 1994 s.24(3).
[439] ibid., s.25(2).

CHAPTER 23

DEBENTURES

NATURE OF A DEBENTURE

Common Law

At common law, there is no precise definition of what constitutes "a debenture".[1]   **23–01**
Chitty J. stated that "a debenture means a document which either creates a debt
or acknowledges it, and any document which fulfils either of these conditions is
a 'debenture'".[2] Thus, in its simplest form, a debenture is an acknowledgement
of debt[3] and apart from the statutory definition considered below, the phrase is
not a technical one.[4]

In the commercial context, the phrase is used to mean an instrument issued by
a company and either acknowledges certain indebtedness or provides for the
repayment of a specified sum on a particular date. Often a debenture is issued in
relation to group companies by a parent or sibling company.

A debenture is a single indivisible instrument. Debenture stock, on the other   **23–02**
hand, if issued by a company, can (unless the articles of the association provide
to the contrary) be transferred in such amounts as the transferor wishes. Debenture stock is thus more flexible and more likely to be held by trustees under a
deed.[5] Convertible debentures are a hybrid, being a mix of debentures (as
undertook above) and shares, containing an option entitling the holder to convert
the debt into ordinary or preference shares of the company at an agreed rate of
exchange.[6] Convertible debentures may, in the meantime, be secured according
to their terms.

The usual reason for issuing a debenture is to secure a loan, most frequently
taken by a company but sometimes by an unincorporated association[7] and, in
such circumstances, it will contain a charge on the borrower's property, thereby
becoming a mortgage debenture (or mortgage debenture stock).[8] However, an

---

[1] See *The British India Steam Navigation Co v IRC* (1881) L.R. 7 Q.B.D. 165 at 168 and 172; *Levy
v Abercorris Slate and Slab Co* (1887) L.R. 37 Ch.D. 260 at 264; *Knightsbridge Estates Trust Limited
v Byre* [1940] A.C. 613 at 621; *NV Slavenburg's Bank v Intercontinental Limited* [1980] 1 All E.R.
955 at 976.

[2] *Levy v Abercorris Slate and Slab Co,* above.

[3] *Edmonds v Blaina Furnaces Co* (1887) L.R. 36 Ch.D. 215; *Lemon v Austin Friars Investment
Trust Ltd* [1926] Ch. 1.

[4] Chitty J. denied that it was a term of art in *Levy v Abercorris Slate and Slab Co,* above.

[5] See para.23–12, below.

[6] Not lower than par—Companies Act 2006 s.580 precludes allotment at a discount.

[7] *Wylie v Carlyon* [1922] 1 Ch. 51.

[8] Unsecured debenture stock is often described as "loan stock" or (if short-term) "loan notes".

ordinary mortgage of freehold property is not a debenture[9] although a floating charge over such security apparently is. A memorandum of the deposit of title deeds as security for borrowings has been held not to be a debenture since it contains no acknowledgement of the debt or a covenant to pay.[10] Where the borrower is a company, the debenture will normally contain a fixed charge on the company's land and a floating charge on its other assets.

Statutory meaning of "debenture"

23–03 Section 738 of the Companies Act 2006[11] defines "debenture" as including "debenture stocks, bonds and any other securities of a company, whether constituting a charge on the assets of the company or not". Accordingly, the statutory definition is broader than the common law definition since it would include a mortgage issued to a single mortgagee.

23–04 Whether a borrowing or a particular document relating to any borrowing by a company constitutes a "debenture" is important since a number of provisions within the Companies Act 2006 relate to debentures.[12] To that end, it is worth noting that under s.739 of the Companies Act 2006, a "debenture" is not invalid by reason that the debenture is made irredeemable or redeemable only upon the happening of a contingency (however remote) or the expiration of a period (however long) "any rule of equity notwithstanding". If one substitutes "mortgage" (which is within the definition) for "debenture" in that section, one can see that the scope for challenging a corporate mortgagor's mortgage on the grounds of a clog on the equity of redemption is thus curtailed insofar as the clog concerns the date of maturity.

23–05 By reason of s.17 of the Bills of Sale Act (1878) Amendment Act 1882, a debenture when issued by a company is also exempt from compliance with the formal registration requirements under the Bills of Sales Acts, which do not apply to companies.[13]

POWER AND AUTHORITY

The company's power to borrow

23–06 Much of the earlier English common law concerned the company's power to borrow. A transaction that exceeded the company's borrowing powers as set out

---

[9] *Knightsbridge Estates Trust Ltd* above, although it can and is a debenture within the statutory definition provided by the Companies Act 2006 s.438—see para.20–03, below.

[10] *Topham v Greenside Glazed Firebrick Co* (1887) L.R. 37 Ch.D. 281.

[11] Replicating the definition in Companies Act 1985 s.744.

[12] In particular ss.423–425 (persons entitled to receive copies of accounts and reports); ss.431, 432 (right to demand copies of accounts and reports); s.739 (perpetual debentures); s.740 (enforcement of contract to subscribe the debentures); s.743 (register of debenture holders); ss.744, 746, 748 and 749 (right to inspect register); s.750 (liability of trustees of debentures); s.752 (power to reissue redeemed debentures—as to which see *Palmer's Company Law* (Sweet & Maxwell, looseleaf), para.13.036); ss.769, 776–778, 782 (a duty of a company as to issue of certificates); and, perhaps most importantly, ss.860–863 which require registration of certain charges, both fixed and floating.

[13] *NV Slavenburg's Bank v Intercontinental Natural Resources* [1980] 1 W.L.R. 1076 (Lloyd J.).

in its memorandum of association was void.[14] Since individuals dealing with a company had constructive notice of its borrowing powers, they could in those circumstances find themselves without contractual rights against the company and left reliant upon their proprietary and restitutionary remedies. This area has long been the subject of statutory intervention, with the current position—namely that a company's capacity to borrow is not to be called into question as a result of anything in its constitution[15]—being reflective of the pre-existing law.[16]

The director's power to borrow

The company's power to borrow is, of course, distinct from the question whether **23–07** the agents of the company have themselves authority to exercise its power to borrow. In order for a binding loan agreement to be entered into, its directors (or those acting on behalf of the company) must have actual or apparent authority to bind it. The modern practice is for the articles of association to permit the directors to exercise all the powers of the company, subject to the provisions of the Companies Act 2006 and its memorandum and articles of association.[17] Moreover, while the directors' authority to borrow is distinct from the capacity of the company, they will inevitably lack actual authority to do something that the company's constitution does not permit them so to do. With regard to those dealing in good faith with corporate borrowers, it should be noted that the power of directors to bind the company or to authorise others to do so is deemed to be free of any limitation under the company's constitution.[18] Where the directors have failed to comply with the constitutional obligations upon them, those advancing moneys in good faith are protected by the rule in *Royal British Bank v Turquand*.[19] In such circumstances the company is bound.

As against directors who have breached their warranty of authority, these **23–08** changes to the ultra vires rule and the doctrine of constructive notice make no difference.[20] Nor does it make any difference as to their liability if they were unaware that they were exceeding their powers.[21]

The power to give security

Even though the company's memorandum of association will commonly contain **23–09** an express power for it to grant security in addition to its power to borrow, the

---

[14] But see *Rolled Steel Products (Holdings) Ltd v British Steel Corp* [1986] Ch. 246; *Halifax Building Society v Chamberlain Martin & Spurgeon* [1994] 2 B.C.L.C. 540.

[15] Companies Act 2006 s.39(1).

[16] See, e.g. the Companies Act 1985 ss.35, 35A and 35B.

[17] Companies Act 1985, Table A (SI 1985/805), reg.70; Companies (Model Articles) Regulations 2008 (SI 2008/3229 Sch.1 (Private Companies limited by shares), reg.3; Sch.2 (Private Companies limited by guarantee), reg.3; Sch.3 (Public Companies), reg.3. Each Schedule allows a special resolution directing the directors to take or refrain from taking specified action(s): reg.4.

[18] Companies Act 2006 s.40(1) re-enacting Companies Act 1985 s.35A(1).

[19] (1856) 6 E.& B. 327.

[20] *Collen v Wright* (1857) 7 El. & Bl. 301.

[21] *Weeks v Propert* (1873) L.R. 8 C.P. 427.

absence of such an express power will not prevent the company giving security; that power is implicit with the power to borrow[22] (albeit articles may expressly authorise the directors to do the same).

FORM AND ISSUE OF DEBENTURES

23-10   As with a mortgage, it is substance, not form, that determines the nature of the document. Since any document in writing, except a bank note, containing a promise to pay, is a promissory note, the distinction between debentures and promissory notes is not clear and the nature of the document may have to be decided on the basis of inferences from surrounding circumstances.[23]

Form

23-11   It is not necessary for a debenture to be issued under the company's seal (depending on its subject matter, a debenture executed under hand would suffice), though such a form of execution was once usual. It is not clear whether the holders of a debenture issued under seal have the powers of sale of a mortgagee by deed under the Law of Property Act 1925 s.101. In *Blaker v Herts and Essex Waterworks Co*,[24] it was held that they did not. However all the cases which follow that decision deal with the right to sell where the property of the company has been acquired under statutory powers for public purposes. If the debenture contains a legal mortgage of land, it must be by deed[25] which itself can be executed under seal or in accordance with the formalities contained in ss.44 to 46 of the Companies Act 2006.

A debenture may be issued to a named individual (by whom it may be transferred—see below) in which case it is payable to the registered holder, or to bearer, or to registered holder with interest coupons payable to bearer, or to bearer but with power for the bearer to have them placed on a register and to have them withdrawn.[26] When a debenture is made payable to its bearer, interest coupons are attached. The principal is payable on presentation of the debenture and the interest on delivery of the coupons. Where it is payable to the registered holder, only he can receive the principal or interest unless the debenture is issued with coupons payable to bearer.

Trust deeds

23-12   The form in which debentures are issued is affected by commercial considerations which dictate (particularly in case of large scale borrowing from a number of individuals or the general public) that the security is vested in trustees for the

---

[22] See *Palmer's Company Law* (Sweet & Maxwell, looseleaf), para.13.027.
[23] *NV Slavenburg's Bank v Intercontinental Natural Resources* [1980] 1 W.L.R. 1076 (Lloyd J.).
[24] (1889) L.R. 41 Ch.D. 399.
[25] Law of Property Act 1925 ss. 85, 86.
[26] See *Palmer's Company Law* (Sweet & Maxwell, looseleaf), paras 13.066 et seq.

debenture holders, rather than in the debenture holders themselves save where the loan is short term or from a bank, where a declaration of trust is often dispensed with.

The debenture trustee is often a trust corporation. The trustees are under an express duty to protect the interests of the debenture holders[27] and the vesting of the security in them greatly simplifies any common action on the part of the debenture holders, particularly the realisation of the security. The trust deed empowers the trustees to appoint a receiver and manager or to enter and realise the security, in the event of the debenture becoming enforceable. Typically, it will contain a covenant for the repayment of the principal on a fixed date, or on the earlier occurrence of certain events (default in payment; winding up, etc.) and to pay interest meanwhile at a specified rate. It will impose a specific charge on the company's realty and a floating charge over all the company's other assets.

The deed will also regulate how the beneficiaries behind the trust can, in certain circumstances, require the trustees to sell the mortgaged property or amend the beneficiaries' rights or the rights of a certain class of those beneficiaries. Usually a large majority is required in order for these rights to be exercised. The beneficiaries may, when casting their votes do so entirely in their own interests provided the whole scheme is fair[28]; secret agreements to acquire the majority of votes are offensive.[29] Unless the deed contains a "majority clause", the sanction of the court will be necessary under s.899 of the Companies Act 2006.

Two aspects merit specific mention:

Remuneration: It will also provide for the remuneration of the trustees, who **23–13** should not have any interest which conflicts with their duties as trustees; hence a debenture trustee should not be a shareholder. The remuneration is not payable in priority to the claims of stockholders, unless the trust deed expressly so provides[30] (which it usually does).

Liability: By s.750(1) of the Companies Act 2006, any provision contained: **23–14**

(1) in a trust deed for securing an issue of debentures;
(2) in any contract with the holder of debentures secured by a trust deed;

not in force on July 1, 1948,[31] is void in so far as it would have the effect of exempting a trustee of the deed from, or indemnifying him against, liability for breach of trust where he fails to show the degree of care and diligence required

---

[27] And must stand up to the company—*Concord Trust v Law Debenture Trust Corp Plc* [2006] 1 B.C.L.C. 616.
[28] *Goodfellow v Nelson Line Ltd* [1912] 2 Ch. 324.
[29] *British America Nickel Corporation v O'Brien* [1927] A.C. 369.
[30] *Hodgson v Accles* (1902) 51 W.R. 57.
[31] See Companies Act 2006 s.751.

of him as a trustee, having regard to the provisions of the trust deed conferring on him any powers, authorities or discretions.

Section 750(2) permits a release in certain circumstances after the event. A debenture trustee may, however, be protected by s.61 of the Trustee Act 1925.

Common terms

23–15 A debenture usually contains a covenant by the company to pay a specified sum, at some specified place, to the registered holder or to a person named. The covenant also provides that payment should be made on a specified date or on the earlier occurrence of certain events, including:

(1) default in payment of interest;

(2) making of an effective order or the passing of a resolution for the winding up of the company or some other insolvency event.

It was also usual to provide for the appointment of a receiver in the event of either occurrence; following the Enterprise Act 2002 and the insertion of Sch.B1 to the Insolvency Act 1986, the debenture will provide for the appointment of an administrator.

A debenture need not, but usually does, embody a charge. Sometimes there is a fixed charge on the company's land, and commonly there is a floating charge on the company's undertaking and all its property, present or future. If a certain class of assets is excepted, the exception applies to those assets from time to time, not merely those in existence at the date of the debenture.[32] All debentures to secure bank and other institutional lending are expressed to be payable on demand. There is sometimes a side letter which restricts the lender from making a demand except in specified circumstances.

Although it can be a single instrument, it is often one of a series. If that is so, it will be stated in the conditions endorsed thereon or annexed thereto, which may also state that all debentures in a series are to rank pari passu[33] as a charge of a specified priority.

Conditions also regulate the holding of meetings of debenture-holders and the validity of resolutions passed so as to bind a dissentient minority.[34] The power to pass resolutions affecting minority rights must be exercised by the majority for the benefit of the class as a whole.

Other common provisions may regulate the effect of set-off and the company's obligation (usually excluded) to enter notice of any trust in the register of debentures (if kept).[35]

---

[32] *Imperial Paper Mills of Canada v Quebec Bank* (1913) 83 L.J.P.C. 67.

[33] *Re Mersey Railwaly Co* [1895] 2 Ch. 287.

[34] *British American Nickel Corporation Ltd v O'Brien* [1927] A.C. 369.

[35] See *Palmer's Company Law* (Sweet & Maxwell, looseleaf), paras 13.073 et seq.

Issue

Issue at a discount

Subject to any provision to the contrary in the company's articles or its memoran-   **23–16**
dum of association, debentures may be issued at a discount.[36] The statutory
provisions[37] which preclude the issue of shares at a discount have no application
to debentures or debenture stock per se. However, the issue of discounted
debentures or debenture stock cannot be used as an alternative method to
circumvent the provisions precluding the issue of shares at a discount[38] by, for
example, permitting the discounted debenture to be converted into shares at
par.

Agreements to issue

Where moneys are advanced to a company upon terms that the company will   **23–17**
issue debentures securing the advance on the undertaking of the company or
upon any specified property of the company, an equitable charge is created.[39]
However, an equitable charge must be registered pursuant to s.860 of the
Companies Act 2006[40] and a failure to comply with the requirements for timeous
registration would have the consequences prescribed by Companies Act 2006
s.874, namely it would be avoided as against the liquidators, administrators and
creditors of the company.[41]

Specific performance

A contract with a company to take up and pay for debentures of the company   **23–18**
may be enforced by an order for specific performance.[42] This right is lost if the
company has forfeited the debentures in question.[43] Furthermore the company is
unable to recover moneys unpaid prior to forfeiture since the same do not
constitute a debt.[44]

Irregular issues

An irregular issue of debentures is capable of being ratified and, in any event,   **23–19**
debentures so issued may be enforced as agreement to issue debentures.[45]

---

[36] *Re Anglo-Danubian Steam Navigation and Colliery Co* (1875) L.R. 20 Eq. 339.
[37] Companies Act 2006 s.580.
[38] *Mosely v Koffyfontein Mines Ltd* [1904] 2 Ch. 108.
[39] *Levy v Abercorris Slate Co* (1887) L.R. 37 Ch.D. 260 at 265; *Tailby v Official Receiver* (1888)
L.R. 13 App. Cas. 523.
[40] As to registration, see para.23–44, below.
[41] See para.23–49, below.
[42] Companies Act 2006 s.740.
[43] *Kuala Pahi Estate v Mobury* (1941) 111 L.T.1072. On forfeiture, the company cannot recover
calls made before forfeiture under s.740—ibid.—nor do moneys due for unpaid instalments on
forfeiture constitute a debt: *South African Territories v Wallington* [1988] A.C. 309 at 315, 316.
[44] *South African Territories v Wallington* [1898] A.C. 309 at 315.
[45] *Re Fireproof Doors* [1916] 2 Ch. 142; cf. *Re Anchor Line (Henderson Brothers) Ltd* [1937] Ch.
483.

Register of debentures

23–20   There is no obligation on a company to keep a register of debenture holders but in the event that it elects so to do, ss.743–745 of the Companies Act 2006 impose certain obligations upon the company. The register must be kept at its registered office or such other place as the Secretary of State may permit under s.1136. Every registered debenture holder and shareholder in the company is entitled to inspect the register of debentures without charge and to take a copy on payment of a fee.[46] Any other person has the right of inspection and the right to acquire a copy but must pay a fee for doing so in both instances.[47] The register may be kept in any form which is capable of reproduction in legible format.

TRANSFER OF DEBENTURES

Form and effect of transfer

23–21   A bearer debenture is a negotiable instrument transferable by delivery[48] and a holder in due course obtains title to it free from equities and from defects in the title of the transferor. Thus it has been held that a holder in due course may demand payment of the principal secured by a bearer debenture which was stolen, or obtained by fraud, or for which the consideration has totally or partially failed.[49] A debenture to a registered holder is transferable in the manner specified therein, subject to the provisions of s.770 of the Companies Act 2006. Section 770(1) states that:

> "A company may not register a transfer of shares in or debentures of the company unless (a) a proper instrument of transfer has been delivered to it, or (b) the transfer is (i) an exempt transfer within the Stock Transfer Act 1982 or (ii) is in accordance with regulations made under Chapter 2 of [Pt I of the Companies Act 2006]."

This applies notwithstanding anything in the company's articles.[50] Thus, it is necessary for the transfer to be effected in writing and, in the case of fully paid registered debentures, the form prescribed by the Stock Transfer Act 1963[51] may be used. The transfer is taken or sent to the office of the company in order that the name of the transferee may be entered into the company's register of members.[52] If a company refuses to register a transfer, it must within two months after the date on which the transfer was lodged with it, send to the transferee

---

[46] Companies Act 2006 s.744; Companies (Company Records) Regulations 2008 (SI 2008/3006).

[47] ibid., s.744(1)(B).

[48] *Edelstein v Schuler & Co* [1902] 2 K.B. 144.

[49] *Bechuanaland Exploration Co v London Trading Bank* [1898] 2 Q.B. 658.

[50] Companies Act 2006 s.770(1). But not if the transfer is via any approved system such as CREST: Uncertified Securities Regulations (No.2) 2001 (SI 2001/3755), reg.51, Sch.7 para.8.

[51] Stock Transfer (Addition and Substitution of Forms) Order 1996 (SI 1996/1571), as amended by SI 2001/3755.

[52] Companies Act 2006 s.772.

notice of its refusal.[53] Section 775 of the Companies Act 2006 (certification of transfers) and s.776 (company's duty to issue certificates) apply.

After notice to the company of the transfer of a registered debenture, the transferee can sue in his own name.

Since a debenture which creates a floating charge over the company's land gives rise to an interest in that land,[54] a contract for the transfer of such an interest must comply with s.2 of the Law of Property (Miscellaneous Provisions) Act 1989 and be in writing, duly signed/exchanged and containing all the terms agreed. In relation to bearer debentures secured on land, where a contract for the disposition of them fails to comply with the 1989 Act, the delivery alone of the debentures will not remedy the defect. The remedy may be an estoppel against the transferor.[55]

Fraudulent transfers

Where a transfer is forged and registered by the company, the company may incur a liability since the registration will not defeat the title of the true owner, who retains a right to require the company to restore his name to the register. The company may, if it discovers that the transfer is a forgery, remove the name of the transferee from the register since no estoppel arises by reason of that registration.[56] However, if the company has issued a certificate to the transferee and a bona fide third party has acted in reliance thereon, the company may be liable in damages to the transferor or third party.[57]

23–22

In the event that the transfer is forged and the transfer effected by the company, the company may not be without remedy itself. A person who procures his registration by the production of a forged instrument of transfer is bound to indemnify the company from its liability to the victim of the transaction even though he acted in good faith.[58] This principle is not limited to a person acting on his own behalf; where a firm of stockbrokers innocently presented a forged transfer for registration, they were held liable to indemnify the company.[59] In order to minimise the danger attendant on the registration of transfers, some companies have adopted the practice of writing to the transferor upon receipt of the deposit of a transfer informing him of that fact and stating that it will be registered unless, by return of post or within a specified period, he objects. While this course will not relieve a company of its obligation to ascertain the authenticity of any deposited transfer it does, in practice, operate as an effective safeguard.

---

[53] ibid., s.771(1).

[54] *Driver v Broad* [1963] 1 Q.B. 744.

[55] *Davis v Bank of England* (1824) 2 Bing. 393; *Barton v L. & N.W. Railway Co* (1888) L.R. 38 Ch.D. 144 at 149.

[56] *Simm v Anglo-American Co* [1879] 5 Q.B.D. 188 at 214.

[57] *Bloomenthal v Ford* [1897] A.C. 156.

[58] *Sheffield Corporation v Barclay* [1905] A.C. 392; *Welsh v Bank of England* [1955] Ch. 508.

[59] *Yeung v Hong Kong & Shanghai Banking Corporation* [1980] 2 All E.R. 599.

THE NATURE OF THE SECURITY: FIXED AND FLOATING CHARGES

Fixed charges

23-23   A debenture which simply creates a specific charge over the property of the company (whether stock in trade or realty) has the same effect as an ordinary mortgage, being immediately effective and binding on the mortgaged property in the hands of any third party taking it from the company. There are three reasons commercially to prefer fixed charges wherever possible. The first is to secure the priority of the chargee against subsequent chargees and mortgagees; a subsequent fixed chargee can take priority over the holder of an earlier floating security while it floats in circumstances where the fixed chargee has no notice of any limitation of the company's powers contained in the floating charge. The second arises out of the statutory provisions that allow a preference to preferential creditors[60] in administrations, administrative receivership and winding-up over the rights of debenture holders with a floating charge to principal or interest. This even extends to unsecured creditors up to a stated financial limit.[61] Thirdly, a fixed chargee will be able to obtain the appointment out of court of an administrator or, in those cases where the procedure remains available after the Enterprise Act 2002, an administrative receiver.

Fixed charges are habitually granted by a company over its fixed and more permanent assets, namely land and interests in land and plant and machinery not otherwise being disposed of in the ordinary course of business.[62] The assets must be unambiguously described in the debenture and be subject to real control by the chargee[63]; from a practical perspective, it is therefore difficult to see how a fixed charge could be taken over a company's circulating capital such as its book debts and stock in trade. These are the subject matter of floating charges, in order to permit the company to dispose of the property in the ordinary course of its business without consulting the holders of the charge until it crystallises and becomes a fixed charge.

Fixed or floating: characteristics and categorisation

23-24   It would be an over simplification to say that a fixed charge cannot be created over assets of a revolving nature such as book debts; but it is fair to say that recent developments before the Privy Council and in the House of Lords have led to a narrowing of the scope of fixed charges.[64] Notwithstanding the decision in *Agnew*, there remains theoretical scope for taking a fixed charge over book debts, though whether the need for sufficient control over the asset in order to constitute

---

[60] See Insolvency Act 1986 ss.40 and 175 and para.65(2) of Sch.B1; Companies Act 2006 s.754.

[61] See Insolvency Act 1986 s.176A.

[62] A charge over machinery to be disposed of in the ordinary course of business would be a floating charge: *Re Geam Cube Products* [2006] B.C.C. 615.

[63] *Agnew v Commissioner of Inland Revenue* [2001] 2 A.C. 710 (JCPC): *Re Spectrum Plus Ltd* [2005] 2 A.C. 680 (HL).

[64] ibid.

the charge a fixed charge can be exercised practically (and thus achieve the desired result) is perhaps open to speculation.

The determination of whether a charge creates a fixed or floating charge was considered by Lord Millett in *Agnew v Commissioner of Inland Revenue*.[65] Lord Millett adopted a two-stage process:

> "At the first stage [the court] must construe the instrument and seek to gather the intentions of the parties from the language they have used. But the object of this stage of the process is not to discover whether the parties intended to create a fixed or a floating charge. It is to ascertain the nature of the rights and obligations which the parties intended to grant each other in respect of the charges assets. Once these have been ascertained, the court can then embark on the second stage process, which is one of categorisation. This is a matter of law. It does not depend on the intention of the parties. If their intention, properly gathered from the language of the instrument, is to grant the company rights in respect of the charged assets which are inconsistent with the nature of a fixed charge, then the charge cannot be a fixed charge however they may have chosen to describe it . . . [I]n construing a debenture to see whether it creates a fixed or floating charge the only intention which is relevant is the intention that the company should be free to deal with the charged assets and withdraw them from the security without the consent of the holder of the charge . . . "

This approach was approved by the Court of Appeal in *Re Spectrum Plus Ltd,*[66] subject to the qualification that the analysis in *Agnew* fails to accommodate the possibility that a charge may be neither fixed nor floating as originally understood, in which case the task of the court was to determine what are its "dominant characteristics" for the purpose of applying insolvency legislation.

Agnew confirmed the decision of the New Zealand Court of Appeal in *Re Brumark Investments Ltd*[67] and held *Re New Bullas Trading Ltd*[68] to have wrongly decided. Thus *Agnew* and the subsequent decision in *Re Spectrum* represent a clear re-statement of the position under English law as to the characteristics and distinctions between fixed and floating charges; earlier authorities must be now read in the light of those cases.[69]

In declaring *Re New Bullas Trading* incorrectly decided, the Privy Council in   **23–25** *Agnew* clearly established that a company's circulating capital can only be the subject of a floating charge, it being illusory to separate a book debt from its monetary proceeds. For a charge to be fixed, there had to be controls which, in the case of book debts, would prevent assignment or factoring and their unrestricted collection and free use of the proceeds. In *Re Spectrum*, the majority held

---

[65] [2001] 2 A.C. 710 (JCPC) at [32], cited in *Arthur D. Little Ltd v Ableco Finance LLC* [2003] Ch. 217, 235 and *Ashborder BV v Green Gas Power Ltd* [2005] 1 B.C.L.C. 263 at [166]. See also *Quicksons (South & West) Ltd v Katz* [2004] EWHC 1638 (Ch) at [116] and *Re Russell Cooke Trust Ltd* [2007] EWHC 1443 (Ch).

[66] *National Westminster Bank v Spectrum Plus Ltd* [2004] Ch. 337, [33]–[34]. The actual decision of the Court of Appeal was reversed by the House of Lords at [2005] 2 A.C. 710.

[67] [2000] 1 B.C.L.C. 353.

[68] [1994] 1 B.C.L.C. 485.

[69] Against this reasoning, the decisions in *Re Atlantic Computer Systems Plc (No.1)* [192] Ch. 505 and *Re Atlantic Medical Ltd* [1992] B.C.C. 653 (which followed it) must be open to serious doubt. In the former case, an assignment "by way of security" on moneys due under certain subleases was held to create a fixed charge; however there was no detailed citation of authority and while *Agnew* and *Spectrum* do not explicitly address the issues considered in *Atlantic Computer Systems*, the reasoning in the latter case must now be viewed as flawed.

that so long as the chargor company had the freedom to draw on the account into which the proceeds of book debts were paid, those book debts could only be the subject of a floating charge. Lord Hope considered that "the company's continued contractual right to draw out sums equivalent to the amounts paid" into its account with the chargee bank was "wholly destructive of the argument that there was a fixed charge over the uncollected proceeds because the account into which the proceeds were to be paid was blocked".[70]

Lord Scott considered that the requirement to pay the proceeds of book debts into a specified account without a restriction on drawing from that account did not give the chargee bank the effect of possession in order to allow the charge to be characterised as a fixed charge, noting that the critical feature of a floating charge was the third characteristic laid down in *Re Yorkshire Woolcombers' Association*,[71] namely that it is contemplated that the company will carry on business in the ordinary way with regard to the assets charged. If a charge possessed that characteristic, Lord Scott considered that it had to be construed as a floating charge and not a fixed charge.[72] This was so even if there was a mechanism enabling the chargee to withdraw the chargor's freedom to collect debts and use them for its business.[73]

It would follow *if* the proceeds of book debt are paid into a genuinely blocked account, then they can be the subject of an appropriately drafted fixed charge. But given the tenor of the speeches in that case,[74] it has been observed that "it would seem that if a chargor is at liberty to draw cheques on that account without the counter-signature of the bank, that the bank is a mandatory having to pay a collecting bank acting on behalf of the payee, without itself being able to counter-demand payment, then this factor of itself ought to be sufficient to render the charge a floating one".[75]

Floating charge

23–26   In *Government Stock Co v Manilla Railway Co*,[76] Lord Macnaughten stated that:

> "A floating security is an equitable charge on the assets for the time being of a going concern. It attaches to the subject charged and the varying conditions in which it happens to be from time to time. It is of the essence of such a charge that it remains dormant until the undertaking charged ceases to be a going concern, or until the person in whose favour the charge is created intervenes. His rights to intervene may

---

[70] [2005] 2 A.C. 680 at [61].

[71] [1903] 2 Ch. 284.

[72] [2005] 2 A.C. 680 at [107].

[73] ibid., [117].

[74] Lord Walker stated that the assets had to be "permanently appropriated" to a charge for it to be fixed: ibid., at [139].

[75] See *Palmer's Company Law* (Sweet & Maxwell, looseleaf), para.13.199, citing Lord Scott in *Spectrum* at [2005] 2 A.C. 680, [119] and Lord Hope in that case at [60]. *Palmer's* goes on to suggest that at the very least, if an account is to be blocked, the chargor's contractual rights to draw cheques without specific permission will have to be withdrawn. The commercial impracticality of such a course is self-evident.

[76] [1897] A.C. 81, 86 (HL).

of course be suspended by agreement. But if there is no agreement for suspension he may exercise his right whenever he pleases after default."

While this description does not take into account the automatic crystallisation provisions now habitually contained in floating charges, it captures their essence. In *Inningworth v Holdsworth*,[77] Lord Macnaughten observed:

> "I should have thought there was not much difficulty in defining what a floating charge is in contrast to what is called a specific charge. A specific charge, I think is one that without more fastens on ascertained and definite property a property capable of being ascertained and defined; a floating charge, on the other hand, is ambulatory and shifting in its nature, hovering over and so to speak floating with the property which it is intended to affect until some event occurs or some act is done which causes it to settle and fasten on the subject of the charge within its reach and grasp."

In *Re Yorkshire Woolcombers' Association*,[78] the Court of Appeal stated that the principle tests to be applied in determining whether a charge was a floating charge were as follows:

(1) Is it a charge upon all of a certain class of assets, present and future?
(2) Will those assets change in the ordinary course of the business of the company?
(3) Is it contemplated that the company will carry on business in the ordinary way with regard to the assets charged?

This is not, of course, a statutory definition but rather a "helpful filter" in determining the characteristics of any particular charge.[79]

Once a specified event occurs—the nature of which is usually set out exhaustively in the relevant documentation—the floating charge becomes fixed or "crystallises".[80] Thereafter, the charge has the characteristics of a fixed charge and the company loses its authority to deal with those assets beneficially in the ordinary course of business.[81] Pending crystallisation:

> "A floating security is not a future security; it is a present security which presently affects all the assets of the company expressed to be included in it. On the other hand, it is not a specific security; the holder cannot affirm that the assets are specifically mortgaged to him. The assets are mortgaged in such a way that the mortgagor can deal with them without the concurrence of the mortgagee. A floating security is not a specific mortgage of the assets, plus a licence to the mortgagor to dispose of them in the ordinary course of his business, but is a floating mortgage applied to every asset comprised in the mortgage, but not specifically affecting any asset until some event occurs or some act on the part of the mortgagee is done which causes it to crystallise into a fixed security."[82]

---

[77] [1904] A.C. 355, 358—see also *Re Brightlife Ltd* [1987] Ch. 200 and *Agnew*, above.
[78] *Re Yorkshire Woolcoombers' Association* [1903] 2 Ch. 284; affirmed *sub nom. Illingworth v Holdsworth* [1904] A.C. 355.
[79] *Re Atlantic Medical* [1992] B.C.C. 653.
[80] *Re Griffin Hotel Co Ltd* [1941] Ch. 129, 135.
[81] *Evans v Rival Granite Quarries Ltd* [1910] 2 K.B. 979 (CA).
[82] ibid., at 999.

Thus, an effective floating charge on the property (both present and future) for the company can be created by any appropriate form of words, a charge on its "undertaking" being the most usual. A charge upon the property now belonging or thereafter acquired by the company creates a floating charge[83] and where a company issues bonds binding itself and its estate property and effects[84] and binding itself and its real and personal estate[85] a floating charge was created, being a charge over both present and future property. Indeed, any such general charge is strongly indicative of the creation of a floating charge since (as the cases cited demonstrate) the charge contemplates the continuance of the company as a going concern and its corresponding commercial activity would be rendered impossible if the charge were to be construed as a fixed charge and not a floating charge. It does not matter that when such a charge is created, the company has little or no assets or, indeed, is a single asset vehicle.[86]

An effective floating charge can be created over simply part of the assets of a company.[87] Those assets may be a specified class or those in a particular geographical location.[88] Whereas a charge over land would ordinarily be considered to be a fixed charge, where land forms part of the trading stock of the company, commonwealth authority has construed such a charge as a floating charge.[89]

The effect of a floating charge prior to crystallisation

23–27   The company has a licence, power or authority to deal with the disposal of the property charged in the ordinary course of its business.[90]

Precisely what was within the ordinary course of dealing of a company for the purposes of a floating charge was considered by the Court of Appeal in *Ashborder BV v Green Gas Power Ltd.*[91] In that case it was submitted that a transaction was only in "the ordinary course of business" of the chargor if it was part of the common flow of business that it carried on with the transaction arising out of no special or particular situation and that accordingly certain transactions with the charged assets would fall outside the permission afforded by the terms of the floating charge. The court held that the starting point for the interpretation of the words "in the ordinary course of [the company's] business" was the meaning which ordinary business people in the position of the parties to the facility and the debentures would expect to give them against the factual and commercial background in which those documents were made; that the question

---

[83] *Wheatley v Silkston & Haigh Moor Coal Co* (1885) L.R. 29 Ch.D. 715.
[84] *Re Florence Land & Public Works Co, Ex p. Moor* (1878–79) L.R. 10 Ch.D. 530.
[85] *Re Colonial Trusts Corp* (1880) L.R. 15 Ch.D. 465.
[86] *Re Croftbell* [1990] B.C.C. 781.
[87] *Re Colonial Trusts Corp* (1880) L.R. 15 Ch.D. 465.
[88] See *National Provincial Bank v United Electric Theatres Ltd* [1916] 1 Ch. 132.
[89] See *Boanbee Bay Pty Ltd v Equus Financial Services Ltd* (1991) 26 N.S.W.L.R. 284.
[90] *Re Bond Worth Ltd* [1980] Ch. 228; *Re Florence Land & Public Works Co,* above; *Re Standard Manufacturing Co* [1891] 1 Ch. 627; *Re Borax Co* [1901] 1 Ch. 326; *Nelson & Co v Fabor & Co* [1903] 2 K.B. 367; *Cretanor Maritime Co Ltd v Irish Marine Management Ltd* [1978] 1 W.L.R. 966 (CA).
[91] [2005] B.C.C. 634 (Etherton J.).

was one of mixed fact and law to be approached in two stages: (a) to ascertain as a matter of fact whether an objective observer with knowledge of the company, its memorandum of association and its business, would view the transaction has having taken place in the ordinary course of its business, and if so; (b) to consider whether, on the proper interpretation of the document creating the floating charge (applying standard techniques of interpretation), the parties nonetheless did not intend that the transaction should be regarded as being in the ordinary course of the company's business for the purpose of the charge. Subject to any special considerations thus arising, the court held there was no reason why an unprecedented or exceptional transaction could not, in appropriate circumstances, be regarded as "in the ordinary course of [the company's] business". Subject to those special circumstances the mere fact that a transaction would, in a liquidation, be liable to be set aside as a fraudulent or otherwise wrongful preference, did not (of itself) necessarily preclude the transaction from being in the ordinary course of the company's business[92] nor did the mere fact that a transaction was made in breach of a fiduciary duty by one or more of the directors of the company necessarily preclude the transaction from being in the ordinary course of the company's business. Transactions intended to bring to an end a company's business were not transactions in the ordinary course of that business.[93]

Prohibition of prior charges

It is common for a floating charge contractually to prohibit the creation of any mortgage or charge ranking in priority to or with the debenture in question. For such a prohibition to be effective against a subsequent encumbrancer, notice of it must be received by those taking that encumbrance because otherwise they are entitled to proceed on the basis that the company has authority to deal with its assets in the ordinary course of its business.[94] Thus, an equitable mortgage arising from the deposit of title deeds can rank ahead of an earlier floating charge[95] even where it forbids their creation[96]; the assignment of a right to receive insurance moneys can defeat an earlier floating charge containing an undisclosed restrictive clause to the extent of that assignment,[97] and a solicitor's lien can also take priority.[98]   **23–28**

Notice

Lenders will hint at the existence of such prohibitory clauses.[99] It is not thought that this gives rise (of itself) to sufficient (constructive) notice.[100] There is a   **23–29**

[92] Applying *Willmott v London Celluloid Co* (1887) L.R. 34 Ch.D. 147.
[93] Permission to appeal the decision in *Ashborder BV* was dismissed: [2005] EWCA Civ 619.
[94] *English & Scottish Mercantile Investment Co v Brunton* [1892] 2 Q.B. 700; *Re Castell & Brown Ltd* [1898] 1 Ch. 315; *Re Valletort Standard Steam Laundry Co* [1983] 2 Ch. 654; cf. *Wilson v Kelland* [1910] 2 Ch. 306.
[95] *Wheatley v Silkstone & Haigh Moor Coal Co,* above.
[96] *Re Valletort Standard Steam Laundry Co,* above. *Re Castell & Brown Ltd,* above.
[97] *English & Scottish Mercantile Investment Co v Brunton* [1892] 2 Q.B. 700.
[98] *Brunton v Electrical Engineering Corp* [1892] 1 Ch. 434.
[99] *Farrar* (1974) 38 Conv. (N.S.) 315, 325.
[100] *Palmer's Company Law* (Sweet & Maxwell, looseleaf), para.13.199.26.

further argument that constructive notice of the charge itself when taken in conjunction with the common practice of inserting clauses prohibiting the creation of prior charges (or those ranking equal to the debenture in question) and the right under s.877 of the Companies Act 2006 to inspect the instrument of charge can give rise to a rebuttable inference of actual knowledge based upon wilful blindness.[101]

It has been said that actual notice of the charge carries with it deemed notice of the restrictive clauses therein.[102] The point, however, remains undecided, largely because notice of the charge by virtue of a search of the appropriate register will either give some notice of the limitation in the register entry itself of the prospective charge will make appropriate and proper enquiries, in either case thus getting actual notice of the provision in the sense of "notice of such facts as [a purchaser] would have discovered if he had taken proper means to investigate them"[103] and the transaction will proceed appropriately in the light of that knowledge.

CRYSTALLISATION OF THE FLOATING CHARGE

Crystallisation at law

23–30   A floating charge crystallises or becomes fixed in accordance with the terms of the debenture creating it or by operation of law when, for example, the company goes into liquidation, whether that liquidation is for the purpose of reconstruction or otherwise.[104] Common prescribed events of crystallisation include the debenture holder taking possession of the company's goods or appointing a receiver in accordance with the terms of the debenture. Crystallisation operates in order to effect an equitable assignment of the assets to the charge holder. However, unless the debenture holder actually takes the necessary steps in accordance with the

---

[101] See *Farrer* (1974) 38 Conv. (N.S.) 315, citing *English & Scottish Mercantile Investment Co v Brunton* [1892] 2 Q.B. 700, 707–708. For the contrary view, see *Gough on Company Charges* (2nd edn, 1996) p.226, citing *Re Standard Rotary Machine Co* (1906) 95 L.T. 829. Also *Welsh v Bowmaker (Ireland) Ltd* [1980] I.R. 251, 256 and *Goode, Legal Problems of Credit & Security*, 4th edn, 2008) paras 2–23 et seq.; *Palmer's Company Law* doubts whether the failure to seek, as a matter of course, a copy of the instrument creating the floating charge itself amounts to wilful blindness and doubts that the other factors mentioned make any difference to the question of notice. See also *Williams v Quebrada Railway Co* [1895] 2 Ch. 751, 755: see below.

[102] *Ian Chisholm Textiles v Griffiths* [1994] B.C.C. 96, a decision which sits at odds with the general rejection of constructive notices in commercial matters; *Manchester Trust v Furness* [1895] 2 Q.B. 39; *Greer v Downs Supply Co* [1927] 2 K.B. 28; *Joseph v Lyons* (1884–85) L.R. 15 Q.B.D. 280.

[103] Other authorities worthy of consideration include *Williams v Quebrada Railway Co* [1895] 2 Ch. 751, 755 where (in the context of an application for disclosure) the creation of a later security ranking in priority to a floating charge was equated to "commercial dishonesty of the very worse type; and that it is fraud". Also *Re Real Meat Co Ltd (in receivership)* [1996] B.C.C. 254, 266 where constructive notice was conceded by the chargee.

[104] *Player v Crompton & Co* [1914] 1 Ch. 954. The appointment of a receiver will cause crystallisation (*Re Florence Land & Public Works Co, Ex p. Moor* (1878–79) L.R. 10 Ch.D. 530) as does the cessation of business or the company ceasing to be a going concern: *Re Woodroffes (Musical Instruments) Ltd* [1986] Ch. 366. See also *Hodson v Tea Co* (1880) L.R. 14 Ch.D. 859 and *Wallace v Universal Automatic Machines Co* [1894] 2 Ch. 547.

terms of the debenture to crystallise the charge, the fact that the holder could crystallise the charge if he so wishes does not limit the company's ability to deal with the assets subject to the floating charge[105] and to dispose of them free of any charge in the ordinary course of business.

Automatic crystallisation

For this reason, the modern tendency is for the terms of the debenture to provide   **23–31** for automatic crystallisation without any steps being required of the debenture holder in certain specified events. Such events habitually include the creation of second or subsequent charges. Despite longstanding Commonwealth authority,[106] it was not until relatively recently that the courts within this jurisdiction have accepted that automatic crystallisation clauses are valid.[107] It would seem, with reference to the dicta in those cases, that the efficacy of an automatic crystallisation clause very much depends upon the true construction of its expressed terms.

Cross-claims and set off

A right of set-off which has accrued to the company's debtor prior to the   **23–32** crystallisation of the debenture holder's charge can be raised against any claim made by a receiver appointed under the debenture against that debtor.[108] Where the cross-claim was assigned to the debtor after the crystallisation of the charge, it affords no defence.[109] The usual rules concerning the right to set off in cases of an assignment of a chose in action apply. Similarly, where the defence comprises a claim for damages by reason of the receiver's repudiation of a contract, the debtor cannot set those damages off against the debt.[110]

Priority of Debentures

The priority of debenture holders[111] depends on a number of factors which   **23–33** include:

(1) The true construction of the instrument or instruments creating the charge.

---

[105] *Evans v Rival Granite Quarries* [1910] 2 K.B. 979 at 986.

[106] *Re Manurewa Transport Limited* [1971] N.Z.L.R. 909.

[107] *Re Brightlife Ltd* [1987] Ch. 200; *Re Permanent Houses (Holdings) Ltd* [1988] B.C.L.C. 56; *Griffiths v Yorkshire Bank Plc* [1994] 1 W.L.R. 1427. See generally *Palmer's Company Law* (Sweet & Maxwell, looseleaf), para.13.199.46.

[108] *Rother Ironworks Ltd v Canterbury Precision Engineers Ltd* [1974] Q.B. 1.

[109] *Robbie v Witney Warehouse Co Ltd* [1963] 1 W.L.R. 1324.

[110] *Business Computers Ltd v Anglo-African Leasing Ltd* [1977] 1 W.L.R. 578.

[111] For general principles see *MacMillan Inc v Bishopsgate Investment Trust Plc (No.3)* [1995] 1 W.L.R. 978.

(2) The status of the debenture as part of a series of debentures which may give rise to the presumption of equality.

(3) The nature of the charge created and the order of creation. A legal charge has priority over an equitable charge and, as between equitable charges, the first in time has priority over latter charges.

(4) The registration or non-registration of the charge pursuant to s.870 of the Companies Act 2006.[112] A failure to comply with the registration requirements imposed by that Act renders the charge void as against creditors, administrators and liquidators of the company[113] although it remains good against the company itself and any purchaser from it.[114]

Presumption of equality

23–34 Debentures created as part of the same series are usually expressed to rank pari passu inter se. In the absence of such an express statement, the courts will readily infer equality. In such circumstances, whether the equality is express or implied, an individual debenture holder will not be permitted to obtain an advantage over his co-debenture holders. Thus, any judgment that a debenture holder obtains, inures for the benefit of all the debenture holders of that particular class[115] and any collateral security that he may obtain is held by him on trust for those individuals.[116]

However, where a number of series of debentures creating floating charges are issued, they rank according to the date of issue unless otherwise expressly provided for.[117] Thus, having issued a series of debentures, the company is precluded from issuing a subsequent series of debentures that rank equally with the first series unless the express terms of the first series of debentures expressly or impliedly so provide.[118] If the terms of the first series merely reserves to the company a power to create subsequent mortgages, that will not suffice for this purpose.[119]

Re-issue of redeemed debentures: Companies Act 2006 s.752

23–35 If a company reissues redeemed debentures,[120] the person entitled to the debentures has, and is always deemed to have had, the same priority as if the

---

[112] Formerly Companies Act 1985 s.395.

[113] See para.23–49 below.

[114] See also *Fever Leather Corp v Johnstone & Sons* [1981] Com. L.R. 251.

[115] *Bowen v Brecon Railway* (1867) L.R. Eq. 541.

[116] *Small v Smith* (1884–85) L.R. 10 App. Cas. 119; *Landowners West of England and South Wales Land Drainage and Inclosure Co v Ashford* (1880–81) L.R. 16 Ch.D. 411.

[117] *Gartside v Silkstone Coal Co* (1882) L.R. 21 Ch.D. 762. *Re Boythorpe Colliery Co* [1890] W.N. 28; *Lister v Henry Lister & Son* (1893) 41 W.R. 330.

[118] ibid.

[119] *Re Benjamin Cope & Son* [1914] 1 Ch. 800.

[120] Assuming the instrument does not preclude this.

debentures had never been redeemed.[121] This is subject to provisions to the contrary in the company's articles of association or in any contract entered into by the company or any resolution of the company or any other act of the company manifesting an intention that the redeemed debentures should be cancelled.[122]

Charges of specific property

Where a company creates a charge on specific property, it will rank ahead of any **23–36** subsequent charge which embraces the same property by reason of the principle that where the equities are equal, the first in time shall prevail. A later fixed charge will take priority over a floating charge if the latter has not crystallised and the former is created by the company in the ordinary course of business.

Where a subsequent chargee obtains a legal mortgage, he will obtain priority over the first equitable charge.[123] Where a specific charge is assigned, the rule that the first in time prevails is displaced by the rule in *Dearle v Hall*[124] which provides that the first assignee to give notice to the debtor is accorded priority over prior assignees provided that the assignee giving notice did not have notice of the earlier assignment.[125]

Priority and postponement agreements

There is no reason why a specific chargee cannot acquire or postpone the priority **23–37** of that charge by agreement.[126]

Floating charges

A debenture which imposes a floating charge on property will be postponed to a **23–38** subsequent fixed mortgage created by the company in the ordinary course of its business because the floating charge, being a floating security, will permit the company to create charges in priority to it in the ordinary course of its business. If there is a prohibition against the creation of such a charge, the subsequent specific chargee may obtain priority for various reasons such as the fact that he obtains the legal estate or he has a better equity.[127] The position will be otherwise if the subsequent specific chargee had actual knowledge or notice of the restrictive clause. In such circumstances his charge will be postponed to the prior charge.[128]

[121] Companies Act 2006 s.752(2).
[122] Companies Act 2006 s.752(1).
[123] *Pilcher v Rawlins* (1871–72) L.R. 7 Ch. App. 259.
[124] (1828) 3 Rush 1, criticised in *Ward v Duncombe* [1893] A.C. 369.
[125] *Gorringe v Irwell India Rubberworks* (1886) L.R. 34 Ch.D. 128.
[126] See *Equiticorp Finance Group Ltd v Cheah* [1991] 1 N.Z.L.R. 299, affirmed [1992] 1 A.C. 472 (JCPC); *Bass Breweries v Delaney* [1994] B.C.C. 851; *Banque Financière de la Cité SA v Parc (Battersea) Ltd* [1999] A.C. 221.
[127] *Re Valletort Sanitary Steam Laundry* [1903] 2 Ch. 654.
[128] See para.23–29.

As indicated above, where there are successive floating charges, the first in time will prevail subject to express agreement to the contrary unless they are part of the same issue of debentures. It would seem that where a second floating charge crystallises prior to an earlier floating charge, the second charge will take priority over the first.[129]

Execution creditors

23–39 Prior to crystallisation, an execution creditor is entitled to the proceeds of the sale of assets of the company seized by the sheriff under a writ of fieri facias.[130] By contrast, if the floating charge has crystallised, it is the debenture holder who has the prior right to the assets taken in execution,[131] at least if the crystallising event has occurred before the sheriff sells the assets.[132] It may be the law that the execution creditor is entitled to the proceeds of sale even if the floating charge crystallises prior to the sheriff making payment.[133] The rationale behind execution creditors ranking ahead of a debenture holder prior to crystallisation arises from the proposition that since the company is entitled to deal with assets under the licence or authority afforded by the floating charge prior to its crystallisation, those assets are liable to the normal civil consequences of the company's conduct, which includes execution.

While third party debt orders (formerly garnishee orders) are, in principle, analogous to execution under a writ of fieri facias,[134] if a floating charge over the debt crystallises prior to payment being made to the beneficiary of such an order, there is authority for the view that the debenture holder is entitled to priority over the beneficiary of the third party debt order if the order is only an interim order.[135]

Preferential creditors

23–40 Sections 175 and 386 and Sch.6 to the Insolvency Act 1986 bestow priority on preferential creditors over a debenture holder whose security was, at the time it was created, a floating charge. In addition, the costs and expenses of the winding up also enjoy that priority.[136]

---

[129] *Griffiths v Yorkshire Bank Plc* [1994] 1 W.L.R. 1427; this decision was made without reference to *Re Woodroffes (Musical Instruments) Ltd* [1986] Ch. 366 where it was held that a first floating charge enjoyed priority to a second floating charge which had crystallised.

[130] *Evans v Rival Granite Quarries Ltd* [1910] 2 K.B. 979.

[131] *Davey & Co v Williamson & Sons* [1898] 2 Q.B. 194; *Re Opera* [1891] 2 Ch. 260; *Taunton v Sheriff of Warwickshire* [1895] 2 Ch. 319; *Standard Manufacturing Co* [1891] 1 Ch. 627; *Simultaneous Colour Printing Syndicate v Foweraker* [1901] 1 K.B. 771; *Duck v Tower Galvanising Co* [1901] 2 K.B. 314; *Re London Pressed Hinge Co* [1905] 1 Ch. 576.

[132] *Evans v Rival Granite Quarries*, above; *Taunton v Sheriff of Warwickshire*, above and *Re Standard Manufacturing Co* above.

[133] *Heaton & Dugard Ltd v Cutting Brothers Ltd* [1925] 1 K.B. 655, 657–658.

[134] See *Evans v Rival Granite Quarries Ltd*, above.

[135] *Norton v Yates* [1906] 1 K.B. 112.

[136] This position, thought to have been established by *Re Barleycorn Enterprises Ltd* [1970] Ch. 465, is now set out in the Insolvency Act 1986 s.176 ZA (reversing *Re Layland DAF Ltd* [2004] 2 A.C. 298) with effect from April 6, 2008.

Where a receiver is appointed by debenture holders whose charge was, when created, a floating charge and the company is not in the course of being wound up, its preferential debts are required to be paid out of the assets coming into the hands of the receiver in priority to the debenture holder's claim and any payments so made shall be re-couped by the debenture holder from the assets available for the payment of the company's general creditors.[137] The priority so accorded only applies to those preferential claims that have accrued prior to the crystallisation of the charge.[138]

Unsecured creditors

With effect from September 15, 2003, s.176A of the Insolvency Act 1986[139] **23–41** provides that where a floating charge relates to the property of a company which enters liquidation, administration or has a provisional liquidator or receiver appointed, the liquidator, administrator or receiver must constitute a separate fund from the company's net property for the purpose of unsecured debts and is satisfying precluded from distributing that part to the proprietor of any floating charge except insofar as it exceeds the amount required for the satisfaction of unsecured debts.[140] Those provisions do not apply if the company's net property is less than the prescribed minimum[141] or where the individual considers the cost of making a distribution to the unsecured creditors will be disproportionate to the benefits that they might receive.[142] The obligation does not arise if and to the extent that it is disapplied by any voluntary arrangement in respect of the company or a compromise or arrangement under Pt 26 of the Companies Act 2006.[143] The court may also disapply the provisions of that section by order. Since the "company's net property" from which the fund is created is defined in s.176A(6) as being property which would, but for the provisions of that section, be available for satisfaction of the claims of holders of debentures secured by, or holders of, any floating charge created by the company, the provisions of the Enterprise Act 2002 which provide for a share of company's assets for unsecured creditors *only* apply in relation to those assets which would otherwise have been available to floating chargees; fixed chargees or those have effective retention of title clauses are unaffected.

The mechanics of the constitution of the fund are set out in the relevant statutory instruments.[144]

---

[137] Insolvency Act 1986 s.40.

[138] *Re Christonette International Ltd* [1982] 1 W.L.R. 1245. The section does not apply to fixed charges (*Re Lewis Merthyr Consolidated Collieries Ltd* [1929] 1 Ch. 498) or where there are fixed and floating charges and a receiver is appointed and sells under s.101 of the Law of Property Act 1925 and who has a surplus under s.105 of that Act: *Re G. L. Saunders Ltd* [1986] 1 W.L.R. 215.

[139] Inserted by the Enterprise Act 2002 s.252.

[140] Insolvency Act 1986 s.176A(2).

[141] Currently £10,000: see SI 2003/2097 para.2.

[142] See *Re Hydroserve Ltd* [2008] B.C.C. 175; *Re Courts Plc* [2008] B.C.C. 917; *Re International Sections Ltd* [2009] B.C.C. 574.

[143] Insolvency Act 1986 s.176A(4).

[144] Insolvency Act 1986 (Prescribed Part) Order 2003 (SI 2003/2097).

Company administrators

23–42   During the course of an administration, no creditor may enforce a security except with the consent of the court or of the administrator.[145] This moratorium applies during the pendency of an application to appoint an administrator,[146] who is free to dispose of the property subject to a charge which, at the time of its creation, was a floating charge.[147]

Liens

23–43   If the goods upon which a bailee claims a general lien came into his possession prior to the crystallisation of the charge, a general lien will prevail over that floating charge. Moreover if they have come into his possession after the crystallisation of the charge but pursuant to a contract entered into before the charge crystallised, the lien will still prevail.[148] A lawful possessory lien is also good against the owner or secured creditor even if the bailment is in breach of the agreement if the lien is created by operation of law.[149]

REGISTRATION OF CHARGES

The register of charges

23–44   The question of the registration of company charges is governed by two sets of statutory provisions. The first are those which provide for all charges affecting the property of a particular company to be kept in a register of charges at the company's registered office. These provisions are contained in ss.875–877 of the Companies Act 2006 and are self-explanatory. They require the company to keep, at its registered office, a register of all charges affecting its property (whether fixed or floating charges) together with a brief description of the asset or property charged, the amount of the sum so secured and (unless the same is a bearer-security) the name(s) of the person(s) entitled to the benefit of the charge. This register is open to inspection by members and creditors without charge and by members of the public on the payment of a modest charge.[150] The second, and by far the most important set of provisions, are those contained in ss.860–874 of the Companies Act 2006 and which require registration of certain charges at Companies House.

---

[145] Insolvency Act 1986 Sch.B1 para.43(2).

[146] ibid., para.44.

[147] ibid., para.70 and s.251.

[148] *George Barker (Transport) Ltd v Eynon* [1974] 1 W.L.R. 462.

[149] *Tappenden v Artus* [1964] 2 Q.B. 185. What matters is the lawfulness (or otherwise) of the leaseholder's possession when the lien arises and will involve questions of the bailee's implied or apparent authority to part with possession.

[150] Companies Act 2006 ss.875–877.

Registration pursuant to ss.860–874 of the Companies Act 2006[151]

Section 860 of the Companies Act 2006 provides that: **23–45**

(a) a charge on land or any interest in land (other than a charge for any rent or other periodical sum issuing out of land),

(b) a charge created or evidenced by an instrument which, if executed by an individual, would require registration as a bill of sale,

(c) a charge for the purposes of securing any issue of debentures,

(d) a charge on uncalled share capital of the company,

(e) a charge on the calls made but not paid,

(f) a charge on book debts of the company,

(g) a floating charge on the company's property or undertaking,

(i) a charge on a ship or aircraft, or any share in a ship and a charge on the goodwill or on any intellectual property,

must be registered at Companies House by delivery of the prescribed particulars together with the instrument (if any) by which the charge is created or evidenced before the end of the period of 21 days beginning with the day the charge was created.[152]

By reason of the definition employed in the Companies Act 2006, a charge includes a mortgage[153] and therefore the scope of charges caught by s.860 is capable of including both legal and equitable security interests in the charges themselves for which registration is prescribed. While s.860 provides that the obligation to procure registration is upon the company, registration may also be effected on the application of the person interested in the charge.[154]

A failure to apply to registration it within the prescribed time (or, to obtain an extension of time under s.873) has the consequence that the charge is void and against the liquidators, administrators and creditors of the company.

Time of creation

Given the obligation to secure its registration within 21 days of creation (if the   **23–46**
efficacy of the charge is to be preserved), it is worth noting that a mortgage or charge is created when the agreement or trust deed providing for the charge is executed and entered into, notwithstanding that any advance is only made subsequently.[155] In relation to a series of debentures unsecured by a trust deed,

---

[151] Formerly, Companies Act 1985 s.395.

[152] Companies Act 2006 s.870(1)(A). For charges created outside the United Kingdom, the period runs from the date when the instrument creating or evidencing the charge could, in due course post and if despatched with due diligence, have been received in the United Kingdom: s.870(1)(B). In the case of a series of debentures, the period runs from the date when the first debenture is executed unless there is a deed containing the charge in which the time runs from execution of that deed: s.870(3).

[153] ibid., s.861(5).

[154] ibid., s.860(2).

[155] *Watson & Co v Spiral Globe Co* [1902] 2 Ch. 209; *Re Harrogate Estates Ltd* [1903] 1 Ch. 498; *Appleyard v New London & Suburban Co* [1908] 1 Ch. 621; *Esberger & Son Ltd v Capital Encounters Bank* [1918] 2 Ch. 366; *Dublin City Distillery v Docherty* [1914] A.C. 823.

it would appear that the time starts to run when the first of the series is issued.[156] An agreement to creating a present obligation to give a mortgage in the future, the same amounts to an equitable charge should be registered within the period following its creation.[157]

In circumstances where the charge is informally granted and is followed by later formal documentation, the latter documentation is also registrable and the failure to effect registration of an earlier manifestation of the charge does not affect its validity if the later document itself is registered.[158] Similarly, a failure to register the formal documentation in circumstances where the earlier informal documentation is properly protected by registration does not affect the validity of the charge.[159]

An agreement to create a charge by way of legal mortgage at a future date[160] or on a contingency[161] has been held not to create a charge.

If the charge permits a substitution of property, no further registration is required if the property is substituted for that originally subject to the charge.[162]

Security arising by operation of law

23–47   Section 860 applies where "a company . . . creates a charge" to which the section applies. Thus, liens (whether in equity or at common law) are not registrable because they are neither charges nor have they been created by the company.[163] A general lien gives a more extensive possessory right than a special lien but since the same still amounts to a possessory right, it should not fall to be treated as a charge.[164] This reasoning extends to a solicitor's liens on company papers and an unpaid vendor's lien.[165] (In the context of registration for purpose of the Land Registration Act 2002, an unpaid vendor's lien must be protected in the register by the vendor by notice against his own title prior to transfer lest he lose priority pursuant to s.29 of that Act since it is a lien that only arises on the exchange of contracts.[166]) A right to subrogation also need not be registered[167]

---

[156] *Watson & Co v Spiral Globe Co,* above; now confirmed by Companies Act 2006 s.870(3).

[157] *Eyre v McDowell* (1861) 9 H.L. 619; *Levy v Abercorris Co* (1887) L.R. 37 Ch.D. 260 at 265.

[158] *Re Colombian Fire Proofing Co* [1910] 2 Ch. 120.

[159] *Cunard SS Co v Hopwood* [1908] 2 Ch. 564; *Re William Hall Ltd (Contractors) (in liquidation)* [1967] 1 W.L.R. 948.

[160] *Williams v Burlington Investments Ltd* (1977) 121 S.J. 424.

[161] *Re Gregory Love & Co* [1916] 1 Ch. 203.

[162] *Tailby v Official Receiver* (1888) 23 App. Cas. 523; *Cunard SS Co v Hopwood* [1908] 2 Ch. 564.

[163] *Brunton v Electrical Engineering Corp* [1892] 1 Ch. 434.

[164] A lien with a power of sale contractually attached to it was held not to be a charge in *Re Hamlet International Plc* [1998] 2 B.C.L.C. 164; cf. *Re Coslett (Contractors) Ltd* [1997] 4 All E.R. 114, where a site owner's power of sale of a contractor's plant was held to be security by way of charge. See also Pickin (1998) 11 Insolvency Intelligence 60. For liens generally, see above paras 1.17 et seq.

[165] *London & Cheshire Insurance Co Ltd v Laplagrene Property Co Ltd* [1971] Ch. 499; *Capital Finance Co Ltd v Stokes* [1969] 1 Ch. 261; *Re Beirnstein* [1925] Ch. 12; *Bank of Ireland Finance v Daly* [1978] I.R. 79, although the point was left open in *Burston Finance Ltd v Speirway Ltd* [1974] 3 All E.R. 735.

[166] *Barclays Bank Plc v Estates & Commercial Ltd (in liquidation)* [1997] 1 W.L.R. 415, 419.

[167] *Burford Finance Ltd v Speirway Ltd,* above.

nor need an interest under a secondary trust arising by operation of law pursuant to which the company must repay moneys paid over for an earmarked primary purpose that has failed.

A charging order on land obtained by a judgment creditor need not be registered.[168]

Meaning of charge

To determine whether an instrument creates "a charge" within the meaning of s.860, the court will have regard to its substance rather than its form[169]; the hallmark of a mortgage or charge is the mortgagor's right to redeem his property and the right to enjoy any surplus in the sale proceeds over and above the sums secured. Thus s.860 does not apply in instances where moneys are held on trust, for example, where retention and escrow funds are constituted.[170] **23–48**

Effect of non-compliance with registration requirements

The sanctions for non-registration are spelt out in s.874—the charge is void (so far as any security on the company's property or undertaking is conferred by it) against the liquidator, an administrator and a creditor of the company. Nonetheless, an unregistered charge remains good against the company itself[171] and against others who are not creditors.[172] **23–49**

Since an unregistered charge remains effective as against the company, prior to its liquidation or entry into administration the charge holder has the remedies available to him pursuant to his charge and generally. Moreover, it is to be noted that it is only the charge which is void pursuant to s.874 and not the debt itself secured thereby.[173] The disappointed chargee may nonetheless prove as an unsecured creditor in circumstances where the charge itself is void.

Rectification of the register and extension of time for registration

The court has power to rectify the register and to extend time for the registration of a charge under ss.870 and 873 of the Companies Act 2006. **23–50**

The effect of registration on priorities

The mere act of registration itself, does not stop the normal rules of priority as between legal and equitable charges continuing to apply. A legal mortgage will prevail over an equitable one unless the legal mortgagee had notice of the prior **23–51**

---

[168] *Re Overseas Aviation Engineering (GB)* [1963] Ch. 24.
[169] *Curtain Dream v Churchill Merchandising* [1990] B.C.L.C. 95.
[170] *Lovell Construction v Independent Estates (in liquidation)* [1994] 1 B.C.L.C. 31.
[171] *Independent Automatic Sales Ltd v Knowles & Foster* [1962] 1 W.L.R. 974.
[172] *Stroud Architectural Systems Ltd v John Laing Construction Ltd* [1994] B.C.C. 18.
[173] *Mercantile Bank of India v Chartered Bank of India, Australia & China* [1937] 1 All E.R. 231.

equitable mortgage. With regard to determining priority between competing legal mortgages and equitable mortgages inter se, the first in time prevails.

Registration pursuant to the Companies Act 2006 affects this position only (a) insofar as it invalidates an unregistered charge which should otherwise be registered, and (b) insofar as it amounts to notice of any prior charge and by that notice, affecting the normal rules of priority. Obviously a subsequent chargee who has searched the register and who knows of the charge has notice and is bound thereby. It has also been held that a subsequent chargee has constructive notice of matters entered on the register.[174] Historically, this has not extended to the terms of the charge[175] but in the case of floating charges which preclude the creation of subsequent fixed charges, the modern practice is to include that prohibition expressly on the register. It would appear that this would amount to constructive notice, although the point has yet to be decided.

DEBENTURES OVER LAND

23–52   Any legal or equitable charge on land is clearly registrable if created by a company registered in England or Wales. An equitable charge by deposit of deeds is registrable[176] although not now capable of valid creation.[177] In circumstances where the charge is secured on land, the normal considerations relating to registration and first registration[178] apply.

Unregistered land

23–53   A charge on unregistered land usually requires to be registered as a land charge[179] in order to preserve its validity against a successor in title. However, by s.3(7) of the Land Charges Act 1972, registration of a land charge for securing money created by a company before January 1, 1970, or so created *at any time* as a floating charge under the provisions of the Companies Acts (as in force from time to time) is sufficient registration for the purposes of the Land Charges Act 1972 and has effect as if the land charge had been registered under that Act. It follows from this that floating charges whenever created need only be registered under the Companies Act 2006 but for all other charges that post-date December 31, 1969, the dual system of registration at Companies House and under the Land Charges Act 1972 operates.

---

[174] *Wilson v Kelland* [1910] 2 Ch. 306. It is open to question whether this extends to all persons dealing with the company, including purchasers. *Palmer* suggests the better view is that constructive notice only extends to those who could fairly be expected to inspect the register: para.13.364.

[175] ibid.

[176] *Re Wallis and Simmonds Builders Ltd* [1974] Q.B. 94.

[177] Since it would fail to comply with Law of Property (Miscellaneous Provisions) Act 1989 s.2; *United Bank of Kuwait Plc v Sahib* [1991] Ch. 107.

[178] The creation of a protected first legal mortgage triggers compulsory registration: Land Registration Act 2002 s.4(1)(g).

[179] Class C(i) (puisne mortgage); Class C(iii) (general equitable charge).

Further, s.198(1) of the Law of Property Act 1925[180] provides that the registration of any instrument or matter under the Land Charges Act 1972, or any enactment which it replaces, in any register kept under the Land Charges Act 1972 or any local land charges register "shall be deemed to constitute actual notice . . . to all persons and for all purposes connected with the land affected". It therefore follows that registration comprises actual notice of a fixed charge on land; however, since floating charges cannot be so registered, there is no deemed actual notice of them.

If a charge on unregistered land is registered under the Land Charges Act 1972 but not under s.860 of the Companies Act 2006, a mortgagee takes free of it since he is a creditor for the purpose of s.860, but a purchaser other than a mortgagee is bound by it.

Registered land

Where a company registered in England or Wales creates a charge on registered land, a purchaser of the land for valuable consideration[181] will not be bound by the charge, even though it is registered at Companies House, unless it is registered or protected in the register of title, or, unusually, it takes effect as an overriding interest by virtue of the occupation of the chargee.[182] This applies to both fixed and floating charges. If a debenture trust deed contains a specific charge capable of taking effect as a legal charge, it can be entered in the register as a registered charge. If it contains a floating charge or an equitable charge, it can be protected by notice.

23–54

REMEDIES OF DEBENTURE HOLDERS

The debenture will contain provisions as to the circumstances when the borrower is in default. In such circumstances, the debenture holder can (subject to any consents required under a trust deed, if any) take steps to protect his position.

23–55

Unsecured debentures

If the debenture is not secured against any of the assets of the company, the debenture holder is confined to the usual steps that may be taken against a recalcitrant debtor: he can commence proceedings and levy execution on any judgment, and petition for the administration of the company or for its winding up. If the debenture is held by trustees, they alone (subject to the terms of the trust) can commence proceedings. If they refuse, the aggrieved beneficiary of the

23–56

---

[180] As amended by the LPA 1969 ss.24(1), 25(2).
[181] "Valuable consideration" does not include marriage consideration or a nominal amount in money: Land Registration Act 2002 s.131(1).
[182] Land Registration Act 2002 s.29.

debenture will have to commence proceedings for the enforcement of the trust in question.

Secured debentures

23–57 A well-drafted debenture will provide expressly for the debenture holder's remedies in the event of default and will usually permit the appointment of a receiver to sell the property of the company. Otherwise, the debenture holder is faced with a choice of four remedies: (a) a debenture holder's action; (b) the appointment of a receiver; (c) foreclosure; or (d) the winding-up of the company.

A debenture holder's action

23–58 Subject to compliance with the terms of the debenture, a debenture holder may commence proceedings on his own behalf and on behalf of any other holders of the same class of debentures[183] in order to claim the repayment of moneys owed or to enforce his security. If the consent of the majority is required and they decline by reason of some special interest adverse to the general interest of the class, the court will intervene and not permit them to benefit at the expense of the minority.[184] The court will regulate the conduct of the action and where a claimant has interests adverse to the other debenture holders, the court may order the substitution of the claimant with another member of the class.[185] Permission to commence such an action is necessary in the event that the winding up has commenced but this is given as of course.[186] Unless the court directs otherwise, any judgment binds all persons represented in the claim.[187]

Receiver

23–59 A receiver and manager can be appointed by the court pursuant to its statutory jurisdiction[188] or pursuant to the terms of the debenture over the company's property. The power of appointment by the debenture holder is a fiduciary one. A receiver's duty is to take possession of and protect the company's property. A receiver and manager has power to carry on the company's business, if the debenture so provides.[189]

Foreclosure

23–60 This remedy is occasionally available in debenture holders' actions[190] but is often seen as impracticable by reason of the fact that all debenture holders and the

---

[183] CPR 19.6 (as amended).
[184] *Mercantile Investment & General Trust Co v River Plate Trust, Loan & Agency Co* [1894] 1 Ch. 578.
[185] *Re Services Club Estate Syndicate Ltd* [1930] 1 Ch. 78.
[186] *Re Joshua Stubbs Ltd* [1891] 1 Ch. 475.
[187] CPR 19.6 (as amended).
[188] Senior Courts Act 1981 s.37.
[189] *Bombaas v King* (1886) 36 Ch.D. 279.
[190] *Sadler v Worley* [1894] 2 Ch. 170.

company must be parties to such a claim and, where the claim is by a legal mortgagee, any subsequent mortgagee must also be a party.[191] If the property has been conveyed to trustees on trust for sale, the remedy is not available.[192]

Winding-up

The appointment of a receiver does not preclude the winding up of the com-   **23–61**
pany[193] and a debenture holder who seeks the winding up of the company is not bound to forsake his security.[194] A debenture holder can petition as a contingent or prospective creditor pursuant to s.124 of the Insolvency Act 1986. A debenture holder who is only a trustee cannot, it appears, petition to wind up the company.[195]

AVOIDANCE OF DEBENTURES

In the appropriate circumstances, a debenture may be open to challenge by an   **23–62**
administrator or a liquidator of a company on the basis that it represents a transaction at an undervalue under s.238 of the Insolvency Act 1986 or it constitutes a preference under s.239 of that Act. In addition, s.423 of the Insolvency Act 1986 permits the court (on the application of an administrator, a liquidator or a victim of a transaction) to make a wide range of orders in order to restore the position in circumstances where the debenture forms part of a transaction which is at an undervalue and thereby defrauds creditors. These sections are of general application in the sense that their subject matter is not confined simply to debentures and are accordingly considered in the chapters on insolvency.[196] The text below considers extortionate credit transactions and the avoidance of certain floating charges under s.245 of the Insolvency Act 1986.

Extortionate credit transactions under the Insolvency Act 1986[197]

Section 244 of the Insolvency Act applies[198] where the company is,[199] or has   **23–63**
been, a party to a transaction for, or involving, the provision of credit to the company.[200] A parallel provision operates in the context of bankruptcy.[201]

---

[191] *Luke v South Kensington Hotel Co* (1879) L.R. 11 Ch.D. 121. This is so even if the subsequent mortgagee has only a floating charge: *Westminster Bank Ltd v Residential Properties Ltd* [1938] Ch. 639.

[192] *Schweitzer v Mayhew* (1863) 31 Beav. 37.

[193] *Re Borough of Portsmouth Tramways* [1892] 2 Ch. 362.

[194] *Moor v Anglo-Italian Bank* (1879) L.R. 10 Ch.D. 681.

[195] *Re Dunderland Iron Ore Co Ltd* [1909] 1 Ch. 446.

[196] Those provisions (including those of s.244, Extortionate Credit Transactions) are of general application.

[197] For consideration of unfair credit relationships under the Consumer Credit Act 1974, see para.16–61.

[198] As does s.238 (transaction at an undervalue)—see s.244(1), (5). It is easy to envisage an extortionate credit transaction also being one at an undervalue.

[199] Thus it catches transactions which are still "live".

[200] ibid., s.244(1).

[201] ibid., s.343.

On the application of the administrator or liquidator, the court may make an order with respect to the transaction if the transaction is or was extortionate and was entered into in the period of three years ending with the day on which the company entered administration or went into liquidation.[202]

A transaction is extortionate if, having regard to the risk accepted by the person providing the credit:

(a) the terms of it are or were such as to require grossly exorbitant payments to be made (whether unconditionally or in certain contingencies) in respect of the provision of the credit, or

(b) it otherwise grossly contravened ordinary principles of fair dealing;

and is presumed, unless the contrary is proved, that a transaction with respect to which an application is made under this section is or, as the case may be, was extortionate.[203] This presumption reflects the analogous provisions of the Consumer Credit Act 1974 and bestows clear advantage on the applicant.

If the court determines that the transaction is extortionate, its order may contain such one or more of the following as the court thinks fit, that is to say:

(a) provision setting aside the whole or part of any obligation created by the transaction;

(b) provision otherwise varying the terms of the transaction or varying the terms on which any security for the purposes of the transaction is held;

(c) provision requiring any person who is or was a party to the transaction to pay to the office-holder any sums paid to that person, by virtue of the transaction, by the company;

(d) provision requiring any person to surrender to the office-holder any property held by him as security for the purposes of the transaction;

(e) provision directing accounts to be taken between any persons.[204]

Avoidance of certain floating charges

23–64   Section 245 of the Insolvency Act 1986 allows the court to avoid certain floating charges. It operates in conjunction with s.238 (transactions at an undervalue)[205] and provides that a floating charge on the company's undertaking or property created at a relevant time is invalid[206] except to the extent of the aggregate of:

---

[202] ibid., s.244(2)

[203] ibid., s.244(3).

[204] ibid., s.244(4).

[205] Again, it is possible to envisage circumstances where a floating charge offends both sections.

[206] But not, it should be noted, the underlying debt for which the creditor may prove in the liquidation as an unsecured creditor. The provisions considered in the text only apply to those charges which post-date the amended s.245's coming into force on September 15, 2003: Sch.11 para.9. For earlier charges, the prior law applies and from June 1, 1991 the unamended s.245.

(a) the value of so much of the consideration for the creation of the charge as consists of money paid, or goods or services supplied, to the company at the same time as, or after, the creation of the charge;

(b) the value of so much of that consideration as consists of the discharge or reduction, at the same time as, or after, the creation of the charge, of any debt of the company[207]; the requirement for the company to be insolvent or to become insolvent does not therefore apply in relation to floating charges created in favour of persons connected with the company. This distinction is aimed particularly at challenging floating charges created in favour of directors, shadow directors and those closely involved with the company's management from procuring enhanced priority as against unsecured creditors. Even where "fresh consideration" is provided by such individuals, the validity of the charge is confined only to the extent of the consideration provided by them at "the same time as or after the creation of the charge" under s.245(2)(a); and

(c) the amount of such interest (if any) as is payable on the amount falling within paragraph (a) or (b) in pursuance of any agreement under which the money was so paid, the goods or services were so supplied or the debt was so discharged or reduced.

For these purposes, the value of any goods or services supplied by way of consideration for a floating charge is the amount of money which at the time they were supplied could reasonably have been expected to be obtained for supplying the goods or services in the ordinary course of business and on the same terms (apart from the consideration) as those on which they were supplied to the company.[208]

Section 245 employs the concept of "a relevant time". It utilises both a temporal test and one as to the effect of the transaction in question. Thus, the temporal requirements thus require for the time at which a floating charge is created by a company to be a relevant time for the charge to be created:

(a) (in the case of a charge which is created in favour of a person who is connected with the company) at a time in the period of two years ending with the onset of insolvency,

---

[207] This provision provides protection where a company grants a floating charge in favour of a bank or other financier to secure further advances and where payments are subsequently made by the bank to other creditors in whose favour cheques have been drawn. Such a charge will qualify for exemption from the effects of the invalidating provision. See (by way of example) under the former provisions contained in the Companies Act 1948 s. 322(1) and *Re Yeovil Glove Co Ltd* [1965] Ch. 148 (CA).

[208] ibid., s.245(6). The requirement for consideration to be measured at "the same time as, or after, the creation of the charge" was considered in *Power v Sharp Investments Ltd* [1993] B.C.C. 609, in which the Court of Appeal stated that the test of contemporaneity is a strict one and that where, in the absence of a pre-existing charge, moneys are paid before the execution of the debenture, they will not qualify for exemption under sub-paragraph (a) "unless the interval between payment and execution is so short that it can be regarded as minimal and execution can be regarded as contemporaneous": ibid., at 620. Perhaps an example is afforded at 619 where reference was made (albeit obiter) to a "coffee break".

(b) (in the case of a charge which is created in favour of any other person) at a time in the period of 12 months ending with the onset of insolvency,

(c) in either case, at a time between the making of an administration application in respect of the company and the making of an administration order on that application; or

(d) in either case, at a time between the filing with the court of a copy of notice of intention to appoint an administrator under paras 14 or 22 of Sch.B1 and the making of an appointment under that paragraph.[209]

Where a company creates a floating charge at a time mentioned in subpara.(b) immediately above and the person in favour of whom the charge is created is not connected with the company, that time is not a relevant time unless the company:

(a) is at that time unable to pay its debts within the meaning of s.123[210] in Ch.VI of Pt IV, or

(b) becomes unable to pay its debts within the meaning of that section in consequence of the transaction under which the charge is created.[211]

23–65 The "onset of insolvency" is defined for the purposes of s.245 and the avoidance of certain floating charges in identical terms to that contained in s.240 for the purposes of s.238 (Transactions at an Undervalue) and s.239 (Preferences).[212]

[209] ibid., s.245(3).

[210] The Act therefore brings in, as the test of the company's inability to pay its debts both the cash-flow basis set out in s.123(1) of the Insolvency Act 1986 and the balance sheet test contained within s.123(2) of the Act.

[211] ibid., s.245(4).

[212] ibid., s.245(5). See paras 34–47 et seq.

CHAPTER 24

AGRICULTURAL MORTGAGES AND CHARGES

THE HISTORICAL BACKGROUND

From about the middle of the 19th century a considerable body of legislation **24–01** came into existence affecting persons engaged in agriculture. This had, among its objects, the improvement of the position of tenants of agricultural land and the provision of finance for farmers over a longer period and on more favourable terms than would have been available from the usual commercial lending institutions. Much of the legislation enacted is outside the scope of this work.

In addition to the normal commercial sources of money, the perceived need for **24–02** long-term finance was provided for by Pt I of the Agricultural Credits Act 1928 ("the 1928 Act"). This established the Agricultural Mortgage Corporation Limited which was encouraged to make loans or mortgages on agricultural land and to make loans under the Improvement of Land Acts 1864 and 1899. Such long term loans were capable of being granted and secured by mortgages over agricultural land where the loan did not exceed two thirds of the value of the mortgaged property. Such mortgages were repayable by yearly or half-yearly instalments of capital and interest over a period of 60 years or on such other terms as the corporation's memorandum or articles might have permitted. Such mortgages were capable of being made irredeemable for the period during which the instalments were repayable.

On September 25, 1991, Pt I of the 1928 Act was repealed subject to a saving **24–03** in relation to mortgages or debentures subsisting the date when the repeal took effect.[1] Despite its repeal Pt I still has practical significance owing to the continued existence of mortgages granted by farmers to secure such advances prior to its repeal. The mortgagee in those circumstances is the Agricultural Mortgage Corporation, a company established under the 1928 Act with all the powers of a company incorporated under the Companies Acts to grant mortgages.[2]

Part II of the 1928 Act makes special provisions for credit by way of charge **24–04**

---

[1] ss.1, 2, 4 repealed by the Agriculture and Forestry (Financial Provisions) Act 1991 s.1(1), (2), Sch. Pt 1; s.3 repealed by the Trustees Investments Act 1961 s.16(2), Sch.5. The latter was, itself, repealed by the Statute Law (Repeals) Act 1974.

[2] Agricultural Credits Act 1928 ss.1 and 2. The limitation on the loan-to-value ratio formerly imposed was repealed by the Agriculture and Forestry (Financial Provisions) Act 1991 s.1(1) and Sch.1.

in favour of a bank over farming stock and assets. These are known as agricultural charges.[3] Prior to considering them, the position outside the 1928 Act merits consideration.

MORTGAGES AND CHARGES OUTSIDE THE 1928 ACT

24-05 It has always been possible to create mortgages of farm stock and agricultural land outside the ambit of the 1928 Act. Such mortgages are governed by the general law of bills of sales and of mortgages, respectively.

However, a number of points of difference between the general law and mortgages of farm stock and agricultural land are to be noted.

The statutory power of leasing

24-06 Before the enactment of s.18 of the Conveyancing Act 1881 (now replaced by s.99 of the Law of Property Act 1925) neither the mortgagor nor the mortgagee alone could make a lease which would be valid against the other unless that power was expressly provided for in the mortgage deed.[4] Since January 1, 1882, the former section and its statutory re-enactment have provided that a mortgagor of land while in possession has the power as against every encumbrancer to make any such lease of the mortgaged land as is authorised by the section. A mortgagee has a similar power as against every prior encumbrancer.[5] Leases authorised by this section include agricultural leases for any term not exceeding 21 years, or in the case of a mortgage made after the commencement of the Law of Property Act 1925, 50 years. This is subject to any contrary intention being expressed in the mortgage deed, or otherwise in writing, and subject to the terms of the deed or of any such writing, and the provisions therein contained.[6]

Where a lease fails to comply with the terms of s.99 but was made in good faith and the lessee has entered the property pursuant to its terms, s.152(1) of the Law of Property Act 1925 provides that the lease shall take effect in equity as a contract for the grant, at the lessee's request of a valid lease of like effect as the invalid lease, subject to such variations as may be necessary in order to comply with the statutory power.[7]

24-07 **Exclusion prior to September 1, 1995:** For mortgages created on and after March 1, 1948 and before September 1, 1995, the statutory power of leasing could not be excluded in the case of a mortgage of agricultural land.[8] Agricultural

---

[3] See paras 24–13 et seq.
[4] *Carpenter v Parker* (1857) 3 C.B.N.S. 206.
[5] Law of Property Act (LPA) 1925 s.99(1), (2).
[6] ibid., s.99(13).
[7] See *Pawson v Revell* [1958] 2 Q.B. 360, and s.152(6); *Rhodes v Dalby* [1971] 1 W.L.R. 1325.
[8] ibid., s.99(13A) inserted by the Agricultural Tenancies Act 1995 s.31 and formerly contained in the Agricultural Holdings Act 1986 s.100, Sch.14 para.12. Previously, the provision had been contained in the Agricultural Holdings Act 1948 s.95, Sch.7 para.2. Also see *National Westminster Bank Plc v Jones* [2001] 1 B.C.L.C 98; affirmed on appeal [2001] 1 B.C.L.C 55.

land is defined by s.1(4) of the Agricultural Holdings Act 1986 and means land used for agriculture which is so used for the purposes of a trade or business.[9]

Exclusion after August 31, 1995:   Unless the land in question remains subject   **24–08** to the Agricultural Holdings Act 1986 by virtue of s.4 of the Agricultural Tenancies Act 1995,[10] there is now no statutory prohibition on the exclusion of the statutory right to lease.

Compensation and the right to charge the holding

In the case where a sum becomes due to a tenant of an agricultural holding in   **24–09** respect of compensation from the landlord and the landlord fails to discharge his liability within the period of one month from the date upon which the sum becomes due, by virtue of the provisions contained in s.85(2) of the Agricultural Holdings Act 1986 the tenant shall be entitled to obtain from the Minister an order charging the holding with payment of the amount due.

By s.2(2) of the Land Charges Act 1972 such a charge is registrable as a Class   **24–10** A Land Charge. Further, by s.87(6) of the Agricultural Holdings Act 1986 such a charge (or likewise a charge under s.74 of the Agricultural Holdings Act 1948)[11] shall rank *in priority* to any other charge however and whenever created or arising. Charges created under these sections rank, as between themselves, in order of their creation. However, generally the charge of a landlord of an agricultural holding for repayment of the payment of compensation by him to his tenant does not rank in priority to other charges.[12]

Growing crops

A mortgagee, whether legal or equitable, who has not taken possession of the   **24–11** holding is not entitled to growing crops which have been removed by the mortgagor between the time of demand and the time of recovery of possession. However, he is entitled to all crops growing on the holding when he takes possession[13] unless under an express contract of tenancy between the mortgagor and the mortgagee, the mortgagor can claim them as emblements.[14] Since the severance of the crops converts them into personal chattels, a mortgagee who has

---

[9] And see Agriculture Act 1947 s.109. The definition of "agriculture" includes horticulture, fruit growing, dairy farming and livestock breeding, see ibid. s.96(1). It is subject to a number of exclusions.

[10] There are various transitional provisions.

[11] This section which dealt with recovery of compensation where a contract of tenancy is not binding on a mortgagee was repealed by s.10(2) and Sch.4 to the Agricultural Holdings Act 1948 which itself was repealed by the Agricultural Holdings Act 1986, but charges created under the 1948 Act are still in existence.

[12] Agricultural Holdings Act 1986 s. 87 makes no provision for the landlord to enjoy priority.

[13] *Bagnall v Villar* (1879) L.R. 12 Ch.D. 812.

[14] *Re Skinner, Ex p. Temple & Fishe* (1882) 1 Gl. and J. 216; *Bagnall v Villar*, above.; *Re Phillips, Ex p. National Mercantile Bank* (1880) L.R. 16 Ch.D. 104. This applies to an equitable mortgagee: *Re Gordon, Ex p. Official Receiver* (1889) 61 L.T. 299.

not taken possession before the mortgagor's bankruptcy has no right to them as against the mortgagor's trustee in bankruptcy.[15]

24–12   If an ordinary mortgage or charge of a holding includes a covenant that a mortgagor shall not without the consent of the mortgagee include any growing crops in an agricultural charge, a breach of that covenant would bring into operation the statutory power of sale pursuant to s.101 of the Law of Property Act 1925.[16]

AGRICULTURAL CHARGES UNDER PART II OF THE 1928 ACT

The nature and creation of an agricultural charge

24–13   Part II of the 1928 Act makes provision for agricultural short-term credits. Section 5 of that Act regulates the nature and mode of creation of agricultural charges on farming stock and assets. Apart from a requirement that an agricultural charge is in writing, the charge may be in any form.[17]

24–14   A farmer[18] who, as tenant or owner of an agricultural holding, cultivates the holding for profit[19] may, notwithstanding any provision in his contract of tenancy to the contrary[20] by instrument in writing create in favour of a bank[21] an agricultural charge on all or any of his farming stock[22] and other agricultural assets[23] as security for sums on short-term credit advanced to him or paid or to be paid on his behalf under any guarantee by the bank and interest, commission and charges thereon.

24–15   An agricultural charge may be either a fixed charge, or a floating charge, or both a fixed and a floating charge.[24] The principal sum secured by an agricultural charge may be either a specified amount, or a fluctuating amount advanced on current account not exceeding at any one time such amount (if any) as may be

---

[15] *Re Phillips,* above.

[16] See below paras 26–39 et seq.

[17] Agricultural Credits Act 1928 s.5(6).

[18] Defined as being any person (not being an incorporated company or society) who as tenant or owner of an agricultural holding cultivates the holding for profit: s.5(7).

[19] "Agriculture" and "Cultivation" shall be deemed to include horticulture, and the use of land for any purpose of husbandry, inclusive of the keeping or breeding of livestock, poultry or bees, and the growth of fruit, vegetables and the like: ibid.

[20] ibid., s.13.

[21] "Bank" means (a) the Bank of England; (b) a person who has permission under Pt 4 of the Financial Services and Markets Act 2000 to accept deposits; (c) an EEA firm of the kind mentioned in para.5(b) of Sch.3 to that Act which has permission under para.15 of that Schedule (as a result of qualifying for authorisation under para.12(1) of that Schedule) to accept deposits or other repayable funds from the public: ibid., s.5(7).

[22] "Farming stock" means crops or horticultural produce, whether growing or severed from the land, and after severance whether subjected to any treatment or process of manufacture or not; livestock, including poultry and bees, and the produce and progeny thereof; any other agricultural or horticultural produce whether subjected to any treatment or process of manufacture or not; seeds and manure; agricultural vehicles, machinery and other parts; agricultural tenant's fixtures and other agricultural fixtures which a tenant is by law authorised to remove, ibid., s.5(7).

[23] "Other agricultural assets" means a tenant's right to compensation under the Agricultural Holdings Act 1986, except under ss.60(2)(b) or 62 for improvements, damage by game, disturbance or otherwise; and any other tenant right, ibid., s.5(7).

[24] ibid., s.5(2).

specified in the charge. In the latter case the charge shall not be deemed to be redeemed by reason only of the current account having ceased to be in debit.[25] An agricultural charge may be in such form and made upon such conditions as the parties may agree and sureties may be made parties to the charge.[26]

Fixed charges and their effect

The property affected by a fixed charge shall be such property forming part of the **24–16** farming stock and other agricultural assets belonging to the farmer at the date of the charge as may be specified in the charge. It may also include in the case of livestock any progeny born after the date of the charge and in the case of agricultural plant any plant which may, while the charge is in force, be substituted for the plant specified in the charge.[27]

A fixed charge shall, so long as the charge continues in force, confer on the **24–17** bank certain rights. These are the following:

(a)   a right upon the happening of any event specified in the charge as being an event authorising the seizure of property subject to the charge, to take possession of any such property;

(b)   where possession of any property has been so taken a right after an interval of five clear days (or such less time as may be allowed by the charge) to sell the property either by auction or, if the charge so provides, by private treaty, and either for a lump sum payment or payment by instalments;

(c)   an obligation, in the event of such prior sale being exercised, to apply the proceeds of sale in or towards the discharge of the moneys and liabilities secured by the charge, and the cost of seizure and sale, and to pay the surplus (if any) of the proceeds to the farmer.[28]

In the absence of the happening of any event specified in the charge the farmer **24–18** is entitled to remain in possession of the property charged and to sell it. However, a number of obligations are imposed upon him so long as the charge continues in force except to such extent that the charge otherwise provides or the bank otherwise allows. Whenever the farmer sells any of the property, or receives any money in respect of other agricultural assets comprised in the charge, or in the event of its receiving any money under a policy of insurance on any of the property comprised in the charge, or any money paid by way of compensation under specified Acts[29] in respect of the destruction of any live stock comprised in the charge, or by way of compensation under the Destructive Insects and Pests Acts, 1877 to 1927 in respect of the destruction of any livestock or crops

---

[25] ibid., s.5(5).
[26] ibid., s.5(6).
[27] ibid., s.5(3).
[28] ibid., s.6(1).
[29] The Act still refers to the Diseases of Animals Acts, 1894 to 1927 and Destructive Insects and Pests Acts, 1877 to 1927.

comprised in the charge, the fixed charge imposes on the farmer the obligation forthwith to pay to the bank the amount of the proceeds of the sale or the money so received in or towards the discharge of the money and liabilities secured by the charge.[30]

24–18   Thus, subject to compliance with the obligations so imposed, a fixed charge shall not prevent the farmer selling any of the property subject to the charge, and neither the purchaser nor (in the case of a sale by auction the auctioneer) shall be concerned to see that such obligations are complied with notwithstanding that he may be aware of the existence of a charge.[31]

24–19   Further, where any proceeds of sale are paid to a person other than the bank which should have been so paid to the bank, the bank has no right to recover such proceeds from that person unless the bank proves that such other person knew that the proceeds were paid to him in breach of such obligation. Notice of the charge does not amount to such knowledge.[32] A farmer who with intent to defraud fails to comply with the obligations as to payment owed to the bank of any money received by him or removes from the holding any property subject to the charge, is guilty of an offence and liable on summary conviction to imprisonment for a term not exceeding six months or a fine not exceeding the prescribed sum, or both, and on conviction on indictment to imprisonment for a term not exceeding three years.[33]

Floating charges and their effect

24–20   The property affected by a floating charge shall be the farming stock and other agricultural assets from time to time belonging to the farmer or such parts of the same as is mentioned in the charge.[34] A floating charge hovers over the assets charged but settles and fixes on no particular asset until some event has happened which converts the charge into a fixed charge. Subject to the consideration set out below an agricultural charge creating a floating charge shall have the like effect as if the charge had been created by a duly registered debenture issued by a company.[35] Assets also not falling under the umbrella of the floating charge would include the farmer's house and furniture and other chattels not connected with the farming business, although he may well have granted a separate legal charge in favour of the bank over the residential premises and such chattels.

24–21   The floating charge is converted into a fixed charge over the property comprised in the charge as existing at the date of its becoming a fixed charge on the occurrence of the following events:

    (a)   upon a bankruptcy order being made against the farmer;

    (b)   upon the death of the farmer;

---

[30] ibid., s.6(2).
[31] ibid., s.6(3).
[32] ibid., s.6(4).
[33] ibid., s.11(1); Criminal Justice Act 1948 ss.1(1), (2); Criminal Law Act 1967 s.1; Magistrates' Courts Act 1980 ss.17, 32, Sch.1 para.20.
[34] ibid., s.5(4).
[35] ibid., s.7(1). As to company debentures, see paras 23–01 et seq.

(c)   upon the dissolution of the partnership in the case where the property charged is partnership property;

(d)   upon notice in writing of that effect being given by the bank on the happening of any event which by virtue of the charge confers on the bank the right to give such notice.[36]

Further, while the status of charge is that of a floating charge, the farmer is subject to the same obligation as under a fixed charge to pay over to the bank money received by him by way of proceeds of sale or money received in respect of other agricultural assets or under policies of insurance or by way of compensation.[37] However, it is not necessary for a farmer to comply with the above obligation to pay over such sums to the bank where the amount so received is expended by him in the purchase of farming stock which on purchase becomes subject to the floating charge.[38]   **24–22**

This means that while the charge remains a floating charge, the farmer is able to pay his way by selling farming stock and using the proceeds of sale in purchasing new farming stock. He is therefore able to pay for the cost of crops, seed, livestock, and plant pro tempore without accounting for the sums received from the sale of farming stock to the bank pursuant to his general obligation to do so. Thus there is one essential difference between a fixed agricultural charge and a floating agricultural charge. In the case of the latter while the charge remains a floating charge the same obligation that the farmer would have if the charge were a fixed charge to pay over to the bank monies received by him is subject to the exception that such sums do not have to be paid over by him to the bank in the case where the amounts so received are expended in the purchase of farming stock.   **24–23**

Registration and priorities of agricultural charges

Registration: Every agricultural charge must be registered within seven clear days after its execution. If it is not so registered it is void against any person other than the farmer. However, if it is proved that omission to register within this period was accidental or inadvertent, the High Court may extend the time for registration.[39]   **24–24**

Registration of an agricultural charge is effected at the Land Registry by sending by post to the Land Registrar a memorandum of the instrument creating the charge together with the prescribed particulars and fee.[40] The Land Registrar is obliged to keep at the Land Registry a register of agricultural charges in such form and containing such particulars as may be prescribed and on receipt of the   **24–25**

---

[36] ibid., s.7 proviso (a) as amended by the Insolvency Act 1985 s.235(1), Sch.8 para.6. As to whether this is an exhaustive list, see *National Westminster Bank Plc v Jones* [2001] 1 B.C.L.C 98; affirmed on appeal [2001] 1 B.C.L.C 55.

[37] ibid., s.7(1)(b).

[38] ibid.

[39] ibid., s.9(1) and proviso.

[40] ibid., s.9(3).

memorandum he shall enter the particulars in the Register and file a memorandum.[41] The Register and memorandum are open to inspection on payment (except where the inspection is made by or on behalf of a bank) of the prescribed fee, and any person inspecting the Register or any such filed memorandum on payment of the prescribed fee may make copies or extracts therefrom.[42]

24–26   Registration of an agricultural charge may be proved by the production of a certified copy of the entry on the Register relating to the charge and the Schedule to the 1928 Act makes special provision as to official searches in the Agricultural Charges Register held at the Land Registry.[43] In favour of a purchaser or intending purchaser and as against persons interested under or in respect of an agricultural charge, the certificate, according to its tenor shall be conclusive, affirmatively or negatively, as the case may be.[44]

24–27   Registration of an agricultural charge is deemed to constitute actual notice of the charge and of the fact of such registration to all persons and for all purposes connected with the property comprised in the charge as from the date of registration or other prescribed date and so long as the registration continues in force.[45] However, where a charge in favour of a bank is expressly made for securing a current account or other further advances, the bank in relation to the making of further advances under the charge is not deemed to have notice of another agricultural charge by reason only that it is so registered if it was not so registered at the time when the first charge was created or when the last search by the bank was made, whichever last happened.[46]

In relation to registered land, the former practice of entering a restriction automatically no longer prevails; a separate application for that purpose is now required.

24–28   **Priorities:**   As to priorities between agricultural charges, it is provided that such charges shall in relation to one another have priority in accordance with the times at which they are respectively registered.[47] Where an agricultural charge creating a floating charge has been made, an agricultural charge purporting to create fixed charge on, or a bill of sale comprising, any of the property subject to the floating charge is void as long as the floating charge remains in force.[48]

---

[41] ibid., s.9(2), (3).

[42] ibid., s.9(4).

[43] Sch. paras 1–3, 5, added by the Land Charges Act 1972 Sch.3 para.7.

[44] Sch. paras 3, 4 as added by the Land Charges Act 1972. Para.6 of the Schedule makes provision for any act of fraud or collusion or wilful negligence on the part of any officer, clerk or other person employed in the Registry who commits any such act or is a party or privy to the same. In such circumstances the offence is punishable on summary conviction with a fine not exceeding the prescribed sum or imprisonment for up to three months or both, and on conviction or indictment with imprisonment for up to two years, and as amended by the provisions of s.32(2) of the Magistrates' Courts Act 1980. Para. 7 of the Schedule further provides that a solicitor, or a trustee, personal representative, agent or other person in a fiduciary position shall not be answerable for any loss that might arise from error in a certificate obtained by him.

[45] ibid., s.9(8).

[46] ibid., s.9(8) proviso.

[47] ibid., s.8(2).

[48] ibid., s.8(3).

Supplemental provisions as agricultural charges

Neither an agricultural charge nor a registered debenture issued by an agricultural society is deemed to be a bill of sale within the meaning of the Bills of Sale Acts 1878 and 1882.[49]   **24–29**

An agricultural charge is no protection in respect of the property included in the charge which but for the charge would have been liable to distress for rent, or (when brought into force) the exercise of the power to use the procedure in Sch.12 to the Tribunals, Courts and Enforcement Act 2007 (taking control of goods) to recover rent, taxes, or rates.[50]   **24–30**

Where a farmer who is adjudged bankrupt has created in favour of a bank an agricultural charge on any of the farming stock or other agricultural assets belonging to him, and the charge was created within three months of the date of the presentation of the bankruptcy petition and operated to secure any sum owing to the bank immediately prior to the giving of the charge, then, unless it is proved that the farmer immediately after the execution of the charge was solvent, the amount which would otherwise have been secured by the charge shall be reduced by the amount of the sum so owing to the bank immediately prior to the giving of the charge, but without prejudice to the bank's right to enforce any other security for that sum or to claim payment thereof as an unsecured debt.[51]   **24–31**

If growing crops are included in an agricultural charge then the rights of the bank in respect of such crops under the charge shall have priority to those of the mortgagee, whether in possession or not, and irrespective of the dates of the mortgage and charge.[52]   **24–32**

Charges on property of registered societies

A debenture issued by a society registered under the Industrial & Provident Societies Act 1965 creating in favour of a bank a floating charge on property which is farming stock may be registered in like manner as an agricultural charge and the charge if so registered shall as respects such property be valid notwithstanding anything in the Bills of Sale Acts 1878 and 1882 and shall not be deemed to be a bill of sale within the meaning of those Acts.[53] Notice of such charges must be signed by the secretary of the society and sent to the central office established under the Friendly Societies Acts 1974 and registered there.[54]   **24–33**

---

[49] ibid., ss.8(1), 14(1).

[50] ibid., s.8(7), the reference to the procedure in Sch.12 to the Tribunals, Courts and Enforcement Act 2007 was inserted by the Tribunals, Courts and Enforcement Act 2007 c.15 Sch.13 para.23 from a date to be appointed.

[51] ibid., s.8(5).

[52] ibid., s.8(6).

[53] ibid., s.14(1). The text of this sub-section refers to the Industrial & Provident Societies' Acts 1893–1928 but these were repealed and replaced by the Industrial & Provident Societies' Act 1965; see ss.4, 77(3).

[54] ibid., s.14(1) proviso. This refers to the Friendly Societies Act 1896 but this was repealed and replaced by the Friendly Societies Act 1974; see s.116, Sch.10 para.2.

Charges on property of agricultural marketing boards

24–34   A debenture may be issued by an agricultural marketing board creating a floating charge on any farming stock in England or Wales which is vested in the board in favour of a bank. Such a charge must be registered in like manner as an agricultural charge under Pt II of the 1928 Act. Section 9 of that Act shall apply to such a charge as it applies to an agricultural charge, and the charge, if so registered, shall, as respects such property, be valid notwithstanding anything in the Bills of Sale Acts, 1878 and 1882, and shall not be deemed to be a bill of sale within the meaning of those Acts.[55]

---

[55] Agricultural Marketing Act 1958 s.15(5). For the purposes of that section, "bank" and "farming stock" have the same meanings respectively as in Pt II of the Agricultural Credits Act 1928.

CHAPTER 25

THE STATUS, RIGHTS AND DUTIES OF THE MORTGAGEE

INTRODUCTION

The essential feature of lending money by means of a mortgage is that the **25-01** mortgagee becomes a secured creditor of the mortgagor. The mortgagee obtains a form of interest in the property and acquires rights both over that property and against the mortgagor which can be enforced in a variety of ways should the mortgagor fall into default. However, in seeking to enforce his rights, the mortgagee must also abide by certain duties owed to the mortgagor and/or to third parties such as subsequent mortgagees.

Because in earlier times the mortgage contract was in essence regarded as an investment by the mortgagee, the principles of law established during the 19th and early 20th centuries effectively permitted the mortgagee complete freedom to realise his security in the event of default on the part of the mortgagor. Most of the mortgagee's rights and remedies have been enshrined in statutory enactments, in particular the Law of Property Act 1925.

These principles, however, must now be viewed in light of more recent **25-02** developments which have tended to temper the strict application of the mortgagee's remedies in the light of changing social policy and expectations. In particular, since the 1930s, and especially since the Second World War, successive governments have placed strong emphasis on home ownership. Concomitant with this has been the growth in lending by the building societies, and latterly by banks and more recently other commercial organisations, which provide funds for the purchase of dwelling-houses secured by way of mortgage. Thus, the traditional rights and remedies of the mortgagee have required some readjustment in order to meet the changing role of the mortgage in society. Substantial restrictions have been placed on the mortgagee's ability to realise his security both by statute and by the courts in order to provide a measure of protection for a mortgagor in the occupation of his own home, the result being to "temper the wind to the shorn lamb."[1]

However, this apparent process of erosion of the mortgagee's remedies should **25-03** not be exaggerated; the mortgagor who defaults on repayment may now be given more opportunity to correct his default than would historically have been the case, but ultimately the courts will uphold a mortgagee's right to protect the security and recover sums due to it under the terms of the agreement between the

---

[1] *Redditch Benefit Building Society v Roberts* [1940] Ch. 415 at 420.

parties. Notwithstanding the enormous growth in institutional lending for home ownership over the past 80 years, and although one of the features of the recession of the late 1980s and early 1990s was a significant increase in the number of mortgage possession cases which pattern has been repeated in cases commenced between 2005 and the beginning of 2010,[2] the number of instances of mortgage defaults remains relatively small in comparison with the total number of mortgaged properties in England and Wales. The reason for this is not that building societies and banks necessarily fail to enforce their security (indeed, there is some evidence that building societies in particular "hold back" to a greater extent in times of crisis) but more that such institutional lenders will, prior to lending, usually make extensive enquiries into the potential borrower's means in order to ensure that he or she can service the level of borrowing. Late twentieth century developments in the mortgage market place and in particular the growth of mortgages where the mortgagor's worth was either not investigated or was "self-certified" by the mortgagor may have been partly responsible for an increase in the proportion of mortgagors in default in the 1990s. However, such mortgages are now far less widely available,[3]contain greater safeguards against dishonesty and abuse, and are therefore unlikely to have a significant impact on the default and enforcement figures in the future.

There are two further points to bear in mind as a precursor to examining the rights, duties and remedies of a mortgagee: first, the nature and extent of the mortgagee's interest in the property; and second, the difference between a mortgagee and a trustee.

Mortgagee's Interest Limited to the Security

25–04   The mortgagor is, in equity, the beneficial owner of the mortgaged property until his interest is lost to him by the realisation of the security or by lapse of time. The corollary is that the mortgagee's interest in the property is solely as a security until he acquires full beneficial ownership by a decree for foreclosure absolute or by lapse of time. This principle was clearly stated in the case of *Thornborough v Baker*[4] where Lord Nottingham held that, in a mortgage of land, if redemption took place after the death of the mortgagee, the redemption monies must be paid to the personal representatives and not to his heir-at-law. At that date the legal title to land necessarily passed to the heir-at-law whereas the title to a contract debt passed to the personal representatives. Lord Nottingham's decision thus meant that the substance of a mortgagee's interest is not his title to the mortgage property which he holds as security but his right to the mortgage monies. Although at law, the mortgagee's title is made absolute by the passing of the contractual date for redemption, in equity it is his beneficial interest in the title which remains his security for enforcing payment of the mortgage debt. Hence, the legal title in the hands of the heir-at-law could not carry any beneficial interest in the mortgage debt which belonged to the personal representatives and

[2] National Statistics published by the Ministry of Justice.
[3] As a result of the Financial Service Authority's intervention in 2009.
[4] (1676) 1 Ch. Cas. 283.

in equity was held on the latter's behalf to enforce the debt. In other words, although at law, his title gives to a mortgagee a right to the property, in equity his interest in the mortgage comprises his debt, his use of the title as security for the debt and nothing more.[5]

MORTGAGEE NOT A TRUSTEE

A mortgagee has, therefore, two titles, the title to the mortgaged property (which he holds subject to the mortgagor's equity of redemption) and his own beneficial interest in the property as a security. At first sight a mortgagee seems to be very like a trustee, for he holds a title to give effect to equitable rights vested in himself and another. However, although there is some analogy between the conceptions of mortgage and trust, a mortgagee is not a trustee.[6] It has been said repeatedly that no fiduciary relationship arises between a mortgagor and a mortgagee until the latter has been paid off.[7] Then, the mortgagee does indeed become a trustee of the legal estate, if the mortgage has been redeemed[8] and of the surplus proceeds of sale if the property has been sold under a power of sale.[9]

25–05

Nor is a mortgagee a trustee of the power of sale, for the power of sale is given to the mortgagee for his own benefit to enable him to realise his security,[10] although such power must be exercised bona fide and with reasonable care.[11] The duty formerly imposed by statute[12] on building societies to take reasonable care to ensure that the price obtained on a sale of a mortgaged property was the best price that could reasonably be obtained has been repealed[13] and any rule of law requiring a mortgagee to take reasonable care to obtain a proper price on true market value is to have effect as if the statute imposing the duty on a building society (and its statutory predecessors) had never been enacted.[14] Thus, until a mortgagee has been satisfied, his interest in the property is essentially adverse to

25–06

---

[5] This position was altered by s.30 of the Conveyancing Act 1881 and the Land Transfer Act 1897 (see Ch.5, paras 5–026 and 5–027), both of which have now been replaced as to deaths after 1925 by the Administration of Estates Act 1925 ss.1(1), 3(1)(ii) (as amended by the Trusts of Land an Appointment of Trustees Act 1996). However, the principle is still of importance.

[6] *Marquis of Cholmondely v Lord Clinton* (1820) 2 J. & W. 1; and see Turner, *Equity of Redemption* (1931), Chap. 8.

[7] *Kennedy v De Trafford* [1897] A.C. 180.

[8] *Taylor v Russell* [1892] A.C. 244; and see *Holme v Fieldsend* [1911] W.N. 111 for the mortgagor's options in those circumstances.

[9] *Rajah Kishendatt Ram v Rajah Mumtaz Ali Khan* (1879) L.R. 6 Ind.App. 145; *Banner v Berridge* (1881) L.R. 18 Ch.D. 254.

[10] See *Warner v Jacob* (1882) L.R. 20 Ch.D. 220 at 224; *Raja v Austin Gray* [2003] 1 E.G.L.R. 91 at 96; *Silven Properties Ltd v Royal Bank of Scotland Plc* [2003] EWCA Civ 1409; [2004] 1 W.L.R. 997; and see below, paras 26–53 et seq. for the various duties of the mortgagee as vendor.

[11] For power of sale see below, paras 26–39 et seq., and see *Cuckmere Brick Co Ltd v Mutual Finance Ltd* [1971] Ch. 949; *Bishop v Bonham* [1988] 1 W.L.R. 742. *Parker-Tweedale v Dunbar Bank* [1991] Ch. 12 (CA); *Downsview Nominees Ltd v First City Corporation Ltd* [1993] A.C. 295; *AIB Finance v Debtors* [1998] 2 All E.R. 929; *Medforth v Blake* [1999] 3 W.L.R. 922 and *Mortgage Express v Mardner* [2004] EWCA Civ 1859.

[12] Building Societies Act 1986 s.13(7) and Sch.4 para.1.

[13] Building Societies Act 1997 s.12(1) with effect from December 1, 1997, SI 1997/2668.

[14] ibid., s.12(2) and see above, Ch.8.

that of the mortgagor. This is never so between a trustee and a cestui que trust.

The suggestion that a mortgagee acts in a fiduciary capacity was strongly attacked by Plumer M.R., in the case of *Marquis of Cholmondely v Lord Clinton*,[15] in a passage which would seem to leave no room for further argument. Yet, in one form or another, the fallacy has reappeared from time to time, and in the later case of *Allen and Clarke v O'Hearne & Co*[16] the Privy Council had occasion again to deny the trusteeship of a mortgagee.

This divergence between the role of a mortgagee and that of a trustee underpins the way in which English law has defined and developed the mortgagee's rights, duties and remedies. It can be seen, for example in the following principles, each of which will be addressed so far as the mortgagee is concerned in more detail below:

> (1) A legal mortgagee has, in general, an absolute right to take possession of the mortgaged property, whereas dispossession of a cestui que trust would be a breach of trust.[17]
>
> (2) Purchases by trustees from their beneficiaries are regarded with the utmost jealousy. However, mortgagees are free to purchase the equity of redemption from the mortgagor as the relationship is considered to be that of vendor and purchaser. This remains so unless and until the mortgagor is able to show any fraud or oppression on the part of the mortgagee or when there is pressure and inequality of bargaining position, and the mortgagee has obtained the property at a nominal or insufficient price. Undervalue alone will not be sufficient to set the transaction aside.[18]
>
> (3) In foreclosure proceedings[19] the court actually assists a mortgagee to acquire the equity of redemption, whereas this is unthinkable in the case of a trustee.
>
> (4) A mortgagee in possession may, while a trustee in possession never can, acquire a title under the statute of limitation.[20]
>
> (5) Apart from his duty to act in good faith and with reasonable care, particularly with regard to the obtaining of a proper price, a mortgagee can elect if and when to exercise his powers in his own interest[21] and need have little regard for the mortgagor's interest, whereas that is the whole duty of the trustee.[22] Certainly a mortgagee need not exercise his

---

[15] (1820) 2 J. & W. 1 at 182 et seq.

[16] [1937] A.C. 213 at 219.

[17] *Marquis of Cholmondely v Lord Clinton* (1820) 2 J. & W. 1, at 183. See paras 26–10 et seq. below.

[18] *Knight v Marjoribanks* (1849) 2 Mac & G. 10; *Ford v Olden* (1867), L.R. 3 Eq. 461, and see below, paras 26–54 et seq.

[19] See below paras 27–24 et seq.

[20] cf. *Re Alison, Johnson v Mounsey* (1879) L.R. 11 Ch.D. 284.

[21] *Rontestone Ltd v Minories Finance Ltd* [1997] 1 E.G.L.R. 123; *Silven Properties Ltd v Royal Bank of Scotland Plc* [2003] EWCA Civ 1409; [2004] 1 W.L.R. 997.

[22] *Davey v Durrant, Smith v Durrant* (1857) 1 De G. & J. 535; but see below, para.26–53 for the mortgagee's duties as vendor.

powers (even if advised to do so) notwithstanding that such an exercise would be highly advantageous to the mortgagor.[23]

(6) A mortgagee in possession is liable to account on the footing of wilful default without it being specially pleaded, whereas a special case must be made out for charging a trustee with wilful default.[24]

Mortgagee's Rights and Duties

The rights and duties of a mortgagee and the remedies available to him in order to enforce those rights or otherwise in the event of default by the mortgagor differ according to whether the mortgage is legal or equitable and whether or not the circumstances of the mortgage are such that statute intervenes to limit his options. Those rights and duties are derived principally from the terms of the mortgage itself overlaid with the provisions of the Law of Property Act 1925 and the principles of equity, which both subject the mortgagee's title to the equity of redemption and provide him with consequent rights and remedies for the protection and realisation of his security. **25–07**

In the case of a legal mortgage, the mortgagee's principal rights are as follows: **25–08**

(1) to take custody of the title deeds (if any);
(2) to maintain his security;
(3) to include fixtures within his security;
(4) to consolidate;
(5) to tack;
(6) to insure;
(7) to appoint or seek the appointment of a receiver;
(8) to realise the security by sale;
(9) to enter into possession[25] or to seek an order for possession;
(10) to seek foreclosure; and
(11) to bring action on the covenant to repay.

Of these, the first six are exercisable by to the mortgagee without involving the court and do not necessarily require any form of default on the part of the mortgagor. Of the remainder, each of which would generally be triggered by the mortgagor's default, (7), (8) and (9) may be pursued either through the court or out of court dependent upon the circumstances of the case. The last two are available only through court proceedings.

An equitable mortgagee[26] has only foreclosure, sale, a limited right to preserve his security, a potential right of possession or the appointment of a receiver with **25–09**

---

[23] *Palk v Mortgage Services Funding Plc* [1993] Ch. 330; *China and South Sea Bank Ltd v Tan* [1990] 1 A.C. 536.

[24] *Dobson v Land* (1850) 8 Hare 216 at 220.

[25] The mortgagee in possession acquires certain additional rights but takes on additional liabilities, as to which see below, paras 26–13 et seq.

[26] See below, Ch.28.

which to protect his entitlement to be repaid, and the rights of an equitable chargee are more limited still.[27]

25-10   As for duties, the law imposes some restraints upon a mortgagee over and above anything set out in the mortgage agreement between the parties. He must act not only in good faith[28] but also with reasonable care,[29] particularly with regard to taking reasonable care to obtain the best price.[30] It has also been said that a mortgagee owes the mortgagor a duty to act fairly,[31] although it is debatable whether this is intended to go further than the duty to act in good faith.[32] He does not, however, owe any duty to explain the security to the mortgagor,[33] although he would be wise to advise a mortgagor to seek independent legal advice. A mortgagee can, if he chooses, disregard his security and simply rely upon the personal covenant to repay.[34]

25-11   Furthermore, the mortgagee who goes into possession of the property thereby takes on additional duties and liabilities.[35] Principal among those are the duty to account, which is otherwise primarily that of the mortgagor, and potential liability for waste or repairs and under certain covenants affecting the property.

25-12   The only other restraints upon the mortgagee which could be said to impose something akin to duties are the equitable rules which establish and regulate the mortgagor's right of redemption. As the mortgagee's only beneficial interest in the property is by way of security for the mortgage debt, so long as any right of redemption still exists,[36] he cannot make any personal profits out of the mortgaged property beyond those which result directly from the mortgage bargain. Thus an accretion to the mortgaged property, for example by the exercise of an option to purchase, benefits the mortgagee by enlarging his security but it

---

[27] See below, paras 28–08 et seq.

[28] *Tomlin v Luce* (1889) L.R. 43 Ch.D. 191; and see *Cuckmere Brick Co Ltd v Mutual Finance Ltd* [1971] Ch. 949; *Downsview Nominees Ltd v First City Corp Ltd* [1993] A.C. 295; *Meretz Investments NV v ACP Ltd* [2006] EWHC 74 (Ch). Examples of breach may be found in *Downsview*, above; *Albany Home Loans Ltd v Massey* [1997] 2 All E.R. 69; *Quenell v Maltby* [1979] 1 W.L.R. 318; *Sadiq v Hussain* (1997) 73 P. & C.R. D44. For an example of discreditable conduct not amounting to bad faith, see *Caricom Cinemas Ltd v Republic Bank Ltd* [2003] UKPC 2.

[29] In *Standard Chartered Bank Ltd v Walker* [1982] 1 W.L.R. 1410 and *American Express International Banking Corporation v Hurley* [1985] F.L.R. 350, the liability of the mortgagee to the mortgagor's guarantor was considered to be a matter of tort. But the relationship between the mortgagee and the guarantor is a matter of contract (see Lord Scarman in *Tai Hing Cotton Mill Ltd v Liu Chong Hing Bank Ltd* [1986] 1 A.C. 80 at 96; *National Bank of Greece S.A. v Pinios (No.1)* [1989] 1 All E.R. 253; *Lancashire & Cheshire Association of Baptist Church Inc. v Howard Seddon Partnership* [1993] 3 All E.R. 467; *Henderson v Merrett Syndicates Ltd* [1995] 2 A.C. 145 and see below, para.26–55.

[30] *Cuckmere Brick Co Ltd v Mutual Finance Ltd* [1971] Ch. 949, in which *Kennedy v De Trafford* [1897] A.C. 180 was explained. See also *Holohan v Friends Provident and Century Life Office* [1966] I.R. 1; *Bishop v Bonham* [1988] 1 W.L.R. 742; and *Silven Properties Ltd v Royal Bank of Scotland Plc* [2003] EWCA Civ 1409; [2004] 1 W.L.R. 997 as to the limits upon steps which one may expect the mortgagee to take . See below, paras 26–54 et seq.

[31] *Palk v Mortgage Services Funding Plc* [1993] Ch. 330; *AIB Finance v Debtors* [1998] 2 All E.R. 929.

[32] See below para.25–14 and *Meretz Investments NV v ACP Ltd* [2007] Ch. 197 for consideration of the impact of the mortgagee's motive.

[33] *Barclays Bank v Khana* [1992] 1 W.L.R. 623; [1993] 1 F.L.R. 343 (CA).

[34] *Cheah Theam Swee v Equiticorp Finance Group Ltd* [1992] 1 A.C. 472.

[35] See below, paras 26–18 et seq.

[36] See above, para.25–04.

actually belongs to the mortgagor.[37] Similarly, any profits from the property, which are intercepted by the mortgagee after exercising his legal right to take possession, must be placed to the credit of the mortgagor.

THE MORTGAGEE'S CHOICE OF RIGHTS AND REMEDIES

Clearly, the mortgagee's decision as to which right(s) he wishes to enforce and by which route(s) in the event of a default by the mortgagor will be significantly influenced by the size of the debt and the value of the security, while he must also bear in mind whatever is known about the financial circumstances of the mortgagor. **25–13**

Some of the mortgagee's options, such as proceedings for foreclosure, sale or a claim on the mortgagor's covenant to pay are generally seen as *final* remedies, their object being to extract the capital and other sums due and to bring the mortgage to an end. Other options are essentially *interim* measures intended to protect the security and to minimise any escalation in the debt while efforts are made either to bring the mortgagor back into line or to identify and effect the most attractive final resolution. Appointment of a receiver or entry into possession by receipt of rents and profits generally fall into this *interim* category. While it is true that a mortgagee in possession, after meeting outgoings and the mortgage interest, is entitled to apply surplus rents and profits to the discharge of the principal, and a receiver appointed by the mortgagee may do the same if so directed, it is rare to find sufficient surplus to enable the principal to be paid off over a period acceptable to the mortgagee. Consequently these options are usually deployed as a preliminary step to the realisation of the security by foreclosure or sale. The mortgagee' claim for possession sits somewhere between the two categories: in itself it does not provide a final remedy, as the mortgagee by obtaining an order for possession or even enforcing such an order has not realised its security so as to clear the mortgage debt. However, it is a more serious and decisive expression of intent than the receipt of rent and profits or appointment of a receiver; while interim in some senses it is generally a clear and substantial step on the road to obtaining payment of that debt from the proceeds of sale of the property as mortgagee in possession.

If the property is worth the sum secured (in theory, at least) by the mortgage or if it is likely to increase in value with good management, foreclosure may be the best course. In other cases, if the property is let to tenants or otherwise produces appreciable income, the appointment of a receiver out of court followed by a sale may provide the simplest means of realising the mortgage. If, however, the mortgagor is in possession, there is nothing for the receiver to receive and the fact that vacant possession cannot be given is an obstacle to sale. Then recourse may be had to proceedings for possession followed by a sale out of court. A personal action on the covenant for payment is always available as an additional remedy where the security is insufficient to meet the mortgage debt, but it may

---

[37] *Nelson v Hannam* [1943] Ch. 59.

be pursued without recourse to the security.[38] It has, of course, particular value where the mortgagor has other property which can be reached once a money judgment has been obtained.

25–14   The mortgagee is entitled to exercise his powers in such a way as to protect his own interests, and may give his interests priority over those of the mortgagor or a subsequent mortgagee. The mortgagee's motive in deciding whether to exercise his rights to seek remedies and, if so, which avenue to pursue is of little relevance. A power is improperly exercised if it is no part of a mortgagee's purpose to recover the debt secured by the mortgage or to protect his security, However, if the mortgagee has a range of motives one of which is genuinely to recover all or part of the secured debt or to protect the security, then the exercise of the power will not be invalidated by the operation of other factors in that decision.[39]

Concurrent exercise of a mortgagee's rights and remedies

25–15   Once the mortgagor is in default the mortgagee is entitled to pursue all his remedies concurrently. He may simultaneously take proceedings to obtain foreclosure or sale, possession or the appointment of a receiver, delivery of the title deeds and payment on the personal covenant.[40] If in the same claim[41] he has any collateral securities, he may also enforce these at the same time.[42] If his mortgage empowers him to sell or to appoint a receiver out of court, he may exercise these powers despite the fact that he has already begun proceedings for foreclosure.[43] There are, however, two qualifications on the right to exercise remedies concurrently. First, once an order nisi for foreclosure has been obtained, the leave of the court is necessary for a sale out of court.[44] Second, if a mortgagee takes proceedings for foreclosure and for payment on the personal covenant concurrently, he must do so in the *same* proceedings. As it is open to him to ask for foreclosure and for judgment on the covenant in the same action, the duplication of the concurrent actions will be regarded as vexatious. He may, as will be seen below, take separate proceedings for foreclosure and payment *successively* but, if he chooses to do so *concurrently*, the action on the covenant will be struck out as vexatious.[45]

Successive exercise of remedies

25–16   A mortgagee may also pursue his remedies successively. The fact that he has enforced one remedy does not prevent him from afterwards pursuing another,

---

[38] *Cheah Theam Swee v Equiticorp Finance Group Ltd* [1992] 1 A.C. 472.
[39] *Meretz Investments NV v ACP Ltd* [2007] Ch. 197 per Lewison J.
[40] *China and South Sea Bank Ltd v Tan* [1990] 1 A.C. 536; *Re BCCI SA (No.8)* [1998] A.C. 214; *Cheah Theam Swee*, above; *Cheltenham & Gloucester Building Society v Grattidge* (1993) 25 H.L.R. 454.
[41] *Dymond v Croft* (1876) L.R. 3 Ch.D. 512.
[42] *Lockhart v Hardy* (1846) 9 Beav. 349; *Palmer v Hendrie* (1859) 27 Beav. 349 at 351.
[43] *Stevens v Theatres Ltd* [1903] 1 Ch. 857.
[44] *Stevens v Theatres Ltd* [1903] 1 Ch. 857.
[45] *Williams v Hunt* [1905] 1 K.B. 512.

unless by enforcing the first he has paid himself off. If a judgment on the covenant is only partially satisfied or, if after a sale there is a deficiency, a mortgagee may still pursue any other remedy that, in the circumstances, is open to him.[46] Even foreclosure absolute does not prevent him from bringing an action on the covenant for payment. If he does so, he reopens the foreclosure because a person cannot receive payment and keep the estate.[47] Only if he sells the estate after foreclosure are his remedies at an end. He can then no longer return the estate and has no further rights against the mortgagor.[48] A secured creditor is, therefore, largely outside the rule that separate proceedings must not be brought for different forms of relief claimed in respect of the same transaction.

---

[46] *Lockhart v Hardy* (1846) 9 Beav. 349 at 355.

[47] *Perry v Barker* (1806) 13 Ves. 198.

[48] *Lockhart v Hardy* (1846) 9 Beav. 349. A bona fide purchaser without notice gets a good title, *Lloyds & Scottish Trust v Britten* (1982) 44 P. & C.R. 249. See also below, paras 27–24 et seq.

CHAPTER 26

THE LEGAL MORTGAGEE—RIGHTS, LIABILITIES AND REMEDIES OUT OF COURT

RIGHT TO CUSTODY OF THE TITLE DEEDS[1]

Registered land

In the case of registered land, there are generally no title deeds of which the first **26–01** legal mortgagee can take possession. Until the Land Registration Act 2002 came into force on October 13, 2003, where a legal mortgage was created over registered land the mortgagor would deposit his land certificate[2] with HM Land Registry, who would then issue a "charge certificate" to the mortgagee as proprietor of the registered charge.[3] Now, by virtue of s.27(2)(f) of the 2002 Act, any legal charge over registered land is required to be completed by registration of that charge against the title of the mortgagor[4] and, since no provision is made for charge certificates, they have been prospectively abolished. Accordingly, instead of title deeds the legal mortgagee will rely upon the registration of his interest against that title and the issue of a new Title Information Document to reflect the existence of the mortgage.

Since March 1998, any mortgage of a freehold or leasehold interest with more than 21 years to run which is supported by documents of title has triggered compulsory registration of the land.[5] Since October 13, 2003, this has been extended to include any mortgage of a leasehold interest with more than seven years to run.[6] Accordingly, the rights discussed below pertaining to possession of documents of title to unregistered land are likely to be of diminishing significance.

Unregistered land

The general rule is that muniments of title follow the legal title, so that the holder **26–02** of the legal title has a prima facie right to custody of the title deeds.[7] Formerly,

---

[1] For what may comprise title deeds, see *Clayton v Clayton* [1930] 2 Ch. 12 at 21.

[2] See Land Registration Act (LRA) 1925 s.27 (now repealed).

[3] Although in practice HM Land Registry did not issue one; there is no question of its storing them nowadays.

[4] See above Chs 3 and 13.

[5] LRA 1925 s.123(2) as amended by LRA 1997 s.1 and see above, Ch.13.

[6] LRA 2002 s.4(1)(g).

[7] As to what is meant by "title deeds" see *Clayton v Clayton* [1930] 2 Ch. 12 at 21. The meaning is used in its widest sense, i.e. all documents necessary to prove title.

this meant that legal mortgagees in fee were, as against the mortgagor, entitled to the deeds[8] but that legal mortgagees by demise including, of course, most mortgagees of leasehold interests were not entitled to custody of the mortgagor's title deeds.[9] However, mortgages of freeholds and leaseholds were required by ss.85 and 86 of the Law of Property Act 1925 to be by demise and those sections, at the same time, provided for the *first* legal mortgagee to have a right to custody of the deeds. Thus, a first legal mortgagee of a freehold interest has the same right to the deeds as if his title included the fee, whereas a first legal mortgagee of a leasehold interest has the same right to custody of the deeds as if his mortgage had been created by assignment of the lease instead of by demise. A mortgagee of a leasehold interest is therefore in a better position than he was before the Act unless he was then a mortgagee by assignment of the lease, which was unusual. An equitable mortgagee, however, not having the legal title, has no right to the deeds as against the mortgagor unless he stipulates for that right in the contract. Such a stipulation is, of course, almost invariably found in a first equitable mortgage. Thus, generally, the non-possession of the title deeds by the holder of the legal title constitutes notice to a subsequent mortgagee that the property in question is subject to a mortgage. Further, the possession of the title deeds by the first legal mortgagee will usually provide difficulties for the mortgagor in raising further finance on the security of the property or otherwise dealing with it to the disadvantage of the first legal mortgagee.

A first legal mortgagee's rights to the deeds, though absolute against the mortgagor, will not prevail against an equitable mortgagee who has already obtained the deeds and of whose encumbrance the legal mortgagee therefore has notice.[10] Nor would it prevail, even against a subsequent equitable encumbrancer in possession of the deeds, if the gross negligence of the legal mortgagee in not obtaining the deeds has induced the equitable encumbrancer to believe that there was no prior legal mortgage.[11] In other words, the right to the deeds may sometimes involve the question of competing priorities and the legal mortgagee's normal right to the custody of the deeds may sometimes be displaced.[12] This is in contrast to the system of priorities in respect of mortgages over registered land, where the negligence of a mortgagee over any title deeds has no impact upon his position in the chain provided he has registered his interest at the appropriate time.[13] It appears that a mortgagee with good title but to whom a forged copy of a genuine deed has been delivered can recover the genuine deed from a subsequent mortgagee.[14]

A mortgagee may require and recover all deeds and documents from any person (bar a mortgagee entitled in priority to him) as soon as the statutory power

---

[8] *Smith v Chichester* (1842) 2 Dr. & War. 393.

[9] *Wiseman & Benley v Westland, Fisher, Benson, Davis & Stanbridge* (1826) 1 Y. & J. 117.

[10] It is just conceivable that the legal mortgagee might have a right to the deeds in such a case, see *Agra Bank v Barry* (1874) L.R. 7 H.L. 135.

[11] See above, paras 11–19 et seq.

[12] Since the Judicature Act 1873, it is in all cases the duty of the court to give complete relief by ordering the delivery of the deeds to the encumbrancer, who has priority. *Re Cooper, Cooper v Vesey* (1882) L.R. 20 Ch.D. 611; *Re Ingham, Jones v Ingham* [1893] 1 Ch. 352.

[13] Land Registration Act 2002, s.48.

[14] *Newton v Beck* (1858) 3 H. & N. 220.

of sale has become exercisable. The deeds and documents to which the mortgagee is entitled are all those which a purchaser may require from him to be delivered.[15]

Liability of the mortgagee in possession of deeds to produce them

For the reasons stated above, there will be ever fewer cases in which the **26–03** mortgagee has the title deeds in his possession. However, the obligation upon the mortgagee who has the deeds under a mortgage to produce them on demand by the mortgagor will still be of some relevance, particularly where there is a long-standing mortgage of unregistered land or where the mortgage was originally created by deposit of the deeds.

Before 1882 a mortgagor could not compel his mortgagee to produce the title deeds for inspection without tendering the mortgage moneys[16] and this was so even though the deeds were required for the purpose of negotiating a loan to pay off the existing mortgage.[17] This rule still applies to any mortgages created before January 1, 1882,[18] but it is reversed with regard to later mortgages by s.96(1) of the Law of Property Act 1925.[19] This provides as follows:

> "A mortgagor, as long as his right to redeem subsists, shall be entitled from time to time, at reasonable times, on his request, and at his own cost, and on payment of the mortgagee's costs and expenses in this behalf, to inspect and make copies or abstracts of or extracts from the documents of title relating to the mortgaged property in the custody or power[20] of the mortgagee."

Moreover, the section expressly forbids any contracting out of the above provision. It will also be noted that the subsection does not entitle the mortgagor to *borrow* the title deeds.

A mortgagee's liability under s.96 is not limited to producing the title deeds only for the mortgagor because "mortgagor" also includes "any person from time to time deriving title under the original mortgagor or entitled to redeem a mortgage according to his estate, interest, or right in the mortgaged property."[21] Presumably, in the case of trust property, the liability is only to produce the deeds to the trustees unless, owing to the default of the trustees, the beneficiaries are admitted to redeem in their place. In the case of settled land the primary liability is, of course, to the life-tenant who holds for all persons entitled under the settlement[22] and he is entitled to production of the title deeds. Whether a vested remainderman has a right to the production of the deeds is uncertain. He certainly had the right before 1926, when his remainder was a legal estate, and it may well

---

[15] Law of Property Act 1925, s.106(4).
[16] *Browne v Lockhart* (1840) 10 Sim. 420.
[17] See Coote, *Mortgages* (9th edn, 1927), Vol.2, p.841.
[18] It is very unlikely that any such mortgages still exist.
[19] Replacing s.16 of the Conveyancing Act 1881.
[20] This includes documents in the mortgagee's solicitor's possession: *Bligh v Benson* (1819) 7 Price 205.
[21] Law of Property Act (LPA) 1925 s.205(1)(xvi).
[22] See the Settled Land Act 1925 s.107(1).

be that this right still exists although his interest is now equitable only. Logically, his right should be confined to the case when he has the consent of the life-tenant to redeem, which he must obtain before he can redeem the mortgaged property.[23]

Delivery of deeds on extinguishment

26–04   A mortgagee whose debt has been satisfied, must at once deliver up any deeds which are in his possession.[24] Again, while this is unlikely to apply to a mortgagee under a modern mortgage, there will for some time yet be historic mortgages which have run their term and in respect of which deeds should have been safely retained for delivery up. When the person redeeming is not the mortgagor, he has a right to keep the mortgage alive for his own benefit, and is entitled to the deeds. However, when it is the mortgagor who redeems, a mortgagee is not always obliged to hand over the deeds to him: on the contrary, if he has notice of puisne encumbrances, it is his duty to deliver the deeds to the encumbrancer next in priority of whom the mortgagee has notice.[25] If he does not do so he is liable to make good any loss resulting to the encumbrancer concerned. In this instance, however, contrary to the general rule that registration is notice, registration under the Land Charges Act 1972 or in a local register is *not* deemed to be equivalent to actual notice. Accordingly, there is no need to make a search before handing over the deeds although a mortgagee is bound to search the appropriate registries before he distributes any surplus after a sale.[26] Thus, a mortgagee is under no liability to persons of whose interest he has neither actual nor constructive notice, even though they have registered their encumbrances.[27] A mortgagor can recover possession of the mortgage and all other title deeds where the mortgagee's title has lapsed by effluxion of time.[28]

Liability for loss of deeds

26–05   A mortgagee whose mortgage includes the deeds, must be ready to give up the deeds when the debt is satisfied.[29] This duty arises from the fact that the deeds are part of the mortgaged property and the mortgagor is entitled to the return of the whole of his property.[30] Thus, a mortgagee's liability for loss of the deeds

---

[23] In *Halsbury's Laws of England* (4th edn, Re-issue, 2005), Vol.32, para.695, the view is expressed that as the vested remainderman has a right to redeem he therefore has the statutory right to production of the title deeds.

[24] See *Graham v Seal* (1918) 88 L.J.Ch. 31.

[25] *Corbett v National Provident Institution* (1900) 17 T.L.R. 5.

[26] See below, paras 26–58 et seq.

[27] See Law of Property (Amendment) Act 1926 s.7 and the Law of Property Act 1925 Schedule of Minor Amendments, which alters LPA 1925 s.96(2) to this extent. See also LPA 1969 s.16(2), [Repealed by Statute Law (Repeals) Act 2004 c. 14 Sch.1(12) para.1 (July 22, 2004)] Sch.2 Pt I; Land Charges Act 1972 s.18(6).

[28] *Lewis v Plunket* [1937] Ch. 306.

[29] See *Schoole v Sall* (1803) 1 Sch. & Lef. 176.

[30] See *Gilligan and Nugent v National Bank* [1901] 2 I.R. 513.

arises, not from breach of contract, nor from negligence as a bailee but from the breach of his duty to return the security of the mortgaged property. This being so, a mortgagor cannot fix the mortgagee with liability, except when he is offering to redeem. This somewhat questionable state of affairs arises as a result of the provisions of s.13 of the Law of Property Act 1925 which, in effect, preserves the principle of the pre-1926 law, which was that the mortgagee, being owner of the land, was also owner of the deeds and could not be liable for losing his own property.[31] During the currency of the security the mortgagor has, it is true, a right to inspect the deeds under s.96 of the Law of Property Act 1925 and presumably might be able to bring an action against the mortgagee for damages for breach of his statutory duty under that section but such damages could not include a sum for the permanent loss of the deeds.[32]

The loss of the deeds does not prevent a mortgagee from pursuing his remedies.[33] It only exposes him to an obligation to make compensation, should the mortgagor offer to redeem.[34] At one time the liability to make compensation was absolute, but now the court has jurisdiction to give relief in cases of accident. The practice appears to be as follows:

(1) When a mortgagor is prevented from redeeming by reason of the absence of the deeds, he has an absolute right to commence proceedings for redemption for the sole purpose of having an inquiry as to the loss of the deeds.[35] The object of the proceedings is to establish the fact of the loss in a way which will satisfy future purchasers from the mortgagor and the mortgagee will be made to bear the costs of the action. The offer of an indemnity is not enough; the Master's inquiry is a protection to which the mortgagor is absolutely entitled.[36] The position is the same when redemption is forced upon the mortgagor in a foreclosure action.[37]

(2) If the Master certifies that the loss was not due to any negligence or wilful default on the part of the mortgagee, the mortgagor is entitled only to an indemnity against future charges and expenses which may result from the absence of the deeds.[38]

(3) If the loss is found to have been due to the negligence or other default of the mortgagee, the mortgagor is entitled both to an indemnity and to immediate compensation.[39] Compensation will cover the expense of procuring new copies of deeds where that is possible and of office-

---

[31] In the case of *Browning v Handiland Group Ltd* (1976) 35 P. & C.R. 345 it was held that a mortgagee owed no duty of care in relation to the documents of title and thus the mortgagor was unable to recover the loss incurred when a projected sale failed as a result of the loss of the deeds.

[32] See *Gilligan and Nugent v National Bank* [1901] 2 I.R. 513.

[33] *Baskett v Skeel* (1863) 11 W.R. 1019.

[34] *Stokoe v Robson* (1815) 19 Ves. 385.

[35] *James v Rumsey* (1879) L.R. 11 Ch.D. 398.

[36] *Lord Midleton v Eliot* (1847) 15 Sim. 531.

[37] *Stokoe v Robson* (1815) 19 Ves. 385; *Shelmardine v Harrop* (1821) 6 Madd. 39.

[38] *Shelmardine v Harrop* (1821) 6 Madd. 39, where the mortgagee was robbed.

[39] *Hornby v Matcham* (1848) 16 Sim. 325. For the form of the indemnity, see *Shelmardine*, above.

copies of any proceedings taken to establish the loss and, in addition, a sum by way of damages for future difficulties in proving title. This last is, however, confined to extra expense in proving title and may not include a speculative amount for possible depreciation of the market value of the estate caused by the lack of the deeds.[40]

(4) If the result of the inquiry is that the deeds are found not to be lost, but to be in the hands of a third party, the mortgagor will be directed to bring an action for their recovery, the expenses of the action to be debited to the mortgagee.[41]

(5) If a mortgagor has given notice to redeem and then been prevented from doing so owing to the loss of the deeds, interest ceases to run from that date when redemption was due to take place, even though he does not hand over his money. He cannot be expected to part with his money except in return for his whole security.[42]

RIGHT TO MAINTAIN THE SECURITY

Rights with regard to title

26-06   A mortgagee is entitled to take all steps necessary to perfect and protect his security and may debit the mortgagor with any costs or charges which he incurs thereby. Thus a legal mortgagee who discovers a defect in his title may call upon the mortgagor to remedy it if that becomes possible.[43] The rule is not, of course, confined to mortgages. "The doctrine of the Court of Chancery," said Cranworth L.C., in the case of *Smith v Osborne*,[44] is "that if a man contracts to convey, or to mortgage, or to settle an estate, and he has not at the time of his contract a title to the estate, but he afterwards acquires such a title as enables him to perform his contract, he shall be bound to do so." On this principle an equitable mortgagee has a right to call for the execution of a legal mortgage and to charge the mortgagor with the costs of preparing it.[45] He may enforce this right, even though the mortgagor has begun proceedings for redemption.[46] Moreover, an equitable mortgagee who has begun proceedings for foreclosure may obtain an interim injunction to prevent dealings with the legal estate intended where there are grounds for believing that the mortgagor intends to do something improper with the legal estate.[47]

A mortgagee may protect the security against third parties who impeach the mortgagor's title by claiming a title paramount; he may take any proceedings necessary to defend the mortgagor's title and may generally add the costs of so

---

[40] ibid.; *Brown v Sewell* (1853) 11 Hare 49.
[41] *James v Rumsey* (1879) L.R. 11 Ch.D. 398.
[42] *Lord Midleton v Eliot* (1847) 15 Sim. 531; *James v Rumsey* (1879) L.R. 11 Ch.D. 398.
[43] *Seabourne v Powel* (1686) 2 Vern. 11.
[44] (1857) 6 H.L.C. 375 at 390.
[45] *National Provincial Bank of England v Games* (1886) L.R. 31 Ch.D. 582.
[46] *Grugeon v Gerrard* (1840) 4 Y. & C. (Ex.) 119.
[47] *London & County Banking Co v Lewis* (1882) L.R. 21 Ch.D. 490.

doing to the mortgage debt.[48] This is, however, subject to the distinction between costs incurred in the preservation of the mortgagor's title from external attack on the one hand and costs incurred in defence of the mortgagee's own rights on the other.[49]

Right to preserve the substance of the security

As against the mortgagor

A mortgagee is also entitled to preserve the substance of his security. A legal mortgagee is to a large extent able to protect his security against the acts of the mortgagor by reason of his legal ownership, but every mortgagee, legal or equitable has a general right in equity, as against the mortgagor, to hold the security undiminished in value.[50] Thus, if a mortgagor is wasting the security by cutting timber,[51] or by removing fixtures included in the security,[52] he may be restrained from doing so, provided that the security is shown to be insufficient. But even when the mortgagor's acts do not amount to waste, they may be restrained if it be shown that the security is insufficient and will be prejudiced. For example, mortgagors of tolls were restrained from reducing the toll fees, the security being insufficient.[53]   26–07

As against other persons or causes

A mortgagee may similarly interfere to prevent depreciation of the security from other causes. He may, for example, restrain by injunction a subsequent encumbrancer from dealing with the property to his prejudice.[54] If the mortgage comprises licensed premises it was historically the case that he could take part in proceedings to obtain the renewal of the licence as a "person aggrieved". However, it seems unlikely that that this right has survived the new regime of the Licensing Act 2003.[55] Again, in a case where part of the mortgagee's security was taken under the Land Clauses Acts, he was entitled to be served with notices, and even to claim compensation for "injurious affection" of other lands.[56] Where the property is to be compulsorily acquired, the mortgagee as well as the mortgagor may be served with the notice to treat and absent such notice will not be prejudiced by the exercise of compulsory powers over the mortgagor's   26–08

---

[48] *Sandon v Hooper* (1843) 6 Beav. 246, on appeal (1844) 14 L.J.Ch. 120, L.C.

[49] See above para.26–05 and paras 27–20 et seq., 33–27 et seq.

[50] *McMahon v North Kent Iron Works Co* [1891] 2 Ch. 148, where the mortgage debt was not even yet due.

[51] *Harper v Aplin* (1886) 54 L.T. 383.

[52] *Ackroyd v Mitchell* (1860) 3 L.T. 236; *Ellis v Glover and Hobson, Ltd* [1908] 1 K.B. 388.

[53] *Lord Crewe v Edleston* (1857) 1 De G. & J. 93; cf. *Re Humber Ironworks Co* (1868) 16 W.R. 667.

[54] *Legg v Mathieson* (1860) 2 Giff. 71 where a judgment creditor had been restrained at the suit of the prior mortgagee, even before the mortgage debt had become due, from taking possession of the property under the legal right acquired by the former elegit.

[55] See *Garrett v St. Marylebone, Middlesex JJ.* (1884) L.R. 12 Q.B.D. 620.

[56] *R. v Clerk of the Peace for Middlesex* [1914] 3 K.B. 259.

interest.[57] Other examples arise in cases where a mortgagee is entitled to take possession of the property in order to prevent deterioration of his security by vandalism,[58] or to prevent injury to the property,[59] or to enforce a restrictive covenant.[60]

A mortgagee's right to take proceedings in respect of damage done to the mortgaged property by third parties largely depends on his title. As a legal mortgagee, or if his contract otherwise gives him a right, he may go into possession and avail himself of all possessory remedies. He may sue for trespass and, whether his mortgage is legal or equitable, the doctrine of trespass by relation back applies to enable him to sue for trespasses committed before his entry.[61] In relation to tenancies created on or after January 1, 1996, a mortgagee in possession can enforce any covenant or right of re-entry that the mortgagor could have enforced.[62] A mortgagee of goods, if he is in possession or has an immediate right to possession, may bring an action in trespass or conversion or seek the recovery of the goods under the provisions of the Torts (Interference with Goods) Act 1977.[63] However, if the mortgagee under the terms of the mortgage is not able either expressly or impliedly to obtain possession until the occurrence of a certain event, for example, a demand for payment on default, proceedings cannot be commenced unless and until the event has occurred.[64] A different picture emerges, however, in the case of an equitable mortgagee. He may stipulate for a right to possession in his contract, but otherwise he can have no right to possession without first enforcing his contract for a legal mortgage.

Although a mortgagee may thus be able to protect his security against third parties, it is not often necessary for him to do so. As a rule, the protection of the property is as much in the interests of the mortgagor as of the mortgagee and action is usually taken by the mortgagor, the mortgagee only being joined as a party where that is necessary.[65] A mortgagor in possession has by virtue of his possession and of the rights given to him in equity and statute, a wide power to take proceedings in defence of the mortgaged property.[66] It is generally only when the mortgagor refuses or is unable to take action that the mortgagee will find it necessary to assert his own rights.[67]

---

[57] *Cooke v L.C.C.* [1911] 1 Ch. 604; *Shewu v Richmond upon Thames and Hackney London Boroughs* (1999) 79 P. & C.R. 47

[58] See *Western Bank Ltd v Shindler* [1977] Ch. 1.

[59] *Matthews v Usher* [1900] 2 Q.B 535 at 538; *Turner v Walsh* [1909] 2 K.B. 484 at 487.

[60] *Fairclough v Marshall* (1878) 4 Ex.D. 37.

[61] *Ocean Accident and Guarantee Corporation v Ilford Gas Co* [1905] 2 K.B. 493.

[62] Landlord and Tenants (Covenants) Act 1995 ss.3–15 as amended by LRA 2002.

[63] But for the recovery of title deeds themselves no action will lie under the 1977 Act.

[64] *Bradley v Copley* (1845) 1 C.B. 685; a future right to possession is not of course enough, so that a mortgagee cannot sue if he has covenanted to give the mortgagor possession until default: ibid. cf. *White v Morris* (1852) 11 C.B. 1015, where the mortgagee was allowed to sue when he was a *trustee* to give the mortgagor possession.

[65] See *Van Gelder, Apsimon & Co v Sowerby Bridge United District Flour Society* (1890) L.R. 44 Ch.D. 374. But see in the case of leasehold interests the mortgagee's right to seek relief from forfeiture under the court's inherent jurisdiction or pursuant to statute, e.g. LPA 1925 s.146(4) above, paras 15–05 et seq. and below, para.26–09.

[66] See LPA 1925 ss.98 and 141(2).

[67] e.g. this may arise in the case where the mortgagee wishes to seek relief from forfeiture under LPA 1925 s.146(4); see above, paras 15–05 et seq.

Right to relief from forfeiture of leasehold security[68]

A mortgagee by sub-demise or a mortgagee by way of legal charge[69] is entitled **26–09**
to claim relief from forfeiture under s.146(4) of the Law of Property Act 1925 in
the same way as if he were an under-lessee.[70] This right exists where the
mortgagee simply has a specifically enforceable right to the creation of a legal
charge or mortgage.[71] A mortgagee can even apply for relief pursuant to s.146(4)
in circumstances where the lease has been disclaimed by a trustee in bankruptcy
of the tenant.[72]

RIGHT TO POSSESSION

The legal title which he obtains by his conveyance gives to a legal mortgagee[73] **26–10**
the immediate right to commence an action for possession of the mortgaged
security subject to any agreement to the contrary. Normally, the right arises at
once on the execution of the conveyance and is based upon the legal estate or
interest which the mortgagee acquires in the property as a result of the mortgage.[74] Once the right has arisen, the court will not by injunction restrain the
mortgagee from exercising his right.[75] This is so even if there has been no default
on the part of the mortgagor[76] or that a bill of exchange has been given for the
debt[77] or that a considerable time has elapsed, provided that the action for
possession is not statute-barred.[78] Alternatively, the mortgagee can enter into
receipt of the rent and profits by serving notice on the tenant to pay their rents to
himself instead of to the mortgagor.[79]

---

[68] See generally *Woodfall, Landlord & Tenant*, paras 17.057–17.178 and see above, paras 15–05 et
seq.
[69] *Grand Junction Co Ltd v Bates* [1954] 2 Q.B. 160; *Belgravia Insurance Co Ltd v Meah* (1964)
1 Q.B. 436.
[70] *Chelsea Estates Investment Trust Co v Marche* (1955) Ch. 328.
[71] *Re Good's Lease* [1954] 1 W.L.R. 309.
[72] *Barclays Bank Plc v Prudential Assurance* [1998] 1 E.G.L.R. 44.
[73] A chargee by way of legal mortgage has a corresponding statutory right by virtue of LPA 1925
s.87(1), and see above, para.26–19.
[74] " . . . before the ink is dry on the mortgage . . . ", per Harman J. in *Four-Maids Ltd v Dudley
Marshall (Properties) Ltd* [1957] Ch. 317 at 320; *Westminster City Council v Haymarket Publishing
Ltd* [1981] 1 W.L.R. 677 at 696. See also *Alliance Perpetual Building Society v Belrum Investments*
[1957] 1 W.L.R. 720; *Western Bank Ltd v Shindler* [1977] Ch. 1; *Mobil Oil Co Ltd v Rawlinson*
(1982) 43 P. & C.R. 221. See further *Credit & Mercantile Plc v Marks* [2004] EWCA Civ 568; [2005]
Ch. 81 and *Ashe v National Westminster Bank Plc* [2008] EWCA Civ 55; [2008] 1 W.L.R. 710.
[75] *Marquis of Cholmondeley v Lord Clinton* (1820) 2 J. & W. 1 at 181; this, of course, is one of
the points of difference between mortgagees and trustees. See also *London Permanent Benefit
Building Society v De Baer* [1969] 1 Ch. 321.
[76] *Birch v Wright* (1786) 1 T.R. 378 at 383; *Four-Maids Ltd v Dudley Marshall (Properties) Ltd*
[1957] Ch. 317; see *Rogers v Grazebrook* (1846) 8 Q.B. 895. But see below, paras 26–11 et seq.
[77] *Bramwell v Eglington* (1864) 5 B. & S. 39.
[78] *Wright v Pepin* [1954] 1 W.L.R. 635.
[79] See below, para.26–13. See also *Horlock v Smith* (1842) 6 Jur. 478; or merely not to pay the rent
to the mortgagor, *Heales v M'Murray* (1856) 23 Beav. 401; see also *Kitchen's Trustee v Madders and
Madders* [1949] Ch. 588, affirmed [1950] Ch. 134; *Mexborough U.D.C. v Harrison* [1964] 1 W.L.R.
733 at 736, 737.

Qualifications and restrictions on the right to enter into possession

26–11   The right of the mortgagee to enter into possession of the mortgaged property[80] is subject to a number of qualifications and restrictions.

(1) As indicated above, the mortgage deed itself may contain an express term under which the mortgagee contracts out of his right to possession of the property for a given term, provided that the mortgagor maintains the repayments due under the mortgage. This may amount to a redemise or merely to a personal covenant by the mortgagee not to interfere with the mortagor's enjoyment.[81]

(2) An agreement restricting the mortgagee's right may be implied into the mortgage deed to the effect that the mortgagee has surrendered his right to take immediate possession of the property. In the absence of an express term it is clear that the court will not lightly restrict the mortgagee's right and it has shown considerable reluctance to do so.[82] It would seem that the court will more readily imply such a term in circumstances where the principal moneys are repayable by instalments which is usual in building society (and bank) mortgages.[83] Once there has been a default, however, on the part of the mortgagor, a term restricting the mortgagee's right to possession, whether express or implied, ceases to operate while the default continues to occur. Then the mortgagee must take into account a number of the following factors before going into possession of the security:

(a) If a security is land which is already let on a lease binding on the mortgagee, either by reason of the fact that the lease was made prior to the creation of the mortgage, or it is a subsequent lease binding upon him, the mortgagee cannot physically go into possession. However, he can enter into receipt of the rents and profits by serving notice on the tenants to pay their rents to himself instead of to the mortgagor.[84]

(b) If the mortgagee desires to seek possession of the premises it is usually advisable to do so by means of court proceedings and not by physically taking possession although at common law he has the right to do so. This is especially so if the mortgage deed contains an attornment clause (for the relationship of landlord and tenant is

---

[80] A right which he has at common law and which is not affected by s.36 of the Administration of Justice Act 1970 in relation to an unoccupied dwelling-house; *Ropaigealach v Barclays Bank* [2000] Q.B. 263. See also *Aurora Leasing Ltd v Morgan* [2009] EWHC 3066 (Ch). Once possession is taken lawfully (without any breach of the criminal law) by a mortgagee on the basis of its common law entitlement any re-entry by a mortgagor is as a trespasser.

[81] *Wilkinson v Hall* (1837) 3 Bing. N.C. 508; *Doe d. Parsley v Day* (1842) 2 Q.B. 147. Such contractual restrictions are not common.

[82] See *Esso Petroleum Co Ltd v Alstonbridge Properties Ltd* [1975] 1 W.L.R. 1474; *Western Bank Ltd v Shindler* [1977] Ch. 1. See [1979] Conv. 266 (R. J. Smith).

[83] See *Birmingham Citizens Permanent Building Society v Caunt* [1962] Ch. 883.

[84] See below, paras 26–13 et seq.

created during the continuance of the security)[85] or if a dwelling-house is the subject of the mortgage in question.[86] If a mortgagee attempts to re-enter premises he *may* be guilty of an offence under the Criminal Law Act 1977.[87] In the case of a dwelling-house an unlawful eviction of a residential occupier *may* also be a criminal offence pursuant to the provisions of the Protection from Eviction Act 1977.[88] However, if the premises are vacant or have been abandoned by the mortgagor and the mortgagee has reasonable cause to believe that the residential occupier has ceased to reside therein, or the mortgagor has consented to the taking of possession, then the mortgagee can take possession. Further, if there is an attornment clause it must be remembered that as the *substance* of the transaction is that of a mortgage, in relation to which the attornment clause plays an ancillary part, the tenancy is outside the protection of the Rent Act 1977, the Protection from Eviction Act 1977, the Agricultural Holdings Act 1986 and the Agricultural Tenancies Act 1995.[89] Also, unless the attornment clause so provides, there is normally no need for the mortgagee to serve a notice to quit or a demand for possession on the mortgagor.[90]

(c) In the case of a mortgage which secures a regulated agreement under the Consumer Credit Act 1974, it is only enforceable pursuant to an order of the court.[91]

(3) Another way in which a mortgagee may find his desire to go into possession obstructed is by the fact that a receiver has already been appointed by the court at the instance of a third party. In such a case he cannot enter into possession unless his right to do so was specially reserved by the court in the order appointing the receiver. His proper

---

[85] See *Regent Oil Co Ltd v J.A. Gregory (Hatch End) Ltd* [1966] Ch. 402. Such clauses are now rare.

[86] Under Administration of Justice Act 1970 s.39, the fact that part of the premises is used for purposes other than residence does not prevent something which would otherwise have been treated as a dwelling house from being so treated. Where user changes, the key date for assessing whether or not premises consist of or include a dwelling is the date on which proceedings are commenced. *Royal Bank of Scotland v Miller* [2001] EWCA Civ 344; (2001) 82 P. & C.R. 396. See further *Ropaigealach v Barclays Bank Plc* [2000] Q.B. 263; *Patel v Pirabakaran* [2006] 1 W.L.R. 3112 and *Polar Park Enterprises Inc v Allason* [2008] 1 P. & C.R. 4.

[87] i.e. of using violence to secure entry, see s.6 (replacing the Forcible Entry Acts 1381–1623 s.13). By virtue of s.6(2) it is no defence that the mortgagee is entitled to possession of the premises.

[88] See ss.2, 3. But there is nothing contained in the Act which affects the jurisdiction of the High Court in possession proceedings in a case where the former tenancy was not binding on the mortgagee (s.9(3)); and see *Bolton Building Society v Cobb* [1965] 1 W.L.R. 1. See also *Midland Bank Ltd v Monobond* [1971] E.G.D. 673 and *London Goldhawk Building Society v Eminer* (1977) 242 E.G. 462.

[89] Except possibly in the case where there was a full rack rent or the mortgagor was required to reside in the premises: see *Portman Building Society v Young* [1951] 1 All E.R. 191; *Alliance Building Society v Pinwill* [1958] Ch. 788; *Peckham Mutual Building Society v Registe* (1980) 42 P. & C.R. 186 *Steyning and Littlehampton B.S. v Wilson* [1951] Ch. 1018 and see above, para.3–36.

[90] *Hinkley Building Society v Henny* [1953] 1 W.L.R. 352. As the status of the mortgagor in possession has been likened to that of a tenant at sufferance who can be ejected without any possession, (see further below, paras 29–13 et seq.).

[91] s.126. See also Goode, *Consumer Credit Law & Practice*, and see generally above Ch.16 et seq. and below, para.27–13.

course is, either to apply to the court for the discharge of the receiver or for leave to bring an action for the recovery of the land.[92] If the mortgagee is prevented from exercising his right by the mortgagor he may bring an action to eject the mortgagor.[93]

(4) A practical factor which tends to inhibit the exercise of the mortgagee's right to possession is the strict liability to account which is placed upon a mortgagee in possession. He is liable to account strictly "on the footing of wilful default." This means that he must account not only for such sums as he actually does receive but also for all that he ought to have received had he managed the property with due diligence.[94]

(5) The claim to an overriding interest by the occupiers of the mortgaged property may inhibit the mortgagee's entry into possession if the mortgagor or some other person claiming a beneficial interest in the property seeks to restrain the mortgagee from taking possession.

(6) A court will not grant an order for possession as against one joint-mortgagor if the other mortgagor is in possession and has an arguable defence,[95] a fortiori, if they are husband and wife.[96]

(7) Reference should also be made to the court's general discretion and its specific statutory discretion to grant a stay in a possession action brought by a mortgagee.[97]

What amounts to possession

26–12   Where a mortgagee is in personal occupation of land or has obtained actual possession of chattels, his possession is beyond argument. But when his alleged entry into possession consists merely of some interference with the mortgaged property it may be doubtful whether or not his acts amount to a taking of possession. Nor is this an academic question, for a mortgagee by entering into possession renders himself liable to account to the mortgagor with considerable strictness for the profits which he has received while in possession.[98] Indeed, for this reason the court will not readily hold a mortgagee to be in possession, unless it is clearly established that such was his position[99] by, for example, giving tenants notice to pay rent to him.[100] In the case of *Noyes v Pollock*[101] the Court of Appeal ruled that to be in possession a mortgagee must have so far interfered

---

[92] *Thomas v Brigstocke* (1827) 4 Russ. 64.
[93] *Doe d. Roby v Maisey* (1828) 8 B. & C. 767.
[94] *Chaplin v Young (No.1)* (1864) 33 Beav. 330 at 337, 338. See also *White v City of London Brewery Co* (1889) L.R. 42 Ch.D. 237 and *Shepherd v Spansheath* (1988) E.G.C.S. 35; and further below, paras 26–18 et seq.
[95] *Albany Home Loans Ltd v Massey* [1997] 2 All E.R. 609.
[96] ibid.
[97] See below, paras 27–12 et seq.
[98] See below, para.26–13.
[99] *Gaskell v Gosling* [1896] 1 Q.B. 669.
[100] *Honlock v Smith* (1842) 11 L.J. Ch. 157.
[101] (1886) L.R. 32 Ch.D. 53; apparently approved in *Berkshire Capital Funding Limited v Street* (2000) 32 H.L.R. 373; but see *Mexborough Urban District Council v Harrison* [1964] 1 W.L.R. 733 at 736, 737, where the mortgagee gave notice to the tenants not to pay rent to the mortgagor.

with the mortgaged property as to take over its control and management. The mortgagee's receipt of certain rents, even by cheques made out by the tenants themselves, was there held not to be enough for it was not shown that he had taken over the power of management.[102] Similarly a mortgagee does not, by foreclosing, render himself liable to account as the mortgagee in possession if the foreclosure is reopened: he must have gone on to control and manage the property, e.g. by giving notice that rent should be paid to him and not the mortgagor.[103] Moreover, even when a mortgagee is admittedly in possession, it must also be shown that he took possession in his capacity as mortgagee without reasonable grounds for believing himself to hold in another capacity.[104] A mortgagee who is in possession as tenant[105] to the mortgagor, or as a life-tenant,[106] or as a purchaser[107] under a sale which turns out to be invalid, cannot be called on to account as a mortgagee in possession, for his possession does not rest on his character as mortgagee. A similar position arose where possession was taken under a forfeiture and not as a mortgagee.[108] On the other hand, once a mortgagee has entered into possession as mortgagee and taken upon himself the burden which is imposed on all mortgagees who are in possession, he must continue to perform the duty and he cannot, when he pleases, elect to give it up. Nor, in the absence of special circumstances, will the court assist him to give it up by appointing a receiver under an express or statutory power.[109]

Where the mortgaged property has a bounded and defined area, entry on to part will be regarded as entry on the whole.[110] However, the mortgagee may limit his possession to part only so as not to render himself liable for default in respect of that part still occupied by the mortgagor.[111]

Additional rights of a mortgagee in possession

Right to receive rents and profits

As long as the mortgagor remains in possession,[112] he is entitled to take all the profits from the security without being in any way obliged either to account for

26–13

---

[102] *Contra* the positions where the mortgagee gives notice to the tenants to pay their rents to him, see *Horlock v Smith* (1842) 11 L.J.Ch. 157. See also *Ward v Carttar* (1865) L.R. 1 Eq. 29 where in the absence of the tenants recognising the mortgagee as landlord, the mortgagee's acts of insuring the premises were held not to amount to possession.

[103] *Re Loom, Fulford v Reversionary Interest Society Ltd* (1910) 2 Ch.D. 230.

[104] *Parkinson v Hanbury* (1867) L.R. 2 H.L. 1; *Gaskell v Gosling* [1896] 1 Q.B. 609 at 691; *Page v Linwood* (1837) 4 Cl. & Finn. 399.

[105] *Page v Linwood* (1837) 4 Cl. & Finn. 399, *qua* tenant.

[106] *Lord Kensington v Bouverie* (1855) 7 De G.M. & G. 156; see also *Whitbread v Smith* (1854) 3 De G.M. & G. 727.

[107] *Parkinson v Hanbury* (1867) L.R. 2 H.L. 1.

[108] *Blennerhassett v Day* (1812) 2 Ball & B. 104 at 125.

[109] *Re Prytherch, Prytherch v Williams* (1889) L.R. 42 Ch.D. 590; *County of Gloucester Bank v Rudry Merthyr Colliery Co* [1895] 1 Ch. 629; but the mortgagee may relieve himself by appointing a receiver under an express or statutory power—see *Refuge Assurance Co v Pearlberg* [1938] Ch. 687. See also below, para.26–30 as to the mortgagee's statutory power.

[110] *Low Moor Co v Stanley Coal Co Ltd* (1876) 34 L.T. 186, CA.

[111] *Soar v Dalby* (1852) 15 Beav. 156; *Simmins v Shirley* (1877) L.R. 6 Ch.D. 173.

[112] See above, paras 26–10 et seq.

them or to apply them in discharging the mortgage interest.[113] However, equally, once the mortgagee goes into possession he is entitled to take the rents and profits by virtue of his legal or equitable ownership conferred upon him by the mortgage[114] and to account for the same.

On such entry into possession the mortgagee is entitled to the rents and profits in respect of any tenancies created before the mortgage or otherwise binding upon the mortgagee under an express or statutory power.[115] This may involve the requirement on the part of the mortgagee to have paid to himself all arrears of rent existing on entry into possession.[116] He may even claim an increased rent despite the fact that the agreement relating to such increase was made after the date of the mortgage.[117]

Where there is in existence a tenancy which is not binding on the mortgagee by virtue of the fact that it has been created after the mortgage and was not pursuant to any express or statutory power,[118] there is no contractual nexus between the tenant and the mortgagee, and thus the mortgagee is not entitled to demand payment of the rents as such from the tenant. However, after notice from the mortgagee the tenant should thereafter pay the rent to the mortgagee and not the mortgagor, since on recovery of possession the mortgagor would be entitled to recover the rents from the tenant as puisne profits.[119] Further, on entry by the mortgagee his possession relates back to the date of the mortgage and he is able to recover any accrued sums in respect of rent due within six years prior to his entry.[120] This position applies despite the fact that strictly the action for recovery of puisne profits is an action in trespass which normally requires the person claiming the sums due to have been in possession during that time.[121]

Although, generally, the mortgagee will be able to recover from the tenant the accrued rents due within six years prior to his entry or commencement of any action brought by him, he can only recover those rents which the tenant had failed to pay to the mortgagor. If the tenant had paid rent to the mortgagor in advance and before it was due, this does not constitute a good payment against the mortgagee in respect of those sums accruing due after notice of the mortgage has been given to the tenant and the tenant is liable to pay those sums over again to the mortgagee.[122]

---

[113] *Trent v Hunt* (1853) 9 Exch. 14.

[114] *Cockburn v Edwards* (1881) L.R. 18 Ch.D. 449 at 457; see LPA 1925 s.141 as amended and disapplied to post 1995 tenancies by the Landlord and Tenant (Covenants) Act 1995.

[115] ibid.

[116] *Moss v Gallimore* (1779) 1 Doug. K.B. 279; *Rogers v Humphreys* (1835) 4 Ad. & El. 299 at 314.

[117] *Burrowes v Gradin* (1843) 1 Dow. & L. 213.

[118] See above, Ch.3 and below, para.32–03.

[119] *Pope v Biggs* (1829) 9 B. & C. 245 at 257; *Underhay v Read* (1887) 20 Q.B.D. 209; and see *Rusden v Pope* (1868) L.R. 3 Exch. 269 at 275.

[120] *Barnett v Earl of Guildford* (1855) 11 Exch. 19; *Ocean Accident & Guarantee Corp. Ltd v Ilford Gas Co* [1905] 2 K.B. 493 at 498; and see Limitation Act 1980 s.19.

[121] See *Turner v Cameron's Coalbrook Steam Coal Co* (1850) 5 Exch. 932; see also *Wheeler v Montefiore* (1841) 2 Q.B. 133.

[122] *De Nicholls v Saunders* (1870) L.R. 5 C.P. 589; *Cook v Guerra* (1872) L.R. 7 C.P. 132; *Lord Ashburton v Knocton* [1915] 1 Ch. 274 at 282; *Smallmas Ltd v Castle* [1932] I.R. 294. *Contra* the position where the tenant has paid a lump sum in satisfaction of all rents accruing during the term and no inquiry of the tenant is made by the mortgagee, he is bound by such payment. See *Green v Rheinberg* (1911) 104 L.T. 149; *Grace Rymer Investments Ltd v Waite* [1958] Ch. 831 at 847.

A mortgagee's object in going into possession is to intercept the profits from the mortgaged property, and to utilise them for the discharge of his claims under the mortgage. Thus, after paying any outgoings, such as rents, rates and taxes, insurance premiums, etc., he may apply the profits to the payment of his interest on the mortgage debt, on the expense of improvements and then, if he so desires, to the reduction of the capital account.[123]

Right to enforce leasehold covenants[124]

At common law, a mortgagee of a leasehold interest does not enjoy privity of **26–14** estate with the lessor since the mortgage from which he derives title is effected by way of sub-demise or by means of a legal charge which has the same effect.[125] Consequently, the mortgagee has, in his capacity solely as mortgagee, no right to require the lessor to perform any of the covenants into which the lessor may have entered with the mortgagor.

Prior to January 1, 1996, statute permitted a mortgagee of a reversionary interest expectant on a term granted by lease to enforce and take advantage of covenants referable to the subject-matter of the lease and any rights of re-entry.[126] A mortgagee of the reversion could re-enter demised premises for breaches of covenant committed prior to the mortgage unless they had been waived or released.[127] A mortgagee in possession of leasehold premises was entitled to the benefits of covenants by the lessor which "touch and concern" the demised premises.[128]

This position has changed[129] with regard to tenancies created on or after January 1, 1996. Thereafter, a mortgagee or chargee in possession of a leasehold interest pursuant to a mortgage or charge granted by the lessee may enforce any covenant which falls to be performed by the lessor unless it is either stated to be personal to any particular individual or would not be enforceable for want of registration.[130] A mortgagee or chargee in possession of premises subject to leasehold interest granted on or after the relevant date can enforce any covenant falling to be complied with by the lessee or any right of re-entry which is enforceable by the mortgagor.[131]

Right to carry on business

A mortgagee in possession has full powers to manage the mortgaged property. In **26–15** the case of business premises the mortgagee may carry on the business for a reasonable time with a view to its sale as a going concern and, for such purpose,

[123] *Re Knight, Ex p. Isherwood* (1882) L.R. 22 Ch.D. 384; *Re Coaks, Coaks v Bayley* [1911] Ch. 171.
[124] For a mortgagee's liability with regard to leasehold covenants, see below, para.26–25.
[125] LPA 1925 ss.86 and 87.
[126] LPA 1925 s.141(1).
[127] ibid., s.141(3).
[128] *Spencer's Case* (1583) 5 Co. Rep. 16a; LPA 1925 s.78.
[129] See the Landlord & Tenant (Covenants) Act 1995 s.15. However, see also *First Penthouse Ltd v Channel Hotels & Properties (UK)* [2003] EWHC 2713 (Ch); [2004] L. & T.R. 16.
[130] ibid., s.15(5), as amended by LRA 2002.
[131] ibid., s.15(1).

he is able to use the name of the firm to do so.[132] Where there is a mortgage of a business as a going concern, the mortgagee in possession is entitled to be recouped in respect of any losses incurred without negligence in carrying it on out of the proceeds of sale.[133] If the mortgage includes the goodwill of the business of a publican, the mortgagee on taking possession is entitled to call upon the mortgagor to concur in obtaining a transfer to the mortgagee of the existing licence.[134] Once the mortgagee enters into possession of the business, he, in effect, becomes the owner of the business and stands in the mortgagor's place,[135] but he does not render himself liable on the existing contracts of the business unless they are specifically adopted so as to effect a novation. It would also seem that the fact that a mortgagee takes possession of a business does not of itself operate as a dismissal of the employees employed in that business.[136] Other contractual and statutory provisions might apply, however, and reference should be made to standard works on employment law and transfer of undertakings, in particular those dealing with the Transfer of Undertakings (Protection of Employment) Regulations.[137]

Right to emblements[138]

26–16   A mortgagee entering into possession of agricultural land is entitled as against the mortgagor or his trustee in bankruptcy to emblements[139] and the mortgagor is not so entitled.[140] The mortgagee on entering into possession is entitled to all the growing crops and the mortgagor, or any person claiming under him, such as his trustee in bankruptcy, may be restrained by injunction from cutting and removing crops on the mortgaged land.[141] However, if the mortgagee has not taken possession of the mortgaged property before the mortgagor's bankruptcy, and the crops had been cut or removed before the bankruptcy, such action converts the crops into personal chattels so that they belong to the mortgagor's trustee in bankruptcy.[142] Further, in the case of an agricultural holding which is occupied under a tenancy not binding on the mortgagee, then the tenant is, as against the mortgagee who takes possession, entitled to any compensation which would otherwise be due to him from the mortgagor with regard to crops, improvements, tillages or other matters connected with the holding pursuant to the provisions of the Agricultural Holdings Act 1986.[143]

---

[132] *Cook v Thomas* (1876) 24 W.R. 427.
[133] *Bompas v King* (1886) L.R. 33 Ch.D. 279.
[134] *Rutter v Daniel* (1882) 30 W.R. 801.
[135] *Chaplin v Young (No.1)* (1864) 33 Beav. 330 at 337.
[136] Per Fry L.J. in *Reid v Explosives Co* (1887) L.R. 19 Q.B.D. 264 at 267, 269.
[137] SI 2006/246.
[138] The growing crops of those plants which are produced by annual cultivation.
[139] *Keech v Hall* (1778) 1 Doug. K.B. 21.
[140] *Birch v Wright* (1786) 1 Trn. Rep. 378 at 383; *Moss v Gallimore* (1779) 1 Doug. K.B. 279 at 283.
[141] *Bagnall v Villar* (1879) L.R. 12 Ch.D. 812.
[142] *Re Phillips, Ex p. National Mercantile Bank* (1880) L.R. 16 Ch.D. 104.
[143] See Agricultural Holdings Act 1986 s.60; see also *Lloyds Bank Ltd v Marcan* [1973] 1 W.L.R. 1387. As for tenancies created on or after September 1, 1995, see generally Pt III of the Agricultural Tenancies Act 1995; Muir, Watt & Moss, *Agricultural Holdings* (14th edn, 1998), Ch.5.

Right to grant and surrender leases[144]

This is an area in which the overlap between the rights of the mortgagee and those of the mortgagor can cause difficulty. It is explored in Chapter 32.   **26–17**

Additional liabilities of a mortgagee in possession

Liability to account

A mortgagee, by taking possession becomes the manager of the property in which the beneficial interest still belongs to the mortgagor.[145] In consequence, he has certain duties to the mortgagor. Thus, he is bound to be diligent in collecting the rents and profits and will have to give the mortgagor credit not only for the rents and profits which he actually receives, but also for the rents and profits which, but for his own gross negligence or wilful default, he might have received.[146] This basis of account applies whether the mortgaged property is tangible or intangible and it appears to extend to the mortgagee's receipt (or otherwise) of the rent and profits of land, the profits of a business[147] and the profits of selling and purchasing of stock which is mortgaged.[148] However, although a mortgagee is bound to be diligent, he is not bound to speculate with the mortgaged property and if he does, he must himself bear the losses.[149] The duty arises when the mortgagee enters into possession *qua* mortgagee[150] and not in another capacity, such as *qua* tenant.[151]   **26–18**

When the duty to account arises: The mortgagee may enter into possession of the property in order to protect his security,[152] in which case he is not liable to account for any notional rent where sale is contemplated within a reasonable period.[153] More frequently however, the mortgagee's object in going into possession is either to sell the property or to intercept the net rents and profits therefrom and to utilise them for the discharge of his claims under the mortgage. After paying any outgoings, he may apply the profits to the payment of his interest, and, if he so desires, to the reduction of the capital account. But a mortgagee   **26–19**

---

[144] See below, Ch.32.

[145] See *Noyes v Pollock* (1886) L.R. 32 Ch.D. 53.

[146] *Hughes v Williams* (1806) 12 Ves. 493. *Medforth v Blake* [2000] Ch. 86; *Parkinson v Hanbury* (1867) L.R. 2 H.L. 1; see also *Chaplin v Young (No.1)* (1864) 33 Beav. 330. A mortgagee must utilise the usual means to recover any arrears of rent if those means may prove effectual; *Duke of Buckingham v Gayer* (1684) 1 Vern. 258.

[147] *Chaplin v Young* (1864) 33 Beav. 330 but not those which do not arise from the premises, see *White v City of London Brewery Co* (1889) L.R. 42 Ch.D. 237.

[148] *Langton v Waite* (1868) L.R. 6 Eq. 165; reversed on another point on appeal (1869) L.R. 4 Ch. App. 402.

[149] *Hughes v Williams* (1806) 12 Ves. 493. See also *Shepherd v Spansheath* (1988) E.G. C.S. 35.

[150] *Parkinson v Hanbury* (1867) L.R. 2 H.L. 1 at 14.

[151] *Page v Linwood* (1837) 4 Cl. & Fin 399.

[152] See, e.g. *Western Bank Ltd v Shindler* [1977] Ch. 1.

[153] *Norwich General Trust v Grierson* [1984] C.L.Y. 2306; see also Law Commission Working Paper No.99: *Land Mortgages* (1986) para.3.25.

cannot, however, be made to accept the return of his capital in instalments,[154] so that if the profits are more than sufficient to meet the interest, he need not apply the surplus in reduction of capital. He may hand over the surplus to the mortgagor, unless he has received notice from a later encumbrancer to divert it to him.[155] If, however, he retains the surplus in his own hands, as he is fully entitled to do, he will have to account for it when the final accounts are taken.[156] The question may then arise whether, by so doing, he is to be held to have gradually reduced the capital indebtedness of the mortgagor, and correspondingly his own claim for interest.

As a mortgagee cannot be made to accept payment by instalments, he cannot be compelled to account until either he attempts to realise his security or the mortgagor seeks to redeem.[157] It makes no difference that the mortgagee is in possession. He cannot be made to render periodical accounts. When the time comes for the mortgage account to be taken, the fact that the mortgagee has been in possession does considerably affect the terms of the order directing the account. The special nature of the account arises from the fact that the mortgagee has in his own interest assumed control over property which, beneficially, does not belong to him.[158]

26–20   Basis of the account[159]:   The first principle of the account is that the mortgagee is entitled to have nothing from the property except his security. He cannot, by going into possession, make a personal profit or reap any personal advantage beyond what is due to him under the mortgage. Although he may have credit for his proper expenditure, he cannot charge a commission for his own time and trouble.[160]

Second, he may have credit only for such expenditure on repairs and outgoings as is reasonably necessary. He may charge for reasonable improvements which permanently increase the value of the property but not for extraordinary improvements made without the consent of the mortgagor.[161] If he could charge for every improvement, he might add so considerably to the mortgagor's indebtedness as to make it impossible for him to redeem and thus "improve" him out of his property altogether.[162]

Third, the mortgagee being under a duty to be diligent[163] is accountable for rents and profits on the footing of wilful default.[164] As Jessel M.R., pointed out

---

[154] *Nelson v Booth* (1858) 3 De G. & J. 119 at 122; *Wrigley v Gill* [1906] 1 Ch. 165.

[155] If notice is received and the moneys paid instead to the mortgagor, the mortgagee is liable to account to the subsequent encumbrance: *Bernsey v Sewell* (1820) 1 Jac. W. 647 at 650.

[156] See generally para.26–13, above.

[157] See *Tasker v Small* (1837) 3 My. & Cr. 63.

[158] *Eyre v Hughes* (1876) L.R. 2 Ch.D. 148 at 162.

[159] See also above, paras 25–11 et seq. and below Ch.33.

[160] *Langstaffe v Fenwick; Fenwick v Langstaffe* (1805) 10 Ves. 405; *Re Wallis, Ex p. Lickorish* (1890) L.R. 25 Q.B.D. 176; but he may stipulate for such payment in the mortgage contract, since now there is no objection to a collateral advantage as such: *Biggs v Hoddinott* [1898] 2 Ch. 307.

[161] *Shepard v Jones* (1882) L.R. 21 Ch.D. 469; see also *Scholefield v Lockwood* (1863) 33 L.J.Ch. 106; *Tipton Green Colliery Co v Tipton Moat Colliery Co* (1877) L.R. 7 Ch.D. 192.

[162] See *Sandon v Hooper* (1844) 14 L.J.Ch. 120.

[163] See *Sherwin v Shakespear* (1854) 5 De G.M. & G. 517.

[164] *Hughes v Williams* (1806) 12 Ves. 493; *Shepherd v Spansheath* (1988) E.G.C.S. 35. See generally para.26–18 above. Wilful default also means he is liable for damage to the corpus of the property. *National Bank of Australasia v United Hand-in-Hand & Co* (1879) 4 A.C. 391, PC.

in *Mayer v Murray*,[165] the case of a mortgagee in possession is the only one in which the charge of wilful default need not be raised in the pleadings. This means that the mortgagor will be credited not only with the profits which the mortgagee in fact received, but also with those which, but for his gross negligence or wilful default, he would have received.[166] A mortgagee who personally occupies the mortgaged property, will be charged a fair occupation rent.[167] For example, a brewer mortgagee, who takes possession of a public house and lets it as a tied house, will be liable to account for the additional rent the house would have commanded as a free house.[168] A mortgagee's duty does not, however, go so far as to compel him to make the most of the mortgaged property: he is not bound to speculate with it[169]; he is not even bound to make special exertions to get the highest possible rent or the largest possible profit.[170] Nor is a mortgagee bound to let the mortgaged property if this might hinder or interfere with an intended sale.[171] He is liable only for gross negligence or wilful default. The fact that the account is on the footing of wilful default need not, therefore, unduly alarm a prudent man of business. Maitland however, sets up a further objection by suggesting[172] that the account against a mortgagee in possession is often taken with annual rests, i.e. that at each half-year[173] if there was an excess of profit of receipts over interest charges, the surplus must be taken to have gone in reduction of the capital debt, so that interest is afterwards allowed only on the reduced amount. However, such an account is only ordered in exceptional circumstances.[174]

Rests: The general rule is that the account of rents and profits runs on from **26–21** beginning to end without reference to the question whether the mortgagee has at any particular time had in his hands more than sufficient to pay the interest. The reason for this is that a mortgagee is not bound to accept payment by instalments and is entitled to have the account taken as a whole. To this rule there appear to be two exceptions: (i) where the mortgagee has claimed the property as his own, thereby denying the mortgagor's right to redeem[175]; and (ii) where the interest

---

[165] (1878) L.R. 8 Ch.D. 424 at 427; see also *Lord Kensington v Bouverie* (1855) 7 De G.M. & G. 134 at 156.

[166] *Brandon v Brandon* (1862) 10 W.R. 287; *Shepherd v Spansheath, ante. Noyes v Pollock* (1886) L.R. 32 Ch.D. 53.

[167] *Lord Trimleston v Hamill* (1810) 1 Ball & B. 377 at 385; *Marriott v Anchor Reversionary Co* (1861) 3 De G.F. & J. 177 at 193, see also *Fyfe v Smith* [1975] 2 N.S.W.L.R. 408; but not, of course, where the premises have no letting value, see *Marshall v Cave* (1824) 3 L.J.(O.S.) Ch. 57; and letting value, *White v City of London Brewery* (1889) L.R. 42 Ch.D. 237 either by reason of their physical condition or a local trading slump. See also Law Commission Working Paper No.99, *Land Mortgages* (1986), para.3.24. A mortgagee who lets a purchaser into possession early is not liable to account: *Shepherd v Jones* (1882) L.R. 21 Ch.D. 469.

[168] *White v City of London Brewery* (1889) L.R. 42 Ch.D. 237 and see *Shepherd v Spansheath*, above.

[169] *Hughes v Williams* (1806) 12 Ves. 493. See also *Shepherd v Spansheath*, above.

[170] See *Wragg v Denham* (1836) 2 Y & C. Ex. 117.

[171] *Downsview Nominees Ltd v First City Corp Ltd* [1993] A.C. 295; *China South Sea Bank Ltd v Tan* [1990] 1 A.C. 536.

[172] Maitland, *Equity* (2nd edn), p.187.

[173] Or at the end of each full year, as the case may be.

[174] *Wrigley v Gill* [1905] 1 Ch. 241; *Ainsworth v Wilding* [1905] 1 Ch. 435.

[175] *National Bank of Australasia v United Hand-in-Hand & Co* (1879) 4 A.C. 391; see *Wrigley v Gill* [1905] 1 Ch. 241 (PC); *Incorporated Society in Dublin v Richards* (1841) 1 Dr. & W. 258.

was not in arrear when the mortgagee went into possession.[176] In the second case the mortgagee is considered to have elected to take his money in instalments, so that he must set off the excess of receipts and interest against the principal[177]: however, once he is in possession, the mere fact that afterwards the interest ceased to be in arrear will not render him liable to make rests. He cannot safely give up possession so that there is no evidence of an intention to take his money in instalments.[178] It is true that in some older cases[179] it is suggested that even when interest was in arrear at the time of entry, the mortgagee must account with rests where the annual profits greatly and notoriously exceed the interest. These cases cannot now be relied on[180] and the true principle seems to be that the court only directs an account with rests by way of penalising the mortgagee when he fails to treat the mortgage property as a security. If he enters when his interest is genuinely in arrears, such a penalty is out of place.[181] If, however, the profits do greatly exceed the interest, the mortgagee must be capable of restoring the property to the mortgagor as soon as his whole debt is satisfied. For, if afterwards he continues in possession, he will have to pay interest to the mortgagor on such further sums as he receives by way of profits.[182] He is not entitled to use the mortgagor's money. Therefore, if the latter can establish that at any particular date the whole debt was paid off, an account will be taken against the mortgagee from that date charging him compound interest on the excess of rents and profits over outgoings with annual rests.[183]

Thus, although the account is taken against a mortgagee in possession with some strictness,[184] this need not deter a mortgagee from enforcing his right if the occasion arises for its exercise and if he keeps in mind that the property does not cease to be the mortgagor's. Mortgagees, particularly building societies, do in practice go into possession a great deal more frequently than is commonly supposed[185] but only as a last resort.

Liability for waste

26–22   Prior to 1926 the mortgagee formerly held the legal estate in fee simple and was thus an absolute owner at law and so was not liable for waste. After 1925 the mortgagee holds by virtue of a term of years but, pursuant to the Law of Property

---

[176] *Shephard v Elliot* (1819) 4 Madd. 254.

[177] This presumption will not be made if, interest not being in arrear, he entered to protect the security; *Patch v Wild* (1861) 30 Beav. 99.

[178] *Davis v May* (1815) 19 Ves. 383; *Latter v Dashwood* (1834) 6 Sim. 462; but if he settles an account with the mortgagor, capitalising the arrears, he must go out of possession or he will be treated as if he had entered when no rent was in arrear; *Wilson v Cluer* (1840) 3 Beav. 136.

[179] E.g. *Uttermare v Stevens* (1851) 17 L.T.(O.S.) 115; see also *Wilson v Cluer* (1840) 3 Beav. 136.

[180] *Nelson v Booth* (1858) 3 De G. & J. 119; *Wrigley v Gill* [1905] 1 Ch. 241.

[181] Per Warrington J. in *Wrigley v Gill* [1905] 1 Ch. 241 at 249.

[182] *Wilson v Metcalfe* (1826) 1 Russ. 530.

[183] *Ashworth v Lord* (1887) L.R. 36 Ch.D. 545 at 551.

[184] For the practice in taking the accounts see below, paras 33–04 et seq.

[185] See Law Commission Working Paper No.99, *Land Mortgages* (1986), para.1.3.

Act 1925, this is normally expressed to be without impeachment of waste.[186] In equity, the mortgagee on redemption must hand back to the mortgagor the property unimpaired and he may not destroy any part of it unless the security is deficient. However, he must make good any such loss to the mortgagor in taking the accounts.[187]

Although a mortgagee will be liable for waste if he causes unnecessary injury to the property, such as cutting timber when the security is not shown to be defective,[188] there may be contractual or statutory provisions entitling him to act in that way which will override the general liability. For example, in the case of cutting timber, if the mortgage is by deed and executed after 1881, s.101(1)(iv) of the Law of Property Act 1925 gives a mortgagee in possession the power to cut and sell timber and other trees ripe for cutting which were not planted or left standing for shelter or ornament. Further, the mortgagee may contract for this to be done on the terms of the contract being completed within one year. The statutory power may be varied or excluded by the mortgage deed,[189] and a felling licence may be necessary.[190] However, even when a mortgagee in possession has no power to cut timber (i.e. the statutory power has been excluded) he will not be restrained by injunction from so doing unless the security is sufficient.[191] This reflects the position prior to 1926 in that the mortgagee of the fee simple might cut timber by virtue of his ownership without committing waste at law, but in equity he would be restrained unless the security was insufficient or defective. All profits from the sale of timber must, of course, be brought into the account for the benefit of the mortgagor. The mortgagee may not open new mines[192] but he has the right to work mines already opened.[193] The court will not interfere if a new mine is opened provided that there is no wanton destruction.[194] Once again, the profits from permitted mining operations must be brought into the account, but if the security is sufficient and new mines are dug without permission, it is likely that all receipts must be brought in without allowance for expenses.[195]

Agricultural land

A mortgagee in possession of such land is liable for damage occasioned by his **26–23** gross negligence with regard to cultivation of that land.[196]

---

[186] See LPA 1925 ss. 85(2), 86(2), 87(1), Sch.1, Pt VII paras 1, 2. Note that as amended by LRA 2002 ss.85(3) and 86(3) state "Subsection (2) does not apply to registered land, but, subject to that, this section applies whether or not the land is registered land and whether or not the mortgage is expressed to be made by way of trust for sale or otherwise".87(4) states "Subsection (1) of this section shall not be taken to be affected by section 23(1)(a) of the Land Registration Act 2002 (under which the owner's powers in relation to a registered estate do not include power to mortgage by demise or sub-demise)". cf. *Downsview Nominees Ltd v First City Corp Ltd* [1993] A.C. 295.

[187] *Millet v Davey* (1862) 31 Beav. 470.

[188] *Withrington v Banks* (1725) Cas temp King 30.

[189] LPA 1925 s.101(3), (4).

[190] Felling licences are obtained from the Forestry Commission.

[191] *Millett v Davey* (1862) 31 Beav. 470.

[192] ibid., at 475.

[193] *Elias v Snowden Slate Quarries Co* (1879) L.R. 4 App.Cas. 454.

[194] *Millett v Davey* (1862) 31 Beav. 470 at 476.

[195] *Hughes v Williams* (1806) 12 Ves 493; *Thorneycroft v Crockett* (1848) 16 Sim 445

[196] *Wragg v Denham* (1836) 2 Y. & C. Ex 117.

Liability for repairs

26–24   The mortgagee is bound to maintain the property in necessary repair but only so far as the rent and profits allow him to do so.[197] He will be liable for any deterioration consequent on his neglect to perform this duty. Provided that such repairs and improvements are necessary and reasonable,[198] the cost of effecting the same will be charged to the mortgagor in the accounts.[199] If the security is leasehold property the rule is especially strict and he will be liable for a forfeiture of the lease occasioned by his breach of a repairing covenant.[200] He need not spend his own money on the upkeep of the security. Accordingly he will only be liable for neglect to effect necessary repairs to the extent of surplus rents and profits after providing for the interest to which he is entitled under the mortgage.[201] A mortgagee may construct new houses in substitution of ruinous old houses,[202] but he is not bound to expend money in rebuilding.[203] Although the mortgagee may without the mortgagor's consent make reasonable and beneficial improvements to the property[204] he cannot make excessive or permanent improvements unless he obtains the mortgagor's consent, or there is acquiescence on the part of the mortgagor after notice to him.[205] The reason for this is that the mortgagee must not improve the mortgagor out of his estate which would have the effect of preventing him from redeeming the property.

Liability under leasehold covenants[206]

26–25   At common law, a mortgagee of a leasehold interest does not enjoy privity of estate with the lessor since the mortgage from which he derives title is effected by way of sub-demise or by means of a legal charge which has the same effect.[207] Consequently, the mortgagee has, in his capacity solely as mortgagee, no liability to the lessor pursuant to the covenants contained in the mortgaged demise. This extends to the payment of rent. However, if the lessor is able to forfeit the demised property for non-compliance with any covenants in the lease, the mortgagee's rights at common law are, if he wishes to maintain his security, of limited benefit.

---

[197] But improvements and repairs not strictly necessary he does at his own risk, unless he first obtains the mortgagor's consent as these may affect the mortgagor's power to redeem, see *Sandon v Hooper* (1844) 14 L.J.Ch. 120.

[198] *Richards v Morgan* (1753) 4 Y. & C.Ex. 570. See also *Moore v Painter* (1842) 6 Jur. 903; *Powell v Trotter* (1861) 1 Drew. & Sm. 388; *Tipton Green Colliery Co v Tipton Moat Colliery Co* (1877–78) L.R. 7 Ch.D. 192.; and *Barclays Bank Plc v Alcorn* [2002] EWHC 498 (Ch); [2002] 2 P. & C.R. DG10.

[199] *Scholefield v Lockwood* (1863) 4 De G.J. & Sm. 22 L.C.; *Tipton Green Colliery Co v Tipton Moat Colliery Co* (1877–78) L.R. 7 Ch.D. 192. See, generally Ch.33.

[200] *Perry v Walker* (1855) 3 Eq.Rep. 721.

[201] *Richards v Morgan* (1753) 4 Y. & C.Ex. 570.

[202] *Hardy v Reeves* (1799) 4 Ves. 466 at 480; *Newman v Baker* (1860) 8 C.B.N.S. 200; *Marshall v Cave* (1824) 3 L.J.(O.S.) Ch. 57.

[203] *Moore v Painter* (1842) 6 Jur. 903.

[204] *Shepard v Jones* (1882) L.R. 21 Ch.D. 469 at 479; see also *Powell v Trotter* (1861) 1 Drew. & Sm. 388.

[205] *Sandon v Hooper* (1844) 14 L.J.Ch. 120; *Bright v Campbell* (1885) 54 L.J.Ch. 1077.

[206] For a mortgagee's rights with regard to leasehold covenants, see above, para.26–14.

[207] LPA 1925 ss.86 and 87 as amended by LRA 2002—see fn.73, above.

Prior to January 1, 1996, a mortgagee of the reversionary interest of a leasehold estate was liable under any covenants entered into by the lessor if they were referable to the subject-matter demised by the lease and if the lessor had power to bind the mortgagee.[208]

In relation to new tenancies created on or after January 1, 1996, s.15 of the Landlord and Tenant (Covenants) Act 1995 has altered the position. A covenant which must be complied with by the lessor is enforceable against any person (other than the reversioner) who is entitled to the rents and profits for the time being of the demised premises. A lessee's mortgagee can enforce such a covenant against the lessor.[209] The new obligations cut both ways: a lessor may also enforce any covenant which is enforceable against the lessee or any right of re-entry to the demised premises[210] against a mortgagee or chargee in possession pursuant to a mortgage or charge granted by the lessee unless the covenant in question is either stated to be personal to any particular individual or would not be enforceable for want of registration.[211]

Liability under freehold covenants

The burden of a positive covenant will not bind a mortgagee. A restrictive **26–26** covenant will, in the appropriate circumstances, be enforceable against the mortgagee as a successor in title of the covenantor.

RIGHT TO APPOINT A RECEIVER

There are two ways in which a mortgagee may obtain the appointment of a **26–27** receiver: (i) by himself making the appointment under a power in the mortgage contract; and (ii) by an application to the court for a receiver to be appointed by the court. This chapter addresses the situation in which a receiver is appointed out of court; appointment by the Court is dealt with in Ch.27 below.[212]

A mortgagee places a receiver in control of the mortgaged property for the same reasons as he goes into possession himself: either the security is in danger of being squandered by the mortgagor; or else he is anxious to intercept the profits and apply them to the discharge of the mortgage debt. Appointing a receiver has a great advantage over going into possession since, by this means the property can be taken out of the mortgagor's control without the mortgagee having to assume any additional responsibilities towards the mortgagor as he would were he to go into possession. There is only one minor disadvantage, which is that lapse of time does not confer a title to the land in the case where a receiver has been appointed.[213]

---

[208] LPA 1925 s.142(1).
[209] Landlord & Tenant (Covenants) Act 1995 s.15(3).
[210] Landlord & Tenant (Covenants) Act 1995 s.15.
[211] ibid., s.15(5)
[212] See below, paras 27–48 et seq.
[213] *Contra* the position in the case of a mortgagee in possession.

History

26–28 Before 1860 a mortgagee had no power to appoint a receiver unless he had expressly stipulated for it in the mortgage. Consequently, if, having no such power, he did appoint a receiver, it was equivalent to going into possession and the receiver was his agent.[214] Well-drawn mortgages, however, invariably contained such a power and also a statement that the receiver, when appointed, was to be considered the agent of the mortgagor and the mortgagee was not liable to account strictly as he would have been if he had taken possession or the receiver had been his agent.[215] In 1860 Lord Cranworth's Act[216] made this power statutory for mortgages created by deed, but the power was confined to the case of rents and profits from land. In 1881, s.19 of the Conveyancing Act widened the scope of the statutory power and this section was replaced by s.101 of the Law of Property Act 1925. All mortgages executed after 1881 are governed by provisions now contained in ss.101 and 109 of the Law of Property Act 1925.

Appointment

Under an express power

26–29 The appointment of a receiver out of court can be made pursuant to an express power contained in the mortgage deed. The appointment may, somewhat unusually, be made at the time of the execution of the mortgage or, more commonly, at some time thereafter. In the latter instance, the appointment is made by the mortgagee by an instrument either in writing or under seal, depending upon the terms of the power bestowed by the mortgage deed. However the appointment is made, it will recite that the receiver is the mortgagor's agent.[217] It is now customary for the receiver expressly to be permitted under the terms of the mortgage deed (and under the instrument appointing him) to have and exercise a number of powers, usually (i) the power to do anything the mortgagor might do; (ii) an irrevocable power of attorney with regard to the execution of deeds and the sale of the mortgaged property; (iii) the power to apply the sums received during the receivership in a specified manner.

Pursuant to statutory powers

26–30 Section 101(1)(iii) of the Law of Property Act 1925 permits a mortgagee, when the mortgage is made by deed to appoint a receiver of the income of the mortgaged property or any part thereof when the mortgage money has become due. Moreover, if the mortgaged property consists of an interest in income or of

---

[214] *Quarrell v Beckford* (1816) 1 Madd. 269.

[215] cf. *Jefferys v Dickson* (1866) 1 L.R. Ch.App. 183 at 190; cf. Rigby L.J., in *Gaskell v Gosling* [1896] 1 Q.B. 669 at 692.

[216] Power of Trustees, Mortgagees, etc. Act 1860.

[217] *Jeffreys v Dixon* (1866) 1 L.R. Ch.App. 183 at 190; *Gaskell v Gosling* [1896] 1 Q.B. 669 at 692.

a rentcharge or an annual or other periodical sum that section permits the mortgagee (where the mortgage is made by deed) to appoint a receiver of that property or any part of it. Section 101 applies only if and as far as a contrary intention is not expressed in the mortgage deed and, in any event, has effect subject to the terms of the mortgage deed and to the provisions contained in it.[218] The statutory power is subject to the limitation that it may not be exercised until the mortgage money has become due pursuant to the terms of the mortgage.[219] Common practice is now for that statutory restriction to be removed and for the receiver's powers to be extended generally and, for example, for a power of the sale to be given to the receiver.[220] The statutory power of appointment may be exercised by the mortgagee in writing under his own hand.[221] A receiver may also be removed and a new receiver appointed by the mortgagee by writing under his hand from time to time.[222] The power to remove a receiver is exercised by a mortgagee even after he has gone into possession.[223]

Mortgagee's duties with regard to the appointment of a receiver

A mortgagee owes a general duty to both the mortgagor and any subsequent **26–31** mortgagees to exercise his powers for the purpose of securing the repayment of any moneys owing to him[224] and further, a duty to act in good faith.[225] The mortgagee, however, has a broad discretion if and when to appoint a receiver having regard to his own peculiar interest, and may exercise his power even though the timing of the appointment of a receiver may be disadvantageous to the mortgagor or any subsequent mortgagees.[226] The distinction, however, should be drawn between an exercise by the mortgagee of his powers in good faith and those which are not so exercised; it would appear arguable that where a mortgagee appoints a receiver in order to frustrate a purpose of the mortgagor or a subsequent mortgagee or who stands by while a receiver acts in such a manner that the exercise of his powers amounts to an abuse of them may be guilty of bad faith.[227]

The mere fact that there exists a dispute with the mortgagor, even of so fundamental a nature as whether or not the security exists or has become enforceable, will not prevent the mortgagee from exercising a right to appoint a

---

[218] LPA 1925 s.101(4).

[219] ibid., s.101(1)(iii). As to the scope of this section, see *Silven Properties Ltd v Royal Bank of Scotland Plc* [2002] EWHC 1976 (Ch); [2003] B.P.I.R. 171.

[220] Such power is, it would appear, an express power rather than an extension of the receiver's statutory powers: *Phoenix Properties v Wimpole Street Nominees* [1992] B.C.L.C. 737.

[221] LPA 1925 s.109(1).

[222] LPA 1925 s.109(5).

[223] *Refuge Assurance Co Ltd v Pearlberg* [1938] Ch. 687 (CA).

[224] Although it seems that this need no longer be the sole purpose for his actions—see *Meretz Investments NV v ACP Ltd* [2006] EWHC 74 (Ch); [2007] Ch. 197.

[225] *Downsview Nominees Ltd v First City Corp Ltd* [1993] A.C. 295.

[226] *Shanji v Johnson Matthey Bankers Ltd* [1986] B.C.L.C. 278 (on appeal [1991] B.C.L.C. 36); *Re Potters Oils Ltd (No.2)* [1986] 1 W.L.R. 201.

[227] *Downsview Nominees Ltd v First City Corp Ltd* [1993] A.C. 295.

receiver. However, the mortgagee will be at risk of damages in the event that the appointment is subsequently shown to have been invalid for such reasons.[228]

The agency of the receiver

26–32   A receiver appointed under the powers conferred by the Law of Property Act 1925 is deemed to be the agent of the mortgagor, who is solely responsible for the receiver's acts or defaults unless the mortgage deed otherwise provides.[229] The agency of the receiver on behalf of the mortgagor is determined by the receiver's subsequent appointment by the court,[230] but not by the mortgagor's death.[231] In circumstances where the mortgagor is dead, the receiver is able to sue in the name of the mortgagor's personal representatives on the provision of a suitable indemnity.[232]

The receiver's position as agent of the mortgagor is different from most types of ordinary agency.[233] His appointment is made by the mortgagee in order to protect the mortgagee's position. However, having been so appointed, the receiver is able by his acts to affect the position of the mortgagor with the objective of benefiting the mortgagee. Furthermore, the mortgagor is obliged to pay the receiver's fees and other expenses but is unable to dismiss him since that is a power reserved to the mortgagee. Notwithstanding his obligation to pay nor the fact that the receiver is able to effect the position of the mortgagor, the mortgagor is unable to instruct the receiver as to how to conduct the receivership.[234] In exercising his powers, a receiver's duties to the mortgagor and anyone else interested in the equity of redemption of the property are not necessarily confined to a duty of good faith. So, when exercising his powers of management, the receiver can owe a duty to manage the mortgaged property with due diligence,[235] subject as ever to his primary duty of advancing the mortgagee's interests in having the secured debt and the interest thereon being paid. So where a receiver decided to continue a business at the mortgaged property, his duties to the mortgagor required him to take reasonable steps to manage it profitably.[236] This duty was one imposed by equity. In *Medforth v Blake*[237] the Vice-Chancellor made it clear that a receiver could not be in breach of his duty of good faith to the mortgagor in the absence of conduct which was otherwise dishonest, improperly motivated or contained an element of bad faith. To make good an allegation

---

[228] *BCPMS (Europe) Ltd v GMAC Commercial Financial Plc* [2006] EWHC 3744 (Ch), *Rushingdale Ltd v Byblos Bank SAL* [1986] 2 B.C.C. 99,549 (CA).

[229] LPA 1925 s.109(2).

[230] *Hand v Blow* [1901] 2 Ch. 721.

[231] *Re Hale, Lilley v Foad* [1899] Ch. 107 (CA).

[232] *Fairhome and Palliser v Kennedy* (1890) 24 L.R. I.R. 498.

[233] See further *Gomba Holdings (UK) Ltd v Homan* [1986] 1 W.L.R. 1301 and as to the character and incidents of a receiver's agency for a mortgagor, see *Silven Properties Ltd v Royal Bank of Scotland* [2004] 1 W.L.R. 997 and *Dolphin Quays Developments Ltd v Mills* [2008] EWCA Civ 385; [2008] 1 W.L.R. 1829.

[234] See generally *Gomba Holdings (U.K.) Ltd v Minories Finance Ltd* [1988] 1 W.L.R. 1231 (CA).

[235] See *Silven v RBS* [2003] EWCA Civ 1409.

[236] *Medforth v Blake* [2000] Ch. 86.

[237] ibid.

of a breach of duty of good faith, the court will require an element such as this to be demonstrated.

The receiver will be treated as an agent of the mortgagee in circumstances where the mortgagee holds the receiver out as being his agent[238] or where the mortgagee directs or interferes with the activities of the receiver.[239] Moreover, the agency of the receiver on behalf of the mortgagor determines if the mortgagor is placed into liquidation and thereafter if the receiver continues to act, he does so as principal unless the mortgagee, by his conduct, ratifies his standing as the mortgagee's agent.[240] Where a receiver is the mortgagee's agent, the mortgagee is liable for his acts and omissions according to the usual rules.[241] Although in the absence of an express exclusion in any contract between the mortgagee and the receiver, the mortgagee is entitled, under an implied term of that contract to an indemnity from the receiver in respect of any negligence on his behalf.[242]

A receiver is under a duty to any guarantor of the mortgagor's debt to take reasonable care to obtain the true market value of the mortgaged property when the same is being realised in the exercise of any power of sale.[243]

Powers of the receiver

Pursuant to statute

A receiver has the statutory powers set forth in s.109 of the Law of Property Act **26–33** 1925. These powers are the power to demand or recover all the income of which he is appointed receiver (whether by action, distress or otherwise) in the name either of the mortgagor or the mortgagee to the full extent of the estate or interest which the mortgagor could dispose of and to give effectual receipts accordingly for that income and to exercise any powers which may have been delegated to him by the mortgagee pursuant to the Law of Property Act 1925.[244] A person paying money to the receiver shall not be concerned to enquire whether any case has happened to authorise the receiver to act.[245]

Statutory powers as to insurance and the application of income

If appointed pursuant to the mortgagee's statutory powers, the receiver shall, if **26–34** so directed in writing by the mortgagee, insure the mortgaged property to the extent, if any, to which the mortgagee might have insured it and keep insured any building, effects or property comprised in the mortgage, whether fixed to the freehold or not, being of an insurable nature against loss or damage by fire out of the money received by him.[246]

---

[238] *Chatsworth Properties Ltd v Effion* [1971] 1 W.L.R. 144.
[239] *American Express International Banking Corp v Hurley* [1985] 3 All E.R. 564.
[240] ibid.
[241] ibid.; *Circuit Systems Ltd v Zuken-Redac (U.K.) Ltd* [1997] 1 W.L.R. 721.
[242] *American Express International Banking Corp v Hurley*, above.
[243] *American Express International Banking Corp v Hurley*, above.
[244] LPA 1925 s.109(3).
[245] ibid., s.109(4).
[246] ibid., s.109(7).

Furthermore, subject to the provisions of the Law of Property Act as to the application of insurance money, the receiver shall apply all money received by him in accordance with s.109(8) of the Law of Property Act 1925. That subsection requires the moneys to be applied as follows:

"(i) in discharge of all rents, taxes, rates and out-goings whatever affecting the mortgage property; and

(ii) in keeping down all annual sums or other payments, and the interest on all principal sums, having priority to the mortgage in right whereof he is receiver; and

(iii) in payment of his commission, and of the premiums on fire, life or other insurance, if any, properly payable under the mortgage deed or under this act, and the cost of executing necessary or proper repairs directed in writing by the mortgagee; and

(iv) in payment of the interest accruing due in respect of any principal money due under the mortgage; and

(v) in or towards discharge of the principal monies so directed in writing by the mortgagee;

and shall pay the residual, if any, of the money received by him to the person who, but for possession of the receiver, would have been entitled to receive the income of which he is appointed receiver, or is otherwise entitled to the mortgaged property."

The statutory powers given to the receiver with regard to the application of income may be extended by the mortgage deed so as to permit, for example, the receiver and manager of a business to pay its unsecured debts.[247] The obligations on the receiver imposed by s.109(8)(iv) and (v) are obligations which ensure for the benefit of both the mortgagor and the mortgagee and, accordingly, a mortgagor may institute proceedings against a receiver if he should fail to perform them.[248]

Express powers

26–35   In any appointment otherwise than pursuant to statute, the receiver only has those powers which are conferred upon him by the mortgage deed or instrument effecting his appointment. The modern practice is for receivers to have extensive powers conferred on them expressly pursuant to the mortgage or charge.

Duties of the receiver to the mortgagor and third parties

26–36   A receiver owes the same duty in equity to the mortgagor and any subsequent mortgagees and guarantors of the mortgagor's liability as the mortgagee does; mainly to exercise his powers in good faith and for the purpose of obtaining repayment of the debt owing to the mortgagee.[249] Sight should not be lost of the

---

[247] *Re Hail, Lilley v Foad* [1899] 2 Ch. 107.

[248] *Leicester Permanent Building Society v Bart Square* [1943] Ch. 308.

[249] *Downsview Nominees Ltd v First City Corp Ltd* [1993] A.C. 215; *American Express International Banking Corp v Hurley* [1985] 3 All E.R. 564; *Standard Chartered Bank v Walker* [1982] 1 W.L.R. 1410; *Silven Properties Ltd v Royal Bank of Scotland Plc* [2003] EWCA Civ 1409, [2004] 1 W.L.R. 997; *Den Norske Bank v Acemex Management Co Ltd* [2003] EWCA Civ 1559; [2003] 2 C.L.C. 910 and see *Medforth v Blake,* above.

fact that the primary duty of any receiver is to the mortgagee and not to the mortgagor.[250] A receiver cannot be in breach of his duty of good faith to the mortgagor in the absence of some dishonesty, improper motive or element of bad faith.[251] A receiver has been held liable for failing to operate rent reviews,[252] but the limited nature of a receiver's obligations to the mortgagor and others is frequently emphasised by the courts.[253]

A receiver owes a duty of care to the guarantor of the debts of the mortgagor and, unless otherwise expressly excluded in any contractual arrangement between the mortgagee and the receiver, owes the mortgagee an indemnity with regard to any acts of negligence committed by the receiver.[254]

Remuneration of the receiver

A receiver is entitled to retain out of any money received by him, for his **26–37** remuneration, and in satisfaction of all costs, charges and expenses incurred by him as receiver, a commission at such rate, not exceeding 5 per cent on the gross amount of all money received, as is specified in his appointment, and if no rate is so specified then at the rate of 5 per cent on the gross amount, or at such other rate as the court thinks fit to allow, on application made by him for that purpose.[255] If a receiver is not appointed pursuant to the statutory powers, the instrument of appointment will usually specify the rate of remuneration that the receiver is entitled to be paid, failing which the receiver will have a remedy in quantum meruit.[256] For obvious reasons, the statutory limit on the remuneration of a receiver is usually excluded and, if necessary, the court can fix the remuneration that is due to a receiver in an account as between the mortgagor and the mortgagee. It seems that in general such costs will be allowed in the account save insofar as the mortgagor can establish that they were unreasonably incurred or unreasonable as to amount.[257] The receiver who runs up costs unreasonably may also be liable to the mortgagor or a guarantor.

Termination of the receivership

Only the mortgagee can terminate the receivership[258] but the receivership is **26–38** determined by a number of other circumstances usually outside the mortgagee's

---

[250] *Downsview Nominees Ltd v First City Corp Ltd*, above; *Gomba Holdings (U.K.) Ltd v Minories Finance Ltd* [1988] 1 W.L.R. 1231.

[251] *Medforth v Blake* [2000] Ch. 86 *Downsview Nominees Ltd v First City Corp Ltd*, above.

[252] *Nike v Lawrence* [1991] 1 E.G.L.R. 143.

[253] *Lloyds Bank Plc v Cassidy* [2004] EWCA Civ 1767; and, in the context of administrative receivers and sale but of more general application to other types of receiver as well, *Bell v Long* [2008] EWHC 1273 (Ch), [2008] 2 B.C.L.C. 706.

[254] *American Express International Banking Corp v Hurley* [1985] 3 All E.R. 564.

[255] LPA 1925 s.109(6). See also *Marshall v Cottingham* [1982] Ch. 82.

[256] *Re Vimbos Ltd* [1900] 1 Ch. 470.

[257] *Gomba Holdings (U.K.) Ltd v Minories Finance Ltd (No.2)* [1993] Ch. 171; *Royal Bank of Scotland v Chandra* [2010] EWHC 105 (Ch); [2010] 1 Lloyd's Rep. 677.

[258] *Gomba Holdings (U.K.) Ltd v Minories Finance Ltd* [1988] 1 W.L.R. 1231.

control: namely, the appointment of a receiver by a prior mortgagee and, where an administration order has been made of an incorporated mortgagor, where the administrator so requires.[259] The liquidation of an incorporated mortgagor does not determine the receiver's appointment or powers but will operate to determine his agency on behalf of the mortgagor.[260] Thereafter it would appear that the receiver would, in the absence of the mortgagee constituting him as his agent, act as principal.[261]

RIGHT TO REALISE THE SECURITY BY SALE OUT OF COURT

History

26–39   A mortgagee of stocks or shares[262] and a mortgagee of personal chattels, who is in possession,[263] have an implied power to sell their security when the mortgagor is in default, unless the contrary is stated in the mortgage. A mortgagee of land, however, has no such implied power and can only sell by virtue of an express or statutory power,[264] or with the mortgagor's consent. Indeed, until the end of the eighteenth century,[265] a mortgage of land could not be realised except through the tedious and expensive medium of proceedings such as foreclosure proceedings in Chancery. Attempts were occasionally made to give the mortgagee power to sell but such attempts, perhaps owing to a doubt whether the power would infringe the rule concerning clogs on the equity of redemption, were not common. In the first years of the nineteenth century more attention was paid to the possibility of realising mortgages out of court through powers expressly given to the mortgagee.[266] The legality of powers of sale was established and, after some doubts about the need for the concurrence of the mortgagor in the sale[267] and some further experiments with trusts, express powers of sale became a regular feature of every mortgage deed.[268] The usual form of an express power permitted the mortgagee and any person subsequently entitled to the mortgage to give a good discharge for the mortgage debt and, at any stage after the moneys became due, to sell the mortgaged property free of encumbrances. The power of sale was often limited in its usage by the requirement for the mortgagor to have been in default in some regard for a specified period. Since the ordinary form of these express

---

[259] Insolvency Act 1986 s.11(2) for administrations commenced before September 15, 2003, and Sch.B1 para.41 for those commenced thereafter (bar cases to which Enterprise Act 2002 s.249 applies).

[260] *American Express International Banking Corp v Hurley* [1985] 3 All E.R. 564.

[261] *Gosling v Gaskell* [1897] A.C. 575.

[262] *Wilson v Tooker* (1714) 5 Bro.Parl.Cas. 193; *Lockwood v Ewer, Child (Lady) v Chanstilet* (1742) 2 Atk. 303; *Kemp v Westbrook* (1749) 1 Ves. Sen. 278; *Deverges v Sandeman, Clark & Co* [1902] 1 Ch. 579; *Stubbs v Slater* [1910] 1 Ch. 632.

[263] *Re Morritt, Ex p. Official Receiver* (1886) L.R. 18 Q.B.D. 222.

[264] *Re Rumney and Smith* [1897] 2 Ch. 351. At common law he could, of course, transfer his mortgage but this would be subject to the mortgagor's equity of redemption and willing purchasers would be difficult to find.

[265] Holdsworth, *History of English Law*, Vol.7, p.160.

[266] It is significant that the delays of the Chancery courts were at their worst during this period.

[267] Set at rest in *Corder v Morgan* (1811) 18 Ves. 344.

[268] cf. *Clarke v Royal Panopticon* (1857) 4 Drew. 26.

powers adequately protected the mortgagor,[269] they were a legitimate improvement of the creditor's remedies for realising his security. At the same time the need to protect the interests of both parties necessitated the insertion of a very elaborately drawn clause until the legislature introduced a statutory power of sale satisfactory to creditors.

Lord Cranworth's Act 1860

This Act largely failed because the power of sale contained in it was less **26–40** satisfactory to creditors than the usual express power and did not induce them to omit the express power. The Act was repealed by the Conveyancing Act 1881 but remains in force for mortgages created between 1860 and 1882.[270] Even then it is only of importance in the exceptional case when the mortgage did not contain an express power.[271]

Power of sale under the Law of Property Act 1925

The statutory power of sale in the Conveyancing Act 1881 was satisfactory to **26–41** creditors and led to the omission of express powers; that Act has, however, been repealed, the relevant provisions being replaced by ss.101–107 of the Law of Property Act 1925. The power of sale contained in the 1925 Act as in the 1881 Act is modelled on the express power of sale in common use before 1882, and is so adequate that the statutory power is almost invariably relied on. It is introduced into all mortgages made by deed[272] created after 1881 and an express power is only found in mortgages made by deed when there is some special reason for departing from the statutory power. There is nothing in the statutory power which inhibits or restricts the use of express powers.[273]

Scope of the power

Section 101(1) of the Law of Property Act 1925 provides as follows: **26–42**

> "A mortgagee, where the mortgage is made by deed, shall, by virtue of this Act, have the following powers, to the like extent as if they had been in terms conferred by the mortgage deed, but not further (namely):
>
> (i) A power, when the mortgage money has become due, to sell, or to concur with any other person in selling, the mortgaged property, or any part thereof, either subject to prior charges or not, and either together or in lots by public auction or by private contract, subject to such conditions respecting title, or evidence of title, or other matter, as the mortgagee thinks fit, with power to vary any contract for sale, and to buy in at an auction, or to rescind any contract for sale, and to resell, without being answerable for any loss occasioned thereby; . . . "

---

[269] By requiring the mortgagor to be given six months' notice of the intention to sell.
[270] *Re Solomon and Meagher's Contract* (1889) L.R. 40 Ch.D. 508.
[271] The number of such mortgages still in existence must now be few.
[272] LPA 1925 s.101(1).
[273] *The Maule* [1997] 1 W.L.R. 528.

This power is ample; the sale may be of the whole property or only of a part; it may be by public auction or by private contract, and the wording of the Act does not mean that the property must first have been put up for auction before the mortgagee can proceed to sell by private contract.[274] The mortgagee may vary or cancel a sale, and an ineffectual attempt to sell does not affect his power to enter into a new contract for sale.[275]

Subsection (2) carries the scope of the power still further where the deed is executed after December 31, 1911,[276] by giving a mortgagee when exercising his power:

"(i) A power to impose or reserve or make binding, as far as the law permits by covenant, condition, or otherwise, on the unsold part of the mortgaged property or any part thereof, or on the purchaser and any property sold, any restriction or reservation with respect to building on or other user of the land, or with respect to mines and minerals, or for the purpose of the more beneficial working thereof, or with respect to any other thing;

(ii) A power to sell the mortgaged property, or any part thereof, or all or any mines and minerals apart from the surface:

(a) With or without a grant or reservation of rights of way, rights of water, easements, rights, and privileges for or connected with building or other purposes in relation to the property remaining in mortgage in any part thereof, or to any property sold; and

(b) With or without an exception or reservation of all or any of the mines and minerals in or under the mortgaged property, and with or without a grant or reservation of powers of working, easements, rights, and privileges for or connected with mining purposes in relation to the property remaining unsold or any part thereof, or to any property sold; and

(c) With or without covenants by the purchaser to expend money on the land sold."

The statutory power of sale set out in s.101 may be varied or extended by the agreement of the parties, and if so varied or extended, will take effect in its altered form just as if the alterations had been part of the provisions contained in the Act.[277] Consequently, it is not necessary to set out an express power unless the mortgagee's requirements are widely different from the statutory power. Finally, although this was already assumed from the law relating to express powers,[278] s.106(2) of the Law of Property Act 1925 distinctly states that the power of sale conferred by the Act does not affect the right of foreclosure. The exercise of the mortgagee's power under s.101 does not amount to a deprivation of the mortgagor's possession such as to violate his rights under art.1 of the First Protocol to the Convention for the Protection of Human Rights and Fundamental Freedom.[279]

---

[274] *Davey v Durrant, Smith v Durrant* (1857) 1 De G. & J. 535.

[275] This had already been decided by the Privy Council: *Henderson v Astwood, Astwood v Cubbold, Cobbold v Astwood* [1894] A.C. 150 at 162 (PC).

[276] If the mortgage was executed before that date, the mortgagee could probably not impose conditions at all but he may sell mines or minerals if he obtains the leave of the court to do so: *Re Hurst's Mortgage* (1890) L.R. 45 Ch.D. 263, *Buckley v Howell* (1861) 29 Beav. 546.

[277] LPA 1925 s.101(3).

[278] *Perry v Keane* (1836) 6 L.J.Ch. 67; *Wade v Hanham* (1851) 9 Hare 62.

[279] *Horsham Properties Group Ltd v Clark* [2009] 1 W.L.R. 1255.

Who may exercise the power

The statutory power may be excluded by agreement but, subject to this, it is **26–43** introduced into every "mortgage" *made by deed*, whether the mortgage is legal or equitable and whether its subject-matter is realty or personalty. It is thus given to a chargee by way of legal mortgage and to the holder of "any charge or lien on property for securing money or money's worth"[280]; it is given also to the proprietor of a registered charge unless a contrary entry has been made on the register.[281] The result is that the holder of *any* mortgage, charge,[282] or equitable lien on any kind of property is entitled to the statutory power so long as the security was created by deed. There is, however, one exception: the statutory power of sale has been held not to be incorporated in a document governed by the Bills of Sale (1878) (Amendment) Act 1882.[283] Subject to this exception, s.101 of the Law of Property Act 1925 applies alike to realty and personalty or any interest in it or anything in action.[284] Section 102 further ensures that the mortgagee of an undivided share in land, who took his security before 1926, shall not lose his statutory or express power of sale by reason of the conversion of his interest into a share in personalty.

An express power of sale is only exercisable by the persons designated for that purpose by the instrument creating it.[285]

Co-mortgagees: The effect of a mortgage to several mortgagees is that, unless **26–44** a contrary intention is expressed in the mortgage deed, the mortgage debt is deemed to be held upon a joint account[286]; this means that the power of sale is exercisable by the original mortgagees jointly and that, if one dies, the survivors may sell without joining his personal representatives in the sale. In the case of land, if the mortgagees exceed four in number, the first four are the statutory trustees on behalf of all the mortgagees and the sale must be made through them, or, if one dies, the survivors of them.[287]

Transferees: The statutory power is exercisable by a transferee of the mort- **26–45** gage debt in the same way as by the original mortgagee, for s.106(1) provides[288]:

[280] LPA 1925 s.205(1)(xvi), which defines "mortgage" to include these.

[281] LRA 1925 s.34(1) and see *Lever Finance v Trustee of the Property of Needleman* [1956] Ch. 375.

[282] Debenture holders in a *public* company have no power of sale, but otherwise debenture holders appear to be entitled to the statutory power: *Deyes v Wood* [1911] 1 K.B. 806. Coote, *Mortgages* (9th edn 1927), p.910, *contra*, following Kay J. in *Blaker v Herts and Essex Waterworks Co* (1889) L.R. 41 Ch.D. 399, but *Deyes v Wood* seems to limit Kay J.'s statement.

[283] *Re Morritt, Ex p. Official Referee* (1886) L.R. 18 Q.B.D. 222; *Calvert v Thomas* (1887) L.R. 19 Q.B.D. 204.

[284] LPA 1925 s.205(1)(xvi), (xx). It may be noted that Lord Cranworth's Act did not extend to personalty, being limited to *hereditaments*.

[285] *Re Crunden and Meux's Contract* [1909] 1 Ch. 690.

[286] ibid., s.111; trustees hold on a joint account. And see Trustee Act 1925 s.18.

[287] LPA 1925 s.34(2) as amended by the Trusts of Land and Appointment of Trustees Act 1996.

[288] In any case s.205(1)(xvi) states that "mortgagee" includes any person from time to time deriving title under the original mortgagee.

"The power of sale conferred by this Act may be exercised by any person for the time being entitled to receive and give a discharge for the mortgage money."

Transferees include sub-mortgagees, who may either sell the mortgage debt only, leaving the original mortgagor's equity of redemption outstanding, or else sell, as assignees of the mortgage and destroy also the original equity of redemption. It is necessary to include a word of warning in circumstances where the power of sale is express and not statutory, since the original mortgage does not in terms extend the power of sale to assignments, the power cannot be transferred.[289] An express power should therefore either incorporate the language of s.106(1) or otherwise provide for assignment of the power.

26–46   **Personal representatives:**   The personal representatives of the mortgagee and, after the necessary assents have been given, the persons beneficially interested in the mortgage moneys may exercise the statutory power of sale, by virtue of s.106(1). Again, this will not be so in the case of an express power unless provided for in the mortgage deed.[290]

Conditions for the power of sale

26–47   **When the power arises:**   There are three conditions which must be fulfilled before the power of sale arises:

(a)   the mortgage must be made by deed (as in the case of all legal mortgages);

(b)   the mortgage money must have become due—i.e. the legal date for redemption must have passed. In most mortgages there is inserted a legal date for redemption but, if there is no such clause and the mortgage debt is repayable by instalments, the power of sale arises as soon as any instalment is in arrear[291]; and

(c)   there is no contrary intention in the mortgage deed.

26–48   **When the power becomes exercisable:**   Although the statutory power of sale *arises* at that time, it cannot—without express variation of the statutory requirements by the parties—*be exercised* unless at least one of the conditions set out in s.103 of the Law of Property Act 1925 has been satisfied, namely:

(a)   notice requiring payment of the mortgage money[292] has been served on the mortgagor or one of two or more mortgagors, and default has been

---

[289] *Re Rumney v Smith* [1897] 2 Ch. 351.

[290] *Re Crunden and Meux's Contract* [1909] 1 Ch. 690.

[291] *Payne v Cardiff Rural District Council* [1932] 1 K.B. 241. But, if the mortgage money is not due (i.e. the interest is in arrear, but the principal is not) the statutory power does not arise, although the court may be able to order a sale in lieu of foreclosure pursuant to LPA 1925 s.91(2). See *Twentieth Century Banking Corporation v Wilkinson* [1977] Ch. 99; *Palk v Mortgage Services Funding Plc* [1993] Ch. 330.

[292] i.e. money or money's worth secured by mortgage—LPA 1925 s.205(1)(xvi).

made in payment of the mortgage money, or of part thereof, for three months after such service[293]; or

(b) some interest under the mortgage is in arrear[294] and unpaid for two months after becoming due[295]; or

(c) there has been a breach of some other provision contained in the mortgage deed[296] or in the 1925 Act,[297] or in an enactment replaced by that Act which should have been observed or performed by the mortgagor or by someone who concurred in making the mortgage.[298]

Although the occurrence of one of these circumstances is normally a condition precedent to the exercise of the statutory power, the mortgage contract may, and usually does, exclude the restrictions. On the other hand, it has been suggested that a clause allowing for sale without any notice might be considered oppressive, and will be so considered, if there is any fiduciary relationship between the parties.[299] Where a mortgage provides for the moneys to be due and payable on a specified date, the power of sale is not exercisable before that date, even if the mortgage is in arrears.[300] Similarly, if the mortgage identifies events after which the mortgagee's power of sale would become exercisable, it will be implied that unless and until such events occur the power is not exercisable.[301]

Form of notice: A notice under s.103 must be served on the mortgagor. The **26–49** notice must be in writing.[302] "Mortgagor" includes any person deriving title under the original mortgagor.[303] Who ought to be served when there are later encumbrancers is an unsettled point; the course generally adopted is to give notice to the mortgagor himself and to the encumbrancer highest in priority.[304] The form of notice contemplated by s.103 is probably a demand for immediate payment, with a threat that if at the end of three months the money has not been paid, the power will be exercised: but a notice is just as good if it is merely a

---

[293] LPA 1925 s.103(i), and see *Barker v Illingworth* [1908] 2 Ch. 20.

[294] It is for the mortgagee to prove affirmatively that the interest is in arrear, and it seems that a mortgagee in possession is not entitled to say that the interest is in arrear merely because he receives nothing on account of interest from the mortgagor. He must show that the interest is in arrear in spite of the receipt of rents and profits: *Cockburn v Edwards* (1881) L.R. 18 Ch.D. 449 at 459, 463; *Wrigley v Gill* [1905] 1 Ch. 241. Capitalisation of arrears may make this difficult to demonstrate: *Davy v Turner* (1970) 21 P. & C.R. 967

[295] LPA 1925 s.103(ii). "Month" means calendar month: Interpretation Act 1978 ss.5, 22(1), Sch.1, Sch.2 para.4(1).

[296] e.g. breach of covenants to repair or insure; see *Braithwaite v Winwood* [1960] 1 W.L.R. 1257.

[297] See *Public Trustee v Lawrence* [1912] 1 Ch. 789 (failure to deliver counterpart of lease as required by s.99(8)).

[298] LPA 1925 s.103(iii).

[299] *Miller v Cook* (1870) L.R. 10 Eq. 641; *Cockburn v Edwards* (1881) L.R. 18 Ch.D. 449; this will not be so if the security was not given for a fresh loan but for obtaining more time for payment: *Pooley's Trustee v Whetham* (1886) L.R. 33 Ch.D. 111.

[300] *Twentieth Century Banking Corp Ltd v Wilkinson* [1977] Ch. 99.

[301] *West Bromwich Building Society v Wilkinson* [2005] UKHL 44; [2005] 1 W.L.R. 2303.

[302] LPA 1925 s.196(1).

[303] ibid., s.205(1)(xvi).

[304] Omission to give notice to an encumbrancer may expose the mortgagee to an action for damages (*Hoole v Smith* (1881) L.R. 17 Ch.D. 434); this decision would appear to apply to the statutory power by virtue of the definition of "mortgagor" given in the text.

notice to pay at the end of three months from the date of the notice,[305] but he must then join in the conveyance to the purchaser.[306] Finally, although a sale cannot take effect until the expiry of the notice required by s.103, the contract of sale may be entered into before that time, the contract being conditional on the mortgagor not discharging the mortgage.[307]

26–50 *Service of the notice:* Section 196 of the Law of Property Act 1925 makes provision for the service of notices under the Act. The notice is sufficiently served if left at the mortgagor's last known place of abode or business or is affixed or left for him on the land or any house or building comprised in the mortgage.[308] It is sufficiently addressed if it is addressed to the mortgagor simply by that designation, without his name, or generally to the persons interested, without any name, and notwithstanding that any person to be affected by the notice is absent, under disability, unborn or unascertained.[309] It is sufficient service if the notice is simply placed through the letterbox of the mortgaged premises, even though those premises were at the time of service vacant, the tenant in person and the normal method of contact being via the tenant's solicitor.[310]

Any notice required or authorised by the Law of Property Act to be served shall also be sufficiently served, if it is sent by post in a registered letter addressed to the mortgagor or other person to be served, by name, at the aforesaid place of abode or business, office, or counting house, and if that letter is not returned through the post-office undelivered; and that service shall be deemed to be made at the time at which the registered letter would in the ordinary course of post be delivered.[311] If the requirements of section 196 are met, the notice is served even if it is never received.[312] A notice left at the farthest place to which a member of the public or postman could obtain access, can constitute service at the mortgagor's place of abode.[313]

Section 196 applies subject to any contrary intention appearing in the deed creating the mortgage or charge.

26–51 **Protection of purchasers:** The importance of the distinction between the power of sale *arising* and the power of sale being *exercisable* cannot be underestimated. If the power has not arisen the mortgagee has no statutory power of sale at all. Any sale by him in purported exercise of the statutory power will not give a good root of title and will not transfer the legal estate to a purchaser. It will, however, operate to transfer his mortgage, i.e. it will only be effective to transfer to the purchaser the rights of mortgagee as mortgagee. Thus, a purchaser must

[305] *Barker v Illingworth* [1908] 2 Ch. 20.
[306] *Selwyn v Garfit* (1888) L.R. 38 Ch.D. 273.
[307] *Major v Ward* (1847) 5 Hare 598.
[308] LPA 1925 s.196(3).
[309] LPA 1925 s.196(2).
[310] *Van Harlaam v Kasner* (1992) 64 P. & C.R. 214.
[311] LPA 1925 s.196(4).
[312] *R. v Westminster Unions Assessment Committee, Ex p. Woodward & Sons* [1917] 1 K.B. 832.
[313] *Henry Smith's Charity Trustees v Kyriakou* [1989] 2 E.G.L.R. 110 (CA).

ascertain whether or not the power of sale has arisen. Since the question of its exercisability is a matter between the mortgagor and the mortgagee, this does not normally concern the purchaser of the legal estate. Thus, if the power of sale has arisen, but is not exercisable, the mortgagee can give a good root of title which is not impeachable and the only recourse open to the mortgagor is a remedy in damages against the person exercising the power of sale.[314] In this regard it is necessary to consider the provisions of s.104(2) of the Law of Property Act 1925 in the light of the case law preceding this legislation. The subsection corresponds with the usual clause in an express power and provides as follows:

> "(2) Where a conveyance is made in exercise of the power of sale conferred by this Act, or any enactment replaced by this Act, the title of the purchaser shall not be impeachable on the ground:
>
> (a) that no case had arisen to authorise the sale; or
> (b) that due notice was not given; or
> (c) where the mortgage is made after the commencement of this Act, that leave of the court, when so required, was not obtained; or
> (d) whether the mortgage was made before or after such commencement, that the power was otherwise improperly or irregularly exercised;
>
> and a purchaser is not, either before or on conveyance[315] concerned to see or inquire whether the case has arisen to authorise the sale, or due notice has been given, or the power is otherwise properly and regularly exercised; but any person damnified by an unauthorised, or improper, or irregular exercise of the power, shall have his remedy for damages against the person exercising the power.[316]
>
> (3) A conveyance on sale by a mortgagee, made after the commencement of this Act, shall be deemed to have been made in exercise of the power of sale conferred by this Act unless a contrary intention appears."[317]

Thus, proof of title is simplified and all that the purchaser need do is to satisfy himself that the power of sale has arisen and he need not inquire whether it has become exercisable.[318] Further a purchaser is under no obligation to make inquiries as to the regularity of the sale and the protection given to him by the terms of the subsection enures to him as soon as the contract is signed and is not dependent on completion having been obtained.[319] The existence of the power of sale is proved by the document creating the power, i.e. the form of the mortgage deed itself, and the redemption date specified in it.

---

[314] See the Law of Property Act 1925, s.104(2).

[315] "Or on conveyance" was inserted to overrule the case of life interests etc.: *Life Interest and Reversionary Securities Corporation v Hand-in-Hand Fire and Life Insurance Society* [1898] 2 Ch. 230.

[316] The reference to a remedy in damages does not create a special statutory remedy, nor does it refer to a common law action for damages. It is a reference to the mortgagor's equitable remedy to hold the mortgagee to account on the footing of wilful default—*McGinnis v Union Bank of Australia Ltd* [1935] V.L.R. 161.

[317] This renders it unnecessary to state in the conveyance that the conveyance is made in exercise of a sale under the statutory power as this is presumed.

[318] *Bailey v Barnes* [1894] 1 Ch. 25 at 35.

[319] s.104 expressly overrules life interests, etc.: *Life Interest and Reversionary Securities Corporation v Hand-in-Hand Fire and Life Insurance Society* [1898] 2 Ch. 230.

However, it now seems clear[320] that when the purchaser (directly or by imputed knowledge) has actual notice or "blind-eye" notice of an irregularity such as a defect in the mortgagee's power to sell,[321] or of facts which make the proposed sale impossible or inconsistent with a proper exercise of the power,[322] the sale will be set aside,[323] and the purchaser's title will be impeached.[324] It has been stated that in the circumstances " . . . to uphold the title of a purchaser who had notice of impropriety or irregularity in the exercise of the power of sale would be to convert the provisions of the statute into an instrument of fraud. . . . ".[325] Constructive notice is not sufficient to displace s.104(2).

In these circumstances it would seem that the present position is as follows: provided that the purchaser does not *actually know* of any irregularity he will obtain a good unimpeachable title and the mortgagor's remedy is in damages against the person exercising the power of sale. Further, it would seem that there is no obligation upon the purchaser to make the inquiries which a suspicious purchaser should make and that the purchaser will not have constructive notice of any irregularity or impropriety in the exercise of the power of sale which would have been revealed by such inquiries. However, the conveyance may be set aside if the purchaser takes with knowledge of any impropriety in the sale, in the sense of what would have come to his knowledge had he not shut his eyes to suspicious circumstances, rather than the usual sense related to failure to inquire, whether that knowledge is his own or properly to be imputed to him.[326]

Exercise of the power of sale

26–52   **Mode of sale:**   The sale will in most cases be made under the provisions of s.101 of the Law of Property Act 1925, without reference to the court.[327] This gives to the mortgagee a wide discretion as to the manner in which he exercises his power. It may be by auction or by private contract. It may be of the whole or part of the property and may be made subject to easements or restrictive covenants. It may include the grant of easements and privileges and may separate the mines and minerals from the ownership of the surface. However, the section

---

[320] *Meretz Investments NV v ACP Ltd* [2006] EWHC 74 (Ch); [2007] Ch. 197.

[321] *Jenkins v Jones* (1860) 2 Giff 99. *Parkinson v Hanbury* (1867) L.R. 2 H.L. 1.

[322] *Selwyn v Garfitt* (1888) L.R. 38 Ch.D. 273; *Bailey v Barnes* [1894] 1 Ch. 25.

[323] *Bailey v Barnes* [1894] 1 Ch. 25.

[324] *Lord Waring v London & Manchester Assurance Co Ltd* [1935] Ch. 310 at 318.

[325] See *Bailey v Barnes* [1894] 1 Ch. 25 at 30, per Stirling J., but note that that statement was made in relation to s.21(2) of the Conveyancing Act 1881, which is reproduced in the first part only of s.104(2). The combination of s.21(2) and s.5(1) of the Conveyancing Act 1911 was addressed in *Holohan v Friends Provident Century Life Office* [1966] I.R. 1.

[326] *Meretz Investments NV v ACP Ltd* [2006] EWHC 74 (Ch); [1007] Ch. 197; see also *Bailey v Barnes* [1894] 1 Ch. 25 at 30, 34; *Holohan v Friends Provident and Century Life Office* [1966] I.R. 1.

[327] There is an exception in the case where a mortgage provides that a power of sale shall be exercisable in the case of bankruptcy. In such a case leave of the court is required but it does not concern the purchaser; see LPA 1925 s.104(2). Also, in those cases where the mortgaged property is occupied by the mortgagor (in particular dwelling-houses) presumably the mortgagee will wish to have vacant possession prior to sale which will normally necessitate court proceedings.

gives no power to sell timber apart from the land,[328] or trade machinery apart from the buildings containing it,[329] nor to grant an option.

The sale may be made either free of or subject to prior charges. This is important when there are successive encumbrancers; a puisne encumbrancer, who is desirous of selling, has two choices: (i) he may sell subject to the prior charges; or (ii) he may sell free of prior charges by arranging to discharge them out of the proceeds of sale. If the latter alternative is adopted he must either obtain the concurrence of the prior encumbrancers in the sale[330] or else he must make use of the procedure provided by s.50 of the Law of Property Act 1925, in which case he obtains leave to pay into court a sum sufficient to cover the requirements of the prior charges, plus any costs or expenses likely to be incurred.

Mortgagee as vendor: The courts have repeatedly affirmed that a mortgagee   **26–53** is not a trustee for the mortgagor until his debt has been satisfied.[331] It follows that a mortgagee, in exercising his power of sale, is not a trustee of the power.[332] He does not owe the mortgagor (or others with an interest in the equity of redemption) a broad duty in this regard; he needs merely to act in good faith in order to protect his security or obtain repayment.[333] The power arises by contract with the mortgagor and forms part of the mortgagee's security so that he is entitled to look after his own interests when making the sale.[334] If the mortgagee does decide in good faith to exercise his power of sale,[335] the timing of that sale is also a matter for him so long as he complies with his duties as to price, and the fact that disadvantage is caused to the mortgagor by the sale does not impede the mortgagee's right.

In *Warner v Jacob*[336] Kay J. stated the general principle at common law of the mortgagee's position thus:

[328] cf. *Cholmeley v Paxton* (1825) 3 Bing. 207.

[329] *Re Yates, Batcheldor v Yates* (1888) L.R. 38 Ch.D. 112.

[330] A complication arises in the case of registered land. The prospective purchaser can insist on the vendor/mortgagee procuring his registration of the charge (see LRA 1925 s.110(5)), but without the concurrence of the *first* mortgagee with whom the Land Certificate may have been deposited this cannot be done.

[331] *Marquis of Cholmondely v Lord Clinton* (1820) 2 J. & W. 1; *Taylor v Russell* [1892] A.C 244; *Sands v Thompson* (1883) L.R. 22 Ch.D. 614; Turner, *Equity of Redemption* (1931), pp.166 et seq.; and see above, paras 26–05 et seq. But even if the mortgagee is not a trustee, he is bound to take reasonable care to obtain a true market value of the mortgaged property, see *Cuckmere Brick Co Ltd v Mutual Finance Ltd* [1971] Ch. 949; *Parker-Tweedale v Dunbar Bank* [1991] Ch. 12 (CA); *Downsview Nominees Ltd v First City Corp Ltd* [1993] A.C. 295; *AIB Finance v Debtors* [1998] 2 All E.R. 929; *Medforth v Blake* [2000] Ch. 86 and see below, paras 26–54 et seq.

[332] *Kennedy v De Trafford* [1897] A.C. 180; *Cuckmere Brick Co Ltd v Mutual Finance Ltd* [1971] Ch. 949.

[333] *Downsview Nominees Ltd v First City Corp Ltd* [1993] A.C. 295; *Meretz Investments NV v ACP Ltd* [2006] EWHC 74 (Ch); [2007] Ch. 197; *Raja v Austin Gray* [2002] EWCA Civ 1965.

[334] *Farrar v Farrars Ltd* (1888) L.R. 40 Ch.D. 395 at 398, per Chitty J.

[335] *Den Norske Bank ASA v Acemex Co Ltd* [2003] EWCA Civ 1559; [2005] 1 B.C.L.C. 274; *China and South Sea Bank Ltd v Tan Soon Gin* [1990] 1 A.C. 536; *Reliance Permanent Building Society v Harwood-Stamper* [1944] Ch. 362 at 372; [1944] 2 All E.R. 75 at 80, per Vaisey J.; *Cuckmere Brick Co v Mutual Finance Ltd*, above at 965, 969; 644, 646. Cf. *Standard Chartered Bank Ltd v Walker* [1982] 1 W.L.R. 1410 at 1415; *Wood v Bank of Nova Scotia* (1979) 10 R.P.R. 156, affd (1980) 112 D.L.R. (3d) 181; *Suskind v Bank of Nova Scotia* (1984) 10 D.L.R. (4th) 101.

[336] (1882) L.R. 20 Ch.D. 220 at 234.

"A mortgagee is, strictly speaking not a trustee of the power of sale. It is a power given to him for his benefit, to enable him the better to realise his debt. If he exercises it bona fide for that purpose, without corruption or collusion with the purchaser, the court will not interfere, even though the sale be very disadvantageous, unless, indeed, the price is so low as in itself to be evidence of fraud."

So strong was this principle that a mortgagee has been held not to be a trustee of the power of sale, even when the mortgage is created in the form of an express trust for sale.[337] However, more recent cases, while recognising and reaffirming the principle that the mortgagee holds the power of sale for his own benefit, have moved away from that apparent suggestion that the mortgagee is virtually totally unfettered in the exercise of his power. So far as it is consistent with the mortgagee's right to put his own interests first,[338] he must act fairly towards the mortgagor or others interested in the equity of redemption and may not unfairly prejudice or wilfully or recklessly damage the interests of those other persons.[339]

26–54   Price: At common law, therefore, the general rule flowing from this principle was that the duty of a mortgagee, exercising his power of sale, merely should act in good faith in the *conduct of the sale*.[340] If the sale was bona fide he need not consult the interests of the mortgagor, so that it would be no ground for setting aside a sale that a larger price could have been obtained if the sale had been delayed.[341] The court would not inquire into a mortgagee's motive for exercising his power,[342] provided the sale itself was fair. Neither spite nor any other indirect motive would invalidate the sale. The mortgagee was not a trustee of the power in any sense.[343] In the absence of evidence of fraud a sale would not be set aside.[344] Indeed, it was well settled that selling at an undervalue did not by itself constitute male fides. In *Adams v Scott*,[345] for example, it was alleged that property sold for £12,000 was worth £20,000, but Wood V.-C., declared that mere undervalue was not enough to justify interference with the sale without proof of fraud. Where there was fraud, however, the court would grant an injunction to restrain the completion of a sale, or would set aside a completed sale.[346] If the

---

[337] *Kirkwood v Thompson* (1865) 2 De G. J. & Sm. 613; *Locking v Parker* (1872) L.R. 8 Ch.App. 30.

[338] *Silven Properties Ltd v Royal Bank of Scotland Plc* [2004] 1 W.L.R. 997.

[339] *Meretz investments NV v ACP Ltd,* above *Raja v Austin Gray* above at 96; *Downsview Nominees Ltd v First City Corp Ltd* [1993] A.C. 295; *Palk v Mortgage Services Funding Plc* [1993] Ch. 330; and see also, for the flexible nature of the duty equity imposes in such circumstances and the applicability of similar duties to receivers who exercise the power of sale, *Medforth v Blake* [2000] Ch. 86.

[340] *Kennedy v De Trafford* [1897] A.C. 180. Lord Herschell, however, deprecated any attempt to define exhaustively the words "acting in good faith".

[341] *Davey v Durrant, Smith v Durrant* (1857) 1 De G. & J. 535.

[342] See *Nash v Eads* (1880) 25 S.J. 95.

[343] *Belton v Bass, Ratcliffe & Gretton Ltd* [1922] 2 Ch. 449; *Nash v Eads* (1880) 25 S.J. 95; *Colson v Williams* (1889) 58 L.J.Ch. 539.

[344] See *Warner v Jacob* (1882) L.R. 20 Ch.D. 220; and see above, paras 26–53 et seq.

[345] (1859) 7 W.R. 213.

[346] *Bettyes v Maynard* (1883) 49 L.T. 389; *Haddington Island Quarry Co Ltd v Hudson* [1911] A.C. 727; *Lord Waring v London and Manchester Assurance Co* [1935] Ch. 310.

property has reached the hands of a purchaser for value without notice of the fraud, an action for damages will lie against the mortgagee.[347]

However, at the same time, obviously the question of the price to be obtained by the mortgagee in respect of the security is of importance to the mortgagor. He is the person interested in the balance of the proceeds of sale after payment of the mortgage debt by the mortgagee exercising his power of sale (and the debt of any other mortgagee interested in the security). In short, the mortgagor's interests must not be sacrificed.

As the law developed, although proof of fraud was essential in order to set aside a sale otherwise executed in accordance with the terms of the mortgagee's power, the mortgagee was made liable to account for his careless handling of the sale. A mortgagee was not to be regarded as a trustee, but he would be treated as a reasonable man of business. Dicta of Lord Herschell L.C.[348] and Lindley L.J.,[349] were sometimes cited in support of the proposition that, in the absence of fraud, a mortgagee was only liable for selling at an undervalue if he wilfully or recklessly sacrifices the property of the mortgagor. This seemed to put the rule too favourably for the mortgagee, for in *Tomlin v Luce*[350] a mortgagee was held responsible for the blunder made by an otherwise competent auctioneer whom he had employed. The Privy Council in *McHugh v Union Bank of Canada*[351] defined the duty of a mortgagee more broadly:

> "It is his duty to behave in conducting the realisation of the mortgaged property as a reasonable man would behave in the realisation of his own property, so that the borrower may receive credit for the fair value of the property sold."

The true rule as it developed was that a mortgagee must use reasonable care to get a fair or proper price,[352] and if he did not, he would be debited in his mortgage account with the full value of the mortgaged property *at the date of the sale*.[353]

It was not until 1971 that this rule finally received full judicial recognition in the English courts. In the case of *Cuckmere Brick Co Ltd v Mutual Finance Ltd*[354] the Court of Appeal held that a mortgagee at common law is under a duty to " . . .

26–55

---

[347] *Dennedy v De Trafford* [1896] 1 Ch. 762 at 772 (CA).

[348] *Kennedy v De Trafford* [1897] A.C. 180 at 185; this dictum does not in fact support the proposition.

[349] *Kennedy v De Trafford* [1896] 1 Ch. 762 at 772 (CA).

[350] (1889) L.R. 43 Ch.D. 191.

[351] [1913] A.C. 299 at 311 (PC).

[352] *Colson v Williams* (1889) 58 L.J.Ch. 539; *Reliance Permanent Building Society v Harwood-Stamper* [1944] Ch. 362.

[353] *Wolff v Vanderzee* (1869) 20 L.T. 350; *Deverges v Sandeman, Clarke & Co* [1902] 1 Ch. 579; for a statement of the measure of the mortgagee's liability, see *Tomlin v Luce* (1889) L.R. 43 Ch.D. 191.

[354] [1971] Ch. 949, explaining *Kennedy v De Tafford* [1897] A.C. 180. See also *Holohan v Friends Provident and Century Life Office* [1966] I.R. 1. The *Cuckmere* principle has since been applied in *Palmer v Barclays Bank Ltd* [1971] 23 P. & C.R. 30; *Bank of Cyprus (London) Ltd v Gill* [1980] 2 Lloyd's Rep. 51; *Standard Chartered Bank Ltd v Walker* [1982] 1 W.L.R. 1410; *Tse Kwong Lam v Wong Chit Sen* [1983] 1 W.L.R. 1349; *Bishop v Bonham* [1988] 1 W.L.R. 742. See also *"The Calm C"*, *Gulf and Fraser Fisherman's Union v Calm C Fish Ltd* [1975] 1 Lloyd's Rep. 189. *Parker-Tweedale v Dunbar Bank* [1991] Ch. 12 (CA); *Downsview Nominees Ltd v First City Corp Ltd* [1993] A.C. 295; *AIB Finance v Debtors* [1998] 2 All E.R. 929; *Medforth v Blake* [2000] Ch. 86.

take reasonable care to obtain the true market value of the mortgaged property."[355] Thus, if a mortgagee in exercising his power of sale in respect of a plot of building land advertises the property and fails to mention that there is in existence planning permission for the erection of 100 flats, he will be accountable to the mortgagor for the difference between the proper price which could have reasonably been obtained and the price actually obtained.[356] This would seem now to place upon *any* mortgagee the same duty of care to obtain the best price reasonably obtainable as has been imposed upon building societies since 1939.

Further decisions in 1982 and 1985 held that this duty of care is also owed to the guarantor of the mortgaged debt as well as to the mortgagor[357] but not to a person beneficially entitled in the property and of whom the mortgagee had notice.[358] The mortgagee's duty of good faith is however owed to the mortgagor and anyone else interested in the equity of redemption.[359] It may be added that in a sale, otherwise bona fide, the price is none the less a fair price, although part, or even the whole of the purchase price is left on mortgage, but the mortgagee must, of course, have debited himself in the mortgage account with the full amount of the purchase price.[360]

The duty formerly imposed by statute[361] on building societies to take reasonable care to ensure that the price obtained on a sale of a mortgaged property was the best price that could reasonably be obtained has been repealed[362] and any rule of law requiring a mortgagee to take reasonable care to obtain a proper price on true market value is to have effect as if the statute imposing the duty on a building society (and its statutory predecessors) had never been enacted.[363]

It is now clear that a mortgagee who decides to sell owes a duty to tale reasonable care to obtain the best price reasonably obtainable for the property at the date of sale, that price also being described as a proper price or the true market value.[364] However, the mortgagee has considerable latitude as to how he is going to seek an appropriate price in the circumstances of the individual case,[365] and will not be in breach of his duty even if another method might have produced a higher price. He is obliged to investigate the possibility of a sale at a higher price, but can legitimately accept a lower firm offer in preference to a potential higher one which has not been formally and firmly made.[366]

---

[355] *Cuckmere Brick Co Ltd v Mutual Finance Ltd* [1971] Ch. 949 at 966, per Salmon L.J.

[356] ibid., per Salmon L.J., who held that the proper price is the same as the true market value.

[357] *Standard Chartered Bank Ltd v Walker* [1982] 1 W.L.R. 1410 (CA), a case where there was a sale by a receiver under a debenture of a private company which was guaranteed by the directors personally; *American Express International Banking Corpn. v Hurley* [1985] 3 All E.R. 564; see also *Downsview Nominees Ltd v First City Corp Ltd* [1993] A.C. 295.

[358] *Parker-Tweedale v Dunbar Bank Plc* [1991] Ch. 12.

[359] *Medforth v Blake* [2000] Ch. 86.

[360] *Davey v Durrant, Smith v Durrant* (1857) 1 De G. & J. 535; *Kennedy v De Trafford* [1897] A.C. 180; *Belton v Bass, Ratcliffe and Gretton Ltd* [1922] 2 Ch. 449.

[361] Building Societies Act 1986., s.13(7) and Sch.4 para.1.

[362] Building Societies Act 1997 s.12(1) with effect from December 1, 1997 (SI 1997/2668).

[363] ibid., s.12(2).

[364] *Silven Properties Ltd v Royal Bank of Scotland* [2004] 1 W.L.R. 997; *Downsview Nominees Ltd v First City Corp Ltd* [1993] A.C. 295; *Michael v Miller* [2004] EWCA Civ 282; *Medforth v Blake* [2000] Ch. 86; and *Raja v Lloyds TSB Bank* [2001] EWCA Civ 210; [2001] Lloyd's Rep. Bank. 113.

[365] *Michael vMiller* [2004] EWCA Civ 282; [2004] 2 E.G.L.R. 151.

[366] *Meftah v Lloyds TSB Bank Plc* [2001] 2 All E.R. Comm 741.

Further, a mortgagee is under no duty to delay the sale in order to obtain a **26–56** better price.[367] Again, the mere fact that a mortgagee in exercising his power of sale omits a material point of which he is ignorant (for example, planning permission) does not of itself justify a finding of negligence.[368] Also the mortgagee is not required to put the property into good repair.[369] So long as one of his motives in selling the property is to recover his debt, the mortgagee is entitled to proceed to a forced sale even if there are other factors also influencing his decision.[370] Provided that he acts bona fide and takes reasonable care to ensure that the price is the best reasonably obtainable *in the circumstances*, and his assessment of the appropriate price falls within a range of acceptable values, then such actions are justifiable. Once he elects to act, however, in a given way by, for example, carrying on business he must take all steps that are reasonably necessary to do so profitably.[371]

The duty of care imposed on a selling mortgagee by the *Cuckmere* and *Silven* principle, being essentially in the nature of an obligation implied by law, is capable, of being excluded by agreement.[372] The courts may not reject exclusion clauses where the exempting words are clear and are susceptible to one meaning only, however unreasonable. The result therefore may be[373] that where such clauses authorise the mortgagee to exercise the power of sale with absolute discretion, the power is nonetheless subject to the implicit restriction that it should be exercised properly within the limits of the general law, that is, with the exercise of reasonable care to obtain a proper price.[374]

If the mortgagee is found to have been in breach of the duty to take reasonable care to obtain the best price reasonably obtainable for the property, the mortgagee will be required to account to the mortgagor (or others interested in the equity of redemption) for the price which should have been received. This is an equitable remedy, the basis for which is that regardless of the mortgagee's strict legal rights it would be unconscionable for him to sell the property at a culpable valuation.[375] It is not an action upon a specialty; the limitation period is therefore six years.

Identity of purchaser: The sale must be a true sale. A mortgagee cannot sell **26–57** to himself, either alone or with others, even though the price be the full value of

---

[367] *Davey v Durrant, Smith v Durrant*, above, at 553; *Bank of Cyprus (London) Ltd v Gill*, above.

[368] *Palmer v Barclays Bank* (1972) 23 P. & C.R. 30.

[369] *Waltham Forest London Borough Council v Webb* (1974) 232 E.G. 461.

[370] *Meretz Investments NV v ACP Ltd* [2006] EWHC 74 (Ch); [2007] Ch. 197; see also for an earlier interpretation of that latitude, *Farrar v Farrars Ltd* (1888) L.R. 40 Ch.D. 395 at 398; and *Adams v Scott* (1859) 7 W.R. 215.

[371] *Medforth v Blake* [2000] Ch. 86 and see above, paras 16–28 et seq.

[372] *Bishop v Bonham* [1988] 1 W.L.R. 742 at 752, per Slade L.J. In the case of building society mortgages *exclusion* of limitability is presently *excluded* see Building Societies Act 1986 Sch.4 para.1(2).

[373] *Photo Production Ltd v Securicor Transport Ltd* [1980] A.C. 827 at 850, per Lord Diplock, cited by Slade L.J. in *Bishop v Bonham* (above); see also *George Mitchell (Chesterhall) Ltd v Finney Lock Seeds* [1983] Q.B. 284 at 312.

[374] *Bishop v Bonham* [1988] 1 W.L.R. 742.

[375] *Raja v Lloyds TSB Bank Plc* [2001] Lloyd's Rep. Bank. 113; *Yorkshire Bank Plc v Hall* [1999] 1 W.L.R. 1713; *Parker-Tweedale v Dunbar Bank Plc* [1991] Ch. 12 and *Downsview Nominees Ltd v First City Corp Ltd* [1993] A.C. 295.

the property sold.[376] Such a sale may restrained or be set aside or ignored.[377] It is not so much that there is the conflict between interest and duty, which prevents a trustee from acquiring the trust property, as the impossibility of the contract. A man cannot make an agreement with himself. Nor can he disguise the fact that he is both buyer and seller by employing an agent or trustee to purchase for him.[378] The same principle prevents a solicitor or other agent employed to conduct the sale from becoming a purchaser.[379] However, a sale by a mortgagee to a company of which he is a shareholder, or even director, or a sale by a mortgagee company to one of its members, is not necessarily invalid.[380] As Lindley L.J. said[381]:

> "A sale by a person to a corporation of which he is a member is not, either in form or in substance, a sale by a person to himself. To hold that it is, would be to ignore the principle which lies at the root of the legal idea of a corporate body, and that idea is that the corporate body is distinct from the persons composing it. A sale by a member of a corporation to the corporation itself is in every sense a sale valid in equity as well as at law."

At the same time, although such a sale is not a nullity, it may be impeached on the ground of fraud or other irregularity[382] and the fact that the mortgagee has a substantial interest in the company will throw upon the mortgagee and the company the burden of affirmatively proving the bona fides of the sale.[383] In *Farrar v Farrars Ltd*[384] this burden was discharged; in *Hodson v Deans*[385] it was not, and the sale was accordingly upset. The sale by a mortgagee to one of its employees will not automatically be viewed as improper, but that degree of connection throws onto the mortgagee a burden to demonstrate the propriety of the sale.[386]

The mortgagor himself may bid at an auction and become the purchaser, and in the case of co-mortgagors one may purchase from the mortgagee without the concurrence of the others. Nor can the others impeach the sale on the ground that they were not notified of the name of the purchaser, for there is no fiduciary relationship between co-mortgagors to render such a notification necessary.[387]

---

[376] *National Bank of Australasia v United Hand-in-Hand and Band of Hope* (1879) L.R. 4 App. Cas. 391; see also *Martison v Clowes* (1882) L.R. 21 Ch.D. 857.

[377] See *Williams v Wellingborough Borough Council* [1975] 1 W.L.R. 1327 where a purported transfer to itself by the local authority was held to be void. A local authority has a statutory power to vest property in itself subject to the court's approval: Housing Act 1985 s.452 and Sch.17.

[378] *Downes v Grazebrook* (1817) 3 Mer. 200; *National Bank of Australasia v United Hand-in-Hand etc., Co* (1879) 4 A.C. 391.

[379] *Martinson v Clowes* (1882) L.R. 21 Ch.D. 857; *Lawrence v Galsworthy* (1857) 30 L.T.(O.S.) 112; *Hodson v Deans* [1903] 2 Ch. 647; but not if the agent was not employed in the conduct of the sale: *Guest v Smythe* (1870) L.R. 5 Ch.App. 551; *Nutt v Easton* [1899] 1 Ch. 873.

[380] *Tse Kwong Lam v Wong Chit Sen* [1983] 1 W.L.R. 1349. See further *Newport Farm Ltd v Damesh Holdings Ltd* [2003] UKPC 54' (2003) 147 S.J.L.B. 1117.

[381] *Farrar v Farrars, Ltd* (1888) L.R. 40 Ch.D. 395 at 409.

[382] *Tse Kwan Lam v Wong Chit Sen* [1983] 1 W.L.R. 1349.

[383] See further *Tse Kwong Lam* [1983] 1 W.L.R. 1349; *Bradford & Bingley Plc v Ross* (2005) 102 (19) LSG. 34; and *Mortgage Express v Mardner* [2004] EWCA Civ 1859.

[384] (1888) L.R. 4 Ch.D. 395.

[385] [1903] 2 Ch. 647.

[386] *Deakin v Corbett* [2002] EWCA Civ 1849; [2003] 1 W.L.R. 964.

[387] *Kennedy v De Trafford* [1897] A.C. 180.

Further, there is no objection to a purchase by a puisne encumbrancer[388] and the effect of such a purchase from a first mortgagee, exercising his power of sale, is quite different from a mere purchase of the first mortgage. The sale carried out in pursuance of a power created by the mortgagor cancels the latter's equity of redemption so that the puisne encumbrancer obtains an absolute irredeemable title.[389]

If the court orders a sale pursuant to statute,[390] the mortgagee may be expressly permitted to buy.[391]

Distribution of surplus proceeds of sale: Sale under a power of sale cancels **26–58** the equitable right to redeem but it by no means destroys the equitable interest of the mortgagor vis-à-vis the mortgagee. Consequently, as on a sale under an express or statutory power of sale, the mortgagee becomes a trustee of the surplus proceeds of sale for the mortgagor and other interested parties.[392] In the case of an express power, he is an express trustee if the mortgage contains an express trust of the proceeds of sale[393]; otherwise he is a constructive trustee.[394] In the case of a statutory power, the Law of Property Act 1925, s.105 expressly states that the mortgagee is a trustee of the purchase-money and provides for its application in this order:

(1) if the sale is "free from encumbrances" and there were some *prior* encumbrancers, in the discharge of their claims;

(2) in the payment of all costs, charges or expenses properly incurred by the mortgagee, incidental to the sale and any attempted sale[395];

(3) in discharging his own debt under the mortgage[396];

(4) the *residue* is to be paid to the person entitled to the mortgaged property, or authorised to give receipts for the proceeds of the sale (i.e. the next encumbrancer, or, if none, the mortgagor).[397]

---

[388] *Parkinson v Hanbury* (1860) 1 Dr. & Sm. 143; affirmed (1867) L.R. 2 H.L. 1; *Rajah Kishendatt Ram v Rajah Mumtaz Ali Khan* (1879) L.R. 6 Ind.App. 145 (PC).

[389] *Shaw v Bunny* (1865) 2 De G. J. & Sm. 468.

[390] LPA 1925 s.91(2).

[391] *Palk v Mortgage Services Funding Plc* [1993] Ch. 330.

[392] *Rajah Kishendatt Ram v Rajah Mumtaz Ali Khan* (1879) L.R. 6 Ind.App. 145 (PC).

[393] *Locking v Parker* (1872) L.R. 8 Ch. 30; *Weld-Blundell v Synott* [1940] 2 K.B. 107.

[394] *Banner v Berridge* (1881) L.R. 18 Ch.D. 254, where Kay J. said that the fiduciary relationship did not arise unless a surplus was proved. cf. *Sands to Thompson* (1883) L.R. 22 Ch.D. 614; *Thorne v Heard and Marsh* [1895] A.C. 495.

[395] Including any statute-barred interest, see para.6–54. A mortgagee who exercises his power of sale may retain *all* arrears of interest out of the proceeds of sale as this is not recovery by action.

[396] This is so irrespective of any cross-claim by the mortgagor against the mortgagee—see *Samuel Keller (Holdings) Ltd v Martin's Bank Ltd* [1971] 1 W.L.R. 43; and see *Inglis v Commonwealth Trading Bank of Australia Ltd* (1972) 126 C.L.R. 161.

[397] The concluding words of s.105 are not accurate in that it states that the residue " . . . shall be paid to the person entitled to the mortgaged property." This literally means the *purchaser* and not any subsequent mortgagee or the mortgagor, if none. It would seem that the phrase must be construed with the following additional words inserted " . . . to the person *who immediately before the sale was entitled to the mortgaged property.*" See *British General Insurance Co Ltd v Att.-Gen.* [1945] L.J.N.C.C.R. 113 at 115. Where the property of a company is subject to a fixed charge and sold, the residue is payable in accordance with s.105 and not to any preferential creditors notwithstanding that the charge may have been a floating charge on creation: *Re G.L. Saunders Ltd (In Liquidation)* [1986] 1 W.L.R. 215.

26–59   When the persons interested in the equity of redemption have lost their titles under the Limitation Act 1980, the mortgagee holds the proceeds of sale free of any obligation to account to them, even if he has purported to sell under the power of sale in the mortgage.[398] However, any person still interested in the residue, whether as a puisne mortgagee or as a holder of the ultimate equity of redemption, is entitled to an account from the mortgagee as to his disbursements under the first three headings. Indeed, the mortgagee must have his accounts settled before he can get a discharge from the person with a first claim on the surplus[399]; if the latter disputes the account, the mortgagee can apply to have the account taken by the court.[400]

26–60   **Destination of the residue:**   The destination of the residue depends on what has happened to the equity of redemption; if there is one person solely entitled, there is no difficulty, but the equity of redemption may have been settled, encumbered, or have devolved upon several persons with partial interests.

(1) Settlement. The money must be paid to the trustees or into court.

(2) Successive encumbrances. The money belongs to the encumbrancers according to their priorities. Each successive encumbrancer holds the balance on trust to satisfy his own claim and to pass on the balance, if any. Accordingly, the mortgagee is liable to any encumbrancer, of whose charge he knows, if he pays over the money to the mortgagor.[401] This means, in the case of a legal mortgage of land, that he must search at the Land Registry, because registration has the same consequences as actual notice.[402] He is not, however, under such a duty to state his accounts correctly to other encumbrancers as to estop him from claiming repayment, if in error he pays over to the second mortgagee more than is in fact left—after discharging his own mortgage.[403] The mortgagee, as a trustee of the money, appears to have three ways of obtaining his discharge. Either he may distribute the whole fund, paying to a puisne encumbrancer only what is due to him on his mortgage[404] or else he may pay the whole fund over to the encumbrancer next entitled and obtain a discharge from him. The latter will then hold the residue on the trusts set out in s.105 of the Law of Property Act 1925.[405] Thirdly, if in doubt as to the priorities, he may pay the money into court.[406]

---

[398] *Young v Clarey* [1948] Ch. 191.

[399] See *Eley v Read* (1897) 76 L.T. 39.

[400] *Chadwick v Heatley* (1845) 2 Coll. 137.

[401] *West London Commercial Bank v Reliance Permanent Building Society* (1885) L.R. 29 Ch.D. 954.

[402] LPA 1925 s.198(1); LRA 2002 254.

[403] *Weld-Blundell v Synott* [1940] 2 K.B. 107.

[404] *Re Bell, Jeffrey v Sayles* [1896] 1 Ch. 1; but, strictly, it is the right of the next encumbrancer to have the whole surplus paid over to him, and therefore his claims must be allowed on that footing, i.e. the first encumbrancer cannot limit him to six years' arrears of interest: *Re Thomson's Mortgage Trust, Thomson v Bruty* [1920] 1 Ch. 508.

[405] cf. s.107(2) which covers such a receipt by a puisne encumbrancer.

[406] *Re Walhampton Estate* (1884) L.R. 26 Ch.D. 391; and see Trustee Act 1925 s.63 (as amended by the Administration of Justice Act 1965 s.36(4), Sch.3). See, generally, CPR Pts 36 and 37.

(3) Several owners of the equity of redemption. Being a trustee, he must regulate his payments in accordance with the strict rights of the parties and give the beneficiaries all proper allowances.[407] In case of difficulty he may apply to the court for guidance.

Finally, if there is a surplus and the mortgagee does not distribute it, he will be charged simple interest on the balance in his hands in favour of persons interested in the equity of redemption; and it will not make any difference that there is delay in applying to have the money paid out.[408] He will not, however, be charged interest if distribution is prevented by disputes concerning priorities.[409]   **26–61**

Effect of a sale: for the persons interested according to their priorities.[410] It vests the whole of the estate of the mortgagor in the purchaser,[411] subject to any prior mortgage but free from the selling mortgagee's mortgage and all subsequent encumbrances, including the mortgagor's equity of redemption. The subsequent interests are overreached and transferred to any capital moneys arising from the transaction if those are paid to the mortgagee.[412] The purchaser will have to register his interest in order to complete the transaction.[413] That the mortgagor's right to redeem is utterly gone is well illustrated by the case of *Shaw v Bunny*,[414] where a puisne encumbrancer purchased the estate from the first mortgagee, selling under an express power. The fact that the purchaser had been under an obligation to allow the mortgagor to redeem the property as to the puisne encumbrance did not prevent his purchase from conferring on him a title absolute and irredeemable. Moreover, under the equitable doctrine of conversion the destruction of the equity of redemption takes place as soon as there is a binding contract for sale (even if it is conditional), not upon completion. In *Lord Waring v London and Manchester Assurance Co*,[415] the court was invited to say that the mortgagor might redeem at any time before the execution of the conveyance: the result would be that a mortgagee could only give a conditional contract for sale and his ability to find a purchaser might be seriously prejudiced. However, the power to sell is a power to bind the mortgagor by sale, and the court had no hesitation in deciding that the contract by itself is enough to defeat the equity of redemption. If the mortgagee has, in exercise of his power of sale, entered into a contract for the sale of property, the mortgagor cannot stop the sale by tendering the moneys due.[416] Further a contract made by the mortgagor has no effect on the mortgagee's power of sale.[417]   **26–62**

[407] *Re Cook's Mortgage, Lawledge v Tyndall* [1896] 1 Ch. 923.

[408] *Eley v Read* (1897) 76 L.T. 39.

[409] *Mathison v Clarke* (1855) 25 L.J.Ch. 29; presumably he would have to account for interest actually produced by the surplus, as, e.g. if he put it to deposit.

[410] *Rajah Kishendatt Ram v Rajah Mumtaz Ali Khan* (1879) L.R. 6 Ind. App. 145.

[411] LPA 1925 ss.88(1), 89(1), 104(1).

[412] ibid., s.2(1)(iii).

[413] LRA 2002 ss.4, 27. A failure to do so within the requisite period or any extension has the consequences specified in s.7.

[414] (1865) 2 De G.J. & Sm. 468; *S.E. Rly Co (Directors, etc.) v Jortin* (1857) 6 H.L.C. 425; (1865) 2 De G.J. & Sm. 468.

[415] [1935] Ch. 310.

[416] ibid., and see *Property and Bloodstock Ltd v Emerton, Bush v Property & Bloodstock Ltd* [1968] Ch. 94. See also below paras 26–59 et seq.

[417] *Duke v Robson* [1973] 1 W.L.R. 267.

26–63   The sale also has consequences for the mortgagee. He has taken steps to realise his security, and therefore the interest ceases to run as from the date of sale so that he cannot charge the mortgagor with an additional six months' interest after the sale.[418] On the other hand, sale is not like foreclosure and does not necessarily put an end to the mortgage debt. If there is a surplus after discharging the debt, the transaction is, of course, concluded, save for the distribution of the surplus. If the amount realised is less than what is due on the mortgage, the mortgagee may still sue on the personal covenant for the deficiency: the rule that a mortgagee disables himself from suing for the debt by putting it out of his power to reconvey does not apply to a sale under a power given by the mortgage.[419]

26–64   **The conveyance: sale under express powers:**   A power to make conveyance on sale is not automatically attendant on a power to sell and it is therefore necessary to consider how the conveyance is made upon a sale by a mortgagee. Formerly, in the case of express powers, the power to sell in a mortgage by conveyance did carry with it the power to convey because the mortgagee was holder of the title. With mortgages of land by demise or sub-demise (the usual method of mortgaging leasehold), the mortgagor's reversion caused a difficulty which was usually got over by declaring the mortgagor a trustee of the reversion for the mortgagee.[420] In equitable mortgages it has been held that the mortgagee, having no legal title, had no power to convey and it was necessary to provide for this by giving the mortgagee a power of attorney to convey the property upon a sale.[421] However, there is some suggestion that the equitable mortgagee may in fact be able to convey the legal estate in light of the difference in wording between the Conveyancing Act 1881, with which the older authority was concerned, and the Law of Property Act 1925.[422] The law is still the same for mortgagees by conveyance of personalty and for equitable mortgagees with express powers.

26–65   *Freehold land:*   After December 31, 1925, legal mortgages of land must be by demise or sub-demise, or by legal charge and whether the power to sell is express or statutory the mortgagor's reversion causes no difficulty, since s.88(1) of the Law of Property Act 1925 provides for mortgages or legal charges of the fee, that whether the mortgagee sells under express or statutory power:

> "(a) the conveyance by him shall operate to vest in the purchaser the fee simple in the land conveyed subject to any legal mortgage having priority to the mortgage in right of which the sale is made and to any money thereby secured, and thereupon;
>
> (b) the mortgage term or the charge by way of legal mortgage and any subsequent mortgage term or charges shall merge or be extinguished as respects the land conveyed; and such conveyance may, as respects the fee simple, be made in the name of the estate owner in whom it is vested."

---

[418] cf. *West v Diprose* [1900] 1 Ch. 337.

[419] *Re McHenry, McDermott v Boyd, Barker's Claim* [1894] 3 Ch. 290.

[420] *London and County Banking Co v Goddard* [1897] 1 Ch. 642.

[421] *Re Hodson and Howes' Contract* (1887) L.R. 35 Ch.D. 668 at 671, per North J. " . . . he can convey all he has; but he cannot convey the legal estate," and see below, para.26–67.

[422] *Re White Rose Cottage* [1965] Ch. 940.

Leasehold interests: Section 89(1) of the Law of Property Act 1925 contains   **26–66**
parallel provisions for mortgages of leasehold interests with one important
difference. The mortgagor's nominal reversion expectant on the mortgagee's
sub-term will vest in the purchaser upon a sale but application may be made to
the court to have the reversion kept alive as a protection to the purchaser against
onerous covenants in the original lease. If the purchaser acquires the whole
leasehold interest formerly vested in the mortgagor, he will be in the position of
an assignee and bound by the covenants under the doctrine in *Spencer's Case.*[423]
Applications to the court under this section will be uncommon and there is no
guidance as to what the court will consider a sufficient reason for allowing a
purchaser to escape from performance of the covenants.[424] Further, where a
licence to assign is required on sale by a mortgagee, such licence shall not be
unreasonably refused.

The conveyance: sale and statutory powers: Conveyances consequent upon   **26–67**
the exercise of *statutory* powers, under which most sales take place, are provided
for by s.104(1) of the Law of Property Act 1925,[425] which states that the
mortgagee shall have power:

> "by deed to convey the property sold *for such estate and interest therein as he is by
> the Act authorised to sell or convey or may be the subject of the mortgage*, freed from
> all estates, interests and rights to which the mortgage has priority, but subject to all
> estates, interests and rights which have priority to the mortgage." [author's
> emphasis]

The words in italics require explanation. Under a statutory power the mortgagee
has the advantage of ss.88(1) and 89(1) of the Law of Property Act 1925, so that
a *legal* mortgagee of leasehold or freehold property may sell and convey a larger
estate than was the subject of the mortgage, i.e. the mortgagor's reversion may
be included; but that in all other cases the mortgagee can only convey the interest
which was mortgaged to him, unless the mortgage gives him powers additional
to that in the statute. This latter point causes no inconvenience to a legal
mortgagee of personalty or to a mortgagee of an equitable interest by assignment.
The mortgagor's whole title is transferred to them and section 104 merely
confirms the right to make a conveyance of a title already vested in them.
However, when the legal owner of land or personalty has created a mere
equitable security by contract, the "subject-matter of the mortgage" is the
equitable interest (i.e. the power over the equity of redemption) transferred to the
mortgagee, and s.104 does not therefore confer[426] a power to convey the mortgagor's legal title to a purchaser.[427] This is a serious disability. It is, however, the
universal practice to provide for this by giving an equitable mortgagee a power

---

[423] (1583) 5 Co.Rep. 16a.

[424] See Wostenholme & Cherry, *Conveyancing Statutes* (13th edn, 1971), Vol.1, p.181.

[425] For a recent consideration of LPA 1925 s104 and its compatibility with the Human Rights Act
1998 see *Horsham Properties Group Ltd v Clark* [2008] EWHC 2327 (Ch); [2009] 1 W.L.R.
1255.

[426] This narrow interpretation was doubted in *Re White Rose Cottage* [1965] Ch. 940 at 951, where
it was suggested that s.104(1) gives an equitable mortgagee power to sell the legal estate.

[427] "The mortgaged property" under LPA 1925 s.101(1)(i).

of attorney to convey on behalf of the mortgagor[428]; indeed, ex abundanti cautela, the mortgagor is usually in addition made a trustee of the legal title for the mortgagee. If no such precaution is taken, the conveyance cannot be made without either the mortgagor's concurrence or an application to the court.

26–68 *Deeds:*   Section 106(4) of the Law of Property Act 1925 provides that when the statutory power has become exercisable, the person entitled to sell may demand and recover from any person (other than someone with a prior interest in the mortgaged property) all deeds or documents relating to the title or to the property which a purchaser might be entitled to demand and recover from him. It should be noticed that this will apply to deeds in the hands of a *prior* mortgagee whose debt is discharged out of the purchase moneys or under s.50 of the Law of Property Act 1925.

26–69 **Injunctions to restrain sale:**   When there is evidence of fraud or some other irregularity in the sale which would justify it being set aside, an injunction will be granted by the court to restrain the sale provided that the purchaser had *actual* notice of the fraud or irregularity or of facts which make the proper exercise of the power impossible.[429] Otherwise the mortgagor will be left to his remedy in damages against the mortgagee.[430]

The court will also restrain a sale when the mortgagee is obstructing redemption by the mortgagor. Thus, if a tender of the mortgage debt has been made and declined[431] or if an offer to redeem has been made and the mortgagee has disputed the right to redeem,[432] the mortgagee will be restrained from *attempting* to exercise his power of sale.[433] Similarly, if, upon application to restrain the sale, the amount claimed is paid into court by the applicant, an injunction will lie.[434] No injunction will be granted if the mortgagor merely expresses an intention to redeem,[435] nor even if he has begun an action for redemption[436] or if the mortgage debt is disputed[437]; it is only on the terms of *payment* that the power of sale will be restrained. Consequently, the court will always, when granting an injunction, insist on payment into court of the amount due as a condition of restraining the sale.[438] Even an order nisi for foreclosure in an action brought by

---

[428] See below, para.28–02.

[429] See above, paras 26–42 et seq.; para.26–51. Note that Fisher & Lightwood para.30.36 takes a different view.

[430] *Prichard v Wilson* (1864) 10 Jur.(N.S.) 330. This is on the assumption that the sale is pursuant to the statutory power which contains the clause for the protection of purchasers (see above paras 26–51 et seq.), or to a well-drawn express power containing such a clause. If the express power contains no such clause then the general doctrine of actual or constructive notice applies.

[431] Even without a tender for costs: *Jenkins v Jones* (1860) 2 Giff. 99.

[432] *Rhodes v Buckland* (1852) 16 Beav. 212; but not if the dispute is only as to the amount due: *Gill v Newton* (1866) 14 L.T. 240.

[433] But note the position if there is in existence a binding contract of sale between the mortgagee and the purchaser in the absence of fraud or some other irregularity, above, para.26–62; fn.416 et seq.

[434] *Whitworth v Rhodes* (1850) 20 L.J.Ch. 105.

[435] *Matthie v Edwards* (1847) 16 L.J.Ch. 405.

[436] *Davies v Williams* (1843) 7 Jur. 663.

[437] *Cockell v Bacon* (1852) 16 Beav. 158.

[438] *Warner v Jacob* (1882) L.R. 20 Ch.D. 220; *Macleod v Jones* (1883) L.R. 24 Ch.D. 289.

the mortgagee does not necessarily put a restraint on the exercise of his power to sell out of court, but until foreclosure absolute he may sell with the leave of the court.[439] Finally, it may be noticed that in special cases, where there is a fiduciary relationship between the mortgagor and mortgagee, the court, without altogether restraining the sale, may interfere and control the rights of the parties.[440]

Implied power of sale at common law of chattels, shares and stocks: The **26–70** mortgagee of personal chattels, if in possession and the mortgagee of stocks and shares has[441] a power of sale implied at common law. When the mortgage is by deed, the common law power is displaced by the power given by s.101 of the Law of Property Act 1925 but the implied power is still serviceable when there is no deed. If the mortgage fixes a day for payment, the implied power is exercisable immediately after default on that date. If no date is fixed, then it is exercisable after the mortgagor has been given reasonable notice to pay the debt and has defaulted.[442] It appears that in a mortgage of shares that a month's notice or even a fortnight's notice may be sufficient.[443]

RIGHT TO FIXTURES

In accordance with general principles, fixtures affixed to mortgaged land form **26–71** part of the security in the land whether affixed before or after the date of the mortgage. They pass automatically to the mortgagee of the land as realty unless a contrary intention appears in the mortgage.[444] Accordingly, the special exceptions ("tenant's fixtures") which have developed in the law of Landlord and Tenant do not apply.[445] Fixtures are considered elsewhere in this work.[446]

RIGHT TO INSURE, CONSOLIDATE AND TACK

These rights are considered elsewhere.[447]   **26–72**

---

[439] *Stevens v Theatres Ltd* [1903] 1 Ch. 857.
[440] *Macleod v Jones* (1883) L.R. 24 Ch.D. 289.
[441] See above, paras 22–82 et seq. generally; above, para.26–41.
[442] *Deverges v Sandeman* [1901] 1 Ch. 70 at 73, per Farwell, J., affirmed [1902] 1 Ch. 579.
[443] *Deverges v Sandeman* [1902] 1 Ch. 579.
[444] *Reynolds v Ashby & Son* [1904] A.C. 466.
[445] See Ch.15 para.15–01. Megarry & Wade, *The Law of Real Property* (7th edn, 2008), paras 23–020.
[446] See Ch.15 paras 15–01 et seq.
[447] See Ch.32 para.32–01 (insurance), Ch.8 para.8–01 (consolidation) and Ch.11 para.11–67 (tacking).

CHAPTER 27

THE LEGAL MORTGAGEE—ENFORCING RIGHTS IN COURT

PROCEEDINGS FOR POSSESSION

A legal mortgagee and a chargee by way of legal mortgage has the right to enter **27–01**
into actual possession of the mortgage security from the moment the mortgage is
created.[1] If the security is land which is already let on leases binding the
mortgagee, he cannot, of course, go into possession physically, but he can enter
into receipt of the rents and profits by serving notice on the tenants to pay their
rents to himself instead of to the mortgagor.[2] Normally, the right arises at once
on the execution of the conveyance, but in practice, some breach of the terms of
the mortgage are required before a mortgagee considers exercising its right to
possession. If, however, (as now rarely happens) the mortgage deed contains a
covenant for quiet enjoyment until default is made on the day fixed for payment
(or any similar provision) the right is suspended.[3] Further once the right has
arisen, the court will not by injunction restrain the mortgagee from exercising his
right.[4]

The right to possession is created by the mortgage and both the time the right
arises and the conditions required for its exercise are determined by construing
the mortgage deed. Any claim for possession issued before the right to possession accrues under the terms of the mortgage will therefore be defective and
vulnerable to attack on that basis. It was formerly common practice for mortgage
deeds to contain an attornment clause whereby the mortgagor agreed to become
the tenant of the mortgagee (whether at well, from year to year or for the duration
of the mortgage depending on the exact terms of the mortgage).[5] Such provisions
rarely appear in modern mortgages. The advantage of such a provision was that
the mortgagee would be able to distrain for non-payment and formerly had access
to procedures that were seen as more efficient (for example, summary

---

[1] See above, paras 26–10 et seq. see also *Horsham Properties Group Ltd. v Clark* [2009] 1 W.L.R.
1255—sale by a receiver without order for possession.
[2] *Horlock v Smith* (1842) 6 Jur. 478; or merely not to pay the rents to the mortgagor: *Heales v
M'Murray* (1856) 23 Beav. 401.
[3] *Wilkinson v Hall* (1837) 3 Bing. N.C. 508; see above, para.26–47.
[4] *Marquis of Cholmondely v Lord Clinton* (1820) 2 J. & W. 1, 181; this, of course, is one of the
points of difference between mortgagees and trustees. See also above, paras 25–05 et seq.
[5] See Woodford, *Law of Landlord and Tenant,* paras 6.078 et seq.

judgment).[6] Some attornment clauses provide for a period of notice to quit to determine the tenancy while others provided that the mortgagee may exercise his rights without giving notice. Where a notice period is required, the right to possession will not arise before such notice has been given and expired. It follows that a claim for possession commenced without the specified notice having expired will be defective. An attornment clause would permit the mortgagor's restrictive covenants to be enforced against his successors in title (because of privity of estate).

The various statutory provisions giving tenants security of tenure do not alter the ability of a mortgagee where the mortgagor has attorned tenant to determine the tenancy and resort to his remedies *qua* mortgagee rather than lessor. The "tenancy" created by such a clause is not seen by the law as the real relationship between the parties and they are not treated as being lessor or lessee or, in the case of a mortgagee of residential premises, the same is not considered to be "let as a dwelling-house".[7] Provided the notional tenancy related in the attornment is determined in accordance with the provisions of the mortgage the fact that the mortgagor has attorned tenant will not act as a bar to a claim for possession.

Procedure

Jurisdiction and location

27–02   As a matter of strict jurisdiction,[8] proceedings by either party to a mortgage[9] can generally be brought either in the High Court or in the county courtcounty court. Both courts have concurrent jurisdiction in relation to (a) property wherever situated and which does not comprise a dwelling house[10] in whole or in part, and (b) property which does comprise a dwelling house in whole or in part which is situated in Greater London.

However, even in purely jurisdictional terms there are a number of important and substantial exceptions to this general statement. First, the county courtcounty court has exclusive jurisdiction in relation to a regulated agreement under the Consumer Credit Act 1974.[11] Secondly, in relation to possession proceedings in

---

[6] The present CPR position is that summary judgment is available in any proceedings save (as relevant for present purposes) proceedings for possession of residential premises against (a) a mortgagor, (b) a tenant or other person holding over at the end of his tenancy whose occupies is protected by the Rent Act 1977 or the Housing Act 1988: CPR 24.3(2)(a).

[7] *Alliance Building Society v Pinwill* [1958] Ch. 788; *Portman Building Society v Young* [1951] 1 All E.R. 191; *Peckham Mutual Building Society v Registe* (1981) 42 P. & C.R. 186.

[8] As opposed to practice which differs markedly after October 15, 2001, when the provisions of CPR Pt 55 came into effect; see below paras 27–04 et seq. The effect of CPR Pt 55 was to remove substantially all mortgage business from the High Court unless there are exceptional reasons to commence in the High Court, notwithstanding it retains full jurisdiction.

[9] With regard to foreclosure proceedings, see also paras 27–24 et seq.

[10] A "dwelling house" includes any building or part of a building so used, and it does not matter that part of it is being used for business, trade or other non-residential purposes: county courts Act 1984 s.21(8).

[11] Consumer Credit Acts 1974 as amended by the Consumer Credit Act 2006. See Consumer Credit Act 1974 s.141.

which there is no claim for sale or foreclosure[12] then unless part of the property is situated in Greater London, the proceedings must be brought in the county court if the claim is for possession of property comprising or including a dwelling house.[13] A claim with a value of less than £25,000 cannot be started in the High Court.[14] A claim with a value of less than £50,000 will generally be transferred to a county court[15] unless it is a claim for fraud or undue influence[16] or the circumstances are such that para.7(5) of the High Court and County Courts Jurisdiction Order 1991 apply.[17] That Order and CPR Part 30.3[18] provide that when a court considers the question of transfer to or from a county court, it shall have regard to, inter alia, the importance of the action and whether it raises questions of general public interest; the complexity of the facts, legal issues, remedies and procedures involved and whether a transfer is more likely to result in a more speedy trial of claim. A claim for possession which the High Court cannot hear and determine (i.e. a claim for possession of a property including a dwelling house outside Greater London) cannot be transferred to the High Court.[19]

In addition to issues where the county court has exclusive jurisdiction (regulated mortgages under the Consumer Credit Act 1974 and possession proceedings involving a dwelling house outside Greater London) the county court has unlimited jurisdiction to hear and determine a claim of any value by a mortgagee for payment of principal and interest.[20] The county court also has an unlimited jurisdiction to make an order on an application by a person who is a trustee of land or has an interest in property subject to a trust of land under s.14 of the Trusts of Land and Appointment of Trustees Act 1996.[21]

The county court has co-extensive jurisdiction with the High Court to hear and determine proceedings which include claims for foreclosure or redemption of any mortgage or for enforcing any charge or lien where the amount owing does not exceed the county court limit[22] or proceedings for relief against fraud or mistake, where the damage sustained does not exceed that limit.[23] The county court limit is currently £30,000.[24] This limit can be extended by a signed agreement by the parties to the proceedings or their legal representatives or agents in certain

---

[12] Such a claim must be a genuine claim. The mere addition of a claim for such relief does not bestow jurisdiction on the High Court (which it otherwise has: county courts Act 1984 s.21(4)): *Trustees of Manchester Unity Life Insurance Collecting Society v Sadler* [1974] 1 W.L.R. 770; *Frost Limited v Green* [1978] 1 W.L.R. 949. The test is to identify the relief which the claimant genuinely seeks: *Trustees of Manchester,* above.

[13] County Courts Act 1984 s.21(3) and (4). See also CPR Pt 55 and below, paras 27–04 et seq.

[14] CPR, Pt 7APD 2.

[15] CPR Pt 29PD 2.2.

[16] ibid., para.2.6.

[17] SI 1991/724 (as amended). Note that this appears to have been revoked by High Court and County Courts Jurisdiction (Amendment) Order 1999 (SI 1999/1014) art.7 (April 26, 1999)—see WB vol.2 pp.2382, however is still referenced in CPR 29PD2.6

[18] See generally CPR Pt 30 and the Practice Direction thereto.

[19] *Yorkshire Bank v Hall* [1999] 1 W.L.R. 1713.

[20] County Courts Act 1984 s.15(1) (as amended).

[21] High Court and County Courts Jurisdiction Order 1991 (SI 1991/724) art.2(1)(p) (as inserted by SI 1996/3141).

[22] County Courts Act 1984 s.23(c).

[23] ibid., s.23(g).

[24] High Court and County Courts Jurisdiction Order 1991 (SI 1999/724) (as amended), reg.2(4)

instances.[25] Where the original mortgage advance exceeded the county court limit but the amount owing had, at the date of the commencement of proceedings, been reduced below that limit, the county court has jurisdiction.[26]

By virtue of CPR Pt 55, (except where the county court does not have jurisdiction), possession claims should be now brought in the county court for the district in which the land or any part of it is situated.[27] Only exceptional circumstances will justify starting a claim in the High Court[28] and these must be certified on the claim form and verified by a statement of truth.[29] Such circumstances may include complicated disputes of fact or points of general importance,[30] they do not normally include the value of the property or the amount of any financial claim, although such factors may be relevant.[31] If a claimant starts a claim in the High Court and the court decides that it should have been started in the county court, the court will normally either strike out or transfer it to the county court on its own initiative. There are real sanctions in such circumstances: not only is there likely to be delay but the court will normally disallow the costs of starting the claim in the High Court and of any transfer.[32]

If, unusually, a possession claim is legitimately to be commenced in the High Court, it is assigned to the Chancery Division.[33] Moreover, Sch.1 to the Senior Courts Act 1981 provides for the assignment of all proceedings for the purposes of, inter alia, the redemption or foreclosure of mortgages and the sale and distribution of the proceeds of property subject to any lien or charge to the Chancery Division.

Commencement

27–03   As well as identifying the correct court in which to commence any proceedings as set out above, the mortgagee wishing to seek a possession order of residential property based on arrears must now ensure that he has complied with the Mortgage Arrears Pre-Action Protocol.[34] A failure to do so in circumstances where the borrower can or may be able to raise matters relevant to the exercise of the court's discretion under s.36 of the Administration of Justice Act 1970[35] appears to give the court power to adjourn to require the lender to comply with the Protocol or to adjourn or suspend on terms; to stay the proceedings for an attempt at ADR, or to disallow the costs of the hearing.[36] However, it does not

[25] County Courts Act 1984 s.24.
[26] *Shields, Whitley and District Amalgamated Model Building Society v Richards* (1901) 84 L.T. 587.
[27] CPR Pt 55PD, para.1.2; CPR Pt 55.3(1).
[28] CPR Pt 55PD, para1.2.
[29] CPR Pt 55.3(1).
[30] ibid., para.1.3.
[31] ibid., para.1.4.
[32] ibid., para.1.2.
[33] CPR 55 APD 1.6.
[34] Reproduced in The White Book Service 2010 at C12. The Protocol came into force on November 19, 2008. The court will be expected at the first hearing to enquire whether or not the Protocol has been followed, and it is advisable to set out both in the Particulars of Claim and in any evidence filed the steps which have been taken to comply.
[35] See below paras 27–12 et seq.
[36] CPR 3PD, Pre-Action PD para.2.3.

affect the legal rights of the respective parties. Two copies of a Compliance Checklist in form N123 dealing with steps taken under the Protocol must be completed and taken to the first hearing in respect of any claim issued after October 2009.[37]

Once the mortgagee is ready to issue, he must take care that his claim form is in the prescribed form and that Particulars of Claim are completed filed and served at the same time including all required details.[38]

As well as the mortgagee and mortgagor, consideration should be given to the need to join any other persons as parties to the claim in the light of the relief sought. For example, anyone with a potential right of occupation separate from that of the mortgagor should generally be named as a party, as should any surety. Where a mortgage of land consists of or includes a dwelling house, a "connected person"[39] to the mortgagor who is able, under the Family Law Act 1996 to meet the mortgagor's liabilities can apply to be joined prior to the final disposal of the matter and may be joined in a party to those proceedings if the court sees no special reason precluding joinder and is satisfied the connected person may be expected to assist in satisfying the mortgagor's liabilities to the mortgagee and where that expectation may affect the outcome of the proceedings or should in any event be considered by the court when exercising its discretion under s.36 of the Administration of Justice Act 1970.[40]

Procedure under CPR 55

Although the detailed procedural considerations and requirements of a mort- **27–04** gagee's possession claim are beyond the scope of this work and the substantive legal aspects concerning the various claims that may be brought and defended are considered elsewhere in the text, in summary the process once a CPR Pt 55 claim has been commenced is as follows:

Service: The date for the hearing will be set when the claim is issued. It will **27–05** generally be at least 28 days but not more than 8 weeks after issue, and the claim form must be served at least 21 days before the hearing date along with notice of that date.[41] If the mortgagee serves the claim form and Particulars of Claim, he must produce a certificate of service at the hearing CPR 6.17(2) does not apply.[42]

In cases involving residential property, within five days of receiving notice of the hearing date the mortgagee must serve by sending to the address of the mortgaged property a notice to occupiers which states that a possession claim for the property has started, shows the name and address of the claimant, the defendant and the court in which proceedings were issued, and gives details of

---

[37] CPR 55 APD para.5.5.
[38] See CPR Pts 55.3(5), 55.4 and 55APD paras 1 & 2. See further CPR 16, with which the Particulars of Claim must also comply.
[39] A spouse, former spouse, co-habitant or former co-habitant.
[40] Family Law Act 1996 s.55(3). See Ch.19, above.
[41] CPR 55.5.
[42] CPR 55.8(6).

the hearing. At the same time, the mortgagee must serve on the housing department of the relevant local authority a similar notice which also includes the full address of the property. At the hearing, the mortgagee will have to produce copies of those notices and evidence that they were served.[43]

27–06 **The mortgagor's response:** The mortgagor is not required to acknowledge service of the claim form and Particulars of Claim.[44] His defence, however, if he wishes to file one must be in the prescribed form[45] and if one is not filed within 14 days, he is not precluded from taking part thereafter in the proceedings but the court may take his failure to file a defence into account when deciding what order should be made concerning costs.[46] CPR Pt 12 (default judgments) does not apply to possession claims.[47] Note that any application by the defendant for a time order under s.129 of the Consumer Credit Act 1974[48] may be made either in his defence or by application notice in the proceedings.[49]

27–07 **The first hearing:** A hearing date will be fixed by the court when the claim form is issued[50] which will generally be not less than 28 days nor more than eight weeks from the date of issue.[51] At that hearing, the court may determine the claim or give case management directions.[52] If the claim is genuinely disputed on grounds which appear to be substantial, the claim will be allocated to either the fast track or the multi-track.[53] When allocating to either of these tracks, the court is to have regard to the matters including those set out in CPR 26.8 (as modified by the relevant Practice Direction) the amount of any arrears of mortgage instalments, the importance to the defendant of retaining possession and the importance to the claimant of obtaining vacant possession.[54] Allocation to the small claims track is only possible by consent.[55]

27–08 **Evidence:** Unless the matter is allocated to the fast track or multi-track or the court orders otherwise, any fact that needs to be proved by evidence at a hearing at which the court decides the claim or gives case management directions may be proved by evidence in writing[56] and each party should wherever possible, include all the evidence he wishes to present in his verified statement of case.[57] The Practice Direction requires the claimant's evidence to include the amount of any mortgage arrears and interest on those arrears, which should (if possible) be up

---

[43] CPR 55.10.
[44] CPR Part 55.7(1).
[45] CPR APD para.1.5.
[46] CPR Pt 55.7(3).
[47] CPR Pt 55.7(4).
[48] See Ch.16 para.16–47.
[49] CPR Pt 55APD, para.7.1.
[50] CPR Pt 55.5(1).
[51] CPR Pt 55.5(3).
[52] CPR Pt 55.8(1).
[53] CPR Pt 55.9. The court will only allocate possession proceedings to the small claims track if all the parties agree (CPR 55.9(2)).
[54] CPR Pt 55.9(1).
[55] CPR Pt 55.9(2).
[56] CPR Pt 55.8(3).
[57] CPR Pt 55APD, para.5.1.

to date to the date of the hearing (if necessary specifying a daily rate of arrears and interest).[58] In addition the Practice Direction states that the defendant should give evidence of (1) the amount of any outstanding social security or housing benefit payments relevant to any mortgage arrears, and (2) the status of any claims for social security or housing benefit about which a decision has not yet been made, and (3) any applications to appeal or review a social security or housing benefit decision where that appeal or review has not yet been concluded.[59]

If the maker of the witness statement does not attend the hearing and the other party disputes material evidence contained in that statement, the court will normally adjourn the hearing so that oral evidence can be given.[60]

All witness statements must be filed and served at least two clear days before the hearing.[61] Thus, if that period includes a Saturday, Sunday, a Bank Holiday, Christmas Day or Good Friday, that day does not count.[62] So, if the hearing is on Tuesday, March 6, the evidence must be served on or before Thursday, March 1.

In addition to the notices and certificates of service identified above, the mortgagee must produce at the hearing either the original charge certificate or an official copy of the Charges Register issued by HM Land Registry, which is admissible in evidence to the same extent as the original.[63] The court will generally also expect to see an official search certificate giving the result of a search under s.56(3) of the Family Law Act 1996.

The court's discretion to order possession

In order properly to understand the purpose and operation of the modern discretion in mortgagee's possession claims which is given by the Administration of Justice Acts 1970 and 1973, it is important to understand its historical context and the steps which preceded it. Socio-economic changes in the United Kingdom and their impact on home-ownership from the 1930s onwards have been addressed above.[64] For the purposes of examining the development of the 1970s statutory discretion, there are two distinct periods which should be considered: before and after the decision of Russell J. in *Birmingham Citizens' Permanent Building Society v Caunt.*[65]   **27–09**

Prior to *Birmingham v Caunt*

Until 1936 it was true to say that a legal mortgagee had an absolute right to possession which he could enforce summarily by obtaining judgment for possession in the King's Bench Division. Thus if it was necessary to commence   **27–10**

---

[58] CPR Pt 55APD, para.5.2. That paragraph further states that CPR Pt 55.8(4) does not prevent such evidence being brought up to date orally or in writing on the day of the hearing if necessary.

[59] ibid., para.5.3.

[60] ibid., para.5.4.

[61] CPR Pt 55.8(4); CPR Pt 2.8(2).

[62] CPR Pt 2.8(4).

[63] Land Registration Act 2002 s. 67 and Land Registration Rules 2003 (SI 2003/1417).

[64] See above paras 25–02 et seq.

[65] [1962] Ch. 883.

proceedings for possession of the mortgaged premises instead of relying upon physical entry, the court would afford to the mortgagee the same summary remedy which he had by virtue of his title to enable him to enforce the security.

An amendment to the Rules of Court in 1936,[66] however, materially affected the enforcement of a mortgagee's right to possession. All proceedings by a mortgagee for payment or for possession were thenceforth assigned to the Chancery Division[67] with the express object of excluding summary proceedings by a mortgagee in the King's Bench Division where no regard was had to the Chancery practice of granting equitable relief to the mortgagor in proper cases. The reason for the amendment was that summary proceedings for possession were usually taken against mortgagor-purchasers of small dwelling-houses and it was desired to give the court discretion to "temper the wind to the shorn lamb."[68] Proceedings for possession therefore had to be taken by writ or originating summons in the Chancery Division and judgment for possession became discretionary but only by leave of the Master. Moreover, practice directions authorised Masters, when the defendant was in arrears with any instalment, to give him an opportunity of paying off the arrears by adjourning the summons if the circumstances warranted such a course. The mortgagee in the case of *Hinckley and South Leicestershire Permanent Benefit Building Society v Freeman*[69] sought to impeach these directions as ultra vires on the ground that they conflicted with a mortgagee's established right to immediate possession but they were upheld by the court. The change in the procedural rules of court thus gave the court some measure of control over the mortgagee's exercise of his right to possession.

This practice, which continued for some 26 years, was terminated abruptly by the decision of Russell J. in *Birmingham Citizens' Permanent Building Society v Caunt*,[70] who declared the court had no power to order an adjournment if the mortgagee objected to such a course, save for a short period of up to 28 days and then only when the mortgagor had reasonable prospects of paying off the whole mortgage debt or otherwise satisfying the mortgagee in full.[71]

Post *Birmingham v Caunt*

27–11   The present position is somewhat obscure, but this discretionary jurisdiction in the High Court would still seem to be extant. If, however, the mortgagor has no reasonable prospect of satisfying the mortgagee within a short period of time, an adjournment will be refused.[72] It should be added that the strict approach of the

---

[66] On the recommendation of the Supreme Court Rule's Committee.

[67] Under RSC 1883, Ord. LV, rr.5A, 5C. Now CPR Pt 55. Also see *Norwich Union Life Assurance Society v Preston* [1957] 1 W.L.R. 813.

[68] *Redditch Benefit Building Society v Roberts* [1940] Ch. 415 at 420.

[69] [1941] Ch. 32.

[70] [1962] Ch. 883.

[71] *Ashley Guarantee Plc v Zacaria* [1993] 1 W.L.R. 62 (CA). See also now the statutory discretion, below, paras 27–12 et seq.

[72] ibid. See also *Robertson v Cilia* [1956] 1 W.L.R. 1502; *Four-Maids Ltd v Dudley Marshall (Properties) Ltd* [1957] Ch. 317; *Braithwaite v Winwood* [1960] 1 W.L.R. 1257.

courts based upon commercial considerations is also exemplified in those deci-sions where despite the fact that the mortgagor has a cross-claim which may exceed the mortgage debt, the courts have still refused an adjournment.[73]

In the case of *Quennel v Maltby*[74] the possibility of a wider equitable discre-tion was raised. There it was held by the Court of Appeal that a mortgagee would not be granted possession by the court if he was seeking to exercise his right for purposes other than the protection or enforcement of his security. In that case the mortgagee was seeking possession of a dwelling-house which, contrary to the terms of the mortgage with Barclays Bank, had been let to students. Thus, while the tenancies enjoyed the protection of the Rent Act 1977 vis-à-vis the mortgagor landlord, their tenancies were not binding on the mortgagee.[75] The mortgagee refused to commence possession proceedings against the tenants. The mortgagor then arranged for his wife to pay off the mortgagee and to take a transfer of the mortgage, thereby becoming the mortgagee. Possession proceedings were then commenced by her to obtain vacant possession of the premises. It was held by the court that she was acting as agent for the landlord mortgagor and thus could not assert the rights of the original mortgagee to evict tenants of the mortgagor. Lord Denning M.R. relied on a wider inherent equitable discretion of the courts to prevent a mortgagee or a transferee from him from obtaining possession of a dwelling-house contrary to the justice of the case when there was an ulterior motive, namely, to gain possession of the premises in order to resell it at a profit.[76] This approach and wider equitable discretion has received recent endorsement by the Court of Appeal.[77] In any event, statute has made provision for the exercise of a discretion by the court.

Statutory discretion under the Administration of Justice Acts 1970 and 1973

Following the recommendations of the Payne Committee,[78] ss.36 to 38 of the **27–12** Administration of Justice Act 1970 were specifically enacted in the case of mortgages of dwelling-houses in order to reverse the decision of *Birmingham Citizens' Permanent Building Society v Caunt*.[79] Whether the action is brought in the High Court or the county court,[80] the Administration of Justice Act 1970, as

---

[73] See *Samuel Keller (Holdings) Ltd v Martins Bank Ltd* [1971] 1 W.L.R. 43; *Mobil Oil v Rawlinson* (1981) 261 E.G. 260; *Citibank Trust Ltd v Aviyor* [1987] 1 W.L.R. 1157; *Barclays Bank Plc v Tennet*, unreported CA (Civ. Div.) Transcript No.242, 1984.

[74] [1979] 1 W.L.R. 318.

[75] See *Dudley and District Benefit Building Society v Emerson* [1949] Ch. 707, *Woolwich Building Society v Dickman* [1996] 3 All E.R. 204; *Barclays Bank Plc v Zaroovabic* [1997] Ch. 321 and below, paras 32–03 et seq.

[76] *Quennel v Maltby* [1979] 1 W.L.R. 318 at 323.

[77] *Albany Home Loans Ltd v Massey* [1997] 2 All E.R. 609.

[78] Report of the Committee on the Enforcement of Judgment Debts 1969 (Cmnd. 3908).

[79] [1962] Ch. 883. These powers are not dependent upon default by the mortgagor: see per Buckley L.J. and Scarman L.J. (*contra* Goff L.J.) in *Western Bank Ltd v Schindler* [1977] Ch. 1.

[80] For the position where the county court has exclusive jurisdiction in mortgage actions, see para.27–02.

amended, provides the court with certain powers to adjourn the proceedings, stay the order for possession, or postpone the date for delivery of possession.[81]

Section 36 of the 1970 Act provides as follows:

"(1) Where the mortgagee under a mortgage of land which consists of or includes a dwelling-house[82] brings an action in which he claims possession of the mortgaged property, not being an action for foreclosure in which a claim for possession of the mortgaged property is also made, the court may exercise any of the powers conferred on it by sub-section (2) below if it appears to the court that in the event of its exercising the power the mortgagor[83] is likely to be able within a reasonable period to pay any sums due under the mortgage[84] or to remedy a default consisting of a breach of any other obligation arising under or by virtue of the mortgage.

(2) The court—

(a) may adjourn the proceedings, or
(b) on giving judgment, or making an order, for delivery of possession of the mortgaged property, or at any time before the execution[85]; of such judgment or order, may—

(i) stay or suspend execution of the judgment or order, or
(ii) postpone the date for delivery of possession,

for such period or periods as the court thinks reasonable.

(3) Any such adjournment, stay, suspension[86] or postponement as is referred to in sub-section (2) above may be made subject to such conditions with regard to payment by the mortgagor of any sums secured by the mortgage or the remedying of any default as the court thinks fit.

(4) The court may from time to time vary or revoke any condition imposed by virtue of this section."

Thus, the purpose of s.36 was to mitigate the severity of the legal rule that a mortgagee is entitled to possession of the mortgaged property by giving some protection to a mortgagor of a dwelling-house who had fallen into temporary financial difficulties over the payment of his instalments in allowing him a reasonable time to make good his default.[87]

---

[81] Unless the mortgage secures a regulated agreement within the meaning of the Consumer Credit Act 1974, in which case the 1974 Act applies (see above, Ch.16).

[82] The key date for determining whether or not the mortgaged property consists of or includes a dwelling house is the date on which the claim is brought: *Royal Bank of Scotland v Miller* [2002] Q.B. 255; [2001] 82 P. & C.R. 396.

[83] By s.39(1) "mortgagee" and "mortgagor" include any person deriving title under the original mortgagee or mortgagor. Thus a tenant of a mortgagor may be able to avail himself of these powers, but *quare* the position where the tenancy has been created after the mortgage and is therefore not binding on the mortgagee.

[84] The amount due for these purposes has been further addressed in respect of instalment mortgages by s.8 Administration of Justice Act 1974—see below paras 27–13 et seq. This aspect of s.36 was originally interpreted so as to mean the arrears due at the date of the hearing: *Middlesbrough Trading and Mortgage Co Ltd v Cunningham* (1974) 28 P. & C.R. 69.

[85] It would seem that these words have overruled the decision in *London Permanent Benefit Building Society v De Baer* [1969] 1 Ch. 321. The court's powers under the section cease once a warrant has been executed: *Cheltenham & Gloucester Building Society v Obi* [1994] C.L.Y. 3297; *National Provincial Building Society v Ahmed* [1995] 38 E.G. 138.

[86] For enforcement of orders and suspended orders in particular, see White Book Vol.2 3A-39.

[87] Per Griffiths L.J. in *Bank of Scotland v Grimes* [1985] Q.B. 1179 at 1190.

Unfortunately, it soon became apparent that those cases in which it was likely that the jurisdiction would be invoked were the very cases where the whole principal sum had become due by reason of the fact that most building society mortgages contain a provision making the whole principal sum due in the case of default. The reference in s.36 to "a reasonable period to pay any sums due under the mortgage" had the effect of confining the operation of the section to relatively few cases where the mortgagor was reasonably likely to be able to pay off the whole of the sums due under the mortgage.[88]

As a result, s.8 of the Administration of Justice Act 1973 was enacted to **27–13** overturn that decision. Section 8, in effect, redefines "sums due under the mortgage" as " . . . such amounts as the mortgagor would have expected to be required to pay if there has been no provision for earlier payment." Thus, s.8 of the 1973 Act restored what was presumed to be the original intention of the 1970 Act, and, in effect, provides that where the mortgage entitles or permits the mortgage debt to be repaid by instalments or otherwise defers payment of the whole or any part of the sum, and there is also a term rendering the whole sum due in the event of a default, then the court may nevertheless exercise its powers pursuant to s.36 of the 1970 Act provided that the mortgagor is likely to be able to pay off the outstanding instalments. Clearly, by virtue of these provisions an instalment mortgage is now included within the terms of the sections where there was a six-month legal date for redemption, and also an endowment mortgage is similarly included as it is a mortgage which otherwise permits deferred repayment.[89]

The court's statutory discretion does not arise if the mortgagee has obtained possession pursuant to his common law right without a court order, since the discretion provided by s.36 of the Administration of Justice Act 1970 only arises in circumstances where the mortgagee has brought an action for possession.[90]

In the case of *Habib Bank Ltd v Tailor*[91] it was held that if the loan is not one which otherwise permits deferred repayment then the statutory discretion does *not* apply. This may have serious consequences for the mortgagor.[92] In that case the mortgagor secured an overdraft on his current account with his bank by a charge on his home, the sums being repayable on demand. As the bank could therefore not sue on a supporting mortgage until such a demand had been made the court held that section 8 of the 1973 Act did not apply as it was not a mortgage which permitted deferred repayment. As a consequence any relief had to be sought under s.36 of the 1970 Act, and as we have seen, this would not be possible unless the mortgagor could demonstrate to the court that he could repay the whole of the debt within a reasonable period. Equally, if the mortgagee grants

---

[88] *Halifax Building Society v Clark* [1973] Ch. 307; but cf. *First Middlesbrough Trading & Mortgage Co Ltd v Cunningham* (1974) 28 P. & C.R. 69 approved in *Cheltenham & Gloucester Building Society v Norgan* [1996] 1 W.L.R. 343 (CA) where this case was not followed.

[89] *Centrax Trustees Ltd v Ross* [1979] 2 All E.R. 952; *Bank of Scotland v Grimes* [1985] Q.B. 1179. The section also empowers the court to adjourn foreclosure actions but not to make suspended orders in such cases.

[90] *Ropaigealach v Barclays Bank Plc* [1999] 3 W.L.R. 17.

[91] [1982] 1 W.L.R. 1218.

[92] But not all mortgages in which the loan is expressed to be on demand fall within this category, see S. Tromans [1984] Conv. 91.

a deferral which is not enforceable against him contractually, by estoppel or otherwise, s.8 will not apply.

In the case of *Western Bank Ltd v Schindler*[93] a majority of the Court of Appeal was even prepared to hold that s.36 of the 1970 Act was applicable even in the absence of a default by the mortgagor.[94] This was an unusual case in that the mortgage made no provision for the payments of capital or interest until 10 years after its execution. The mortgagor, however, failed to pay the premium due on the life assurance policy and the policy lapsed. The debt was therefore inadequately secured and in the event it was held that it was not a proper case for the exercise of statutory discretion in the mortgagor's favour. But, the contrary opinion of Goff L.J. is probably to be preferred in that he was of the view that s.36 of the 1970 Act had no application in any event.

However, once a possession order has been made and executed, the court no longer retains a discretion under s.36 unless that execution was oppressive or an abuse of process or the hearing is a subsequent appeal to a judge against a district judge's refusal to suspend the warrant of possession before its execution.[95]

Exercising the court's discretion under the Administration of Justice Acts

27-14 The conditions for the grant of an adjournment are strict. The court's discretionary powers are only exercisable if there is a likelihood of the mortgagor being able to pay the sums due (i.e. the arrears and also the current instalments) within a reasonable period, or that he will seek a speedy sale of the mortgaged property to discharge the arrears and the mortgage debt.[96] Thus, the court should not grant an indefinite adjournment and the period must be fixed or ascertainable.[97] In any event, these powers are *not* exercisable where the mortgagor is unable to comply with the original payment schedule and pay off the arrears by reasonable instalments.[98] Thus the court has no power to order payment of instalments at a reduced level, for example, payment of interest only.

In assessing how long it would be appropriate to postpone the mortgagee's right of possession, the starting point in determining that period is (in the absence of unusual circumstances) the outstanding term of the mortgage.[99] The court

---

[93] [1977] Ch. 1.

[94] ibid., at 12, 13, 15, 19, 26. See also *Royal Trust Co of Canada v Markham* [1975] 1 W.L.R. 1416.

[95] See *Mortgage Express v Da Rocha-Afodu* [2007] EWHC 297 (QB); *London Borough of Lambeth v Hughes* (2001) 33 H.L.R. 33.

[96] *Royal Trust Company of Canada v Markham* [1975] 1 W.L.R. 1416. *Mobil Oil v Rawlinson* (1982) 43 P. & C.R. 221; *Bank of Scotland v Grimes* [1985] Q.B. 1179; *Citibank Trust Ltd v Aviyor* [1987] 1 W.L.R. 1157; *National & Provincial Building Society v Lloyd* [1996] 1 All E.R. 630; *Cheltenham & Gloucester Building Society v Krausz* [1996] 1 W.L.R. 1558; *Target Home Loans Ltd v Clothier* [1994] 1 All E.R. 439.

[97] The usual time given for possession if no order is made under the Administration of Justice Acts 1970–1973, is 28 days after service, see *Barclays Bank v Bird* [1954] Ch. 274 at 282, per Harman J.

[98] *First National Bank Plc v Sayed* [1991] 2 All E.R. 250; *National Westminster Bank plc v Skelton* [1993] 1 W.L.R. 72; *Ashley Guarantee Plc v Zacaria* [1993] 1 W.L.R. 62; *Halifax Plc v Okin* [2007] EWCA Civ 567.

[99] *Cheltenham & Gloucester Building Society v Norgan* [1996] 1 W.L.R. 343.

should, at the outset, resolve any disputes over the apportionment of any instalments ordered to be paid by the mortgagor as between the interest accrued on the mortgage debt and the outstanding principal and ask itself whether the mortgagee's security was likely to be put at risk by the delay in possession occasioned by the court's order.[100]

In assessing whether a mortgagor is able to comply with the terms of any proposed suspended order for possession, the court is entitled to rely on the mortgagor's witness statements or those of his solicitor.[101] While a counterclaim by a mortgagee cannot amount to a defence to a claim for possession per se, the existence and quantum of any counterclaim is relevant for the purposes of the exercise of the court's discretion pursuant to statute.[102] Since a counterclaim can also operate as a set-off to reduce the arrears due on the mortgage debt it is thus relevant in ascertaining the material level of indebtedness and the manner in which the court may exercise its discretion.[103]

In determining what is a reasonable period under s.36, the court (when considering the evidence before it) will consider the following factors[104]:

> "(a) How much can the borrower reasonably afford to pay, both now and in the future?
> (b) If the borrower has a temporary difficulty in meeting his obligations, how long is the difficulty likely to last?
> (c) What was the reason for the arrears which have accumulated?
> (d) How much remains of the original term?
> (e) What are relevant contractual terms, and what type of mortgage is it, *i.e.* when is the principal due to be repaid?
> (f) Is it a case where the court should exercise its powers to disregard accelerated payment provisions (section 8 of the Act of 1973)?
> (g) Is it reasonable to expect the lender, in the circumstances of the particular case, to recoup the arrears of interest (1) over the whole of the original term, or (2) within a shorter period, or even (3) within a longer period, *i.e.* by extending the repayment period? Is it reasonable to expect the lender to capitalise the interest or not?
> (h) Are there any reasons affecting the security which should influence the length of the period for repayment?
>
> In the light of the answers above the court can proceed to exercise its overall discretion taking account also of any further factors which may arise in a particular case."

Once a reasonable period has been determined by the court and the mortgagor **27–15** then fails to show that there is likelihood that he can pay off such arrears as may have accumulated within that time, the court has no jurisdiction under s.36 to suspend the possession order.[105]

[100] ibid.

[101] *Cheltenham & Gloucester Building Society v Grant* (1994) 26 H.L.R. 703.

[102] *National Westminster Bank Plc v Skelton* [1993] 1 W.L.R. 72; *Ashleigh Guarantee Plc v Zacaria* [1993] 1 W.L.R. 62.

[103] cf. *Household Mortgage Corp Plc v Pringle* (1997) 30 H.L.R. 250 where the court disregarded the counterclaim for unliquidated damages.

[104] *Cheltenham & Gloucester Building Society v Norgan* [1996] 1 W.L.R. 343 at 357.

[105] *Town & Country Building Society v Julien* (1992) 24 H.L.R. 312; *Abbey National Mortgages Plc v Bernard* [1995] N.P.C. 118.

The court also has the jurisdiction to postpone a possession order in circumstances where it is apparent that the mortgagors do not have the available funds to meet any of the liabilities other than by selling the mortgaged property[106] and where, on the evidence, the court is satisfied that a sale would be more readily effected if the house was occupied by the mortgagor rather than repossessed by the mortgagee.[107] It would seem that the mortgagor must adduce evidence relating to the actual marketing of his property[108] and that the mortgagor has not set too high a sale price.[109] The period of postponement that the court will grant is not necessarily confined to a very short period, and a period of up to a year has been considered to be potentially reasonable.[110] Where there has been considerable delay in attempting to sell the property or it is clear that the sale price of the property would be barely sufficient to discharge the debt secured on it, the court will order immediate possession or else only allow a particularly short postponement.[111]

If the proceeds of sale of the mortgaged property will be insufficient to redeem the mortgage, the jurisdiction under s.36 cannot arise since there will be no prospect of the mortgagor paying all the sums due under the mortgage within a reasonable time. In such circumstances the mortgagor may have to consider any remedies that he may have under s.91 of the Law of Property Act 1925.[112]

It should also be added that where the mortgage falls within the provisions of s.8 of the 1973 Act, the court's discretion also extends to foreclosure actions whether or not possession is also sought in the same proceedings.[113]

Consumer Credit Act 1974[114]

27–16   The Consumer Credit Act 1974 have provided a complex series of safeguards in many different types of credit transactions. In addition to requiring strict compliance with detailed requirements as to the paperwork required for the valid creation of such mortgages, the Act provides for the service of default notices and an opportunity for the mortgagor to comply with them before possession proceedings can be brought. The court has a wide discretion to make a "time order" under s.129(1) of the 1974 Act, under which the mortgagor is given time to pay by such instalments and at such time as the court having regard to the means of the mortgagor, considers reasonable. The court can also make a suspended order for possession under s.135 of the 1974 Act.[115]

---

[106] See para.27–14, fn.96.

[107] *Target Home Loans Ltd v Clothier* [1994] 1 All E.R. 439 (CA).

[108] cf. *Mortgage Service Funding Plc v Steele* (1996) 72 P. & C.R. 40, where the evidence was described as "utterly flimsy".

[109] *Royal Trust Bank of Canada v Markham* [1975] 1 W.L.R. 1416.

[110] *National & Provincial Building Society v Lloyd* [1996] 1 All E.R. 630.

[111] *Bristol & West Building Society v Ellis* (1997) 73 P. & C.R. 159.

[112] See *Palk v Mortgage Services Funding Plc* [1993] Ch. 330; *Cheltenham & Gloucester Building Society v Krausz* [1997] 1 W.L.R. 1558 and paras 27–37 et seq.

[113] Administration of Justice Act 1973 s.8(3), and see *Lord Marples of Wallasey v Holmes* (1975) 31 P. & C.R. 94.

[114] See generally Ch.16.

[115] For a fuller explanation of the terms of the Consumer Credit Act 1974, see Ch.16 above.

Regulated mortgages under the Rent Act 1977[116]

Finally, mention should be made of the provisions of the Rent Act 1977 (as **27–17** amended)[117] which impose special statutory restrictions on the right of a mortgagee to take possession of mortgaged premises in the case of regulated mortgages. A regulated mortgage is a legal mortgage or charge by way of legal mortgage[118] of land consisting of or including a dwelling-house which is let on or subject to a regulated tenancy which binds the mortgagee[119] and which is not exempted under s.131(2) of the Act. These mortgages are now rare as the provisions of the 1977 Act generally have no application unless the mortgage was created before the relevant date.[120] Thus these complex provisions are of limited importance and it is suggested that further reference be made to the standard works on the Rent Act 1977.[121]

Possession orders and execution

An order for immediate possession will be in the prescribed form[122] as will a **27–18** suspended order for possession.[123] An order for possession in a mortgage case is generally made so as to take effect 28 days later. It requires the mortgagor to deliver up vacant possession of the mortgaged premises[124] in accordance with the terms of the order. The order should, wherever practicable, express the last date for compliance as a calendar date and include the time of the day by which the possession must be delivered up.[125] The parties can agree to vary the specified date by an agreement contained in writing.[126]

In the event that the mortgagor does not deliver up possession of the mortgaged property in accordance with the terms of the order and the mortgagee wishes to enforce the order for possession, the mortgagee must file a request[127] certifying that the property has not been vacated in accordance with the order for possession and provide the prescribed details.[128] A warrant of possession will then be issued.[129] Permission is required to issue a warrant of possession where

---

[116] Controlled mortgages were abolished by the Housing Act 1980 s.152 and Sch.26.

[117] Rent Act 1977 ss.131, 132, as amended by the Housing Act 1980 s.152 and Sch.25, 26.

[118] ibid., s.131(4).

[119] ibid., s.131(1).

[120] Usually December 8, 1965, but in any event no later than August 14, 1974.

[121] See, e.g. Megarry, *The Rent Acts* (11th edn, 1988), Woodfall, *Law of Landlord and Tenant*.

[122] Form N.26:

[123] Form N.31:

[124] *National Union Life Insurance Society v Preston* [1957] 1 W.L.R. 813.

[125] CPR Pt 2.9(1).

[126] CPR Pt 2.11.

[127] Under CCR Ord. 26 r.17 in Form N325. Note that this is the procedure in the county court. In the event of a mortgagee's possession order in the High Court, a writ of possession is required. The relevant provisions are contained in RSC Ord. 46, and the applicable forms are N66 and N66A.

[128] CPR, Sch.2, CCR Ord. 26, r.17.

[129] In Form N49.

inter alia,[130] where more than six years has elapsed since the date of the order[131] or the party entitled to enforce the order or the party against whom the order falls to be enforced has died.[132] If an application for permission is necessary, the application is made in accordance with CPR Pt 23 and must be accompanied by a witness statement of evidence containing the prescribed information.[133]

A warrant of execution may be issued,[134] with the permission of the court, in aid of any warrant of possession.[135] The application is made without notice and must be supported by evidence of the wrongful re-entry into possession following the execution of the warrant of possession plus such further facts as would permit the issue of a writ of restitution in the High Court.[136]

On execution of a warrant of possession by the bailiff, a representative of the mortgagee should be in attendance in order to take possession of the property from the bailiff and secure it.

An order for possession or any warrant for possession can be set aside even after the warrant has been executed if (a) the order giving rise to the warrant is set aside,[137] or (b) the warrant has been obtained by fraud, or (c) there has been an abuse of process or oppression in its execution.[138]

Possession and sale where only part of the beneficial interest stands charged

27–19   The court will not, in general, make an order for possession against only one of two or more mortgagors in possession of the mortgaged property since such an order is of little benefit to the mortgagee, especially where the mortgagors are husband and wife. So where, for example, the mortgagors are husband and wife and the former admits the validity of the mortgage as against his beneficial interest in the mortgaged property and the latter disputes the validity as against her beneficial interest alleging, for example, undue influence, the court will adjourn the mortgagee's proceedings for possession as against the husband with permission for the mortgagee to restore the same in the event that the wife leaves the mortgaged property or an order for possession is made against her.[139]

---

[130] See CPR, Sch. 2, RSC Ord. 26, r.5.

[131] ibid., r.5(1)(a). Note that it is possible to apply to enforce a judgment more than six years old, but obtaining permission to do so is not a formality. The test is whether the circumstances are such that it would be demonstrably just to grant the application and that there should be a departure from the general rule: *Society* of *Lloyds v Longtin* [2005] EWHC 2491 (Ch); [2005] 2 C.L.C. 774; *Duer v Fraser* [2001] 1 W.L.R. 919.

[132] ibid., r.5(1)(b).

[133] ibid., r.4.

[134] In Form N50.

[135] CPR, Sch.2, CCR Ord. 26, r.17(4).

[136] CPR, Sch.2, CCR Ord. 26, r.17(5).

[137] *Peabody Donation Fund Governors v Haly* (1986) 19 H.L.R. 145.

[138] *Hammersmith & Fulham London Borough Council v Hill* (1995) 27 H.L.R. 368.See also *Mortgage Express v Da Rocha-Afodu* [2007] EWHC 297 (QB); *London Borough of Lambeth v Hughes* (2001) 33 H.L.R. 33

[139] *Albany Home Loans Limited v Massey* [1997] 2 All E.R. 609.

An order for sale would, in such circumstances, require the mortgagee to invite the court to exercise its discretion under s.14 of the Trusts of Land and Appointment of Trustees Act 1996. In *The Mortgage Corporation v Shaire*,[140] Neuberger J. concluded that the enactment of that Act had substantially altered the matters to which the court is now to have regard when exercising its discretion and that any authorities decided under s.30 of the Law of Property Act 1925 (which was repealed by the 1996 Act) should be treated with caution since they were "unlikely to be of great, let alone decisive, assistance".[141] Thus the approach previously adopted by the courts pursuant to which a sale of property would be ordered save other than in exceptional circumstances[142] is no longer good. Instead the court will have regard to all the circumstances of the case and the factors to which it is, by s.15 of the Act, directed to consider. Section 15 provides:

> "(1) The matters to which the Court is to have regard in determining an application for an order under section 14 include—
>
> (a) The intentions of the person or persons (if any) who created the trust,
> (b) The purposes for which the property subject to the trust is held,
> (c) The welfare of any minor who occupies or might reasonably be expected to occupy any land subject to the rust at his home, and
> (d) The interest of any secured creditor of any beneficiaries.
>
> (2) . . . .
> (3) . . . the matters to which the court is to have regard also include the circumstances and wishes of any beneficiaries of full age and entitled to an interest in possession of the property subject to the trust or (in the case of dispute) of the majority (according to the value of their combined interests)."[143]

Neuberger J. in *The Mortgage Corporation v Shaire* held that the inclusion of s.15(1)(d) on an equal footing with s.15(1)(a)–(c) removed the creditor's preferred status under s.30 of the Law of Property Act 1925, as typified in authorities such as *Lloyds Bank Plc v Byrne*.[144] Thus now, when considering whether a property held subject to a trust of land should be sold, the court will have regard to a number of factors, including those laid down in s.15. In *The Mortgage Corporation v Shaire*, Neuberger J. further considered the mortgagee's commercial position and security if a sale was not ordered, the hardship that Mrs Shaire (who was, in effect, the innocent party by reason of the forging of her signature to a number of documents) would suffer in the event of an order for sale being made and what other property Mrs Shaire might be able to acquire in the event that a sale was sold and her equity realised.[145] Accordingly, a mortgagee which only enjoys security over part of the beneficial interest in a jointly-owned property cannot be certain that an order for sale will now be made in its favour;

---

[140] [200] 1 F.L.R. 973. See also *Bank of Ireland Home Mortgages v Bell* [2001] 3 F.C.R. 134 and *C Putnam & Sons v Taylor* [2009] EWHC 317 (Ch).

[141] ibid., at 991B–C.

[142] See *Re Ciro* [1991] Ch. 142; *Lloyds Bank Plc v Byrne* (1993) 1 F.L.R. 369.

[143] s.15(4) provides that "This section does not apply to an application if section 335A of the Insolvency Act 1986 (which . . . relates to applications by a trustee of a bankrupt) applies to it."

[144] [1993] 1 F.L.R. 369.

[145] In fact there was no evidence of this before the court but Neuberger J. clearly considered it to be significant see [2000] 1 F.L.R. at 973 993G–995C.

much depends on the overall circumstances of each particular case. In the4 event that the party whose interest is charged has been adjudged bankrupt, a mortgagee can rely on the provisions of the Insolvency Act 1986, which provide the court with a more limited discretion.[146]

In considering whether or not make an order under s.14, there are a number of factors which the courts have expressly mentioned including:

(1) whether the creditor is being properly compensated for being kept out of his money where payment is overdue,[147]

(2) whether the debt exceeded the realisable sale value of the property and was increasing and whether the delay to the mortgagee would be unconscionable,[148]

(3) the hardship caused to a long-term resident being forced to leave property,[149]

(4) whether leasehold property is in fact being put at risk by the mortgagor's conduct.[150]

Others include the respective shares in the property of the mortgagee and the occupiers; whether (upon the refusal of a sale) provision could be made for the mortgagee to have control over repairs to the property and keep it insured; whether the accommodation provided is excessive given the needs of the occupiers; whether the sum likely to be obtained by the occupiers on sale would enable them to find other accommodation; and the income of those occupiers and their ability and willingness to pay the mortgagee in the meanwhile. Where the court decides that an order for sale is appropriate, it is best if the sale process can be underway either before, or while, any disputes between beneficial owners can be resolved.[151]

The factors to which the court is to have regard under s.15 and their consideration (express or otherwise) is sufficient for the purposes of the Human Rights Act 1998.[152]

Costs against the mortgagor[153]

Recovery from the security

27–20   A mortgagee has an equitable right to obtain reimbursement from the security that he holds for those costs which he has reasonably and properly incurred in proceedings between the mortgagee and mortgagor and the mortgagor's surety[154]

---

[146] See Insolvency Act 1986 s.335A and generally Ch.34.

[147] See *Pritchard Englefield v Steinberg* [2001] EWHC 1908 (Ch); [2005] 1 P. & C.R. DG2.

[148] *Bank of Ireland Home Mortgages v Bell* [2001] 2 All E.R. (Comm) 920. *(a)*.

[149] *Shaire* [2000] 1 F.L.R. at 973 *(a)*.

[150] *Pritchard Englefield* above *(a)*.

[151] *Wilcox v Tait* [2006] EWCA Civ 1867; [2007] 2 F.L.R. 871.

[152] See *C Putnam & Sons v Taylor* [2009] EWHC 317 (Ch); [2009] B.P.I.R. 769; *Close Invoice Finance Limited v Pile* [2008] B.P.I.R 1465; *National Westminster Bank v Rushmer* [2010] EWHC 554 (Ch).

[153] See also paras 33–12 and 33–27.

[154] *Parker-Tweedale v Dunbar Bank plc (No.2)* [1991] Ch. 26; *Gomba Holdings Ltd v Minories Finance Ltd (No.2)* [1993] Ch. 171.

and the same are not usually within the discretion of the court unless misconduct is charged and proved.[155] Moreover, most well-drawn mortgages also make express provision for the mortgagee to add all and any costs that he has incurred to his security, often on an indemnity basis, thereby augmenting the equitable right. In the absence of special agreement, they are not a personal debt of the mortgagor.[156] In addition, at the conclusion of any proceedings, the court has a discretion to award costs in a party's favour.[157] Generally, the court will order costs to be paid by the unsuccessful party to the successful party[158] but, having regard to all the circumstances and in particular the parties' conduct,[159] the court may make a different order if justice so requires.[160]

Interrelationship between the mortgagee's rights and the court's discretion[161]

The following principles emerge.

27–21

(1) The court's exercise of its discretion under the Civil Procedure Rules remains a matter solely within its remit having regard to the appropriate circumstances of each case.

(2) However, and generally speaking, an order for costs pursuant to the court's discretion should be made in such terms as reflects the mortgagee's contractual entitlement.[162]

(3) The court may deny a mortgagee the benefit of his equitable or contractual rights to add his costs to the security in circumstances where such an outcome would be appropriate.[163] A mortgagee's right to recover his costs by adding them to the mortgage security arises from the jurisdiction inherent in a court of equity to fix the terms on which the mortgagor may redeem the mortgaged security.[164] Accordingly, it follows that a court may disallow the mortgagee's costs if to permit them to be recovered from the mortgage debt would be inequitable as an exercise of its statutory discretion to award costs[165] or of its equitable discretion to fix the terms upon which the mortgagor can redeem the mortgaged security or both.[166]

---

[155] *Charles v Jones* (1886) L.R. 33 Ch.D. 80.
[156] *Frazer v Jones* (1846) 5 Hare 475; *Sinfield v Sweet* [1967] 1 W.L.R. 1489.
[157] See generally CPR Pt 44.3.
[158] CPR Pt 44.3(2).
[159] CPR Pt 44.3 (4) and (5).
[160] CPR Pt 44.3(6). *BCCI SA v Ali (No.3)* (1999) 149 N.L.J. 1734.
[161] See CPR 48PD, 50.3 50.4; *Gomba Holdings Ltd v Minories Finance*, above; *Forcelux Ltd v Binnie* [2010] C.P. Rep. 7 or [2009] EWCA Civ 1077; [2010] H.L.R. 20.
[162] *Gomba Holdings Ltd v Minories Finance Ltd (No.2)* [1993] Ch. 171: a contractual provision for costs on an indemnity basis was reflected in an order for taxation/assessment.
[163] See paras 33–12 and 33–27.
[164] *Parker-Tweedale v Dunbar Bank Plc (No.2)* [1991] Ch. 26; *Gomba Holdings Ltd v Minories Finance Ltd (No.2)* [1993] Ch. 171.
[165] Senior Courts Act 1981 s.51 (as amended); CPR Pt 44.3.
[166] *Parker-Tweedale v Dunbar Bank Plc (No.2)* [1991] Ch. 26; *Gomba Holdings Ltd v Minories Finance Ltd (No.2)* [1993] Ch. 171.

(4) In order for a mortgagee to be deprived of his equitable or contractual right to add his costs to the security, the court should determine that issue specifically with reference to the mortgagee's specific rights; an adverse order for costs against a mortgagee will not be sufficient to deprive the mortgagee of his rights.[167]

27–22   Assessment of costs: The basis of the assessment of the mortgagee's costs (whether in the taking of an account or on a detailed assessment) should correspond to that contained in the mortgage deed,[168] although problems arise if the mortgage deed appears to produce a result which is neither akin to the standard nor the indemnity basis.[169] If the mortgage deed is silent in that regard, the standard basis is the appropriate basis[170] unless the court, in the exercise of its discretion, considers that the mortgagee's costs of any litigation should be assessed on the indemnity basis. In practice, even if the mortgagee's costs are assessed on an indemnity basis, he will not necessarily recover all his costs. A mortgage deed will never be construed so as to require the payment by the mortgagor of all the mortgagee's costs, charges and expenses even if improperly or unreasonably incurred or improper or unreasonable in amount; an express provision to that effect would be open to serious question on public policy grounds[171] or under the provisions governing unfair contractual terms.

27–23   Recovery from the mortgagor personally: Generally, a mortgagor is not personally liable for the mortgagee's costs in the absence of special agreement to that effect[172]; however, most modern mortgages are drafted so as to impose that liability.

If the mortgagor raises a defence which fails and the mortgage security is insufficient to bear those costs, the mortgagor must pay the unsecured balance of those costs personally.[173] If the mortgagor brings a redemption action and then fails to redeem, he is liable personally to pay the costs of that action, which will be dismissed.[174]

PROCEEDINGS FOR FORECLOSURE OR JUDICIAL SALE

Generally

27–24   Equity, having created the equity of redemption, also provides the means whereby a mortgagee may free his title from the equity. Otherwise a mortgagee would suffer a serious injustice since, even when in urgent need of his capital, he

---

[167] ibid.

[168] *Gomba Holdings Ltd v Minories Finance Ltd (No.2)* [1993] Ch. 171.

[169] As these are the two assessment options available to the court under CPR 44.4 and CPR 48.3.

[170] *Re Adelphi Hotel (Brighton) Ltd* [1953] 1 W.L.R. 955.

[171] *Gomba Holdings Ltd v Minories Finance Ltd (No.2)* [1993] Ch. 171 at 187–188.

[172] *Frazer v Jones* (1846) 5 Hare 475; *Sinfield v Sweet* [1967] 1 W.L.R. 1489.

[173] *Liverpool Marine Credit Co v Wilson* (1872) L.R. 7 Ch. App. 507.

[174] *Mutual Life Assurance Society v Langley* (1886) L.R. 32 Ch.D. 460.

would have no means of compelling its restoration.[175] He might go into possession or appoint a receiver but even so, the rents and profits might do no more than
pay him his interest. Consequently, although jealous to protect the equity of
redemption, the court allows a mortgagee to destroy the equitable right to redeem
with its own assistance. This assistance takes the form of an order either for
foreclosure or for a judicial sale. By the former, a mortgagee's title is made
absolute by the court, the effect of which is to transfer the legal estate from the
mortgagor to the mortgagee.[176] By the latter, the security is, under the supervision of the court, sold freed from the equity of redemption. In the Republic of
Ireland, foreclosure orders have never been favoured[177] and there judicial sale is
the remedy for a mortgagee as well as for a chargee. In England, on the other
hand, the natural remedy given by the court to a mortgagee is foreclosure, and
judicial sale is available to him only as an alternative which the court may in its
discretion grant him in the course of proceedings for foreclosure.[178] The realisation of his security in court in one of these two ways is, historically, the primary
remedy of a mortgagee. However, today a mortgagee will nearly always possess
either an express or statutory power to sell out of court[179] and will not be obliged
to seek the court's assistance. Further, the courts have shown a reluctance to
order foreclosure. Consequently, it is a remedy which now has only limited
importance and it has been suggested that it should be replaced by the simple
remedy to order a judicial sale as in the Republic of Ireland.[180] On the other hand,
the power of the court to order foreclosure is still of some interest, since a
mortgagee may desire to retain the mortgaged property in his own hands and to
obtain the balance of its value.[181]

The right of foreclosure

Notwithstanding the Law Commission's recommendation that the right to fore-   **27–25**
closure be abolished,[182] in England and Wales the right to foreclose remains and
is inherent in the nature of mortgage[183] and in no other form of security. It was
for this reason that the test of a security as to whether it was a mortgage rather

---

[175] *Campbell v Holyland* (1877) L.R. 7 Ch.D. 166 at 171, per Jessel, M.R.

[176] i.e. by vesting the mortgagor's fee simple or term of years in the mortgagee, see Law of
Property Act (LPA) 1925 ss.88(2), 89(2). In the case of registered land an order for foreclosure is
completed by registration of the proprietor of the charge as proprietor of the land and by cancellation
of the charge and all encumbrances and entries inferior thereto: Land Registration Rules 2003 r.112.
Prior to 1925 the remedy of foreclosure terminated the mortgagor's equity of redemption leaving the
mortgagee with an unencumbered interest.

[177] *Re Cronin* [1914] 1 I.R. 23, 29; *Harpur v Buchanan* [1919] 1 I.R. 1, 4; but the jurisdiction to
give foreclosure, though not exercised, appears to exist: *Shea v Moore* [1894] 1 I.R. 158 at 163, n,
per Porter, M.R.

[178] LPA 1925 s.91(2) and see below, para.27–37.

[179] See above, paras 26–39 et seq. In practice a mortgagee will only seek the remedy of foreclosure
where the security is deficient but there is a prospect that the value of the property will improve.

[180] Transfer of Land—Land Mortgages 1991, Law Com. No.204, paras 7.26, 7.27

[181] For a modern case illustrating the difficulties which can be encountered in foreclosure proceedings, see *Lloyds & Scottish Trust Ltd v Britten* (1982) 44 P. & C.R. 249.

[182] Transfer of Land—Land Mortgages 1991, Law Com. No.204, paras 7.26, 7.27.

[183] *Re Bogg* [1917] 2 Ch. 239 at 255.

than a mere charge was determined by the availability to the creditor of the remedy of foreclosure. The only exceptions being (i) the old Welsh mortgage, in which any realisation of the security is impossible,[184] (ii) mortgages given by public utility companies where the impossibility of foreclosure arises not from the form of mortgage but from the property being in public use,[185] and (iii) mortgages granted by the Crown, against which foreclosure is not available.[186] In instances where the Crown is the mortgagor, the court will simply order a sale and rely upon the Crown conveying.[187] All other mortgages, whether their subject-matter is realty or personalty[188] and whether the mortgage is legal or equitable, give rise to this remedy. Thus an equitable mortgagee of a legal estate by express contract or by deposit of title deeds may foreclose,[189] while a mortgagee of an equitable interest in property may foreclose the equitable interest leaving the legal title outstanding in a third party.[190] Similarly, a mortgagee of personal chattels[191] and of a share in a partnership,[192] and a debenture holder[193] may foreclose as may a mortgage of policies of insurance[194] and pensions[195] and of reversionary as well as present interests.[196] However, apart from statute, the remedy of a chargee is sale, not foreclosure.[197]

Court's control of the loss of the equity of redemption

27–26   Foreclosure is the prerogative only of a mortgagee because foreclosure presupposes a title in the creditor which has become absolute at law through the breach of a condition.[198] Under his contract a mortgagee's title to the property becomes absolute when the mortgagor fails to redeem in accordance with the terms of the proviso for redemption. Equity then intervenes on behalf of the mortgagor to give him a right to redeem notwithstanding that failure, and thus puts a stop on the absolute title of the mortgagee. However, there has to be a stage at which a mortgagee can finally enforce his security and the mortgagor's equitable rights brought to an end. Foreclosure, as Jessel M.R. indicated,[199] is no more than the court's removal from the mortgagee's title of the stop which the court itself has imposed. Foreclosure is therefore always an act of the court: today a mortgagee

---

[184] See *Coote on Mortgages* (9th edn, 1927), Vol.1, Ch.III, p.35.
[185] *Gardner v London, Chatham and Dover Rly Co* (1867) L.R. 2 Ch. App. 201.
[186] *Hodge v Attorney-General* (1839) 3 Y. & G. Ex 342.
[187] *Hancock v Attorney-General* (1864) 10 Jur. N.S. 557; *Bartlett v Rees* (1871) L.R. 12 Eq. 395.
[188] *General Credit and Discount Co v Glegg* (1883) L.R. 22 Ch.D. 549.
[189] *Pryce v Bury* (1853) 2 Drew 41; *Frail v Ellis* (1852) 16 Beav. 350.
[190] cf. *Slade v Rigg* (1843) 3 Hare 35.
[191] *Kemp v Westbrook* (1749) 1 Ves.Sen. 278.
[192] *Redmayne v Forster* (1866) L.R. 2 Eq. 467.
[193] *Sadler v Worley* [1894] 2 Ch. 170.
[194] *Re Kerr's Policy* (1869) L.R. 8 Eq. 331.
[195] *James v Ellis* (1871) 19 W.R. 319.
[196] *Slade v Rigg* (1843) 3 Hare 35.
[197] *Tennant v Trenchard* (1869) L.R. 4 Ch. 537.
[198] *Bonham v Newcomb* (1684) 1 Vern. 232 affirmed (1689) 1 Vern. 233 (HL).
[199] " . . . the court simply removes the stop it has itself put on." per Jessel M.R. in *Carter v Wake* (1877) L.R. 4 Ch.D. 605 at 606. See also *Heath v Pugh* (1882) 2 A.C. 235.

usually has power to sell his security out of court but he cannot become the beneficial owner of the security except under the authority of the court. In *Re Farnol, Eades, Irvine & Co*[200] Warrington J. said:

> "Foreclosure as a thing which can be done by a person has no meaning. Foreclosure is done by the order of the court, not by any person. In the strict legal sense it is nothing more than the destruction of the equity of redemption which previously existed."

It follows that the right to foreclosure cannot arise until the mortgagor is in default under the proviso for redemption[201] and repayment has become due at law. The importance of this is that not every breach of his contract by a mortgagor will give a mortgagee the right of foreclosure: the breach must bring into effect the condition rendering the mortgagee's title absolute and therefore must concern the proviso for redemption. This is illustrated by *Williams v Morgan*,[202] where a mortgage made in 1900 contained a covenant for the payment of the principal in 1914 (with interest half-yearly in the meanwhile) but the proviso for redemption permitted redemption in 1914 on payment of the capital and of such interest as might then be due and unpaid. The mortgagor defaulted in payment of interest before 1914 but Swinfen-Eady J. held that under this deed no right to foreclose could arise until 1914. The covenant for payment and the proviso for redemption were distinct stipulations, and it would have been altering the plain language of the deed to incorporate the terms of the covenant for payment into the proviso for redemption. The mortgagor's default did not, therefore, constitute a default under the proviso for redemption, so that the mortgagee was not entitled to a foreclosure.

However, this does not mean that the mortgagor's default must be in the repayment of capital. Even when the mortgagee has debarred himself from calling in the capital for a definite period of years, default in the payment of any instalment of interest will entitle him to foreclose if the proviso for redemption was made conditional on the punctual payment of interest.[203] The point is that the terms of the covenant for payment of interest must have been incorporated into the proviso for redemption. The same principle applies to a mortgagor's other covenants. Ultimately, it is a question of construction of the mortgage terms.[204] Thus, in a mortgage of leaseholds, the mortgagor's breach of his covenant to observe the terms of the lease will give rise to a right of foreclosure only if the performance of the covenant was expressly incorporated in the proviso for redemption.[205] If such a covenant and the proviso for redemption are expressed

---

[200] [1915] 1 Ch. 22 at 24.

[201] In a mortgage of a legal estate, a proviso for redemption is not strictly necessary since by mere payment the mortgage term becomes a satisfied term: therefore a forfeiture clause would be sufficient. However, a proviso for redemption is often found in practice. *Contra* bank mortgages, which are usually payable on demand and contain no such proviso.

[202] [1906] 1 Ch. 804.

[203] *Burrowes v Molloy* (1845) 2 Jo. & Lat. 521; *Edwards v Martin* (1856) 25 L.J.Ch. 284; *Kidderminster Mutual Benefit Building Society v Haddock* [1936] W.N. 158; *Twentieth Century Banking Corporation Ltd v Wilkinson* [1977] Ch. 99.

[204] *Mohamedali Jaffer Karachiwalla v Noorally Rattanshi Rajan Nanji* [1959] A.C. 518, JCPC.

[205] cf. *Seaton v Twyford* (1870) L.R. 11 Eq. 591; if in an equitable mortgage by contract to create a legal mortgage the mortgagee agrees not to foreclose for a given period, the court will imply that this is conditional on the performance of covenants. ibid.

as distinct stipulations, the court will not, by construction, incorporate the covenant into the proviso for redemption.[206]

The time when foreclosure becomes available is therefore the moment the mortgagor makes default under the proviso for redemption. The default which usually calls into being the right of foreclosure is the failure to repay the principal on the date named in the contract for redemption which is usually six months after the execution of the mortgage deed. If no date is fixed or if the money is repayable on demand, then the right arises after a demand has been made and a reasonable time has been allowed for compliance with the demand.[207] As a rule, the right to foreclose and the equitable right to redeem arise simultaneously on the passing of that date without redemption. There is, however, no objection to a mortgagee precluding himself from foreclosing during any period of whatever length or on whatever terms and the mortgagor need not be under a corresponding obligation not to redeem.[208] As a mortgagee requires no protection when making the agreement, he cannot obtain relief on the ground of want of mutuality even when he has not made his agreement to forbear conditional on the punctual payment of interest.[209] Therefore he almost invariably makes forbearance conditional on such payment of interest in order that a failure to pay interest may lift the bar to foreclosure.[210] Nor will he afterwards lose his right to foreclose by merely accepting payment of the interest: to revive the bar he must actually waive the breach of the condition.[211]

If there is only an agreement to execute a mortgage, equity takes on that as done which ought to be done and permits the mortgagee to foreclose after nonpayment by the mortgagor in accordance with the terms of the agreement or after demand and a reasonable time for compliance.[212]

The right to foreclose, once it has arisen, continues to be available so long as any part of the mortgage debt remains unpaid.[213]

Persons entitled to seek foreclosure

27–27   Foreclosure is available to a legal or equitable mortgagee and to the holder either of a registered charge or a charge by way of legal mortgage. The right to

---

[206] *Turner v Spencer* (1894) 43 W.R. 153.

[207] *Fitzgerald's Trustee v Mellersh* [1892] 1 Ch. 385; *Balfe v Lord* (1842) 2 Dr. & War. 480.

[208] *Ramsbottom v Wallis* (1835) 5 L.J.Ch. 92; *Kreglinger v New Patagonia Meat & Cold Storage Co Ltd* [1914] A.C. 25.

[209] *Burrowes v Molloy* (1845) 2 Jo. & Lat. 521.

[210] The way such an agreement is framed is to have the ordinary proviso for redemption putting the mortgagor in default after six months followed by a separate covenant not to call in the money for the period specified, the covenant being made conditional on the regular payment of interest.

[211] *Keene v Biscoe* (1878) L.R. 8 Ch.D. 201. However, receipt of interest will be one factor to which the court will have regard in determining whether or not the breach has been waived: *Seal v Gimson* (1914) 110 L.T. 583.

[212] *Fitzgerald's Trustee v Mellersh* [1892] 1 Ch. 385.

[213] A foreclosure decree will not, however, be made in respect of costs or interest only: *Drought v Redford* (1827) 1 Moll. 572.

foreclose also belongs to persons who become entitled to the mortgage by assignment or devolution and is available to a trustee in bankruptcy.[214] Thus, in addition to an encumbrancer solely entitled, the following persons may foreclose:

(1) Express assignees of the mortgagee. The assignee's right is, however, subject to the state of the accounts between mortgagor and mortgagee at the date of the assignment and also to any equities then existing in the mortgagor's favour.[215] An assignment of the debt without the security leaves the right to foreclose in the original mortgagee.[216]

(2) Sub-mortgagees are assignees and may foreclose on the original mortgagor on similar terms.[217] They may also foreclose on encumbrances ranking below them.[218]

(3) Co-mortgagees. Each must foreclose the whole mortgage not merely his own share.[219] Co-ownership of land involves a trust of land and co-mortgagees of land ought presumably to foreclose through the trustees.

(4) Trustees. The beneficiaries must proceed through their trustees.[220]

(5) Personal representatives, before assent or transfer.[221]

(6) Trustees in bankruptcy, in the case of the bankruptcy of a mortgagee.[222]

Parties to the action

If there are several persons beneficially interested in the mortgage moneys, they   **27–28** must all be represented in the action; and in accordance with the general rule, trustees and personal representatives sufficiently represent the persons for whom they act so that none of the beneficiaries need be joined.[223] In the case of co-mortgagees *all* must be joined[224]; if they are willing to concur in the proceedings, they will be made claimants; if not, they must be made defendants.[225] If

---

[214] A judgment creditor who has obtained a charging order under the Charging Orders Act 1979 is in the position of an equitable mortgagee. See Ch.20.

[215] *Withington v Tate* (1869) L.R. 4 Ch. App. 288; *Turner v Smith* [1901] 1 Ch. 213.

[216] *Morley v Morley* (1858) 25 Beav. 253; he will, however, be a trustee of the security for the assignee.

[217] See *Hobart v Abbott* (1731) 2 P.Wms. 643; *Norrish v Marshall* (1821) 5 Madd. 475.

[218] *Rose v Page* (1829) 2 Sim. 471; *Slade v Rigg* (1843) 3 Hare 35.

[219] *Davenport v James* (1847) 7 Hare 249; *Luke v South Kensington Hotel Co* (1879) L.R. 11 Ch.D. 121; as to the effect of decree in the case of an equitable mortgage, see *Re Continental Oxygen Co, Elias v Continental Oxygen Co* [1897] 1 Ch. 511.

[220] *Wood v Williams* (1819) 4 Madd. 186.

[221] Administration of Estates Act 1925 ss.1, 3 as amended.

[222] As to insolvency generally, see Chs 34–35.

[223] CPR Pts 64 and 19.

[224] *Davenport v James* (1847) 7 Hare 249.

[225] See *Luke v South Kensington Hotel Co Ltd* (1879) L.R. 11 Ch.D. 121.

land has been mortgaged to several co-mortgagees, there will be a trust of land[226] and foreclosure must take place through the trustees. Clearly, when the money was advanced out of a joint account (as in the case of trustee-mortgagees), the personal representatives of a deceased co-mortgagee need not be joined. Moreover under s.111 of the Law of Property Act 1925 co-mortgagees are to be deemed joint tenants—subject to any statement to the contrary—both when the money is expressed to be advanced out of a joint account and when the mortgage is merely made to them jointly. Even in the rare case when a mortgage of land is not made upon a joint account, the personal representatives of a deceased co-mortgagee probably need not be joined, since foreclosure will always take place through the trustees of the land, who are necessarily joint tenants. In a mortgage of personalty, however, the fact that the money neither was, nor could be deemed to be, advanced out of a joint account would necessitate the joinder of the personal representative because personalty is not subject to the trust of land imposed by statute.[227] It may be added that in an action by debenture holders all must be before the court either as claimants or defendants[228]; this is usually achieved by a representative action under CPR 19.6.

In foreclosure actions, all persons interested in the equity of redemption *must* be before the court in order that they may be bound by the accounts. In general, beneficiaries are sufficiently represented by their trustees.[229] However, so anxious is the court that no party shall be deprived of his opportunity to redeem that it will readily allow beneficiaries to be joined if it appears that the trustees may be unable to redeem.[230] The determination of who, in general, has a right to redeem and is entitled to be joined as defendant will be investigated at length in connection with redemption and with the maxim, *redeem up, foreclose down.*[231] The details need not be repeated here but the general principle is that all persons must be joined who will be affected by the accounts taken in the action, so that in a foreclosure action all persons acquiring interests in the property subsequent to the mortgage must be joined.[232] Thus, a mortgagee must foreclose not only on the mortgagor but on all persons claiming through him, including puisne encumbrancers.[233] He may, however, foreclose without, at the same time, claiming to redeem *prior* encumbrancers[234]; one may not redeem up without foreclosing down, but one may foreclose down without redeeming up because prior encumbrancers will not be affected by the accounts taken in the foreclosure. On the same principle a mortgagee may foreclose on the mortgagor without at the same time redeeming his own sub-mortgage.

---

[226] LPA 1925 s.34(2).

[227] cf. *Vickers v Cowell* (1839) 1 Beav. 529.

[228] *Re Continental Oxygen Co, Elias v Continental Oxygen Co* [1897] 1 Ch. 511; *Westminster Bank Ltd v Residential Properties Improvement Co Ltd* [1938] Ch. 639.

[229] CPR Pts 64 and 19.

[230] *Goldsmid v Stonehewer* (1852) 9 Hare, App. XXXVIII.

[231] See Ch.29.

[232] A person entitled to redeem who has not been made a defendant will not be bound by the foreclosure: *Gee v Liddell* [1913] 2 Ch. 62.

[233] See *Keith v Butcher* (1884) L.R. 25 Ch.D. 750.

[234] *Rose v Page* (1829) 2 Sim. 471; *Slade v Rigg* (1843) 3 Hare 35.

Procedure in foreclosure actions

Jurisdiction

If the amount actually advanced does not exceed the county court limit,[235]   **27–29**
proceedings for foreclosure may be taken in the county court[236]; otherwise
foreclosure proceedings must be brought in the High Court and are assigned by
the Senior Courts Act 1981 to the Chancery Division.[237] The exclusive jurisdiction of a county court in relation to proceedings for possession of property
compromising a dwelling-house outside Greater London[238] does not apply to an
action for foreclosure or sale in which a claim for possession of the mortgaged
property is also made.[239] Thus, a mortgagee in a foreclosure action is under no
compulsion to commence proceedings in the county court when his advance is
less than £30,000. However, and importantly, the action for foreclosure or sale
must be a genuine one for that relief and the claim for foreclosure or sale not
merely added as a device to take the proceedings outside the county court's
exclusive jurisdiction in possession proceedings.[240] Often a claim will include
payment, possession of the mortgaged property, foreclosure of sale together with
other relief in the same proceedings. The mere claim for foreclosure or sale,
however, does not itself render the action one for foreclosure or sale. The test is
to have regard to the nature of the relief which the claimant genuinely seeks.
Thus a claim for possession under a mortgage is usually treated as an action for
recovery of land within s.21 of the County Courts Act 1984 and not as an action
for foreclosure within s.23.[241] If the claim is in reality one for possession, the
mortgagee must comply with the provisions of CPR 55.

A claim for foreclosure, whether in the High Court or county court, is begun
by a Part 8 Claim Form unless there is a dispute of fact, in which case the Pt 7
procedure may be used instead.[242]

A mortgagee may bring his claim for foreclosure only, so that his claim is
merely that an account be taken of what is due to him on the mortgage in respect
of principal, interest and costs, and that the court may foreclose the mortgage. In
such a claim the court may, at the instance of any interested party, direct a sale,
although the claim is for foreclosure. However, the mortgagee himself may
favour a sale and then his claim is for an account and for foreclosure or sale.

---

[235] At present £30,000 (unless extended by agreement): see County Courts Act 1984 s.23; High
Court and County Courts Jurisdiction Order 1991 (SI 1991/724). Where the sum originally advanced
exceeded the county court limit but is reduced by payment or otherwise, to below that sum, the county
court would appear to have jurisdiction to hear the action—see *Shields, Whitley and District
Amalgamated Model Building Society v Richards* (1901) 84 L.T. 587.

[236] i.e. the court for the district in which the land or any part of it is situate; where the mortgage
comprises property other than land action may be commenced in the court or the district in which the
defendant resides or carries on business.

[237] s.61(1). This remains the case under CPR Pt 55.

[238] See above, para.27–02.

[239] See the County Courts Act 1984 ss.21, 147(1) (replacing the Administration of Justice Act 1970
s.37(2)).

[240] *The Trustees of Manchester Unity Life Insurance Collecting Society v Sadler* [1974] 1 W.L.R.
770.

[241] *West Penwith Rural District Council v Gunnell* [1968] 1 W.L.R. 1153.

[242] CPR 8 PD.

Furthermore, if he is a mortgagee in possession his claim for an account must refer to that fact and he should make a specific claim to be allowed such sums as have been properly expended by him on the mortgaged property. If a mortgagee is not in possession and is asking for foreclosure rather than sale, an order for possession will be necessary when the mortgagor proves obstructive. The court has jurisdiction to make an order for possession without any demand for such an order having been made in the claim form,[243] and may make the order even after the foreclosure decree has been made absolute.[244] Nevertheless, if the mortgagor is expected to prove obstructive, it is advisable to claim the order specifically, since the court will not make the order without notice where it was not asked for in the claim form.[245] Again, a mortgagee is entitled to pursue all his remedies concurrently and will frequently combine with his foreclosure action a claim for judgment on the mortgagor's personal covenant to pay the mortgage debt. Such actions must be commenced in the Chancery Division if the High Court is the appropriate forum.[246] However, it must be remembered that if a mortgagee sues on the personal covenant *after* foreclosing he reopens the foreclosure.[247]

A mortgagee who starts proceedings for foreclosure cannot bring an action on the personal covenant concurrently in the Queen's Bench Division, since it was open to him to combine this remedy with his foreclosure suit.[248] Thus, such an action will be treated as vexatious and will be stayed.[249] Further, although a mortgagee may obtain judgment for payment and foreclosure in the same action, the two claims are quite distinct. For example, a foreclosure decree gives the mortgagor six months in which to redeem but the judgment on the covenant is for immediate payment as there is no rule in equity that a sum of money immediately payable at law shall not be payable until after six months have elapsed.[250]

The witness statement in support of the Pt 8 Claim or the Particulars of Claim if the matter is commenced under Pt 7 should provide particulars of all necessary terms affecting or giving rise to the relief claimed (e.g. that the date fixed for redemption has passed). Additional matters which require consideration are such aspects which may affect the taking of any accounts, such as whether the mortgagee has gone into possession of the mortgaged property.

Order in a foreclosure action for account to be taken

27–30   Since a mortgagor is entitled to have an account, the decree will first direct that the appropriate account be taken unless, of course, the parties have already

---

[243] *Salt v Edgar* (1886) 54 L.T. 374.

[244] *Jenkins v Ridgley* (1893) 41 W.R. 585.

[245] *Le Bas v Grant* (1895) 64 L.J.Ch. 368.

[246] Senior Courts Act 1981 Sch.1.

[247] See below, paras 27–36 et seq.

[248] A claim for payment was only a "mortgage action" within CPR, Sch.1, RSC Ord. 88, r.1 (repealed with effect from October 15, 2001) if the claimant was relying upon the mortgage to make his claim: *National Westminster Bank v Kitch* [1996] 1 W.L.R. 1316. Thus a claim by a bank for moneys due on the account alone could (and presumably still can) be properly brought in the Queen's Bench Division.

[249] *Earl Poulett v Viscount Hill* [1893] 1 Ch. 277; *Williams v Hunt* [1905] 1 K.B. 512.

[250] *Farrer v Lacy, Hartland & Co* (1885) L.R. 31 Ch.D. 42; see also *Dymond v Croft* (1876) L.R. 3 Ch.D. 512.

agreed to it. Although a mortgagor has this right to an account, the court in exceptional cases will stay the taking of it unless he is prepared to give security for the costs of the account because if it is highly improbable that the mortgaged property will prove sufficient to satisfy the mortgage debt, it is unfair to the mortgagee to increase the costs of his foreclosure unnecessarily.[251] The court's direction for the account is subject to variation to meet the special circumstances of the mortgage. For example, a mortgagee in possession must account for rents and profits and there may be a claim for special allowances or expenses. The court order will also contain a direction for all necessary further accounts and inquiries which arise from the mortgagee's possession.[252] In any event, if a claim on the personal covenant has been joined with a foreclosure action it is necessary to have two distinct accounts, one for the sum recoverable on the personal covenant and one to determine what must be paid in order to redeem. The reason for this is obvious. A foreclosure decree allows six months for redemption and the foreclosure account will include an allowance of six months' additional interest. However, in an action on the personal covenant a mortgagee will obtain judgment for immediate payment of the sum due and correspondingly will not be entitled to additional interest. Again, if the mortgagee is in possession, judgment for the payment on the covenant cannot include in the amount to be paid any allowances or expenses in connection with the mortgaged property.[253] Similarly, judgment on the covenant carries with it a right only to the costs of proceedings on the covenant and the costs of a foreclosure must therefore go into the mortgage account only. Plainly, the two accounts must be taken separately.[254]

Foreclosure nisi[255]

A foreclosure decree is granted in stages and in a normal case, redemption of the mortgaged property by the mortgagor is still possible until the end of a period of six months from the date when the mortgage account is certified by the Master. The decree is thus an order nisi which will be made absolute on a subsequent application provided that in the meanwhile the right to redeem has not been exercised. A foreclosure order absolute will never be granted in the first instance unless the persons interested in the equity of redemption agree to that course.[256]   **27–31**

Form: The order nisi will generally begin with a declaration as to the validity   **27–32** of the security, if there has been any issue in that regard, and the respective rights of the interested parties. If the latter remain to be determined, it may provide for an appropriate inquiry.

---

[251] *Exchange and Hop Warehouses Ltd v Association of Land Financiers* (1886) L.R. 34 Ch.D. 195.

[252] For the details of the account, see below, Ch.33 generally; above, paras 26–18 et seq.

[253] These are a charge upon the property, but are not a personal debt of the mortgagor: *Frazer v Jones* (1846) 5 Hare 475.

[254] *Farrer v Lacy, Hartland & Co* (1885) L.R. 31 Ch.D. 42.

[255] The CPR has not abolished this terminology as it has, for example, in relation to charging orders.

[256] *Patey v Flint* (1879) 48 L.J.Ch. 696.

After such preamble, the order may take this form[257]:

> "It is directed that upon the payment of the sum certified by the Master on a day six months after the date of this certificate and at the time and place specified therein, the mortgagee shall give the defendant a receipt in accordance with the provisions of section 115 of the Law of Property Act 1925[258] and shall deliver up the title deeds but that in default of such payment, the defendant shall be foreclosed."

The order (unless the court otherwise directs) requires the mortgagor to give seven days' notice of his intention to attend and redeem and, in the absence of such notice and if the mortgagor does attend, the order will provide for seven days' extension to the period allowed for redemption. If the mortgagee has applied for possession, there will be added a direction that the defendant shall deliver up possession to the claimant. Only in the case of an equitable mortgagee, is there also a special direction for the conveyance of the legal title to the mortgagee.[259]

However, as in redemption actions, there may be several parties before the court with distinct rights to redeem, and the decree must provide in detail for the exercise of those rights. Questions may arise as to priority and as to successive periods for redemption because foreclosure means the destruction of the equity of redemption of every person who acquired an interest in the property subsequently to the claimant's mortgage.[260] The determination of these questions, however, proceeds in decrees for foreclosure on the same lines as in decrees for redemption and the rules will not be repeated here.[261] It should be added that it is also possible for the court to give the mortgagees successive periods of redemption, the party first entitled to redeem being allowed six months, and each of the others successive periods of three months more[262] after which the rights of any mortgagee not redeeming would be extinguished.[263] This is now rarely seen unless special circumstances exist to justify it. In the event that a subsequent mortgagee redeems, proceedings are thereafter for foreclosure between him and the mortgagor who, in order to redeem, will have to pay that which the mortgagee has paid to redeem together with the amounts outstanding on the mortgage with the subsequent mortgagee.

In the case of dwelling-houses the court in foreclosure actions now has a statutory discretion to adjourn the proceedings, or to suspend executions of its

---

[257] Originally prescribed by Practice Direction [1955] 1 W.L.R. 36; that practice direction has been repealed by the Chancery Division Practice Directions which are silent in this regard. It is anticipated that the old form remains in use however.

[258] LPA 1925 s.115 is applied with qualifications by the Building Societies Act 1986 s.6c, Sch.2A (as inserted by the Building Societies Act 1997). See above, para.6–02 and below, Ch.29.

[259] *Lees v Fisher* (1882) L.R. 22 Ch.D. 283; the order must also be preceded by a declaration of the equitable mortgage in such a case: *Marshall v Shrewsbury* (1875) L.R. 10 Ch. 250.

[260] See *Briscoe v Kenrick* (1832) 1 L.J.Ch. 116.

[261] See below, paras 30–36 et seq.

[262] *Smithett v Hesketh* (1840) L.R. 44 Ch.D. 161; *Platt v Mendel* (1884) L.R. 27 Ch.D. 246.

[263] In instances where there are successive subsequent mortgagees, this formula can lead to substantial delay. Accordingly the Master's order will usually only permit one period for subsequent mortgagees to redeem and will allow them to apply to determine their rights inter se: *Bartlett v Rees* (1871) L.R. 12 Eq. 395; *Doble v Manley* (1885) L.R. 28 Ch.D. 664; *Smith v Olding* (1884) L.R. 25 Ch.D. 462.

order, or to postpone the date for delivery of possession as it thinks fit whether or not possession is sought in the same proceedings.[264]

Foreclosure absolute

After the order nisi, the accounts are taken and certified by the Master, and the Master's certificate fixes the time and place for redemption. However, a mortgagor's failure to pay on this date in accordance with the certificate does not automatically complete the mortgagee's title. The equity of redemption is not finally destroyed until a further decree, the foreclosure absolute, has been obtained making the mortgagee the sole owner both in law and in equity and free from any subsequent mortgages but subject to any prior encumbrances.[265] In consequence a foreclosure nisi is by itself no defence to an action for redemption.[266]

27–33

Moreover, although the mortgagor's further default entitles the mortgagee as of course to have his order nisi made absolute, the court will require the fact of non-payment to be strictly proved by the mortgagee by witness statement verified in accordance with CPR Pt 22 or, if he chooses, by affidavit.[267] The evidence must be verified or sworn by the mortgagee (or by the person who acted on his behalf) to the effect that attendance was made at the time and place fixed by the certificate, and that the mortgagor did not appear[268]; in addition, there must be a positive statement by the mortgagee himself that he has not paid. Evidence to that effect by his attorney is insufficient and even in the case of co-mortgagees an affidavit or witness statement by one on behalf of the others will not be accepted except where a mortgagee is out of the jurisdiction.[269] In any case a mortgagee, who has received rents or other profits after the decree nisi but before default was made, must inform the court of this and *cannot* proceed to a decree absolute: such a receipt reopens the account and a new date for redemption will be allowed.[270] If, however, the receipt of profits did not occur until *after* the mortgagor's default under the decree nisi, the account is not reopened and the mortgagee (upon producing the proper evidence) may obtain an order absolute.[271] The actual application for an order absolute should be made in accordance with CPR, Pt 23. Notice of the proceedings must be served on the owner of the equity of redemption, but, with one exception, the application may be made without notice. The exception is the case of a deceased defendant, when the court will insist on the presence of a properly appointed representative of the deceased.[272]

---

[264] Administration of Justice Act 1973 s.8(3), and see above, para.27–13.

[265] LPA 1925 ss.88(2), 89(2). See also *Sheriff v Sparks* (1737) Westtemp. Hard. 130.

[266] *Senhouse v Earl* (1752) 2 Ves.Sen. 450.

[267] *Patey v Flint* (1879) 48 L.J.Ch. 696.

[268] *Moore and Robinson's Nottinghamshire Banking Co v Horsfield* [1882] W.N. 43.

[269] *Barrow v Smith* (1885) 52 L.T. 798; *Docksey v Else* (1891) 64 L.T. 256; *Kinnaird v Yorke* (1889) 60 L.T. 380.

[270] *Prees v Coke* (1871) L.R. 6 Ch. 645; nor will the mortgagor be put under conditions as to payment of arrears of interest.

[271] *National Permanent Mutual Benefit Building Society v Raper* [1892] 1 Ch. 54.

[272] *Aylward v Lewis* [1891] 2 Ch. 81.

27–34   **Form:**   A foreclosure order absolute takes the form of a recital of the decree nisi and of the mortgagor's default thereunder, the evidence in support of the order and an order absolutely debarring and foreclosing him from all equity of redemption in the mortgaged property. In addition, the court will order the delivery to the claimants of any title deeds to the property which are still in the defendant's hand. Any deeds, which were executed subsequently to the claimant's mortgage, and which therefore relate only to the equity of redemption, will not be included in such an order, although their possession may be of advantage to the claimant.[273] The effect of foreclosure absolute, it must be repeated, is merely to destroy the equity of redemption and transfer the beneficial ownership to the mortgagee; it is not a conveyance of the legal title. Consequently, in the case of an equitable mortgage, if the mortgagor is obstructive, the order absolute must provide for the transfer of the legal title to the claimant.[274] This is achieved by a declaration that the mortgagor is a trustee for the mortgagee, followed by a vesting order in favour of the mortgagee-beneficiary under s.44 of the Trustee Act 1925. For the same reason an order absolute is not enough to give the claimant possession of the mortgaged property. For some purposes a foreclosure action is an action for the recovery of land,[275] but it is not an action for the recovery of the possession of land, and is not enforceable by writ of possession under CPR, Sch.1, RSC Ord. 45, r.3.[276] If, however, application is made, the court will add an order for possession to the order absolute, whether or not the order nisi directed delivery of possession, and whether or not such an order was asked for in the statements of case.[277] Indeed, an order for possession will even be made, as ancillary to the judgment, after decree absolute.[278]

Until July 8, 2003, an order for foreclosure absolute required to be stamped as if it were a conveyance upon a sale of the mortgaged property.[279] Accordingly, the evidence in support of the application for an order for foreclosure absolute under that regime had to contain the necessary details and the appropriate certificate for stamp duty purposes in order for the same to be included in the order absolute. If the effect of the order for foreclosure absolute was such that it vested the reversion of the interest in the mortgaged land automatically in the mortgagee, the order itself needed to be produced to the Commissioners of Inland Revenue for stamping.[280]

This regime was replaced in 2003 by Stamp Duty Land Tax.[281] A foreclosure order is liable to ad valorem duty as a conveyance or transfer on sale.

In circumstances where an estate in fee simple has been mortgaged either by the creation of a term of years absolute or by a charge by way of legal mortgage, an order for foreclosure absolute operates to vest in fee simple in the mortgagee

---

[273] *Greene v Foster* (1882) L.R. 22 Ch.D. 566.

[274] *Lees v Fisher* (1882) L.R. 22 Ch.D. 283.

[275] *Pugh v Heath* (1880–81) L.R. 6 Q.B.D. 345, affirmed (1881–82) L.R. 7 App. Cas. 235.

[276] *Wood v Wheater* (1882) L.R. 22 Ch.D. 281.

[277] *Salt v Edgar* (1886) 54 L.T. 374; see also *Best v Applegate* (1887) L.R. 37 Ch.D. 42; *Keith v Day* (1888) L.R. 39 Ch.D. 452.

[278] *Keith v Day* (1888) L.R. 39 Ch.D. 452; an order for possession should so describe the property that the sheriff may identify it from the terms of the order: *Thynne v Sarl* [1891] 2 Ch. 79.

[279] Finance Act 1898 s.6.

[280] Finance Act 1931 s.28 (as amended).

[281] Under the Finance Act 2003.

(subject to any legal mortgage having priority to the mortgage in light of which the foreclosure was obtained and to any money thereby secured) and thereupon the mortgage term, if any, merges with the fee simple and any subsequent mortgage term or charge by way of legal mortgage which is bound by the order for foreclosure absolute is extinguished.[282] In the case of a sub-mortgage by a sub-demise out of an estate in fee simple, the same principles apply as if the sub-mortgage had itself been carved out of the fee simple so as to enlarge the principal term and extinguish the derivative term created by the sub-mortgage.[283]

Where a term of years absolute has been mortgaged by the creation of another term of years absolute limited out of it or by a charge by way of legal mortgage and an order for foreclosure absolute is obtained, the order operates (unless it provides to the contrary) to vest the leasehold reversion affected by the mortgage and any subsequent mortgage in the mortgagee subject to any legal mortgage having priority to the mortgage in the light of which the foreclosure was obtained and to any money thereby secured and thereupon the mortgage term and any subsequent mortgage term or charge by way of legal mortgage which is bound by the order shall, subject to any express provision to the contrary contained in the order, merge in such leasehold reversion or be extinguished.[284]

In the case of a sub-mortgage by sub-demise of a term limited out of a leasehold reversion, the provisions of s.89 of the Law of Property Act 1925 apply mutatis mutandis. The statutory vesting of the leasehold reversion in the mortgagee does not give the lessor of the mortgaged property a right to forfeit the term of years for want of licence to assign.

Where the order is made in respect of registered land, the mortgagee in whom the interest has been vested should then apply to be registered as proprietor of that title, attaching a copy of the order absolute. The registrar must then cancel the registration of the charge in respect of which the order was made, cancel all entries relating to interests over which the charge had priority, and enter the applicant as registered proprietor of the estate.[285]

Costs of foreclosure proceedings

These are dealt with elsewhere.[286]

27–35

Re-opening foreclosure

The effect of a foreclosure absolute is to constitute the mortgagee beneficial owner of the property, so that he may at once deal with it as owner. The proceedings between the parties, theoretically, are at an end and, apart from an ancillary order for possession, the court cannot add to its decree as, for example,

27–36

---

[282] LPA 1925 s.88(2).
[283] LPA 1925 s.88(5).
[284] LPA 1925 s.89(2).
[285] Land Registration Rules 2003 r.112.
[286] See below, paras 33–12 et seq.

by appointing a receiver.[287] Nevertheless, as Jessel M.R. pointed out,[288] the finality of a decree absolute is nearly as illusory as the mortgage contract itself, since the court reserves for itself a discretion to discharge the final decree if the mortgagor makes out a special case for indulgence.[289] Of course, a decree absolute, like any other decree, is liable to be set aside for actual fraud or oppression by the mortgagee which will be sufficient to reopen the foreclosure. Again, the mortgagee himself may cause the foreclosure to be opened by suing the mortgagor or guarantor[290] on his personal covenant, for this automatically revives the right to redeem as would a sale by the mortgagee under his power of sale rather than qua absolute owner.[291] In such circumstances, the mortgagee is liable to account for any surplus sale proceeds; the purchaser's title is not affected.[292] Even so, there is an absolute discretion in the court to reopen the foreclosure[293] and fix a new date for redemption, without the mortgagee having been guilty of misconduct or having taken collateral proceedings against the mortgagor. In truth, the court's tenderness towards a mortgagor is so extreme that it is prepared in special circumstances to treat his property as still essentially security, even after decree absolute and to give him a last chance of redeeming. When the court exercises its discretion, the procedure is not immediately to vacate the decree, but to fix a new date for redemption, notwithstanding the decree, and to discharge the decree if redemption then takes place.[294] However, since a mortgagor is not entitled, as of course, to an enlargement of time for redemption before the decree absolute, a fortiori he must make out a special case for the opening of foreclosure absolute.

The opening of a foreclosure is completely within the court's discretion and no precise rules have been laid down. In *Campbell v Holyland*,[295] however, Jessel M.R. made some valuable comments on the exercise of the discretion which indicate clearly the grounds on which it is exercised which merit repetition in full. He said:

> "On what terms is that judicial discretion to be exercised? It has been said by the highest authority that it is impossible to say *a priori* what are the terms. They must depend on the circumstances of each case. . . . There are certain things which are intelligible to everybody. In the first place the mortgagor must come, as it is said, promptly; that is within a reasonable time. He is not to let the mortgagee deal with the estate as his own—if it is a landed estate, the mortgagee being in possession of it and using it—and then without any special reason come and say, 'Now I will redeem.' He cannot do that; he must come within a reasonable time. What is a reasonable time? You must have regard to the nature of the property. As has been stated in more than one of the cases, where the estate is an estate in land in

---

[287] *Pugh v Heath* (1880–81) L.R. 6 Q.B.D. 345, affirmed (1881–82) L.R. 7 App. Cas. 235; *Wills v Luff* (1888) L.R. 38 Ch.D. 197.

[288] *Campbell v Holyland* (1877) L.R. 7 Ch.D. 166 at 171.

[289] Even possibly after sale of the property, but this would be most unusual especially if the purchaser had no notice of the circumstances.

[290] *Lloyds and Scottish Trust Ltd v Britten* (1982) 44 P. & C.R. 249, and see below, paras 27–42 et seq.

[291] *Perry v Barker* (1806) 13 Ves. 198; *Lockhart v Hardy* (1846) 9 Beav. 349.

[292] *Stevens v Theatres Ltd* [1903] 1 Ch. 857.

[293] See *Quarles v Knight* (1820) 8 Price 630; *Eyre v Hansom* (1840) 2 Beav. 478.

[294] *Ford v Wastell* (1848) 6 Hare 229.

[295] (1877) L.R. 7 Ch.D. 166 at 172.

possession—where the mortgagee takes it in possession and deals with it and alters the property, and so on—the mortgagor must come much more quickly than where it is an estate in reversion, as to which the mortgagee can do nothing except sell it. So that you must have regard to the nature of the estate in ascertaining what is to be considered a reasonable time.

Then again was the mortgagor entitled to redeem, but by some accident unable to redeem? Did he expect to get the money from a quarter from which he might reasonably hope to obtain it, and was he disappointed at the last moment? Was it a very large sum, and did he require a considerable time to raise it elsewhere? All those things must be considered in determining what is a reasonable time.

Then an element for consideration has always been the nature of the property as regards value. For instance, if an estate were worth £50,000, and had been foreclosed for a mortgage debt of £5,000, the man who came to redeem that estate would have a longer time than where the estate was worth £5,100, and he was foreclosed for £5,000. But not only is there money value, but there may be other considerations. It may be an old family estate or a chattel, or picture, which possesses a special value for the mortgagor, but which possesses not the same value for other people; or it may be, as has happened in this instance, that the property, though a reversionary interest in the funds, is of special value to both the litigants; it may possess not merely a positive money value, but a peculiar value, having regard to the nature of title and other incidents, so that you cannot set an actual money value upon it. . . . All this must be taken into consideration."

These dicta suggest that three points will be likely to influence the court in favour of opening foreclosure: (i) promptness of application; (ii) the special value of the estate, whether monetary or otherwise; and (iii) the fact that the mortgagor had a reasonable expectation of redeeming, but was disappointed in his attempt to obtain the money. It seems that the court would also expect an explanation of why the mortgagor failed to pay sums due at the proper time, and would be likely to require the mortgagor to reimburse the mortgagee for any sums expended since the order absolute was obtained.[296] It may be added that there is little chance of obtaining the court's indulgence unless it can be shown at the time of the application that the security is reasonably sufficient and that there is a reasonable expectation of the money being obtained.[297] In any case, it is now the practice to make it a condition of opening a foreclosure that the mortgagor pay up immediately or within, at the most, one month, all arrears of interest and costs reported to be due. On failure to comply with this condition the foreclosure remains absolute.[298] Delay in applying for relief will prejudice the chance of reopening a foreclosure unless it can be explained; if the mortgagee deals with the estate or expends money on it, laches in the mortgagor will be fatal.[299]

However, mere dealing with the estate by the mortgagee will not prevent the revival of the right to redeem because a purchaser of a foreclosed estate must be taken to know that a foreclosure may be reopened and if he purchases soon after the decree, the foreclosure may be reopened as against him. In *Campbell v Holyland*[300] Jessel M.R. explained the position of a purchaser thus:

[296] *Thornhill v Manning* (1851) 1 Sim (N.S.) 451; *Coombe v Stewart* (1851) 13 Beav 111.
[297] *Patch v Ward* (1867–68) L.R. 3 Ch. App. 203; and see *Lancashire and Yorkshire Reversionary Interest Co Ltd v Crowe* (1970) 114 S.J. 435.
[298] See *Eyre v Hansom* (1840) 2 Beav. 478; *Holford v Yate* (1855) 1 K. & J. 677.
[299] See *Thornhill v Manning* (1851) 1 Sim.(N.S.) 451.
[300] (1877) L.R. 7 Ch.D. 166 at 173.

"Then it is said that you must not interfere against purchasers ... there are purchasers and purchasers. If the purchaser buys a freehold estate in possession after the lapse of a considerable time from the order of foreclosure absolute, with no notice of any extraneous circumstances which would induce the court to interfere, I for one should decline to interfere with such a title as that; but if the purchaser bought the estate within twenty-four hours after the foreclosure absolute, and with notice of the fact that it was of much greater value than the amount of the mortgage debt, is it to be supposed that a court of equity would listen to the contention of such a purchaser that he ought not to be interfered with? He must be taken to know the general law that an order for foreclosure may be opened under proper circumstances, and under a proper exercise of discretion by the court; and if the mortgagor in that case came the week after, is it to be supposed a court of equity would so stultify itself as to say that a title so acquired would stand in the way? I am of opinion it would not."

Judicial sale pursuant to the Law of Property Act 1925 s.91

27-37 Both generally and in a claim for foreclosure, the court has jurisdiction to order a sale of the property pursuant to s.91 of the Law of Property Act 1925. In a foreclosure action the court's jurisdiction to order a sale in lieu of foreclosure[301] does not depend on a sale having been asked for in the Particulars of Claim. Under s.91(2) of the Law of Property Act 1925, the court, on the request of the mortgagee or of any interested person[302] may direct a sale (a "judicial sale") on such terms as it thinks fit, including the deposit in court of a sum to meet the expenses of sale and to secure performance of the terms at any time prior to an order absolute.[303] The jurisdiction is entirely discretionary both as to making the order for sale and as to the terms of the sale. The court may order the sale notwithstanding the dissent of non-appearance of any person[304] and without allowing time for redemption.[305]

If a sale is requested, the order is not given as a matter of course, but a special case has to be made out for the exercise of the court's discretion.[306] It is unusual for the court to order an immediate sale unless the mortgagor consents. The rule is not to direct a sale unless it will confer a benefit on one of the parties sufficient to justify the expenses of a sale.[307] Nor will a sale be ordered if it will prejudice the position of any person interested.[308] Conversely, if the mortgagee's refusal to sell the mortgaged property would cause the mortgagor prejudice, the court may order a sale in order to protect him from potential prejudice.[309]

---

[301] The county court's jurisdiction is limited to circumstances where, at the commencement of proceedings, the amount owing does not exceed £30,000: LPA 1925 s.91(8).

[302] e.g. a subsequent mortgagee or the mortgagor and see *Twentieth Century Banking Corporation v Wilkinson* [1977] Ch. 99.

[303] *Union Bank of London v Ingram* (1882) L.R. 20 Ch.D. 463.

[304] Which includes the mortgagee, and see *Wade v Wilson* (1882) L.R. 22 Ch.D. 235.

[305] Or determining the priorities of interested parties: LPA 1925 s.91(4).

[306] *Provident Clerks' Mutual Life Assurance Association v Lewis* (1892) 62 L.J. Ch. 89.

[307] *Lloyds Bank v Colston* (1912) 106 L.T. 420.

[308] *Merchant Banking Co of London v London & Hanseatic Bank* (1886) 55 L.J. Ch. 479; *Silsby v Holliman* [1955] Ch. 552.

[309] *Palk v Mortgage Services Funding Plc* [1993] Ch. 330; *Cheltenham & Gloucester Plc v Krausz* [1997] 1 W.L.R. 1558; *AIB Finance Limited v Debtors* [1997] 4 All E.R. 677; *Yorkshire Bank Plc v Hall* [1999] 1 W.L.R. 1713, distinguishing *Palk*. See also *GMAC-RFC Ltd v Pearson* [2005] EWCA Civ 330.

The usual direction given is that accounts be certified and a period allowed to the mortgagor for redemption.[310] Indeed, if the claim is for foreclosure only, the court will not order sale at all unless the mortgagor has been notified of the application for sale.[311] An immediate sale may be directed if the property is small and the security deficient.[312] The actual application for a sale may be made at any stage of the proceedings[313] and upon an interlocutory application,[314] the court's jurisdiction to order the sale being only terminated by decree absolute.[315]

Circumstances in which a sale may be ordered

Usually the court will order a sale where the mortgagee is seeking to foreclose **27–38** and the property is worth more than the amount secured by the mortgage and the mortgagor is unable to raise the sum required to redeem the property in order to obtain the advantage of securing the surplus sale proceeds for his own ends.[316] However, the jurisdiction to order a sale is not limited to such circumstances and may be used in order to relieve one party from the potentially prejudicial consequences of the other party's proposed course of conduct.[317] The jurisdiction may also be exercised in circumstances where foreclosure is sought by one mortgagee in circumstances where there are sufficient numbers of subsequent encumbrances so as to make the exercise of foreclosure excessively slow or burdensome.[318] An order for sale will be refused in circumstances where there is no evidence before the court as to the value of the property[319] or where the sale would necessarily involve the disposition of property not subject to the mortgage in question.[320]

Conduct of the sale

The conduct and conditions of sale are always within the court's discretion.[321] **27–39** The general practice is to give the conduct of the sale to the mortgagor since he is the person whose interest is to obtain the best price[322]; on the same principle, if the mortgagor declines the privilege, the conduct of the sale will be given to the encumbrancer lowest in priority in preference to the mortgagee.[323] It seems, moreover, that this course will sometimes be followed, even when the first mortgagee has objected and claimed the right to carry out the sale.[324] However,

---

[310] *Green v Biggs* (1885) 52 L.T. 680; see also *Smith v Robinson* (1853) 1 Sm. & G. 140.
[311] See *Union Bank of London v Ingram* (1882) L.R. 20 Ch.D. 463.
[312] *Palk v Mortgage Services Funding Plc* [1993] Ch. 330.
[313] *Palk*, above.
[314] *Palk*, above.
[315] *Smithett v Hesketh* (1890) L.R. 44 Ch.D. 161.
[316] *Gibbs v Haydon* (1882) 30 W.R. 726.
[317] CPR 40–15–17, 3A8–13, PD 400–1.
[318] *South Western District Bank v Turner* (1882) 31 W.R. 113.
[319] *Oldham v Stringer* (1884) 33 W.R. 251; but cf. *Hopkinson v Miers* (1889) 34 S.J. 128.
[320] *Union Bank of London v Ingram* (1882) L.R. 20 Ch.D. 463.
[321] *Woolley v Coleman* (1882) L.R. 21 Ch.D. 169.
[322] *Davis v Wright* (1886) L.R. 32 Ch.D. 220; cf. *Re Jordan, Ex p. Harrison* (1884) L.R. 13 Q.B.D. 228 and see *Cheltenham & Gloucester Plc v Krauscz* [1997] 1 W.L.R. 1558
[323] *Norman v Beaumont* [1893] W.N. 45.
[324] e.g. *Brewer v Square* [1892] 2 Ch. 111.

if the security is deficient, a first mortgagee's claim to be given the conduct of the sale will be allowed[325]; again, the court may prefer the first mortgagee's claim, on the ground that the expense may be saved by allowing the person in possession of the deeds to conduct the sale.[326] Thus, there is no rule that the mortgagor must conduct the sale although the general practice very much favours that course.[327] Furthermore, the court will readily permit the sale to take place altogether out of the court, the proceeds of the sale being ordered to be paid into a court: but in such cases the order must be prefaced by a declaration that all interested parties are before the court.[328] The fact that a first mortgagee does not agree to the mortgagor having the conduct of the sale will affect the terms on which the order is made; the mortgagor (or the puisne encumbrancer) will usually have to deposit a sum to cover the expenses of an ineffectual attempt to sell and the court will fix a reserved price sufficient to cover the first mortgagee's claim.[329] If the first mortgagee's objection arises from the fact that he is himself anxious to exercise his powers of realising the security, the court will fix a time within which the sale must take place and, on default, the mortgagee may proceed to realise the security.[330] If no objection has been made to the sale by the first mortgagee, the mortgagor will not be made to give security for the expenses of the sale[331] but if the sale is to take place altogether out of the court, special directions will be given as to a reserved price and other conditions. A reserved price will also be fixed if the first mortgagee is given leave to bid at auction for the property.[332] Whoever conducts the sale acts primarily for himself and is not liable for improper activities of other parties to the action.[333] Any party who wishes to buy the property should apply to the court for permission to do so.[334]

A vesting order conveying the property

27–40   In order to effect a sale of the mortgaged property, the court may, in favour of the purchaser, make a vesting order conveying the mortgaged property, or appoint a person to do so, subject or not to any encumbrance, as it thinks fit; or, in the case of an equitable mortgage, may create and vest a mortgage term in the mortgagee to enable him to carry out the sale as if the mortgage had been made by deed by

---

[325] *Cheltenham & Gloucester Plc v Krausz* [1997] 1 W.L.R. 1558; *Re Jordan, Ex p. Harrison* (1884) L.R. 13 Q.B.D. 228; but not if a sum is deposited in court as a guarantee against loss: *Norman v Beaumont* [1893] W.N. 45.

[326] *Hewitt v Nanson* (1858) 28 L.J. Ch. 49.

[327] *Christy v Van Tromp* [1886] W.N. 111; the language of Chitty J. goes further than the cases warrant.

[328] See *Cumberland Union Banking Co v Maryport Hematite Iron & Steel Co* [1892] 1 Ch. 92.

[329] *Whitbread v Roberts* (1859) 28 L.J. Ch. 431; *Brewer v Square* [1892] 2 Ch. 111.

[330] ibid.

[331] *Davies v Wright* (1886) L.R. 32 Ch.D. 220; but the mortgagor is personally liable for the expenses.

[332] *Re Commercial bank of London* (1864) 9 L.T.(N.S.) 782.

[333] *Union Bank of London v Munster* (1887) L.R. 37 Ch.D. 51.

[334] See *Palk*, above.

way of legal mortgage.[335] Such a vesting order conveying the mortgaged property has the effect of rendering the conveyance beyond impeachment.[336] An order under this sub-section will only be made in exceptional circumstances and any applicant for such an order must provide the court with sufficient evidence upon which it may exercise its discretion.[337] An order will only be made if the court is satisfied that the prospects of the mortgagor impeaching the sale are utterly remote; that the conduct of the mortgagor, both during the application as well as before it is such as to justify the apprehension that he will not hesitate to threaten proceedings against the purchaser if that could spoil the proposed sale; and that the mortgagee's fear that the sale will be lost unless an order is obtained is not unreasonable.[338] Otherwise, the court will leave the mechanics of the sale to the mortgagee pursuant to his own power.

Application of the proceeds of sale

The proceeds of a judicial sale are applied in the same way and in the same order   **27–41** as the proceeds arising from a sale out of the court under a power of sale. The rules governing the distribution of the proceeds of sale will therefore be set out elsewhere.[339]

ACTION ON THE PERSONAL COVENANT TO REPAY

A creditor's primary remedy to recover his money is to bring a personal action   **27–42** against his debtor[340] on the contract of loan, for a creditor by taking security only reinforces his personal remedy. As Maitland said,[341] a mortgagee is not the less a creditor because he is a secured creditor. All well-drawn mortgages[342] contain an express covenant by the mortgagor to pay both principal and interest. Even when there is no such covenant, a promise to pay is implied in law from the acceptance of the loan so that a simple contract debt is created. Every mortgage, therefore, contains within itself a personal liability to repay the amount advanced,[343] which the mortgagee may enforce by an action on the contract.

Accrual and demand

The covenant to pay normally fixes a date on which payment is to be made and   **27–43** thus no right of action on the personal covenant accrues to the mortgagee until

---

[335] LPA 1925 s.91(7).
[336] LPA 1925 s.104(2).
[337] *Alba Bank Plc v Mercantile Holdings Ltd* [1994] Ch. 71.
[338] ibid.
[339] See paras 26–39 et seq. and Ch.33.
[340] This includes a guarantor, see *Lloyds & Scottish Trust Ltd v Britten* (1982) 44 P. & C.R. 249.
[341] Maitland, *Equity* (2nd edn), p.182.
[342] The personal liability of the mortgagor to pay is sometimes registered by the mortgage deed itself.
[343] *Sutton v Sutton* (1882) L.R. 22 Ch.D. 511 at 515, per Jessel M.R.

non-payment on the day named, for the affirmative covenant to pay implies a negative promise by the lender not to sue before that date.[344] If, on the other hand, the principal is made payable on demand, and there is no express or implied provision for notice to be given,[345] the right to sue on the personal covenant of the mortgagor to whom the moneys have been advanced arises immediately on the execution of the mortgage,[346] and it is not even necessary to make a demand before beginning the action. If the covenant is to pay the debt of another (e.g. secures another's overdraft with a bank) and is thus collateral to the indebtedness, a demand is necessary to found a claim.[347] In *Kotonou v National Westminster Bank Plc*[348] a demand under the guarantee which warned that the mortgage would be enforced unless payment was made was held not to be sufficient demand under the mortgage itself. In the case of an instalment mortgage, a written demand *is* necessary by reason of the alterations in the nature of the debtor's obligations from payment by instalments to the whole capital sum.[349] Any mode of service is sufficient which enables a mortgagor to realise that a demand has been made.[350] A well-drawn covenant stipulates expressly for payment of both principal and interest, so that the right to sue for interest is quite distinct from the right to sue for principal and the actions may be brought separately.[351]

Even where demand has been made, if the mortgage includes a list of events the occurrence of which entitles the mortgagee to appoint a receiver or to sell, it is implicit that those powers cannot be exercised and the debt is not repayable until one of the events has occurred.[352]

Parties to a claim

27–44   If a mortgagee assigns the mortgage debt, the assignee will be able to sue on the personal covenant. He can sue in his own name if the assignment meets the requirements of s.136 of the Law of Property Act 1925; otherwise he must join the original mortgagee.[353] On the mortgagee's death the right to sue on the covenant passes to his personal representatives and, after assent, to his legatees,

---

[344] *Bolton v Buckenham* [1891] 1 Q.B. 278; *Twentieth Century Banking Corporation Ltd v Wilkinson* [1977] Ch. 99. But it is possible that a demand should be first made, see *Re Tewkesbury Gas Co, Tysoe v Tewkesbury Gas Co* [1912] 1 Ch. 1.

[345] *Esso Petroleum Co Ltd v Alstonbridge Properties Ltd* [1975] 1 W.L.R. 1474. If there is such a provision an actual demand in writing must be made before the right of action accrues, see *Lloyds Bank v Margolis* [1954] 1 W.L.R. 644. See also Limitation of Actions, paras 6–35 et seq. It is also necessary to make a demand in writing if the covenant is merely *collateral* to the security, e.g. if the right is being enforced against a surety, see *Re Brown's Estate, Brown v Brown* [1893] 2 Ch. 300 at 304.

[346] *Evans v Jones* (1839) 5 M. & W. 295.

[347] *Lloyds Bank Ltd v Margolis* [1954] 1 W.L.R. 644; *Habib Bank Ltd v Tailor* [1982] 1 W.L.R. 1218.

[348] *Kotonou v National Westminster Bank Plc* [2006] EWHC 1021 (Ch).

[349] *Esso Petroleum Co Ltd v Alstonbridge Properties Ltd* [1975] 1 W.L.R. 1474. In practice a demand is usually made before action is commenced in any event.

[350] *Worthington & Co Ltd v Abbott* [1910] 1 Ch. 588.

[351] *Dickenson v Harrison* (1817) 4 Pri. 282.

[352] *West Bromwich Building Society v Wilkinson* [2005] 1 W.L.R. 2303.

[353] See above, paras 22–45 et seq.

provided that the latter give notice of the assent to the debtor.[354] The claim may be brought against the covenantee and any person who stands as surety to that person.[355]

If two people are together described as the mortgagor and the covenant is to pay "all sums or money . . . advanced to the mortgagor by the Bank", they are each liable for any sums advanced to them jointly or to either of them individually. Thus, if A and B are joint mortgagors under such a covenant, A can be sued for all sums advanced to A, B or A+B.

Loss of the right to sue

The right to sue on the personal covenant may be lost by the mortgagee's **27–45** inability to reconvey the mortgaged property. Although a mortgagor's covenant for repayment is usually absolute in form and is not expressed to be conditional on the reconveyance of the security, equity treats a mortgagor's liability to pay and a mortgagee's obligation to reconvey as reciprocal. A mortgagee will therefore be restrained from suing on the covenant if, without authority from the mortgagor, he has parted with the property mortgaged.[356] If the mortgagee is only temporarily disabled from making the reconveyance by, for example allowing his solicitor to obtain a lien on the title deeds, he is restrained from suing on the covenant until the disability has been removed by, for example, the discharge of the lien.[357] If he forecloses, he cannot afterwards sue on the personal covenant to make up the deficiency unless he still retains the mortgaged property in his hands.[358] In other words, a sale of the property after foreclosure extinguishes the mortgagor's liability for the contract debt.[359] It is for the same reason that if a mortgagee sues on the personal covenant after foreclosing, he reopens the foreclosure[360]: he cannot require the mortgagor or guarantor to repay his loan unless he is himself ready and willing to surrender the security.[361]

This rule still applies although the mortgagor has assigned his equity of redemption. A mortgagor cannot assign his personal liability, but if he is sued on the contract debt after assigning the equity of redemption he is still entitled to the reconveyance of his security.[362] Consequently, any bargain between an assignee of the equity of redemption and the mortgagee which prevents reconveyance will

---

[354] Administration of Estates Act 1925 ss.1(1), 3(1)(ii), 36.

[355] *Esso Petroleum Co Ltd v Alstonbridge Properties Ltd* [1975] 1 W.L.R. 1474.

[356] *Walker v Jones* (1866) L.R. 1 P.C. 50; *Palmer v Hendrie (No.2)* (1860) 28 Beav. 341; this principle applies equally to mortgages of personalty, though its application there may be more flexible: *Ellis & Co's Trustee v Dixon-Johnson* [1925] A.C. 489.

[357] *Schoole v Sall* (1803) 1 Sch. & Lef. 176.

[358] *Perry v Barker* (1806) 13 Ves. 198; a puisne mortgagee does not, however, lose his right to sue on the personal covenant by consenting to a decree for foreclosure absolute in favour of a prior mortgagee: *Worthington v Abbott* [1910] 1 Ch. 588.

[359] *Lockhart v Hardy* (1846) 9 Beav. 349; *Gordon, Grant & Co v Boos* [1926] A.C. 781; see also *Lloyds and Scottish Trust Ltd v Britten* (1982) 44 P. & C.R. 249.

[360] *Perry v Barker* (1806) 13 Ves. 198, and see above, paras 27–36 et seq.

[361] See *Lloyds and Scottish Trust Ltd v Britten* (1982) 44 P. & C.R. 249.

[362] *Kinnaird v Trollope* (1888) L.R. 39 Ch.D. 636, subject, of course, to the equity of redemption. For the form of conveyance, see *Pearce v Morris* (1869) L.R. 5 Ch.App. 227.

discharge the original mortgagor from his liability on the contract of loan.[363] On the other hand, a mortgagor surrenders his right to recover his security by authorising the mortgagee to part with it. Thus, a mortgagee does not lose his right to sue on the personal covenant if he sells the mortgaged property either with the express concurrence of the mortgagor or under an express or implied power of sale in the mortgage deed.[364] Nor does he lose his right if, when realising his security, he asks the court for a judicial sale instead of for fore-closure. Such a sale is a sale by the court and not by the mortgagee, so that although the mortgagee can no longer reconvey, he is entitled to recover any deficiency from the mortgagor by suing on the covenant.[365]

Limitation

27–46   This is considered elsewhere in this work.[366]

Cause of action estoppel

27–47   A mortgagee who obtains judgment for possession of the mortgaged property and for the sums expressed to be due under the mortgage cannot bring a subsequent claim for any money due under a guarantee which is also secured by that mortgage since the latter claim is one which should properly have been raised in the proceedings for possession and for the monetary judgment previously obtained.[367] However, it would appear that if a mortgagee obtains an unopposed order for possession and payment of sums claimed to be due under the mortgage, the mortgagee is not estopped thereby from bringing a subsequent claim for payment.[368] Equally, where proceedings seeking repayment from guarantors have been struck out for delay, while it would be an abuse of process to bring a further claim for repayment, the mortgagee is not precluded from commencing a claim for possession and sale of the guarantors' property.[369] The mortgagee who has failed in a possession claim against the mortgagor on the basis of undue influence raised by the mortgagor's spouse may still sue the mortgagor on his personal covenant to repay with a view to bankrupting him, even though that might lead to the trustee in bankruptcy seeking again to sell the mortgaged property against the interests of the spouse.[370]

---

[363] *Palmer v Hendrie* (1859) 27 Beav. 349.

[364] *Rudge v Richens* (1872–73) L.R. 8 C.P. 358.

[365] *Gordon Grant & Co v Boos* [1926] A.C. 781. This is a particularly strong case, as the mortgagee had obtained leave to bid and had actually bought the mortgage property, subsequently reselling it at an enhanced value.

[366] See Ch.6, above.

[367] *Arnold v National Westminster Bank Plc* [1991] 2 A.C. 93; *Talbot v Berkshire County Council* [1994] Q.B. 290; *Lloyds Bank v Hawkins* [1998] 47 E.G. 137.

[368] *UCB Bank Plc v Chandler* (1999) 79 P & C R 270 (CA).

[369] *Securum Finance Ltd v Ashton* [2001] Ch. 291.

[370] *Alliance & Leicester Plc v Slayford* [2001] 1 All E.R. (Comm) 1.

APPOINTMENT OF A RECEIVER BY THE COURT

Before the Judicature Act 1873, courts of equity always acted on the principle **27–48** that they would never grant a receiver where the party applying for the receiver had a legal right to the possession. The effect of this principle is that an equitable mortgagee could obtain the appointment of a receiver, but a legal mortgagee could not.[371] However, s.25(8) of that Act, which is now replaced by s.37 of the Senior Courts Act 1981,[372] empowered the court to grant a receiver by interlocutory orders whenever it should appear just or convenient to do so.[373] The Court of Appeal has decided that a receiver will now be granted at the instance of a legal mortgagee in the same way as at the instance of an equitable mortgagee because, although a legal mortgagee has power to take possession, there are obvious conveniences in granting a receiver: for example, by relieving a legal mortgagee from assuming the responsibilities of a mortgagee in possession.[374] It should be added, however, that the statutory power and the express inclusion of such power in the mortgage agreement usually renders it unnecessary to apply to the court.[375]

Although the court may now appoint a receiver in all cases in which such a course appears just or convenient, the principles on which this jurisdiction is exercised are well defined. The appointment of a receiver will be made with a view to preserving the corpus of the mortgaged property or to receive the income generated by that property in order to meet the mortgagor's liabilities to the mortgagee or to create a fund sufficient to meet that or other liabilities. Except in very special cases,[376] the court will not make an appointment, unless an action is pending. If an action is pending, so that the parties are already at arm's length, it is preferable that the appointment should be made by the court in all cases, rather than that the mortgagee himself should appoint under a power.[377] It appears that a mortgagee is entitled to a receiver in any of the following cases:

(1) if the property would be in jeopardy if left in the mortgagor's possession until the hearing of the action[378];

(2) if default has been made in payment of the principal[379];

---

[371] *Berney v Sewell* (1820) 1 J. & W. 647; *Sollory v Leaver* (1869) L.R. 9 Eq. 22 at 25.

[372] Although the power to appoint a receiver and manager under subs.(1) is wide, the duty of maintaining houses owned by a local authority is expressly entrusted to the local authority under the Housing Act 1957 s.111 (now repealed and replaced, with amendment, by Housing Act 1985 s.21), and the court will not usurp that duty by appointing a receiver and manager: *Parker v Camden London Borough Council* [1986] Ch. 162.

[373] As to the power of the court to appoint receivers, see generally CPR 69.2 and PD 69.

[374] *Anglo-Italian Bank v Davies* (1878) L.R. 9 Ch.D. 275; *Re Pope* (1886) L.R. 17 Q.B.D. 743 at 749, per Cotton L.J.

[375] LPA 1925 s.101(iii); see above paras 26–27 et seq. See also *Bank of Credit & Commerce International SA v BRS Kumar Bros* [1994] 1 B.C.L.C. 211.

[376] e.g. where the mortgagee is a patient under the Mental Health Act 1983. Or a person who lacks capacity under the Mental Capacity Act 2005.

[377] *Tillett v Nixon* (1883) L.R. 25 Ch.D. 238.

[378] *Stevens v Lord* (1838) 2 Jur. 92; *Re Victoria Steamboats, Ltd* [1897] 1 Ch. 158; *Re London Pressed Hinge Co Ltd* [1905] 1 Ch. 576.

[379] *Curling v Marquis of Townshend* (1816) 19 Ves. 628 at 633.

(3) if any interest is in arrear[380]; nor does it make any difference that the mortgagee has covenanted not to call in his loan until some future date.[381]

Subsequent mortgagees

27–49   When there are two or more mortgagees, later mortgagees may obtain the appointment of a receiver without prejudice to the rights of prior mortgagees.[382] Nevertheless, if the order appointing the receiver does not contain an express reservation of the rights of prior encumbrancers, the latter cannot interfere with the receiver without an application to the court, for the receiver is an officer of the court.[383] When a prior legal mortgagee has already gone into possession, the court will not appoint a receiver at the instance of a later encumbrancer who is not offering to redeem the legal mortgagee.[384] If a mortgagee in possession cannot assert on oath or by a witness statement verified in accordance with CPR Pt 22 that there is something still due to him on his mortgage, the court will appoint a receiver at the instance of a later encumbrancer.[385]

Nominating a receiver

27–50   Although the selection of a receiver appointed by the court is in its discretion, a nomination by the party applying for the appointment will usually be accepted. One person will not, however, be appointed, namely, the mortgagee's solicitor, for it is his duty to check the accounts of the receiver.[386] By contrast, when the mortgagee himself appoints a receiver under a power, he frequently appoints his own solicitor to act as receiver.

Duties of a receiver

27–51   The duties of a receiver appointed by the court cannot be exhaustively discussed here,[387] but it may be observed that, while they include similar obligations to act in good faith, avoid conflicts of interest, and to obtain the best price reasonably possible if selling the property, in some important aspects they differ substantially from those of a receiver appointed by the mortgagee out of court. Thus, a receiver appointed by the court is an officer of the court rather than an agent for either party to the mortgage, and is personally liable for what he does as receiver: Consequently, the court almost invariably[388] requires him to give security before

---

[380] *Strong v Carlyle Press* [1893] 1 Ch. 268.
[381] *Burrowes v Molloy* (1845) 2 J. & L. 521.
[382] *Berney v Sewell* (1820) 1 J. & W. 647.
[383] *Aston v Heron* (1834) 2 My. & K. 390.
[384] *Berney v Sewell* (1820) 1 J. & W. 647.
[385] *Quarrell v Beckford* (1807) 13 Ves. 377.
[386] *Re Lloyd* (1879) L.R. 12 Ch.D. 447.
[387] See *Halsbury's Laws of England*, Vol.39(2), Receivers.
[388] CPR 69.2 and PD69.

entering into office. Indeed, his appointment is normally incomplete until he has actually given security.[389] His duties are regulated by the terms of the order appointing him but in general he is bound to assume possession of the mortgaged property,[390] to get in the rents and profits, and to pay these, after deducting outgoings and his own salary (determined by the court), into court or according to the court's direction. Not being the mortgagor's agent, it is his duty to take possession himself and to compel tenants to attorn to himself. He must keep down outgoings, and has power to grant leases for a term not exceeding three years[391] and to do necessary repairs; for any other repairs, he should first obtain the leave of the court. If he requires any further powers not specially sanctioned by the terms of the order appointing him, such as a power to sell the property, he must make an application to the court for an order permitting him to do so. A receiver, for example, has no power to carry on a business, and, if such a power is desired, the court must be asked to appoint a receiver and manager.[392]

Registration of a receiver's appointment

The appointment of a receiver should be protected by registration of a restriction **27–52** against the title to registered land[393]; with regard to unregistered land, the order may be protected by the registration of a land charge, whether the appointment was by court order or under the mortgagee's powers.[394]

---

[389] *Edwards v Edwards* (1876) L.R. 2 Ch.D. 291.

[390] But not generally to take charge of any business conducted from the mortgaged property unless that is also part of the security—see *Whitley v Challis* [1892] 1 Ch. 64.

[391] *Daniel's Chancery Practice* (8th edn), p.1443. But see *Stamford Banking Co v Keeble* [1913] 2 Ch. 96 at 97, where it was laid down that no lease can be granted without leave of the court. The court, however, can approve the granting of any lease which it concludes is necessary for the protection of or making fruitful the mortgaged property. See also *Re Cripps* [1946] Ch. 265.

[392] See *Re Manchester & Milford Rly Co* (1880) L.R. 14 Ch.D. 645 at 653.

[393] LRA 1925 ss.43 and 87; Land Registration Rules 2003 r.172.

[394] Land Charges Act 1972 s.6(1)(b); see also *Clayhope Properties Ltd v Evans* [1986] 1 W.L.R. 1223.

CHAPTER 28

THE EQUITABLE MORTGAGEE OR CHARGEE—RIGHTS AND REMEDIES

EQUITABLE MORTGAGEES[1]

Foreclosure

Since the equitable mortgagee has no legal estate, foreclosure is his primary **28–01** remedy. It is available whether the charge relates to land[2] or to personalty.[3] His right to foreclosure is based upon an express or implied agreement on the part of the mortgagor to execute a legal mortgage over the property.

The procedure to be followed by an equitable mortgagee seeking foreclosure is similar to that adopted by the legal mortgagee.[4] However, in the case of an equitable mortgage of land as the mortgagee has no legal estate, the foreclosure order absolute will direct the mortgagor to convey the land in question freed from any right to redeem.[5] In the case of a chose in action the court will direct the execution by the mortgagor of a power of attorney.[6] In the case of a chose in action, it is available, for example, in the case of the deposit of the share certificates,[7] policies of insurance,[8] and of a share in a partnership.[9]

Sale

The statutory power of sale[10] applies only where the mortgage was made by **28–02** deed.[11] Thus, it is usual for equitable mortgages to be made by deed. Even so,

---

[1] See generally Ch.14 with regard to equitable mortgages of land.
[2] *Re Owen* [1894] 3 Ch. 220.
[3] *London & Midland Bank v Mitchell* [1899] 2 Ch. 161; *Harrold v Plenty* [1901] 2 Ch. 314.
[4] As to which see paras 27–29 et seq. above.
[5] *James v James* (1873) L.R. 16 Eq. 153. Foreclosure of an equity of redemption also occurs occasionally through the dismissal of an action for redemption, see *Cholmley v Countess of Oxford* (1741) 2 Atk. 267.
[6] *James v Ellis* (1871) 19 W.R. 319.
[7] See *Harrold v Plenty* [1901] 2 Ch. 314.
[8] See *Re Kerr's Policy* (1869) L.R. 8 Eq. 331 at 336.
[9] See *Redmayne v Forster* (1866) L.R. 2 Eq. 467.
[10] See above, para.26–42.
[11] Law of Property Act (LPA) 1925 s.101(1).

there still may be difficulties for the reasons expressed elsewhere[12] arising from the decision in *Re Hodson & Howes Contract*,[13] in that the mortgagee can sell only the interest which he himself holds.[14]

Therefore, in order to avoid such difficulties, the practice has arisen of employing either or both of two conveyancing devices which enables the mortgagee, in effect, to convey the legal estate:

(1) Power of attorney. A power of attorney is inserted into the mortgage deed granting a power of attorney to the mortgagee or his assigns[15] to convey the legal estate which remains vested until sale in the mortgagor. It is usual for such a power to be expressed to be irrevocable and under s.4(1) of the Powers of Attorney Act 1971 this is permissible since the power is given for value to secure a proprietary interest of the donee of the power. Thus, neither the mortgagee nor any purchaser from him will be affected by any act on the part of the mortgagor or by his death.[16] Accordingly, by virtue of s.5(3) of the 1971 Act, such persons are protected, as they are entitled to assume that the power is incapable of revocation.[17]

(2) Declaration of trust. A clause is inserted in the mortgage deed whereby the mortgagor declares that he holds the legal estate on trust for the mortgagee and authorises the mortgagee to appoint himself or his nominee as trustee in place of the mortgagor.[18] By this method the mortgagee can vest the legal estate in himself or in a purchaser.[19]

It goes without saying that an equitable mortgagee is subject to the same duties and restrictions on sale of the mortgaged property as a legal mortgagee.[20]

28–03   *Equitable mortgages not by deed:*   In the case of other equitable mortgages not made by deed, there is no statutory power of sale out of court. However, by virtue of s.91(2) of the Law of Property Act 1925, the court itself has the power to order a judicial sale on the application of the mortgagee or of any interested person and may vest a legal term of years in the mortgagee so that he can sell as if he were a legal mortgagee.[21] This power of the court should not be affected by s.23(1)(a) of the Land Registration Act 2002, as that provision restricts only the ability of the *owner* of land to create a mortgage by devise.

---

[12] See above, para.5–18.

[13] (1887) L.R. 35 Ch.D. 668.

[14] But this interpretation has been doubted in the case of *Re White Rose Cottage* [1965] Ch. 940 at 951.

[15] See Powers of Attorney Act 1971, as amended.

[16] See Powers of Attorney Act 1971, as amended

[17] See *Re White Rose Cottage* [1965] Ch. 940.

[18] See *London and County Banking Co v Goddard* [1897] 1 Ch. 642.

[19] Under the Trustee Act 1925 s.40.

[20] See above, paras 26–47 et seq.

[21] LPA 1925 ss.90, 91(7), and see above, paras 27–37 et seq.; *Oldham v Stringer* (1884) 33 W.R. 251.

Possession

Right to take possession

The position with regard to the right of an equitable mortgagee to take possession **28–04** of the mortgaged property is unclear. It is generally stated in the authorities (including the second edition of Waldock, *The Law of Mortgages*) that an equitable mortgagee has no right to take possession.[22] It is clear that the equitable mortgagee has no right to take possession at law, for he has no legal estate in the land.[23] However, it is also clear that an equitable mortgagee can take possession if there is an express provision in the agreement giving him that right.[24] Thus, many agreements contain a clause empowering the mortgagee to take possession in the event of a default by the mortgagor. Another device is to insert into the equitable mortgage a clause granting a power of attorney to the mortgagee making available to him all the rights and remedies of a legal mortgagee including the right to take possession of the mortgaged property. Further, the mortgagor may, by express permission, give the equitable mortgagee the right to take possession,[25] and the right to appoint a receiver may take effect as a right to take possession.[26]

What remains unclear is whether or not an equitable mortgagee has the right to take possession absent any of the above factors. In Megarry & Wade, *The Law of Real Property*[27] it is urged that in equity an equitable mortgagee should be entitled to the same rights as if he had a legal mortgage and that there would seem to be no reason why he should not take possession under the doctrine of *Walsh v Lonsdale*,[28] as the basis of an equitable mortgage is the creation of an immediate relationship of mortgagor and mortgagee, rather than a mere contract for a future mortgage.[29] However, it is possible that an equitable mortgage is an interest in property which is independent of the doctrine of *Walsh v Lonsdale*. Further, it must be remembered that if this doctrine applies to equitable mortgages, it may produce a number of substantial difficulties with regard to the question of priority.[30] The argument that the absence of a right to take possession is founded on an implied term to that effect is unattractive and appears contrary to authority.[31]

---

[22] Coote, *Law of Mortgages* (9th edn, 1927), p.823; Halsbury, *Laws of England* (4th edn, 1980), Vol.32 (re-issue, 2005), p.291; Waldock, *The Law of Mortgages* (2nd edn, 1950) pp.5, 235; and see *Barclays Bank Ltd v Bird* [1954] Ch. 274 at 280. See also the discussion in (1954) 70 L.Q.R. 161, and (1955) 71 L.Q.R. 204, where the authorities are reviewed.

[23] *Doodes v Gotham* [2006] 1 W.L.R. 729—overturned on appeal, but not on this point [2007] 1 W.L.R. 86.

[24] *Ocean Accident and Guarantee Corp Ltd v Ilford Gas Co* [1905] 2 K.B. 493.

[25] *Re Postle, Ex p. Bignold* (1835) 2 Mont. & A. 214.

[26] *Vacuum Oil Co Ltd v Ellis* [1914] 1 K.B. 693.

[27] 7th edn, 2008, paras 25–046—25–048.

[28] (1882) L.R. 21 Ch.D. 9.

[29] And as indicated an action for the recovery of land will not be defeated merely for want of the legal estate, see *General Finance Mortgage and Discount Co v Liberator Permanent Benefit Building Society* (1878) L.R. 10 Ch.D. 15 at 24). *Re O'Neill* [1967] N.I. 129.

[30] See Fairest, *Mortgages* (2nd edn, 1980), p.109.

[31] Megarry & Wade, *The Law of Real Property* (7th edn, 2008), para.25–046 n.335.

Thus, the equitable mortgagee's right to take possession is uncertain. The court may in any event award him possession.[32] There is also some authority which indicates that the equitable mortgagee may take possession in his own right,[33] but the basis of the legality of such a right is uncertain. Unfortunately, the subject is not merely academic, for if there is such a right for an order for possession the statutory discretion pursuant to the provisions of the Administration of Justice Acts 1970 and 1973 would apply.[34]

Collection of rents

28–05   As there is no privity of estate or tenure between an equitable mortgagee and the tenants of the mortgagor, the equitable mortgagee has no right to direct the tenants of the mortgagor to pay over their rents to himself, nor to collect such rents,[35] without an order of the court.[36] If the tenants do pay the rents to the equitable mortgagee, his receipt will not discharge them from liability. However, at the same time, the tenants cannot demand the return of the rent if payment has been made under no mistake of fact.[37] Moreover, if a prior legal mortgagee is already in possession, the equitable mortgagee can intercept the surplus rents and profits of the prior legal mortgagee by requiring them to be paid over to himself instead of to the mortgagor.[38]

Appointment of receiver

28–06   In a proper case an equitable mortgagee can apply to the court for the judicial appointment of a receiver[39] and an equitable mortgagee has also the statutory power to appoint a receiver if the mortgage is by deed.[40] The statutory power usually renders it unnecessary to apply to the court to appoint a receiver.

Protection of security, etc.

28–07   The equitable mortgagee will not have the right to possess the title deeds unless he has stipulated for that right in the contract. His rights to fixtures, to con-

---

[32] *Barclays Bank Ltd v Bird* [1954] Ch. 274; *Re O'Neill* [1967] N.I. 129.

[33] Megarry & Wade, *The Law of Real Property* (7th edn, 2008), para.25–046 n.335.

[34] See above, paras 27–12 et seq.

[35] *Re Pearson, Ex p. Scott* (1838) 3 Mont. and A. 592; *Finck v Tranter* [1905] 1 K.B. 427; *Vacuum Oil Co Ltd v Ellis* [1914] 1 K.B. 693.

[36] The appropriate order is for the appointment of a receiver by way of equitable execution, see *Vacuum Oil Co Ltd v Ellis* [1914] 1 K.B. 693 at 703.

[37] *Finck v Tranter* [1905] 1 K.B. 427.

[38] *Parker v Calcraft, Dunn v Same* (1821) 6 Madd. 11.

[39] Senior Courts Act 1981 s.37; and see above, para.27–48.

[40] LPA 1925 s.101(1)(iii); and see above, paras 26–27 et seq.

solidate, tack and insure will be broadly in line with those of the legal mortgagee, and are addressed elsewhere.[41]

If the mortgage is equitable and a third party with inferior title proposes to dispose of the legal estate, an injunction will lie to restrain that party.[42] It has also been held that where a mortgagee of land loses his security through failure to register and a subsequent unencumbered sale by the mortgagor without his consent, he retains against the mortgagor an interest in the proceeds of sale under a constructive trust.[43]

EQUITABLE CHARGEES

An equitable chargee, which includes a judgment creditor who has obtained a charging order, has no right to take possession.[44] Further, an equitable chargee cannot foreclose, as he has no express or implied agreement to create a legal mortgage over the property in his favour.[45] His primary remedies are to apply to the court for an order for sale or for the appointment of a receiver.[46] However, as the statutory definition of a mortgage extends to a charge,[47] an equitable chargee by deed will have the same statutory powers as an equitable mortgagee with regard to sale and the appointment of a receiver out of court. **28–08**

In exercising its discretion to order sale in respect of any property held on trust, the court will consider the matters identified in ss.14 and 15 of the Trusts of Land and Appointment of Trustees Act 1996. While the interests of the secured creditor have lost their former pre-eminent status since the introduction of the 1996 Act, the fact that a chargee will be kept out of his money unless sale is ordered will be a powerful consideration.[48] **28–09**

Note that where a judgment creditor has obtained a charging order, enforcement of that order is not subject to the provisions of s.20(1) and (5) of the Limitation Act 1980.[49]

Furthermore, an equitable chargee may obtain relief from forfeiture of the charged leasehold property even though he has no entitlement to possession or any legal or equitable interest in the property. The right arises from an implied obligation upon the chargor to preserve the security, which includes an obligation **28–10**

---

[41] See paras 26–71, 8–01, 11–67 and 32–01 respectively.

[42] *London & County Bank Co v Lewis* (1882) L.R. 21 Ch.D. 490.

[43] *Barclays Bank Plc v Buhr*[2001] EWCA Civ 1223; [2002] 1 P. & C.R. DG7.

[44] *Garfitt v Allen, Allen v Longstaffe* (1887) L.R. 37 Ch.D. 48 at 50.

[45] *Tennant v Trenchard* (1869) L.R. 4 Ch. App. 537; *Re Lloyd, Lloyd v Lloyd* [1903] 1 Ch. 385 at 404; *Croydon (Unique) Ltd v Wright* [2001] Ch. 318; and *Doodes v Gotham* [2006] 1 W.L.R. 729—overturned on appeal, but not on this point [2007] 1 W.L.R. 86.

[46] *Tennant v Trenchard* (1869) L.R. 4 Ch. App. 537; *Re Owen* [1894] 3 Ch. 220. Sale is also the remedy for the holder of an equitable lien, see *Neate v Duke of Marlborough* (1838) 3 My. & C. 407.

[47] See LPA 1925 ss.101(1), 205(1)(xvi).

[48] *Bank of Ireland Home Mortgages Ltd v Bell* [2001] 3 F.C.R. 134; *First National Bank Plc v Achampong* [2004] 1 F.C.R. 18.

[49] *Yorkshire Bank Finance Ltd v Mulhall* [2008] EWCA Civ 1156; [2009] 2 All E.R. (Comm)

on the chargor to obtain relief from forfeiture.[50] It seems that an equitable chargee holding under a charging order is able to obtain relief under s.146(4) of the Law of Property Act 1925 on the basis that he is seen as a mortgagee for the purposes of the subsection.[51] Both the chargor and the chargee should be parties to any application for relief from forfeiture.[52]

---

[50] *Bland v Ingram's Estates Ltd* [2001] 24 E.G. 163 (CA), where the court required the chargee to make payment directly to the lessor of all outstanding rent costs.

[51] *Ladup v William and Glynn's Bank Plc* [1985] 1 W.L.R. 851; *Croydon (Unique) Ltd v Wright* [2001] Ch. 318; [1999] 4 All E.R. 257. An equitable chargee can obtain relief in reliance on the implied obligation of the equitable chargor to preserve the charged security: *Bland v Ingram's Estates Ltd* [2001] 24 E.G. 163.

[52] *Bland v Ingram's Estates Ltd*, above.

CHAPTER 29

THE EQUITY OF REDEMPTION AS AN INTEREST IN PROPERTY

MORTGAGOR AS EQUITABLE OWNER

In *Kreglinger v New Patagonia Meat Co*[1] Lord Parker pointed out that the **29–01** equitable right to redeem which arises on failure to exercise the contractual right must be carefully distinguished from the equitable interest, which, from the first, remains in the mortgagor and is sometimes referred to as an equity of redemption. The equitable *right* to redeem does not exist until the mortgagor is in default and the mortgagee's estate has become absolute at law.[2] The equitable *interest*, on the other hand, arises simultaneously with the execution of the mortgage, since in equity the mortgage conveyance does not have the effect of transferring to the mortgagee the whole beneficial interest in the security, but separates the legal from the equitable ownership. Equity from the outset treats the mortgagor as continuing to be the owner of the property which he has conveyed away, subject only to the mortgagee's charge.[3] By like reasoning a mortgagee's interest is, in equity, not a right to the mortgaged property, but to the mortgage debt, and his beneficial interest in the security is only as a means for enforcing his right to the debt.[4] He is a mere encumbrancer.

The equity of redemption is therefore not only an equitable right but also an interest in property.[5] When personal chattels are the subject-matter of the security, the mortgagor's equity is an interest in personalty similar to any other equitable interest in a fund of personalty. Similarly, when the subject-matter is land, the equity of redemption is an equitable interest in land, which before 1926 was termed an equitable estate.[6] Since a mortgagor *held* the same interest in equity as he had at law before the mortgage if he had mortgaged a legal estate in land, he retained afterwards a corresponding equitable estate. Lord Hardwicke, in

---

[1] [1914] A.C. 25 at 48.
[2] *Brown v Cole* (1845) 14 Sim. 427.
[3] *Casborne v Scarfe* (1738) 1 Atk. 603; *Finch v Earl of Winchelsea* (1715) 1 P.Wms. 277; cf. *English Sewing Cotton Co v IRC* (1947) 63 T.L.R. 306 at 307.
[4] *Thornborough v Baker* (1675) 1 Ch.Cas. 283.
[5] A mortgagor has a title in equity "equitable right inherent in the land," per Hale C.B. in *Pawlett v Att.-Gen.* (1667) Hard. 465 at 469. See also *Lloyd v Lander* (1821) 5 Madd. 282. In view of s.1 of the Law of Property Act (LPA) 1925, it may now be safer to term it an equitable interest, or perhaps a mere equity.
[6] *Casborne v Scarfe* (1738) 1 Atk. 603.

Casborne v Scarfe,[7] drew attention to the conception of the equity of redemption as an estate in the following well-known passage:

> "An equity of redemption has always been considered as an estate in the land, for it may be devised, granted, or entailed with remainders, and such entail and remainders may be barred by a fine and recovery, and therefore cannot be considered as a mere right only, but such an estate whereof there may be a seisin."

In *Casborne v Scarfe*,[8] Lord Hardwicke gave a husband an estate by the curtesy in his wife's equity of redemption,[9] and his decision resulted in the equity of redemption being placed on the same footing as the equity of a cestui que trust. A mortgagor's equity of redemption is therefore not only his right to redeem but also his title to the beneficial ownership of the mortgaged property during the continuance of the mortgage. Having this equitable title he may deal with the beneficial ownership just as if he had never made a mortgage; he may sell it, settle it, create charges upon it, demise it. Thus he may do anything he pleases with it, subject only to the mortgagee's encumbrance. Moreover, he will continue to have an equitable title to the property until his title is terminated by lapse of time, release, sale under a power of sale or by a judgment of the court.[10]

29–02   This view of the equity of redemption was reasserted in the case of *Re Sir Thomas Spencer Wells*.[11] A company mortgaged certain leaseholds by assigning to the mortgagees the residue of the terms, subject to a proviso for redemption. In 1910 a liquidator was appointed, who, believing the equities of redemption to be then valueless, neither surrendered them to the mortgagees nor made any attempt to sell them. In 1916 the company was dissolved. By 1931 the leaseholds had appreciated in value so considerably that the equities of redemption were claimed by the Crown as bona vacantia. Farwell J., at first instance, held[12] that whereas there was, immediately prior to the dissolution of the company, a legal entity entitled to redeem, that legal entity had ceased to exist, with the result that the leaseholds were vested in the mortgagee free of any right in any one to redeem. Such a result could be reached only by treating the equity of redemption, not as a title, but as a personal equity, and the Court of Appeal had no hesitation in reversing the decision and allowing the claim of the Crown. Lawrence L.J.[13] put the matter thus:

> "In equity the mortgagor is regarded as the owner of the mortgaged land subject only to the mortgagee's charge, and the mortgagor's equity of redemption is treated as an equitable estate in the land of the same nature as other equitable estates . . . . It would be just as unconscionable for a mortgagee to set up a claim to hold the land comprised in his mortgage free from the equity of redemption as it would be for a trustee to set up a claim to retain the trust property in his hands for his own use. Consequently, the reasoning which has induced the Court to hold that a trustee cannot on failure of the trusts set up his legal title so as to defeat the Crown's claim to bona

---

[7] ibid., at 605.
[8] (1738) 1 Atk. 603
[9] Curtesy was abolished by Administration of Estates Act 1925 s.45.
[10] cf. *Weld v Petre* [1929] 1 Ch. 33 at 42, per Russell J.
[11] [1933] Ch. 29.
[12] [1932] 1 Ch. 380.
[13] [1933] Ch. 29 at 52, 53.

vacantia applies with equal force to a mortgagee of leaseholds where the mortgagor, being an individual, has died intestate without next of kin, or being a company, has been dissolved."

EQUITY OF REDEMPTION UNDER THE LAW OF PROPERTY ACT 1925

In the case of *Re Sir Thomas Spencer Wells*[14] the Court of Appeal did not refer **29–03** to the effect of the Law of Property Act 1925 on the nature of a mortgagor's rights although some reference to the transitional provisions[15] of that Act might not have been inappropriate. The mortgagor's position has, in the case of mortgages of legal estates, been technically changed by ss.85 and 86 of the Law of Property Act 1925 which alter the formal methods of creating such mortgages.[16] A mortgagor now possesses not merely his equitable title but also a legal reversion. Under ss.85 and 86, mortgages of both freeholds and leaseholds are created by demise, so that a mortgagor necessarily retains for himself at least a nominal reversion. Freeholds can no longer be mortgaged by the conveyance of the fee simple. Now on mortgaging a fee simple, for example, the mortgagor possesses simultaneously a legal reversion expectant on a 3,000 year lease and an equitable interest in the 3,000 year term. It is contended in *Halsbury's Laws of England*,[17] that the equitable interest in the term is co-extensive with and therefore cannot exist at the same time as the legal reversion so suggesting something akin to a merger occurs. For this premise it is concluded that "instead of the [mortgagor's] equity of redemption constituting an equitable estate or interest, it subsists only as a right in equity to redeem the property, this right being attached to his legal freehold estate."[18] No doubt this view of the equity of redemption avoids any conveyancing complications and corresponds with the broad policy of the 1925 legislation. It may be questioned whether the statement in *Halsbury* provides a completely satisfactory explanation of the position of the equity of redemption in mortgages by demise. Certainly the equity of redemption, viewed simply as the equitable title arising from the right to pay off the mortgagee and recover the mortgaged property after the passing of the contract date, is co-extensive with the legal reversion. If, however, the equitable interest in the 3,000 year lease is also to disappear by being merged in the fee, how is the mortgagor's right to the beneficial ownership of the lease before redemption to be accounted for? Even if the mortgagee takes possession under the lease, the mortgagor is in equity beneficially entitled to the profits, a fact which cannot be explained by reference to the fee simple title since this is *subject to the lease*. In other words, the equity of redemption in the lease appears to be essentially distinct from, and additional to, the nominal legal reversion. For this reason there does not seem to be a merger as such of the equitable interest in the fee,[19] and

[14] [1933] Ch. 29.
[15] Sch.1 Pt 7.
[16] These provisions do not apply to registered land, see Land Registration Act (LRA) 2002 s.23(1)(a).
[17] Vol.77, para.302.
[18] Citing *Selby v Alston* (1797) 3 Ves 339, *Re Selous, Thomas v Selous* [1901] 1 Ch. 921.
[19] Turner, *Equity of Redemption* (1931) pp.186, 187. See also *Young v Clarey* [1948] Ch. 191 at 198, where Harman J., seems to have regarded the reversion as a distinct interest.

it is considered that the statement in *Halsbury* is too broad an interpretation. The view is preferred that ss.85 and 86 of the Law of Property Act 1925 are concerned only with conveyancing and do not effect any essential change in the character of the equity of redemption. It is clear that the substance of the mortgagor's rights is still his equitable right of redemption and that his legal reversion is a nominal estate meeting the requirements of the modern system of conveyancing. At the same time, the legislature undoubtedly regarded the equity of redemption and the legal reversion as inseparable interests and the view in *Halsbury* that the equity of redemption is now attached to the legal reversion is perhaps correct. Otherwise, the two-fold nature of the mortgagor's interest might cause conveyancing complications.

DISPOSITION AND DEVOLUTION OF THE EQUITY OF REDEMPTION

Disposition inter vivos and by will

29–04   Since a mortgagor through the protection of equity remains substantially the owner of the property which he has mortgaged, he has as much power to deal with it as if he had never executed the conveyance though the dealings will generally be subject to the mortgagee's charge.[20] Thus, an equity of redemption may be sold, leased,[21] settled, mortgaged, assigned for the benefit of creditors, or disposed of by will. Dispositions by will must, of course, be in accordance with the provisions of the Wills Act 1837 and conveyances of equities of redemption, being conveyances of equitable interests, must be in writing under s.53(1)(c) of the Law of Property Act 1925. When the subject-matter of the mortgage is land, the equity of redemption is an interest in land and thus any contract to assign it must contain all the terms of the parties' agreement and be signed by both or both must sign a copy and exchange them.[22] Moreover, in the case of land, although s.53(1)(c) only requires the conveyance of an equity of redemption to be in writing, it will usually be by deed. This is because on a mortgage of freehold or leasehold property the mortgagor necessarily retains, at least, a nominal reversion which he will convey to his assignee, together with the equity of redemption.

The assignee of encumbered property generally takes it subject to the mortgagee's charge. The Law of Property Act 1925, however, provides special machinery, whereby a person selling or exchanging land which is subject to a charge, may transfer it free of the charge. Under s.50 an application may be made to the court to allow a fund to be brought into court to meet the charge, interest

---

[20] Provision is made by LPA 1925 s.50 for the discharge of an encumbrance on the sale or exchange of land, if there is paid into court a sum sufficient to meet the mortgagee's claim.

[21] *Tarn v Turner* (1888) L.R. 39 Ch.D. 456 (CA). When a mortgagor has no power to create leases binding on the mortgagee, a lease granted by him is valid on the principle of estoppel and confers on the lessee an interest in the equity of redemption sufficient to entitle him to redeem. See below, para.32–03.

[22] Law of Property (Miscellaneous Provisions) Act 1989 s.2. Contracts entered into prior to September 27, 1989, were simply required to be evidenced by a memorandum in writing signed by the party to be charged or his lawful agent: LPA 1925 s.40. *Massey v Johnson* (1847) 1 Exch. 241.

on it, if any, plus all necessary costs and then to have the property declared free from the encumbrance. If the application is granted, the court may make appropriate vesting orders or orders for conveyance and give directions concerning the investment of the fund in court. The advantage of this machinery is that it enables land to be sold free of an encumbrance in cases when, by the terms of the charge, the encumbrance cannot immediately be paid off, for example, where an annual sum is charged on land or where a capital sum is due on some future date. It is true that the encumbrancer loses the security of the land, but the fund in court is not his only protection; for, if by the depreciation of its investments the fund proves insufficient, the deficiency must be made up by the vendor. The fund is thus not substituted for the charge but is a security for it, and consequently, if there is a surplus after discharging the encumbrance, the surplus belongs to the vendor.[23]

Settlement of the equity of redemption

Since a large proportion of family estates are to some extent mortgaged, the **29–05** settlement of an equity of redemption was a common occurrence. Even before 1926, an equity of redemption in freehold land, being an equitable estate of inheritance, could be entailed[24] and the entail could be barred under the Fines and Recoveries Act 1833; the mortgaging of freehold estates did not therefore interrupt the continuity of a strict settlement. Section 130(1) of the Law of Property Act 1925 enabled an equity of redemption to be entailed whether the subject-matter of the mortgage be real or personal property. With the enactment of the Trusts of Land and Appointment of Trustees Act 1996 that ability was abolished along with the ability to create any entailed interest.

When entails or other successive interests were created in an equity of redemption, the question arose as to how far the tenant for life was obliged to keep down the interest on the mortgage debt. The general principle is that a tenant for life is bound on all paramount encumbrances to keep down the interest accruing during his period of enjoyment to the extent of the profits received by him.[25] Thus, if a tenant for life allowed the interest to get into arrear when the rents and profits were sufficient to meet it, the persons subsequently entitled could bring an action to have the arrears discharged and could enforce their right against the life tenant's personal representatives after his death.[26] Moreover, if encumbered and unencumbered property was included in the same settlement the tenant for life was bound to employ the profits from all the properties in discharging the interest on the encumbered portion.[27] Tenants in tail in possession, however, were not within the rule. Although they were tenants for life for the purposes of the Settled Land Act 1925, they were not under an obligation to

---

[23] *Re Wilberforce's Trusts* [1915] 1 Ch. 94.

[24] *Casborne v Scarfe* (1738) 1 Atk. 603.

[25] *Revel v Watkinson* (1748) 1 Ves.Sen. 93.

[26] *Lord Kensington v Bouverie* (1859) 7 H.L.C. 557; *Makings v Makings* (1860) 1 De G.F. & J. 355.

[27] *Frewen v Law Life Assurance Society* (1896) 2 Ch. 511; *Honeywood v Honeywood* [1902] 1 Ch. 347.

keep down the interest on encumbrances, because by the power of breaking the entail they always had the reversioner and the remaindermen at their mercy.[28]

The duty of a life tenant to keep down interest on charges is not owed to the encumbrancer; it exists only between the life tenant and persons subsequently entitled.[29] Consequently, when the income from the settled property is insufficient to meet the claim for interest, and the life tenant makes up the deficiency out of his own pocket, he does not necessarily obtain a charge on the property for the amount of the deficiency. He is presumed to intend a benefit to the inheritance, unless he intimates to those next entitled his intention to reserve a charge on the property before he meets the claim for interest.[30]

Equity of redemption as an asset for the payment of debts

29–06   An equity of redemption is part of the mortgagor's assets available for the payment of his debts and therefore on his bankruptcy vests in his trustee for that purpose and, on his death, in his personal representatives. An equity of redemption may also be taken by a judgment creditor to satisfy his judgment, the process varying with the nature of the property.

When the equity of redemption arises from the mortgage of land the appropriate remedy is for the judgment creditor to register his judgment in the Register of Writs and Orders at the Land Charges Register pursuant to the Land Charges Act 1972.[31] If title to the land is registered and the charging order would have been registrable as a land charge, it should be protected by a notice in the same way as in the case of unregistered land, otherwise it can be protected by a restriction.[32] In the case of unregistered land a charging order is in principle registrable, but not solely over the beneficial interest. The reason for this is that

---

[28] *Amesbury v Brown* (1750) 1 Ves.Sen. 477; *Chaplin v Chaplin* (1734) 3 P.Wms. 245. An infant tenant in tail cannot, of course, break the entail during his minority, and the interest must be kept down during that period: *Sergeson v Sealey* (1742) 2 Atk. 412; *Burgess v Mawbey* (1823) 1 T. & R. 167.

[29] *Re Morley* (1869) L.R. 8 Eq. 594.

[30] *Lord Kensington v Bouverie* (1859) 7 H.L.C. 557. cf. *Re Warwick's Settlement Trusts* [1937] Ch. 561.

[31] Power is given to the High Court and to any county court for the purpose of enforcing any judgment or order of those courts for the payment of money to any person, to impose by order a charge on any such land or interest in land of the debtor as may be specified in the order, and for securing the payment of moneys due or to become due under the judgment order. Such an order may be made absolute or on conditions, see Charging Orders Act 1979 ss.1(1), 3(2), as amended by Land Registration Act (LRA) 2002 s.133, Sch.11 para.15, and 6(1). A charging order has the same effect as if it were an equitable charge created by the debtor by writing under his hand, ibid., 3(4). Formerly a mere interest under a trust for sale was not an interest in "land" for this purpose, see *Irani Finance Ltd v Singh* [1971] Ch. 59. Since the Charging Orders Act 1979, the court is now empowered to make an order charging a debtor's beneficial interest under any trust including therefore a trust for land as such an interest now is (see *National Westminster Bank v Stockman* [1981] 1 W.L.R. 67 and *First National Securities Ltd v Hegarty* [1985] Q.B. 850). Under s.6 (as amended by the Trusts of Land and Appointment of Trustees Act 1996), however, no writ or order affecting an interest under a trust for land may be registered in the Register of Writs and Orders. See also Ch.20.

[32] LRA 2002 s.34; Land Registration Rules 2003 r.93(k)—any person with the benefit of a charging order over a beneficial interest in registered land held under a trust of land can apply for a restriction in Form K. Formerly, under the LPA 1925, this would have been protected by a caution. See also Ch.4, above.

the definition of "land" for the purposes of the Land Charges Act 1972 does not extend to an undivided share.[33] The chargee is not an estate owner.[34] Registration can only be effected in such circumstances where the charging order is imposed over land held by the chargee beneficially or on land held by trustees.[35]

A charging order is enforceable by sale of the interest or by the appointment of a receiver.[36] A judgment creditor holding a charging order over the beneficial interest in land may seek an order for sale under s.14 of the Trusts for Land and Appointment of Trustees Act 1996. Alternatively, the judgment creditor can obtain the appointment of a receiver by way of equitable execution (which the High Court and any county court is empowered to do in appropriate circumstances in relation to land and interests therein).[37] It also relates to personal property such as stocks and shares. The receiver gains an interest in the equity of redemption once the mortgaged property has been delivered to the judgment creditor in execution by registration of the order appointing the receiver.[38] The power may be exercised whether or not a charging order has been imposed under the Charging Orders Act 1979 and CPR Pt 69 and is in addition to and not in derogation of any power of the court to appoint a receiver in proceedings by enforcing a charge created by a charging order.[39] The appointment of a receiver by way of equitable execution does *not* of itself create a charge on the property and will be void if not registered under the Land Charges Act 1972.[40] In the case of registered land the order appointing the receiver is protected by a restriction.[41]

When the equity of redemption is in personal chattels which have been mortgaged the mortgagee can still redeem even after the mortgagee has seized the goods as long as they still remain in the mortgagee's possession.[42] In the case where the personal chattels have been mortgaged by a bill of sale, the chattels cannot be taken by the sheriff under a writ of *fi. fa.*, since the property in them has already passed to the holder of the bill of sale.[43] The judgment creditor may apply to the court for a sale of the chattels and will be entitled to any sum which is realised in excess of the amount due to the holder of the bill of sale. If it is doubtful whether there will be any excess, the court will not order a sale unless the creditor indemnifies the mortgagee against loss, while if it is certain that there will be no excess, an order for sale will not be granted.[44]

---

[33] See *Perry v Phoenix Assurance Plc* (1988) 1 W.L.R. 940.

[34] See Charging Orders Act 1979 s.6(1), (1A) as inserted by Trusts for Land and Appointment of Trustees Act 1996 6(2), s.25(1), Sch.3 para.12(3).

[35] ibid., s. 6(1).

[36] See CPR 73.10, and see *Midland Bank Plc v Pike* [1988] 2 All E.R. 434, at 435.

[37] Senior Courts Act 1981 s.37; County Courts Act 1984 s.107; and see CPR Pt 69. See also paras 26–29 et seq. for the power to appoint a receiver under LPA 1925.

[38] See *Mildred v Austin* (1869) L.R. 8 Eq. 220; *Earl of Cork v Russell* (1871) L.R. 13 Eq. 210. See also *Hood Barrs v Cathcart* [1895] 2 Ch. 411, 414.

[39] CPR Pt 73.

[40] ibid., s.6(1)(b). It will not, however, be void if an order has also been made under the Charging Orders Acts 1979 (see CPR Pt 69).

[41] See Land Charges Act 1972 s.6(1)(b); LRA 2002 s.87(2).

[42] *Johnson v Diprose* [1893] 1 Q.B. 512.

[43] *Scarlett v Hanson* (1883) L.R. 12 Q.B.D. 213.

[44] *Stern v Tegner* (1898) 1 Q.B. 37.

Devolution of equity of redemption on intestacy

29–07   Since a mortgagor continues in equity to be the owner of the mortgaged property, the mortgage does not affect the devolution of the property after the mortgagor's death. Thus, before 1926, an equity of redemption in freehold belonged to the heir-at-law, while an equity of redemption in chattels real or in pure personalty belonged to the next of kin. Moreover, in the case of land, if any special custom of descent was applicable to the land as, for example, gavelkind, the custom governed the descent of an equity of redemption in the land.[45] Today, succession to an equity of redemption, whether of chattels or realty, is governed by the provisions of the Administration of Estates Act 1925.[46] Consequently, on the death of a mortgagor intestate, the equity of redemption passes to his personal representatives together with the rest of his property.

Incidence of the mortgage debt

29–08   A mortgagor's liability for the mortgage debt has two aspects—his personal liability on the express or implied promise to pay and his encumbered property's liability to be taken by the mortgagee. Liabilities under a contract cannot be assigned without consent,[47] and consequently, in the event of a mortgagor assigning his equity of redemption (even if the assignee undertakes personal liability[48]) the assignee does not become personally liable to pay the mortgage debt,[49] although the mortgagee may, of course, still take the property to satisfy his debt. Moreover, even though an assignment is made subject to the mortgage debt, the original mortgagor is still liable to be sued on the personal covenant[50] and thus usually takes an indemnity from his assignee to meet that contingency.[51] Of course, the mortgagee may consent to the assignee, and not the original mortgagor taking over the liability to pay, by the assignee entering into a fresh covenant with the mortgagee.

The case is more complicated when the equity of redemption is transferred, not inter vivos, but on the death of the mortgagor, for his personal representatives succeed to the liability in contract,[52] whereas the encumbered property may devolve upon or be devised to beneficiaries who have not that liability. Until the law was altered by Locke King's Acts,[53] a deceased's personal estate was

---

[45] *Fawcett v Lowther* (1751) 2 Ves. Sen. 300.
[46] ss.45–52 as amended by the Family Law Reform Act 1987 ss.1, 18 and 33(1).
[47] See generally *Chitty on Contracts*, 30th edn, Ch.19.
[48] *West Bromwich Building Society v Bullock* (1936) 80 S.J. 654.
[49] *Oxford (Earl) v Lady Rodney* (1808) 14 Ves. 417; *Re Errington, Ex p. Mason* [1894] 1 Q.B. 11.
[50] *Kinnaird v Trollope* (1888) L.R. 39 Ch.D. 636; subsequent proceedings (1889) L.R. 42 Ch.D. 610.
[51] Even if he does not (see *Mills v United Counties Bank Ltd* [1912] 1 Ch. 231), when the whole mortgaged property is assigned subject to the mortgage, such an indemnity will be implied (*Bridgman v Daw* (1891) 40 W.R. 253) unless it is not made for value (*Re Best* [1924] 1 Ch. 42). See also Romer L.J. in *Re Mainwaring's Settlement Trusts* [1937] 1 Ch. 96 at 103.
[52] *Bartholomew v May* (1737) 1 Atk. 487.
[53] Real Estates Charges Acts 1854, 1867 and 1877.

primarily liable to satisfy a debt charged upon land, so that an heir-at-law or a devisee was entitled to call on the personalty to exonerate lands from the debts charged upon them.[54] The rule was displaced if the deceased had signified a contrary intention[55] and, being based upon succession to the deceased's contractual liability, it only applied on the death of the original mortgagor. An assignee of an equity of redemption had not himself created the charge and was not therefore under any personal liability.[56]

The current position: Today, however, the rule is reversed. Unless the deceased **29–09** mortgagor has signified a contrary intention, the primary liability to satisfy charges upon his property is, as between persons claiming beneficially under him, upon the encumbered property. The personal estate is still, of course, liable to satisfy a mortgagee's claim in contract against the deceased, but, if called on to do so, has a right to be compensated out of the mortgaged property. This change was first effected in 1854 but the Administration of Estates Act 1925[57] extends the new rule to encumbered *personalty* as well as realty. Thus, specific personalty which has been mortgaged or pledged will not, after 1925, be entitled to exoneration at the expense of the general assets of the deceased, unless the latter has shown an intention by will, deed or other document to that effect. Under the Administration of Estates Act 1925, as under Locke King's Acts, the deceased's contrary direction in favour of exoneration must be clear and unambiguous. Thus, a general direction for the payment of debts, or even of *all* debts, out of the deceased's personal or residuary estate will not be sufficient to exonerate property mortgaged or charged[58] nor will a direction to charge all debts upon the personal or residuary estate. In fact, an intention to exonerate must be signified by words referring clearly to mortgage debts, and not to debts generally.[59] Such an intention can be shown in any document such as a letter.[60] It may be partial in that it applies to mortgages and not to liens[61] but it is not enough to make a specific demise of one property comprised in a mortgage and not the whole.[62]

These provisions do not in any way affect a mortgagee's right to satisfy himself, either out of the encumbered property or, by suing on the personal promise, out of the deceased mortgagor's general assets. The changed incidence of the debt does not alter the mortgagee's remedies.[63] They do not apply to a person who is given the right to purchase part of the estate by will. He is not a devisee or legatee, but a purchaser.[64]

[54] *Cope v Cope* (1710) 2 Salk. 449; *Galton v Hancock* (1742) 2 Atk. 436.
[55] *Morrow v Bush* (1785) 1 Cox. 185; *Forrest v Prescott* (1870) L.R. 10 Eq. 545; *Hancox v Abbey* (1805) 11 Ves. 179.
[56] *Scott v Beecher* (1820) 5 Madd. 96; *Butler v Butler* (1800) 5 Ves. 534; *Earl of Ilchester v Earl of Carnarvon* (1839) 1 Beav. 209.
[57] ss.35, 55(1)(xvii); this largely restates the old law.
[58] s.35(2).
[59] *Re Valpy* [1906] 1 Ch. 531.
[60] See *Re Campbell* [1898] 2 Ch. 206; *Re Wakefield* (1943) 87 S.J. 371, CA; *Re Birmingham* [1959] Ch. 523.
[61] *Re Beirnstein* [1925] Ch. 12.
[62] *Re Neeld* [1962] Ch. 643, overruling *Re Biss* [1956] Ch. 243.
[63] s.35(3).
[64] *Re Fison's Wills Trust* [1950] Ch. 394.

Contribution

29–10   When several estates, held in different ownership, are subject to the same mortgage, any one owner, who discharges the common debt, has a right to contribution from the others pro rata according to the value of their securities. The primary equitable rule is that, where different properties are charged with the same debt, the burden shall be distributed proportionately among the various properties.[65] Thus the mortgagee may pursue his remedies against any estate he pleases but he cannot, by so doing, throw the whole liability on the owner of one estate.[66] The same rule applies when a mortgagor has mortgaged several estates to secure the same debt and then, on his death, the estates pass into the hands of several owners. Under s.35 of the Administration of Estates Act 1925, all the encumbered properties are responsible for the debt and if one owner discharges the whole liability, he has a right to contribution against the other properties.[67] The fundamental requirement for this right to contribution is that all the properties shall be subject to a common liability *of the same degree*.[68] It is not enough that a creditor has a charge on more than one property; the properties must, as between themselves, be equally liable. For example, a property specifically charged with a debt has no right to contribution from property over which the creditor has only a general lien. It is for this reason that the owner of encumbered property, who is also under a personal obligation to pay a common debt, cannot claim contribution from another whose property is subject to the same encumbrance, but who has no personal liability in respect of the debt.[69] Nor must it be forgotten that the doctrine of marshalling may have the result of throwing the primary liability for a common debt upon one only of the mortgaged estates, so that the owner of that estate, not having an equal liability, will lose his right to contribution.[70] Again, even in the case of joint mortgagees there may be no right of contribution because of the special circumstances of the mortgage. For example, of two co-mortgagors one may be acting as surety for the other so that, as between themselves, the primarily liability is upon the principal debtor.[71] In all these cases, where the primary liability is upon one debtor or property, the others are not only bound to contribute but if they in fact discharge the debt, they have a right to be compensated.[72] This is important if a mortgagor mortgages two estates to cover the same debt and afterwards assigns one of the estates. Under the principles just stated, the primary liability is upon the assignor so that, if he does not intend to exonerate his assignee's estate, he must be careful to preserve his own right to contribution.[73] This right he will preserve if he assigns the estate *subject to the mortgage*, because by so doing he shows that the primary liability

---

[65] per Tomlin J. in *Re Best* [1924] 1 Ch. 42 at 44.

[66] *Aldrich v Cooper* (1803) 8 Ves. 382; *Johnson v Child* (1844) 4 Hare 87.

[67] See *Carter v Barnardiston* (1718) 1 P.Wms. 505; *Middleton v Middleton* (1852) 15 Beav. 450.

[68] *Re Dunlop* (1882) 21 Ch.D. 583.

[69] *Re Darby's Estate* [1907] 2 Ch. 465.

[70] *Bartholomew v May* (1737) 1 Atk. 487.

[71] *Marquess of Bute v Cunynghame* (1826) 2 Russ. 275.

[72] *Re Best* [1924] 1 Ch. 42.

[73] ibid.

is not to be all on the property which he retains, and thus restores the fundamental rule of equity which requires the imposition of proportionate burdens on properties charged with the same debt.[74] On the other hand, the assignment of one estate subject to the mortgage does not, by itself, shift the *whole* burden of the whole mortgage to the property assigned. Only an express indemnity covering the whole mortgage debt will have that effect.[75]

MORTGAGOR'S BENEFICIAL ENJOYMENT OF THE SECURITY

The notion that the mortgagor is the real owner of the security is carried in equity **29–11** as far as it can be, without actually infringing the rights vested in the mortgagee by virtue of his legal estate. The mortgagee is not a trustee for the mortgagor, for he has an interest in the mortgaged property adverse to that of the mortgagor.[76] In equity, however, that interest is rigidly confined to a right to hold the property as a security. A mortgagor, until his equity of redemption is lost to him by foreclosure, sale under a power of sale, lapse of time or release, is entitled to the full beneficial enjoyment of the land. He is regarded as the owner of the land[77] subject to a mere encumbrance. It is true that a mortgage contract usually confers on the mortgagee a legal right to take possession of the property immediately and without regard to the state of the mortgage debt but equity treats this right as part of his security and not as a right to beneficial enjoyment. Thus, if a mortgagee does take possession of his security, he will be called on to account with strictness for his use of it and for the profits which he has taken or ought to have taken from the property.[78] For example, if the mortgagee occupies land the mortgagor is entitled to be credited with a fair occupation rent.[79] In consequence, not only is a mortgagee prevented from making any profit out of the mortgage property, but he is, by the strictness of the account, discouraged from exercising his legal right to take possession except as a measure to preserve his security.[80] Equity stops short of restraining the mortgagee from taking possession by granting an injunction, but, if possession is taken, the mortgagor is considered as being entitled to the profits, subject only to the mortgagee's right to devote them to the satisfaction of the mortgage debt.

On the other hand, if, as generally happens, the mortgagor remains in posses- **29–12** sion, he is entitled to take all the profits from the security without being in any way obliged either to account for them or to apply them in discharging the mortgage interest.[81] This is so even though the security is insufficient. Thus, in

---

[74] *Re Mainwaring's Settlement Trusts* [1937] 1 Ch. 96.

[75] ibid.

[76] *Dobson v Land* (1850) 8 Hare 216.

[77] See Lord Denning in *Westminster City Council v Haymarket Publishing Ltd* [1981] 1 W.L.R. 677 at 680 B–C and 681 C–E.

[78] *Hughes v Williams* (1806) 12 Ves. 493; *Shepherd v Spansheath* (1988) E.G.C.S. 35; *Chaplin v Young (No.1)* (1864) 33 Beav. 330; *Parkinson v Hanbury* (1867) L.P. 2 H.L. 1.

[79] *Marriott v Anchor Reversionary Co* (1861) 3 De G.F. & J. 177 at 193.

[80] It is in the nature of the transaction that the mortgagor shall continue in possession. per Lord Selborne, *Pugh v Heath* (1881–82) L.R. 6 Q.B.D. 345 at 359.

[81] *Trent v Hunt* (1853) 9 Exch. 14; *Pugh v Heath* (1881–82) L.R. 6 Q.B.D. 345 at 359, per Lord Selborne; affirmed (1881–82) L.R. 7 App. Cas. 235 (HL).

a case[82] where the property mortgaged was land let out on lease and the mortgagor went bankrupt, Lord Eldon refused to compel the assignee in bankruptcy to account for past rents received by him. He insisted that a mortgagor does not receive the rents for the mortgagee and that there is no instance of a mortgagor being directly called on to account for rents. Again, a mortgagor of land may cut and sell timber, and in so doing may even waste the inheritance provided that he does not thereby render the security insufficient.[83] A mortgagor in possession cannot therefore be considered a bailiff of the mortgagee. He is equitable owner of the property and as such is not liable to pay an occupation rent to the mortgagee.[84] Correspondingly, he has the ordinary liabilities of an owner and is, for example, responsible for the maintenance of dykes and sea walls.[85]

MORTGAGOR IN POSSESSION

General

29–13   Although in equity a mortgagor remains owner of the property, by the mortgage conveyance he parts with an estate or interest which carries with it the immediate right to possession.[86] While it is true that he usually remains in occupation and that equity discourages the mortgagee from going into occupation, the fact remains that the mortgagee holds the legal title to possession, and that the court will never prevent him from insisting on his title.[87] It follows that as a mortgagee has the immediate right to possession, the mortgagor can only lawfully remain in occupation as the mortgagee's tenant and that in the absence of any special agreement the tenancy will be precarious. For unless the mortgage contract makes express provision for the mortgagor's continued possession of the property, his tenancy depends solely on his de facto possession and is terminable by the mortgagee at any moment. The exact nature of this precarious tenancy is a subject of controversy, with three distinct theories being put forward: (i) that the mortgagor is a tenant at will[88]; (ii) that he is a tenant at sufferance[89]; and (iii) that as a tenant he is sui generis and cannot be assigned to any of the well-known classes.[90] The first theory has frequently been criticised[91] and can scarcely be

---

[82] *Ex p. Wilson* (1813) 2 v & B. 252; cf. *Colman v Duke of St. Albans* (1796) 3 Ves. 25; *Hele v Lord Bexley* (1855) 20 Beav. 127.

[83] *Usborne v Usborne* (1740) 1 Dick. 75; *Hippesley v Spencer* (1820) 5 Mad. 422; *Harper v Aplin* (1886) 54 L.T. 383.

[84] *Yorkshire Banking Co v Mullan* (1887) L.R. 35 Ch.D. 125.

[85] *Reg. v Baker* (1867) 2 Q.B. 621.

[86] Thus, under the old law a heriot could not be taken from a mortgagor because he was not seised: *Copestake v Hoper* [1908] 2 Ch. 10.

[87] per Plumer, M.R., *Marquis Cholmondely v Lord Clinton* (1817) 2 Mer. 171 at 359; *Pope v Biggs* (1829) 9 B. & C. 245.

[88] Lord Mansfield in *Keech v Hall* (1778) 1 Doug. 21; cf. *Moss v Gallimore* (1779) 1 Doug.K.B. 279; Fortescue, M.R., in *Leman v Newnham* (1747) 1 Ves.Sen. 51.

[89] Lord Ellenborough, *Thunder v Belcher* (1803) 3 East. 449 at 451; Vaughan-Williams J. in *Scobie v Collins* [1895] 1 Q.B. 375. See Turner, *Equity of Redemption* (1931), p.102.

[90] Parke B. in *Litchfield v Ready* (1850) 20 L.J.(N.S.) Ex. 51 at 52; Turner, *Equity of Redemption* (1931), p.110.

[91] e.g. by Buller J. in *Birch v Wright* (1786) 1 Term. 378 at 381.

correct because a mortgagee may bring ejectment against a mortgagor without any previous demand for possession[92] and a mortgagor, when ejected, is not entitled to emblements.[93] It is not, of course, suggested that a mortgagor is never a tenant at will of the mortgagee because he may be made such a tenant by actual agreement,[94] or by the mortgagee expressly or impliedly recognising him as a tenant. The receipt of interest by the mortgagee is, however, referable to the mortgage and is by itself no recognition of a tenancy in the mortgagor.[95] The second theory has more to recommend it because the position of a mortgagor in possession, who has not been recognised as a tenant, largely corresponds to that of a tenant at sufferance: he begins lawfully, holds over without title, may be ejected without previous demand for possession and is not entitled to emblements. Moreover, there are clear statements by Lord Ellenborough[96] and Lord Tenterden[97] that the mortgagor is at most a tenant at sufferance. On the other hand, unlike a tenant at sufferance, a mortgagor in possession, who pays his interest, will not find time running in his favour under the Limitation Act 1980,[98] although he is not thereby recognising the mortgagee as his landlord. Furthermore, statute[99] has given to a mortgagor in possession wide powers of bringing actions in respect of the mortgaged property and of granting leases without the concurrence of the mortgagee, so that his position is, in fact, rather different from that of a tenant at sufferance. In the past,[100] analogies from tenancies at will or at sufferance may have influenced judges in deciding questions concerning the mortgage relationship, but today the rights, powers and interests of mortgagor and mortgagee are well settled.[101] Therefore, while recognising that the closest analogy to the possession of a mortgagor is the possession of a tenant at sufferance,[102] it is sufficient to describe mortgagors as being in possession as mortgagors.[103]

A mortgagor, when his contract makes no provision for his continued occupation, holds precariously from the mortgagee, being liable to be ejected not only without notice, but without even a previous demand for possession. In fact it is then at the option of the mortgagee to treat his mortgagor in possession, either as **29–14**

---

[92] *Doe* d. *Griffith v Mayo* (1828) 7 L.J.(O.S.) K.B. 84; *Jolly v Arbuthnot* (1859) 4 De G. & J. 224.

[93] per Buller J. in *Birch v Wright* (1786) 1 Term. 378 at 387; *Christophers v Sparke* (1820) 2 Jac. & W. 223. Even Lord Mansfield, who is chiefly responsible for the description of the mortgagor as tenant at will, was constrained by these differences to admit that he is a tenant at will only *quodam modo*: *Moss v Gallimore* (1779) 1 Doug.K.B. 279.

[94] e.g. by the mortgagor attorning tenant to the mortgagee. See above, para.26–11.

[95] *Doe* d. *Rogers v Cadwallader* (1831) 2 B. & Ad. 473; *Scobie v Collins* [1895] 1 Q.B. 375.

[96] *Weaver v Belcher* (1803) 3 East 449.

[97] *Doe* d. *Roby v Maisey* (1828) 8 B. & C. 767; cf. Littledale J. in *Pope v Biggs* (1829) 9 B. & C. 245.

[98] See paras 6–56 et seq.

[99] Now LPA 1925 ss.98 and 99. See paras 26–08 et seq., 32–04.

[100] Turner, *Equity of Redemption* (1931), p.104.

[101] Thus Buller J. in *Birch v Wright* (1786) 1 Term. 378 at 383, said, perhaps somewhat prematurely: "A mortgagor and mortgagee are characters as well known and their rights, powers and interests are well settled, as any in the law."

[102] See I. Smith, *Leading Cases* (13th edn), p.594; Turner, *Equity of Redemption* (1931), Ch.5.

[103] Turner, *Equity of Redemption* (1931), p.110.

his tenant or as a trespasser.[104] It is by no means uncommon however, for a mortgagor to stipulate in the mortgage the right to continue in possession of the security.[105] Such a stipulation will sometimes amount to a redemise of the property, sometimes only to a personal covenant by the mortgagee not to interfere with the mortgagor's enjoyment, and, if the language is not precise, it is not always easy to distinguish between a redemise and a mere covenant. The cases suggest the following propositions:

(1) If there is an *affirmative* covenant[106] for the mortgagor's enjoyment of the property and a determinate period[107] is indicated as the length of the term, the mortgage contract operates as a redemise for a term.

(2) If the agreement contains an affirmative covenant that the mortgagor shall continue in possession, or have quiet enjoyment until he makes default on the date fixed for repayment, he is a tenant for the intervening period.[108]

(3) In either case, if the mortgagor remains in occupation after the term has expired, he becomes a tenant at sufferance.[109]

(4) If the mortgagor is expressed to hold at the will and pleasure of the mortgagee, a tenancy at will is created and it may still be a tenancy at will, although a yearly rent is payable.[110] On the other hand, the tenancy may be a periodic tenancy, although the mortgagee reserves a right to determine it without notice.[111] In each case it is a question of the true intention of the parties.

(5) If there is a covenant, which is negative, for example, that the mortgagee shall not interrupt the mortgagor's possession, or which does not indicate any period for the lease, it will be a personal covenant and no demise is made thereby.[112] In such cases a mortgagor is tenant as mortgagor and his position is very like that of a tenant at sufferance.

Right of a mortgagor in possession to bring actions in respect of the mortgaged property

29–15   Although the tenancy of a mortgagor is usually precarious, it is plain that when he is in possession of the mortgaged property, he will have the protection which

---

[104] *Partridge v Bere* (1822) 5 B. & Ald. 604; *Hitchman v Walton* (1838) 4 M. & W. 409; *Moss v Gallimore* (1779) 1 Doug.K.B. 279; *Re Ind, Coope & Co Ltd* [1911] 2 Ch. 223.

[105] This is sometimes effected by an "attornment clause," by which the mortgagor attorns tenant to the mortgagee. If there is such an attornment clause it can have certain consequences in a mortgagor's claim for possession. See above, para.26–11.

[106] *Wilkinson v Hall* (1837) 3 Bing.N.C. 508; *Doe d. Parsley v Day* (1842) 2 Q.B. 147.

[107] *Doe d. Roylance v Lightfoot* (1841) 8 M. & W. 553; *Doe d. Parsley v Day* (1842) 2 Q.B. 147.

[108] *Wilkinson v Hall* (1837) 3 Bing. N.S. 508. See Coote, *Law of Mortgages* (9th edn, 1927), p.677 (n.).

[109] *Gibbs v Cruickshank* (1873) L.R. 8 C.P. 454.

[110] *Doe d. Bastow v Cox* (1847) L.R. 11 Q.B. 122.

[111] *Re Knight, Ex p. Voisey* (1882) L.R. 21 Ch.D. 442; *Re Threlfall, Ex p. Queen's Benefit Building Society* (1880) L.R. 16 Ch.D. 274.

[112] *Doe d. Parsley v Day* (1842) 2 Q.B. 147.

the law always affords to a possessory title.[113] Except against the person entitled, a disseisor or a tenant at sufferance has all the remedies, legal or equitable, which the true owner has to protect his property.[114] So, too, has a mortgagor who is in personal occupation. However, when the mortgage property is let out on lease, the mortgagor is, of course, only a reversioner, though technically still in possession. As owner of the property in equity he has always had available to him equitable remedies to protect his interest.[115] Thus, he may bring an action for an injunction against his lessee or against a third party to prevent an injury to the property,[116] or to enforce a restrictive covenant.[117] Legal remedies, however, at common law attach only to the legal estate and in days when mortgages were usually created by assignment, passed with the legal estate to the mortgagee.[118] A mortgagor was, indeed, allowed to recover the rents from his lease, and even distrain for them on the basis that he had an implied authority from the mortgagee[119] but that, at common law, was the limit of his rights. Having at law no estate he was unable, against third parties, to bring an action for damages for injury to the reversion[120] and having parted with the reversion to the mortgagee he was unable against his lessee to bring ejectment or any action on the covenants in the lease.[121] His course was either to induce the mortgagee to sue or to ask the court to compel the mortgagee to lend his name to the action. However, this he could do only on the terms of offering to redeem.[122]

The power of a mortgagor in possession of mortgaged land to sue in respect **29–16** of the land was, however, considerably enlarged by s.25(5) of the Judicature Act 1873 and s.10 of the Conveyancing Act 1881, which are now replaced by, respectively, ss.98 and 141 of the Law of Property Act 1925 and, in relation to the enforcement of leasehold covenants in leases granted on or after January 1, 1996, s.15 of the Landlord and Tenant (Covenants) Act 1995. These sections apply to all mortgages, whether made before or after January 1, 1926, and their effect is as follows—so long as the mortgagee has not given an effective[123] notice of an intention to take possession or to enter into receipt of the rent and profits, a mortgagor may, in his own name, sue for possession or for the recovery of rents and profits, and may bring an action for damages against a trespasser or against any other wrongdoer.[124] Similarly, while still a mortgagor in possession, he may, in his own name, enforce all covenants and conditions which are contained in

---

[113] *Perry v Clissold* [1907] A.C. 73.

[114] *Graham v Peat* (1801) 1 East. 244; *Asher v Whitlock* (1865) L.R. 1 Q.B. 1.

[115] per Channel J. in *Turner v Walsh* [1909] 2 K.B. 484 at 487.

[116] *Van Gelder, Apsimon & Co v Sowerby Bridge, & United District Flour Society* (1890) L.R. 44 Ch.D. 374.

[117] *Fairclough v Marshall* (1878) 4 Ex. D. 37; *Rogers v Hosegood* [1900] 2 Ch. 388.

[118] *Doe* d. *Marriot v Edwards* (1834) 5 B. & Ad. 1065. But if the mortgage was made *before* the lease there was no difficulty.

[119] ibid., cf. also *Trent v Hunt* (1853) 9 Ex. 14.

[120] per Bramwell B., at Assizes, *Rumford v Oxford, Worcester & Wolverhampton Rly Co* (1856) 1 H. & N. 34.

[121] *Matthews v Usher* [1900] 2 Q.B. 535. See also *Molyneux v Richard* [1906] 1 Ch. 34.

[122] per Farwell L.J. in *Turner v Walsh* [1909] 2 K.B. 484 at 495.

[123] Possession proceedings which are defective by means of a technicality are not sufficient, see *Kitchen's Trustee v Madders and Madders* [1949] Ch. 588 affirmed [1950] Ch. 134.

[124] s.98(1).

leases of the mortgaged land.[125] It is immaterial whether the mortgage[126] or lease[127] was made before or after the statutory amendment. Finally, these statutory powers do not in any way prejudice a mortgagor's right to bring actions which may be vested in him independently of the Act, for example, by virtue of the possession of a legal estate.

---

[125] s.141(2) in relation to leases prior to 1996; Landlord and Tenant (Covenants) Act 1995 s.15 in relation to leases after 1995.
[126] s.98(3).
[127] s.141(4) in relation to leases prior to 1996; Landlord and Tenant (Covenants) Act 1995 s.15 in relation to leases after 1995.

CHAPTER 30

THE RIGHTS, DUTIES AND REMEDIES OF THE MORTGAGOR OR CHARGOR

THE RIGHT OF REDEMPTION

Legal right to redeem

The legal right to redeem is the right specifically reserved to the mortgagor in the   **30–01**
mortgage contract to recover his property upon discharging the obligations which
the mortgage was created in order to secure. At law the contract is construed
strictly so that a mortgagor exercising his legal right to redeem must comply
punctiliously with the proviso for redemption. Thus, a mortgage to secure a
money loan ordinarily fixes a definite date for repayment and at law repayment
must be made precisely on that date. Before the stipulated date the mortgagor has
no right to redeem either at law or in equity,[1] nor has the mortgagee, in the
absence of a special agreement to that effect, any right to call in his money. Even
the fact that the mortgagor is in default upon other covenants not touching the
proviso for redemption will not accelerate the mortgagee's right to call in his
money.[2] After the stipulated date the mortgagor ceases at law to have any right
to redeem his property.

The date for redemption usually prescribed by the mortgage contract is six
months after the date of its execution. The period before which the property may
be redeemed at law may, however, be shorter and indeed the mortgage may be
made redeemable and repayable on demand, in which case the demand fixes the
date for redemption. Normally the period is a short one because it is an advantage
to the mortgagee to place the mortgagor in default as soon as possible. However,
at law there is no restriction upon the parties making their own arrangements.
Accordingly the date for repayment and redemption may be suspended for any
period, however long, provided that the mortgage contract does not infringe the
equitable rules for the protection of the equity of redemption discussed below.
Broadly, the position under these rules is that there is no limit to the length of a
mortgage contract if the date for redemption is fixed genuinely upon an investment basis and the contract is neither a device to render the right of redemption
illusory nor otherwise a cloak for an unconscionable bargain.[3]

---

[1] *Brown v Cole* (1845) 14 Sim. 427.
[2] *Williams v Morgan* [1906] 1 Ch. 804.
[3] *Knightsbridge Estates Trust Ltd v Byrne* [1939] Ch. 441; see below, paras 30–02 et seq. and paras
30–23 et seq.

Equitable right to redeem

30–02   The equitable right to redeem[4] is the right of a mortgagor to recover his security by discharging his obligations under the mortgage despite the time fixed by the contract for the performance of those obligations having passed and even though under the express terms of his agreement the security may be stated to be the absolute property of the mortgagee. Similarly, in the case of a charge it is the right to have the security freed from the charge although default was made at the time fixed by the contract for the performance of the obligations in respect of which the charge was given. The right to redeem in equity is therefore a right given in contradiction to the declared terms of the contract between the parties.[5] Today, however, the nature of the equitable right to redeem is so well known that when a mortgage is made in the usual form to secure a money payment on a certain day it may generally be taken to be a term of the real bargain between the parties that the property is to remain redeemable after default on the day named.[6] As Maitland said,[7] the common form of mortgage by conveyance "is one long *suppressio veri* and *suggestio falsi*".

The equitable right to redeem is thus the right to recover the mortgaged property *after* the expiry of the legal right to redeem through its non-exercise on the contract date.[8] After the passing of the contract date equity superimposes on the mortgage agreement a condition giving the mortgagor a continuing right to redeem which he may exercise at any time before the right is destroyed by foreclosure, sale, release, or lapse of time. In general, this equitable right is dependent on the mortgagor giving the mortgagee reasonable notice of his intention to redeem and on his fully performing his obligations under the mortgage. In special cases the mortgagor is absolved from giving notice[9] and sometimes may even be allowed to recover his security on giving the mortgagee less than that to which he is entitled under the provisions of the mortgage.[10]

CONTROL BY THE COURT

Excluding the right

30–03   However, in every case the terms of redemption in equity[11] are imposed on the parties ab extra by the settled custom of the court which regulates every mortgage

---

[4] The equitable right to redeem should be distinguished from the "equity of redemption," which has a wider meaning. See above, para.29–01.

[5] per Lord Bramwell in *Salt v Marquess of Northampton* [1892] A.C. 1 at 18.

[6] per Lord Parker in *Kreglinger v New Patagonia Meat and Cold Storage Co Ltd* [1914] A.C. 25 at 50.

[7] *Equity* (2nd edn), p.182.

[8] The right can arise *before* the legal date for redemption if the mortgagee has demanded payment, e.g. by entering into possession of the security, see *Bovill v Endle* [1896] 1 Ch. 648.

[9] See below, paras 30–38 et seq.

[10] e.g. in the case of a mortgage executed under undue influence.

[11] These terms are set out in full, below, paras 30–38 et seq.

contract. Nor can the court's control be ousted by any agreement in the mortgage itself. Lord Eldon in *Seton v Slade*[12] said:

"I take it to be so in the case of a mortgage; that you shall not by special terms alter what this Court says are the special terms of that contract."

Accordingly, if property is transferred with the object of providing security and with the intention that it should be restored to the mortgagor, it is not competent for the parties so to frame their bargain that the mortgagee has a right under its terms to obtain an absolute title to the property overriding the equity of redemption. Thus, a person who has taken property by way of security will not be allowed to deprive the mortgagor of his equity of redemption by formulating the bargain as a conditional sale or by any similar device.[13] The jurisdiction of the court over mortgages cannot be ousted by any trick of conveyancing. Moreover, the question whether a transaction is a mortgage is one of substance, not of form, so that the court will freely admit parol evidence for the purpose of establishing that the true intention was merely to give a security, even if the parol evidence contradicts the plain terms of a deed.[14] The equity of redemption is thus an inseparable incident of a contract of mortgage. As counsel said in *Howard v Harris*,[15] a mortgage can no more be made irredeemable than a distress for a rentcharge can be irrepleviable. The one statutory exception to this principle is now set out in s.739 of the Companies Act 2006. This specifically authorises the creation of irredeemable mortgages in the form of irredeemable debentures[16] or those redeemable only on the happening of a contingency or the expiration of a period of time.[17]

Equity, therefore, interferes directly with freedom of contract between mortgagor and mortgagee. Today this interference is sometimes explained as being an illustration of the principle that equity looks to the intent rather than to the form. Historically, however, the Chancellor's intervention was the result partly of a desire to extend his jurisdiction[18] and partly of the position held by mortgages in the life of the 16th and 17th centuries. During that period mortgages were very generally securities taken by creditors from persons in circumstances of financial embarrassment such that the mortgagors were not free agents in making their

30–04

[12] (1802) 7 Ves. 265 at 273.

[13] *Barnhart v Greenshields* (1853) 9 Moo.P.C.C. 18.

[14] *England v Codrington* (1758) 1 Eden 169; *Lincoln v Wright* (1859) 4 De G. & J. 16. In the latter case, Turner L.J. puts this upon the general principle that in equity parol evidence will be admitted to prove a fraud. cf. *Rochefoucauld v Boustead* [1897] 1 Ch. 196. See also *Barton v Bank of New South Wales* (1890) 15 App. Cas. 379; *Grangeside Properties Ltd v Collingwoods Securities Ltd* [1964] 1 W.L.R. 139 (an assignment of a lease treated as a mortgage so as to enable the assignee—mortgagee to claim relief from forfeiture of the lease by the head-lessor).

[15] (1683) 1 Vern. 191 at 192.

[16] Although, strictly, an irredeemable debenture is not a mortgager; (see *Samuel v Jarrah Timber and Wood Paving Corporation Ltd* [1904] A.C. 323 at 330) it is within the statutory definition under Companies Act 2006, s.738. See also below, paras 30–05 and 30–06.

[17] It replaces the former provision contained in Companies Act 1985 s.193.

[18] Turner, *Equity of Redemption* (1931), p.42, thinks that this was the main reason for the development of the equity of redemption.

contracts.[19] At first the Chancellor justified his interference either on the ground of protecting the mortgagor against an unscrupulous creditor or on the ground that relief should be given to a debtor who had been prevented from discharging his obligation only by reason of some mistake, accident or special hardship. At the same time and for the same reasons he was giving similar relief against penal clauses in bonds. Early in the 17th century, however, the Chancellor[20] decided to give relief against penal conditions in all cases even though no special ground for relief could be shown and the equity of redemption became part of the settled custom of the court.

PROTECTION OF THE RIGHT TO REDEEM

30–05 However, the protection of embarrassed mortgagors could not be achieved by the mere creation of the equitable right of redemption. As soon as the practice in equity to allow redemption after the contract date became known, mortgagees sought to defeat the intervention of equity by special provisions in the mortgage deed. These provisions were designed either to render the legal right to redeem illusory, thus preventing the equity of redemption from arising at all, or to defeat or clog the equity of redemption after it had arisen. For example, the mortgage contract might provide for an option for the mortgagee to purchase the mortgaged property, thus defeating both the legal and equitable right to redeem, or might allow redemption after the contract date only upon payment of an additional sum or upon performance of some additional obligation. Consequently, the Chancellor began to relieve mortgagors against such restrictions and fetters on the legal and equitable rights to redeem imposed by special covenants in the mortgage.

"Once a mortgage always a mortgage"

30–06 The protection of a mortgagor against all attempts to defeat or clog his right of redemption involved the creation of subsidiary rules of equity, invalidating the various contrivances which ingenious conveyancers devised. So, for example, while it is possible for redemption to be postponed in certain circumstances, an agreement made at the time of the mortgage as part of that particular transaction cannot extinguish the right. These rules are sometimes summed up in a maxim of equity "once a mortgage always a mortgage".[21] This means that once a contract is seen to be a mortgage no provision in the contract will be valid if it is inconsistent with the right of the mortgagor to recover his security on discharging his obligations. Provisions offending against the maxim may either touch the

---

[19] "For necessitous men are not, truly speaking, free men, but, to answer a present exigency, will submit to any terms the crafty may impose on them" per Lord Northington in *Vernon v Bethell* (1761) 2 Eden 110 at 113.

[20] Turner, *Equity of Redemption* (1931), p.32, suggests that the Chancellor who took this step was none other than Lord Bacon.

[21] per Lord Eldon L.C. in *Seton v Slade* (1802) 7 Ves. 265 at 273.

contractual terms of redemption thereby rendering the right to redeem illusory or they may touch only the equitable right to redeem after the passing of the contract date hampering the exercise of the right. Provisions of the latter kind are termed "clogs" on the equity of redemption. The mortgagee is not permitted to include any term or other requirement in the mortgage transaction which prevents the mortgagor getting back that which he mortgaged (although the focus of the courts is clearly on the substance rather than the form of the transaction).[22] Greene M.R. in *Knightsbridge Estates v Byrne*, emphasised that provisions touching the *contractual right* to redeem are not properly to be classed as clogs on the equity of redemption. However, it is evident that such provisions are in substance clogs on the equity of redemption since they tend to defeat it altogether. In *Jones v Morgan*, Lord Phillips M.R. expressed the view that "the doctrine of a clog on the equity of redemption is, so it seems to me, an appendix to our law which no longer serves a useful purpose and would be better excised."[23] The reluctant view of the Court of Appeal in that case and that the doctrine remains in existence[24] and has not been subject to statutory or other revision.

Provisions infringing the equitable principle "once a mortgage always a mortgage" are invalid not merely against the mortgagor but against any person subsequently interested in the equity of redemption. For although the object of the rules against clogs on the equity of redemption is the protection of the mortgagor himself, the operation of the rules is to invalidate altogether any provisions which offend against them. The reason for this was clearly explained by Lord Tomlin in the case of *Mehrban Khan v Makhna*[25]:

> " . . . the provisions in question, being a clog upon the equity of redemption, were void and could have no more binding force against the assign of the mortgagor than they had against the mortgagor himself. They are not provisions of general validity avoided against the mortgagor personally by reason of pressure or undue influence brought to bear on him. They are provisions which, when forming part of the actual mortgage contract, have under the general law no validity at all. If it were otherwise, an illogical result would follow. The mortgagor, if he redeemed, would escape from the burden, but, if he sold to another he would necessarily bear the burden, as the validity of the provisions as against the assign would be reflected in the price which he received."[26]

The parties' freedom to contract

Formerly the court's jurisdiction to intervene in mortgage contracts was wider **30–07** than it is today owing to the existence of the usury laws. The court, in mortgages

[22] *Jones v Morgan* [2001] Lloyd's Rep. Bank 323.
[23] See further below at paras 30–08 et seq.
[24] See *Warnborough Ltd v Garmite Ltd* [2004] 1 P. & C.R. DG8 where the Court of Appeal reinstated the original decision of Master Bowman dismissing an application for summary judgment on the basis that given that the question as to whether part of (or a separate) transaction constituted a clog was one as to the substance of the transaction and no appropriate for summary judgment. Jonathan Parker L.J. concluded at [72] that the "unruly dog" that is the doctrine of clogs on the equity of redemption was "still alive" (although one might perhaps reasonably expect its venerable age to inhibit it straying too far or too often from its kennel) and that " . . . however desirable an appendectomy might be thought to be, no such relieving operation has as yet been carried out."
[25] (1930) 57 Ind. App. 168.
[26] ibid., at 172.

securing money loans, asserted a general jurisdiction to invalidate the contractual terms of redemption if inconsistent with the policy of those laws. The economic fact that in the seventeenth and eighteenth centuries a mortgagee had an ascendancy over a mortgagor was taken into account by courts of equity as well as by the legislature, resulting in a jealous scrutiny of the terms of redemption. The usury laws were, however, repealed in 1854.

Today, the parties to a mortgage are free to make what bargain they like, subject to the protection extended by the court to a mortgagor: (i) through the special equitable rules safeguarding the right to redeem; (ii) in cases of undue influence or duress at common law and under general equitable principles; (iii) in transactions falling within the provisions of the Consumer Credit Act 2006[27] as on unfair credit relationships or as regulated mortgages; and (iv) other instances where the court will intervene pursuant to its statutory or equitable jurisdiction.[28] Chief among the statutory provisions to which the court will have regard will be the Unfair Terms: Consumer Contracts Regulations, considered elsewhere.[29]

Special equitable rules against clogs on the equity of redemption

30–08   The following are the special equitable rules protecting the right of redemption which permit the mortgagor to redeem regardless of the terms of the mortgage.

A mortgage must be redeemable

30–09   A mortgage may not be framed with the design to render the security irredeemable.[30] It is the essence of a mortgage, in the conception of equity, that it shall be redeemable and the rule cannot be evaded by dressing up the mortgage as a conditional sale or by any other conveyancing device.[31] Equally, it cannot be circumvented by a provision which, while not extinguishing the equity of redemption, has the result of making the right nugatory. Therefore in *Fairclough v Swan Brewery Co Ltd*,[32] where the security was a lease with 210 months still to run and the mortgage was made redeemable only by 209 monthly payments, the mortgagor was permitted to disregard the instalment arrangement and to redeem at once on giving reasonable notice. In substance the leasehold security was made irredeemable by the terms of the mortgage. This rule, as previously stated,[33] no longer applies to debentures for s.739 of the Companies Act 2006 provides that debentures shall not be invalid by reason only that they are made irredeemable, or redeemable only on the happening of a contingency, however remote. Otherwise the only limitation upon the principle appears to be that where a short-lived asset, such as a lease or insurance policy, is mortgaged to secure a

---

[27] See Ch.16, above.
[28] See e.g. Insolvency Act 1986 ss.244, 245—see Ch.16 above; *Evans v Cherry Tree Finance Ltd* [2008] EWCA Civ 331 and see above, paras 2–09 et seq.
[29] See paras 16–08, above.
[30] *Newcomb v Bonham* (1681) 1 Vern. 7; *Re Sir Thomas Spencer Wells* [1933] Ch. 29 at 52.
[31] And see above, para.1–04.
[32] [1912] A.C. 562.
[33] See below, para.30–02.

longer dated obligation, the fact that the property owing to its nature will not be restored to the mortgagor freed from the mortgage is not enough by itself to invalidate the mortgage contract.[34]

Accordingly, any condition in a mortgage is invalid if its effect is to vest the security absolutely in the mortgagee on any event whatsoever.[35] The mortgage must not only begin by being redeemable, it must continue so. Lord Northington said in *Vernon v Bethell*[36]:

> "This Court as a Court of conscience is very jealous of persons taking securities for a loan and converting such securities into purchases, and therefore I take it to be an established rule that a mortgagee can never provide, at the time of making the loan, for any event or condition on which the equity of redemption shall be discharged and the conveyance absolute."

A condition which confines redemption to any particular person or period is therefore void. In *Howard v Harris*[37] although the agreement only allowed redemption by the mortgagor or his heir male, yet it was held that *any* heir might redeem. Again, where life policies were mortgaged and redemption was confined to a period covering the life of the mortgagor himself it was held that his executor might redeem.[38]

Insofar as the time for redemption is concerned, where the debt is repayable on demand by the mortgagee and no specific date for redemption is set out in the agreement, it appears that the mortgagor can redeem at any point of his choosing. This appears to be the case where the mortgagee has specifically agreed a date before which he will not call in the mortgage.[39] Where the covenant for repayment provides a date for repayment (in the absence of any other specified date for redemption) the mortgagor can redeem only terms set by the mortgagee. Further, a mortgagor may not redeem in equity while contingent liabilities exist or are capable of arising which are secured by the mortgage unless the contractual terms permit—it being critical to ensure that the terms of redemption in equity should be not be more favourable either to the mortgagor or the mortgagee than the contractual terms.[40]

Obtaining an option

Similarly, a mortgagee cannot by a stipulation in the mortgage contract obtain for himself an option on the property mortgaged. A contract cannot at once be a mortgage and a conditional sale even if the transaction is not oppressive.[41] In the   **30–10**

---

[34] *Knightsbridge Estates Trust Ltd v Byrne* [1939] Ch. 441, 462; [1940] A.C. 613.

[35] *Toomes v Conset* (1745) 3 Atk. 261.

[36] (1761) 2 Eden 110 at 113.

[37] (1583) 1 Vern. 32 and 190; cf. *Spurgeon v Collier* (1758) 1 Eden 55.

[38] *Salt v Marquess of Northampton* [1892] A.C. 1. See also *Newcomb v Bonham* (1681) 1 Vern. 7.

[39] *G A Investments Party Ltd v Standard Insurance Co Ltd* [1964] W.L.R. 264—the only notice that needed to be given was that which enabled the mortgagee to receive the money and bank it.

[40] *Re Rudd and Son Ltd* [1986] 2 B.C.C. 98,955, *Estoril Investments Ltd v Westpac Banking Group* (1993) A.C.L.R. 295 N.S.W. 24 and *The Law Debenture Trust Corporation plc v Concord Trust* [2007] EWHC 1380 (Ch).

[41] *Samuel v Jarrah Timber and Wood Paving Corporation Ltd* [1904] A.C. 323; cf. *Jennings v Ward* (1705) 2 Vern. 520; *Price v Perrie* (1702) Free.Ch. 258; *Re Edwards' Estate* (1861) 11 Ir.Ch.R. 367.

case of *Jones v Morgan*,[42] after an extensive review of the authorities prior to the case of *Kreglinger v New Patagonia Meat & Cold Storage Co Ltd*,[43] it was restated by the Court of Appeal that the court must consider whether or not the transaction is, in substance, a transaction of mortgage. That could only be viewed in the light of the nature and substance of the transaction and not its form—in particular (following Vaughan Williams L.J. in *Reeve v Lisle*)[44] the Court of Appeal stated that the question in each case is whether the arrangement made after the mortgage has been granted is "in substance and in fact subsequent to and independent of the original bargain".[45] The court found no difficulty in concluding that an option entered into in 1997 was a clog on the equity of redemption despite it being entered into some three years after the original 1994 mortgage transaction. In the particular circumstances it was entirely artificial to regard the 1997 option as being independent of the 1994 mortgage transaction.[46] So, too, if a mortgagor holds an option to purchase the fee or to renew a lease and assigns it to a mortgagee by way of security, the mortgagee cannot exercise the option and then claim the purchased property or new lease as against the mortgagor. In *Nelson v Hannam*,[47] the mortgage comprised an assignment of a 99 years' building lease plus the option to purchase the freehold. The mortgagee exercised the option after he had taken out a summons for foreclosure but before the decree had become absolute. The Court of Appeal held that the mortgagor was entitled—and, indeed, bound if called upon—to redeem not merely the lease but also the freehold reversion. Greene M.R. stated that if an option is an essential part of a mortgage transaction, whether as the sole security or merely as one element in the security, the mortgagee cannot retain against the mortgagor what is directly the fruit of the mortgaged property. The mortgagee may improve his security by exercising the option and may add the expense incurred in so doing to the mortgage account, but he cannot thus defeat the mortgagor's right to recover the fruit of the option. The court, in so deciding, acted on the analogy of cases dealing with mortgages of renewable leases, in which it has consistently been held that a mortgagee who exercises the right to renew must hold the renewed lease subject to the same equity of redemption as existed in relation to the original lease.[48]

Purchase by the mortgagee

30–11 The maxim "once a mortgage always a mortgage," does not, however, mean that a mortgagee can never purchase the mortgaged property while the relationship of mortgagor and mortgagee subsists. If the contract for the purchase of the

---

[42] [2001] Lloyd's Rep. Bank. 323.
[43] [1914] A.C. 25.
[44] [1902] A.C. 461
[45] ibid., [69].
[46] See also *Bannerman v Murray* [1972] N.Z.L.R. 411, *Jones v Morgan* (supra). In *Warnborough Ltd v Garmite Ltd* [2007] 1 P. & C.R. 2. the Court of Appeal having held that the issue of whether or not an option granted to the mortgagee was a clog or not was not appropriate for summary judgment simply by reference to the transaction documentation—the critical question being as to the true nature of the bargain.
[47] [1943] Ch. 59.
[48] *Rakestraw v Brewer* (1729) 2 P.W. 511; *Re Biss* [1903] 2 Ch. 40 at 62.

mortgaged property is a transaction independent of the mortgage or genuinely collateral to the mortgage, the mortgagee is fully entitled either to buy it or to obtain an option for himself[49] provided that the agreement cannot be struck down as being in restraint of trade or is unfair or unconscionable.[50]

Similar considerations probably apply to a right of pre-emption[51] for a mortgagee may take a release of the equity of redemption from the mortgagor without in any way being subject to the stringent rules which affect purchases by a trustee from his cestui que trust.[52] It makes no difference that the only consideration for the release is the discharge of the mortgage debt itself.[53] It follows a fortiori that the mortgagee of a lease containing no option to purchase the fee or renew the lease should on principle be entitled to purchase or obtain an option on the fee or obtain a renewal for his own account from a third party without being liable to have the new title redeemed by the mortgagor of the lease even if it wholly or partially destroys the equity of redemption.[54] An option is also plainly valid if it was obtained *before* the execution of the mortgage.[55] However, in a case where the executors of a deceased mortgagee sought to call in a loan and the mortgagor procured the transfer of the mortgage to a new mortgagee, it was held (following the principles set out in *Samuel v Jarrah Timber and Wood Paving Corporation Ltd*)[56] that the options to purchase part of the mortgaged property imposed as a condition of the transfer by the new mortgagees were void. In effect, it was a new loan purportedly made subject to an option to purchase.[57]

Suspension of the right to redeem

A stipulation postponing or suspending the right to redeem until some date in the **30–12** future longer than the customary six months may not be framed with the design of rendering the right illusory under the rule just explained. In addition it may not be so framed as to be actually repugnant to the expressed right to redeem. Such a stipulation is otherwise valid unless it forms part of a mortgage contract which was extorted from the mortgagor oppressively, unconscionably or through undue influence in which the contract will be set aside under the general equitable principles applying to such cases discussed elsewhere.[58]

---

[49] See *Reeve v Lisle* [1902] A.C. 461 (where the option was granted to the mortgagee some 10 days after the mortgage itself). However, see also *Lewis v Frank Love Limited* [1961] 1 All E.R. 446, applied in *Jones v Morgan*, above.

[50] See below, para.30–14 and Ch.31 and *Brighton & Hove City Council v Audus* [2010] 1 All E.R. (Comm) 343.

[51] *Orby v Trigg* (1722) 9 Mod. 2.

[52] *Knight v Marjoribanks* (1849) 2 Mac. & G. 10.

[53] *Melbourne Banking Co v Brougham* (1882) L.R. 7 App. Cas. 307.

[54] For a case where there was a lease by the claimants to an oil company and a re-lease at a higher rent by the oil company to the directors with an exclusive tie to sell the oil company's products after the grant of mortgage which was redeemed by the new arrangement, see *Alec Lobb (Garages) Ltd v Total Oil (Great Britain) Ltd* [1985] 1 W.L.R. 173, approving *Multiservice Bookbinding Ltd v Marden* [1979] Ch. 84. See also *Davies v Directloans Ltd* [1986] 1 W.L.R. 823.

[55] *London and Globe Finance Corporation v Montgomery* (1902) 18 T.L.R. 661.

[56] [1904] A.C. 323. See also *Bonham v Fishwick* [2008] 2 P. & C.R. DG6.

[57] See *Lewis v Frank Love Ltd* [1961] 1 W.L.R. 261.

[58] See below, Ch.31; cf. *Cowdry v Day* (1859) 1 Giff. 316.

Stipulations postponing or suspending the contractual right to redeem for a period of years clearly have a tendency to defeat the equity of redemption or render it illusory and until recently the court adopted a reserved attitude towards any considerable postponement or suspension of redemption.[59] Nevertheless, in individual cases the court did accept postponement of the right to redeem for five years[60]; eight years[61]; 10 years[62] and 14 years.[63] In all these cases, however, the obligation to continue the mortgage was *mutual*, i.e. the mortgagee could not call in his money during the period when the mortgagor was precluded from redeeming. Moreover, the dicta in the cases suggested the equitable principle to be that a suspension of the right to redeem must be shown to be reasonable between the parties in the circumstances of the particular mortgage and that the mutuality of the obligation is the best evidence of reasonableness.[64] In *Morgan v Jeffreys*[65] Joyce J. held invalid a postponement of the right to redeem for 28 years unaccompanied by a corresponding forbearance on the part of the mortgagee during the same period. Again, in *Davis v Symons*[66] Eve J. was prepared to uphold a postponement for 20 years, but only if the covenant for postponement was genuinely mutual and the longer the period of postponement the more closely the ostensible mutuality required, he thought, to be scrutinised. In the particular case two insurance policies were mortgaged, and redemption was postponed for a period of 20 years during which the mortgagee was not to call in his money. The mortgage provided, however, that on maturity the policy moneys were to be paid over to the mortgagee and applied in the reduction of the mortgage debt. Both policies were due to mature before the end of the 20-year period, one four years and the other eight days before that time. This provision was held by the learned judge to destroy the mutuality[67] and to render the postponement of redemption invalid.

The modern position with regard to postponement or suspension

30–13   Recognition of the fact that modern mortgages are normally genuine investments and not oppressive exactions from the mortgagor has already caused a considerable relaxation in the court's attitude towards postponement or suspension of redemption. Thus, that Eve J. could envisage a genuinely mutual postponement for 20 years as unobjectionable. In *Knightsbridge Estates Trust Ltd v Byrne*[68] it led the Court of Appeal entirely to reject the view that a postponement of the

---

[59] See e.g. *Fairclough v Swan Brewery Co Ltd* [1912] A.C. 562, (redemption allowed after only three years).
[60] *Biggs v Hoddinott* [1898] 2 Ch. 307.
[61] *Re Hones Estate* (1873) 8 I.R.Eq. 65.
[62] *Re Fortescue's Estate* (1916) 1 I.R. 268.
[63] *Williams v Morgan* [1906] 1 Ch. 804.
[64] e.g. Sir Edward Burtenshaw Sugden L.C. in *Lawless v Mansfield* (1841) 1 Dr. & W. 557 at 598.
[65] [1910] 1 Ch. 620.
[66] [1934] Ch. 442 at 448.
[67] This provision rendered part of the security irredeemable but more owing to the nature of the security than to the contrivance of the mortgagee.
[68] [1939] Ch. 441; affirmed on other grounds [1940] A.C. 613.

contractual right to redeem is only permissible if reasonable between the parties.[69] In that case, a large estate company mortgaged freehold properties to the trustees of a friendly society to secure a loan of £310,000. The mortgagor covenanted to repay the principal and interest in 80 half-yearly instalments, combining principal and interest, redemption being thus suspended for 40 years. The mortgagees in turn covenanted that if the mortgagor made no default in respect of any of its covenants, the money would only be called in by the 80 half-yearly instalments. There was thus mutuality in the covenant to continue the mortgage for 40 years and the contract was made between two powerful corporations at arm's length. The only reason why the mortgagor desired a release from their covenant was that they had miscalculated the future trend of interest rates and that money was now obtainable at easier rates than the mortgage rate. A less meritorious claim to the protection of equity it would be difficult to imagine and the court upheld the postponement for 40 years on the grounds that (i) as the covenant did not render the right to redeem illusory[70] or form part of an oppressive or unconscionable bargain[71] the court could not interfere; and (ii) the covenant was in any event reasonable between the parties. Although the court thus upheld this long suspension even upon the test of reasonableness, the main ground for their decision was that only a covenant which renders redemption illusory or alternatively forms part of an oppressive or unconscionable mortgage is bad. Greene M.R. who delivered the judgment of the court, stated roundly that the proposition that a postponement of the contractual right of redemption is only permissible for a reasonable time is ill-founded. He denied that there is any general jurisdiction to reform mortgage transactions because the court considers them unreasonable—a view which is undoubtedly correct.[72]

Although the covenant postponing redemption in the instant case was as a **30–14** matter of fact mutual, by rejecting the test of reasonableness the Court of Appeal appears also to have rejected mutuality as essential to the validity of a postponement of redemption. The absence of mutuality may in a particular case be confirmatory evidence of an oppressive or unconscionable bargain but the covenant will not be invalidated unless the mortgage in its totality is found to be oppressive or unconscionable.

In the course of a discussion of the earlier authorities, Greene M.R. also emphasised that a covenant suspending redemption may be invalid for actual repugnancy to the legal and equitable rights to redeem set up by the proviso for redemption. This will be so when, as in *Morgan v Jeffreys*[73] and *Davis v Symons*,[74] there is an express proviso for redemption after a few months followed by a stipulation binding the mortgagor not to redeem for a longer period. Neither

---

[69] See e.g. the explanation of the judgments in *Fairclough v Swan Brewery Co Ltd* ([1912] A.C. 565) in [1939] Ch. 441 at 460–462.

[70] ibid., at 456, 457.

[71] ibid., at 463.

[72] Subject now to the provisions of the Consumer Credit Act 1974 (as amended by the Consumer Credit Act 2006) and the Insolvency Act 1986 (as amended), the Unfair Terms in Consumer Contracts Regulations 1999. The Unfair Contract Terms Act 1977 does not apply to contracts for the disposition of an interest in land; see s.1(2), Sch.1 para.1(b).

[73] [1910] 1 Ch. 620.

[74] [1934] Ch. 442.

of the two judges who decided those cases made this feature of the mortgages a ground of their decision but it was on this ground of repugnancy to the legal and equitable rights to redeem that the Court of Appeal alone thought that the decisions in the two older cases could be supported.

When *Knightsbridge Estates Trust Ltd v Byrne*[75] came before the House of Lords, it was unanimously decided that the mortgage constituted a debenture within the meaning of the Companies Act 1929 so that the long postponement of redemption was in any event covered by the statutory authority to create irredeemable debentures contained in s.74 of that Act. The House of Lords vouchsafed no opinion on the correctness of the views expressed by the Court of Appeal—an omission to be regretted as the matter is of general importance to conveyancers. Although it is difficult to accept the Court of Appeal's explanation of the earlier authorities, as never having intended the word "reasonable" to denote anything more than "not unconscionable" or "not rendering the right to redeem illusory," it is considered that the principles stated by the Court of Appeal can be confidently accepted as representing the true modern doctrine of equity concerning postponement of the right to redeem. These principles are fully in accord with the opinions expressed by the House of Lords in *Kreglinger v New Patagonia Meat and Cold Storage Co Ltd*[76] upon the rules concerning the validity of collateral advantages.

30–15   The House of Lords in *Knightsbridge Estates Trust Ltd v Byrne*,[77] and both the courts below, were unanimous in holding that the rule against perpetuities has no application to a covenant in a mortgage suspending the contractual right to redeem for more than 21 years. The result therefore is that the modern principles concerning suspension of redemption are such that provided that a covenant suspending redemption is framed genuinely on an investment basis, not as a cloak for oppression, it will be valid unless (i) it renders the right to redeem illusory, or (ii) it is directly repugnant to the contractual and equitable rights to redeem.

In many of the more recent cases there has been the added factor to be considered of a contract made in unlawful restraint of trade in which the mortgagor has been "tied" by a "solus agreement" to sell the mortgagee's products for the duration of the mortgage. In *Esso Petroleum Co Ltd v Harper's Garage (Stourport) Ltd*[78] it was held that a covenant by a mortgagor to sell only the mortgagee's brand of petrol for 21 years and not to redeem the mortgage which was repayable by instalments over a 21-year period before the expiry of 21 years was void as it was in unreasonable restraint of trade. The mortgage was therefore redeemable.

It seems, however, that a postponement for a shorter period may be valid (as in *Texaco Ltd v Mulberry Filling Station*[79]). Further, if the tying provisions and

[75] [1940] A.C. 613, and see now Companies Act 2006 s.739.
[76] [1914] A.C. 25.
[77] [1940] A.C. 613.
[78] [1968] A.C. 269, following and extending the decision in *Petrofina (Great Britain) Ltd v Martin* [1966] Ch. 146; see also *Hill v Regent Oil Co Ltd* [1962] E.G.D. 452 and *Regent Oil Co Ltd v J. A. Gregory (Hatch End) Ltd* [1966] Ch. 402 (an earlier case reported later), in which the doctrine of restraint of trade was not mentioned.
[79] [1972] 1 W.L.R. 814.

the mortgage are separate and independent transactions, the restrictions being freely negotiated prior to the mortgage, the tie may well be valid provided that it is not unreasonable in duration.[80] It should also be added that in the *Esso* case[81] the House of Lords held valid a tie in respect of another garage owned by Harpers Ltd. But in this case the tie was for four-and-a-half years and no mortgage was involved.

Further, it has been stated that the doctrine only applies to an agreement where a person is required to give up an existing freedom to trade as opposed to a position where there was no such previous right.[82]

Ancillary matters—nature of the obligation secured

In conclusion it should be noticed that sometimes the very nature of the obliga-   **30–16** tion secured by a mortgage may render the security irredeemable for a considerable period without the mortgage being invalidated. Thus a mortgage may be made to secure an annuity during the life of some person or as an indemnity against contingent charges or for some other object not capable of immediate pecuniary valuation. Redemption in these cases is necessarily suspended for an uncertain period.[83]

Penalties: stipulations for enhanced sums due on redemption

A covenant is invalid if it imposes a penalty on the mortgagor for his failure to   **30–17** redeem on the contract date. Equity grants relief against penalties[84] in all kinds of contracts, but in the case of mortgages there is the added consideration that such covenants are designed, or at any rate calculated, to render redemption more difficult and are, therefore, clogs on the equity of redemption. Consequently, any additional sum expressed to be due from the mortgagor by reason of his default on the contract date is not recoverable by the mortgagee.[85] This principle does not, however, avoid a stipulation which obliges the mortgagor, when he redeems, to pay in respect of principal a sum greater than that actually advanced. This is not automatically unenforceable but falls to be considered in the same way as any other collateral advantage whether as a bonus or commission for making the advance, or possibly because either interest has been added to the advance[86] or because the principal is index-linked.[87] It is possible even that a premium might

---

[80] *Re Petrol Filling Station, Vauxhall Bridge Road* (1968) 20 P. & C.R. 1.

[81] [1968] A.C. 269.

[82] See *Esso Petroleum Ltd v Harper's Garage (Stourport) Ltd* [1968] A.C. 269 at 298, 306–309, 316–317. See also *Alec Lobb (Garages) Ltd v Total Oil (Great Britain) Ltd* [1985] 1 W.L.R. 1735 and contra, *Cleveland Petroleum Ltd v Dartstone Ltd* [1969] 1 W.L.R. 116. There is the somewhat questionable practice imposed by some finance houses which provides that if the mortgagor redeems within two or three years he pays three or six months additional "penalty" interest in any event and not in lieu of notice. Whether or not such a clause is a clog is yet to be decided.

[83] *Fleming v Self* (1854) 3 De G. M. & G. 997 at 1024; cf. Lindley L.J. in *Secretary of State in Council of India v British Empire Mutual Life Assurance Co* (1892) 67 L.T. 434 at 439.

[84] See Snell's *Principles of Equity* (30th edn, 2000), paras 36–01 to 36–14.

[85] *Booth v Salvation Army Building Association (Ltd)* (1897) 14 T.L.R. 3.

[86] *Cityland v Property (Holdings) Ltd v Dabrah* [1968] Ch. 166.

[87] *Multiservice Bookbinding Ltd. v Marden* [[1979] Ch. 84

be added in place of interest where the rate represented by the premium is reasonable.[88] Obviously, the size of that premium may of itself render the right of redemption illusory. It must be born in mind that the court may, in circumstances where the provision is unreasonable (and, as a consequence, not payable), order the payment of interest at a rate fixed by the court. Since the repeal of the usury laws there is no objection to such a stipulation if the mortgage is not otherwise unconscionable.[89]

Enhanced interest rates

30–18   An analogous rule invalidates a provision whereby the rate of interest is unreasonably increased if it is not paid punctually. Such a provision can constitute a penalty and is accordingly void.[90] However, in *Lordsvale Finance Plc v Bank of Zambia*,[91] Colman J. held that there was no reason why a contractual provision, the effect of which was to increase the interest rate that was payable under an executory contract on the default of one party, should be struck down if the increase could in the circumstances be commercially justified provided its dominant purpose was not to deter the other party from breach. Thus an increase in interest of one per cent per annum upon the default of the paying party was held to be unenforceable by reason of the increased credit risk of a borrower in default. Furthermore, there is no objection to a provision which stipulates for a higher rate of interest *reducible on punctual payment* to the rate agreed by the parties.[92] Nor does the rule invalidate a stipulation for compound interest. Formerly objection was taken to such stipulations on the ground of usury,[93] but after the abolition of the usury laws in 1854 and their subsequent replacement by the Moneylenders Acts 1900–1927, objection was no longer taken (unless the transactions fell within the provisions of the latter Acts which, inter alia, forbade the charging of compound interest in moneylending transactions).

Now, in addition to the courts' general equitable jurisdiction to interfere with a mortgage transaction where one of the terms is oppressive and unconscionable,[94] since the repeal of the Moneylenders Acts the courts have had a statutory jurisdiction to interfere in extortionate credit bargains under the Consumer Credit Act 1974 and now enjoy a broader discretion to do so under the amended provisions of that Act where it is satisfied of the existence of an unfair credit relationship.[95]

---

[88] *Cityland v Property (Holdings) Ltd v Dabrah* (above).

[89] *Potter v Edwards* (1857) 26 L.J.Ch. 468; *Mainland v Upjohn* (1889) L.R. 41 Ch.D. 126; cf. *James v Kerr* (1889) L.R. 40 Ch.D. 449 where in all the circumstances the mortgage itself was unconscionable; *Bucknell v Vickery* (1891) 64 L.T. 701.

[90] *Holles v Wyse* (1693) 2 Vern. 289.

[91] [1996] Q.B. 752.

[92] *Strode v Parker* (1694) 2 Vern. 316; this provision is construed strictly against the mortgagor, so that his payments must be exactly punctual if he is to be entitled to pay the lower rate, *Maclaine v Gatty* [1921] 1 A.C. 376.

[93] *Clarkson v Henderson* (1880) L.R. 14 Ch.D. 348.

[94] See para.30–35.

[95] See above, para.30–08.

Conclusion

The present approach to clogs (quite apart from judicial comments referred to **30–19**
above to the effect that the doctrine is an appendix to the law which no longer
serves a useful purpose) is best illustrated by the decision of the Morgan J. in
Brighton & City Council v Audus.[96] The Council was the proprietor of a
registered charge taken in 2008 over Mrs Bull's leasehold flat to cover the
reimbursement of nursing home fees incurred by Mrs Bull and paid by the
Council. The charge ranked third behind two earlier charges both created in 1998.
The first covered the payment to Mrs Bull by Mr Audus (her nephew) of the
purchase price of the grant of the lease to Mrs Bull under the Right to Buy
Legislation. The second charge, said to be a supplemental deed, provided that if
the principal charge was ever redeemed, Mrs Bull would be obliged to pay to Mr
Audus the whole of the difference between the principal charge and the market
value of the property. The Council sought declaratory relief to the effect that the
second charge was either repugnant to the right to redeem created by the
principal charge or made that illusory. On the facts, Mrs Bull had remained in the
flat rent and service charge free, the agreement being that on her death the flat
would belong to Mr Audus.

The judge referred to *Warnborough Ltd v Garmite Ltd*[97] saying that " ...
where there is a composite transaction, which includes as one of its elements a
genuine mortgage, it is open to the Court to assess the overall character of the
composite transaction and identify that character as being other than that of
mortgage."[98] He concluded that although there was an admitted mortgage, the
reality of the transaction was that Mr Audus would buy and own the flat but his
rights were to be postponed to the right of Mrs Bull to live in the flat for life. The
concomitant conclusion was that the transaction was not in fact a loan or security
for a loan at all—the scheme was the unfortunate "brainchild" of Mr Audus's
solicitor at the time. The very difficulty in discerning the difference between a
transaction which includes an admitted mortgage but which overall either is or is
not a transaction of mortgage, will, it seems, make it easier for the courts to
abrogate the doctrine of clogs on the equity without the need for the "appendectomy" referred to above particularly in cases where no unfairness on the part of
the mortgagee is alleged.

Collateral advantages

A stipulation which, being a term of a mortgage, secures to the mortgagee an **30–20**
advantage outside his principal and interest is invalid if it (i) defeats or renders
illusory the right to redeem, under the propositions discussed above, (ii) is
repugnant to the right to redeem under the second rule; (iii) clogs the equity of
redemption; or (iv) forms part of a mortgage contract obtained oppressively or

[96] [2010] 1 All E.R. (Comm) 343, above at fn.50.
[97] *Warnborough Ltd v Garmite Ltd* [2007] 1 P. & C.R. 2.
[98] At [55].

through undue influence under the rules discussed elsewhere.[99] These rules do not however prevent a mortgagor from including advantageous clauses which either do not affect the property or which affect the property but which cease on redemption.

The position before 1854

30–21   Before the repeal of the usury laws, equitable principles concerning collateral advantages were somewhat obscured by the existence of absolute limitations on the rate of interest which might legally be charged for a loan: for a mortgagee who insisted on an advantage additional to his interest might well appear to be evading the usury laws. At any rate, it appears that before 1854 collateral advantages were not enforceable. Thus in *Jennings v Ward*[100] Trevor M.R. said:

> "A man shall not have interest for his money and a collateral advantage besides for the loan of it, or clog the redemption with any by-agreement."

30–22   It is evident that this much quoted dictum propounds two distinct principles: (i) that a mortgagee may not obtain an advantage additional to his interest; (ii) a collateral covenant must not operate to impede redemption. If the first proposition is correct, the second is unnecessary; but there is ample authority that the first proposition is no longer law.

The modern position

30–23   In *Biggs v Hoddinott*[101] the Court of Appeal went so far as to declare that in all previous cases in which a collateral advantage had been disallowed it had been such as either to clog the equity of redemption or to render the mortgage oppressive. The court went on to decide that following the repeal of the usury laws collateral advantages are not in themselves objectionable and that they will be valid provided that: (i) they do not make the bargain harsh and unconscionable; and (ii) they do not clog the equity of redemption. As to the first test, we shall see that a mortgage is not unconscionable merely because it appears unduly favourable to the mortgagee and is therefore unreasonable as regards the mortgagor. Collateral advantages will not be considered unconscionable unless they were extorted from the mortgagor by active exploitation of his weakness through oppression or undue influence. It is the application of the second test which is here mainly discussed, namely, when a collateral advantage "clogs" the equity of redemption.

Collateral a financing advantage

30–24   A collateral stipulation is plainly a clog if its effect is to render the security irredeemable on any event whatever. In these cases, which have already been

[99] See below, para.30–35.
[100] (1705) 2 Vern. 520 at 521.
[101] [1898] 2 Ch. 307. When considering collateral advantages which restrain trade, see above, paras 17–07 et seq. and below, para.30–33.

explained, the collateral stipulation may be repugnant not only to the equitable but also to the legal right to redeem.[102] For example, the grant of an option to purchase is inconsistent with the contractual right to redeem, as well as with the equity of redemption, when the option is exercisable before the contract date for redemption. On the other hand, it is equally evident that a collateral advantage is no clog if it ceases to affect both the security and the mortgagor the moment the legal or the equitable right to redeem is exercised. Thus, in *Biggs v Hoddinott*, a hotel was mortgaged to a brewery company with mutual covenants by mortgagor and mortgagee to continue the mortgage for five years. In addition, the mortgagor covenanted that during the five years and afterwards, while any money was still due on the mortgage, he would purchase from the company all the beer sold or consumed at the hotel. The court held that (i) five years was in the circumstances a reasonable period for the suspension of the contractual right to redeem; and (ii) the equity of redemption was not in any way clogged by a covenant which was to be operative only until redemption took place. This decision has received the emphatic approval of the House of Lords.[103]

Collateral advantages secured on the property

But what if the collateral stipulation is expressed to bind the mortgagor abso- **30–25** lutely during a specified period while the mortgage allows for redemption before the end of that period, i.e. before the expiry of the period at the end of which the collateral advantage ceases? Is the mortgagor to be bound until the end of the named period, or do the doctrines of equity demand that he be automatically released from the stipulation if he redeems before that time?[104] For a covenant may be so framed that the collateral advantage is as much charged on the security as the principal and interest itself, in which case the mortgagor, by the contract, is not entitled to a reconveyance of his security until the end of the period during which the collateral advantage is intended to operate. Thus in *Santley v Wilde*,[105] the tenant of a theatre borrowed £2,000 at 6 per cent on a mortgage of her lease which still had 10 years to run. In addition she agreed to pay to the mortgagee during the rest of the lease one-third of the net profits to be derived from any underleases of the theatre. Moreover, she gave an express covenant that even if she repaid the loan the mortgage should continue in existence to secure the payment of the share of profits.

The Court of Appeal pointed out that a mortgage can be redeemed only when **30–26** all the obligations have been discharged for which the mortgage was given; and that in this case redemption, by the contract of the parties, could not take place until the covenant to pay a share of the profits had been fully performed. The covenant was a business agreement between parties at arm's length and was

---

[102] *Kreglinger v New Patagonia Meat and Cold Storage Co Ltd* [1914] A.C. 25 at 50, per Lord Parker.

[103] *Noakes and Co Ltd v Rice* [1902] A.C. 24; *Bradley v Carritt* [1903] A.C. 253; *Kreglinger v New Patagonia Meat and Cold Storage Co Ltd* [1914] A.C. 25.

[104] The stipulation is never void ab initio, unless it is actually unconscionable; it is void, if at all, only after redemption.

[105] [1899] 2 Ch. 474.

upheld. Lindley M.R. in a classic passage,[106] explained the doctrine of clogs on the equity of redemption:

30-27   "A mortgage is a conveyance of land or an assignment of chattels as a security for the payment of a debt or the discharge of some other obligation for which it is given. This is the idea of a mortgage: and the security is redeemable on the payment or discharge of such debt or obligation, any provision to the contrary notwithstanding. . . . Any provision inserted to prevent redemption on payment or performance of the debt or obligation for which the security was given is what is meant by a clog or fetter on the equity of redemption, and is therefore void. It follows from this that 'once a mortgage always a mortgage'; but I do not understand that this principle involves the further proposition that the amount or nature of the further debt or obligation, the payment or performance of which is to be secured, is a clog or fetter within the rule. . . . Of course, the debt or obligation may be impeachable for fraud, oppression or overreaching. . . . But putting such cases out of the question, when you get a security for a debt or obligation, that security can be redeemed the moment the debt or obligation is paid or performed, but on no other terms."

The principles stated by Lindley M.R. in the above passage have frequently been approved, although the actual decision in *Santley v Wilde* was strongly criticised by Lords Macnaghten and Davey in *Noakes v Rice*.[107] It is open to the objection that it takes no account of the fact that the mortgagor was prevented from discharging his obligations until a time when his security ceased to exist. The collateral covenant made the security irredeemable and there is thus some difficulty in reconciling the decision with that of the House of Lords in *Fairclough v Swan Brewery Co Ltd*.[108] Although there is no objection in principle to a mortgagee retaining a security for the performance of a collateral stipulation even *after* payment of principal and interest, the covenant, it is submitted, must not be such as to defeat or render illusory the right to redeem nor such as to be repugnant to it. In the light of later cases, the only way in which it seems possible to support the admittedly desirable decision in *Santley v Wilde*[109] is by holding that the transaction was not in essence one of mortgage, but a partnership agreement to share in the profits of the theatre.[110]

Collateral advantage not secured upon the property

30-28   Normally the collateral advantage is not made a charge on the security. Although the additional stipulation is expressed to be binding until a named date, redemption is allowed *before* that date on payment of principal, interest and costs without more, leaving the collateral advantage outstanding. In consequence, the performance of the collateral stipulation is not one of the terms of redemption. Thus, in *Noakes v Rice*[111]:

---

[106] ibid., at 475.
[107] [1902] A.C. 24.
[108] [1912] A.C. 565.
[109] [1899] 2 Ch. 474.
[110] See Waldock, *Law of Mortgages* (2nd edn, 1950), p.187.
[111] [1900] 2 Ch. at 445 and [1902] A.C. 24 (HL).

"On mortgaging the lease of a public-house a mortgagor covenanted that during the whole remainder of the lease (which still had twenty-six years to run) no beer would be sold at the public-house, except beer bought from the mortgagees. The mortgage moneys, on the other hand, were made repayable on demand by either side, and there was an express proviso for reconveyance of the security on payment of principal, interest and costs."

The House of Lords decided unanimously that the collateral advantage was a clog upon redemption because it was repugnant to the mortgagor's right to recover his security *intact and unimpaired by the mortgage*. The covenant turned a free public-house into a tied house. In this case the fetter on the mortgaged property was direct but a covenant will, it seems, be just as much a clog if it indirectly impairs the enjoyment of the property not by fettering the property itself but by imposing personal obligations on the mortgagor which make it advisable (though not compulsory) for him to enjoy his property in a particular way. In *Bradley v Carritt*[112] the defendant, who had a controlling interest in a tea company, mortgaged his shares to the claimant, who was a tea-broker, and, as part of the consideration, covenanted to use his best endeavours always thereafter to secure that the company should continue to employ the mortgagee as their broker; if the company should cease to do so he was to pay to the mortgagee the amount of commission the latter would have earned had his services been retained. The collateral stipulation was personal to the mortgagor and its performance was not made a charge on the security.

The mortgagor redeemed his shares and the House of Lords (Lords Lindley and Shand dissenting) decided that the collateral covenant was no longer binding since it was a clog on the equity of redemption. The difference of opinion between the majority of the court (Lords Macnaghten, Davey and Robertson) and Lords Lindley and Shand, lay not so much in the principle to be applied as in its application to the particular case.[113] Thus, Lord Macnaghten found in the covenant a contrivance calculated to impede redemption because, by making it advisable for the mortgagor to retain control of his shares after redemption, the covenant indirectly fettered his right to recover his security unimpaired by the mortgage. Lord Lindley, on the other hand, was unable to comprehend how the covenant, which was purely personal to the mortgagor and did not *bind* him to deal with the shares in any particular way, could possibly clog the equity of redemption when it was open to the mortgagor to recover his security merely by paying up principal, interest and costs.

The modern position

The difficulty in reconciling *Bradley v Carritt* with the later decision of the **30–29** House of Lords in *Kreglinger v New Patagonia Meat Co Ltd*[114] has led some writers to treat the earlier case as no longer of any importance. But, although

---

[112] [1903] A.C. 253.

[113] cf. Lord Parker in *Kreglinger v New Patagonia Meat Co* [1914] A.C. 25 at 59.

[114] [1914] A.C. 25 at 59; applied in *Re Cuban Land and Development Co (1911) Ltd* [1921] 2 Ch. 147 and *Brighton & Hove City Council v Audus* [2010] 1 All E.R. (Comm) 343.

some of the dicta of Lords Macnaghten and Davey in *Bradley v Carritt*[115] are disapproved by the judges in *Kreglinger v New Patagonia Meat Co Ltd*, the decisions in the two cases are not irreconcilable. Consequently the earlier case must, it is submitted, still be treated as laying down that a collateral covenant, which is a term of the mortgage and may endure *after* redemption, may constitute a clog on the equity although it imposes a purely personal obligation on the mortgagor.

In *Bradley v Carritt*, Lords Macnaghten and Davey both expressed the opinion that collateral advantages are only another form of interest and therefore must come to an end when the principal sum is repaid. Consequently it appeared to have been settled that in no circumstances could a collateral advantage survive redemption. In *Kreglinger*'s case, however, this reasoning was decisively rejected by a unanimous court who pointed out that it was unnecessary for the decision in *Bradley v Carritt*.

30–30   *The test of severability:*   In *Kreglinger*'s case the House of Lords refused to admit that a covenant clogged the equity of redemption merely because it was contained in a mortgage deed and by its nature might continue to impose obligations on the mortgagor after redemption. *Kreglinger*'s case appears to decide that, just as equity looks at the substance of a transaction rather than at its form to see if the transaction is really a mortgage and even admits parol evidence to explain the deed, so it will look at the intention of the parties rather than at the form of the documents to see if a collateral covenant was intended to be truly a constituent element of the mortgage or an independent severable bargain linked to a mortgage in a larger business transaction but not constituting a term of the mortgage. In the latter case the collateral covenant does not touch the mortgage relationship and stands entirely outside the equitable principles protecting the right to redeem.

This principle will more easily be understood if regard is had to the case of *De Beers Consolidated Mines Ltd v B.S.A. Co.*[116] De Beers, who had already lent the B.S.A. Co £112,000 and were proposing to lend a further £100,000, contracted for the grant of a licence to work diamond mines in consideration of "the assistance rendered and to be rendered" by them to the company. The contract was not itself a mortgage but contained a provision enabling the company, in lieu of repayment, to cover the loan by issuing debenture stock and assigning an appropriate amount of stock to De Beers. The grant of the loan was not, however, conditional on the issue of the debentures. The company issued debentures and assigned to De Beers sufficient stock to cover the loan. Subsequently they redeemed the debentures and claimed that the licence was no longer binding on them.

30–31   The House of Lords had no hesitation in rejecting this claim. The licence had been obtained by a contract independent of and preliminary to the mortgage transaction. This contract did not even compel the company to grant a mortgage, but, when they did so, they could only mortgage assets which were already bound by the licence. The protection of the equity of redemption does not require the

---

[115] [1903] A.C. 253.
[116] [1912] A.C. 52.

court to free a man of pre-existing obligations when he mortgages his property to the obligee. Similarly, the court in *Kreglinger*'s case[117] held that there were two independent contracts, a contract for the grant of an option and a contract of mortgage. The separation of the mortgage from the other contract was by no means so obvious as in *De Beers v British South Africa Co.*[118]

The facts of *Kreglinger*'s case were these: the appellants, a firm of wool-brokers, consented to lend £10,000 to the respondents, a meat company, in consideration of obtaining an option on such sheep skins as the respondents might have for sale to the public. The £10,000 was lent at 6 per cent. and was secured by a floating charge on the assets of the meat company. If the latter paid the interest punctually, the appellants were not to call in their money for five years. The terms of the option[119] were that it was to extend over a period of five years, *but this period was not co-extensive with that during which the appellants were not to call in their loan.* The price to be paid for the skins was to be equal to the best price offered by anyone else, while the respondents were to pay a commission of 1 per cent on any skins sold to other buyers at the best market price. The respondents repaid the loan after only two years and claimed to be at once relieved of their obligation to offer their sheep skins to the appellants.

The House of Lords decided unanimously that the option continued to bind the mortgagors notwithstanding the termination of the mortgage. The construction placed upon the transaction by the court was that it contained two distinct bargains—the sale of an option and the loan of money on security—and that although these two bargains were contemporaneous and in fact formulated in the same deed, they were intended by the parties to be independent of each other. Thus, although the sale of the option was a condition precedent to the grant of the *loan* it was not intended to form a term *in the mortgage* but rather to be a separate contract as much outside the terms of the mortgage as the grant of the licence in *De Beers v B.S.A. Co.*[120] In short, the collateral covenant was not repugnant to the mortgagor's right to recover his security unfettered *by the mortgage* because, in the intention of the parties, the mortgage was the grant of a security already subject[121] to the option.

Applying the test of severability

The question whether a collateral stipulation is a condition independent of the **30–32** mortgage, not touching equitable principles concerning redemption of mortgages, or an actual term of the mortgage is, of course, a question of the intention of the parties in each case such that no one case will be a precise authority for another. *Bradley v Carritt*[122] and *Kreglinger*'s case[123] can be reconciled on this ground although it must be admitted that the majority judges in *Bradley v Carritt*

---

[117] [1914] A.C. 25 and see and *Brighton & Hove City Council v Audus* [2010] 1 All E.R. (Comm) 343.
[118] [1912] A.C. 52.
[119] Perhaps a right of pre-emption.
[120] [1912] A.C. 52.
[121] Or at any rate, made subject to the option by an independent agreement.
[122] [1903] A.C. 253.
[123] [1914] A.C. 25.

held views widely divergent from those of the unanimous court in *Kreglinger's* case. The earlier case represents the high-water mark of the old conception of a mortgage as an exaction from a man who is not a free agent. *Kreglinger's* case,[124] by excluding from equitable doctrines concerning mortgages those cases where collateral covenants do not in the true intention of the parties constitute a term of the mortgage, has to this extent prevented genuine commercial bargains between equal parties at arm's length from being upset by technical doctrines framed to defeat usury and oppression.

Ultimately, it may be that the distinction to be drawn between the cases rests on the reluctance of the courts on the one hand to interfere in commercial transactions freely negotiated at arm's length (albeit unfair to one party), and the vigilance of the courts on the other hand to protect individuals who have been persuaded to enter into a disadvantageous trading transaction as a condition of the grant of the loans. However, even this interpretation does not lay at rest the difficulties of reconciling the various cases—purportedly based on the balance between advantages which are consideration for the loan on the one hand (which are lawful), and those which are collateral. Those decisions turn on the substance (and not the form) of the transaction and require an investigation of the real nature of the bargain. Perhaps the view expressed by Megarry and Wade in *The Law of Real Property*[125] that the "severability" test introduced in the *Kreglinger* case "provides a convenient but indefinable rule for dealing with such cases on their merits" sums up the difficulties in the attempts to reconcile the differences.

Restraint of trade clauses

30–33   It should also be noted that it was not until *Esso Petroleum Co Ltd v Harper's Garage (Stourport) Ltd*[126] that the issue of restraint of trade was raised in the "tie" cases with a mortgage element. Thus neither in *Biggs v Hoddinott*[127] nor in *Noakes v Rice*[128] was this issue canvassed with the result that they should now perhaps be regarded as of doubtful authority on their particular facts. As a result of the *Esso* case, such covenants in mortgages will be prima facie void unless they are shown to be reasonable[129] in the light of the circumstances irrespective of whether or not they are rendered void in accordance with equitable principles.[130]

Conclusion

30–34   Thus, if a mortgagee intends to impose the burden of a collateral advantage on the mortgagor for a specified period without also suspending redemption during

---

[124] ibid.

[125] (7th edn, 2008), para.25–098 See also para.3.35 Law Commission's Working Paper No.99, "Land Mortgages".

[126] [1968] A.C. 269; and see above, para.30–15.

[127] [1898] 2 Ch. 307.

[128] [1902] A.C. 24; nor indeed, in *Hills v Regent Oil Co Ltd* [1962] E.G.D. 452 and *Regent Oil Co Ltd v J. A. Gregory (Hatch End) Ltd* [1966] Ch. 402.

[129] A more simple test than having regard to equitable principles.

[130] It is also possible that mortgage terms could be challenged on the grounds that they infringe the competition provisions under EU law. See also *Courage Ltd v Crehan* [1999] 2 E.G.L.R. 145.

that period, the deed or deeds must be so drawn that the court can reasonably infer an intention to keep the collateral advantage outside the terms of the mortgage.[131] For although the substance of the agreement is the determining factor, the language of the deeds is, of course, the best evidence of the actual intention. Viscount Haldane L.C. indeed suggested in *Kreglinger*'s case that[132]:

> "the validity of the bargain in such cases as *Bradley v Carritt* and *Santley v Wilde* might have been made free from serious question if the parties had chosen to seek what would have been substantially the same result in a different form."

Accordingly, it is submitted that a covenant giving a mortgagee advantages beyond his principal and interest is valid if:

(1) the covenant is truly collateral to the mortgage in the sense that the covenant, as a matter of construction, is not one of the terms of the mortgage; or

(2) the covenant, though a term of the mortgage, does not conflict with the three preceding equitable rules for the protection of the equity of redemption and does not form part of a mortgage extorted by oppression or undue influence; and

(3) the stipulation is not in restraint of trade; and

(4) it is not otherwise oppressive or unconscionable.[133]

REDEMPTION OF OPPRESSIVE AND UNCONSCIONABLE MORTGAGES

Equity will permit an individual to redeem a mortgage which affects his property **30–35** and which has been obtained unconscionably or by the exercise of undue influence and, on occasions, to do so without charge. The law concerning such mortgages and other instances where a mortgagor may not be bound are discussed elsewhere.[134]

REDEMPTION IN COURT

Generally

Redemption takes place when a mortgagor, either under the terms of his covenant **30–36** or under the principles of equity, discharges the obligations imposed by the mortgage and thus becomes entitled to have his property revested in him free of

---

[131] Although the point is not noted in the judgments, it is submitted that in *Kreglinger*'s case it would have been more difficult to construe the sale of the option as an independent bargain if the period during which the option was to be exercisable had been coincident with the period during which the mortgagees were not to call in their money.

[132] [1914] A.C. 25 at 43.

[133] See para.30–35.

[134] See Ch.31.

the charge. Until the debt has been paid and the money accepted, however, the mortgage remains in being.[135] The mortgagor's right is to have his property returned to him contemporaneously with the due discharge of his obligations, so that it is the duty of the mortgagee at once to execute the instruments necessary to terminate the mortgage. In *Graham v Seal*,[136] Swinfen Eady M.R. said:

> "The obligation of a mortgagee is, as against payment of what is due to him, to reconvey and deliver up the deeds of the mortgaged premises. It is like the obligation of a vendor to convey and hand over the title deeds and the conveyance as against payment of the purchase-money. It contemplates that the handing over of the conveyance and payment of the purchase-money shall be a simultaneous transaction, so that neither party is at risk for any time without either the money or the estate; so in the paying off of a mortgage a mortgagee is not entitled to insist upon payment of the mortgage money with a view to his reconveying at some future time."

Consequently, if a mortgagee has been fully satisfied and refuses to reconvey the security, he will have to pay the costs of any proceedings taken by the mortgagor to recover his property.[137] Even a valid tender of the mortgage debt is not, however, *equivalent* to payment. Although a tender may have the effect of stopping the running of interest and of throwing the risk of the costs of a redemption action on the mortgagee,[138] the mortgagor's obligations are not finally discharged until his tender has been accepted, or if not accepted, the money is set aside.[139] Thus, in the case of a mortgage with a deposit of title deeds, if the mortgagee improperly refuses a tender, an action for trespass to goods or wrongful interference with goods under the Torts (Interference with Goods) Act 1977 will probably not lie for the deeds at the suit of the mortgagor (but, of course, would in the event of payment).[140] If the mortgagor disputes the amount claimed by the mortgagee, his only remedy[141] is to bring an action for redemption.

Exercising the right

30–37   A mortgagor exercises his right to redeem in one of two ways—either (i) out of court, by inducing the mortgagee to accept a tender of the money due under the mortgage; or (ii) by bringing the mortgagee into court in an action for redemption and afterwards complying with the court's order for the payment of the mortgage debt. He has, of course, no right whatever to redeem, either at law or in equity,

---

[135] *Samuel Keller (Holdings) Ltd v Martins Bank Ltd* [1971] 1 W.L.R. 43.

[136] (1918) 88 L.J.Ch. 31 at 35.

[137] *Walker v Jones* (1866) L.R. 1 P.C. 50.

[138] See Lindley M.R. in *Greenwood v Sutcliffe* [1892] 1 Ch. 1 at 10; *Graham v Seal* (1918) 88 L.J.Ch. 31; *Harmer v Priestly* (1863) 16 Beav 569; *Bank of New South Wales v O'Connor* (1889) L.R. 14 App. Cas. 273 (PC).

[139] *Barratt v Gough-Thomas (No.3)* [1951] W.N. 309; and see below, paras 30–49 et seq.

[140] *Bank of New South Wales v O'Connor* (1889) L.R. 14 App. Cas. 273, where a claim for detinue was rejected. Similarly, a mortgagee cannot be held liable for negligence for loss of the deeds, see *Browning v Handiland Group Ltd* (1978) 35 P. & C.R. 345.

[141] He is, however, advised to make a tender in order to put the responsibility for the extra costs on the mortgagee: *Greenwood v Sutcliffe* [1892] 1 Ch. 1.

until the day named in the mortgage as the date for repayment.[142] Before that date he cannot maintain an action for redemption against the mortgagee, while if he tenders to the mortgagee a sum representing principal and full interest right up to the contract date, plus costs, the latter is not bound to reconvey the security nor, indeed, to accept the money. The case is, however, different if the mortgagee by demanding payment or by taking steps to enforce payment (for example, by taking possession) himself disturbs the relation between the parties set up by the contract. The mortgagor may then redeem at once and need only tender the amount of the principal, plus interest *up to the date of the tender* and costs.[143]

Notice of intention to redeem

At law

A mortgagor who is redeeming on the contract date need not give notice of his **30–38** intention to redeem.[144] He need only attend on the day named and tender to the mortgagee the full amount of the mortgage debt, plus costs, observing any conditions there may be as to time and place of payment. If the contract allows the mortgagor to redeem on demand he need do no more than give the mortgagee a reasonable opportunity to look up the deeds and prepare the instrument for the discharge of the mortgage.[145] Moreover, redemption may be made on demand in all cases where the mortgage contains no proviso for redemption or express covenant for payment. Equitable mortgages by deposit of title deeds do not, as a rule, fix any date either for redemption or repayment and either party may terminate the mortgage on demand.[146] A mortgage can no longer be created by mere deposit.[147]

In equity

However, if, as usually happens, the mortgagor allows the contract date for **30–39** payment to pass without redeeming so that at law he is in default, it is a settled rule of equity that he must give the mortgagee six months' notice of his intention to redeem.[148] In practical terms, the majority of modern mortgages contain express notice provisions which provide the necessary period. The reason for this is that the mortgagor, having lost his estate at law, will only be allowed to redeem in equity on the terms that he does equity to the mortgagee by giving the latter a reasonable opportunity to find a new investment for his money.[149] A mortgagee

---

[142] *Brown v Cole* (1845) 14 Sim. 427.

[143] *Bovill v Endle* [1896] 1 Ch. 648.

[144] See *Crickmore v Freeston* (1870) 40 L.J.Ch. 137.

[145] *Toms v Wilson* (1863) 4 B. & S. 442.

[146] *Fitzgerald Trustees v Mellersh* [1892] 1 Ch. 385.

[147] Law of Property (Miscellaneous Provisions) Act 1989 s.2, and see *United Bank of Kuwait v Sahib* [1997] Ch. 107.

[148] *Shrapnell v Blake* (1737) West. T. Hard. 166. *Smith v Smith* [1891] 3 Ch. 550; cf. Maugham J. in *Cromwell Property Investment Co v Western and Toovey* [1934] Ch. 322 at 331, 332.

[149] *Browne v Lockhart* (1840) 10 Sim. 420 at 424, per Shadwell V.-C.

may, of course, agree to accept repayment at shorter notice but his right is to a clear six months' notice. Even though it may be possible to find suitable investments in less than six months, it appears to remain the settled practice that a mortgagee is entitled to that amount of notice regardless of the nature of the property mortgaged.[150] Exceptions to the rule have been allowed when a mortgagee either demands his money (athough a mortgagee cannot claim interest in lieu of notice where he has waived that right by his own action),[151] or takes proceedings (for example, foreclosure proceedings)[152] or steps to enforce payment[153] (for example, by taking possession). The mortgagor may then redeem at any moment by paying up the principal, plus interest up to the date of payment and costs[154] and he is not deprived of this right even if he has previously given notice of an intention to redeem in six months' time.[155] It need scarcely be said that a mortgagor may always dispense with the giving of notice, subject to the precise contractual terms, by offering to pay six months' interest in lieu of notice.[156]

Failure to redeem on notice date

30–40   Since a mortgagee is entitled to have six months' notice of the date of payment, it follows that if the mortgagor fails to tender the amount due on the date fixed by his notice he is bound either to give a fresh notice, or its equivalent in additional interest (whether or not the notice was given by him or by the mortgagor) save in circumstances where notice was given by the mortgagor and there is a proper explanation for the non-payment.[157] Otherwise the mortgagee might be put to inconvenience and loss in finding a new investment. In this instance, however, there is no rigid rule that the further period of notice must be one of six months. At the most the mortgagee is entitled to a reasonable amount of further notice. Thus, in one case,[158] a mortgagee had agreed to take payment if he were given three months' notice. Notice was duly given but owing to conveyancing difficulties payment could not be made on the due date. Maugham J. held that the mortgagee was entitled in the circumstances to the benefit of only three months' further notice. He also pointed out that even this period of notice

---

[150] *Cromwell Property Investment Co v Toovey* [1934] Ch. 322 at 331, 332, *Centrax Trustees Ltd v Ross* [1979] 2 All E.R. 952 at 955–956—both decisions at first instance. *Querie* whether should be the practice in the investment environment of the 21st century.

[151] *Banner v Berridge* (1881) L.R. 18 Ch.D. 254).

[152] *Hill v Rowlands* [1897] 2 Ch. 361 at 363; or, e.g. giving the mortgagor notice to repay the debt so as to entitle the mortgagee to sell on default being made, *Edmondson v Copland* [1911] 2 Ch. 301.

[153] per Romer J. *Smith v Smith* [1891] 3 Ch. 550 at 552.

[154] *Bovill v Endle* [1896] 1 Ch. 648; *Letts v Hutchins* (1871) L.R. 13 Eq. 176; the same rule applies in the case of a bill of sale: *Ex p. Wickens* [1898] 1 Q.B. 543.

[155] *Re Alcock* (1883) L.R. 23 Ch.D. 372 at 376. Although the court would have considered the point had the mortgagee altered his financial position as a result of the mortgagors' notice.

[156] *Johnson v Evans* (1889) 61 L.T. 18. As to those contractual terms and the Unfair Terms in Consumer Contract Regulations 1999 (SI 1999/2083), see also Ch.16, above.

[157] *Bartlett v Franklin* (1867) 15 W.R. 1077; *Re Moss* (1885) L.R. 31 Ch.D. 90; *Edmund v Copland* [1911] 2 Ch. 30.

[158] *Cromwell Investment Co v Western and Toovey* [1934] Ch. 322.

would not have been allowed if the mortgagor had not failed to communicate with the mortgagee for several days after the expiry of the first notice. He declared that the right to further notice is by no means automatic. If the mortgagor gives a reasonable explanation of the reason why a short delay is necessary and keeps the mortgagee advised as to when payment may be expected, redemption will be allowed on payment of principal, plus the interest due only up to the actual date of payment, plus, of course, costs. In any case, a mortgagee will not be entitled to six months' further notice where the security is a fund in court and he has been a party to an order directing payment of his debt out of that fund. By accepting the order he assents to be governed by all the contingencies to which the completion of the order may be subject.[159]

Redemption and interest

Once the contract date has passed, the mortgagor insisting on redemption must **30–41** pay interest on the loan. This applies even if the mortgage makes no provision for the payment of interest, and it includes statute-barred interest.[160] If necessary, the court will fix the rate of such interest.[161] He must also pay the mortgagee's proper costs in any redemption action brought by the mortgagor including any expenses incurred by the mortgagee in protecting his security.[162] These costs are not payable personally by the mortgagor[163] but are added to the secured debt and are payable as a condition of redemption. This forms a single debt with the principal and interest, payable in the same priority.[164]

Persons entitled to redeem[165]

The right to redeem is not confined to the mortgagor or even to those claiming **30–42** through him. It is exercisable by any person who either has an interest in the mortgaged property[166] or is under a liability to pay the mortgage debt[167] irrespective of the size of their interest.[168] The mortgagor himself does not lose his right

---

[159] *Re Moss* (1886) 31 Ch.D. 90, above.

[160] See paras 6–53 et seq.

[161] See *Cityland and Property (Holdings) Ltd v Dabrah* [1968] Ch. 166; *Congresbury Motors Ltd v Anglo-Belge Finance Co Ltd* [1970] Ch. 294' [1969] 3 All ER 545; *Finance and Investment Pty Ltd v Van Kempen* (1986) 6 N.S.W.L.R. 305 (CA) and also *Wallersteiner v Moir (No.2)* [1975] Q.B. 373, 508n, and *Bartlett v Barclays Bank Trust Co Ltd (No.2)* [1980] Ch. 515.

[162] See *Sinfield v Sweet* [1967] 1 W.L.R. 1489. Absent an express term a mortgagor, however, is not personally liable for these expenses unless the redemption claim is dismissed because the mortgagor fails to redeem (*Mutual Life Assurance Society v Langley* (1886) L.R. 32 Ch.D. 460).

[163] *Sinfield v Sweet* [1967] 1 W.L.R. 1489.

[164] *Barnes v Racster* (1842) 1 Y&C Ch Cas 401; *Pollock v Lands Improvement Co* (1888) L.R. 37 Ch.D. 661 and *White v City of London Brewery Co* (1889) L.R. 42 Ch.D. 237.

[165] A stranger has no right to redeem. But a person who is entitled to redeem the mortgage may, instead of redeeming, insist that the mortgage be transferred to a stranger who is discharging the mortgage debt; Law of Property Act (LPA) 1925 s.95. See below, paras 30–53 et seq.

[166] *Pearce v Morris* (1869) L.R. 5 Ch. App. 227.

[167] *Green v Wynn* (1869) L.R. 4 Ch. App. 204.

[168] *Hunter v Macklew* (1846) 5 Hare 238.

to redeem until he has made an absolute assignment of his equity of redemption.[169] Even then his right will revive if he is sued on the personal covenant,[170] in which event he may redeem notwithstanding that the assignee has created fresh charges in favour of the mortgagee. If he assigns his equity of redemption by way of mortgage only, he does not lose his right to redeem the first mortgage, but he does alter his position to some extent, because the maxim "redeem up, foreclose down", prevents him from redeeming a prior mortgagee *by action* without at the same time redeeming all intermediate encumbrancers.[171] The right to redeem is not available to a Rent Act statutory tenant.[172]

Present owners of the ultimate equity of redemption have the same right to redeem as the original mortgagor whom they replace[173] even if they are statute-barred[174] and it makes no difference whether they are purchasers for value[175] or mere volunteers.[176] If the property is only subject to one encumbrance, their right to redeem is the only right to redeem but if there are successive encumbrances the primary right to redeem the first encumbrance is in the holder of the second and so on, and it is only the ultimate equity of redemption which remains in the mortgagor or those who represent him.[177] Consequently the latter can only redeem a first mortgage after the other encumbrancers have had the opportunity of exercising their prior rights. Persons who may redeem as holders of the ultimate equity of redemption[178] are:

(1) Assignees.[179] It makes no differences that the assignee acquires only a partial or limited interest in the property.[180] For example, a lessee under a lease, which is not binding on the mortgagee, may redeem.[181]

(2) Persons taking the equity of redemption under an intestacy or under a will.[182] On the death of a mortgagor the right to redeem first belongs to his personal representatives but will pass to the persons beneficially interested when an assent has been made in their favour.

(3) Trustees of land and life tenants under the Settled Land Act 1925. On the mortgage of land subject to a trust of land or of settled property,[183] the primary right to redeem is in either the trustees or, in the case of

---

[169] *Moore v Morton* (1886) W.N. 196.

[170] *Kinnaird v Trollope* (1888) L.R. 39 Ch.D. 636.

[171] See below, paras 30–43 et seq.

[172] *Britannia Building Society v Earl* [1990] 2 All E.R. 469.

[173] *Fell v Brown* (1787) 2 Bro.C.C. 276.

[174] *Cotterell v Price* [1960] 1 W.L.R. 1097.

[175] A purchaser for value, if he redeems, has no right to a conveyance of the legal estate from the mortgagee, or to delivery of the title deeds, unless he has already accepted his assignor's title: *Pearce v Morris* (1869) L.R. 5 Ch. App. 227.

[176] *Thorne v Thorne* (1683) 1 Vern. 182; *Howard v Harris* (1683) 1 Vern. 191; *Rand v Cartwright* (1664) 1 Cas. in Ch. 59.

[177] *Teevan v Smith* (1882) 20 Ch.D. 724 at 730.

[178] Subsequent encumbrancers can redeem as well but subject to particular rules: see para.30–44.

[179] *Kinnaird v Trollope* (1889) 58 L.J.Ch. 556.

[180] *Hunter v Maclew* (1846) 5 Hare 238.

[181] *Tarn v Turner* (1888) L.R. 39 Ch.D. 456.

[182] Administration of Estates Act 1925 ss.1 and 2.

[183] No new settlements of land may be made after January 1, 1997, see Trusts of Land and Appointment of Trustees Act 1996 s.2.

settled land, the estate owners. Consequently, when an equity of redemption is in settlement the beneficiaries, though they may redeem, must do so through their trustees or through the life tenant.[184] It is only when the trustees or estate owners are in collusion with the mortgagee, or otherwise refuse improperly to act, that the beneficiaries may take proceedings for redemption.[185] In any case, it must be remembered that a remainderman cannot redeem if the tenant for life objects.[186]

(4) Joint tenants and tenants in common. Each co-owner has a right to redeem provided that he discharges the whole debt and does not claim to redeem merely his own share.[187] Since 1925, however, co-ownership of land involves statutory trusts and presumably the rule that beneficiaries ought to redeem through their trustees applies. Consequently, in the case of land, a co-owner of the equity of redemption should proceed through the trustees.[188]

(5) In the case of two properties mortgaged to secure one debt, the owner of each property has an individual right to discharge the whole debt; indeed, since the mortgagee cannot be made to accept payment in instalments, if only one owner redeems he must redeem the whole mortgage and not merely his own share.[189]

(6) A surety or any person whose property is under any liability to satisfy the mortgage debt will be allowed to redeem.[190] For example, the doctrine of consolidation may render the purchaser of an equity of redemption in Blackacre liable to discharge a mortgage on Whiteacre in addition to that on Blackacre. This entitles him to redeem Whiteacre.

(7) A stranger, who has no title to the equity of redemption, *cannot* redeem; against him the mortgagee's title is absolute.[191]

(8) Creditors. General creditors of a mortgagor cannot redeem except in special circumstances, as when there is collusion between mortgagor and mortgagee.[192] Similarly, when the mortgaged property has been assigned to a trustee for the benefit of creditors, creditors who were parties to the deed must proceed through their trustee, but if the latter acts improperly they will be admitted to redeem.[193] Again, a judgment creditor, as such, has no right to redeem but will become entitled to do so if he has obtained a charging order[194] or he has obtained the

---

[184] *Troughton v Binkes* (1801) 6 Ves. 573; *Mills v Jennings* (1880) L.R. 13 Ch.D. 639.

[185] *Troughton v Binkes* (1801) 6 Ves. 573. It may also be possible for the beneficiaries to apply for relief under s.14 of the Trusts of Land and Appointment of Trustees Act 1996—see s.6.

[186] *Prout v Cock* [1896] 2 Ch. 808.

[187] *Marquis of Cholmondeley v Lord Clinton* (1820) 2 J. & W. 1 at 134; *Pearce v Morris* (1869) L.R. 5 Ch. App. 227.

[188] See Trustees of Land and Appointment of Trustees Act 1996 s.5, and Sch.2 para.7.

[189] *Hall v Heward* (1886) L.R. 32 Ch.D. 430.

[190] *Green v Wynn* (1869) L.R. 4 Ch. App. 204.

[191] *James v Biou* (1813) 3 Swanst. 234.

[192] *White v Parnther* (1829) 1 Knapp 179; but see *Beckett v Buckley* (1874) L.R. 17 Eq. 435.

[193] *Troughton v Binkes* (1801) 6 Ves. 573.

[194] See Charging Orders Act 1979 ss.1, 2(2)(*a*), 3(2), (4); the Land Charges Act 1972 s.6 (as amended); and the Land Registration Act 2002 ss. 42(1)(c) and 42(4).

appointment of a receiver by way of equitable execution provided that the order making the appointment is similarly registered.[195] It should also be born in mind that a judgment creditor has been permitted to make a payment to save an estate in a case where the debtor's representatives do not do so.[196]

(9) Bankruptcy. Bankruptcy divests a mortgagor of his right to redeem and it passes to the trustee[197]; creditors of a bankrupt can thus only redeem through the trustee.[198] The mortgagee has the option to either prove in the bankruptcy as a secured creditor, in which case he puts a value on the security and proves for the deficiency,[199] or else to stand outside the bankruptcy and rest on his security. If he elects to do the former, the trustee may redeem at the valuation[200]; if he does the latter, the trustee can only redeem on the terms of an ordinary redemption. It appears that if the body of creditors wish the trustee to redeem by action but he refuses to do so, a creditor may do so (albeit at his own risk on costs) but the right to redeem will be given to the trustee prior to the creditor.[201]

(10) The Crown. If the equity of redemption is left vacant, whether by a failure of persons entitled to take on intestacy or by the dissolution of a company, the right to redeem vests in the Crown by reason of its right to bona vacantia. For the equity of redemption, being an estate or interest and not a mere personal equity, is not extinguished by a failure of persons representing the mortgagor.[202]

(11) Spouses.[203] Where a spouse has matrimonial home rights under the Family Law Act 1996, that spouse will be entitled to redeem the mortgage as a person interested in the equity of redemption if able to do so.[204] Further the spouse is entitled to make such payments, inter alia, in respect of the mortgage due from the other spouse in respect of the matrimonial home.[205] Also the spouse is entitled to be made a party to any action brought by the mortgagee to enforce his security if such person is able to meet the mortgagor's liabilities under the mortgage and the court does not see any special reason against it. Further the

---

[195] As to equitable execution, see Senior Court Act 1981 s.37 and CPR, Sch.1, RSC Ord. 51 (as amended). Also *Wells v Kilpin* (1874) L.R. 18 Eq. 298; *Beckett v Buckley* (1874) L.R. 17 Eq. 435.

[196] *Blagrave v Chann* (1706) 2 Vern 576; *Frederick v Anyscombe* (1739) Atk 392.

[197] *Spragg v Binkes* (1800) 5 Ves. 583; see below, para.30–46.

[198] *Troughton v Binkes* (1801) 6 Ves. 573.

[199] The mortgagee must prove in the bankruptcy in accordance with Insolvency Act 1986 s.332. See Ch.34.

[200] The trustee may redeem upon 28 days' notice at the mortgagee's value, subject to the mortgagee's right to revalue (Insolvency Rules 1986 (SI 1986/1925) rr.6115, 6.117). It is also subject to the trustees' right to sell the property if he considers that the mortgagee's value is excessive (r.6.118).

[201] *Francklyn v Fern* (1740) Barn Ch. 30.

[202] *Re Sir Thomas Spencer Wells* [1933] 1 Ch. 29; Administration of Estates Act 1925 s.46 as amended, and Intestates' Estate Act 1952 s.4 and Sch.1.

[203] See Ch.32.

[204] If the court is satisfied that the spouse is likely to be able to pay off the mortgage, see *Hastings and Thanet Building Society v Goddard* [1970] 1 W.L.R. 1544.

[205] Family Law Act 1996 s.30(3) as amended by the Civil Partnership Act 2004.

court must be satisfied that the spouse may be expected to make such payments towards the mortgagor's liabilities which might affect the outcome of the proceedings.[206] The spouse is also entitled to be served with notice of the action if a Class F land charge has been registered at the Land Charges Registry (in the case of unregistered land) or a registration of a notice at the Land Registry (in respect of registered land).[207]

Redemption by action

In earlier chapters it was emphasised that once default is made under the contract relations between mortgagor and mortgagee are strictly regulated by the practice of the court. This does not, however, mean that redemption invariably, or even usually, takes place in court. On the contrary, the parties, as a rule, agree to the accounts out of court and the mortgage is discharged by payment of the agreed sum. It is only when there is a dispute that an action is necessary. Nevertheless, it is convenient to deal first with redemption by action, since the practice in redemption suits largely controls the rights of the parties in settlements out of court.

30–43

Parties

All persons interested in the equity of redemption are entitled to redeem and this means that persons with very diverse interests in the mortgaged property may have such a right. The importance of this rule in actions for redemption is considerable since the general principle is that all persons with a right to redeem must be represented in the action.[208] The reason is that the mortgagee has a right to account once and for all as against all persons other than those with paramount title. This entails the presence of all persons who are entitled to an account.[209] Thus the person who issues the claim must himself have a proper right to redeem and if it can be shown that he does not have title, he will not be allowed to redeem even on his own risk.[210] It follows that all persons known to have any interest in the equity of redemption must be joined as parties either personally or through their representatives. It is no excuse that the interest of an omitted person is very small.[211] The result is that if a co-mortgagor or other person with only a partial interest seeks to redeem, the remaining mortgagors or interested parties ought to be joined.[212]

30–44

---

[206] ibid., s.55, if a dwelling-house.

[207] A caution may no longer be lodged: s.33(11).

[208] *Fell v Brown* (1787) 2 Bro.C.C. 276; *Johnson v Holdsworth* (1850) 1 Sim. N.S. 106.

[209] *Palk v Clinton* (1805) 12 Ves. 48.

[210] *Lomax v Bird* (1683) 1 Vern 182; *Francklyn v Fern* (above).

[211] *Hunter v Maclew* (1846) 5 Hare 238. The court will not however refuse redemption because of the absence of a party who cannot be located provided that the mortgagee is not prejudiced (*Faulkner v Daniel* (1843) 3 Hare 199).

[212] *Marquis of Cholmondeley v Lord Clinton* (1820) 2 J. & W. 1 at 134; *Bolton v Salmon* [1891] 2 Ch. 48.

The only exception to the rule that interested parties ought to be joined is when a life tenant, trustees, executors, administrators or the trustee under a deed of assignment represent the persons for whom they act.[213] Even then it is in the discretion of the court to allow beneficiaries to be made parties if their rights cannot adequately be protected by the decree (for example in the case of an administrator appointed to act only during the minority of an executor). It is not often necessary to allow this in redemption actions but in foreclosure actions the court will always bring in beneficiaries if there is a danger of the trustees having insufficient funds for redemption.[214] Again, all persons interested in the mortgage debt are necessary parties.[215] If there are co-mortgagees all must be joined. If the right to the mortgage money has been assigned or otherwise passed into different hands, the new owners are the proper persons to be redeemed. If there has been a sub-mortgage the original mortgagor, in bringing his action, must join the sub-mortgagee; the mortgagee may, however, redeem the sub-mortgage without adding the mortgagor. Although all persons known to be interested ought to be joined, the joinder of the parties is in the discretion of the court, which will sometimes allow the action to proceed without the representation of a party who cannot be found, provided that the mortgagee runs no risk.[216] In such a case the decree will expressly preserve the rights of the absent us party.[217]

"Redeem up, foreclose down"

30–45   The rule that a mortgagee is entitled to account once and for all is of the utmost importance where there are successive encumbrances since it prevents a puisne encumbrancer from redeeming an earlier mortgagee by action without at the same time foreclosing on subsequent mortgagees and on the mortgagor.[218] The subsequent encumbrancers and the mortgagor have successive[219] rights to redeem and the accounts taken in the puisne encumbrancer's action for redemption will inevitably fix the price at which any later redemption can be effected. Therefore it is essential that in the puisne encumbrancer's action all persons with later rights to redeem should be before the court in order that they may be bound by the accounts. On the other hand, it would be onerous to the mortgagor and to the later encumbrancers to allow them to be dragged before the court merely that they might watch the accounts being taken.[220] Indeed, they cannot be joined for this limited purpose. It is the rule that a puisne encumbrancer who redeems an earlier mortgage by action must at the same time foreclose on all later encumbrancers and on the mortgagor—the insistence of the Court being that all interests are settled in one action. For the same reason, anyone who redeems an

---

[213] See CPR 11.9, 19.2 and 64.

[214] *Goldsmit v Stonehewer* (1852) 9 Hare App. xxxviii.

[215] *Wetherell v Collins* (1818) 3 Mad. 255.

[216] *Faulkner v Daniel* (1843) 3 Hare 199.

[217] *Francis v Harrison* (1889) L.R. 43 Ch.D. 183.

[218] *Fell v Brown* (1787) 2 Bro. C.C. 276.

[219] The first right to redeem a first mortgage is in the second mortgagee, the next right in the third mortgagee and so on: *Teevan v Smith* (1882) L.R. 20 Ch.D. 724.

[220] *Ramsbottom v Wallis* (1835) 5 L.J. N.S. Ch. 92; *Slade v Rigg* (1843) 3 Hare 35; *Rose v Page* (1829) 2 Sim. 471; *Briscoe v Kenrick* (1832) 1 L.J.Ch. 116.

earlier mortgage, which is not the immediately preceding encumbrance, must also redeem any intermediate mortgages. If, for example, a third mortgagee redeems the first, it is obvious that the first mortgagee's account will affect the rights of the second. The latter must therefore be joined as a party and redeemed.[221] This principle applies also in foreclosure actions with this result—a mortgagee who forecloses must join all persons with interests in the security subsequent to his,[222] since his account will fix the price of redemption for them all. Foreclosure on the mortgagor means foreclosure also on intermediate mortgagees. The general result is that actions to discharge encumbrances are multiple actions, and this is commonly expressed by the maxim, *redeem up, foreclose down*. Two consequences of this principle should be noticed in relation to the right to redeem: (i) a puisne mortgagee cannot redeem an earlier mortgage in court without at the same time exposing himself to redemption by the mortgagor and later encumbrancers; (ii) there cannot be a redemption action in the absence of the mortgagor, such that a puisne mortgagee, who, by stipulating not to call in his money for a stated period, has precluded himself from bringing the mortgagor before the court, cannot during that period bring a redemption action against any prior mortgagee.[223]

Procedure[224]

In either the High Court of the county court,[225] the proceedings are brought by **30–46** a claim form using the CPR Pt 7 or Pt 8 procedure as appropriate.[226] Any person who has the right to redeem any mortgage, whether legal or equitable, can, as of course seek redemption, reconveyance and delivery of possession.[227]

In a redemption action the claim is for an account and for redemption. If the parties wish to redeem, the statement of case or the evidence in support must expressly or by implication contain an offer to redeem, and, if the claimant makes out a case for redemption without such an offer, he will be compelled to amend his plea[228] or at any rate to give an undertaking to redeem.[229] It is only in exceptional circumstances that a mortgagor can bring the mortgagee into court without offering to redeem him,[230] namely:

---

[221] *Teevan v Smith* (1882) L.R. 20 Ch.D. 724.

[222] See above, paras 17–28 et seq.

[223] *Ramsbottom v Wallis* (1835) 5 L.J. N.S. Ch. 92; there is, however, no objection to the prior mortgagee being paid off out of court; indeed, the prior mortgagee ought to accept payment in such circumstances: *Smith v Green* (1844) 1 Coll. 555.

[224] See generally Ch.27.

[225] The county court has jurisdiction where the amount owing on the mortgage at the time of the claim—*Shields, Whitley and District Amalgamated Model Building Society v Richards* (1901) 84 L.T. 587—does not exceed the county court limit (currently £30,000).

[226] There are no specific rules relating to the commencement or progression of redemption actions per se. Prior rules (CPR Sch.1, RSC Ord. 88 and CPR Pt 8, Practice Direction A3) concerning them and the manner in which they should progress (Pt 8 claim) have been repealed. The choice between a Pt 7 claim and a Pt 8 claim will depend on the individual facts of each case and whether there is likely to be a substantial dispute of fact.

[227] In general, a mortgagor has to pay the costs of a redemption action, but there are occasions when the mortgagee by his conduct renders himself liable to pay the costs.

[228] *Palk v Lord Clinton* (1805) 12 Ves. 48.

[229] *Balfe v Lord* (1842) 2 Dr. & W. 480.

[230] *Tasker v Small* (1837) 3 My. & Cr. 63.

(1) if he claims a sale instead of redemption;

(2) when the proceedings are merely for the purpose of determining questions of the construction of the mortgage deed[231]; and

(3) when the mortgagee is a party to a trust deed affecting the equity of redemption, for the trust may be enforced without an offer to redeem[232];

(4) (possibly) where the mortgagee is not exercising his power of sale bona fide.

Nor need the mortgagor offer to redeem if he denies the existence of the mortgage, or is asking that it be avoided.[233] However, in such a case the existing authorities state that if the mortgage is upheld, he cannot redeem in the same action unless he has pleaded in the alternative for redemption.[234]

Sale in lieu of redemption

30–47   A mortgagor in his plea may claim a sale in lieu of redemption. This requires further explanation, since neither the mortgage contract nor the rules of equity give him this right. Section 91(1) of the Law of Property Act 1925 provides as follows:

> "Any person entitled to redeem mortgaged property may have a judgment or order for sale, instead of for redemption in an action brought by him, either for redemption alone, or for sale alone or for sale or redemption in the alternative."

The language of this subsection would appear to confer an absolute right on a claimant to apply for a sale in lieu of redemption, rather than to give a discretionary power to the court to order a sale.[235] It is submitted that the subsection must be so interpreted, although under the Conveyancing Act 1881, Kekewich J. undoubtedly treated the whole question of sale as a matter of discretion.[236] Section 91 does, on the other hand, provide that, when a person interested in the equity of redemption is a claimant asking for a sale the court may, on the application of any defendant, direct the claimant to give security for costs and may give the conduct of the sale to any defendant, with appropriate directions as to costs. Moreover, although, as we have suggested, the court may have no discretion to refuse an order for sale in lieu of redemption the terms of the order for sale are very much within its discretion. Section 91 further provides:

[231] *Re Nobbs* [1896] 2 Ch. 830.

[232] *Jefferys v Dickson* (1866) L.R. 1 Ch. 183.

[233] Such a claim may, nonetheless, be treated as a redemption claim: *Powell v Roberts* (1869) L.R. 9 Eq. 169. As to redemption when the claim concerns successors in title to the original parties (mortgagor's successor seeking possession against purchaser from mortgagee), *Murugaser Marimuttu v De Soysa* [1891] A.C. 69 (JCPC).

[234] *Martinez v Cooper* (1826) 2 Russ. 198; *Bagot v Easton* (1877) L.R. 7 Ch.D. 1. Whether those authorities remain good procedural law following the introduction of the Civil Procedure Rules must be open to question. cf. CPR Pt 1.1 (Overriding objective) and 16.2(5). Practically, the mortgagor may encounter obstacles by the lateness of any proposed amendment: see *The White Book*, (2010 Service), Vol.1, para.17.3.8.

[235] *Clarke v Pannell* (1884) 29 S.J. 147.

[236] *Brewer v Square* [1892] 2 Ch. 111.

"In any action, whether for foreclosure, or for redemption, or for sale, or for the raising and payment in any manner of mortgage money, the court on the request of the mortgagee, or of any person interested, either in the mortgage money or in the right of redemption, and notwithstanding that—

(a) any other person dissents; or
(b) the mortgagee or any person so interested does not appear in the action;

and without allowing any time for redemption or for payment of any mortgage money, may direct a sale of the mortgaged property on such terms as it thinks fit, including the deposit in Court of a reasonable sum fixed by the Court to meet the expenses of sale and to secure performance of the terms."

The practice in sales by the court has already been considered,[237] but here it may be said that in redemption actions the order for sale may be made at any time before the final decree for redemption and may, indeed, be made on an interlocutory application before the trial.[238]

Order

In the ordinary case, assuming that any dispute as to the existence of the right of **30–48** redemption is resolved in favour of the claimant, the court's order is that an account be taken of what is due to the mortgagee in respect of his mortgage, including the costs of the redemption action and that upon the mortgagor paying to the mortgagee the amount certified by the Master to be due within six (calendar[239]) months[240] after the date of his certificate and at a time and place to be appointed in the certificate the mortgagee shall surrender his mortgage term or give a receipt in accordance with s.115 of the Law of Property Act 1925 and deliver up the title deeds. The order further directs that if the mortgagor makes default in such payment his action is to stand dismissed with costs.[241] The order may be varied by an order for sale in lieu of redemption. It may be necessary to add an order for possession if the mortgagee has exercised his right to take possession. Again, the circumstances may make it necessary to give special directions for the account. For example, if the order for redemption is made after the mortgagee has refused a proper tender, the account must be stopped on the date of the tender and there must be alternative orders to meet the possibilities that the tender may or may not have been sufficient. Similarly, if the mortgagee is in possession, the account must be taken on the footing of wilful default and further variations in the order will be necessary if the mortgagee in possession has been charged with waste, improper management or improper sale of the security. The order must also accommodate the more usual consideration(s) of rents and profits. Moreover, the account of a mortgagee in possession may sometimes be ordered with annual rests. The accounts taken between mortgagor

---

[237] See above, paras 33–12 et seq.
[238] *Woolley v Colman* (1882) L.R. 21 Ch.D. 169.
[239] CPR 2.10.
[240] But see para.33–11 above re: six months' notice.
[241] See Seton, *Judgments and Orders* (7th edn), Vol.3, p.1853.

and mortgagee are considered elsewhere in detail in connection with the mortgagee's interest.[242]

Successive redemptions

30–49   Special directions will be necessary when there are several parties to the action with successive rights to redeem; the order must not only notice their priorities[243] but must also provide distinctly for the possibility of any party redeeming or failing to redeem. To take a simple case, if a second mortgagee is claiming to redeem the first and to foreclose on the mortgagor, the order is: on payment by the claimant of the amount due to the first mortgagee within six months of the certificate, the first mortgagee to surrender his mortgage term or give the statutory receipt—in default the claim to be dismissed with costs; if the claimant shall pay off the first mortgagee, interest to be computed on what he shall pay, and an account to be taken of what is due on the claimant's own mortgage and for his costs of the claim; and, on payment by the mortgagor within three months of the certificate of the amount reported due to the claimant, the claimant to surrender his mortgage term or give a statutory receipt to the mortgagor—in default, the mortgagor to be foreclosed. The introduction of other parties further complicates the order which, as we said, will provide for every contingency.

Two further points must be noticed in the form of the order given above: (i) when a mesne encumbrancer brings the claim for redemption and fails to redeem, not only is his action dismissed but he is made to pay the costs both of the first mortgagee and also of the mortgagor[244]; (ii) in special circumstances the mortgagor may be given a longer period to redeem.[245] The limitation of a successive period for redemption in case an intermediate encumbrancer redeems is obviously necessary since a new account has to be taken, but in the redemption of a first mortgage, when the claimant is the mortgagor or a third or later encumbrancer, the question will arise whether distinct periods are to be allotted to each party for the redemption of the *first mortgage*.

Formerly the practice was to give a period of six months to the person entitled to the first equity of redemption and further periods of three months to each later encumbrancer with an additional three months for the mortgagor. This rule applied only to encumbrancers so that a life tenant and remainderman under a settlement of the equity of redemption had only one period between them.[246] Nor did it even apply to encumbrancers when their mortgages were created on the same day,[247] or when it was plain that the security would be insufficient to give anything to the later encumbrancers.[248]

30–50   It is not, however, going too far to say that the practice of the court today is the reverse.[249] A mortgagee may be seriously inconvenienced by the delay

---

[242] See below, paras 33–11 et seq.

[243] *Jones v Griffith* (1845) 2 Coll. 207; *Duberly v Day* (1851) 14 Beav. 9.

[244] *Hallett v Furze* (1885) L.R. 31 Ch.D. 312.

[245] See *Lewis v Aberdare and Plymouth Co* (1884) 53 L.J.Ch. 741.

[246] *Beevor v Luck* (1867) L.R. 4 Eq. 537.

[247] *Long v Storie* (1849) 3 De G. & Sm. 308.

[248] *Cripps v Wood* (1882) 51 L.J.Ch. 584.

[249] *Bartlett v Rees* (1871) L.R. 12 Eq. 395; *Smith v Olding* (1884) L.R. 25 Ch.D. 462; *Platt v Mendel* (1884) L.R. 27 Ch.D. 246.

caused by allowing successive periods for redemption and now, as a general rule, one period only of six months will be allotted to the puisne encumbrancers and the mortgagor together: if there is any ground for successive periods the encumbrancers must appear and make out a special case for such an order.[250] The mortgagor himself cannot apply for the special order because he cannot enlarge his own time for redemption by merely dealing with the equity of redemption.[251] It follows that a special order will never be made if the puisne encumbrancers are not before the court. To make an order in such a case would be equivalent to giving judgment between co-defendants without their having asked for it.[252] Nor will a special order be made when the priorities are in dispute. The determination of the priorities will cause delay and is a question in which the first mortgagee has no interest.[253] But where, as is now usual, there is only one period of six months for all the defendants there is, of course, liberty to apply to the court in case any one of the defendants shall redeem. The court will then determine the rights of the defendants inter se.

If a special order for successive periods is made, the procedure is as follows. The first right to redeem is in the second mortgagee and if he defaults he is foreclosed; a further three months' interest is then added to the mortgage account and the person next entitled has an opportunity to redeem, and so on. If a puisne encumbrancer does redeem the action continues between him and later encumbrancers and the mortgagor; his own debt is added to the first mortgage debt together with an allowance of three months' interest and the person next entitled must redeem or be foreclosed, and so on.

Effect of an order

The rules for payment by the mortgagor and for the execution of the necessary instruments by the mortgagee are the same whether redemption takes place under the order of the court or by agreement. It must, however, be emphasised that in redemption actions payment has to be made strictly in accordance with the terms of the order. In foreclosure actions the court will readily grant an extension of time for redemption but not so when the proceedings are initiated by the mortgagor. He comes of his own volition to the court professing to have his money ready. If he has not, he cannot claim the indulgence which he receives when the mortgagee is pressing him for payment. Consequently, a failure to pay on the date specified results in the final dismissal of the action.[254] This is so even when after his default the mortgagor has made a tender of the full amount reported due with subsequent interest.[255] It is only in the rare case of a bona fide

30–51

---

[250] *Platt v Mendel* (1884) L.R. 27 Ch.D. 246; *Doble v Manley* (1885) L.R. 28 Ch.D. 664.

[251] ibid., at 248.

[252] *Doble v Manley* (1885) L.R. 28 Ch.D. 664.

[253] *Bartlett v Rees* (1871) L.R. 12 Eq. 395; *General Credit and Discount Co v Glegg* (1883) L.R. 22 Ch.D. 549; *Lordsvale Finance Plc v Bank of Zambia* [1996] Q.B. 752.

[254] *Novosielski v Wakefield* (1811) 17 Ves. 417.

[255] *Faulkner v Bolton* (1835) 7 Sim. 319.

mistake, as when the court's order is misunderstood, that any enlargement may be obtained.[256]

Dismissal of the action

30–52 The dismissal of an action for redemption is obtained as of course upon production of the certificate of the amount due and of an evidence of attendance for payment resulting in no payment. In the case of a legal mortgage the dismissal of the action for any cause, except want of prosecution,[257] operates as a decree for foreclosure absolute against the plaintiff. As James L.J. said[258]:

> "The mortgagor, by filing the bill, admits the title of the mortgagee, and admits the mortgage debt, and the dismissal of the bill operates as a decree for foreclosure, because he cannot afterwards file another bill for the same purpose; he is not allowed thus to harass the mortgagee."

The claimant's equity of redemption is extinguished. In the case of a legal mortgage this completes the mortgagee's title and the court may grant an order for possession in the same claim.[259] In the case of an equitable mortgage the effect is somewhat different. Although the claimant is not allowed to take subsequent proceedings for the same purpose, a mere dismissal of his action cannot complete the mortgagee's title. The mortgagee must either rely on the acquisition of a title by lapse of time under the Limitation Act 1980,[260] which is only possible if he is in possession, or else must take fresh proceedings in order to obtain a conveyance and possession. It is just possible that after 1925, even in the case of a legal mortgage, the mortgagee does not acquire the mortgagor's whole title. Although ss.89 and 90 of the Law of Property Act 1925 carefully provide that a foreclosure decree is to pass the mortgagor's legal reversion to the mortgagee, there is no similar provision for the dismissal of an action for redemption.

The dismissal of the action operates against the claimant only and therefore, in the case of successive encumbrancers if the mortgagor is the claimant, the dismissal of his action places the final equity of redemption in the last encumbrancer who becomes quasi-mortgagor.[261] If a puisne encumbrancer is the claimant and fails to redeem, he is not only foreclosed but must pay the costs of all parties including the mortgagor, whom he must, of course, have made a defendant.[262]

---

[256] *Collinson v Jeffery* [1896] 1 Ch. 644.

[257] *Hansard v Hardy* (1812) 18 Ves. 455.

[258] *Marshall v Shrewsbury* (1875) L.R. 10 Ch. App. 250 at 254.

[259] While there was previously express provision in this regard (CPR Pt 50, Sch.1 and RSC Ord. 88, r.7, following the revocation of RSC Ord. 88 there has been no indication that the former practice will cease.

[260] See para.6–29.

[261] *Cottingham v Shrewsbury* (1843) 3 Hare 627.

[262] *Hallett v Furze* (1885) L.R. 31 Ch.D. 312.

Possession by the mortgagee pursuant to a judgment given in a foreclosure action is a good defence to an action to redeem.[263] The circumstances in which foreclosure can be re-opened are considered elsewhere.[264]

Finally, it must be remembered that proceedings for redemption are a pending action, and therefore the dismissal will not bind an assignee for value between the date of the claim form and the dismissal unless the action has been registered as a pending action.

REDEMPTION OUT OF COURT

Generally

This is effected by an accord and satisfaction out of court, which usually resolves itself into a tender of the mortgage moneys and an acceptance of the tender. For the most part the conditions under which redemption may be claimed out of court are the same as those under which it is allowed in an action. Thus, the right to make a tender only arises at the same time as the right to redeem by action and the mortgagee, after default, is entitled to six months' notice, or to six months' interest in lieu of notice,[265] unless the mortgage contract otherwise provides. Similarly, tender must be made by someone entitled to redeem, for, as stated above, a mortgagee's estate is absolute against a stranger.[266] A mortgagee may, if he pleases, transfer his mortgage to a stranger but he cannot be compelled to accept payment from anyone who is not entitled to bring an action for redemption. **30–53**

The maxim "redeem up, foreclose down" does not apply to redemption out of court. That maxim is founded on the court's anxiety to make a complete decree which will bind all parties interested in the estate and redemption out of court is not governed by the same considerations. On the contrary, it is well established that a prior mortgagee ought to accept a proper tender of his money if it is made by any person interested in the equity of redemption and that he rejects such a tender at the peril of paying the costs of a redemption action.[267] Consequently, a puisne mortgagee or any person claiming through the mortgagor may redeem the first mortgage by payment out of court without at the same time discharging intermediate encumbrances. Of course, a satisfied mortgagee is strictly a trustee for the persons entitled to the equity of redemption such that he must be careful to preserve the rights of such other persons of whose interests he has notice. This does not, however, prevent him from being under an obligation to transfer his mortgage to the person who has redeemed him, subject to an express reservation of the rights of the other interested parties of whom he knows.[268] If several persons are claiming to redeem the first mortgagee at the same time, the right to

---

[263] *Nichols v Short* (1713) 2 Eq. Cas. Abr. 608.
[264] See para.27–36, above.
[265] But see para.30–40 above.
[266] *James v Biou* (1818) 3 Swanst. 234 at 237.
[267] *Smith v Green* (1844) 1 Coll. 555.
[268] *Pearce v Morris* (1869) L.R. 5 Ch. App. 227.

redeem first out of court clearly belongs to the puisne encumbrancer whose charge has priority.[269] While accounts which have been agreed out of court are not conclusive against third parties, they are binding on all persons interested until they are impeached. They may be impeached for error or fraud and then in a proper case the court will set aside the settled account.

Tender

30–54 In order to be effective a tender must be made to the mortgagee himself (which is to say the person named in the mortgage deed for the purpose of payment), and not to his solicitor, or other agent,[270] unless the agent has been expressly authorised or is otherwise legally entitled to receive payment of the money and to reconvey the estate.[271] However, under s.69 of the Law of Property Act 1925 the validity of a tender cannot be questioned if it was made to the mortgagee's solicitor,[272] who at the time produced a deed executed by the mortgagee and attached to it a receipt for the mortgage moneys.[273] A person properly authorised to do so as agent of a trustee may receive trust money under s.11 of the Trustee Act 2000 including money due under a loan by the trustees secured on a mortgage.[274] Again, a tender on the contract date must conform strictly to any conditions as to time and place of payment which may have been fixed by the mortgage deed if it is to stop interest running.[275] If a particular hour has been appointed for payment the mortgagor may appear to make his tender at any time during the currency of the hour named, because in law a named hour is not an individual moment of time but the whole hour.[276] For the same reason, if the mortgagee does not appear or is late, the mortgagor himself must continue to attend during the whole hour or his tender will be bad.[277] Today, when the fact that a mortgage is redeemable after default is well known, it is unusual to find a special hour or place for payment fixed by the mortgage deed. If, as usually happens, payment is not made until after the contract date, or, in any case, if no place is named for payment, the mortgagor must seek out the mortgagee and tender the money either to him personally or to his authorised agent. Tender on the mortgaged land is not sufficient, because mortgage moneys are a sum in gross and do not issue out of the land like a rent.[278] Consequently, a mortgagor will, as a rule, suggest a time and place for payment when he notifies the mortgagee of

---

[269] *Teevan v Smith* (1882) L.R. 20 Ch.D. 724.

[270] *Withington v Tate* (1869) L.R. 4 Ch. App. 288.

[271] *Cliff v Wadsworth* (1843) 2 Y. & C Ch 598; *Bourton v Williams* (1870) L.R. 5 Ch. App. 655; and see *Bonham v Maycock* (1928) 138 L.T. 736.

[272] And licensed conveyancer, see Administration of Justice Act 1985 s.34(1). A forged reconveyance will not suffice: *Jared v Walker* (1902) 18 T.L.R. 569.

[273] This is not the case (whether in relation to interest or principal) in circumstances where the solicitor simply by virtue of possession of the security (*Jared v Walker* (above)) or (in relation to principal) merely has authority to receive interest (*Withington v Tate* (1869) L.R. 4 Ch. App. 288).

[274] Subject to the restrictions in s.12.

[275] *Gyles v Hall* (1726) 2 P.Wms. 378.

[276] *Knox v Simmons* (1793) 4 Bro. C.C. 433.

[277] *Bernard v Norton* (1864) 10 L.T. 183.

[278] Co.Lit. Vol.II, 210 b.

his intention to redeem. Then, if the suggested place is reasonably near the mortgagee's residence or is for other reasons convenient to the mortgagee and if the latter has made no objection, an effective tender may be made at that place.[279] A tender must, of course, be a "legal tender" in the proper currency. Except by special agreement, the mortgagor is not entitled to deduct any sum by way of set-off from the amount of principal, interest and costs.[280]

Again, a tender must not be clogged with a condition[281] but must be unconditional; for example, the tender of a sum on condition that it is accepted in full satisfaction of all claims is a bad tender even though the sum tendered turn out to be all that is due.[282] An offer to pay into an escrow account is not an unconditional tender but a "conditional tender par excellence".[283] However, a tender is not rendered invalid by reason of the tenderer reserving the right to tax the costs of the mortgagee and to review the account. A tender may thus always be made under protest, the mortgagor reserving a right afterwards to dispute the mortgagee's claim.[284] Nor is a tender conditional if the mortgagor does no more than demand what he is by law entitled to. Thus, a demand that a reconveyance be executed at the time of the tender does not invalidate the tender because, on payment, a mortgagor's right is to the immediate discharge of the mortgage.[285] In any case a tender, otherwise invalid, will be good if the mortgagee makes no objection except to dispute the amount of the mortgage debt.[286]

Payment to joint creditors

Creditors who advance money on a joint mortgage are, in equity, entitled in **30–55** common[287] even if the legal estate was conveyed to them as joint tenants. Consequently, although at law payment to one joint creditor discharges the debt to all,[288] in equity (absent any special authority to receive it) a receipt from one creditor does not release the debtor from the claims of the others.[289] The receipt must, therefore, be taken from all the creditors. Formerly, a conveyancing difficulty arose when one of the creditors died. Since his interest was an interest in severalty it passed to his personal representatives[290] who must also, therefore,

---

[279] Coote, *Mortgages* (9th edn, 1927), Vol.1, p.739; it has, indeed, been said that a tender for redemption need not always be such as would afford a defence to an action at law on the covenant: *Manning v Burges* (1663) 1 Cas. in Ch. 29; *Webb v Crosse* [1912] 1 Ch. 323.

[280] *Searles v Sadgrave* (1855) 5 E. & B. 639. In general, the money must actually be produced; but see *Dickinson v Shee* (1801) 4 Esp. 67.

[281] *Jennings and Turner v Major* (1837) 8 C. & P. 61.

[282] *Strong v Harvey* (1825) 3 Bing. 304 (an insurance case).

[283] per Lewison J. in *The Law Debenture Trust Corp Plc v Conrad Trust* [2007] EWHC 1380 (Ch).

[284] *Manning v Lunn and Thrupp* (1845) 2 C. & K. 13; *Greenwood v Sutcliffe* [1892] 1 Ch. 1.

[285] *Rourke v Robinson* [1911] 1 Ch. 480.

[286] *Jones v Arthur* (1840) 8 Dowl.P.C. 442.

[287] *Vickers v Cowell* (1839) 1 Beav. 529.

[288] *Rigden v Vallier* (1751) 2 Ves.Sen. 252 at 258.

[289] *Husband v Davis* (1851) 10 C.B. 645.

[290] *Matson v Dennis* (1864) 4 De G.J. & S. 345; *Powell v Brodhurst* [1901] 2 Ch. 160. The case would, of course, be different if one creditor was specially authorised by the others to receive payment for them all.

join in the receipt.[291] This would obviously be inconvenient in the case of mortgages by trustees and so it was customary to insert in the mortgage a statement that the moneys were advanced on a *joint account* (a "joint account clause") in order that on the death of one trustee the receipt of the survivors would be sufficient to release the mortgagor. Although the joint account clause is still frequently included in a joint mortgage, it is no longer necessary. Section 111 of the Law of Property Act 1925 provides that in all joint mortgages, not merely those of trustees, the moneys shall be deemed to have been advanced on a joint account unless the deed expresses a contrary intention. Consequently, in such cases, unless the mortgage contract otherwise provides payment may safely be made to the survivors (or survivor) of joint mortgagees. This enables the surviving mortgagees to overreach the beneficial interests in the mortgaged property. However it does not affect the right of the mortgagees inter se nor does it alter the presumptions as to a tenancy in common. Section 56 of the Land Registration Act 2002 now provides that where a charge is registered in the name or two or more proprietors, those registered proprietors or the survivor(s) of the registered proprietors or the personal representatives of the last survivor can give a receipt for moneys secured by the charge.

Effect of a proper tender when refused

30–56   A mortgagee is bound to know the state of the mortgage debt so that if a proper tender (actual tender of money due) is made he rejects it at his peril.[292] By the contract and by the practice of the court while a mortgagee is entitled to all the costs of the mortgage, including those of redemption, he cannot be allowed to swell the costs and thereby render redemption more difficult. He will have to reimburse the mortgagor for such additional costs (usually the costs of a redemption action)[293] as the latter may be put to by the refusal of his tender. Clearly, therefore, even if it is known that a proper tender will be rejected it is of the first importance that the tender should be made and the risk of further expense placed upon the mortgagee. As Lindley L.J. said[294]:

> "What is the object of a tender? It is not necessarily to put an end to all controversy. It may have that effect and very often has, but its main object is to throw the risk of further controversy on the other party."

Apart from the question of costs, a tender may have the effect of terminating the mortgagee's right to interest. It is true that a tender by itself will not altogether stop the running of interest because tender is not equivalent to payment. A mortgagor who continues to have the use of the mortgagee's money will have to pay interest for its use.[295] But if, after tender, the mortgagor continues to keep the

---

[291] *Petty v Styward* (1632) 1 Rep. Ch. 31; no survivorship; *Vickers v Cowell* (1839) 1 Beav. 529.

[292] Provided they were created after December 31, 1881.

[293] *Harmer v Priestly* (1853) 16 Beav. 569.

[294] *Greenwood v Sutcliffe* [1892] 1 Ch. 1 at 10.

[295] *Edmondson v Copland* [1911] 2 Ch. 301.

money set aside[296] and available for payment of the mortgage debt the running of interest is absolutely stopped as from the date of tender.[297] Interest will continue to run on proof that that a proper tender of the whole sum has not been made, or that the money had ceased to be available for payment without profit being made.[298] Further, a proposal by the mortgagor to set off against the mortgage sums due to him from the mortgagee on another account will not stop interest running.[299] Presumably he need not keep the money completely idle and if, for example, he places it to deposit, he will only have to account to the mortgagee for the interest earned by the money while on deposit.[300] Even if he does not keep the money available, his tender afterwards enables him to enforce redemption without giving any further notice to the mortgagee by payment of the principal plus interest *only up to the date of payment*.[301] If the mortgagee unequivocally refuses a proposed tender, this is equivalent to a waiver by the mortgagee and a formal tender is not necessary.[302]

Effect of a proper tender when accepted

Usually a proper tender is accepted and the mortgage thereby discharged. The **30–57** mortgagee is then bound to execute such instruments as are necessary to release the security from the debt. Accordingly, he must be given a reasonable time in which to prepare and execute the deeds, especially when he is not the original mortgagee but a derivative holder of the mortgage. The cost of preparing these deeds falls on the mortgagor, as being part of the general costs of the mortgage and this is true even when the costs have been increased by complications in the title caused by the mortgagee's activities. For example, in a case where one trustee-mortgagee absconded the cost of obtaining a vesting order from the court vesting the estate in the remaining trustees was included in the general costs of the mortgage and added to the mortgage debt.[303]

---

[296] ibid., at 310.

[297] *Rourke v Robinson* [1911] 1 Ch. 480.

[298] *Gyles v Hall* (1726) 2 P. Wms. 378.

[299] *Barclays Bank Plc v Buhr* [2002] 1 P. & C.R. DG7.

[300] *Edmondson v Copland* [1911] 2 Ch. 301, per Joyce J. at 310. See also *Barratt v Gough-Thomas* [1951] 2 All E.R. 48.

[301] *Edmondson v Copland* [1911] 2 Ch. 301 at 307.

[302] *Chalikani Venkatarayanim v Zaminder of Tun* (1922) L.R. Ind. App. 41.

[303] In the case of several encumbrances, the person *immediately* entitled to the equity of redemption, is, of course, the second encumbrancer. For discharge of mortgages, see below, Ch.6.

CHAPTER 31

VOID AND IMPERFECT SECURITIES

COMMON DEFENCES TO CLAIM

The most common remedy sought by mortgagees in proceedings is an order for **31–01** sale of a dwelling-house, although that remedy may be pursued either in conjunction with a claim for repayment of the debt itself or on its own. The right to possession, arising out of the mortgagee's interest in the land,[1] is a powerful tool in the mortgagee's armoury and is an entitlement recognised by the common law as arising even if the mortgagor is not in default.[2] The courts will, however, prevent the taking of possession if the exercise of that right is not genuinely (that is to say, in good faith) being used as a means of enforcing or preserving security for the mortgagee's liability.[3] While the courts will not restrict the rights of the mortgagee without real caution,[4] the contractual (whether express or implied) terms in circumstances where the sum lent is repayable by instalments will usually provide that the mortgagee will not be entitled to possession until default. There are also statutory restrictions on the exercise of the right to possession.[5]

The vast majority of mortgagees' possession claims are undefended. Nevertheless there are a number of challenges to the efficacy of a mortgagee's security (and thus his claimed rights) which are frequently encountered and, while not confined to possession actions, are often raised in response to a claim by a mortgagee for possession.

---

[1] See *Western Bank Ltd v Schindler* [1977] Ch. 1; *National Westminster Bank Plc v Skelton* [1993] 1 All E.R. 242; *Credit & Mercantile Plc v Marks* [2005] Ch. 81 and *Ashe v National Westminster Bank Plc* [2008] 1 W.L.R. 71.

[2] *Western Bank Ltd v Schindler* (above). See above, para.26–11. The mortgagee is entitled to possession without notice or demand and (subject to the contractual terms and statutory protection afforded to the mortgagor) without a court order (see *Ropeaigelach v Barclays Bank Plc* [2000] Q.B. 263. The mortgagee is entitled to seek possession even where he has transferred beneficial ownership of the charge to a third party—*Paragon Finance Plc v Pender* [2005] 1 W.L.R. 3412. .

[3] *Quennell v Maltby* [1979] 1 W.L.R. 318; *Midland Bank Plc v McGrath* [1996] EGCS 61.

[4] *Western Bank Ltd v Schindler* (above); *Ashley Guarantee Plc v Zacaria* [1993] 1 All ER 254; *Credit & Mercantile v Marks* (above); *Ashe v National Westminster Bank Plc* (above).

[5] See above, paras 26–11 et seq.

No Liability—Debt Discharged or Released

Debt repaid

31–02   Once the debt secured by a mortgage is repaid or the liability secured by the mortgage is satisfied, the mortgagor is entitled to seek redemption of the mortgage in order for his interest in the property to be released from the mortgagee's charge.[6] A dispute about the amount of the debt or the true amount of any repayments made or the recoverability of part or all of the debt[7] may provide a defence to the claim for possession if it can be established that the whole of the debt has been satisfied or is unenforceable. Such a defence, when coupled with a counterclaim for redemption, may result in the release of the mortgage. However, a challenge to the amount owed which merely reduces the claim but does not extinguish it will not provide an answer to a claim for possession, although it may be relevant to the immediacy and terms of the order made.[8]

The position of sureties

31–03   A surety who is under a liability for the mortgage debt or whose property is subject to the debt,[9] has a right to redeem in circumstances either where he pays the debt or where the mortgagor refuses to do so. Thus, where a surety secures his obligations under a guarantee he gave by the provision of a mortgage, if he is able to establish that the principal debtor is not liable to repay the debt or that the guarantee was not valid as against him, he will have a defence to a claim for possession and will be entitled to seek redemption of his property from the mortgagee's charge.[10] Where the debt ceases to exist as a matter of law, the creditor cannot preserve any right against the surety. The same result is achieved whether the creditor novates such that the principal debtor is released and a new person is accepted as debtor in his place. A release by operation of law (for example, in bankruptcy or upon a deed of composition voluntarily entered into between the creditor and debtor[11]) does not release the surety. Notwithstanding the fact that as between the primary debtor and mortgagee the debt or part of it is outstanding, a surety will also have a defence to a claim for payment or possession of any property mortgaged to secure his guarantee if he can establish that his liability under the guarantee has been released.

---

[6] See above, paras 30–36 et seq.

[7] For instance where a court exercises its powers under s.140A-D of the Consumer Credit Act 1974 (see further Ch.16), on the basis that the interest rate charged arose in an unfair relationship as between creditor and debtor.

[8] See Administration of Justice Act 1970 s.36. See above, paras 27–12 et seq.

[9] *Green v Wynn* (1869) L.R. 4 Ch. App. 204; *Gedye v Matson* (1858) 25 Beav 310. Note that the surety does not have the right to redeem if he has given up his right of subrogation: *Royal Trust Co Mortgage Corp v Nudnyk Holdings Ltd* (1974) 4 O.R. (2d) 721 Note further that it is unclear whether the former distinction between a creditor giving the debtor an absolute release (thereby releasing the surety) and a creditor agreeing not to sue (which would not release the surety) can still be maintained: *Johnson v Davies* [1999] Ch. 117.

[10] *National Westminster Bank v Skelton* [1993] 1 W.L.R. 72.

[11] Insolvency Act 1986 s.281(7).

In the absence of express provision to the contrary,[12] the personal liability of the surety under a guarantee may be released when the mortgagee/creditor, without the consent of the surety in question, grants a variation of the contract with the principal debtor or an indulgence to the principal debtor or another surety,[13] such that the surety's position is prejudiced without his agreement.[14] Accordingly the surety is, in such circumstances, released from his obligations.

An indulgence includes a material alteration of the principal contract[15] under which the debt arises, the giving of time to the principal debtor[16] or waiving of part of the liability.

The release of any co-surety or alternative security, whether wholly or in part, may have the same effect of releasing a surety from his liability to pay under the guarantee and therefore entitling him to seek redemption of any mortgage obtained to secure his guarantee. The question of release, in the case of joint and several liability, is determined by the construction of the agreement between the creditor and the co-surety, in particular as to whether the creditor intended to preserve his rights against the other co-surety.[17] This approach is also now used where the liability is joint only.[18] It is not clear whether this approach is also correct in the case of several liability only, it is thought that such would be the case subject only to the likely reluctance of the court to construe an agreement with one debtor as releasing others. In some instances, the existence or liability of co-sureties and/or other securities are effectively conditions[19] of the original contract of guarantee. In those circumstances it seems that the release of any element of the whole transaction will release the surety in question from any liability[20] without the need to establish that the change is a material alteration.

The release of such a co-surety or security would be a breach of a condition and probably therefore a repudiation of the suretyship since the alteration to the surety's risk extends beyond that which was agreed—it being considered inappropriate that the surety should not be made responsible for an altered contract The surety is also released where changes in the law effect a material change in

[12] Which is almost invariably included in modern agreements to the usual effect that any indulgence granted to the principal debtor (whether by extension of time or otherwise) does not amount to a waiver of any rights against the surety. Note that a consolidation of mortgages given by the principal debtor with the fixing of a later date for payment will operate as a giving of time and discharge the surety: *Bolton v Buckenham* [1891] 1 Q.B. 278; *Bolton v Salmon* [1891] 2 Ch. 48.

[13] *Whitcher v Hall* (1826) 5 B. & C. 269; *Holme v Briskill* (1877) L.R. 3 Q.B.D. 496; *National Provincial Bank of Nigeria Ltd v Awolesi* [1964] 1 W.L.R. 1311; *West Horndon Industrial Park Ltd v Phoenix Timber Group Plc* [1995] 1 E.G.L.R. 77; *Howard de Walden Estates Ltd v Pasta Place Ltd* [1995] 1 E.G.L.R. 79.

[14] See *Chitty on Contracts* (30th edn, 2008), paras 44–067 and 44–104. See also *Associated British Ports v Ferryways NV* [2009] 1 Lloyd's Rep. 595 and *Royal Bank of Scotland Plc v Chandra* [2010] 1 Lloyd's Rep. 677.

[15] *Holme v Brunskill* (1878) L.R. 3 Q.B.D. 495. See also *Egbert v National Crown Bank* [1918] A.C. 903; *Credit Suisse v Borough Council of Allerdale* [1995] 1 Lloyd's Rep. 315; *National Bank of Nigeria v Awolesi* [1964] 1 W.L.R. 1311. See also *Chitty on Contracts* (30th edn, 2008), paras 44–091 et seq.

[16] *Nisbet v Smith* (1789) 2 Bro. C.C. 579; *Swire v Redman* (1876) L.R. 1 Q.B.D. 536.

[17] The old approach whereby an agreement that took effect as a release of the debtor on the one hand or a covenant not to sue on the other has been superseded.

[18] *Johnson v Davies* (above).

[19] See *Chitty on Contracts* (30th edn, 2008), para.44–062.

[20] ibid. (30th edn, 2008), paras 44–104/44–105.

his position.[21] However, where the surety either did not know of the other elements of the transaction or, notwithstanding his knowledge, they were not conditions to the provision of his suretyship, it is likely that the creditor's release of other elements (even if not sufficient to secure the release of the surety) may have a more limited effect. Such a release, although not a breach of a condition of the suretyship, has the effect of increasing the potential liability of the surety and can have the effect of releasing the surety to the extent to which his position is prejudiced thereby.[22]

Counterclaim and set-off

31–04   A counterclaim (whether simpliciter or by way of a cross-claim for unliquidated damages) for a sum that equals or exceeds the amount of the debt secured, if it amounts to a set-off, can be a defence to any claim for repayment of the debt. However, such a defence to the money claim does not amount to a defence to a claim for possession brought against the mortgagor or any surety of his.[23] In such cases, the counterclaim advanced by the party from whom possession is claimed should include in the counterclaim a claim for redemption of the mortgage. The entire counterclaim should then be prosecuted quickly to ensure that judgment on the counterclaim is secured, to enable the redemption of the mortgage to occur prior to the mortgagee's claim for possession being concluded. Practically this may present the mortgagor with grave difficulties.

Alteration of the mortgage deed

31–05   Where a mortgagee or his agent, without the knowledge or consent of the mortgagor, alters or mutilates the mortgage instrument after execution, the mortgagee loses the right to enforce that instrument and the mortgagor is discharged.[24] An alteration of the repayment date and interest dates would be sufficient alteration for these purposes. In such circumstances the mortgagee will usually have a restitutionary claim for the money advanced but will have no claim directly against the property itself.[25]

WANT OF FORMALITY

Writing

31–06   Where a purported contract for the grant of a mortgage on or after September 26, 1989. fails to comply with the requirements of s.2 of the Law of Property

---

[21] *Mortgage Insurance Corp Ltd v Pound* (1894) 64 L.J.Q.B. 394 and (1895) L.J.Q.B. 129 (HL).

[22] *Carter v White* (1883) L.R. 25 Ch.D. 666 and *Chitty on Contracts* (30th edn, 2008), para.44–105.

[23] *Samuel Keller (Holdings) Ltd v Martins Bank Ltd* [1971] 1 W.L.R. 43; *Ashley Guarantee Plc v Zacaria* [1993] 1 W.L.R. 62.

[24] *Goss v Chilcott* [1996] A.C. 788; *Piggot's Case* (1614) 11 Co. Rep. 286.

[25] *Goss v Chilcott*, above.

(Miscellaneous Provisions) Act 1989, no mortgage will be created and, notwithstanding any oral agreement or deposit of title deeds, the creditor will have no interest in or rights over the debtor's land.[26] It follows that the failure to comply with s.2 will provide a defence to any claim for possession pursuant to a mortgage. A creditor in such circumstances may nevertheless have a right to claim repayment of the debt and, upon securing judgment, he may then seek to levy execution against the land. With regard to mortgages executed prior to September 26, 1989, and which fail to satisfy the formalities then applicable,[27] they could nevertheless result in the creation of a mortgage by reason of the doctrine of part performance and thus provide the foundation of a claim to possession.

This does not, however, prevent a party relying on a proprietary estoppel which would effectively negate the effect of s.2(1). In *Kinane v Mackie-Conteh*[28] the court concluded that a defendant encouraging a claimant (whether by words or conduct) to believe that an agreement for the disposition of an interest in land was valid and binding could meet the requirement that that the defendant encouraged the claimant to believe that he would acquire an interest in land.

Where a mortgage is provided to secure a surety's liability under a guarantee, the requirement for formality arises in relation to both the guarantee and mortgage. To be a valid contract of guarantee, it must be evidenced in writing so as to satisfy the requirements of the Statute of Frauds 1677.[29] Generally, if the formalities required by s.2 of the Property (Miscellaneous Provisions) Act 1989 have been complied with for the purposes of the supporting mortgage there should be no difficulty. However, errors falling foul of those provisions can be fatal to the validity of both guarantee and mortgage: for instance, the omission of the principal debtor's name, the lack of a date and the failure to include the agreed limit.[30]

Registration

A failure to register a mortgage at HM Land Registry does not affect its validity. **31–07** However, it may affect the mortgagee's rights as against third parties[31] in the event of an attempt to secure vacant possession. A mortgage granted by a company over its property must be registered with the Registrar of Companies within 21 days. The failure to register does not give the mortgagor company a defence to a claim under the mortgage but merely renders the mortgage invalid as against any liquidator or creditor of the company.[32]

---

[26] See above, para.14–06 and *United Bank of Kuwait v Sahib* [1997] Ch. 107. The former provision in the Law of Property Act (LPA) 1925 rendered the contract unenforceable rather than void.

[27] LPA 1925 s.40(1).

[28] [2005] 2 P. & C.R. DG3.

[29] Statute of Frauds 1677 s.4.

[30] *State Bank of India v Kaur* [1996] 5 Bank. L.R. 158. See also Andrew, *Law of Guarantees* (5th edn) pp.70 onwards.

[31] See above, paras 13–02 et seq.

[32] Companies Act 2006 ss.860–861. See above, paras 23–45 et seq.

NON EST FACTUM, INCLUDING FORGERY[33]

Generally

31–08   Where an apparent signatory can establish that the signature on a contract or deed (including a loan agreement or mortgage) is not his, either because it has literally been signed by a third party without his authority or because, despite the fact he physically signed the document, he can establish sufficient absence of consent for the law to treat the document as if it were not his, the transaction in question will be void (as opposed to voidable). In the context of a mortgage there may, where there was a loan agreement or guarantee separate from the legal charge, be two documents, either or both of which are challenged.

31–09   The fact that a successful plea of non est factum results in a finding that the transaction attacked was void can be particularly important for two reasons. First, it gives the defendant protection against the totality of the claimant's claim, even though the claimant may be an entirely innocent party to the void contract and notwithstanding that the wrongdoer may be a family member or joint owner with the innocent party or principal debtor. Where a third party, typically the principal debtor, forges a signature or otherwise secures a signature thereby giving rise to a successful plea of non est factum, it matters not that the other party to the contract (usually a bank) had no knowledge, whether actual or constructive, of those matters and was not in any way at fault.[34] Secondly, it gives protection against innocent third parties even when they purport to acquire an interest in the property for value. That aspect is particularly important since it is often many years before the dealings that are challenged are discovered and other transactions may have taken place in the intervening period. While the detail of the law surrounding the alteration and rectification of the Register at HM Land Registry in cases of registered land is outside the scope of this work,[35] circumstances frequently arise[36] where, following the initial void transaction, an innocent third party has relied on the void transaction, and for instance, acquired an interest in the property based on the belief that the void transaction was in fact genuine, only to find that the transaction will still not bind the purported signatory.

31–10   The law has long recognised the need to keep the plea of non est factum within narrow confines so as to ensure the confidence of those who, in the course of all manner of transactions regularly, rightly and of necessity, rely on signatures where they have no reason to question them.[37] Not surprisingly, given the extent to which the law in this area is seeking to strike a fair balance between two or more innocent parties whose interests are diametrically opposed, the principles underpinning the defences are narrowly defined and strictly applied, since, if the

---

[33] See generally *Chitty on Contracts* (30th edn, 2008) at paras 5–101–5–106 and *Karsten v Markham* [2010] 1 F.C.R. 523..

[34] *United Dominion Trust Ltd v Western* [1976] Q.B. 513.

[35] See Ruoff & Roper, *Registered Conveyancing* (Sweet and Maxwell, looseleaf, Ch.46), Land Registration Act (LRA) 2002 Sch.4.

[36] Where the wronged party remains in possession of the land, for example.

[37] See the dicta of Lord Reid in *Saunders v Anglia Building Society* [1971] A.C. 1004, 1015G, and Donovan L.J. in *Muskham Finance Ltd v Howard* [1963] 1 Q.B. 904, 912.

plea succeeds, the law is favouring the innocent party who, in a sense, would have been in the best position to avoid the difficulty in the first instance.

Non est factum—by forgery

A defence based on the allegation that the contract or deed was not signed by the **31–11** defendant but by a third party forging his signature is a plea of non est factum in its simplest form, turning as it does on one finding of fact. Generally it will be necessary for such a defence to be supported by expert handwriting evidence or other forensic evidence showing that someone other than the defendant signed the document or that the signature or the signature of the defendant was not originally physically attached to that particular document. If a party to a document, while not signing himself, authorised the person who did sign to do so in his name and/or on his behalf he will of course be bound, notwithstanding the fact that the signature is not literally his. If an agent fails to read or understand the document signed, the principal is unlikely to be able to raise successfully a plea of *non est factum*. In such circumstances the named party would probably be found to have accepted the risk of his agent's actions.[38]

Where a forged signature relates to a mortgage and any monies advanced under its terms comprised the funds for all or part of the purchase price for an interest in property which was conveyed into the name of the innocent party or which redeemed a binding prior mortgage by which the innocent party was bound, he cannot rely on the forgery to escape the mortgage and the mortgage debt entirely while at the same time claiming the benefit of the interest in his name. A claim by the victim of the forgery for a declaration setting aside the legal charge over the property will not be successful where the effect would be to leave the victim unjustly enriched by retaining property acquired with the mortgagee's money.[39]

Although registration vests the legal estate in a transferee regardless of the forgery of that transferee's signature, the person whose signature was forged can apply to rectify the register.[40] However, where a transfer from one party to a second occurs by reason of the forgery of a signature and the receiving party then mortgages the property to a third, the person whose signature was forged does not appear to be able to seek rectification against the mortgagee.[41] Where the register is rectified and a third party suffers loss as a result (which does not arise because of his fraud or lack of proper care), that third party may be able claim an indemnity from the registrar in respect of some or all his loss.[42]

---

[38] *Norwich Building Society v Steed* [1993] Ch. 116, per Scott L.J. at 127–128 (where a son's lack of care in ensuring his mother understood the nature and effect of a power of attorney he granted to her prevented him from relying upon her ignorance of that power when executing a transfer of his property). See also para.31–15.

[39] See below, Ch.7 generally.

[40] LRA 2002 Sch.4.

[41] *Barclays Bank v Guy* [2008] 2 E.G.L.R. 74 .

[42] LRA 2002 Sch.8; *Norwich and Peterborough Building Society v Steed* [1993] Ch. 116 and *Commercial Acceptances Ltd v. Sheikh* [2001] N.P.C. 83.

Where property is in multiple ownership and one or more of the joint owners was a genuine signatory to a mortgage, equity will treat as done that which ought to have been done under the transaction. In those circumstances the transaction will be binding as far as possible against the interest of those who participated in it. Usually therefore, the beneficial interests of those who were parties to the transaction will be subject to an equitable charge to secure repayment of the money advanced.[43] In the most frequently occurring factual scenario, a husband raises finance on the marital home without telling his wife and by forging her signature. In such a situation the forgery will not bind the wife (subject to the possibility that the charge will bind the wife until rectification pursuant to Sch.4 of Land Registration Act 2002) but will take effect as an equitable charge against the husband's interest alone.[44]

Non est factum—where the defendant in fact signed the document

31–12   A plea of non est factum may be open to someone who, while intending to sign a particular document or type of document and who actually does sign the document in question, was actually misled into executing that deed or contract, believing it to be of an essentially different nature.

The difference required

31–13   In *Saunders v Anglia Building Society*[45] the House of Lords considered, for the purpose of a plea of non est factum, the necessary difference between the document actually signed and the document the defendant intended to sign. The House of Lords did not draw a distinction, for these purposes, between the nature and the content of the document. In order to establish the plea, it held that it is necessary to show "a radical or fundamental difference between what [the defendant] signed and what he thought he was signing".[46] An "all monies charge" has been found to be sufficiently different from a guarantee relating to monies borrowed to fund a particular purchase.[47]

Those under a disability

31–14   Since the sixteenth century, the plea of non est factum has been extended to protect those who are particularly vulnerable. Originally, the extension was understood to assist those who were forced to rely upon others to inform them of

---

[43] *First National Securities v Hegerty* [1985] Q.B. 850; *Ahmed v Kendrick* (1988) 56 P. & C.R. 120. Any equitable joint tenancy is severed—*Ahmed* (above).
[44] See *Mortgage Corporation v Shaire* [2000] 1 F.L.R. 973; *First National Bank Plc v Achampong* [2004] 1 F.C.R. 18; *Edwards v Lloyds TSB Bank Plc* [2005] 1 F.C.R. 139 and *Filby v Mortgage Express (No.2) Ltd* [2004] 2 P. & C.R. DG16.
[45] [1971] 1 A.C. 1004, affirming sub nom *Gallie v Lee* [1969] 2 Ch. 17.
[46] ibid., per Lord Reid at 1017.
[47] *Lloyds Bank Plc v Waterhouse* [1993] 2 F.L.R. 97.

the nature and content of a document they signed, being unable to read through blindness or illiteracy. However, it is now clear that the defence can extend to those who "are permanently or temporarily unable through no fault of their own to have any real understanding of the purport of a particular document without explanation, whether that be from defective education, illness or innate incapacity".[48] The extent of a defendant's disability was considered in *Lloyds Bank Plc v Waterhouse*,[49] where the Court of Appeal identified three crucial elements to such a defence. First, the defendant must establish he is under a disability which prevents him from having any real understanding without assistance. Second, the defendant must establish that the document signed was sufficiently different from that which he intended to sign. Third, even those acting under a disability are required to establish that they were not careless in failing to take proper precautions to establish the significance of the document actually signed.

Blank documents

It follows, theoretically at least, that those who sign blank documents (or hand **31–15** them to another leaving that other to fill in the details and complete the transaction[50]) could potentially raise a successful plea of non est factum.[51] However, in balancing the interests of the person signing such a document and those who may later rely on that signature, the court will have regard to how the defendant's signature came to be on a document, the content of which was not known or understood. It is a matter for anyone signing or authorising the signing of a document to consider what they need to know about its content and to what extent they should understand it properly before it is executed. The onus is clearly on those who sign blank documents to show that they have acted carefully and done all they prudently and reasonably could to protect their own interests.[52] For this reason, it is unlikely that those of full capacity signing blank documents, including loan agreements and mortgages, will be able successfully to rely on a plea of non est factum. It should be remembered that such a person is generally bound by his signature to a document which he has not read or which he is ignorant of its precise legal effect.[53]

UNDUE INFLUENCE

During the 1990s there was a marked escalation in mortgage possession claims **31–16** defended on the basis that the mortgagor had the right to set the mortgage and/or the underlying loan agreement aside as a result of a vitiating factor such as undue

---

[48] *Saunders v Anglia Building Society* [1971] 1 A.C. 1004, per Lord Reid at 1016 and *Norwich Building Society v Steed*, above.
[49] [1993] 2 F.L.R. 97.
[50] See further *Chitty* (above) at para.5–105.
[51] *United Dominions Trust v Western* [1976] Q.B. 513.
[52] per Lord Reid at 1016; *Norwich Building Society v Steed*, above.
[53] *L'Estrange v F. Graucob Ltd* [1934] 2 K.B. 394.

influence[54] or misrepresentation. It is valuable to bear in mind at the outset that the particular context within which a party may seek to set aside a mortgage are, in essence, two-fold. The first is the two party situation, where the mortgagee exercises undue influence over the mortgagor.[55] The second, involving three parties, sees undue influence exercised either by one of a number of mortgagors over another mortgagor. In this second circumstance the mortgagee does not exercise any undue influence. The most obvious example, and the one which has enabled to courts in recent years to develop this area of the law considerably, sees the husband exercise undue influence over his wife in the course of (re-)mortgaging the marital home. However, the position can be yet one step more complicated by the fact that the wrongdoer, the perpetrator of the undue influence or misrepresentation, is not the mortgagor, or possibly, is not even a party to any aspect of the transaction but someone associated with the mortgagor and who had an interest in the transaction proceeding. It follows that consideration of the various factors that can render a mortgage or the underlying loan agreement voidable involves two stages. First, it is necessary to identify the factor or wrong which would justify setting aside the transaction. Secondly, it is necessary to ascertain whether that factor justifies the transaction being set aside as against the mortgagee, where the mortgagee is not the wrongdoer.

The nature of undue influence

31–17   Unlike duress, where the justification for the setting aside of the transaction is the duress preventing the party constrained from forming a full and independent resolution to enter into the transaction, the essence of undue influence is the absence of true consent to the contract by a party to that contract because his agreement was obtained by the inappropriate use of influence over him. Equity operates both to prevent the wrongdoer taking the benefit of his wrongdoing and to protect those who are vulnerable against having advantage taken of them by another in order to prevent the wrongdoer from benefiting from his wrongdoing. Where one person has abused their position of influence or domination over another, thereby procuring the "victim" to enter into a transaction, that transaction may be voidable and the court can set it aside. The principle has been described as a "fetter placed on the conscience of the recipient . . . and one that arises out of public policy and fair play".[56] It follows that when undue influence is raised as a defence, it is not the defendant's understanding of the agreement that is in question, rather, it is the reasons for the defendant's acquiescence that are relevant. Unlike misrepresentation, the contracting party could understand the transaction correctly and yet be entering it as a result of undue influence rather than as a result of the exercise of their own free will. Equity should not however be understood as protecting those who act foolishly or without any regard for their own interests, or those who choose to take a financial risk in order to help

---

[54] See most recently *Strydom v Vendside Ltd* [2009] EWHC 2130 (QB); [2009] 6 Costs L.R. 886 and *Royal Bank of Scotland v Chandra* [2010] 1 Lloyd's Rep. 677.

[55] For example, *Nel v Kean* [2003] P. & C.R. D19.

[56] *Allcard v Skinner* (1887) L.R. 36 Ch.D. 145.

those they care about. Further, it should be noted that in practice, the actions of the wrongdoer in influencing the defending party are often alleged to involve elements of misrepresentation as well as pressure and influence.

Establishing undue influence

Undue influence can be established either as a matter of fact (actual undue **31–18** influence) or it may arise from the relationship between two parties. Historically, the position in equity has been addressed as follows, Cotton L.J. describing the two types of undue influence in *Allcard v Skinner* as:

> "First, where the court has been satisfied that the gift was the result of influence expressly used by the donee for the purpose; second, where the relations between the donor and donee have at or shortly before the execution of the gift been such as to raise a presumption that the donee had influence over the donor.... The first class of cases may be considered as depending on the principle that no one shall be allowed to retain any benefit arising from his own fraud or wrongful act. In the second class of cases the court interferes, not on the ground that any wrongful act has in fact been committed by the donee, but on the ground of public policy, and to prevent the relations which existed between the parties and the influence arising therefrom being abused."[57]

Thus, the focus of an allegation of actual undue influence will be upon the events that actually occurred, whereas presumed undue influence focuses on the relationship between the parties and the potential for abuse of that relationship.

In the first class of undue influence the complainant must show that the he or she entered into the transaction of which complaint is made not as a result of his or her own free will but as a result of actual undue influence.[58] The second class of cases arise where there is a relationship which the law recognises as involving trust and confidence. It is not necessary for the complainant to prove trust and confidence. Obvious examples are parent and child; solicitor and client, medical practitioner and patient; engaged couples and the like. The relationship between husband and wife (or co-habiting couples of any type) is not such a relationship. The existence of the relationship does not of itself give rise to a presumption of undue influence. However, where it can be shown that such a relationship existed and the transaction is not readily explained by that relationship, the complainant succeeds in transferring the evidential burden to the other party. Past discussions about whether husbands and wives (or other cohabiting couples) should form a separate and distinct category[59] have been disapproved as unhelpful.[60]

Actual undue influence

Actual undue influence has been described as a species of fraud.[61] In order to **31–19** establish a defence based on actual undue influence, it is necessary to establish

---

[57] ibid., at 171.
[58] For example, *Drew v Daniel* [2005] 2 F.C.R. 365.
[59] Class 2B.
[60] *Royal Bank of Scotland v Etridge (No.2)* [2002] 2 A.C. 773.
[61] *CIBC Mortgages Ltd v Pitt* [1994] 1 A.C. 200.

that the defendant entered into the particular transaction as a result of actual coercion, illegitimate pressure or such domination or control by the wrongdoer that the defendant's ability to make an independent decision was defeated. The defendant has the burden of proving that:

    (a)   the wrongdoer has the capacity to influence the defendant;

    (b)   that influence was exercised;

    (c)   the exercise was undue; and

    (d)   the exercise of that influence actually brought about the transaction.[62]

It is impossible to give an exhaustive definition of what may amount to undue influence.[63] While "importunity and pressure . . . [are] neither always necessary nor sufficient",[64] the critical question is whether the complainant was permitted to exercise independent and informed judgment. The courts have repeatedly stressed the need for this jurisdiction to remain flexible so that its usefulness as an inhibitor of wrongful behaviour and a protection to the vulnerable is not fettered by exactly defined limits.[65] Nevertheless it is clear that not all actual influence, pressure or encouragement is undue influence. In *Royal Bank of Scotland v Etridge (No.2)*, Stuart-Smith L.J. said[66]:

> "In our view the doctrine of undue influence should not be applied so as to shield persons from the consequences of external forces in the absence of some sort of fraud, victimisation or coercion practised by the alleged wrongdoer sufficient to affect his conscience . . . "

The court had previously described the sort of substantial pressures many may be subjected to without being able to establish they had been a victim of undue influence:

> "Legitimate commercial pressure brought by a creditor, however strong, coupled with proper feelings of family loyalty and a laudable desire to help a husband or son in financial difficulty, may be difficult to resist. They may be sufficient to induce a reluctant wife or mother to agree to charge her home by way of collateral security, particularly if they are accompanied by family pressure or emotional scenes. But they are not enough to justify the setting aside of the transaction unless they go beyond what is permissible and lead the complainant to execute the charge not because, however reluctantly, she is persuaded that it is the right thing to do, but because the wrongdoer's importunity has left her with no will of her own."[67]

It follows that the ability to establish that the defending mortgagor did not make the decision to enter the transaction himself but had lost the ability to exercise

---

[62] *Bank of Credit and Commercial International SA v Aboody* [1990] 1 Q.B. 923, per Slade L.J. at 967.

[63] At first instance in *Royal Bank of Scotland v Bennett* [1997] 1 F.L.R. 801, 822–826, Mr James Mumby Q.C. (sitting as a deputy judge of the Chancery Division) provided a detailed analysis of various ways the Courts had sought to define and describe incidents of actual undue influence.

[64] *Etridge (No.2)* [1998] 4 All E.R. 705 at 712.

[65] *Bank of Credit and Commerce International SA v Aboody* [1990] 1 Q.B. 923.

[66] [1998] 4 All E.R. 705 at 746, [23].

[67] *Royal Bank of Scotland v Etridge (No.2)*, above, at 713, [10].

free will because of another's acts is central to a finding of actual undue influence.

Establishing such a proposition will require a detailed consideration of a **31–20** number of factors, including the circumstances surrounding the transaction, the relationship between the relevant parties (particularly when the transaction was concluded), any discussions or advice given leading up to the transaction and the reasons or motives of both the defendant and the alleged wrongdoer in wishing to bring about the traction in question. While the nature of the transaction and the extent to which it is to the defendant's manifest disadvantage seems not to be a necessary element[68] of actual undue influence, it will be of highly significant evidential value in relation to a finding of actual undue influence if the defendant's acts have caused him manifest disadvantage. The causal link between the undue influence and entry into the transaction is critical; but the proposition in *Aboody*[69] that it would not be appropriate for the court to set aside a transaction where the evidence establishes that on the balance of probabilities the complainant would have entered into the transaction in any event has been disapproved. In *UCB Corporate Services Ltd v Williams*[70] concluded that it is the fact that the complainant has been deprived of the opportunity to make a free choice that founds the equity to set aside the transaction. The *Aboody* proposition was "flatly inconsistent with Lord Browne-Wilkinson's propositions in *CIBC Mortgages v Pit.*"[71] By analogy with fraud, it appears to be sufficient to establish that the influence exercised was a significant reason for the entry into the transaction rather than the predominant or only reason.

Presumed undue influence

By recognising that certain types of relationship will make some categories of **31–21** people particularly vulnerable to undue influence and give others the opportunity to take advantage of such relationships, a presumption of undue influence will arise in certain situations. The evil that presumed undue influence focuses upon is subtly different to that addressed by actual undue influence. Presumed undue influence addresses the potential for abuse of relationships of trust, rather than a particular instance of undue influence. Hence it becomes the nature of the relationship and potential for abuse by one party of another for his own or a third party's advantage that is the primary factor which gives rise to the presumption rather than the actual cause of the entry into the particular transaction.

The categories of presumed undue influence

Historically the classes of cases in which undue influence was presumed were **31–22** divided into two. These two categories of cases involving presumed undue

---

[68] *CIBC Mortgages Ltd v Pitt*, above, per Lord Browne-Wilkinson at 209; *Royal Bank of Scotland v Etridge (No.2)*, above, at 713, [11]–[12].
[69] *BCCI v Aboody* [1990] 1 Q.B. 923.
[70] [2002] 3 F.C.R. 448.
[71] [1994] 1 A.C. 180.

influence were most clearly classified by Lord Browne-Wilkinson in *Barclays Bank Plc v O'Brien*[72] as class 2A and class 2B, class 1 cases being those involving actual undue influence.

Class 2A: Where there is a transaction between two people who are in a certain type of relationship, or where one party to such a relationship is induced to enter a transaction with a third party by the other party to the relationship, undue influence will be presumed;

Class 2B: Where it is established that as between the particular defendant and the other contracting party, or the person who secured the defendant's entry into the transaction, there was actually a relationship such that the defendant "reposed trust and confidence" in the wrongdoer, undue influence will be presumed.

The difference was tolerably clear: class 2A cases required the defendant to adduce evidence of the existence of a certain relationship; class 2B cases required evidence of the reposing of trust and confidence outside a relationship which, per se, can give rise to the presumption of undue influence.

The relationships that gave rise to the first class of a presumption of undue influence include that of parent and child,[73] guardian and ward,[74] solicitor and client,[75] doctor and patient,[76] and religious adviser and follower or parishioner if role of adviser has been adopted.[77] Other relationships which are properly characterised as fiduciary in nature or confidential can similarly give rise to the presumption.[78]

Relationships giving rise to a presumption of influence: The courts have made clear that they do not consider this historical division to be of any great assistance.[79] The critical questions are whether there is (i) a relationship of trust and confidence, and (ii) a transaction that cannot reasonably be accounted for on the grounds of friendship, relationship, charity or the ordinary motives on which ordinary men act.[80] Each member of the House of Lords in *Etridge (No.2)* made clear that the distinctions between two classes of presumed undue influence are problematic because they do not assist in identifying what it is about a particular transaction that arouses the suspicions of the court and accordingly either "confuse" or cloud the issue.

However, it does remain clear that at least the above categories of relationship remain ones where the court will not require the complainant to show that he or she in fact reposed trust and confidence in the wrongdoer. The very fact of that relationship is sufficient to cause the court to consider the second question (whether the transaction can reasonably be accounted for). In those cases Lord

---

[72] [1994] A.C. 180 at 189.

[73] *Lancashire Loans Ltd v Black* [1934] Ch. 380; *Wright v Vanderplank* (1855) 2 K. & J. 1; *Archer v Hudson* (1844) 7 Beav. 551.

[74] *Hylton v Hylton* (1804) 2 Ves. Sen. 547; *Taylor v Johnston* (1882) L.R. 19 Ch.D. 603; *Powell v Powell* [1900] 1 Ch. 243.

[75] See *Chitty on Contracts* (30th edn, 2008), para.7–076; *Wright v Carter* [1903] 1 Ch. 27; *Demerara Bauxite v Hubbard* [1923] A.C. 673; *McMaster v Byrne* [1952] 1 All E.R. 1362.

[76] *Mitchell v Homfray* (1881) L.R. 8 Q.B.D. 587; *Radcliffe v Price* (1902) 18 T.L.R. 466.

[77] *Lyon v Home* (1868) 6 L.R. Eq. 655; *Allcard v Skinner* (1887) L.R. 36 Ch.D. 145.

[78] *Tate v Williamson* (1866) 2 L.R. Ch. App. 55, 61.

[79] *Royal Bank of Scotland v Etridge* (above).

[80] *Turkey v Awadh* [2005] 2 F.C.R. 7.

Nicholls said in *Etridge (No.2)* that "the law presumes, irrebutably, that one party had influence over the other."

There are of course, other relationships by virtue of which it will (by degree) be easier to persuade a court that there was a reposition of trust and confidence[81] and that, as a result, the court should look further into the nature of the transaction in order to decide whether or not to set it aside. When considering such of relationships it does not matter whether one party has acquired a dominating influence over the mind of the other. The former "two-fold" analysis must treated with very real caution—the two "groups" are little more than differing instances of relationships in which a transaction which cannot readily be accounted for give rise to an inference that the transaction was procured by undue influence and, unless that inference is rebutted, the transaction should be set aside. It may be that the factor which underlies both "groups" of relationships is simply that the level of trust and confidence reposed by the "victim" is sufficient to warrant suspicion rather than the fact that the relationship is of a particular type.

Transaction not explicable by ordinary motives

Notwithstanding the stated absence in *Barclays Bank Plc v O'Brien*[82] of any requirement that the transaction in question should involve manifest disadvantage to the innocent party in order for undue influence to be presumed, the historical position was (and since *Barclays Bank Plc v O'Brien* has been) that a presumption of undue influence would not arise unless the relevant transaction has to be shown to have been manifestly disadvantageous to the party allegedly influenced and that "manifest disadvantage" for those purposes was that which was clear and obvious and more than de minimis.[83] The present position, reverting to Lindley L.J.'s view in *Allcard* (above), is that the essence of the test is whether the transaction is one which calls for explanation. Upon the court concluding that the relationship was one of trust and confidence and the transaction is one that does call for explanation, the evidential burden shifts to the party about whose conduct complaint is made to rebut the presumption of undue influence. Obviously, the clearer the disadvantage in the transaction to the complainant, the easier it will be to persuade a court that the transaction is not readily explicable (and, by the same token, the harder it will be for the wrongdoer to rebut the presumption).

31–23

This re-casting of the test has perhaps arisen because of the difficulty in deciding in the "normal" husband and wife case whether the transaction was either an advantage or disadvantage to the wife—the reality being that there was probably an element of both. If, on the other hand, when the transaction is looked at, it calls for explanation the balancing of the competing advantages and disadvantages would have been addressed and resolved.

---

[81] See, for example, *Markham v Karsten* [2007] B.P.I.R. 1109.

[82] *Barclays Bank Plc v O'Brien*, above, at 189; *Royal Bank of Scotland v Etridge (No.2)*, above, at 713–714, para.11–13.

[83] *Barclays Bank Plc v Coleman* [2001] Q.B. 20. This appeal was heard by the House of Lords together with the others in *Royal Bank of Scotland v Etridge* (above).

Since the decision in *Etridge (No.2)*, this particular question has caused the courts to think twice. In *Mortgage Agency Services Number Two Ltd v Chater*,[84] the Court concluded that a test which required a transaction "only" explicable on the basis of undue influence; the preferable route was that of Lord Nicholls in *Etridge* who suggested that the test was whether the transaction was one which called for an explanation. HHJ Cooke QC in *Turkey v Awadh*,[85] in the midst of rather unusual facts, considered that the question was whether " . . . given the circumstances and the nature of the transaction, it says to the unbiased observer that absent explanation it must represent the beneficiary taking advantage of his position." What is clear beyond doubt is that the transaction must be look at as a whole and in its proper context in order to see what it tried to achieve for the parties.

The shifting burden

31–24 The effect of establishing a presumption of undue influence is that the onus of proof then shifts to the other party to the transaction to show that it was in fact entered into as a result of the exercise of "full, free and informed consent" of the complainant in order to avoid a finding of undue influence.[86] In order to establish that presumption the complainant will have to provide evidence of the nature of the alleged undue influence; the personality of the various parties; the nature of their relationship; and the reasons why the transaction cannot readily be accounted for. Once established, the Defendant must adduce evidence to rebut the presumption and persuade the Court not to set aside the transaction. It must explain, in the context of the nature of the parties and their relationship why and how it is that the transaction can properly be explained.[87] As Lord Millett made clear in *National Commercial Bank (Jamaica) Ltd v Hew*,[88] "Unless the ascendant party has exploited his influence to obtain some unfair advantage from the vulnerable party there is no ground for equity to intervene. However commercially disadvantageous the transaction may be to the vulnerable party, equity will not set it aside if it is a fair transaction as between the parties to it."

Rebutting the presumption of undue influence

31–25 Evidence that the defendant acted independently and with a full appreciation of what he was doing will rebut a presumption of undue influence.[89] Given the nature of undue influence it is not enough to simply show that the defendant understood the transaction correctly, or indeed that when signing the defendant

---

[84] [2004] 1 P. & C.R. 4.
[85] [2005] 2 F.C.R. 7.
[86] *Zamet v Hyman* [1961] 1 W.L.R. 1442 at 1444; *Etridge (No.2)* at [21]–[31]; *Barclays Bank Plc v Boulter* [1999] 1 W.L.R. 1919.
[87] See *Hogg v Hogg* [2008] 1 P. & C.R. DG7 and *Shaw v Finnimore* [2009] EWHC 376 (Ch).
[88] [2003] UKPC 51.
[89] *Inche Noriah v Shaik Allie Bin Omar* [1929] A.C. 127 at 135.

actually intended to sign the document that was executed.[90] The critical aspect is that the complainant was free from the influence of the wrongdoer. The most obvious way to demonstrate the necessary degree of independence is for the wrongdoer to show that the transaction was explained to the complainant by an independent and properly qualified person who knew of all the material facts. It is insufficient for the giver of a gift to state in a witness statement that he had not been put under any pressure by the donee.[91]

Independent legal advice: The most common way of seeking to rebut the **31–26** presumption is to establish that the complainant had the benefit of independent legal advice. The consideration of whether the defendant had the benefit of legal advice may arise when (1) establishing undue influence, and (2) considering whether the transaction ought to be set aside against the other contracting party, even if they were not the actual wrongdoer. At the first stage, its relevance will be as evidence to rebut the presumption of undue influence (or even possibly as part of the evidence to be considered in deciding whether any actual undue influence was the cause of the entry into the transaction). At that point, again, the question of whether appropriate legal advice was given and its effect must be considered objectively by reference to what in fact occurred. At the second stage, the provision of legal advice will be relevant to the question whether, for instance, the claimant bank had constructive notice of the undue influence and thus whether as between the bank and the "victim" the transaction ought to be set aside. Again, at that second stage the matter is to be considered only from the other contracting party's point of view and on the basis of what was properly known or is assumed to have been known by that party.

Often the advice given by a solicitor[92] to a client contemplating a loan agreement and/or mortgage will simply be to explain to the defendant the nature, effect and potential consequences of the transaction. The view of the Court of Appeal in *Royal Bank of Scotland v Etridge (No.2)*[93] was the subject of specific criticism by the members of the House of Lords. Stuart-Smith L.J. had set out his view that:

> " . . . a solicitor who is asked to advise a client who may be subject to the undue influence of another 'takes upon himself no light nor easy task': see *Wright v Carter* [1903] 1 Ch. 27 at 57, *per* Stirling L.J. How far he should go in probing the matter in order to satisfy himself that his client is able to make a free and informed decision and is not merely agreeing to do what the wrongdoer wants is a matter of professional judgment: see *Massey v Midland Bank plc* [1995] 1 All E.R. 929 at 934, *per* Steyn L.J. It must depend on all the circumstances of the case. Independent advice may be desirable but it is not always necessary. It depends on the nature of the proposed transaction and the relationship between the parties. Where there is a real conflict of interest, and certainly where there is a possibility that he may be called on to advise the wife not to enter into the proposed transaction, a solicitor should decline to act

---

[90] *Royal Bank of Scotland v Etridge (No.2)*, above, at 714, para.11–13; *Powell v Powell* [1900] 1 Ch. 243, 247.

[91] *Goodchild v Bradbury* [2006] All E.R. (D) 247.

[92] Or a legal executive: see *Barclays Bank Plc v Coleman* [2001] Q.B. 20, and heard on appeal to the House of Lords together with *Royal Bank of Scotland v Etridge (No.2)* (above).

[93] [1998] 4 All E.R. 705 at 716.

if he is also acting (otherwise than in a purely ministerial capacity) for another party to the transaction."

Lord Nicholls made it clear that it is not for the solicitor to advise whether or not the complainant should enter into the transaction (other, it seems, than in circumstances where it is glaringly obvious that the transaction would result in a grievous wrong to the complainant where the solicitor should refuse to continue to act if the complainant wishes to continue with the transaction). The decision whether to proceed is that of the complainant.

It follows that in considering whether the independent legal advice (the precise advice which is appropriate will differ from case to case) was sufficient to rebut the presumption of undue influence, it will be relevant to consider what advice was given, whether the defendant was specifically told that he/she must make his/her own decision about whether to enter the transaction and whether, having done so, that was as a result of an independent and free decision so to do. In particular, it will be important that the solicitor explains to the complainant both the reasons why it is that he has become involved and the fact that in the event of some future complaint the mortgagee will rely on the fact of advice having been given to counter any suggestion that the complainant either did not understand the transaction or did not enter into it freely after proper advice. The solicitor must confirm that the complainant wishes him to act and then give the necessary advice. If the solicitor does not have a full and proper understanding of the factual background to the transaction (and, so realising, does not ask any questions or receive adequate answers) the advice may be treated as inadequate.

Thus, as a bare minimum, it is thought that the advice (which should be in non-technical language and given in a face to face meeting at which no other party should be present) ought to contain the following:

    (i) an explanation of the nature of the documentation that the complainant is being asked to sign and the practical consequences for the complainant if he or she does sign;

   (ii) a discussion of the risks which will arise upon signing the documentation and the implications for the complainant upon such signature;

  (iii) if the solicitor considers that the transaction is not in the complainant's best interests, he should advise accordingly; and

  (iv) a clear statement that the complainant has a choice. The nature of that choice should be explained both in the event that the documents are signed and in the event that they are not.

The solicitor should then confirm whether or not the complainant wishes to sign the documents and whether or not the solicitor can write to the mortgagee to state that he has explained the nature of the documentation and the practical implications for the complainant. This must not be done without the express authority of the complainant.

Further, there will be occasions when it will be necessary for the advice to go further so as to identify the information that the defendant should ascertain before making a decision, or even so far as to make a recommendation whether or not the transaction should be entered into. The absence of independence in any sense on the part of the solicitor would clearly diminish the value of evidence of his involvement to rebut the presumption. Thus, where the solicitor was advising the wife of a company director who was securing that company's borrowings against the jointly owned matrimonial home and the solicitor was also the company's secretary the bank was put on enquiry and could not avoid constructive notice of the company director's undue influence over his wife.[94] If the entry into the transaction by the defendant was in accordance with the advice given by a solicitor and that advice was sufficient and independent, the presumption is likely to be rebutted, or, at the very least, the bank will not be fixed with constructive notice of it.

The position is rather more difficult in circumstances where the defendant was given independent legal advice and ignored or rejected it. In such circumstances there are good arguments that this is sufficient; however that argument will not always present itself. In some instances it can be argued that the ignoring of advice not to enter the transaction is actually an example of just how strong the undue influence was. In practice, a solicitor should withdraw if not satisfied that his client is exercising free will. Unless he does so, his client will (at a later stage) struggle to establish that the presumption should operate unless he can show that his solicitor had been negligent. By the same token, the mere involvement of an independent solicitor will not, without more, prevent a plea of undue influence succeeding.[95]

Other circumstances: It is, of course, open to a court to conclude on the facts,   **31–27** even without independent advice having been given, that the presumption is rebutted. Other professionals' advice (e.g. a financial adviser) could suffice and, of course, the court may conclude that despite the relationship the transaction was a product of the complainant's "full, free and informed will" nonetheless. Clearly instances of the latter will be difficult to establish.

<h2 style="text-align:center">MISREPRESENTATION AND OTHER VITIATING FACTORS</h2>

Misrepresentation

As with any other contract, if a defendant can establish that he was induced to   **31–28** enter a loan agreement and/or mortgage by a misrepresentation (whether made by the mortgagee or a third party[96]) he may have a right to set that agreement aside.[97] While in order to succeed the defendant will need to establish a misrepresentation of fact which was the effective cause of his entry into the contract, the misrepresentation need not have been the sole cause. It need only be one of

---

[94] *National Westminster Bank v Breeds* [2001] Lloyd's Rep. Bank. 98.

[95] *Niersmans v Pesticcio* [2004] N.P.C. 55.

[96] See *Kings North Trust Ltd v Bell* [1961] 1 W.L.R. 119; *Royal Bank of Scotland v Etridge (No.2)* (above).

[97] See *Chitty on Contracts* (30th edn, 2008), Ch.6; *Macdonald v Myerson* [2001] 6 E.G. 162 (C.S.).

the inducing causes. In the context of mortgages, the misrepresentation is most often about the circumstances in which liability or enforcement will occur or the extent of that liability. If the defendant did not actually hear or understand the misrepresentation so that it was not operating on his mind in order to induce the decision to contract, it would not have been an effective cause.[98] The misrepresentation must still be effective at the time of entry into the transaction; if by that point the defendant is aware of the true position, the earlier misrepresentation does not give rise to a defence. Even if the claimant is unaware of the inaccuracy of the representation at the time of entry into the transaction, if it can be established that the defendant would in fact have entered the transaction even if the truth were known, a defence based on misrepresentation will fail.[99]

Where a right to set aside a mortgage is established on the basis that the terms of the loan agreement or mortgage were misrepresented, the right to set aside is not qualified or limited to a right to convert the loan agreement or mortgage to an agreement on the terms it was understood were being agreed to. So, for instance, where the right to set aside arose as a result of a misrepresentation to the defendant that the liability secured by the charge was limited to £15,000 the mortgagee's contention that the original mortgage should be set aside on terms that a limited charge or mortgage be granted was rejected and the mortgage was simply set aside.[100] However, where the transaction consists of several distinct parts, for instance where separate advances were made at different times and the matters that give rise to the right to set aside only affect one distinct part of the transaction, the transaction can be severed so that the distinct part can be set aside and the rest survive.[101]

Other vitiating factors

31–29   Similarly, loan agreements and mortgages can also be challenged on the basis of a right to set them aside arising as a result of any other vitiating factor that provides a defence to a contractual claim. It follows that if a mortgagor can establish mistake or duress, the security may be ineffective as against a mortgagee depending on the complainant's ability to establish that any right to set the underlying agreement aside is effective as against the mortgagee, whether he is the wrongdoer or not. An 'innocent' mortgagee would have to have notice of the wrongdoing to be affected by the complainant's equity.

EXERCISING THE RIGHT TO SET ASIDE

As against the mortgagee

31–30   Once a mortgagor has established that his entry into a transaction was brought about by a vitiating factor such as undue influence or misrepresentation, a right

---

[98] *Horsfall v Thomas* (1862) 1 H. & C. 90.
[99] *Industrial Properties Ltd v Associated Electrical Industries Ltd* [1977] Q.B. 580; *Pan Atlantic Insurance Co Ltd v Pine Top Insurance Co Ltd* [1995] 1 A.C. 501.
[100] *TSB Bank Plc v Camfield* [1995] 1 W.L.R. 430.
[101] *Barclays Bank Plc v Caplan* [1998] 1 F.L.R. 532.

to set aside the transaction will arise as between the mortgagor and the wrong-doer. If the mortgagee is, in fact or vicariously, the wrongdoer, the right to set aside the transaction arises directly against the mortgagee.

Mortgages of reversionary interests and expectancies

The courts have a general equitable jurisdiction to interfere and set aside mort-   **31–31**
gages of reversionary interests and expectancies (and to modify the terms of redemption modified) if it is established that the mortgagor has been over-reached.[102] This jurisdiction may also operate where the mortgagor is poor and ignorant or in weak health.[103] This is considered elsewhere in this work.[104]

Control under the Consumer Credit Act 1974[105]

By reason of the 1974 Act the court has a general and additional power to make   **31–32**
a range of remedial orders[106] in respect of unfair relationships[107] between creditors and debtors if the debtor or mortgagor is an "individual" as defined.[108] Finally, it must be remembered that in relatively few cases, where the mortgage is a "regulated agreement" within the meaning of s.189(1) of the Consumer Credit Act 1974, the mortgagor has an overriding right of redemption exercisable at any time.[109] The extent of the 1974 Act is considered elsewhere in this work.[110]

As against an "innocent" third party

Clearly, transactions may be set aside as result, for example, of the undue   **31–33**
influence of the one of the contracting parties or a third party. In the three party

---

[102] In the sense of having been overpowered, see *Croft v Graham* (1863) 2 De G. J. & S. 155.

[103] *Bromley v Smith* (1859) 26 Beav. 644; *Croft v Graham*, above; *Fry v Lane* (1889) L.R. 40 Ch.D. 312; *Cresswell v Potter* [1978] 1 W.L.R. 255.

[104] See Chs 26 and 27.

[105] As amended by the Consumer Credit Act 2006.

[106] Consumer Credit Act 2006 s.140B

[107] Consumer Credit Act ss.19–22 repealed and replaced ss.137–140 of the 1974 Act. Sections 140A–140D relate to "unfair relationships" between creditors and debtors and replace the previous provisions concerning extortionate credit transactions. Those powers came into force on April 6, 2007, but the provision in para.15(1) of Sch.3 makes expressly clear that the repeal of ss.137–140 do not affect the power of the court to reopen an existing agreement under those sections. See generally, Ch.26.

[108] Section 189 (as amended by the 2006 Act) makes clear that an "individual" extends to a partnership (of two or three partners not all of whom are bodies corporate) and an unincorporated body of persons which does not consist entirely of bodies corporate and is not a partnership and any other form of legal entity which is not a body corporate. This definition applies from April 6, 2007, onwards in relation to agreements made after that date. The powers are contained in s.140B. See also the similar powers of the court under the Insolvency Act 1986 s.244 in the case of companies and s.343 in the case of bankrupts.

[109] See above Ch.26 and paras 30–01 et seq.

[110] See Ch.26.

scenario referred to at the start of this section,[111] it is more often than not the influence of the husband which is exerted over the wife which enables the wife to set aside the transaction as against the mortgagee. Prior to *Barclays Bank v O'Brien*,[112] the basis on which she could do so was not clear. The first theoretical basis was agency—the wrongdoer was regarded as the agent of the third party and thus the third party could be in no better position that his agent when it came to enforcing the transaction against the complainant. This view is now best disregarded. The second theory was notice—the third party had actual or constructive notice of the equity upon which the wife relied to set aside the transaction. This is clearly the better view in circumstances where the husband borrows against the matrimonial home. It is quite wrong to view him as the agent of the bank, whether the lending is to be used by him personally or his corporate manifestation.

Actual notice to the mortgagee of the undue influence or duress presents few problems. The critical area for consideration is that of constructive notice. The law of undue influence has developed specifically in the context of mortgages and title questions. The essence of the doctrine is that where there exists a standard procedure for investigating title, the lender will be fixed with constructive notice of that which he would have discovered had he followed that procedure. The doctrine goes further, though, in that it applies whenever a party is put on inquiry as to the existence of another's rights. If no inquiry is made, he is again fixed with notice of that which he would have discovered if had made reasonable inquiry.[113]

It is not surprising given the nature of the defences concerned that equity has developed principles that involve establishing an element of culpability on the part of the third party before imposing the consequences on that third party of the wrongdoer's actions. If not the wrongdoer itself, the mortgagee must be knowingly taking advantage of the wrongdoing or have conducted itself in a way that justifies treating it as if it knew that it was taking advantage of the wrongdoing. There are a number of ways in which the mortgagee's conscience can be affected.

Actual notice of the vitiating factor

31–34   The concept of actual notice speaks for itself and will of course be a question of fact. If it is possible to show that the mortgagee or its employee were actually informed or observed for themselves that undue influence was being exercised in order to secure the mortgagor's entry into the loan agreement or other vitiating circumstances were present, the mortgagor's right to set the agreement aside will be effective against the mortgagee. Such cases are rare.

---

[111] The mortgage of the matrimonial home by husband and wife to a bank to secure the business or other indebtedness of the husband or his company.
[112] ibid.
[113] *Etridge (No.2)* (above) at [33]–[43].

Imputed notice of the vitiating factor

A small number of cases turned on the notion of imputed notice—where the **31–35** knowledge of the agent is imputed to the principal. One obvious area of concern is the knowledge of a solicitor who acts for both the third party and the wrongdoer. That said, the third party will not be troubled by notice of anything the solicitor knows unless that knowledge was acquired when the solicitor was acting for the third party when he acquired it.[114]

Constructive notice of the vitiating factor

The courts have been heavily engaged in considering the ambit of constructive **31–36** notice in the context of undue influence and misrepresentation as defences to mortgagees' claims. The doctrine of constructive notice represents an attempt by the courts to ensure a fair allocation of the risk of the consequences of a third party's wrongdoing between the two innocent parties, namely the defendant mortgagor and the mortgagee. The starting point is that the mortgagee should be alert to indications that the mortgagor may have a right to set aside the transaction. If put on inquiry by such indications as are available to it, a mortgagee will be deemed to have constructive notice of that wrongdoing and would not be entitled to take the benefit of the transaction. If, having been initially put on inquiry, the mortgagee takes reasonable steps to inquire further and ensures that the risk of wrongdoing is largely dispelled, the mortgagee may avoid a finding of constructive notice. The initial burden of establishing constructive notice lies with the mortgagor seeking to set aside the transaction.[115]

In recent times the doctrine has seen significant revision. In *Barclays Bank v O'Brien* (above), the House of Lords started to clarify what is required. Their Lordships made clear that there was no special equity protecting wives and that the surety wife could not set aside the transaction merely because she did not understand it. Lord Browne-Wilkinson set out that there was a substantial risk that a wife would act as surety when the transaction was not to her advantage because of some equitable or legal wrong on the part of her husband. Thus, where the creditor knew that the debtor and surety were husband and wife and the transaction was not, on its face, to the surety's financial advantage, the mortgagee would be fixed with constructive notice of any undue influence unless it took reasonable steps to satisfy itself that the obligations being undertaken by the surety were undertaken freely and with knowledge of the true facts.

This position was reconsidered in *Etridge (No.2)*. Lord Nicholls made clear that *O'Brien* was an unconventional use of the doctrine of constructive notice because the law imposes no obligation on one party to check whether the other party's consent was obtained by undue influence. In *Etridge (No.2)*, the steps suggested were such that the bank can reduce or eliminate the risk of entry into a transaction as a result of undue influence. As a result of the decision in *Etridge*

---

[114] LPA 1925 s.199(1)(ii)(b); *Halifax Mortgage Services Ltd v Stepsky* [1996] Ch. 207.
[115] *Barclays Bank Plc v Boulter* [1999] 2 F.L.R. 986.

(No.2), the lender is now to be viewed as being put on inquiry by the combination of a non-commercial relationship between the surety and the lender *and* a transaction which on its face is disadvantageous to the surety. Clearly the first element is satisfied if the lender is aware of the relationship between the parties—whether they are husband and wife, an unmarried couple, parent and child. The second element does not arise where the money is advanced jointly, unless the lender is aware that the advance is to be used for the husband's purposes only. However, where the wife stands as surety for a company whose shares are held by husband and wife (even in equal shares), the lender is put on inquiry.

Lord Nicholls went on to reiterate that the lender will need "to bring home to the wife the risk she is running by standing as surety and to advise her to take independent legal advice."[116] However, he then went on to state that for the future 'the lender will satisfy the requirement if it insists that the wife attend a private meeting with a representative of the lender at which she is told of the extent of her liability as surety; warned as to the risk she is running and urged to take independent legal advice. He stated that if the lender prefers that task to be undertaken by a solicitor it would usually be sufficient to rely on a confirmation from the solicitor, acting for the wife, that he has advised the wife appropriately.

31–37   A fundamental factor that underpins the court's approach to the involvement of a solicitor is that a mortgagee is obviously not entitled to inquire into exactly what passes between the solicitor and the mortgagor but is entitled to assume that the solicitor acted properly and professionally[117] and so gave sufficient advice and was sufficiently independent.[118] Further, as indicated above,[119] a solicitor advising someone who may be entering a transaction as a result of undue influence or something similar has a duty to address that and to ensure that the entry into the transaction is as a result of a free and informed decision or to withdraw from acting for that person. Where a potential mortgagor does not approach the mortgagee through a solicitor or appear to have a solicitor, the mortgagee can generally avoid a finding of constructive notice if it urges the mortgagor to take independent legal advice and, if advice is taken, receives confirmation from a solicitor that the transaction has been explained to the mortgagor.[120]

31–38   When giving advice to a potential mortgagor, a solicitor acts exclusively as that individual's solicitor regardless of who actually instructed or retained the solicitor in relation to that advice or the transaction as a whole.[121] In those circumstances, the entitlement to make the assumption that a solicitor who did not withdraw acted properly amounts to an assumption that the vitiating factor

---

[116] *Etridge (No.2)* (above) at [50].

[117] *Royal Bank of Scotland v Etridge*, above.

[118] *Massey v Midland Bank Plc* [1995] 1 All E.R. 929; *Bank of Baroda v Rayarel*, above; *Royal Bank of Scotland v Etridge*, above.

[119] See para.31–25.

[120] *Massey v Midland Bank Plc* above; *Bank of Baroda v Rayarel*, above; *Royal Bank of Scotland v Etridge*, above.

[121] *Bank of Baroda v Rayarel ante*; *Royal Bank of Scotland v Etridge*, above.

has been addressed.[122] In the absence of express confirmation from a solicitor that he has undertaken the work he was instructed to do, a mortgagee is not entitled to assume that the mortgagor has been properly advised. So for instance, where a solicitor has simply witnessed the mortgagor's signature, the mortgagee will not avoid having constructive notice of undue influence.[123] However, it is not necessary for the confirmation to be full or detailed. Where the confirmation is inadequate, at most the mortgagee is put on inquiry as to whether the mortgagor has been properly advised and the mortgagor will only succeed in establishing the mortgagee had constructive notice if he was not properly advised *and* the mortgagee fails to make further inquiries or secure clearer confirmation.[124] Where a mortgagee is aware of material facts that would be relevant to the decision to enter the transaction and is aware that a solicitor does not have knowledge of those matters, the mortgagee will not be able simply to rely on the fact that a solicitor was instructed to advise and confirmed that he had so acted.[125] Where a solicitor instructed to advise the mortgagor acquires information in the course of that retainer, the mortgagee is not imputed with that knowledge, even if it was the mortgagee that instructed the solicitor.[126]

THE LOSS OF THE RIGHT TO SET ASIDE

Contracts obtained by undue influence, misrepresentation and duress are voidable rather than void ab initio. Where a contract is voidable, the innocent party to the contract has a choice of electing whether to rescind or affirm the contract. In determining whether the right to set aside a transaction is lost, the underlying test (as approved by Stuart-Smith L.J. in *Royal Bank of Scotland v Etridge*[127] can be stated thus: **31–39**

> "Upon whatever precise basis it is sought to uphold a transaction which was originally obtained by undue influence it is an essential ingredient that it would be inequitable to allow the influenced party to set aside the transaction."

Various recognised factors can deny a complainant the right to set a transaction aside.

Affirmation

If, after the complainant is free of the effects of the vitiating factor, a choice/ election is made to affirm the contract, the right to avoid/rescind such a contract **31–40**

---

[122] *Northern Rock Building Society v Archer* (1998) 78 P.& C. R. 65; *Bank of Scotland v Hill* [2003] 1 P. & C.R. DG7, *UCB v Williams* [2003] 2 P. & C.R. 168. For a case where a personal interview was required, see *Wright v Cherry Tree Finance Ltd* [2001] EWCA Civ 449.

[123] *Scottish Equitable Life Plc v Virdee* [1999] 1 F.L.R. 863.

[124] *Royal Bank of Scotland v Etridge*, above.

[125] *Royal Bank of Scotland v Etridge*, above, at 722; see also *Credit Lyonnaise Bank Nederland v Burch*, above.

[126] *Halifax Mortgage Services Ltd v Stepsky* [1996] Ch. 207; *Royal Bank of Scotland v Etridge*, above.

[127] [1998] 4 All E.R. 705, approving *Goldworthy v Brickell* [1987] Ch. 378.

may be lost.[128] In the case of a right to set aside based on misrepresentation, that would generally mean simply that the defendant knows that the representation made was false. The position is more complex where the vitiating factor is undue influence. In such circumstances, as a matter of principle, it is suggested that it should not be sufficient merely to establish the cessation of the pressure applied which initially secured the impugned transaction. Almost inevitably that particular pressure will end once the transaction has been completed. In order to be free of the undue influence so as to make an election, it is necessary for the innocent party to have moved out of the reach of the influential relationship. This necessarily involves the ending of the relationship between the two people or the changing of the nature of the relationship so that it is no longer possible for such influence to be exercised. Although it appears that it is not a rigid rule, generally a party will not be treated as having affirmed such a contract unless, with knowledge of both (1) the facts which give rise to the election, and (2) the existence of his right to elect, he unequivocally demonstrates to the other contracting party that he intends to proceed with the contract.[129] Affirmation may be by an express statement that the right to set aside is not being exercised or by reliance still being placed on the contract and the obligations arising thereunder. Alternatively, the affirmation may occur when the party with the right to set aside the contract continues to conduct himself in a manner that is consistent with the continued existence of the contract.

Delay and estoppel

31–41 Delay in itself is not a bar to a claim to set aside a contract for undue influence or misrepresentation.[130] Evidence of delay after the cessation of the influential relationship and with actual knowledge of both the facts that give rise to and of the existence of the possible right to set aside may be the basis of an inference that the party has subsequently acquiesced in the contract[131] so that affirmation would be made out. It is to be noted that the courts do not easily draw such an inference even when there is evidence that a mortgagor with actual knowledge of the possible right to set aside acts in a way that demonstrates an attitude inconsistent with the claim to set aside.[132] Delay coupled with some actions that can be construed as a representation that the contract is continuing will more readily result in an inference that the mortgagor is acquiescing in the continuation of the contract. Alternatively, if the mortgagee acts in reliance on a belief that the contract remains in place, the delay and actions of the mortgagor can form the

---

[128] *Hatch v Hatch* (1804) 9 Ves. Jr. 292; *Allcard v Skinner* (1887) L.R. 36 Ch.D. 145, 187, 191. See *Chitty on Contracts* (30th edn, 2008) Ch.24, para.24–003.

[129] *Peyman v Lanjani* [1985] 1 Ch. 457.

[130] *Armstrong v Jackson* [1917] 2 K.B. 822, 830; *Allcard v Skinner*, above, at 174, 191. Except where the misrepresentation is innocent: see *Leaf v International Galleries* [1950] 2 K.B. 86.

[131] *Allcard v Skinner*, above, at 174–175, 187, 193; *Bullock v Lloyds Bank Ltd* [1955] Ch. 317 at 327; *Re Pauling's Settlement Trusts* [1964] Ch. 303 at 353.

[132] *Bullock v Lloyds Bank Ltd*, above, at 327; *Re Pauling's Settlement Trusts*, above, at 353.

basis of an estoppel barring any attempt by the mortgagor to set aside the contract.

Restitutio in integrum

Where a defendant has received a benefit under the transaction, the transaction **31–42** can only be set aside if the defendant gives back that benefit. The setting aside of a transaction is a restitutionary remedy which can only be granted if both parties to the transaction are, inter se, put back into the position they were in prior to the transaction.[133] In the context of mortgages, it is often the case that the mortgagor is acting as surety for a principal debtor so that the mortgagor himself received no benefit. In those circumstances, the contract can be set aside without the money secured being repaid.

The Effect of Setting Aside a Transaction

In circumstances where a party succeeds in setting aside a mortgage as against **31–43** the mortgagee, a number of consequences flow. First, the successful party's beneficial interest will (subject to the matters raised below) be freed from the obligations that would otherwise be imposed upon it by the transaction that has been impeached. Secondly, in circumstances where the successful party is one of two registered proprietors and the transaction is binding on the other proprietor (for example, where the other proprietor is, in fact, the wrongdoer and has forged or otherwise obtained the successful party's signature to the transaction), the beneficial interest of the successful party remains freed from the obligations that would otherwise have been imposed upon it by the impeached transaction (again subject to the matters raised below) while the wrongdoer's beneficial interest in the property remains subject to the terms of the transaction which the wrongdoer himself has duly executed.[134]

From the successful party's point of view this can have a number of consequences. First, the wrongdoer's execution of a mortgage or charge over his beneficial interest in the property will operate to sever any beneficial joint tenancy that may exist in relation to that property.[135] Secondly, the mortgagee is able to exercise all its remedies against the beneficial interest in the property that

---

[133] *Dunbar Bank Plc v Nadeem* [1998] 3 All E.R. 876; *Society of Lloyd's v Khan* [1999] 1 F.L.R. 246. See *Chitty on Contracts* (30th edn, 2008), para.7–098 and Goff & Jones, (7th edn, 2007), *The Law of Restitution*, paras 11–10 et seq.

[134] *First National Securities v Hegarty* [1985] Q.B. 850; *Mortgage Corporation v Shaire* (above); *First National Bank Plc v Achampong* (above) and *Edwards v Lloyds TSB Bank Plc* (above). No interest passes if the transaction is intended by both parties to it to be a sham (*Penn v Bristol & West Building Society* [1995] 2 F.L.R. 938).

[135] *Ahmed v Kendrick* (1988) 56 P. & C.R. 120.

is properly charged to it. Such remedies obviously include taking possession of the property[136] and obtaining an order for sale. Obviously, a mortgagor can only mortgage the estate in the property that he in fact has. So where a mortgagor purports to mortgage a larger estate that he has, the conveyance[137] or disposition[138] passes only that interest.

---

[136] Possession will not be given of a dwelling-house to the mortgagee while a party enjoys an arguable defence to any claim (e.g. is asserting a defence of undue influence), particularly if the defendants are husband and wife: *Albany Home Loans Limited v Massey* [1997] 2 All E.R. 609. However, once the strength of that defence has been determined, the usual considerations with regard to granting an order for possession apply. In practical terms, when a mortgagee seeks possession of a jointly owned and jointly mortgaged property and only one of the two mortgagors has a defence to the claim, the claim against the mortgagor with no defence should be adjourned until the other mortgagor leaves the property or has a possession order made against him. Alternatively, a possession order can be made, subject to an undertaking not to enforce until, again, the other mortgagor leaves the property or has a possession order made against him.

[137] In the case of unregistered land includes a mortgage, charge, lease, assent, vesting declaration, vesting instrument, disclaimer, release and every other assurance of property or of an interest therein by any instrument except a will.

[138] Pursuant to LRA 2002 s.23(1)(a), the powers of the owner consist of (a) power to make a disposition of any kind permitted by the general law in relation to an interest of that description other than a mortgage by demise or sub-demise, and (b) power to charge the legal estate at law with the payment of money. These take effect as charges by way of legal mortgage (s.51). The grant of a legal charge is a registrable disposition pursuant to s.27(2)(f) and must be created by deed (LPA 1925 ss.85 and 86).

CHAPTER 32

MATTERS INCIDENTAL TO THE SECURITY

INSURANCE[1]

By virtue of s.101 of the Law of Property Act 1925[2] the mortgagee has the statutory power to insure and keep insured the mortgaged property at the expense of the mortgagor in order to preserve his security in respect of loss or damage by fire.[3] The premiums paid for any such insurance shall be a charge on the mortgaged property with the same priority and carrying interest at the same rate as the mortgage debt. However, the premiums cannot be recovered from the mortgagor as a debt in the absence of any express covenant. The power is exercisable as soon as the mortgage is made.[4] It is worth bearing in mind that if a life policy falls within the security, the premiums paid by the mortgagee in order to keep the policy alive can be added to the debt (even in circumstances where the mortgagee covenanted to pay those premiums[5]).

32–01

The disadvantages of the statutory power arise not only by virtue of this express restriction as to loss or damage by fire, but also from the terms of s.108(1)[6] of the Law of Property Act 1925 in that the power is limited to an insurance not exceeding the amount specified in the mortgage deed, or if no amount is so specified, two-thirds of the sum necessary to restore the mortgaged property in the event of total destruction. Further, by s.108(2) the statutory power cannot be exercised by the mortgagee:

> "(i) where there is a declaration in the mortgage deed that no insurance is required;
> (ii) when an insurance is kept by or on behalf of the mortgagor in accordance with the mortgage deed;
> (iii) where the mortgage deed contains no stipulation respecting insurance, and an insurance is kept up by or on behalf of the mortgagor with the consent of the mortgagee to the amount to which the mortgagee is by the Act authorised to insure."

---

[1] See also paras 16–08 et seq.

[2] Law of Property Act (LPA) 1925 ss.101(1)(ii), 108, replacing (with slight variations) the Conveyancing Act 1881 ss.18(1)(ii), 23.

[3] The power may be varied or extended by the mortgage deed, and the section only applies if and so far as a contrary intention is not expressed in the deed—LPA 1925 s.101(3), (4).

[4] LPA 1925 s.101(1)(ii).

[5] *Shaw v Scottish Widows' Fund Assurance Society* (1917) 87 L.J. Ch. 76.

[6] LPA 1925 s.108(3).

The mortgagee may require that the insurance moneys received be applied by the mortgagor in making good the loss or damage in respect of which it has been paid.[7]

32–02   Thus, owing to the inadequacy of the statutory power it is usual for the mortgage deed to contain an express covenant on the part of the mortgagor to insure the security for a specified amount, or for the full value of the property. The covenant also usually contains an agreement by the mortgagor to produce receipts for the premiums on demand, and to repay to the mortgagee any sums paid by him in respect of those premiums.

The effect of such an express covenant on the part of the mortgagor enables the mortgagee, in the case of default by the mortgagor, to recover those sums paid by the mortgagee in respect of premiums as a debt and as a breach of the covenant by the mortgagor instead of having to add such premiums to the mortgage debt which occurs in the case of the statutory power. Breach of such a covenant is a default which at once sets up the mortgagee's statutory power of sale.

Further, and without prejudice to any obligation to the contrary imposed by law or by special contract, a mortgagee may require that all money received under an insurance effected as mentioned above be applied by the mortgagor in or towards the discharge of the mortgage money.[8] The covenant operates to grant to the mortgagee a charge over the proceeds. This position arises even if the insurance is taken out in the name of the mortgagor.[9] As a direct result of the fact that the interest of the mortgagee is only to secure the mortgage debt, where a policy is in the mortgagee's name he is legally entitled to the proceeds but only to that extent. He must account to the mortgagor (and following mortgagees) in respect of any surplus.[10] Where the mortgagor takes out a policy in his own name in compliance with the terms of a covenant to insure, he is legally entitled to the proceeds but subject to the same interest of the mortgagee (i.e. to secure the mortgage debt). The interest of the mortgagee operates as a partial equitable assignment (protection being subject to the standard rule of note to the insurance company[11]).

However, if the mortgagor has effected a further insurance which is independent of the security, the mortgagee will not be entitled to its benefit.[12] Thus, if the insurance policy contains a clause limiting the insurers' liability in the event of the security in question being the subject of any other insurance, the result may

---

[7] LPA 1925 s.101(1)(ii).

[8] LPA 1925 s.108(4). In the case of loss or damage by fire and reinstatement of the mortgaged property from the insurance proceeds the position is somewhat complicated, see the Fire Prevention (Metropolis) Act 1774 s.83, the operation of which is not confined to the metropolis. It is generally assumed that the mortgagee's rights under s.108(4) or the mortgagee's contractual rights are subsumed to the rights of "any person interested" under s.83 of the 1774 Act to require the insurance company to utilise the insurance proceeds towards reinstatement of the building (see, e.g. Fisher & Lightwood, *Law of Mortgage* (12th edn, 2006), para.7.21; but see MacGillivray and Parkington, *Insurance Law* (11th edn, 2008), paras 20–31 et seq.). Even if this is a correct interpretation of the law in relation to fire insurance, a third party with no interest in the mortgagee but who is a "person interested" under s.83 of the 1774 Act, can insist on reinstatement.

[9] *Colonial Mutual Insurance Co Ltd v ANZ Banking Insurance Group (New Zealand) Ltd* [1995] 1 W.L.R. 1140.

[10] ibid.

[11] *Dearle v Hall* (1828) 3 Russ 1.

[12] See *Halifax Building Society v Keighley* [1931] 2 K.B. 248.

be that the amount payable to the mortgagee is diminished and the mortgagee will have no right to the benefit of the further insurance moneys.[13]

POWER TO GRANT LEASES

Generally

The power of a mortgagor to grant and enforce leases well illustrates the compromise between the equitable ownership of the mortgagor and the legal rights inherent in the title of the mortgagee.[14] Having parted with his legal right to possession by demise or legal charge and merely retaining the reversion subject to a long term of years[15] (together with the equity of redemption), the mortgagor might be expected to have no power to grant leases to take effect during the continuance of the mortgage. There are, however, a number of circumstances in which a mortgagor can grant leases which will bind the mortgagee, irrespective of the position of the tenant. Three of these relate directly to the mortgagee, namely where the mortgagee either consents to the lease or treats the tenant as his own,[16] or where the mortgage expressly empowers the mortgagor to grant leases; the fourth is a statutory power. **32–03**

Unless he has actually been dispossessed by the mortgagee, he can create legal tenancies which are binding on himself and his lessee upon the principle of estoppel.[17] For a tenant is estopped from denying his landlord's title and a landlord from denying the validity of his lease. Consequently, the mortgagor may sue or distrain for rent.[18] Such a lease will not, however, be binding on the mortgagee, if the latter asserts his paramount title to possession.[19] That is the position even where, before completion of a purchase and associated mortgage, a purchaser of the legal estate purports to grant a lease of the land he has contracted to purchase.[20]

Where a purchase and the grant of a mortgage occur at the same time, for instance where a purchaser relies on a mortgage to fund all or part of the purchase price, the purchaser will only ever acquire the equity of redemption so there is no

---

[13] ibid.

[14] For the position with regard to leases granted *before* the mortgage, see above, Ch.17.

[15] See above, paras 12–02 et seq.

[16] *Stroud Building Society v Delamont* [1960] 1 All E.R. 749.

[17] *Doe d. Marriot v Edwards* (1834) 6 C. & P. 208; *Webb v Austin* (1844) 7 Man. & G. 701; *Cuthbertson v Irving* (1860) 4 H. & N. 742 at 754, affirmed (1860) 6 H. & N. 135); *Trent v Hunt* (1853) 9 Exch. 14.

[18] *Trent v Hunt* (1853) 9 Ex. 14; and see above, paras 29–15 et seq.

[19] *Rogers v Humphreys* (1835) 4 Ad. & El. 299; *Trent v Hunt* (1853) 9 Ex. 14; unless, of course, the lease was authorised by the mortgagee; *Corbett v Plowden* (1884) L.R. 25 Ch.D. 678; or his concurrence in the tenancy could be implied from some act or conduct on his part, *e.g.* by the acceptance of the mortgagees' tenant, see *Stroud Building Society v Delamont* [1960] 1 W.L.R. 431, approved in *Chatsworth Properties Ltd v Effiom* [1971] 1 W.L.R. 144. But such a tenancy binding the mortgagee will not arise merely because the mortgagee does not object, (*Re O'Rourke's Estate* (1889) 23 L.R. Ir. 497); or the mortgagee fails to evict the tenant, (*Parker v Braithwaite* [1952] W.N. 504), even though the mortgagor was in default at the time, (*Taylor v Ellis* [1960] Ch. 368); see also *Barclays Bank v Kiley* [1961] 1 W.L.R. 1050.

[20] *Abbey National Building Society v Cann* [1991] A.C. 56; *Hardy v Fowle* [2007] EWHC 2423 (Ch.)

scintilla temporis when the estoppel affecting him can be fed by his acquisition of the legal estate, and thus give rise to a tenancy binding on the mortgagee.[21] However, circumstances may arise where the lease may have priority and bind the mortgagee, even when the contractual tenancy ends and only a statutory tenancy remains.[22]where a mortgagee either fails to register a mortgage of registered land and a tenancy is granted in breach of the terms of the mortgage before its registration, or the mortgagor purports to grant a lease prior to completion of a purchase at a time when he has only an equitable interest (such that on completion the estoppel by which the tenancy exists is fed) and the charge is executed after the completion of the purchase.[23]

32–04   Thus, apart from in the limited circumstances explained above, or pursuant to an express or statutory power, a mortgagor cannot grant leases which bind the mortgagee without the privity of the mortgage because he has conveyed away the title to possession. Further,[24] although the mortgagor may remain in possession of the mortgaged property and receive the rents and profits and sue in his own name[25] until demand by the mortgagee, it is the mortgagee who is always entitled to take possession or after an effective demand[26] to require the rent including any arrears[27] to be paid to himself.[28] This right to possession on the part of the mortgagee cannot be fettered by the mortgagor[29] and against the mortgagee the tenant has no defence,[30] even where as between tenant and mortgagor the tenant has the benefit of statutory protection.[31]

The corollary to this ought to be that the mortgagee, having the legal title to possession, should be able to create legal tenancies to the full extent of the estate mortgaged to him, though, of course, the exercise of the power would mean that he took possession of the security. Equity, however, in pursuance of the principle that the mortgagee's estate belongs to him only as a security, refuses to recognise that leases granted by him are binding on the mortgagor after redemption.[32] Consequently, unless special powers of leasing are granted in the mortgage there may be difficulty in the management of the property, since during the continuance of the mortgage it is impossible for either mortgagor or mortgagee to grant an indefeasible term without the concurrence of the other. The result was that mortgage contracts frequently contained express powers to grant leases

---

[21] See also *Nationwide Anglia Building Society v Ahmed* (1995) 70 P. & C.R. 381; *Whale v Viasystems* [2002] EWCA Civ 480; *Redstone Mortgages Plc v Welch* [2009] 36 E.G. 98.

[22] *Barclays Bank Plc v Zaroovabli* [1997] Ch. 321.

[23] *Rust v Goodale* [1957] Ch. 33.

[24] See above, paras 29–11 et seq.

[25] LPA 1925 s.98, and see above, para.29–16.

[26] See *Kitchen's Trustee v Madders and Madders* [1950] Ch. 134.

[27] *Moss v Gallimore* (1779) 1 Doug. K.B. 279.

[28] *Pope v Biggs* (1829) 9 B. & C. 245.

[29] See *Thunder* d. *Weaver v Belcher* (1803) 3 East. 449.

[30] *Rogers v Humphreys* (1835) 4 Ad. & El. 299; *Dudley and District Benefit Building Society v Emerson* [1949] Ch. 707; *Rust v Goodale* [1957] Ch. 33.

[31] *Britannia Building Society v Earl* [1990] 1 W.L.R. 422.

[32] *Franklinski v Ball* (1864) 33 Beav. 560; and see *Chapman v Smith* [1907] 2 Ch. 97 at 102. LPA 1925 s.99 empowers a mortgagee to make certain leases which will bind the mortgagor even after redemption: a lease made ultra vires these powers would still, however, be void against the mortgagor after redemption.

binding on both parties and this practice eventually received statutory recognition.[33]

Statutory power

The Law of Property Act 1925[34] makes elaborate provision for the creation of indefeasible tenancies by a mortgagor in possession and by a mortgagee who has gone into possession. In essence a mortgagee in possession has the same statutory powers of leasing as a mortgagor[35] in possession.[36] However, the distinction must be drawn between a mortgagor of land in possession[37] who has, as against every encumbrancer, the power to make any lease authorised by the section, and a mortgagee of land in possession which has that power as against all prior encumbrancers. Where the mortgage contract does not limit the statutory powers of leasing[38] and was itself executed after December 31, 1881,[39] the mortgagor in possession[40] or the mortgagee if he is in possession[41] or has appointed a receiver who is still acting[42] (in which case the mortgagee's powers of leasing may be delegated in writing to the receiver) is vested by section 99 with the power to grant leases[43] so that they will bind all persons.

32–05

Duration

A lease may be granted for the following terms:

32–06

(1) agricultural or occupation leases for any term not exceeding 50 years[44];

(2) building leases for any term not exceeding 999 years.[45]

No power is, however, given to create mining leases.

---

[33] Conveyancing Act 1881 s.18; and now LPA 1925 s.99.

[34] s.99.

[35] It is critical to bear in mind that for the purpose of ss.99 and 100, "mortgagor" does not include an "encumbrancer" deriving title under the original mortgagor (see s.99(18) and s.100(12)).

[36] Section 99 and 100(2). cf *Berkshire Capital Funding v Street* (199) 32 HLR 273; and in the context of s.99(13), *Julian S Hodge & Co Ltd v St Helen's Credit Ltd* [1965] EGD 143.

[37] NB: a prospective purchaser who happens also to be a prospective mortgagor is not in possession: *Hughes v Waite* [1957] 1 All E.R. 603.

[38] See s.99(13) as amended by the Agricultural Holdings Act 1986 s.100, Sch.14 para.12 and Landlord and Tenant Act 1954 s.36(4). See also *Lavin v Johnson* [2002] EWCA Civ 1138. The section has effect subject to the terms of the mortgage deed or any such writing.

[39] The Conveyancing Act of that year first introduced the statutory powers; in cases where a mortgage was executed before 1822, the parties may now by agreement introduce the statutory powers in the mortgage.

[40] LPA 1925 s.99(1).

[41] ibid., s.99(2).

[42] ibid., s.99(19).

[43] The provisions of this section extend to agreements for a lease as well as to leases, and specific performance of such agreements will therefore be decreed.

[44] 21 years if the mortgage was executed before January 1, 1926. See LPA 1925 s.99(3)(i).

[45] 99 years if the mortgage was executed before January 1, 1926. See LPA 1925 s.99(3)(ii). As to building leases, see further s.99(9) and (10).

Conditions

32–07 All leases within the terms of the statute must comply with the following conditions:

(1) the lease must be limited to take effect in possession not later than 12 months after its date[46];

(2) the lease must reserve the best rent that can reasonably be obtained[47] regard being had to the particular circumstances of the case,[48] and with certain qualifications no fine may be taken[49] though in a building lease the rent may be nominal for the first five years[50];

(3) the lease must contain a covenant by the lessee for the payment of rent, and a condition of re-entry on the rent not being paid within a specified time not exceeding 30 days[51];

(4) in the case of a building lease there must be a covenant by the lessee that within five years improvements will be effected on the land in connection with buildings, repairs to buildings, or building purposes[52];

(5) a counterpart of the lease must be executed by the lessee and delivered to the lessor[53];

(6) where it is the mortgagor who grants the lease, he must within one month deliver to the mortgagee, first in priority, a counterpart of the lease duly executed by the lessee.[54]

The provisions of the section extend to agreements for a lease.[55] Some doubt has been raised as to whether the covenant by the lessee for the payment of rent and the condition of re-entry in the event of rent not being paid can apply in the case of an oral letting. In any event such a condition, if imposed, will be strictly construed.[56]

A lease by the mortgagor of agricultural land does not cease to be such if it includes chattels and sporting rights not included in the mortgage.[57] But it will

[46] LPA 1925 s.99(5).
[47] *Feakins v DEFRA* [2007] B.C.C. 54.
[48] *Coutts v Sommerville* [1935] Ch. 483.
[49] ibid., s.99(6).
[50] ibid., s.99(10).
[51] ibid., s.99(7).
[52] ibid., s.99(9).
[53] ibid., s.99(8).
[54] ibid., s.99(11). The lessee is not, however, concerned to see that this provision has been complied with. Non-compliance does not invalidate the lease although it renders the power of sale exercisable; see *Public Trustee v Lawrence* [1912] 1 Ch. 789; and see *Rhodes v Dalby* [1971] 1 W.L.R. 1325.
[55] LPA 1925 s.99(17), " . . . as far as circumstances admit . . . [the definitions of lease] . . . to an agreement, whether in writing or not, for leasing or letting."
[56] See *Pawson v Revell* [1958] 2 Q.B. 360; *Rhodes v Dalby* [1971] 1 W.L.R. 1325; Wolstenholme & Cherry, *Conveyancing Statutes* (13th edn, 1971), pp.198, 200. But even if the letting does not comply with the statutory requirements, provided that it is made in good faith and the tenant has taken possession it may be effective in equity at the tenant's option as a contract for a lease subject to such variations as may be necessary to comply with the above conditions; see LPA 1925 s.152, replacing the Leases Acts 1849, 1850.
[57] *Brown v Peto* [1900] 2 Q.B. 653.

not bind the mortgagee if it comprises both the mortgaged land and other land at a single inclusive rent.[58]

Contrary agreement

The above powers are subject to exclusion[59] or extension[60] by the mortgage agreement (which in fact frequently does modify the mortgagor's statutory power[61]) or otherwise in writing by the parties. But the statutory power cannot be excluded in any mortgage of agricultural land after March 1, 1948,[62] and in the case of business premises the exclusion of the statutory power does not prevent the court from ordering the grant of a new tenancy.[63] It is important to bear in mind that where the statutory powers are modified such that consent is required there is no implied obligation on the mortgagee not to refuse consent unreasonably (subject it seems only to the possibility of complaint where the refusal of consent is made in bad faith.[64]

32–08

Leases not made under the statutory power

Section 99 of the Law of Property Act 1925 does not, however, take away the mortgagor's ordinary power, outside the statute, to create leases binding on himself by estoppel although not binding on the mortgagee, should the latter assert his paramount title to possession.[65] Thus, if the mortgage deed altogether excludes the statutory power to grant leases binding on the mortgagee, the mortgagor may still create leases effective between himself and his lessee.[66] The same is true if, as frequently happens, the mortgage deed merely restricts the statutory power by making its exercise subject to the previous consent of the mortgagee. Indeed, in a case where the mortgagors had covenanted not to exercise the statutory power without the previous consent of the mortgagees and had then created a yearly tenancy without their consent, Farwell J. held that the mortgagors must be assumed to have been exercising their general power to

32–09

---

[58] *King v Bird* [1909] 1 K.B. 837.

[59] LPA 1925 s.99(13).

[60] ibid., s.99(14).

[61] As, for instance, by requiring the mortgagee's consent before the powers can be exercised; *Iron Trades Employers Insurance Association Ltd v Union of Land & House Investors Ltd* [1937] 1 Ch. 313. Present day mortgages normally make an express provision that a failure to obtain consent is a breach of the mortgage terms (see for instance *Bishop v Blake* [2006] 17 E.G. 113 (C.S.)).

[62] Initially by reason of the Agricultural Holdings Act 1986 s.100, Sch.14 para.12, since 1995 by reason of amendments to LPA 1925 s.99 made by the Agricultural Tenancies Act 1995. See also *Pawson v Revell* [1958] 2 Q.B. 360; *Rhodes v Dalby* [1971] 1 W.L.R. 1325 and *National Westminster Bank Plc v Jones* [2000] B.P.I.R. 1092.

[63] Landlord and Tenant Act 1954 s.36(4).

[64] See *Citibank International Plc v Kessler* [1999] Lloyd's Rep. Bank. 123 (CA); *Starling v Lloyds TSB Bank Plc* (2000) 79 P. & C.R. D12.

[65] See above, para.27–47.

[66] *Dudley and District Benefit Building Society v Emerson* [1949] Ch. 707. *Rust v Goodale* [1957] Ch. 33.

create leases by estoppel and had therefore not committed a breach of the covenant.[67]

Consequently, at the very least, a demise by a mortgagor in possession will create a lease which is effective between the parties.[68] Thus the mortgagor can distrain for rent and enforce the covenants and his interest will pass to his personal representatives or to assignees, so as to enable them to sue upon the covenants.[69] The lessee, on his side, may not only enforce the lease but obtains an interest in the equity of redemption which is sufficient to entitle him to redeem.[70] He cannot insist that the mortgagee shall accept him as tenant but he may, if he thinks fit, take over the mortgage by redeeming. If he does not redeem and is dispossessed by the mortgagee, his only relief against the mortgagor is an action for damages because the court will not compel a mortgagor to redeem for the purpose of giving efficacy to his lease.[71] The mortgagee's right to eject the mortgagor's lessee by estoppel is absolute, for he is asserting a title to possession paramount to that of the mortgagor himself. There is no contractual nexus of any kind between the lessee and the mortgagee so that the latter is not, for example, a landlord for the purpose of the Rent Act 1977[72] and the lessee cannot claim the protection of the Act.[73]

32–10   Thus, it is now usual for the mortgage deed to contain a clause not only excluding the statutory power of leasing but also a clause which makes the grant of any lease or tenancy or otherwise parting with possession of the mortgaged property a breach of the mortgagor's obligations under the mortgage.[74]

The importation of such a clause will cause the power of sale to arise in the event of any breach on the part of the mortgagor.

If the mortgage permits the mortgagor to exercise the statutory power of leasing with the consent of the mortgagee, the onus is on the lessee to prove that the mortgagee gave his consent.[75] If the deed provides that the proposed lessee shall not be concerned to inquire as to such consent, the mortgagee is estopped from denying the lease was made with his consent.[76] Similarly, and as set out above, if a lease is granted without consent but the mortgagee accepts the lessee as his own, the lease will bind him.[77]

The result is that a mortgagor's power to grant leases will either be expressly stated by the agreement or will depend on s.99 of the Law of Property Act 1925. Leases granted in conformity with the express or statutory power will be binding on the mortgagee and, equally, on his assuming possession, the benefit of the

---

[67] *Iron Trades Employers Insurance Association Ltd v Union of Land & House Investors Ltd* [1937] 1 Ch. 313.

[68] This appears to be so whether or not the lease discloses on its face the existence of the mortgage: *Morton v Woods* (1869) L.R. 4 Q.B. 293.

[69] *Cuthbertson v Irving* (1860) 6 H. & N. 135.

[70] *Tarn v Turner* (1888) L.R. 39 Ch.D. 456 (CA).

[71] *Howe v Hunt* (1862) 31 Beav. 420.

[72] *Dudley and District Benefit Building Society v Emerson* [1949] Ch. 707; *Rust v Goodale* [1957] Ch. 33. *Quaere* whether a statutory tenant can claim the protection of the Act, see dicta in *Jessamine Investment Co Ltd v Schwartz* [1978] Q.B. 264 at 273; and see P. W. Smith (1977) Conv. 197.

[73] See for example *Britannia Building Society v Earl* [1990] 2 All E.R. 469.

[74] See for example *Bishop v Blake* (above).

[75] *Taylor v Ellis* [1960] Ch. 368.

[76] *Lever Finance Ltd v Needlemans Property Trustee* [1956] Ch. 375.

[77] See *Mann v Nijar* (1998) 32 HLR 223.

covenants will pass to the mortgagee by virtue of s.141 of the Law of Property Act 1925[78] in relation to leases created before January 1, 1996, and, by virtue of s.15 of the Landlord and Tenants (Covenants) Act 1995, in relation to leases created after that date.[79] By the same token, the mortgagees' powers set out in the statute are restrictive and are often the subject of extension (for example such that they may be exercised without the mortgagee going into possession.

POWER TO ACCEPT SURRENDER OF LEASES

Complementary to the power to grant leases is the power given by s.100 of the **32–11** Law of Property Act 1925 to the mortgagor or mortgagee to accept surrenders of leases. This power was first introduced by the Conveyancing Act 1911[80] and now extends to all mortgages executed after December 31, 1911. Its purpose is to allow a mortgagee or mortgagor to accept a surrender in order to enable another lease (whether authorised under s.99 or by the deed) to be granted.

The surrender may be accepted:

(1) by the mortgagee, if he is in possession[81] or has appointed a receiver who is still acting[82] (in which case the mortgagee may delegate his powers of accepting surrenders to the receiver in writing[83]);

(2) by the mortgagor, if he is in possession.[84]

For the surrender to be valid the following conditions must apply:

(a) a fresh authorised lease of the property concerned must be granted to take effect within one month of the surrender; and

(b) the new lease must be for a term not less than the unexpired term of the surrendered lease; and

(c) the rent must be at least equivalent to the rent reserved in the surrendered lease.[85]

These provisions also apply to agreements for a lease and are subject to the parties expressing a contrary intention either in the mortgage deed or otherwise in writing.[86] However, the power may be extended by an agreement in writing between the parties whether in the mortgage or not.[87] A surrender which does not comply with these conditions is void.[88]

---

[78] *Municipal Permanent Investment Building Society v Smith* (1888) L.R. 22 Q.B.D. 70.

[79] See above, para.26–14.

[80] s.3. Prior to the 1911 Act a mortgagor who had granted a lease under his statutory powers could not accept its surrender unless the mortgagee consented.

[81] LPA 1925 s.100(2).

[82] ibid., s.100(13).

[83] ibid.

[84] ibid., s.100(1).

[85] ibid., s.100(5).

[86] ibid., s.100(7).

[87] ibid., s.100(10).

[88] *Barclays Bank v Stasek* [1957] Ch. 28; *Rhyl U.D.C. v Rhyl Amusements Ltd* [1959] 1 W.L.R. 465 applied in *Camden LBC v Shortlife Community Housing Ltd* (1992) 90 L.G.R. 358.

Chapter 33

THE MORTGAGE DEBT AND THE MORTGAGE ACCOUNT

General

The key question for the mortgagee when contemplating enforcement of his rights will generally be the extent of the relevant debt both present and contingent and the relative value of the property as security for that debt. Accordingly, before examining the various options available to a mortgagee, it is important to understand how the mortgage debt is made up and which sums will ultimately be recoverable by the mortgagee from his security when the final mortgage account is taken. **33–01**

The extent of the mortgage debt depends primarily on the terms of the mortgage agreement but the rules of equity and court practice also come into play. The mortgage debt is to be calculated and an account taken either upon the date of discharge of the mortgage or the date of realisation of the security. It is often the case that enforcement through court process will require the taking of an account,[1] but the respective rights of mortgagor and mortgagee are generally sufficiently well defined in the mortgage agreement that the account itself can be taken and agreed out of court. It is only in cases of dispute that the account need be brought into court, and then the account will generally be directed to be taken by a Master or District Judge.[2] Moreover, a mortgagor cannot bring his mortgagee to court for the purpose of having the accounts taken unless either he is offering to redeem or he is seeking to recover surplus proceeds of sale.[3] The court directs an account only in actions for redemption, foreclosure, judicial sale, or for the recovery of moneys resulting from the exercise of a power of sale. **33–02**

The obligation to account is not, as is sometimes thought, a liability only of the mortgagee, but also of the mortgagor. Indeed, save in cases where a mortgagee has gone into possession of the property and has therefore taken on additional liabilities,[4] the account is primarily taken "against" the mortgagor in the sense **33–03**

---

[1] Even in a foreclosure action (in which the mortgagee asks for the cancellation of the right to redeem) an account is required, because the court will not order foreclosure without first giving the mortgagor an opportunity to redeem, while permitting later encumbrancers to assert against the first mortgagee within that account any challenge which the mortgagor might himself assert: *Mainland v Upjohn* (1889) L.R. 41 Ch.D. 126; *Close Asset Finance Ltd v Derek Allan Taylor* [2006] EWCA Civ 788, (2006) 150 SJLA 708.
[2] CPR 40PD, para.9.2.
[3] *Troughton v Binkes* (1801) 6 Ves. 573; *Tasker v Small* (1837) 3 My. & Cr. 63.
[4] As to which, see paras 26–18 to 26–21.

that the exercise is concerned with how much he must pay to the mortgagee under various headings in order to compel the release of the security.

33–04   In *Re Wallis*,[5] Fry L.J. stated that a mortgagee's claim may comprise the following five elements:

(1) the principal debt;
(2) the interest thereon;
(3) his costs in proceedings for redemption or foreclosure of the security;
(4) all proper costs, charges and expenses incurred by the mortgagee in relation to the mortgage debt or the mortgage security; and
(5) the cost of litigation properly undertaken by the mortgagee in reference to the mortgage debt or security.

Of these elements, which will be addressed in turn below, the first three are automatically included in the account unless it is established that there has been misconduct on the part of the mortgagee; the last two items will also be allowed if a case is made out for them. However, CPR 40 APD.4 provides that in taking any account directed by any judgment or order, all "just allowances" shall be made without any express direction to that effect. It is now settled that the words "all just allowances" cover all payments to which a mortgagee is entitled under the terms of his security, i.e. all payments properly incurred in the enforcement of the rights given to him by the terms of his mortgage.[6]

33–05   Accordingly, the costs of proceedings taken to obtain possession, or of proceedings by an equitable mortgagee to compel the execution of a legal mortgage and the costs of all necessary repairs and outgoings will be allowed to the mortgagee as part of the secured debt without the court having made any special direction to that effect. However, care must be taken in respect of other categories of legal costs incurred for reasons apparently connected with the mortgage, many of which may require debate as to whether or not they can truly be said to have been incurred in connection with the enforcement of rights under the mortgage.[7]

33–06   If a mortgagee has taken unusual steps in relation to the property, for example where "permanent improvements" have been made by a mortgagee in possession, or extraordinary litigation has been pursued by the mortgagee in defence of the mortgage security, and the mortgagee wishes to add his expenses in that regard to the secured debt, the facts justifying an extraordinary allowance must be pleaded in any relevant statement of case and a special direction will be given as to the taking of any necessary inquiries and the inclusion or otherwise of such sums from the account.[8]

33–07   A further situation in which the account may be complicated arises where the mortgagee has gone into possession of the property or has appointed a receiver.

---

[5] (1890) L.R. 25 Q.B.D. 176 at 181.
[6] *Blackford v Davis* (1869) L.R. 4 Ch. App. 304; *Wilkes v Saunion* (1877) L.R. 7 Ch.D. 188.
[7] As to which see *Kotonou v National Westminster Bank Plc* [2006] EWHC 1021 (Ch).
[8] *Bolingbroke v Hinde* (1884) L.R. 25 Ch.D. 795.

In such circumstances the items standing to the mortgagee's credit will be offset in part by his receipt of rents and profits and by any other liability which he has incurred to the mortgagor.

PRINCIPAL DEBT

The original advance and stipulated sums

Under this heading a mortgagee is entitled not merely to the sums actually **33–08** advanced, but also to any bonus, premium, or commission for which he has legitimately stipulated by way of a fee for advancing the money.[9] The bonus or other fee in the nature of a bonus is provided for in the mortgage either by the mortgagee deducting the amount of the bonus from the sum expressed to be advanced,[10] or else by a condition that the mortgagor shall only be able to redeem on payment of a sum larger than that actually advanced.[11] The former is the usual method, but the latter is employed when the security is a reversionary interest whose immediate value is small. Whichever course is adopted, the mortgagee is entitled to recover the full amount for which he contracted and where the mortgage deed states the sum advanced and includes an acknowledgement or receipt for that advance, the deed is prima facie evidence of an advance of that sum and the principal debt is proved by the production of the deed.[12] Again, where a mortgage is payable by instalments, and the instalments represent partly capital and partly interest—as in building society mortgages—commission or fines may payable on default upon a single instalment are not within the rule against penalties, and may be included in the account for principal.[13] Finally, if a bonus or other such sum is not claimed as part of the principal, it may be claimed specially as a "just allowance".[14]

Note, however, that a mortgagor is not precluded from asserting in the context of an account that sums recorded in the mortgage were not in fact advanced to him, even where the mortgage includes a "receipt clause". Provided the mortgagor or someone claiming under him can show sufficient circumstantial evidence to suggest that there is a serious question as to whether or not the mortgage was genuinely security for the stated loan, the court may order an inquiry as to what, if any, principal sum was in fact advanced.[15]

---

[9] *Potter v Edwards* (1857) 26 L.J.Ch. 468; cf. *Bradley v Carritt* [1903] A.C. 253, per Lord Davey. See above Ch.30 for consideration of such sums as collateral advantage or clogs on the equity of redemption.

[10] See *Mainland v Upjohn* (1889) L.R. 41 Ch.D. 126.

[11] *Webster v Cook* (1867) L.R. 2 Ch. 542.

[12] *Piddock v Brown* (1734) 3 P. Wms. 288.

[13] *General Credit and Discount Co v Glegg* (1883) L.R. 22 Ch.D. 549.

[14] *Bucknell v Vickery* (1891) 64 L.T. 701.

[15] *Close Asset Finance Ltd v Derek Allan Taylor* [2006] EWCA Civ 788; (2006) 150 S.J.L.B. 708, applying *Minot v Eaton* (1826) 4 LJOS Ch 134, and *Mainland v Upjohn* (1889) L.R. 41 Ch.D. 126.

Future advances

33–09   A mortgagee not infrequently makes further advances upon the security of property already mortgaged to him and such advances, if proved, go into the account for principal due on the original mortgage—at any rate, as against the mortgagor. Whether a puisne encumbrancer is subject to the further advances depends on the law of tacking contained in s.94 of the Law of Property Act 1925.[16]

However, the further advance must be shown to have been in fact made upon the faith of the security.[17] Where further advances are contemplated, it is usual for the first mortgage to be taken on the understanding that it will cover future advances either up to a specified amount or to the amount indicated by the stamp. If a sum is so specified, it is a question of construction whether the sum named stands for principal only or for the total amount of the mortgage debt.[18]

Current accounts

33–10   The mortgage may be taken to secure not isolated advances but rather the general balance of an account; the burden of proving that the security is intended to operate on such a running basis is upon the mortgagee,[19] but if he establishes this he may prove the amount due by extrinsic evidence. If the requisite evidence is not forthcoming when an inquiry is undertaken, the mortgagor can only be charged to the extent of his own admissions.[20]

Special questions arise if the account is taken between a first mortgagee, who holds the mortgagor's current account, and a puisne encumbrancer. If the latter acted wisely and gave notice to the first mortgagee, the first mortgage becomes as against him security only for the amount due at the date of the notice unless the first mortgagee is under an obligation to make those subsequent advances. Further advances by the first mortgagee will thereafter only rank as a third mortgage. Unless the first mortgagee took the precaution of closing the first account upon receipt of the notice, he may find that, as against the puisne encumbrancer, his priority for principal has been seriously reduced by the operation of the rule in *Clayton's Case,*[21] which provides that subsequent payments into the account by the mortgagor must be set against the first advances to him. Thus, all fresh payments in, as against the puisne encumbrancer, reduce the amount secured by the first mortgage, while any further withdrawals add to the debt which now can only rank after the second mortgage.[22] Banks who, of

---

[16] As amended by the Land Registration Act 2002 (LRA 2002). See, above, paras 11–67 et seq. for consideration of tacking. A puisne encumbrancer who is subject to the further advances should be able, in appropriate circumstances, to challenge the amounts claimed under the *Close Asset v Taylor* principle.

[17] *Ex p. Knott* (1806) 11 Ves. 609.

[18] See *Blackford v Davis* (1869) L.R. 4 Ch. App. 304.

[19] *Re Boys* (1870) L.R. 10 Eq. 467.

[20] *Melland v Gray* (1843) 2 Y. & C.C.C. 199.

[21] (1816) 1 Mer. 572.

[22] *Deeley v Lloyds Bank* [1912] A.C. 756, see above, Ch.30.

course, hold many securities for current accounts, direct their officials to close the account at once on receipt of notice of a subsequent encumbrance, thus obviating this risk.

INTEREST

The rules as to allowance of interest within the account may be shortly stated as **33–11** follows:

(a) Except in cases of undue influence or where the bargain is extortionate or unfair under the Consumer Credit Act 1974 (as amended), there is no rule to prevent a mortgagee from obtaining the agreed rate of interest, however high.[23]

(b) Similarly, there is no objection to compound interest,[24] but it will only be allowed if it was contracted for in the mortgage.[25] Such a term may be either express or implied from the usage of a trade or business.[26] Compound interest will also be chargeable when, though not a term of the mortgage agreement itself, it has been agreed to subsequently for a fresh consideration, for example, in consideration of the mortgagee's forbearance.[27]

(c) If there is no mention of interest in the mortgage, an agreement to pay interest will be implied.[28] The rate formerly allowed was 5 per cent (4 per cent for equitable mortgages).[29] The court will undoubtedly order a more commercial rate today to be compounded at appropriate intervals.[30] The only exception to this rule is when the mortgage agreement expressly indicates that no interest is to be paid.[31] Whether the fact that the proviso for reconveyance is upon payment only of principal is

---

[23] See Ch.30 and in particular para.16–65. Bargains will not be interfered with merely because they are unreasonable (*Knightsbridge Estates v Byme* [1939] Ch. 441 at 457) unless the provisions relating to interest could be seen as an unreasonable collateral advantage (see *Cityland and Property Holdings Ltd v Dabrah* [1968] Ch. 166). The Unfair Terms in Consumer Contracts Regulations 1999 (SI 1999/2083) have no impact in this context as they do not apply to terms as to the adequacy of price or remuneration: see para.16–15, above and *OFT v Abbey National Plc* [2010] 1 A.C. 696.

[24] *Clarkson v Henderson* (1880) L.R. 14 Ch.D. 348.

[25] *Daniell v Sinclair* (1880–81) L.R. 6 App. Cas. 181.

[26] *Fergusson v Fyffe* (1841) 8 Cl. & F. 121; *National Bank of Greece S.A. v Pinios (No.1)* [1990] 1 A.C. 637 (HL).

[27] *Blackburn v Warwick* (1836) 2 Y. & C. Ex. 92.

[28] *Mendl v Smith* (1943) 169 L.T. 153; and see *Wallersteiner v Moir (No.2)* [1975] Q.B. 373; *Bartlett v Barclays Bank Trust Co Ltd (No.2)* [1980] Ch. 515; *International Military Services Ltd v Capital and Counties Plc* [1982] 1 W.L.R. 575; *Matthews v T.M. Sutton Ltd* [1994] 1 W.L.R. 1455. See also *Al-Wazir v Islamic Press Agency Inc* [2001] EWCA 1276 (Ch); [2002] 2 P. & C.R. 12.

[29] *Re Kerr's Policy* (1869) L.R. 8 Eq. 331; *Re Drax* [1903] 1 Ch. 781.

[30] *Cityland and Property Holdings Ltd v Dabrah* [1968] Ch. 166; *Wallersteiner v Moir (No.2)* [1975] Q.B. 373; *Matthew v T.M. Sutton Ltd* [1994] 1 W.L.R. 1455. The practice of the commercial court is to award interest at base rate plus 1% unless it is shown that would be unfair to one or other party; *Shearson Lehman Hutton Inc v Maclaine Watson & Co Ltd (No.2)* [1990] All E.R. 723; and see *Claymore Services Ltd v Nautilus Properties Ltd* [2007] EWHC 805 (TCC); [2007] B.L.R. 452.

[31] *Thompson v Drew* (1855) 20 Beav. 49.

sufficient to amount to such an express indication now appears doubtful.[32]

(d) If the mortgage provides for payment of a stated rate down to the date named for repayment of the loan,[33] but nothing is said of interest to be paid afterwards, no agreement will be implied to continue payment of interest at the mortgage rate after default. Interest will, however, be recoverable for the period after default not strictly as mortgage interest, but by way of damages for detention of the debt,[34] pursuant to statute. The former practice was to allow the mortgage rate, if not in excess of 5 per cent, but to limit it to 5 per cent in other cases. The rate awarded today will presumably be the current High Court rate.[35] This rule applies to foreclosure and redemption, as well as to an action on the personal covenant: Fry J. in *Wallington v Cook*[36] pointed out that in foreclosure and redemption proceedings interest could not properly be awarded as damages but decided that it could be awarded by way of consideration for allowing the loan to remain unpaid. Thus, equity once again follows the law.[37]

(e) A well-drawn mortgage deed provides for payment of interest at the mortgage rate after default so long as the security continues but even so, the mortgage rate will not be allowed after a judgment has been obtained upon the personal covenant. The mortgagee's personal right merges in his judgment and judgments carry interest only at the statutory rate.[38] This rule only affects actions on the personal cove-nant[39] and does not reduce the mortgagee's claim for interest in redemption or foreclosure accounts. The fact that he obtains a personal judgment does not alter his right to retain his security and the mortga-gor cannot redeem except on the terms of payment of all that he contracted for in the mortgage.[40] Where on the true construction of the covenant, it is a covenant to pay interest on principal moneys remain-ing due on the security of the mortgage, the covenant remains enforce-able after judgment.[41]

(f) A stipulation for a higher rate of interest in case the agreed rate is not punctually paid is a penalty and void unless it is commercially justifi-able and provided its dominant purpose is not to deter the other party

---

[32] *Mendl v Smith* (1943) 169 L.T. 153.

[33] *Cook v Fowler* (1874) L.R. 7 H.L. 27.

[34] See Senior Courts Act 1981 s.35A; County Courts Act 1984 s.69. See generally Civil Procedure (The White Book Service 2010) notes in CPR Pts 7.0.9 et seq.

[35] *Re Roberts* (1880) L.R. 14 Ch.D. 49.

[36] (1878) 47 L.J.Ch. 508 at 510.

[37] *Re Sneyd* (1883) L.R. 25 Ch.D. 338.

[38] The rate under the Judgment Act 1838 has, since April 1, 1993, been 8%. In the county court, interest is not payable on judgments less than £5,000 (County Courts (Interest on Judgment Debts) Order 1991 (SI 1991/1184)) or on a judgment which grants a suspended order for possession of a dwelling house (ibid., at 2(B)(b)(ii)). Note the discussion as to merger after judgment in *Director General of Fair Trading v First National Bank Plc* [2001] UKHL 52.

[39] Even to that extent it may be avoided by stipulation for the agreed rate to be paid "as well before as after any judgment."

[40] *Economic Life Assurance Society v Usborne* [1902] A.C. 147.

[41] *Popple v Sylvester* (1882) L.R. 22 Ch.D. 98.

from breach.[42] Certainly a subsequent agreement for a higher rate, made in consideration of the mortgagee's further forbearance, is enforceable.[43] In any case, the higher rate is always obtainable by the simple device of drawing the covenant in the form that the higher rate is the agreed rate, but is reducible upon punctual payment.[44]

(g) In redemption actions the mortgagor must give six months' notice of his intention to redeem or else give six months' interest in lieu of notice[45]; the only exceptions are: (i) if the mortgagee refuses a proper tender,[46] or otherwise improperly obstructs redemption[47]; (ii) if the mortgagee takes steps to obtain payment[48]; (iii) where the mortgage is payable on demand.[49]

(h) Whether the mortgage is of land or of personalty, no more than six years' arrears of interest are recoverable on the covenant for payment.[50] The rule does not, however, apply in actions for redemption nor in foreclosure.[51]

(i) When a mortgagor is in arrears with his interest, the mortgagee may, as a condition of his further forbearance, require that the arrears be capitalised and added to the principal, so that they too may bear interest.[52] Such an arrangement is enforceable, provided that the mortgagor's positive assent to it is proved. Mere absence of protest is not enough, and there must at least be evidence from which the court can infer that he agreed to the proposal.[53] In any case, capitalisation of arrears will not bind a mesne encumbrancer, of whose charge the first mortgagee had notice before the capitalisation occurred. To allow the first mortgagee the advantage of capitalisation in those circumstances would be to allow him to tack a further charge with notice.[54] Capitalisation often takes place when a mortgage is transferred to a third party, but it does not then bind the mortgagor without his concurrence.[55]

(j) If interest has been paid on an amount which subsequently is shown to be greater than that due, any overpayment of interest is not treated as

---

[42] *Lordsvale Finance Plc v Bank of Zambia* [1996] Q.B. 752 where an increase of 1% was permitted. See further *Murray v Leisureplay Plc* [2005] EWCA Civ 963; [2005] I.R.L.R. 946 and *General Trading Company (Holdings) Ltd v Richmond Corp Ltd* [2008] EWHC 1479 (Comm); [2008] 2 Lloyd's Rep. 475.

[43] See *Law v Glenn* (1866–67) L.R. 2 Ch. App. 634.

[44] *Union Bank of London v Ingram* (1880) L.R. 16 Ch.D. 53.

[45] *Johnson v Evans* (1889) 61 L.T. 18. *Quaere,* whether this requirement persists in the modern investment age (a paid-off mortgagee can readily, it must be supposed, re-invest). A contractual term to this extent, however, may not fall foul of the Unfair Terms in Consumer Contracts Regulations 1999 (SI 1999/2083) reg.6(2)(b). See *OFT v Abbey National Plc* [2010] 1 A.C. 696.

[46] *Rourke v Robinson* [1911] 1 Ch. 480, only if the money is kept available.

[47] e.g. by losing the deeds.

[48] *Bovill v Endle* [1896] 1 Ch. 648.

[49] *Fitzgerald's Trustee v Mellersh* [1892] 1 Ch. 385.

[50] Limitation Act 1990 s.20(5), *Bristol & West v Bartlett* [2002] EWCA Civ 1181.

[51] See above, para.6–54.

[52] As to the difference between capitalisation of arrears and compound interest, see *Re Morris, Mayhew v Halton* [1922] 1 Ch. 126.

[53] *Tompson v Leith* (1858) 4 Jur.(N.S.) 1091.

[54] *Digby v Craggs* (1762) Amb. 612.

[55] *Agnew v King* [1902] 1 I.R. 471.

a payment reducing the capital outstanding[56] but may be refunded to the mortgagor.[57] If there has been an underpayment of interest, that may be required to be made up by the mortgagor.[58]

COSTS OF PROCEEDINGS FOR REDEMPTION OR FORECLOSURE

33–12   A mortgagee's right to his costs, charges and expenses reasonably and properly incurred in enforcing or preserving the security (including costs of litigation)[59] is an equity arising from his contract and is not therefore within the usual discretion of the court as to costs.[60] The right is not, however, contractual in the sense that the mortgagor is under a personal contract to pay the costs. Liability to pay the costs is rather part of the price which he must pay for being permitted to redeem, so that the costs are a charge upon the property but not (without special agreement) a personal debt of the mortgagor.[61] Similarly, the right to costs being an equitable right, the mortgagee may forfeit his right by misconduct.[62]

33–13   Misconduct by the mortgagee, when proved, puts the costs in the discretion of the court,[63] whose order may be either that he be merely deprived of his costs or else be made to pay the costs of the mortgagor as well.[64] In the latter case the costs are generally not paid to the mortgagor direct, but are credited to him in the mortgage account.[65] The following are the main instances upon which the court will depart from the normal rule as to costs although the court retains an overall discretion.[66]

Mortgagee's failure to accept a proper tender

33–14   This may occur because the tender is refused, or the mortgagee has lost the deeds,[67] or because he is not ready with his receipt or conveyance.[68] On a proper

---

[56] *Blandy v Kimber (No.2)* (1858) 25 Beav. 537.

[57] *Gregory v Pilkington* (1856) 8 De G.M. & G. 616.

[58] *Universities Superannuation Scheme Ltd v Marks & Spencer Plc* [1998] E.G.C.S. 168.

[59] *Parker-Tweedale v Dunbar Bank Plc (No.2)* [1991] Ch. 26; *Gomba Holdings Ltd v Minories Finance Ltd (No.2)* [1993] Ch. 171.

[60] See below, para.27–20. The costs are within the discretion of the court only when a charge of misconduct has been *made and proved*: *Charles v Jones* (1886) L.R. 33 Ch.D. 80. See *Parker-Tweedale v Dunbar Bank Plc*, above; *Gomba Holdings Ltd v Minories Finance (No.2)* above. See also acceptance of the general principle that the discretion on costs is to be exercised in accordance with the contract, although the circumstances of the case may mean that it is appropriate to depart from the contractual terms in *Forcelux Ltd v Binnie* [2009] EWCA Civ 1077; [2010] C.P.Rep 7.

[61] *Frazer v Jones* (1846) 5 Hare 475; *Sinfield v Sweet* [1967] 1 W.L.R. 1489.

[62] *Cottrell v Stantton* (1872) L.R. 8 Ch. App. 295 at 302. See *Parker-Tweedale v Dunbar Bank Plc*, above; *Gomba Holdings Ltd v Minories Finance (No.2)*, above; *Forcelux Ltd v Binnie*, above.

[63] *Charles v Jones* (1886) L.R. 33 Ch.D. 80.

[64] *Detillin v Gale* (1802) 7 Ves. 583; *Kinnaird v Trollope* (1889) L.R. 42 Ch.D. 610.

[65] *Wheaton v Graham* (1857) 24 Beav. 483.

[66] under CPR Pt 44.3.

[67] *Stokoe v Robson* (1815) 19 Ves. 385; *Greenwood v Sutcliffe* [1892] 1 Ch 1 (CA); *Fletcher and Campbell v City Marine Finance Ltd* [1968] 2 Lloyd's Rep. 520.

[68] *Rourke v Robinson* [1911] 1 Ch. 480.

tender, a mortgagor is entitled to have his mortgage discharged and the mortgagee must pay the costs of subsequent litigation necessary to enforce that discharge.[69] However, it is not enough necessarily to save the costs if the mortgagor merely offers to pay what he considers to be due without actually tendering that sum, even if he is subsequently found to have been correct in his calculation.[70]

Mortgage already paid off

If, after receiving the full amount of his debt, a mortgagee either takes proceedings for foreclosure or defends an action for redemption, he will be made to pay the costs of the proceedings.[71] On the same principle a mortgagee, who is paid off after he has instituted proceedings, must pay any costs consequent on his failure to discontinue the action.[72] **33–15**

Untenable claim

A mortgagee, who raises a foreclosure claim or defence to an action for redemption which is untenable for some other reason than payment in full, may also be deprived of his costs or even made to pay the mortgagor's costs. Nor is it a question of male fides.[73] If he sets up an unfounded claim to tack[74] or consolidate, or if he claims the conveyance to be absolute[75] and not by way of mortgage,[76] or otherwise denies or improperly obstructs the right to redeem,[77] he will be made responsible for the costs thus occasioned. However, he will not, it seems, be deprived of costs which would have been incurred in any event.[78] Moreover, he will not be penalised if his claim, though mistaken, was fairly open to argument.[79] Beyond redemption and foreclosure actions, the attitude of the court to the costs discretion in other forms of mortgage proceedings is more fluid and there is perhaps a greater tendency now to order an unsuccessful mortgagee to pay the costs of mortgage proceedings than has historically been the case.[80] **33–16**

---

[69] *Graham v Seal* (1918) 88 L.J.Ch. 31.

[70] *Hodges v Croydon Canal Co* (1840) 3 Beav. 86.

[71] *Barlow v Gains* (1856) 23 Beav. 244; *National Bank of Australasia v United Hand in Hand Co* (1878–79) L.R. 4 App. Cas. 391; unless the mortgagor makes allegations against the mortgagee which he fails to substantiate when no order will be made.

[72] *Gregg v Slater* (1856) 22 Beav. 314.

[73] *Credland v Potter* (1874) L.R. 10 Ch. App. 8.

[74] ibid.; *Kinnaird v Trollope* (1889) L.R. 42 Ch.D. 610.

[75] *Squire v Pardoe* (1891) 66 L.T. 243.

[76] *England v Codrington* (1758) 1 Ed. 169.

[77] See *Whitfield v Parfitt* (1851) 4 De G. & Sm. 240; *Ashworth v Lord* (1887) L.R. 36 Ch.D. 545; *Hall v Heward* (1886) L.R. 32 Ch.D. 430; *Heath v Chinn* [1908] W.N. 120.

[78] *Harvey v Tebbutt* (1820) 1 J. & W. 197.

[79] *Bird v Wenn* (1886) L.R. 33 Ch.D. 215.

[80] See, for example, *National Westminster Bank v Kotonou* [2006] EWHC 1785 (Ch) where the bank was ultimately ordered to pay the costs of the unsuccessful proceedings dealing with issues of construction of the mortgage albeit without, it seems, contesting the point.

Vexatious or oppressive conduct

33–17 If the mortgage transaction is shown to have been tainted with fraud,[81] or if the mortgagee's subsequent conduct has been unreasonable or oppressive, he may be made to pay costs. For example, if he refuses to account or obstructs the taking of an account[82]; if he fails to allow the mortgagor a reasonable opportunity of tendering the mortgage moneys[83]; if he harasses the mortgagor by bringing simultaneous actions for foreclosure and for judgment on the personal covenant in separate proceedings[84]; in any of these cases he will have to pay the costs occasioned by his misconduct. On the other hand, not every mistake made by the mortgagee is oppression; for example, mere over-statement of his claim is not a sufficient ground for refusing him his costs.[85]

Improper joinder of parties

33–18 A mortgagee is liable for all costs resulting from the wrongful joinder of parties, whether as defendants or claimants.[86] This rule is of special importance for parties whose interest in a security is worthless owing to prior claims. A person who is made a party but disclaims before delivering any defence will be entitled to his costs after the date of disclaimer if the mortgagee insists on taking him to the hearing.[87] It is not, however, the mortgagee's duty to invite a defendant to disclaim.[88]

Conclusion

33–19 The general rule, it may be repeated, is that a mortgagee is entitled to his costs of action and that only misconduct can deprive him of that right. Judges have said time and again that the court is reluctant to depart from the normal rule.[89] However, the court is by no means so favourable to a mortgagee who has sold the security and retains in his hands surplus proceeds of sale. He is a trustee for the persons next entitled and if his conduct makes it necessary to bring an action to recover the money, he will be liable for the costs of the action.[90] In *Williams v Jones*,[91] Eve J. said expressly that the general rule allowing a mortgagee his costs of action does not apply to an action for an account against a mortgagee who has exercised his power of sale.

[81] *Baker v Wind* (1748) 1 Ves.Sen. 160; *Morony v O'Dea* (1809) 1 Ball & B. 109.
[82] *Detillin v Gale* (1802) 7 Ves. 583.
[83] *Cliff v Wadsworth* (1843) 2 Y. & C.C.C. 598.
[84] *Williams v Hunt* [1905] 1 K.B. 512.
[85] *Cotterell v Stratton* (1872) L.R. 8 Ch. App. 295; *Re Watts* (1882) L.R. 22 Ch.D. 5.
[86] *Pearce v Watkins* (1852) 5 De G. & Sm. 315.
[87] *Greene v Foster* (1882) L.R. 22 Ch.D. 566; *Ridgway v Kynnerslly* (1865) 2 Hem. & M. 515.
[88] *Maxwell v Wightwick* (1886) L.R. 3 Eq. 210.
[89] e.g. *Cotterell v Stratton* (1872) L.R. 8 Ch. App. 295 at 302, per Selborne, L.C.
[90] See *Tanner v Heard* (1857) 23 Beav. 555; *Charles v Jones* (1887) L.R. 35 Ch.D. 544.
[91] (1911) 55 S.J. 500.

COSTS, CHARGES AND EXPENSES INCURRED IN RELATION TO THE MORTGAGE
DEBT OR SECURITY

Disbursements under this heading are for the most part within the terms of the   **33–20**
mortgage contract as applied in equity, and will, therefore, be included in the
account as "just allowances" within CPR 40APD.4. They are not a personal debt
of the mortgagor, for they are only one of the equitable terms of redemption and
are not covered by the covenant for payment unless expressly brought within it
by the contract. There are four main grounds on which disbursements are
admitted as "just allowances".

Perfecting the security

An equitable mortgagee is entitled to specific performance and will be allowed   **33–21**
the costs of completing his security by the execution of a legal mortgage. These
costs cover the preparation of the mortgage and the correspondence relating
thereto; they do not include the investigation of title, because an equitable
mortgagee only contracts to transfer such title as he himself possesses.[92] On the
same principle a mortgagee has been allowed the costs of obtaining a stop order
against a fund in court.[93] On the other hand, the costs of negotiating the loan and
of preparing the original mortgage cannot be brought into the mortgage account
without express contract. Farwell J. in *Wales v Carr*[94] said that such costs are a
simple contract debt and a personal liability of the mortgagor, but are not part of
the price fixed for redemption in equity. These costs may, however, be brought
into the account by express contract,[95] indeed, it is the usual practice to deduct
the amount of the initial expenses from the sum advanced.

Maintenance of property

A mortgage is generally entitled to preserve his security and to add to the debt   **33–22**
expenses incurred in so doing. A mortgagee of leaseholds may bring into the
account payments for rent, ground-rents[96] or renewal fines.[97] A mortgagee whose
security includes an insurance policy may pay the premiums to prevent default.[98]
Where the payments are not merely to protect but to salve the security, a puisne
encumbrancer who makes the payments is entitled to a charge for such payments
in priority even to the first mortgage.[99] A mortgagee's right to add fire insurance

[92] *National Provincial Bank v Games* (1886) L.R. 31 Ch.D. 582. See *Pryce v Bury* (1853) 2 Drew.
41.
[93] *Waddilove v Taylor* (1848) 6 Hare 307.
[94] [1902] 1 Ch. 860.
[95] *Blackford v Davis* (1869) L.R. 4 Ch. App. 304.
[96] *Brandon v Brandon* (1862) 10 W.R. 287; *Shepherd v Spansheath* (1988) E.G.C.S. 35.
[97] *Lacon v Mertins* (1743) 3 Atk. 4; *Hamilton v Denny* (1809) 1 Ball & B. 199.
[98] *Bellamy v Brickenden* (1861) 2 J. & H. 137; *Gill v Downing* (1874) L.R. 17 Eq. 316; *Re Leslie*
(1883) L.R. 23 Ch.D. 552.
[99] *Angel v Bryan* (1845) 2 Jo. & Lat. 763; but it must really have been a case of salvage:
Landowners, etc. Drainage and Inclosures Co v Ashford (1880) L.R. 16 Ch.D. 411.

premiums to the mortgage debt will in general be provided for by s.101 of the Law of Property Act 1925, which gives that right to all mortgagees whose security is by deed, unless the mortgagor is keeping up a sufficient policy.[100] If the terms of the contract do not allow for the mortgagee insuring and the mortgagor paying for such insurance, it appears that any insurance policy he takes out is effected for his own benefit and that he cannot charge the premiums in the account.[101]

Management

33–23   A mortgagee in possession is entitled to bring into the account the reasonable expenses of managing the property. He will thus be credited with the amount of any wages paid to such servants or agents as would reasonably be employed by an owner of the property[102]; and in most cases he will be allowed the salary or commission of a bailiff or other general agent employed to look after the whole property.[103]

Similarly, a mortgagee will be reimbursed expenditure incurred in running a business,[104] or working existing mines.[105] It appears also that, although as a rule he will only be allowed to balance his losses against his receipts, yet if a business is mortgaged as a going concern, losses may be made a charge upon the corpus of the mortgaged property.[106] However, a mortgagee is not, apart from express contract, allowed to make any charge for his own time and trouble.[107] He may not charge commission for collecting rents[108] or for any other business done in connection with the mortgaged property.[109] Formerly, an express contract that such commission should be allowed made no difference, because the agreement for commission was held to come within the rule against collateral advantages.[110] After the decision in *Biggs v Hoddinott*[111] it is clear that collateral advantages are not bad as such, and so an agreement for commission is valid, provided the bargain is not otherwise unconscionable.[112] In any case, by virtue of s.58 of the Solicitors Act 1974[113] solicitor mortgagees may charge the usual professional

---

[100] Law of Property Act (LPA) 1925 s.108(2); and see para.32–01.

[101] *Dobson v Land* (1850) 8 Hare 216; but a mortgagee in possession may include such payments as part of his management expenses under just allowances: *Scholefield v Lockwood* (1863) 11 W.R. 555.

[102] *Brandon v Brandon* (1862) 10 W.R. 287; *Shepherd v Spansheath* (1988) E.G.C.S. 35.

[103] *Bank of London v Ingram* (1880) L.R. 16 Ch.D. 53; *Leith v Irvine* (1883) 1 My. & Cr. 277.

[104] *Bompas v King* (1886) L.R. 33 Ch.D. 279.

[105] *County of Gloucester Bank v Rudry, Merthyr Steam and House Colliery Co* [1895] 1 Ch. 629; but not for working new mines: *Hughes v Williams* (1806) 12 Ves. 493; *Shepherd v Spansheath* (1988) E.G.C.S. 35.

[106] *Bompas v King* (1886) L.R. 33 Ch.D. 279.

[107] *Bonithon v Hockmore* (1685) 1 Vern. 316; *Nicholson v Tutin* (1857) 3 K. & J. 159; cf. *Re Wallis* (1890) 25 Q.B.D. 176.

[108] *Langstaffe v Fenwick* (1805) 10 Ves. 405.

[109] *Leith v Irvine* (1883) 1 My. & Cr. 277.

[110] See *Chambers v Goldwin* (1804) 9 Ves 254.

[111] [1898] 2 Ch. 307.

[112] See *Bucknell v Vickery* (1891) 64 L.T. 701 at 702, though the case is not absolutely in point; *Barrett v Hartley* (1866) L.R. 2 Eq. 789.

[113] Formerly Mortgagees' Legal Costs Act 1895 s.3.

fees for all business done in relation to the security, whether or not the mortgage contains an express stipulation to that effect.

Where the powers of management yield profits for which the mortgagee must account, he will be allowed the cost of obtaining them.[114] If the mortgage expressly permits this item of expenditure and any moneys yielded by the expenditure do not exceed the costs incurred, the balance may be charged against the property[115] or permitted out of the proceeds of sale.[116]

Improvements

A mortgagee may also include in his account sums expended on repairs, **33–24** improvements and other outgoings. He has, for example, been allowed the amount of compensation payable to a tenant at the end of his tenancy.[117] Repairs and improvements require careful examination. Concerning "necessary repairs" there is no doubt: a mortgagee in possession is under a duty to execute them and will be entitled to his expenditure under the heading of just allowances.[118] However, the mortgagee is not under a duty to carry out repairs where the cost of doing so exceeds the likely increase in value of the security that would result from those repairs, and may in fact be seen as acting unreasonably if he undertakes the repairs in those circumstances. Accordingly, substantial repairs or permanent improvements will generally only be allowed if the value of the property has been increased to a suitable extent by carrying out those works.[119] In any event a special case must be made out for their allowance at the hearing, or no inquiry will be directed. Jessel M.R. in *Shepard v Jones*[120] stated the established practice to be that the mortgagee must plead that he has made a lasting improvement, and then, if he adduces evidence of laying out money and that the works were prima facie lasting improvements, he will be entitled to an inquiry. The older cases[121] suggest that even an admitted improvement, if substantial, will not be allowed to a mortgagee unless it was consented to by a mortgagor. The reason for this was that a mortgagee by increasing the price of redemption might prevent redemption altogether. But the Court of Appeal in *Shepard v Jones*[122] greatly modified this doctrine, and stated the following rules:

(1) If the improvement is reasonable and produces a benefit, the mortgagor's consent is unnecessary.

---

[114] *Bompas v King* (1886) L.R. Ch.D. 279.
[115] *Norton v Cooper* (1854) 5 De G.M. & G. 728.
[116] *Bompas v King,* above; *White v City of London Brewery Co* (1889) L.R. 42 Ch.D. 237.
[117] *Oxenham v Ellis* (1854) 18 Beav. 593.
[118] *Tipton Green Colliery Co v Tipton Moat Colliery Co* (1877) L.R. 7 Ch.D. 192.
[119] *Barclays Bank Plc v Alcorn* [2002] EWCA Civ 817. Different considerations apply if the nature of the property is altered: *Moore v Painter* (1842) 6 Jur. 903.
[120] (1882) L.R. 21 Ch.D. 469 at 476.
[121] e.g. *Sandon v Hooper* (1843) 6 Beav. 246.
[122] (1882) L.R. 21 Ch.D. 469.

(2) If the improvement is unreasonable and produces no benefit it will be allowed, if the mortgagor either expressly agreed to it or did what in law amounted to acquiescing to it.

(3) If the improvement is unreasonable and was not agreed to, it will not be allowed in any circumstances. The mortgagee cannot force the improvement on the mortgagor by merely serving a notice upon him, whatever the terms of the notice.

Finally, it must be observed that repairs and improvements are not "salvage" advances and do not entitle a mesne encumbrancer, who executes them, to priority for his expenditure over earlier mortgagees.[123]

Appointing a receiver

33–25   The mortgagee will be entitled to recover his expenses of appointing a receiver save insofar as they were unreasonably incurred or unreasonable in amount. The burden rests on the mortgagor to establish the unreasonableness of such expenses.[124]

Exercising his power of sale

33–26   A mortgagee is entitled to claim in the account the expenses not merely of an actual sale, but also of an abortive attempt to sell.[125] In accordance with the general principle that he may not charge for his own time and trouble, he may not, if he is an auctioneer,[126] or a broker,[127] be credited with a commission on the sale, unless he has expressly contracted for such commission.[128]

Costs of Litigation in Connection with the Mortgage[129]

33–27   In *Dryden v Frost*[130] Cottenham L.C. expressed the rule thus:

"This Court, in settling the account between a mortgagor and mortgagee, will give to the latter all that his contract, or the legal or equitable consequences of it entitle

---

[123] *Landowners West of England & South West Drainage and Inclosure Co v Ashford* (1880) L.R. 16 Ch.D. 411.

[124] *Gomba Holdings (UK) Ltd v Minories Finance Ltd (No.2)* [1993] Ch. 171; *Royal Bank of Scotland v Chandra* [2010] EWHC 105 (Ch); [2010] 1 Lloyd's Rep. 677.

[125] *Corsellis v Patman* (1867) L.R. 4 Eq. 156; *Farrer v Lacy, Hartland & Co* (1885) L.R. 31 Ch.D. 42.

[126] *Matthison v Clarke* (1854) 3 Drew. 3.

[127] *Arnold v Garner* (1847) 2 Ph. 231.

[128] *Biggs v Hoddinott* [1898] 2 Ch. 307. But after redemption he cannot insist on being made auctioneer of the property when it is to be sold; the clause allowing him commission must terminate at redemption: *Browne v Ryan* [1901] 2 I.R. 635.

[129] See paras 27–32 et seq.

[130] (1838) 3 My. & Cr. 670 at 675.

him to receive, and all the costs properly incurred in ascertaining or defending such rights."[131]

That does not mean, however, that the court has no jurisdiction in this regard. The modern inter-relationship between the court's discretion and the mortgagee's contractual and equitable entitlement is considered elsewhere. In other words, the litigation must have been reasonable and if it is, the costs that are reasonably and properly incurred in that litigation are allowable.[132] Usually, such costs are the mortgagee's costs of obtaining possession but the mortgagee is entitled his costs of a claim to recover the mortgage debt from the mortgagor or his surety[133] or for example, administrating the deceased mortgagor's estate if necessary to recover the debt.[134] Costs of litigation, with one exception, will not be allowed unless they have been specially pleaded and claimed at the hearing.[135] The one exception is costs of proceedings to obtain possession which are included under "just allowances".[136]

Costs may be allowed to the mortgagee whether he is claimant or defendant in the litigation. If his title is impeached by the mortgagor, he is entitled to be fully reimbursed, so that if he was successful and received costs in the action, he may still recover the difference between the assessed costs and his actual costs.[137] Similarly, if the mortgagor's title to the mortgaged property is questioned, the mortgagee may defend it and charge his full costs in the account.[138] But if his own title qua mortgagee is attacked by third parties, he must pay his own expenses, for the mortgagor cannot be made to bear the loss caused by the litigious activities of third parties.[139] Where a sub-mortgagee is a party to any proceedings and has, of necessity been joined, the sub-mortgagee's costs will be payable by the mortgagee who may than add them to his own debt and so recover them as against the mortgagor.[140] The mortgagee's right so to do will only arise in relation to sub-mortgagees claiming under him; the costs of parties claiming under the mortgagor (e.g. a trustee in bankruptcy) cannot be so recovered.[141] The mortgagor entitled to the costs of an ejectment against third parties.[142] Similarly, the costs of an ejectment against the mortgagor and of a judgment on the personal covenant previously obtained may be included in the account.

---

[131] The decision in this case was that litigation is not properly undertaken when an equitable mortgagee institutes an action available only to a legal mortgagee, and in another case a mortgagee was refused his costs when, in exercising his power of sale, he brought an action against the purchaser for specific performance and lost because of errors in the description of the property sold; see *Peers v Ceeley* (1852) 15 Beav. 209.

[132] *Parker-Tweedale v Dunbar Bank Plc (No.2)* [1991] Ch. 26.

[133] *National Provincial Bank of England v Games* (1886) L.R. 31 Ch.D. 582. It does not matter that the claim against the surety is unproductive; *Ellison v Wright* (1827) 3 Russ. 458.

[134] *Ward v Barton* (1841) 11 Sim. 534; but see also *Saunders v Duncan* (1878) L.R. 7 Ch.D. 825.

[135] *Millar v Magor* (1818) 3 MADP 433.

[136] *Wilkes v Saunion* (1877) L.R. 7 Ch.D. 188.

[137] *Ramsden v Langley* (1706) 2 Vern. 536. cf. also *Re Leighton's Conveyance* [1937] Ch. 149.

[138] *Parker-Tweedale v Dunbar Bank Plc (No.2)* [1991] Ch. 26.

[139] *Parker-Tweedale v Dunbar Bank Plc (No.2)*, above; see also *Gomba Holdings Ltd v Minories Finance Ltd (No.2)* [1993] Ch. 171.

[140] *Smith v Chichester* (1842) 2 Dr. & War. 393.

[141] *Hunter v Pugh* (1839) 1 Hare 307; *Clarke v Wilmot* (1843) 1 Ph. 276.

[142] *Owen v Crouch* (1857) 5 W.R. 545.

It is, however, necessary to distinguish carefully between costs incurred in cases where third parties are attacking or dealing vexatiously with the mortgagor's title and cases where the mortgagee's own title to the security is impeached by third parties. In the latter situation the mortgagee must bear the cost of defending himself.[143] An unusual application of this rule occurred in the case of *Re Smith's Mortgage, Harrison v Edwards*[144] in which a first mortgagee sold under his power of sale and realised a sufficient sum to provide something for the second mortgagee. The mortgagor, however, impeached the sale and the first mortgagee incurred costs in establishing its validity. He was not, as against the second mortgagee, allowed to add these costs to his mortgage debt, for he was defending himself rather than the title to the mortgaged property. In *Parker-Tweedale v Dunbar (No.2)*[145] the Court of Appeal denied a mortgagee his costs out of the security in an action where a third party impugned the mortgagee's title to the mortgage, even though the costs had been reasonably and necessarily incurred and the third party was interested in the equity of redemption. Similarly, in *Kotonou v National Westminster Bank*[146] the mortgagee was not permitted to treat the costs of proceedings to establish the liability of a guarantor as "costs incurred in connection with the enforcement of the mortgage" and thus to add them to the mortgage debt.

Taking the Account

Mortgagee out of possession

33–28   The general rule for taking a mortgage account is to take it as a continuous debtor and creditor account. A mortgagor, apart from express contract, is never compelled to pay interest on interest in arrear[147] so that, when the mortgagee is not in possession, there is no occasion for stopping the account. At the end of the account the amount of unpaid interest is added to the principal, and the resulting sum, plus any special allowances, is the price of redemption. Where the mortgagee is not in possession, the only possible exceptions to the rule are when the parties have themselves struck a balance at some date during the currency of the mortgage[148] or when part of the mortgaged property has previously been sold. In the latter case the proceeds are applied first in discharging the expenses of sale and any interest already accrued due at the date of the sale, and then the residue, if it was not handed over to the mortgagor, must be taken to have satisfied the

---

[143] *Parker v Watkins* (1859) John 133; *Parker v Tweedale v Dunbar Bank Plc (No.2)* [1991] Ch. 26. But where beneficiaries seek, unsuccessfully, to impeach a mortgage by the trustees, the mortgagee is a party, the mortgagee will (apparently) be permitted his costs; *Laughton v Laughton* (1855) 6 De G.M. & G. 30. See further *Kali Ltd v Chawla* [2007] EWHC 2357 (Ch); [2008] B.P.I.R. 415 as to the difficulties of bringing costs into the security where there is a subrogation claim.
[144] [1931] 2 Ch. 168.
[145] [1991] Ch. 26 (CA).
[146] *Kontonou v National Westminster Bank Plc* [2006] EWHC 1021 (Ch).
[147] *Parker v Butcher* (1867) L.R. 3 Eq. 762.
[148] *C. Wilson v Cluer* (1840) 3 Beav. 136.

principal debt pro tanto. Thus, in the final account interest will only be allowed, as from the date of the sale, on the diminished amount of the principal.[149]

Mortgagee in possession

In most cases, the general rule applies equally to the account of a mortgagee in possession since it is only in special circumstances that the court will direct the account to be taken against the mortgagee with rests. On the other hand, a mortgagee's entry into possession always complicates the account because he must be debited with the amount of rents and profits which he actually received or which, but for his wilful default,[150] he ought to have received. In practice, it means that the account is split into three distinct amounts: **33–29**

(1) The account of principal, interest and costs.[151]
(2) The account of the mortgagee's expenditure in managing, repairing or improving the property, plus interest on the expenditure.
(3) The account of rents, profits and other sums received by the mortgagee or which, but for his wilful default, he ought to have received.

The price of redemption is, of course, calculated by adding together the first two accounts and then deducting the third from the aggregate so obtained Again, the continuity of the account may be interrupted either by the parties having struck a balance during the currency of the mortgage or by a sale of part of the security. In the latter case the net proceeds are appropriated first to the discharge of the interest in account number (1) and then to the reduction of the principal debt with a consequent reduction in the amount of interest due in account number (1). However, the rest in that account is not accompanied by a simultaneous rest in the other accounts. The mere fact of the sale cannot entitle the mortgagor at the date of the sale to have the amount of the rents and profits received before the sale immediately set off against the mortgage debt. In other words, without a general direction for rests throughout the account, the mortgagor has no right to have the items of account number (1) in any way affected by the state of account number (3) until the final accounts are taken.[152] **33–30**

Since the account of a mortgagee in possession is in the normal case a continuous debtor and creditor account, the mortgagee will derive an indirect profit from his possession if the amount of his receipts exceeds that of the interest due. He may retain the balance and have the use of the money without debiting himself with interest upon it. If, on the other hand, the receipts are less than the interest, the mortgagor does not pay interest on the unpaid arrears of interest, and

---

[149] *Thompson v Hudson* (1870) L.R. 10 Eq. 497; here the mortgagee was in possession, but the reasoning of Romilly M.R. applies generally.

[150] *Downsview Nominees Ltd v First City Corporation Ltd* [1993] A.C. 295; *Adamson v Halifax Plc* [2002] EWCA Civ 1134. Note that the situation is different if a receiver is appointed: default by the receiver may instead give rise to a claim by the mortgagor against the receiver: *Medford v Blake* [2000] Ch. 86.

[151] Interest is usually allowed.

[152] *Wrigley v Gill* [1905] 1 Ch. 241; *Ainsworth v Wilding* [1905] 1 Ch. 435.

so he has the advantage.[153] The object and effect of directing the account to be taken with periodic rests is to prevent the mortgagee from deriving any advantage from an excess of receipts over interest due. Such a direction is unusual and operates to only penalise the mortgagee.[154] The procedure then is to strike a balance at the end of each year or half-year, as the case may be, and to appropriate at once the surplus receipts—after discharging the interest—to the reduction of the principal debt with a consequent reduction in the future interest due on the debt. Furthermore, if by this method of accounting it is found that the whole mortgage debt had been satisfied before the end of the account, the result is that the periodic rests make the mortgagee liable to account for the subsequent receipts with compound interest in favour of the mortgagor.[155]

Procedure for taking the account

33–31   An account or any necessary inquiries can obviously be ordered by the court at trial. Such an order can also be made pursuant to CPR Pt 24[156] and CPR Pt 25.[157] In the former instance, where a claimant seeks an account or brings a claim which necessarily involves the taking of an account, he can apply for a summary order that all necessary accounts be taken and inquiries made. Alternatively, an order for the taking of an account or making of an inquiry can also be made by the court pursuant to its jurisdiction to order interim remedies under CPR Pt 25. The court can, on application or of its own initiative (whether before or after judgment), make an order directing that any necessary account be taken or inquiries made.[158] In either case, the procedural provisions of CPR 40APD also apply.

That Practice Direction states that the court may give directions generally as to the manner in which the account is to be taken and verified or the inquiry is to be conducted,[159] and provides that the court may at any stage during the taking of an account or an inquiry order the resolution of any issue that has arisen and may order the service of Points of Claim and Points of Defence and give other directions for that purpose.[160] Verification of an account can now be by affidavit or witness statement.[161]

The account will be taken or the inquiry conducted by a Master or District Judge in the High Court and by a District Judge in the county court, unless the court orders otherwise.[162] In the Chancery Division of the High Court, while accounts are generally retained by the Master, inquiries which are estimated to last more than two days and involve very large sums of money or strongly

---

[153] *Union Bank of London v Ingram* (1880) L.R. 16 Ch.D. 53 at 56, per Jessel M.R.
[154] *Wrigley v Gill* [1905] 1 Ch. 241; cf. *Cowens v Francis* [1948] 2 L.R. 567.
[155] Seton, *Judgments and Orders* (7th edn), Vol.3, p.1885.
[156] CPR 24PD.6.
[157] CPR 25.1(1)(o).
[158] CPR 25.1(1)(n) and 25.1(1)(o); CPR 25.2.
[159] CPR 40APD, para.1.1.
[160] CPR 40APD, para.5.
[161] CPR 40APD, para.2.
[162] CPR 40APD para.9.

contested issues of fact or difficult points of law may be directed to be heard by a judge.[163] Within the taking of the account issues concerning the quantum of recoverable costs are frequently directed to be determined by a Costs Judge of the Senior Court Costs Office.

Effect of an account having been taken

In the absence of fraud, in which case an account may be re-opened after a **33–32** substantial number of years have passed,[164] a settled account is prima facie binding on all parties to the action in which it was taken and on any other persons interested in the equity of redemption and will not, save in limited circumstances, be disturbed.[165] A party wishing to challenge a settled account must either show that there are sufficient grounds to set the account aside and to establish a right for an order for a new account to be taken or, alternatively, demonstrate that certain aspects of the account are inaccurate and that he should be given liberty "to surcharge and falsify" some of the items and charges contained in that account.

Re-opening an account in its entirety

As indicated, an account will only be opened altogether in the case of fraud or **33–33** where, in the absence of fraud, it would be inequitable for one party to take advantage of it by reason of the manner in which the account took place or the nature of any error contained in it.[166] An account will be reopened if it contains considerable errors both in number and amount. What amounts to a sufficient degree of error to re-open an account is a question of fact but where a fiduciary relationship exists between the accounting parties, it would seem that fewer errors are sufficient in order to persuade the court to re-open the account.[167] In *Pritt v Clay*[168] a single error of a substantial amount was held to be sufficient for the re-opening of the whole account but, in the absence of any evidence to demonstrate that that error was likely to be repeated elsewhere in the account, it would seem that such a single incident should give rise to leave to surcharge and falsify.[169] In order to re-open an account, clear allegations of fraud or specific error must be made and proved.[170]

Liberty to surcharge and falsify

If leave is given to surcharge and falsify an account, the settled account is **33–34** permitted to stand but the specific errors that it has been shown to contain can be

---

[163] Chancery Guide 2009, Ch.9.19.
[164] *Vernon v Vawdrey* (174) 2 Atk. 119; *Allfrey v Allfrey* (1849) 1 Mac. & G. 87.
[165] *Newen v Wetten* (1862) 31 Beav. 315.
[166] *Coleman v Mellersh* (1850) 2 Nac. & G. 309; *Re. Webb* [1894] 1 Ch. 73.
[167] *Willamson v Barbour* (1877) L.R. 9 Ch.D. 529.
[168] (1843) 6 Beav. 503.
[169] *Gething v Keighley* (1878) L.R. 9 Ch.D. 547.
[170] *Needler v Deeble* (1677) 1 Ch. Cas. 299.

corrected. It is thus a more limited (and perhaps more focused) challenge to an account. Liberty to surcharge and falsify will be given provided that at least one error is specifically charged and proved to court's satisfaction.[171] The error alleged may be either that of fact or law.[172]

If an account is admitted to contain and error and other accounts are pending between the same parties, that error can be "purged" by the setting-off in the subsequent accounts of the error that is admitted to be contained in the settled account.[173]

[171] *Parkinson v Hanbury* (1867) L.R. 2 H.L. 1.
[172] *Roberts v Kuffn* (1740) 2 Atk. 112.
[173] *Lawless v Mansfield* (1841) 1 Dr. & War. 557.

CHAPTER 34

INSOLVENCY OF THE MORTGAGOR

INTRODUCTION

A mortgagee can usually face the insolvency of the mortgagor with greater **34–01** confidence than that which unsecured creditors experience. Even so, the insolvency of a mortgagor can cause difficulties for the mortgagee and in this chapter, consideration will be given to the impact of a mortgagor's insolvency on the mortgagee and his security, rights and remedies.

For the purposes of the Insolvency Act 1986, a company is deemed unable to pay its debts and is therefore insolvent in circumstances where a statutory demand has been served upon it in the sum exceeding £750 and it has, for three weeks thereafter, neglected to pay the sum or to secure or compound for it to the reasonable satisfaction of the creditor,[1] if execution or other process issued on a judgment, decree or order of any court in favour of a creditor of the company is returned unsatisfied in whole or in part,[2] or if it is proved to the satisfaction of the court that the company is unable to pay its debts as the fall due.[3] A company is also deemed unable to pay its debts if it is proved to the satisfaction of the court that the value of its assets is less than the amount of its liabilities, taking into account its contingent and prospective liabilities.[4] In connection with an individual, an individual is insolvent if he is unable to pay his debts[5]; the test for an individual is therefore the ability to pay debts as and when they fall due.[6]

The general perception of insolvency is that it involves bankruptcy if one is an **34–02** individual or compulsory winding up in the case of a company. However, there are many more options available to or in respect of an insolvent person or entity and the impact of that insolvency upon a mortgagee may differ according to which option is taken. The principal ways of addressing an insolvency situation in respect of an individual debtor are an Individual Voluntary Arrangement (known as an IVA) or a bankruptcy order, obtained on the petition of either a creditor or the debtor himself. In the case of an insolvent corporate entity, the options are more numerous and apart from any consensual general moratorium which its creditor may agree, comprise a Company Voluntary Arrangement

---

[1] Insolvency Act (IA) 1986 s.123(1)(a).
[2] ibid., s.123(1)(b).
[3] ibid., s.123(1)(e).
[4] ibid., s.123(2).
[5] ibid., s.272(1).
[6] See *Re Coney* [1998] B.P.I.R. 333; *Paulin v Paulin* [2009] B.P.I.R. 572.

(known as a CVA), a Scheme of Arrangement,[7] the appointment of a receiver, administration, and liquidation, whether compulsory (by order of the court) or voluntary at the instance of the members or creditors of the company.

If a partnership is insolvent, the available options involve various combinations of corporate and individual insolvency procedures.[8]

In essence, a partnership may be wound up as an unregistered company, with or without the presentation of bankruptcy petitions against any one or more of the individual partners; in addition, there may be bankruptcy petitions against partners without seeking also to wind up the partnership as a whole; the partners or a creditor may seek an administration order; or there may be a Partnership Voluntary Arrangement ("PVA"). The consequences for a mortgagee who has an insolvent partnership as mortgagor will generally flow in a similar fashion to those set out below in respect of individual or corporate mortgagors for the relevant procedure. In the case of an LLP, the choices are broadly as for an insolvent registered company.[9]

Non-Corporate Mortgagors

Individual Voluntary Arrangements[10]

34–03   An IVA may be entered into by a debtor who is either an undischarged bankrupt or is able to petition for his own bankruptcy.[11] The details of the procedure that must be followed are beyond the scope of this work,[12] but it is in essence an agreement between the debtor and his creditors that those creditors will accept less than the full sums due to them and/or will permit the debtor an extended period in which to pay. If he wishes to protect his position while the terms of the IVA are being negotiated with his creditors, the debtor may apply to the court for an interim order pending the approval of the IVA.[13] The effect of such an application is to permit the court to stay any action, execution or other legal process against the property or person of the debtor.[14] While any interim order

[7] Formerly under the Companies Act 1986 s.425, now restated in ss.895–899 of the Companies Act 2006. Due to the complexity of this procedure such schemes are now relatively rare, as CVAs provide a much more straightforward process. Therefore Schemes of Arrangement are not considered further in this work.

[8] Insolvent Partnerships Order 1994 (SI 1994/2421) (as amended).

[9] Limited Liability Partnerships Act 2000 and Limited Liability Partnerships Regulations 2001 (SI 2001/1090).

[10] Under Pt VIII of IA 1986 ss. 252–263G.

[11] IA 1986 s.255(1)(b).

[12] Reference should be made to the specialist texts: *Muir Hunter on Personal Insolvency; Lawson, Individual Voluntary Arrangements* (2010). Note also that substantive procedural changes have been made under the Insolvency (Amendment) Rules 2010 (SI 2010/686) and the Insolvency (Amendment) (No.2) Rules 2010 (SI 2010/734) and the Legislative Reform (Insolvency) (Miscellaneous Provisions) Order 2010 (SI 2010/18) which significantly updated the Insolvency Rules 1986 with effect from April 6, 2010. Some elements of those changes will have retrospective effect upon insolvencies which predated their implementation. See Sch.4 to the Insolvency (Amendment) Rules 2010 in this regard.

[13] *Fletcher v Vooght* [2000] B.P.I.R. 435.

[14] IA 1986 s.254(1). Note that this section and many others in Pt VIII dealing with IVAs were amended by the Insolvency Act 2000 with effect from January 1, 2003.

has effect, no bankruptcy petition relating to the debtor may be presented or proceeded with and no other proceedings and no execution or other legal process may be commenced or continued against the debtor or his property except with leave of the court.[15] Unless extended, an interim order remains in force for 14 days beginning with the day upon which the order is made.[16]

During the currency of the interim order, the nominee will prepare a proposal to place before the court which may, if it considers that the proposal should be placed before a meeting of the debtor's creditors, extend the period in which the interim order is in force to enable such a meeting to be held,[17] in order to secure the creditors' approval of the IVA at that meeting. The creditors may modify the proposal with the debtor's consent[18] and, if they approve the proposal (whether amended or not), it takes effect as if made by the debtor at the meeting and binds every person who, in accordance with the Insolvency Rules, had notice of and was entitled to vote at the meeting (whether or not he was present or represented at it) as if he were a party to the arrangement.[19] An IVA which unfairly prejudices the interests of a creditor or in which there has been some material irregularity at or in relation to the creditors' meeting may be challenged.[20] The court may revoke or suspend any approval given to an IVA upon such an application or may give direction as to the summoning of a further meeting of the creditors.[21]

Effect of an interim order

The terms of s.252 of the Insolvency Act 1986 are quite clear; once an interim **34–04** order has been made "no other proceedings, and no execution or other legal process, may be commenced or continued against the debtor or his property except with leave of the court". Accordingly, once an order is made, a mortgagee will, during its currency, be governed by its terms and precluded from continuing or commencing any proceedings (whether for possession or otherwise) or enforcing any judgment that it may have in its favour with the court's permission.[22]

The creditors' meeting

A person who holds any security for a debt owed to him (whether by way of **34–05** mortgage, charge, lien or other security) is a "secured creditor"[23] for the purposes of, inter alia, the provisions governing an IVA and is entitled to notice of

---

[15] IA 1986 s.252.
[16] IA 1986 s.255(6).
[17] IA 1986 s.256(5).
[18] IA 1986 s.258(2).
[19] IA 1986 s.260(2).
[20] IA 1986 s.262.
[21] IA 1986 s.262(4).
[22] For guidance on when the court may give such permission see *Re Atlantic Computer Systems* [1992] Ch. 505 and para.34–30 below.
[23] IA 1986 s.383(2). However, note that this does not apply to the creditor who has obtained an interim charging order but not yet been able to obtain a final charging order. He is not a secured creditor, and must seek permission of the court if he wishes to pursue his application for a final order. See *Clarke v Coutts & Co* [2002] B.P.I.R. 916.

the creditors' meeting[24] and to vote at that meeting.[25] A secured creditor is thus bound by the result of the meeting, albeit that s.258 contains important safeguards in relation to the enforcement against the security. As a result of the changes to the IVA process brought about by the Insolvency Act 2000 with effect from January 1, 2003, a creditor who should have been given notice of the meeting will be bound by its decision even if in fact he did not receive such notice, although he would also be able to challenge that decision for irregularity.

Section 258: the preservation of the liability of a mortgagee to enforce against the security

34–06   The creditors' meeting "shall not approve any proposal or modification which affects the right of a secured creditor of the debtor to enforce his security, except with the concurrence of the creditor concerned".[26] Thus, while the mortgagee may be precluded from enforcing his security during the period for which an interim order is in force, the rights and remedies that he would otherwise have pursuant to the terms of the security are preserved in the event that the IVA is approved unless he consents to their limitation as a matter of construction of the IVA's terms.[27]

However, the mortgagee's right to sue for the debt under the personal covenant to repay will be suspended while the IVA is in effect. Obviously, if the IVA is not approved, the mortgagee's rights remain unaffected after the expiry of the interim order.

Any creditor must take care in the manner in which he conducts himself in relation to the creditors' meeting and any decision arising therefrom. In *Re Millwall Football Club and Athletic Co (1985) Plc (in admin)*[28] the administrator dismissed an employee of the company after his appointment. Subsequently a company voluntary arrangement was proposed. The terms of that arrangement were such that creditors of the company as at the date of the appointment of the administrator (i.e. prior to the employee's dismissal) were only to be paid a much reduced dividend. The employee voted in favour of the CVA and subsequently sought to argue that since the company's liability to him for his wrongful dismissal arose on that dismissal and thus after the administrator's appointment, he would not be bound by the reduced dividend provisions. Rimer J. rejected this argument. He held that the obligation arose from the contract of employment that was in place at the administrator's appointment and the liability for wrongful dismissal could be properly characterised as a future, prospective or contingent liability incurred prior to the administrators appointment and thus subject to the reduced dividend provisions. More importantly (and perhaps of more general application) Rimer J. held that the creditor was estopped from denying that he

---

[24] IA 1986 s.257(2).
[25] Insolvency Rules (IR) 1986 r.5.17(1).
[26] IA 1986 s.258(4).
[27] *Khan v Permayer* [2001] B.P.I.R 95; *Whitehead v Household Mortgage Corporation Plc* [2003] 1 W.L.R. 1173; *Rey v FNCB Ltd* [2006] B.P.I.R. 1260.
[28] [1999] B.C.C. 455.

was bound by the dividend provisions since both he and the administrator had proceeded right down to the creditors' meeting on the basis that he was and, on that footing, the administrator had not proposed any variation of the terms of the proposal before it was approved. An estoppel by convention had arisen.

Thus, a secured creditor may find that its rights to enforce its security may be lost by an estoppel arising from its conduct or by its "concurrence", which may (depending on the facts) amount to something less than its express consent.

Negative equity

The provisions that prevail in a bankruptcy and which permit a secured creditor **34–07** to realise his security and prove for the balance or to re-value his security or for the security to be redeemed at the value attributed thereto by the secured creditor[29] do not apply to an IVA. A secured creditor who has notice of a proposal for an IVA and who envisages that the security may be worth less than the sum secured may wish for the express incorporation of some or all of the appropriate bankruptcy provisions in the proposal.[30] The same considerations would apply in a company voluntary arrangement.

Bankruptcy

Bankruptcy differs from any other form of insolvency in that all property owned **34–08** by the insolvent passes not just into the control but into the ownership of another person. Upon the making of a bankruptcy order, the bankrupt's estate vests in the trustee in bankruptcy on his appointment or, in the case of the official receiver, on his becoming trustee. The estate vests without any conveyance, assignment or transfer.[31] The bankrupt's estate consists of, inter alia, "all property belonging to or vested in the bankrupt at the commencement of the bankruptcy",[32] i.e. the day upon which the bankruptcy order is made, and not the date on which the petition was presented.[33] The making of a bankruptcy order does not affect the mortgagee's right to enforce his security[34] unless the security is over goods held by way of pledge, pawn or other security and the official receiver has exercised his rights to inspect them.[35] In such circumstances, the court's permission is required to sell those goods unless a reasonable opportunity has been given for the estate to redeem them.[36] Similarly, a right to appoint a receiver which becomes exercisable upon the making of a bankruptcy order cannot be exercised without the permission of the court.[37]

---

[29] IR 1986 rr.6.109, 6.115 and 6.117.
[30] See *Lawson, Individual Voluntary Arrangements* (2010).
[31] IA 1986 s.306. For consideration of the way in which property is held and controlled in other insolvency situations, see Ch.35 Insolvency of the Mortgagee, below.
[32] IA 1986 s.283(1).
[33] IA 1986 s.278(a).
[34] IA 1986 s.285(4).
[35] IA 1986 s.285(5).
[36] ibid.
[37] Law of Property Act (LPA) 1925 s.110 (as amended).

Proof of debts

34–09   A secured creditor has, when faced with the bankruptcy of the mortgagor, a variety of options. First, he can decline to prove at all in the bankruptcy and must, in such circumstances, rely on his security alone. Second, he may surrender his security to the trustee and prove for his debt in full as an unsecured creditor.[38] Third, he may realise his security and prove for the unsecured balance remaining due to him.[39] Fourth, he may value his security and prove for the unsecured balance.[40]

In the last instance, a trustee who is unsatisfied with the value placed upon the security by the mortgagee may either give the creditor 28 days' notice that he intends to redeem the security at the value placed on it by the creditor in his proof[41] or require the property to be sold, and if the sale is by auction. the trustee and the creditor may bid.[42] A secured creditor may, with the agreement of the trustee or the leave of the court alter the value placed by him upon the security in his proof of debt unless he is the petitioning creditor and has valued the security in his petition or has voted in respect of the unsecured balance. In such instances, only the leave of the court will do.[43]

Failure to disclose security:

34–10   A creditor that does not disclose in his proof that he holds security is required to surrender that security for the general benefit of the creditors unless relieved therefrom by the court on the ground that the omission was inadvertent or the result of an honest mistake.[44]

Amount of proof

34–11   This must be limited to what was due by way of principal and interest at the date that the bankruptcy order was made, after deducting from the amount outstanding the value of the security[45] the proceeds of any sale.[46]

Interest

34–12   A secured creditor remains entitled to look to his security to meet the contractual rate of interest agreed with the bankrupt. However, a mortgagee cannot prove for interest that has accrued due since the bankruptcy order was made[47] and, in the

---

[38] IR 1986 r.6.109(2). Such a surrender will not release a surety: *Rainbow v Juggins* (1880) L.R. 5 Q.B.D. 422.

[39] IR 1986 r.6.109(1).

[40] IR 1986 r.6.93(4).

[41] IR 1986 r.6.117.

[42] IR 1986 r.6.118.

[43] IR 1986 r.6.115. See *Rey v FNCB* [2006] B.P.I.R. 1260.

[44] IR 1986 r.6.116; *Re Maxson* [1919] 2 K.B. 330.

[45] IR 1986 r.6.93(4).

[46] *Re London, Windsor & Greenwich Hotels Co* [1892] 1 Ch. 639; *Re William Hall (Contractors) Ltd (in liq)* [1967] 1 W.L.R. 948.

[47] IA 1986 s.322(2).

event that he wishes to prove for interest that has accrued prior to the commencement of the bankruptcy, he can only do so if the requirements of r.6.113 are satisfied.[48]

A debt due under a written instrument and payable at a certain time will attract interest at the rate specified under the Judgment Act 1838 at the date of the bankruptcy order from the time that the debt is due to the date of the bankruptcy order. Debts that are due otherwise will only attract interest for any period prior to the bankruptcy order if demand is made prior to the presentation of the petition and notice given that interest is payable.[49] However, in the unusual event that a surplus remains after payment of the bankruptcy debts, the trustee must apply such surplus to pay interest on those debts from the commencement of the bankruptcy if it would have been due under the contract but for the intervention of the bankruptcy order.[50]

Sale of the mortgaged property

When a trustee in bankruptcy applies, on behalf of the estate, for the sale of a property jointly owned by the bankrupt and any third party, s.335A of the Insolvency Act 1986 applies and creates a statutory assumption that after the end of the period of one year beginning with the first vesting of the bankrupt's estate in a trustee, the interests of the creditors outweigh all other considerations and a sale of the property will be ordered save other than in exceptional circumstances.[51] Where the trustee is unable for the time being to realise the matrimonial home, he may also apply to the court for a charging order over that property for the benefit of the estate.[52] Such an order has effect as if the bankrupt had granted an equitable charge, but the right to receive the money under it does not arise until an order for sale is made.[53]   **34–13**

If a mortgagee wishes to cause the property to be sold, he may apply to the court for a order directing that the property be sold[54] and, upon that application, the court may order that the land or any part of it is sold with vacant possession in such manner as the court may direct.[55] If sale is by public auction, the court may permit the mortgagee to appear and bid on his own behalf.[56] Conduct of the sale is generally given to the trustee unless the proceeds are unlikely to exceed the secured debt, in which the mortgagee will be given conduct.[57]   **34–14**

Prior to any sale, the court may order that all necessary accounts and inquiries are made as to the outstanding principal, interest and costs due under the   **34–15**

---

[48] See *El Anjou v Stern* [2007] B.P.I.R. 693 for a discussion of r.6.113.
[49] IR 1986 r.6.113(2), (3).
[50] IA 1986 s.328(4).
[51] Such as ill-health see *Re Raval* [1998] B.P.I.R. 389; *Claughton v Charalamabous* [1998] B.P.I.R. 558. See *Turner v Avis* [2008] B.P.I.R. 1143 for consideration of the ambit of exceptional circumstances, adopting the definition applied by Paul Morgan QC in *Hosking v Michaelides* [2006] B.P.I.R. 1193.
[52] IA 1986 s.313.
[53] *Gotham v Doodes* [2007] 1 W.L.R. 86.
[54] IR 1986 r.6.197(1).
[55] IR 1986 r.6.198.
[56] IR 1986 r.6.198(4).
[57] *Re Jordan, Ex p. Harrison* (1884) L.R. 13 Q.B.D. 228.

mortgage and, if the mortgage has been in possession, the moneys received by him or on his behalf.[58] The procedure adopted in the Chancery Division with regard to accounts and inquiries may be applied.[59]

34–16   The proceeds of the sale shall be applied in the payment of the trustees expenses of and occasioned by the application to the court, of the sale and attendance thereat and of any costs arising from the taking of accounts and the making of such inquiries as the court may have directed under the Insolvency Rules 1986 r.6.197.[60]

Disclaimer

34–17   A trustee in bankruptcy can disclaim "onerous property", notwithstanding that he has taken possession of it, endeavoured to sell it or otherwise exercised rights of ownership in relation to it.[61] "Onerous property" is defined as being any unprofitable contract and any other property comprised in the bankrupt's estate which is unsaleable or not readily saleable, or is such that it may give rise to a liability to pay money or perform any other onerous act. Such a disclaimer determines the rights, interests and liabilities of the bankrupt and his estate in relation to the property disclaimed, but does not (save insofar as it is necessary for releasing the bankrupt from his liability) affect the rights or liabilities of any other person.[62] Any person who suffers loss by reason of a disclaimer may prove to that extent as an unsecured creditor in the bankruptcy.[63]

34–18   Leasehold property is more likely than freehold property to be viewed as onerous, given that all leases are likely to include obligations to pay money and perform onerous acts. If leasehold property is to be disclaimed, a copy of the disclaimer must be served on every person claiming under the bankrupt as underlessee or mortgagee and either (1) no application is made for a vesting order before the end of 14 days beginning with day upon which the notice is served, or (2) (where such an application is made) the court orders that the disclaimer is to take effect notwithstanding the application.[64] Note that it is not possible for the trustee to disclaim only part of the property comprised in a lease; the choice is to keep or disclaim the demised property as a whole.[65]

Where leasehold land is disclaimed, a mortgagee is one of the persons who may apply under s.320 of the Insolvency Act 1986 for a vesting order. Such an order causes the property which has been disclaimed to be vested in the successful applicant without conveyance, assignment or transfer.[66] The mortgagee, along with any subtenants, falls into the top category of priority in the event that

---

[58] IR 1986 r.6.197(2).
[59] IR 1986 r.6.197(4); see Ch.33.
[60] IR 1986 r.6.199.
[61] IA 1986 s.315.
[62] IA 1986 s.315(3). See *Hindcastle v Barbara Attenborough Associates* [1997] A.C. 70 for the definitive analysis of the effects of disclaimer, and recent consideration on the impact of disclaimer upon a guarantor's liability in *Shaw v Doleman* [2009] EWCA Civ 279.
[63] IA 1986 s.315(5). See *Christopher Moran Holdings v Bairstow* [2000] 2 A.C. 172.
[64] IA 1986 s.317(1).
[65] *Re Fussell, Ex p. Allen* (1882) L.R. 20 Ch.D. 341.
[66] IA 1986 s.320(6).

multiple applications are made by different interested persons.[67] The court will make an order if it is just to do so but, in the case of leaseholds, will only make the order on terms that the mortgagee is subject to the same liabilities and obligations as the bankrupt was on the day that the petition was presented or (in exceptional circumstances if it thinks fit) subject to the same liabilities and obligations as the mortgagee would have been subject to if the lease had been assigned to him on that day.[68]

CORPORATE MORTGAGORS

The general moratorium

Mention has been made above of a "general moratorium" which is effected by agreement between the company and all its creditors that they will not pursue their claims for a period of time to enable the company to attempt to trade its way out of difficulty. The conduct of such a moratorium is generally under the supervision of an insolvency practitioner or accountant. It is an informal arrangement in the sense that it does not involve any statutory protection of the insolvent's assets and generally has no enforceable contractual basis. The mortgagee can thus only be prevented from enforcing his rights in full to the extent that he has contractually bound himself to hold off or his conduct could otherwise be said to have estopped him from pursuing some or all of his options. **34–19**

Company Voluntary Arrangements[69]

As the name suggests, this is the corporate equivalent of the IVA. Again, it is beyond the scope of this work to consider the procedure in any detail, and reference should be made to the specialist texts, bearing in mind also the impact of the Insolvency (Amendment) Rules 2010, the Insolvency (Amendment) (No.2) Rules 2010 and the Legislative Reform (Insolvency) (Miscellaneous Provisions) Order 2010. The directors of a company which is not in administration or being wound up may make a proposal to the company and its creditors for a CVA; if the company is in administration that right rests with the administrator, and if it is in liquidation only the liquidator may make the proposal.[70] A nominee must be appointed to act in relation to the proposal.[71] **34–20**

If the nominee is not the administrator or liquidator of the company, he must report to the court within 28 days of being given notice of the proposal stating whether, in his opinion, the proposed CVA has a reasonable prospect of being approved and implemented, whether a meeting of the company's creditors should

---

[67] *Re AE Realisations Ltd* [1987] 3 All E.R. 83.
[68] IA 1986 s.321(1). *Re Walker, Ex p. Mills* (1895) 64 L.J.Q.B. 783.
[69] Under Pt 1 of the Insolvency Act 1986, as repeatedly amended.
[70] IA 1986 s.1.
[71] IA 1986 s.1(2).

be summoned and, if so, when and where that meeting should be held.[72] A liquidator or administrator acting as nominee can simply summon a meeting to consider the proposal without recourse to the court.[73] At the meeting of the company's creditors, the proposal may be approved or rejected or modified.[74] Once approved, the CVA has a similar effect on the company and its creditors to that set out above in respect of IVAs.[75] A CVA which unfairly prejudices the interests of a creditor or in which there has been some material irregularity at or in relation to the creditors' meeting may be challenged.[76]

34–21   The principal difference between a CVA and an IVA is that there is no generally applicable provision for interim protection for a company equivalent to the making of an interim order in respect of an insolvent individual. However, if the company satisfies at least two of the tests to define a "small company" and is eligible,[77] it is now able to apply for a statutory moratorium[78] either before or after a proposal has been made to creditors. The procedure for obtaining such a moratorium and provisions which deal with managing and investigating the company's affairs while it is in force are set out in Sch.A1 to the Insolvency Act 1986 (as amended).

The creditors' meeting

34–22   The persons to be summoned to a creditors' meeting are every creditor of the company of whose claim and address the person summoning the creditors' meeting is aware.[79] A "secured creditor" in relation to a company means a creditor of the company who holds in respect of his debt a security over the property of the company.[80] As with IVAs, the changes implemented on January 1, 2003, mean that a creditor who should have been given notice of the meeting will be bound by its decision even if in fact he did not receive such notice, although he would also be able to challenge that decision for irregularity.[81]

Section 4: the preservation of the ability of a mortgagee to enforce against the security

34–23   The creditors' meeting "shall not approve any proposal or modification which affects the right of a secured creditor of the debtor to enforce his security, except

---

[72] IA 1986 s.2(2).

[73] IA 1986 s.3(2).

[74] IA 1986 s.4.

[75] Above, paras 34–03 et seq. and IA 1986 s.5.

[76] IA 1986 s.6. For the power to intervene in such circumstances, see *Sisu Capital Fund Limited v Tucker* [2006] 1 All E.R. 167.

[77] Companies Act 2006 ss.381ab–384, and Ia 1986 Sch.A1 paras 4A–K: Certain companies are thereby excluded.

[78] IA 1986 s.1A.

[79] IA 1986 s.3(3).

[80] IA 1986 s.248(a). However, as with all other forms of insolvency process, note that this does not apply to the creditor who has obtained an interim charging order but not yet been able to obtain a final charging order. He is not a secured creditor, and if a moratorium is in place must seek permission of the court if he wishes to pursue his application for a final order. See *Clarke v Coutts & Co* [2002] B.P.I.R. 916.

[81] IA 1986 ss.5(2) and 6.

with the concurrence of the creditor concerned".[82] Accordingly, save in respect of the right to enforce a mortgagor's personal covenant to pay, unless the terms of the CVA are such that a secured creditor is taken to have approved a fetter on his rights to enforce his security, those rights remain unaffected by the implementation of a CVA. The caveat expressed above[83] arising from the decision in *Re Millwall Football Club and Athletic Co (1985) Plc (in admin)*[84] is applicable in the case of a CVA as well as that of an IVA.

Receivers

There are two forms of receiver whose appointment may be considered where a mortgagor is insolvent: a Law of Property Act receiver and an administrative receiver. The former is addressed elsewhere in this work.[85] The latter was created by the Insolvency Act 1986 with the aim of providing an option under which the company's board's powers and ability to manage the company were merely suspended insofar as they were inconsistent with the administrative receiver's powers to realise sufficient funds to pay off the debenture holder who appointed him. However, the amendments effected by the Enterprise Act 2002 now restrict the use of administrative receivers to floating charges created in connection with transactions in capital markets, and they are unlikely to be seen very often in the context of mortgages. Instead, it is intended that debenture holders will utilise the new broader and more flexible system of administration in respect of an insolvent corporate grantor.   **34–24**

Administration[86]

So radical were the amendments to the law concerning the administration of companies effected by Pt 10 of the Enterprise Act 2002, that it is fair to view the implementation date of September 15, 2003, as marking the watershed between two different systems. Virtually all administrations commenced after that date are governed by the "new" system, and it is therefore only to the post-September 2003 position that this work refers. Once again, it is recommended that reference is made to specialist texts for detailed analysis of the law in this area; what follows is no more than an overview.   **34–25**

The idea of administration is to suspend the rights of all creditors, whether secured or not, while an attempt is made through an insolvency practitioner to manage, continue and, where necessary restructure the company's business.

The company may be placed into administration by the court on application by the company, its directors or any creditor [87] provided the court is satisfied that (1)   **34–26**

---

[82] IA 1986 s.4(3). See *Thomas v Ken Thomas Ltd* [2007] B.P.I.R. 959.
[83] See above paras 34–06 et seq.
[84] [1988] 2 B.C.L.C. 272.
[85] See paras 26–27 et seq.
[86] Under Pt II of the Insolvency Act 1986 as amended and Sch.B1.
[87] IA 1986 Sch.B1 para.12. For the procedure see IR 1986 rr.2.2 (as amended) et seq., and for the court's powers on hearing the application see IA 1986 Sch.B1 para.13.

the company is or is likely to become unable to pay its debts (within the meaning ascribed to that expression by s.123 of the Insolvency Act 1986), and (2) that an order would be reasonably likely to achieve the statutory purpose of administration.[88] Under the new regime the company, its directors or the holder of a floating charge in respect of its property who is empowered by that charge in a relevant way may also appoint an administrator directly without applying to the court for an order to that effect.[89] Note that the court hearing an application for an administration order by the holder of a qualifying floating charge may also make an order in circumstances where the company is still solvent but the holder of the charge would have been able to make a direct appointment[90] under its terms.

34-27   The "purpose of administration" is (a) to rescue the company as a going concern, or (b) to achieve a better result for the company's creditors as a whole than would be likely if the company were to be wound up without first being in administration, or (c) to realise property in order to make a distribution to one or more secured creditors. The administrator is obliged to look first to achieving (a) and can move on to (b) only if he concludes that (a) is not reasonably practicable or (b) would achieve a better result for the creditors as a whole. He may only make (c) his objective if he has concluded that it is not reasonably practicable to achieve either of (a) and (b) and, if in so doing, he does not unnecessarily harm the interests of the creditors as a whole.[91] This reflects the status of an administrator as an officer of the court regardless of the instigator and manner of his appointment.[92] Where the real motive for an administration application was to prevent a secured creditor who had already appointed a receiver from realising his security through the sale of the property and instead to give the company a chance to sell it at a higher price, it was held to be inappropriate to make an administration order.[93]

Interim moratorium

34-28   Where an application to the court for an administration order has been made but not yet determined, or where a notice of intention to appoint an administrator has been filed but the appointment has not yet taken effect, there is an automatic moratorium on the commencement of insolvency proceedings and on taking any other form of legal process or step to enforce security without the permission or the court.[94]

Moratorium during administration

34-29   Once an administrator has been appointed by the court, a slightly different form of moratorium comes into being. In most cases, any existing winding up petition

[88] IA 1986 Sch.B1 para.11. See below.
[89] IA 1986 Sch.B1 paras 14 et seq. for the holder of a floating charge and 22 et seq. for the company or its directors.
[90] IA 1986 Sch.B1 para.35.
[91] IA 1986 Sch.B1 para.3.
[92] IA 1986 Sch.B1 para.5.
[93] *Doltable Ltd v Lexi Holdings Plc* [2006] 1 B.C.L.C. 384.
[94] IA 1986 Sch.B1 para.44, applying the provisions of paras 42–43 save as to consent of the administrator.

will be dismissed and any administrative receiver will vacate office.[95] If the administrator was appointed out of court by the holder of a floating charge, any winding up petition will generally be suspended. The company and its directors are not able to appoint an administrator where a petition is already pending.

Regardless of the manner of the administrator's appointment, once he takes office, no resolution may be passed to wind up the company and no winding up order will be made unless the petition was presented on certain limited grounds.[96] No other step may be taken to enforce security or to initiate or continue any other form of legal process against the company unless the administrator consents or permission to do so is obtained from the court.[97]

Obtaining permission to bypass the moratorium

The court will, on an application by a secured creditor to enforce his rights, **34–30** undertake a balancing exercise between that creditor's rights and the interests of the other creditors in the light of the administrator's proposals. A detailed analysis of the authorities is beyond the scope of this work[98] but in general, where the exercise of the right would not impede the purpose of the administration, permission is generally given.[99] The principles to be applied are those derived from the judgment of Nicholls L.J. in *Re Atlantic Computer Systems Plc*,[100] wherein he felt bound "to make some general observations regarding cases where leave is sought to exercise existing proprietary rights, including security rights, against a company in administration". His Lordship observed[101]:

> "(1) It is in every case for the person who seeks permission to make out a case for him to be given permission.
> (2) the prohibition (now contained in Schedule B1 paragraph 43) is intended to assist the company, under the management of the administrator, to achieve the purpose for which the administration order was made. If granting leave to a person with security to exercise his rights is unlikely to impede the achievement of that purpose, leave should normally be given.
> (3) In other cases when a secured creditor seeks possession the court has to carry out a balancing exercise, balancing the legitimate interests of the secured creditor. This is not a mechanical exercise but a matter of judgment seeking to give effect to the purpose of the statutory provisions with regard to the parties' interests and the circumstances of the case. The purpose of the power to give permission is to enable the court to relax the prohibition where it would be inequitable for the prohibition to apply.
> (4) In carrying out the balancing exercise great importance, or weight, is normally to be given to the proprietary interests of the secured creditor. So far as possible, the administration procedure should not be used to prejudice those who were secured creditors when the administration order was made in lieu of

[95] IA 1986 1986, Sch.B1 paras 40, 41.
[96] IA 1986 Sch.B1 para.42.
[97] IA 1986 Sch.B1 para.43.
[98] See generally, *Palmer's Company Law*, paras 14.024–14.026.2.
[99] *Metro Nominees (Wandsworth) Ltd v Rayment* [2008] B.C.C. 40; *Innovate Logistics Ltd (in admin) v Sunberry Properties Ltd* [2009] 1 B.C.L.C. 145.
[100] [1992] Ch. 505 (CA).
[101] ibid., 542.

a winding up order. The underlying principle is that an administration for the benefit of unsecured creditors should not be conducted at the expense of those who have proprietary rights which they are seeking to exercise, save to the extent that this may be unavoidable and even then this will usually be acceptable only to a strictly limited extent.

(5) It will normally be a sufficient ground for the grant of leave if significant loss would be caused to the secured creditor by a refusal. For this purpose loss comprises any kind of financial loss, direct or indirect, including loss by reason of delay, and may extend to loss which is not financial. However, where substantial loss would be caused to others if permission were to be granted, that may outweigh the loss to the secured creditor were permission to be refused.

(6) In assessing these respective losses the court will have regard to matters such as: the financial position of the company, its ability to pay the rental arrears and the continuing rentals, the administrator's proposals, the period for which the administration order has already been in force and is expected to remain in force, the effect on the administration if leave were given, the effect on the applicant if leave were refused, the end result sought to be achieved by the administration, the prospects of that result being achieved, and the history of the administration so far.

(7) In considering these matters it will often be necessary to assess how probable the suggested consequences are. Thus if loss to the applicant is virtually certain if leave is refused, and loss to others a remote possibility if leave is granted, that will be a powerful factor in favour of granting leave.

(8) The conduct of the parties may be material

(9) The above considerations may be relevant not only to the decision whether leave should be granted or refuse, but also to a decision to impose terms if leave is granted.

(10) In the case of a mortgagee seeking to enforce his security, an important consideration will often be whether the applicant is fully secured. If he is, delay in enforcement is likely to be less prejudicial than in cases where his security is insufficient.

(12) In some cases there will be a dispute over the existence, validity or nature of the security which the applicant is seeking leave to enforce. It is not for the court on the leave application to seek to adjudicate upon that issue, unless the issue raises a short point of law which it is convenient to determine without further ado. Otherwise the court needs to be satisfied only that the applicant has a seriously arguable case."

Thus it can be seen that the court will not normally permit unsecured creditors to obtain a benefit by the administration of a company at the expense of a secured creditor save to the extent that this may be unavoidable and proportionate. Permission will usually be granted to a mortgagee who wishes to take steps to enforce his security in circumstances where he would otherwise experience a significant loss, unless the loss that would be occasioned by the unsecured creditors in the event that permission was granted would be out of all proportion to that which the secured creditor may suffer.

The administrator's power to deal with charged property

34–31   The administrator may dispose of or take action relating to property which is subject to a floating charge as if it were not subject to the charge, and may apply to the court for an order permitting him to dispose of property subject to other forms of security as if it were not subject to that security.[102] The court may only make such an order if it thinks that disposal of the property would be likely to promote the purpose of administration in respect of the company. The order will be subject to conditions that the net proceeds of sale of the property be applied towards discharging the secured sums and further payments be made as necessary to bring the proceeds up to a determined market value. Where the order relates to more than one security, the proceeds and additional sums will be applied in order of priority of those securities. Accordingly, it can be seen that the distinction between what was a fixed or floating charge on its creation is important.[103]

In *Re A R V Aviation Ltd*,[104] the court emphasised the need to have proper valuation evidence before it as to the value of the security in question (the secured creditor was alleging that the administrator's valuation was overly optimistic) and held that "the sums secured by the security" extended to interest and (subject to the court's discretion) the secured creditor's costs. Where the administrator is considering a challenge to the validity of the security and wishes to cause property subject to a fixed charge to be sold prior to any such challenge being commenced, it seems that the court has no jurisdiction under Sch.B1 para.71 to authorise sale and the retention of the proceeds in a designated account. The preferable course would be to commence the challenge and seek directions within those proceedings.[105]

Schedule B1 paras 73 and 74: protection of the interest of secured and other creditors

New provision has been made for the protection of secured and preferential creditors by the inclusion of Sch.B1 para.73. This precludes an administrator from making proposals which affect the rights of a secured creditor to enforce his security unless he consents to that aspect of the proposals.   **34–32**

Furthermore, any creditor of a company in administration may apply to the court for relief under para.74 of Sch.B1 if he considers that the administrator is acting or has acted or proposes to act so as unfairly to harm the interests of the applicant. The court is given a broad range of powers to control the administrator in such circumstances and may make such order as it thinks fit,[106] although it cannot impede or prevent the implementation of a CVA or a compromise or scheme under Pt 26 of the Companies Act 2006 or a cross-border merger, or (if the application was more than 28 days after the approval of any proposals or revised proposals by the creditors in the administration) the implementation of those proposals.[107]   **34–33**

---

[102] IA 1986 Sch.B1 paras 70 and 71

[103] See paras 23–23 et seq. It does not matter, for the purposes of s.15(1) that the charge has crystallised.

[104] (1988) 4 B.C.C. 708.

[105] *Re Newman Shopfitters (Cleveland) Limited* [1991] B.C.L.C. 407. This case was decided under the former regime (IA 1986, s.15) but should apply equally to the "new" paragraph 71 power.

[106] IA 1986 Sch.B1 para.74(3)(e).

[107] IA 1986 s.27(3).

Liquidation

Stay of proceedings

34–34 At any time after the presentation of a winding up petition and before a winding up order is made, the company or any creditor or contributory may apply to the court for an order staying or restraining any proceedings against the company.[108] Unless there are special circumstances, the court will exercise its discretion to ensure an equal distribution of assets.[109]

Upon the making of a winding up order or the appointment of a provisional liquidator, no action or proceeding shall be proceeded with or commenced against the company or its property, except by leave of the court and subject to such terms as the court may impose.[110] In determining whether leave should be given, the court will undertake a balancing exercise and seek to do what is right and just in all the circumstances. A lessor has been permitted to take proceedings to re-enter demised premises where there has been a breach of covenant.[111] A mortgagee seeking to obtain possession would, it is submitted, enjoy equal rights and prospects.

Proof of debts

34–35 Similar provisions to those which prevail in bankruptcy[112] apply in the event that a company is wound up[113] and accordingly, do not merit repetition.

Interest

34–36 There are corresponding statutory provisions governing interest in a winding up[114] to those which apply in a bankruptcy.[115]

Disclaimer

34–37 A liquidator's powers to disclaim onerous property are similar to those given to the trustee in bankruptcy addressed above.[116] A mortgagee is equally able to seek a vesting order in the case of a disclaimer of a leasehold property by a liquidator.[117]

---

[108] IA 1986 s.126. In a voluntary winding up similar provisions apply: IA 1986 s.112.

[109] *Bowkett v Fuller United Electric Works Ltd* [1923] 1 K.B. 160.

[110] IA 1986 s.130(2).

[111] *Re Strand Hotel Co* [1868] W.N. 2.

[112] See above, paras 34–09 et seq.

[113] See IR 1986 r.4.88 (proving for the balance/whole debt due to a secured creditor) and Ch.10 of the Insolvency Rules, rr.4.95–4.99 (valuation of security; surrender for non-disclosure; redemption by the liquidator; test of value; realisation by the creditor).

[114] IA 1986 s.189 and IR 1986 r.4.93.

[115] See above, para.34–12.

[116] See above, paras 34–17 et seq. and, for the provisions relating to liquidation IA 1986 s.178 (power to disclaim), s.179 (disclaimer of leaseholds), s.180 (land subject to a rentcharge), s.181 (powers of court (general)) and s.182 (powers of court (leasehold)).

[117] IA 1986 s.182(3).

Dissolution of the company

Dissolution is not a separate form of corporate insolvency; it is the ultimate **34–38** conclusion of the liquidation of a limited company. Once the liquidation has been completed, the company is dissolved and thus ceases to exist.[118] Dissolution can follow upon the completion of the winding up process, in which the company's assets are realised and its creditors paid, with any surplus being distributed to its contributories. Section 205 of the Insolvency Act provides for the dissolution of the company at the expiry of a period of three months after either the final meeting of creditors and the vacation of office by the liquidator or notice from the official receiver that the winding up is complete.[119] Section 201 makes similar provision in the case of a voluntary winding up: dissolution generally occurs three months after the registration of the liquidator's final account and return.

However, a company may also be subject to early dissolution where it appears **34–39** that the realisable assets of the company are insufficient to cover the expenses of the winding up and that the affairs of the company do not require further investigation.[120] The official receiver and any creditor or contributory may object to early dissolution,[121] however, unless effective objection is made the effect of early dissolution is that the company's assets will not be realised as they would have been if the liquidation ran its course. Accordingly, those assets would, on dissolution pass as bona vacantia.[122]

Absent any form of winding up, the registrar of companies may initiate a **34–40** procedure in relation to a company which he has cause to believe is no longer carrying on business or in operation which, at its conclusion, similarly results in its dissolution.[123] Upon dissolution on this basis, the company's property passes as bona vacantia.[124]

The court may restore a dissolved company to the register in accordance with **34–41** its statutory powers.[125]

Bona vacantia

On dissolution all property and rights whatsoever vested in or held on trust for **34–42** the company immediately before its dissolution (including leasehold property, but not including property held by the company on trust for any other person) are deemed to be bona vacantia and accordingly belong to the Crown or to the Duchy of Lancaster or to the Duke of Cornwall for the time being (as the case may be), and vest and may be dealt with in the same manner as other bona vacantia accruing to the Crown or to the Duchy of Lancaster or to the Duke of Cornwall.[126]

---

[118] IA 1986 Ch.IX (ss.201–205).
[119] IA 1986 s.205(1)(a), (b).
[120] IA 1986 s.202(2).
[121] IA 1986 s.203.
[122] Companies Act 2006 s.1012, replacing Companies Act 1985 s.654.
[123] ibid., ss.1000–1002.
[124] ibid., s.1012.
[125] ibid., ss.1024–8 and 1029–1032.
[126] ibid., s.1012(1).

The equity of redemption is an interest which the mortgagor can convey, devise, entail, lease, mortgage, or settle[127] and thus it has been held that the equity of redemption in leasehold premises subject to a mortgage can pass as bona vacantia upon the dissolution of a corporate mortgagor.[128]

The Crown, the Duchy of Lancaster and the Duke of Cornwall can disclaim property that has vested as bona vacantia.[129] If the company is restored to the register, the property is deemed never to have vested in the Crown, and any disclaimer is deemed not to have occurred, although a disposition of that property made while it was held as bona vacantia will stand and the Crown will make a compensatory payment to the company in its place.[130]

CHALLENGING TRANSACTIONS

Avoidance of property dispositions: ss.127 and 284

34–43   If an individual mortgagor is adjudged bankrupt, any disposition of property which he made from the day on which the petition was presented until the day on which his estate vested in the trustee in bankruptcy is void save to the extent that it was made with the consent of the court or subsequently ratified by the court.[131] This does not provide a remedy against any person:

    (a)   in respect of any property or payment which he received before the commencement of the bankruptcy in good faith, for value and without notice that the petition had been presented, or

    (b)   in respect of any interest in property which derives from an interest in respect of which there is thus no remedy.

34–44   In the case of a corporate mortgagor which is wound up by the court, any disposition of the company's property and any transfer of shares or alteration in the status of the company's members made after the commencement of the winding up[132] will be void unless the court otherwise orders or the act in question was undertaken by an administrator while the winding up petition was suspended.[133]

Other routes

34–45   In addition to those provisions rendering dispositions automatically void, where a mortgagor becomes insolvent there are various ways in which his recent prior

---

[127] *Pawlett v Att.-Gen.* (1667) Hard, 465, 469; *Fawcett v Lowther* (1751) 2 Ves. Sen. 300.
[128] *Re Wells* [1933] Ch. 29.
[129] Companies Act 2006 ss.1013–1014.
[130] *Allied Dunbar Assurance Plc v Fowler* [1994] 2 B.C.L.C. 197. See also Companies Act 2006 ss.1028, 1032 and 1034.
[131] IA 1986 s.284. Note that this does not apply to dispositions made by the bankrupt of property held by him on trust for someone else.
[132] Being the time of the presentation of the petition: IA 1986 s.129(2).
[133] IA 1986 s.127 as amended. See also IA 1986 s.88 (voluntary winding up).

transactions may be susceptible to challenge. If that mortgagor, being an individual, is adjudged bankrupt, such matters are governed by Pt IX Ch.V of the Insolvency Act 1986.[134] If a company is in administration or liquidation, the relevant provisions are contained in Ch.X Pt VI.[135]

In respect of any individual or company, transactions at an undervalue for the purpose of putting assets beyond the reach of someone who is making or might make a claim against them or otherwise prejudicing the interests of such a person in relation to their claim may also be challenged using the provisions of s.423. An application to the court on this basis may be made by a "victim of the transaction"[136] even if the individual or company is not bankrupt, being wound up or in administration, nor even necessarily insolvent, and is also available to the victim or the supervisor where a voluntary arrangement is in place.[137]

The three forms of challenge which are most likely to be of interest in relation to mortgages are those relating to transactions at an undervalue,[138] preferences,[139] and those dealing with transactions at an undervalue where the purpose is debt avoidance.[140]   **34–46**

Transactions at an undervalue

The administrator or the liquidator of a company or the trustee in bankruptcy of   **34–47**
an individual[141] may apply to the court where the insolvent debtor has at a "relevant time"[142] entered into a transaction with any person at an undervalue. On such an application, the court shall make such order as it thinks fit for restoring the position to what it would have been if the company or individual had not entered into that transaction.[143]

A transaction is entered into at an undervalue if:

(a) the debtor makes a gift to that person or otherwise enters into a transaction with that person on terms that provide for the debtor to receive no consideration, or

(b) the debtor enters into a transaction with that person for a consideration the value of which, in money or money's worth, is significantly less than the value, in money or money's worth, of the consideration provided by the debtor, or

---

[134] IA1986 ss.339–349. See also the provisions of Ch.VI as to bankruptcy offences.

[135] IA 1986 ss.238–246, as amended

[136] That is to say a person who is, or is capable of being prejudiced by the transaction—s.423(5).

[137] IA 1986 s.424(1).

[138] IA 1986s.238 with regard to companies in administration or liquidation and s.339 in respect of bankrupt individuals.

[139] IA 1986 s.239 with regard to companies in administration or liquidation and s.340 in respect of bankrupt individuals.

[140] IA 1986 ss.423 et seq.

[141] But not a receiver or the supervisor of a CVA or IVA.

[142] Defined in IA 1986 ss.240 and 341 and considered in paras 34–54 et seq. below.

[143] In this regard, the court retains a discretion whether to make an order; *Re Paramount Airways (In Administration)* [1993] Ch. 223, 239; *Singla v Brown* [2008] Ch. 357.

(c)   in the case of an individual debtor, he or she enters into a transaction with that person in consideration of marriage or the formation of a civil partnership.[144]

The statutory provisions require either an outright gift or some element of dealing between the parties to the transaction in order for it to be treated as being at an undervalue.[145] Thus, for example, if the debtor was forced to liquidate stock at a heavily discounted price in order to improve its cash flow, such transactions would be unlikely to be susceptible to challenge in any subsequent administration, liquidation or bankruptcy unless there was some further aspect which cast doubt on their veracity. There is no statutory definition of "consideration" nor is there any requirement as to the identity or relationship of the person to whom the consideration is to be provided.[146] The authorities demonstrate that the general concept of consideration in the context in the formation of contracts is the one to which the courts have regard, but there is no reason why the value of a collateral agreement entered into by the debtor with a third party as part of the overall transaction should not fall within the purview of the court's scrutiny.

34–48   A debenture created as part of a transaction to prevent an unsecured overdraft being called in has generally not been treated as a transaction at an undervalue within subpara.(b) above, since the mere creation of a security does not deplete the debtor's assets and therefore the debtor has not provided a consideration measured in money or money's worth as required by those provisions.[147] However, this approach has recently been questioned (albeit in a case on s.423 of the Insolvency Act 1986) by Arden L.J., in circumstances where she thought the value to the creditor was a right to have recourse to security, which should not invariably be left out of account when assessing the respective considerations given by the parties.[148]

34–49   In the case of a corporate debtor, the court will not make an order in respect of a transaction at an undervalue if it is satisfied:

(a)   that the company which entered into the transaction did so in good faith and for the purpose of carrying on its business, and

(b)   that at the time it did so there were reasonable grounds for believing that the transaction would benefit the company.[149]

---

[144] ibid., s.238(4) and s.339(3).

[145] *Re Taylor Sinclair (Capital) Ltd* [2001] 2 B.C.L.C. 176.

[146] Any sums paid before the execution of the transaction are, however, discounted as amounting to "past consideration" for the benefit to be provided in return: see *Re Bangla Television Ltd* [2007] 1 B.C.L.C. 609.

[147] *Re MC Bacon Ltd* [1990] B.C.C. 78; [1990] B.C.L.C. 234; *Re Mistral Finance Limited* [2001] B.C.C. 27. See also *Weisgard v Pilkington* [1995] B.C.C. 1108; *Re Exchange Travel (Holdings) Ltd* [1996] B.C.C. 933, affirmed sub non *Katz v McNally* [1997] B.C.C. 784; *Re Corfe Joinery Ltd* [1997] B.C.C. 511; *Re Agriplant Services Limited* [1997] B.C.C. 842; *Re Brian D. Pierson (Contractors) Limited* [1999] B.C.C. 26.

[148] *Hill v Spread Trustee Co Ltd* [2007] 1 W.L.R. 2404.

[149] ibid., s.238(5). As to sub-para.(b), see *Phillips v Brewin Dolphin Bell Lawrie Limited* [2001] 1 W.L.R. 143.

Preferences

The administrator or liquidator of a company or the trustee in bankruptcy of an **34–50** individual may also apply to the court where that company or individual has at a "relevant time"[150] given a preference to any person, and the court shall on such an application, make such order as it thinks fit for restoring the position to what it would have been if the company or individual had not given that preference.[151]

A corporate or individual debtor gives a preference to a person if: **34–51**

(a) that person is one of the debtor's creditors or a surety or guarantor for any of the debtor's debts or other liabilities, and

(b) the debtor does anything or suffers anything to be done which (in either case) has the effect of putting that person into a position which, in the event of the debtor going into insolvent liquidation or becoming bankrupt, will be better than the position he would have been in if that thing had not been done.[152]

Motive is of importance in respect of preferences regardless of whether the debtor is a company or an individual. The court will not make an order in respect of a preference given to any person unless the corporate or individual debtor was influenced in deciding to give it by a desire to produce in relation to that person the effect set out in sub-para.(b) immediately above.[153]

To assist those bringing such claims, the Act raises various presumptions, one **34–52** of which is that a company which has given a preference to a person connected with the company[154] (otherwise than by reason only of being its employee) at the time the preference was given is presumed, unless the contrary is shown, to have been influenced in deciding to give it by that desire.[155] A similar presumption is raised where an individual gives a preference to a person who at that time was an associate of his (otherwise than by reason only of being his employee).[156]

A preference will be voidable if the desire to create the advantage in question is at least present as an operative force in the mind of the debtor, even if the desire is not the dominant intention. However, in circumstances where the debtor yields to the genuine commercial pressure applied by a creditor and makes payment or does some other act which places the creditor in a better position than he would have been if the act had not been done, the court may determine that the necessary "desire" is absent because a transaction was not, on the facts, destined to produce that result.

---

[150] Defined in IA 1986 ss.240 and 341 and considered in paras 34–54 et seq. below.

[151] ibid., s.239(2), (3) and s.340(1) and (2). For the appropriate limitation period, see para.34–58 below. The court also retains a discretion in the case of preferences whether to make an order at all: *Re Paramount Airways (in admin)* [1993] Ch. 223, 239; *Singla v Brown* [2008] Ch. 357.

[152] ibid., s.239(4) and s.340(3).

[153] ibid., s.239(5) and s.340(3).

[154] See para.34–56, below.

[155] ibid., s.239(6).

[156] ibid., s..340(5). For instances where the presumption has been rebutted on the evidence (in whole or in part) see *Re Beacon Leisure Ltd* [1991] B.C.C. 213; *Re Fairway Magazines Ltd* [1992] B.C.C. 924 and *Re Oxford Pharmaceuticals Ltd* [2009] 2 B.C.L.C. 485.

34–53   In *Re MC Bacon Ltd*[157] the court held that the use of the word "desire" required a far stronger and more positive state of mind on the part of the company alleged to have given the preference than was signified by the previous statutory formulation, which had merely required "intention". In order to show that a transaction was a voidable preference, it was necessary to show that the debtor was influenced by a desire to produce the effect set out in s.239(4)(b) or 340(3)(b). That "desire" was subjective, and a debtor would not be taken to desire all the necessary consequences of its acts, as there were acts which might have to be carried out against the interests of the debtor but which could be regarded as the unavoidable price of obtaining the sought-after advantage.

While there was no need to produce direct evidence of the desire to prefer the creditor, what had to be proved was that at the time the debtor decided to enter into the transaction in question it was influenced by a desire to achieve the effect in s.239(4)(b) or 340(3)(b). It was not necessary to prove that had the desire not been present the company would not have entered into the transaction. So where the debtor had succumbed to the pressure of its bankers to execute a mortgage debenture in the bank's favour over its fixed and floating assets as a condition of the bank's continued support of the debtor in circumstances where a report by bank officials had concluded that the debtor was insolvent but that there were reasonable grounds for thinking it could trade out of its difficulties, the court concluded that the debtor had no choice but to grant the bank's security if it wanted to continue to trade as the bank's support was necessary to prevent it from entering insolvent liquidation. Accordingly there was no "desire" on the part of the debtor to put the bank into a position which in the event of liquidation would be better than would otherwise have been the case. The debenture was therefore held not to be void as a preference. The case is also illustrative of the court's approach to consideration, the consideration in that particular instance being provided by the bank's forbearance from calling in the overdraft facility.

"Relevant time"

34–54   The court is empowered to inspect and adjust transactions at an undervalue and preferences under these provisions only when they have occurred at a 'relevant time'. This requires consideration both of the date at which the transaction took place and also of the debtor's circumstances at that time. The test differs dependent upon whether the debtor is a company or an individual.

Corporate debtor

34–55   In respect of a corporate debtor, the time at which that company enters into a transaction at an undervalue or gives a preference is a "relevant time" if the transaction is entered into or the preference given:

---

[157] [1990] B.C.C. 78; [1990] B.C.L.C. 324.

(a) in the case of a transaction at an undervalue or of a preference which is given to a person who is connected with the company[158] (otherwise than by reason only of being its employee) within the period of two years ending with the onset of insolvency;

(b) in the case of a preference which is not such a transaction and is not so given, at a time in the period of six months ending with the onset of insolvency;

(c) in either case, at a time between the making of an administration application in respect of the company and the making of an administration order on that application; and

(d) in either case, at a time between the filing with the court of a copy of notice of intention to appoint an administrator under para.14 or 22 of Sch.B1 and the making of an appointment under that paragraph.[159]

As to the need to consider the debtor's circumstances for the purposes of ascertaining whether it is a "relevant time", where a company enters into a transaction at an undervalue or gives a preference at a time mentioned in paras (a) or (b) immediately above, that time is *not* a relevant time unless the company:

(a) is at that time unable to pay its debts within the meaning of s.123[160] in Ch.VI of Pt IV of the Insolvency Act 1986; or

(b) becomes unable to pay its debts within the meaning of that section in consequence of the transaction or preference.[161]

However, the Act further provides that the company is presumed to be unable to **34–56** pay its debts or to have become unable to pay its debts in relation to any transaction at an undervalue[162] which is entered into by a company with a person who is connected with the company unless the contrary is shown.[163]

The Act defines the "onset of insolvency" in s.240(3) as:

(a) in a case where s.238 or 239 applies by reason of an administrator of a company being appointed by administration order, the date on which the administration application is made,

(b) in a case where s.238 or 239 applies by reason of an administrator of a company being appointed under para.14 or 22 of Sch.B1 following filing with the court of a copy of a notice of intention to appoint under that paragraph, the date on which the copy of the notice is filed,

---

[158] Defined above., ss.249 and 435. A person is connected with the company if he is its director or shadow director or an associate of either or an associate of the company (as to which, see also s.435).

[159] ibid., s.240(1).

[160] The Act therefore brings in, as the test of the company's inability to pay its debts both the cash-flow basis set out in IA 1986 s.123(1) and the balance sheet test contained within s.123(2) of the Act.

[161] ibid., s.240(2).

[162] But not a preference.

[163] ibid., s.240(2).

(c)   in a case where s.238 or 239 applies by reason of an administrator of a company being appointed otherwise than as mentioned in the immediately preceding paras (a) or (b), the date on which the appointment takes effect,

(d)   in a case where s.238 or 239 applies by reason of a company going into liquidation either following conversion of administration into winding up by virtue of art.37 of the EC Regulation[164] or at the time when the appointment of an administrator ceases to have effect, the date on which the company entered administration (or, if relevant, the date on which the application for the administration order was made or a copy of the notice of intention to appoint was filed), and

(e)   in a case where s.238 or 239 applies by reason of a company going into liquidation at any other time, the date of the commencement of the winding up.[165]

Individual debtor

34–57   The time at which an individual debtor enters into a transaction at an undervalue or grants a preference is a relevant time if the transaction is entered into or the preference is given:

(a)   in the case of a transaction at an undervalue, at a time in the period of five years ending with the day of the presentation of the bankruptcy petition on which the individual is adjudged bankrupt,

(b)   in the case of a preference which is not a transaction at an undervalue and is given to a person who is an associate of the individual (otherwise than by reason only of being his employee) at a time in the period of two years ending with that day, and

(c)   in any other case of a preference which is not a transaction at an undervalue, at a time in the period of six months ending with that day.[166]

Where the individual enters into a transaction at an undervalue or gives a preference at one of those times, save in circumstances where the transaction in question is at an undervalue and occurred within two years ending on the day of presentation of the petition, the trustee wishing to challenge it must also establish that either the individual was insolvent at the time of the transaction or preference or he became insolvent in consequence of the transaction or preference.[167] Once again, where the beneficiary of the transaction or preference is an associate[168] of the debtor, it is presumed that the debtor was or became insolvent unless the contrary is shown.

---

[164] EC Regulation on Insolvency. 1346/2000, [2000] O.J. L160/1 (as amended).
[165] As to which see IA 1986 s.129.
[166] ibid., s.341(1)
[167] ibid., s.341(2). Note that insolvency for these purposes is defined in s.340(3) and includes both the cash-flow and the balance sheet tests.
[168] Defined in IA 1986 s.435 subject to the employee qualification in s.340(5).

Limitation

Applicants to set aside transactions under ss.238 to 241 and 339 to 342 of the **34–58** Insolvency Act 1986 are generally actions on a specialty within s.8(1) of the Limitation Act 1980. Accordingly, a 12-year period of limitation applies commencing on the date upon which an application could have been brought. However, where the substance of the claim is in effect to recover a sum of money rather than to set aside a transaction, the period is six years.[169]

The fact that something has been done in pursuance of the order of a court does not, without more, prevent the doing or suffering of that thing from constituting the giving of a preference.[170]

Preferences and transactions at an undervalue: relief available

The starting point is that the court has the express jurisdiction under ss.238 and **34–59** 239 in respect of companies and ss.339 and 340 in respect of individual debtors to make such orders as it sees fit.

Nevertheless, without prejudice to that generality, ss.241 and 342 provide that **34–60** the court may:

(a) require any property transferred as part of the transaction, or in connection with the giving of the preference, to be vested in the company or the trustee of the bankrupt's estate;

(b) require any property to be so vested if it represents in any person's hands the application either of the proceeds of sale of property so transferred or of money so transferred;

(c) release or discharge (in whole or in part) any security given by the corporate or individual debtor;

(d) require any person to pay, in respect of benefits received by him from the corporate or individual debtor, such sums to the office-holder/trustee as the court may direct;

(e) provide for any surety or guarantor whose obligations to any person were released or discharged (in whole or in part) under the transaction, or by the giving of the preference, to be under such new or revived obligations to that person as the court thinks appropriate;

(f) provide for security to be provided for the discharge of any obligation imposed by or arising under the order, for such an obligation to be charged on any property and for the security or charge to have the same priority as a security or charge released or discharged (in whole or in part) under the transaction or by the giving of the preference; and

(g) provide for the extent to which any person whose property is vested by the order in the company or the trustee of the bankrupt's estate, or on whom obligations are imposed by the order, is to be able to prove in the

---

[169] *Re Priory Garage (Walthamstow) Ltd* [2001] B.P.I.R. 144.
[170] ibid., s.239(7) and s.340(6).

winding up of the company or the bankruptcy of the individual for debts or other liabilities which arose from, or were released or discharged (in whole or in part) under or by, the transaction or the giving of the preference.

34–61   The court may also, when making an order, affect the property of, or impose any obligation on, any person whether or not he is the person with whom the corporate or individual debtor in question entered into the transaction or (as the case may be) the person to whom the preference was given.[171] However, any such order:

(a)   shall not prejudice any interest in property which was acquired from a person other than the corporate or individual debtor and was acquired in good faith and for value, or prejudice any interest deriving from such an interest, and

(b)   shall not require a person who received a benefit from the transaction or preference in good faith and for value to pay a sum to the office-holder/trustee, except where that person was a party to the transaction or the payment is to be in respect of a preference given to that person at a time when he was a creditor of the corporate or individual debtor.

34–62   Where a person has acquired an interest in property from a person other than the debtor or has received a benefit from the transaction or preference, and at the time of that acquisition or receipt:

(a)   he had notice of the relevant surrounding circumstances and of the relevant proceedings, or

(b)   he was connected with, or was an associate of, either the debtor or the person with whom the debtor entered into the transaction or to whom the debtor gave the preference,

then, it is presumed (unless the contrary is shown) for the purposes of either sub-para.(a) or (b) in the immediately preceding paragraph above that the interest was acquired or the benefit was received otherwise than in good faith.[172]

The "relevant surrounding circumstances" are (as the case may require):

(a)   the fact that the corporate or individual debtor in question entered into the transaction at an undervalue; or

(b)   the circumstances which amounted to the giving of the preference by the corporate or individual debtor in question.[173]

34–63   As for the requirement that a person who acquired an interest had notice of the relevant proceedings, the precise matters of which he must have had notice in

---

[171] ibid., s.241(2) and s.342(2).

[172] ibid., s.241(2A) and s.342(2)(A). This provision was introduced in relation to interests acquired and benefits received after July 26, 1994, when the Insolvency (No.2) Act 1994 came into force.

[173] ibid., s.241(3).

order to raise the presumption will depend upon the form of insolvency into which the debtor has entered.

Where the debtor is a company in administration, a person has notice of the relevant proceedings if he has notice that:

(a) an administration application has been made,
(b) an administration order has been made,
(c) a copy of a notice of intention to appoint an administrator under para.14 or 22 of Sch.B1 has been filed, or
(d) notice of the appointment of an administrator has been filed under para.18 or 29 of that Schedule.[174]

Where the debtor company has gone into liquidation at the time when the appointment of an administrator of the company ceases to have effect, a person has notice of the relevant proceedings if he has notice that:

(a) an administration application has been made,
(b) an administration order has been made,
(c) a copy of a notice of intention to appoint an administrator under para.14 or 22 of Sch.B1 has been filed,
(d) notice of the appointment of an administrator has been filed under para.18 or 29 of that Schedule, or
(e) the company has gone into liquidation.[175]

In any other case where the company has gone into liquidation, a person has notice of the relevant proceedings if he has notice :

(a) where the company goes into liquidation on the making of a winding-up order, of the fact that the petition on which the winding-up order is made has been presented or of the fact that the company has gone into liquidation;
(b) in any other case, of the fact that the company has gone into liqui-dation.[176]

Where the debtor is an individual who has been adjudged bankrupt, a person has notice of the relevant proceedings if he has notice:

(a) of the fact that the petition on which the individual in question is adjudged bankrupt has been presented; or
(b) of the fact that the individual in question has been adjudged bank-rupt.[177]

---

[174] ibid., s.241(3A), as amended.
[175] ibid., s.241(3b), as amended.
[176] ibid., s.241(3C).
[177] ibid., s.342(5).

Transactions defrauding creditors

34–64 Section 423 of the Insolvency Act 1986 relates to transactions[178] entered into by either a corporate or an individual debtor at an undervalue designed to put assets out of the reach of creditors. A debtor enters into such a transaction with another person:

(a) he makes a gift to the other person or he otherwise enters into a transaction with the other on terms that provide for him to receive no consideration;

(b) he enters into a transaction with the other in consideration of marriage or the formation of a civil partnership[179]; or

(c) he enters into a transaction with the other for a consideration the value of which, in money or money's worth, is significantly less than the value, in money or money's worth, of the consideration provided by himself.[180]

If the court is satisfied that the transaction was entered into by a debtor for the purpose:

(a) of putting assets beyond the reach of a person who is making, or may at some time make, a claim against him, or

(b) of otherwise prejudicing the interests of such a person in relation to the claim which he is making or make.[181]

The court[182] may make such order as it thinks fit for restoring the position to what it would have been if the transaction had not been entered into, and protecting the interests of persons who are victims of the transaction.[183] The requirement that these objectives represent the "purpose of" the person entering into the transaction has been held to have the effect of making it a requirement that the intention of putting assets beyond the reach of a person or otherwise prejudicing his interests must have been the dominant purpose in the context of the transaction in question.[184] However, this does not sit comfortably with the weight of more recent authority under this provision and s.238.[185] Furthermore, the purpose need not have been to put assets beyond the reach or otherwise prejudicing the

---

[178] What constitutes a "transaction" is approached with a degree of flexibility and can encompass a formal agreement or an informal understanding. See *Feakins v Defra* [2006] B.P.I.R. 895.

[179] This element applies in the case of an individual debtor only, of course.

[180] ibid., s.423(1).

[181] ibid., s.423(3).

[182] "The court" means the High Court or, if the person entering into the transaction is an individual, any other court which would have jurisdiction in relation to a bankruptcy petition relating to him or if that person is a body capable of being wound up under IA 1986 Pt IV or V, any other court having jurisdiction to wind it up—s.423(4).

[183] ibid., s.423(2).

[184] *Chohan v Saggar* [1992] B.C.C. 306 and [1992] B.C.C. 750.

[185] See, for example, *Hashmi v IRC* [2002] B.P.I.R. 974; *Kubiangha v Ekpenyong* [2002] 2 B.C.L.C. 597.

interests of the particular victim who makes the application; it is enough that the debtor had this purpose in respect of some person or class of persons.[186]

An application for an order under s.423 can only be made in relation to a **34–65** transaction:

(a) in a case where the debtor[187] is an individual who has been adjudged bankrupt or is a body corporate which is being wound up or is in administration, by the official receiver, by the trustee of the bankrupt's estate or the liquidator or administrator of the body corporate or (with the leave of the court)[188] by a victim of the transaction[189];

(b) in a case where a victim of the transaction is bound by a voluntary arrangement approved under Pt I or Pt VIII of the Insolvency Act 1986 by the supervisor of the voluntary arrangement or by any person who (whether or not so bound) is such a victim; or

(c) in any other case, by a victim of the transaction.[190]

Any application made is treated as made on behalf of every victim of the transaction.[191]

Without prejudice to the generality of s.423 and the express power thereunder **34–66** to make such orders as it thinks fit for the stated purposes, the court may (subject as follows)[192]:

(a) require any property transferred as part of the transaction to be vested in any person, either absolutely or for the benefit of all the persons on whose behalf the application for the order is treated as made;

(b) require any property to be so vested if it represents, in any person's hands, the application either of the proceeds of sale of property so transferred or of money so transferred;

(c) release or discharge (in whole or in part) any security[193] given by the debtor;

(d) require any person to pay to any other person in respect of benefits received from the debtor such sums as the court may direct;

(e) provide for any surety or guarantor whose obligations to any person were released or discharged (in whole or in part) under the transaction to be under such new or revived obligations as the court thinks appropriate;

(f) provide for security to be provided for the discharge of any obligation imposed by or arising under the order, for such an obligation to be

---

[186] *Hill v Spread Trustee Co Ltd* [2007] 1 W.L.R. 2404.

[187] The person entering the transaction: s.423(5).

[188] As to which, see *Dora v Simper* [2002] 2 B.C.L.C. 561. There appears to be some judicial dispute as to whether or not a retrospective grant of leave is possible—cf. *Godfrey v Torpey (No.2)* [2007] B.P.I.R. 1538 and *Seal v Chief Constable of South Wales* [2001] 1 W.L.R. 1910.

[189] The "victim" of the transaction is the person who is, or is capable of being prejudiced by the transaction: s.423(5).

[190] ibid., s.424(1).

[191] ibid., s.424(2).

[192] ibid., s.425(1).

[193] In s.425, "security" means any mortgage, charge, lien or other security: s.425(4).

charged on any property and for such security or charge to have the
same priority as a security or charge released or discharged (in whole
or in part) under the transactions.

The limitation on those powers is expressed in s.425(2). An order under s.423
may affect the property of, or impose any obligation on, and person whether or
not he is the person with whom the debtor entered into the transaction; but such
an order:

> (a) shall not prejudice any interest in property which was acquired from a
> person other than the debtor and was acquired in good faith, for value
> and without notice of the relevant circumstances,[194] or prejudice any
> interest deriving from such an interest, and
>
> (b) shall not require a person who received a benefit from the transaction
> in good faith, for value and without notice of the relevant circum-
> stances to pay any sum unless he was a party to the transaction.

34–67   In *Barclays Bank Plc v Eustace*[195] the Court of Appeal held that the court can
order disclosure of documents that would otherwise enjoy the benefit of legal
professional privilege if these relate to a transaction which is a subject of an
application for avoidance under s.423 and where there is a strong prima facie
case that the requirements of the section are fulfilled.[196] In performing the
balancing exercise between the applicant's rights and the public policy that
persons should be able to contact their legal advisers in confidence without fear
of their communications having to be disclosed, the principle that legal advice
sought or given for the purpose of effecting an inequity should not enjoy
privilege ultimately prevailed. Clearly, in the context of an application in relation
to a mortgage or charge over land, the involvement of a legal adviser is usual (if
not inevitable), and this authority has significant practical importance.

---

[194] "The relevant circumstances" in relation to a transaction defrauding creditors are the circumstances by virtue of which an order under s.423 may be made in respect of the transaction:
s.425(3).

[195] [1995] 1 W.L.R. 1238.

[196] This is to be contrasted with *Royscot Spa Leasing Ltd v Lovett* [1995] B.C.C. 502, where such
an order was refused in circumstances where the applicants had failed to show a prima facie case that
the requirements of s.423 were fulfilled.

Chapter 35

INSOLVENCY OF THE MORTGAGEE

Introduction

The mortgagor who is abiding by the terms of his mortgage agreement should **35–01** experience little impact from the insolvency of the mortgagee.[1] He is most unlikely to be a creditor of the mortgagee, and therefore will have no need or ability to claim on the estate or protect himself within the administration or voluntary arrangement. The only thing which is likely to change is the ownership of the charge over his property and consequently the identity of the company or individual to whom he is obliged to make payments.

However, life may become more complicated for a mortgagor in arrears whose mortgagee enters into some form of insolvency process. A new and independent person in at least substantial control of the mortgagee's business, motivated by a desire and a duty to maximise the available assets for the benefit of some or all of the creditors, may adopt a less generous approach to dealing with those who owe the mortgagee money than had been the case before his appointment. Employees of the mortgagee who wish to see the business survive may need to change their tone in dealing with its non-compliant customers. A purchaser of the portfolio may wish to cut losses on those mortgages where arrears have mounted by repossessing properties at an early stage.

The various different forms which insolvency may take and the consequences of each option for a creditor of the insolvent have been addressed in the previous chapter.[2] A debtor of the insolvent mortgagee will be principally concerned with the identity and powers of the person now dealing with matters in place or on behalf of the insolvent individual, partnership or company to whom he owes money. In outline, the position for each form of insolvency is as follows.[3]

---

[1] Unless, irrespective of his compliance, the mortgagee can and does call upon him to repay his indebtedness.

[2] See paras 34–02 et seq.

[3] Reference should be made to the specialist texts for a detailed analysis of this complex area.

NON-CORPORATE MORTGAGEES

Individual Voluntary Arrangements[4]

35–02 When a debtor wishes to make a proposal for an IVA he must identify an insolvency practitioner[5] to act as nominee and assist with the preparation of his statement of affairs. If an interim order has been obtained, or if it seems that the debtor is an undischarged bankrupt or able to petition for his own bankruptcy, the IP must also produce a report for the court at that early stage.[6] In the event that the creditors' meeting ultimately approves the proposal, it will confer upon the nominee the various functions set out in the proposal. From that point on, the nominee (or another IP as his replacement) is known as the supervisor of the IVA.

35–03 Although the supervisor is an officer of the court[7] and obliged to report to the court, there is no schedule to the Insolvency Act setting out his powers as there is for other insolvency situations. Therefore it is important that the full extent of his powers and obligations is expressed in the proposal itself. It is to this that the mortgagor must have regard.

35–04 As soon as reasonably practicable after the approval of the IVA the debtor or, where the debtor is an undischarged bankrupt, the official receiver or the debtor's trustee, must do all that is required for putting the supervisor into possession of the assets included in the arrangement.[8] The supervisor is able to apply to the court for directions in relation to any matter arising under the IVA,[9] but is otherwise free to manage the assets of the debtor in accordance with the terms of the IVA. If the debtor, any of his creditors or any other person is dissatisfied by any act, omission or decision of the supervisor he may apply to the court which may confirm, reverse or modify any act or decision of the supervisor, give him directions or make such other order as it thinks fit.[10] The court is not able to give directions which would have the effect of varying the IVA itself.[11]

35–05 Although the supervisor is put into possession of the relevant assets, and is therefore likely to be the person managing the bank accounts into which mortgage instalments are paid and to be the person making decisions about how to deal with a mortgagor in default or a mortgagor seeking to negotiate new terms, he does not become the owner of the charge. Any new agreement with the mortgagor or any transfer of the charge to a third party should therefore include the debtor himself as a party, and any step to enforce the mortgagee's rights under the mortgage should be taken in the name of the debtor rather than that of the supervisor.

---

[4] Under Pt VIII of the Insolvency Act (IA) 1986 ss.252–263G and Pt 5 of the Insolvency Rules (IR) 1986, as amended.

[5] Although where the debtor is already an undischarged bankrupt the Official Receiver may act as nominee and supervisor of a Fast-track IVA under IA 1986 s.263B and IR 1986 Ch.7: a new scheme introduced by the Enterprise Act 2002.

[6] IA 1986 s.256; IR 1986 r.5.11; IA 1986 s.256A; IR 1986 r.5.14.

[7] *King v Anthony* [1998] 2 B.C.L.C. 517.

[8] IR 1986 5.26(1).

[9] IA 1986 s.263(4).

[10] IA 1986 s.263(3).

[11] *Re Alpa Lighting Ltd* [1997] B.P.I.R. 341; *Raja v Rubin* [1999] B.P.I.R. 575.

Bankruptcy

Bankruptcy differs from any other form of insolvency in that all property owned   **35–06**
by the insolvent passes not just into the control but into the ownership of another
person. Upon the making of a bankruptcy order, the bankrupt's estate vests in the
trustee in bankruptcy on his appointment or, in the case of the official receiver,
on his becoming trustee. The estate vests without any conveyance, assignment or
transfer.[12] The bankrupt's estate consists of, inter alia, "all property belonging to
or vested in the bankrupt at the commencement of the bankruptcy",[13] i.e. the day
upon which the bankruptcy order is made (*not* the date on which the petition was
presented).[14] However, it will not include any property held by the bankrupt
entirely on trust for another person.

Because the bankrupt mortgagee's entire interest in the property will have
passed automatically to his trustee, from that point onwards it is the trustee rather
than the mortgagee who can exercise any remedies in respect of the mortgage.
This includes the right to bring a claim for foreclosure,[15] possession/or the sale
or to sue the mortgagor on the covenant to pay. A transfer of an interest in
property by operation of law on the bankruptcy of the proprietor is expressly
excluded from the general requirement that a disposition be completed by
registration at HM Land Registry.[16] There is therefore no need for the trustee to
be registered as proprietor of the charge. However, it is wise for the creditor or
trustee to ensure that some entry on the register reflects the presentation of the
petition and/or subsequent bankruptcy order, as the bankrupt may otherwise be
able to transfer the charge to a third party acting in good faith and without
notice.[17]

The powers of the trustee in bankruptcy are considerable. They are set out in   **35–07**
Pt IX of and Sch.5 to the Insolvency Act 1986. His function is to get in, realise
and distribute the bankrupt's estate in accordance with the provisions of the Act
and may use his discretion in so doing.[18] Save where the Official Receiver acts
as trustee, the bankrupt's creditors in general meeting may establish a committee
to supervise the trustee.[19] The trustee may apply to the court for directions in
relation to any particular matter arising under the bankruptcy.[20] If the bankrupt or
any of his creditors or any other person is dissatisfied by any act, omission or
decision of the trustee of the bankrupt's estate, he may apply to the court which
may confirm, reverse or modify any act or decision of the trustee and may give
him such directions or make such other order as it thinks fit.[21] The trustee may
also be held liable to repay, restore or account for moneys or to pay compensation
in the event that he has misapplied or retained or become accountable for any

---

[12] IA 1986 s.306.
[13] IA 1986 s.283(1).
[14] IA 1986 s.278(a).
[15] *Waddell v Toleman* (1878) L.R. 9 Ch.D. 212.
[16] Land Registration Act (LRA) 2002 s.27(5).
[17] LRA 2002 s.86(5). A notice is usually entered.
[18] IA 1986 s.305(2).
[19] IA 1986 s.301(1).
[20] IA 1986 s.303(2).
[21] IA 1986 s.303(1).

money or other property comprised in the bankrupt's estate, or that the bankrupt's estate has suffered any loss in consequence of any misfeasance or breach of fiduciary or other duty by a trustee in the carrying out of his functions.[22]

CORPORATE MORTGAGEES

35–08   A "general moratorium" agreed between the parties thereto addresses the position as between an insolvent or troubled company and its creditors. It is therefore unlikely to have any significant impact upon the relationship between an insolvent mortgagee and its mortgagor, save in the sense that the mortgagee may feel an increased sense of pressure to demonstrate that it is dealing properly with its portfolio so as to maximise the cash available to satisfy those forbearing creditors. There is no change of ownership of the mortgagee's assets. There may be an insolvency practitioner or accountant involved in the business during the period of the moratorium, but that business will continue to be conducted by and in the name of the mortgagee.

Company Voluntary Arrangements[23]

35–09   The process of obtaining a CVA and the role of the insolvency practitioner who acts as nominee/supervisor are broadly in line with those applicable to an IVA, save for the differences in respect of the applications for an interim order/moratorium addressed in the previous chapter.[24] The tasks which the IP must undertake and the detail of his conduct of the CVA process will also differ dependent upon whether the CVA has the benefit of a moratorium or not.[25]

35–10   Again, the supervisor is an officer of the court and obliged to report to the court, but there is no statutory schedule of his powers. Instead they should be defined in the proposal and approved by the creditors so as to form part of the CVA itself.

35–11   As soon as reasonably practicable after the effective decision approving the CVA the directors or, where the company is already in liquidation or administration and someone other than the IP who has been responsible for that liquidation or administration is appointed as supervisor, that IP must do all that is required for putting the supervisor into possession of the assets included in the arrangement.[26] The supervisor is able to apply to the court for directions in relation to any matter arising under the CVA and is one of the persons who may apply for the company to be wound up or placed into administration,[27] but is otherwise free

[22] IA 1986 s.304(1). Note that the applicants for such an order may be any of the Official Receiver, the Secretary of State, a creditor of the bankrupt or the bankrupt himself, provided he obtains leave of the court—s.304(2). Liability is limited by s.304(3).

[23] Under IA 1986 Pt 1 as repeatedly amended.

[24] See para.34–21. See also observations on the duties of the supervisor in *Appleyard Ltd v Ritecrown Ltd* [2009] B.P.I.R. 235.

[25] Much of the detail of the process is set out in IR 1986 Pt 1, supporting Pt 1 of the Act.

[26] IR 1986 1.23(1).

[27] IA 1986 s.7(4). See *Re Federal-Mogul Aftermarket Ltd* [2008] B.P.I.R. 846.

to manage the assets of the debtor in accordance with the terms of the CVA. If any of the company's creditors or any other person is dissatisfied by any act, omission or decision of the supervisor he may apply to the court which may confirm, reverse or modify any act or decision of the supervisor, give him directions or make such other order as it thinks fit.[28] The court is not able to give directions which would have the effect of varying the CVA itself.[29] However, in appropriate circumstances the court may feel able to extend the scheme of the CVA to include persons who did not participate in the meetings.[30]

As with an IVA, although the supervisor is put into possession of the relevant **35–12** assets, and is therefore likely to be the person managing the bank accounts into which mortgage instalments are paid and making decisions about how to deal with a mortgagor in default or a mortgagor seeking to negotiate new terms, he does not become the owner of the charge. Any new agreement with the mortgagor or any transfer of the charge to a third party should therefore include the company itself as a party, and any step to enforce the mortgagee's rights under the mortgage should be taken in the name of the company rather than that of the supervisor.

Receivers

Two forms of receivership may be of relevance where a mortgagee is insolvent: **35–13** a receiver appointed under the Law of Property Act 1925 and an administrative receiver. Each is addressed elsewhere in this work.[31] The precise powers of a receiver will depend upon the terms of his appointment, but are likely to include a power to receive payments from mortgagors. The ultimate ownership of the charge and entitlement to payment of the debt will generally remain with the mortgagee, the receiver standing as the mortgagee's agent for the purposes of carrying out his functions.

Administration[32]

The previous chapter includes an introduction to the post-2003 administration **35–14** regime and the opportunities which it provides to protect the insolvent estate by means of a moratorium.[33] Once a company is in administration, the administrator is empowered to do anything necessary or expedient for the management of the affairs, business and property of the company.[34] He also has the specific powers set out in Sch.1 to the 1986 Act, which include powers to:

[28] IA 1986 s.7(3).
[29] *Re Alpa Lighting Ltd* [1997] B.P.I.R. 341; *Raja v Rubin* [1999] B.P.I.R. 575.
[30] *Re FMS Financial Management Systems Ltd* (1989) 5 B.C.C. 191.
[31] See above paras 26–27 et seq. in respect of LPA Receivers and para.34–24 for Administrative Receivers.
[32] Under IA 1986 Pt II (as amended) and Sch.B1.
[33] See above paras 34–25 et seq.
[34] IA 1986 Sch.B1 para.59(1).

- take any proceedings which seem to him to be expedient to take possession of, collect and get in property belonging to the company;
- sell any of the company's property;
- bring or defend any legal proceedings in the name and on behalf of the company;
- do all acts and to execute in the name of the company any deed, receipt or other document;
- do all such things as may be necessary for the realisation of the company's property;
- carry on the business of the company;
- transfer to subsidiaries the whole or any part of the business and property of the company;
- make any arrangement or compromise on behalf of the company;
- rank and claim in the bankruptcy or other insolvency of any person indebted to the company; and
- do all other things incidental to the exercise of the specific powers.

Once a company has entered administration, neither the company itself nor any officer of the company can exercise any management power (i.e. one which could be exercised so as to interfere with the exercise of the administrator's powers) without the consent of the administrator.[35] The administrator takes control of all the property to which he thinks the company is entitled and manages its affairs, business and property as its agent in accordance with the proposals and any subsequent directions or approved revisions.[36] He must act at all times with the objective of meeting the purpose of the administration.[37]

35–15   Accordingly, while any transaction or agreement into which the mortgagor might wish to enter with his insolvent mortgagee will need to be undertaken in the name of the mortgagee itself, the person with whom the mortgagor will be dealing and who will have the power to decide whether to consent thereto on behalf of mortgagee will generally be the administrator. If the mortgagor, or any other person deals with the administrator in good faith and for value, he is not obliged to inquire whether the administrator is acting within his powers.[38]

Liquidation

35–16   The precise provisions governing the impact of a liquidation differ dependent upon whether it is a voluntary winding up by members of the company[39] or its creditors[40] or a winding up by the court[41] pursuant to a petition by the company, its directors, a creditor, a contributory or various existing office holders. A voluntary winding up commences at the instant the resolution is passed and the

---

[35] IA 1986 Sch.B1 para.64.
[36] IA 1986 Sch.B1 paras 67, 68 and 69.
[37] See above para.34–27 and IA 1986 Sch.B1 para.3.
[38] IA 1986 Sch.B1 para.59(3).
[39] IA 1986 ss.84–96 and 107–116.
[40] IA 1986 ss.84–90 and 97–116.
[41] IA 1986 ss.117 et seq.

company must therefore immediately cease to carry on its business except so far as may be required for its beneficial winding up.[42] A liquidator will be appointed and will get in and apply the company's assets in accordance with the statutory provisions.

If the company is wound up by the court, its winding up is generally deemed **35–17** to have commenced at the date of presentation of the petition.[43] While the company is able to continue in business during the period between presentation and the winding up order,[44] any disposition of its property during that period will be void unless the court orders otherwise.[45] Once in post, the liquidator under a compulsory liquidation is obliged to secure that the assets of the company are gathered in, realised and distributed to the company's creditors and, if there is a surplus, to the persons entitled thereto. In order to do so, he is to take into his custody or under his control all the property and things in action to which the company is or appears to be entitled.[46] However, unless he seeks and obtains from the court a vesting order,[47] the property remains in the ownership of the company in liquidation.

The powers and duties of liquidators are set out in ss.165 and 166 of the **35–18** Insolvency Act 1986 and in Sch.4 to that Act. Some may be exercised only with the sanction of the company (in a members' voluntary winding up), the liquidation committee or creditors' meeting (in a creditors' voluntary winding up), or the liquidation committee or the court (in a winding up by the court).[48]

Powers which the liquidator may exercise without sanction in any winding up include those powers to:

- sell any of the company's property by public auction or private contract;
- do all acts and to execute in the name and on behalf of the company any deeds, receipts or other documents;
- rank and claim in the bankruptcy or other insolvency of any person indebted to the company; and
- do all such other things as may be necessary for winding up the company's affairs and distributing its assets.

In a voluntary winding up, the liquidator may without sanction also bring or defend any action or other legal proceeding in the name and on behalf of the company and may carry on the business of the company so far as may be necessary for its beneficial winding up. The liquidator in a compulsory liquidation also has those powers but requires the sanction of the court or the liquidation committee to exercise them. The liquidator in his capacity as an officer of the

---

[42] IA 1986 ss.86–87.
[43] IA 1986 s.129.
[44] At least as a matter of law; practically the presentation and certainly the advertisement of a petition can have profoundly adverse commercial consequences.
[45] IA 1986 s.127.
[46] IA 1986 ss.143–144.
[47] IA 1986 s.145.
[48] See IA 1986 ss.165–168 for the identification of those powers in each category.

court is also given the same powers as a receiver appointed by the High Court to support him in the exercise of his duties on behalf of the court.[49]

35–19   The appointment of a liquidator does not automatically remove the directors of a company from office in a voluntary winding up, but their powers to deal with the company or its assets cease save insofar as the continuance of any of those powers is sanctioned.[50] Where a company is wound up by the court, the appointments of all directors are automatically terminated.[51] Accordingly, the mortgagor whose mortgagee in the process of being wound up is likely to be required to deal with the liquidator, and should assume that the liquidator is in control of the company's business unless and until told otherwise. However, the charge remains the property of the mortgagee company and the debt is owed to that company and not to the liquidator, albeit that he has authority to receive and deal with the mortgage moneys paid by the mortgagor. While the liquidator is likely to have at least ostensible authority to bind the company to any agreement reached with a mortgagor, that agreement needs to be entered into between the mortgagor and the company itself through the agency of the liquidator.

Dissolution

35–20   As explained in the previous chapter,[52] dissolution is not itself a separate form of insolvency but rather the ultimate conclusion of the liquidation of a limited company, leading to the passing of any remaining assets bona vacantia to the Crown, the Duchy of Lancaster or the Duke of Cornwall. When a corporate mortgagee is dissolved, any remaining charges it holds and rights against its mortgagors will therefore pass bona vacantia, without the need for any form of assignment or consent.[53]

---

[49] IA 1986 ss.148 and 160; IR 1986 r.4.179.
[50] IA 1986 ss.91 and 103.
[51] *Measures Brothers Ltd v Measures* [1910] 2 Ch. 248.
[52] See above paras 34–38 et seq.
[53] Under Companies Act 2006 s.1012. See *Re Strathblaine Estates Ltd* [1948] 1 Ch. 228.

INDEX

LEGAL TAXONOMY
FROM SWEET & MAXWELL

This index has been prepared using Sweet and Maxwell's Legal Taxonomy. Main index entries conform to keywords provided by the Legal Taxonomy except where references to specific documents or non-standard terms (denoted by quotation marks) have been included. These keywords provide a means of identifying similar concepts in other Sweet & Maxwell publications and online services to which keywords from the Legal Taxonomy have been applied. Readers may find some minor differences between terms used in the text and those which appear in the index. Suggestions to *taxonomy@sweetandmaxwell. co.uk.*